38
185
191
116
123
156
163
170

American Casebook Series
Hornbook Series and Basic Legal Texts
Nutshell Series

of

WEST PUBLISHING COMPANY
P.O. Box 43526
St. Paul, Minnesota 55164
January, 1984

ACCOUNTING

Faris' Law and Accounting in a Nutshell, approximately 392 pages, 1984 (Text)

Fiflis, Kripke and Foster's Teaching Materials on Accounting for Business Lawyers, 3rd Ed., approximately 784 pages, 1984 (Casebook)

Siegel and Siegel's Accounting and Financial Disclosure: A Guide to Basic Concepts, 259 pages, 1983 (Text)

ADMINISTRATIVE LAW

Davis' Cases, Text and Problems on Administrative Law, 6th Ed., 683 pages, 1977 (Casebook)

Davis' Basic Text on Administrative Law, 3rd Ed., 617 pages, 1972 (Text)

Davis' Police Discretion, 176 pages, 1975 (Text)

Gellhorn and Boyer's Administrative Law and Process in a Nutshell, 2nd Ed., 445 pages, 1981 (Text)

Mashaw and Merrill's Introduction to the American Public Law System, 1095 pages, 1975, with 1980 Supplement (Casebook)

Robinson, Gellhorn and Bruff's The Administrative Process, 2nd Ed., 959 pages, 1980, with 1983 Supplement (Casebook)

ADMIRALTY

Healy and Sharpe's Cases and Materials on Admiralty, 875 pages, 1974 (Casebook)

Maraist's Admiralty in a Nutshell, 400 pages, 1983 (Text)

Sohn and Gustafson's Law of the Sea in a Nutshell, approximately 250 pages, 1984 (Text)

AGENCY PARTNERSHIP

Fessler's Alternatives to Incorporation for Persons in Quest of Profit, 258 pages, 1980 (Casebook)

Henn's Cases and Materials on Agency, Partnership and Other Unincorporated Business Enterprises, 396 pages, 1972 (Casebook)

Reuschlein and Gregory's Hornbook on the Law of Agency and Partnership, 625 pages, 1979, with 1981 pocket part (Text)

Seavey's Hornbook on Agency, 329 pages, 1964 (Text)

Seavey and Hall's Cases on Agency, 431 pages, 1956 (Casebook)

Seavey, Reuschlein and Hall's Cases on Agency and Partnership, 599 pages, 1962 (Casebook)

Selected Corporation and Partnership Statutes and Forms, 556 pages, 1982

Steffen and Kerr's Cases and Materials on Agency-Partnership, 4th Ed., 859 pages, 1980 (Casebook)

Steffen's Agency-Partnership in a Nutshell, 364 pages, 1977 (Text)

AMERICAN INDIAN LAW

Canby's American Indian Law in a Nutshell, 288 pages, 1981 (Text)

Getches, Rosenfelt and Wilkinson's Cases on Federal Indian Law, 660 pages, 1979, with 1983 Supplement (Casebook)

ANTITRUST LAW

Gellhorn's Antitrust Law and Economics in a Nutshell, 2nd Ed., 425 pages, 1981 (Text)

Gifford and Raskind's Cases and Materials on Antitrust, 694 pages, 1983 (Casebook)

LAW SCHOOL PUBLICATIONS—Continued

ANTITRUST LAW—Continued

Oppenheim, Weston and McCarthy's Cases and Comments on Federal Antitrust Laws, 4th Ed., 1168 pages, 1981 (Casebook)

Posner and Easterbrook's Cases and Economic Notes on Antitrust, 2nd Ed., 1077 pages, 1981, with 1982–83 Supplement (Casebook)

Sullivan's Hornbook of the Law of Antitrust, 886 pages, 1977 (Text)

See also Regulated Industries, Trade Regulation

ART LAW

DuBoff's Art Law in a Nutshell, approximately 290 pages, 1984 (Text)

BANKING LAW

Lovett's Banking and Financial Institutions in a Nutshell, 409 pages, 1984 (Text)

White's Teaching Materials on Banking Law, 1058 pages, 1976, with Case and Statutory Supplement (Casebook)

BUSINESS PLANNING

Epstein and Scheinfeld's Teaching Materials on Business Reorganization Under the Bankruptcy Code, 216 pages, 1980 (Casebook)

Painter's Problems and Materials in Business Planning, 2nd Ed., approximately 1035 pages, 1984 (Casebook)

Selected Securities and Business Planning Statutes, Rules and Forms, 485 pages, 1982

CIVIL PROCEDURE

Casad's Res Judicata in a Nutshell, 310 pages, 1976 (text)

Cound, Friedenthal and Miller's Cases and Materials on Civil Procedure, 3rd Ed., 1147 pages, 1980 with 1984 Supplement (Casebook)

Ehrenzweig, Louisell and Hazard's Jurisdiction in a Nutshell, 4th Ed., 232 pages, 1980 (Text)

Federal Rules of Civil-Appellate-Criminal Procedure—West Law School Edition, 343 pages, 1983

Hodges, Jones and Elliott's Cases and Materials on Texas Trial and Appellate Procedure, 2nd Ed., 745 pages, 1974 (Casebook)

Hodges, Jones and Elliott's Cases and Materials on the Judicial Process Prior to Trial in Texas, 2nd Ed., 871 pages, 1977 (Casebook)

Kane's Civil Procedure in a Nutshell, 271 pages, 1979 (Text)

Karlen's Procedure Before Trial in a Nutshell, 258 pages, 1972 (Text)

Karlen, Meisenholder, Stevens and Vestal's Cases on Civil Procedure, 923 pages, 1975 (Casebook)

CIVIL PROCEDURE—Continued

Koffler and Reppy's Hornbook on Common Law Pleading, 663 pages, 1969 (Text)

McBaine's Cases on Introduction to Civil Procedure, 399 pages, 1950 (Casebook)

Park's Computer-Aided Exercises on Civil Procedure, 2nd Ed., 167 pages, 1983 (Coursebook)

Shipman's Hornbook on Common-Law Pleading, 3rd Ed., 644 pages, 1923 (Text)

Siegel's Hornbook on New York Practice, 1011 pages, 1978 with 1981–82 Pocket Part (Text)

See also Federal Jurisdiction and Procedure

CIVIL RIGHTS

Abernathy's Cases and Materials on Civil Rights, 660 pages, 1980 (Casebook)

Cohen's Cases on the Law of Deprivation of Liberty: A Study in Social Control, 755 pages, 1980 (Casebook)

Lockhart, Kamisar and Choper's Cases on Constitutional Rights and Liberties, 5th Ed., 1298 pages plus Appendix, 1981, with 1983 Supplement (Casebook)—reprint from Lockhart, et al. Cases on Constitutional Law, 5th Ed., 1980

Vieira's Civil Rights in a Nutshell, 279 pages, 1978 (Text)

COMMERCIAL LAW

Bailey's Secured Transactions in a Nutshell, 2nd Ed., 391 pages, 1981 (Text)

Epstein and Martin's Basic Uniform Commercial Code Teaching Materials, 2nd Ed., 667 pages, 1983 (Casebook)

Henson's Hornbook on Secured Transactions Under the U.C.C., 2nd Ed., 504 pages, 1979 with 1979 P.P. (Text)

Murray's Commercial Law, Problems and Materials, 366 pages, 1975 (Coursebook)

Nordstrom and Clovis' Problems and Materials on Commercial Paper, 458 pages, 1972 (Casebook)

Nordstrom and Lattin's Problems and Materials on Sales and Secured Transactions, 809 pages, 1968 (Casebook)

Nordstrom, Murray and Clovis' Problems and Materials on Sales, 515 pages, 1982 (Casebook)

Nordstrom's Hornbook on Sales, 600 pages, 1970 (Text)

Selected Commercial Statutes, 1379 pages, 1983

Speidel, Summers and White's Teaching Materials on Commercial and Consumer Law, 3rd Ed., 1490 pages, 1981 (Casebook)

Stockton's Sales in a Nutshell, 2nd Ed., 370 pages, 1981 (Text)

Stone's Uniform Commercial Code in a Nutshell, 507 pages, 1975 (Text)

Uniform Commercial Code, Official Text with Comments, 994 pages, 1978

LAW SCHOOL PUBLICATIONS—Continued

COMMERCIAL LAW—Continued

UCC Article 8, 1977 Amendments, 249 pages, 1978

UCC Article 9, Reprint from 1962 Code, 128 pages, 1976

UCC Article 9, 1972 Amendments, 304 pages, 1978

Weber and Speidel's Commercial Paper in a Nutshell, 3rd Ed., 404 pages, 1982 (Text)

White and Summers' Hornbook on the Uniform Commercial Code, 2nd Ed., 1250 pages, 1980 (Text)

COMMUNITY PROPERTY

Mennell's Community Property in a Nutshell, 447 pages, 1982 (Text)

Verrall and Bird's Cases and Materials on California Community Property, 4th Ed., 549 pages, 1983 (Casebook)

COMPARATIVE LAW

Barton, Gibbs, Li and Merryman's Law in Radically Different Cultures, 960 pages, 1983 (Casebook)

Glendon, Gordon, and Osakwe's Comparative Legal Traditions in a Nutshell, 402 pages, 1982 (Text)

Langbein's Comparative Criminal Procedure: Germany, 172 pages, 1977 (Casebook)

COMPUTERS AND LAW

Mason's An Introduction to the Use of Computers in Law, approximately 200 pages, 1984 (Text)

CONFLICT OF LAWS

Cramton, Currie and Kay's Cases-Comments-Questions on Conflict of Laws, 3rd Ed., 1026 pages, 1981 (Casebook)

Scoles and Hay's Hornbook on Conflict of Laws, Student Ed., 1085 pages, 1982 (Text)

Scoles and Weintraub's Cases and Materials on Conflict of Laws, 2nd Ed., 966 pages, 1972, with 1978 Supplement (Casebook)

Siegel's Conflicts in a Nutshell, 469 pages, 1982 (Text)

CONSTITUTIONAL LAW

Engdahl's Constitutional Power in a Nutshell: Federal and State, 411 pages, 1974 (Text)

Lockhart, Kamisar and Choper's Cases-Comments-Questions on Constitutional Law, 5th Ed., 1705 pages plus Appendix, 1980, with 1983 Supplement (Casebook)

Lockhart, Kamisar and Choper's Cases-Comments-Questions on the American Constitution, 5th Ed., 1185 pages plus Appendix, 1981, with 1983 Supplement (Casebook)—reprint from Lockhart, et al. Cases on Constitutional Law, 5th Ed., 1980

CONSTITUTIONAL LAW—Continued

Manning's The Law of Church-State Relations in a Nutshell, 305 pages, 1981 (Text)

Miller's Presidential Power in a Nutshell, 328 pages, 1977 (Text)

Nowak, Rotunda and Young's Hornbook on Constitutional Law, 2nd Ed., Student Ed., 1172 pages, 1983 (Text)

Rotunda's Modern Constitutional Law: Cases and Notes, 1034 pages, 1981, with 1983 Supplement (Casebook)

Williams' Constitutional Analysis in a Nutshell, 388 pages, 1979 (Text)

See also Civil Rights

CONSUMER LAW

Epstein and Nickles' Consumer Law in a Nutshell, 2nd Ed., 418 pages, 1981 (Text)

McCall's Consumer Protection, Cases, Notes and Materials, 594 pages, 1977, with 1977 Statutory Supplement (Casebook)

Selected Commercial Statutes, 1379 pages, 1983

Spanogle and Rohner's Cases and Materials on Consumer Law, 693 pages, 1979, with 1982 Supplement (Casebook)

See also Commercial Law

CONTRACTS

Calamari & Perillo's Cases and Problems on Contracts, 1061 pages, 1978 (Casebook)

Calamari and Perillo's Hornbook on Contracts, 2nd Ed., 878 pages, 1977 (Text)

Corbin's Text on Contracts, One Volume Student Edition, 1224 pages, 1952 (Text)

Fessler and Loiseaux's Cases and Materials on Contracts, 837 pages, 1982 (Casebook)

Freedman's Cases and Materials on Contracts, 658 pages, 1973 (Casebook)

Friedman's Contract Remedies in a Nutshell, 323 pages, 1981 (Text)

Fuller and Eisenberg's Cases on Basic Contract Law, 4th Ed., 1203 pages, 1981 (Casebook)

Hamilton, Rau and Weintraub's Cases and Materials on Contracts, approximately 950 pages, 1984 (Casebook)

Jackson and Bollinger's Cases on Contract Law in Modern Society, 2nd Ed., 1329 pages, 1980 (Casebook)

Keyes' Government Contracts in a Nutshell, 423 pages, 1979 (Text)

Reitz's Cases on Contracts as Basic Commercial Law, 763 pages, 1975 (Casebook)

Schaber and Rohwer's Contracts in a Nutshell, 2nd Ed., approximately 409 pages, 1984 (Text)

Simpson's Hornbook on Contracts, 2nd Ed., 510 pages, 1965 (Text)

COPYRIGHT

See Patent and Copyright Law

LAW SCHOOL PUBLICATIONS—Continued

CORPORATIONS

Hamilton's Cases on Corporations—Including Partnerships and Limited Partnerships, 2nd Ed., 1108 pages, 1981, with 1981 Statutory Supplement and 1984 Supplement (Casebook)

Hamilton's Law of Corporations in a Nutshell, 379 pages, 1980 (Text)

Henn's Cases on Corporations, 1279 pages, 1974, with 1980 Supplement (Casebook)

Henn and Alexander's Hornbook on Corporations, 3rd Ed., Student Ed., 1371 pages, 1983 (Text)

Jennings and Buxbaum's Cases and Materials on Corporations, 5th Ed., 1180 pages, 1979 (Casebook)

Selected Corporation and Partnership Statutes, Regulations and Forms, 556 pages, 1982

Solomon, Stevenson and Schwartz' Materials and Problems on the Law and Policies on Corporations, 1172 pages, 1982 with 1983 Supplement (Casebook)

CORPORATE FINANCE

Hamilton's Cases and Materials on Corporate Finance, approximately 882 pages, 1984 (Casebook)

CORRECTIONS

Krantz's Cases and Materials on the Law of Corrections and Prisoners' Rights, 2nd Ed., 735 pages, 1981, with 1982 Supplement (Casebook)

Krantz's Law of Corrections and Prisoners' Rights in a Nutshell, 2nd Ed., 384 pages, 1983 (Text)

Popper's Post-Conviction Remedies in a Nutshell, 360 pages, 1978 (Text)

Robbins' Cases and Materials on Post Conviction Remedies, 506 pages, 1982 (Casebook)

Rubin's Law of Criminal Corrections, 2nd Ed., 873 pages, 1973, with 1978 Supplement (Text)

CREDITOR'S RIGHTS

Bankruptcy Code and Rules, Law School Ed., 438 pages, 1984

Epstein's Debtor-Creditor Law in a Nutshell, 2nd Ed., 324 pages, 1980 (Text)

Epstein and Landers' Debtors and Creditors: Cases and Materials, 2nd Ed., 689 pages, 1982 (Casebook)

Epstein and Sheinfeld's Teaching Materials on Business Reorganization Under the Bankruptcy Code, 216 pages, 1980 (Casebook)

Riesenfeld's Cases and Materials on Creditors' Remedies and Debtors' Protection, 3rd Ed., 810 pages, 1979 with 1979 Statutory Supplement and 1981 Case Supplement (Casebook)

CRIMINAL LAW AND CRIMINAL PROCEDURE

Cohen and Gobert's Problems in Criminal Law, 297 pages, 1976 (Problem book)

Davis' Police Discretion, 176 pages, 1975 (Text)

Dix and Sharlot's Cases and Materials on Criminal Law, 2nd Ed., 771 pages, 1979 (Casebook)

Federal Rules of Civil-Appellate-Criminal Procedure—West Law School Edition, 343 pages, 1983

Grano's Problems in Criminal Procedure, 2nd Ed., 176 pages, 1981 (Problem book)

Israel and LaFave's Criminal Procedure in a Nutshell, 3rd Ed., 438 pages, 1980 (Text)

Johnson's Cases, Materials and Text on Substantive Criminal Law in its Procedural Context, 2nd Ed., 956 pages, 1980 (Casebook)

Kamisar, LaFave and Israel's Cases, Comments and Questions on Modern Criminal Procedure, 5th ed., 1635 pages plus Appendix, 1980 with 1983 Supplement (Casebook)

Kamisar, LaFave and Israel's Cases, Comments and Questions on Basic Criminal Procedure, 5th Ed., 869 pages, 1980 with 1983 Supplement (Casebook)—reprint from Kamisar, et al. Modern Criminal Procedure, 5th ed., 1980

LaFave's Modern Criminal Law: Cases, Comments and Questions, 789 pages, 1978 (Casebook)

LaFave and Scott's Hornbook on Criminal Law, 763 pages, 1972 (Text)

Langbein's Comparative Criminal Procedure: Germany, 172 pages, 1977 (Casebook)

Loewy's Criminal Law in a Nutshell, 302 pages, 1975 (Text)

Saltzburg's American Criminal Procedure, Cases and Commentary, 2nd Ed., 1193 pages, 1984 (Casebook)

Uviller's The Processes of Criminal Justice: Investigation and Adjudication, 2nd Ed., 1384 pages, 1979 with 1979 Statutory Supplement and 1983 Update (Casebook)

Uviller's The Processes of Criminal Justice: Adjudication, 2nd Ed., 730 pages, 1979. Soft-cover reprint from Uviller's The Processes of Criminal Justice: Investigation and Adjudication, 2nd Ed. (Casebook)

Uviller's The Processes of Criminal Justice: Investigation, 2nd Ed., 655 pages, 1979. Soft-cover reprint from Uviller's The Processes of Criminal Justice: Investigation and Adjudication, 2nd Ed. (Casebook)

Vorenberg's Cases on Criminal Law and Procedure, 2nd Ed., 1088 pages, 1981 (Casebook)

LAW SCHOOL PUBLICATIONS—Continued

CRIMINAL LAW AND CRIMINAL PRO-CEDURE—Continued

See also Corrections, Juvenile Justice

DECEDENTS ESTATES

See Trusts and Estates

DOMESTIC RELATIONS

Clark's Cases and Problems on Domestic Relations, 3rd Ed., 1153 pages, 1980 (Casebook)

Clark's Hornbook on Domestic Relations, 754 pages, 1968 (Text)

Krause's Cases and Materials on Family Law, 2nd Ed., 1221 pages, 1983 (Casebook)

Krause's Family Law in a Nutshell, 400 pages, 1977 (Text)

Krauskopf's Cases on Property Division at Marriage Dissolution, 250 pages, 1984 (Casebook)

EDUCATION LAW

Alexander and Alexander's The Law of Schools, Students and Teachers in a Nutshell, approximately 395 pages, 1984 (Text)

Morris' The Constitution and American Education, 2nd Ed., 992 pages, 1980 (Casebook)

EMPLOYMENT DISCRIMINATION

Player's Cases and Materials on Employment Discrimination Law, 2nd Ed., approximately 675 pages, 1984 (Casebook)

Player's Federal Law of Employment Discrimination in a Nutshell, 2nd Ed., 402 pages, 1981 (Text)

See also Women and the Law

ENERGY AND NATURAL RESOURCES LAW

Rodgers' Cases and Materials on Energy and Natural Resources Law, 2nd Ed., 877 pages, 1983 (Casebook)

Selected Environmental Law Statutes, 768 pages, 1983

Tomain's Energy Law in a Nutshell, 338 pages, 1981 (Text)

See also Environmental Law, Oil and Gas, Water Law

ENVIRONMENTAL LAW

Bonine and McGarity's Cases and Materials on the Law of Environment and Pollution, approximately 892 pages, 1984 (Casebook)

Findley and Farber's Cases and Materials on Environmental Law, 738 pages, 1981, with 1983 Supplement (Casebook)

Findley and Farber's Environmental Law in a Nutshell, 343 pages, 1983 (Text)

ENVIROMENTAL LAW—Continued

Hanks, Tarlock and Hanks' Cases on Environmental Law and Policy, 1242 pages, 1974, with 1976 Supplement (Casebook)

Rodgers' Hornbook on Environmental Law, 956 pages, 1977 (Text)

Selected Environmental Law Statutes, 768 pages, 1983

See also Energy and Natural Resources Law, Water Law

EQUITY

See Remedies

ESTATES

See Trusts and Estates

ESTATE PLANNING

Kurtz' Cases, Materials and Problems on Family Estate Planning, 853 pages, 1983 (Casebook)

Lynn's Introduction to Estate Planning, in a Nutshell, 3rd Ed., 370 pages, 1983 (Text)

See also Taxation

EVIDENCE

Broun and Meisenholder's Problems in Evidence, 2nd Ed., 304 pages, 1981 (Problem book)

Cleary and Strong's Cases, Materials and Problems on Evidence, 3rd Ed., 1143 pages, 1981 (Casebook)

Federal Rules of Evidence for United States Courts and Magistrates, 327 pages, 1983

Graham's Federal Rules of Evidence in a Nutshell, 429 pages, 1981 (Text)

Kimball's Programmed Materials on Problems in Evidence, 380 pages, 1978 (Problem book)

Lempert and Saltzburg's A Modern Approach to Evidence: Text, Problems, Transcripts and Cases, 2nd Ed., 1296 pages, 1983 (Casebook)

Lilly's Introduction to the Law of Evidence, 486 pages, 1978 (Text)

McCormick, Elliott and Sutton's Cases and Materials on Evidence, 5th Ed., 1212 pages, 1981 (Casebook)

McCormick's Hornbook on Evidence, 3rd Ed., Student Ed., approximately 1006 pages, 1984 (Text)

Rothstein's Evidence, State and Federal Rules in a Nutshell, 2nd Ed., 514 pages, 1981 (Text)

Saltzburg's Evidence Supplement: Rules, Statutes, Commentary, 245 pages, 1980 (Casebook Supplement)

FEDERAL JURISDICTION AND PROCEDURE

Currie's Cases and Materials on Federal Courts, 3rd Ed., 1042 pages, 1982 (Casebook)

LAW SCHOOL PUBLICATIONS—Continued

**FEDERAL JURISDICTION AND PROCE-
DURE**—Continued

Currie's Federal Jurisdiction in a Nutshell,
2nd Ed., 258 pages, 1981 (Text)

Federal Rules of Civil-Appellate-Criminal
Procedure—West Law School Edition,
343 pages, 1983

Forrester and Moye's Cases and Materials
on Federal Jurisdiction and Procedure,
3rd Ed., 917 pages, 1977 with 1981 Supplement (Casebook)

Redish's Cases, Comments and Questions on
Federal Courts, 878 pages, 1983 (Casebook)

Vetri and Merrill's Federal Courts, Problems
and Materials, 2nd Ed., approximately
250 pages, 1984

Wright's Hornbook on Federal Courts, 4th
Ed., Student Ed., 870 pages, 1983 (Text)

FUTURE INTERESTS

See Trusts and Estates

**HOUSING AND URBAN DEVELOP-
MENT**

Berger's Cases and Materials on Housing,
2nd Ed., 254 pages, 1973 (Casebook)—
reprint from Cooper et al. Cases on Law
and Poverty, 2nd Ed., 1973

See also Land Use

IMMIGRATION LAW

Weissbrodt's Immigration Law and Procedure in a Nutshell, approximately 337
pages, 1984 (Text)

INDIAN LAW

See American Indian Law

INSURANCE

Dobbyn's Insurance Law in a Nutshell, 281
pages, 1981 (Text)

Keeton's Cases on Basic Insurance Law, 2nd
Ed., 1086 pages, 1977

Keeton's Basic Text on Insurance Law, 712
pages, 1971 (Text)

Keeton's Case Supplement to Keeton's Basic
Text on Insurance Law, 334 pages, 1978
(Casebook)

Keeton's Programmed Problems in Insurance Law, 243 pages, 1972 (Text Supplement)

York and Whelan's Cases, Materials and
Problems on Insurance Law, 715 pages,
1982 (Casebook)

INTERNATIONAL LAW

Henkin, Pugh, Schachter and Smit's Cases
and Materials on International Law, 2nd
Ed., 1152 pages, 1980, with Documents
Supplement (Casebook)

INTERNATIONAL LAW—Continued

Jackson's Legal Problems of International
Economic Relations, 1097 pages, 1977,
with Documents Supplement (Casebook)

Kirgis' International Organizations in Their
Legal Setting, 1016 pages, 1977, with
1981 Supplement (Casebook)

Weston, Falk and D'Amato's International
Law and World Order—A Problem Oriented Coursebook, 1195 pages, 1980,
with Documents Supplement (Casebook)

Wilson's International Business Transactions
in a Nutshell, 2nd Ed., 476 pages, 1984
(Text)

INTERVIEWING AND COUNSELING

Binder and Price's Interviewing and Counseling, 232 pages, 1977 (Text)

Shaffer's Interviewing and Counseling in a
Nutshell, 353 pages, 1976 (Text)

INTRODUCTION TO LAW

Dobbyn's So You Want to go to Law School,
Revised First Edition, 206 pages, 1976
(Text)

Hegland's Introduction to the Study and
Practice of Law in a Nutshell, 418 pages,
1983 (Text)

Kelso and Kelso's Studying Law: An Introduction, approximately 585 pages, 1984
(Coursebook)

Kinyon's Introduction to Law Study and Law
Examinations in a Nutshell, 389 pages,
1971 (Text)

See also Legal Method and Legal System

JUDICIAL ADMINISTRATION

Carrington, Meador and Rosenberg's Justice
on Appeal, 263 pages, 1976 (Casebook)

Nelson's Cases and Materials on Judicial
Administration and the Administration of
Justice, 1032 pages, 1974 (Casebook)

JURISPRUDENCE

Christie's Text and Readings on Jurisprudence—The Philosophy of Law, 1056
pages, 1973 (Casebook)

JUVENILE JUSTICE

Fox's Cases and Materials on Modern Juvenile Justice, 2nd Ed., 960 pages, 1981
(Casebook)

Fox's Juvenile Courts in a Nutshell, 3rd Ed.,
approximately 290 pages, 1984 (Text)

LABOR LAW

Gorman's Basic Text on Labor Law—Unioni-
zation and Collective Bargaining, 914
pages, 1976 (Text)

Leslie's Labor Law in a Nutshell, 403 pages,
1979 (Text)

Nolan's Labor Arbitration Law and Practice
in a Nutshell, 358 pages, 1979 (Text)

LAW SCHOOL PUBLICATIONS—Continued

LABOR LAW—Continued

Oberer, Hanslowe and Andersen's Cases and Materials on Labor Law—Collective Bargaining in a Free Society, 2nd Ed., 1168 pages, 1979, with 1979 Statutory Supplement and 1982 Case Supplement (Casebook)

See also Employment Discrimination, Social Legislation

LAND FINANCE

See Real Estate Transactions

LAND USE

Hagman's Cases on Public Planning and Control of Urban and Land Development, 2nd Ed., 1301 pages, 1980 (Casebook)

Hagman's Hornbook on Urban Planning and Land Development Control Law, 706 pages, 1971 (Text)

Wright and Gitelman's Cases and Materials on Land Use, 3rd Ed., 1300 pages, 1982 (Casebook)

Wright and Webber's Land Use in a Nutshell, 316 pages, 1978 (Text)

See also Housing and Urban Development

LAW AND ECONOMICS

Goetz' Cases and Materials on Law and Economics, 547 pages, 1984 (Casebook)

Manne's The Economics of Legal Relationships—Readings in the Theory of Property Rights, 660 pages, 1975 (Text)

See also Antitrust, Regulated Industries

LAW AND MEDICINE—PSYCHIATRY

Cohen's Cases and Materials on the Law of Deprivation of Liberty: A Study in Social Control, 755 pages, 1980 (Casebook)

King's The Law of Medical Malpractice in a Nutshell, 340 pages, 1977 (Text)

Shapiro and Spece's Problems, Cases and Materials on Bioethics and Law, 892 pages, 1981 (Casebook)

Sharpe, Fiscina and Head's Cases on Law and Medicine, 882 pages, 1978 (Casebook)

LEGAL HISTORY

Presser and Zainaldin's Cases on Law and American History, 855 pages, 1980 (Casebook)

See also Legal Method and Legal System

LEGAL METHOD AND LEGAL SYSTEM

Aldisert's Readings, Materials and Cases in the Judicial Process, 948 pages, 1976 (Casebook)

LEGAL METHOD AND LEGAL SYSTEM—Continued

Bodenheimer, Oakley and Love's Readings and Cases on an Introduction to the Anglo-American Legal System, 161 pages, 1980 (Casebook)

Davies and Lawry's Institutions and Methods of the Law—Introductory Teaching Materials, 547 pages, 1982 (Casebook)

Dvorkin, Himmelstein and Lesnick's Becoming a Lawyer: A Humanistic Perspective on Legal Education and Professionalism, 211 pages, 1981 (Text)

Fryer and Orentlicher's Cases and Materials on Legal Method and Legal System, 1043 pages, 1967 (Casebook)

Greenberg's Judicial Process and Social Change, 666 pages, 1977 (Coursebook)

Kempin's Historical Introduction to Anglo-American Law in a Nutshell, 2nd Ed., 280 pages, 1973 (Text)

Kimball's Historical Introduction to the Legal System, 610 pages, 1966 (Casebook)

Mashaw and Merrill's Introduction to the American Public Law System, 1095 pages, 1975, with 1980 Supplement (Casebook)

Murphy's Cases and Materials on Introduction to Law—Legal Process and Procedure, 772 pages, 1977 (Casebook)

Reynolds' Judicial Process in a Nutshell, 292 pages, 1980 (Text)

See also Legal Research and Writing

LEGAL NEGOTIATION

Edwards and White's Problems, Readings and Materials on the Lawyer as a Negotiator, 484 pages, 1977 (Casebook)

Williams' Legal Negotiation and Settlement, 207 pages, 1983 (Coursebook)

LEGAL PROFESSION

Aronson's Problems in Professional Responsibility, 280 pages, 1978 (Problem book)

Aronson and Weckstein's Professional Responsibility in a Nutshell, 399 pages, 1980 (Text)

Mellinkoff's The Conscience of a Lawyer, 304 pages, 1973 (Text)

Mellinkoff's Lawyers and the System of Justice, 983 pages, 1976 (Casebook)

Pirsig and Kirwin's Cases and Materials on Professional Responsibility, 4th Ed., approximately 650 pages, 1984 (Casebook)

Schwartz and Wydick's Problems in Legal Ethics, 285 pages, 1983 (Casebook)

Selected Statutes, Rules and Standards on the Legal Profession, 249 pages, 1984

Smith's Preventing Legal Malpractice, 142 pages, 1981 (Text)

LEGAL RESEARCH AND WRITING

Cohen's Legal Research in a Nutshell, 3rd Ed., 415 pages, 1978 (Text)

LAW SCHOOL PUBLICATIONS—Continued

LEGAL RESEARCH AND WRITING—Continued

Cohen and Berring's How to Find the Law, 8th Ed., 790 pages, 1983. Problem book by Foster and Kelly available (Casebook)

Cohen and Berring's Finding the Law, 8th Ed., Abridged Ed., 556 pages, 1984 (Casebook)

Dickerson's Materials on Legal Drafting, 425 pages, 1981 (Casebook)

Felsenfeld and Siegel's Writing Contracts in Plain English, 290 pages, 1981 (Text)

Gopen's Writing From a Legal Perspective, 225 pages, 1981 (Text)

Mellinkoff's Legal Writing—Sense and Nonsense, 242 pages, 1982 (Text)

Rombauer's Legal Problem Solving—Analysis, Research and Writing, 4th Ed., 424 pages, 1983 (Coursebook)

Squires and Rombauer's Legal Writing in a Nutshell, 294 pages, 1982 (Text)

Statsky's Legal Research, Writing and Analysis, 2nd Ed., 167 pages, 1982 (Coursebook)

Statsky's Legislative Analysis: How to Use Statutes and Regulations, 2nd Ed., 217 pages, 1984 (Text)

Statsky and Wernet's Case Analysis and Fundamentals of Legal Writing, 2nd Ed., 441 pages, 1984 (Text)

Teply's Programmed Materials on Legal Research and Citation, 334 pages, 1982. Student Library Exercises available (Coursebook)

Weihofen's Legal Writing Style, 2nd Ed., 332 pages, 1980 (Text)

LEGISLATION

Davies' Legislative Law and Process in a Nutshell, 279 pages, 1975 (Text)

Nutting and Dickerson's Cases and Materials on Legislation, 5th Ed., 744 pages, 1978 (Casebook)

Statsky's Legislative Analysis: How to Use Statutes and Regulations, 2nd Ed., 217 pages, 1984 (Text)

LOCAL GOVERNMENT

McCarthy's Local Government Law in a Nutshell, 2nd Ed., 404 pages, 1983 (Text)

Michelman and Sandalow's Cases-Comments-Questions on Government in Urban Areas, 1216 pages, 1970, with 1972 Supplement (Casebook)

Reynolds' Hornbook on Local Government Law, 860 pages, 1982 (Text)

Stason and Kauper's Cases and Materials on Municipal Corporations, 3rd Ed., 692 pages, 1959 (Casebook)

Valente's Cases and Materials on Local Government Law, 2nd Ed., 980 pages, 1980 with 1982 Supplement (Casebook)

MASS COMMUNICATION LAW

Gillmor and Barron's Cases and Comment on Mass Communication Law, 4th Ed., approximately 1100 pages, 1984 (Casebook)

Ginsburg's Regulation of Broadcasting: Law and Policy Towards Radio, Television and Cable Communications, 741 pages, 1979, with 1983 Supplement (Casebook)

Zuckman and Gayne's Mass Communications Law in a Nutshell, 2nd Ed., 473 pages, 1983 (Text)

MILITARY LAW

Shanor and Terrell's Military Law in a Nutshell, 378 pages, 1980 (Text)

MORTGAGES

See Real Estate Transactions

NATURAL RESOURCES LAW

See Energy and Natural Resources Law, Environmental Law, Oil and Gas, Water Law

OFFICE PRACTICE

Hegland's Trial and Practice Skills in a Nutshell, 346 pages, 1978 (Text)

Strong and Clark's Law Office Management, 424 pages, 1974 (Casebook)

See also Legal Interviewing and Counseling, Legal Negotiation

OIL AND GAS

Hemingway's Hornbook on Oil and Gas, 2nd Ed., Student Ed., 543 pages, 1983 (Text)

Huie, Woodward and Smith's Cases and Materials on Oil and Gas, 2nd Ed., 955 pages, 1972 (Casebook)

Lowe's Oil and Gas Law in a Nutshell, 443 pages, 1983 (Text)

See also Energy and Natural Resources Law

PARTNERSHIP

See Agency—Partnership

PATENT AND COPYRIGHT LAW

Choate and Francis' Cases and Materials on Patent Law, 2nd Ed., 1110 pages, 1981 (Casebook)

Miller and Davis' Intellectual Property—Patents, Trademarks and Copyright in a Nutshell, 428 pages, 1983 (Text)

Nimmer's Cases on Copyright and Other Aspects of Law Pertaining to Literary, Musical and Artistic Works, 2nd Ed., 1023 pages, 1979 (Casebook)

POVERTY LAW

Brudno's Poverty, Inequality, and the Law: Cases-Commentary-Analysis, 934 pages, 1976 (Casebook)

LAW SCHOOL PUBLICATIONS—Continued

POVERTY LAW—Continued

LaFrance, Schroeder, Bennett and Boyd's Hornbook on Law of the Poor, 558 pages, 1973 (Text)

See also Social Legislation

PRODUCTS LIABILITY

Noel and Phillips' Cases on Products Liability, 2nd Ed., 821 pages, 1982 (Casebook)

Noel and Phillips' Products Liability in a Nutshell, 2nd Ed., 341 pages, 1981 (Text)

PROPERTY

Aigler, Smith and Tefft's Cases on Property, 2 volumes, 1339 pages, 1960 (Casebook)

Bernhardt's Real Property in a Nutshell, 2nd Ed., 448 pages, 1981 (Text)

Boyer's Survey of the Law of Property, 766 pages, 1981 (Text)

Browder, Cunningham and Smith's Cases on Basic Property Law, 4th Ed., approximately 1368 pages, 1984 (Casebook)

Bruce, Ely and Bostick's Cases and Materials on Modern Property Law, approximately 1000 pages, 1984 (Casebook)

Burby's Hornbook on Real Property, 3rd Ed., 490 pages, 1965 (Text)

Burke's Personal Property in a Nutshell, 322 pages, 1983 (Text)

Chused's A Modern Approach to Property: Cases-Notes-Materials, 1069 pages, 1978 with 1980 Supplement (Casebook)

Cohen's Materials for a Basic Course in Property, 526 pages, 1978 (Casebook)

Cunningham, Whitman and Stoebuck's Hornbook on the Law of Property, Student Ed., approximately 928 pages, 1984 (Text)

Donahue, Kauper and Martin's Cases on Property, 2nd Ed., 1362 pages, 1983 (Casebook)

Hill's Landlord and Tenant Law in a Nutshell, 319 pages, 1979 (Text)

Moynihan's Introduction to Real Property, 254 pages, 1962 (Text)

Phipps' Titles in a Nutshell, 277 pages, 1968 (Text)

Uniform Land Transactions Act, Uniform Simplification of Land Transfers Act, Uniform Condominium Act, 1977 Official Text with Comments, 462 pages, 1978

See also Housing and Urban Development, Real Estate Transactions, Land Use

REAL ESTATE TRANSACTIONS

Bruce's Real Estate Finance in a Nutshell, 292 pages, 1979 (Text)

Maxwell, Riesenfeld, Hetland and Warren's Cases on California Security Transactions in Land, 3rd Ed., approximately 710 pages, 1984 (Casebook)

REAL ESTATE TRANSACTIONS—Continued

Nelson and Whitman's Cases on Real Estate Transfer, Finance and Development, 2nd Ed., 1114 pages, 1981, with 1983 Supplement (Casebook)

Osborne's Cases and Materials on Secured Transactions, 559 pages, 1967 (Casebook)

Osborne, Nelson and Whitman's Hornbook on Real Estate Finance Law, 3rd Ed., 885 pages, 1979 (Text)

REGULATED INDUSTRIES

Gellhorn and Pierce's Regulated Industries in a Nutshell, 394 pages, 1982 (Text)

Morgan's Cases and Materials on Economic Regulation of Business, 830 pages, 1976, with 1978 Supplement (Casebook)

Pozen's Financial Institutions: Cases, Materials and Problems on Investment Management, 844 pages, 1978 (Casebook)

See also Mass Communication Law, Banking Law

REMEDIES

Dobbs' Hornbook on Remedies, 1067 pages, 1973 (Text)

Dobbs' Problems in Remedies, 137 pages, 1974 (Problem book)

Dobbyn's Injunctions in a Nutshell, 264 pages, 1974 (Text)

Friedman's Contract Remedies in a Nutshell, 323 pages, 1981 (Text)

Leavell, Love and Nelson's Cases and Materials on Equitable Remedies and Restitution, 3rd Ed., 704 pages, 1980 (Casebook)

McCormick's Hornbook on Damages, 811 pages, 1935 (Text)

O'Connell's Remedies in a Nutshell, 364 pages, 1977 (Text)

York and Bauman's Cases and Materials on Remedies, 3rd Ed., 1250 pages, 1979 (Casebook)

REVIEW MATERIALS

Ballantine's Problems

Black Letter Series

Smith's Review Series

West's Review Covering Multistate Subjects

SECURITIES REGULATION

Hazen's Hornbook on The Law of Securities Regulation, approximately 520 pages, 1984 (Text)

Ratner's Securities Regulation: Materials for a Basic Course, 2nd Ed., 1050 pages, 1980 with 1982 Supplement (Casebook)

Ratner's Securities Regulation in a Nutshell, 2nd Ed., 322 pages, 1982 (Text)

Selected Securities and Business Planning Statutes, Rules and Forms, 485 pages, 1982

LAW SCHOOL PUBLICATIONS—Continued

SOCIAL LEGISLATION

Brudno's Income Redistribution Theories and Programs: Cases-Commentary-Analyses, 480 pages, 1977 (Casebook)—reprint from Brudno's Poverty, Inequality and the Law, 1976

Hood and Hardy's Workers' Compensation and Employee Protection Laws in a Nutshell, 274 pages, 1984 (Text)

LaFrance's Welfare Law: Structure and Entitlement in a Nutshell, 455 pages, 1979 (Text)

Malone, Plant and Little's Cases on Workers' Compensation and Employment Rights, 2nd Ed., 951 pages, 1980 (Casebook)

See also Poverty Law

TAXATION

Dodge's Federal Taxation of Estates, Trusts and Gifts: Principles and Planning, 771 pages, 1981 with 1982 Supplement (Casebook)

Garbis and Struntz' Cases and Materials on Tax Procedure and Tax Fraud, 829 pages, 1982 with 1984 Supplement (Casebook)

Gunn's Cases and Materials on Federal Income Taxation of Individuals, 785 pages, 1981 with 1983 Supplement (Casebook)

Hellerstein and Hellerstein's Cases on State and Local Taxation, 4th Ed., 1041 pages, 1978 with 1982 Supplement (Casebook)

Kahn's Handbook on Basic Corporate Taxation, 3rd Ed., Student Ed., 614 pages, 1981 with 1983 Supplement (Text)

Kahn and Gann's Corporate Taxation and Taxation of Partnerships and Partners, 2nd Ed., approximately 1300 pages, 1984 (Casebook)

Kragen and McNulty's Cases and Materials on Federal Income Taxation, Vol. I: Taxation of Individuals, 3rd Ed., 1283 pages, 1979 with 1983 Supplement (Casebook)

Kragen and McNulty's Cases and Materials on Federal Income Taxation, Vol. II: Taxation of Corporations, Shareholders, Partnerships and Partners, 3rd Ed., 989 pages, 1981 with 1983 Supplement (Casebook)

McNulty's Federal Estate and Gift Taxation in a Nutshell, 3rd Ed., 509 pages, 1983 (Text)

McNulty's Federal Income Taxation of Individuals in a Nutshell, 3rd Ed., 487 pages, 1983 (Text)

Posin's Hornbook on Federal Income Taxation of Individuals, Student Ed., 491 pages, 1983 (Text)

Rice's Problems and Materials in Federal Estate and Gift Taxation, 3rd Ed., 474 pages, 1978 (Casebook)

Rice and Solomon's Problems and Materials in Federal Income Taxation, 3rd Ed., 670 pages, 1979 (Casebook)

TAXATION—Continued

Rose and Raskind's Advanced Federal Income Taxation: Corporate Transactions—Cases, Materials and Problems, 955 pages, 1978 (Casebook)

Selected Federal Taxation Statutes and Regulations, 1255 pages, 1983

Sobeloff and Weidenbruch's Federal Income Taxation of Corporations and Stockholders in a Nutshell, 362 pages, 1981 (Text)

TORTS

Christie's Cases and Materials on the Law of Torts, 1264 pages, 1983 (Casebook)

Green, Pedrick, Rahl, Thode, Hawkins, Smith and Treece's Cases and Materials on Torts, 2nd Ed., 1360 pages, 1977 (Casebook)

Green, Pedrick, Rahl, Thode, Hawkins, Smith, and Treece's Advanced Torts: Injuries to Business, Political and Family Interests, 2nd Ed., 544 pages, 1977 (Casebook)—reprint from Green, et al. Cases and Materials on Torts, 2nd Ed., 1977

Keeton, Keeton, Sargentich and Steiner's Cases and Materials on Torts, and Accident Law, 1360 pages, 1983 (Casebook)

Kionka's Torts in a Nutshell: Injuries to Persons and Property, 434 pages, 1977 (Text)

Malone's Torts in a Nutshell: Injuries to Family, Social and Trade Relations, 358 pages, 1979 (Text)

Prosser and Keeton's Hornbook on Torts, 5th Ed., Student Ed., approximately 1052 pages, 1984 (Text)

Shapo's Cases on Tort and Compensation Law, 1244 pages, 1976 (Casebook)

See also Products Liability

TRADE REGULATION

McManis' Unfair Trade Practices in a Nutshell, 444 pages, 1982 (Text)

Oppenheim, Weston, Maggs and Schechter's Cases and Materials on Unfair Trade Practices and Consumer Protection, 4th Ed., 1038 pages, 1983 (Casebook)

See also Antitrust, Regulated Industries

TRIAL AND APPELLATE ADVOCACY

Appellate Advocacy, Handbook of, 249 pages, 1980 (Text)

Bergman's Trial Advocacy in a Nutshell, 402 pages, 1979 (Text)

Binder and Bergman's Fact Investigation: From Hypothesis to Proof, approximately 350 pages, 1984 (Coursebook)

Goldberg's The First Trial (Where Do I Sit?) (What Do I Say?) in a Nutshell, 396 pages, 1982 (Text)

Hegland's Trial and Practice Skills in a Nutshell, 346 pages, 1978 (Text)

LAW SCHOOL PUBLICATIONS—Continued

TRIAL AND APPELLATE ADVOCACY—Continued

Hornstein's Appellate Advocacy in a Nutshell, approximately 270 pages, 1984 (Text)

Jeans' Handbook on Trial Advocacy, Student Ed., 473 pages, 1975 (Text)

McElhaney's Effective Litigation, 457 pages, 1974 (Casebook)

Nolan's Cases and Materials on Trial Practice, 518 pages, 1981 (Casebook)

Parnell and Shellhaas' Cases, Exercises and Problems for Trial Advocacy, 171 pages, 1982 (Coursebook)

Sonsteng, Haydock and Boyd's The Trialbook: A Total System for Preparation and Presentation of a Case, Student Ed., approximately 400 pages, 1984 (Coursebook)

TRUSTS AND ESTATES

Atkinson's Hornbook on Wills, 2nd Ed., 975 pages, 1953 (Text)

Averill's Uniform Probate Code in a Nutshell, 425 pages, 1978 (Text)

Bogert's Hornbook on Trusts, 5th Ed., 726 pages, 1973 (Text)

Clark, Lusky and Murphy's Cases and Materials on Gratuitous Transfers, 2nd Ed., 1102 pages, 1977 (Casebook)

Gulliver's Cases and Materials on Future Interests, 624 pages, 1959 (Casebook)

Gulliver's Introduction to the Law of Future Interests, 87 pages, 1959 (Casebook)—reprint from Gulliver's Cases and Materials on Future Interests, 1959

McGovern's Cases and Materials on Wills, Trusts and Future Interests: An Introduction to Estate Planning, 750 pages, 1983 (Casebook)

TRUSTS AND ESTATES—Continued

Mennell's Cases and Materials on California Decedent's Estates, 566 pages, 1973 (Casebook)

Mennell's Wills and Trusts in a Nutshell, 392 pages, 1979 (Text)

Powell's The Law of Future Interests in California, 91 pages, 1980 (Text)

Simes' Hornbook on Future Interests, 2nd Ed., 355 pages, 1966 (Text)

Turrentine's Cases and Text on Wills and Administration, 2nd Ed., 483 pages, 1962 (Casebook)

Uniform Probate Code, 5th Ed., Official Text With Comments, 384 pages, 1977

Waggoner's Future Interests in a Nutshell, 361 pages, 1981 (Text)

WATER LAW

Getches' Water Law in a Nutshell, approximately 400 pages, 1984 (Text)

Trelease's Cases and Materials on Water Law, 3rd Ed., 833 pages, 1979, with 1984 Supplement (Casebook)

See also Energy and Natural Resources Law, Environmental Law

WILLS

See Trusts and Estates

WOMEN AND THE LAW

Kay's Text, Cases and Materials on Sex-Based Discrimination, 2nd Ed., 1045 pages, 1981, with 1983 Supplement (Casebook)

Thomas' Sex Discrimination in a Nutshell, 399 pages, 1982 (Text)

See also Employment Discrimination

WORKERS' COMPENSATION

See Social Legislation

XII

CASES AND PROBLEMS

ON

DOMESTIC RELATIONS

THIRD EDITION

By

HOMER H. CLARK, Jr.
Professor of Law, University of Colorado

AMERICAN CASEBOOK SERIES

ST. PAUL, MINN.
WEST PUBLISHING CO.
1980

Library of Congress Cataloging In Publication Data

Clark, Homer Harrison, 1918–
    Cases and problems on domestic relations.

    (American casebook series)
    Includes index.
    1.   Domestic relations—United States—Cases.
I. Title. II. Series.
KF504.C545   1980   346.7301'5   80–19763

ISBN 0–8299–2104–4

Clark, Cs on Dom.Rel.3rd Ed. A.C.B.

2nd Reprint—1984

ACKNOWLEDGMENTS

One of the advantages of editing a revised edition of a casebook is that the generosity of colleagues who used earlier editions enables the editor to make improvements which otherwise might be missed. This edition has benefited especially from the informed criticisms and suggestions of Professor Paul M. Kurtz of the University of Georgia Law School and I am deeply grateful for his assistance. As with earlier editions, Professor Norton Steuben has reviewed and criticized the material on taxation, help which is particularly welcome to a non-tax lawyer. My appreciation also goes to my two student research assistants, Rhonda Smith and Kenton Kuhlman, whose work saved me many hours of labor in the library.

The staff of the University of Colorado law library, Professor Oscar Miller, Lois Calvert, Rhonda Carlson and others, have been unfailingly cooperative in obtaining materials and making them easily available for use in this book. I am most grateful to them.

Major assistance at all stages of the writing of this edition has been provided by my wife, Jean Clark. Her unfailing encouragement was largely responsible for my being able to meet the publisher's deadline and her energetic review of the manuscript corrected many errors.

I should like to acknowledge with gratitude the permission to quote from their works which has been generously extended by the following authors and publishers:

Professor Robert J. Levy, The Rights of Parents, 1976 B.Y.U.L.Rev. 693.

Professor Bruce Hafen, Children's Liberation and the New Egalitarianism: Some Reservations About Abandoning Youth to Their "Rights", 1976 B.Y.U.L.Rev. 606.

Professor Michael Wald, State Intervention on Behalf of "Neglected" Children: A Search for Realistic Standards, 27 Stan.L.Rev. 985 (1975).

Professor Sanford Katz, Freeing Children for Permanent Placement Through a Model Act, 12 Fam.L.Q. 203 (1978). Reprinted with the permission of Sanford N. Katz, Editor-in-Chief of the Family Law Quarterly.

HOMER H. CLARK, JR.

July, 1980

*

SUMMARY OF CONTENTS

*

TABLE OF CONTENTS

TABLE OF CONTENTS

TABLE OF CONTENTS

*

TABLE OF CASES

The principal cases are in italic type. Cases cited or discussed are in roman type. References are to Pages.

TABLE OF CASES

TABLE OF CASES

TABLE OF CASES

TABLE OF CASES

TABLE OF CASES

TABLE OF CASES

TABLE OF CASES

TABLE OF CASES

CASES AND PROBLEMS

ON

DOMESTIC RELATIONS

INTRODUCTION

"Of all actions of a mans life, his marriage does least concerne other people, yet of all accons of our life tis most medled with by other people." John Selden, Table Talk, 75 (Pollock ed. 1927).

A. SCOPE OF THE COURSE

Domestic relations, or family law as it is often called nowadays, is, perhaps more than other subjects in the law school curriculum, defined differently by different persons and by different casebooks. One reason for this is that the law impinges on family relationships at so many different points that in order to keep a course on domestic relations within workable limits large segments of this law have to be allocated to other subjects and other courses. So, for example, it is accepted that the law of wills and estates is not included in such courses even though its importance for families is obvious. The same is true of the law of community and other joint interests in property, the law of workmen's compensation, the law of social security or the law of estate and gift taxation. On the other hand, there is disagreement on what should be done with the large and still growing body of law concerning juvenile courts and juvenile delinquency, whose direct impact on the family is plain. There is similar disagreement over how far questions of the conflict of laws should be permitted to intrude into courses on domestic relations. These questions are resolved for the present edition of this casebook by including those aspects of juvenile law and of conflicts which have the closest and most direct relation to family problems. With respect to the law of conflicts especially this approach is based on the strongly held opinion that the conflict of laws problems of marriage and divorce can be more satisfactorily solved by concentrating on their effects on the family rather than on analogies to conflicts rules relating to contracts or torts or general principles of jurisdiction. In other words, the pressures operating are family law pressures rather than broad considerations taken from other applications of conflict of laws.

For different reasons there is also a perennial debate over the extent to which domestic relations is a proper subject for lawyers at all. In practice the question is to what extent and how people with various kinds of training other than legal should participate in the administration of the divorce laws, the juvenile laws, the adoption laws and other aspects of domestic relations. In the law school world the debate, now of nearly forty years' duration, has concerned the extent and method of injection of non-legal materials into the course on domestic relations. It is odd that this debate has not after so long produced any generally accepted solutions to the questions of course content and method. Diversity still flourishes. That is not a bad thing except so far as it diverts attention to method from more important matters. The first edition of this casebook included a few non-legal materials, but they proved largely ineffective for teaching purposes. The use of any such materials is full of risks in the hands of anyone not expert in the particular subject. Superficiality is the most obvious risk, but there is always the danger that one will fail to take account of the hostilities among the various schools of psychiatry, say, or between psychiatry and psychology, or that the significance of recent developments will be overemphasized or not sufficiently appreciated, or that one isolated expert opinion will be taken as representative of all. Some of these risks have to be run because no one concerned with domestic relations can shut out what is going on in the other disciplines which study that subject. Attitudes of caution and scepticism are essential, and are reflected in the questions which this edition raises concerning both legal and non-legal materials. In addition, the effort has been made to apply the non-legal materials as precisely as possible to specific legal problems, so that their relevance and soundness can be tested as thoroughly as is possible for a layman.

The heart of domestic relations has been viewed in this book as the formation, internal conflicts and dissolution of families. The legal categories are antenuptial contracts, marriage, divorce, adoption, and such hard to classify cases as intra-family torts, interference with consortium, claims for maintenance and support asserted by one member of the family against another, conflicts between parents and children, and the legal capacities of children and married women. Some subjects, like breach of promise of marriage, which were covered at some length in the first edition have either been eliminated or, by means of text discussion, drastically reduced in scope, on the theory that they are no longer of practical importance. In all sections there has been an attempt to raise the claims that are being made concerning sex roles in society, even at the risk that many of these issues which look so important to us now may, in view of the insubstantial and faddish nature of American society, turn out to be ephemeral after all.

The arrangement of the book is suggested by experience in using the first edition. Very broadly, it may be seen that there are two subjects here. One is marriage and divorce, the relationship between the spouses. The other is the welfare of children. Obviously there is more than enough material in the book for a single course, the purpose being to offer some opportunity for variety in coverage and emphasis. In one year one might emphasize marriage and divorce, while in another the major part of the time available might be spent on Chapter 5, most of which is devoted to parent-child relationships and to the state's power over those relationships.

The book is also designed to leave a substantial part of the learning to the student, both by the textual discussion of some subjects and by the inclusion of problems which should illuminate the main cases if the student spends the time required to work them out. The intention is to leave to the instructor a large amount of leeway in what he spends class time on, and at the same time to give the student the materials with which to acquire a broad acquaintence with the subject of domestic relations.

B. HISTORICAL BACKGROUND OF MARRIAGE AND DIVORCE

A brief review of some of the historical sources of this subject is desirable, even in this unhistorical age, to show by what steps we arrived at the present state of the law and, more importantly, to expose the roots of some of the emotions and prejudices we all bring to discussions of marital questions. This might begin with Roman law. Under the Republic, in the centuries before Christ, marriage was a matter of fact rather than a matter of law. What this meant was that the consent of the parties to live together produced a marriage. No prescribed forms were necessary. In addition, however, marriage was usually accompanied by the transfer of the woman from the family of her father into that of her husband, and subject to the power of her husband. This transfer could be accomplished either by a religious ceremony, or by a ritual purchase of the wife by the husband, or by the wife's remaining married to the husband without interruption for one year. Any of these forms of transfer had the effect of giving the husband broad powers over the wife's property and over her person. In this early period divorce also could be accomplished without legal formalities, merely by the separation of the parties with the intention of ending the marriage. But the power of the husband over the wife's person and property could only be dissolved by certain formalities, generally available at this early period only to the husband, and as a result divorce was uncommon.

By the time of Augustus (A.D. 14) marriage and divorce had become wholly free, the subjection of the wife to the husband having largely disappeared and the ceremonies by which her transfer into his power was effected having fallen into disuse. The wife's property remained her own. The marriage occurred through the consent of the parties without more, although there was often a ceremony of betrothal and ceremonies marking the occurrence of the marriage. Certain relationships by blood or marriage, not very different from later English incest prohibitions, were held to disqualify individuals from marriage. Divorce during this period could be accomplished at the will of either party without legal proceedings, and was quite common.

Roman marriages, both the early patriarchal and the later free versions, were monogamous. Husbands could and sometimes did have concubines, but it was generally forbidden to have simultaneously both a wife and a concubine. Concubinage was socially but not legally recognized. The concubine did not have the status of a wife, nor were her children legitimate.

The appearance of Christianity in the Roman Empire produced changes in the law of marriage and divorce, although these did not occur all at once, and did not go so far as to revolutionize the Roman law. Marriage remained a matter of consent alone, but the circumstances creating impediments to marriage, such as relationships by affinity, were increased. Perhaps the most striking change concerned the Roman law's attitude to divorce. Divorce continued to be available, but attempts were made to discourage it by imposing various penalties such as restrictions upon remarriage or loss of property.

Although Roman law left perceptible traces in the marriage and divorce law of European countries, the canon law, based upon Biblical precepts as elaborated by learned exegesis, was the dominant influence in those countries. That law took the odd position that people ought to marry only in a religious ceremony after publication of banns, but at the same time that a private consensual marriage was valid, as binding as a ceremonial marriage. This was the rule at least from the Twelfth Century until 1563. At that date the Council of Trent, a part of the movement known as the Counter-Reformation, ordained that marriages were not valid unless contracted in the presence of a priest and two witnesses. Until the Reformation, and after it in countries remaining in the Catholic faith, divorce was not permitted.

In England the Catholic Church's law largely displaced earlier, now obscure, Teutonic marriage customs, although as Mssrs. Pollock and Maitland demonstrated, the ceremony of marriage still used in many weddings bears a surprising resemblance to that of the Anglo-Saxons. From a time as early as the Seventh Century the Church's teachings were reflected in the English law. What were those teachings? The two of greatest significance were, first, that matrimony was a divine institution, a sacrament, and, second, that it should therefore be the exclusive province of the spiritual courts. The second of these teachings was not fully accepted in England until after the Conquest, but by the middle of the Twelfth Century the ecclesiastical courts had made good their claim to exclusive jurisdiction over marriage and its incidents. This jurisdiction passed to the Anglican Church at the time of the English Reformation in 1534 and continued until the passage of the Matrimonial Clauses Act of 1857. The effect of these two doctrines was to ensure an extraordinarily conservative body of law, one which was most resistant to change until the middle of the Nineteenth Century and which even then only changed slowly.

The English ecclesiastical law, both before and after the Reformation, regulated marriage in considerable detail. This law recognized as valid not only marriages celebrated by formal religious ceremonies, but two types of informal marriages as well, thereby perhaps evidencing the influence of the Roman law of consensual marriage. One such informal marriage, called sponsalia per verba de praesenti, occurred when the parties made an agreement presently to have each other as husband and wife. This form of marriage based on nothing more than present consent, was entirely valid and would prevail over a later ceremonial marriage which one of the parties attempted to contract with someone else. The other type of informal marriage, known as sponsalia per verba de futuro, required an exchange of promises to marry in the future, followed by later consummation. The marriage was considered effective when it was consummated. Obviously the distinction between these two kinds of informal marriage could be difficult to draw in practice. Considerable litigation in the ecclesiastical courts was concerned with the terms and the meaning of the words which had been exchanged and with the question of whether the parties had consummated their relationship. Clandestine marriages could also be contracted by employing unscrupulous itinerant clergymen to perform them. The area of London near the Fleet prison was the center of this trade in quick marriages to such an extent that they became known as Fleet marriages.

By the middle of the Eighteenth Century it was widely recognized that secret marriages of both the informal and the Fleet variety had produced abuses, such as fraudulent claims that marriage had or had not occurred, bigamous marriages, and great uncertainty in marital relations and in the property rights which often turned on marriage. Since the Council of Trent did not occur until after the English had severed ties with the Catholic Church, its teachings never became effective in England, and these informal and secret marriages continued to be recognized in England until 1753. In that year Lord Hardwicke's Act, 26 Geo. II, c. 33, was passed. That Act required, as a condition upon contracting a valid marriage, that banns be published for three Sundays preceding the ceremony, that marriages be contracted only by religious ceremony in church and that persons under the age of twenty-one obtain the consent of parents or guardians before marrying. The publication of banns could be avoided by obtaining a special license.

Regina v. Millis, 10 Cl. & F. 534, 8 Eng.Rep. 844 (1843) contains opinions stating that informal marriages were never recognized as valid in English law, but the historical evidence, as is demonstrated by Pollock and Maitland in Chapter VII of the second volume of their History of English Law, is to the contrary. Lord Hardwicke's Act did not apply to marriages contracted in Scotland even by English persons, and clandestine marriages continued to be contracted there. The tale of the impecunious fortune-hunter who persuades a young heiress to run off to the Scottish border town of Gretna Green in order to contract a secret marriage, hotly pursued by the lady's father, became part of the folklore of the late Eighteenth and early Nineteenth Centuries.

The canon law also regulated the capacity to marry, imposing numerous disabilities based upon relationships by blood or marriage between the spouses. Broad early rules were narrowed in 1215 to the proposition that marriages within the fourth degree of consanguinity, as computed by the canon law system, were invalid. Somewhat similar prohibitions applied to relationships by affinity, on the theory that one is related to his spouse's relatives. And finally the relation of spiritual kinship, between godfather and godchild or between godfather's daughter and godson might be a disqualification. Marriages could often be found defective under these restrictions and ended by divorce a vinculo, or as we would say today, by annulment. The prohibited degrees of relationship were further narrowed in the reign of Henry VIII, by a statute, 32 Henry VIII, c. 38 (1541), which provided that marriages outside the Levitical degrees would be valid. The reference is to the Eighteenth Chapter of Leviticus, whose graphic but inexplicit language is taken to announce the Biblical incest prohibitions. These roughly include the ascending and descending lines, by consanguinity and affinity, certain collaterals such as uncle-niece and aunt-nephew, and of course siblings of half and whole blood, related by consanguinity or affinity.

The canon law also invalidated marriages for insanity, impotence and nonage—the relevant ages being fourteen for males and twelve for females—though such marriages were voidable only, not void. Bigamous marriages were of course forbidden.

The subordinate position of married women in English law, pursuant to which their husbands acquired broad powers over their property, was almost as resistant to change as other aspects of English family law. Not until the Seventeenth and Eighteenth Centuries did equity succeed in protecting the married woman's rights in her real and personal property. Partly as a cause and partly no doubt as an effect of the wife's subordinate position, marriages until the Seventeenth Century and sometimes even later were largely arranged and among the upper classes were predominantly financial transactions. For daughters marriage was the only respectable career. In order to ensure an advantageous marriage, a father had to provide a marriage portion, which was used as a bargaining counter to obtain a corresponding jointure from the bridegroom's father to protect the bride during widowhood. The relative size of the two funds was the subject of strenuous negotiation. There is some evidence that marriages contracted in this fashion were unstable in a sizeable proportion of cases, notwithstanding the formidable obstacles to divorce.

Divorce as we know it did not exist in England until 1857, except briefly and doubtfully in the late Sixteenth Century and perhaps in Cromwell's time, but there were a few ways, even under the rigidly monogamous canon law, in which to escape from an uncomfortable marriage. One way was to have the marriage invalidated for the reason that the parties were related within the forbidden degrees, though this was less readily available after 1535. In the Twelfth Century Eleanor of Aquitaine ended her marriage to Louis VII of France by this device thereby freeing herself for marriage to the man who became Henry II of England. And Henry VIII used this method to get rid of Catherine of Aragon in order to marry Ann Boleyn. The appropriate action in the ecclesiastical court was often referred to as a divorce a vinculo matrimonii, but in today's terminology it would be called an annulment, since it declared that no valid marriage between the parties had ever existed.

Limited divorce, or divorce a mensa et thoro was also available from the ecclesiastical courts on the ground of cruelty or adultery, and, after certain other proceedings, for desertion. But this form of divorce merely authorized the parties to live apart, did not free them to contract other marriages, and therefore cannot be considered the equivalent of true divorce.

After 1660 one other avenue of escape from marriage came to be available but only to a very few of the richest and most powerful people in Britain. This was the divorce by special Parliamentary act, given only for adultery and only after a successful suit for criminal conversation against the co-respondent and after the wronged spouse succeeded in obtaining a divorce a mensa et thoro from the ecclesiastical court. Not only was this kind of divorce confined to the rich, it was also largely the prerogative of men, only four being granted to wives during one hundred and fifty years. There are some indications that the virtually complete absence of any legal method for terminating marriages led large segments of the society to adopt non-legal methods for this purpose, that is, to separate and contract subsequent marriages without benefit of divorce.

Although the American colonies never had ecclesiastical courts, they did receive the English ecclesiastical rules concerning marriage. The English form of the marriage ceremony was generally adopted in this country. That type of informal marriage called sponsalia per verba de praesenti was also recognized and under the label of common law marriage became a useful but often misunderstood institution until it was abolished by statute in a majority of states during the Twentieth Century. The various impediments to marriage, such as consanguinity and affinity, insanity, impotence or nonage, all became parts of American domestic relations law, to be administered by the common law or equity courts. Fortunately, however, the Catholic and Anglican doctrine that marriage is of divine origin and indissoluble did not prevail in those colonies settled by Protestants. The Protestants in Europe, Luther and Calvin, for example, did countenance divorce as a legal matter, and colonies like Massachusetts Bay had general divorce statutes from earliest times. On the other hand, the colonies strongly influenced by Anglicanism, those in the middle Atlantic and southern parts of the country, generally followed the English example. The strength of the English influence may be measured by the fact that South Carolina had no general divorce statute at all until 1942, and that New York's statute limited divorce to the ground of adultery from 1787 to 1966. At the same time the pernicious institution of the legislative divorce was imported from England into many colonies and survived until well into the Nineteenth Century.

The grounds for divorce in those colonies which recognized the action included not only adultery and desertion but grounds which we would consider applicable to annulment, such as bigamy, or impotence or consanguinity. These latter grounds are still found in the divorce statutes of a few states. Cruelty also appeared in the laws of some New England states as a ground for divorce, more often in other states as a ground for divorce a mensa et thoro, this action having been borrowed from England along with other ecclesiastical doctrines and practices, such as, for example, the doctrine of recrimination. Recrimination's effect was to deny a divorce to a plaintiff if he had also been guilty of conduct which would be grounds for divorce.

The settlement of the American West had some effect on the law of divorce during the second half of the Nineteenth Century. In general, the western states administered their divorce law with greater liberality than the older states, although Connecticut's 1849 act was very broad, authorizing divorce for conduct which would defeat the purpose of the marriage. By the 1860's and 1870's some western states had even begun to reach out for divorce business from the eastern states and the now familiar American institution of migratory divorce appeared. Two legal factors contributed to this development, the omnibus clause on grounds for divorce and a relatively brief requirement for residence. The omnibus clause authorized divorces, in addition to the usual list of grounds, for any other cause which the courts might deem proper. Indiana was a pioneer in the use of this clause, but the forces of righteousness forced its removal and the reform of Indiana's divorce law in the 1870's. Utah for a short time also had such a clause. Near the end of the century North and South Dakota, primarily by virtue of a three-month residence requirement, enjoyed divorce booms for relatively short periods. The business was never developed with the thoroughness nor publicized with the imagination which have characterized Twentieth Century divorce mills, however.

Contemporary accounts indicate that the second half of the Nineteenth Century saw nearly as much popular discussion of marriage and divorce as has our own time. The discussion accompanied and was intensified by drastic social changes. Women had begun to work outside the home and their legal disabilities vis-a-vis their husbands had begun to be removed. Most important of all, the function of the family was changing. From an economically productive and child training unit it was being converted into an organization whose primary functions were psychological and whose economic significance was solely as a consumer. A liberalized divorce law was one of the reforms advocated by the women's suffrage movement, just as abortion reform has been taken up by women's groups today. The short-lived Mormon experience with polygamy made the only serious inroad on the nation's conservative adherence to the Christian ideal of monogamous marriage. This ended with the territorial statutes outlawing polygamy which were upheld against constitutional attack in Reynolds v. United States, 98 U.S. 145, 25 L.Ed. 244 (1878). The divorce rate gradually rose in many states, leading to agitation for more specific definition of grounds, statutes requiring corroboration of testimony, prohibitions on remarriage, and uniform divorce legislation. Church organizations were prominent in this movement and some statutory changes were made. The drive for uniformity produced a uniform act which was only enacted in three states. This relative failure was followed by attempts at constitutional amendment which would give Congress authority to enact a federal law of divorce, attempts which, despite a complete lack of success, continued for more than fifty years. It is difficult to imagine what sort of a divorce law might have received Congressional approval if the constitutional amendment had passed, but in all likelihood it would have been more restrictive than the statutes of many states.

Along with the movements for women's suffrage and for the improvement of the legal position of women generally during the Nineteenth Century came the demand for greater dissemination and availability of information about birth control as a way to the social and economic betterment of women. Jeremy Bentham, Francis Place and Annie Besant in England and Charles Knowlton in the United States were leaders in this campaign. The response of government in both England and the United States was to attempt to repress all such discussion or information. Criminal prosecutions under the obscenity laws were brought against the leaders. In the 1870's Anthony J. Comstock and his followers were able to persuade Congress to pass statutes, known as the Comstock Laws, prohibiting both the importation and the transmittal through the mails of birth control devices and of written material describing such devices. The Comstock laws contained criminal sanctions. Similar statutes were passed by the legislatures of some important states. Prosecutions under these statutes often occurred and they were undoubtedly effective in hampering the spread of information and techniques among people desiring birth control. These laws remained in the statute books for nearly a hundred years, long after they ceased to be enforced in any systematic way.

The women's rights movement succeeded in reducing the legal disabilities of married women by bringing about the enactment of Married Women's Property Acts during the Nineteenth Century. The purpose of these Acts was to place married women on an equal footing with their husbands with respect to contracts, earnings and the ownership of property, but as they were construed by the courts they often failed to accomplish the intended reforms. It was not until the 1960's that a vigorous and effective attack upon sex discrimination began to eliminate all the married woman's legal disabilities. This was done by federal legislation, state legislation, the Supreme Court's broader application of the Equal Protection Clause of the Fourteenth Amendment, and the adoption of Equal Rights Amendments in about seventeen states. These amendments to state constitutions generally provide that equal rights under the law shall not be denied or abridged on the ground of sex. A federal Equal Rights Amendment has also been proposed as the Twenty-Seventh Amendment to the United States Constitution and has currently been approved by thirty-five of the required thirty-eight states.

The first sixty years of this century saw increasingly lax judicial treatment of grounds for divorce, the development of large scale divorce mills in a few jurisdictions, and some legislative tinkering with marriage and divorce statutes, all of these legal activities being accompanied by substantial increases in the rate of divorce. The divorce rate for the United States rose from .7 divorces per one thousand population in 1900 to 4.4 per thousand in 1946, the high rate due no doubt to the dislocations of World War II. The rate then declined to 2.3 per thousand in 1956, but rose steadily from 1965 to the high rate of 5.1 per thousand population in 1977. The latest available figures from the Monthly Vital Statistics Report of the Department of Health, Education and Welfare for June 16, 1978 show a rate for the twelve months ending in March, 1978 of 5.0 divorces per thousand of the population. The same publication shows a slight decline in the rate of marriages in the United States over the past three years.

Much of the increase in the rate of divorce during the first half of the Twentieth Century was accounted for by expansion in the application of cruelty as a ground for divorce. By 1950 in many states proof of cruelty had come to be a formality, involving a bit of exaggeration, a little perjury at times, and a judicial atmosphere tolerant of both in the interest of processing the maximum number of divorces per hour. Although the official dogma was that divorce might not be granted by default and that the parties were required to prove statutory grounds even when the case was uncontested, this requirement and the standard of proof became legal fictions, at least where cruelty was alleged.

As we have seen, some states developed into divorce mills in the Nineteenth Century in response to the demand created by the limited grounds for divorce existing in other states. Nevada led in the expansion of the business after 1900 as a result of its three-month residence requirement. In 1931 it reduced the requirement to six weeks, where it remains. Citizens of New York were good Nevada customers until the New York grounds were broadened in 1967. Of course this was class discrimination of the most egregious kind, since only wealthy people could afford the cost of a Nevada divorce. Other states and territories have been in the divorce business from time to time, including Idaho, Florida, Arkansas, Alabama and the Virgin Islands. Alabama's effort was unusual in that no period of residence whatever was required, so that with the connivance of its bar and judiciary it was able to offer divorces to New Yorkers at an expenditure of only a day or two of time. Its business prospered through the 1950's and then was largely cut off when one of its divorces was invalidated by Hartigan v. Hartigan, 272 Ala. 67, 128 So.2d 725 (1961). The Virgin Islands for a time also offered divorces without a period of residence if both parties would appear in the action, but its statute was held unconstitutional in 1955. Mexico provided one-day divorces which New York declared valid in 1965 if both parties participated in the suit, but the Mexican law was changed in 1971 so as to make such divorces impossible. When this occurred, Haiti and the Dominican Republic took Mexico's place as a purveyor of quick divorces. The enactment of liberal "no-fault" divorce laws in many states has drastically reduced the migratory divorce traffic, since in these states it is no longer necessary to leave home in order to obtain a divorce. Migratory divorce seems now to have become less important than in the past.

There were no dramatic changes in marriage and divorce statutes until 1969, although criticism of the divorce law was constant, sharp and often well informed. In particular the traditional grounds came under attack from sociologists and psychologists who thought that such activities as adultery, cruelty or desertion were merely symptoms, not causes, of marital failure. They argued that fault itself was out of place in divorce, and that marriages broke up in a context of conflicts in attitude, personality or other difficulty on both sides rather than as a result of fault by one spouse and innocence by the other. Some states began to insert non-fault grounds into their divorce statutes, the most common being the ground of living separate and apart for a prescribed time, usually one to three or five years. But because of the time required this ground was not much used in states where it was enacted.

Criticism from another quarter complained of the law's failure to limit or reduce the number of divorces. One response to this criticism was to bring counselling into the legal process, either in the form of a conciliation court, as in Los Angeles, or by having trained counsellors on the court staff, as in New York and New Jersey. This did not produce a spectacular reduction in the divorce rate, although it may in many cases have reduced the hostility of litigants, thereby benefiting them and their children.

Sustained and substantial efforts at divorce reform finally were exerted in the late 1960's on several fronts. Oddly enough, one book which was influential in this movement was the report of a group in England appointed by the Archbishop of Canterbury to study the grounds for divorce. This report, entitled *Putting Asunder,* published in 1966, advocated "marriage breakdown" as the sole ground for divorce. Another study of divorce was made by a commission appointed by the governor of California. Finally, and most important, the National Conference of Commissioners on Uniform State Laws appointed a special committee on divorce which, with Professor Robert J. Levy as director, made a study of existing divorce laws published as an extensive monograph in 1969, and later drafted a Uniform Marriage and Divorce Act which in 1971 was approved by the Commissioners. This statute adopts irretrievable marriage breakdown as the sole ground for divorce. Commencing in 1969 with California, about thirty-three states have adopted marriage breakdown or incompatibility as a ground or the only ground for divorce. As those statutes are currently being applied in the courts, the effect is that when either party wishes the divorce, it will be granted. Since the states having marriage breakdown as a ground and those having separation as a ground comprise nearly all American jurisdictions, it is accurate to say that fault has largely been eliminated from the question whether a divorce is to be granted in a particular case. The Uniform Marriage and Divorce Act also reduces the period of residence for divorce jurisdiction to ninety days, imposes some limits on the occasions in which alimony may be granted, and makes fault irrelevant in assessing alimony.

The English, not to be outdone, have also made irretrievable marriage breakdown the sole ground for divorce, in the Matrimonial Causes Act of 1973. But the statute requires as evidence of the breakdown proof of various fault grounds, so that its reforms are not as striking as might otherwise appear.

Another significant uniform statute, the Uniform Child Custody Jurisdiction Act, approved in 1968 and now in force in forty-one states, establishes jurisdictional rules for custody litigation whose purpose is to reduce inter-state conflicts in jurisdiction, to provide for the enforcement of custody orders, and to avoid wherever possible the relitigation of custody disputes. The wide influence of this statute is in large part due to the work of the Reporter for the Act, Professor Brigitte Bodenheimer.

Contemporaneously with the abolition of fault from divorce and the increase in the rate of divorce, the United States has seen many changes in attitudes toward marriage and sex. The courts and legislatures have not been inactive respecting these changes, many of which have been reflected in the repeal of old statutes and the development of new judicial doctrines. For example the rate of illegitimate births has risen to about fifteen percent of all births in recent years, and among some classes constitutes fifty percent of all births. The Supreme Court has attempted to respond to this development by eliminating on constitutional grounds some of the traditional disabilities of the illegitimate child. The Supreme Court has also held that the Constitution forbids many of the statutory restrictions on contraception and abortion which were enacted in the Nineteenth Century, thereby recognizing that substantial segments of public opinion favor control by individuals over procreation. But federal and state statutes and judicial decisions limiting access to abortion and contraception by withholding public funds for such purposes are evidence that society is still far from complete agreement on the morality and wisdom of these processes.

The growing numbers of people who live together without being married have influenced the courts to give such unions legal recognition for some purposes. The most widely publicized of the cases, Marvin v. Marvin, reproduced infra at page 38, authorized the enforcement of contracts between men and women living together out of wedlock where the contracts regulated property or financial relationships. The same case also intimated that there could be property or financial responsibilities between such persons even in the absence of contract. This case and others like it will doubtless tend to legitimate such non-marital unions, giving them greater respectability and consequently leading to an increase in their occurrence.

The last couple of decades have seen significant changes in the law of domestic relations, making a sharp contrast with previous centuries of relatively little change. The changes in the law will certainly affect and be affected by further rapidly changing contemporary attitudes toward marriage, divorce, sex, population growth and family relations. The legal materials presented by this book should be analyzed critically with this background in mind. In addition the student might find it intriguing to make his own forecasts of future developments both legal and non-legal.

NOTES AND QUESTIONS

1. In Maynard v. Hill, 125 U.S. 190, 205 (1888) the Supreme Court said: "Marriage, as creating the most important relation in life, as having more to do with the morals and civilization of a people than any other institution, has always been subject to the control of the legislature." The New

York Court of Appeals, in Fearon v. Treanor, 272 N.Y. 268, 272, 5 N.E.2d 815, 816 (1936) made a similar statement: "Marriage is more than a personal relation between a man and a woman. It is a status founded on contract and established by law. It constitutes an institution involving the highest interests of society. It is regulated and controlled by law based on principles of public policy affecting the welfare of the people of the state." More recently the United States Supreme Court has said, in Griswold v. Connecticut, 381 U.S. 479, 486 (1965): "Marriage is a coming together for better or for worse, hopefully enduring, and intimate to the degree of being sacred. It is an association that promotes a way of life, not causes; a harmony in living, not political faiths; a bilateral loyalty, not commercial or social projects. Yet it is an association for as noble a purpose as any involved in our prior decisions." And in Boddie v. Connecticut, 401 U.S. 371, 376 (1971) the Court wrote: "As this Court on more than one occasion has recognized, marriage involves interests of basic importance in our society. * * * It is not surprising, then, that the States have seen fit to oversee many aspects of that institution. Without a prior judicial imprimatur, individuals may freely enter into and rescind commercial contracts, for example, but we are unaware of any jurisdiction where private citizens may covenant for or dissolve marriages without state approval. Even where all substantive requirements are concededly met, we know of no instance where two consenting adults may divorce and mutually liberate themselves from the constraints of legal obligations that go with marriage, and more fundamentally the prohibition against remarriage, without invoking the State's judicial machinery."

(a) Are these statements historically correct, so far as you can tell from the foregoing brief historical sketch? Is it true, as the courts' statements indicate, that marriage and divorce have always been extensively regulated by law? How do you account for the paradox referred to in the quotation from John Selden, supra page 1, that this most private of relationships is "most medled with" by the state?

(b) What would you say were the purposes or functions of the marriage and divorce law of Rome, of England, and of the United States at the various periods described in the introduction? To what extent did that law or does that law accomplish those purposes?

(c) To what extent, if any, did our law of marriage and divorce enforce principles of sexual morality? To what extent does our law presently attempt to do this?

(d) What similarities and what differences do you see between Roman, English and American regulation of marriage and divorce, and in society's response to that regulation? How do you account for the differences?

(e) From what you know of contemporary marriage and divorce, can you formulate a legal definition of marriage today? How would it differ from the definition of a hundred years ago? Is Mr. Justice Douglas' definition in the quotation from Griswold v. Connecticut adequate or satisfactory?

(f) The author of an interesting article has recently suggested that we are presently seeing a decline in the importance of the nuclear family, that is, the family composed of husband, wife and their children, and at the same time an increase in the importance of the employment relationship.

Evidence for this idea is supplied by the law's permitting a quick and easy dissolution of marriage, while it has made the dissolution of the employment relation more difficult. Glendon, The New Family and the New Property, 53 Tul.L.Rev. 697 (1979). Would you agree with this analysis? If so, what would you suppose the legal and social consequences of this development might be?

2. The following books and articles give helpful accounts of the history of marriage and divorce and insight into contemporary developments. They are listed here rather than as footnotes to the introductory essay:

J. Barnett, Divorce and the American Divorce Novel (1939).

J. Bishop, Marriage, Divorce and Separation, Vol. I, 108–114 (1891).

N. Blake, The Road to Reno (1962).

J. Bryce, Marriage and Divorce Under Roman and English Law, 3 Select Essays on Anglo-American Legal History, 782 (1909).

W. Buckland, A Text-Book of Roman Law, Ch. III (3rd ed. Stein 1963).

H. Carter and P. Glick, Marriage and Divorce (1970). A statistical study.

H. Clark, The New Marriage, 12 Willamette L.J. 441 (1976).

M. Glendon, The New Family and the New Property, 53 Tul.L.Rev. 697 (1979).

R. Helmholz, Marriage Litigation in Medieval England (1974).

W. Holdsworth, History of English Law, Vol. I, 622–624; Vol. II, 87–90; Vol. IV, 34–42 (1903–1914).

G. Howard, A History of Matrimonial Institutions (1904).

W. D. Howells, A Modern Instance (1881). A novel of marriage and divorce.

P. Jacobson, American Marriage and Divorce (1961). An excellent statistical study.

H. Jolowicz and B. Nicholas, Historical Introduction to the Study of Roman Law (3d ed. 1972).

S. Kitchin, A History of Divorce (1912).

R. Leage, Roman Private Law, 98–114 (1961).

J. Lichtenberger, Divorce, 19–140 (1931).

O. McGregor, Divorce in England (1957).

A. Mueller, Inquiry Into the State of a Divorceless Society, 18 U.Pitt. L.Rev. 545 (1957).

B. Nicholas, An Introduction to Roman Law, 80–90 (1962).

F. Pollock and F. Maitland, The History of English Law, Ch. VII (2d ed. 1898, reissued in paperback, 1968, by the Cambridge University Press).

L. Stone, Marriage Among the English Nobility, 3 Comparative Studies in Society and History, 182 (1960), reprinted in R. Coser, The Family, 153 (1964).

L. Stone, The Family, Sex and Marriage in England 1500–1800 (1977).

Chapter 1

PRE–MARITAL CONTRACTS

SECTION 1. BREACH OF PROMISE

The action for breach of promise to marry has become an anachronism in American law, perhaps because engagement is now recognized for what it should be, that is, a period of increased intimacy in which the parties can make the final decision whether to marry without worrying about the possibilities of a lawsuit if one of them should choose not to go through with the marriage. Or the reason may be that engagement itself as a well defined stage on the road to marriage is less common. At any rate for whatever reason very few breach of promise cases arise today. Therefore that subject, as well as a discussion of the impact of "heart balm statutes" abolishing breach of promise which have been enacted in some states have been omitted from this work. They are described in H. Clark, Law of Domestic Relations, Ch. 1 (1968). Stanard v. Bolin, 88 Wash.2d 614, 565 P.2d 94 (1977), after a full consideration of the merits and demerits of the suit for breach of promise, refused to abolish it by judicial decision, but did limit recoverable damages by excluding the loss of expected financial and social position as an element of damage.

SECTION 2. CONTRACTS RESTRAINING OR PROMOTING MARRIAGE

COWAN v. COWAN

Supreme Court of Iowa, 1956.
247 Iowa 729, 75 N.W.2d 920.

THOMPSON, Justice. On May 12, 1954, the parties hereto had been wife and husband for approximately twenty years. There had been pending at that time for about five months a separate maintenance action instituted by the plaintiff. Both parties were communicants of the Roman Catholic Church. Their marital difficulties, according to the testimony of the plaintiff, were caused by the misconduct of the defendant with one Thelma Julius. Plaintiff says Thelma Julius admitted having "relations" with the defendant, this admission being made in defendant's presence. Although he took the witness stand, defendant made no denial of this evidence.

On or about the date above set forth, the parties to the pending separate maintenance action entered into a stipulation settling their property rights, plaintiff amended the prayer of her petition to ask a divorce, and offered evidence upon which a decree was granted to her. The stipulation above referred to was apparently incorporated in the divorce decree. The parties were farm people, and the property involved was substantial, as was the share awarded to the plaintiff.

On the same date—May 12, 1954—the parties entered into another contract, in the nature of a supplement to the formal stipulation above referred to. It was not filed in the court records or made a part of the divorce decree. It is denominated a "Collateral Agreement", and by its terms is a "collateral agreement and stipulation to the stipulation to be filed in the matter". The litigation here arises from Paragraph 3 of this second or supplemental agreement, which we set out:

"3. If either party hereto shall remarry prior to the time the youngest child of the parties, Charles Cowan, attains the age of twenty one years, or prior to his sooner emancipation, such party shall forfeit and be indebted to the other in the sum of $10,000, and judgment may enter accordingly."

The parties had three sons, of whom Charles, the youngest, was 13 years of age at the time of the agreement. The defendant remained on his farm and the sons have at all times lived there with him, except that the oldest has now married and maintains his own home. On December 15, 1954, the defendant married Thelma Julius. The plaintiff thereupon made application to modify the divorce decree by incorporating therein the "collateral agreement." Defendant resisted, a hearing was had with evidence taken, and the trial court modified the decree as prayed and entered judgment for plaintiff for $10,000, with interest and costs.

Appellant states two propositions relied upon for reversal, which we shall consider in order. They are 1, that "The court erred in failing to find that Paragraph III of the 'Collateral Agreement' is contrary to public policy and, therefore, void or unenforceable"; *

*   *   *

I. There is no doubt that Iowa follows the universal rule that contracts in general restraint of marriage are against public policy and so are void. * * * But there are exceptions, occasioned by varying factual situations; or perhaps it is more nearly correct to say there are facts to which the rule does not apply. Thus, it is often said, in fact it is well established, that restraints against second marriages are not invalid. We said in McCoy v. Flynn, page 632 of 169 Iowa, page 468 of 151 N.W.: "That contracts in restraint of a second marriage are valid is everywhere affirmed." * * *

If the contract under examination here was in restraint of marriage, it was clearly of a second marriage. But the appellant says

---

* The husband's second contention, also rejected, was that the agreement was unenforceable because it amounted to a penalty or forfeiture. (Ed. note.)

that, even with second marriages, the restraint must serve some purpose other than merely that of preventing the marriage. Many of the cases concern wills, in which the testator limits a gift to his spouse so long as she does not remarry. It is universally held a reasonable limitation, the manifest intent being to support her until she has acquired another provider. In the case at bar the appellant thinks the restriction is a restraint only and has no other apparent or actual object.

Without holding that all restraints upon second marriage are valid—that is, that under no circumstances may they offend against public policy—we hold that no such invalidity appears here.   *   *   *

The problem before us, in the light of the rule last quoted, is one of facts and the reasonable conclusions to be drawn from them. Some reference to authorities from other jurisdictions may be helpful. In Barnes v. Hobson, 250 S.W. 238, 242, 243 (Tex.Civ.App.1923), the governing principle is thus stated:

"We are inclined to think, in the light of all the authorities, and having in mind the basis of the rule, to wit, the interest the public has in the matter, that the term 'general restraint' as used in the rule should be construed to mean restraint which binds a competent person not to marry any one at any time, and that the validity of a contract, where the restraint it imposes is only against marrying a particular person, or a person of a particular class, or within a specified limited time, should be determined with reference to the reasonableness of such restraint under the circumstances of the particular case."

     *   *   *

Nunn v. Justice, 278 Ky. 811, 129 S.W.2d 564, 566 (1939), concerned a factual situation in which a well-to-do father and mother deeded substantially all their property to their two daughters, each deed containing this provision:

" 'First party shall hold and control any or all property mentioned in this deed as long as they live, so long as neither marries again. If either member of the first party marries again that member shall lose all control of the property.' "

The mother having died and the father remarried, the Kentucky Court of Appeals held that the deeds amounted to a contract, that the provision terminating the father's interest upon remarriage was valid, and the daughters were entitled to the full interest in and control of the property.

In Perreault v. Hall, 94 N.H. 191, 49 A.2d 812 (1946), an employe had contracted to remain with her employer as business assistant and adviser, and "give her full attention to said [the] business by not becoming married". This restraint was held to be reasonable and the contract valid.

6 Williston, Contracts (Rev.Ed.), section 1741, at page 4926, states the rule in these terms:

"The modern law regards bargains and conditions in restraint of marriage as only prima facie illegal and will accord them validity if the restraint is shown to be reasonable under the circumstances. For example, reasonable contracts involving the performance of services which are inconsistent with matrimony have been upheld."

* * *

We conclude that not all restraints, even of first marriages, are of necessity invalid. They will be upheld if they are not general and unlimited and if they serve a reasonable purpose. The tendency is also to uphold restraints on second marriages, either because it is said the "public policy" rule does not apply to such marriages, or on the more limited ground, found in the facts of the cases, that the restraints imposed are under the circumstances reasonable and intended to serve a proper and meritorious purpose. We think the facts in the instant case bring it within the latter rule.

* * *

The reason for the rule that general and unlimited restraints on marriage offend against public policy lies in the universal belief that marriage is the proper way of life, and must be encouraged. But there are clearly some marriages not made in Heaven, which a just and informed public opinion must condemn rather than approve. Such a marriage is that between a divorced husband and the woman with whom his misconduct left his blameless wife no alternative but to resort to the divorce courts.

A remarriage under these circumstances is strongly disapproved by the defendant's church. The plaintiff testified that under these circumstances "the individual that remarries is eliminated or ousted, in plain speaking, from the Catholic Church."

It is evident that, far from basking in the warmth of public sanction, a marriage such as the defendant contracted here meets with general disapproval and the strongest condemnation from the church of his choice. The reason for the rule making general restraints on marriage void and unenforceable fails here, and where the reason for a rule no longer exists, the rule should not be applied. This is but another way of saying that restraints which are reasonable under the existing circumstances and conditions are valid and will be enforced.

We have pointed out that the defendant, as a witness upon the hearing, did not deny his improper conduct with the woman Thelma Julius. The plaintiff testified, without objection, that she wished Paragraph 3 to be included in the agreement in the hope the defendant would not marry the Julius woman so long as her sons were living in his home. She feared the effect of a woman of such evident loose morals upon them. It will be noted the restriction upon marriage is not general—that is, unlimited as to time, but only for a period of seven or eight years, at the most, until the youngest son becomes of age or is sooner emancipated. In view of the undenied misconduct of the defendant and Thelma Julius, the purpose seems laudable and the restraint reasonable. The defendant had been once married; he voluntarily signed a contract subjecting himself to loss if he chose to remarry; the restraint imposed was not general, but limited in time, and its object was a proper and reasonable one. The defendant received the benefit of the signing of the stipulation-in-chief and the supplemental or "collateral" agreement, and so of the adjustment of property rights in the pending litigation. He made his contract, and we think it was a valid one.

    *   *   *

We find no error. Affirmed.

NOTES AND QUESTIONS

1. What interests of what people is this agreement designed to achieve? What general social interests persuaded the court to hold the agreement valid? Was it the general interest in freedom of contract? Of what value is the interest which the court protects?

2. If the general rule is assumed, that is, that general restraints on marriage are invalid, what basis, if any, is there for saying that restraints on second marriages are nevertheless enforceable? Why the distinction between first and second marriages? In view of the fact that most divorced persons remarry, should the law allow such second marriages to be discouraged in this fashion? Cf. P. Jacobson, American Marriage and Divorce, 82, 83 (1961); H. Carter and P. Glick, Marriage and Divorce, 239 (1970).

3. This court accepts the common view that "reasonable" restraints on marriage are enforceable. What does "reasonable" mean in this context? For example:

(a) Is a restraint on marriage outside a particular religious faith "reasonable"? Shapira v. Union Nat. Bank, 39 Ohio Misc. 28, 315 N.E.2d 825, 68 O.O.2d 187 (1974); Koresic v. Grand Carniolian Slovenian Catholic Union, 138 Kan. 261, 25 P.2d 355 (1933).

(b) Would an agreement be "reasonable" if it were made between the parties in the *Cowan* case and provided that the husband would be obligated to pay to the wife the sum of $10,000 if he should ever marry Thelma Julius? What would be the result under such a contract if the husband subsequently lived with Thelma Julius without marrying her?

(c) Would a conveyance of land be "reasonable" if it provided that the land must be reconveyed to the grantor if the grantee should marry? Winters v. Miller, 23 Ohio Misc. 73, 261 N.E.2d 205 (1970). Would it matter in such a case that the grantor's purpose was to provide for the support of a daughter until her marriage?

4. Some restraints upon marriage in employment contracts are phrased to apply only to women. For example, many airlines formerly would employ only unmarried stewardesses, although they would employ married male flight attendants. This sort of restriction is generally held to violate section 703(a)(1) of Title VII of the Civil Rights Act of 1964, 42

U.S.C.A. § 2000e–2(a)(1), which provides: "It shall be an unlawful employment practice for an employer—(1) to fail or refuse to hire or to discharge any individual, or otherwise to discriminate against any individual with respect to his compensation, terms, conditions, or privileges of employment, because of such individual's race, color, religion, sex, or national origin. * * *" Sprogis v. United Air Lines, Inc., 444 F.2d 1194 (7th Cir. 1971), cert. den. 404 U.S. 991 (1971); Annot., Distinctions Based on Marital Status As Constituting Sex Discrimination Under § 703(a) of Civil Rights Act of 1964 (42 U.S.C.A. § 2000e–2(a)), 34 A.L.R.Fed. 648 (1977). In order to be lawful under the statute, the Supreme Court has said that the condition must be shown to be a bona fide qualification which is reasonably necessary to normal operation of the particular business or enterprise. Phillips v. Martin Marietta Corp., 400 U.S. 542 (1971). What would be the result if the provision concerning marriage were applied to a woman working for a dating service?

5. The proposed Twenty-Seventh Amendment to the United States Constitution provides, in relevant part: "Equality of rights under the law shall not be denied or abridged by the United States or by any State on account of sex. * * * This amendment shall take effect two years after the date of ratification." United States Code Congressional and Administrative News No. 3, April 20, 1972, 835, reproducing H.R.J.Res. 208, passed by the Congress on March 22, 1972. The proposal required ratification within seven years. At the present writing the amendment has been approved by thirty-five states, three short of the needed thirty-eight. U.S.C.A., Const., Amendments 14 to End, 1102. An extension of the deadline for ratification until June 30, 1982 was approved by the House of Representatives on August 15, 1978, and by the Senate on October 6, 1978. H.J.Res. 638, 95th Cong., 2d Sess., 124 Cong.Rec. H8664–5, S17318. For the legislative history of the amendment see Report of the House Judiciary Committee, H.R.Rep. No. 92–359, 92d Cong., 2d Sess. (1971); Equal Rights for Men and Woman, S.R. No. 92–689, 92d Cong., 2d Sess., Senate Committee on the Judiciary (1972); C. Stimpson, ed., Women and the "Equal Rights" Amendment (1972). For the extensive debates on the validity of the extension of time for ratification see 124 Cong.Rec. H8597–H8665, S17283–17319 (1978).

Seventeen state constitutions forbid discrimination by the state on the basis of sex. These states are Alaska, Colorado, Connecticut, Hawaii, Illinois, Louisiana, Maryland, Massachusetts, Montana, New Hampshire, New Mexico, Pennsylvania, Texas, Utah, Virginia, Washington and Wyoming. Kurtz, The State Equal Rights Amendments and Their Impact on Domestic Relations Law, 11 Fam.L.Q. 101 (1977); Treadwell and Page, Equal Rights Provisions: The Experience Under State Constitutions, 65 Cal.L.Rev. 1086 (1977).

Would the existence of this sort of constitutional provision affect the restraints upon marriage applicable to women described in paragraph four, supra?

6. A school board adopted a regulation prohibiting a married female student from participating in any school activities other than classes carrying credit for graduation. In holding the regulation unconstitutional, the court had this to say: "* * * it now seems settled beyond peradventure that the right to marry is a *fundamental* one as that term is applied in the area of federal constitutional law * * * The signification of a "funda-

mental" constitutional right is great in the present context, for it determines the constitutional standard according to which the regulation under attack must be judged: any infringement by a state or an arm thereof * * * upon a fundamental right of its citizens is subject to the closest judicial scrutiny. Any such infringement is constitutionally impermissible unless it is shown to be *necessary* to promote a *compelling* state interest." Holt v. Shelton, 341 F.Supp. 821, 822 (M.D.Tenn.1972); Beeson v. Kiowa County School District RE–1, 39 Colo.App. 174, 567 P.2d 801 (1977).

(a) Would the result in the *Cowan* case be affected by this case? Is state action involved in the *Cowan* case? Cf. Shelley v. Kraemer, 334 U.S. 1 (1948); Barrows v. Jackson, 346 U.S. 249 (1953); Reitman v. Mulkey, 387 U.S. 369 (1967); Moose Lodge No. 107 v. Irvis, 407 U.S. 163 (1972); Jackson v. Metropolitan Edison Co., 419 U.S. 345 (1974); L. Tribe, American Constitutional Law § 18–2, 18–6 (1978); Black, Foreword: "State Action", Equal Protection, and California's Proposition 14, 81 Harv.L.Rev. 69, 95, 100–109 (1967).

(b) Do any of the foregoing restraints survive this doctrine?

7. The courts have dealt with other forms of discrimination against married women with mixed results. Cleveland Bd. of Educ. v. LaFleur, 414 U.S. 632 (1974) held that a school board regulation was unconstitutional in requiring a pregnant teacher to take maternity leave five months before the child's birth and for three months thereafter. The Court took the position that the regulation restricted the freedom of personal choice in the family and marriage without a sufficiently rational relation to the state's interest. On the other hand Geduldig v. Aiello, 417 U.S. 484 (1974) held that a California statute was constitutional when it excluded pregnancy related disabilities from disability insurance coverage. And General Electric Co. v. Gilbert, 429 U.S. 125, rehearing denied 429 U.S. 1079 (1976) held that an employer's disability plan did not violate the Civil Rights Act of 1964 when it excluded pregnancy from the list of covered disabilities. But Nashville Gas Co. v. Satty, 434 U.S. 136 (1977) held that an employer violated Title VII of the Civil Rights Act when it deprived women taking pregnancy leave of their accumulated job seniority. See also Barkett, Pregnancy Discrimination—Purpose, Effect, and Nashville Gas Co. v. Satty, 16 J.Fam.L. 401 (1978); Note, Pregnancy and the Constitution: The Uniqueness Trap, 62 Cal.L.Rev. 1532 (1974).

8. Would an employer's refusal to hire married persons of either sex for a particular position or positions be an invalid restraint upon marriage, under either the *Cowan* or *Holt* cases? Stroud v. Delta Air Lines, 544 F.2d 892, rehearing denied 548 F.2d 356 (5th Cir. 1977); Keckeisen v. Independent School District, 509 F.2d 1062 (8th Cir. 1975), cert. den. 423 U.S. 833 (1975) (nepotism rule); Southwestern Community Action Council, Inc. v. Community Services Administration, 462 F.Supp. 289 (S.D.W.Va.1978) (nepotism rule); Sanbonmatsu v. Boyer, 45 A.D.2d 249, 357 N.Y.S.2d 245 (4th Dep't 1974), appeal dismissed 36 N.Y.2d 871, 370 N.Y.S.2d 926, 331 N.E.2d 701 (1975), motion to vacate dismissal denied 37 N.Y.2d 749, 374 N.Y.S.2d 623, 337 N.E.2d 134 (1975), motion for leave to appeal denied 37 N.Y.2d 705, 374 N.Y.S.2d 1026 (1975), aff'd 39 N.Y.2d 914, 386 N.Y.S.2d 404, 352 N.E.2d 591 (1976) (nepotism rule); Note Conflicts of Interest and the Changing Concept of Marriage: The Congressional Compromise, 75 Mich.L.Rev. 1647 (1977) (conflicts arising when one spouse is a member of

Congress and the other in a high level position in industry or the executive branch of the government.)

9. Should contracts which promote, rather than restrain, marriage be held invalid? Does computerized matchmaking, a service offered by some firms, raise any problems under the foregoing cases and authorities? See 6 Corbin, Contracts 884 (1951); Annot., Validity and Construction of Testamentary Gift Conditioned on Beneficiary's Remaining Married, 28 A.L.R. 3d 1325 (1969).

SECTION 3. ANTENUPTIAL AGREEMENTS

KOSIK v. GEORGE

Supreme Court of Oregon, 1969.
253 Or. 15, 452 P.2d 560.

HAMMOND, Justice (Pro Tempore). This suit for declaratory relief is brought by plaintiff as the daughter and only child of Earl Robert George against the defendant individually and as administratrix of the estate of Earl Robert George. Defendant is the widow of Mr. George. Plaintiff asks that the court declare that the defendant has waived and released all rights as surviving widow of the decedent in and to his estate by virtue of the execution of a prenuptial agreement. Defendant asks that the prenuptial agreement be declared void.

Plaintiff appeals from a decree declaring the prenuptial agreement void and of no effect.

In 1943, defendant, then Marian F. Stevenson, met Earl Robert George when he, as a real estate broker, handled a transaction wherein the Stevensons purchased a home. Defendant and Mr. George saw each other after that on occasion until 1952. Defendant was divorced from Mr. Stevenson in 1955 and Mr. George and his then wife were divorced in 1956.

On Palm Sunday in 1957 Mr. George called defendant on the telephone for reasons related by defendant as:

"A He had heard that I was free, and he had gotten a divorce from Faye George, and he wanted to know if he could come out and see me."

Defendant was then clerking in an east Portland department store and Mr. George was running his real estate business in the same city.

Although the parties had not seen each other for five years, Mr. George spoke of marriage the first night they were together. The couple were together every evening after that first meeting until their marriage eight days later. Wednesday night Mr. George brought out a diamond engagement ring, put it on defendant's finger and she accepted it. Either that evening or the next the parties talked about a prenuptial agreement but they did not discuss their respective worth or holdings.

On Friday evening Mr. George took defendant to the home of his attorney so that they could sign an agreement that the attorney had prepared at his request, which agreement is the subject of this controversy. The prenuptial agreement was signed by the parties and they were married the following Monday. The agreement was recorded by Mr. George the next day. The parties remained married until the death of Mr. George March 13, 1967.

At the time of the marriage the defendant's resources had a value of approximately $4,000, while Mr. George was worth about $100,000. After the marriage Mr. George bought the parties a home valued at about $14,500. Title was taken by the couple as tenants by the entirety. Defendant also became the beneficiary of a $5,000 policy on the life of her husband. The decedent's estate was appraised at $89,515.46. He left no will.

Defendant states that the couple did not discuss their financial worth or their properties before the marriage. She said she knew that Mr. George had on [sic] office, a ranch and some beach property, but other than that she knew nothing of his holdings. When asked about their conversations defendant stated:

"Q   Now during this week—from Palm Sunday to Easter Sunday —and you being together every day of the week, or every evening, did you discuss your individual affairs?

"A   Are you referring to my personal money, or—

"Q   Yes, I'm referring to your worldly goods and his.

"A   No, sir.

"Q   You didn't discuss it at all?

"A   No, sir.

"Q   It wasn't mentioned?

"A   How much he was worth and how much I was worth, not once."

Defendant could not remember when she learned that Mr. George was worth approximately $100,000, but a witness called by plaintiff testified that she met defendant at the store where she worked and that defendant told her that she was going to marry Earl George, a wealthy real estate man, and that she didn't have to work any more or worry about her children.

The attorney who drew the prenuptial agreement had been Mr. George's lawyer for several years. He testified about his instructions from Mr. George and about preparing this agreement as follows:

"A   He came and told me he was getting married. He wanted to know what he could do to keep his estate in his own name after he was married.

"Now Mr. George was in the real estate business. He knew all about dower and curtesy, and that type of thing.

"He asked me if there was any way to keep his estate separate, and I told him he could enter into a prenuptial agreement.

"Q Did he state anything in that conversation about his intended spouse and her rights?

"A All he told me was she had her own property, and he had his, and he didn't tell me the extent of either one of them.

    " * * *

"A He called me later on the telephone and told me to write it up, and I did.

"Q And what did you write up?

"A The agreement I have in my hand.

"Q In the form that appears there?

"A Yes, I took this form out of an Oregon Supreme Court case that I just read. Randall Kester wrote the opinion, and I wrote it word for word, except changing the name,—which I did.

"Q And is that the Moore versus Schermerhorn case?

"A Yes. I think that's the name of the case all right.

"Q Then what is the next thing that happened?

"A The next thing that happened, Mr. George called me and asked if I would take my seal home, that he and Mrs. Stevenson—the intended Mrs. George—would come by the house and sign the agreement."

Defendant did not consult a lawyer before signing the agreement and was not asked by Mr. George's attorney whether she had an attorney nor was she told that she had a right to have independent counsel. She had a high school education and very limited business experience. She did read the prenuptial agreement before she signed it, but it appears clear from the record that she received no copy of the agreement. She related her understanding of the agreement as follows:

"Q Is this a fair statement of what your understanding was: That the agreement proposed that the property he had before his marriage, he could dispose of it as he saw fit, and your property you had before your marriage, you could dispose of as you saw fit, but you understood you would be taken care of?

"A Yes, sir."

She spoke of her motive for signing the agreement in this testimony:

"Q Now after that first—when Mr. George asked you if you would sign this agreement, what did you tell him?

"A I told him yes. I trusted him. Why not?

"Q In other words, it was all right with you at that point that each of you would have a right to dispose of your own properties as you saw fit?

"A He said it would be just like any other married couple."

It does not appear from the record that any detailed explanation of the prenuptial agreement was made to defendant by anyone. The attorney could remember no specific explanation being made, but when asked whether he made any explanation to the defendant about dower or curtesy the following explanation was given:

" 'Answer: * * * I might have told her—I might have explained that, because there's only one purpose of this agreement, and that's to avoid dower and courtesy [sic], and if the question came up I might have explained it to her along those lines, I don't know. But my recollection is that my understanding was that Earl had explained all of this prior. My function was to prepare the papers, and certainly, as I remember the situation very vividly, there were no problems * * *. It was cut and dried. I mean it was something that they worked out and I was just writing up the papers.' "

It is now important to recall the testimony of Mr. George's attorney who stated that the prenuptial agreement executed by Earl Robert George and Marian F. Stevenson (except for the names of the parties and date of execution) conforms exactly to the wording of the agreement set out in Moore v. Schermerhorn, 210 Or. 23, 307 P.2d 483, 308 P.2d 180 (1957), 65 A.L.R.2d 715 (1959). In view of the availability in *Moore* of a complete duplicate of the agreement now in question, we see no reason to publish it again *in haec verba*, but summarize the agreement to provide: A. That the husband's right of curtesy in the wife's separate estate is barred; B. That the wife's right of dower in the husband's separate estate is barred; and C. Each party agrees to make no claim to the separate property of the other at any time thereafter.

While there is no record here regarding any advice being given defendant about the effect of the prenuptial agreement she was asked to sign, we may conclude that if the attorney advised her at all it was as quoted above, "* * * [T]here's only one purpose of this agreement, and that's to avoid dower and courtesy [sic], and if the question came up I might have explained it to her along those lines, I don't know." Such advice, if given, would have been *contra* to the decision in Moore v. Schermerhorn, supra, since the thrust of the opinion in that case was that the agreement did act to bar a surviving spouse's right to claim property exempt from execution under ORS 116.010, but the opinion left undecided whether dower and curtesy were also barred.

It is obvious, therefore, that more than dower and curtesy were involved in the agreement presented to the defendant.

The relationship between the parties to a prenuptial agreement is fiduciary in character if the agreement was entered into after the parties became engaged. *   *   *

Where, by the terms of a prenuptial agreement, the provision for the wife as the survivor is clearly disproportionate to the husband's wealth, it raises a presumption of designed concealment, and places the burden on those claiming under it in his right to show that there was a full knowledge and understanding on the part of the wife at the time of execution of all the facts materially affecting her interests, viz., the extent of his wealth and her rights in his property as his survivor, and how modified by the proposed agreement. *   *   *

Mr. George was a man of extensive business background, described by his attorney to have been a very brilliant man in his field of work. It was his duty to see that defendant was fully informed concerning the rights she was surrendering. *   *   * See Annotation, Lindey, Separation Agreements and Ante-Nuptial Contracts 638, 652 (1937), and Note, 55 Dick.L.Rev. 382–91 (1950–1951).

We deem it unnecessary to decide whether defendant had adequate knowledge of the worth of Mr. George before she signed the prenuptial contract and before entering into the marriage, but we do hold that George breached the fiduciary relationship existing between him and defendant by securing her signature to the proposed agreement without first according to defendant a reasonable opportunity to learn what property rights she would have as his wife (and potentially as his widow) that would be altered or extinguished by the agreement.

The fact that the parties were engaged, coupled with a wide disparity in their business experience, knowledge and financial worth, invoked a responsibility in George and his attorney to fully inform defendant regarding the consequences of executing the agreement proffered to her, a duty that was neglected. The agreement was therefore invalid.

Affirmed.

NOTES AND QUESTIONS

1. As in the *Kosik* case, these agreements are usually made when the persons proposing to marry are older, have substantial property, and have children of prior marriages or other obligations such that they wish to limit the property passing to the new spouse on death. Since life expectancies have risen, and since the American divorce rate is high and may go higher, the circumstances in which antenuptial contracts will be used can be expected to become more common, and lawyers should be familiar with their implications.

2. In most states antenuptial agreements are held to be within the Third Clause of the Statute of Frauds, that which requires that contracts made in consideration of marriage must be in writing, signed by the party to be charged. See the cases collected in Annot., 75 A.L.R.2d 633 (1961).

In addition, some states have statutes which impose other formalities for antenuptial agreements, such as Del.Code Ann. tit. 13, § 301 (1975), which requires two witnesses, acknowledgment of the contract, and that it be executed at least ten days before the celebration of the marriage. See Hill v. Hill, 269 A.2d 212 (Del.1970), and Annot., 16 A.L.R.3d 370 (1967). For the rules governing the waiver of widow's allowance or other claims against decedents' estates, see Uniform Probate Code § 2–204, 8 Unif.L.Ann. 337 (1972); Annot., 30 A.L.R.3d 858 (1970).

3. The *Kosik* case makes it clear that antenuptial agreements are generally valid if there is a full disclosure of the parties' worth and an adequate provision for the spouses. See Clark, Antenuptial Contracts, 50 Univ. of Colo.L.Rev. 141 (1979); Hartz v. Hartz, 248 Md. 47, 234 A.2d 865 (1967); In re Estate of Broadie, 208 Kan. 621, 493 P.2d 289 (1972), and other cases cited in Annot., 27 A.L.R.2d 883 (1953), and Whitney v. Seattle-First Nat. Bank, 90 Wash.2d 105, 579 P.2d 937 (1978), 54 Wash.L.Rev. 135 (1978). This "rule" suggests various questions:

(a) Why should the courts hold that there is a confidential relationship between the parties in this situation? Is this a relic of sex prejudice based upon the assumption that women are not competent to evaluate such contracts?

(b) If there is an adequate disclosure, should the agreement be invalidated on the ground that the provision for the wife is inadequate in relation to the husband's wealth? Del Vecchio v. Del Vecchio, 143 So.2d 17 (Fla.1962). Conversely, if the provision for the wife is adequate, is the contract invalidated by the husband's failure to make a full disclosure? In re Estate of Strickland, 181 Neb. 478, 149 N.W.2d 344 (1967). Who should have the burden of proof as to these matters? In re Estate of Hillegass, 431 Pa. 144, 244 A.2d 672 (1968).

(c) What should be the result when a full and fair disclosure has not been made, but the contract contains the following provision: "Each party to this agreement owns real and personal property, the extent of which has been disclosed by each to the other. Each party understands said disclosure, has read and understood this agreement, and agrees that this written agreement contains the whole agreement between the parties, to the exclusion of any side agreements, promises or representations." Cf. In re Estate of Harris, 431 Pa. 293, 245 A.2d 647 (1968), cert. den. 393 U.S. 1065 (1969). What further provisions should be inserted in the agreement, or what further steps should be taken to ensure that the agreement would not be upset?

(d) If a lawyer is consulted by the prospective spouses together, with the request that he prepare an antenuptial agreement, what should be his response? Would you handle the case in the way Mr. George's lawyer did in the *Kosik* case? ABA Code of Professional Responsibility, DR 5–105, EC 5–15 and 5–16 (1969); 2 A. Lindey, Separation Agreements and Ante-Nuptial Contracts, § 90–36 (1964); Cathey, Ante-Nuptial Agreements in Arkansas—A Drafter's Problem, 24 Ark.L.Rev. 275, 279 (1970).

4. Where property is transferred by one prospective spouse to the other at the time the antenuptial agreement is executed, in consideration for a release of marital property claims, a gift tax may be due. Merrill v. Fahs, 324 U.S. 308 (1945); Commissioner v. Wemyss, 324 U.S. 303 (1945). For

other possible tax implications of such transfers, see Clark, Antenuptial Contracts, 50 Univ. of Colo.L.Rev. 141, 157 (1979), and Note, Federal Tax Consequences of Antenuptial Contracts, 53 Wash.L.Rev. 105 (1977).

POSNER v. POSNER *

Supreme Court of Florida, 1970.
233 So.2d 381.

ROBERTS, Justice.　This cause is before the court on rehearing granted on petition for certiorari to review the decision of the Third District Court of Appeal in Posner v. Posner, 206 So.2d 416 (Fla.App. 1968).　Both parties had appealed to the appellate court for reversal of the decree of the Chancellor entered in a divorce suit—the wife having appealed from those portions of the decree awarding a divorce to the husband and the sum of $600 per month as alimony to the wife pursuant to the terms of an antenuptial agreement between the parties, and the husband having attacked, by cross-appeal, the award of $600 per month support money for each of the two minor children of the parties.

The three appellate judges who considered the appeals agreed upon the affirmance of the decree of divorce to the husband and the award for child support of $1,200 per month.　However, each took a different position respecting the antenuptial agreement concerning alimony.　Their respective views were (1) that the parties may validly agree upon alimony in an antenuptial agreement but that the trial court is not bound by their agreement;　(2) that such an agreement is void as against public policy;　and (3) that an antenuptial agreement respecting alimony is entitled to the same consideration and should be just as binding as an antenuptial agreement settling the property rights of the wife in her husband's estate upon his death. They have certified to this court, as one of great public interest, the question of the validity and binding effect of an antenuptial agreement respecting alimony in the event of the divorce or separation of the parties.　We have concluded that jurisdiction should be accepted, as authorized by Section 4(2), Article V, Florida Constitution, F.S.A.

At the outset we must recognize that there is a vast difference between a contract made in the market place and one relating to the institution of marriage.

It has long been the rule in a majority of the courts of this country and in this State that contracts intended to facilitate or promote the procurement of a divorce will be declared illegal as contrary to public policy.　*　*　*　The reason for the rule lies in the nature of the marriage contract and the interest of the State therein.

---

* The *Posner* case is noted in 3 Rutgers Camden L.Rev. 175 (1971), 4 Creighton L.Rev. 180 (1970), 23 U.Fla.L.Rev. 113 (1970), and 73 W.Va.L.Rev. 339 (1971).

At common law, the so-called "matrimonial causes", including divorce, were cognizable only in the Ecclesiastical Courts. Because of the Church's view of the sanctity of the nuptial tie, a marriage valid in its inception would not be dissolved by an absolute divorce *a vinculo matrimonii,* even for adultery—although such divorces could be granted by an Act of Parliament. Therefore, the divorce was only from bed and board, with an appropriate allowance for sustenance of the wife out of the husband's estate. * * * We have, of course, changed by statute the common-law rule respecting the indissolubility of a marriage valid in its inception; but the concept of marriage as a social institution that is the foundation of the family and of society remains unchanged. * * * Since marriage is of vital interest to society and the state, it has frequently been said that in every divorce suit the state is a third party whose interests take precedence over the private interests of the spouses. * * *

The state's interest in the preservation of the marriage is the basis for the rule that a divorce cannot be awarded by consent of the parties, as well as the doctrine of corroboration applicable in divorce suits. * * * In the *Underwood* case [12 Fla. 434 (1869)] this court said that it "would be aiming a deadly blow at public morals to decree a dissolution of the marriage contract merely because the parties requested it;" and in the *Pickston* case [109 So.2d 577 (Fla.App. 1959)] it was noted that the "prime object of the corroboration doctrine is to prevent collusion and to forestall any attempt which might otherwise be made to destroy the marital relationship falsely."

And it is this same public policy that is the basis for the rule that an antenuptial agreement by which a prospective wife waives or limits her right to alimony or to the property of her husband in the event of a divorce or separation, regardless of who is at fault, has been in some states held to be invalid. * * * The reason that such an agreement is said to "facilitate or promote the procurement of a divorce" was stated in Crouch v. Crouch, [53 Tenn.App. 594, 385 S.W.2d 288 (1964)] as follows:—

"Such contract could induce a mercenary husband to inflict on his wife any wrong he might desire with the knowledge his pecuniary liability would be limited. In other words, a husband could through abuse and ill treatment of his wife force her to bring an action for divorce and thereby buy a divorce for a small fee less than he would otherwise have to pay."

Antenuptial or so-called "marriage settlement" contracts by which the parties agree upon and fix the property rights which either spouse will have in the estate of the other upon his or her death have, however, long been recognized as being conducive to marital tranquility and thus in harmony with public policy. See Del Vecchio v. Del Vecchio, 143 So.2d 17 (Fla.1962), in which we prescribed the rules by which the validity of such antenuptial or postnuptial property settlement agreements should be tested. Such an agreement has been upheld after the death of the spouse even though it contained also a provision settling their property rights in the event of divorce or separation—the court concluding that it could not be said this provision "facilitated or tended to induce a separation or divorce." See In re Muxlow's Estate, 367 Mich. 133, 116 N.W.2d 43 (1962).

In this view of an antenuptial agreement that settles the right of the parties in the event of divorce as well as upon death, it is not inconceivable that a dissatisfied wife—secure in the knowledge that the provisions for alimony contained in the antenuptial agreement could not be enforced against her, but that she would be bound by the provisions limiting or waiving her property rights in the estate of her husband—might provoke her husband into divorcing her in order to collect a large alimony check every month, or a lump-sum award (since, in this State, a wife is entitled to alimony, if needed, even though the divorce is awarded to the husband) rather than take her chances on being remembered generously in her husband's will. In this situation, a valid antenuptial agreement limiting property rights upon death would have the same meretricious effect, insofar as the public policy in question is concerned, as would an antenuptial divorce provision in the circumstances hypothesized in Crouch v. Crouch, 53 Tenn.App. 594, 385 S.W.2d 288 (1965).

There can be no doubt that the institution of marriage is the foundation of the familial and social structure of our Nation and, as such, continues to be of vital interest to the State; but we cannot blind ourselves to the fact that the concept of the "sanctity" of a marriage—as being practically indissoluble, once entered into—held by our ancestors only a few generations ago, has been greatly eroded in the last several decades. This court can take judicial notice of the fact that the ratio of marriages to divorces has reached a disturbing rate in many states; and that a new concept of divorce—in which there is no "guilty" party— is being advocated by many groups and has been adopted by the State of California in a recent revision of its divorce laws providing for dissolution of a marriage upon pleading and proof of "irreconcilable differences" between the parties, without assessing the fault for the failure of the marriage against either party.

With divorce such a commonplace fact of life, it is fair to assume that many prospective marriage partners whose property and familial situation is such as to generate a valid antenuptial agreement settling their property rights upon the death of either, might want to consider and discuss also—and agree upon, if possible—the disposition of their property and the alimony rights of the wife in the event their marriage, despite their best efforts, should fail. In Allen v. Allen, 150 So. at page 238, this court said that the agreements relating to divorce that are held to be illegal as contrary to public policy are those "withdrawing opposition to the divorce or not to contest it or to conceal the true cause thereof by alleging another" and that they "have no reference to bona fide agreements relating to alimony or the adjustment of property rights between husband and wife, though in contemplation of divorce, if they are not directly conducive to the procurement of it."

We know of no community or society in which the public policy that condemned a husband and wife to a lifetime of misery as an alternative to the opprobrium of divorce still exists. And a tendency to recognize this change in public policy and to give effect to the antenuptial agreements of the parties relating to divorce is clearly discernible. Thus, in Hudson v. Hudson, 350 P.2d 596 (Okl.1960), the court simply applied to an antenuptial contract respecting alimony the rule applicable to antenuptial contracts settling property rights upon the death of a spouse and thus tacitly, if not expressly, discarded the contrary-to-public-policy rule.

     *   *   *

In re Muxlow's Estate, 367 Mich. 133, 116 N.W.2d 43 (1962), was a contest between the heirs of the deceased spouses, in which the heirs of the deceased husband relied upon an antenuptial agreement limiting the husband's financial obligations to the wife in the event of divorce and the share of his estate to which she would be entitled at his death. *The agreement was upheld*, the court stating that it could not be held that any effective provision in the agreement "provided for, facilitated, or tended to ind'ce a separation or divorce *   *   * ."

Strandberg v. Strandberg, 33 Wis.2d 204, 147 N.W.2d 349 (1967), was a divorce case in which an antenuptial agreement providing for the division of property in the event of divorce or separation was held to be void; however, it was held, also, that it could be admitted into evidence "and considered for a limited purpose as one of the circumstances in determining the equities of the division."

The trend of recent cases involving postnuptial agreements is well summarized by the court in Schulz v. Fox, 136 Mont. 152, 345 P. 2d 1045, 1050 (1959), as follows:—

"The conclusion to be drawn from these cases is that any agreement the purpose of which is to facilitate the granting of a divorce without proper grounds existing, is void, but that where proper grounds do exist, an agreement with respect to a property settlement, when not brought about by duress or coercion, cannot be said to perpetrate a fraud upon the court and will not be held void. *   *   * All of the well reasoned cases we have read look to the collusive intent, that is, as to whether the divorce was on proper grounds and as to whether the Court's interest in the continuity of the marriage status or support of spouse and children has been protected."

We have given careful consideration to the question of whether the change in public policy towards divorce requires a change in the rule respecting antenuptial agreements settling alimony and property rights of the parties upon divorce and have concluded that such agreements should no longer be held to be void *ab initio* as "contrary to public policy." If such an agreement is valid when tested by the stringent rules prescribed in Del Vecchio v. Del Vecchio, supra, 143 S.2d 17 (Fla.1962), for ante- and post-nuptial agreements settling the property rights of the spouses in the estate of the other upon death, and if, in addition, it is made to appear that the divorce was prosecuted in good faith, on proper grounds, so that, under the rules applicable to post-nuptial alimony and property settlement agreements referred to above, it could not be said to facilitate or promote the procurement of a divorce, then it should be held valid as to conditions existing at the time the agreement was made.

The question of the future binding effect of such antenuptial agreements when presented to the Chancellor for approval and incorporation in the final decree, and the question of the modification thereof upon a showing of a change in circumstances after the entry of the decree of divorce, should be decided under applicable statutory law and judicial decisions relating to postnuptial contracts settling the alimony and/or property rights of the parties.

Section 61.14, Florida Statutes, F.S.A. (ch. 16780, 1935) among other things, provides:—

"(1) When a husband and wife have entered or hereafter enter into an agreement for payments for, or instead of, support, maintenance or alimony, whether in connection with an action for divorce or separate maintenance or with any voluntary property settlement or when a husband is required by court order to make any payments to his wife, and the circumstances of the parties or the financial ability of the husband has changed since the execution of such agreement or the rendition of the order, either party may apply to the circuit court of the circuit in which the parties, or either of them, resided at the date of the execution of the agreement or reside at the date of the application or in which the agreement was executed or in which the order was rendered, for a judgment decreasing or increasing the amount of support, maintenance or alimony, and the court has jurisdiction to make orders as equity requires with due regard to the changed circumstances and the financial ability of the husband, decreasing or increasing or confirming the amount of separate support, maintenance or alimony provided for in the agreement or order."

We must assume that the parties to this litigation knew of the existence of § 61.14, Florida Statutes, F.S.A., when they made their agreement in 1960 and that their capacity to make the agreement was and is limited by same.

In summary, we hold that the antenuptial agreement, if entered into under the conditions outlined in Del Vecchio v. Del Vecchio, 143

So.2d 17 (Fla.1962), was a valid and binding agreement between the parties at the time and under the conditions it was made, but subject to be increased or decreased under changed conditions as provided in § 61.14, Florida Statutes, F.S.A.

Accordingly, the decision under review is quashed with instructions to the District Court of Appeal, Third District, to vacate that portion of the final decree of the trial court relating to alimony and support money and remand same for further proceedings in the trial court not inconsistent with this opinion.

NOTES AND QUESTIONS

1. As the *Posner* case concedes, the prior cases nearly universally held that the parties, by their antenuptial agreement, could not validly regulate the disposition of property or the award of alimony on divorce. Any agreement attempting to accomplish this was declared to be contrary to public policy and void. See, e. g., Reiling v. Reiling, 474 P.2d 327 (Or.1970), citing other cases, and Annot., 57 A.L.R.2d 942 (1958). In re Muxlow's Estate, 367 Mich. 133, 116 N.W.2d 43 (1962), relied on by *Posner,* does not stand for a contrary rule. One earlier and inadequately reasoned case, Hudson v. Hudson, 350 P.2d 596 (Okl.1960), does support *Posner.*

The leading case for the position that such contracts are void is Fricke v. Fricke, 257 Wis. 124, 42 N.W.2d 500 (1950), which contains the following language: "There are three parties to a marriage contract—the husband, the wife, and the state. The husband and wife are presumed to have, and the state unquestionably has an interest in the maintenance of the relation which for centuries has been recognized as a bulwark of our civilization. That unusual conditions have caused a marked increase in the divorce rate does not require us to change our attitude toward the marital relation and its obligations, nor should it encourage the growth of a tendency to treat it as a bargain made with as little concern and dignity as is given to the ordinary contract * * * The court should not look with favor upon an agreement which may tend to permit a reservation in the mind of the husband when he assumes the responsibility of maintaining his spouse in such comfort as he is able to provide and until his death or the law relieves him of it * * *. At least a majority, if not all of the courts which have considered the matter have held that any antenuptial contract which provides for, facilitates, or tends to induce a separation or divorce of the parties after marriage, is contrary to public policy and is therefore void. Quite generally the courts have said that the contract itself invites dispute, encourages separation and incites divorce proceedings * * *."

(a) What arguments may be made to support either the *Posner* case or the *Fricke* case?

(b) Does the contract in the *Posner* case invite dispute, encourage separation and incite divorce? In deciding this point, the facts in the *Posner* case may be relevant. As revealed by the Florida Supreme Court in a later opinion in the case (Posner v. Posner, 257 So.2d 530 (Fla.1972), and by the dissent in the District Court of Appeal (206 So.2d 416, 420), they were that the wife had sued for alimony and the husband counterclaimed for divorce, the divorce being granted to the husband on the ground of extreme cruelty. The husband had been reluctant to marry, and the wife, in order to persuade him to marry her, had urged the execution of the antenuptial agreement, which provided for alimony of six hundred dollars per month in the event of divorce, and a payment of $21,600 on the husband's death. At the time of the marriage the husband was a life beneficiary of a trust in the amount of $8,600,000. The trustees could, in their discretion, invade principal for his benefit. He had other assets worth about $1,600,000. The parties had been married six years and had two children. The wife was represented when the antenuptial agreement was signed. The Florida Supreme Court, in the second opinion cited above held that the husband had failed to disclose to the wife that he might receive distributions from the corpus of the trust to maintain his standard of living, that he failed to disclose the amount of income from the trust, and that this was in addition to the $1,600,000 held outside the trust. The court then held that since the provision for the wife was disproportionate to the husband's means, this imposed upon him the burden of showing he had made a full disclosure of his property, and he had failed to sustain this burden. The case was remanded for the determination of permanent alimony in the light of the holding, the court at the same time awarding the wife $146,400.00 as temporary alimony, this being arrived at at the rate of $3,000 per month from the date of the divorce decree, less credit for the $600 per month which the husband had paid under the agreement.

Cases which agree with *Posner* include Volid v. Volid, 6 Ill.App.3d 386, 286 N.E.2d 42 (1972); Tomlinson v. Tomlinson, —— Ind.App. ——, 352 N. E.2d 785 (1976); Buettner v. Buettner, 89 Nev. 39, 505 P.2d 600 (1973); In re Marriage of Ingels, —— Colo.App. ——, 596 P.2d 1211 (1979). A case which refused to follow *Posner* is Connolly v. Connolly, —— S.D. ——, 270 N.W.2d 44 (1978), 24 S.D.L.Rev. 495 (1979). A case which takes an equivocal position on the question is Marriage of Dawley, 17 Cal.3d 342, 131 Cal. Rptr. 3, 551 P.2d 323 (1976). In this case the parties' antenuptial agreement was made with the understanding that they would be divorced and provided that the earnings and property acquired during the marriage would remain the separate property of each. The court held that their "subjective contemplation" that they would be divorced did not invalidate the agreement, but that the agreement would be invalid if its terms should encourage or promote dissolution.

2. Husband and wife are married when they are both twenty-three. Before marriage they execute a written antenuptial agreement which provides that if they should be divorced, neither would seek alimony (either temporary or permanent) from the other, and that the property owned by both would be aggregated and divided in half, one half going to each. At the time of their marriage neither has any property and both are working. Fifteen years later, when the wife has stopped working and is caring for their two children, they find they cannot get along together and agree to get a divorce. In the meantime they have accumulated no property. Assuming that there was full disclosure and full representation on the part of both parties when the antenuptial agreement was made, and that the *Posner* case controls, does this agreement incite divorce? Are there any other objections to enforcing it in the divorce action? Should it be enforced?

Belcher v. Belcher, 271 So.2d 7 (Fla.1972). If not enforced might it be admitted in evidence for the court to consider? Moats v. Moats, 168 Colo. 120, 450 P.2d 64 (1969). Would you advise parties in this situation to execute such an agreement?

3. Husband and wife execute an antenuptial agreement which provides that wife waives her right to elect a share in the husband's estate, in return for which he agrees to leave her $50,000 in his will. Assume that there is full disclosure and no overreaching. Later the parties are divorced, after which the husband dies without a will. What should be the result? Would the result be different if the wife obtained an annulment on the ground that the marriage was void because the parties were uncle and niece under the law of the state of celebration? Cf. Sims v. Sims, 186 Neb. 780, 186 N.W.2d 491 (1971), with In re Estate of Simms, 26 N.Y.2d 163, 309 N. Y.S.2d 170, 257 N.E.2d 627 (1970), 9 Duq.L.Rev. 135 (1970).

4. H-1 and W, both well along in life, each with children of former marriages, make an antenuptial agreement that they will make reciprocal wills. The agreement is that each will make a will leaving all of his property to the other, with the further provision that the spouse dying last will leave to the children of the other spouse all of the property received via the will of the other spouse. Thus if H-1 should die first, his will would leave all his property to W, and her will would leave that property to the children of H-1. The wills are made in accordance with the agreement. H-1 dies, leaving all his property to W. W then marries H-2 and dies. There are two children of H-1 who would be entitled to take under W's will the property which she received by the will of H-1, which is substantially all the property she owns at her death. May H-2 take a statutory forced share of the estate of W, against her will, thereby pro tanto depriving the children of H-1? Would you draft an antenuptial agreement in this way? How else might the same thing be better done?

You should assume that this problem arises in a particular state and deal with it on the basis of a specific forced share statute. The relevant sections of the Uniform Probate Code are §§ 2–202, 2–508, 8 Unif.L.Ann. 333, 353 (1972). See also Rubinstein v. Mueller, 19 N.Y.2d 228, 278 N.Y.S.2d 845, 225 N.E.2d 540 (1967); Simpson v. Dodge, 220 Ga. 705, 141 S.E.2d 532 (1965); In re Estate of Stewart, 69 Cal.2d 296, 70 Cal.Rptr. 545, 444 P.2d 337 (1968). For possible tax implications see Saul Kampf, 56 T.C. 293 (1971).

5. Draft an antenuptial agreement which will accomplish the purposes of the prospective spouses described as follows. H and W propose to marry. Since they are about fifty years old and have been married before, with children of the earlier marriages, they wish to retain as the separate property of each of them all property brought into the marriage and any property either may acquire during the marriage. There is one exception to this intention, however, in the form of their residence. They propose to buy, using the funds of both of them, a valuable piece of residential real estate in which they will live. They wish this real estate or any other real estate purchased as a residence to remain separate property in proportion to the contributions of each of them. But they also wish to make sure that when either dies, the other may continue living in the home until he or she dies or no longer wishes to remain.

See Marriage of Dawley, 17 Cal.3d 342, 131 Cal.Rptr. 3, 551 P.2d 323 (1976); Williams v. Williams, 569 S.W.2d 867 (Tex.1978), 56 Tex.L.Rev. 861 (1978).

6. You are consulted by H and W, a young couple proposing to be married, who wish to have an antenuptial agreement dealing with many of the aspects of their marriage in addition to property or financial matters. Both are twenty-seven years old. W, having spent several years in an advertising agency after college, decided to become a lawyer and is in her first year of law school. H has completed a management training course with a large corporation and works for that corporation in a minor executive capacity. He believes that he can look forward to promotions and a successful career with the company. He agrees to support both of them during W's law school years, including her expenses for tuition, books and fees. After her graduation from law school they will contribute equally to the household expenses, since both expect to work. If they should be divorced before W completes law school, H agrees to support W through law school in the same way. After her graduation W agrees that she will reimburse H for all expenses attributable to law school. They both agree that they will not have children for the first four years of marriage, birth control being the responsibility of both. At the end of that time they will have two children, one or two years apart. Sexual relations will occur only upon mutual consent. W will continue to work except during those brief periods when pregnancy and birth of a child make work impossible. H and W will share equally in child care or in providing child care by baby sitters or day care centers. They will decide where they will live by mutual agreement, giving due consideration to the careers of both. W's parents are elderly and in poor health. H and W agree that W's parents will not be invited to live with them. On a more conventional level, H and W agree that the earnings of each will remain the separate property of each, that each will contribute equally to the education of any children, and that neither will seek alimony in the event of divorce.

(a) Would you draft a contract embodying these understandings on behalf of H and W? If you would do so, should you represent only one of them, or could you represent both?

(b) If you would draft such a contract, would you provide for any sanctions in the event of a violation? If one provision were violated, would that excuse performance of other provisions?

(c) Would you include in such a contract a provision for arbitration in the event of any dispute over performance?

The foregoing question obviously owes much to the thorough and influential article by Professor Weitzman, Legal Regulation of Marriage: Tradition and Change, 62 Cal.L.Rev. 1169 (1974). See also Note, Marriage Contracts for Support and Services: Constitutionality Begins at Home, 49 N. Y.U.L.Rev. 1161 (1975), making an argument that the constitution requires the courts to enforce such contracts. For a somewhat earlier example of a similar agreement, see William Congreve, The Way of the World, Act IV, Scene 1 (1700).

MARVIN v. MARVIN *

Supreme Court of California, In Bank, 1976.
18 Cal.3d 660, 134 Cal.Rptr. 815, 557 P.2d 106.

TOBRINER, Justice.   During the past 15 years, there has been a substantial increase in the number of couples living together without marrying.[1]   Such nonmarital relationships lead to legal controversy when one partner dies or the couple separates.   Courts of Appeal, faced with the task of determining property rights in such cases, have arrived at conflicting positions: two cases (In re Marriage of Cary (1973) 34 Cal.App.3d 345, 109 Cal.Rptr. 862; Estate of Atherley (1975) 44 Cal.App.3d 758, 119 Cal.Rptr. 41) have held that the Family Law Act (Civ.Code, § 4000 et seq.) requires division of the property according to community property principles, and one decision (Beckman v. Mayhew (1975) 49 Cal.App.3d 529, 122 Cal.Rptr. 604) has rejected that holding.   We take this opportunity to resolve that controversy and to declare the principles which should govern distribution of property acquired in a nonmarital relationship.

We conclude: (1) The provisions of the Family Law Act do not govern the distribution of property acquired during a nonmarital relationship; such a relationship remains subject solely to judicial decision. (2) The courts should enforce express contracts between nonmarital partners except to the extent that the contract is explicitly founded on the consideration of meretricious sexual services.   (3) In the absence of an express contract, the courts should inquire into the conduct of the parties to determine whether that conduct demonstrates an implied contract, agreement of partnership or joint venture, or some other tacit understanding between the parties.   The courts may also employ the doctrine of quantum meruit, or equitable remedies such as constructive or resulting trusts, when warranted by the facts of the case.

In the instant case plaintiff and defendant lived together for seven years without marrying; all property acquired during this period was taken in defendant's name.   When plaintiff sued to enforce a

---

* The point in the course at which the *Marvin* case should be discussed is a matter as to which there may be legitimate disagreement.   It is placed here because the first branch of the case involves a contract and because the practitioner's response to the case will doubtless be a recommendation that parties living together make a contract before undertaking their relationship.   It has obvious connections with maintenance and the division of property on divorce, and with the nature and obligations of marriage, and may be discussed in conjunction with those sections of the course.   For the sake of simplicity and out of a dislike for splitting judicial opinions, the entire opinion is printed at this point even though parts of it may be discussed later on. [Ed. note.]

1. "The 1970 census figures indicate that today perhaps eight times as many couples are living together without being married as cohabited ten years ago." (Comment, In re Cary: A Judicial Recognition of Illicit Cohabitation (1974) 25 Hastings L. J. 1226.)

contract under which she was entitled to half the property and to support payments, the trial court granted judgment on the pleadings for defendant, thus leaving him with all property accumulated by the couple during their relationship. Since the trial court denied plaintiff a trial on the merits of her claim, its decision conflicts with the principles stated above, and must be reversed.

1. *The factual setting of this appeal.*

Since the trial court rendered judgment for defendant on the pleadings, we must accept the allegations of plaintiff's complaint as true, determining whether such allegations state, or can be amended to state, a cause of action. We turn therefore to the specific allegations of the complaint.

Plaintiff avers that in October of 1964 she and defendant "entered into an oral agreement" that while "the parties lived together they would combine their efforts and earnings and would share equally any and all property accumulated as a result of their efforts whether individual or combined." Furthermore, they agreed to "hold themselves out to the general public as husband and wife" and that "plaintiff would further render her services as a companion, homemaker, housekeeper and cook to * * * defendant."

Shortly thereafter plaintiff agreed to "give up her lucrative career as an entertainer [and] singer" in order to "devote her full time to defendant * * * as a companion, homemaker, housekeeper and cook;" in return defendant agreed to "provide for all of plaintiff's financial support and needs for the rest of her life."

Plaintiff alleges that she lived with defendant from October of 1964 through May of 1970 and fulfilled her obligations under the agreement. During this period the parties as a result of their efforts and earnings acquired in defendant's name substantial real and personal property, including motion picture rights worth over $1 million. In May of 1970, however, defendant compelled plaintiff to leave his household. He continued to support plaintiff until November of 1971, but thereafter refused to provide further support.

On the basis of these allegations plaintiff asserts two causes of action. The first, for declaratory relief, asks the court to determine her contract and property rights; the second seeks to impose a constructive trust upon one half of the property acquired during the course of the relationship.

Defendant demurred unsuccessfully, and then answered the complaint. Following extensive discovery and pretrial proceedings, the case came to trial. Defendant renewed his attack on the complaint by a motion to dismiss. Since the parties had stipulated that defendant's marriage to Betty Marvin did not terminate until the filing of a final decree of divorce in January 1967, the trial court treated defendant's motion as one for judgment on the pleadings augmented by the stipulation.

After hearing argument the court granted defendant's motion and entered judgment for defendant. Plaintiff moved to set aside the judgment and asked leave to amend her complaint to allege that she and defendant reaffirmed their agreement after defendant's divorce was final. The trial court denied plaintiff's motion, and she appealed from the judgment.

2. *Plaintiff's complaint states a cause of action for breach of an express contract.*

In Trutalli v. Meraviglia (1932) 215 Cal. 698, 12 P.2d 430 we established the principle that nonmarital partners may lawfully contract concerning the ownership of property acquired during the relationship. We reaffirmed this principle in Vallera v. Vallera (1943) 21 Cal.2d 681, 685, 134 P.2d 761, 763, stating that "If a man and woman [who are not married] live together as husband and wife under an agreement to pool their earnings and share equally in their joint accumulations, equity will protect the interests of each in such property."

In the case before us plaintiff, basing her cause of action in contract upon these precedents, maintains that the trial court erred in denying her a trial on the merits of her contention. Although that court did not specify the ground for its conclusion that plaintiff's contractual allegations stated no cause of action, defendant offers some four theories to sustain the ruling; we proceed to examine them.

Defendant first and principally relies on the contention that the alleged contract is so closely related to the supposed "immoral" character of the relationship between plaintiff and himself that the enforcement of the contract would violate public policy. He points to cases asserting that a contract between nonmarital partners is unenforceable if it is "involved in" an illicit relationship, or made in "contemplation" of such a relationship. A review of the numerous California decisions concerning contracts between nonmarital partners, however, reveals that the courts have not employed such broad and uncertain standards to strike down contracts. The decisions instead disclose a narrower and more precise standard: a contract between nonmarital partners is unenforceable only *to the extent* that it *explicitly* rests upon the immoral and illicit consideration of meretricious sexual services.

[At this point in its opinion the court briefly stated Trutalli v. Meraviglia, 215 Cal. 698, 12 P.2d 430 (1932); Bridges v. Bridges, 125 Cal.App.2d 359, 270 P.2d 69 (1954); and Croslin v. Scott, 154 Cal. App.2d 767, 316 P.2d 755 (1957). All three cases contained language stating that a contract concerning property made by persons living together but not married was valid so long as an immoral relationship was not made a consideration of the contract.]

Numerous other cases have upheld enforcement of agreements between nonmarital partners in factual settings essentially indistinguishable from the present case.[5]

Although the past decisions hover over the issue in the somewhat wispy form of the figures of a Chagall painting, we can abstract from those decisions a clear and simple rule. The fact that a man and woman live together without marriage, and engage in a sexual relationship, does not in itself invalidate agreements between them relating to their earnings, property, or expenses. Neither is such an agreement invalid merely because the parties may have contemplated the creation or continuation of a nonmarital relationship when they entered into it. Agreements between nonmarital partners fail only to the extent that they rest upon a consideration of meretricious sexual services. Thus the rule asserted by defendant, that a contract fails if it is "involved in" or made "in contemplation" of a nonmarital relationship, cannot be reconciled with the decisions.

The three cases cited by defendant which have *declined* to enforce contracts between nonmarital partners involved consideration that was expressly founded upon an illicit sexual services. In Hill v. Estate of Westbrook, supra, 95 Cal.App.2d 599, 213 P.2d 727, the woman promised to keep house for the man, to live with him as man and wife, and to bear his children; the man promised to provide for her in his will, but died without doing so. Reversing a judgment for the woman based on the reasonable value of her services, the Court of Appeal stated that "the action is predicated upon a claim which seeks, among other things, the reasonable value of living with decedent in meretricious relationship and bearing him two children * * *. The law does not award compensation for living with a man as a concubine and bearing him children. * * * As the judgment is, at least in part, for the value of the claimed services for which recovery cannot be had, it must be reversed." (95 Cal.App.2d at p. 603, 213 P.2d at p. 730.) Upon retrial, the trial court found that it could not sever the contract and place an independent value upon the legitimate services performed by claimant. We therefore

---

5. Defendant urges that all of the cited cases, with the possible exception of In re Marriage of Foster, supra, 42 Cal.App.3d 577, 117 Cal.Rptr. 49, and Bridges v. Bridges, supra, 125 Cal. App.2d 359, 270 P.2d 69, can be distinguished on the ground that the partner seeking to enforce the contract contributed either property or services additional to ordinary homemaking services. No case however, suggests that a pooling agreement in which one partner contributes only homemaking services is invalid, and dictum in Hill v. Estate of Westbrook (1950) 95 Cal.App.2d 599, 603, 213 P. 2d 727, states the opposite. A promise to perform homemaking services is, of course, a lawful and adequate consideration for a contract (see Taylor v. Taylor (1954) 66 Cal.App.2d 390, 398, 152 P.2d 480)—otherwise those engaged in domestic employment could not sue for their wages —and defendant advances no reason why his proposed distinction would justify denial of enforcement to contracts supported by such consideration. (See Tyranski v. Piggins (1973) 44 Mich.App. 570, 205 N.W.2d 595, 597.)

affirmed a judgment for the estate. (Hill v. Estate of Westbrook (1952) 39 Cal.2d 458, 247 P.2d 19.)

In the only other cited decision refusing to enforce a contract, Updeck v. Samuel (1964), 123 Cal.App.2d 264, 266 P.2d 822, the contract "was based on the consideration that the parties live together as husband and wife." (123 Cal.App.2d at p. 267, 266 P.2d at p. 824.) Viewing the contract as calling for adultery, the court held it illegal.

The decisions in the *Hill* and *Updeck* cases thus demonstrate that a contract between nonmarital partners, even if expressly made in contemplation of a common living arrangement, is invalid only if sexual acts form an inseparable part of the consideration for the agreement. In sum, a court will not enforce a contract for the pooling of property and earnings if it is explicitly and inseparably based upon services as a paramour. The Court of Appeal opinion in *Hill*, however, indicates that even if sexual services are part of the contractual consideration, any *severable* portion of the contract supported by independent consideration will still be enforced.

The principle that a contract between nonmarital partners will be enforced unless expressly and inseparably based upon an illicit consideration of sexual services not only represents the distillation of the decisional law, but also offers a far more precise and workable standard than that advocated by defendant. Our recent decision in In re Marriage of Dawley (1976) 17 Cal.3d 342, 551 P.2d 323, offers a close analogy. Rejecting the contention that an antenuptial agreement is invalid if the parties contemplated a marriage of short duration, we pointed out in *Dawley* that a standard based upon the subjective contemplation of the parties is uncertain and unworkable; such a test, we stated, "might invalidate virtually all antenuptial agreements on the ground that the parties contemplated dissolution * * * but it provides no principled basis for determining which antenuptial agreements offend public policy and which do not." (17 Cal.3d 342, 352, 551 P.2d 323, 329.)

Similarly, in the present case a standard which inquires whether an agreement is "involved" in or "contemplates" a nonmarital relationship is vague and unworkable. Virtually all agreements between nonmarital partners can be said to be "involved" in some sense in the fact of their mutual sexual relationship, or to "contemplate" the existence of that relationship. Thus defendant's proposed standards, if taken literally, might invalidate all agreements between nonmarital partners, a result no one favors. Moreover, those standards offer no basis to distinguish between valid and invalid agreements. By looking not to such uncertain tests, but only to the consideration underlying the agreement, we provide the parties and the courts with a practical guide to determine when an agreement between nonmarital partners should be enforced.

Defendant secondly relies upon the ground suggested by the trial court: that the 1964 contract violated public policy because it impaired the community property rights of Betty Marvin, defendant's lawful wife. Defendant points out that his earnings while living apart from his wife before rendition of the interlocutory decree were community property under 1964 statutory law (former Civ.Code, §§ 169, 169.2) [7] and that defendant's agreement with plaintiff purported to transfer to her a half interest in that community property. But whether or not defendant's contract with plaintiff exceeded his authority as manager of the community property (see former Civ.Code, § 172), defendant's argument fails for the reason that an improper transfer of community property is not void *ab initio,* but merely voidable at the instance of the aggrieved spouse.

In the present case Betty Marvin, the aggrieved spouse, had the opportunity to assert her community property rights in the divorce action. The interlocutory and final decrees in that action fix and limit her interest. Enforcement of the contract between plaintiff and defendant against property awarded to defendant by the divorce decree will not impair any right of Betty's, and thus is not on that account violative of public policy.[8]

Defendant's third contention is noteworthy for the lack of authority advanced in its support. He contends that enforcement of the oral agreement between plaintiff and himself is barred by Civil Code section 5134, which provides that "All contracts for marriage settlements must be in writing * * * ." A marriage settlement, however, is an agreement in contemplation of marriage in which each party agrees to release or modify the property rights which would otherwise arise from the marriage. (See Corker v. Corker (1891) 87 Cal. 643, 648, 25 P. 922.) The contract at issue here does not conceivably fall within that definition, and thus is beyond the compass of section 5134.[9]

---

7. Sections 169 and 169.2 were replaced in 1970 by Civil Code section 5118. In 1972 section 5118 was amended to provide that the earnings and accumulations of *both* spouses "while living separate and apart from the other spouse, are the separate property of the spouse."

8. Defendant also contends that the contract is invalid as an agreement to promote or encourage divorce. (See 1 Witkin, Summary of Cal.Law (8th ed.) pp. 390–392 and cases there cited.) The contract between plaintiff and defendant did not, however, by its terms require defendant to divorce Betty, nor reward him for so doing. Moreover, the principle on which defendant relies does not apply when the marriage in question is beyond redemption (Glickman v. Collins (1975) 13 Cal.3d 852, 858–859, 120 Cal.Rptr. 76, 533 P.2d 204); whether or not defendant's marriage to Betty was beyond redemption when defendant contracted with plaintiff is obviously a question of fact which cannot be resolved by judgment on the pleadings.

9. Our review of the many cases enforcing agreements between nonmarital partners reveals that the majority of such agreements were oral. In two cases (Ferguson v. Schuenemann, supra, 167 Cal.App.2d 413, 334 P.2d 668; Cline v. Festersen, supra, 128 Cal.App.2d 380, 275 P.2d 149), the court expressly rejected defenses grounded upon the statute of frauds.

*   *   *

In summary, we base our opinion on the principle that adults who voluntarily live together and engage in sexual relations are nonetheless as competent as any other persons to contract respecting their earnings and property rights. Of course, they cannot lawfully contract to pay for the performance of sexual services, for such a contract is, in essence, an agreement for prostitution and unlawful for that reason. But they may agree to pool their earnings and to hold all property acquired during the relationship in accord with the law governing community property; conversely they may agree that each partner's earnings and the property acquired from those earnings remains the separate property of the earning partner. So long as the agreement does not rest upon illicit meretricious consideration, the parties may order their economic affairs as they choose, and no policy precludes the courts from enforcing such agreements.

In the present instance, plaintiff alleges that the parties agreed to pool their earnings, that they contracted to share equally in all property acquired, and that defendant agreed to support plaintiff. The terms of the contract as alleged do not rest upon any unlawful consideration. We therefore conclude that the complaint furnishes a suitable basis upon which the trial court can render declaratory relief. The trial court consequently erred in granting defendant's motion for judgment on the pleadings.

3. *Plaintiff's complaint can be amended to state a cause of action founded upon theories of implied contract or equitable relief.*

As we have noted, both causes of action in plaintiff's complaint allege an express contract; neither assert any basis for relief independent from the contract. In In re Marriage of Cary, supra, 34 Cal.App.3d 345, 109 Cal.Rptr. 862, however, the Court of Appeal held that, in view of the policy of the Family Law Act, property accumulated by nonmarital partners in an actual family relationship should be divided equally. Upon examining the *Cary* opinion, the parties to the present case realized that plaintiff's alleged relationship with defendant might arguably support a cause of action independent of any express contract between the parties. The parties have therefore briefed and discussed the issue of the property rights of a nonmarital partner in the absence of an express contract. Although our conclusion that plaintiff's complaint states a cause of action based on an express contract alone compels us to reverse the judgment for defendant, resolution of the *Cary* issue will serve both to guide the parties upon retrial and to resolve a conflict presently manifest in published Court of Appeal decisions.

Both plaintiff and defendant stand in broad agreement that the law should be fashioned to carry out the reasonable expectations of the parties. Plaintiff, however, presents the following contentions: that the decisions prior to *Cary* rest upon implicit and erroneous notions of punishing a party for his or her guilt in entering into a non-marital relationship, that such decisions result in an inequitable distribution of property accumulated during the relationship, and that *Cary* correctly held that the enactment of the Family Law Act in 1970 overturned those prior decisions. Defendant in response maintains that the prior decisions merely applied common law principles of contract and property to persons who have deliberately elected to remain outside the bounds of the community property system.[11] *Cary*, defendant contends, erred in holding that the Family Law Act vitiated the force of the prior precedents.

As we shall see from examination of the pre-*Cary* decisions, the truth lies somewhere between the positions of plaintiff and defendant. The classic opinion on this subject is Vallera v. Vallera, supra, 21 Cal.2d 681, 134 P.2d 761. Speaking for a four-member majority, Justice Traynor posed the question: "whether a woman living with a man as his wife but with no genuine belief that she is legally married to him acquires by reason of cohabitation alone the rights of a co-tenant in his earnings and accumulations during the period of their relationship." (21 Cal.2d at p. 684, 134 P.2d at p. 762.) Citing Flanagan v. Capital Nat. Bank (1931) 213 Cal. 664, 3 P.2d 307, which held that a nonmarital "wife" could not claim that her husband's estate was community property, the majority answered that question "in the negative." (21 Cal.2d pp. 684–685, 134 P.2d 761.) *Vallera* explains that "Equitable considerations arising from the reasonable expectation of the continuation of benefits attending the status of marriage entered into in good faith are not present in such a case." (P. 685, 134 P.2d p. 763.) In the absence of express contract, *Vallera* concluded, the woman is entitled to share in property jointly accumulated only "in the proportion that her funds contributed toward its acquisition." (P. 685, 134 P.2d p. 763.) Justice Curtis, dissenting, argued that the evidence showed an implied contract under which each party owned an equal interest in property acquired during the relationship.

---

11. We note that a deliberate decision to avoid the strictures of the community property system is not the only reason that couples live together without marriage. Some couples may wish to avoid the permanent commitment that marriage implies, yet be willing to share equally any property acquired during the relationship; others may fear the loss of pension, welfare, or tax benefits resulting from marriage (see Beckman v. Mayhew, supra, 49 Cal.App.3d 529, 122 Cal.Rptr. 604). Others may engage in the relationship as a possible prelude to marriage. In lower socioeconomic groups the difficulty and expense of dissolving a former marriage often leads couples to choose a nonmarital relationship; many unmarried couples may also incorrectly believe that the doctrine of common law marriage prevails in California, and thus that they are in fact married. Consequently we conclude that the mere fact that a couple have not participated in a valid marriage ceremony cannot serve as a basis for a court's inference that the couple intend to keep their earnings and property separate and independent; the parties' intention can only be ascertained by a more searching inquiry into the nature of their relationship.

The majority opinion in *Vallera* did not expressly bar recovery based upon an implied contract, nor preclude resort to equitable remedies. But Vallera's broad assertion that equitable considerations "are not present" in the case of a nonmarital relationship (21 Cal.2d at p. 685, 134 P.2d 761) led the Courts of Appeal to interpret the language to preclude recovery based on such theories. (See Lazzarevich v. Lazzarevich (1948) 88 Cal.App.2d 708, 719, 200 P.2d 49; Oakley v. Oakley (1947) 82 Cal.App.2d 188, 191–192, 185 P.2d 848.) [12]

Consequently, when the issue of the rights of a nonmarital partner reached this court in Keene v. Keene (1962) 57 Cal.2d 657, 21 Cal.Rptr. 593, 371 P.2d 329, the claimant forwent reliance upon theories of contract implied in law or fact. Asserting that she had worked on her partner's ranch and that her labor had enhanced its value, she confined her cause of action to the claim that the court should impress a resulting trust on the property derived from the sale of the ranch. The court limited its opinion accordingly, rejecting her argument on the ground that the rendition of services gives rise to a resulting trust only when the services aid in acquisition of the property, not in its subsequent improvement. (57 Cal.2d at p. 668, 21 Cal.Rptr. 593, 371 P.2d 329.) Justice Peters, dissenting, attacked the majority's distinction between the rendition of services and the contribution of funds or property; he maintained that both property and services furnished valuable consideration, and potentially afforded the ground for a resulting trust.

This failure of the courts to recognize an action by a nonmarital partner based upon implied contract, or to grant an equitable remedy, contrasts with the judicial treatment of the putative spouse. Prior to the enactment of the Family Law Act, no statute granted rights to a putative spouse. [13] The courts accordingly fashioned a variety of remedies by judicial decision. Some cases permitted the putative spouse to recover half the property on a theory that the conduct of the parties implied an agreement of partnership or joint venture. Others permitted the spouse to recover the reasonable value of rendered services, less the value of support received. (See Sanguinetti v. Sanguinetti (1937) 9 Cal.2d 95, 100–102, 69 P.2d 845.) [14] Finally, deci-

---

12. The cases did not clearly determine whether a nonmarital partner could recover in quantum meruit for the reasonable value of services rendered. But when we affirmed a trial court ruling denying recovery in Hill v. Estate of Westbrook, supra, 39 Cal.2d 458, 247 P.2d 19, we did so in part on the ground that whether the partner "rendered her services because of expectation of monetary reward" (p. 462, 247 P.2d p. 21) was a question of fact resolved against her by the trial court—thus implying that in a proper case the court would allow recovery based on quantum meruit.

13. The Family Law Act, in Civil Code section 4452, classifies property acquired during a putative marriage as "quasi-marital property," and requires that such property be divided upon dissolution of the marriage in accord with Civil Code section 4800.

14. The putative spouse need not prove that he rendered services in expectation of monetary reward in order to recover the reasonable value

sions affirmed the power of a court to employ equitable principles to achieve a fair division of property acquired during putative marriage. (Coats v. Coats (1911) 160 Cal. 671, 677–678, 118 P. 441; Caldwell v. Odisio (1956) 142 Cal.App.2d 732, 735, 299 P.2d 14.) [15]

Thus in summary, the cases prior to *Cary* exhibited a schizophrenic inconsistency. By enforcing an express contract between nonmarital partners unless it rested upon an unlawful consideration, the courts applied a common law principle as to contracts. Yet the courts disregarded the common law principle that holds that implied contracts can arise from the conduct of the parties.[16] Refusing to enforce such contracts, the courts spoke of leaving the parties "in the position in which they had placed themselves", just as if they were guilty parties "in pari delicto."

Justice Curtis noted this inconsistency in his dissenting opinion in *Vallera,* pointing out that "if an express agreement will be enforced, there is no legal or just reason why an implied agreement to share the property cannot be enforced." (21 Cal.2d 681, 686, 134 P. 2d 761, 764; see Bruch, Property Rights of De Facto Spouses Including Thoughts on the Value of Homemakers' Services (1976) 10 Family L.Q. 101, 117–121.) And in Keene v. Keene, supra, 57 Cal.2d 657, 21 Cal.Rptr. 593, 371 P.2d 329, Justice Peters observed that if the man and woman "were not illegally living together * * * it would be a plain business relationship and a contract would be implied." (Diss. opn. at p. 672, 21 Cal.Rptr. at p. 602, 371 P.2d at p. 338.)

Still another inconsistency in the prior cases arises from their treatment of property accumulated through joint effort. To the ex-

---

of those services. (Sanguinetti v. Sanguinetti, supra, 9 Cal.2d 95, 100, 69 P.2d 845.)

15. The contrast between principles governing nonmarital and putative relationships appears most strikingly in Lazzarevich v. Lazzarevich, supra, 88 Cal.App.2d 708, 200 P.2d 49. When Mrs. Lazzarevich sued her husband for divorce in 1945, she discovered to her surprise that she was not lawfully married to him. She nevertheless reconciled with him, and the Lazzareviches lived together for another year before they finally separated. The court awarded her recovery for the reasonable value of services rendered, less the value of support received, until she discovered the invalidity of the marriage, but denied recovery for the same services rendered after that date.

16. "Contracts may be express or implied. These terms, however, do not denote different kinds of contracts, but have reference to the evidence by which the agreement between the parties is shown. If the agreement is shown by the direct words of the parties, spoken or written, the contract is said to be an express one. But if such agreement can only be shown by the acts and conduct of the parties, interpreted in the light of the subject-matter and of the surrounding circumstances, then the contract is an implied one." (Skelly v. Bristol Sav. Bank (1893) 63 Conn. 83, 26 A. 474, 475, quoted in 1 Corbin, Contracts (1963) p. 41.) Thus, as Justice Schauer observed in Desny v. Wilder (1956) 46 Cal.2d 715, 299 P.2d 257, in a sense all contracts made in fact, as distinguished from quasi-contractual obligations, are express contracts, differing only in the manner in which the assent of the parties is expressed and proved. (See 46 Cal.2d at pp. 735–736, 299 P.2d 257.)

tent that a partner had contributed *funds* or *property,* the cases held that the partner obtains a proportionate share in the acquisition, despite the lack of legal standing of the relationship. Yet courts have refused to recognize just such an interest based upon the contribution of *services.* As Justice Curtis points out "Unless it can be argued that a woman's services as cook, housekeeper, and homemaker are valueless, it would seem logical that if, when she contributes money to the purchase of property, her interest will be protected, then when she contributes her services in the home, her interest in property accumulated should be protected." (Vallera v. Vallera, supra, 21 Cal.2d 681, 686–687, 134 P.2d 761, 764 (diss. opn.); see Bruch, op. cit. supra, 10 Family L.Q. 101, 110–114; Article, Illicit Cohabitation: The Impact of the Vallera and Keene Cases on the Rights of the Meretricious Spouse (1973) 6 U.C. Davis L.Rev. 354, 369–370; Comment (1972) 48 Wash.L.Rev. 635, 641.)

Thus as of 1973, the time of the filing of In re Marriage of Cary, supra, 34 Cal.App.3d 345, 109 Cal.Rptr. 862, the cases apparently held that a nonmarital partner who rendered services in the absence of express contract could assert no right to property acquired during the relationship. The facts of *Cary* demonstrated the unfairness of that rule.

Janet and Paul Cary had lived together, unmarried, for more than eight years. They held themselves out to friends and family as husband and wife, reared four children, purchased a home and other property, obtained credit, filed joint income tax returns, and otherwise conducted themselves as though they were married. Paul worked outside the home, and Janet generally cared for the house and children.

In 1971 Paul petitioned for "nullity of the marriage." Following a hearing on that petition, the trial court awarded Janet half the property acquired during the relationship, although all such property was traceable to Paul's earnings. The Court of Appeal affirmed the award.

Reviewing the prior decisions which had denied relief to the homemaking partner, the Court of Appeal reasoned that those decisions rested upon a policy of punishing persons guilty of cohabitation without marriage. The Family Law Act, the court observed, aimed to eliminate fault or guilt as a basis for dividing marital property. But once fault or guilt is excluded, the court reasoned, nothing distinguishes the property rights of a nonmarital "spouse" from those of a putative spouse. Since the latter is entitled to half the "quasi marital property" (Civ.Code, § 4452), the Court of Appeal concluded that, giving effect to the policy of the Family Law Act, a nonmarital cohabitator should also be entitled to half the property accumulated during an "actual family relationship." (34 Cal.App.3d at p. 353, 109 Cal.Rptr. 862.)

* * *

If *Cary* is interpreted as holding that the Family Law Act requires an equal division of property accumulated in nonmarital "actual family relationships," then we agree with Beckman v. Mayhew that *Cary* distends the act. No language in the Family Law Act addresses the property rights of nonmarital partners, and nothing in the legislative history of the act suggests that the Legislature considered that subject. The delineation of the rights of nonmarital partners before 1970 had been fixed entirely by judicial decision; we see no reason to believe that the Legislature, by enacting the Family Law Act, intended to change that state of affairs.

But although we reject the reasoning of *Cary* and *Atherley,* we share the perception of the *Cary* and *Atherley* courts that the application of former precedent in the factual setting of those cases would work an unfair distribution of the property accumulated by the couple. Justice Friedman in Beckman v. Mayhew, supra, 49 Cal.App.3d 529, 535, 122 Cal.Rptr. 604, also questioned the continued viability of our decisions in *Vallera* and *Keene*; commentators have argued the need to reconsider those precedents. We should not, therefore, reject the authority of *Cary* and *Atherley* without also examining the deficiencies in the former law which led to those decisions.

The principal reason why the pre-*Cary* decisions result in an unfair distribution of property inheres in the court's refusal to permit a nonmarital partner to assert rights based upon accepted principles of implied contract or equity. We have examined the reasons advanced to justify this denial of relief, and find that none have merit.

First, we note that the cases denying relief do not rest their refusal upon any theory of "punishing" a "guilty" partner. Indeed, to the extent that denial of relief "punishes" one partner, it necessarily rewards the other by permitting him to retain a disproportionate amount of the property. Concepts of "guilt" thus cannot justify an unequal division of property between two equally "guilty" persons.

Other reasons advanced in the decisions fare no better. The principal argument seems to be that "[e]quitable considerations arising from the reasonable expectation of * * * benefits attending the status of marriage * * * are not present [in a nonmarital relationship]." (Vallera v. Vallera, supra, 21 Cal.2d at p. 685, 134 P.2d 761, 763.) But, although parties to a nonmarital relationship obviously cannot have based any expectations upon the belief that they were married, other expectations and equitable considerations remain. The parties may well expect that property will be divided in accord with the parties' own tacit understanding and that in the absence of such understanding the courts will fairly apportion property accumulated through mutual effort. We need not treat nonmarital partners as putatively married persons in order to apply principles of implied contract, or extend equitable remedies; we need to treat them only as we do any other unmarried persons.[22]

The remaining arguments advanced from time to time to deny remedies to the nonmarital partners are of less moment. There is no more reason to presume that services are contributed as a gift than to presume that funds are contributed as a gift; in any event the better approach is to presume, as Justice Peters suggested, "that the parties intend to deal fairly with each other." (Keene v. Keene, supra, 57 Cal.2d 657, 674, 21 Cal.Rptr. 593, 603, 371 P.2d 329, 339 (dissenting opn.).).

The argument that granting remedies to the nonmarital partners would discourage marriage must fail; as *Cary* pointed out, "with equal or greater force the point might be made that the pre-1970 rule was calculated to cause the income producing partner to avoid marriage and thus retain the benefit of all of his or her accumulated earnings." (34 Cal.App.3d at p. 353, 109 Cal.Rptr. at p. 866.) Although we recognize the well-established public policy to foster and promote the institution of marriage, perpetuation of judicial rules which result in an inequitable distribution of property accumulated during a nonmarital relationship is neither a just nor an effective way of carrying out that policy.

In summary, we believe that the prevalence of nonmarital relationships in modern society and the social acceptance of them, marks this as a time when our courts should by no means apply the doctrine of the unlawfulness of the so-called meretricious relationship to the instant case. As we have explained, the nonenforceability of agreements expressly providing for meretricious conduct rested upon the fact that such conduct, as the word suggests, pertained to and encompassed prostitution. To equate the nonmarital relationship of today to such a subject matter is to do violence to an accepted and wholly different practice.

We are aware that many young couples live together without the solemnization of marriage, in order to make sure that they can successfully later undertake marriage. This trial period, preliminary to marriage, serves as some assurance that the marriage will not subsequently end in dissolution to the harm of both parties. We are aware, as we have stated, of the pervasiveness of nonmarital relationships in other situations.

The mores of the society have indeed changed so radically in regard to cohabitation that we cannot impose a standard based on alleged moral considerations that have apparently been so widely abandoned by so many. Lest we be misunderstood, however, we take this occasion to point out that the structure of society itself largely de-

---

22. In some instances a confidential relationship may arise between nonmarital partners, and economic transactions between them should be governed by the principles applicable to such relationships.

pends upon the institution of marriage, and nothing we have said in this opinion should be taken to derogate from that institution. The joining of the man and woman in marriage is at once the most socially productive and individually fulfilling relationship that one can enjoy in the course of a lifetime.

We conclude that the judicial barriers that may stand in the way of a policy based upon the fulfillment of the reasonable expectations of the parties to a nonmarital relationship should be removed. As we have explained, the courts now hold that express agreements will be enforced unless they rest on an unlawful meretricious consideration. We add that in the absence of an express agreement, the courts may look to a variety of other remedies in order to protect the parties' lawful expectations.[24]

The courts may inquire into the conduct of the parties to determine whether that conduct demonstrates an implied contract or implied agreement of partnership or joint venture, or some other tacit understanding between the parties. The courts may, when appropriate, employ principles of constructive trust (see Omer v. Omer (1974) 11 Wash.App. 386, 523 P.2d 957) or resulting trust (see Hyman v. Hyman (Tex.Civ.App.1954) 275 S.W.2d 149). Finally, a nonmarital partner may recover in quantum meruit for the reasonable value of household services rendered less the reasonable value of support received if he can show that he rendered services with the expectation of monetary reward. (See Hill v. Estate of Westbrook, supra, 39 Cal.2d 458, 462, 247 P.2d 19.)[25]

Since we have determined that plaintiff's complaint states a cause of action for breach of an express contract, and, as we have explained, can be amended to state a cause of action independent of allegations of express contract,[26] we must conclude that the trial court erred in granting defendant a judgment on the pleadings.

The judgment is reversed and the cause remanded for further proceedings consistent with the views expressed herein.

* * *

24. We do not seek to resurrect the doctrine of common law marriage, which was abolished in California by statute in 1895. (See Norman v. Thomson (1898) 121 Cal. 620, 628; 54 P. 143; Estate of Abate (1958) 166 Cal.App.2d 282, 292, 333 P.2d 200.) Thus we do not hold that plaintiff and defendant were "married," nor do we extend to plaintiff the rights which the Family Law Act grants valid or putative spouses; we hold only that she has the same rights to enforce contracts and to assert her equitable interest in property acquired through her effort as does any other unmarried person.

25. Our opinion does not preclude the evolution of additional equitable remedies to protect the expectations of the parties to a nonmarital relationship in cases in which existing remedies prove inadequate; the suitability of such remedies may be determined in later cases in light of the factual setting in which they arise.

26. We do not pass upon the question whether, in the absence of an express or implied contractual obligation, a party to a nonmarital relationship is entitled to support payments from the other party after the relationship terminates.

NOTES AND QUESTIONS

1. Justice Clark dissented from the second part of the *Marvin* opinion. He agreed that a contract between the parties should be enforced, but he did not think that in the absence of a contract an award should be made in reliance upon "general equitable principles."

The *Marvin* case has been noted in many law reviews, among them 14 Cal.West.L.Rev. 485 (1978); 90 Harv.L.Rev. 1708 (1977); 16 J.Fam.L. 331 (1978); 66 Ky.L.J. 707 (1978); 62 Minn.L.Rev. 449 (1978); 10 S.W.U.L. Rev. 699 (1978); 30 Stan.L.Rev. 359 (1978); 53 Wash.L.Rev. 145 (1977). See also Kay and Amyx, Marvin v. Marvin, Preserving the Options, 65 Cal. L.Rev. 937 (1977); and G. Douthwaite, Unmarried Couples and the Law (1979).

Upon remand to the trial court, the factual issues in the case were tried before Judge Arthur K. Marshall. On April 18, 1979, after a long trial, Judge Marshall rejected Ms. Marvin's claim to half of the defendant's property, but awarded her $104,000, the equivalent of $1,000 per week for two years. New York Times, April 19, 1979, page 1, col. 5. The complete text of Judge Marshall's memorandum opinion is reproduced in 5 Fam.L. Rptr. 3077. A comment on both the Supreme Court and the Superior Court opinions is Foster and Freed, Marvin v. Marvin: New Wine in Old Bottles, 5 Fam.L.Rptr. 4001 (1979). Judge Marshall found no express contract between the parties, no basis for a constructive trust or a resulting trust, but made his award in the following language:

> "The court is aware that Footnote 25, Marvin v. Marvin, supra, p. 684, urges the trial court to employ whatever equitable remedy may be proper under the circumstances. The court is also aware of the recent resort of plaintiff to unemployment insurance benefits to support herself and of the fact that a return of plaintiff to a career as a singer is doubtful. Additionally, the court knows that the market value of defendant's property at time of separation exceeded $1,000,000.

> In view of these circumstances, the court in equity awards plaintiff $104,000 for rehabilitation purposes so that she may have the economic means to re-educate herself and to learn new, employable skills or to refurbish those utilized, for example, during her most recent employment and so that she may return from her status as companion of a motion picture star to a separate, independent but perhaps more prosaic existence."

(Footnotes omitted. 5 Fam.L.Rptr. 3085.)

2. Although statements have been made that seventeen states have followed Marvin and only four have rejected it, Foster and Freed, supra, point out that this is somewhat misleading. The first branch of Marvin, which holds that contracts between cohabitants may be enforced, has been the law in several states both before and after Marvin. E. g., Latham v. Latham, 274 Ore. 421, 547 P.2d 144 (1976); Kozlowski v. Kozlowski, 80 N.J. 378, 403 A.2d 902 (1979). Cases the other way are Rehak v. Mathis, 239 Ga. 541, 238 S.E.2d 81 (1977), 12 Ga.L.Rev. 361 (1978); McCall v. Frampton, 99 Misc.2d 159, 415 N.Y.S.2d 752 (Sup.Ct.1979). The second branch of the case, holding that there may be property claims arising out of such relationships even in the absence of any contract, has not been accepted in many

states. A case which does follow *Marvin* on this point is Carlson v. Olson, 256 N.W.2d 249 (Minn.1977). A case contra Marvin is Hewitt v. Hewitt, 77 Ill.2d 49, 31 Ill.Dec. 827, 394 N.E.2d 1204 (1979).

An Oregon case, Beal v. Beal, 282 Ore. 115, 577 P.2d 507 (1978), achieves the Marvin result on somewhat different facts by adopting the principle that the property disputes between a man and woman living together out of wedlock should be determined on the basis of the "express or implied intent of those parties". The court in this case was apparently not relying upon contract in the usual sense, but seems to have been trying to reach the result the parties would have wished if they had thought about the possibility of a breakup in their relationship before it occurred. Their intent was deduced from such evidence as the manner in which the property was acquired, the extent to which each party contributed to household expenses or other financial arrangements between them. The case is noted in 58 Ore.L.Rev. 245 (1979).

3. At the outset of the opinion Judge Tobriner emphasizes the increase in the number of people living together out of wedlock. The government statistics on this question are contained in Bureau of Census, U.S. Dep't. of Commerce, Current Population Reports, Marital Status and Living Arrangements, Series P–20, No. 306, at pp. 4, 5, Table F (1977). That document indicates that the number of household heads living with an unrelated person of the opposite sex doubled between 1970 and 1976. The total of such households in 1976 was 660,000, involving 1.3 million persons. This of course is not an overwhelming proportion in a total population of about 200 million persons. In fact the same document states that it represents only about 4% of all heads of household who have no relatives living in the household, and only about 1% of all heads of household. Finally, the document contains this statement: "* * * data users who make inferences about the nature of the relationships between unrelated adults of the opposite sex who share the same living quarters should be made aware that the data on this subject are aggregates which are distributed over a spectrum of categories including partners, resident employees and roomers."

The foregoing suggests some questions:

(a) What conclusions, if any, can be drawn from this data concerning relationships between men and women in the United States in the 1970's?

(b) What conclusions are drawn from the data by the California Supreme Court?

(c) In general terms, what is the relevance for judicial decision of data of this kind?

4. What would have been the result in the *Marvin* case if the parties had had a written contract providing that they would live together as if they were husband and wife, would engage in sexual relations when mutually desired, that Ms. Marvin would keep house and be a companion to Mr. Marvin, and that Mr. Marvin would support them both and that any property acquired by him would be shared equally? Is this contract any more "illicit" than the contract alleged by the plaintiff in the case? If, as the court indicates, the mores of society have changed radically as to cohabitation, what difference does it make whether the parties expressly agree to engage in sexual relations or leave that aspect of their relationship unspoken?

5. What would be the result under the *Marvin* decision if a contract similar to that alleged by the plaintiff were made between two homosexuals who were living together?

6. What would have been the result in this case if Lee and Betty Marvin had still been married when the plaintiff claimed half of the property?

7. Is it possible to make an argument that the Statute of Frauds should apply to the *Marvin* type of contract? If not, should the legislature amend the Statute of Frauds to apply to such contracts?

8. When the California Supreme Court appears to approve a recovery based upon an "implied contract", is the court referring to a contract implied in fact or a contract implied in law? What role do the "reasonable expectations of the parties" play in granting recovery? If there is no contract, express or implied in fact, how would the court determine what the reasonable expectations of the parties were?

9. At the end of the opinion the court adds that even in the absence of contract the courts may grant relief on the basis of other legal theories, referring to an implied partnership contract, constructive trust, resulting trust, quantum meruit, and, in footnote 25, "additional equitable remedies".

(a) What is a constructive trust? 5 A. Scott, The Law of Trusts §§ 404.2, 440.1 (3d ed. 1967); Restatement, Restitution § 160 (1937).

(b) What is a resulting trust? 5 A. Scott, The Law of Trusts § 404 (3d ed. 1967); Restatement, Restitution § 160 b (1937).

(c) How is quantum meruit defined? 5 A. Corbin, Contracts §§ 1109–1115 (1964); 12 S. Williston, Contracts § 1459 (3d ed. Jaeger 1970).

(d) How do these doctrines apply to the *Marvin* situation?

(e) What do you suppose the court means by "additional equitable remedies"? For a discussion of all of the foregoing questions, see Folberg and Buren, Domestic Partnership: A Proposal For Dividing the Property of Unmarried Families, 12 Willamette L.J. 453 (1976).

(f) Are you persuaded by the court's statement in footnote 24 that it does not seek to resurrect common law marriage, which had been abolished by statute in California?

(g) What is the basis for this branch of the opinion? Is it that the plaintiff should be awarded compensation for services rendered? Or is it that the parties had a relationship which so resembled marriage that the property rights attendant upon marriage should apply to it?

10. What are some of the implications of the *Marvin* opinion's creation of equitable remedies?

(a) Suppose that Lee Marvin had not had a large amount of property, but had been earning a large salary. Under the court's opinion, would the trial court have been justified in awarding the plaintiff periodic payments resembling alimony or maintenance? Cf. McCullon v. McCullon, 96 Misc. 2d 962, 410 N.Y.S.2d 226 (Sup.Ct.1978). Notice that in footnote 26 the court expressly refuses to decide whether the plaintiff would be entitled to support. Does that mean that the trial court exceeded its mandate when it gave the plaintiff the $104,000 "for rehabilitation purposes"? "Rehabilitative alimony" is an incident to divorce in some states. See, e. g., Cann v. Cann, 334 So.2d 325 (Fla.App.1976); Turner v. Turner, 158 N.J.Super.

313, 385 A.2d 1280 (1978). Does it matter for purposes of determining its validity or its character whether it is to be paid all at once or in installments?

(b) What would be the result under the *Marvin* case if the man were killed in an industrial accident while the parties were still living together? Could the woman collect workers' compensation benefits? Could she inherit his property? If he were killed as the result of negligence, could she recover for wrongful death? Does the opinion provide a rationale for answering these questions?

(c) What would have been the result in the *Marvin* case if the parties had lived together only two years instead of five and one-half years? One year? Six months? What principles can be found in the opinion which would help to answer these questions?

(d) If you had a client who was contemplating entering upon a Marvin-type of relationship, what legal advice would you give him or her? Would you recommend the execution of some sort of contract? If so, what should it provide? For example, suppose your client was a lady of sixty, about to begin living with a man of similar age, both of them having had earlier marriages and both having substantial property. Or suppose that a daughter of a wealthy client proposes to live with an indigent and itinerant construction worker. Or that two ill paid school teachers set up housekeeping together, each planning to contribute to the household expenses.

(e) What do we call the relationship in the *Marvin* case? Cohabitation? Mateship? Pseudo-marriage? De facto marriage?

11. What are some of the tax implications of the *Marvin* situation? Consider the following:

(a) Would the man be entitled to deduct the woman's medical expenses if he paid them? I.R.C. §§ 151, 152 (a)(9), 152 (b)(5); Cassius L. Peacock v. Commissioner, T.C.M. 1978–30; John J. Whalen, Jr. v. Commissioner, T.C.M. 1976–137.

(b) If a man is living with a woman to whom he makes gifts of cash for her living expenses, does she realize taxable income in the amount of such gifts? Lyna Kathryn Jones v. Commissioner, T.C.M. 1977–329.

(c) If Mr. Marvin should comply with the trial court's judgment by transferring to Ms. Marvin appreciated property, will he have a taxable gain on the difference between his basis and the fair market value of the property at the time of transfer? See United States v. Davis, 370 U.S. 65 (1962), reproduced infra at page 981. Does Ms. Marvin realize taxable income when she receives the payment? Rev.Rul. 67–221, 1967–2 C.B. 63; Treas.Reg. § 1.102–1(a) (1956). The foregoing and other questions are discussed in Randall, Living Together Can Be Very Taxing, 1 Fam.L.Advocate 2 (1979).

12. Tom and Mary begin living together when Tom is a graduate student in a state which does not recognize common law marriage. Mary, by working as a secretary, helps to support him. Tom finally gets a degree in physics and finds a lucrative job with a large corporation. Tom and Mary continue living together for several years, but at the end of that time Tom meets and falls in love with the daughter of the president of the company. He tells Mary that since they were never married and never intended to be

husband and wife, he has no responsibilities with respect to her. He moves out of the apartment and marries the president's daughter. Tom has by this time accumulated real and personal property worth $50,000, and has a salary of $30,000 per year. What claim or claims might Mary make against Tom, and how should they be disposed of? The student might consult Walker v. Walker, infra, page 216, in addition to the *Marvin* case.

13.   Do you see situations like that in *Marvin*, or that in paragraph 12 as presenting social problems with which the legislature should deal? If so, draft a statute which in your opinion deals with the problems in a satisfactory way. California of course does have a statute which is aimed at giving some relief to people who mistakenly think that they are married, a statute which is referred to in footnote 13 of the *Marvin* opinion. This is Cal.Civ.Code § 4452 (Supp.1979), providing in substance that when a marriage is determined to be void or voidable and either or both parties believe it is a valid marriage, the court shall declare the party so believing to be a putative spouse and make certain divisions of property. For further discussion of the putative spouse doctrine, see page 116, infra.

14.   The *Marvin* opinion is at pains to disclaim any intention to "derogate" from the institution of marriage, adding the customary acknowledgment of the value and importance of marriage to society. If the *Marvin* case should be followed, what consequences, if any, will it have for the law of marriage? What consequences for people's behavior? Do you see any relationship between the doctrines of the *Marvin* case and the English law of marriage before 1753?

Chapter 2

DOMICILE

INTRODUCTORY NOTE

The first question which occurs to one who confronts the confusing concept of domicile is, why must we be concerned with it? The answer is that, given the multitude of governing units which exist in the United States, the diversity of their laws, and the propensity of Americans to move about, we need a body of rules by which we can determine which governing unit has the authority to regulate the legal relations of individuals in certain ways. To take an obvious example, it would be unworkable for all of the fifty states to tax the income of every American. Some legal principle for determining which states may assert such a tax and which may not is essential to orderly government. Likewise do we require rules establishing the place in which a person may vote. Or, when a person dies leaving property, there must be some accepted principle by which the probate courts may decide how the property is to be distributed, whether according to the law of the place where the property happens to be, or the place in which the deceased lived, or some other place.

In the law of domestic relations the courts and legislatures of the various states have long felt that each state has an interest in the marriage and family relations of its citizens. This is reflected specifically in rules governing jurisdiction to grant divorces, annulments, custody orders, and adoption decrees. It is also reflected in rules relating to the choice of law to be applied to certain kinds of suits, such as suits for negligence between husband and wife or between parent and child. Given this assumption, and the fact that there is not uniformity among the states with respect to the substantive doctrines of divorce, annulment, custody, adoption and intrafamily suits, here again we must have a set of principles designed to tell us what sort of relation between the individual person and the state will warrant the state in asserting jurisdiction over his family relations or in applying its law to his tort claims.

The concept which the courts have chosen for these purposes is domicile. Broadly speaking, the state of a person's domicile may impose certain taxes upon him, may permit him to vote in its elections, may determine how certain kinds of his property pass on his death, may grant him a divorce or an annulment, and may enter decrees concerning the custody or adoption of his children, although all of these statements are subject to qualification. To put it differently, domicile is the judicially formulated link between a person and a place which justifies granting to or imposing upon that person certain legal rights and liabilities.

In earlier times domicile could be defined in quite specific terms and was subject to quite specific rules, a highly desirable state of affairs in view of the function of domicile. That is no longer true, but the concept can best be understood by first looking at these rules, and then exploring the extent to which they have been changed or diluted in recent years. The rules are set out and to some degree discussed in Restatement, Second, Conflict of Laws, §§ 11–20 (1971). See also H. Clark, Law of Domestic Relations, Ch. 4 (1968).

Domicile was, and still is subdivided into three categories, domicile of choice, domicile of origin and domicile by operation of law. Domicile of choice is the form of domicile which we generally think about. It consists of the place in which a person having legal capacity has been physically present with the contemporaneous intention of making that place his home. One's domicile of origin is his domicile at birth, which is the domicile of his father, for a legitimate child, and the domicile of his mother for an illegitimate child. Domicile by operation of law is the domicile assigned by the law to persons who do not have legal capacity to choose their own domicile, such as minors, incompetents and, at common law, married women.

Traditionally domicile was a unitary concept. At a particular moment a person could have only one domicile, which would be his domicile for all purposes. Conversely, every person had a domicile at all times. And everyone was held to retain his existing domicile until he should acquire a new one.

The foregoing have been characterized as the traditional or conventional rules of domicile, implying that they have undergone changes recently. The extent of those changes is hard to measure. For example a recent Wisconsin case has stated the rules as if nothing substantial had changed. In re Estate of Daniels, 53 Wis.2d 611, 193 N.W.2d 847 (1972). It is reasonably clear, however, that a person's domicile will not be adjudged the same by all courts for all purposes. Thus the courts of two different states may find that a person is domiciled in two different places, and if this is done, no constitutional principle is violated. A. Ehrenzweig, Conflict of Laws, 240 (1962); H. Goodrich, Conflict of Laws (Scoles 4th ed. 1964); H. Clark, Law of Domestic Relations, 144–146 (1968). Since the considerations of policy vary, depending on the purposes for which domicile is being determined, different conclusions as to the location of a person's domicile may also be reached for different purposes. Reese, Does Domicile Bear a Single Meaning? 55 Colum.L.Rev. 589 (1955); Restatement, Second, Conflict of Laws, § 11, comments m, n, o (1971); Weintraub, An Inquiry Into the Utility of "Domicile" as a Concept in Conflicts Analysis, 63 Mich.L.Rev. 961 (1965). To a great extent these differences arise by virtue not of differences in the rules, but of differences in application of the rules to the facts and in evaluating the evidence.

A further source of uncertainty in the law of domicile is produced by the inexplicable reluctance of legislatures to use the term "domicile" when enacting statutes. Instead they use the term "residence". An exception is the Uniform Marriage and Divorce Act § 302, 9 Unif.L.Ann. 418 (Supp.1978), which bases jurisdiction for divorce upon ninety days' domicile in the state. Generally but not universally, when residence is referred to in divorce statutes, the courts construe it to mean domicile. Reese and Green, That Elusive Word, "Residence", 6 Vand.L.Rev. 561 (1963); H. Clark, Law of Domestic Relations 286 (1968). Even when the courts hold that "residence" does not mean "domicile, they sometimes define residence in terms indistinguishable from domicile. Garrison v. Garrison, 107 Ill.App.2d 311, 246 N.E.2d 9 (1969). But the initial question in construing all such statutes still remains whether "residence" means "domicile" or something else.

STEVENS v. STEVENS

Court of Appeals of Washington, 1971.
4 Wash.App. 79, 480 P.2d 238.

HOROWITZ, Acting Chief Judge. This court has heretofore granted petitioner's application for a writ of certiorari to review the court's decree granting a divorce to the parties and awarding to respondent custody of the two minor children of the parties. The matter is now before us on the merits.

The parties were originally domiciled in Washington. While so domiciled, they married in Seattle on May 6, 1967. Petitioner husband was a Boeing Co. employee. In September of 1967, the parties moved to Texas where petitioner continued to work for Boeing. The parties took their mobile home to Texas but left with relatives in Washington the possessions for which they did not have room. While in Texas they lived in their mobile home. While in Texas, both family cars were licensed there and petitioner obtained a Texas driver's license. Both parties registered to vote in Texas, and voted in federal elections there; however, according to the testimony below, only petitioner voted in local elections. Copies of the voting registration papers were not offered in evidence. Additionally, both petitioner and respondent enrolled in college there as Texas residents.

Petitioner took pre-med courses there and decided to go to medical school. He applied for admission to a school in South Africa. While the application was pending, petitioner's job ran out and in January of 1969 he, his wife and children returned to Seattle. The evidence as to the purpose of the return to Seattle was conflicting. Petitioner testified that he returned there to await word from the South African school and once admitted, to take care of the possessions left in Seattle prior to going to Africa. Respondent testified, however, that the parties returned so that petitioner could work at Boeing in Seattle. Petitioner's application to medical school was denied. In September of 1969, he made plans to return to Texas and continue his medical training there. At this time, however, petitioner and respondent became estranged and respondent decided to stay in Seattle. They agreed that petitioner should have custody of their two minor children, both under the age of 4 at the time of trial. * * * Petitioner then returned to Texas for a brief period, then came back to Seattle, then left for Montana to find employment, and eventually moved to California where he is now working.

Respondent filed her complaint for divorce on December 3, 1969. At that time respondent had been physically present in the state since January 7, 1969, a period of less than 11 months. Petitioner contends that the marital domicile changed to Texas when they moved there, and that consequently, respondent did not satisfy the jurisdictional requirements, set forth in RCW 26.08.030 that all plaintiffs in divorce actions "reside" in the state for one year.

Residence, as used in the statute, means domicile. * * * The statute as construed requires that the person filing the complaint must have been domiciled in Washington for 1 year, or more, prior to the date the complaint is filed; any period of residence after the date of filing cannot be used in computing the year. * * * If the statute is to be satisfied under the facts here, it must be shown that respondent's domicile was in Washington during the period that she and her husband lived in Texas.

To establish a domicile requires the physical presence at the place of intended domicile accompanied by the intention of making that place one's home. * * * A domicile, once established, is not destroyed by a temporary absence no matter how long continued. * * * Once acquired, domicile is presumed to continue until changed and the change must be shown by substantial evidence. * * * It is the generally accepted rule that a woman at marriage loses her own domicile, and acquires that of her husband, although she may acquire a separate domicile when living apart from her husband. * * *

In the instant case, the question for determination is whether the petitioner changed the matrimonial domicile to Texas and the answer depends primarily upon his intent. Intent is generally determined by objective events, and not the parties' subjective state of mind. * * * However, the existence of domiciliary intent is an ultimate question of fact to be determined by the trial court. * * * The trial court found that respondent was domiciled in Washington for the required 1 year period. We believe that finding is supported by substantial evidence. The parties' domiciles of origin and original marital domicile were in Seattle. They had family ties there. They retained a lot there which was originally purchased as a site for a house. Petitioner and respondent moved to Texas as a result of an interdivisional company transfer and the job in Texas was, at its inception, of a specific duration. It is a permissible inference from the evidence that petitioner's sojourn to Texas was temporary in nature and that he intended to keep Washington as his home. It is true that the uncontroverted evidence indicated that petitioner voted in federal, state and local elections while in Texas. However, under the weight of authority, the act of voting is not necessarily controlling in determining domicile. It is only one factor, albeit an important one, to be considered in reaching a determination on domicile; it is sometimes persuasive, sometimes not, depending upon all the facts. * * * The trial court's finding as to domicile was supported by substantial evidence.

* * *

The judgment is affirmed.

NOTES AND QUESTIONS

1. If the trial court had found, in the *Stevens* case, that the parties had acquired a Texas domicile, would the Court of Appeals have affirmed that finding?

2. If this court had held that the parties had acquired a Texas domicile, but had reacquired a Washington domicile when they brought their mobile home back to Seattle, where, if anywhere, could the wife have obtained her divorce? If there was no place in which she could meet the jurisdictional requirements for divorce, might that have influenced the court to reach the result it did with respect to their Washington domicile?

3. The Restatement, Second, Conflict of Laws § 18 (1971) describes the intention required for the acquisition of a domicile of choice to be that the person intends to make a place his home, for the time at least. The same section's comments state that the intention must be determined from the person's declarations and other conduct. Using this section as the governing principle, would you have decided the *Stevens* case as the court did?

4. If, as seems to be true, "residence" in voting statutes means domicile (Reese and Green, That Elusive Word, "Residence", 6 Vand.L.Rev. 561, 571 (1953)), what becomes of the idea that a person has only one domicile at any one time? Does this case suggest that these parties were domiciled in Texas for voting purposes, but in Washington for divorce purposes?

5. H and W were married and lived in Michigan, where H was president of a medium sized industrial corporation. In 1969 after several quarrels they separated, W accusing H of having an affair with another woman. In June of 1970 H went to Reno, Nevada, where he rented an apartment, signed a year's lease, registered his car, registered as a voter, bought a small amount of stock in a local gambling casino, and bought a few acres of land. He stayed in Reno, except for two trips on business back to Michigan, until January, 1971, when he brought an ex parte suit for divorce in Nevada. The Nevada statute provides that in order to sue for divorce in the state a person must have been a resident of Nevada for six weeks preceding the action. His Nevada attorney told him that this statute required

a six-week Nevada domicile, and assured H that he had been domiciled in Nevada for the prescribed time. As soon as he obtained the divorce, H married W–2. They continued to live together in Nevada until April, 1971, except for three trips by H back to Michigan to attend to his business affairs. During this time he retained his position as president of the Michigan corporation. When he wrote to W of his divorce and second marriage, her Michigan attorney responded by informing H that Michigan would not recognize the divorce because under its law H had not acquired a Nevada domicile. In April of 1971 H and W–2 left on a trip around the world, at the end of which, in March, 1972, they returned to Michigan, bought a new home and settled down there.

(a) If the Nevada divorce were attacked by W in a Michigan proceeding, by what law would the existence of a Nevada domicile be determined? Restatement, Second, Conflict Laws, § 13 (1971); H. Clark, Law of Domestic Relations, 146 (1968). Cf. Ziady v. Curley, 396 F.2d 873 (4th Cir. 1968), where the question of domicile was raised for purposes of determining diversity of citizenship.

(b) What arguments on the question of the Nevada domicile would you make? Are there other facts which you would like to know? Would your attitude toward the situation be different if H had gone to California rather than Nevada, had done the same things indicating his relation to the state, and had complied with the California statute concerning length of stay in the state before obtaining the divorce? Cf. Henry v. Henry, 362 Mich. 85, 106 N.W.2d 570 (1960); In re Estate of March, 426 Pa. 364, 231 A.2d 168 (1967); Korn v. Korn, 398 F.2d 689 (3d Cir. 1968); Milbank v. Milbank, 36 A.D.2d 292, 320 N.Y.S.2d 436 (1st Dep't 1971), aff'd per curiam 29 N.Y.2d 844, 327 N.Y.S.2d 856, 277 N.E.2d 788 (1971).

6. H was employed by a corporation in Des Moines, Iowa, and was transferred by them to their Chicago office. He and W packed up their furniture and put it in storage until they could find housing in Chicago. H then went to Chicago to look for a house, while W took their two children to California, where her parents lived, to remain until H could find a suitable house. Before H could find a house in Illinois, W wrote to him that she had decided she could not live with him any longer and would not come to Illinois to join him.

(a) Where is H domiciled for divorce purposes? Cf. Julson v. Julson, 255 Iowa 301, 122 N.W.2d 329 (1963), 49 Iowa L.Rev. 1318 (1964); Puissegur v. Puissegur, 220 So.2d 547 (La.App.1969).

To what extent is H's choice of a domicile affected by the fact that his employer brought about the move? Would the case be different if he were in the army and moved pursuant to military orders? Collins v. Collins, 472 P.2d 696 (Colo.App.1970); Marcus v. Marcus, 3 Wash.App. 370, 475 P. 2d 571 (1970); Jizmejian v. Jizmejian, 16 Ariz.App. 270, 492 P.2d 1208 (1972); Clauss v. Clauss, 459 P.2d 369 (Wyo.1969); Restatement, Second, Conflict of Laws § 17 (1971).

7. W, a middle-aged widow, owned a large and valuable apartment house. She met H, a man her own age, also unmarried, and their acquaintance progressed to an engagement, and then marriage. H had some knowledge of the construction business, and he supervised and paid for extensive improvements upon W's apartment house. H and W then moved into an

apartment in the building. After some years of marital harmony, H and W fell into disharmony and finally W moved out of the apartment because of their inability to get along together. W then brought suit in the appropriate court to evict H from the apartment. What should be the result? Would the result be different if H owned the building and W had continued to remain in the apartment after they quarreled and after H had moved out? Cf. Owens v. Owens, 38 Del.Ch. 220, 149 A.2d 320 (1959).

8. What rule of domicile governs when a person lives on the state line? Aldabe v. Aldabe, 84 Nev. 392, 441 P.2d 691 (1968), cert. den. 393 U.S. 1042 (1969).

JOLICOEUR v. MIHALY

Supreme Court of California, In Bank, 1971.
5 Cal.3d 565, 96 Cal.Rptr. 697, 488 P.2d 1.

PETERS, Justice. In these proceedings we are called upon to determine whether the newly enfranchised young people of this state residing apart from their parents shall be treated like other voters for purposes of acquiring a voting residence or, on the contrary, shall be presumed to reside with their parents. We conclude that for state officials to treat minor citizens differently from adults for any purpose related to voting would violate the Twenty-Sixth Amendment to the United States Constitution. We also conclude that strong state policies require that voters participate in elections where they reside and, in accordance with California law permitting a minor to be emancipated for residential or other purposes, that California law requires that minors of 18 years of age or older be treated as emancipated and hence as adults for voting purposes in light of the Twenty-Sixth Amendment.

Petitioners are nine individual unmarried minors and two organizations. The nine individuals sought to register to vote in the jurisdiction they claim to be their actual permanent residence. Registrars of voters in the City and County of San Francisco, Alameda County, Santa Barbara County, San Diego County, and Los Angeles County refused to register the individual petitioners because they did not register at their parents' address pursuant to the California Attorney General's opinion of February 17, 1971 (Opn. No. 70/213, 54 Adv. Ops.Cal.Atty.Gen. 7, 12), in which he concluded that "for voting purposes the residence of an unmarried minor [whether student or not] * * * will normally be his parents' home" regardless of where the minor's present or intended future habitation might be.

In reliance upon this opinion, respondent Mihaly told petitioner McConville, whose parents live in Argentina, that he could not vote in local elections at all unless he became a *married* minor. Petitioners Pang and Fruchtendler were told that they would have to register to vote in Hawaii and Arizona, respectively. The six other individual petitioners were told to register in other California jurisdictions up to

700 miles away from their claimed permanent residences. Petitioners Jolicoeur and King, who are fully self-supporting and work full-time, were told that these facts were irrelevant to their capacity to establish a legal residence for voting purposes. Petitioner Randell, who has *never* lived at his parents' current domicile, and is not familiar with any political issues pertinent to that area, was told that he must vote there and not where he lives.

Petitioners invoke the original jurisdiction of this court seeking writs of mandate directed to the respondent registrars ordering respondents to register petitioners according to the same procedures and qualifications that are followed with respect to adult registrants, pursuant to Elections Code, sections 14280–14292.

The Twenty-Sixth Amendment: On June 22, 1970, President Nixon signed into law the Voting Rights Act of 1970 (P.L. 91–285, 84 Stats. 314), title III of which purported to lower the voting age to 18 for all federal, state, and local elections. After the United States Supreme Court held unconstitutional that part of title III which applied to nonfederal elections (Oregon v. Mitchell, 400 U.S. 112, 118, 91 S. Ct. 260, 27 L.Ed.2d 272 (1970)), Congress passed Senate Joint Resolution 7 on March 23, 1971, submitting a proposed constitutional amendment to the states for ratification, pursuant to article 5 of the federal Constitution. On June 30, 1971, Ohio became the 38th state to ratify the Twenty-Sixth Amendment to the United States Constitution, and it became law.

Section 1 of the Twenty-Sixth Amendment provides: "The right of citizens of the United States, who are eighteen years of age or older, to vote shall not be denied *or abridged* by the United States or by any State on account of age." (Italics added.)

The Twenty-Sixth Amendment prohibits abridging the right to vote on account of age. The word "abridge" means diminish, curtail, deprive, cut off, reduce.   *   *   *

Compelling young people who live apart from their parents to travel to their parents' district to register and vote or else to register and vote as absentees burdens their right to vote no less than the State of Mississippi burdened its poor people in *Gray*. [Gray v. Johnson, 234 F.Supp. 743 (S.D.Miss.1964)] Such young people would be isolated from local political activity, with a concomitant reduction in their political influence and information. The burden placed on youth would be different than that placed on other absentee voters. The youth, unlike other absentee voters, claims his current residence as his domicile but would be disqualified solely "on account of age."
     *   *   *

An unmarried minor must be subject to the same requirements in proving the location of his domicile as is any other voter. Fears of the way minors may vote or of their impermanency in the community may not be used to justify special presumptions—conclusive or otherwise—that they are not bona fide residents of the community in which they live.

*   *   *

It is clear that respondents have abridged petitioners' right to vote in precisely one of the ways that Congress sought to avoid—by singling minor voters out for special treatment and effectively making many of them vote by absentee ballot. The Senate Report indicates that Congress not only disapproved of such treatment, but feared that it would give youth "less of a sense of participation in the election system" and "might well serve to dissuade them from participating in the election," a result inconsistent with the goal of encouraging "greater political participation on the part of the young."

Respondents' policy would clearly frustrate youthful willingness to accomplish change at the local level through the political system. Whether a youth lives in Quincy, Berkeley, or Orange County, he will not be brought into the bosom of the political system by being told that he may not have a voice in the community in which he lives, but must instead vote wherever his parents live or may move to. Surely as well, such a system would give any group of voters less incentive "in devising responsible programs" in the town in which they live. Only the most dedicated partisan would travel from Oakland to San Diego (or Tucson) in order to exercise effectively his First Amendment rights of political association and expression.

America's youth entreated, pleaded for, demanded a voice in the governance of this nation. On campuses by the hundreds, at Lincoln's Monument by the hundreds of thousands, they voiced their frustration at their electoral impotence and their love of a country which they believed to be abandoning its ideals. Many more worked quietly and effectively within a system that gave them scant recognition. And in the land of Vietnam they lie as proof that death accords youth no protected status. Their struggle for recognition divided a nation against itself. Congress and more than three-fourths of the states have now determined in their wisdom that youth "shall have a new birth of freedom"—the franchise. Rights won at the cost of so much individual and societal suffering may not and shall not be curtailed on the basis of hoary fictions that these men and women are children tied to residential apron strings. Respondents' refusal to treat petitioners as adults for voting purposes violates the letter and spirit of the Twenty-Sixth Amendment.

California Law: California law also compels respondents to treat citizens of 18 years of age or older as adults for all purposes related to voting.

Petitioners sought to register at addresses they claim to be their residences for voting purposes. If petitioners *are* residents of the districts they claim, the integrity of our state's political system demands that they be allowed to vote in those areas.

* * *

The rules announced by respondents not only would deny to some residents the right to vote where they live, but could also serve to give an unmarried minor a series of voting residences which he has never seen. The 18-year-old who lives and works in San Francisco for the three years he is a voting minor might well wind up voting in turn for the Mayor of Seattle, the Governor of Maine, and school bonds in Oshkosh, Wisconsin, only to be disenfranchised completely on the local level when his parents move permanently to Paris.

It may be objected that to allow unmarried minors to establish a domicile where they live may swell the rolls of college town electorates. It is contended that college students may "take over" a town by all voting the same way, that they are not "truly" residents in that many of them will move to other areas after they leave school, and that local governments have a legitimate interest in excluding such persons from the local polity.[1]

In many states special rules are applied in determining the voting residence of students. (Singer, Student Power at the Polls (1970) 31 Ohio St.L.J. 703, 721–723.) The underlying rationale of these various tests is that students are apt to be transient inhabitants of the community, little concerned about long-term policies and problems, and often may not pay local property taxes. (But see Note, Restrictions on Student Voting: An Unconstitutional Anachronism? (1970) 4 U.Mich.J.Law Reform 215.) The possible transiency, penury, or ignorance of students did not, however, impress the California Legislature, which has expressly provided that the law "shall not be construed to prevent a student at an institution of learning from qualifying as an elector in the locality where he resides while attending that institution, when in fact the student has abandoned his former residence." (Elec.Code, § 14283.) Student status is therefore a neutral fact in determining residence for voting purposes.

The Legislature has thus determined that differential treatment of students for voting purposes may not be condoned as a legitimate governmental policy. No reason appears for construing differential treatment of minors in a more favorable light.

The second major evil accomplished by allowing or forcing voters to vote in districts not their own is that voters of other districts have

---

1. The fear of a deluge is more theoretical than real. In Berkeley, for example, some 51,464 votes were cast in the recent municipal election. (Oakland Tribune, April 7, 1971.) Of 27,000 students at the University of California, no more than 9,000 (freshmen through juniors) are likely to be in the 18–20 age group. If typical registration percentages adhere, no more than 5,000–6,000 of these minors would register to vote. Even if every single one of these minors registered in Berkeley, which is highly unlikely, and even if every one then voted (which is more unlikely), the *vote* total would be increased no more than 10 percent, and the rolls an even lesser percentage. Nor, among this highly educated group, is it very probable that all 5,000 minors would vote the same way on any issue.

inflicted upon them a voter with no stake or interest in the outcome of the election. The extent of the evil is not only that residents of California would be asked to decide issues in Arizona or Hawaii. Small towns in California would be especially affected by such a rule, since the number of young people from the town who have left for other areas may be substantial in comparison to the town's total population. Allowing unmarried minors who reside elsewhere to vote may effectively turn a small town over to the control of unconcerned outsiders. Over a century ago we recognized the wisdom of requiring voters to be residents of the jurisdiction: "[C]itizens   *   *   * should not deal with public questions through the ballot box until they at least [have] the benefit of an opportunity to learn the public wants, of concerting measures the best calculated to provide for them, and of selecting proper men to carry those measures into effect;   *   *   * " (Bourland v. Hildreth, 26 Cal. 161, 179 (1864).) Allowing minors to vote at fictional residences would compromise the integrity of the political process.

*   *   *

Respondents apparently do apply section 14282 in determining the residence of a married minor (who may be considered an adult for some purposes, but would still be a minor under state law for voting purposes; see Civ.Code, § 25). They appear to refuse as a matter of policy, however, to accept affidavits of residence from unmarried minors, unless the residence claimed is that of the parents. Even considering state law alone, this policy may be sustained, in light of the Elections Code, and the strong state policies discussed above, only if unmarried minors are generally incapable of having a domicile of their own. Subject to some unspecified objections, the Attorney General so believed (54 Adv.Ops.Cal.Atty.Gen., supra, at pp. 11–12), relying on Government Code, section 244, subdivisions (d) and (f), which provide that an unmarried minor's residence is that of his parents, and cannot be changed by his own act alone.[2]

The Attorney General has misapplied section 244 by failing to view it in light of other pertinent statutes and decisions governing parent-child relations. Specifically, under California law a minor may be emancipated partially or completely by his parents or by operation of law. It is possible that a minor of 18 years of age or older, living apart from his parents, will be emancipated for all purposes; it is substantially probable that he will be emancipated for purposes of residence; and the minor is necessarily emancipated for all purposes

2. Government Code, section 244, subdivision (d) provides: "The residence of the father during his life, and after his death the residence of the mother, while she remains unmarried, is the residence of the unmarried minor child, provided that when the parents are separated, the residence of the parent with whom an unmarried minor child maintains his place of abode is the residence of such unmarried minor child." Subdivision (f) further provides: "The residence of an unmarried minor who has a parent living cannot be changed by his own act."

related to voting when he is given the vote in his own right, without regard to the consent of his parent or guardian. In light of this California law regarding the emancipation of minors, we conclude that minors over 18 years of age must be treated as adults for voting purposes, and the location of their domiciles may not be questioned on account of their age.

Although section 244 is couched in absolute terms, it has not been so applied. Our courts have long held, for example, that the minor's residence does not follow that of the parent when the parent has abandoned him. * * * Similarly, although section 244, subdivision (e) baldly states that "[t]he residence of the husband is the residence of the wife," the section has not been applied where the wife obviously maintained a separate domicile from that of her husband, to whom she was apparently happily married. * * *

Section 244's proviso that an unmarried minor's residence is that of his parents and cannot be changed by his own act must be construed in light of other statutes governing parent-child relations. In particular Civil Code, section 211 provides in pertinent part: "The parent * * * may relinquish to the child the right of controlling him. * * *" Such relinquishment constitutes emancipation of the minor, and may be express or implied, complete or partial, conditional or absolute. * * * The emancipated child "is in all respects his own man." * * * To the extent he is emancipated he becomes *sui juris*, with the same independence as though he had attained majority. * * * After consenting to the emancipation of a child old enough to work and care for himself, the parent has no right to custody or control. * * * "A parent not entitled to the custody of a child has no right to control his residence." [3] * * *

Nor must a child be fully emancipated in order to acquire a domicile of choice. California law recognizes that emancipation for specific purposes is effective. * * *

Whether the minor has been emancipated for residential purposes is ordinarily a question of fact. * * * Establishment of a separate abode is evidence of emancipation. * * * In addition, it is common sense to believe that a good many minors over the age of 18 living apart from their parents *are* emancipated for these purposes. Eighteen is the age when most minors graduate from and

---

3. The great preponderance of authority from other jurisdictions similarly holds that an emancipated minor, being *sui juris*, may acquire his own domicile. (See, e. g., Bonneau v. Russell, 117 Vt. 134, 85 A.2d 569, 570 (1952); Cohen v. Delaware, Lack. & Western R. R. Co., 150 Misc. 450, 269 N.Y.S. 667, 673–675 (1934); Bjornquist v. Boston & A. R. Co., 250 F. 929, 932–933 (1st Cir. 1918); Spurgeon v. Mission State Bank, 151 F.2d 702, 705 (8th Cir. 1945), cert. den. 327 U.S. 782, 66 S.Ct. 682, 90 L.Ed. 1009 (1946); Appelt v. Whitty, 286 F.2d 135, 137 (7th Cir. 1961); 28 C.J.S. Domicile § 12, p. 21; Rest., Conflict of Laws, § 31; Rest.2d, Conflict of Laws, § 22.) As provided in Restatement Second of Conflict of Laws, section 22, comment f: "A parent has no power to control the domicil of an emancipated child. * * *"

leave school, when many get full time jobs and become self-support-ing, when the state ceases to limit the number of hours they may work * * * when they may smoke cigarettes * * * and when criminal proceedings begin to be brought in adult rather than juve-nile courts. * * * It is an age when males register for the draft and females may get married without the consent of either parent. * * * A minor 18 to 21 years old who lives apart from his parents will usually consider his house to be home.

Not only is there a substantial likelihood that a minor over the age of 18 living apart from his parents has been emancipated for all purposes or at least for purposes of residence; it is also clear that when the minor is given the right to vote he is emancipated for all purposes relating to voting. Obviously in giving the minor the right to vote, it was never contemplated that the parent or guardian should be able to control whether or not the minor should be permitted to vote or how he should exercise the franchise. It was necessarily the intention to accept him as a responsible member of the community, capable of participating in its political affairs, directing its policies, and choosing its leaders. For these purposes, he must be free entire-ly of parental control, and unless he is, the right to vote granted to him would be meaningless.

* * *

We hold today that both the Twenty-Sixth Amendment to the United States Constitution and California law require respondent reg-istrars to treat all citizens 18 years of age or older alike for all pur-poses related to voting. We do not imply that registrars may not question a citizen of any age as to his true domicile. However, the middleaged person who obtains a job and moves to San Francisco from San Diego, and the youth who moves from his family home in Grass Valley to Turlock to attend college must be treated equally. Whether either of them acquires a new domicile or retains the old one is governed by sections 14280–14292 of the Elections Code. We hold only that registrars may not specially question the validity of an affiant's claim of domicile on account of his age or occupational sta-tus.

Let the peremptory writ of mandate issue directing respondent voting registrars to determine each individual petitioner's residence for voting purposes, strictly in accordance with Elections Code, sec-tions 14280–14292, and by the same standards, tests, and procedures as are applied to persons 21 years of age or older.

NOTES AND QUESTIONS

1. The *Jolicoeur* case has been noted in 9 San Diego L.Rev. 329 (1972) and 60 Geo.L.J. 115 (1972). See also Note, 81 Yale L.J. 35 (1971). In the similar case of Wilkins v. Bentley, 385 Mich. 670, 189 N.W.2d 423 (1971) eight University of Michigan students were granted mandamus or-dering the clerk at Ann Arbor to permit them to register to vote there.

The Michigan statute provided that no one should be deemed to have gained or lost a residence for voting while a student at any institution of learning. This had been construed to create a rebuttable presumption that a student was not a resident at the university he was attending. The Michigan Supreme Court held that the statute as construed violates the Equal Protection Clause of the Fourteenth Amendment to the United States Constitution. See also Anderson v. Brown, 332 F.Supp. 1195 (S.D.Ohio 1971); Gordon v. Steele, 376 F.Supp. 575 (W.D.Pa.1974); Liberty Mut. Ins. Co. v. Craddock, 26 Md.App. 296, 338 A.2d 363 (1975); Hershkoff v. Board of Registrars of Voters of Worcester, 366 Mass. 570, 321 N.E.2d 656 (1974) (holding that college students had acquired domiciles at college for voting purposes "even if they intend to move later on", and notwithstanding that they were committed to a period of military service after graduation); Gorenberg v. Onondaga County Bd. of Elections, 38 A.D.2d 145, 328 N.Y.S.2d 198 (4th Dep't 1972); Hall v. Wake County Bd. of Elections, 280 N.C. 600, 187 S.E.2d 52 (1972).

What were the two classes of people treated unequally here? In what respects was treatment not "equal"?

2. Since the decision in Jolicoeur the California statutes have been amended so as to reduce the age of majority for all purposes from twenty-one to eighteen. Cal.Civ.Code §§ 25, 25.1 (Supp.1979). A similar lowering of the age of majority has occurred in most other states.

3. At common law, and generally today, an unemancipated minor child is considered incapable of acquiring a domicile and takes the domicile of his father, if the child is legitimate. If his parents are subsequently separated or divorced, he takes the domicile of the parent in whose custody he is placed, or with whom he lives. If he lives with someone other than a parent, his domicile remains that of his parent unless a guardian is appointed or the parents are dead or have abandoned him, in which case his domicile is that of the guardian or of those persons with whom he lives. Restatement, Second, Conflict of Laws § 22 (1971); H. Clark, Law of Domestic Relations, 151–153 (1968); In re Huck, 435 Pa. 325, 257 A.2d 522 (1969), cert. den. 397 U.S. 1040 (1970).

4. Was the opinion of the California Attorney General, as quoted in the Jolicoeur case at page 67, correct on the basis of the law as it existed before the decision in this case? Did that opinion mean that all minors, regardless of their circumstances, were domiciled at the domicile of their parents? Restatement, Second, Conflict of Laws, § 22, comment f (1971).

5. Were the students in the Jolicoeur case emancipated minors?

6. Does the case hold that all minors, whether emancipated or not, must be permitted to vote where they attend college? Does the case hold that all minors, whether emancipated or not, must be permitted to vote at the place where they acquire a domicile of choice pursuant to the rules applicable to adults?

7. Is the Jolicoeur case of significance only for voting purposes? Or would the courts of California now have to hold, for example, that petitioner McConville, whose parents lived in Argentina, was domiciled in California for purposes of paying in-state tuition at the University? Cf. Lev v. College of Marin, 22 Cal.App.3d 488, 99 Cal.Rptr. 476 (1971); Hayes v. Board of Regents of Kentucky State University, 495 F.2d 1326 (6th Cir.

1974); Arizona Bd. of Regents v. Harper, 108 Ariz. 223, 495 P.2d 453 (1972); Florida Bd. of Regents v. Harris, 338 So.2d 215 (Fla.App.1976). On the residence of school children for tuition purposes, see Spriggs v. Altheimer Arkansas School Dist. No. 22, 385 F.2d 254 (8th Cir. 1967).

8. Assume that the student does have capacity to choose his domicile, under Jolicoeur. To require that he be permitted to vote at the location of the university, would it be sufficient that he merely sign an affidavit stating that he considered the university his place of residence? Or would additional evidence be required? If so, of what kind? If the evidence indicated that the student intended merely to stay at the university until his course of study had been completed, but had no plans beyond that period, should the university be his domicile? If so does this dilute the concept of domicile? Cf. Alves v. Alves, 262 A.2d 111 (D.C.Ct.App.1970).

9. What effect, if any, does *Jolicoeur* have upon the rules of domicile for persons who are not students, not emancipated and are under eighteen? Consider the following facts: H and W are married and live in Kansas. W obtains a divorce in Kansas, the decree giving her custody of their son, S, and moves with S to Ohio, obtaining a domicile there. W is killed in an auto accident and S, then sixteen years old, chooses to live with his maternal uncle in Kansas.

(a) If H consents to S's living with the uncle, where is S domiciled?

(b) Would the result be different if H did not consent, but instead demanded that S live with him?

See In re Robben, 188 Kan. 217, 362 P.2d 29 (1961); Restatement, Second, Conflict of Laws § 22 (1971); Tureson v. Tureson, 281 Minn. 107, 160 N.W.2d 552 (1968).

10. Where is the domicile under the following circumstances? A, a youth of seventeen, lives in a panel truck which he drives around the country. From time to time his family sends him money, and he does occasional odd jobs to earn additional sums. He sometimes remains in one city for several months but he often moves on after only a few days or weeks in one place. He sometimes revisits places where he has been before. Would your answer to the question be affected by the purpose for which it is asked, for example, whether for voting or tax purposes or for the purposes of custody litigation? Is it possible that legally A has no domicile at all? Restatement, Second, Conflict of Laws, §§ 11, 16, 19, comment c (1971). If we say that his domicile of origin or some other domicile continues until a new one is chosen, does that not make a farce out of the principle that intent to make a home in the place is essential to acquisition of a domicile, since this person has no such intent and attribution of such an intent to him on these facts is fictional? But if we say he has no domicile, how and where can his legal rights and obligations be determined?

11. As has been indicated, the general rule is that the legitimate child at birth takes the domicile of his father, while the illegitimate child takes the domicile of his mother. See In re Estate of Moore, 68 Wash.2d 792, 415 P.2d 653 (1966). Can this rule survive Levy v. Louisiana; Labine v. Vincent; Stanley v. Illinois; and Weber v. Aetna Casualty & Surety Co., reproduced, infra, pages 328, 342, 432, and 369?

12. At common law the married woman took the domicile of her husband. Vestiges of this rule remained in the law until quite recently, for ex-

ample, some cases holding that the married woman could only choose her own domicile when living apart from her husband due to his misconduct. Today, however, several cases have held that she may choose her own domicile in the same fashion as any other competent adult. E. g., In re Marriage of Rinderknecht, —— Ind.App. ——, 367 N.E.2d 1128 (1977). In other states the married woman is given this right by statute. E. g., Colo.Rev. Stat. § 14–2–210 (1973); N.Y.Dom.Rel.L. § 61 (1974). In those states listed supra at page 21 which have enacted state equal rights amendments the married woman clearly has a constitutional right to choose her own domicile. It seems equally clear that the effect of the Supreme Court's decisions on discrimination against women under the Equal Protection Clause of the Fourteenth Amendment is that married women cannot constitutionally be restricted in their capacity to acquire a domicile. See, e. g., Reed v. Reed, 404 U.S. 71 (1971); Frontiero v. Richardson, 411 U.S. 677 (1973); Cleveland Bd. of Educ. v. LaFleur, 414 U.S. 632 (1974); Taylor v. Louisiana, 419 U.S. 522 (1975); Weinberger v. Wiesenfeld, 420 U.S. 636 (1975); Califano v. Goldfarb, 430 U.S. 199 (1977).

13. After reading and thinking about the materials on domicile, do you conclude that domicile is a concept adequate to the task for which it has been used? Why or why not? If not, what concept do you suggest in its place? Could you draft a statute which would satisfactorily define the concept? See Weintraub, An Inquiry Into The Utility of "Domicile" as a Concept in Conflicts Analysis, 63 Mich.L.Rev. 961 (1968).

Chapter 3

MARRIAGE

SECTION 1. THE EXTENT OF STATE POWER

GRISWOLD v. CONNECTICUT

Supreme Court of the United States, 1965.
381 U.S. 479, 85 S.Ct. 1678, 14 L.Ed.2d 510.

Mr. Justice DOUGLAS delivered the opinion of the Court.

Appellant Griswold is Executive Director of the Planned Parenthood League of Connecticut. Appellant Buxton is a licensed physician and a professor at the Yale Medical School who served as Medical Director for the League at its Center in New Haven—a center open and operating from November 1 to November 10, 1961, when appellants were arrested.

They gave information, instruction, and medical advice to *married persons* as to the means of preventing conception. They examined the wife and prescribed the best contraceptive device or material for her use. Fees were usually charged, although some couples were serviced free.

The statutes whose constitutionality is involved in this appeal are §§ 53–32 and 54–196 of the General Statutes of Connecticut (1958 rev.). The former provides:

"Any person who uses any drug, medicinal article or instrument for the purpose of preventing conception shall be fined not less than fifty dollars or imprisoned not less than sixty days nor more than one year or be both fined and imprisoned."

Section 54–196 provides:

"Any person who assists, abets, counsels, causes, hires or commands another to commit any offense may be prosecuted and punished as if he were the principal offender."

The appellants were found guilty as accessories and fined $100 each, against the claim that the accessory statute as so applied violated the Fourteenth Amendment. The Appellate Division of the Circuit Court affirmed. The Supreme Court of Errors affirmed that judgment. 151 Conn. 544, 200 A.2d 479 (1964). We noted probable jurisdiction. 379 U.S. 926, 85 S.Ct. 328, 13 L.Ed.2d 339 (1964).

[At this point the Court held that the appellants had standing to raise the constitutional issues.]

* * *

Coming to the merits, we are met with a wide range of questions that implicate the Due Process Clause of the Fourteenth Amendment. Overtones of some arguments suggest that Lochner v. New York, 198 U.S. 45, 25 S.Ct. 539, 49 L.Ed. 937 (1904), should be our guide. But we decline that invitation. * * * We do not sit as a super-legislature to determine the wisdom, need, and propriety of laws that touch economic problems, business affairs, or social conditions. This law, however, operates directly on an intimate relation of husband and wife and their physician's role in one aspect of that relation.

The association of people is not mentioned in the Constitution nor in the Bill of Rights. The right to educate a child in a school of the parents' choice—whether public or private or parochial—is also not mentioned. Nor is the right to study any particular subject or any foreign language. Yet the First Amendment has been construed to include certain of those rights.

By Pierce v. Society of Sisters, [268 U.S. 510, 45 S.Ct. 571, 69 L. Ed. 1070 (1925)] the right to educate one's children as one chooses is made applicable to the States by the force of the First and Fourteenth Amendments. By Meyer v. Nebraska, [262 U.S. 390, 43 S.Ct. 625, 67 L.Ed. 1042 (1923)] the same dignity is given the right to study the German language in a private school. In other words, the State may not, consistently with the spirit of the First Amendment, contract the spectrum of available knowledge. The right of freedom of speech and press includes not only the right to utter or to print, but the right to distribute, the right to receive, the right to read (Martin v. City of Struthers, 319 U.S. 141, 143, 63 S.Ct. 862, 863, 87 L.Ed. 1313 (1943)) and freedom of inquiry, freedom of thought, and freedom to teach (see Wieman v. Updegraff, 344 U.S. 183, 195, 73 S. Ct. 215, 220, 97 L.Ed. 216 (1952))—indeed the freedom of the entire university community. Sweezy v. New Hampshire, 354 U.S. 234, 249–250, 261–263, 77 S.Ct. 1203, 1211, 1217–1218, 1 L.Ed.2d 1311 (1957); Barenblatt v. United States, 360 U.S. 109, 112, 79 S.Ct. 1081, 1085, 3 L.Ed.2d 1115 (1959); Baggett v. Bullitt, 377 U.S. 360, 369, 84 S.Ct. 1316, 1321, 12 L.Ed.2d 377 (1964). Without those peripheral rights the specific rights would be less secure. And so we reaffirm the principle of the *Pierce* and the *Meyer* cases.

In NAACP v. Alabama, 357 U.S. 449, 462, 78 S.Ct. 1163, 1172 (1958), we protected the "freedom to associate and privacy in one's associations," noting that freedom of association was a peripheral First Amendment right. Disclosure of membership lists of a constitutionally valid association, we held, was invalid "as entailing the likelihood of a substantial restraint upon the exercise by petitioner's members of their right to freedom of association." In other words, the First Amendment has a penumbra where privacy is protected from governmental intrusion. In like context, we have protected forms of "association" that are not political in the customary sense but pertain to the social, legal, and economic benefit of the members.

NAACP v. Button, 371 U.S. 415, 430–431, 83 S.Ct. 328, 336–337 (1963). In Schware v. Board of Bar Examiners, 353 U.S. 232, 77 S. Ct. 752, 1 L.Ed.2d 796 (1957), we held it not permissible to bar a lawyer from practice, because he had once been a member of the Communist Party. The man's "association with that Party" was not shown to be "anything more than a political faith in a political party" (id., at 244) and was not action of a kind proving bad moral character. Id., at 245–246.

Those cases involved more than the "right of assembly"—a right that extends to all irrespective of their race or ideology. DeJonge v. Oregon, 299 U.S. 353, 57 S.Ct. 255, 81 L.Ed. 278 (1937). The right of "association," like the right of belief (Board of Education v. Barnette, 319 U.S. 624, 63 S.Ct. 1178 (1943)), is more than the right to attend a meeting; it includes the right to express one's attitudes or philosophies by membership in a group or by affiliation with it or by other lawful means. Association in that context is a form of expression of opinion; and while it is not expressly included in the First Amendment its existence is necessary in making the express guarantees fully meaningful.

The foregoing cases suggest that specific guarantees in the Bill of Rights have penumbras, formed by emanations from those guarantees that help give them life and substance. See Poe v. Ullman, 367 U.S. 497, 516–522, 81 S.Ct. 1752, 6 L.Ed.2d 989 (1961) (dissenting opinion). Various guarantees create zones of privacy. The right of association contained in the penumbra of the First Amendment is one, as we have seen. The Third Amendment in its prohibition against the quartering of soldiers "in any house" in time of peace without the consent of the owner is another facet of that privacy. The Fourth Amendment explicitly affirms the "right of the people to be secure in their persons, houses, papers, and effects, against unreasonable searches and seizures." The Fifth Amendment in its Self-Incrimination Clause enables the citizen to create a zone of privacy which government may not force him to surrender to his detriment. The Ninth Amendment provides: "The enumeration in the Constitution, of certain rights, shall not be construed to deny or disparage others retained by the people."

The Fourth and Fifth Amendments were described in Boyd v. United States, 116 U.S. 616, 630, 6 S.Ct. 524, 532, 29 L.Ed. 746 (1886), as protection against all governmental invasions "of the sanctity of a man's home and the privacies of life." * We recently

* The Court said in full about this right of privacy:

"The principles laid down in this opinion [by Lord Camden in Entick v. Carrington, 19 How.St.Tr. 1029] affect the very essence of constitutional liberty and security. They reach farther than the concrete form of the case then before the court, with its adventitious circumstances; they apply to all invasions on the part of the government and its employes of the sanctity of a man's home and the privacies of life. It is not the breaking of his doors, and the rummaging of his

referred in Mapp v. Ohio, 367 U.S. 643, 656, 81 S.Ct. 1684, 1692, 6 L. Ed.2d 1081 (1961), to the Fourth Amendment as creating a "right to privacy, no less important than any other right carefully and particularly reserved to the people." * * *

We have had many controversies over these penumbral rights of "privacy and repose." See, e. g., Breard v. Alexandria, 341 U.S. 622, 626, 644, 71 S.Ct. 920, 923, 933, 95 L.Ed. 1233 (1951); Public Utilities Comm'n v. Pollak, 343 U.S. 451, 72 S.Ct. 813, 96 L.Ed. 1068 (1952); Monroe v. Pape, 365 U.S. 167, 81 S.Ct. 473, 5 L.Ed.2d 492 (1961); Lanza v. New York, 370 U.S. 139, 82 S.Ct. 1218, 8 L.Ed.2d 384 (1962); Frank v. Maryland 359 U.S. 360, 79 S.Ct. 804, 3 L.Ed.2d 877 (1959); Skinner v. Oklahoma, 316 U.S. 535, 541, 62 S.Ct. 1110, 1113, 86 L.Ed. 1655 (1942). These cases bear witness that the right of privacy which presses for recognition here is a legitimate one.

The present case, then, concerns a relationship lying within the zone of privacy created by several fundamental constitutional guarantees. And it concerns a law which, in forbidding the *use* of contraceptives rather than regulating their manufacture or sale, seeks to achieve its goals by means having a maximum destructive impact upon that relationship. Such a law cannot stand in light of the familiar principle, so often applied by this Court, that a "governmental purpose to control or prevent activities constitutionally subject to state regulation may not be achieved by means which sweep unnecessarily broadly and thereby invade the area of protected freedoms." NAACP v. Alabama, 377 U.S. 288, 307, 84 S.Ct. 1302, 1314, 12 L.Ed. 2d 325 (1964). Would we allow the police to search the sacred precincts of marital bedrooms for telltale signs of the use of contraceptives? The very idea is repulsive to the notions of privacy surrounding the marriage relationship.

We deal with a right of privacy older than the Bill of Rights— older than our political parties, older than our school system. Marriage is a coming together for better or for worse, hopefully enduring, and intimate to the degree of being sacred. It is an association that promotes a way of life, not causes; a harmony in living, not political faiths; a bilateral loyalty, not commercial or social projects.

drawers, that constitutes the essence of the offence; but it is the invasion of his indefeasible right of personal security, personal liberty and private property, where that right has never been forfeited by his conviction of some public offence,—it is the invasion of this sacred right which underlies and constitutes the essence of Lord Camden's judgment. Breaking into a house and opening boxes and drawers are circumstances of aggravation; but any forcible and compulsory extortion of a man's own testimony or of his private papers to be used as evidence to convict him of crime or to forfeit his goods, is within the condemnation of that judgment. In this regard the Fourth and Fifth Amendments run almost into each other." 116 U.S. at 630.

Yet it is an association for as noble a purpose as any involved in our prior decisions.

Reversed.

Mr. Justice GOLDBERG, whom The CHIEF JUSTICE and Mr. Justice BRENNAN join, concurring.

I agree with the Court that Connecticut's birth-control law unconstitutionally intrudes upon the right of marital privacy, and I join in its opinion and judgment. Although I have not accepted the view that "due process" as used in the Fourteenth Amendment incorporates all of the first eight Amendments * * *, I do agree that the concept of liberty protects those personal rights that are fundamental, and is not confined to the specific terms of the Bill of Rights. * * *

The Court stated many years ago that the Due Process Clause protects those liberties that are "so rooted in the traditions and conscience of our people as to be ranked as fundamental." Snyder v. Massachusetts, 291 U.S. 97, 105, 54 S.Ct. 330, 332, 78 L.Ed. 674 (1934). * * *

This Court, in a series of decisions, has held that the Fourteenth Amendment absorbs and applies to the States those specifics of the first eight amendments which express fundamental personal rights. The language and history of the Ninth Amendment reveal that the Framers of the Constitution believed that there are additional fundamental rights, protected from governmental infringement, which exist alongside those fundamental rights specifically mentioned in the first eight constitutional amendments.

The Ninth Amendment reads, "The enumeration in the Constitution, of certain rights, shall not be construed to deny or disparage others retained by the people." The Amendment is almost entirely the work of James Madison. It was introduced in Congress by him and passed the House and Senate with little or no debate and virtually no change in language. It was proffered to quiet expressed fears that a bill of specifically enumerated rights could not be sufficiently broad to cover all essential rights and that the specific mention of certain rights would be interpreted as a denial that others were protected.

* * * the Framers did not intend that the first eight amendments be construed to exhaust the basic and fundamental rights which the Constitution guaranteed to the people.

While this Court has had little occasion to interpret the Ninth Amendment, "[i]t cannot be presumed that any clause in the constitution is intended to be without effect." Marbury v. Madison, 1 Cranch 137, 174, 2 L.Ed. 60 (1803). In interpreting the Constitution, "real effect should be given to all the words it uses." Myers v. United States, 272 U.S. 52, 151, 47 S.Ct. 21, 37, 71 L.Ed. 160 (1926). The Ninth Amendment to the Constitution may be regarded by some as a recent discovery and may be forgotten by others, but since 1791 it has been a basic part of the Constitution which we are sworn to uphold. To hold that a right so basic and fundamental and so deep-rooted in our society as the right of privacy in marriage may be infringed because that right is not guaranteed in so many words by the first eight amendments to the Constitution is to ignore the Ninth Amendment and to give it no effect whatsoever. Moreover, a judicial construction that this fundamental right is not protected by the Constitution because it is not mentioned in explicit terms by one of the first eight amendments or elsewhere in the Constitution would violate the Ninth Amendment, which specifically states that "[t]he enumeration in the Constitution, of certain rights, shall not be *construed* to deny or disparage others retained by the people." (Emphasis added.)

* * * I do not take the position of my Brother BLACK in his dissent in Adamson v. California, 332 U.S. 46, 68, 67 S.Ct. 1672, 1683, 91 L.Ed. 1903 (1947), that the entire Bill of Rights is incorporated in the Fourteenth Amendment, and I do not mean to imply that the Ninth Amendment is applied against the States by the Fourteenth. Nor do I mean to state that the Ninth Amendment constitutes an independent source of rights protected from infringement by either the States or the Federal Government. Rather, the Ninth Amendment shows a belief of the Constitution's authors that fundamental rights exist that are not expressly enumerated in the first eight amendments and an intent that the list of rights included there not be deemed exhaustive. As any student of this Court's opinions knows, this Court has held, often unanimously, that the Fifth and Fourteenth Amendments protect certain fundamental personal liberties from abridgment by the Federal Government or the States. * * * The Ninth Amendment simply shows the intent of the Constitution's authors that other fundamental personal rights should not be denied such protection or disparaged in any other way simply because they are not specifically listed in the first eight constitutional amendments. * * * In sum, the Ninth Amendment simply lends strong support to the view that the "liberty" protected by the Fifth and Fourteenth Amendments from infringement by the Federal Government or the States is not restricted to rights specifically mentioned in the first eight amendments. * * *

In determining which rights are fundamental, judges are not left at large to decide cases in light of their personal and private notions. Rather, they must look to the "traditions and [collective] conscience of our people" to determine whether a principle is "so rooted [there] * * * as to be ranked as fundamental." Snyder v. Massachusetts, 291 U.S. 97, 105, 54 S.Ct. 330, 332 (1934). The inquiry is whether a right involved "is of such a character that it cannot be denied without violating those 'fundamental principles of liberty and justice which lie at the base of all our civil and political institutions' * * *."

Powell v. Alabama, 287 U.S. 45, 67, 53 S.Ct. 55, 63, 77 L.Ed. 989 (1932). "Liberty" also "gains content from the emanations of * * * specific [constitutional] guarantees" and "from experience with the requirements of a free society." Poe v. Ullman, 367 U.S. 497, 517, 81 S.Ct. 1752, 1763, 6 L.Ed.2d 989 (1961) (dissenting opinion of Mr. Justice DOUGLAS).

I agree fully with the Court that, applying these tests, the right of privacy is a fundamental personal right, emanating "from the totality of the constitutional scheme under which we live." Id., at 521, 81 S.Ct. at 1765.

The Connecticut statutes here involved deal with a particularly important and sensitive area of privacy—that of the marital relation and the marital home. * * *

The entire fabric of the Constitution and the purposes that clearly underlie its specific guarantees demonstrate that the rights to marital privacy and to marry and raise a family are of similar order and magnitude as the fundamental rights specifically protected.

Although the Constitution does not speak in so many words of the right of privacy in marriage, I cannot believe that it offers these fundamental rights no protection. The fact that no particular provision of the Constitution explicitly forbids the State from disrupting the traditional relation of the family—a relation as old and as fundamental as our entire civilization—surely does not show that the Government was meant to have the power to do so. Rather, as the Ninth Amendment expressly recognizes, there are fundamental personal rights such as this one, which are protected from abridgment by the Government though not specifically mentioned in the Constitution.

* * *

The logic of the dissents would sanction federal or state legislation that seems to me even more plainly unconstitutional than the statute before us. Surely the Government, absent a showing of a compelling subordinating state interest, could not decree that all husbands and wives must be sterilized after two children have been born to them. Yet by their reasoning such an invasion of marital privacy would not be subject to constitutional challenge because, while it might be "silly," no provision of the Constitution specifically prevents the Government from curtailing the marital right to bear children and raise a family. While it may shock some of my Brethren that the Court today holds that the Constitution protects the right of marital privacy, in my view it is far more shocking to believe that the personal liberty guaranteed by the Constitution does not include protection against such totalitarian limitation of family size, which is at complete variance with our constitutional concepts. Yet, if upon a showing of a slender basis of rationality, a law outlawing voluntary birth control by married persons is valid, then, by the same reasoning, a law requiring compulsory birth control also would seem to be valid. In my view, however, both types of law would unjustifiably intrude upon rights of marital privacy which are constitutionally protected.

In a long series of cases this Court has held that where fundamental personal liberties are involved, they may not be abridged by the States simply on a showing that a regulatory statute has some rational relationship to the effectuation of a proper state purpose. "Where there is a significant encroachment upon personal liberty, the State may prevail only upon showing a subordinating interest which is compelling," Bates v. Little Rock, 361 U.S. 516, 524, 80 S.Ct. 412, 417, 4 L.Ed.2d 480 (1960). The law must be shown "necessary, and not merely rationally related, to the accomplishment of a permissible state policy." McLaughlin v. Florida, 379 U.S. 184, 196, 85 S.Ct. 283, 290, 13 L.Ed.2d 222 (1964).

Although the Connecticut birth-control law obviously encroaches upon a fundamental personal liberty, the State does not show that the law serves any "subordinating [state] interest which is compelling" or that it is "necessary * * * to the accomplishment of a permissible state policy." The State, at most, argues that there is some rational relation between this statute and what is admittedly a legitimate subject of state concern—the discouraging of extra-marital relations. It says that preventing the use of birth-control devices by married persons helps prevent the indulgence by some in such extra-marital relations. The rationality of this justification is dubious, particularly in light of the admitted widespread availability to all persons in the State of Connecticut, unmarried as well as married, of birth-control devices for the prevention of disease, as distinguished from the prevention of conception, see Tileston v. Ullman, 129 Conn. 84, 26 A.2d 582 (1948). But, in any event, it is clear that the state interest in safeguarding marital fidelity can be served by a more discriminately tailored statute, which does not like the present one, sweep unnecessarily broadly, reaching far beyond the evil sought to be dealt with and intruding upon the privacy of all married couples. * * * The State of Connecticut does have statutes, the constitutionality of which is beyond doubt, which prohibit adultery and fornication. See Conn.Gen.Stat. §§ 53–218, 53–219 et seq. These statutes demonstrate that means for achieving the same basic purpose of protecting marital fidelity are available to Connecticut without the need to "invade the area of protected freedoms." * * *

Finally, it should be said of the Court's holding today that it in no way interferes with a State's proper regulation of sexual promiscuity or misconduct. * * *

In sum, I believe that the right of privacy in the marital relation is fundamental and basic—a personal right "retained by the people" within the meaning of the Ninth Amendment. Connecticut cannot constitutionally abridge this fundamental right, which is protected by the Fourteenth Amendment from infringement by the States. I agree with the Court that petitioners' convictions must therefore be reversed.

*   *   *

NOTES AND QUESTIONS

1. In addition to the opinions quoted, Mr. Justice Harlan concurred in the judgment, but on the ground that the Connecticut statute infringed the Due Process Clause of the Fourteenth Amendment because it violated basic values implicit in the concept of ordered liberty. He conceded that the result might be aided by resort to one or more provisions of the Bill of Rights, but thought that it would not be dependent upon them, and especially disagreed with the notion that the Fourteenth Amendment's incorporation of the Bill of Rights could be used to restrict the category of rights applied to the states by that Amendment.

Mr. Justice White also concurred in the judgment, employing more traditional Fourteenth Amendment analysis. In his view the statute deprived married couples of liberty without due process by interfering with a fundamental right, that is, the right to participate in family life, without sufficient justification.

Mr. Justice Black and Mr. Justice Stewart dissented. Their view was that the Due Process Clause of the Fourteenth Amendment does not restrict the states' powers to legislate beyond the limitations imposed by the Bill of Rights. They found none of the Bill of Rights involved in this case.

Although the Court voted 7–2 against the validity of the Connecticut statute, no single opinion obtained the adherence of a majority. Mr. Justice Douglas was joined by Mr. Justice Clark in writing for the Court. Mr. Justice Goldberg, Chief Justice Warren and Mr. Justice Brennan indicated agreement with the Douglas opinion, although they also joined in Mr. Justice Goldberg's separate concurrence. It therefore seems accurate to say that five of the justices agreed broadly on the rationale of the case (but with differences in detail and in emphasis), two favored a different rationale, and two dissented.

2. The *Griswold* case has been noted in more than twenty-five law reviews, among which are 1966 Duke L.J. 562; 79 Harv.L.Rev. 162 (1965); 6 J.Fam.L. 371 (1966); 64 Mich.L.Rev. 197 (1965); 30 U.Colo.L.Rev. 267 (1966); and 1966 Wis.L.Rev. 979.

3. Precisely what is the rationale of the Douglas and Goldberg opinions? Can you outline it in logical fashion? Does Mr. Justice Douglas hold that there is an area of marital privacy, which the state may not invade under any circumstances? What does Mr. Justice Goldberg's opinion say on this point? Do these two opinions spell the end of the view that the Due Process Clause guarantees "freedom from all substantial arbitrary impositions and purposeless restraints," as Mr. Justice Harlan put it in Poe v. Ullman, 367 U.S. 497, 522, 543 (1961) or, as Mr. Justice Traynor said in Perez v. Lippold, 32 Cal.2d 711, 198 P.2d 17 (1948), that it ensures that "no law within the broad areas of state interest may be unreasonably discriminatory or arbitrary"?

4. Are these opinions, in their general approach to regulation of marriage, historically accurate, at least so far as appears from the historical sketch supra at pages 3–13? Cf. Boddie v. Connecticut, 401 U.S. 371, 376, 389 (1971).

5. Griswold raises many questions about the extent to which the states may regulate marriage. Some such questions are as follows:

(a) H and W, having lived together for more than a year, decide to marry. They are willing to obtain a marriage license and execute a marriage certificate, but they reject the notion that the state should be able to control the relationship of marriage. They therefore plan a ceremony in which they will gather with their friends, refreshments will be served (and perhaps smoked), and at some point a particular friend will come before the group, read from the works of Kahlil Gibran and then give a short account of the lives of H and W, concluding as follows: "And so, H and W, who have lived together for one year, have come here with their friends to show their desire to become man and wife. I now request them to exchange rings," (upon which H and W do so) and the friend will continue, "I now pronounce H and W man and woman." In a state requiring solemnization of marriage before a minister, priest or rabbi, or some civil officer, would Griswold invalidate the requirement and make this marriage valid? Cf. Holt v. Shelton, 341 F.Supp. 821 (M.D.Tenn.1972), briefly summarized supra, page 21?

(b) Many states have statutes making sodomy a crime. Would such statutes be unconstitutional under Griswold so far as they are applied to adult homosexuals engaged in private sexual conduct? Doe v. Commonwealth's Attorney for City of Richmond, 403 F.Supp. 1199 (E.D.Va.1975), affirmed without opinion 425 U.S. 901 (1976), rehearing denied 425 U.S. 985 (1976). Justices Brennan, Marshall and Stevens thought that probable jurisdiction should be noted and the case set down for oral argument. Would the result be the same if such a statute, or a statute forbidding "lewd and lascivious acts" were applied to conduct occurring in private between husband and wife? Cotner v. Henry, 394 F.2d 873 (7th Cir. 1968); State v. Bateman, 113 Ariz. 107, 547 P.2d 6 (1976), cert. den. 429 U.S. 864 (1976). What state interests are promoted by such statutes? See also Lovisi v. Slayton, 539 F.2d 349 (4th Cir. 1976), cert. den. 429 U.S. 977 (1976). Would the result be the same if the acts were performed by a consenting man and woman in private but they were not married to each other? State v. Pilcher, 242 N.W.2d 348 (Iowa 1976), 1977 Wash.U.L.Q. 337; State v. Saunders, 75 N.J. 200, 381 A.2d 333 (1976).

(c) A city ordinance provides that in a particular zone there may only be single family dwellings, and that only families may live in such dwellings. A "family" is defined to include only persons related by blood, marriage or adoption. A man and woman living together but not married wish to buy a house in a neighborhood covered by the ordinance and are told that they would violate it by living together in the house. Does *Griswold* have any effect upon this controversy? Would the result be different if the man and woman were married but they wished to have live with them an elderly woman who had been the wife's nurse years before? Village of Belle Terre v. Boraas, 416 U.S. 1 (1974); Moore v. City of East Cleveland, Ohio, 431 U.S. 494 (1977); Atkisson v. Kern County Housing Auth., 59 Cal.App. 3d 89, 130 Cal.Rptr. 375 (1976); Annot., What Constitutes a "Family"

Within Meaning of Zoning Regulation or Restrictive Covenant, 71 A.L.R.3d 693 (1976).

(d) Contemplating the Griswold case in general terms, would you conclude that it has been and will be a charter of freedom for the individual in marriage? Did it liberate us from the sort of "meddling" about which John Selden wrote, supra page 1, in the Seventeenth Century? Cf. Glendon, Marriage and the State: The Withering Away of Marriage, 62 Va.L. Rev. 663 (1976); Goode, State Intervention and the Family: Problems of Policy, 1976 B.Y.U.L.Rev. 715. Does the case signal a revolution in marriage and the family comparable to the extensive changes leading to the male dominated nuclear family which emerged in the English upper and middle classes during the Sixteenth and Seventeenth Centuries? Cf. L. Stone, The Family, Sex and Marriage in England 1500–1800 Ch. 5 (1977).

ZABLOCKI v. REDHAIL

Supreme Court of the United States, 1978.
434 U.S. 374, 98 S.Ct. 673, 54 L.Ed.2d 618.

Mr. Justice MARSHALL, delivered the opinion of the Court.

At issue in this case is the constitutionality of a Wisconsin statute, Wis.Stat. §§ 245.10(1), (4), (5) (1973), which provides that members of a certain class of Wisconsin residents may not marry, within the State or elsewhere, without first obtaining a court order granting permission to marry. The class is defined by the statute to include any "Wisconsin resident having minor issue not in his custody and which he is under an obligation to support by any court order or judgment." The statute specifies that court permission cannot be granted unless the marriage applicant submits proof of compliance with the support obligation and, in addition, demonstrates that the children covered by the support order "are not then and are not likely thereafter to become public charges." No marriage license may lawfully be issued in Wisconsin to a person covered by the statute, except upon court order; any marriage entered into without compliance with § 245.10 is declared void; and persons acquiring marriage licenses in violation of the section are subject to criminal penalties.

After being denied a marriage license because of his failure to comply with § 245.10, appellee brought this class action under 42 U. S.C.A. § 1983, challenging the statute as violative of the Equal Protection and Due Process Clauses of the Fourteenth Amendment and seeking declaratory and injunctive relief. The United States District Court for the Eastern District of Wisconsin held the statute unconstitutional under the Equal Protection Clause and enjoined its enforcement. 418 F.Supp. 1061 (1976). We noted probable jurisdiction, 429 U.S. 1089, 97 S.Ct. 1096, 51 L.Ed.2d 534 (1977), and we now affirm.

I

Appellee Redhail is a Wisconsin resident who, under the terms of § 245.10, is unable to enter into a lawful marriage in Wisconsin or elsewhere so long as he maintains his Wisconsin residency. The facts, according to the stipulation filed by the parties in the District Court, are as follows. In January 1972, when appellee was a minor and a high school student, a paternity action was instituted against him in Milwaukee County Court, alleging that he was the father of a baby girl born out of wedlock on July 5, 1971. After he appeared and admitted that he was the child's father, the court entered an order on May 12, 1972, adjudging appellee the father and ordering him to pay $109 per month as support for the child until she reached 18 years of age. From May 1972 until August 1974, appellee was unemployed and indigent, and consequently was unable to make any support payments.

On September 27, 1974, appellee filed an application for a marriage license with appellant Zablocki, the County Clerk of Milwaukee County, and a few days later the application was denied on the sole ground that appellee had not obtained a court order granting him permission to marry, as required by § 245.10. Although appellee did not petition a state court thereafter, it is stipulated that he would not have been able to satisfy either of the statutory prerequisites for an order granting permission to marry. First, he had not satisfied his support obligations to his illegitimate child, and as of December 1974 there was an arrearage in excess of $3,700. Second, the child had been a public charge since her birth, receiving benefits under the Aid to Families with Dependent Children program. It is stipulated that the child's benefit payments were such that she would have been a public charge even if appellee had been current in his support payments.

On December 24, 1974, appellee filed his complaint in the District Court, on behalf of himself and the class of all Wisconsin residents who had been refused a marriage license pursuant to § 245.-10(1) by one of the county clerks in Wisconsin. Zablocki was named as the defendant, individually and as representative of a class consisting of all county clerks in the State. The complaint alleged, among other things, that appellee and the woman he desired to marry were expecting a child in March 1975 and wished to be lawfully married before that time. The statute was attacked on the grounds that it deprived appellee, and the class he sought to represent of equal protection and due process rights secured by the First, Fifth, Ninth, and Fourteenth Amendments to the United States Constitution.

A three-judge court was convened pursuant to 28 U.S.C.A. §§ 2281, 2284. * * *

The three-judge court handed down a unanimous decision on August 31, 1976. The court ruled, first, that it was not required to abstain from decision under the principles set forth in Huffman v. Pursue, Ltd., 420 U.S. 592, 95 S.Ct. 1200, 43 L.Ed.2d 482 (1975), and Younger v. Harris, 401 U.S. 37, 91 S.Ct. 746, 27 L.Ed.2d 669 (1971), since there was no pending state-court proceeding that could be frustrated by the declaratory and injunctive relief requested. Second, the court held that the class of all county clerks in Wisconsin was a proper defendant class under Rule 23(a) and b(2), and that neither Rule 23 nor due process required prejudgment notice to the members of the plaintiff or the defendant class.

On the merits, the three-judge panel analyzed the challenged statute under the Equal Protection Clause and concluded that "strict scrutiny" was required because the classification created by the statute infringed upon a fundamental right, the right to marry.[7] The court then proceeded to evaluate the interests advanced by the State to justify the statute, and, finding that the classification was not necessary for the achievement of those interests, the court held the statute invalid and enjoined the county clerks from enforcing it.

Appellant brought this direct appeal pursuant to 28 U.S.C.A. § 1253, claiming that the three-judge court erred in finding §§ 245.-10(1), (4), (5) invalid under the Equal Protection Clause. Appellee defends the lower court's equal protection holding and, in the alternative, urges affirmance of the District Court's judgment on the ground that the statute does not satisfy the requirements of substantive due process. We agree with the District Court that the statute violates the Equal Protection Clause.[9]

---

7. 418 F.Supp., at 1068–1071. The court found an additional justification for applying strict scrutiny in the fact that the statute discriminates on the basis of wealth, absolutely denying individuals the opportunity to marry if they lack sufficient financial resources to make the showing required by the statute. Id., at 1070, citing San Antonio School District v. Rodriguez, 411 U.S. 1, 20, 93 S.Ct. 1278, 1289, 36 L.Ed.2d 16 (1973).

9. Counsel for appellee informed us at oral argument that appellee was married in Illinois some time after argument on the merits in the District Court, but prior to judgment. Tr. of Oral Arg., at 23, 30–31. This development in no way moots the issues before us. First, appellee's individual claim is unaffected, since he is still a Wisconsin resident and the Illinois marriage is consequently void under the provisions of §§ 245.10(1), (4), (5). See State v. Mueller, supra (§ 245.10 has extraterritorial effect with respect to Wisconsin residents). Second, regardless of the current status of appellee's individual claim, the dispute over the statute's constitutionality remains live with respect to members of the class appellee represents, and the Illinois marriage took place well after the class was certified. See Franks v. Bowman Transp. Co., 424 U.S. 747, 752–757, 96 S.Ct. 1251, 1258–1261, 47 L.Ed.2d 444 (1976); Sosna v. Iowa, 419 U.S. 393, 397–403, 95 S.Ct. 553, 556–559, 42 L. Ed.2d 532 (1975).

After argument in this Court, the Acting Governor of Wisconsin signed into law a comprehensive revision of the State's marriage laws, effective February 1, 1978. 1977 Wis. Laws 597, ch. 105. The revision added a new section (§ 245.105) which appears to be a somewhat narrower version of § 245.10. Enactment of this new provision also does not moot our inquiry into the constitutionality of § 245.10. By its terms, the new section "shall be enforced only when the provisions of § 245.10 and utilization of the procedures, thereunder are stayed or enjoined by the order of any court." § 245.105 (8). As we read this somewhat unusual proviso, and as it was explained to us at argument by the representative of the Wisconsin Attorney General, Tr. of Oral Arg., at 4–10, the new section is meant only to serve as a stopgap during such time as enforcement of § 245.10 is barred by court order. Were we to vacate the District Court's injunction on this

II

In evaluating §§ 245.10(1), (4), (5) under the Equal Protection Clause, "we must first determine what burden of justification the classification created thereby must meet, by looking to the nature of the classification and the individual interests affected." Memorial Hospital v. Maricopa County, 415 U.S. 250, 253, 94 S.Ct. 1076, 1079, 1080, 39 L.Ed.2d 306 (1974). Since our past decisions make clear that the right to marry is of fundamental importance, and since the classification at issue here significantly interferes with the exercise of that right, we believe that "critical examination" of the state interests advanced in support of the classification is required.

The leading decision of this Court on the right to marry is Loving v. Virginia, 388 U.S. 1, 87 S.Ct. 1817, 18 L.Ed.2d 1010 (1967). In that case, an interracial couple who had been convicted of violating Virginia's miscegenation laws challenged the statutory scheme on both equal protection and due process grounds. The Court's opinion could have rested solely on the ground that the statutes discriminated on the basis of race in violation of the Equal Protection Clause. Id., at 11–12, 87 S.Ct., at 1823–1824. But the Court went on to hold that the laws arbitrarily deprived the couple of a fundamental liberty protected by the Due Process Clause, the freedom to marry. The Court's language on the latter point bears repeating:

"The freedom to marry has long been recognized as one of the vital personal rights essential to the orderly pursuit of happiness by free men.

"Marriage is one of the 'basic civil rights of man,' fundamental to our very existence and survivial." Id., at 12, 87 S.Ct., at 1824, quoting Skinner v. Oklahoma, 316 U.S. 535, 541, 62 S.Ct. 1110, 1113, 86 L.Ed. 1655 (1942).

Although *Loving* arose in the context of racial discrimination, prior and subsequent decisions of this Court confirm that the right to marry is of fundamental importance for all individuals. Long ago, in Maynard v. Hill, 125 U.S. 190, 8 S.Ct. 723, 31 L.Ed. 654 (1888), the Court characterized marriage as "the most important relation in life," id., at 205, 8 S.Ct., at 726, and as "the foundation of the family and of society, without which there would be neither civilization nor progress," id., at 211, 8 S.Ct., at 729. In Meyer v. Nebraska, 262 U.S. 390, 43 S.Ct. 625, 67 L.Ed. 1042 (1923), the Court recognized that the right "to marry, establish a home and bring up children" is a central part of the liberty protected by the Due Process Clause, id., at 399, 43 S.Ct., at 626, and in Skinner v. Oklahoma, 316 U.S. 535, 62 S. Ct. 1110, 86 L.Ed. 1655 (1942), marriage was described as "funda-

appeal, § 245.10 would go back into full force and effect; accordingly, the dispute over its validity is quite live.

We express no judgment on the constitutionality of the new section.

mental to the very existence and survival of the race," id., at 541, 62 S.Ct., at 1113.

More recent decisions have established that the right to marry is part of the fundamental "right of privacy" implicit in the Fourteenth Amendment's Due Process Clause. In Griswold v. Connecticut, 381 U.S. 479, 85 S.Ct. 1678, 14 L.Ed.2d 510 (1965), the Court observed:

"We deal with a right of privacy older than the Bill of Rights— older than our political parties, older than our school system. Marriage is a coming together for better or for worse, hopefully enduring, and intimate to the degree of being sacred. It is an association that promotes a way of life, not causes; a harmony in living, not political faiths; a bilateral loyalty, not commercial or social projects. Yet it is an association for as noble a purpose as any involved in our prior decisions." Id., at 486, 85 S.Ct., at 1682.

Cases subsequent to *Griswold* and *Loving* have routinely categorized the decision to marry as among the personal decisions protected by the right of privacy. For example, last Term in Carey v. Population Services International, 431 U.S. 678, 97 S.Ct. 2010, 52 L.Ed.2d 675 (1977), we declared:

"While the outer limits of [the right of personal privacy] have not been marked by the Court, it is clear that among the decisions that an individual may make without unjustified government interference are personal decisions 'relating to marriage, Loving v. Virginia, 388 U.S. 1, 12, 87 S.Ct. 1817, 1823, 18 L.Ed.2d 1010 (1967); procreation, Skinner v. Oklahoma, 316 U.S. 535, 541–542, 62 S.Ct. 1110, 1113–1114, 86 L.Ed. 1655 (1942); contraception, Eisenstadt v. Baird, 405 U.S. [438], at 453–454, 92 S.Ct. [1029], at 1038–1039, 31 L.Ed.2d 349; id., at 460, 463–465, 92 S.Ct. at 1042, 1043–1044 (White, J., concurring in result); family relationships, Prince v. Massachusetts, 321 U.S. 158, 166, 64 S.Ct. 438, 442, 88 L.Ed. 645 (1944); and child rearing and education, Pierce v. Society of Sisters, 268 U.S. 510, 535, 45 S.Ct. 571, 573, 69 L.Ed. 1070 (1925); Meyer v. Nebraska, [262 U.S. 390, 399, 43 S.Ct. 625, 67 L.Ed. 1042 (1923)].'"

*   *   *

It is not surprising that the decision to marry has been placed on the same level of importance as decisions relating to procreation, childbirth, child-rearing, and family relationships. As the facts of this case illustrate, it would make little sense to recognize a right of privacy with respect to other matters of family life and not with respect to the decision to enter the relationship that is the foundation of the family in our society. The woman whom appellee desired to marry had a fundamental right to seek an abortion of their expected child, see Roe v. Wade, supra, or to bring the child into life to suffer the myriad social, if not economic, disabilities that the status of illegitimacy brings. Surely, a decision to marry and raise the child in a traditional family setting must receive equivalent protection. And, if appellee's right to procreate means anything at all, it must imply some right to enter the only relationship in which the State of Wisconsin allows sexual relations legally to take place.[11]

By reaffirming the fundamental character of the right to marry, we do not mean to suggest that every state regulation which relates in any way to the incidents of or prerequisites for marriage must be subjected to rigorous scrutiny. To the contrary, reasonable regulations that do not significantly interfere with decisions to enter into the marital relationship may legitimately be imposed. See Califano v. Jobst, 434 U.S. 47, 98 S.Ct. 95, 54 L.Ed.2d 228, No. 76–860, 1977; n. 12, infra. The statutory classification at issue here, however, clearly does interfere directly and substantially with the right to marry.

Under the challenged statute, no Wisconsin resident in the affected class may marry in Wisconsin or elsewhere without a court order, and marriages contracted in violation of the statute are both void and punishable as criminal offenses. Some of those in the affected class, like appellee, will never be able to obtain the necessary court order, because they either lack the financial means to meet their support obligations or cannot prove that their children will not become public charges. These persons are absolutely prevented from getting married. Many others, able in theory to satisfy the statute's requirements, will be sufficiently burdened by having to do so that they will in effect be coerced into foregoing their right to marry. And even those who can be persuaded to meet the statute's requirements suffer a serious intrusion into their freedom of choice in an area in which we have held such freedom to be fundamental.[12]

11. Wisconsin punishes fornication as a criminal offense:
"Whoever has sexual intercourse with a person not his spouse may be fined not more than $200 or imprisoned not more than 6 months or both." Wis.Stat. § 944.15 (1973).

12. The directness and substantiality of the interference with the freedom to marry distinguish the instant case from Califano v. Jobst, 434 U.S. 47, 98 S.Ct. 95, 54 L.Ed.2d 228, No. 76–860, 1977. In Jobst, we upheld sections of the Social Security Act providing, inter alia, for termination of a dependent child's benefits upon marriage to an individual not entitled to benefits under the Act. As the opinion for the Court expressly noted, the rule terminating benefits upon marriage was not "an attempt to interfere with the individual's freedom to make a decision as important as marriage." Id. at 54, 98 S.Ct., at 99. The Social Security provisions placed no direct legal obstacle in the path of persons desiring to get married, and —notwithstanding our Brother Rehnquist's imaginative recasting of the case, see dissenting opinion, post, at 692—there was no evidence that the laws significantly discouraged, let alone made "practically impossible," any marriages. Indeed, the provisions had not deterred the individual who challenged the statute from getting married, even though he and his wife were both disabled. See Califano v. Jobst, supra, at 48, 98 S.Ct. at 96. See also id., at 57, n. 17, 98 S.Ct., at 101, (because of availability of other federal benefits, total payments to the Jobsts after marriage were only $20 per month less than they would have been had Mr. Jobst's child benefits not been terminated).

III

When a statutory classification significantly interferes with the exercise of a fundamental right, it cannot be upheld unless it is supported by sufficiently important state interests and is closely tailored to effectuate only those interests. Appellant asserts that two interests are served by the challenged statute: the permission-to-marry proceeding furnishes an opportunity to counsel the applicant as to the necessity of fulfilling his prior support obligations; and the welfare of the out-of-custody children is protected. We may accept for present purposes that these are legitimate and substantial interests, but, since the means selected by the State for achieving these interests unnecessarily impinge on the right to marry, the statute cannot be sustained.

There is evidence that the challenged statute, as originally introduced in the Wisconsin Legislature, was intended merely to establish a mechanism whereby persons with support obligations to children from prior marriages could be counselled before they entered into new marital relationships and incurred further support obligations.[13] Court permission to marry was to be required, but apparently permission was automatically to be granted after counselling was completed.[14] The statute actually enacted, however, does not expressly require or provide for any counselling whatsoever, nor for any automatic granting of permission to marry by the court,[15] and thus it can hardly be justified as a means for ensuring counselling of the persons within its coverage. Even assuming that counselling does take place—a fact as to which there is no evidence in the record—this interest obviously cannot support the withholding of court permission to marry once counselling is completed.

With regard to safeguarding the welfare of the out-of-custody children, appellant's brief does not make clear the connection between the State's interest and the statute's requirements. At argument, appellant's counsel suggested that, since permission to marry cannot be granted unless the applicant shows that he has satisfied his court-determined support obligations to the prior children and that those children will not become public charges, the statute provides incentive for the applicant to make support payments to his children. Tr. of

13. See Wisconsin Legislative Council Notes, 1959, reprinted following Wis. Stat.Ann. § 245.10 (Cum.Supp.1977); 5 Wisconsin Legislative Council, General Report 68 (1959).

14. See 5 Wisconsin Legislative Council, supra, n. 14, at 68.

15. Although the statute as originally enacted in 1959 did not provide for automatic granting of permission, it did allow the court to grant permission if it found "good cause" for doing so, even in the absence of a showing that support obligations were being met. 1 [1958–1959] Wis. Sess.Laws c. 595, § 17 (1959). In 1961, the good-cause provision was deleted, and the requirement of a showing that the out-of-custody children are not and will not become public charges was added. 1 [1961] Wis.Sess.Laws c. 505, § 11.

Oral Arg., at 17–20. This "collection device" rationale cannot justify the statute's broad infringement on the right to marry.

First, with respect to individuals who are unable to meet the statutory requirements, the statute merely prevents the applicant from getting married, without delivering any money at all into the hands of the applicant's prior children. More importantly, regardless of the applicant's ability or willingness to meet the statutory requirements, the State already has numerous other means for exacting compliance with support obligations, means that are at least as effective as the instant statute's and yet do not impinge upon the right to marry. Under Wisconsin law, whether the children are from a prior marriage or were born out of wedlock, court-determined support obligations may be enforced directly via wage assignments, civil contempt proceedings, and criminal penalties.[16] And, if the State believes that parents of children out of their custody should be responsible for ensuring that those children do not become public charges, this interest can be achieved by adjusting the criteria used for determining the amounts to be paid under their support orders.

There is also some suggestion that § 245.10 protects the ability of marriage applicants to meet support obligations to prior children by preventing the applicants from incurring new support obligations. But the challenged provisions of § 245.10 are grossly underinclusive with respect to this purpose, since they do not limit in any way new financial commitments by the applicant other than those arising out of the contemplated marriage. The statutory classification is substantially overinclusive as well: given the possibility that the new spouse will actually better the applicant's financial situation, by contributing income from a job or otherwise, the statute in many cases may prevent affected individuals from improving their ability to satisfy their prior support obligations. And, although it is true that the applicant will incur support obligations to any children born during the contemplated marriage, preventing the marriage may only result in the children being born out of wedlock, as in fact occurred in appellee's case. Since the support obligation is the same whether the child is born in or out of wedlock, the net result of preventing the marriage is simply more illegitimate children.

The statutory classification created by §§ 245.10(1), (4), (5) thus cannot be justified by the interests advanced in support of it. The judgment of the District Court is, accordingly,

Affirmed.

---

16. Wisconsin statutory provisions for civil enforcement of support obligations to children from a prior marriage include §§ 247.232 (wage assignment), 247.265 (same), and 295.03 (civil contempt). Support obligations arising out of paternity actions may be civilly enforced under §§ 52.21(2) (wage assignment) and 52.40 (civil contempt). See also § 52.39. In addition, failure to meet support obligations may result in conviction of the felony offense of abandonment of a minor child, § 52.05, or the misdemeanor of failure to support a minor child, § 52.055.

NOTES AND QUESTIONS

1. Justices White, Blackmun, Brennan and Chief Justice Burger joined in Justice Marshall's opinion, making up the majority. Justice Stewart wrote a separate concurrence in which he said that this was not an Equal Protection case, but that the result could be upheld on the ground that the Due Process Clause of the Fourteenth Amendment protects freedom of choice in marriage, and that the Wisconsin statute abridged that freedom in a manner not warranted by the state's interest in enforcing support obligations. He found that "* * * the State's legitimate concern with the financial soundness of prospective marriages must stop short of telling people they may not marry because they are too poor or because they might persist in their financial irresponsibility. The invasion of constitutionally protected liberty and the chance of erroneous prediction are simply too great." 434 U.S. at 395.

Justice Powell also concurred separately on the ground that under either the Due Process Clause or the Equal Protection Clause the Wisconsin statute was invalid because it did not allow for those without the means to comply with their child support obligations. He expressed the view that as applied to those who were able to pay child support but merely were shirking their obligation the statute was constitutional.

Justice Stevens' concurrence took the position that the defect in the statute was that the distinctions it made had no rational relation to its purpose. For example, it did not apply at all to those least likely to be supporting their children, that is, those so poor that no support order was made in the divorce proceeding. On the other hand it did prevent the marriage of an indigent parent even though he was proposing to marry someone who would improve his financial position, and so presumably would be able to pay his child support. He characterized the statute as either futile or perverse so far as it applied to remarriages which produce no children, or to couples who will have illegitimate children if they are refused permission to marry. He also seems to have placed some weight on the fact that the statute discriminated between rich and poor.

Justice Rehnquist dissented on the ground that this case was controlled by Califano v. Jobst, 434 U.S. 47 (1977). That case held constitutional a provision of the Social Security Act which terminated the entitlement of a disabled dependent of a wage earner when he married another disabled person who was not entitled to social security benefits, although the payments would not have been terminated under the Act if the marriage had been contracted with another disabled person who was entitled to social security benefits. The statutory distinction between the two classes of marriage, turning on whether the new spouse was or was not a beneficiary of social security the Court found to be rational, partly because it was "a reliable indicator of probable hardship" and partly as a matter of administrative convenience. The Court in this case gave little attention to the issue of whether such a classification placed an unconstitutional restriction upon the liberty of choice in marriage. Justice Rehnquist found both the Social Security Act and the Wisconsin statute to be rational devices for the administration of social welfare programs.

2. Since the Wisconsin statute was unique and others like it not likely to be enacted, the Court's invalidation of it is of less importance than the

reasoning by which the Court reached that result. That reasoning raises some questions which may have an impact upon cases arising in the future:

(a) Why is it that the decision to marry is a "fundamental right"? Does this follow, as the Court seems to say, from the Griswold case?

(b) If the right to marry is "fundamental", what follows from that in cases in which a state regulation of marriage is challenged?

3. What effect, if any, would the *Zablocki* decision have on the questions raised in paragraph 5, supra, page 82? Does the decision have any effect on regulations made by public employers against the hiring of married couples in some circumstances, as in the cases cited in paragraph 8, supra, page 22.

4. As indicated, infra, chapter 6, section 6, the federal income tax rates are so arranged that under some circumstances a man and woman who both have income will pay less income tax when they are single than when they are married. In other words the tax rates create a disincentive to marry. Would this provision of the Internal Revenue Code be unconstitutional under the *Zablocki* case for this reason?

5. (a) What would be the result under the *Zablocki* decision if the Wisconsin statute were redrafted to provide that an indigent person would not be prevented from marrying, but that a person who was subject to an outstanding child support order could not obtain a marriage license if it were proved at a hearing that he was able to pay the child support but that he had not done so? Cf. Utah Code Ann. § 30–1–28 (1976).

(b) The Court, 434 U.S. at 386–7, writes:

"By reaffirming the fundamental character of the right to marry, we do not mean to suggest that every state regulation which relates in any way to the incidents of or prerequisites for marriage must be subjected to rigorous scrutiny. To the contrary, reasonable regulations that do not significantly interfere with decisions to enter into the marital relationship may legitimately be imposed. * * * The statutory classification at issue here, however, clearly does interfere directly and substantially with the right to marry."

What does this mean?

(c) What state interests was this statute intended to promote?

(d) Why were these interests not sufficient to sustain the constitutionality of the statute?

6. The *Zablocki* decision seems to make it necessary for the courts to look into the effect of a challenged regulation upon the decision to marry. This in turn requires some consideration of why people marry at a particular time and why they marry a particular person. The application of economic analysis to these questions has lately been described by G. Becker, The Economic Approach to Human Behavior, ch. 11 (1976). The premises for his analysis are there outlined as being that since marriage is voluntary, it can be expected to occur when the persons making the decision expect to achieve a utility in excess of what it would be if they remained single. And since there is competition for marriage partners, he postulates a market in mates in which each person searches for the best mate available. The consequences of these premises are worked out in detail. The same analysis is printed in T. Schultz, ed., Economics of the Family 299–344

(1973), followed by commentary on the thesis by a sociologist and an economist. To what extent is this way of looking at marriage useful for lawyers who face the sort of questions raised in the *Zablocki* decision?

SECTION 2.   THE FORMALITIES OF CELEBRATION

Statutory Regulation of Marriage

As the introductory chapter to this book indicates, the American states have from earliest days asserted the power to regulate marriage. This power is implied by the language often found in statutes to the effect that "marriage is a personal relation arising out of a civil contract   *   *   *". See Cal.Civ.Code § 4100 (Supp.1979), and, similarly, N.Y.Dom.Rel.L. § 10 (1977).

In all states a license to marry must be procured in order to have a ceremonial marriage, usually from some such public official as the county clerk or a clerk of court. Where "common law marriage" or some other form of informal marriage is recognized, this as well as other statutory requirements may be by-passed. The license must be procured either in the county where the marriage is to occur, or where the parties reside, or, under some statutes, anywhere in the state where the marriage is to be performed. Both parties usually appear to apply for the license, but this is not always required. The information which must be furnished in order to obtain a license to marry includes the names, ages, relationship if any, and prior marriages of the parties. See, e. g., Cal.Civ.Code §§ 4201, 4202 (Supp. 1979); N.Y.Dom.Rel.L. § 15 (1977). The issuing officer may have more than a ministerial function in issuing licenses, and may be required to satisfy himself of the truth of the statements made by the applicants and of their right under the statutes to be issued a license to marry.

A waiting period is generally imposed by statute, to run between the application for the license and its issuance or between the issuance of the license and the marriage. In spite of the frequently heard suggestion that many marriages are hasty and ill considered, the waiting periods imposed continue to be minimal, on the order of three to five days. A partial response to this problem has been undertaken in the California statute which provides that the parties to a marriage of a person under eighteen must be ordered to participate in premarital counselling if the court deems such counselling necessary. The counselling is to relate to the social, economic and personal responsibilities incident to marriage, Cal.Civ.Code § 4101 (Supp.1979). For a proposal of much broader impact, see Note, Preventive Law and Family Law: Pre-Marital Phases and Purposes, 12 Vill.L.Rev. 839 (1967).

A physical examination is also generally required as a condition upon obtaining a marriage license. The examination is usually limited to tests for the discovery of venereal disease, but in some states it may be broadened to include tests for tuberculosis, epilepsy, drug addiction and alcoholism and variously described mental defects. Colorado has recently also begun to require tests of women of childbearing age for rubella and also to require blood grouping, including RH type. Colo.Rev.Stat.Ann. § 14–2–106 (Supp.1978).

Marriages may be solemnized under most statutes by ministers, priests and rabbis, and in addition by such named public officers as judges of courts of record or justices of the peace. Some statutes also authorize marriages to be solemnized in accordance with the rules of any denomination. Wis.Stat.Ann. § 245.16 (Supp.1979–1980). The Uniform Marriage and Divorce Act, § 206, authorizes marriages to be solemnized in accordance with the customs of any Indian Nation, Tribe or Native Group. In some states the person seeking to solemnize marriages must obtain a certificate of his authority. See Paramore v. Brown, 84 Nev. 725, 448 P.2d 699 (1968) and Galloway v. Truesdell, 83 Nev. 13, 422 P.2d 237 (1967).

Marrying people can be a lucrative business in some places. In Las Vegas, for example, the two justices of the peace were making $100,000 per year each not long ago by performing marriages. Wall Street Journal, February 27, 1967, page 1, col. 4. Unfortunately, however, the state legislature spoiled things by authorizing marriages to be performed by county clerks and their deputies, and by limiting their compensation. Nev.Rev.Stat. §§ 122.171–122.181 (1977). Apparently Clintwood, Virginia also enjoys a quickie marriage business. Wall Street Journal, March 24, 1972, page 1.

The fact that a marriage is solemnized by a person not authorized to do so does not invalidate the marriage if either or both parties are not aware of the disqualification. Knapp v. Knapp, 149 Md. 263, 131 A. 329 (1925); Helfond v. Helfond, 53 Misc.2d 974, 280 N. Y.S.2d 990 (Sup.Ct.1967).

A few states have statutes which make minimal requirements as to the form of the marriage ceremony. Thus in New York no form is prescribed, but the parties must solemnly declare, in the presence of the officiating person and witnesses that they take each other as husband and wife. N.Y.Dom.Rel.L. § 12 (1977). See also Wis.Stat. Ann. § 245.16 (Supp.1979–1980). For the form which the religious ceremony of marriage takes in the various faiths, see, e. g., Book of Common Prayer Authorized for Use in the Protestant Episcopal Church, 300 ff. (1928); St. Joseph Daily Missal, 1300 (1953).

A case which discusses the definition of ceremonial marriage is Hames v. Hames, 163 Conn. 588, 316 A.2d 379 (1972). There the parties, who were Catholic, had formerly been married and divorced. They decided to remarry each other, obtained a license, and the husband took it to a priest who signed the certificate of marriage on the form and the husband then filed the certificate in the proper office.

The court held that this did not constitute a valid ceremonial marriage according to state law although it apparently did satisfy the requirements of Catholic canon law. The court said that the requirement of a ceremony implied at the least a present manifestation of the parties' consent before a religious group or functionary.

Most statutes require two witnesses for marriage, whose names or signatures appear on the marriage certificate. The certificate must usually be filled out by the person solemnizing the marriage and sent to the place of recording. Marriage certificates are then kept as public records.

A properly solemnized marriage is generally held valid even though it is not consummated. See Berdikas v. Berdikas, 4 Storey 297, 178 A.2d 468 (1962). "Consummation" in this context means the physical act of coition, although the word is occasionally misused by courts and lawyers.

The question sometimes arises whether a marriage which is solemnized without a license, or under a defective license, is valid. Most cases hold that such marriages are valid, as in De Potty v. De Potty, 226 Ark. 881, 295 S.W.2d 330 (1956); Parker v. Saileau, 213 So.2d 190 (La.App.1968). See also N.Y.Dom.Rel.L. § 25 (1977).

For more detailed discussion of marriage regulations, see H. Clark, Law of Domestic Relations, § 2.3 (1968).

TACZANOWSKA (orse. ROTH) v. TACZANOWSKI

Court of Appeal.
[1957] P. 301, 2 All Eng.Rep. 563.

Petition for Decree of Nullity.

The following facts are taken from the judgment of Hodson, L. J., in the Court of Appeal. The parties, Krystyna Roth, spinster, and Stanislaw Taczanowski, went through a form of marriage in the Parish Church of the Resurrectionists in Rome on July 16, 1946. They were Polish nationals, the bride being a civilian refugee who had been staying in a convent in Rome, and the bridegroom an officer in the Polish 2nd Corps, then serving in Italy, in the course of his military duties. The ceremony was performed by a Roman Catholic priest then serving as a Polish army chaplain. There was no question but that the parties intended to enter into marriage. They lived together until 1950, having from the early part of 1947 lived in England, where it was pleaded that they were domiciled at the time of the institution of the present proceedings by the wife on June 15, 1955, for a decree of nullity of marriage. In November, 1947, a child was born.

*   *   *

1957. June 6. The following judgments were read.

HODSON, L. J., stated the facts and continued: The petitioner alleged that the ceremony was null and void because in form it did not comply with the lex loci, namely, Italian law. She relied upon the rule established by the decision of Sir Edward Simpson, sitting in the Consistory Court of London, in Scrimshire v. Scrimshire.[1] The principle is there clearly stated that in administering the law of this country the rights of the parties are to be determined by our law which applies foreign law in such a case, since by entering into the marriage contract in another country the parties subject themselves to have the validity of the contract determined by the laws of that country.

* * * Lord Dunedin, giving his advice in the Privy Council in Berthiaume v. Dastous,[2] said: "If the so-called marriage is no marriage in the place where it is celebrated, there is no marriage anywhere, although the ceremony or proceeding if conducted in the place of the parties' domicile would be considered a good marriage." Thus, so far as forms and ceremonies are concerned, the general rule is that where parties contract marriage in a country other than their own, they are taken to subject themselves to the law of that other country.

The wife contended that the law of Italy regulating form had not been complied with. It was conceded that the municipal law of Italy had not been followed in that articles 143, 144 and 145 of the Civil Code were not read over to the parties by the officiating priest, and in that the ceremony was not registered in the civil register of marriage as required by Italian law. Italian law would, however, according to article 226 of the General Provisions preliminary to the Italian Civil Code, recognize the validity of the marriage if it was valid by Polish law, since that was at the material date the national law of both spouses.

By the old law of Poland prior to the establishment of the Lublin Government the marriage would have been valid. * * *

On July 5, 1945, His Majesty's Government recognized the new Government of Poland, the so-called Lublin Government, and Dr. Nissim, an Italian lawyer who gave evidence, stated that in his opinion the same recognition had been accorded by the Government of Italy before the marriage of the parties. On September 25, 1945, the Lublin Government introduced a new matrimonial law, with effect from January 1, 1946, which provided that only a marriage contracted before an official of civil status should be valid in the eyes of the State. By article 1 of the Introductory Provisions it was provided that all previous provisions dealt with by the national law should cease to have effect and point 20 of the Statute of November 28, 1926, was expressly repealed. By a note dated July 14, 1946, the Polish Ministry of Foreign Affairs stated that as from that date the Polish forces abroad could no longer be considered units of the Polish Army.

1. (1752) 2 Hag.Con. 395.   2. [1930] A.C. 79, 83; 45 T.L.R. 607.

I agree with the reasoning of the judge and with his conclusion, having heard evidence from eminent Polish lawyers, when he found, notwithstanding an ingenious theory put forward by Dr. Block in support of the marriage, that there was no escape from the finding that by Polish law the ceremony of marriage in question was invalid. Professor Kuratowski, whose evidence was accepted, was emphatically of this opinion. *   *   *

There remains the argument put forward by the Queen's Proctor, and supported by counsel for the appellant husband, that the ceremony was valid at common law, and the requirements of the lex loci as to form did not apply. At the material date the Polish land forces in Italy were forces in belligerent occupation of Italian territory and therefore, it is said, exempt from the requirements of the lex loci. Karminski J. pointed out that the position of such persons has always been recognized by English law as requiring special consideration with regard to formalities. It is true that they may, in fact, submit to the lex loci, but there is no evidence that the parties did so. The ceremony was indeed performed in an Italian church, but by a Polish Army chaplain acting as a member of the Polish Forces, and no attempt was made to comply with the local law.

*   *   *

Lord Stowell in Ruding v. Smith did not found his judgment on the proposition now contended for, although he said nothing to the contrary, and it is therefore necessary to consider the judgment in some detail. The suit was for nullity to set aside a marriage celebrated in a room in a private house between British subjects at the Cape of Good Hope on October 2, 1796, by the chaplain of the English forces, by virtue of a licence or permission from the general officer commanding the British forces in the colony. Drs. Jenner and Phillimore argued that the general principle of the lex loci could not apply to persons at the Cape as British subjects, under the protection of the British forces then in possession of the settlement by virtue of the recent surrender, even though in that case the terms of the capitulation might have preserved to the inhabitants the enjoyment of their former laws. *   *   *

Lord Stowell held that the terms of the capitulation, preserving the prerogatives which the Dutch enjoyed, were not binding on the conquerors. He rejected the submission that the lex loci applied to the said parties. *   *   *

He added: "It is true, indeed, that English decisions have established this rule, that a foreign marriage, valid according to the law of the place where celebrated, is good everywhere else; but they have not è converso established that marriages of British subjects, not good according to the general law of the place where celebrated, are universally, and under all possible circumstances, to be regarded as invalid in England. It is therefore certainly to be advised that the safest course is always to be married according to the law of the country, for then no question can be stirred; but if this cannot be done on account of legal or religious difficulties, the law of this country does not say that its subjects shall not marry abroad. And even in cases where no difficulties of that insuperable magnitude exist, yet, if a contrary practice has been sanctioned by long acquiescence and acceptance of the one country, that has silently permitted such marriages, and of the other, that has silently accepted them, the courts of this country, I presume, would not incline to shake their validity, upon these large and general theories, encountered, as they are, by numerous exceptions in the practice of nations."

His conclusion was, however, of a guarded and limited nature, for he said at the conclusion of his judgment: "In my opinion, this marriage (for I desire to be understood as not extending this decision beyond cases including nearly the same circumstances) rests upon solid foundations. On the distinct British character of the parties—on their independence of the Dutch law, in their own British transactions—on the insuperable difficulties of obtaining any marriage conformable to the Dutch law—on the countenance given by British authority, and British ministration to this British transaction—upon the whole country being under British dominion—and upon the other grounds to which I have adverted; and I therefore dismiss this libel, as insufficient, if proved for the conclusion it prays."

* * *

Lord Stowell laid emphasis on the British character of the parties, but there is, as Karminski J. also pointed out, nothing in the judgment in Ruding v. Smith which would indicate that he would necessarily have refused to take the same view in the case of a foreigner. Lord Stowell's observations in the course of his judgment show that he relied to a great extent on the mere fact of the position of a conquering army in a conquered country—a situation which exists in this case, and I do not see in principle why, if this consideration is taken into account, it should not prevail even though the possibility of submitting to the laws of the conquered exists.

The principle in Scrimshire's case, that parties by entering into a marriage contract in a foreign country subject themselves to have the validity of it determined by the laws of that country, does not apply in the case of a contract performed in an occupied country by a member of the occupying forces. * * *

This reasoning has no application when one is considering the position of a conquering army in a conquered country. This case is not complicated by any terms of capitulation and there was no evidence that in 1946 the Allied Forces in Italy were in any way subject to the laws of that country. I see no reason, therefore, why the validity of the ceremony in form should be governed by the lex loci in the case we are now considering. If it be said that since the parties are not British subjects, the common law of England does not apply to them, my answer is that such is the law prima facie to be administered in the courts of this country.   There is no question here of personal incapacity to marry or any other consideration apart from form for which one would look to the law of the domicile, and there would be a grave difficulty in applying the law of the domicile or nationality, amounting to an impossibility in some cases, where a marriage had been celebrated between persons of different nations or different domiciles.

        *   *   *

The common law conception of marriage knows no distinction of race or nationality. The effect of the decision in Reg. v. Millis is that such a marriage to be valid must be celebrated before an episcopally ordained clergyman.   A priest of the Church of Rome is in the same position as an Anglican clergyman. *   *   *

The ceremony of marriage here fulfils all the essentials of a common law marriage, and in my opinion should be recognized as such notwithstanding the foreign nationality and domicile of the parties at the date of the ceremony.

The same conclusion was reached in Savenis v. Savenis and Szmeck, a decision of Mayo J., where the facts have some similarity to those with which we are here concerned.   The parties were Lithuanians who were married on November 1, 1945, in Bavaria in a Roman Catholic church according to the ritual of that church without complying with the German law as to form.   Lithuania was then incorporated in the U.S.S.R. and warfare with Germany had ceased. Compliance with the local law was impossible, since no registrars were available.   Mayo J., having regard to Ruding v. Smith and other cases, said: "If the matter be res integra, in circumstances where a marriage cannot be lawfully solemnized in accordance with the laws of some territory owing to chaotic conditions brought about (inter alia) by warfare, and if the country in which the parties are, or were formerly, domiciled is itself overrun, the government being taken over by an alien power then in such a case, so far as our courts are concerned, I think it would be proper to extend (if it be necessary) the area of legal recognition given to marriages that conform to our own common law: compare Lord Herschell's remarks in Alexander v. Jenkins.   Apart from local measures, such as provision for the licensing of celebrants, and for the recording of marriages, which do not go to the fundamentals of the actual rite, the ceremony performed on November 1, 1945, was such as would be given legal recognition in all civilized countries, or at least in many such.   The marriage was given ecclesiastical sanction.   If in such circumstances a marriage is to be regarded as null and void, that will have to be laid down elsewhere." Thus Mayo J., having rejected the lex loci for the reasons he gave, looked not to the law of the domicile (Lithuania) but to the common law.

* * *

ORMEROD L. J. I agree, and would only wish to add a few words on the question of the validity of this marriage as a common law marriage. As the judge has found, the parties went through a ceremony of marriage in Rome not only with the desire of entering into a valid marriage, but in the belief that the ceremony was effective; and they lived together as man and wife for a period of four years after the marriage, during which time a child was born to them. He felt compelled, however, to declare the marriage null and void on the ground that on the authorities the law governing the case must be the lex loci celebrationis. As I understand this judgment, he based his decision on the view that the lex loci must prevail unless a marriage by that law was impossible or at least contrary to conscience, and referred to the words in the final paragraph of the judgment of Lord Stowell in Ruding v. Smith, where undoubtedly one of the reasons for declaring the marriage to be valid was the insuperable difficulty of obtaining any marriage conformable to the Dutch law. But Lord Stowell clearly had in mind the fact that the husband had gone to the Cape under orders as a member of an occupying authority. * * * It was necessary for Lord Stowell, in the circumstances of Ruding v. Smith, to decide that the lex loci should not apply on the ground that the parties should not be deemed to have submitted to the laws of the country in which the marriage took place.
* * *

If the true reason for application of the lex loci is based on the principle that the parties shall be deemed to have submitted to it, then it seems difficult to apply that principle to a case such as the one at present under consideration, where the husband is in Italy not from choice but under the orders of his military superiors as a member of an occupying army. There can, I think, be no doubt on the judge's findings that this marriage was in a form recognized by the courts of this country as a common law marriage, and if the lex loci does not apply in this case—and in my view it does not—then for the reasons which have already been given in the judgments which have been read I agree that this marriage should be declared to be valid, and that the appeal should be allowed.

NOTES AND QUESTIONS

1. Other cases reaching similar results are Preston (orse Putynski) v. Preston (orse Basinska), [1963] 2 All Eng.Rep. 405, [1963] P. 411; Kochanski v. Kochanska [1958] P. 147. In Lazarewicz v. Lazarewicz, [1962] P. 171 the parties were married at a civilian refugee camp in Italy by a Catholic priest in 1945. The marriage was not valid by either Polish law (the husband being Polish, the wife Italian) or Italian law. They lived together in England until 1956. The court held the marriage invalid. It recognized the principle of the *Taczanowska* case, but held that it did not apply where, as in this case, the parties clearly did choose to submit to Italian law, and that therefore the general rule of the lex loci applied.

2. Would you characterize the application of the English common law to this marriage as "odd"? Cf. 20 Mod.L.Rev. 505 (1957), 20 Mod.L.Rev. 641 (1957), 74 L.Q.Rev. 326 (1958), and (1957) Camb.L.J. 126. Was English common law applied because the forum was an English court? Or because this was, at the time of the suit, an English marriage? Or for some other reason? See A. Ehrenzweig, Conflict of Laws, 379 (1962).

3. Does this case turn on an issue of fact, that is, that the Roman Catholic priest who married the parties was the equivalent of an Anglican clergyman? Would the same result have been reached if the parties had been married in Italy by a Unitarian minister?

4. Restatement, Second, Conflict of Laws, § 283 (1971) states that the "validity of a marriage is to be determined by the local law of the state which, with respect to the particular issue, has the most significant relationship to the spouses and the marriage * * *". § 6 of the same work lists as factors bearing on the question of significant relationship (a) the needs of the interstate and international systems; (b) the relevant policies of the forum; (c) the relevant policies of other interested states and the relative interests of those states in the determination of the particular issue; (d) the protection of justified expectations; (e) the basic policies underlying the particular field of law; (f) certainty, predictability and uniformity of result; (g) ease in the determination and application of the law to be applied.

(a) Does the result in Taczanowska support the Restatement's view?

(b) Could it have been said, at the time this marriage was contracted, that English law had any relationship whatever to the spouses or to the marriage?

(c) Which of the listed factors are controlling in Taczanowska? If the influence of one or more factors conflicts with others, how does one determine which has the greater weight?

(d) When the Restatement speaks of protecting expectations, whose expectations does it refer to?

For a critique of the Restatement's approach to this and similar issues, see Baade, Marriage and Divorce in American Conflicts Law: Governmental Interests Analysis and the Restatement (Second), 72 Colum.L.Rev. 329 (1972).

5. Can this case be explained as merely indicating a preference for divorce rather than annulment as a way of terminating marriage?

6. What should be the result if the parties left the state of their domicile and went to another state to be married, for the express purpose of evading requirements as to marriage formalities existing in their domicile, intending to return to their domicile immediately after being married? Cf. Cal.Civ.Code § 4104 (1970) with Wis.Stat.Ann. § 245.04 (Supp.1979–1980), and Lyannes v. Lyannes, 171 Wis. 381, 177 N.W. 683 (1920).

SECTION 3.   INFORMAL MARRIAGES

A.   "COMMON LAW MARRIAGE"

As the introduction to this book indicates, the English ecclesiastical courts recognized until a statute of 1753 a form of marriage called "sponsalia per verba de praesenti", entered into without a ceremony.   Such a marriage was held valid to the extent of prevailing over a subsequent ceremonial marriage meeting all the formal requirements, although the common law courts would not recognize it for purposes of awarding dower to the woman who was married in this fashion.   A second type of informal marriage, "sponsalia per verba de futuro" was also recognized by the ecclesiastical courts, but never took root in the United States.   See Engdahl, English Marriage Conflicts Law Before the Time of Bracton, 15 Am.J.Comp.L. 109 (1967).

The leading case of Dalrymple v. Dalrymple, 2 Hagg.Cons. 53, 161 Eng.Rep. 665 (1811) contains this language: " * * * the consent of two parties expressed in words of present mutual acceptance constituted an actual and legal marriage technically known by the name of sponsalia per verba de praesenti * * *".   No further requirements were made, the court later in its opinion stating that such a marriage was valid without the need for proof of consummation. Further discussion may be found in Koegel, Common Law Marriage (1922) and II Pollock and Maitland, History of English Law, 364–392 (1898).

With this background, the courts of some of the states also recognized informal marriages, at least where the applicable statutes did not foreclose such recognition.   The term "common law marriage" was coined to describe such marriages, although it was somewhat inappropriate since they originated in the ecclesiastical law rather than the common law.   The term presumably refers to their non-statutory origin.

At the present writing, thirteen states and the District of Columbia continue to recognize common law marriages as valid.   They are Alabama, Colorado, Georgia, Idaho, Iowa (but see Iowa Code Ann. § 595.11), Kansas, Montana, Ohio, Oklahoma, Pennsylvania, Rhode Island, South Carolina and Texas.   New York, although after much vacillation it no longer recognizes common law marriage, does recognize a marriage contracted by a written, signed, witnessed and acknowledged document.   N.Y.Dom.Rel.L. § 11(4) (1977).   Thirty-seven states refuse to recognize common law marriage, the latest to take this position being Florida.   Fla.Stat.Ann. § 741.211 (Supp. 1979).

A Nevada statute provides that Indians may contract a valid marriage in accordance with tribal customs. See Nev.Rev.Stat. § 122.170 (1977) and Ponina v. Leland, 185 Nev. 263, 454 P.2d 16 (1969) holding that Indians living together off the reservation were validly married, although they had no ceremony, under circumstances resembling common law marriage.

IN RE ESTATE OF FISHER

Supreme Court of Iowa, 1970.
176 N.W.2d 801.

REES, Justice. Decedent, Wilson Paul Fisher, Jr., died intestate on November 21, 1968, a resident of Polk county. On the petition of decedent's mother, appellant who here claims to be the common-law wife of decedent was appointed administrator. The divorced former wife of decedent, acting as the mother and next-friend of two minor children of decedent, filed application to remove administrator, and trial court ordered removal and appointed decedent's former wife, Cheryl Joy Pepin, as administrator, from which order this appeal is taken. We are unable to agree with the trial court, and reverse and remand for the entry of orders in keeping herewith.

The appellees, Cary Laurence Fisher and Christian Louis Fisher, are the issue of the marriage of Wilson Paul Fisher, Jr., and Cheryl Joy Fisher, one of said children being the issue of the marriage by natural birth and the other by adoption. The parties were married in June, 1965, and the marriage relationship terminated by divorce in August, 1967. The two children, Cary Laurence Fisher and Christian Louis Fisher, are identified in the record as appellees, and are represented by their mother and next-friend, Cheryl Joy Fisher Pepin. The custody of the children by the terms of the decree of divorce was vested in the mother. About October of 1967 the decedent became acquainted with the appellant, Carroll Sue Vanderpool Perdue, who was then married to one Platt Perdue, who was serving in Germany as a member of the Armed Forces. Platt and Carroll Perdue were the parents of one child, born in January of 1967. In October, 1967, the decedent and the appellant started dating each other, and in June, 1968, they took up residence together in a house at 1919 Capitol in Des Moines. Earlier in 1968 the appellant had filed a petition for divorce in the district court of Dallas county. Prior to the entry of a decree of divorce, a child which the record establishes was the issue of the relationship between the appellant and the decedent, Wilson Paul Fisher, Jr., was born on August 27, 1968. A decree of divorce was entered September 9, 1968. The child who is referred to above as the issue of the relationship between the decedent and the appellant was delivered at Broadlawns Hospital in Des Moines, and just prior to its birth the appellant was taken to the hospital by the decedent. When she entered the hospital the appellant identified herself as Carroll Sue Fisher, and at the time of the birth of the child the birth certificate identified the child as Wilson Paul Fisher, III. The record discloses that the administrative officer of the hospital was subsequently advised that the mother of the child was married to Platt Perdue, and caused to be filed a substitute or amended birth certificate identifying the child as Wilson Paul Perdue. The birth certificate first filed identified Wilson Paul Fisher, Jr., as the father of the child, and the amended or substituted certificate of birth indicated that the father of the child was Platt Perdue.

Following the entry of the decree of divorce on September 9, 1968, the appellant and the decedent continued to live together, removing from the residence at 1919 East Capitol, in late October, to a rented house in or near Granger, Iowa. During all the time the parties lived together and until early September, 1968, the appellant received an allotment out of the service pay of her husband, Platt Perdue. These allotment payments terminated in September of 1968. At the time the appellant filed her petition for divorce, and during its pendency, she at no time advised her husband of the fact of her pregnancy, nor did she advise the court at the time the divorce was proved up of the fact that she had been delivered of a child not the issue of her marriage to her husband.

On September 16, 1968, the appellant purchased a policy of life insurance on her own life, the agent for the insurance company having been summoned to the home at 1919 East Capitol by the decedent. The application for insurance showed that Wilson P. Fisher, Jr., was her husband, and the record discloses that during the time the information was being furnished the agent by the appellant the decedent Fisher was personally present, and that the initial monthly payment was paid to the agent by the decedent by his personal check.

On October 26, 1968, the appellant and the decedent opened a joint checking account in Brenton State Bank, Granger, Iowa, under the names "W. P. or Carroll Fisher, Jr.", and the authorized signatures on the bank record card indicated that Wilson Paul Fisher, Jr., or Carroll Fisher were authorized to check on the account.

The record discloses that at the time the agent for the life insurance company was at the Fisher home in Des Moines completing the application for life insurance on the life of the appellant, one Betty Jean Hopkins, a foster sister of the decedent, and her husband was present. It appears that Mr. & Mrs. Hopkins owned a set of rings, a wedding band and an engagement type ring, which that night they sold to the decedent who in their presence gave the rings to the appellant and she put the rings on her hand and continued to wear them throughout the relationship of the decedent and appellant.

[Deceased was killed in an auto accident on November 21, 1968. His alleged common law wife, Carroll Sue, was appointed administrator of his estate. His first wife, Cheryl, now seeks to have Carroll

Sue removed as administrator and to have herself appointed. The trial court found no common law marriage had been contracted, removed Carroll Sue and appointed deceased's first wife as administrator of deceased's estate.]

Concededly, the appellant, Carroll Sue Fisher, whose marriage to Platt Perdue, was terminated by a decree of divorce on September 9, 1968, could not have prior to that date entered in to a valid marriage relationship with the decedent. We therefore need concern ourselves in the main with the record insofar as it establishes or fails to establish a common-law marriage relationship commenced on or subsequent to the date of her decree of divorce. We may of course consider the entire record of the relationship of the parties for the purpose of determining the ultimate question which is here before us. Section 595.19, Code, 1966, provides,

"Marriages between the following persons shall be void: * * * 4. Between persons either of whom has a husband or wife living, but, if the parties live and cohabit together after the death or divorce of the former husband or wife, such marriage shall be valid."

Iowa has recognized common-law marriage for well over a century. * * * "Where recognized, common-law marriages are as fully valid as ceremonial marriages * * * however, the courts do not look on such marriages with favor, and * * * where a common-law marriage is claimed, the courts will carefully scrutinize the evidence and require that the marriage be established by clear and convincing evidence." C.J.S. Marriage § 6, p. 818. If any of the essentials of a common-law marriage are lacking, the relationship is illicit and meretricious and is not a marriage. * * * Thus, in order to establish a common-law marriage, all of the essential elements of such a relationship must be shown by clear, consistent and convincing evidence, especially must all of the essential elements of such a relationship be shown when one of the parties is dead; and such marriage must be proved by a preponderance. * * * The elements and conditions necessary to establish the existence of a common-law marriage have been outlined by this court as: (1) intent and agreement in praesenti as to marriage on the part of both parties together with continuous cohabitation and public declaration that they are husband and wife; (2) the burden of proof is on the one asserting the claim; (3) all elements of relationship as to marriage must be shown to exist; (4) a claim of such marriage is regarded with suspicion, and will be closely scrutinized; (5) when one party is dead, the essential elements must be shown by clear, consistent and convincing evidence. * * *

The purpose and intention of Carroll Perdue in her relationship with Wilson Paul Fisher, Jr., were of the greatest importance as bearing on the fact of marriage. Likewise the purpose and intention of decedent in his relationship with Carroll were of equal importance. Carroll Perdue Fisher as a witness would have been incompetent to testify to any transactions or communications with the deceased amounting to a mutual agreement to marry, but she was not incompetent to testify as to her own purposes and intentions and the circumstances under which their cohabitation was begun and continued. * * * It is well settled that where cohabitation is in its beginning illicit affirmative proof of a subsequent present intention to change that relationship into legitimate relationship of husband and wife is essential to establish a common-law marriage. * * * While the record is in some respects conflicting it tends to show a willingness on the part of the decedent and Carroll Perdue that they be considered husband and wife, both before and after the entry of the decree of divorce in Dallas county by which Carroll Perdue was divorced from her former husband, Platt Perdue. When she checked into the hospital just prior to the delivery of her child in August of 1968, she was accompanied by the decedent, who supplied the general information taken on her admission to the hospital, and was cognizant of the fact that the name appearing on the admission records was Fisher. He acquiesced in the use of his own family name by which the child was known. Shortly after the entry of the divorce decree in Dallas county, he introduced Carroll as his wife to a gas appliance man at Granger. The gas man, a Mr. Biondi, had been acquainted with Carroll and knew that she was married to Platt Perdue, and asked the decedent if he was Mr. Perdue. Biondi was then advised that Carroll had divorced Perdue and that Wilson Paul Fisher, Jr. "is her husband now". On October 21, 1968, the decedent introduced Carroll to a friend, Melvin Moore, as "my wife, Carroll". On August 2, 1968, the decedent made application for employment at Iowa Clay Pipe Company, and on his written application for employment and in his own handwriting he indicated his marital status as "married", and directed in case of accident or injury Carroll Fisher of 1919 Capitol should be notified. This was of course prior to the entry of the decree of divorce by which the appellant was divorced from her prior husband but is significant with respect to the relationship of the parties. The purchase of the rings by the decedent and his gift of them to the appellant is also a significant circumstance as bearing upon their relationship to each other. The rings were a wedding band and an engagement type ring, and as both parties had been ceremonially married to others before, they certainly recognized the significance of the custom of giving and receiving wedding and engagement type rings. After the divorce decree by which the appellant was divorced from her former husband, the decedent accompanied the appellant's parents to a grocery store in Des Moines and introduced them as "my mother-in-law and father-in-law". The willingness of the decedent to recognize the appellant as his wife during the relatively short time following the entry of the decree of divorce in appellant's favor on

September 9, 1968, and the death of the decedent on November 21, 1968, runs through the entire record.

There are of course, as in all cases, inconsistencies. His former wife, the appellee here, indicated there were discussions of a reconciliation between the decedent and herself in June, 1968. She knew the decedent and appellant were living together, but testified the decedent had never indicated to her that he was married to the appellant or for that matter to anyone else. On balance, however, we find the preponderance of the evidence establishes that the conduct of the decedent, as the record discloses, was consistent with the existence of the claimed common-law marriage relationship.

Marriage is a civil contract, requiring the consent of the parties capable of entering into other contracts * * *. Section 595.1, Code 1966. Mutuality of consent means just what it means in ordinary civil contracts. * * * No particular form or ceremony is necessary, and all that is required is that the minds of the parties meet in mutual consent, and this is accomplished if they live together and in so doing intend to sustain the relationship of husband and wife but neither such intention nor consent can be inferred from cohabitation alone. * * * A common-law marriage may be proven by circumstantial evidence. * * *

That the appellant and the decedent were planning a ceremonial marriage in futuro seems to be established in the record without question. We recognize that a contract per verba futuro which implies no more than that the parties will marry each other at a later time is not sufficient to establish a common-law marriage in the absence of other circumstances. * * *

The conduct of the decedent in summoning an insurance agent to his home to secure life insurance upon the life of the appellant at which time he either represented himself to be her husband or acquiesced in her statements that such was the case, is indicative of a present intention on the part of the decedent to recognize the marriage relationship. The representation of the appellant to the insurance agent on her own part that she was the wife of the decedent made in the presence of the decedent and either acquiesced in by him or not denied, is a strong circumstance evidencing that the minds of the parties had met, and that there was mutuality of consent to establish a marriage relationship. Introduction of one party by the other as the wife or husband is in and of itself an acknowledgment of the marital relation, and while it may not be in and of itself proof of a present agreement and intent, it may support other evidence and is important in cases of the kind. * * *

Appellant suggests arguendo that had the decedent Fisher not died, and had the appellant here instituted a suit for divorce against him that Fisher could not have successfully denied the existence of the marriage relationship. We agree, assuming the record in the trial court in such a hypothetical situation reflected the same facts as were established in the instant case.

* * * We conclude the marriage relationship was shown by clear, consistent and convincing evidence.

The case is reversed and remanded to the trial court for an entry of further orders in the Estate of Wilson Paul Fisher, Jr., deceased, in keeping herewith.

Reversed and remanded.

NOTES AND QUESTIONS

1. Some other cases finding that a common law marriage had been contracted include Roy v. Industrial Commission, 97 Ariz. 98, 397 P.2d 211 (1964); Graham v. Graham, 130 Colo. 225, 274 P.2d 605 (1954); In re Estate of Alcala, 188 So.2d 903 (Fla.App.1966); Chaachou v. Chaachou, 73 So.2d 830 (Fla.1954); In the Matter of Foster, 77 Idaho 26, 287 P.2d 282 (1955); Stathos v. La Salle Nat. Bank, 65 Ill.App.2d 398, 210 N.E.2d 828 (1965), 15 DeP.L.Rev. 486 (1966); Gammelgaard v. Gammelgaard, 247 Iowa 979, 77 N.W.2d 479 (1956); Chivers v. Couch Motor Lines, Inc., 159 So.2d 544 (La.App.1964); Hill v. Shreve, 448 P.2d 848 (Okl.1968); Campbell v. Christian, 235 S.C. 102, 110 S.E.2d 1 (1959); Howard v. Howard, 459 S.W.2d 901 (Tex.Civ.App.1970).

Some cases holding no common law marriage had been proved are In re Estate of Malli, 260 Iowa 252, 149 N.W.2d 155 (1967), 17 Drake L.Rev. 264 (1968); Schrader v. Schrader, 207 Kan. 349, 484 P.2d 1007 (1971); Sullivan v. Sullivan, 196 Kan. 705, 413 P.2d 988 (1966); Whetstone v. Whetstone, 178 Kan. 595, 290 P.2d 1022 (1955); Miller v. Sutherland, 131 Mont. 175, 309 P.2d 322 (1957); Quinton v. Webb, 207 Okl. 133, 248 P.2d 586 (1952); Ex Parte Threet, 160 Tex. 482, 333 S.W.2d 361 (1960).

2. How should counsel go about proving the existence of a marriage, whether ceremonial or common law, in any suit in which the marriage may be relevant? VII Wigmore, Evidence, §§ 2082–2088 (3d ed. 1940).

3. The court in the *Fisher* case, at page 106, states that Carroll Sue would have been incompetent to testify to transactions or communications with the deceased amounting to a mutual agreement to marry. Is the court correct in this? Why or why not? Iowa Code Ann. §§ 622.4, 622.5 (Supp.1972); II Wigmore, Evidence, § 578 (3d ed. 1940); Berger v. Kirby, 105 Tex. 611, 153 S.W. 1130 (1913); Brown v. Brown, 115 S.W.2d 786 (Tex.Civ.App.1938); Estate of McCausland, 52 Cal. 568 (1878); In re McKanna's Estate, 106 Cal.App.2d 126, 234 P.2d 673 (1951); In re Long's Estate, 251 Iowa 1042, 102 N.W.2d 76 (1960); In re Wagner's Estate, 398 Pa. 531, 159 A.2d 495, 82 A.L.R.2d 681 (1960).

4. The *Fisher* case imposes, in addition to certain evidentiary rules, the requirement that (a) there be a present intent and agreement to be married; (b) there be continuous cohabitation and public declaration that they are man and wife; and (c) all elements of marriage must exist. Why does the court add these other conditions to the simple requirement of agreement found in the Dalrymple case? What would be the result under the Fisher decision if there were clear evidence of present agreement to be man and wife, but the parties never told people they were married? In re

Estate of Dallman, 228 N.W.2d 187 (Iowa 1975). Conversely, what would be the result if there were no evidence (or little evidence) of agreement, but the parties were thought by their friends and relatives to be married, the parties referred to each other as husband and wife in official documents or otherwise? In re Marriage of Winegard, 257 N.W.2d 609 (Iowa 1977); In re Estate of Benjamin, 34 N.Y.2d 27, 355 N.Y.S.2d 356, 311 N.E.2d 495 (1974).

The Texas Family Code, § 1.91(a)(2) (1975) provides that the marriage may be proved by evidence that the parties "agreed to be married, and after the agreement they lived together in this state as husband and wife and there represented to others that they were married." And in subsection (b) of the same section it is provided that "the agreement of the parties may be inferred if it is proved that they lived together as husband and wife and represented to others that they were married."

5. In the *Fisher* case, the parties began living together at a time when, as they both knew, they could not be married because Carroll Sue was still married to her first husband. At what point after the divorce, which occurred on September 9, 1968, did they presently agree to be husband and wife? Or is that agreement inferred from the fact that they just went on living together as before? If, as the court concedes, they were planning a marriage ceremony in the future, how could it be said that they presently had agreed to be husband and wife? Does the cited Iowa statute explain the court's position on this point? What significance should be attached to the purchase of the rings?

Most cases agree that where the spouses begin living together at a time when there is an impediment to their marriage, usually a prior existing marriage, and they continue after the impediment is removed, as by divorce or death, a common law marriage results if one or both parties began living together in bona fide ignorance of the impediment. See, e. g., In re Walls' Estate, 358 Mich. 148, 99 N.W.2d 599 (1959); Mass.Gen.L.Ann.C. 207, § 6 (1969); Wis.Stat.Ann. § 245.24 (Supp.1979–1980); Note, Common Law Marriage and Annulment, 15 Vill.L.Rev. 134 (1969). But where the parties begin living together with full knowledge that they cannot marry because of a prior existing marriage, the cases are divided. Leading cases holding that such conduct cannot result in a valid common law marriage without proof of a subsequent express consent to be man and wife are Metropolitan Life Ins. Co. v. Chase, 294 F.2d 500 (3d Cir. 1961); Dandy v. Dandy, 234 So.2d 728 (Fla.App.1970); Anderson v. Anderson, 235 Ind. 113, 131 N.E.2d 301 (1956) (semble); Howard v. Howard, 459 S.W.2d 901 (Tex.Civ.App. 1970) (semble). A leading case validating the marriage without additional expression of consent is Matthews v. Britton, 112 U.S.App.D.C. 397, 303 F. 2d 408 (1962), the court there saying, "It is not to be expected that parties once having agreed to be married will deem it necessary to agree to do so again when an earlier marriage is terminated or some other bar to union is eliminated." Which of these positions does the *Fisher* case take? Which position is the correct one? Why? Is there any relation to morality in these cases? For example, in *Fisher* Carroll Sue was clearly guilty of adultery, and if she intended or attempted to contract a second marriage before September 9, 1968, she was also a bigamist. Does the court's decision in this case condone or reward her criminal conduct?

What would have been the result in this case if neither the deceased nor Carroll Sue had learned of the divorce, but had gone on living together on the assumption that Carroll Sue's first marriage was still in existence? Kersey v. Gardner, 264 F.Supp. 887 (M.D.Ga.1967).

6. What would be the result, under the *Fisher* case or the Texas statute, in the following situations:

(a) H and W, young graduate students, strongly feel that marriage is productive of hypocrisy, is based upon a demeaning view of human nature, and is an immoral restraint on individual freedom. They begin living together in a state which recognizes common law marriage. In order to avoid unpleasant reactions from their parents, their landlord, and some friends, to simplify such matters as bank accounts and income tax returns, they represent themselves to be husband and wife. Since W is a nonresident and H a resident, W is also motivated by the desire to obtain the lower resident tuition at the University by appearing to be married. Their names are given as Mr. and Mrs. on their apartment, checking account and auto registration. They file a joint income tax return. After living in this way for three years, H is killed through the negligence of D in the operation of an automobile. Assuming a wrongful death statute in the state which gives to a surviving spouse a cause of action for negligently causing death, may W recover from D? Cf. Schrader v. Schrader, 207 Kan. 349, 484 P.2d 1007 (1971). If you represented W, how would you try the case? May W take H's property against his will? Would W have been entitled to alimony and a divorce from H? If W or H had consulted you after they began living together in this way, what would you have advised them about their legal rights?

(b) H and W were divorced after many years of marriage. Shortly after the divorce H became seriously ill with cancer. When this occurred, H and W discovered that their affection for each other still continued and they resumed living together, agreeing that they would be man and wife, on the mistaken impression that they could by this agreement nullify their divorce. Due to H's illness sexual relations were impossible. A month thereafter H died. During that month few of their friends knew of this reconciliation and no documents were executed indicating their marital status. Evidence of their agreement was contained in an exchange of letters.

Assuming that the state recognizes common law marriage, and that it has a statute giving to a surviving spouse the entire estate of one dying intestate, may W take H's estate? Cf. Beck v. Beck, 286 Ala. 692, 246 So.2d 420 (1971); In re Estate of Soeder, 7 Ohio App.2d 271, 220 N.E.2d 547 (1966); In re Wagner's Estate, 398 Pa. 531, 159 A.2d 495, 82 A.L.R.2d 681 (1960); In the Matter of Peterson's Estate, 148 Colo. 52, 365 P.2d 254 (1961).

KENNEDY v. DAMRON

Court of Appeals of Kentucky, 1954.
268 S.W.2d 22.

CULLEN, Commissioner. Eula Mae Kennedy (Damron) sought a share in the estate of J. R. Damron, deceased, on the ground that she was his widow. The court found that she had not been married to J.

R. Damron, either by a ceremonial or common-law marriage, and she now appeals from a judgment denying her claim.

* * *

The evidence shows that Eula Mae and Mr. Damron commenced a clandestine relationship in 1937, in West Virginia, when Mr. Damron was married to another. In 1939, Mr. Damron's wife obtained a divorce and he and Eula Mae then moved to Kentucky, where they lived together secretly until late in 1940, when Mr. Damron's mother died. Thereafter, until the spring of 1949, they lived together openly in Kentucky, and there is evidence that during this period they held themselves out to the public as man and wife. In 1949, Mr. Damron and his brother-in-law purchased a farm in Ohio, and the brother-in-law took occupancy of the main dwelling on the farm. Mr. Damron and Eula Mae visited the farm from time to time during 1949 and 1950, and during part of this time they lived in a converted chicken house on the farm. There was evidence that during the last nine months of 1950 they spent more time in Ohio than in Kentucky, but ordinarily they did not spend more than one week at a time in Ohio, and they never spent more than one month at a time in Ohio. In 1951, they remained in Kentucky, where Mr. Damron died in December 1951.

During the period Mr. Damron and Eula Mae were visiting and living at the farm in Ohio, Mr. Damron continued to maintain his dwelling in Kentucky. He did not have the utilities cut off, and he arranged with the neighbor to look after the house and receive the mail. He and Eula Mae left most of their clothing in the Kentucky dwelling, taking to Ohio only enough for their temporary needs. He continued to vote in Kentucky and do his banking there. He also continued to maintain a post office box in Kentucky, and during 1950 he maintained a garden in connection with his Kentucky dwelling.

Under the evidence, the chancellor clearly was correct in finding as a fact that Mr. Damron and Eula Mae never became residents of Ohio. Accordingly, Travers v. Reinhardt, 205 U.S. 423, 27 S.Ct. 563, 51 L.Ed. 865 (1907), so confidently relied upon by counsel for Eula Mae, is not applicable. In that case, the parties had established a permanent residence in a state in which common-law marriages were valid. * * *

The relation of husband and wife is inseparably identified with the home. We think that if the relation is to be presumed from conduct and reputation, it must be in identification with an established home. That this is the law of Ohio is apparent from the language in the Dibble case, 100 N.E.2d 451, 457 (1951), referring to conduct and reputation " 'in the community in which they reside.' " We do not intend to say that there must be a legal domicile in the common-law state, in the sense of residence with intent to remain permanently, but we are of the opinion that there must be an established place of abode with which the parties may be identified as members of the community.

Upon the evidence in the case before us, the chancellor was justified in concluding that Mr. Damron and Eula Mae were merely visitors in Ohio, with no abode by which they established themselves as members of the community. It is true that they occupied a dwelling for a time, but only in the character of transients, and their holding themselves out as man and wife, in Ohio, was principally as to tradesmen with whom they had casual dealings. They did not become an established part of the community.

A further impediment to Eula Mae's claim of a common-law marriage arises from the fact that she insisted at all times that she and Mr. Damron were ceremonially married in West Virginia. Her position is shown by the following excerpt from the testimony:

"Q. Did you ever say to one another that you would take him for your husband and he would take you for his wife? A. No, we didn't in the State of Ohio. We were married in West Virginia.

"Q. You don't claim you entered into a marriage relationship in Ohio? A. No, not in the State of Ohio."

Under the law of Ohio, an agreement *in praesenti* to be man and wife is essential to establish a common-law marriage, although such an agreement may be implied from the conduct of the parties in holding themselves out to the public as man and wife, in the community in which they reside. Dibble v. Dibble, 88 Ohio App. 490, 100 N.E.2d 451 (1951); Markley v. Hudson, 143 Ohio St. 163, 54 N.E.2d 304 (1944). It will be obvious that if the parties lived together under the belief that they were ceremonially married, there would have been no occasion for them to make an express agreement to be man and wife; by the same token, their living together would not be evidence of an implied agreement.

In Carroll v. Carroll, Ky., 251 S.W.2d 989 (1952), we pointed out that a claim of a ceremonial marriage is entirely inconsistent with the existence of a common-law marriage. In that case we held that a common-law marriage in Florida was not established, where the putative wife had pitched her case on a ceremonial marriage in Ohio.

Another similarity between the present case and the *Carroll* case is that in neither case did the putative wife plead specifically a common-law marriage. The pleadings of Eula Mae in the present case merely allege cohabitation and public recognition as man and wife in Ohio, without alleging an agreement in Ohio to be man and wife.

We are unable to distinguish this case from the *Carroll* case, and therefore we conclude that the chancellor correctly adjudged there was no marriage.

NOTES AND QUESTIONS

(1) The facts in In re Schneider's Will, 206 Misc. 18, 131 N.Y.S.2d 215 (Surr.Ct.1954), were as follows: H-2 and W were married ceremonially in 1938 in New York, W having been divorced in New York by a decree which forbade her to remarry. They lived together in all respects as man and wife until H-2's death in 1952. They remained domiciled in New York during this time, but from time to time they visited in New Jersey and Florida. At these times both New Jersey and Florida recognized common law marriage. The court held that they were validly married and that W could take, as a widow, an intestate share of H-2's estate. The court said that a valid common law marriage was contracted either in New Jersey or in Florida, the New York ceremonial marriage being invalid because in violation of W's divorce decree. The court rejected both of the arguments on which the Kentucky court in Kennedy v. Damron, supra, had held the marriage invalid, holding that it did not matter that no new agreement was proved, and that a valid common law marriage could be found to have occurred during the visits to Florida or New Jersey.

(a) Which court is correct on the issue of the absence of a new agreement to be man and wife? Cf. In the Matter of the Estate of Fisher, supra, page 103, and Travers v. Reinhardt, 205 U.S. 423 (1907). In the latter case the parties lived together in various states which did not recognize common law marriage. They finally moved to New Jersey and acquired a domicile there. Since New Jersey did recognize common law marriage, the Supreme Court held that they were married in that state, although there was no evidence of any new agreement to be husband and wife after moving to that state, and they only lived in New Jersey a short time until the husband died. Mr. Justice Holmes' dissent contains the remark that "To live in New Jersey and think you are married does not constitute a marriage by the law of that state." Would you agree with him?

(b) Which court is correct on the issue of allowing visits to another state to produce a valid common law marriage? Cases agreeing with *Schneider's Will* on this issue are In re Frost's Estate, 35 A.D.2d 1069, 316 N.Y.S.2d 372 (4th Dep't 1970); Ventura v. Ventura, 53 Misc.2d 881, 280 N.Y.S.2d 5 (Sup.Ct.1967); Metropolitan Life Ins. Co. v. Holding, 293 F. Supp. 854 (E.D.Va.1968); and perhaps Albina Engine & Machine Works v. J. J. O'Leary, 328 F.2d 877 (9th Cir. 1964), though there were other facts in support of the holding here. Cases agreeing that visits are not sufficient to support a finding of common law marriage are Walker v. Hildebrand, 243 Or. 117, 410 P.2d 244 (1966); Bridgman v. Stout, 485 P.2d 1101 (Or.App.1971).

(c) What law controls on these questions? For example, in the *Kennedy* case, is it Ohio law or Kentucky law? Shea v. Shea, 294 N.Y. 909, 63 N.E.2d 113 (1945); Metropolitan Life Ins. Co. v. Holding, 293 F.Supp. 854 (E.D.Va.1968); Restatement, Second, Conflict of Laws, § 283, comment g (1971).

(d) Would the result be different if the parties were domiciled in a state which did not recognize common law marriage but paid a visit to a common law marriage state for the purpose of contracting such a marriage, did so in compliance with the law of the common law state, and then immediately returned to the state of their domicile? See Vaughn v. Hufnagel,

473 S.W.2d 124 (Ky.1971), cert. den. 405 U.S. 1041 (1972); In re Vetas' Estate, 110 Utah 187, 170 P.2d 183 (1946).

(e) If the result of the *Schneider's Will* case is accepted, how much of a stay in the common law marriage state would suffice to bring a valid common law marriage into existence? A two-week stay on a summer or winter holiday? An overnight stay? A drive through the state without stopping overnight? An hour's flight over the state in an airplane, en route to some other place?

(f) Are the answers to these questions affected by the view that one takes of the wisdom of common law marriage as an institution? Should they be so affected? Are the answers affected by the appeal made by the proponent of the marriage in the particular case, as where the proponent is an elderly widow seeking social security or workmen's compensation payments to support herself in old age? Should this factor affect the finding of validity of the marriage? To what extent should the law individualize results in this context? Cf. Or.Rev.Stat. § 656.226 (1971), which provides that where an unmarried man and woman live together in Oregon for more than a year, and have children, the wife and children are entitled to workmen's compensation as if there had been a legal marriage, Oregon being a state which has repudiated common law marriage.

2. The disrepute in which common law marriage as an institution is held is attested by the fact that a large majority of states have abolished it, and by the hostility to it revealed in the cases. As in the *Fisher* case, supra, claims of common law marriage are regarded with suspicion and are closely scrutinized by the courts. Judge Bok, in Wagner's Estate, 398 Pa. 531, 159 A.2d 495 (1960) refers to it "as a fruitful source of perjury and fraud". In re Erickson's Estate, 75 S.D. 345, 64 N.W.2d 316 (1954), looks with disfavor on common law marriages, tolerating but not encouraging them. Similar attitudes are revealed by social scientists. See, e. g., Baber, Marriage and the Family, 69–71 (2d ed. 1953); Kephart, The Family, Society and the Individual, 415 (1961). Is there anything to be said in favor of common law marriage, or are all these authorities right in the view that it is a pernicious institution? Precisely how does it lead to fraud and perjury? And precisely how does it place honest matrimony and mere meretricious relationships on a level with each other, as some courts maintain? In this connection consider Seagriff v. Seagriff, 21 Misc.2d 604, 195 N.Y.S. 2d 718 (Dom.Rel.Ct.1960): H and W lived together from 1921 to 1957, in all respects as if married. Before 1928 W was married to another, and after that time she was forbidden to remarry by a divorce decree. They visited at times in Massachusetts, but Massachusetts did not recognize common law marriage. In 1957 H abandoned W and she sued for non-support. The court held the parties were not married and therefore that W had no legal remedy. Would the recognition of a legal status here lead to fraud and perjury, or cause honest marriage to resemble mere meretricious cohabitation?

Or consider People v. Allen, 27 N.Y.2d 108, 261 N.E.2d 637, 313 N.Y.S. 2d 719 (1970): Under section 812 of the New York Family Court Act the Family Court is given exclusive jurisdiction over disorderly conduct or assault between members of a family or household. One of the defendants was convicted in the criminal court of assault on a woman with whom he had been living for about eleven years and by whom he had had two children, and contended that the case should have been brought in the Family

Court, the purpose of the statute being to substitute conciliation or other forms of assistance for prison terms in intra-family disputes. But the New York Court of Appeals held that statute only applicable where a legal marriage exists, and since no common law marriage is recognized in New York, there was no legal marriage here. In what way would the recognition of common law marriage, and the handling of such cases by the Family Court result in perjury and fraud, or the honoring of meretricious relationships?

For a comprehensive discussion of the arguments pro and con common law marriage, see W. Weyrauch, Informal Marriage and Common Law Marriage, in R. Slovenko, Sexual Behavior and the Law 297 (1965).

3. What is or should be the relation between the common law marriage cases and the doctrine of Marvin v. Marvin, supra, page 38? If a particular state has abolished common law marriage, presumably because of the social evils which it produced, should the state follow the Marvin case? Or if the rules described in the preceding paragraphs by which common law marriage is rather strictly circumscribed are followed in the state, should the courts, by adopting the Marvin principle, give a spouse the financial advantages of marriage? Cf. Note, Common Law Marriage and Unmarried Cohabitation: An Old Solution to a New Problem, 39 U.Pitt.L.Rev. 579 (1978).

B.　PROXY MARRIAGE

Proxy marriage is a marriage contracted or celebrated through agents who are representing one or both parties. It may take the form either of a ceremonial marriage or a common law marriage. If the parties attempt a ceremony by proxy, the validity of the marriage will depend upon a construction of the statutes governing the obtaining of a license and the performance of the ceremony. In many states these statutes are construed to require the presence of both parties, in which event the proxy marriage as a ceremonial marriage is not valid. The cases on this are not numerous. See Barrons v. U. S., 191 F.2d 92 (9th Cir. 1951); Annot. 170 A.L.R. 947 (1947); Morris Plan Co. of California v. Converse, 15 Cal.App.3d 399, 93 Cal. Rptr. 103 (1971); State v. Anderson, 239 Or. 200, 396 P.2d 558 (1964); H. Clark, Law of Domestic Relations, § 2.5 (1968); Howery, Marriage by Proxy and Other Informal Marriages, 13 U.Kan.City L.Rev. 48 (1944).

Proxy marriages may or may not qualify as valid common law marriages in states which recognize common law marriage. If, as is generally the case in the United States, cohabitation is necessary for a valid common law marriage, and if the parties to the proxy marriage do not live together after celebrating the marriage, then the marriage cannot qualify as a common law marriage. Since the proxy marriage is usually relied upon because one party is unable to be present at the ceremony, this means that most proxy marriages cannot amount to valid common law marriages. Cf. Hardin v. Davis, 16 Ohio Supp. 19 (Ohio Com.Pl.1945).

Section 206 of the Uniform Marriage and Divorce Act expressly authorizes proxy marriages.

C. PUTATIVE MARRIAGE

Putative marriage was adopted from the Napoleonic Code in those states having a civil law tradition, such as California, Louisiana and Texas. The purpose of the doctrine is to protect parties to invalid marriages. Putative marriage occurs when a marriage is contracted at a time when an existing impediment makes the purported marriage void or voidable and when one or both of the parties are ignorant of the impediment. Under these circumstances a party who entered the marriage in the good faith belief that it was valid is entitled to assert financial or property claims based upon the marriage, such as the claim to share in community property, the right to inherit from the putative spouse, the right to sue for wrongful death, or the right to social security benefits. No requirement of cohabitation (as for common law marriage) is made. It is sufficient if a marriage was contracted in good faith. See, e. g., Aubrey v. Folsom, 151 F. Supp. 836 (N.D.Cal.1957); Speedling v. Hobby, 132 F.Supp. 833 (N. D.Cal.1955); Adduddell v. Board of Administration, 8 Cal.App.3d 243, 87 Cal.Rptr. 268 (1970); Sancha v. Arnold, 114 Cal.App.2d 772, 251 P.2d 67 (1952); Succession of Pigg, 228 La. 799, 84 So.2d 196 (1955); Succession of Marinoni, 183 La. 776, 164 So. 797 (1935); Texas Co. v. Stewart, 101 So.2d 222 (La.App.1958); Note, The Rights of the Putative and Meretricious Spouse in California, 50 Cal. L.Rev. 866 (1962); Note, The Putative Marriage Doctrine in Louisiana, 12 Loy.L.Rev. 89 (1967); Borah and Cook, Marriage and Legitimacy in Mexican Culture: Mexico and California, 54 Cal.L.Rev. 946 (1966).

In those states recognizing common law marriage, putative marriage benefits may be based upon the good faith contracting of a common law marriage. Sancha v. Arnold, 114 Cal.App.2d 772, 251 P.2d 67 (1952); Curtin v. State, 155 Tex.Cr.R. 625, 238 S.W.2d 187 (1951).

Some states have adopted putative marriage by statute. See, e. g. Cal.Civ.Code § 4452 (Supp.1979); Smith v. Smith, 52 Wis.2d 262, 190 N.W.2d 174 (1971); Uniform Marriage and Divorce Act § 209, 9A Unif.L.Ann. 115 (1979).

SECTION 4. SUCCESSIVE MARRIAGES AND THE PRINCIPLE OF MONOGAMY

PARKER v. AMERICAN LUMBER CORP.

Supreme Court of Appeals of Virginia, 1949.
190 Va. 181, 56 S.E.2d 214.

BUCHANAN, Justice. The Industrial Commission has denied compensation to the appellant, Mollie D. Parker, as the widow of Hezekiah Parker, and on this appeal the question presented is whether she was legally his wife.

Hezekiah Parker died March 5, 1948, as the result of an injury suffered in the course of his employment. The appellant filed an application for a hearing claiming compensation as his widow and sole dependent. In it she stated that the case could not be settled by agreement because "my husband was not married previously as far as I know. My former statement was a mistake." She had apparently stated to the employer that her husband had four children.

At a hearing on June 2, 1948, she filed a certified copy of a marriage license showing her marriage to Parker on August 23, 1941, in Northampton county, Virginia. She then testified that she had thought these children were her husband's, but after his death his brother told her they were the brother's children, and that the children she referred to were all grown. She first met her husband, she said, in Conway, North Carolina, about five years before they were married; that he was not married at that time and to the best of her knowledge and belief he had never been married before. Two other witnesses testified that Parker had said he had never been married before he married Mollie, and that he had never said anything about having children. There were no children of his marriage with Mollie.

As a result of this hearing an award was made to Mollie as the widow and only dependent of the deceased. Subsequently Sylvia Hill filed an affidavit stating that she had married Parker on August 4, 1923, in Edgecombe county, North Carolina, filing a certificate of marriage to Carl Parker, who was the same person as Hezekiah Parker, she said; that nine children were born of this marriage, two of whom (Viola and Lillie Mae) were under eighteen, as shown by certificates of their birth which were filed. She also stated that she and Hezekiah Parker separated thirteen or fourteen years ago, and that she had since married and was living with Henry Hill. Thereafter, by order of September 8, 1948, the commission restored the case to the hearing docket.

A second hearing was held November 11, 1948. Sylvia then testified that Carl Parker, whom she married in 1923, was the same person as Hezekiah Parker, and there was other evidence to the same effect. She said she and Hezekiah separated some eleven or twelve years before, which would be 1937 or 1936, "because he was not so good to me and my children." The only time she ever saw him afterwards was when he came to see the children for a few minutes in 1941, and said he was expecting to be called for military duty. He was called later but his military record did not show he had any children or was married. Sylvia also testified that she married Hill about two and one-half years after her separation from Hezekiah, but that she had never got a divorce from Hezekiah and had not heard anything about his getting a divorce from her, and that no divorce papers or summons of any kind had been served on her.

At the conclusion of this hearing the commission vacated the former award and held that Mollie's marriage to Hezekiah was biga- mous and void and that she was not entitled to compensation. It also held that Sylvia was not entitled to compensation but that Viola and Lillie Mae, the two infant children of Sylvia and Hezekiah, were his only surviving dependents, and made an award in their favor. The correctness of that ruling depends on whether in legal contemplation Hezekiah was divorced from Sylvia at the time he married Mollie.

Appellant contends that under Code 1942 (Michie), section 5074, the marriage license of Hezekiah and Mollie furnishes prima facie ev- idence that he was divorced from Sylvia. On the application for that license, required by said section, Hezekiah stated on oath (declared by the statute to be material on prosecution for perjury) that he was divorced, having been previously married once. The statute does not, however, make that statement prima facie a fact. Said section also requires that the minister celebrating the marriage shall make his own certificate of the time and place of the marriage, which shall be returned to the clerk, who is required to record it by section 5076 of the Code. Section 5074 provides that when the certificate of the minister is so recorded, the record thereof shall be prima facie evi- dence of the facts stated therein. This clearly applies to the minis- ter's certificate, and does not include statements made in the applica- tion for the license.

Appellant's main contention is that there is a legal presumption that her marriage to Hezekiah was valid; that the burden was on the appellees to overcome that presumption, that is, to show that Hezek- iah was not divorced; that the evidence was not sufficient for that purpose and, hence, that the finding of the commission was without sufficient evidence to support it.

The decided weight of authority, and we think the correct view, is that where two marriages of the same person are shown, the sec- ond marriage is presumed to be valid; that such presumption is stronger than and overcomes the presumption of the continuance of the first marriage, so that a person who attacks a second marriage has the burden of producing evidence of its invalidity. Where both parties to the first marriage are shown to be living at the time of the second marriage, it is presumed in favor of the second marriage that the first was dissolved by divorce. These presumptions arise, it is said, because the law presumes morality and legitimacy, not immoral- ity and bastardy. *   *   *

The cases are not entirely in harmony as to the force and effect to be given to the presumption in favor of the validity of the second marriage. Generally, it is said to be a strong presumption but one that may be rebutted by evidence of invalidating facts. In 55 C.J.S., supra, Marriage, § 45e, page 918, many cases are cited in support of the statement that in order to overcome this presumption of validity, "the evidence must be strong, distinct, satisfactory, and conclusive". A less stringent and, as we think, a more logical and better supported rule is this, from the case of Brokeshoulder v. Brokeshoulder, 84 Okl. 249, 204 P. 284, 291, 34 A.L.R. 441, at page 452 (1922):

"The presumption arising in favor of the validity of a second marriage is not a conclusive presumption, but is what is known as a rebuttable presumption, and the one contending against the legality of the second marriage is not required to make plenary proof of a negative averment. It is enough that he introduce such evidence as, in the absence of all counter testimony, will afford reasonable grounds for presuming that the allegation is true, and when it is done the onus probandi will be thrown on his adversary." * * *

Applying these principles to this case we have this situation: The marriage of Parker to Mollie, his second marriage, was duly proved. The burden was then on appellees to produce evidence to show the invalidity of that marriage. They proved the former marriage to Sylvia, and she testified that she had not divorced him and had never had any notice of any divorce obtained by him. Nevertheless, within two and one-half years from the time they separated she married again and was living with her second husband when Parker married Mollie and on down to the time of his death. There was no other attempt to prove there had been no divorce. In the eleven or twelve years of their separation, Sylvia made no claim that Parker was her husband. She neither saw nor heard from him in that period except the one time in 1941 when he came to see the children.

In the meantime, Parker had lived, for times of uncertain duration, in North Carolina, New Jersey and Maryland, and in Virginia around Norfolk, Suffolk and in Franklin. On August 23, 1941, some five years after he left Sylvia, and after she had married again, he married Mollie and lived with her until he died seven years later. On his application for license to marry Mollie he made oath that he had been married once before and was divorced. If that statement was not true, he was guilty of perjury, and of bigamy when he married. She signed that oath with him, and, of course, knew the statement was made.

It is true that she stated in the application for license that she was single, when in fact she was a widow; and it is also true that on the first hearing she denied knowledge of his previous marriage and that there were children of that marriage. This was evidently untrue and done, no doubt, for the purpose of securing all the compensation for herself. This was reprehensible, of course, but it does not add to or subtract from the question of whether Parker was divorced from Sylvia at the time he married Mollie. That issue remains to be decided on the weight of the presumption that he was divorced from Sylvia, coupled with his sworn statement that he was so divorced, as against the statement of Sylvia that she did not divorce him and did not know of his divorcing her, coupled with the fact that two and one-half years after their separation she married another man.

* * *

We hold the evidence adduced to be insufficient to support the finding that Mollie was not Parker's lawful wife.

The award is, therefore, reversed to the extent that it denies compensation to the appellant, and the case is remanded to the commission with direction to amend its award to include the appellant as the widow of deceased and to divide the compensation between her and the two dependent children of his first marriage, as provided by law.

Reversed and remanded.

NOTES AND QUESTIONS

1. It goes without saying that monogamy is the controlling principle of Anglo-American marriage law. A person may have but a single spouse at a time. In the civil law this is expressed by statutes which state that a subsequent marriage contracted by one having a living spouse from whom he has not been divorced is void. Cal.Civ.Code § 4401 (1970). The case law is in accord. Beaudin v. Suarez, 365 Mich. 534, 113 N.W.2d 818 (1962). The criminal law expresses the same principle by imposing penalties for bigamy, the crime of attempting to contract a marriage when a prior marriage remains undissolved, or for bigamous cohabitation, the crime of living with a person of the opposite sex as a spouse when there is an earlier marriage still in existence. See, e. g., N.Y.Penal L. §§ 255.15, 255.20 (1967); Cal.Penal Code §§ 281, 282 (1970); Model Penal Code § 230.1 (Proposed Official Draft 1962); Colo.Rev.Stat.Ann. § 18–6–201 (1978); Tenn.Code Ann. § 39–701 (1975).

Having announced the principle, we must at once recognize that it is so riddled with exceptions as to leave one in doubt as to how much of it is left. To begin with we know that the criminal law is seldom enforced against bigamists, although one famous case, Williams v. North Carolina, I and II, 317 U.S. 287 (1942) and 325 U.S. 226 (1945) did involve a bigamy prosecution. Suggestions are even being made that bigamy and polygamy should not be prosecuted. Slovenko, The De Facto Decriminalization of Bigamy, 17 J.Fam.L. 297 (1978). On the civil side there are several doctrines which dilute the force of the monogamy principle. The presumption of the validity of the later marriage is one such doctrine. In many of the cases applying this presumption no divorce ended the earlier marriage, but the court presumed a divorce without great concern that one or both of the parties was a bigamist. And the teaching of Marvin v. Marvin, supra page 38, is that a married man may have financial responsibilities to a woman with whom he is living which resemble the responsibilities of a spouse, even though he is currently married to someone else. People who enjoy coining phrases might call this de facto bigamy. Other doctrines which have the effect of imposing obligations to more than one "spouse" at a time are described in H. Clark, Law of Domestic Relations § 2.6 (1968).

Polygamy, or more specifically, polygyny, is also practiced in a few places in the United States. This is a form of marriage permitted by some religious sects in which a man marries and lives at one time with several wives and their children. Technically it is also bigamy, but generally the bigamist only lives with one spouse at a time and so bigamy and polygamy refer to essentially different relationships. In 1953 news stories were filed concerning polygamy in a small town on the Arizona-Utah border among some fundamentalist Mormons. The events are described in Hearings Before the Subcommittee to Investigate Juvenile Delinquency of the Committee on the Judiciary of the U.S. Senate, 84th Congress, 1st Sess., pursuant to S.Res. 62 (1955). Beyond various legal proceedings and a good deal of rhetoric, little was done about the situation. Newspaper accounts continue to describe polygamous groups, suggesting that their numbers are increasing in the western United States, especially in Utah. One such account estimates that twenty to thirty thousand people live in polygamous families. New York Times, October 9, 1977, page 1, col. 1.

There are many other countries and societies in the world where monogamy is not the rule. Polygamous marriages may be contracted in many parts of Africa, and in Islamic countries. It is striking that as our law seems to be growing more tolerant of infringements on the principle of monogamy, other societies seem to be retreating from polygamy. In Africa fewer polygamous marriages seem to be contracted and in India polygamy was abandoned in 1955. See W. Goode, World Revolution and Family Patterns, 187, 188 (1963); Hartley, Polygamy and Social Policy, 32 Mod.L.Rev. 155 (1969); Zabel, Hyde v. Hyde in Africa: A Comparative Study of the Law of Marriage in the Sudan and Nigeria, 1969 Utah L.Rev. 22.

For an economic analysis of polygamy, see G. Becker, The Economic Approach to Human Behavior 238–241 (1976).

The latest assault on monogamy comes from the much publicized but not widespread institution of communal living. Various kinds of communes existed in America in the Nineteenth Century, some of them rejecting monogamy but others adhering to it as a form of marriage. The same is true of contemporary communes. Some of them are little more than loose aggregations of mates with their children. Others, however, are sufficiently advanced in their social views to reject marriage and the nuclear family. In these the communal family is felt in some vague way to be a unit, but there is no generally accepted structure. Sexual relations may occur among all the members and if so, children are considered to be the children of the entire group. Some communes admit new members freely while others do not. At the moment most such groups seem to have relatively short lives, but it is too early to make any reliable generalizations about them. For an enlightening study of American communes, old and new, see R. Kanter, Commitment and Community, Communes and Utopias in Sociological Perspective (1972).

2. "My theory is that mature woman is physically polygamous but emotionally monogamous, while mature man is emotionally polygamous but physically monogamous." Alan Brien, Anyone for Polygamy, New Statesman, December 6, 1968, page 787, column 1. Would you agree?

3. Some other cases holding, on a variety of facts, that the presumption of the later marriage was not rebutted include:

Yarbrough v. United States, 169 Ct.Cl. 589, 341 F.2d 621 (1965): Uncorroborated testimony by one party that he did not obtain a divorce does not rebut the presumption. The presumption is described as very strong.

Wilson v. Wilson, 1 Ariz.App. 77, 399 P.2d 698 (1965): Evidence that no divorce was procured in three Texas counties during a period of six years while the first wife had no contact with the husband (later deceased) failed to rebut the presumption. A divorce could have been procured in other places.

Spears v. Spears, 178 Ark. 720, 12 S.W.2d 875 (1928): Proof that the deceased had not obtained a divorce in any of the counties of his residence did not rebut the presumption, since he could have obtained a divorce in other counties.

Yarbrough v. Celebrezze, 217 F.Supp. 943 (M.D.N.C.1963): W–1's testimony that she searched the divorce records of various states without finding any divorce obtained by H failed to rebut the presumption.

Eygabrood v. Gruis, 247 Iowa 1346, 79 N.W.2d 215 (1956): Evidence of no divorce in counties of presumed residence was held not sufficient, reversing the trial court's decision that the presumption was rebutted.

Commonwealth ex rel. Alexander v. Alexander, 445 Pa. 406, 289 A.2d 83 (1971): In a suit by W–2 against H for non-support, the court held that the presumption of validity of the marriage to W–2 was not rebutted by H's self-serving declaration that he had not been divorced from W–1 before marrying W–2.

Many other cases are collected in Annot., 14 A.L.R.2d 7 (1950) and Note, 30 Harv.L.Rev. 500 (1917).

4. Should the presumption apply to a later common law marriage? Warner v. Warner, 76 Idaho 399, 283 P.2d 931 (1955); Anderson-Tully Co. v. Wilson, 221 Miss. 656, 74 So.2d 735 (1954); Texas Employers' Ins. Ass'n v. Elder, 155 Tex. 27, 282 S.W.2d 371 (1955).

5. What is the basis for the presumption of validity of the later marriage? Is it that the probabilities favor the validity of that marriage? Or is it some consideration of social policy?

6. Is it possible that in those cases where the presumption of validity of the later marriage is relied upon the courts are construing "wife" or "husband" as meaning de facto rather than de jure wife or husband? Why would they do this? Is such a construction justified? See Dawson v. Hatfield Wire & Cable Co., 59 N.J. 190, 280 A.2d 173 (1971).

7. Is there any logical or philosophical relationship between the *Parker* case and Taczanowska v. Taczanowski, supra, page 95?

8. Other presumptions may flow from the fact that a marriage has been proved. These include the presumption that the marriage was contracted in good faith, that it was performed by a person having authority, and that the parties had capacity to marry. In other words, the marriage is presumed valid, the party attacking it having the burden of proving it invalid. See Annot., 34 A.L.R. 464 (1925) and H. Clark, Law of Domestic Relations, § 2.7 (1968).

DOLAN v. CELEBREZZE

United States Court of Appeals Second Circuit, 1967.
381 F.2d 231.

FRIENDLY, Circuit Judge:

Elizabeth Dolan brought this action in the District Court for the Eastern District of New York under 42 U.S.C.A. § 405(g), to review a decision of the Secretary of Health, Education and Welfare which denied her application for insurance benefits as the widow of John J. Dolan, 42 U.S.C.A. § 402(e). Section 216(c) of the Social Security Act, 42 U.S.C.A. § 416(c), defines "widow" as the surviving wife of an insured individual; under § 216(h)(1)(A) of the Act the test is whether "the courts of the State in which such insured individual * * * was domiciled at the time of death," here New York, "would find that such applicant and such insured individual were validly married * * * at the time he died." The Hearing Examiner thought that on the evidence here they would but the Appeals Council disagreed and this action followed. Both parties having moved for summary judgment, the District Court granted the Secretary's motion; we think it should have granted Mrs. Dolan's and so order.

It is undisputed that the claimant married Dolan on May 14, 1914. A son, John Howard, was born of the marriage. Three years later Dolan left for Peru to work as an electrician. He returned in 1920 or 1921, stayed for six months, then renewed his employment contract and took his wife and son with him to Peru. Since Mrs. Dolan did not like the climate, she and the son came back to New York, where Dolan joined them in 1925 or 1926. A year later he returned to South America. For the first year of his absence they received news and support from him; when these ceased, Mrs. Dolan inquired about her husband and was told by his employer that Dolan had left its employ and his whereabouts were unknown.

Having little or no money Mrs. Dolan and her son lived for a time with various members of her family. In the mid-1930's she became acquainted with James Reilly, an engineer for the Long Island Railroad, and took up living with him in a home he provided for her and John Howard. Dolan returned to New York in 1936 and got in touch with his son. For a year and a half they worked together in an art gallery but Dolan made no effort to disrupt the ménage; in fact he did not see his wife. In his employment and social security forms he listed himself as "single"—not "divorced"—and named John Howard Dolan, described as a "nephew," as his beneficiary, as the son knew. John Howard testified that during this period his father never said he had gotten a divorce from Mrs. Dolan; "he still felt that he was married to her but he was just separated," and he told the people at the art gallery that he was separated and that John Howard was the son of the marriage. John Howard lost touch with his father in 1939. Three years later Reilly and Mrs. Dolan decided upon matrimony. The application for a license recited she was a widow, and a ceremony was performed in St. Patrick's Cathedral. Mrs. Dolan testified she thought that after seven years of separation without support she was free to remarry; the statement as to Dolan's death, acknowledged to be without basis, is understandable in view of the parties' desire for a Catholic religious ceremony. Reilly died in 1949 and Mrs. Dolan, representing herself to be his widow, obtained from the Railroad Retirement Board the lump sum annuity payable under 45 U.S.C.A. § 228e(f)(2). Two years later Dolan appeared at her home, stayed overnight on several occasions and finally took up living there and contributing to the support of the household. After his death* the son claimed a lump sum payment for Dolan's burial expenses under 42 U.S.C.A. § 402(i) as a nephew, the role in which his father had cast him. The application stated that Dolan had been married in 1913 to an unknown person and that the marriage had ended in divorce, the date and place of which were also unknown. The son collected the pay due to Dolan at the date of death, making an affidavit that he was a nephew and the sole living relative.

Mrs. Dolan denied she had ever initiated or received notice of a proceeding for divorce, and a search of the County Clerk's records of Bronx, New York and Queens Counties covering the years 1912 to 1942 disclosed no evidence of a divorce or annulment. When her claim as Dolan's widow under the Social Security Act led the Railroad Retirement Board to seek recovery of its payment to her as Reilly's, she acknowledged her indebtedness but pleaded inability to repay; the Retirement Board took no action, see 45 U.S.C.A. § 228i(c).

* * *

The Council relied heavily on what it characterized as "a strong presumption in favor of the validity of a second or subsequent marriage" recognized by the New York courts which, in its view, "can be rebutted only by evidence demonstrating that the prior marriage was still in effect at the time of the later marriage." Examination of the New York decisions convinces us that both the Council and the District Court considerably overestimated the demonstration New York would require in a case like this.

* * *

[At this point in its opinion the court stated and discussed in detail several cases from the lower courts of New York holding that the presumption of validity of the later marriage had been rebutted.]

In contrast to these cases holding the presumption to have been rebutted, the decisions that have held the subsequent marriage to be

---

* Dolan died in 1962. Dolan v. Celebrezze, 250 F.Supp. 932, 933 (E.D.N.Y.1966). (Editor's footnote.)

valid on the basis of the presumption are explicable in terms of effectuating a particular public policy such as upholding legitimacy, favoring the participation in the decedent's estate of one who lived with him as his spouse, and preserving the validity of a marriage where no strong public policy would be served by doing otherwise.   *   *   * We have found no decision of a New York appellate court which declared a prior marriage to have been dissolved and a subsequent one valid where this would have had the effect of disinheriting a spouse of the earlier marriage without any offsetting advantage in terms of the legitimacy of children or the sharing in the estate by the spouse or children of the second marriage. Mindful of Chief Judge Cardozo's admonition to beware "the presumption   *   *   * gone mad," Matter of Findlay, 253 N.Y. 1, 13, 170 N.E. 471 (1930), we are satisfied that in a case like the present the only force New York would give it would be to place on Mrs. Dolan the burden—here amply satisfied—of coming forward with evidence reasonably supporting the continuity of the first marriage. Only to attain important human values do the New York courts extend the presumption of validity of a subsequent marriage beyond the logical core that most people do not knowingly commit bigamy; we are confident they would be surprised to find it invoked by a government agency to deny benefits to an old lady convincingly shown to have remained the widow of the first marriage when no spouse or child of the second can be adversely affected.   *   *   *

The summary judgment in favor of the defendant is reversed, with instructions to enter judgment in favor of the plaintiff.

NOTES AND QUESTIONS

1. The Federal Rules of Civil Procedure, Rule 56 provides that summary judgment may be granted where "there is no genuine issue as to any material fact and   *   *   * the moving party is entitled to judgment as a matter of law". Would you say that in the *Dolan* case there was no genuine issue as to any material fact? Or was the whole argument about a material fact, that is, whether Elizabeth Dolan was married to Dolan when he died? Is the question whether the presumption was rebutted a question of fact? Is the availability of summary judgment affected by the fact that both parties filed cross motions for summary judgment? See Rains v. Cascade Industries, Inc., 402 F.2d 241 (3d Cir. 1968).

2. Is the *Dolan* decision based on the assumption that the only issue in the case was the strength of the New York version of the presumption, and that this was an issue of law, not of fact?

3. Suppose that this case had arisen in 1949, after the death of James Reilly, as a result of Elizabeth's claim to a lump sum annuity from the Railroad Retirement Board as the widow of Reilly. What disposition do you think this court would have made of that claim?

4. Is your answer to Question 3, supra, inconsistent with the court's opinion in the *Dolan* case?

5. What does the *Dolan* case suggest concerning the purpose and the limits of the presumption of validity of the later marriage? Could you write an opinion on the *Dolan* facts which would make that purpose and those limits more explicit than the court's opinion did?

6. What arguments and what decision would you make in the following case:

H and W–1 were married in 1954. One child of the marriage was born in 1955. W–1 went to live with her mother late in 1956, but she and H continued to live together sporadically until August of 1957, at which time she moved to a new address not known to H and got an unlisted telephone so that he would not be able to call her. He did discover where she was and learned her telephone number, however, but he did not try to call her for eight years, until 1965. W–1 never saw him after 1957 and only heard from him once, in 1965, when he telephoned her. She did not know where he lived or what he was doing. After 1957, H never made any attempt to support W–1 or their child.

In October, 1956, H married W–2 in a ceremonial marriage in Mexico. Two children were born of this marriage, one in 1957 and one in 1961. H and W–2 lived together continuously from the date of their marriage until H was killed in an industrial accident in 1966. In 1962 H and W–2 went through another wedding ceremony in their home state, which W–2 explained by saying, "I might as well be married in the United States as well as in Mexico." Both W–1 and W–2 made claims for workmen's compensation death benefits which were payable as a result of H's death. At the hearing, W–1 testified that she had never known of the marriage to W–2 until after H's death, and W–2 testified that she had not known of H's earlier marriage. W–1 also testified that she had never obtained a divorce or annulment from H. An appeal is taken from the trial court's decision in favor of W–1. Cf. Sparling v. Industrial Commission, 48 Ill.2d 332, 270 N. E.2d 411 (1971).

7. What effect does the principle of monogamous marriage have upon these situations, i. e., the *Dolan* case and the problem case?

8. Other cases holding the presumption of validity of the later marriage rebutted include:

Gainey v. Flemming, 279 F.2d 56 (10th Cir. 1960): Rebuttal by a search of the divorce records in two places (Denver and New Orleans) which revealed no divorce.

Tatum v. Tatum, 241 F.2d 401 (9th Cir. 1957): Rebuttal found on evidence that one spouse had obtained no divorce and had been served with no divorce papers, together with some other evidence. This case states the California version of the presumption to be that it merely requires the proponent of the earlier marriage to establish by competent evidence a prima facie case of a regularly solemnized prior marriage, and if this is done, the ultimate burden rests upon the proponent of the second marriage to prove the termination of the first.

Dixon v. Gardner, 302 F.Supp. 395 (E.D.Pa.1969): Rebuttal was largely based on letters from four counties where the spouse had resided to the effect that no divorce had been granted in any of these counties.

Henderson v. Finch, 300 F.Supp. 753 (W.D.La.1969): The presumption was rebutted by a search of eleven counties in which the spouse had lived, in none of which was a divorce granted.

Dorsey v. Dorsey, 259 Ala. 220, 66 So.2d 135 (1953): Rebuttal was based upon evidence that no divorce had been obtained in the counties in which the parties to the first marriage had lived, together with testimony of one of those parties that she had not obtained a divorce plus the refusal of the other party to testify.

Cole v. Cole, 249 Ark. 824, 462 S.W.2d 213 (1971): The presumption, characterized as one of the strongest in our law, was held rebutted by testimony of both spouses that they had never obtained a divorce, plus a search of the records in the one county in which a divorce suit might have been brought which disclosed no divorce.

Quinn v. Miles, 124 So.2d 883 (Fla.App.1960): Evidence from the records of counties in which the first spouse lived after the separation showed no divorce and this was held sufficient for rebuttal.

In re Estate of Watt, 409 Pa. 44, 185 A.2d 781 (1962): The presumption was held rebutted by proof that a divorce ending the first marriage was set aside for fraud and by evidence of a resumption of marital relations.

Other cases are cited in Annot., 14 A.L.R.2d 7 (1950).

9.   There is one situation in which the presumption that the later marriage is valid usually can be rebutted and yet which causes considerable hardship to the parties. This is the *Enoch Arden* case so named after Tennyson's poem. H–1 and W are married and some time later H–1 disappears, often as a result of army service or being listed as missing in action. W waits a considerable time and then on the assumption that H–1 is dead marries H–2. Later H–1 returns. Since both W and H–1 are available to testify that they have not obtained a divorce, the presumption is rebutted. In those circumstances the principle of monogamy dictates that the first marriage is still in force and the second of no effect. From an early date an English statute protected the wife in such cases from a bigamy prosecution by providing that a second marriage after seven years' absence of the first spouse, without any knowledge of his whereabouts, would not be bigamous. But this statute does not ensure the validity of the second marriage, although many laymen have the erroneous impression that it does. Some American states have enacted similar statutes, sometimes reducing the period to five years. See, e. g., Cal.Penal Code § 282 (1970).

Several states have attempted to deal with the Enoch Arden problem by statute, by providing for a proceeding to be brought by the spouse who wishes to remarry, as in New York and Pennsylvania, in which a court may make a finding that the first spouse has died. See N.Y.Dom.Rel.L. §§ 220, 221 (1964); Pa.Stat.Ann. tit. 48, §§ 1–8 (1965). See also Ann.Cal. Civ.Code § 4401 (1970), making the subsequent marriage valid until annulled. In re Lemont's Estate, 7 Cal.App.3d 437, 86 Cal.Rptr. 810 (1970).

10.   Harold and Wilma were married and lived in the State of Holmes. Four years later, their relationship having become impossible to both, Wilma left to visit some friends on the West Coast, and from there went to Detroit, where she established a home and got a job. Five years after Wilma left, Harold married Mary in Holmes. They had no children. Wilma knew

nothing of this second marriage, and Mary knew nothing about Harold's first marriage. Harold's second marriage was not a success either. After six years Harold sued Mary for annulment, on the ground of his prior subsisting marriage, and Mary counterclaimed for divorce on the ground of cruelty. The court granted the divorce, holding the marriage valid and awarding Mary alimony. Three years later Harold died, leaving an estate of $250,000. Wilma heard of his death from a friend, and returned to Holmes, where she claimed one-half of Harold's estate under the Holmes statute providing that a surviving spouse shall take one-half of a decedent's estate notwithstanding the provisions of decedent's will. Mary offered a will for probate which was properly executed by Harold, leaving his entire estate "to my wife Mary." Appropriate legal proceedings were brought by Mary, and both she and Wilma moved for summary judgment. What arguments on this motion should be made on both sides? Cf. Williamson v. Williamson, 9 Terry 277, 101 A.2d 871 (Del.1954); Headen v. Pope & Talbot, 252 F.2d 739 (3d Cir. 1958).

Appeal of O'Rourke, 310 Minn. 373, 246 N.W.2d 461 (1976) held that the presumption of validity of the later marriage would not overcome the presumption that the earlier marriage continued where the later marriage was of very short duration.

Recognition of Polygamous Marriages

The principle of monogamy, defined as "the voluntary union for life of a man and a woman to the exclusion of all others", by Hyde v. Hyde (1866) L.R. 1 P. & D. 130, 133, was so strongly adhered to by Anglo-American judges in the Nineteenth Century that it was generally held, *Hyde* being the leading case, that polygamous marriages would not be recognized even though valid by the law of the place where they were contracted, where the parties were domiciled at the time of the marriage and where they intended to make their married home. In Hyde the marriage was contracted in Salt Lake City at a time when Mormon polygamous marriages were still recognized as valid in Utah. The *Hyde* case denied a divorce in such circumstances on the ground that this was not a marriage as known to English law. It likewise stood for the proposition that a marriage was to be characterized as polygamous if it was potentially so under the law of the place of contract, even though the husband at no time had more than one wife. See also Zwerling v. Zwerling, 270 S.C. 685, 244 S.E.2d 311 (1978). Hyde is still occasionally cited, but the decision has little force today. Thus it has been held that non-matrimonial relief may be granted even though the marriage was polygamous. In In re Dalip Singh Bir's Estate, 83 Cal.App.2d 256, 188 P.2d 499 (1948) such a marriage was recognized for purposes of intestate succession. In Ali v. Ali, [1968] P. 564 it was held that where the husband in a potentially polygamous marriage changes his domicile to a country such as England in which only monogamous marriages may be contracted, his marriage becomes monogamous, and this permits the courts to take jurisdiction of it for all purposes. And in Radwan v. Radwan

(No. 2), [1973] Fam. 35, the court held that a polygamous marriage would be recognized as valid for purposes of granting a divorce. In that case the marriage was contracted before the Egyptian Consulate in Paris. The husband was an Egyptian domiciled in Cairo, the wife an English national domiciled in England. The husband already had one wife so that the marriage was actually, and not merely potentially, polygamous, and was valid according to Egyptian law. The court was persuaded to find the marriage valid because the wife had decided before the marriage to give up her English domicile and to live with her husband in Egypt. The result of the decision and its emphasis upon the intended matrimonial domicile are approved in Jaffey, The Essential Validity of Marriage in the English Conflict of Laws, 41 Mod.L.Rev. 38 (1978).

In Australia the problem has been dealt with in part by statute, Matrimonial Causes Act 1965, section 3, and by various state statutes. D. Hambly and J. Turner, Cases and Materials on Australian Family Law 34–37 (1971).

Now that the American domestic relations law has gone far toward abandoning monogamy, at least in the strict sense defined by Hyde v. Hyde, there seems little reason why potentially polygamous marriages should not be recognized for all purposes. For extensive discussion of American and English cases on this point, see Bartholomew, Recognition of Polygamous Marriages in America, 13 Int. & Comp.L.Q. 1022 (1964); Hartley, Polygamy and Social Policy, 32 Mod.L.Rev. 155 (1969); Pearl, Muslim Marriages in English Law, 30 Camb.L.J. 120 (1972). See also Restatement, Second, Conflict of Laws, §§ 283, 284 (1971).

SECTION 5. CAPACITY TO MARRY

A. HOMOSEXUAL MARRIAGE

BAKER v. NELSON

Supreme Court of Minnesota, 1971.
291 Minn. 310, 191 N.W.2d 185.
Appeal dismissed 410 U.S. 810, 93 S.Ct. 37, 34 L.Ed.2d 65 (1972).

PETERSON, Justice. The questions for decision are whether a marriage of two persons of the same sex is authorized by state statutes and, if not, whether state authorization is constitutionally compelled.

Petitioners, Richard John Baker and James Michael McConnell, both adult male persons, made application to respondent, Gerald R. Nelson, clerk of Hennepin County District Court, for a marriage license, pursuant to Minn.St. 517.08. Respondent declined to issue the license on the sole ground that petitioners were of the same sex, it being undisputed that there were otherwise no statutory impediments to a heterosexual marriage by either petitioner.

The trial court, quashing an alternative writ of mandamus, ruled that respondent was not required to issue a marriage license to petitioners and specifically directed that a marriage license not be issued to them. This appeal is from those orders. We affirm.

1. Petitioners contend, first, that the absence of an express statutory prohibition against same-sex marriages evinces a legislative intent to authorize such marriages. We think, however, that a sensible reading of the statute discloses a contrary intent.

Minn.St. c. 517, which governs "marriage," employs that term as one of common usage, meaning the state of union between persons of the opposite sex.[1] It is unrealistic to think that the original draftsmen of our marriage statutes, which date from territorial days, would have used the term in any different sense. The term is of contemporary significance as well, for the present statute is replete with words of heterosexual import such as "husband and wife" and "bride and groom" (the latter words inserted by L.1969, c. 1145, § 3, subd. 3).

---

1. Webster's Third New International Dictionary (1966) p. 1384 gives this primary meaning to marriage: "1 a: the state of being united to a person of the opposite sex as husband or wife."

Black, Law Dictionary (4 ed.) p. 1123, states this definition: "Marriage * * * is the civil status, condition, or relation of one man and one woman united in law for life, for the discharge to each other and the community of the duties legally incumbent on those whose association is founded on the distinction of sex."

We hold, therefore, that Minn.St. c. 517 does not authorize marriage between persons of the same sex and that such marriages are accordingly prohibited.

2. Petitioners contend, second, that Minn.St. c. 517, so interpreted, is unconstitutional. There is a dual aspect to this contention: The prohibition of a same-sex marriage denies petitioners a fundamental right guaranteed by the Ninth Amendment to the United States Constitution, arguably made applicable to the states by the Fourteenth Amendment, and petitioners are deprived of liberty and property without due process and are denied the equal protection of the laws, both guaranteed by the Fourteenth Amendment.

These constitutional challenges have in common the assertion that the right to marry without regard to the sex of the parties is a fundamental right of all persons and that restricting marriage to only couples of the opposite sex is irrational and invidiously discriminatory. We are not independently persuaded by these contentions and do not find support for them in any decisions of the United States Supreme Court.

The institution of marriage as a union of man and woman, uniquely involving the procreation and rearing of children within a family, is as old as the book of Genesis. Skinner v. Oklahoma ex rel. Williamson, 316 U.S. 535, 541, 62 S.Ct. 1110, 1113, 86 L.Ed. 1655, 1660 (1942), which invalidated Oklahoma's Habitual Criminal Sterilization Act on equal protection grounds, stated in part: "Marriage and procreation are fundamental to the very existence and survival of the race." This historic institution manifestly is more deeply founded than the asserted contemporary concept of marriage and societal interests for which petitioners contend. The due process clause of the Fourteenth Amendment is not a charter for restructuring it by judicial legislation.

Griswold v. Connecticut, 381 U.S. 479, 85 S.Ct. 1678, 14 L.Ed.2d 510 (1965), upon which petitioners rely, does not support a contrary conclusion. A Connecticut criminal statute prohibiting the use of contraceptives by married couples was held invalid, as violating the due process clause of the Fourteenth Amendment. The basic premise of that decision, however, was that the state, having authorized marriage, was without power to intrude upon the right of privacy inherent in the marital relationship. Mr. Justice Douglas, author of the majority opinion, wrote that this criminal statute "operates directly on an intimate relation of husband and wife," 381 U.S. 482, 85 S.Ct. 1680, 14 L.Ed.2d 513 (1965), and that the very idea of its enforcement by police search of "the sacred precincts of marital bedrooms for telltale signs of the use of contraceptives * * * is repulsive to the notions of privacy surrounding the marriage relationship," 381 U.S. 485, 85 S.Ct. 1682, 14 L.Ed.2d 516 (1965). In a separate opinion for three justices, Mr. Justice Goldberg similarly abhorred this state disruption of "the traditional relation of the family—a relation as old and as fundamental as our entire civilization." 381 U.S. 496, 85 S.Ct. 1688, 14 L.Ed.2d 522 (1965).[2]

The equal protection clause of the Fourteenth Amendment, like the due process clause, is not offended by the state's classification of persons authorized to marry. There is no irrational or invidious discrimination. Petitioners note that the state does not impose upon heterosexual married couples a condition that they have a proved capacity or declared willingness to procreate, posing a rhetorical demand that this court must read such condition into the statute if same-sex marriages are to be prohibited. Even assuming that such a condition would be neither unrealistic nor offensive under the Griswold rationale, the classification is no more than theoretically imperfect. We are reminded, however, that "abstract symmetry" is not demanded by the Fourteenth Amendment.

Loving v. Virginia, 388 U.S. 1, 87 S.Ct. 1817, 18 L.Ed.2d 1010 (1967), upon which petitioners additionally rely, does not militate against this conclusion. Virginia's antimiscegenation statute, prohibiting interracial marriages, was invalidated solely on the grounds of its patent racial discrimination. As Mr. Chief Justice Warren wrote for the court (388 U.S. 12, 87 S.Ct. 1824, 18 L.Ed.2d 1018 (1967)):

"Marriage is one of the 'basic civil rights of man,' fundamental to our very existence and survival. Skinner v. Oklahoma, 316 U.S. 535, 541, 62 S.Ct. 1110, 86 L.Ed. 1655 (1942). See also Maynard v. Hill, 125 U.S. 190, 8 S.Ct. 723, 31 L.Ed. 654 (1888). To deny this fundamental freedom on so unsupportable a basis as the racial classifications embodied in these statutes, classifications so directly subversive of the principle of equality at the heart of the Fourteenth Amendment, is surely to deprive all the State's citizens of liberty without due process of law. The Fourteenth Amendment requires that the freedom of choice to marry not be restricted by invidious racial discriminations."

Loving does indicate that not all state restrictions upon the right to marry are beyond reach of the Fourteenth Amendment. But in commonsense and in a constitutional sense, there is a clear distinction between a marital restriction based merely upon race and one based upon the fundamental difference in sex.

We hold, therefore, that Minn.St. c. 517 does not offend the First, Eighth, Ninth, or Fourteenth Amendments to the United States Constitution.

Affirmed.

2. The difference between the majority opinion of Mr. Justice Douglas and the concurring opinion of Mr. Justice Goldberg was that the latter wrote extensively concerning this right of marital privacy as one preserved to the individual by the Ninth Amendment. He stopped short, however, of an implication that the Ninth Amendment was made applicable against the states by the Fourteenth Amendment.

NOTES AND QUESTIONS

1. Pending the appeal to the Minnesota Supreme Court Baker and McConnell were able to get a marriage license and were married by a minister. Baker then sought Veterans' Administration benefits for a dependent spouse, but these were denied on the authority of Baker v. Nelson in McConnell v. Nooner, 547 F.2d 54 (8th Cir. 1976). The *Baker* case is discussed in a Note, The Legality of Homosexual Marriage, 82 Yale L.J. 573 (1973).

2. Jones v. Hallahan, 501 S.W.2d 588 (Ky.1973) also held that two female homosexuals could not obtain a marriage license or contract a valid marriage. Anonymous v. Anonymous, 67 Misc.2d 982, 325 N.Y.S.2d 499 (Sup.Ct.1971), dealing with a transsexual, likewise held that same-sex marriage was not permitted by state law. In M.T. v. J.T., 140 N.J.Super. 77, 355 A.2d 204 (1976), cert. den. 71 N.J. 345, 364 A.2d 1076 (1976) the court upheld a marriage between a person who was born with male sex organs but was psychologically a female and who had had a transsexual operation to become physically a female, and a man. In the course of its opinion the court indicated that lawful marriage requires that the parties be male and female. But Corbett v. Corbett, [1970], 2 All Eng.Rep. 33, [1970] 2 W.L.R. 1306 annulled a marriage on the ground that a transsexual was not a woman and therefore not able to contract a valid marriage to a man. See also Holloway, Transsexuals—Their Legal Sex, 40 U.Colo.L.Rev. 282 (1968).

3. Homosexuality may be broadly defined as a sexual attraction between members of the same sex. As with heterosexual attraction, homosexuality may or may not result in overt sexual behavior. It is now clear that a substantial percentage of the general population has, at some time during life, often in adolescence, some homosexual feelings and some homosexual experience. Kinsey attempted to classify homosexuals and found that four percent of white males in the United States are exclusively homosexual (by his method of classification) throughout their lives. Much larger percentages obtained for less exclusively homosexual men, for example, those who had had some homosexual experience at some time during their lives. The proportion for females he found to be lower, with the further difference that the homosexual experiences of females occurred mostly with one or two partners, whereas long term homosexual relationships between males were notably few. It therefore seems clear that a minority group substantial in numbers but small in relation to the total population is concerned with the issues in the *Baker* case. Kinsey, Pomeroy, Martin, Sexual Behavior in the Human Male, Ch. 21 (1948); Kinsey, Pomeroy, Martin, Gebhard, Sexual Behavior in the Human Female, Ch. 11 (1953). See also, G. Westwood, A Minority, A Report on the Life of the Male Homosexual in Great Britain, Ch. 5 (1960).

In the past most religious teachings have condemned homosexuality. A. Karlen, Sexuality and Homosexuality ch. 4 (1971); D. Bailey, Homosexuality and the Western Christian Tradition (1975). Some changes in this attitude have recently begun to appear, however, and individual theologians are beginning to take a more tolerant view of it. See New York Times, December 3, 1967, page E 7, column 4, reporting the views of various religious authorities on homosexuality, and W. Tobin, Homosexuality and Marriage

(1964), and Barrett, Legal Homophobia and the Christian Church, 30 Hastings L.J. 1019 (1979).

Public attitudes toward homosexuality have paralleled the religious teachings. Homosexuality has been regarded with strong emotional aversion by the American public, an aversion which has been vividly expressed by criminal statutes in nearly all states imposing severe penalities for homosexual activities, by refusal by many employers, including the state and federal governments, to hire homosexuals, and in many other ways. See Note, Government Employment and the Homosexual, 45 St. John's L.Rev. 303 (1970); Note, Homosexuals and the Law: Why the Status Quo? 5 Cal. Western L.Rev. 232 (1969). A comprehensive review of all aspects of the legal treatment of the homosexual is found in Rivera, Our Straight-Laced Judges: The Legal Position of Homosexual Persons in the United States, 30 Hastings L.J. 799 (1979). Some attacks on employment discrimination against homosexuals are now being made, and some lessening of public hostility is perceptible, but barely so. See Wall Street Journal July 15, 1968, page 1, column 1. Reforms of the criminal law eliminating the penalties for homosexual conduct between consenting adults are beginning to appear, in Britain, under the Sexual Offences Act, 1967, § 1(1), in the Model Penal Code, § 213.2 and comment (Proposed Official Draft 1962), in Illinois and the recently redrafted Colorado Criminal Code. The changes in the criminal law were to a great extent precipitated by the recommendation in the Report of the Committee on Homosexual Offences and Prostitution, Cmnd. No. 247 (1957) at 115, usually known as the Wolfenden Report, from the name of the committee chairman, to the effect that "homosexual behavior between consenting adults in private be no longer a criminal offence."

The etiology of homosexuality remains a subject of disagreement among the physicians, psychiatrists, biologists and geneticists who have studied the question. Psychoanalysis has attempted to explain male homosexuality as the result of the child's having a dominating mother, no satisfactory father, and thus a childhood which aggravates Oedipal conflicts to a degree making heterosexual relations difficult or impossible later on. D. West, Homosexuality, Ch. VIII (1967). Other theories of malfunctioning endocrine systems or genetic tendencies have been advanced but not well substantiated. No theories seem to offer wholly satisfactory explanations. The lack of agreement is perhaps not unconnected with the emotional reactions which homosexuality sets up in all persons, making it difficult even for scientists to look at the subject without bias or prejudice. There is a tendency, even among such educated persons as the members of the Wolfenden Committee, to be concerned with such irrelevancies as whether homosexuality is to be considered a "disease", whether it is "natural" or "unnatural" and similar matters. A more satisfactory way of looking at homosexuality would seem to recognize that it is not uncommon in varying degrees, that it is largely beyond the person's control, that in some persons it is a source of great tensions, conflicts and unhappiness, while other homosexuals have managed to work out an adjustment to their sex drives which is as stable and secure as that of the average heterosexual person. One source of the tension and conflict, or at least of their aggravation, is undoubtedly the social disapproval expressed by the criminal law. Even though that law is enforced very unevenly, and hardly ever against women, its effect cannot be disregarded. Obviously it can be devastating when it is enforced. For discussion of these questions, together with citations to other authorities, see M. Baisden, The Dynamics of Homosexuality (1975); W. Barnett, Sexual Freedom and the Constitution chs. 6, 7 (1973); E. Goode, ed., Sexual Deviance and Sexual Deviants chs. IV, V (1974); A. Karlen, Sexuality and Homosexuality ch. 28 (1971).

One of the few points of agreement among those who have studied homosexuality is that the homosexual should not marry a person of the other sex in the hope of curing his homosexuality. Most such marriages apparently fail, in the process inflicting suffering on both parties, and on the children if there are any. D. West, Homosexuality, 239–241 (1967); Tobin, Homosexuality and Marriage, 74 (1964).

4. The student should look back at this point to Griswold v. Connecticut, supra, page 73, and Zablocki v. Redhail, supra, page 83. Does the court in the *Baker* case give an accurate account of the rationale of *Griswold*? Does the doctrine of that case and of *Zablocki* support the decision in Baker v. Nelson?

5. Would it be correct to say that *Griswold* and *Zablocki* recognize a right of privacy in marriage which is fundamental and is in part deduced from the Ninth Amendment though not expressly mentioned there, and that they then hold that such fundamental rights may only be abridged upon proof of compelling subordinating interest by the state? If so, what state interests underlie the refusal to permit homosexual marriage? Are these interests "compelling"?

6. The proposed Twenty-Seventh Amendment provides, "Equality of rights under the law shall not be denied or abridged by the United States or by any State on account of sex." See page 21, supra. Several states have added similar provisions to their state constitutions. Does such a constitutional provision overrule the *Baker* case? Why or why not? Singer v. Hara, 11 Wash.App. 247, 522 P.2d 1187 (1974).

B. NONAGE

Statutory Regulations of Marriageable Age

English law after the Reformation classified the various factors involving incapacity or lack of consent to marry as either canonical or civil. The canonical disabilities were said to make marriages voidable, and included consanguinity, affinity and impotence. "Voidable" in this context apparently meant that the marriage could only be attacked during the lifetime of the parties. The civil disabilities included age, prior marriage, insanity and perhaps fraud and duress, and these defects were said to make the marriages void, meaning that an attack could be made upon them even after the death of a party. See 1 Bishop, Marriage, Divorce and Separation, 112, 113 (1891); Elliott v. Gurr, 2 Phill.Ecc. 16, 161 Eng.Rep. 1064 (1812); and Tolstoy, Void and Voidable Marriages, 27 Mod.L.Rev. 385, 387 (1964). The void-voidable distinction was carried over and survived in American marriage law to a substantial extent, although the terms void and voidable may carry meanings quite different from those of early English law. These terms raise particularly troublesome questions in connection with attacks on marriage for nonage. The student, as he reads the cases, should be concerned with (a) what is meant by calling a marriage void or voidable; and (b) whether these labels may sensibly be applied in specific cases.

By the Engish law before the settlement of the United States, a child under 7 was held entirely incapable of contracting a marriage, any attempt to do so being deemed void. At the age of seven the child might consent, but the marriage continued inchoate and imperfect until the age of 14 for boys and 12 for girls. The effect of this was that during the interval between 7 and either 14 or 12 the party could declare the marriage void without obtaining a decree of nullity. This was the limited meaning of "void" in that context. If the marriage were not declared void, it became valid and unassailable when the ages of 14 and 12 were reached.

Today the marriageable ages have changed in two ways. Statutes generally set higher ages for marriage, and they establish the same age for the marriage of males and females. The consensus seems to be that people should be permitted to marry at age eighteen. See, e. g., Ariz.Rev.Stat.Ann. § 25–102 (1976); Cal.Civ.Code § 4101 (Supp.1978); Minn.Stat.Ann. § 517.02 (Supp.1979); N.Y.Dom.Rel.L. §§ 7, 15 (1964 and Supp.1978); Tex.Fam.Code Ann. § 1.51 (Supp. 1978–1979); Utah Code Ann. § 30–1–9 (Supp.1977). The Uniform Marriage and Divorce Act §§ 203, 208, 9A Unif.L.Ann. 102, 110 (1979) likewise sets the marriageable age at eighteen. The statutes in the very few states which continue to set different ages for the marriages of men and women are probably unconstitutional under Stanton v. Stanton, 421 U.S. 7 (1975), which held that a Utah statute was unconstitutional when it provided that the age of majority for males was twenty-one and for females eighteen, for purposes of requiring support by their parents. See also Phelps v. Bing, 58 Ill.2d 32, 316 N.E.2d 775 (1974).

The nearly universal adoption of eighteen as the minimum age for marriage in the various states was perhaps related to the passage of the Twenty-Sixth Amendment to the United States Constitution, which lowered the voting age to eighteen, and to the widespread sentimentality with which youth was treated in the late 1960's and early 1970's. It reflects a somewhat dubious social policy, in view of the statistics which show that the highest divorce rate is for those who marry between ages fifteen and nineteen or, in other words, that the stability of marriages is generally less for youthful marriages, Furlong, Youthful Marriage and Parenthood: A Threat to Family Stability, 19 Hastings L.J. 105, 109 (1967); H. Carter and P. Glick, Marriage and Divorce: A Social and Economic Study, 235, 236 (1970), and in view of the fact that a sensible population policy in our present state of over-population dictates postponing marriages rather than encouraging earlier ones.

The nonage statutes also frequently require, for persons below certain ages, but above the statutory age limit for valid marriage, consent of a parent or guardian. The consent may have to be given in writing and with prescribed formalities. See, e. g., Ariz.Rev.Stat. Ann. § 25–102 (1976); Colo.Rev.Stat.Ann. § 14–2–106 (1973); Mass. Ann.L. ch. 207, § 7 (Supp.1978); N.Y.Dom.Rel.L. §§ 7, 15 (1977). The Uniform Marriage and Divorce Act, § 208, 9A Unif.L.Ann. 110 (1979), requires the consent of a parent or guardian if the person seeking to be married is sixteen or seventeen years of age. Requirements of this sort are usually made a condition upon obtaining a marriage license, and for this reason the cases hold that failure to get the parent's consent does not invalidate the marriage, so long as the parties are above the minimum marriageable age. Noble v. Noble, 299 Mich. 565, 300 N.W. 885 (1941); Needam v. Needam, 183 Va. 681, 33 S.E.2d 288 (1943), 31 Va.L.Rev. 210 (1944). Lack of parents' consent does invalidate the marriage under the Uniform Marriage and Divorce Act § 208(b)(3), however.

Under the statutes of some states the minimum age for marriage may be waived by order of a court, the usual ground for this being the woman's pregnancy. See, e. g., Ga.Code Ann. § 53–102 (Supp. 1978); Burns' Ind.Stat.Ann. § 31–1–1–1 (Supp.1978); N.C.Gen.Stat. § 51–2 (1976). The Uniform Marriage and Divorce Act §§ 205, 208, 9A Unif.L.Ann. 105, 110 (1979), provides that a person under sixteen may marry with the consent of parents or guardian and the approval of a court. The court may only approve the marriage if it finds the underage party is able to assume the responsibilities of marriage and that the marriage will serve his best interests. The Act specifically provides that pregnancy alone does not establish that the party's best interests will be served. This recognizes the obvious fact that premarital pregnancy does not of itself constitute a good reason for marrying, notwithstanding older notions about "giving the child a name".

The California statute also provides that a person under eighteen must have both the parents' consent and court approval in order to marry. If the court deems it necessary, it may condition approval upon the underage party's engaging in premarital counselling concerning the responsibilities of marriage. Cal.Civ.Code § 4101 (Supp.1979). Does this requirement of counselling survive the constitutional doctrines of Griswold, supra, page 73, and Zablocki, supra, page 83?

It is usually held that the child need not wait to reach full age before suing to annul his marriage on the ground of nonage. In re Anonymous, 32 N.J.Super. 599, 108 A.2d 882 (1954). The child himself is the real party plaintiff in such cases, but under the practice in many states the child sues "by his next friend", generally a parent. Unless a statute expressly authorizes it, the parent cannot bring the action in his own name, however. Kirby v. Gilliam, 182 Va. 111, 28

S.E.2d 40 (1943). Statutes which do authorize the parent to sue include Cal.Civ.Code § 4426(a) (1970); N.Y.Dom.Rel.L. § 140(1977); and Uniform Marriage and Divorce Act § 208(b)(3), 9A Unif.L.Ann. 110 (1979).

Difficult questions of the conflict of laws have arisen where underage marriages are contracted in a state other than that of the parties' domicile. One such case, Wilkins v. Zelichowski, 26 N.J. 370, 140 A.2d 65 (1958), held that where the parties lived in New Jersey, where the woman was too young to contract a valid marriage, but ran away to Indiana and contracted a marriage which was valid by Indiana law, New Jersey would grant the woman an annulment. The court recognized that its result was contrary to the usual rule that the law of the place where the marriage is contracted controls its validity, but said that its result was consistent with New Jersey's policy of protecting its young people against the tragic consequences of such immature conduct. A case reaching the other result is State v. Graves, 228 Ark. 378, 307 S.W.2d 545 (1957). The conflicts cases are extensively cited and discussed in Annot., 71 A.L.R.2d 687 (1960); Baade, Marriage and Divorce in American Conflicts Law: Governmental-Interests Analysis and the Restatement (Second), 72 Colum. L.Rev. 329, 358–360 (1972); Mpiliris v. Hellenic Lines, Ltd., 323 F. Supp. 865, 876 (S.D.Tex.1970), aff'd p.c. 440 F.2d 1163 (5th Cir. 1971); Restatement, Second, Conflict of Laws § 283 (1971); A. Ehrenzweig, Conflict of Laws 376–387 (1962).

NOTES AND QUESTIONS

1. By the statutes of most states the marriage of a person who is under age is characterized as voidable, at least where the age is in the range of 16 to 20. In a few states the statute provides that the marriage of a person under age is void. For example Mich.Stat.Ann. § 25.21 (1974) states that the marriage of a female under 16 is void. N.H.Rev.Stat.Ann. § 457:4 (1968) states that a marriage of a male under 14 or a female under 13 is null and void. If the marriage is "void", at least one case has held that a spouse who is over the statutory age may have it annulled where the other spouse is under age, Evans v. Ross, 309 Mich. 149, 14 N.W.2d 815 (1944), although this seems clearly wrong in terms of the policy underlying the statute. And even though the marriage is labeled void by the statute, it should be capable of ratification if the parties live together beyond the statutory age. Cf. Powell v. Powell, 97 N.H. 301, 86 A.2d 331 (1952).

Some other questions of greater difficulty may be raised, however:

(a) Where the marriage is labeled "void" by the statute, what should be the result if the spouse under age sued the spouse over age for nonsupport? Could the adult spouse attack the marriage as non-existent and thereby avoid any support liability?

(b) Where the marriage is "void" under the statute, what would be the result if a girl, under age, married a man of 22, and after they had been married one month he was killed in an automobile accident? Could his collateral relatives prevent her from taking his estate by intestacy, on the ground the marriage was "void", i. e. non-existent?

(c) What does "void" mean in this context?

2. In those jurisdictions, the great majority, where the marriage of a person under the specified age is "voidable", what should be the result in the following cases:

(a) H, 17, married W, 20. The statutory age of consent to marry is 18. H obtained a marriage license by lying to the clerk about his age. He also lied about his age to the minister who married them. At the time of his marriage H was emancipated and held a full-time job, the wages from which were adequate to support him and his wife. H and W lived together in an apartment, which H had obtained, for about six months. At the end of that time, H still being 17, H met another girl, X, became strongly attracted to her, and moved out of his apartment and began living with X. When W protested at this, H sued her for annulment. W filed a counterclaim for divorce. What arguments should be made for H and for W? What should be the result? Cf. Ruiz v. Ruiz, 6 Cal.App.3d 58, 85 Cal.Rptr. 674 (1970); Duley v. Duley, 151 A.2d 255 (D.C.Mun.Ct.App.1959). What should be the result on these facts under § 208 of the Uniform Marriage and Divorce Act, which provides, "The * * * court shall enter its decree declaring the invalidity of a marriage entered into under the following circumstances:", including among the circumstances a marriage by a person 16 or 17 years old without parental consent or judicial approval? Assume no such consent or approval was obtained here.

(b) H, 17 years old, married W, 28. He obtained a marriage license by lying to the clerk about his age and presenting forged papers which showed him to be 18. H's parents knew nothing of his marriage until after it occurred. They then attempted to persuade H that the marriage was a mistake and that he should have it annulled. He refused, saying he loved W, and wished to remain married to her. His parents then brought suit for a declaration of invalidity of the marriage. Assume the Uniform Marriage and Divorce Act applies, containing the provision quoted in paragraph (a) above, and also the following: "A declaration of invalidity * * * may be sought by any of the following persons * * *: (3) for the reason set forth in subsection (a)(3), by the underaged party, his parent or guardian, prior to the time the underaged party reaches the age at which he could have married without satisfying the omitted requirement." Should H be made a party defendant in the case? What arguments should be made on behalf of H and of his parents? What should be the result?

8. Mr. and Mrs. John Smith, residents of Holmes, an imaginary state of the United States, consult you, giving you the following information and asking your advice: They have a daughter Jane, 15 years old, a high school student. She has been going steady with Tom Jones, who is 18 and also in high school. They have just learned that Jane is pregnant, and that, by her account at least, only Tom could be the father of the child. Both Jane and Tom are eager to be married. Holmes has the Uniform Marriage and Divorce Act, which provides, in § 205, that a person under the age of 16 may marry if he or she has the consent of both parents and also if a court finds that he or she is capable of assuming the responsibilities of marriage and the marriage would serve his or her best interests. It also provides that pregnancy alone does not establish that the best interests of the party

would be served. Mr. and Mrs. Smith have learned that the law of the nearby state of Maryland (Md.Code Ann. art. 62, § 9 (Supp.1978)) is that a person under 16 may be married with consent of both parents upon certification by a physician that the girl is pregnant. Mr. Smith is very reluctant to give his consent to such a marriage, while Mrs. Smith thinks Tom and Jane should marry and is willing to give her consent.

Holmes also has a statute on juvenile delinquency, which provides that the commission of any act by a person under 18 which, if committed by an adult, would constitute a crime amounts to delinquency, and also provides that any person under 18 who so behaves as to injure or endanger the morals or health of himself or others is a juvenile delinquent. Holmes' criminal law makes it a crime for one to have sexual intercourse with a person not his spouse. Finally, the Holmes statute imposing criminal penalties on adults for contributing to delinquency of persons under eighteen provides, "No person shall aid, abet, cause, encourage or contribute to the dependency or delinquency of a child under 18 or act in any way tending to cause delinquency."

How would you advise Mr. and Mrs. Smith? Whom do you represent in such a case? In thinking about this problem you might consider the availability of abortion and the possibility of placing Jane's baby for adoption. Cf. State v. Gans, 168 Ohio St. 174, 151 N.E.2d 709 (1958); State of New Jersey in the Interest of S. I., 68 N.J.Super. 598, 173 A.2d 457 (Juv. and Dom.Rel.Ct.1961); People v. Benu, 87 Misc.2d 139, 385 N.Y.S.2d 222 (Crim.Ct.1976); Annots., 68 A.L.R.2d 745 (1959), 84 A.L.R.2d 1254 (1962).

C. MENTAL INCOMPETENCE

Mental incompetence is generally a disqualification for marriage in the United States, the rule being expressed in statutes which make it a ground for annulment. The statutes label the disqualification in a variety of ways as insanity, idiocy, lunacy and other unscientific and old-fashioned terms. See, e. g., Mich.Stat.Ann. § 25.81 (1974). In the hands of the courts, however, most of the terms come to about the same thing, which is that a person may not marry if he so lacks understanding as to be incapable of assenting to the marriage. A few statutes express this requirement. N.Y.Dom.Rel.L. § 7(2) (1977); Wis.Stat.Ann. § 247.03(1) (Supp.1979–1980); Uniform Marriage and Divorce Act § 208(a)(1) (mental incapacity). Or, as a leading case put it, " * * * if the party possesses sufficient mental capacity to understand the nature, effect, duties, and obligations of the marriage contract into which he or she is entering, the marriage contract is binding, * * * " Larson v. Larson, 42 Ill.App.2d 467, 192 N.E.2d 594 (1963). The standard is a rather low one, however, as the *Larson* case demonstrates, since the marriage there was upheld even though the wife had had a history of mental illness, with several commitments to institutions. In Johnson v. Johnson, 104 N.W.2d 8 (N.D.1960) the marriage was upheld even though the spouse was concededly incompetent to manage his business affairs. The extraordinary case of DeMedio v. DeMedio, 215 Pa.Super. 255, 257 A.2d 290 (1969) seems to hold that there must be evidence of mental incompetence at the time of the wedding ceremony, not before or after that moment, before a marriage can be annulled on this ground. Other cases are collected in McCurdy, Insanity as a Ground for Annulment or Divorce in English and American Law, 29 Va.L.Rev. 771 (1943), and Note, 15 Syra.L.Rev. 42 (1963).

The policy underlying these statutes and the cases which apply them is obviously the prevention of marriages where one of the parties is incapable of giving an understanding consent to the responsibilities of marriage. Another possible policy, that of preventing marriages where one of the parties is incapable of carrying out those responsibilities, including the responsibility of caring for children, seems generally ignored, except possibly in the Pennsylvania statute which forbids a marriage license to be issued to mental incompetents unless a judge finds its issuance is in the best interests of the applicant and of the public. Pa.Stat.Ann. art. 48, § 1–5 (Supp.1979–1980).

In the somewhat similar situation, where a person is so intoxicated that he is unable to understand the nature and consequences of a marriage ceremony, or where he is in that condition as the result of drug use, he may have the marriage annulled. Dobson v. Dobson, 86 Cal.App.2d 13, 193 P.2d 794 (1948), and cases cited in Annot., 57 A.L. R.2d 1246 (1958).

The void-voidable distinction has caused the same sort of confusion and meaningless discussion in relation to the marriages of insane persons as where nonage is concerned. For example, Mich.Stat.Ann. § 25.81 (1974) makes the marriage of an insane person or an "idiot" "absolutely void". At common law the marriage of an insane person was held void. Wightman v. Wightman, 4 Johns.Ch. 343 (N.Y.1820). This seems to mean in consequence that the marriage may be attacked by either spouse or by a third person either collaterally or directly and would not be ratifiable even by cohabitation after the mental illness was cured. See Ivery v. Ivery, 258 N.C. 721, 129 S.E.2d 457 (1963). Presumably some courts would not give "void" its full meaning in such situations, but one cannot be sure. In any event, this gives the insane party little protection, which is quite inconsistent with those divorce statutes which list insanity as a ground for divorce, since they generally provide many safeguards for the rights of the insane party. There is little point in protecting the mental incompetent in a divorce action but not in an annulment action. The Washington Court recognizes this by making divorce the exclusive remedy, Saville v. Saville, 44 Wash.2d 793, 271 P.2d 432 (1954) and Jones v. Minc, 77 Wash.2d 381, 462 P.2d 927 (1969).

On the other hand, marriages of insane persons are described as merely voidable by the statutes of some jurisdictions. E. g., Cal.Civ. Code § 4425 (1970); N.Y.Dom.Rel.L. § 7(2) (1977). Patey v. Peaslee, 99 N.H. 335, 111 A.2d 194 (1955), held that in such circumstances the marriage could not be attacked after the death of one of the parties. Annot., 47 A.L.R.2d 1388 (1955). Where the marriage is voidable, it has been held that the competent party may not sue for annulment. Hoadley v. Hoadley, 244 N.Y. 424, 155 N.E. 728 (1927).

In general more satisfactory results are attained if the statute omits the void-voidable distinction and deals specifically and directly with the issues of parties, collateral attack, death of a spouse and similar problems. Draft statutes which do this are Vernon, Annulment of Marriages in New Mexico: Part II—Proposed Statute, 2 Nat.Res.J. 270, 283 (1962), and Uniform Marriage and Divorce Act, § 208. It should also be remembered that a divorce statute which is not limited to the traditional grounds based upon fault, but includes broad non-fault grounds enables the courts and parties to avoid some of the hardships of the technical annulment rules.

For a complete citation of the various state statutes on mental incompetency, see Note, The Right of the Mentally Disabled to Marry: A Statutory Evaluation, 15 J.Fam.L. 463 (1977). For further discussion of mental incompetence and marriage, see H. Clark, Law of Domestic Relations § 2.15 (1968).

D. IMPOTENCE AND OTHER CONDITIONS OF HEALTH

The impotence of either party was a canonical disability making their marriage voidable according to the English ecclesiastical law. In this country by statute impotence is made a ground for annulment in most states, the statutes usually providing that the impotence must be incurable and must arise from physical causes. Impotence in this context means the inability to engage in sexual intercourse. Sterility or barrenness, the inability to have children, is not impotence. Notwithstanding the requirement that the impotence must proceed from physical causes, several cases have held that impotence arising from psychogenic causes, if incurable, is a ground for annulment. The leading case is Tompkins v. Tompkins, 92 N.J.Eq. 113, 111 A. 599 (1920), granting the annulment where the impotence was psychogenic in origin and pertained solely to the spouse. See also Rickards v. Rickards, 3 Storey (50 Del.) 134, 166 A.2d 425 (Del.1960) and Helen v. Thomas, 2 Storey (52 Del.) 1, 150 A.2d 833 (1959). An interesting case brought under N.J.Stat.Ann. § 2A:34–1(c) (Supp.1979–1980) which requires that the impotence be "physical", held that the impotence of the wife, proceeding from vaginismus of apparently psychological origins could be the basis for annulment even though the wife had become pregnant and had miscarried. T v. M, 100 N.J.Super. 530, 242 A.2d 670 (1968).

The requirement that impotence be incurable may cause the court to deny annulment where the only evidence is that for a given time the defendant was unable to engage in intercourse. This was the case in Dolan v. Dolan, 259 A.2d 32 (Me.1969). But there is an old common law rule that failure to consummate the marriage for three years creates a presumption of impotence, or as some authorities put it, persistent refusal to consummate is evidence of impotence. Annot., 28 A.L.R.2d 499, 514 (1953).

Since it is generally held that impotence makes the marriage voidable only, it may only be attacked directly in a suit to annul, not collaterally. There is some authority that the impotent party may get the annulment if he or she did not know of the impotence before marriage. D v. C, 91 N.J.Super. 562, 221 A.2d 763 (1966), 52 Iowa L.Rev. 767 (1967). If the plaintiff knew of the impotence, or if he continued to live with the defendant for a long time after learning of the condition, the annulment will be denied. D v. D, 2 Terry (41 Del.) 263, 20 A.2d 139 (1941); Annot., 15 A.L.R.2d 706 (1951). The Uniform Marriage and Divorce Act, § 208(a)(2) and (b)(2), 9A Unif.L.Ann. 110 (1979), authorizes a declaration of invalidity of the marriage where a party lacks physical capacity to consummate, permits the suit to be brought by either spouse, but requires it to be brought no later than one year after the petitioner learns of the impotence.

Many states have statutes requiring tests for venereal disease as a condition on obtaining a marriage license. Although a few of them go on to provide that marriages contracted in violation of such statutes are invalid, in most states non-compliance with the statute would not affect the validity of the marriage. A few states impose other conditions relating to health upon entry into marriage, by forbidding the marriage of epileptics, or persons having pulmonary tuberculosis. See H. Clark, Law of Domestic Relations, §§ 2.10, 2.11 (1968). Are such statutes constitutional under the *Griswold* and *Zablocki* cases, supra, pages 73 and 83?

E. MISCEGENATION

In 1967 there were sixteen states in which statutes prohibited inter-racial marriages, a small remnant of a much larger group of states which had earlier enacted such legislation. All such statutes were declared unconstitutional in that year by Loving v. Virginia, 388 U.S. 1 (1967). That case had been foreshadowed by McLaughlin v. Florida, 379 U.S. 184 (1964), which held unconstitutional a Florida criminal statute imposing penalties for the habitual occupation of a room at night by a negro and a white person who were not married. Much earlier the landmark case of Perez v. Lippold, 32 Cal.2d 711, 198 P.2d 17 (1948), 58 Yale L.J. 472 (1949), had held that the California miscegenation statute violated both the Equal Protection Clause of the Fourteenth Amendment and the Religious Freedom Clause of the First Amendment to the United States Constitution.

Although miscegenation statutes are therefore past history in the United States, they may still on occasion have harsh effects. For example, Vetrano v. Gardner, 290 F.Supp. 200 (N.D.Miss.1968) held that no common law marriage had been contracted in Mississippi because the parties (a black woman and a white man) had not openly cohabited as husband and wife. At the time of their alleged common law marriage such cohabitation would have been criminal under the Mississippi miscegenation statute, and so they had been forced to keep their relationship secret. The result was a denial of certain social security benefits. The implication is that if they had so cohabited, their marriage would have been validated by the subsequent holding that the miscegenation statute was unconstitutional. The case thus for a limited purpose gives *Loving* a retroactive application, since it seems to say that a miscegenous common law marriage contracted in Mississippi before *Loving* would be valid if the usual elements of a common law marriage occur. It goes on to take what seems an unnecessarily strict view of common law marriage, however, by imposing upon the parties a standard of conduct which would have caused them to incur both prohibitive social sanctions and criminal penalties.

Interracial marriage has been relatively rare between white and black persons, at least before *Loving*. Even before that case, there were many states in which there was no legal impediment to such marriages, and yet they were not numerous. H. Carter and P. Glick, Marriage and Divorce: A Social and Economic Study, 117–129 (1970). Marriages involving "other races" have been more common. The effect of *Loving*, and of other changes in white-black relations, may be to increase the numbers of marriages between blacks and whites, however. Such marriages still face pervasive and forbidding prejudices in both white and black communities throughout the United States. See, e. g., Furlong, Interracial Marriage is a Sometime Thing, New York Times Magazine, June 9, 1968, page 44, describing in detail the difficulties faced by people in mixed marriages.

Problem on Miscegenation

H and W were domiciled in Virginia. In 1964 they decided to get married and since H was a black man and W a white woman, and since Virginia had a statute prohibiting and making void interracial marriages, they went to the District of Columbia which had no such statute, and went through a marriage ceremony which complied in all respects with the law of the District of Columbia, intending to return to Virginia to live immediately after the ceremony. They did return and lived together secretly in Virginia for a short time, but their marriage was not a success. In 1965 H sued for and obtained an annulment on the ground that the marriage was void under the Virginia miscegenation statute. A year or so later H contracted a second marriage in Virginia to a black woman. In 1968, after the decision in Loving v. Virginia, 388 U.S. 1 (1967), W found herself in needy circumstances. She learned that H had prospered greatly and sued him for non-support, alleging that they were still married.

(a) Assuming that the foregoing facts are proved, and that Virginia law gives a wife the right to be supported by her husband when she is in need, and that this right is enforceable in a direct civil suit against him, what should be the result? See Naim v. Naim, 197 Va. 80, 87 S.E.2d 749 (1955), remanded 350 U.S. 891 (1955), adherence to former decision, 197 Va. 734, 90 S.E.2d 849 (1956), motion to set case down for oral argument on the merits denied 350 U.S. 985 (1956); Norton v. Shelby County, 118 U.S. 425, 442 (1886); Chicot County Drainage District v. Baxter State Bank, 308 U.S. 371, 374 (1940), Note 42 Yale L.J. 779 (1933); Coleman v. Mitnick, 137 Ind. App. 125, 202 N.E.2d 577 (1964), petition for rehearing denied 137 Ind.App. 125, 203 N.E.2d 834 (1965); Linkletter v. Walker, 381 U.S. 618, 622–629 (1965); Wellington, Common Law Rules and Constitutional Double Standards: Some Notes on Adjudication, 83 Yale L.J. 221, 254–261 (1973).

(b) Assume that the marriage occurred under the circumstances outlined above, but that instead of obtaining an annulment, H just left W, upon the advice of his lawyer, who told him that an interracial marriage was void in Virginia when contracted in another state for the purpose of evading the domicile's miscegenation statute. If W should then sue H for non-support, after H had married a second time, and after the decision in *Loving*, what result? Would H be a bigamist?

(c) Assume that the marriage occurred under the circumstances outlined above, but that H and W lived together as husband and wife until 1972, at which time H died intestate, leaving considerable property. In a contest between W and H's collateral relatives over H's estate, who should prevail?

F. CONSANGUINITY OR AFFINITY

IN RE MAY'S ESTATE

Court of Appeals of New York, 1953.
305 N.Y. 486, 114 N.E.2d 4.

LEWIS, Chief Judge. In this proceeding, involving the administration of the estate of Fannie May, deceased, we are to determine whether the marriage in 1913 between the respondent Sam May and the decedent, who was his niece by the half blood—which marriage was celebrated in Rhode Island, where concededly such marriage is valid—is to be given legal effect in New York where statute law declares incestuous and void a marriage between uncle and niece. Domestic Relations Law, § 5. * * *

The question thus presented arises from proof of the following facts: The petitioner Alice May Greenberg, one of six children born of the Rhode Island marriage of Sam and Fannie May, petitioned in 1951 for letters of administration of the estate of her mother Fannie May, who had died in 1945. Thereupon, the respondent Sam May, who asserts the validity of his marriage to the decedent, filed an objection to the issuance to petitioner of such letters of administration upon the ground that he is the surviving husband of the decedent and accordingly, under section 118 of the Surrogate's Court Act, he has the paramount right to administer her estate. Contemporaneously with, and in support of the objection filed by Sam May, his daughter Sirel Lenrow and his sons Harry May and Morris B. May—who are children of the challenged marriage—filed objections to the issuance of letters of administration to their sister, the petitioner, and by such objections consented that letters of administration be issued to their father Sam May. .

The petitioner, supported by her sisters Ruth Weisbrout and Evelyn May, contended throughout this proceeding that her father is not the surviving spouse of her mother because, although their marriage was valid in Rhode Island, the marriage never had validity in New York where they were then resident and where they retained their residence until the decedent's death.

The record shows that for a period of more than five years prior to his marriage to decedent the respondent Sam May had resided in Portage, Wisconsin; that he came to New York in December, 1912, and within a month thereafter he and the decedent—both of whom were adherents of the Jewish faith—went to Providence, Rhode Island, where, on January 21, 1913, they entered into a ceremonial marriage performed by and at the home of a Jewish rabbi. The certificate issued upon that marriage gave the age of each party as twenty-six years and the residence of each as "New York, N.Y." Two weeks after their marriage in Rhode Island the respondent May and the decedent returned to Ulster County, New York, where they lived as man and wife for thirty-two years until the decedent's death in 1945. Meantime the six children were born who are parties to this proceeding.

A further significant item of proof—to which more particular reference will be made—was the fact that in Rhode Island on January 21, 1913, the date of the marriage here involved, there were effective statutes which prohibited, the marriage of an uncle and a niece, *excluding,* however, those instances—of which the present case is one—where the marriage solemnized is between persons of the Jewish faith within the degrees of affinity and consanguinity allowed by their religion.

In Surrogate's Court, where letters of administration were granted to the petitioner, the Surrogate ruled that although the marriage of Sam May and the decedent in Rhode Island in 1913 was valid in that State, such marriage was not only void in New York as opposed to natural law but is contrary to the provisions of subdivision 3 of section 5 of the Domestic Relations Law. Accordingly the Surrogate concluded that Sam May did not qualify in this jurisdiction for letters of administration as the surviving spouse of the decedent.

At the Appellate Division the order of the Surrogate was reversed on the law and the proceeding was remitted to Surrogate's Court with direction that letters of administration upon decedent's estate be granted to Sam May who was held to be the surviving spouse of the decedent. * * *

We regard the law as settled that, subject to two exceptions presently to be considered, and in the absence of a statute expressly regulating within the domiciliary State marriages solemnized abroad, the legality of a marriage between persons *sui juris* is to be determined by the law of the place where it is celebrated. * * *

In Van Voorhis v. Brintnall, the decision turned upon the civil status in this State of a divorced husband and his second wife whom he had married in Connecticut to evade the prohibition of a judgment of divorce which, pursuant to New York law then prevailing, forbade his remarriage until the death of his former wife. In reaching its decision, which held valid the Connecticut marriage there involved, this court noted the fact that in the much earlier case of Decouche v. Savetier, 3 Johns.Ch. 190, 211 (1817), Chancellor Kent had recognized the general principle " * * * that the rights dependent upon nuptial contracts, are to be determined by the *lex loci*." Incidental to the decision in Van Voorhis v. Brintnall, supra, which followed the general rule that " * * * recognizes as valid a marriage considered valid in the place where celebrated", Id., 86 N.Y. at page 25, this court gave careful consideration to, and held against the application of two exceptions to that rule—viz., cases within the prohibition of positive law; and cases involving polygamy or incest in a degree regarded generally as within the prohibition of natural law.

We think the Appellate Division in the case at bar rightly held that the principle of law which ruled Van Voorhis v. Brintnall and kindred cases cited, supra, was decisive of the present case and that neither of the two exceptions to that general rule is here applicable.

The statute of New York upon which the appellants rely is subdivision 3 of section 5 of the Domestic Relations Law which, insofar as relevant to our problem, provides:

"§ 5.   *Incestuous and void marriages*

"A marriage is incestuous and void whether the relatives are legitimate or illegitimate between either:

"1. * * *

"2. * * *

"3.   An uncle and niece or an aunt and nephew. * * *"

Although the New York statute quoted above declares to be incestuous and void a marriage between an uncle and a niece and imposes penal measures upon the parties thereto, it is important to note that the statute does not by express terms regulate a marriage solemnized in another State where, as in our present case, the marriage was concededly legal. In the case at hand, as we have seen, the parties to the challenged marriage were adherents of the Jewish faith which, according to Biblical law and Jewish tradition—made the subject of proof in this case—permits a marriage between an uncle and a niece; they were married by a Jewish rabbi in the State of Rhode Island where, on the date of such marriage in 1913 and ever since, a statute forbidding the marriage of an uncle and a niece was expressly qualified by the following statutory exceptions appearing in 1913 in Rhode Island General Laws, tit. XXIV, ch. 243, §§ 4, 9; now tit. XXXVI, ch. 415, §§ 4, 9:

"§ 4. The provisions of the preceding sections shall not extend to, or in any way affect, any marriage which shall be solemnized among the Jews, within the degrees of affinity or consanguinity allowed by their religion."

*   *   *

As section 5 of the New York Domestic Relations Law (quoted supra) does not expressly declare void a marriage of its domiciliaries solemnized in a foreign State where such marriage is valid, the statute's scope should not be extended by judicial construction. *   *   * Indeed, had the Legislature been so disposed it could have declared by appropriate enactment that marriages contracted in another State— which if entered into here would be void—shall have no force in this State. *   *   * Although examples of such legislation are not wanting, we find none in New York which serve to give subdivision 3 of section 5 of the Domestic Relations Law extraterritorial effectiveness. *   *   * Accordingly, as to the first exception to the general rule that a marriage valid where performed is valid everywhere, we conclude that, absent any New York statute expressing clearly the Legislature's intent to regulate within this State marriages of its domiciliaries solemnized abroad, there is no "positive law" in this jurisdiction which serves to interdict the 1913 marriage in Rhode Island of the respondent Sam May and the decedent.

As to the application of the second exception to the marriage here involved—between persons of the Jewish faith whose kinship was not in the direct ascending or descending line of consanguinity and who were not brother and sister—we conclude that such marriage, solemnized, as it was, in accord with the ritual of the Jewish faith in a State whose legislative body has declared such a marriage to be "good and valid in law", was not offensive to the public sense of morality to a degree regarded generally with abhorrence and thus was not within the inhibitions of natural law.

*   *   *

The decree of the Surrogate's Court should be affirmed, with one bill of costs to respondents, payable out of the estate.

DESMOND, Judge (dissenting). It is fundamental that every State has the right to determine the marital status of its own citizens. * * * Exercising that right, New York has declared in section 5 of the Domestic Relations Law that a marriage between uncle and niece is incestuous, void and criminal. Such marriages, while not within the Levitical forbidden degrees of the Old Testament, have been condemned by public opinion for centuries * * *, and are void, by statute in (it would seem) forty-seven of the States of the Union (all except Georgia, * * * and except, also, that Rhode Island, one of the forty-seven, exempts from its local statute "any marriage which shall be solemnized among the Jews, within the degrees of affinity or consanguinity allowed by their religion", Gen.L. of R. I., ch. 415, § 4). It is undisputed here that this uncle and niece were both domiciled in New York in 1913, when they left New York for the sole purpose of going to Rhode Island to be married there, and that they were married in that State conformably to its laws (see above) and immediately returned to New York and ever afterwards resided in this State. That Rhode Island marriage between two New York residents, was, in New York, absolutely void for any and all purposes, by positive New York law which declares a strong public policy of this State. * * *

The general rule that "a marriage valid were solemnized is valid everywhere" (see Restatement, Conflict of Laws, § 121) does not apply. To that rule there is a proviso or exception, recognized, it would seem, by all the States as follows: "unless contrary to the prohibitions of natural law or the express prohibitions of a statute". * * * New York, as a sovereign State with absolute powers over the marital status of its citizens, has enacted such legislation, but we, by this decision, are denying it efficacy.

* * * This court's opinion in the *Van Voorhis* case, while stating the general rule that the validity of a marriage depends on the law of the place of marriage, noted that there are exceptions thereto in cases of incest within the prohibition of natural law, and "prohibition by positive law". * * * Section 5 of the Domestic Relations Law, the one we are concerned with here, lists the marriages which are "incestuous and void" in New York, as being those between parent and child, brother and sister, uncle and niece, and aunt and nephew. All such misalliances are incestuous, and all, equally, are void. The policy, language, meaning and validity of the statute are beyond dispute. It should be enforced by the courts.

* * *

NOTES AND QUESTIONS

1. The Rhode Island statute permitting Jews to contract marriages within the degrees of relationship permitted by their religion is now R.I. Gen.L. § 15–1–4 (1970). Does this statute violate the United States Constitution under the *Griswold* and *Zablocki* cases, supra, pages 73 and 83?

2. The Uniform Marriage and Divorce Act § 207, 9A Unif.L.Ann. 108 (1979), also forbids uncle-niece and aunt-nephew marriages, "except

* * * marriages permitted by the established customs of aboriginal cultures". Does this violate the principles of the *Griswold* and *Zablocki* cases, or of Loving v. Virginia, 388 U.S. 1 (1967)?

3. The present New York provision on incestuous marriage is N.Y. Dom.Rel.L. § 5 (1977), reading as follows:

"§ 5. Incestuous and void marriages

"A marriage is incestuous and void whether the relatives are legitimate or illegitimate between either:

"1. An ancestor and a descendant;

"2. A brother and sister of either the whole or the half blood;

"3. An uncle and niece or an aunt and nephew.

"If a marriage prohibited by the foregoing provisions of this section be solemnized it shall be void, and the parties thereto shall each be fined not less than fifty nor more than one hundred dollars and may, in the discretion of the court in addition to said fine, be imprisoned for a term not exceeding six months. Any person who shall knowingly and wilfully solemnize such marriage, or procure or aid in the solemnization of the same, shall be deemed guilty of a misdemeanor and shall be fined or imprisoned in like manner. L.1909, c. 19."

The California law, Cal.Civ.Code § 4400 (1970) is similar.

4. What social purpose is served by the New York prohibition against the marriage of uncle and niece? Does the result in the *May* case advance or frustrate that social purpose? So far as appears from the case, did the parties go to Rhode Island solely for the purpose of evading the New York prohibition on their marriage? If the New York prohibition is to be taken seriously as a reflection of some social policy, should it be avoidable by a trip to Rhode Island? Is this case inconsistent with Wilkins v. Zelichowski, supra at page 138? Can you justify the result in the *May* case on grounds other than the purpose of the statute? Cf. Restatement, Second, Conflict of Laws §§ 6, 283 (1971).

5. What should be the result if this marriage had been invalid in Rhode Island, but valid in New York?

6. What should have been the result in this case if Sam May had brought a suit against Fannie to annul their marriage a few years after their return to New York?

7. What should be the result in this case if at the time of the marriage Fannie had been domiciled in Rhode Island and Sam in New York? Restatement, Second, Conflict of Laws §§ 283, 6 (1971); Catalano v. Catalano, 148 Conn. 288, 170 A.2d 726 (1961).

8. The Uniform Marriage Evasion Act, in effect in about fifteen states, would prevent the result of the *May* case. See Wis.Stat.Ann. § 245.-04 (Supp.1979–1980), which is a slightly broader version of the Marriage Evasion Act, since it applies to marriages prohibited *or* declared void by the law of the state of residence. Which result is preferable, that of *May* or the Uniform Marriage Evasion Act?

9. All states have statutes prohibiting marriages between persons related by consanguinity, most but not all of such statutes providing that the prohibited marriages are void. But cf. Uniform Marriage and Divorce Act

§ 208(c). All statutes prohibit marriages in the ascending and descending line, between brother and sister, of the half blood as well as the whole blood, illegitimates as well as legitimates. Nearly all statutes prohibit the marriages of uncle and niece and of aunt and nephew. About half the states prohibit the marriages of first cousins, and about nineteen states prohibit marriages between persons related in various ways by affinity, that is, by marriage exclusively. See Vernon, Annulment of Marriage, 12 J.Pub.L. 143, 151 (1963).

For additional discussion of incest prohibitions, see H. Clark, Law of Domestic Relations § 2.8 (1968).

ISRAEL v. ALLEN

Supreme Court of Colorado, En Banc, 1978.
—— Colo. ——, 577 P.2d 762.

PRINGLE, Chief Justice. This is an appeal from a decision of the District Court of Jefferson County holding a provision of the Colorado Uniform Marriage Act unconstitutional as violative of equal protection of the laws. We affirm.

Plaintiffs, Martin Richard Israel and Tammy Lee Bannon Israel, are brother and sister related by adoption and are not related by either the half or the whole blood.

Raymond Israel (the natural father of Martin Richard Israel) and Sylvia Bannon (the natural mother of Tammy Lee Bannon Israel) were married on November 3, 1972. At the time of their marriage, Martin was 18 years of age and was living in the State of Washington; Tammy was 13 years of age and was living with her mother in Denver, Colorado. Raymond Israel adopted Tammy on January 7, 1975.

Plaintiffs desire to be married in the State of Colorado. Defendant, Clerk and Recorder of Jefferson County, however, denied plaintiffs a license to marry based on section 14–2–110(1)(b), C.R.S.1973:

"*Prohibited marriages.* (1) The following marriages are prohibited: * * * (b) A marriage between an ancestor and a descendant or between a brother and sister, whether the relationship is by the half or the whole blood or by adoption; * * *".

A complaint seeking declaratory relief was filed in the district court. The district court found that marriage is a fundamental right and that no compelling state interest is furthered by prohibiting marriage between a brother and sister related only by adoption. Thus, the court held that that part of section 14–2–110(1)(b) which prohibited the marriage of a brother and sister by adoption was unconstitutional as a denial of equal protection and, therefore, severed from the statute the words "or by adoption."

I

At the outset, there is an issue as to whether or not marriage is a fundamental right in Colorado. If it is, defendant must show a compelling state interest in order to justify the unequal treatment of adopted brothers and sisters under the statute. Since we find, however, that the provision prohibiting marriage between adopted children fails even to satisfy minimum rationality requirements, we need not determine whether a fundamental right is infringed by this statute.

While the practice of adoption is an ancient one, the legal regulation of adoptive relationships in our society is strictly statutory in nature. The legislative intent in promulgating statutes concerning adoption was, in part, to make the law affecting adopted children in respect to equality of inheritance and parental duties *in pari materia* with that affecting natural children. It is clear, however, that adopted children are not engrafted upon their adoptive families for all purposes. See, e. g., the criminal incest statute, section 18–6–301, C.R. S.1973, which does not include sexual relationships between adopted brother and sister.

Nonetheless, defendant argues that this marriage prohibition provision furthers a legitimate state interest in family harmony. See, section 14–2–102(2)(a), C.R.S.1973. We do not agree. As the instant case illustrates, it is just as likely that prohibiting marriage between brother and sister related by adoption will result in family discord.[2] While we are not, strictly speaking, dealing with an affinity based relationship in this case,[3] we find the following analysis equally applicable to the situation presently before us:

"According to the English law, relationship by affinity was an impediment to marriage to the same extent and in the same degree of consanguinity. While this principle, derived from the ecclesiastically administered canon law, still strongly persists in England, in the United States the statutory law governing the marriage relationship nowhere so sweepingly condemns the marriage of persons related only by affinity. * * * The objections that exist against consanguineous marriages are not present where the relationship is merely by affinity. The physical detriment to the offspring of persons related by blood is totally absent. The natural repugnance of people toward marriages of blood relatives, that has resulted in well-nigh uni-

2. Plaintiff's parents filed affidavits indicating that they had no objection to the proposed marriage and, in fact, were in favor of the marriage. In addition, Bishop Evans of the Roman Catholic Archdiocese of Denver filed an affidavit stating that the Church had no objection to the proposed marriage.

3. An affinity based relationship is that which one spouse because of marriage has to blood relatives of the other. Black's Law Dictionary (4th ed.).

versal moral condemnation of such marriages, is quite generally lacking in application to the union of those related only by affinity. It is difficult to construct any very logical case for the prohibition of marriage on grounds of affinity　*　*　*". 1 Vernier, American Family Laws 183.

We hold that it is just as illogical to prohibit marriage between adopted brother and sister.

II

Defendant next argues that the trial court erred in its holding that the provision of section 14–2–110(1)(b), C.R.S.1973, in question here is severable from that portion of section 14–2–110(1)(b), C.R.S. 1973, prohibiting marriage between a brother and sister related by the half or whole blood. We disagree.

This court has consistently stated that:

"When portions of a statute are held unconstitutional, the remaining provisions will remain valid if they are complete in themselves and are not dependent on the invalid parts." Shroyer v. Sokol, Colo., 550 P.2d 309, 311 (1976).

The prohibition against marriage between a brother and sister related by the half or whole blood is complete in itself and in no way depends upon the stricken provision. Thus, the trial court did not err in holding that this statute was severable.

The judgment of the district court is affirmed.

NOTES AND QUESTIONS

1. The court in Israel relies on a quotation from Vernier's treatise concerning relationship by affinity. Is the relationship involved in Israel affinal or consanguineous or something else? For a list of the relationships generally dealt with by the older statutes on affinity, see 1 Vernier, American Family Laws 184–187 (1931).

2. Why do you suppose statutes in the Anglo-American world universally prohibit the marriage of brother and sister? Why do we have any incest prohibitions in the law? Much writing in the social sciences has been devoted to the origins of the incest taboos, without reaching any broad consensus. A representative selection would include Parker, The Precultural Basis of the Incest Taboo: Toward a Biosocial Theory, 78 American Anthropologist, 285, 286, 288–289, 299 (1976); G. Murdock, Social Structure, 292–313 (1949); H. Maisch, Incest, 81–85 (1972); T. Parsons, The Incest Taboo, 5 British J. of Sociology 101 (1954); Schwartzman, The Individual, Incest, and Exogamy, 37 Psychiatry 171 (1974).

3. Does incest have harmful genetic consequences? W. Bodmer and L. Cavalli-Sforza, Genetics, Evolution and Man, ch. 11 (1976); C. Stern, Principles of Human Genetics, 607, 625 (3d ed. 1973).

4. Are the genetic harms caused by inbreeding, if any, the sole basis for our incest prohibitions?

5. Why is it "illogical" or irrational to prohibit the marriage of adopted brother and sister? Do the purposes underlying incest taboos have any application to this relationship? Wadlington, The Adopted Child and Intra-Family Marriage Prohibitions, 49 Va.L.Rev. 478 (1963). The Commissioners' Note to § 207 of the Uniform Marriage and Divorce Act, 9A Unif.L.Ann. 109 (1979) contains the following: "Marriages of brothers and sisters by adoption are prohibited because of the social interest in discouraging romantic attachments between such persons even if there is no genetic risk." Why do you suppose the court in *Israel* did not address itself to this Note?

6. The court in *Israel* states that adopted children do not become members of their adoptive families for all purposes, citing the criminal incest statute. State v. Rogers, 260 N.C. 406, 133 S.E.2d 1 (1963) is in accord, holding no criminal violation occurred when a father had sexual relations with his adopted daughter. But Colo.Rev.Stat.Ann. § 19–4–113 (1973) provides: "After the entry of a final decree of adoption, the person adopted shall be, to all intents and purposes, the child of the petitioner. He shall be entitled to all the rights and privileges and be subject to all the obligations of a child born in lawful wedlock to the petitioner." Does this provision affect the issue in the *Israel* case?

7. Does the result in *Israel* mean that the provision in Colo.Rev.Stat. Ann. § 14–2–110(1)(b) (1973) which prohibits the marriage of father with adopted daughter is likewise unconstitutional? See State v. Lee, 196 Miss. 311, 17 So.2d 277 (1944), holding that a statute forbidding the marriage of parent and child does not apply to marriages of parent and adopted child. The case has been overruled by Miss.Code Ann. § 93–1–1 (1973).

8. Some states have statutes which still forbid marriages between some classes of persons related by affinity. See, e. g., Iowa Code Ann. § 595.19 (1950); Mass.Gen.L.Ann. c. 207, §§ 1, 2 (1969); Miss.Code Ann. § 93–1–1 (1973). If *Israel* were followed, would these be unconstitutional?

9. Incest within the nuclear family has generally been a problem of father-daughter sexual exploitation in this country. Attempted marriages of persons within the nuclear family have been virtually non-existent. But in 1979 a brother-sister marriage came to light. It occurred in Massachusetts and apparently will be prosecuted as a crime. The husband supposedly intends to obtain a vasectomy so that there will be no risk of genetic harm. Time Magazine, July 2, 1979, page 76, col. 1. If he should do this, would this make the statute unconstitutional as applied to this couple, as a result of the *Israel* case?

10. Would a criminal statute which imposed more severe penalties for father-daughter incest than for mother-son or brother-sister incest violate the Equal Protection Clause of the Fourteenth Amendment to the United States Constitution? Would such a statute violate a state's Equal Rights Amendment, forbidding the abridgment of rights on account of sex? See People v. Yocum, 66 Ill.2d 211, 5 Ill.Dec. 665, 361 N.E.2d 1369 (1977); People v. Boyer, 63 Ill.2d 433, 349 N.E.2d 50 (1976), cert. den. 429 U.S. 1063 (1977).

SECTION 6. THE INTENT TO MARRY

A. INTENT

The authorities agree that "Marriage being a contract is of course consensual * * * for it is of the essence of all contracts to be constituted by the consent of parties." Dalrymple v. Dalrymple, 2 Hagg.Cons. 53, 62, 161 Eng.Rep. 665, 668 (1811). This implies in general terms that the consent be freely and voluntarily given. Religious teaching has emphasized that the marriage contract requires a free consent. See, e. g., Encyclical Letter on Christian Marriage of Pope Pius XI, Association of American Law Schools, Selected Essays on Family Law 132, 133 (1950). But many ambiguities lie concealed in that apparently simple statement. The cases which follow in this section attempt to explore those ambiguities, raising such questions as whether duress or fraud vitiate consent to marriage, and whether intent to marry for one purpose but not others is sufficient.

B. DURESS

If duress is the inducing cause of a marriage, there is not that voluntary consent to the marriage contract which is essential to its validity. For this reason most states have statutes providing that marriages brought about by duress are invalid, generally voidable rather than void. In applying these statutes the courts have held that the effect of the duress must have been perceptible at the time of the marriage ceremony and must have been of such severity that the complaining party was unable to act as a free agent in entering the marriage. See Kingsley, Duress as a Ground for Annulment of Marriage, 33 So.Cal.L.Rev. 1 (1959); Annot., 91 A.L.R. 414 (1934). Most cases seem to make the test a subjective one, that is, the question is whether the particular individual (whether reasonably or not) was entering the marriage only through fear of the consequences if he did not. Duress may be a ground for annulment even though exerted by someone other than the defendant and without the defendant's participation. H. v. H., [1954] P. 258.

Much discussion recently has centered around what one author has called duress by operation of law. Wadlington, Shotgun Marriage by Operation of Law, 1 Ga.L.Rev. 183 (1967). Between thirty and forty states have statutes imposing criminal penalties for seduction of a female under promise of marriage. Note, Coercive Power of the Criminal Seduction Statute, 16 S.D.L.Rev. 166 (1971). Of these statutes many have express provisions that marriage of the defendant with the complaining witness is a defense to the prosecution. Even without such a provision, it is often the case that prosecutions for this and other sex crimes, like fornication or statutory rape, will be dropped if the defendant agrees to marry the girl. Although such marriages are anything but voluntary, the courts have generally refused to annul them, the reason apparently being that they feel that some valuable social policy is attained by forcing the defendant to make amends in this fashion. Annot., 16 A.L.R.2d 1430 (1951); Brown, The Shotgun Marriage, 42 Tulane L.Rev. 837 (1968). If the prosecution is not brought in good faith or with reasonable basis, however, the marriage may be annulled. See, e. g., Buckland v. Buckland, [1967] 2 All Eng.Rep. 300, 29 Mod.L.Rev. 622 (1966), in which a member of a British police force in Malta, forced to marry a Maltese girl by a trumped up charge of seduction, was granted an annulment by an English court.

It seems obvious, and has often been pointed out, that such forced marriages are not likely to be successful or to last, and do not in fact accomplish anything useful either for the parties or the society. The Model Penal Code, § 213.3 (Proposed Official Draft 1962) has taken some steps toward improving the situation by removing the defense of marriage from the crime of seduction, and also by requiring proof that the seduction was accomplished by a promise of marriage not made in good faith. But this is of little real consequence so long as the crime exists since marriage can always be forced by offering to drop the prosecution if the defendant agrees to marry. Another possible remedy may lie in the proposed Twenty-Seventh Amendment to the United States Constitution, which may outlaw criminal seduction statutes on the ground that they apply only to men, thereby abridging men's equality of rights.

The Uniform Marriage and Divorce Act, § 208 omits any mention of duress as a ground for declaring a marriage invalid, presumably intending that marriages entered into as result of duress should not be declared invalid. There may be some difficulty with this, however, since it has been held that equity has inherent jurisdiction, without the aid of statutory authority, to annul marriages for duress. Worthington v. Worthington, 234 Ark. 216, 352 S.W.2d 80 (1962). Without statutory language expressly abolishing duress as a ground for annulment, it may therefore survive.

C. FRAUD

MASTERS v. MASTERS

Supreme Court of Wisconsin, 1961.
13 Wis.2d 332, 108 N.W.2d 674.

Action for annulment of marriage instituted by the plaintiff Edward Masters against the defendant Ramona Masters.

The material facts brought out in the testimony are set forth in the following findings of fact of the trial court:

"During November 1959 and prior to the 28th day thereof and to induce the plaintiff to marry her, said defendant represented to the plaintiff that she was pregnant with child by him, displaying to him a certificate (of her pregnancy of several months standing) by a local well-known doctor and such representation was made by her to him upon several occasions during the first twenty-eight days of said month of November, 1959 and before said marriage. Such representations were made to the plaintiff by the defendant deliberately and intentionally to induce him to marry her. The plaintiff believed said representations to be true and was induced thereby to marry the defendant in reliance thereon. Had such representations not been made to him he would not have married the defendant. The representations of her pregnancy by the plaintiff or anybody else were false and not true.

"On Tuesday, January 26, 1960, the plaintiff discovered that the defendant's representations of her pregnancy aforesaid were false and untrue and fraudulent and thereafter and upon such discovery he had no marital relation with the defendant, renounced her as his wife, and left their said residence. Since such discovery the plaintiff did nothing to confirm said marriage."

Upon the basis of such findings of fact the trial court entered the following conclusion of law:

"The defendant's representations of her pregnancy with child by the plaintiff although intentional and false and fraudulent and the sole means of procuring the marriage of the parties hereto is not sufficiently material under the applicable statutes to constitute cause for annulment of said marriage even though the plaintiff sues as the innocent and injured party who has done no act to confirm such marriage after his discovery of the character of such representations."

Judgment was accordingly entered under date of October 17, 1960, dismissing the plaintiff's complaint. From such judgment the plaintiff has appealed.

CURRIE, Justice. The controlling statute in the instant action for annulment of marriage is sec. 247.02, Stats., which reads in part as follows:

"No marriage shall be annulled or held void except pursuant to judicial proceedings. A marriage may be annulled for any of the following causes existing at the time of the marriage: * * *

"(4) Fraud, force or coercion, at the suit of the innocent and injured party, unless the marriage has been confirmed by the acts of the injured party."

* * *

The Wisconsin case closest in point from the standpoint of the factual situation is Winner v. Winner, 171 Wis. 413, 177 N.W. 680, 11 A.L.R. 919 (1920). In that case the parties had illicit intercourse and the defendant falsely represented to the plaintiff that she was pregnant and that he was the cause thereof. The plaintiff believed such representation and by reason thereof married the defendant. Five months and fourteen days from the first act of intercourse between the parties the defendant gave birth to a fully developed full-term child, thus establishing the falsity of her representation that the plaintiff was the cause of her pregnancy. The plaintiff upon the birth of such child refused to cohabit further with the defendant and thereafter commenced an action to have the marriage annulled. The trial court refused to grant the annulment, but upon appeal this court reversed and held that the plaintiff was entitled to an annulment.

In the opinion in the Winner case there was cited the case of DiLorenzo v. DiLorenzo, 174 N.Y. 467, 67 N.E. 63, 63 L.R.A. 92 (1903). As in the instant case, the false representations in the *DiLorenzo* case, which had induced the plaintiff husband to marry the defendant, were that she was pregnant by reason of having had illicit intercourse with him, when in fact she was not pregnant. The New York court granted an annulment of the marriage. * * *

There is a fairly even division in authorities as to whether a false representation by the defendant woman that she is pregnant by the plaintiff man, when actually she is pregnant by another, is sufficient to support a cause of action for annulment of marriage. However, in fact situations in which the woman's false representation is that she is pregnant by the man whom she induces thereby to marry her, when in fact she is not pregnant, the New York courts stand alone in granting an annulment of the marriage. * * *

We have carefully reviewed the cases from other jurisdictions, which have denied annulment to husbands victimized by the same type of fraud as was perpetrated upon the instant plaintiff by the defendant, to ascertain the reasons advanced in support of such a determination. There appear to be two such reasons. One is that, because the parties indulged in illicit intercourse before marriage, the parties stand in *pari delicto* so that the defendant comes into court with "unclean hands." The second is that the false representation was not material, which is the view adopted by the trial court in the case at bar.

The argument that the parties stand *in pari delicto* was advanced by the defendant wife in Winner v. Winner, supra, and was rejected by this court. With respect to such contention the opinion pointed out that such intercourse constituted a mere misdemeanor. We are of the opinion that the punishment inflicted by denying an annulment in cases of this kind is out of all proportion to the offense committed. In so holding, we do not condone in the least the plaintiff's infraction of the moral code. Furthermore, by refusing an annulment the plaintiff would not be punished for the illicit intercourse, but rather for his laudable conduct in seeking to rectify a wrong he believed would result unless he did marry the defendant. There may be aggravated situations in which the doctrine of *in pari delicto* ought to be applied, such as was present in Gonduin v. Gonduin, 14 Cal.App. 285, 111 P.

756 (1910), in which the man induced the woman to submit to intercourse by his promise to marry her. This is not such a case.

Whether to apply the doctrine of *in pari delicto* poses a question of public policy. The lone justification which we can perceive for here invoking such doctrine is that it might act as a future deterrent to unmarried persons engaging in illicit intercourse. If the thought of the unpleasant consequences, which are likely to befall the male participant should pregnancy result, or the fear of a criminal prosecution for fornication, are insufficient to deter him, we doubt very much that the example which would be afforded by denying an annulment in the instant fact situation would be any more effective. On the other hand, to deny an annulment would reward the defendant for a palpable fraud and punish the plaintiff for being victimized thereby in an effort on his part to right a wrong, which he was induced by the fraud to think would result if he did not marry the defendant. When the competing policy factors are so weighed, the scales of justice tip in but one direction. Therefore, we refuse here to apply the principle of *in pari delicto*.

The reason why some courts have held that fraudulent representations of the character of those perpetrated by the instant defendant are not material is well stated in Helfrick v. Helfrick, 246 Ill.App. 294, 295 (1927), as follows:

"The fraudulent representations for which a marriage may be annulled must be of something essential to the marriage relation—of something making impossible the performance of the duties and obligations of that relation, or rendering its assumption and continuance dangerous to health or life."

In Varney v. Varney, 52 Wis. 120, 8 N.W. 739, 741 (1881), a wife sued for divorce, and the husband counterclaimed for an annulment. The allegations of the counterclaim were that the wife prior to marriage had fraudulently represented that she was a chaste and virtuous woman, and had fraudulently concealed the fact that she had given birth to an illegitimate child which had subsequently died. This court held that such allegations were not sufficient to state a cause of action for annulment and quoted with approval the following statements by the Massachusetts court made in Reynolds v. Reynolds, 3 Allen 605, 607, 85 Mass. 605, 607 (1862):

" 'While, however, marriage by our law is regarded as a purely civil contract, which may well be avoided and set aside on the ground of fraud, it is not to be supposed that every error or mistake into which a person may fall concerning character or qualities of a wife or husband, although occasioned by disingenuous or even false statements or practices, will afford sufficient reason for annulling an executed contract of marriage. In the absence of force or duress, and where there is no mistake as to the identity of the person, any error or misapprehension as to personal traits or attributes, or concerning the position or circumstances in life of a party, is deemed wholly immaterial, and furnishes no good cause for divorce. Therefore no misconception as to the character, fortune, health, or temper, however brought about, will support an allegation of fraud on which a dissolution of the marriage contract, when once executed, can be obtained in a court of justice.' "

It is arguable that this court in Varney v. Varney, supra, by its approval of the foregoing quotation, adopted the same test of materiality as stated by the Illinois court in Helfrick v. Helfrick supra. However, while a false representation, that one is pregnant when she is not, might be classified as a representation with respect to health, it extends far beyond that. This is because such a false representation is not calculated to impress the man involved with the desirability of the woman as a wife, as an inducement to marriage, but to cause him to enter into a marriage against his will in an attempt to right a wrong and legitimatize the supposed unborn child.

Sec. 247.02, (4), Stats., contains no limitation that would restrict its application to only those cases of fraud which makes impossible the performance of the duties and obligations of marriage, or renders marriage dangerous to health or life. In the absence of such a legislative command, we do not deem it advisable that we adopt such a restrictive interpretation of the statute and thus tie the hands of this court so as to prevent it from annulling a marriage in such an aggravated case of fraud as this record presents.

The decisions of this court in Varney v. Varney, supra, and Wells v. Talham, 180 Wis. 654, 194 N.W. 36, 33 A.L.R. 827 (1923), make it plain that a much stricter rule is followed in annuling [sic] marriages for fraud than is followed in rescinding ordinary contracts. In Wells v. Talham, supra, the court declared at page 662, 194 N.W. at page 39:

"It will be seen from the decisions that this court early adopted the view, which has been adhered to, that, although marriage is purely a civil contract, false representations which would set aside ordinary civil contracts are not necessarily sufficient to void the contract of marriage. This policy depends not alone on the vital importance of the dissolution of the marriage relation to the parties directly concerned. It rests on the deep concern of the state that the integrity of the marriage contract shall, so far as possible, be preserved. This is shown by the careful provision of our statute regulating marriage and divorce, including the statute providing for the appointment of divorce counsel in each county to represent the public, whose duty it is to appear and investigate the merits in such actions for the prevention of collusion, fraud, and imposition upon the court."

Because of these considerations courts should be hesitant to annul marriages on the ground of fraud perpetrated upon one of the parties by the other, unless thoroughly convinced that the defrauded party would not have entered into the marriage contract except for such fraud. In the instant case the trial court has found that, had the defendant's fraudulent representations not been made, the plaintiff would not have married the defendant. We deem the character of such false representations to be such as to be material as a matter of law, if they in fact caused the marriage to be entered into under circumstances that no marriage would have taken place absent such false representations. Therefore, the plaintiff is entitled to a decree annulling the marriage.

We deem it advisable to point out that there may be situations of marriages induced by material fraudulent representations in which an annulment should be denied for policy reasons. An illustration of this would be a false representation of financial worth. Insofar as the instant case is concerned, we have hereinbefore reviewed the policy factors, in passing on the application of the doctrine of *in pari delicto*, and have concluded that the annulment should not be denied for reasons of policy.

*   *   *

Judgment reversed and cause remanded with directions to enter a judgment annulling the marriage of the parties.

NOTES AND QUESTIONS

1. The *Masters* case is noted in 45 Marq.L.Rev. 447 (1962). For citation and discussion of the earlier cases, see Kingsley, Fraud as a Ground for Annulment of Marriage, 18 So.Cal.L.Rev. 213 (1945). A similar case granting annulment is Parks v. Parks, 418 S.W.2d 726 (Ky.1967), 57 Ky. L.J. 272 (1968), 21 Vand.L.Rev. 567 (1968), 9 Ariz.L.Rev. 481 (1968). See also Note, 13 S.D.L.Rev. 146 (1968).

2. The *Reynolds* case quoted at page 159, in the *Masters* case, is the leading early authority for the view that fraud must relate to the "essentials" of marriage in order to constitute grounds for annulment. In that case the wife concealed her pregnancy, by a man other than the husband, from her husband. The parties had had no pre-marital sexual relations. The reasoning of the *Reynolds* case leading to a decree annulling the marriage seems to be summarized in the following quotation, 3 Allen (85 Mass.) 605, 607: "The great object of marriage in a civilized and Christian community is to secure the existence and permanence of the family relation, and to insure the legitimacy of offspring. It would tend to defeat this object, if error or disappointment in personal qualities or character was allowed to be the basis of proceedings on which to found a dissolution of the marriage tie. The law therefore wisely requires that persons who act on representations or belief in regard to such matters should bear the consequences which flow from contracts into which they have voluntarily entered, after they have been executed, and affords no relief for the results of a " 'blind credulity, however it may have been produced' ".

(a) Does the *Masters* case adhere to the rule that the fraud must relate to the essentials of the marriage in order to justify an annulment? If so, how does it define essentials? How does the *Reynolds* case define essentials? See also Patey v. Peaslee, infra, page 200.

(b) Does the *Masters* case adopt the rule that the fraud must be material in order to justify an annulment? What does "material" mean? Does it mean that the falsehood must have concerned a matter sufficiently important to induce the ordinary reasonable man to marry? Or does it mean that the falsehood must have been such that the ordinary reasonable man would have been deceived, and would not have investigated and discovered the truth? Or does it mean both of these things? Was Edward Masters negligent in not insisting that Ramona have medical tests for pregnancy before he married her? What rules of materiality govern the disaffirmance of commercial contracts for fraud? See, e. g., Restatement of Contracts §§ 476(1), 471 (1932); 12 Williston, Contracts, § 1490 (3d ed. Jaeger 1970).

(c) The *Reynolds* case as quoted above seems to base its limited view of the kind of fraud justifying annulment on the ground that this is necessary in order to secure the existence and permanence of the family relation. Would denial of the annulment in the *Masters* case have secured the existence and permanence of the family relation?

(d) What should be the result in the *Masters* case if the wife had stated she was pregnant thinking in good faith that she was, and had found after the marriage ceremony that she was not? See 12 Williston, Contracts, § 1510 (3d ed. Jaeger 1970).

(e) What should be the result if no representations at all were made, but after the marriage it appeared that the wife was pregnant by a man other than her husband? Hardesty v. Hardesty, 193 Cal. 330, 223 P. 951 (1924).

(f) What result should the court reach if the wife persuades the husband to marry her by telling him she is pregnant and that he is the father of the child when the fact is that another man is the father? Gard v. Gard, 204 Mich. 255, 169 N.W. 908 (1918), 28 Yale L.J. 516 (1919); B. v. S., 99 N.J.Super. 429, 240 A.2d 189 (1968). Should the court respond to his claim by telling him that he should have waited until the baby was born and then insisted upon blood grouping tests to determine non-paternity before marrying, and that he was negligent in accepting the wife's statements at face value? Cf. Goree v. Goree, 187 Neb. 774, 194 N.W.2d 212 (1972). There may be a defense of ratification if the husband lives with his wife after marriage, and after learning of her falsehood, McLarty v. McLarty, 433 S.W.2d 722 (Tex.Civ.App.1968), 21 Baylor L.Rev. 391 (1969).

(g) Assuming that pre-marital sexual relations constitute a crime, as is true in many states including apparently Wisconsin at the time of the *Masters* case, was the court in that case, and would the court in the case in paragraph (f) above be warranted in rejecting a defense of *in pari delicto*? Why or why not?

(h) If Edward Masters in the *Masters* case had been suspicious of Ramona's statement that she was pregnant and had inquired of her physician about her condition, would the physician be authorized to respond to such an inquiry? See Curry v. Corn, 52 Misc.2d 1035, 277 N.Y.S.2d 470 (Sup.Ct. 1966).

KOBER v. KOBER

Court of Appeals of New York, 1965.
16 N.Y.2d 191, 211 N.E.2d 817, 264 N.Y.S.2d 364.

VAN VOORHIS, Judge. This is an annulment suit. * * *

The material portions of this cause of action allege that the parties were married at New York City on June 28, 1963 (this annul- *CASE* ment action was begun April 22, 1964) and that at and before the marriage the defendant husband falsely and fraudulently concealed from the plaintiff that he had been an officer in the German Army and a member of the Nazi party during World War II, and "was fanatically anti-Semitic; that he believed in, advocated, approved and even applauded Hitler's 'Final Solution' of the Jewish question, namely the extermination of the Jewish people; and that he would require plaintiff to 'weed out' all of her Jewish friends and to cease socializing with them." The next paragraph alleges that plaintiff married defendant believing him to be without fanatic anti-Semitism and without the belief that the Jewish people should be exterminated, "all of which he had at the date thereof, and during the marriage and all of which he expressed after and during the marriage so as to make the marital relationship unworkable." The next paragraph further alleges: "That plaintiff relied on defendant's apparent normal character, high moral beliefs and absence of fanatic anti-Semitism and would not have married him had she known prior to the aforementioned marriage that the defendant had been a member of the Nazi Party, was fanatically anti-Semitic, believed that all Jews should be exterminated, and that he would require plaintiff to cease socializing with all her Jewish friends, and had the defendant not been guilty of said fraudulent concealment."

A pleading, the sufficiency of which is being tested, "is deemed to allege whatever can be implied from its statements by fair intendment and the whole of it must be considered." * * * All of the allegations, for the purpose of such a motion, must be assumed to be true, and the cause of action must stand "If in any aspect upon the facts stated the plaintiff is entitled to a recovery" * * *

Bearing these principles in mind, we hold that this portion of the amended complaint states a cause of action. In Shonfeld v. Shonfeld *C/A* (260 N.Y. 477, 184 N.E. 60 (1933)) an annulment was granted under section 1139 of the Civil Practice Act (now Domestic Relations Law, Consol.Laws, c. 14, § 140, subd. [e]), husband against wife, where the former had stated that he was in no position to marry because he was not able to make a living, in response to which the defendant had stated fraudulently that, if it was merely a matter of sufficient money to establish him in a business of his own, she had enough, if such an opportunity presented itself. The opportunity did arise, but she refused to advance the money before marriage, and the trial court had found as facts that the representations thus made were false, were believed and relied upon, and induced the plaintiff's consent to the marriage, and that if they had not been made he would not have consented. The case reached this court in the posture that a decree of annulment had been refused upon the ground that these representations did not go "to the essence of the marriage contract."

The decree was granted in this court upon the ground that, if the true facts had been known to the husband, he would not have entered into the marriage. "The obligation of a husband to support a wife is no less lightly to be entered into than the other obligations of the marital relation. The ability to support is correspondingly important. * * * The business which defendant's mythical money was to establish was plaintiff's only prospect of supporting her. The misrepresentation was not a mere exaggeration or misstatement of her means or prospects, which might or might not be an incentive to marriage. It was a definite statement of an existing fact without which, as defendant clearly understood, no marriage was presently practicable" (supra, p. 482, 184 N.E. p. 62).

The development of the law of annulment was reviewed, the court pointing out (pp. 479–480, 184 N.E. p. 61) that the fraud need no longer "necessarily concern what is commonly called the essentials of the marriage *relation*—the rights and duties connected with cohabitation and consortium attached by law to the marital status. * * * Any fraud is adequate which is 'material, to that degree that, had it not been practiced, the party deceived would not have consented to the marriage' * * * and is 'of such a nature as to deceive an ordinarily prudent person.' * * * Although it is not enough to show merely that one partner married for money and was disappointed (Woronzoff-Daschkoff v. Woronzoff-Daschkoff, 303 N.Y. p. 512, 104 N.E.2d p. 880), and the decisions upon the subject of annulment of marriage have not always been uniform, there have been circumstances where misrepresentation of love and affection, with intention to make a home, were held sufficient (Schinker v. Schinker, 271 App.Div. 688, 68 N.Y.S.2d 470 (1947)), likewise in case of fraudulent misrepresentations concerning the legitimacy of children of the wife by a supposedly prior marriage (Domschke v. Domschke, 138 App.Div. 454, 122 N.Y.S. 892 (1910)), or concerning prior marital status (Smith v. Smith, 273 App.Div. 987, 77 N.Y.S.2d 902 (1948)). Concealment of prior marital status was held to be sufficient in Costello v. Costello (155 Misc. 28, 279 N.Y.S. 303 (1935)), concealment of affliction with tuberculosis in Yelin v. Yelin (142 Misc. 533, 255 N.Y.S. 708 (1932)) and Sobol v. Sobol (88 Misc. 277, 150 N.Y.S. 248 (1914)); failure to reveal treatment of a mental disorder (schizophrenia, catatonic type) was held to be enough in Schaeffer v. Schaeffer (20 Misc.2d 662, 192 N.Y.S.2d 275 (1959)); material misrepresentation of age in Tacchi v. Tacchi (47 Misc.2d 996, 195 N.Y.S. 2d 892 (1959)); fraudulent promise to become a United States citizen in Siecht v. Siecht, Sup., (41 N.Y.S.2d 393 (1943)), where after years of married life the husband learned that his wife was a member of the Deutsche Bund and that her failure to become a citizen had been deliberate because of disloyalty to the United States. In Laage v. Laage (176 Misc. 190, 26 N.Y.S.2d 874 (1941)), an annulment was granted to a wife by reason of the husband's false representation that he was a naturalized American citizen, after she had stated to him that she would not marry a German-born alien. In Brillis v. Brillis (207 Misc. 104, 137 N.Y.S.2d 32 (1955), affd. 3 A.D.2d 662, 158 N.Y. S.2d 780 (1957)), a marriage was annulled where the evidence established that the defendant did not intend, at the time when he induced plaintiff's consent to the marriage, to establish a home for his wife and to support her, and that his purpose in entering into the marriage, unknown to plaintiff, was to facilitate his re-entry into the United States from Greece as a nonquota immigrant. In Harris v. Harris (201 App.Div. 880, 193 N.Y.S. 936 (1922)), an annulment was granted on account of the concealment by the husband of previous criminal activities. A recent annulment suit in this court was Sophian v. Von Linde (22 A.D.2d 34, 253 N.Y.S.2d 496 (1964), affd. 16 N. Y.2d 785, 262 N.Y.S.2d 505, 209 N.E.2d 823 [July 9, 1965]). Although a third cause of action was sustained that the defendant misrepresented his intentions to have normal sexual relations with his wife, the first cause of action was also sustained (see opinion at Appellate Division, p. 35, 253 N.Y.S.2d p. 497) based on misrepresentation by the defendant of his age, origin and ancestry. We affirmed, notwithstanding the dissent of two Justices at the Appellate Division based on Lapides v. Lapides (254 N.Y. 73, 80, 171 N.E. 911 (1930)) and other decisions holding or purporting to hold that misrepresentations of the nature alleged in the Sophian first cause of action were not vital to the marriage relationship.

Marriage is a civil contract (Domestic Relations Law, § 10) and, as stated in Shonfeld v. Shonfeld (supra, 260 N.Y. p. 479, 184 N.E. p. 61): "The essentials of marriage as a civil *contract* are, therefore, (a) consent by (b) parties having statutory capacity to give it. Any lack in those essentials makes the marriage void (Domestic Relations Law, §§ 5 and 6) or voidable (Id. § 7). If either party consents by reason of fraud there is no reality of consent. Hence the marriage is voidable (Id. § 7, subd. 4) and an action may be maintained to annul it."

Under these principles, if the facts stated in the second cause of action of this amended complaint are true (as we are bound to assume for the purposes of this appeal) the trier of the fact might well conclude that there was no reality to the consent of plaintiff to this marriage. Allowing the pleading the broad construction to which it is entitled under the law, defendant had not merely been a member of the Nazi party and an officer in the German Army during World War II, which in themselves would be insufficient to sustain an annulment, but also, as an individual, he was fanatically anti-Semitic and supported the extermination of the Jewish people. In spite of the fact that he believed in, advocated and approved such genocide, he nevertheless, during courtship, according to the complaint, maintained an "apparent * * * absence of fanatic anti-Semitism" from which it would appear that, if true, he put on a false front to obtain plaintiff's hand in that he dissembled his genocidal beliefs by seemingly associating agreeably with Jews.

Plaintiff alleges that she relied on this, and would not have married him had she known his true nature, in these respects, which he manifested "after and during the marriage so as to make the marital relationship unworkable."

These allegations go beyond merely requiring "a wife, in order to preserve marital harmony, to give up friendships which she had made in the past", or asking the courts to "lay down a viable line of separation between political and philosophical views too extreme to be concealed during the courting relationship from those not so extreme which may be concealed intentionally or inadvertently without impairing the agreement to marry" as said by the Appellate Division majority (22 A.D.2d, p. 471, 256 N.Y.S.2d p. 618). A fanatical conviction, to be effectuated where possible through the mobilization of superior force, that a race or group of people living in the same community should be put to death as at Auschwitz, Belsen, Dachau or Buchenwald, evinces a diseased mind and makeup which parallels the ground for annulment stated in subdivision (c) of section 140 of the Domestic Relations Law, where a party to the marriage is an idiot or lunatic.

The continuation of defendant's addiction to this anti-social and fanatical objective after and during marriage, which had been concealed and inferentially misrepresented during courtship, would so plainly make the marital relationship unworkable in this jurisdiction, where the marriage was contracted, that it would depart from the realities to conclude that it was not essential to this married relationship, or that, to defendant's knowledge, plaintiff would have consented to the marriage without its concealment. At least the trier of the fact could so find if evidence is adduced to sustain the allegations of the second cause of action in this pleading. As was said in the dissenting opinion at the Appellate Division, quoting from Justice Loreto at Special Term, " 'These are more than distasteful beliefs; they are absolutely repugnant and insufferable * * *. A fraud with respect to such beliefs, inducing marriage, is one affecting a vital aspect of the marital relationship. At least, it may be so determined upon a trial. It might well be found to be "material to that degree that, had it not been practiced, the party deceived would not have consented to the marriage" and is of such a nature as to deceive an "ordinarily prudent person" * * *.' "

We are not called upon at this stage of the litigation to determine whether plaintiff will succeed in establishing these allegations at the trial. She should not be denied her day in court, however, on the basis that it could not be found at the trial that the facts alleged, if established by evidence, would go to the essence of her consent to marry him.

The order appealed from should be reversed and that of Special Term reinstated, without costs.

DYE, FULD, and BERGAN, JJ., concur with VAN VOORHIS, J.

DESMOND, C.J., and BURKE and SCILEPPI, JJ., dissent and vote to affirm upon the majority opinion at the Appellate Division.

NOTES AND QUESTIONS

1. The *Kober* case has been noted in 32 Bklyn.L.Rev. 419 (1966), 35 Ford.L.Rev. 125 (1966); 11 Vill.L.Rev. 632 (1966), and 12 Wayne L.Rev. 661 (1966).

2. The willingness of New York courts to grant annulments for fraud was, to an extent not precisely measurable, due to the fact that until 1967 the only ground for divorce in New York was adultery. Some substitute for divorce was needed in addition to the trip to Reno and annulment was the obvious answer. The only ground for annulment susceptible to expansion was fraud. This development of the law of annulment for fraud is documented in Note, Annulments for Fraud—New York's Answer to Reno? 48 Colum.L.Rev. 900 (1948). Whether the New York courts' hospitality to annulments for fraud will continue now that the state has a more sensible divorce statute remains to be seen. Cf. Gleason v. Gleason, 26 N.Y.2d 28, 256 N.E.2d 513, 308 N.Y.S.2d 347 (1970).

3. What general principle does the *Kober* case adopt to govern the grant or denial of annulments for fraud? Is this different from or similar to the principle announced in the *Masters* case?

4. The court in the *Kober* case seems to make a distinction between a case in which the husband had been "merely" a member of the Nazi party and an officer in the German army, in which circumstances no annulment would be granted, and this case, in which the husband was in addition a fanatical anti-Semite who supported the extermination of the Jews. Why this distinction? Is this case a holding that concealment of a mental condition equivalent to insanity is sufficient fraud on which to base annulment? Or is the basis for the case that the husband's adherence to such beliefs would make the marriage intolerable to the wife, so that the court was in effect putting an end to the marriage on the ground of mental cruelty? The opinion of the Appellate Division in the case, 22 A.D.2d 468, 256 N.Y.S.2d 615 (1965), states that the complaint does not allege whether the plaintiff was Jewish. Would it make a difference whether or not she was Jewish?

5. (a) H and W were married in 1965 and separated in 1973. W had been married before, but told H that her first husband was dead, which was not true, she having been divorced from him before the marriage to H. W knew he was not dead, but told H he was because H was a Catholic and had told W he could not marry her if she had been divorced. After the parties

separated, H learned that W's first husband was still alive and sued W to annul their marriage. What should be the result? Is the test for fraud as a ground for annulment one which is subjective as related to the plaintiff, or is it objective? Would it matter if the facts were that W was also mistaken about her first husband's being alive and thought in good faith that he was dead until she learned otherwise in 1974? See Wolfe v. Wolfe, 62 Ill.App.3d 498, 19 Ill.Dec. 306, 378 N.E.2d 1181 (1978).

(b) H and W were married when both were 35 years old. H failed to disclose to W that he had been married five times before, but instead told her he had been married and divorced once. W learned the truth a month after they were married. Would the *Kober* case be authority for granting W an annulment? Would it make a difference that H was paying alimony to two of his former wives and that he also failed to disclose this fact to W before their marriage? Cf. Sanderson v. Sanderson, 212 Va. 537, 186 S.E. 2d 84 (1972); Fortin v. Fortin, 106 N.H. 208, 208 A.2d 447 (1965); Annot., 15 A.L.R.3d 759 (1967).

6. Consider the effect of the *Kober* case on the following facts: H, 36 years old, was an impecunious native of a small Middle Eastern country who made a meager living in Paris by escorting lonely women to the theater, night clubs, restaurants. He had acquired several languages, a manner of rather artificial charm, and the ability to be agreeable to women. He was a frequent user of amphetamines to the point where his health was affected. He had been arrested and served short prison terms on two occasions for fraud and for passing bad checks. He met W, a woman of 21 from California who had just inherited substantial property, and succeeded in convincing her that he was a poor but honest descendant of a noble Hungarian family who had been driven out of Hungary by the Communists. He represented himself as 28 years old. He also convinced her that he was very much in love with her, which was true in the sense that he was in love with one quality of hers, namely wealth. They went to England together and were married there, and from there went to California where they intended to live. W then discovered the truth about H's past, and about his motives in marrying her. Assuming that the English law is that annulment may only be granted if the defendant had a communicable venereal disease at the time of marriage, or if the defendant was pregnant by a man other than her husband, Matrimonial Causes Act of 1965, § 9(c), (d), what arguments might be made in a suit by W against H in California for annulment? Cf. Woronzoff-Daschkoff v. Woronzoff-Daschkoff, 303 N.Y. 506, 104 N.E.2d 877 (1952); Douglass v. Douglass, 148 Cal.App.2d 867, 307 P.2d 674 (1957); Brown v. Scott, 140 Md. 258, 117 A. 114 (1922); Husband v. Wife, 257 A.2d 765 (Del.Super.1969); Costello v. Porzelt, 116 N.J.Super. 380, 282 A.2d 432 (1971); Potter v. Potter, 27 A.D.2d 634, 275 N.Y.S.2d 499 (4th Dep't 1966); Sophian v. Von Linde, 22 A.D.2d 34, 253 N.Y.S.2d 496 (1st Dept. 1964), aff'd p. c. 16 N.Y.2d 785, 209 N.E.2d 823, 262 N.Y.S. 2d 505 (1965).

7. Relying on either the *Masters* case or the *Kober* case, what arguments might one make in an annulment suit brought by the husband where the evidence showed that the wife had had sexual relations with many men before her marriage and had failed to disclose this to the husband, but had made no affirmative misstatements about her past life? Would you agree with the *Reynolds* case, 3 Allen (85 Mass.) 605, 609 (1862), that the follow-

ing reason would dictate denying an annulment in such a case: "Certainly it would lead to disastrous consequences if a woman who had once fallen from virtue could not be permitted to represent herself as continent, and thus restore herself to the rights and privileges of her sex, and enter into matrimony without incurring the risk of being put away by her husband on discovery of her previous immorality." Or should it be argued that in view of Kinsey's findings that nearly 50% of the women he interviewed had had premarital sexual relations, Kinsey, Sexual Behavior in the Human Female 286 (1953), premarital chastity can no longer be a material circumstance to parties entering marriage? Should the same arguments be made, with the same effect, if it were the husband who had been engaged in numerous premarital sexual exploits? Should the answer to these questions depend upon the attitudes of the parties toward premarital chastity? See Annot., 64 A.L.R.2d 742 (1959). Should people in such a situation make a full disclosure of their past lives as a foundation for an honest and lasting marital relationship? Cf. Sheresky and Mannes, A Radical Guide to Wedlock, The Saturday Review, July 29, 1972, page 33. If that is desirable, should the law insist upon such a disclosure on pain of granting an annulment when it is not made?

8. Does either the *Masters* case or the *Kober* case throw any light on the case which arises when W, a deeply and sincerely religious woman, marries H, who professes also to be religious, but who, W finds after their marriage, is an atheist who asserts there is no God and that all religions are delusions? Should W obtain an annulment on this ground? See State Compensation Fund v. Foughty, 13 Ariz.App. 381, 476 P.2d 902 (1971), 22 Syra.L.Rev. 1180 (1971), 1971 Wash.U.L.Q. 469; Annot. 44 A.L. R.3d 972 (1972).

9. Do these cases suggest what ought to be the result when W sues H for annulment on the ground that H had concealed from her before their marriage his intention not to have children? Williams v. Witt, 98 N.J.Super. 1, 235 A.2d 902 (1967); Heup v. Heup, 45 Wis.2d 71, 172 N.W.2d 334 (1969); Zoglio v. Zoglio, 157 A.2d 627 (D.C.Mun.Ct.App.1960). Misrepresentation of one's ability to have children has been held grounds for annulment. Aufort v. Aufort, 9 Cal.App.2d 310, 49 P.2d 620 (1935). Where one of the parties misrepresents or fails to disclose an intention not to consummate the marriage, the courts have generally granted the annulment. Bernstein v. Bernstein, 25 Conn.Sup. 239, 201 A.2d 660 (1964); Lopez v. Lopez, 102 N.J.Super. 253, 245 A.2d 771 (1968); Handley v. Handley, 179 Cal. App.2d 742, 3 Cal.Rptr. 910 (1960).

10. Can you devise any reasonably clear statutory provisions which would assist the courts to arrive at sensible decisions on the types of misrepresentation or non-disclosure justifying annulment for fraud? Do the cases and problems discussed leave you with the suspicion that the courts are willing to tolerate a good deal of fraud in the process of courtship and marriage? If so, what becomes of the idea expressed at the beginning of this section that marriage must be entered into freely and voluntarily? If a satisfactory statute cannot be drafted, what arguments might be made in favor of the abolition of fraud as a ground for annulment, as apparently is the intention of the Uniform Marriage and Divorce Act, § 208, 9A.Unif.L. Ann. 110 (1979), and comment thereto?

D. MARRIAGE IN JEST

Mutual promises expressed in a context which indicates that the parties are joking, and which are so understood or would be so understood by a reasonable person in the particular circumstances, do not result in a legally binding contract. 1 Corbin, Contracts, § 34 (1950). The same is true for marriage contracts. In Davis v. Davis, 119 Conn. 194, 175 A. 574 (1934), for example, the man and woman were nineteen years old and were in a group of other young people out for a party. After the girl dared the young man to marry her, and some joking about it, the group drove to another state and went through a marriage ceremony. The marriage was never consummated. The court held that since there was no consent to enter the relationship, and no consummation, the marriage would be annulled. The result would very likely be otherwise if the marriage were consummated. It is not clear why consummation should make such a difference to the courts. Perhaps it is because consummation of the marriage tends to prove the ceremony was taken seriously after all and was not in jest. Jests aside, an unconsummated ceremonial marriage is as much of a marriage as any other, although there are unsupported statements in a few cases to the contrary. H. Clark, Law of Domestic Relations, 40–41 (1968).

For further discussion of marriage in jest, see H. Clark, Law of Domestic Relations, § 2.14 (1968).

E. SHAM MARRIAGE

SCHIBI v. SCHIBI

Supreme Court of Errors of Connecticut, 1949.
136 Conn. 196, 69 A.2d 831.

BROWN, Judge. This action was brought pursuant to General Statutes, § 7341, for the annulment of a marriage which the plaintiff claims never existed, for lack of mutual consent. * * * The court rendered judgment for the defendant. The plaintiff has appealed and there is no appearance on behalf of the defendant. The facts found by the court are undisputed before us. The plaintiff has resided in Connecticut for many years and in September, 1946, became acquainted with the defendant, who was then staying in New Hartford. Late in 1946 she told the plaintiff that she was pregnant by him. In response to a Torrington attorney's letter, the parties met in his office and agreed that there would be a marriage ceremony in New York and that the defendant would apply for an annulment of the marriage six weeks after the ceremony. The intention of the parties was to give a name to the unborn child. The plaintiff did not intend that they would live together, or cohabit, or assume the relationship of husband and wife after the ceremony, but on the contrary intended to live separate and apart from the defendant, which intentions were known to her.

Thereafter, the parties consulted an attorney in New York City and the defendant retained him to proceed with the annulment after the marriage ceremony. Subsequently, on January 26, 1947, the parties went through a marriage ceremony in New York City, pursuant to the plan agreed upon. Following this, the plaintiff returned to New Hartford. The defendant remained in New York City for a time, as she was employed there, and later returned to New Hartford to live. The parties have not cohabited since the marriage. 'A child, Frederick F. Schibi, Jr., was born to the defendant on July 1, 1947, in Winsted. The plaintiff makes no claim that he is not the father of the child. He has paid the expenses incident to the child's birth, contributed to his support and expressed an intention to continue to do so. The defendant refused to bring the annulment proceeding and informed the New York attorney not to proceed with it. The plaintiff's sole claim was that the marriage should be annulled because it lacked the element of mutual consent of the parties, having been "ostensible" and entered into only to give the unborn child a name. The court concluded that the parties were legally married and that it would be against public policy to find the marriage void.

The law is clear that mutual consent is essential to a valid marriage. * * * It is unquestioned that mutual consent by these parties was requisite to validity under the law of New York, where the ceremony was performed, and that without it the marriage was void and the Superior Court had jurisdiction so to decree. * * * In his complaint, the plaintiff alleges as the only basis for relief that at the time of the ceremony there was neither consent nor intent to incur the obligations of a marriage contract, and his prayers for relief are that the purported marriage be annulled and declared void. The sole question presented to the court for determination was whether the marriage was void because there was no mutual consent of the parties. That there was such mutual consent is implicit in the court's conclusion that the parties were legally married. Whether this conclusion is supported by the subordinate facts is the question decisive of the appeal.

In the trial court there was no appearance by the defendant, and the only evidence was the testimony of the plaintiff himself, which was not subjected to cross-examination. Since the case was uncontested, it was particularly incumbent upon the trial court to satisfy itself fully that the plaintiff had sustained the burden of proving the lack of mutual consent which he claimed vitiated the marriage. * * * In so far as the consent and intent of the defendant to enter into a binding marriage are concerned, the court's conclusion cannot be disturbed. In determining whether the same holds true as to the plaintiff, mention may be made of the court's finding that he did not intend to live and cohabit with the defendant or to enter into the re-

lationship of husband and wife with her after the marriage, but on
the contrary intended to live separate and apart from her and that
they did not in fact cohabit thereafter. While it is true that in passing upon a petition to annul a marriage, courts may well take into
consideration whether there has been cohabitation or not, the fact
that there has been none subsequent to the marriage ceremony is not
of controlling importance, and particularly is this true where there
has been prior sexual intercourse. * * * The fact that, in accord
with the plaintiff's intent, the parties did not cohabit after the ceremony, while possibly evidential of a lack of intent on his part to consent to and enter into a binding marriage with the defendant, did not
require a finding to that effect. This necessarily follows from the
fact, alleged in the plaintiff's complaint and found by the court upon
his request, that prior to the marriage he and the defendant agreed
that she would apply for an annulment "six weeks after the ceremony." Since that was the situation, it is apparent that regardless of
any specific intent which the plaintiff had with regard to his future
cohabitation with the defendant, in entering into the marriage ceremony as he did he was contemplating the creation of the status of
marriage for at least the limited period and purpose stated. He must
be held charged with the legal implications arising from the status;
* * * such, for example, as the rights of survivorship in the event
he or the defendant died during that interval. In principle, it would
make no difference whether the status so created by the terms of the
agreement was to continue for six weeks or six years. It is of even
greater significance that the parties married "to give the child a
name," that is, to give it the status incident to a legitimate birth. To
annul the marriage would render it void ab initio and so defeat this
very purpose. The court was amply warranted in its conclusion that
the consent and intent essential to afford the mutuality of a valid
contract of marriage existed upon the part of the plaintiff. * * *

     * * * The court reached the further conclusion, fortified by
the plaintiff's failure to claim an order or judgment of any nature
with relation to his child, that to decree the marriage void would be
against public policy. This was undoubtedly sound. * * * It was
not, however, essentially involved in the judgment upon this record.
The result reached is in accord with this general principle relative to
the effect of prenuptial agreements: "Once a marriage has been
properly solemnized and the obligations of married life undertaken,
its validity cannot be affected by an antenuptial agreement not to live
together nor by an agreement previously entered into that the marriage should not be valid and binding, nor because one or even both
of the parties did not intend it to be a permanent relation." Keezer,
Marriage & Divorce (3d Ed.) § 3. That prenuptial agreements designed to negative the effect of a marriage are generally void as
against public policy is well exemplified by these authorities: Po-
pham v. Duncan, 87 Colo. 149, 285 P. 757, 70 A.L.R. 824 (1930), note

826; French v. McAnarney, 290 Mass. 544, 546, 195 N.E. 714, 98 A. L.R. 530 (1935); Cumming v. Cumming, 127 Va. 16, 29, 102 S.E. 572; note, 98 A.L.R. 533 (1920).

There is no error.

*   *   *

NOTES AND QUESTIONS

1. This and similar cases are discussed in Note, Sham Marriages, 20 Univ.Chi.L.Rev. 710 (1953). A more recent case discussing the problem inadequately is Bishop v. Bishop, 62 Misc.2d 436, 308 N.Y.S.2d 998 (Sup.Ct. 1970).

2. What law should govern the validity of this marriage, that of New York, where the ceremony occurred, or that of Connecticut, where the parties were domiciled? Why do you suppose they went to New York to be married?

3. The court in the *Schibi* case mentions the need for mutual consent to form a valid marriage. In what sense, if any, can it be said that there was mutual consent to marry in this case? Does the ambiguity lie in "consent" or in "marry"?

4. Should other considerations influence the result in this case? For example, is the court saying that marriage is a ceremony of such seriousness that it must not be performed for ulterior motives, and if it is, the parties will not be heard to say that they really did not intend to contract a binding relationship? See Mpiliris v. Hellenic Lines, Ltd., 323 F.Supp. 865, 881–882 (S.D.Tex.1970), aff'd p. c. 440 F.2d 1163 (5th Cir. 1971): "* * * by reason of the strong social interests in protecting the integrity of the marital status, when two persons, otherwise qualified voluntarily go through a marriage ceremony, albeit for a limited purpose, with the intention, mutual understanding and anticipation that the marriage is to be accorded legal significance, the marriage is binding and, therefore, not subject to attack in a collateral proceeding." Is this analysis inconsistent with the cases on marriage in jest?

5. Would this case have been decided differently if Connecticut had had a statute, as most states do, providing that the child of a void or voidable marriage is deemed legitimate? For a typical provision, see Cal.Civ. Code § 4453 (1970).

6. Would the result in this case be easier to support if the state had had a statute authorizing divorce for irretrievable breakdown of a marriage, such as the Uniform Marriage and Divorce Act, §§ 302, 305, 9A. Unif.L.Ann. 121, 132 (1979)?

UNITED STATES v. DIOGO

United States Court of Appeals, Second Circuit, 1963.
320 F.2d 898.

WATERMAN, Circuit Judge. Appellants Jose Diogo, Manuel Gonzalez and Domingo Costa, are alleged to have entered into sham marriages with American citizens in order to obtain non-quota immigrant status under 8 U.S.C.A. § 1101(a)(27)(A). After a trial upon a twelve count indictment in the district court below, each of the aliens was convicted of (1) falsely representing to the Immigration authorities, in violation of 18 U.S.C.A. §§ 1001 and 1546, that he was actually married, and (2) entering into a conspiracy with the alleged instigator of the scheme, Adria Gonzalez, and others, to commit the substantive offenses charged. 18 U.S.C.A. § 371.

Appellants attack the convictions on the grounds, *inter alia,* that the evidence failed, as a matter of law, to prove the offenses charged, and that the trial judge erred in his instructions to the jury. We hold that the convictions must be reversed and the indictment dismissed as to each appellant.

Considering only the evidence most favorable to the Government's contentions, a jury might have found the following facts: In 1951, Jose Diogo, a Portuguese citizen, entered the United States as a business visitor under a temporary permit. In March 1957, he was introduced by Adria Gonzalez, an American of Puerto Rican descent, to Clara Heredia, also an American citizen. At that time Diogo, inasmuch as he had exceeded the time allotted for his stay in this country was about to be deported. Adria asked Clara Heredia if she would be willing to marry Diogo so that he could remain in the United States. Clara agreed, upon the assurance that she would receive a sum of money and that no sexual relations would be involved.

Pursuant to this understanding, Diogo and Clara were "married" at Newark, New Jersey, on April 6, 1957. Shortly after the ceremony Diogo gave Adria $500 which she shared with Clara. Thereafter, Diogo did not live with Clara and they did not consummate the marriage. On the basis of his representations regarding his change in marital status, the deportation proceedings against Diogo were reopened and he was ultimately found to qualify for non-quota status as the spouse of an American citizen. On January 4, 1958, Clara obtained a Mexican divorce from Diogo.

On February 9, 1960, Manuel Gonzalez, a Spanish citizen, entered the United States under a temporary permit. Shortly thereafter, Adria Gonzalez (who was not related to Manuel) again arranged for a "marriage" to permit the alien to remain in the United States. Yvette Garces, the daughter of Clara Heredia, agreed to marry Manuel for this purpose, upon the understanding that she would be paid for her cooperation and that she and Manuel would not live together as man and wife. Their marriage ceremony took place in Queens, New York, on February 24, 1960. Thereafter, Yvette received $500 from Manuel, but the couple neither lived together nor consummated their marriage. On April 28, 1960, Gonzalez applied to become a permanent resident by virtue of his marriage to an American citizen and his application was granted. Yvette obtained an Alabama divorce in August of 1961.

Appellant Domingo Costa is a Portuguese citizen and the brother of Jose Diogo. On November 9, 1956, Costa was deported from the United States for having overstayed a limited permit to enter this country while he was purportedly in transit to Venezuela. In the summer of 1957, Adria Gonzalez contacted Emma Mercado, an American citizen, and, according to Emma, "asked me if I would like to take a trip to Europe (where) I will meet some young man and that we may get married and that the future will be more rosy for me, that I wouldn't have to work any more." It is conceded by the Government that Emma subsequently agreed in all good faith to marry Costa. No money was mentioned or paid in consideration for the marriage and there never was any suggestion that the marriage would not be consummated or that it would be entered into in contemplation of a divorce. In the latter part of 1957 Emma went to Lisbon, Portugal, where she met Costa and where she remained for some two months while her visa and passport documents were being processed. The couple were married in Lisbon on January 21, 1958, and the marriage was consummated by sexual intercourse. Shortly thereafter Emma returned to the United States; Costa, having received a non-quota immigrant visa as Emma's spouse, entered this country on August 15, 1958. On May 10, 1960, Costa was granted a divorce from Emma in the New York courts.

Upon these facts we have no doubt that appellants may be deportable from the United States under 8 U.S.C.A. §§ 1251(a)(1) or 1251(c).[1] This, however, was a criminal prosecution, not a deportation proceeding.

We turn, therefore, to the question whether the Government has failed, as a matter of law, to prove violations of the criminal provisions under which appellants stand convicted: 18 U.S.C.A. § 1001 (false statements generally), 18 U.S.C.A. § 1546 (false statement in application for visa, etc.), and 18 U.S.C.A. § 371 (conspiracy to commit offense or to defraud United States). The statutory pattern re-

---

1. Under 8 U.S.C.A. § 1251(c) an alien is deportable if

"(1) hereafter he or she obtains any entry into the United States with an immigrant visa or other documentation procured on the basis of a marriage entered into less than two years prior to such entry of the alien and which, within two years subsequent to an entry of the alien into the United States shall be judicially anulled or terminated, unless such alien shall establish to the satisfaction of the Attorney General that such marriage was not contracted for the purpose of evading any provisions of the immigration laws; or (2) it appears to the satisfaction of the Attorney General that he or she has failed or refused to fulfill his or her marital agreement which in the opinion of the Attorney General was hereafter made for the purpose of procuring his or her entry as an immigrant."

8 U.S.C.A. § 1251(a) provides that an alien is deportable if he

"(1) at the time of entry was within one or more of the classes of aliens excludable by the law existing at the time of such entry;"

Under 8 U.S.C.A. § 1182(a)(21), each appellant was excludable from the United States at the time of his entry if he was not, in fact, "the spouse of a citizen of the United States," within the proper interpretation of that phrase under the immigration law.

veals that acts sufficient to constitute violation of the relevant clause of 18 U.S.C.A. § 1546 will also constitute a violation of 18 U.S.C.A. § 1001. Moreover, there is no suggestion in the indictment that the alleged conspiracies failed to achieve their supposed objective, the commission of the substantive offenses charged. It is clear, therefore, that the counts in the indictment charging violations of 18 U.S.C.A. § 1001 constitute the cornerstone of these prosecutions. If, as appellants contend, the Government has failed to prove violations of this provision, their convictions on all counts of the indictment must fall.

Section 1001 of Title 18 U.S.C.A., provides:

"§ 1001. Statements or entries generally

"Whoever, in any matter within the jurisdiction of any department or agency of the United States knowingly and willfully falsifies, conceals or covers up by any trick, scheme, or device a material fact, or makes any false, fictitious or fraudulent statements or representations, or makes or uses any false writing or document knowing the same to contain any false, fictitious or fraudulent statement or entry, shall be fined not more than $10,000 or imprisoned not more than five years, or both."

It is well established that this section encompasses within its proscription two distinct offenses, concealment of a material fact and false representations. * * * The objective of both offenses may be the same, to create or foster on the part of a Government agency a misapprehension of the true state of affairs. * * * What must be proved to establish each offense, however, differs significantly. False representations, like common law perjury, require proof of actual falsity; concealment requires proof of wilful nondisclosure by means of a "trick, scheme or device."

It is conceded by the Government that the basic substantive offense with which the present indictment charges each of the appellants is that of making false representations with respect to his marital status. The jury was so instructed below. We are brought, thus, to the question whether the Government has established that the statements of each appellant regarding his marital status were false, and that these statements were known by the appellants to be false at the time they were made.

Appellants maintain that neither the secret reservations of Costa, nor the limited purpose for which Diogo and Gonzalez married their respective spouses, renders these marriages invalid under the domestic relations law of New York or of most other American jurisdictions. * * *

The Government does not deny the "formal" validity of appellants' marriages. Relying upon Lutwak v. United States, 344 U.S. 604, 73 S.Ct. 481, 97 L.Ed. 593 (1953) and United States v. Rubenstein, 151 F.2d 915 (2 Cir. 1945), cert. denied 326 U.S. 766, 66 S.Ct. 168, 90 L.Ed. 462, however, the Government contends that the validity of the marriages under state law is immaterial to these prosecutions. The Government argues that, for the purposes of a criminal prosecution such as this one, if two persons, as part of an effort to circumvent the immigration laws, agree to a marriage "only for the sake of representing it as such to the outside world and with the understanding that they will put an end to it as soon as it has served its purpose to deceive," they were never married at all. * * *

Even by the strict standards of validity which the Government would have us adopt as determinative of this criminal prosecution, the marriage of Domingo Costa and Emma Mercado was valid at the time Costa represented to the immigration authorities that he was the spouse of an American citizen. Far from having entered into the marriage "with the understanding that they will put an end to it as soon as it has served its purpose to deceive," Emma married Costa in all good faith and with no knowledge of his ulterior motives. Therefore, there having been no false representation, Costa's conviction must be reversed and the indictment dismissed as to him.

By applying the same strict standards of marriage validity, the Government also contends that the convictions of Diogo and Gonzalez must be affirmed. Whether Rubenstein and Lutwak are dispositive of the issues presented by these appeals, however, raises difficult questions of interpretation.

In United States v. Rubenstein, supra, appellant, a New York attorney, was alleged to have arranged a sham marriage between an alien and an American citizen for purposes of evading the immigration laws. The indictment upon which he was convicted closely paralleled that in the case at bar, save that there concealment of a material fact, as well as affirmative false representations, was charged to have been an objective of the conspiratorial scheme. On appeal Rubenstein claimed that the allegedly sham marriage was valid under state law and that the representations with respect to it were true. This court rested an affirmance of Rubenstein's conviction upon two grounds: (1) that the validity of the marriage was immaterial to the charge of concealment of material facts, but (2) that the marriage was, in fact, a nullity under traditional requirements of mutual consent in the law of contract.

[At this point in its opinion the court discussed and quoted from Lutwak v. United States, 344 U.S. 604 (1953), concluding that the basis for the conviction in that case was a finding that the defendants had concealed their intention to separate immediately after their marriages, and that the Supreme Court had held that the validity or invalidity of the marriages was not material. The court thus emphasized the distinction that in *Lutwak* concealment of material facts was alleged in addition to false representations, while in this case only false representations were alleged.]

* * * We return thus to the question whether the representations of marriage made by Diogo and Gonzalez were literally false

and were known by appellants to be false at the time they were made to the immigration authorities.

It is undeniable, we believe, that neither of these questions may be answered until the *meaning* of the statements in issue has been ascertained. When he claimed to be the "spouse of" or to be "married to" an American citizen, each appellant purported to state the legal significance of a fact situation. Each representation was rendered ambiguous, however, by the quite understandable failure of appellants to specify the jurisdiction to which their legal conclusions referred. Assuming that New York domestic relations law is as appellants claim it to be, the mere addition of a parenthetical qualification— "under New York law"—would clearly have rendered blameless appellants' marital representations to the immigration authorities. By the same token, the statement that they were married "in the customary sense of the term as intended by Congress" would have rendered appellants culpable, assuming that they were apprised of the proper interpretation of Congressional intent. Therefore, the problem of ascertaining the law under which the validity of appellants' marriage is to be determined in a federal prosecution for false representations, is not, in the first instance, an issue of either federal intramural or federal conflict of laws doctrine. It is a question, rather, of the proper interpretation of appellants' statements.

In construing these statements it is well established that we must look to the meaning intended by the appellants themselves, rather than to the interpretation of the statements which the immigration authorities *did in fact make,* or even to the interpretation which the authorities *might reasonably have made.* * * *

We do not suggest that a court must accept as conclusive the meaning which a defendant, in a prosecution such as this, ascribes to the words he has used. If this were the rule to be applied, every person accused of perjury or false representations could assert his understanding of the words used in such a way as to preclude any possibility of conviction. * * * In a prosecution for perjury or false representation, absent fundamental ambiguity of the kind found in Lattimore, the question of what a defendant meant when he made his representation will normally be for the jury. * * * Where, as here, however, no evidence is presented on the question, it is incumbent upon the Government to negative any reasonable interpretation that would make the defendant's statement factually correct.

Here appellant asserts that their marital representations were true under the law of New York. The marriages of both Diogo and Gonzalez were initially arranged in New York. Gonzalez's marriage was celebrated in that jurisdiction. Both appellants were domiciliaries of New York at the time the representations were made to the immigration authorities. It is as reasonable to suppose, therefore, that appellants' statements were made with the New York law in mind as that they were made with the Congressional intent that prompted the enactment of 8 U.S.C.A. § 1101(a)(27)(A) in mind.

Under the law of New York a defective marriage may be either void or voidable. Voidable marriages are valid for all purposes until annulled by a court of competent jurisdiction. N.Y. Domestic Relations Law, § 7. * * * Parties to an absolutely void marriage may procure a judicial declaration of nullity, N.Y.Civil Practice Act, § 1132, but as their "marriage" never existed in contemplation of the law, such a declaration effects no change in the unmarried status of the two persons. * * *

The only provisions of the New York statutes which absolutely void a marriage are those contained in Sections 5, 6 and 11 of the Domestic Relations Law. * * * Sections 5 and 6 concern incestuous and bigamous marriages. Section 11 provides for the invalidity of a marriage not solemnized as therein required. It is uncertain whether these provisions encompass all grounds for voidity (either as a matter of substantive law or for purpose of conferring jurisdiction upon the courts of the state). * * * No case has been discovered, however, in which the New York courts have issued a declaration of nullity, as distinguished from the grant of an annulment, because of the absence of contractual intent or because both parties with limited purposes negating their acts entered into a formal marriage relationship.[2] Indeed, the New York courts have repeatedly held allegedly "sham" or "limited purpose" marriages to be neither void nor voidable, and thus to be dissolvable only by a decree of divorce.[3]

In Gregg v. Gregg, 133 Misc. 109, 231 N.Y.S. 221 (Sup.Ct.1928), the defendant spouse in an action for separation set up, by way of defense and counterclaim, the voidity of the parties' marriage. He alleged that they agreed to go through the "farce and mockery" of a French wedding ceremony with the understanding that they would not cohabit, that the defendant would not contribute to the plaintiff's

2. Our research reveals but two instances in which the New York courts have granted an annulment upon facts similar to those at bar, Dorgeloh v. Murtha, 92 Misc. 279, 156 N.Y.S. 181 (Sup.Ct.1915) and Amsden v. Amsden, 202 Misc. 391, 110 N.Y.S.2d 307 (Sup.Ct.1952). In each, by operation of the doctrine of "relation back," the decree of annulment was held to render the marriage void *ab initio*. These cases do not support the Government's contention that appellants' marriages were absolutely void, however, for they contain no suggestion that the parties to the defective marriage relationships might have disregarded their relationships absent the decree of annulment issued by a court of competent jurisdiction.

3. Where the "limited purpose" exists in the mind of only one of the parties to a marriage the marriage is ordinarily held to be voidable under N.Y. Domestic Relations Law, § 7(4) at the instance of the innocent party. See, e. g., Pastore v. Pastore, 199 Misc. 435, 100 N.Y.S.2d 552 (Sup.Ct.1950); Ernst v. Ernst, 32 N.Y.S.2d 759 (Sup. Ct.1941); Miodownik v. Miodownik, 259 App.Div. 851, 19 N.Y.S.2d 175 (1940); Lederkremer v. Lederkremer, 173 Misc. 587, 18 N.Y.S.2d 725 (Sup. Ct.1940).

support, and that he would be free to cohabit with other women. Dismissing the counterclaim, the court stated:

"In this state the parties to a marriage may not vary or diminish the obligations which the law attaches to the relationship by private agreements between themselves.

* * *

"The parties here concededly went through a marriage ceremony. Any private reservations they may have made in regard to their respective obligations under the marital status which resulted are void and of no effect.

* * *

" * * * even if it be assumed that the averments of the defense do sufficiently establish the absence of a contractual intention, that would at most give the defendant the right to maintain an annulment action.

"Sections 5 and 6 of the Domestic Relations Law, defining void marriages, include only incestuous marriages and those contracted by a person whose husband or wife by a former marriage is living. The 'marriage' referred to in the defense is valid until annulled by judicial decree." (231 N.Y.S. at 223–224).

In Erickson v. Erickson, 48 N.Y.S.2d 588 (Sup.Ct.1944) the parties entered into a marriage solely for the purpose of legitimizing a child which subsequently died at birth. It was understood that the marriage would take place only in form and that the parties would never cohabit. Denying the wife's uncontested petition for annulment, the court stated:

"In view of the fact that the child had died; that marriage was never consummated by cohabitation; that there is no hope of the parties ever living together and creating a family home, we agree * * * that it would be much better * * * if some legal termination to this difficult relationship could be had. We reluctantly reach the conclusion that the plaintiff's application must be denied. * * * If a fraud has occurred, they are the parties who purposely and intentionally brought it about. It may be unfortunate for them and the public generally that the law governing these conditions does not permit this half-marriage to be wiped out. However, divorces and annulments are only granted in those cases where the law specifically provides therefor, and no stretching of the statutes of this State can possibly be made to include the case here presented." 48 N.Y.S. 2d at 589–590. * * *

We are not called upon to rule, on the authorities cited above, that neither appellants nor their respective spouses could secure declarations of nullity with respect to their alleged marriages in the New York courts. It is sufficient to hold, as we now do, that the Government has failed, as a matter of law, at the trial below, to sustain its burden of there proving that the marriages were void at the time appellants' representations concerning marital status were made.[4]

* * *

The judgment of the district court is reversed and the cause is remanded with instructions that the indictment be dismissed as to all appellants.

CLARK, Circuit Judge (dissenting). I am unable to perceive why this case is not precisely governed by Lutwak v. United States, 344 U.S. 604 (1953), and by our own earlier decision of United States v. Rubenstein, 2 Cir., 151 F.2d 915, cert. denied 326 U.S. 766 (1945), cited with approval in Lutwak. In fact the more my brothers protest that there is some (unclear) distinction between the cases, the more they disclose the essential identity. In Lutwak three justices dissented, making essentially the same point my brothers stress, namely, that proof was lacking that the marriages were invalid or at least only voidable where made. But the six-man majority held expressly that the validity of the marriages was immaterial. Among other things Justice Minton said, 344 U.S. 604, at pages 611, 612: "Thus, when one of the aliens stated that he was married, and omitted to explain the true nature of his marital relationship, his statement did, and was intended to, carry with it implications of a state of facts which were not in fact true." Why my brothers quote this with apparent approval is not clear, since it is so directly applicable to our present case.

While I cannot discover what distinction my brothers are actually advancing, I gather that they are attempting to fragmentize the facts so as to look for small differences in the representations made by these defendants from those appearing in the earlier cases. They are not successful; for the differences at best are trifling as well as immaterial on the evidence. Here appellants Diogo and Gonzalez hired defendant Adria Gonzalez to procure for them women who for hire went through sham weddings which were never consummated and by which appellants fooled the immigration authorities as to their marital status and staved off deportation until the true facts were brought out on investigation. What more precise testimony of obviously and knowingly making a false claim against the government could be imagined! And on this basis the laborious attempt to determine the New York law of marriage is without point; whatever ideas these appellants may have had as to that law, they knew enough about the federal law of deportation to make quite an investment in an endeavor to evade it.

4. Although the New Jersey authorities are not as numerous as those of New York, no different conclusion would be demanded as to Diogo if we were to consider New Jersey law to be controlling in his case. Cf. e. g., Woodward v. Heichelbeck, 97 N.J.Eq. 253, 128 A. 169; Lindquist v. Lindquist, 130 N.J.Eq. 11, 20 A.2d 325 (1941).

* * *

I excepted appellant Costa from the above statement because his case is somewhat different from the others. In his case the evidence tends to show that the woman he procured went into the marriage in good faith, without knowledge of his intent, and that the marriage was consummated. How far inner reservations as to intent of only one party to a marriage may be used to show a false claim to secure immigration advantages is a problem. I would not be greatly troubled to accept the view that a marriage thus at least partially valid should not be inquired into further as a matter of public policy. But examining the rationale of the Lutwak and Rubenstein cases, I find stress upon the deportee's intent; hence although the case seems not free from doubt, I am constrained to conclude that Costa, too, was properly convicted on the evidence.

* * *

It is to be noted that Adria Gonzalez, the procuress of the women and the pivot about whom the conspiracy revolved, was convicted and sentenced to seven years' imprisonment and has not appealed. So she must do time for a crime which my brothers hold does not exist. But at any rate her business has been validated; and it may be expected that others, too, may take up this occupation, now that a real gap in the immigration laws has been found at hand for convenient exploitation.

NOTES AND QUESTIONS

1. A later case in the Second Circuit is based upon the distinction made in the *Diogo* case between misrepresentation of the marriage relation and concealment, and affirmed a conviction where the jury found that the defendants had concealed antenuptial agreements to pay for the marriage and to get a divorce two years later after the immigration authorities had been properly deceived. In addition there were false representations that the parties had lived together as husband and wife. United States v. Pantelopoulos, 336 F.2d 421 (2d Cir. 1964). The validity of the marriage was not an issue in the case.

2. In Johl v. United States, 370 F.2d 174 (9th Cir. 1967) the defendant, a citizen of India, was charged with concealment from the Immigration and Naturalization Service the fact that he had married solely for the purpose of obtaining the status of permanent resident alien, with the understanding that he and his purported spouse would not live together as husband and wife. The court upheld the indictment, on the authority of Lutwak v. United States, 344 U.S. 604 (1952), which had stated that the validity or invalidity of the marriage was irrelevant, and which contained the following language: "The common understanding of a marriage, which Congress must have had in mind when it made provision for 'alien *spouses*' in the War Brides Act, is that the two parties have undertaken to establish a life together and assume certain duties and obligations. Such was not the case here, or so the jury might reasonably have found. Thus, when one of the aliens stated that he was married, and omitted to explain the true nature of his marital relationship, his statement did, and was intended to, carry with it implications of a state of facts which were not in fact true." The *Johl* opinion then goes on to say that *Lutwak* means that the immigration law is

not talking about the legality of marriage, but about the relationship of marriage itself, with which separation or an agreement to separate is wholly inconsistent. So the government was concerned with the parties' purpose, not the normality of their relationship. The relationship here was then labelled a "sham". For somewhat similar reasoning, see United States v. Sacco, 428 F.2d 264 (9th Cir. 1970), cert. den. 400 U.S. 903 reh. den. 401 U.S. 926 (1971).

This and the *Lutwak* case raise the following questions:

(a) Does a legal definition of marriage have any relevance in these cases? Or are the courts concerned exclusively with the construction and purposes of the immigration laws?

(b) Do these cases mean that an alien spouse admitted to the United States because married to a United States citizen would be guilty of violation of 18 U.S.C.A. § 1001 in that he "did wilfully * * * conceal * * * by trick, scheme and device a material fact in a matter within the jurisdiction of the Immigration and Naturalization Service", assuming that no question of the validity of their marriage could be raised, solely on the ground that at the time of admission the spouses had agreed that their marriage was broken, had separated, and had intended to get a divorce at the earliest opportunity? Or is all the talk in the *Lutwak* and *Johl* cases just an elaborate and intellectually devious method of avoiding the question of the validity of the marriages?

3. Judging from the reported cases, there is frequent use of marriage as a way of circumventing the immigration laws. The principle announced in Lutwak seems to have been generally followed by the lower federal courts, rather than the analysis in Diogo, although Diogo has not been overruled. In other words the immigration cases tend to define "marriage" as meaning that the parties did not merely go through a technically valid ceremony, but that when they did so they had the intention of establishing a life together. Such cases include Whetstone v. Immigration and Naturalization Service, 561 F.2d 1303 (9th Cir. 1977); Bark v. Immigration and Naturalization Service, 511 F.2d 1200 (9th Cir. 1975); De Figueroa v. Immigration and Naturalization Service, 501 F.2d 191 (7th Cir. 1974); McLat v. Longo, 412 F.Supp. 1021 (D.V.I. 1976), 15 J.Fam.L. 602 (1977).

4. What would have been the result in the *Diogo* case if Clara had subsequently married someone else, without bothering to obtain a divorce from Diogo? Would such a marriage have made her liable to a conviction for bigamy?

5. What would have been the result if, after marrying Diogo, Clara had sued him in New York for separation or non-support, under N.Y.Dom. Rel.L. § 200 which authorizes such an action when the husband neglects or refuses to provide for his wife? Silver (orse Kraft) v. Silver, [1955] 2 All Eng.Rep. 614, [1955] 1 W.L.R. 728, 69 Harv.L.Rev. 768 (1956).

6. What would have been the result if, after the marriage of Clara and Diogo, Diogo had been killed in an industrial accident and Clara had filed a claim as his widow under the applicable workmen's compensation law? Cf. Mpiliris v. Hellenic Lines, Ltd., 323 F.Supp. 865, 879–882 (S.D. Tex.1970), aff'd p. c. 440 F.2d 1163 (5th Cir. 1971).

7. In the Encyclical Letter on Christian Marriage of Pope Pius XI, reprinted in Association of American Law Schools, Selected Essays on Fam-

ily Law, at page 132 (1950), at page 133, there is the following: "For each individual marriage, inasmuch as it is a conjugal union of a particular man and woman, arises only from the free consent of each of the spouses; and this free act of the will, by which each party hands over and accepts those rights proper to the state of marriage, is so necessary to constitute the true marriage that it cannot be supplied by any human power. This freedom, however, regards only the question whether the contracting parties really wish to enter upon matrimony or to marry this particular person; but the nature of matrimony is entirely independent of the free will of man * * *." Judged by this test, was the necessary consent present in the Diogo marriage? Is the law's requirement different from that of Pope Pius XI?

8. Look back at the brief account of the reasoning in *Lutwak* and *Johl* in paragraph 2, supra. The courts in those cases seemed to emphasize that the parties had not undertaken to assume the duties and obligations of marriage, although they had gone through a marriage ceremony. But is it not true, as the Pope's Encyclical and as the final paragraph of the *Schibi* case state, that once fully qualified parties voluntarily engage in a marriage ceremony, the legal consequences of marriage immediately attach, irrespective of whether the parties intend to assume them or not? Therefore would it not follow that for purposes of determining the validity of a marriage it is of no consequence whether the parties undertook to assume the duties of marriage? Or should the law be otherwise and say that only if the parties knowingly undertake all the marital obligations are they married? But how are they to know what all the obligations are?

9. Would a better solution to the various cases result if we frankly recognize that whether or not a valid marriage exists depends largely upon the context in which the question arises? Consider the following case: Frank was charged with murder and the question arose in the course of his trial whether Rose could testify in the case. A statute provided that a wife might not testify for or against her husband without his consent. Rose and Frank had gone through a civil marriage ceremony in Italy which was concededly valid by Italian law. There was evidence that the ceremony was held for the purpose of enabling Frank to get into the United States, that he and Rose intended to have a religious ceremony later on, and that only after the religious ceremony would they consider themselves to be man and wife. The court, after characterizing the marriage as cold, inanimate and lifeless, held that Rose and Frank were never husband and wife within the meaning of the evidence statute, concluding this section of its opinion by saying, "Our decision here is limited to an application of the statute to the facts as disclosed by this record." Archina v. People, 135 Colo. 8, 28, 307 P.2d 1083, 1094 (1957); United States v. Mathis, 559 F.2d 294 (5th Cir. 1977); United States v. Apodaca, 522 F.2d 568 (10th Cir. 1975). Does this suggest that for purposes of the testimonial privilege parties might not be married, while for other purposes they might be married? Does it imply that the statute would not apply to persons undeniably married but living estranged and apart? On this and other marital privileges, see 8 J. Wigmore, Evidence §§ 2227, 2230, 2231, 2334 (McNaughton rev. ed. 1961).

10. If greater certainty is desirable, and a single, unified definition of marriage is needed, draft a statute which embodies such a definition, dealing with the questions of intent raised by the cases.

Chapter 4

THE SUIT TO ANNUL

SECTION 1. PROBLEMS OF JURISDICTION

PERLSTEIN v. PERLSTEIN

Supreme Court of Errors of Connecticut, 1964.
152 Conn. 152, 204 A.2d 909.

KING, Chief Justice. The plaintiff husband instituted this action against the defendant wife, claiming an annulment of their purported marriage. While the complaint lacks clarity, the allegations of fact in the plaintiff's answer to the defendant's plea in abatement, admitted by the defendant's demurrer to that answer, make it clear that the annulment is claimed on the ground that the defendant was legally married to another at the time she went through the marriage ceremony with the plaintiff in Hartford, Connecticut, on August 25, 1959.

The court sustained the demurrer to the plaintiff's answer to the plea in abatement, the plaintiff chose not to plead over, and judgment was thereupon rendered that the action abate. * * *

I

The ground of the jurisdictional attack was that this action was for the annulment of a bigamous marriage and could be maintained only if the defendant, who was a resident of the state of New Jersey at the time of the institution of the action, was personally served within Connecticut. Service had been constructive, by registered mail addressed to the defendant in New Jersey.

At the outset, it should be noted that the defendant's claim is concerned with jurisdiction of the person, that is, jurisdiction to affect the rights of this particular nonresident defendant, in this particular action, on the basis of the particular service of process utilized. There is no doubt that the Superior Court has jurisdiction over the subject matter of annulment where, as here, the plaintiff is domiciled in Connecticut, and this is so whether the ground relied upon would make the marriage void or voidable. General Statutes, § 46–28; Restatement, Conflict of Laws § 115(1); id., §§ 109–111 and § 113 as amended in the 1948 Sup., p. 111. Indeed, the defendant does not seem seriously to contest the court's jurisdiction of the subject matter.

The rule denying that jurisdiction over this nonresident defendant can be acquired by constructive service outside Connecticut appears to be the majority rule today. Note, 128 A.L.R. 61, 73; 43 A. L.R.2d 1086; * * * It is set forth perhaps as well as anywhere in the case of Owen v. Owen, 127 Colo. 359, 257 P.2d 581, 43 A.L.R.2d 1081 (1953). In essence, in a case seeking annulment of a bigamous marriage, the majority rule proceeds upon two grounds. The first relates to the situation during the pendency of the action and prior to the rendition of the decree of annulment. The second applies to the action upon the rendition of the decree of annulment.

A

1. The first ground is that, by instituting an action for the annulment of a marriage on the claim that it is bigamous, the plaintiff necessarily claims that the marriage is "void"; [1] that, therefore, there can on the plaintiff's own claims, be no marriage status, and, consequently, no res; and that without a res the action is necessarily in personam. Admittedly, in personam jurisdiction cannot be acquired over a nonresident defendant by constructive service without the state.

One vice in the reasoning of this first ground is that it presupposes that the marriage status, in the constitutional sense, can be changed by a plaintiff's claims. Obviously, status either exists or it does not exist, and a plaintiff cannot create it or destroy it by his claims as to the validity or invalidity of the marriage.

Another vice in the reasoning is that it overlooks the fact that the terms "in rem" and "in personam" are not apt in describing the character of an action seeking to affect marital status. Such an action is neither an action merely in personam nor a true action in rem. In the constitutional sense it requires, in the forum state, the domicil of at least one of the parties to the marriage. In the determination of jurisdiction to render a decree affecting the marriage status, the search must be for a domicil, not for a status or res. Williams v. North Carolina, 317 U.S. 287, 297, 63 S.Ct. 207, 212, 87 L.Ed. 279 (1942). Manifestly, domicil cannot be affected by the type of action instituted.

Moreover, the status of marriage is an intangible res, entirely different from the tangible res of real estate or personal property within the jurisdiction upon which a true in rem action can be based as in cases such as Harris v. Weed, 89 Conn. 214, 221, 93 A. 232, 234 (1915), or a quasi in rem action as in cases such as Pezas v. Pezas, 151 Conn. 611, 614, 201 A.2d 192, 193 (1964). Thus, if the parties are domiciled in separate states, jurisdiction over the marriage status exists in each state, and under the "res" theory, the res necessarily

---

1. Where the marriage sought to be annulled is voidable, as distinguished from being "void", it is generally agreed that the marriage status does persist unless and until a decree of annulment is rendered.

exists in each state. The res is not, nor can it be, independently ascertainable as such, apart from domicil. The existence of the status or "res" in the forum state stems solely from the fact that the domicil of at least one party to the marriage is in that state. * * * If domicil exists in a state, jurisdiction to affect the status of marriage exists in that state, regardless of whether the status does or does not fit into the classic concept of a "res". * * *

A marriage ceremony, especially if apparently legally performed, gives rise to a presumptively valid status of marriage which persists unless and until it is overthrown by evidence in an appropriate judicial proceeding. No mere claim of bigamy, whether made in a pleading or elsewhere, would establish that a marriage was bigamous. * * * Seldom, if ever, would a party to a bigamous marriage, in the face of the presumption of its validity, feel free to treat the marriage as a nullity without a decree of annulment. Nor do we believe any attorney would advise such a course of conduct. The state's concern in the marriage status of its domiciliaries imperatively demands that the invalidity of the purported marriage be judicially determined before that invalidity be accepted. * * * If judicial action is needed, it must be because, in some degree at least, a status of marriage exists. If it does exist, then to that extent at least it is a res, as far as there is any res in a status action, and must be treated as such. Even theoretically, it is inaccurate to state that in this case there is no "res" during the pendency of the annulment action.

B

The second ground on which the majority rule proceeds is that upon the rendition of a decree of annulment the marriage is made void retroactively from its inception, and, therefore, there can be and is no status or res on which the court could act.

Under this theory, whether or not a status exists prior to a decree of annulment, upon the rendition of such a decree the court necessarily determines that such a status does not exist and, ab initio, never did exist, and thereby ousts itself, by its very decree, of any jurisdiction to render that decree against a nonresident defendant constructively served by mail. Owen v. Owen, 127 Colo. 359, 365, 257 P.2d 581, 584, 43 A.L.R.2d 1081 (1953).

"Despite the legal fiction that a judgment in [an annulment] case relates back to the inception of the marriage, for some purposes, such a judgment involves and vitally affects the status of the parties from a logical, legal and practical standpoint." Buzzi v. Buzzi, 91 Cal.App.2d 823, 825, 205 P.2d 1125, 1126 (1949), cert. denied 338 U.S. 894, 70 S.Ct. 244, 94 L.Ed. 549. The legal fiction that an annulment relates back to destroy the marriage ab initio is one applied only as the "purposes of justice" require. Gaines v. Jacobsen, 308 N.Y. 218, 225, 124 N.E.2d 290, 294, 48 A.L.R.2d 312 (1954). Certainly, neither justice nor this state's interest in the marriage status of its domiciliary would be advanced by the application of such a legal fiction here.

Our annulment statute itself (§ 46–28), although referring to "void or voidable" marriages, provides that the court may grant alimony, and custody and support orders for any minor child, as in the case of divorce. Public Acts 1963, No. 105, amended the section by adding a sentence declaring that "[t]he issue of any void or voidable marriage shall be deemed legitimate." These provisions are irreconcilable with the theory that even a marriage claimed to be void is, or upon the rendition of a decree of annulment retroactively becomes, an absolute nullity ab initio so that nothing in the way of a status or res ever flowed from the marriage. See Gaines v. Jacobsen, supra.

In the instant case the plaintiff's Connecticut domicil would give jurisdiction for a decree of divorce even upon constructive service on a nonresident defendant. We agree with the California court in Buzzi v. Buzzi, supra, that the same jurisdictional requirements apply in the case of an action for annulment. We further hold that this is so whether the action is based on a ground which, if established, would make the marriage "void" or "voidable". Any other rule would leave it in the power of a party to a bigamous marriage, by removing himself to a jurisdiction in a remote part of the world, to force an innocent Connecticut party, domiciled in this state, to resort to the tribunals (if any) of that jurisdiction in order to secure relief (if any were there obtainable) from the obviously intolerable situation of a subsisting marriage bigamous in fact. Public policy does not support or countenance such a rule, and no hypertechnical, unrealistic and inaccurate definitions of the terms "status" and "res" make it constitutionally necessary to follow such a rule. * * *

Indeed in this very case, it is admitted that both parties were domiciled in Connecticut when and before the marriage was celebrated, and that this joint domicil continued until the defendant moved to New Jersey not long prior to the institution of this action.

II

It perhaps should be pointed out that our statute (§ 46–28) conferring jurisdiction on the Superior Court to render a judgment of annulment contains no particular residence requirement, nor any particular requirement as to service of process. Mazzei v. Cantales, 142 Conn. 173, 176, 112 A.2d 205, 207 (1955). It follows that the statute (§ 52–68) generally governing service by publication on a nonresident defendant properly applies to an annulment action where, as here, the plaintiff is domiciled in Connecticut. See cases such as Hartley v. Vitiello, 113 Conn. 74, 81, 154 A. 255, 258 (1931). That statute was followed in the instant case and resulted in actual notice within a few days. Thus, no question can arise as to conformity with the statutory requirements of the forum with respect to residence or manner of service of process.

III

Lastly, the defendant makes much of the case of Mazzei v. Cantales, supra. It is true that that case contains dicta (p. 178, 112 A.2d 205) supporting the majority rule, which we have rejected. The actual holding of that case, however, is stated on page 179 of the opinion, 112 A.2d on page 208 in the following language: "Where both parties to an action for annulment of a void marriage are nonresidents and the defendant is not served with process within this state or does not appear and submit to the jurisdiction of the * * * court, the fact that the marriage was performed within this state does not empower the court to obtain jurisdiction over the defendant by constructive service and to render a judgment annulling the marriage." * * * This holding is not inconsistent with the position which we take in this case. Here, the plaintiff is, and at all times has been, a domiciliary of Connecticut.

[handwritten margin note: disting. both non-residents]

IV

There is error, the judgments erasing and abating the action for lack of jurisdiction are set aside and the case is remanded for further proceedings in conformity with this opinion.

In this opinion the other judges concurred.

NOTES AND QUESTIONS

1. After the remand by the Supreme Court of Errors, the plaintiff died, but the Superior Court held that the action did not thereby abate. Perlstein v. Perlstein, 26 Conn.Sup. 257, 217 A.2d 481 (1966).

2. This and the next case are concerned with jurisdiction to hear and decide annulment suits. What does jurisdiction mean? Why need we be concerned with it here, or in any other connection?

3. There are some kinds of lawsuits, e. g. the ordinary personal injury suit, which are customarily labeled in personam actions. For jurisdiction to be acquired in such actions, personal service upon the defendant must be made within the state, or certain equivalent events must occur, as by the defendant's entering a general appearance in the case. Why should our law make this requirement for this kind of suit? See Pennoyer v. Neff, 95 U. S. 714, 720 (1877): "The authority of every tribunal is necessarily restricted by the territorial limits of the State in which it is established. Any attempt to exercise authority beyond those limits would be deemed in every other forum, as has been said by this court, an illegitimate assumption of power, and be resisted as mere abuse." Is this the reason for the requirement? Or is the requirement merely an elaborate way of ensuring notice of the suit to the defendant under guarantees of procedural due process made by the Fourteenth Amendment?

4. The Restatement of Judgments, § 32, comment a. (1942) defines proceedings in rem as follows: "Where a thing is subject to the power of a State, a proceeding may be brought to affect the interests in the thing not merely of particular persons but of all persons in the world. Such a pro-

ceeding is called a proceeding in rem, as distinguished from a proceeding brought to affect the interests in the thing of particular persons only, which is called a proceeding quasi in rem." The courts, (vide Owen v. Owen, 127 Colo. 359, 257 P.2d 581 (1953) cited in Perlstein), sometimes assume that the reason and justification for the creation of a class of actions called "in rem" actions is that a thing or res is located within the state, on which the court's judgment may operate. Is this correct? Or is there some other reason for establishing a class of actions in which personal service on defendants within the jurisdiction is not required? See, e. g., in addition to *Pennoyer*, supra, paragraph 3, Tyler v. Judges of the Court of Registration, 175 Mass. 71, 73, 55 N.E. 812, 813 (1900).

5. The court in *Perlstein* concedes that the "majority rule" holds that jurisdiction over a nonresident defendant in an annulment suit may not be acquired by constructive service. What is the rationale for this rule? Does it turn on the classification of annulment as either in personam or in rem?

6. What reasons does the Connecticut court give for rejecting the "majority rule"? Does the court's decision raise constitutional questions? Is the finding of a "res" essential to the constitutionality of the result in this case?

7. The court in *Perlstein* cites the earlier Connecticut case of Mazzei v. Cantales, 142 Conn. 173, 112 A.2d 205 (1955), holding that where neither party was a domiciliary of Connecticut, but the marriage had been contracted there, constructive service could not be the basis for annulment jurisdiction. Is the court here correct in holding that its decision is not inconsistent with *Mazzei*? Many early cases agree with *Mazzei* that the state where the marriage occurred has subject matter jurisdiction in annulment. Why should this be? Cf. Foster v. Nordman, 244 S.C. 485, 137 S.E.2d 600 (1964).

8. Would it be desirable to solve the problem of this case by statute? If so, what should the statute provide? If the statutes of a state include comprehensive regulations of marriage and annulment, as for example does the Uniform Marriage and Divorce Act, but say nothing about service of process or personal jurisdiction, what inferences should the courts draw? Should they assume that the rule of *Perlstein* governs, or that annulment has been made an in personam action in all circumstances, or that some other rule prevails?

9. H and W have been living together purportedly as husband and wife for about a year, for the most part in State A, which does not recognize common law marriage. They have, however, spent time in State B, where common law marriage is recognized. They have never engaged in a marriage ceremony. At the end of this time H leaves W, telling her he does not think they are married and that he has no obligation to her. Since H has considerable property, and since W has been telling people they were married, the existence of a marriage is important to her. She brings suit in State A, where she is domiciled, seeking a declaration that the marriage is valid, and serving H by registered mail in State B, where he now lives. H files a special appearance, and a motion to dismiss the suit for lack of jurisdiction. What arguments should be made on either side? See Gardner v. Gardner, 98 U.S.App.D.C. 144, 233 F.2d 23 (1956); Annot., 92 A.L.

R.2d 1102 (1963). If you had represented W, would you have advised her to take some other action than this suit in State A?

WHEALTON v. WHEALTON

Supreme Court of California, In Bank, 1967.
67 Cal.2d 656, 432 P.2d 979, 63 Cal.Rptr. 291.

TRAYNOR, Chief Justice. Defendant appeals from a default *Case* judgment annulling her marriage to plaintiff on the ground of fraud.

Plaintiff, a petty officer on active duty with the United States Navy, married defendant at Bel Air, Maryland, on June 15, 1964. Thereafter his military duties took him from place to place on the east coast until he was assigned to the U.S.S. *Repose* at the San Francisco Naval Shipyard. He arrived in California on July 14, 1965. *F* Plaintiff and defendant lived together for only six or seven weeks on the east coast.

On September 3, 1965, plaintiff filed this action for annulment of the marriage. Summons was issued and an order for publication of summons was filed on the same day. Publication of the summons was accomplished as prescribed by law. Defendant received a copy of the summons by mail at her home in Maryland on September 7, 1965. On September 11, 1965, she wrote the court that she was having difficulty obtaining legal counsel, but that she wished "it known that it is my earnest desire and intent to contest this complaint." On October 11, 1965, the court entered her default, heard testimony in *Default* support of the complaint, and entered a judgment annulling the marriage. On October 19, 1965, defendant made a motion to set aside the default and the judgment by default and to permit the filing of an answer and a cross-complaint. The motion was denied on November 9, 1965.

Defendant contends that the default judgment must be reversed on the grounds that it was prematurely entered and that the court did not have jurisdiction of the subject matter.

Since defendant resides outside the state, the summons could be served by publication (Code Civ.Proc. §§ 412, 413). "When publication is ordered, personal service of a copy of the summons and complaint out of the State is equivalent to publication and deposit in the post office. Service is complete upon the making of such personal service or at the expiration of the time prescribed by the order of publication, whichever event shall first occur." (Code Civ.Proc. § 413.) Defendant had 30 days after service was complete to appear and answer (Code Civ.Proc. § 407) and would not be in default until the expiration of that time (Code Civ.Proc. § 585, subd. 3; Foster v. Vehmeyer, 133 Cal. 459, 460, 65 P. 974 (1901); Grewell v. Henderson, 5 Cal. 465, 466 (1855); Burt v. Scrantom, 1 Cal. 416, 417

(1851).) Since she was not personally served [1] the 30-day period could not begin before September 25, 1965, the earliest date on which service of publication could be deemed completed. (See Code Civ. Proc. § 413; Gov.Code, § 6064.) The entry of default and the default judgment entered on October 11, 1965, only 16 days later, are therefore void.

Even if the default judgment were not premature, it would have to be reversed, for neither the pleadings nor the evidence establish that either party was a domiciliary of California. The court therefore lacked jurisdiction to award an ex parte annulment.

In ex parte divorce actions, a bona fide domicile of at least one of the parties within the forum state is necessary for jurisdiction. (Williams v. State of North Carolina, 325 U.S. 226, 229, 238, 65 S.Ct. 1092, 1094, 1099, 89 L.Ed. 1577 (1945); Crouch v. Crouch, 28 Cal.2d 243, 249, 169 P.2d 897 (1946); see D. Currie, Suitcase Divorce in the Conflict of Laws: Simons, Rosenstiel, and Borax (1966) 34 U.Chi.L. Rev. 26, 45; Developments—Jurisdiction (1960) 73 Harv.L.Rev. 909, 966; Rest., Conflict of Laws, § 111.) This rule reflects due process considerations involved in adjudicating rights of an absent party in an inconvenient forum; it also reflects the interests of the several states in regulating the marital status of their domiciliaries and limits forum shopping for self-serving substantive divorce law. (See Williams v. State of North Carolina, supra, 325 U.S. 226, 229–230, 65 S.Ct. 1092, 89 L.Ed. 1577 (1945); Crouch v. Crouch, supra, 28 Cal.2d 243, 251, 169 P.2d 897 (1946); see von Mehren & Trautman, Jurisdiction to Adjudicate: A Suggested Analysis (1966) 79 Harv.L.Rev. 1121, 1130; Developments—Jurisdiction, supra, 73 Harv.L.Rev. 909, 967–968, 973–974.)

Civil Code section 128 implements this rule by requiring that at least one of the parties to an action for divorce be a resident of the state for a year before the action is commenced. (See also Civ.Code, § 128.1.) In this context the statutory terms "residence" and "domicile" are synonymous.[2] (Haas v. Haas, 227 Cal.App.2d 615, 617, 38

---

1. Receipt of the mailed summons on September 7, 1965, was not personal service. The requirements of a personal service are strictly construed; a mere showing that a party had notice in fact is insufficient. (Lettenmaier v. Lettenmaier (1962) 203 Cal. App.2d 837, 843–844, 22 Cal.Rptr. 156 (1962); Sternbeck v. Buck (1957) 148 Cal.App.2d 829, 832, 307 P.2d 970 (1957).

2. A majority of the states use length of residence as a basis for jurisdiction. Equating domicile with residence should be unnecessary to fulfill due process requirements. A reason-able length-of-residence test alone would obviate the necessity for an often spurious inquiry into intent and would demonstrate as clearly as domicile that the forum state has an interest in adjudicating the marital status. (See D. Currie, Suitcase Divorce in the Conflict of Laws: Simons, Rosenstiel, and Borax, supra, 34 U.Chi. L.Rev. 26, 64; Powell, And Repent at Leisure (1945) 58 Harv.L.Rev. 930, 1008–1010.) Several states have statutes permitting resident servicemen to obtain divorces without inquiry into domicile. These states apply their own law. (See Cheatham, Griswold, Reese and Rosenberg (5th ed.

Cal.Rptr. 811 (1964); Ungemach v. Ungemach, 61 Cal.App.2d 29, 36, 142 P.2d 99 (1943); see Smith v. Smith, 45 Cal.2d 235, 239, 288 P.2d 497 (1955).)

In Millar v. Millar, 175 Cal. 797, 807, 167 P. 394, L.R.A.1918B (1917), this court held that the statutory residence requirement for divorce did not apply to annulment proceedings. In that case, however, since both parties were before the court and the marriage had been entered into in California, the court had no occasion to and did not consider on what basis a state may constitutionally declare void a marriage of prima facie validity when one of the parties is not before the court.

Ex parte divorces are a striking exception to the rule that a court must have personal jurisdiction over a party before it may adjudicate his substantial rights. (See von Mehren & Trautman, Jurisdiction to Adjudicate: A Suggested Analysis, supra, 79 Harv.L.Rev. 1121, 1129–1130.) The legal fiction that explains the exception by regarding the marital status as a res present at the permanent home of either of the spouses provides doctrinal consistency with other rules governing jurisdiction over things, but the appellation "in rem" is unnecessary to support the conclusion that jurisdiction is properly assumed.[3] (Williams v. State of North Carolina, 325 U.S. 226, 232, 65 S.Ct. 1092, 89 L.Ed. 1577 (1945).) *Williams* does hold, however, that due process requires something more than mere presence of a party within a jurisdiction before that party can invoke the legal process of the forum to force an absent spouse to defend her marital status in an inconvenient forum and to subvert the policies of other interested jurisdictions in preserving marriages. When the forum state is also the domicile of one of the parties, however, its interest and that of its domiciliary justify subordinating the conflicting interests of the absent spouse and of any other interested jurisdiction.

Jurisdiction to grant annulments has followed an analogous, but somewhat divergent course. An annulment differs conceptually from a divorce in that a divorce terminates a legal status, whereas an annulment establishes that a marital status never existed. The absence of a valid marriage precluded reliance on the divorce cases in formulating a theory of ex parte jurisdiction in annulment, for no res or status could be found within the state. (See Comment (1927) 16 Cal.L.Rev. 38.) The courts, however, did not let jurisdictional concepts of in personam and in rem dictate results in annulment actions.

1964) Cases on Conflict of Laws 855–856; Leflar, Conflict of Laws and Family Law (1960) 14 Ark.L.Rev. 47, 49–50.)

3. Terms such as in rem, quasi in rem, and in personam, seldom solve jurisdictional problems and are often a misleading shorthand for the result.

Such terms in statutes, however, may be invoked in their traditional meanings to expand or contract jurisdiction. (See, e. g., Code Civ.Proc., § 417; Traynor, Is This Conflict Really Necessary? (1959) 37 Tex.L.Rev. 657, 662–663; Atkinson v. Superior Court, 49 Cal.2d 338, 344–346, 316 P.2d 960 (1957).)

They recognized a state's interest in providing a forum for some annulment actions even though the court lacked personal jurisdiction over one of the parties. (Buzzi v. Buzzi, 91 Cal.App.2d 823, 205 P.2d 1125 (1949); Bing Gee v. Chan Lai Yung Gee, 89 Cal.App.2d 877, 202 P.2d 360 (1949); Comment, Jurisdiction to Annul (1953) 6 Stan. L.Rev. 153.) The crucial question, then, is whether there are sufficient factors to justify the court's exercising ex parte annulment jurisdiction.[4] Although we write on a slate free of legislative directives regarding annulment jurisdiction (Millar v. Millar, supra, 175 Cal. 797, 167 P. 394, L.R.A.1918B), we are bound by constitutional limitations.

We need not dwell on a resolution of any conflict between the interests of California and Maryland. The primary issue under the facts of this case is whether due process concepts of fairness to defendant permit plaintiff to choose a forum inconvenient to her absent personal jurisdiction over her. Although a rule that requires a party who is in California and who had been fraudulently induced into a marriage to travel to an inconvenient forum to obtain legal recognition of the nullity of that status works a hardship on that party, such a rule is essential to preclude a transient plaintiff from choosing a forum that would make defense difficult or impossible simply because of physical distance. We find no factor here that would justify an exception to the general rule requiring personal jurisdiction and thereby shift the burden of inconvenience to defendant. The marriage ceremony took place elsewhere, defendant lives elsewhere, the matrimonial domicile was elsewhere, and witnesses are likely to be located elsewhere. Although domicile of a plaintiff here would afford jurisdiction to award an ex parte annulment,[5] plaintiff in this case did not plead or prove that he was a domiciliary of California when the default judgment was entered. The court was therefore without jurisdiction to enter the default judgment.

Since the entry of the judgment, however, defendant has appeared in the action. We must therefore determine for purposes of proceedings on retrial whether the court may award an annulment

---

4. See D. Currie, Suitcase Divorce in the Conflict of Laws: Simons, Rosenstiel and Borax, supra, 34 U.Chi.L. Rev. 26, 39–40; Developments—Jurisdiction, supra, 73 Harv.L.Rev. 909, 975–976.

5. Buzzi v. Buzzi, supra, 91 Cal.App.2d 823, 205 P.2d 1125 (1949); Bing Gee v. Chan Lai Yung Gee, supra, 89 Cal. App.2d 877, 883, 202 P.2d 360 (1949); Comment Jurisdiction to Annul, supra, 6 Stan.L.Rev. 153, 155–159; cf. Williams v. State of North Carolina, supra, 325 U.S. 226, 65 S.Ct. 1092, 89 L.Ed. 1577 (1945). It is true that "instant" domicile carries a danger of fraud on the court of a higher magnitude than does a year's residence requirement, which weighs the objective fact of presence more heavily than a declared intent. The bona fides of the intent to make permanent a California residence can be attacked, however, to provide relief against those who would abuse the court's jurisdiction. (Crouch v. Crouch, 28 Cal.2d 243, 249, 169 P.2d 897 (1946); cf. Civ.Code, § 150.2.)

when both parties are before it, even though neither is a domiciliary of the state.

The primary basis for jurisdiction to resolve disputes between parties is their presence before the court. Plaintiff initiated this action in the only jurisdiction practically available to him because of his military service. Although defendant was not within the jurisdiction of the court when the default was erroneously entered, she voluntarily appeared while the action was before the court. Her appearance was not limited to challenging the jurisdiction of the court, but included a request for relief on the merits by way of an answer and cross-complaint for separate maintenance. (Judson v. Superior Court, 21 Cal.2d 11, 13, 129 P.2d 361 (1942); Harrington v. Superior Court, 194 Cal. 185, 189, 228 P. 15 (1924); Olcese v. Justice's Court, 156 Cal. 82, 88, 103 P. 317 (1909).)

Since both parties are properly before the court, we confront the questions whether we may treat the action as a transitory cause (see Westerman v. Westerman, 121 Kan. 501, 247 P. 863 (1926); Avakian v. Avakian, 69 N.J.Eq. 89, 60 A. 521, 525 (1905), affd. 69 N.J.Eq. 834, 66 A. 1133; Storke, Annulment in the Conflict of Laws (1959) 43 Minn.L.Rev. 849, 852) and whether the interest of another state compels us to refuse to hear this cause.

The rule that domicile is a prerequisite to a valid divorce, even when the parties are before the court, may be justified by the superior interests of the domiciliary jurisdiction. Such jurisdiction is primarily concerned with the status of its domiciliaries and the application of its own law in preserving or terminating marriages in accord with its social policies. (See Developments—Jurisdiction, supra, 73 Harv.L.Rev. 909, 975–976.) When both parties to a divorce action are before the court, however, it is questionable whether domicile is an indispensable prerequisite for jurisdiction. If the moving party's mobility is greatly restricted, for instance, access to a domiciliary forum may be practically unavailable. (Ibid; D. Currie, Suitcase Divorce in the Conflict of Laws: Simons, Rosenstiel and Borax, supra, 34 U.Chi.L.Rev. 26, 48.) Moreover, when parties secure a divorce without the prerequisite domicile in the forum state, it may not be attacked at a later date by either of them. (Sutton v. Leib, 342 U.S. 402, 72 S.Ct. 398, 96 L.Ed. 448 (1952); Cook v. Cook, 342 U.S. 126, 72 S.Ct. 157, 96 L.Ed. 146 (1951); Johnson v. Muelberger, 340 U.S. 581, 71 S.Ct. 474, 95 L.Ed. 552 (1951); Coe v. Coe, 334 U.S. 378, 68 S.Ct. 1094, 92 L.Ed. 1451 (1948); Sherrer v. Sherrer, 334 U.S. 343, 68 S.Ct. 1087, 92 L.Ed. 1429 (1948).) Hence, the prerequisite of domicile may be easily avoided at the trial by parties wishing to invoke the jurisdiction of a court, with little fear in most instances that the judgment will be any less effective than if a valid domicile in fact existed. (See Laflar [sic], Conflict of Laws and Family Law (1960) 14 Ark.L.Rev. 47, 51.)

However valid the rationale for the domicile prerequisite may be in divorce actions, it does not apply to annulment actions. In divorce actions, the applicable substantive law changes as parties change their domicile, but in annulment actions courts uniformly apply the law of the state in which the marriage was contracted. (Colbert v. Colbert, 28 Cal.2d 276, 280, 169 P.2d 633 (1946); McDonald v. McDonald, 6 Cal.2d 457, 58 P.2d 163, 104 A.L.R. 1290 (1936); Civ.Code, § 63; See Storke, Annulment in the Conflict of Laws (1959) 43 Minn.L.Rev. 849, 866.) Moreover, no jurisdictional bar prevents defendant in this case from continuing to press her claim for separate maintenance (see Goodwine v. Superior Court, 63 Cal.2d 481, 483, 47 Cal.Rptr. 201, 407 P.2d 1 (1965)) and plaintiff may defend on the ground that no valid marriage exists (see Hudson v. Hudson, 52 Cal. 2d 735, 742, 344 P.2d 295 (1959); Dimon v. Dimon, 40 Cal.2d 516, 537, 254 P.2d 528 (1953); DeYoung v. DeYoung, 27 Cal.2d 521, 528, 165 P.2d 457 (1946); Patterson v. Patterson, 82 Cal.App.2d 838, 842–843, 187 P.2d 113 (1947)). We conclude, therefore, that the interests of the state of celebration of the marriage or the state of domicile of either party do not preclude a court that has personal jurisdiction over both parties from entertaining an annulment action.

It does not follow that because a court may exercise that jurisdiction it must do so in all cases. In the present case plaintiff was under a special disability in terms of access to any forum other than California.[6] Moreover, defendant was not caught inadvertently within California, and personal jurisdiction was not exercised on a territorial power theory but was obtained over defendant through her consent. Hence, we assume that no undue burdens are placed on her by the trial of the action in California. In other annulment actions where personal jurisdiction is the sole jurisdictional basis, however, the doctrine of *forum non conveniens* might well be invoked by one of the parties, or asserted by the court, to cause a discretionary dismissal when fairness and the interests of judicial administration so demand. (See Developments—Jurisdiction, supra, 73 Harv.L.Rev. 909, 968.)

Plaintiff raises a procedural ground to preclude setting aside the judgment. When defendant filed her motion to set aside the default judgment and sought to file her cross-complaint for separate maintenance, plaintiff was outside of the United States by reason of military orders. His attorney filed a request for a stay of proceedings under the Soldiers' and Sailors' Civil Relief Act of 1940.[7] That act provides

6. Several states considering this disability have enacted legislation permitting servicemen to obtain divorce based on residence. See note 2 supra.

7. "At any stage thereof any action or proceeding in any court in which a person in military service is involved, either as plaintiff or defendant, during the period of such service or within sixty days thereafter may, in the discretion of the court in which it is pending, on its own motion, and shall, on application to it by such person or some person on his behalf,

that at any state of any proceeding in which a military person is either plaintiff or defendant the court must on his application stay the proceedings "unless, in the opinion of the court, the ability of plaintiff to prosecute the action or the defendant to conduct his defense is not materially affected by his military service." Plaintiff's attorney urged that because of his absence due to military service plaintiff could not assist him in opposing defendant's efforts to set aside the default judgment or appear as a witness in such further hearings as might be held and that the proceedings must therefore be stayed.

When plaintiff's attorney requested a stay, a default judgment had been entered in favor of plaintiff, and defendant had asked to set it aside and also had requested separate maintenance. Different considerations are involved in regard to each of defendant's requests in ascertaining whether plaintiff's ability to prosecute his action is materially affected by his military service. The grounds urged for setting aside the default judgment, the only issue we reach today, were that it was premature and that the California court was without jurisdiction. Although we have upheld defendant's contentions as to the default judgment, we do not find that plaintiff's military service in any way interfered with his ability to defend that judgment. The facts—dates of publication and actual notice—were not in dispute and were a matter of first-hand knowledge to his attorney as well as to plaintiff. The disputed question was one of law that plaintiff's attorney could take charge of without plaintiff's presence. It is therefore our opinion that plaintiff's prosecution of the case at this stage has not been "materially affected by reason of his military service." When the case is again before the trial court, plaintiff can decide whether to proceed with his action for an annulment. If defendant pursues her cross-complaint, plaintiff can still request a stay. The trial court will then have an opportunity to rule on the request.

The judgment is reversed.

McCOMB, PETERS, TOBRINER, MOSK, BURKE and SULLIVAN, JJ., concur.

NOTES AND QUESTIONS

1. *Whealton* has been noted in 22 Ark.L.Rev. 509 (1968) and 4 San Diego L.Rev. 401 (1968).

2. Is all of the *Whealton* opinion dictum after the paragraph in which the court decided that the entry of the default was too early and therefore void? Is it all dictum after the paragraph in which the court decided that since neither party was apparently domiciled in California the court lacked jurisdiction to grant an ex parte annulment?

be stayed as provided in this Act unless, in the opinion of the court, the ability of plaintiff to prosecute the action or the defendant to conduct his defense is not materially affected by reason of his military service." (Soldiers' and Sailors' Civil Relief Act of 1940 (50 U.S.C.A.App. § 521).)

3. When Judge Traynor says that the court was without jurisdiction to enter an ex parte annulment because neither spouse was domiciled in California, is he using "jurisdiction" in a sense different from that in *Perlstein?*

4. As Judge Traynor indicates, in California and in other states, there are statutes requiring that at least one of the parties must have been domiciled in the state for a period, usually a year, before the courts of the state may grant a divorce.

(a) Do such statutes impose requirements of "jurisdiction"? Jurisdiction in what sense?

(b) Why are there no such statutes applicable to annulment, in California and in many other states? For example, why does the recently drafted Uniform Marriage and Divorce Act have no such provision with respect to annulment, when it does have a provision, § 302, 9A Unif.L.Ann. 121 (1979), requiring ninety days' residence, for divorce? Does this imply that for annulment, called by that statute declaration of invalidity of marriage, the Uniform Act permits the suit to be brought by anyone, whether or not a resident? If you were drafting a statute on the subject of marriage and divorce, would you include a comprehensive provision on annulment jurisdiction?

(c) Why should there be any rules at all, either statutory or otherwise about the domicile (expressed in statutes as residence) of persons suing for annulment? Is it because the action is in rem and the "res" is located at the domicile of one of the parties? Or is all that talk about a "res" just a fiction concealing some other governmental purpose?

(d) As Judge Traynor indicates, earlier California cases had held that the statute requiring residence for divorce actions was not applicable to annulment. Why should that be? Does not annulment terminate the marriage? Would it not be sensible to say that both actions end marriages and therefore both should be governed by the same statute? Or is there a crucial distinction between a decree that a valid marriage is henceforth terminated, and a decree that there never was a valid marriage?

5. What does the *Whealton* opinion reveal about the relationship between rules of personal service and rules of subject matter jurisdiction, where annulment suits are concerned? What does the United States Constitution have to do with this relationship? Cf. Currie, Suitcase Divorce in the Conflict of Laws: Simons, Rosenstiel, and Borax, 34 Univ.Chi.L.Rev. 26, 39 (1966): "But the talismanic labels 'in rem' and 'in personam' are rapidly giving way to a general test of fairness in terms of state interests and minimum contacts with interested parties."

6. Judge Traynor concludes by holding that the trial court may hear this case even if neither party is domiciled in California, on the ground that the court has personal jurisdiction over both parties, the wife having filed a general appearance and a cross-complaint for separate maintenance.

If the "general test of fairness in terms of state interests and minimum contacts" is applied to this situation, what should be the result? What interest does California have in the marital status of these two persons?

7. H and W lived in New Hampshire and were married there. Immediately after the marriage H was drafted and sent to an army post in California. W then visited him in California, during which visit H learned that W had been twice convicted of felonies and had had an illegitimate child. He forthwith brought suit in California to annul their marriage, serving W personally at the airport just before she boarded the plane to return to New Hampshire. Assume that the law of California might, under these circumstances, support an annulment for fraud, while the law of New Hampshire would not.

(a) Under Professor Currie's "general test of fairness in terms of state interests and minimum contacts with interested parties", would the California court have jurisdiction to hear the annulment suit? Is this a minimum standard for jurisdiction, or a comparative standard requiring a scrutiny of the contacts with other states to see whether they might be more numerous?

(b) Under *Whealton* would the California court have jurisdiction? Cf. Annot., 9 A.L.R.3d 545 (1966).

8. Herb and Wendy, both 17, were Connecticut residents. Herb came from a wealthy family and had considerable assets in his own name. During the summer before they started as freshmen at the University of Connecticut, they traveled together to Berkeley, California, where they went through a civil marriage ceremony, falsely stating that they were both 21. They had talked a good deal about their future and had agreed that they would have no children for two years, but at that time would start raising a family. They returned to school, where they lived off-campus together. At the end of that school year, their relationship had deteriorated. They quarreled a lot, each accusing the other of immaturity and unrealistic attitudes. Herb told Wendy that he was never going to have children, at least by her, and this led to an intense quarrel and their separation. Wendy went home to Hartford for the summer. Herb went out to California in June. In July he initiated annulment proceedings in California, alleging that he was domiciled there and causing Wendy to be served by registered mail. He claimed that the marriage was invalid under California law because of the age of the parties. Wendy did not appear and an annulment was granted to Herb in late August. The court filed no opinion in the case. Herb transferred to the University of California at Berkeley, where he is now a student.

When Wendy was served with notice of the annulment proceeding in July, she went to a lawyer who told her to disregard it. With his assistance she filed, in early August, a suit for annulment in Connecticut, causing Herb to be served by registered mail. She requested alimony, intending to collect it out of valuable Connecticut real estate owned by Herb. Herb has appeared in the Connecticut suit and moved to dismiss the complaint. Wendy has since been in an automobile accident in which she suffered permanent injury to both hands, which will apparently limit her opportunity for employment and education very severely. Prepare to argue this motion for either party.

9. In addition to the problems of jurisdiction just discussed, there may be questions under the local law as to what court, if any, has authority to grant annulment decrees. This was a question of some difficulty in earlier times, since only the ecclesiastical courts had this authority in England and in this country we had no such courts. It was sometimes said that

since the ecclesiastical jurisdiction never was adopted in the United States, in the absence of statute there was no court having authority to hear suits for annulment. An intermediate solution reached by some courts was to say that the American courts of equity had inherent jurisdiction to hear annulments where the ground was one of the civil disabilities, but not where the canonical disabilities were involved. Or, to put it somewhat differently, equity courts could annul marriage contracts for fraud, duress and perhaps insanity by an analogy to their powers with respect to contracts generally, but they could not annul for other reasons. Chancellor Kent was the leading exponent of this view. See, e. g., Wightman v. Wightman, 4 Johns.Ch. 343 (N.Y.1819), and Burtis v. Burtis, 1 Hopk.Ch. 557 (N.Y.1825). It is also expressed in the notorious Romatz v. Romatz, 355 Mich. 81, 94 N.W.2d 432 (1959).

Other courts take the position that principles of marriage law and annulments came to this country as part of the common law of England, and could be applied by our courts notwithstanding their ecclesiastical origins. Le Barron v. Le Barron, 35 Vt. 365 (1862); Harper v. Dupree, 185 Kan. 483, 345 P.2d 644 (1959). This problem is no longer of great importance since most states have, either by statute or decision, placed annulment powers in one court or another. For a thorough discussion of the problem see Speca, The Development of Jurisdiction in Annulment of Marriage Cases, 22 Univ. of Kan. City L.Rev. 109 (1954). There still may be a question whether the courts of a state have authority to grant annulments on particular grounds, where no statutory authority exists, as for example in the case of impotence. It has been held by one case that if the marriage disability is canonical, statutory authority is a prerequisite to annulment. D. v. D., 2 Terry (41 Del.) 263, 20 A.2d 139 (1941).

SECTION 2. SOME PROCEDURAL ASPECTS OF ANNULMENT SUITS

PATEY v. PEASLEE

Supreme Court of New Hampshire, Merrimack, 1955.
99 N.H. 335, 111 A.2d 194.

Petition, for the annulment of the marriage of the defendant and the late Winifred P. Peaslee brought by her heirs-at-law [on the ground of mental incompetence and fraud]. The petition also seeks to debar the defendant from inheriting any rights in the estate of the late Winifred P. Peaslee. The defendant, reserving the right to answer the petition further, filed a motion to dismiss. A hearing on the merits was not held but the Court after hearing granted the defendant's motion to dismiss. The plaintiffs' exception thereto was reserved and transferred by Wheeler, C.J.

KENISON, Chief Justice. At common law the marriage of an insane person was absolutely void. * * * Since the marriage was void, it could be challenged in a collateral proceeding and the surviving spouse could take no interest in the marital property. * * * Where the common-law rule has not been modified by statute, a collateral attack upon such a marriage after the death of a spouse has been allowed. * * * If, however, such a marriage is regarded as voidable, it can be attacked only in a direct proceeding during the lifetime of both spouses. * * *

In this state the Legislature has specifically provided that biga-mous marriages and marriages within certain degrees of consanguini-ty or affinity of the parties are void. * * * Likewise the mar-riage of males less than fourteen years of age and females of less than thirteen years of age are declared "null and void." * * * While certain other marriages are prohibited or made illegal for rea-sons of age or mental incompetency, these statutes have been consist-ently construed as making the marriage voidable and not void. * * * R.L. c. 338, § 10, as amended by Laws 1949, c. 121, reads as follows: "No woman under the age of forty-five years, or man of any age,—except he marry a woman over the age of forty-five years,—ei-ther of whom is epileptic, imbecile, feeble-minded, idiotic or insane, shall hereafter intermarry or marry any other person within this state unless permitted by the state department of health." This stat-ute was construed as making a marriage in violation of its terms only voidable. "As the marriage was not void and the husband is dead, no inquiry can now be made into its validity." Lau v. Lau, 81 N.H. 44, 45, 122 A. 345, 346 (1923); * * *.

Of course the Legislature may prescribe that the marriage of a person with any degree of mental incompetency shall be void but it is plain that they have been careful not to do so. * * * The rule of Lau v. Lau, 81 N.H. 44, 122 A. 345 (1923), that the marriage of an incompetent is voidable and free from attack after death has been fol-lowed in many cases including some recent ones. * * *

There is a Hobson's choice whether the Legislature declares the marriage void which favors the heirs or declares the marriage voida-ble which favors the surviving spouse. The former method may al-low the heirs to step forward after death and claim the fruit of their own neglect. The latter method may allow a scheming suitor to mar-ry for money. "It is apparent that the question presented here is an important one and that grave inequities might result from either in-terpretation. If it is held that such a marriage is voidable only and cannot be attacked after the death of the allegedly incompetent party then a situation arises where fraud could easily be perpetrated. For example, a designing person could effect a marriage with a known imbecile a few days or hours before the latter's death and there would seem to be no way to prevent such a person from profiting un-justly by his designing acts. On the other hand if it is held that such a marriage is absolutely void and can be collaterally attacked even after the death of the alleged incompetent it would be possible for de-signing heirs to set aside the sacred vows of matrimony and deprive the surviving spouse of valuable property to which he or she might otherwise be legally and morally entitled to receive." Vance v. Hinch, supra, 261 S.W.2d 414 (1953).

In urging that a marriage procured by fraud and misrepresentation is invalid, the plaintiffs rely on Gatto v. Gatto, 79 N.H. 177, 106 A. 493, decided in 1919, for the proposition that fraud with respect to any matter material to the marriage relation will be sufficient ground to annul a marriage contract. In 1932, that case was reconsidered in a fifteen-page opinion "to consider if the reasoning of the case is to receive credit as accepted and established authority." Heath v. Heath, 85 N.H. 419, 421, 159 A. 418, 419 (1932). The broad language of the former case was disapproved and it was indicated that the holding of the case was to be confined to its own particular and peculiar facts. * * * Although many annulment cases have been considered since that time, it has never been cited as an authority in this court in any subsequent case. The annulment of a marriage contract for fraud and misrepresentation is governed by the principles laid down in the Heath case. "Whatever the differences in definition of the kind and nature of fraud required to warrant an annulment, deception by one of the parties as to character, morality, habits, wealth, or social position is generally held insufficient." * * * Annulment is not granted for any and every kind of fraud. "Premarital falsehoods as to love and affection are not enough, nor disclosure that one partner 'married for money.'" Woronzoff-Daschkoff v. Woronzoff-Daschkoff, 303 N.Y. 506, 512, 104 N.E.2d 877, 880 (1952). To justify annulment the fraud must relate to conditions making "normal marital relations * * * morally impossible" and the representations " 'must be of * * * something making impossible the performance of the duties' " of the marriage relation. * * * It is the function of the Legislature and not of the judiciary "to invent new grounds" for the annulment of marriages. * * *

While the plaintiffs allege fraud upon themselves as well as their intestate, they seek no relief except that which would result from annulment of the marriage. Apart from an order of nullity, an order "debarring" the defendant from inheritance could be entered only in plain disregard of the statutes relating to the rights of surviving husbands. Whether "ordinary fraud", Heath v. Heath, supra, 85 N.H. 430, 159 A. 418 (1932), differing in kind and nature from the fraud which would warrant an annulment, might nevertheless justify exercise of equity jurisdiction to impose a constructive trust with respect to property acquired from the decedent, Ibey v. Ibey, 93 N.H. 434, 43 A.2d 157 (1945); Latham v. Father Divine, 299 N.Y. 22, 85 N.E.2d 168, 11 A.L.R.2d 802 (1949); Pomeroy, Equity Jurisprudence (5th Ed.) §§ 155, 1053; Scott on Trusts, § 488, is an issue not presented in this case. Similarly, although the plaintiffs' petition alleges that the defendant's conduct after his marriage to the plaintiffs' intestate "hastened her death," no felonious conduct is alleged such as might be claimed to warrant application of the rule applied in some jurisdictions and, supported by statute in others, that an heir or spouse will not be permitted to profit from his own homicidal conduct. * * *

We conclude that the plaintiffs have not stated a cause for annulment which is cognizable in the courts of this state, because the marriage was voidable rather than void, and the proceedings were not brought "during the lives of both the contracting parties." * * * The petition fails to state any other cause which would prevent operation of the statutes establishing the rights of a surviving spouse in the estate of his deceased wife. * * *

Petition dismissed.

* * *

NOTES AND QUESTIONS

1. Compare with this case Sophian v. Von Linde, 22 A.D.2d 34, 253 N.Y.S.2d 496 (1st Dep't 1964), aff'd p. c. 16 N.Y.2d 785, 209 N.E.2d 823, 262 N.Y.S.2d 505 (1965). See Cal.Civ.Code § 4426(c) (1970); Uniform Marriage and Divorce Act § 208(b), 9A Unif.L.Ann. 110 (1979).

2. (a) What would have been the result in this case if Winifred's relatives (and expectant heirs-at-law) had sued to annul Winifred's marriage *before* her death? Would they have had standing to sue?

(b) Would the answer to (a) be different if the statute provided that the marriages of mental incompetents are void?

(c) If an attack on the marriage by one not a party to it would not be permitted during the life of the spouse, should it be permitted after her death?

3. Where the ground for annulment is nonage, the question of standing to sue is determined by the wording of the particular statute, but in general only the party under age may obtain the annulment. The question of who may sue may be affected by labelling the marriage void or voidable. See Evans v. Ross, 309 Mich. 149, 14 N.W.2d 815 (1944). A few statutes specifically authorize the parent or guardian of the person under age to bring the suit, e. g. Uniform Marriage and Divorce Act, § 208(b)(3); Cal.Civ.Code § 4426(a) (1970). In the absence of such specific authorization the parent is not permitted to sue. H. Clark, Law of Domestic Relations, § 2.9 (1968).

Where the ground for annulment is mental incompetence, again the statutes control the question of standing to sue, with some providing that either spouse may have the marriage annulled, such as Minn.Stat.Ann. § 518.03 (Supp.1977); Tex.Fam.Code § 2.45 (1975); Uniform Marriage and Divorce Act § 208(b)(1), and others providing that only the insane party or his guardian may sue, as in Cal.Civ.Code § 4426(c)(1970). N.Y.Dom.Rel.L. § 140(c) (Supp.1978–1979) permits an interested relative of the mental incompetent to sue, and also permits the mental incompetent to sue after restoration to a sound mind and even permits the sane spouse to sue during the continuance of the mental illness if he did not know of the illness at the time of the marriage.

Annulments for impotence are generally brought by the capable party as the party "injured" by the condition, but there is some English authority that the impotent party may also sue. Harthan v. Harthan [1948] 2 All Eng.Rep. 639 (C.A.), 76 L.Q.Rev. 267 (1960). The Uniform Marriage and Divorce Act, § 208(b)(2) also authorizes either party to sue.

Either party is usually entitled to annul marriages where the defect is one based on relationship of the parties, such as incest or prior subsisting marriage.

For cases on the right to attack a marriage after the death of a party, see Annot., 47 A.L.R.2d 1393 (1956).

4. What should be the result if an annulment action is begun when both spouses are living, but one of them dies pending the suit? Should the action survive under a statute which provides as follows: "All actions in law whatsoever, save and except actions for slander or libel, or trespass for injuries done to the person, and actions brought for the recovery of real estate, shall survive to and against executors, administrators and conservators." Merrick v. Merrick, 314 Ill.App. 623, 42 N.E.2d 341 (1942); Dibble v. Meyer, 203 Or. 541, 278 P.2d 901 (1955); Rattray v. Raynor, 10 N.Y.2d 494, 225 N.Y.S.2d 39, 180 N.E.2d 429 (1962).

5. What arguments might be made for or against the proposition that a guardian should be entitled to sue for the annulment of the marriage of his incompetent ward, where no statute expressly authorizes him to do so? Would the case be different if the remedy sought were divorce for mental incompetence rather than annulment? See Jones v. Minc, 77 Wash.2d 381, 462 P.2d 927 (1969).

6. H and W-1 were married and lived in New York. H became dissatisfied with W-1 and obtained a Mexican mail-order divorce, a type of divorce which New York's courts do not recognize as valid. H then married W-2 in New York, and they took up their domicile in New Jersey. W-1, still a resident of New York, brings suit in New York to annul the marriage of H and W-2, on the ground that it is bigamous, serving H and W-2 by registered mail.

(a) What arguments should be made in the event that H and W-2 moved to dismiss the complaint on the ground that there was no jurisdiction in the New York court? See Sacks v. Sacks, 47 Misc.2d 1050, 263 N.Y.S.2d 891 (Sup.Ct.1965).

(b) What arguments should be made if a motion to dismiss were filed by the defendants on the ground that W-1 had no standing to attack their marriage? See N.Y.Dom.Rel.L. § 140(a) (1977); Uniform Marriage and Divorce Act § 208(c) (Alternative A), 9A Unif.L.Ann. 110 (1979). If the suit had been brought in New Jersey, what arguments should be made?

(c) If you were consulted by W-1 after H's Mexican divorce and remarriage, what legal action would you advise her to take?

(d) If H and W-2 had a child, C, whose status might be affected by the decree in the case, must C be made a party defendant? Cf. Roe v. Roe, 49 Misc.2d 1070, 269 N.Y.S.2d 40 (Sup.Ct.1966).

7. If the defendant in the annulment is, at the time of the suit, but not at the time of the marriage, mentally incompetent, should that foreclose the plaintiff from bringing the suit? Should it matter, for purposes of deciding this question, what the ground for annulment is? Goldstein v. Gold-

stein, 220 Cal.App.2d 369, 33 Cal.Rptr. 857 (1963); Annot., 97 A.L.R.2d 483 (1964).

8. Under the law of some states a decree of annulment may not be granted on the uncorroborated testimony of one of the parties. The rule originated in the ecclesiastical law and has been embodied in statutes in some jurisdictions. Generally, with some exceptions, the rule does not prevail without a statute. See generally Annot., 71 A.L.R.2d 620 (1960). A similar rule applies to divorce in many states. H. Clark, Law of Domestic Relations, §§ 3.3, 13.7 (1968).

STATTER v. STATTER

Court of Appeals of New York, 1957.
2 N.Y.2d 668, 143 N.E.2d 10.

BURKE, Judge. On February 16, 1953 Humphrey Statter commenced an action for separation against his wife, Amy Statter, charging cruelty and abandonment. An extension of time to answer was granted the wife on her attorney's representation that further time was required to establish the existence of a prior marriage by the husband, the fact of which would serve as a defense and basis for affirmative relief in the separation action. Despite this extension, however, when the answer was filed it contained neither affirmative defense nor counterclaim. Instead, the wife's pleading admitted the marriage's validity and denied the allegations as to cruelty and abandonment. After a trial of the issues, both parties having appeared, the cause of action alleging cruelty was dismissed on consent but the cause based on abandonment was sustained and a judgment in favor of the husband entered. The court's decision contained a finding that the husband and wife were validly married.

More than two years later the wife initiated the present suit. Her complaint alleges two causes of action: the first based upon the existence of a valid, undissolved marriage between the husband and one Kate Oglesby that rendered the husband's purported marriage to the complainant void; the second claiming that the wife's consent was fraudulently procured by the husband who falsely represented to her that he had not previously been married.

The husband has moved under subdivision 4 of rule 107 of the Rules of Civil Practice to dismiss the complaint on the ground that the existing final judgment of separation is determinative as to any issue of the marriage's validity. The wife's principal argument is to the effect that the causes of action for annulment and separation are "different" and that, therefore, only issues actually contested, i. e., issues controverted by the pleadings, are barred in the second action. She concludes that since the marriage's validity was never actually litigated in that sense, the court's determination on the question is not preclusive. In explanation of her failure to raise the questions now presented during the earlier action, the wife alleges that although she was then in possession of a Mexican divorce decree which purported to dissolve a marriage between a Humphrey Statter and one Kate Oglesby, and a Massachusetts birth certificate for a child born to "Kate Oglesby Statter of New York and Humphrey Statter, a lawyer, born in Iowa", she was then unable to establish that the Humphrey Statter who married Kate Oglesby was the same Humphrey Statter (also a lawyer) who was plaintiff in the separation action. She assigns as at least a contributing cause for her failure to raise the questions in the earlier action the fact that her husband, when confronted with the evidence of the marriage, denied that he had been married to the woman mentioned in the birth certificate or that he was the father of the child. According to the wife, she has since that time acquired additional evidence sufficient to make out the causes of action she now pleads.

The question on this appeal is whether the prior separation judgment should be deemed *res judicata* on the question of the marriage's validity, thereby precluding a reopening of that issue in this subsequent and separate proceeding.

Although there is probably no area of our law less susceptible of rigid formulation and definition than that of *res judicata*, some criteria have been traditionally and consistently employed. Such is the nature of the statement of the rule as it appears in the oft-cited case of Pray v. Hegeman, 98 N.Y. 351, 358 (1885). It was there said that the estoppel of a former judgment extends to all matters "comprehended and involved in the thing expressly stated and decided, whether they were or were not actually litigated or considered [citations omitted]. It is not necessary to the conclusiveness of a former judgment that issue should have been taken on the precise point controverted in the second action. Whatever is necessarily implied in the former decision, is for the purpose of the estoppel deemed to have been actually decided". Another statement of the rule, in substantially similar terms was cited and relied upon by us in the case of Ripley v. Storer, 309 N.Y. 506, 517, 132 N.E.2d 87, 93 (1956). * * * This principle points the way in the present case.

Guided by the rule in the *Pray* case, supra, our inquiry here is directed not to the forms of the two actions * * *, but rather toward a determination as to whether the questions presented by the suit before us were necessarily involved in and determined by the first judgment. Examination reveals that they were. The subject of the present suit is, of course, the validity or invalidity of the marriage. By virtue of section 1161 of the Civil Practice Act, the first action for separation could be maintained only "by a husband or wife against the other party to the marriage". It is clear beyond dispute that this section makes the existence of a valid marriage a condition precedent to the successful maintenance of a cause for separation * * *, and that a judgment of separation establishes the existence of a valid and subsisting marriage between the parties * * *. We said as much, though in a different context, when we decided the case of Garvin v. Garvin, 306 N.Y. 118, 116 N.E.2d 73 (1954). In the words of the Pray case the validity of the marriage was "comprehended and involved in the thing * * * decided"; it was "necessarily implied in the former decision" * * *. It follows that *res judicata* bars a second trial on the issue of the marriage's validity. As already indicated this is true despite the fact that no clash or controversy surrounded the issue and that it was found on the basis of an admission in the pleading. * * * The essence of *res judicata* is the fact that a court has already been presented with the subject sought to be litigated and has rendered a judicial determination thereon. The question of what evidence has been actually produced is immaterial. It may be that in seeking to ascertain whether the two issues are the same a comparison of the evidence needed to establish the respective questions may be an appropriate criterion. But assuming the issues in the two cases to be the same, whether or not it has been determined in no wise depends upon whether it has been the subject of stubborn contention or has been found by way of concession (2 Freeman on Judgments 5th Ed., § 660, pp. 1390–1391; Last Chance Min. Co. v. Tyler, Min. Co., 157 U.S. 683, 691–692, 15 S.Ct. 733, 39 L.Ed. 859 (1895)). In either case the public policy which underlies the doctrine of *res judicata* is applicable.

The famous statement of then Chief Judge Cardozo in Schuylkill Fuel Corp. v. B. & C. Nieberg Realty Corp., 250 N.Y. 304, 165 N.E. 456 (1929), leads us to the same conclusion. It was there indicated, as it had been in the Pray case, supra, that further judicial consideration in a second action should be denied if the subject of the second suit is so inextricably involved with that of the first that it must have entered into the composition of the first judgment. Chief Judge Cardozo said: " A judgment in one action is conclusive in a later one, not only as to any matters actually litigated therein, but also as to any that might have been so litigated, when the two causes of action have such a measure of identity that a different judgment in the second would destroy or impair rights or interests established by the first" (250 N.Y. 304, 306–307, 165 N.E. 456, 457 (1929)). Since the primary fact to be established in the separation action was the existence of a valid marriage, it cannot be gainsaid that a decision in the pending annulment action declaring the marriage invalid would undermine and devitalize completely the earlier separation judgment by depriving it of the very basis upon which it was rendered. The inconsistent determination would result in the alteration or dissolution of the status and concomitant rights and interests already declared to exist. To avoid this threatened impairment and inconsistency the law imposes the bar of *res judicata* * * *.

We see no real conflict between the rule of "collateral estoppel by judgment" urged by the wife and adopted by the court below, and the conclusion here reached. That principle revolves about a determination of which causes of action are the "same" and which are "different" * * *. But causes of action in this setting are not different by virtue merely of their form or the relief sought. If we apply the standard propounded in the Schuylkill case, supra, causes of action are the same when the second judgment could result in an impairment of the one obtained in the first suit. It follows, however, that if the question or questions in the second action were material and necessarily involved in the first determination the threat of impairment must be present. As has already been pointed out a judgment of nullity could not now be granted without thereby undermining the judgment of separation which rests upon the fact of marriage. Since this is so, even if we were to insist upon the statement of the rule as it appears in the opinion of the Appellate Division, we would have to hold that the causes of action are the same for the purposes of the rule and that accordingly relevant matters not raised in the separation action on the question of the marriage's validity are now precluded.

Concluding as we have that the question of the marriage's validity was determined by the earlier separation judgment attempted avoidance of that judgment in this action constitutes a collateral attack (Restatement, Judgments, § 11, comment a, p. 65). As such, the wife's argument that the husband's concealment of his prior marriage constituted fraud would not be a sufficient basis upon which to deprive the earlier judgment of its conclusive effect. * * *

The claim of "newly discovered evidence" is equally inappropriate. It is commonly held that the mere discovery of fresh evidence is no answer to the defense of *res judicata* when raised in a subsequent, separate cause of action * * *.

A number of factors militate in favor of the principle, demonstrated by these cases, that a valid judgment should not be subject to a collateral attack, i. e., in other ways than by proceeding against the original judgment directly. Perhaps the most relevant factor here is the law's desire to secure stability and consistency of judicial determinations. To this end, in order to obviate the possibility that a second court in a separate action shall reach a decision contrary to one already achieved, the law requires, with few exceptions, that objections, other than jurisdictional be raised in the same proceeding or in a separate proceeding to dissolve the first judgment. Thus if the court has been mistaken in the law there is a remedy by way of appeal. If the court or jury has been mistaken in the facts the remedy is by a motion for a new trial. If there has been evidence discovered since the trial the law makes appropriate provision by way of motion in the first proceeding. By relegating questions such as the one here, where possible, to remedies in the original proceeding the law secures the integrity of determinations and at the same time provides that justice may be accomplished in the individual case. The method is a well-established one * * * the operation and effect of which is exampled by the circumstances of this case. If we refuse to apply the doctrine of *res judicata* or permit collateral attack of the separation judgment on the grounds urged and the annulment action is subsequently prosecuted to judgment for the wife, a situation would be created whereby a judgment of separation would be extant simultaneously with a judgment of annulment between the same parties. Further confusion might thereby be engendered in already complex areas of law. On the other hand our law supplies a procedure by virtue of which any injustice claimed by the wife in this case might have been alleviated without the undesirable result of separate and inconsistent judicial determinations. Under section 552 of the Civil Practice Act if a party has acquired material evidence since the time of trial, which evidence was not earlier uncovered despite the exercise of due diligence, a motion can be made for a new trial on that basis. There appears to be no reason why the wife thereby could not have obtained a full measure of relief if, as she maintains, the only reason she did not make a defense in the earlier action was because the necessary evidence was, at the time, unavailable to her.

In any event, our law closes the door to attack upon the judgment already obtained by the method the wife has chosen to employ.

There remains one further and final consideration. The wife urges that since the claim here made, if established, would render the marriage void *ab initio* the doctrine of *res judicata* is not applicable. In effect she would have us engraft upon the doctrine an absolute exception in favor of actions such as the one before us. Neither of the courts below has suggested such a total immunity and it appears to be unwarranted by either principle or precedent. The considerations that underlie and inspire the doctrine and particularly those mentioned here, are relevant to actions for a decree of nullity as to any area of law. * * *

The order of the Appellate Division should be reversed and the complaint dismissed; the question certified answered in the negative.

DESMOND, Judge. I dissent. The principle of *res judicata* is misapplied when it results without independent proof in holding that a marriage is dissolved or that a void divorce is valid or an illegal marriage legal. Estoppel by judgment is a rule of public policy but it is not the whole of our public policy and it must give way when it collides with a stronger and more fundamental policy * * *. Much more basic than the need for finality in litigation is the State's insistence that the marriage status is not to be altered by consent or default directly or indirectly * * *. The reason for this ancient rule is that marriage is a public institution in which the public is deeply interested and the State, regulating marriage for the benefit of the community, is a party to every divorce and annulment suit * * *.

If the existence of a valid marriage between plaintiff and defendant had actually been tried out in the earlier separation suit, the demands of public policy would be satisfied and the resulting judgment would be safe from collateral attack. But there never has been a judicial investigation of that question. The wife's failure in that separation action to deny that she was married to defendant produced automatically a formal finding without any supporting proof that the parties were husband and wife. To make that finding conclusive is to permit the impermissible * * *. It forever bars defendant from showing that plaintiff defrauded her into a void marriage. Proper public policy will be enforced by ordering a trial of plaintiff's allegations that defendant was still married to another woman when he went through a marriage ceremony with plaintiff.

The order appealed from should be affirmed and the certified question answered in the affirmative.

*   *   *

NOTES AND QUESTIONS

1. Broadly speaking, what reasons underlie legal doctrines of res judicata?

2. Although few legal subjects are as resistant to black letter treatment as the law of judgments, the American Law Institute has made and is making a manful effort to organize the subject through the Restatement of Judgments (1942) and the drafting of the Restatement, Second, Judgments. Some of its definitions provide a helpful approach to the decisions, and the Reporter's notes and comments contain useful citations. The general rules of res judicata are summarized by the Restatement, Second, Judgments, § 47 (Tent. Draft No. 1, 1973) to the effect that when a valid and final personal judgment is given for the plaintiff, he cannot thereafter sue on the claim, nor, in any action by the plaintiff, can the defendant raise defenses he might have raised in the original action. This principle is labeled merger. Conversely, under § 48 of the same work, the rule is stated to be that a valid and final personal judgment in favor of a defendant bars another action by the plaintiff on the same claim. This is the rule of bar. And, under § 68, the judgment is conclusive against either party in any subsequent suit, with respect to issues of fact or law actually litigated. Restatement, Second, Judgments § 68 (Tent. Draft No. 4, 1977). This principle is called issue preclusion. It is sometimes referred to in the cases as collateral estoppel.

(a) Are the actions for separation and annulment the same, so that the wife in Statter, having lost in the first suit, should be foreclosed from bringing the second? Do §§ 47 and 48 of the Restatement, Second have any application to this situation? Or is this an appropriate situation for applying "issue preclusion"? Restatement, Second, Judgments § 68, comment e (Tent. Draft No. 4, 1977).

(b) Could the husband, after winning in the separation suit, have brought an action to annul?

(c) The wife in the separation suit could presumably have counterclaimed for an annulment, at least if she had known about the prior marriage and the invalid divorce. Is the controlling principle here that since she failed to do so, she is now foreclosed from making the claim she might have made in the former suit? But Restatement, Second, Judgments § 56.-1 (Tent. Draft No. 1, 1973) states that where the defendant fails to interpose a counterclaim when he might have done so, he is not precluded from later asserting his claim, except where the relationship between claim and counterclaim is such that success in the second action would impair rights secured in the first. See also comments b and f to that section.

(d) If none of these principles applies, just what is the basis for the *Statter* result? Is it an extension of the Restatement's position, holding that collateral estoppel applies not merely to issues which were actually litigated, as the Restatement indicates, but also to issues which might have been litigated? How do the reasons given in paragraph 1, supra, operate in *Statter*? How are they reflected in the rules outlined by the Restatement of Judgments?

(e) Or is the rationale for *Statter* the argument that, as the court points out on page 208, "If there has been evidence discovered since the trial the law makes appropriate provision by way of motion in the first proceeding"? That is, is the court saying that since the wife had a remedy, in the form of a motion to reopen the separation judgment, she need not be given the remedy she seeks of an annulment? See N.Y.Civ.Prac.L. & R., Rule 5015 (1963).

3. In Schoenbrod v. Siegler, 20 N.Y.2d 403, 230 N.E.2d 638, 283 N.Y. S.2d 881 (1967), the facts were as follows: H and W, New York residents, were married in Grenada, British West Indies. Two years later they executed a separation agreement in New York, and then H obtained a Mexican divorce. H appeared personally in the Mexican suit, W appearing by attorney. Later H discovered that the person who married them had had no authority to perform marriages. He repudiated the separation agreement and moved to vacate the Mexican divorce. The Mexican court refused relief, on the ground that it had no power to reopen the divorce decree for any reason. In the meantime W sued in New York for arrears due under the separation agreement, and H then sued in New York for a declaratory judgment that the separation agreement was void, apparently on the theory that the parties had never been married. W then moved to dismiss this action on the ground that the Mexican divorce decree made the validity of the marriage res judicata. The New York Court of Appeals held that since in its view the Mexican law was that the Mexican divorce could have been collaterally attacked in Mexico, although it could not have been reopened by a motion in the original proceeding, it could also be collaterally attacked in New York. In other words it would not have been res judicata of the validity of the marriage in New York. *Statter* was distinguished on the ground that in that case there was another remedy, namely the motion for new trial on the ground of newly discovered evidence. The court also held that it need give no more conclusive effect to the Mexican divorce decree than Mexico would give. The conflicts aspects of this case are discussed in Peterson, Foreign Country Judgments and The Second Restatement of Conflict of Laws, 72 Colum.L.Rev. 220, 252 (1972). See also Restatement, Second, Conflict of Laws § 115 (1971), and Psaroudis v. Psaroudis, 27 N.Y.2d 527, 261 N.E.2d 108, 312 N.Y.S.2d 998 (1970).

4. Assuming for the moment that *Statter* reached the correct result on general principles of res judicata, should those principles apply with full force in matrimonial litigation? Or is it arguable that such litigation involves rights and obligations of such importance to the parties and to society that they should be fully and correctly adjudicated notwithstanding earlier litigation which may have reached erroneous results?

5. Other defenses to annulment include that of estoppel, which may also be called ratification, waiver or laches. This defense takes various forms, depending in part upon the ground for annulment which is asserted. Thus if annulment is sought for nonage, it is a defense that the plaintiff continued to live with the defendant after reaching full age. In the case of fraud, it is a defense that cohabitation continued after discovery of the false representation. H. Clark, Law of Domestic Relations, § 3.3 (1968); Moore, Defenses Available in Annulment Actions, 7 J.Fam.L. 239 (1967).

One other application of estoppel occurs where the ground for annulment is a prior subsisting marriage. Usually, though not always, the plaintiff is asserting that a divorce purporting to end the prior marriage was void for lack of jurisdiction, thereby invalidating the subsequent marriage. The defendant often then asserts that the plaintiff is estopped to make this claim, either because the plaintiff himself obtained the void divorce, or because the plaintiff or others relied on the divorce's validity. Analytically these cases are closely related to problems of jurisdiction over the subject matter of divorce, and therefore they will be found in that section of the book, infra, Chapter 6, Section 1.

A somewhat similar defense is that of laches, in the sense of delay in suit. Due to the highly unsatisfactory state of annulment statutes, it is rare to find statutes of limitations which apply to annulment. Should general omnibus statutes of limitations apply? Or should laches alone be relied upon, in the usual sense of delay plus a change of position by the other party? See Annot., 52 A.L.R.2d 1163 (1957). The Uniform Marriage and Divorce Act, § 208(b), 9A Unif.L.Ann. 110 (1979), sets periods of limitations for each of the different grounds for declaring marriages invalid, as does the proposed annulment statute in Vernon, Annulment in New Mexico, 2 Nat.Res.J. 270, 279 ff. (1962). See also Cal.Civ.Code § 4426 (1970).

The fact that the divorce statutes of many states include as grounds for divorce what would normally also be grounds for annulment raises still another possible defense to annulment. Such statutes provide, for example, that a prior subsisting marriage is a ground for divorce, Ohio Rev.Code § 3105.01 (1972), or that duress, fraud, impotence or mental incapacity are grounds for divorce. Ga.Code Ann. § 30–102 (Supp.1978). The question is thereby raised whether the remedy afforded by the divorce statute is to be exclusive, barring a suit for annulment on this ground. What arguments might be made for or against this result? Eggleston v. Eggleston, 156 Ohio St. 422, 103 N.E.2d 395 (1952); Abelt v. Zeman, 173 N.E.2d 907 (Ohio Com.Pl.1961); Schwartz v. Schwartz, 113 Ohio App. 275, 173 N.E.2d 393 (1960), 23 Ohio St.L.J. 774 (1962); Saville v. Saville, 44 Wash.2d 793, 271 P.2d 432 (1954); Jones v. Minc, 77 Wash.2d 381, 462 P.2d 927 (1969).

SECTION 3. THE INCIDENTS OF ANNULMENT

CLAYTON v. CLAYTON

Court of Appeals of Maryland, 1963
231 Md. 74, 188 A.2d 550.

HENDERSON, Judge. This appeal challenges the authority of the divorce court to award alimony to a wife incident to a decree of divorce on the ground that her husband had another wife living at the time of the marriage. It was alleged, and proved, that the parties were married by a religious ceremony on September 6, 1933, and that there are four children of the marriage. She alleged that she discovered that the appellant had been married on January 24, 1926, to one Adelaide Magruder, although Adelaide obtained a divorce on February 15, 1945. The appellee filed her bill on May 24, 1961. The Chancellor awarded her alimony and support for a minor child. It is conceded that the effect of the decree was to legitimate the children under Code (1957), Art. 16, Sec. 27 and the award of support for the minor child is not challenged.

One of the grounds for a divorce *a vinculo*, set out in Code (1962 Suppl.), Art. 16, Sec. 24, is "secondly, for any cause which by the laws of this State, render a marriage null and void ab initio". The purpose and application of this clause are not free from doubt. * * * But we think it clearly covers the case of bigamy and establishes another prevenient ground of divorce, as distinguished from annulment under Code (1962 Suppl.) Art. 16, Sec. 22 * * *, and now under Rule S76, following a conviction of bigamy under Code (1957) Art. 27, Sec. 18. Whether there could be a bigamy prosecution in the instant case is a question we need not consider. Code (1957), Art. 16, Sec. 3 provides: "In cases where a divorce is decreed, alimony may be awarded".

* * *

The appellant argues, however, that alimony is an incident of marriage and dependent upon that relationship. Hence, when it is judicially determined that there has been no marriage, or in the words of the statute the marriage is null and void ab initio, he contends that there can be no alimony as defined in such cases as Staub v. Staub, 170 Md. 202, 208, 183 A. 605 (1936). The holding in the Staub case, however, was that a right to alimony would not survive the dissolution of a marriage, without reservation in the decree. * * * It is true that in Yake v. Yake, 170 Md. 75, 78, 183 A. 555, 556 (1936), it was said, citing 2 Bishop, Marriage, Divorce and Separation, § 855, that alimony "cannot be predicated upon, or granted in consequence of, an annulment of marriage." But in that case the marriage had been annulled on the ground of fraud (the husband, a disabled veteran, claimed to have been insane at the time of the ceremony), and the holding was that a partial assignment of his pension rights was invalid under the Act of Congress (three judges dissenting). In Townsend v. Morgan, 192 Md. 168, 173, 63 A.2d 743, 745 (1949), it was said that "[a] second marriage contracted while a first *rule* marriage exists undissolved is a nullity without the passage of any judicial decree declaring it void." But the case is distinguishable on its facts.

The key to the instant case, as we see it, is the legislative declaration that alimony is allowable whenever there is a decree for divorce. We read "alimony" not in the technical sense of the word, but as commensurate with "support". The inclusion of prevenient invalidity as a ground for divorce must be ascribed some meaning, and we think it shows a legislative intent to permit an award of alimony in a proper case. The writers and cases recognize that the problem is one of statutory construction. In the absence of statute, alimony is generally not allowed in any case where the marriage is declared to be null and void ab initio. * * * The cases are collected in a note 54 A.L.R.2d 1410. But by statute in many states, support for the putative wife is allowed in all cases of divorce or annulment. In other states, the same result is reached, by construction of the divorce statutes to permit an award of alimony, even where the ground of divorce is that the marriage is a nullity. * * * We take the same view. If other questions relating to voidable marriages and annulments are left unanswered, that is a matter for legislative consideration, as suggested by Professor Strahorn in the articles cited, supra, and by Judge Hammond in his concurring opinion in Johnson v. Johnson, supra.

Decree affirmed, with costs.

NOTES AND QUESTIONS

1. As the *Clayton* case says, it is generally held that permanent alimony may not be granted in annulment suits, absent specific statutory authority. Wigder v. Wigder, 14 N.J.Misc. 880, 188 A. 235 (1936); Annot., 54 A.L.R.2d 1410 (1957); Note, The Aftereffects of Annulment: Alimony, Property Division, Provision for Children, 1968 Wash.U.L.Q. 148, 152. The reasoning of the cases is that since alimony is a substitute for the support which a husband owes to his wife, and since the annulment decree declares that no marriage ever existed, the support basis for alimony is likewise declared never to have existed. Thus the effect of the annulment decree, in holding the marriage void ab initio, is logically to eliminate any claim for alimony. Where the wife is the plaintiff in the annulment suit, there is the additional argument that in seeking alimony she is taking an inconsistent position. She is on the one hand asserting there is no marriage, and on the other claiming the benefit of one of the incidents of marriage.

(a) Could you advance any arguments in favor of granting alimony in annulment suits? Consider the following hypothetical situation: H and W–2 are married after H's first marriage ended in a Reno divorce which was obtained by H's first wife. H has no reason to think the divorce was invalid. Some years later H consults his attorney, who tells him the divorce was void for lack of jurisdiction, whereupon H sues W–2 for annulment. Assuming that the annulment would be granted, as it would in some cases, is W–2 in a position which should entitle her to alimony? How is her position any different in its practical aspects from what it would be if H had sued her for divorce?

(b) If alimony is not given in annulment suits, and if some grounds for annulment, such as bigamy, are also grounds for divorce, what effect does that have on the question whether divorce should be the exclusive remedy?

2. Some states have statutes expressly authorizing permanent alimony to be ordered in annulment where such an award would be equitable. Alaska Stat.Ann. § 09.55.210 (1973); Cal.Civ.Code § 4455 (Supp.1979); Colo. Rev.Stat.Ann. § 14–10–111(6) (1973); Conn.Gen.Stat.Ann. § 46b-60 (Supp. 1979); Iowa Code Ann. § 598.32 (Supp.1979–1980) (court may decree the innocent party "compensation"); N.H.Rev.Stat.Ann. § 458.19 (1968); N. Y.Dom.Rel.L. § 236 (1977); Wash.Rev.Code Ann. §§ 26.09.080, 26.09.090 (Supp.1978); Wis.Stat.Ann. § 247.26 (Supp.1979–1980). The Uniform Marriage and Divorce Act § 208(e) 9A Unif.L.Ann. 110 (1979) contains an unusual provision. It states that the declaration of invalidity of a marriage is to make the decree retroactive, unless the court finds that the interests of justice would be served by making it not retroactive. If it is made not retroactive, then alimony (called maintenance in this statute) may be granted as in the action for dissolution of marriage.

In addition to the foregoing states, there are also states in which grounds ordinarily appropriate for annulment are made grounds for divorce by statute. Where that is done, as in *Clayton*, alimony may be granted as in divorce. This may mean, however, that if both parties are responsible for the condition which invalidates the marriage, no alimony will be granted. Burger v. Burger, 166 So.2d 433 (Fla.1964) and Brown v. Brown, 186 So.2d 510 (Fla.1966). But see Johnson v. Johnson, 295 N.Y. 477, 68 N.E.2d 499 (1946).

3. A graphic illustration of the difficulties facing women who try to collect maintenance, either in annulment or divorce, is provided by Roe v. Doe, 68 Misc.2d 833, 328 N.Y.S.2d 506 (Sup.Ct.1972).

4. The wife's claim for temporary alimony, or alimony pendente lite, in annulment also runs into logical difficulties. If she is the plaintiff, her position is as self-contradictory as when she is seeking permanent alimony, since temporary alimony has as its purpose the support of the wife during the pendency of the suit. She is thus claiming a) that she is not a wife, and b) she wants the support to which a wife is entitled. Even if the wife is not attacking the marriage, but is upholding it, the husband can make the argument that if he is forced to pay her temporary alimony and later wins the suit, he will be unable to recover the payments, so that he will then be in the position of having been required to support a woman who never was his wife. Here again the essence of the difficulty is the ex post facto effect of the annulment decree. The cases seem to solve the problem by denying temporary alimony to the wife when she is plaintiff, Jones v. Brinsmade, 183 N.Y. 258, 76 N.E. 22 (1905), and granting it to her when she is upholding the marriage, provided she is able to make a prima facie showing of the validity of the marriage. State ex rel. Reger v. Superior Court, 242 Ind. 241, 177 N.E.2d 908 (1961); Bell v. Bell, 122 W.Va. 223, 8

S.E.2d 183 (1940). Other cases are cited in Annot., 110 A.L.R. 1283 (1937). Statutes in several states expressly authorize temporary alimony and attorney fees or "suit money" to the wife. Cal.Civ.Code §§ 4455, 4456 (Supp.1979) (putative spouse may get temporary alimony); Colo.Rev.Stat. Ann. § 14–10–111(6) (1973); N.Y.Dom.Rel.L. § 236 (1977); Wis.Stat.Ann. § 247.23 (Supp.1979–1980). See Note, The Aftereffects of Annulment: Alimony, Property Division, Provision for Children, 1968 Wash.U.L.Q. 148, 149.

WALKER v. WALKER

Supreme Court of Michigan, 1951.
330 Mich. 332, 47 N.W.2d 633.

BOYLES, Justice. This case is a follow-up from our decision in Walker v. Walker, 323 Mich. 137, 35 N.W.2d 146, 147 (1949), where we denied this plaintiff a divorce from a common-law marriage because the defendant had a lawful wife living at the same time the plaintiff claimed to be his wife. We entered a decree affirming the circuit judge in finding that the alleged common-law marriage was void *ab initio,* but reversed the decree entered below "insofar as it undertakes to settle the property rights of the parties." In so doing, this Court wrote (italics supplied):

"She is left to pursue her remedies *under the general chancery jurisdiction* which as we have seen cannot be invoked in a divorce action. Plaintiff does not request of us permission to amend her bill of complaint so as to invoke general chancery jurisdiction instead of the limited jurisdiction conferred by the divorce statutes; nor does she claim that she made a request of the lower court for such permission.

"Our refusal to make an award of property rights to plaintiff in this suit is without prejudice to her right to file and maintain a different suit."

Thereupon plaintiff filed the instant bill of complaint asking for a decree determining her interest in the personal property and real estate accumulated during the alleged common-law marriage, that the court determine the value of her services as housekeeper for the defendant, that the defendant be required to account for the money she had contributed toward the purchase on contract of a home with apartments, for household furniture and equipment, asked that the same be made a lien on the property, and that the defendant be enjoined from disposing of or encumbering said real estate until the lien was discharged. The trial court, after a hearing and taking testimony, entered a decree finding the defendant guilty of misrepresentation and fraud by concealing the fact that he had a wife living at the time he contracted the common-law marriage, ordered that the defendant pay $1,000 as the reasonable value of plaintiff's services and the amount she had contributed toward the home and property, and decreed a lien on the real estate for its payment. The defendant appeals.

* * * The record establishes that in June or July, 1941, these parties entered into a relationship which would have been a valid common-law marriage except for the fact that the defendant had a lawful wife living. They lived and cohabited together until 1947, at which time the divorce case hereinbefore referred to was begun, resulting as above stated. Plaintiff did not know that the defendant had a wife living, until the answer in the divorce case was filed. The record is plain that the defendant concealed that fact from the plaintiff and that the services rendered by the plaintiff and the contributions made by her were under the mistaken belief that she was his common-law wife. Concealment of material facts may constitute actionable fraud. * * *

During the 6 years these parties lived together as husband and wife the plaintiff cooked meals for the defendant, did his laundry, performed other services, made substantial contributions toward the purchase of the home on land contract, toward the household goods, and contributed to later payments on the land contract. In the decree in the divorce case the trial judge attempted to award plaintiff an undivided half interest in the real estate and in the household furniture and equipment, having determined the value of said interest to be $1,000. The testimony in that case, stipulated to apply to the instant case, as well as testimony taken in the case at bar, amply supports the present decree granting plaintiff a lien on the real estate for that amount.

The defendant mainly relies for reversal on a claim that plaintiff has an adequate remedy at law, wherefore the equity court should not take jurisdiction. More weight might be given the claim were it not for the fact that this Court in the divorce case indicated that we left plaintiff to pursue her remedies *under the general chancery jurisdiction*. However, these parties were, at least to some extent, in a confidential relationship after the defendant induced the plaintiff to enter into the supposed status of a common-law marriage. The defendant has been unjustly enriched to the extent of plaintiff's contributions to the value of the property he seeks to retain. Justice requires that the Court dispose of the property rights of these parties without further multiplicity of suits. Under the circumstances of this case, defendant's claim that equity does not have jurisdiction stands only as a stumbling block in the path of justice, without substantial merit, and we are not in accord with the defendant's claim that plaintiff's sole remedy is in the law side of the Court. "Appellant claims that plaintiff could obtain full relief, if entitled thereto, in an action of replevin, and that equity has no jurisdiction if plaintiff has an adequate remedy at law. However, the test of equitable jurisdiction is not whether there is an alternative remedy at law, but whether the remedy at law is as adequate, complete and certain as the relief in equity. * * * Equity has jurisdiction in cases of fraud where the remedy at law would be doubtful, incomplete or otherwise inadequate, * * *, and also to prevent a multiplicity of suits, * * *."

While cases from other jurisdictions are not in full accord, it has been held that equity has jurisdiction to adjudicate the property rights between the parties although the marriage was void. * * *

In Buckley v. Buckley, 50 Wash. 213, 96 P. 1079, 1081, 126 Am. St.Rep. 900 (1907), two cases were consolidated for trial—a suit for divorce or annulment of marriage on the ground that the spouse already had a wife, and another suit by the supposed wife for a division of property acquired while living in the marital relation. In affirming both the judgment and the decree, the court held: "Where a woman in good faith enters into a marriage contract with a man, and they assume and enter into the marriage state pursuant to any ceremony or agreement recognized by the law of the place, which marriage would be legal except for the incompetency of the man which he conceals from the woman, a status is created which will justify a court in rendering a decree of annulment of the attempted and assumed marriage contract upon complaint of the innocent party; and where in such a case the facts are as they have been found here, where the woman helped to acquire and very materially to save the property, the court has jurisdiction, as between the parties, to dispose of their property as it would do, under section 5723, Ballinger's Ann. Codes & St. (Pierce's Code, § 4637), in a case of granting a divorce, awarding to the innocent, injured woman such proportion of the property as, under all the circumstances, would be just and equitable."

* * *

Affirmed, with costs.

* * *

NOTES AND QUESTIONS

1. For a case similarly ordering a property division on the basis of an opinion containing some unconscious humor, see Sclamberg v. Sclamberg, 220 Ind. 209, 41 N.E.2d 801 (1942). Other cases are collected in Annot., 31 A.L.R.2d 1255 (1953); Annot., 11 A.L.R. 1394 (1921); Annot., 111 A.L.R. 348 (1937).

2. What factors does the court find relevant in deciding whether the plaintiff should be given part of the defendant's property in this case? In considering these factors is the court trying to determine who owns what property? Or is it arriving at the wife's share on some other basis? Is there any relation to the alimony cases here?

3. Does the award to the plaintiff in this case constitute an abandonment of the "relation back" effect of annulment, amounting to an admission that there is no difference between annulment and divorce?

4. The court emphasizes that while the parties lived together the plaintiff performed various services in the household, implying that she ought to be compensated therefor. But was she not supported by the de-

fendant during this time? Was this sufficient compensation for her services?

5. Is the court in the *Walker* case relying upon the same principles as the court in Marvin v. Marvin, supra, page 38? Is the *Walker* case an example of putative marriage as described, supra, page 116?

6. The logical consequence of the usual view of annulment is that since it declares that no marriage ever existed, any children of the parties are illegitimate. Fortunately this harsh logic has been overridden by statute in nearly every state, except possibly Rhode Island, where a statute provides that the children of certain void marriages are illegitimate. R.I.Gen.L. § 15–1–5 (1970). The statutes saving the legitimacy of children take several forms, of varying breadth. Some provide that the children of marriages which are annulled are legitimate. E. g., Tenn.Code Ann. § 36–832 (1977). A much larger number provides that the children of any void or voidable marriage are legitimate. E. g., N.J.Stat.Ann. § 2A:34–20 (Supp.1979–1980); N.Y.Dom.Rel.L. § 24 (1977). The Uniform Parentage Act § 4, 9 Unif.L.Ann. 523 (Supp.1978), now in force in several states, provides that a man is presumed to be the father of a child born during an invalid marriage under described circumstances. Section 2 of the same Act provides that the parent-child relationship extends to every child and every parent, regardless of the parents' marital status.

The type of statute which legitimizes the children of void or voidable marriages has generally been given a broad and liberal construction with the obvious purpose of protecting children whenever possible. Thus in State v. Bragg, 152 W.Va. 372, 163 S.E.2d 685 (1968) it was held that a child of a common law marriage contracted in a state which did not recognize common law marriage was legitimate, as a child of a marriage "null in law" under the statute, and so entitled to support by virtue of the criminal non-support statute. And a bigamous common law marriage, known by both spouses to be bigamous and therefore invalid, contracted in Ohio, which recognizes common law marriage, was held to result in legitimate offspring for Social Security Act purposes in Wolf v. Gardner, 386 F.2d 295 (6th Cir. 1967). Another case, turning to some extent on an unusual Virginia statute, held that a bigamous common law marriage, in a state which does not recognize common law marriage, legitimated a child for social security purposes. Kasey v. Richardson, 331 F.Supp. 580 (W.D.Va.1971). A case the other way is Crenshaw v. Gardner, 277 F.Supp. 427 (D.N.J.1967).

Statutes in many states also empower the courts in annulment suits to order the support and provide for the custody of children of annulled marriages. E. g., Cal.Civ.Code Ann. § 4454 (1970); N.Y.Dom.Rel.L. § 240 (1977); Wis.Stat.Ann. § 247.24 (Supp.1979–1980). See also the Uniform Marriage and Divorce Act § 208(e), 9A Unif.L.Ann. 110 (1979). Even without statutory authority the courts have power by virtue of their responsibility to protect children to enter custody and maintenance orders for children of annulled marriages. Cardenas v. Cardenas, 12 Ill.App.2d 497, 140 N.E.2d 377 (1957); Annots., 63 A.L.R.2d 1008 (1959) and 63 A.L.R.2d 1029 (1959); Note, The Aftereffects of Annulment: Alimony, Property Division, Provision for Children, 1968 Wash.U.L.Q. 148, 159.

For a discussion of the current status of the illegitimate child, see chapter 5, section 2, infra.

GAINES v. JACOBSEN

Court of Appeals of New York, 1954.
308 N.Y. 218, 124 N.E.2d 290, 48 A.L.R.2d 312.

FULD, Judge. The question in this case is whether, under a separation agreement requiring annual payments for plaintiff's support "until she shall remarry", defendant husband's obligation to make the payments terminates permanently with the wife's "remarriage" or is revived by a later annulment of that "remarriage." The trial court, deciding that the agreement "contemplated a valid marriage," held that defendant's obligation was revived as of the date the second "marriage" was annulled. On appeal, the Appellate Division reversed, finding that plaintiff did remarry, within the meaning of the agreement, and that defendant's obligations were thereupon permanently extinguished, despite the later annulment.

Plaintiff and defendant, married in 1927, separated and entered into a separation agreement in March of 1944. The agreement provided, *inter alia,* that defendant was to pay to plaintiff $1,668 a year for her support and maintenance, during her life "or until she shall remarry"; it also required that defendant maintain a $10,000 insurance policy on his life for the benefit of plaintiff, "unless and until * * * [she] shall remarry." The agreement, it was specified, was to survive any decree of divorce and all questions relating to its "validity, interpretation and enforcement" were to "be construed and determined in accordance with the law of the State of Connecticut."

Two months later, plaintiff wife was granted an absolute divorce from defendant in Nevada, the decree providing, with respect to support and maintenance, that the parties be left to their agreement. Defendant husband remarried in August of 1944 and plaintiff married one George W. Harragan five years later. Upon her marriage to the latter, plaintiff advised defendant that she "had been married" and that he could "quit making * * * the payments".

Harragan had obtained a divorce in Nevada from his former wife Rosalind prior to his marriage to plaintiff. Soon after that marriage, however, Rosalind instituted suit for divorce against Harragan in this state on grounds of adultery. The New York court, finding that there was no prior decree of divorce between them "by any court having jurisdiction to grant the same," awarded Rosalind an absolute divorce. With this turn of events, plaintiff left Harragan and brought suit in this state for an annulment on the ground that he was married at the time of his alleged marriage to her. The action resulted in a judgment of annulment, "declaring the alleged marriage * * * a nullity".

Plaintiff made no request for alimony in the annulment action having been advised by her attorney that Harragan was so burdened with debts and alimony payments to Rosalind that the court would make no award against him.[1] Neither did she make any claim that defendant resume payments under the agreement until about a year and a half later, feeling, as she put it, that "I got myself in trouble and I would take care of myself." In February of 1953, however, she commenced this present action against defendant (1) to recover support and maintenance payments allegedly in arrears under the separation agreement and (2) to require defendant to provide and maintain the $10,000 insurance policy for her benefit.

Although the agreement stipulates that Connecticut law should govern its construction and effect, the Appellate Division, concluding that the question posed had never arisen in the courts of that state, rested its determination on New York law. In so doing, it was correct. In the absence of proof to the contrary, we must assume that the law of Connecticut is the same as the law of New York, * * *, and, indeed, both parties, as well as the Appellate Division, agree that the major question in this case is whether our decision in Sleicher v. Sleicher, 251 N.Y. 366, at page 369, 167 N.E. 501, 502, is controlling.

In the Sleicher case, a separation agreement, incorporated in a Nevada decree of divorce, provided for payments to the wife "so long as she remains unmarried"; the wife's subsequent remarriage was later annulled because of the second husband's insanity. The court held that the first husband's obligation to make the payments was not terminated by the invalid remarriage, resting the decision on the doctrine of "relation" back or "rescission from the beginning"—that is, as the court put it, that an "annulment when decreed, puts an end to [the marriage] from the beginning * * *. It is not dissolved as upon divorce. It is effaced as if it had never been." 251 N.Y. at page 369, 167 N.E. at page 502. Accordingly, the husband was required to pay all installments due from the date of the annulment. The court, however, rejected the wife's claim that she was also entitled to the payments which fell due during the period of the second marriage and before its annulment. In that connection, it observed that the " 'doctrine of relation is a fiction of law adopted * * * solely for the purposes of justice' " and that it is "not * * * without limits, prescribed by policy and justice", which "have their typical application to the rights and duties of a stranger." 251 N.Y. at page 369, 167 N.E. at page 502. Accordingly, since the "purpose of an award of alimony is support for a divorced wife not otherwise supported", 251 N.Y. at page 371, 167 N.E. at page 503, and since the wife was supported by her second husband until their marriage was annulled, the court denied recovery from her first husband for the period during which the second marriage continued.

At the time of the Sleicher decision, it was impossible for a wife to obtain alimony or other support upon annulment of a marriage; it

---

1. We are advised of the fact—not in the record—that Harragan died in   December, 1953, following the trial of the present action.

followed inexorably, from the theory that an annulled marriage never existed, that such a marriage created no subsequent duty of support. * * * To have held otherwise than the court did in Sleicher would, therefore, have deprived the wife in that case of any source of support whatsoever. However, since that time, the legislature has enacted section 1140–a of the Civil Practice Act, which provides that

"When an action is brought to annul a marriage or to declare the nullity of a void marriage, the court may give such direction for support of the wife by the husband as justice requires".

This new provision, respondent urges, by removing the primary and underlying motivation for the Sleicher decision, distinguishes that case from the one before us and justifies us in reaching a different conclusion. Appellant, on the other hand, contends that there is no basis for distinguishing Sleicher, and that it is dispositive of this appeal.

While resolution of the dispute may not be easy, it is our opinion that the new enactment, after the date of the Sleicher decision, alters the situation before us so materially that it calls for a different result in this case.

Since the function of alimony payments is to provide support for a wife not otherwise supported, the reason for such payments fails when the wife acquires a new source of support by remarrying, cf. Civ.Prac.Act, § 1172–c. And by a ceremonial marriage she receives the right to support—even though the circumstances are such that grounds for annulment exist—for the entire period that the parties live together as husband and wife, unless and until there is an actual judicial declaration of annulment. * * *

The subsequent fortunes of the remarriage, and whether or not it is later terminated, are in no way material to the agreement; the husband's obligations are by its terms to continue only until she remarries, and there is nothing in the agreement which can serve as a basis for subsequently reviving those obligations. No one contends that they would be revived if the remarriage ended in divorce, * * *, and it is difficult to see any reason for a different result when it ends in annulment. It is certainly unlikely that the parties intended the result to turn upon whether an unsuccessful remarriage is deemed in law void—as is the one in this case, Domestic Relations Law, Consol.Laws, c. 14, § 6—or voidable, Domestic Relations Law, § 7, or valid, until dissolved by a decree of divorce. Rather, the understanding must have been that, upon the wife's remarriage, the husband could regard himself as free of the duty to support her. He could then assume new obligations—he could himself remarry, if he were of a mind to, but his means limited—without remaining forever subject to the possibility that his first wife's remarriage would be annulled and the burden of supporting her shifted back to him. And the wife, too, must have understood that by remarrying she abandoned her rights to support under the agreement, for better or for worse, in favor of whatever support would be furnished her by her second mate.

These arguments were, of course, available to the husband at the time of the Sleicher case, but, as already noted, the fact situation was materially altered in the interim. In 1929, when Sleicher was decided, there was no section 1140–a, with the consequence that, if the remarriage ended in annulment rather than divorce, no alimony could have been awarded against the second spouse. If the court had determined that the wife had lost her rights under the agreement as well, she would have had no source of support whatsoever. To avoid this harsh result, the court had recourse to the doctrine that annulment relates back to destroy the marriage from the beginning—fully recognizing that it was " 'a fiction of law adopted * * * solely for the purposes of justice' "—to hold that there was no "remarriage" under the terms of the agreement. At the same time, however, in order to deny recovery for the period that the second marriage continued, the court acknowledged that the doctrine was "not * * * without limits, prescribed by policy and justice." 251 N.Y. at page 369, 167 N.E. at page 502.

Today, through the operation of section 1140–a, the wife can receive support from the husband of the annulled marriage, where "justice requires," and there is no more reason to revive the obligation of the first husband—a stranger to the annulment—than there would be if the remarriage were terminated by divorce. The "purposes of justice" now dictate that his discharge, effected when the wife goes through a second marriage, be permanent, that he be not required to stand perpetually ready to resume her support should the remarriage some day be annulled. The interests of justice require, too, that, as between successive husbands, the wife look to the last one for support, and, certainly, that she be given neither two sources of support nor the ability to choose between her first and second husbands for the more profitable. The court put it most aptly in Sleicher, when it wrote, "To say that the judgment of annulment has put the defendant in default through the fiction of relation is to say that the plaintiff shall have support or an equivalent from each of two men during the same period of time, and this by force of a fiction subservient to justice." 251 N.Y. at page 370, 167 N.E. at page 503.

Not only does the practical justification for the Sleicher decision fall with the enactment of section 1140–a, but its doctrinal basis becomes extremely questionable as well. The fiction that annulment effaces a marriage "as if it had never been" is sometimes given effect and sometimes ignored, as the "purposes of justice" are deemed to require. The courts and the legislature have, accordingly, attached to annulled marriages, for certain purposes, the same significance that a valid marriage would have, when a more desirable result is thereby achieved. Thus, although a distinction is sometimes made between void and voidable marriages, the annulled marriage has been given sufficient vitality to constitute valid consideration for a gift in contemplation of the marriage, * * * ; to make a remarriage by one of the parties during its continuance bigamous, * * * ; and, by statute in this state, to legitimatize any children born of the union, Civ.Prac.Act, § 1135.

By writing section 1140–a into the law, the legislature has chosen, without regard to whether the marriage is void or voidable, to attach to annulled marriages sufficient validity and significance to support an award of alimony, in other words, to serve, the same as any valid marriage would, as the foundation of a continuing duty to support the wife after the marriage is terminated. See Johnson v. Johnson, 295 N.Y. 477, 68 N.E.2d 499 (1946). It has declared, in effect, that, for the purpose of sustaining a right to support after annullment, the annulled marriage is no longer to be deemed a nullity, "effaced as if it had never been." In so doing, the legislature has destroyed the very foundation of the Sleicher decision. To give an annulled marriage this effect, and yet stamp it a nullity for the purpose of terminating the first husband's duty of support under the agreement, would fly in the face of logic and consistence.

It is true, as plaintiff points out, that an affirmance places her in a less than happy position because Harragan has died; she can no longer ask the court in the annulment action to amend the decree and exercise its discretion, under section 1140–a, to provide for alimony payments from him. Such a consideration cannot, however, affect our decision. In the ordinary case, it is far more likely that justice will be served by not disturbing the first husband's discharge, and by leaving the wife to seek support, from her second husband, in the annulment action. That the second husband has died is unfortunate, but plaintiff's plight is no different from that of any woman whose source of support has come to an end through death. Having remarried, she chose to abandon her right to support from defendant in favor of Harragan. Plaintiff could not retain both husbands as sources of support; having made her choice, she is bound by it, although subsequent events prove it to have been an improvident one.

The judgment appealed from should be affirmed.

* * *

NOTES AND QUESTIONS

1. The *Gaines* case is noted in 54 Colum.L.Rev. 1162 (1954), 41 Corn. L.Q. 141 (1955), and 68 Harv.L.Rev. 1076 (1955). For a collection of cases on this question see Annot., 45 A.L.R.3d 1033 (1972).

2. The leading case contra *Gaines* is Sutton v. Leib, 199 F.2d 163, 33 A.L.R.2d 1451 (7th Cir. 1952), on remand from 342 U.S. 402, 72 S.Ct. 398, 96 L.Ed. 448 (1952), noted in 26 So.Cal.L.Rev. 448 (1953), applying Illinois law. W had obtained a divorce decree from her first husband, the decree awarding her alimony to continue as long as she remained unmarried. She

then married H–2, and three years later obtained an annulment of this marriage on the ground of H–2's prior subsisting marriage. On notification by W's counsel, H–1 had stopped paying alimony when W married H–2. The court held that not only did H–1's alimony obligation revive after the annulment, but that H–1 was also required to pay to W the forty monthly installments of alimony which had accrued while she was living with H–2, the reason being that W had had no legal right to support from H–2 because her marriage to him was wholly void. A case seeming to reach the same result is Reese v. Reese, 192 So.2d 1 (Fla.1966).

For other cases see Annot., 48 A.L.R.2d 270, 298 (1956).

3. What is the rationale of the *Gaines* case? In answering this question, you might consider the following questions:

(a) Could the plaintiff have obtained alimony in her annulment suit against H–2? Does this matter?

(b) H–1 and W were divorced in New York, a separation agreement which they executed providing that the wife was to receive $50 per week so long as she did not remarry. H–1 remarried. About two or three years later W married H–2, who had been married to H–1's sister, and they took up residence in New Jersey. After her remarriage W made no demand for the payments under the separation agreement. Six months later H–2's first wife sued him in New Jersey to set aside the Mexican divorce which H–2 had obtained. The New Jersey court declared the Mexican divorce void, and after this H–2 was convicted in New Jersey of bigamy. New Jersey does not permit alimony to be granted in annulment suits. H–1 apparently instigated the legal actions which upset W's second marriage and led to the bigamy prosecution. After her marriage to H–2 was annulled, W separated from him and demanded that H–1 resume the payments called for by their separation agreement. H–1 thereupon sued in New York for a declaratory judgment that his obligations under the separation agreement did not revive. What should be the result, on your theory of the reasoning underlying *Gaines?* Denberg v. Frischman, 24 A.D.2d 100, 264 N.Y.S.2d 114 (1st Dep't 1965), aff'd on the opinion of the Appellate Division, with dissent by Judge Keating, 17 N.Y.2d 778, 217 N.E.2d 675, 270 N.Y.S.2d 627 (1966).

(c) Should the *Gaines* and *Denberg* cases turn on a "construction" of the separation agreement?

(d) Is the issue in the two cases the determination of what was the intent of the parties when they made the separation agreement? Cf. Dodd v. Dodd, 210 Kan. 50, 499 P.2d 518 (1972).

4. H–1 and W are divorced in New York with alimony to W to continue until her remarriage. W marries H–2 in New Jersey, where they become domiciled. H–2 has been married before, but his first marriage has been dissolved by a bilateral Mexican divorce, that is, one in which he went to Mexico and brought the proceeding, and his first wife was represented by Mexican counsel, who filed a general appearance on her behalf. W obtains an annulment in New Jersey on the grounds that H–2's Mexican divorce was invalid and that his marriage to W was bigamous. W now demands that H–1 resume the alimony payments, and when he refuses, she brings suit against him in New York asking that he be ordered to resume the payments. H–1 moves to dismiss her suit on the ground that under New York law the Mexican divorce obtained by H–2 is valid, so that W is

still married to H–2. Assume that New York does hold such divorces valid, but that New Jersey does not.

(a) May H–1 make this defense? Does it depend on whether the annulment suit is characterized as in personam or in rem? Which is it? Cf. Perlstein v. Perlstein, supra, page 185 and Whealton v. Whealton, supra, page 191; Restatement, Second, Judgments § 74, comment a (Tent.Draft No. 3, 1976); Presbrey v. Presbrey, 6 A.D.2d 477, 179 N.Y.S.2d 788 (1st Dep't 1958), aff'd p.c. 8 N.Y.2d 797, 201 N.Y.S.2d 807, 168 N.E.2d 135 (1960); Cecil v. Cecil, 11 Utah 2d 155, 356 P.2d 279 (1960); Hallford v. Industrial Commission, 63 Ariz. 40, 159 P.2d 305 (1945).

(b) Which law controls this question, that of New York or that of New Jersey? Restatement, Second, Conflict of Laws § 94 (1971).

(c) What would be the result in this case if the states involved had the following statute: "A judgment of nullity is conclusive only as to the parties to the proceeding and those claiming under them"? Cal.Civ.Code § 4451 (1970). Would you advocate the enactment of such a statute in states which did not have it?

SEFTON v. SEFTON

Supreme Court of California, In Bank, 1955.
45 Cal.2d 872, 291 P.2d 439.

SHENK, Justice. This action was brought by Mrs. Sefton to enforce the alimony provisions of a property settlement agreement.

The facts are not disputed. On December 6, 1951, Mrs. Sefton was granted a final decree of divorce from the defendant. The decree confirmed and incorporated by reference a property settlement agreement which obligated the defendant to pay Mrs. Sefton $275 monthly for her support and maintenance. This obligation was to continue until the death or remarriage of Mrs. Sefton. The defendant made the regular monthly payments pursuant to the agreement through June 5, 1953.

On June 12, 1953, Mrs. Sefton entered into a ceremonial marriage with one Ross C. Marble. Thereafter she commenced an action to annul this marriage, alleging as the ground for annulment a species of fraud which would make the marriage voidable only. Marble appeared on the same day and consented that the annulment could be heard as a default matter. On June 19, 1953, Mrs. Sefton's marriage to Marble was decreed null and void.

Civil Code section 139, as amended in 1951, provides: "Except as otherwise agreed by the parties in writing, the obligation of any party in any decree, judgment or order for the support and maintenance of the other party shall terminate upon the death of the obligor or upon the remarriage of the other party." The agreement here involved adopted language substantially the same as section 139 as amended and provided that the husband make payments for the support and maintenance of the wife "* * * until her death or remarriage * * *." The sole issue is whether the annulment decree effectively revived the defendant's obligation to pay alimony, or whether Mrs. Sefton's voidable marriage to Marble was a "remarriage" within the meaning of that term as employed in section 139 as amended and in the property settlement agreement of the parties.

It has been said that an annulment decree has the effect of declaring a marriage void *ab initio.* A divorce in this state merely dissolves the existing marriage, leaving intact the marriage relationship between the time of the marriage ceremony and the entry of the final decree. An annulment, on the other hand, has been said to "relate back" and erase the marriage and all its implications from the outset. * * * If the "relation back" theory is given strict application, as Mrs. Sefton contends it should be, then her marriage to Marble never existed, she has not remarried as the property settlement agreement contemplates, and she would remain entitled to the alimony provided in the agreement.

Despite this contention, the doctrine of "relation back" is not without its exceptions. The doctrine was fashioned by our courts to do substantial justice as between the parties to a voidable marriage. It is a mere legal fiction which has an appeal when used as a device for achieving that purpose. The test for determining the applicability of the doctrine as applied to voidable marriages is whether it effects a result which conforms to the sanctions of sound policy and justice as between the immediate parties thereto, their property rights acquired during that marriage and the rights of their offspring. Certain rights of the purported spouses living under the color of a voidable marriage have been recognized as paramount to the doctrine in appropriate cases. It is well settled, for example, that a party who in good faith enters into a voidable or even an invalid marriage is entitled, upon annulment or other termination of the relationship, to have the property acquired during the purported marriage considered the same as community property and treated as such upon the dissolution of the marriage. * * * The doctrine has similarly yielded to permit temporary alimony, court costs, attorney fees and appeal expenses. These may be ordered where appropriate in annulment actions. * * *

However, in cases involving the rights of third parties, courts have been especially wary lest the logical appeal of the fiction should obscure fundamental problems and lead to unjust or ill-advised results respecting a third party's rights. Thus the exceptions to the theory of "relation back" should have their typical application to situations affecting an innocent third party. * * * Logic has long ago yielded to principle in the solution of the problem of determining the status of the children of annulled marriages. While a strict application of the doctrine of relation would reach back to deprive those children of their legitimate status, they are, of course, protected

against the stain of illegitimacy not only where the marriage is voidable,   *   *   *, but also where the marriage is totally void.
*   *   * The doctrine has been held similarly without application to
other transactions involving the rights of third parties.   *   *   *
Therefore, whatever may be said for the fiction of "relation back" as
a general principle in annulment cases, it must be deemed to apply
only where it promotes the purposes for which it was intended. It is
apparent that Mrs. Sefton's contention would not lead to those results. By the celebration of marriage she held herself out as having
remarried. The defendant was entitled to rely upon her apparent
marital status after the ceremony. If Mrs. Sefton's new marriage
was subject to annulment for fraud as provided for in subdivision
four of section 82 of the Civil Code, or for the incapacity of her new
husband to enter upon the marriage state as provided for in subdivision six, or for any reason stated in subdivisions one, three and five
of that section, the marriage would be voidable only. Redress by
way of annulment might never be sought by the offended party and
the marital status might thus continue indefinitely. The causes for
annulment thus provided for by statute are ordinarily known to or
concern only the individual contracting parties. The divorced spouse,
the defendant here, may never know of the circumstances which
make his former wife's new marriage voidable. Certainly knowledge
of such voidability may not be imputed to him. After the ceremony
took place he could properly assume, in accordance with section 139
and the property settlement agreement, that his obligation to pay alimony had ceased. He was then entitled to recommit his assets previously chargeable to alimony to other purposes. Under such circumstances it would be improper to reinstate his alimony obligation.
While it is true that both the plaintiff and defendant may be deemed
to be innocent parties, it accords with the policy of the law to look
less favorably upon the more active of two innocent parties when by
reason of such activity a loss is sustained as the result of the misconduct of a stranger. Here it is clear that Mrs. Sefton was the active
party who brought herself and the defendant into their present situation. Accordingly, it is she who should assume the responsibility for
it.

Counsel for Mrs. Sefton rely strongly on the case of Sleicher v.
Sleicher, supra, 251 N.Y. 356, 167 N.E. 501 (1929), which reached a
contrary result.   *   *   *. Following the decision in that case the
New York legislature enacted section 1140–a of the Civil Practice Act
which provided that "When an action is brought to annul a marriage
or to declare the nullity of a void marriage, the court may give such
direction for support of the wife by the husband as justice requires."
Soon after the enactment of that law the same question as that involved in the Sleicher case came before the same court in 1954 in
Gaines v. Jacobsen, 308 N.Y. 218, 124 N.E.2d 290, 293 (1954). In
that case it was decided in effect that whatever the "doctrinal basis"

for the holding in the Sleicher case, it faded away by the enactment of the new code section. The court then entered upon a discussion of the fundamental problem which obviously detracted from the soundness of the opinion in the Sleicher case and which lends support for the conclusion herein.

It is noted that in both of the New York cases a wife sought to reinstate alimony claimed not to have been terminated by a marriage later annulled. The wife was successful in the Sleicher case but unsuccessful in the Gaines case. The court considered the two situations in view of the new statute. However in the Gaines case the court recognized that the new statutory provision did not afford the wife in that case any advantage. In fact she did not invoke it because the husband of the annulled marriage could not have furnished her any support. And the court, while considering the statutory change, nevertheless departed from the application of "relation back" as employed in the Sleicher case when it considered it to be important that a divorced husband's obligations under the property settlement agreement were to furnish support until his former wife should remarry. The court held that "there is nothing in the agreement which can serve as a basis for subsequently reviving those obligations"; that they would not "be revived if the remarriage ended in divorce * * * and it is difficult to see any reason for a different result when it ends in annulment"; that it must have been the intent of the parties that upon the wife's remarriage the husband would be free of his duty for support and could assume new marital and economic obligations "without remaining forever subject to the possibility that his first wife's remarriage would be annulled, and the burden of supporting her shifted back to him"; that the "wife, too, must have understood that by remarrying she abandoned her rights to support under the agreement, for better or for worse, in favor of whatever support would be furnished her by her second mate"; and that the plaintiff "could not retain both husbands as sources of support; having made her choice, she is bound by it, although subsequent events prove it to have been an improvident one." It is obvious that the reasoning in the *Gaines* case has deprived the *Sleicher* case of any present persuasive authority. * * *

The foregoing dictates the conclusion that the ceremony of remarriage in this case terminated the alimony obligation.

The judgment is affirmed.

* * *

NOTES AND QUESTIONS

1. Does the California court in *Sefton* correctly assess the reasoning in Gaines v. Jacobsen? Cf. Robbins v. Robbins, 343 Mass. 247, 178 N.E.2d 281 (1961); Gerrig v. Sneirson, 344 Mass. 518, 183 N.E.2d 131 (1962).

2. What is the rationale of Sefton v. Sefton? How long did Mrs. Sefton's second marriage last? Would Mr. Sefton be likely to "recommit

his assets * * * to other purposes" in that time? If not, does that impair the reasoning of the case?

3. In Gaines v. Jacobsen the annulment was granted on the ground of a prior subsisting marriage, that is, that the wife's second marriage was bigamous, while in *Sefton* the second marriage was annulled for fraud. Does this make the cases distinguishable? Would the alimony payments be revived when the second marriage was void, even though they would not when it was merely voidable? Cf. Bridges v. Bridges, 217 So.2d 281 (Miss.1969); and cf. Flaxman v. Flaxman, 57 N.J. 458, 273 A.2d 567 (1971) with Minder v. Minder, 83 N.J.Super. 159, 199 A.2d 69 (1964); Ballew v. Ballew, 187 Neb. 397, 191 N.W.2d 462 (1971); Berkely v. Berkely, 269 Cal.App.2d 872, 75 Cal.Rptr. 294 (1969); Broadus v. Broadus, 361 So. 2d 582 (Ala.App.1978); Kelley v. Kelley, 350 So.2d 11 (Fla.App.1977).

4. How would you characterize the following reasoning: "To us, the provisions of the decree concerning alimony seem perfectly clear and unambiguous, providing, as they do, that '* * * in the event of her remarriage said payments shall cease.' By the decree, cessation of alimony did not turn on the status of the remarriage as being valid. It simply provided that in a certain event, alimony would cease; the event occurred and the alimony ceased." Chavez v. Chavez, 82 N.M. 624, 485 P.2d 735 (1971). In this case the second marriage had been annulled for fraud.

5. Should the result be different in these cases if the wife were peculiarly unable to support herself, for example because she was mentally incompetent? Cecil v. Cecil, 11 Utah 2d 155, 356 P.2d 279 (1960); Minder v. Minder, 83 N.J.Super. 159, 199 A.2d 69 (1964).

6. If the annulment of the second marriage is obtained in a state like New Jersey, which does not authorize alimony in annulment suits, is there any other remedy which the wife might have against her second "husband"? See Flaxman v. Flaxman, 57 N.J. 458, 273 A.2d 567 (1971).

7. What should be the effect on an alimony decree if the ex-wife makes no pretense of marrying, but just lives with another man? Is no marriage at all equivalent for this purpose to a void marriage? What is a void marriage if it is not a complete absence of marriage? Conversely, what is the effect of Marvin v. Marvin, supra, page 38, on this question? The question is discussed in more detail in connection with the modification of alimony decrees, infra, chapter 6, section 7.

8. What should be the result if W is divorced from H–1 with an award of alimony terminable upon her death or remarriage, and she then marries H–2, later divorcing H–2 on the ground of a prior subsisting marriage, as would be possible, for example, under Ohio Rev.Code Ann. § 3105.-01(A) (1972)?

FOLSOM v. PEARSALL

United States Court of Appeals, Ninth Circuit, 1957.
245 F.2d 562.

Before STEPHENS, BONE and POPE, Circuit Judges.

BONE, Circuit Judge. In October 1952, appellee began to receive mother's insurance benefits as she was the unremarried widow of Delbert L. Pearsall, a deceased wage earner, such payments being made according to 42 U.S.C.A. § 402(g). These payments to her terminated as of June, 1954, because of a marriage that month to one Frank Richard. On November 19, 1954, appellee filed in an appropriate California court a "Complaint for Annulment and/or Divorce" against Richard. * * * Richard defaulted, and the court issued its decree of annulment on December 9, 1954.

After this decree of annulment appellee requested reinstatement of her mother's insurance benefits. The Bureau of Old Age and Survivors Insurance, Social Security Administration, refused reinstatement. Appellee then had a hearing before a referee of the Office of the Appeals Council. The decision of this particular hearing was that appellee was not entitled to reinstatement of mother's insurance benefits as a result of the annulment of the marriage to Richard. Appellee's request for a review by the Appeals Council of the Referee's decision was denied, the decision thus becoming final.

Appellee commenced this action for a judicial review of the final administrative decision, as provided in 42 U.S.C.A. § 405(g). Both parties moved for summary judgment. In a memorandum opinion the lower court reversed the administrative decision. Pearsall v. Folsom, 138 F.Supp. 939 (D.C.N.D.Cal.1956). Following a motion for reconsideration, the district judge filed a supplemental memorandum opinion affirming the prior decision. 138 F.Supp. 939, 943. Judgment was entered, from which appellant appeals.

Appellant and appellee agree on the question presented to this Court: "Whether the District Court erred in holding that the present appellee, whose mother's insurance benefits as the unremarried widow of a deceased wage earner had been terminated by her remarriage in accordance with Section 202(g) of the Act (42 U.S.C.A. § 402(g)), was entitled to reinstatement of those benefits upon the annulment of her remarriage on the ground that such was a voidable marriage."[1]

The statute, 42 U.S.C.A. § 402(g)(1), reads:

"The widow * * * of an individual who died a fully or currently insured individual after 1939, if such widow * * *

"(A) has not remarried,

* * *

"(D) has filed application for mother's insurance benefits,

"(E) at the time of filing such application has in her care a child of such individual entitled to a child's insurance benefit, and

"(F) * * * shall be entitled to a mother's insurance benefit for each month, beginning with the first month after August 1950 in which she becomes so entitled to such insurance benefits *and ending* with the month preceding the first month in which any of the following occurs: * * * *she remarries* * * *." (Emphasis supplied.)

Agency determination of questions of law are entitled to weight, although not conclusive. * * * We have given serious and weighty consideration to the referee's decision, but we believe the judgment of the district court should be affirmed. * * *

Appellant urges that "remarries" is a term used in a Federal statute, and that its meaning must be interpreted in the context of that law. While we agree, we do not find a definition of "remarries" in the statute. "The scope of a federal right is, of course, a federal question, but that does not mean that its content is not to be determined by state, rather than federal law. [Citations omitted.] This is especially true where a statute deals with a familial relationship; there is no federal law of domestic relations, which is primarily a matter of state concern." * * *

By California law an annulment of a marriage means that no valid marriage ever existed, even though the marriage be only voidable.[1] * * * This doctrine of "relation back" to declare the marriage void from the beginning is not applied by the California courts in every instance. "The test for determining the applicability of the doctrine as applied to voidable marriages is whether it effects a result which conforms to the sanctions of sound policy and justice as between the immediate parties thereto, their property rights acquired during that marriage and the rights of their offspring * * *." Sefton v. Sefton, 45 Cal.2d 872, 875, 291 P.2d 439, 441 (1955). In the Sefton case, the court decided "* * * it would be improper to reinstate * * *" the alimony obligation of a divorced husband following the annulment of a marriage by the divorced wife made subsequent to the divorce, on the theory that after the "celebration of marriage" the divorced husband "* * * was then entitled to recommit his assets previously chargeable to alimony * * *." At pages 876–877 of 45 Cal.2d, at page 442 of 291 P.2d. But we believe there is a manifest difference between an alimony paying divorced husband and appellant and the Board of Trustees of the Federal Old-Age and Survivors Insurance Trust Fund.

We believe, as did the district court, that decisions of state courts involving state workmen's compensation statutes and termination of benefits upon remarriage are sufficiently analogous to guide this Court in this case involving the Social Security Act. While the language of state workmen's compensation statutes vary among the states and all differ to some extent from the Social Security Act, we believe the problems sufficiently similar for the cases to be of relevance here.

1. The annulment decree involved in this case reads, in part:
　　"Now, therefore, it is ordered, adjudged and decreed that Plaintiff is entitled to an annulment; and that the marriage between the said plaintiff Gretta Richard, and the said defendant Frank Richard, be and the same is hereby declared wholly null and void from the beginning; * * *."

In Eureka Block Coal Co. v. Wells, 83 Ind.App. 181, 147 N.E. 811 (1925), the court decided that the annulment related back to the time of marriage, and that it was proper under the State's statute for the Industrial Board to restore to the widow payments which were terminated on her remarriage. In First National Bank in Grand Forks v. North Dakota Workmen's Compensation Bureau, 68 N.W.2d 661, 665 (N.D.1955), the Court stated the daughter of the deceased workman, following the annulment of her marriage, should "* * * receive payment from the Workmen's Compensation Bureau as though no marriage ceremony ever took place * * *." Southern Ry. Co. v. Baskette, 175 Tenn. 253, 133 S.W.2d 498 (1939), followed the decision in Eureka Block Coal Co. v. Wells, supra. See Southern Pacific Co. v. Industrial Commission, 54 Ariz. 1, 91 P.2d 700 (1939), where the court reached the same conclusion, though the plaintiff lost the suit because the court held the annulment invalid.

Appellant seeks to mitigate the import of these decisions by urging that "dependency" determines rights to benefits under workmen's compensation statutes whereas "status" is determinative of rights to benefits under the Social Security Act. Even if there is such a distinction, and we express no opinion thereon, we believe such a distinction is insufficient, on the facts of this case, to require a difference in result. Appellant urges that turning to state law for the meaning of "remarries" means that application of the Federal law may vary among the states. While this may be so, we believe this to be a matter for Congressional consideration.

By looking to California law for the "content" of the word "remarries" used in the Federal law, we believe that, as appellee's California marriage was annulled by a California court and the marriage decreed null and void from the beginning so that under California law no valid marriage ever existed, appellee may receive the mother's insurance benefits of the Social Security Act.

The judgment of the District Court remanding the case to the Department of Health, Education and Welfare for further proceedings in conformity with its decision is affirmed.

NOTES AND QUESTIONS

1. Does Folsom v. Pearsall correctly state the rationale of Sefton v. Sefton?

2. What guides does this court furnish for the determination of "sound policy and justice" in particular cases? For example, consider the following situations:

(a) What would have been the result in the *Pearsall* case if Mrs. Pearsall's second marriage had been annulled for her own fraud? Cf. State Compensation Fund v. Reed, 12 Ariz.App. 317, 470 P.2d 465 (1970).

(b) What would have been the result in the *Pearsall* case if Mrs. Pearsall's second marriage had been annulled because the husband had a prior subsisting marriage, that is, on the ground of bigamy?

(c) H and W are married. W requires an operation and is hospitalized, incurring expenses of $3,000 for room, nursing, operating room and other charges. On admission H was listed as W's husband and was indicated as the person responsible for her expenses. Shortly thereafter H obtains an annulment of their mariage on the ground that it was bigamous. Is he liable for the hospital bill? Kurtis v. DeSiervo, 46 Misc.2d 1014, 261 N.Y. S.2d 679 (County Ct.1965).

(d) W is injured through H's negligence. After the injury W obtains an annulment of the marriage. In a state which does not permit actions for personal injury between husband and wife, may W sue H in tort? Callow v. Thomas, 322 Mass. 550, 78 N.E.2d 637 (1948); Gordon v. Pollard, 207 Tenn. 45, 336 S.W.2d 25 (1960), 28 Tenn.L.Rev. 573 (1961).

(e) H conveyed to W substantial amounts of property in consideration for her agreement to marry him. They were married, but W subsequently had the marriage annulled for H's fraud. May H recover the property on the ground that there has been a failure of consideration? Would it make a difference if H had obtained the annulment on the ground of W's fraud? American Surety Co. v. Conner, 251 N.Y. 1, 166 N.E. 783 (1929); In re Estate of Simms, 26 N.Y.2d 163, 257 N.E.2d 627, 309 N.Y.S.2d 170 (1970), 9 Duq.L.Rev. 135 (1970).

(f) N, a wealthy man and a "jilted suitor" of D, set up a trust in his will for D, under which she was to receive $500 per month for life or until her marriage. N died and payments to D began. D later married M, lived with him for three years, and then obtained an annulment on finding that M was already married to someone else. During the three years the trust payments had stopped. Is D entitled to a resumption of the trust payments and also to payments for the period during which she lived with M? Stoner v. Nethercutt, 8 Cal.App.3d 667, 87 Cal.Rptr. 659 (1970).

(g) W's first husband was killed in an industrial accident and she was awarded workmen's compensation benefits in Idaho. W was domiciled in Utah. The compensation payments were to continue until her remarriage. Some time later W married H–2 in Utah, where they lived together. About six months later W obtained an annulment in Utah on the ground that H–2 had a prior subsisting marriage. The workmen's compensation payments were discontinued at the time of W's marriage to H–2 and after the annulment decree was entered W sought to have them resumed, and to obtain the payments which would have accrued to her during the six months of her "marriage" to H–2. What result? See In re Duncan's Death, 83 Idaho 254, 360 P.2d 987 (1961).

(h) W and H–1 were married, but decided to separate and obtain a divorce. As part of the property settlement agreement made incident to the divorce, H–1 set up a trust, the provisions of which W accepted in lieu of alimony. The trust provided for payments of income to W, but the income was to be reduced in the event of her remarriage. About two years later W married H–2 and notified the trustee to that effect, whereupon the payments were reduced. Within a year W learned that H–2 had another wife from whom he had not been divorced, and she then obtained an annulment of the marriage. The trustee then sued for a declaratory judgment to determine the rights of W to the income of the trust. What result? What law should govern if the annulment was in Arizona, the trust set up in Kansas and the bigamous second marriage occurred in Wyoming? See Johnson County Nat. Bank & Trust Co. v. Bach, 189 Kan. 291, 369 P.2d 231 (1962).

(i) H and W are divorced, the decree ordering H to pay $200 per month for the support of the parties' daughter, C, until C should reach majority or be emancipated. C was fifteen at the time of the divorce and a month later she married X. Two months after the ceremony C's marriage was annulled for nonage, under the applicable state statute. Must H resume making child support payments? Must he make the payments for the two months during which C was "married"?

(j) M became pregnant as a result of intercourse with F, whom she was dating. When she informed him of the pregnancy, F agreed to marry M and they were married. Three months later M had the marriage annulled for fraud. Three months after the annulment decree the child was born. Is the child legitimate, under the statute which provides, "Where a man having by a woman a child or children shall afterwards intermarry with such woman, such child or children shall thereby be legitimated * * *"? Home of Holy Infancy v. Kaska, 397 S.W.2d 208 (Tex.1965), 44 Tex.L.Rev. 1028 (1966).

NOTT v. FLEMMING

United States Court of Appeals, Second Circuit, 1959.
272 F.2d 380.

WATERMAN, Circuit Judge. Under section 202(e) of the Social Security Act, 42 U.S.C.A. § 402(e), the widow of an insured wage earner is entitled to survivor's benefits. This case presents the issue of whether a widow who has lost her right to survivor's benefits by virtue of a subsequent ceremonial marriage regains this right when that marriage has been annulled by a decree of a New York state court.

The undisputed facts are as follows:

Appellant, Sophie Nott, was born on January 17, 1894. On November 6, 1915, she married Max Nott, with whom she lived until his death on September 14, 1949. In January 1955 she married Louis Klein. After three months Klein and appellant separated. In July 1955 Klein instituted an action for annulment in the Supreme Court of the State of New York, Bronx County. The asserted ground for annulment was appellant's failure to consummate the marriage. An interlocutory decree of annulment was entered January 25, 1956. The decree became final on April 25, 1956. On October 8, 1956 Mrs. Nott filed an application for a widow's benefits under the Social Security Act as the widow of Max Nott, who had been a fully insured wage earner. The application was denied on January 10, 1957. Having exhausted her administrative remedies, on November 4, 1957 appellant instituted an action in the District Court under 42 U.S.C.A. § 405(g), for judicial review of the adverse determination. Both parties filed motions for summary judgment. The district court granted

TC for D
SJ for D

summary judgment for defendant, Nott v. Folsom, 161 F.Supp. 905 (D.C.S.D.N.Y.1958), and Mrs. Nott appeals.

We are called upon to construe Section 202(e) of the Social Security Act, 42 U.S.C.A. § 402(e), the relevant sections of which are as follows:

"(e)(1) The widow * * * of an individual who died a fully insured individual after 1939, if such widow—

"(A) Has not remarried,

* * *

"(E) * * * shall be entitled to a widow's insurance benefit for each month, beginning with the first month after August 1950 in which she becomes so entitled to such insurance benefits and ending with the month preceding the first month in which any of the following occurs: she remarries * * *."

Resolution of the present case, then, depends upon the definitions given the words "remarried" and "remarries." These words are not defined in the Act and we must seek a meaning for them.

We agree with the district court's disposition of the present case, but for reasons to be set forth subsequently in this opinion we are not fully in accord with the emphasis which the district judge placed upon New York law in determining whether Mrs. Nott had "remarried" within the meaning of section 202(e). The court below relied upon Gaines v. Jacobsen, 308 N.Y. 218, 124 N.E.2d 290, 48 A.L.R.2d 312 (1954). There the New York Court of Appeals held that the first husband's alimony obligation, terminable upon the wife's remarriage, was not revived when the wife's second marriage was annulled. The Court of Appeals reasoned that the annulment decree did not relate back to annul the second marriage *ab initio*. Nevertheless, in the Gaines case the Court of Appeals recognized that the doctrine of the "relation back" of an annulment decree is a fiction whose applicability depends upon the particular problem at hand.[1] It is clear that the factors[2] which may lead to a holding that an annulment decree does not relate back to revive a former husband's alimony obligation might be totally irrelevant in the event that a state court should be confronted with the issue of whether an annulment decree should relate back to revive a right to Social Security benefits. See Folsom v. Pearsall, 245 F.2d 562, 565 (9 Cir., 1957). It is also clear that this issue of whether social security benefits should be revived will be faced only by federal courts, never by state courts. It seems most

1. In United States v. Dininny, 261 F. 2d 517, 518 (2d Cir., 1958), in view of the circumstances present there, we accepted the view that under New York law an annulment decree *did* relate back to prevent the wife's taking the proceeds of her former husband's National Service Life Insurance.

2. In the *Gaines* case the court recognized that once the divorced wife has been a party to a subsequent ceremonial marriage the former husband will feel free to reallocate his funds upon the reasonable assumption that the ceremonial event forthwith terminated his alimony obligations.

unlikely that Congress intended that eligibility for social security
benefits should depend upon a body of state law that can never come
into existence.

Furthermore, we believe that the congressional purpose in terminating a widow's eligibility for social security benefits upon her remarriage is reasonably clear. A widow of a wage earner is made eligible for benefits in order that she may be assured of the continuance
of that minimal level of support which the Social Security system is
designed to provide; but by the act of remarriage she elects to accept
the financial support of her second husband [3] and Congress apparently concluded that she should not be entitled thereafter to supplemental support from the Social Security Fund. Thus reference to state
law is necessary, but only for the narrow purpose of determining
whether the widow has entered into a relationship that will entitle
her under state law to support from her second husband. It is clear
that in New York a female participant in a ceremonial marriage is
entitled to support from her ostensible husband not only during the
official existence of the marriage but also after its formal dissolution.
Under section 1140–a of the New York Civil Practice Act (enacted
Sept. 1, 1940) the court awarding an annulment decree may affix
such directions for support "as justice requires." This provision has
been authoritatively construed to permit even the "guilty" party to
receive alimony. Johnson v. Johnson, 295 N.Y. 477, 68 N.E.2d 499
(1946). As the district court pointed out below, it is still possible for
Mrs. Nott by petition to the New York courts to obtain alimony from
Louis Klein. Thus the state law applicable here differs from that applicable in the cases upon which appellant relies—Folsom v. Pearsall,
245 F.2d 562 (9 Cir., 1957), affirming 138 F.Supp. 939 (D.C.N.D.Cal.
1956); Mays v. Folsom, 143 F.Supp. 784 (D.C.D.Idaho 1956); Sparks
v. United States, 153 F.Supp. 909 (D.C.D.Vt.1957). In those cases
it was clear that, though the ostensible husband may have had an
obligation to support during the time the marriage was formerly
in effect, it was also clear that no obligation to support could be enforced against him after the marriage had been dissolved by the annulment decree.

Judgment affirmed.

NOTES AND QUESTIONS

1. Does the court in Nott v. Flemming agree with *Sefton* as to the rationale of Gaines v. Jacobsen? If not, which is correct?

3. In Sparks v. United States, 153 F.
Supp. 909 (D.C.D.Vt.1957), Judge Gibson suggested that unless annulment
were held to revive a widow's benefits, a widow who was forced to remarry at gun point would be forever
disqualified. Indeed such a widow
should receive widow's benefits. We
do not reach that problem here. We
construe "remarried" as stating a relationship based upon some modicum
of consent to living with the new
husband and accepting his support.

2. Is it desirable to have benefits under the Social Security Act, a national system of old age insurance, vary, depending upon the place of domicile of the wage earner? What is the solution to this problem? Seidelson and Bowler, Determination of Family Status in the Administration of Federal Acts: A Choice of Law Problem for Federal Agencies and Courts, 33 G.W.L.Rev. 863 (1965).

3. Would the results of the various problems outlined in paragraph 2, supra, page 233, be the same in New York as in California?

4. The Social Security Act, 42 U.S.C.A. § 402 gives the divorced wife certain disability and other benefits under certain circumstances. In 42 U. S.C.A. § 416(d)(4) the Act states that the terms "divorce" and "divorced" refer to a divorce a vinculo matrimonii. Would a woman whose marriage had been annulled qualify as "divorced" under this statute, in either California or New York?

5. Are the results of the line of cases beginning with Gaines v. Jacobsen reasonably satisfactory? Would the problem be better solved by statute? If so, what should the statute say?

(a) Is a satisfactory treatment achieved by the following statute which is the Uniform Marriage and Divorce Act § 208(e), 9A Unif.L.Ann. 110 (1979)?

"(e) Unless the court finds, after a consideration of all relevant circumstances including the effect of a retroactive decree on third parties, that the interests of justice would be served by making the decree not retroactive, it shall declare the marriage invalid as of the date of the marriage. The provisions of this Act relating to property rights of the spouses, maintenance, support and custody of children on dissolution of marriage are applicable to nonretroactive decrees of invalidity."

Would you anticipate that the trial court's finding with respect to the retroactivity of the decree would be held a matter within its discretion, to be reviewed only where that discretion is abused? What factors would be relevant on the question whether the "interests of justice" are to be served by retroactivity?

(b) Is this statute satisfactory? Colo.Rev.Stat.Ann. § 14–10–11(5) (1973): "Marriages declared invalid under this section shall be so declared as of the date of the marriage."

(c) Would it be desirable for the statute to provide that there shall be no such action as annulment or declaration of invalidity of marriages, and that in all cases in which such defects as nonage, impotence, mental incompetence, incest, fraud, duress and the like occur, the only remedy shall be an action for dissolution of the marriage or divorce?

Chapter 5

THE FAMILY

___

SECTION 1. ABORTION, CONTRACEPTION AND STERILIZATION *

ROE v. WADE

Supreme Court of the United States, 1973.
410 U.S. 113, 93 S.Ct. 705, 35 L.Ed.2d 147.

Mr. Justice BLACKMUN delivered the opinion of the Court.

This Texas federal appeal and its Georgia companion, Doe v. Bolton, post, p. 179, present constitutional challenges to state criminal abortion legislation. The Texas statutes under attack here are typical of those that have been in effect in many States for approximately a century. The Georgia statutes, in contrast, have a modern cast and are a legislative product that, to an extent at least, obviously reflects the influences of recent attitudinal change, of advancing medical knowledge and techniques, and of new thinking about an old issue.

* * *

I

The Texas statutes that concern us here are Arts. 1191–1194 and 1196 of the State's Penal Code.[1] These make it a crime to "procure

___

*At this point the student should reread Griswold v. Connecticut, supra, page 73.

1. "Article 1191. Abortion
"If any person shall designedly administer to a pregnant woman or knowingly procure to be administered with her consent any drug or medicine, or shall use towards her any violence or means whatever externally or internally applied, and thereby procure an abortion, he shall be confined in the penitentiary not less than two nor more than five years; if it be done without her consent, the punishment shall be doubled. By 'abortion' is meant that the life of the fetus or embryo shall be destroyed in the woman's womb or that a premature birth thereof be caused.
"Art. 1192. Furnishing the means

"Whoever furnishes the means for procuring an abortion knowing the purpose intended is guilty as an accomplice.
"Art. 1193. Attempt at abortion
"If the means used shall fail to produce an abortion, the offender is nevertheless guilty of an attempt to produce abortion, provided it be shown that such means were calculated to produce that result, and shall be fined not less than one hundred nor more than one thousand dollars.
"Art. 1194. Murder in producing abortion
"If the death of the mother is occasioned by an abortion so produced or by an attempt to effect the same it is murder."
"Art. 1196. By medical advice
"Nothing in this chapter applies to an abortion procured or attempted by medical advice for the pur-

an abortion," as therein defined, or to attempt one, except with respect to "an abortion procured or attempted by medical advice for the purpose of saving the life of the mother." Similar statutes are in existence in a majority of the States.

[At this point in its Opinion the Court described the plaintiffs. Plaintiff Jane Roe was an unmarried pregnant woman who wanted a safe, physician-performed abortion in Texas. Plaintiff James Hallford was a physician under prosecution for performing abortions. Plaintiffs John and Mary Doe were a married couple without children who had been advised by their physician that Mrs. Doe should not have children until her "neural-chemical disorder" had improved, although a pregnancy would not have presented a serious risk to her life. The District Court had held that Roe and Hallford had standing to sue but the Does did not. On the merits it then held that the Texas statute was unconstitutionally vague and also infringed plaintiffs' Ninth Amendment rights.

The Supreme Court held that Jane Roe had standing to sue, that her case presented a case or controversy, and it was not moot, even though it was obvious that her pregnancy, which had existed in 1970 when the suit was brought, must have long since ended. The Court based its holding on mootness on the ground that it was essential to any effective review of the case.

James Hallford's suit was dismissed under the rule of Younger v. Harris, 401 U.S. 37, 91 S.Ct. 746, 27 L.Ed.2d 669 (1971), on the ground that without evidence of harassment or bad faith a state criminal defendant may not affirmatively challenge by injunction or declaratory judgment in federal court the statute under which he is being prosecuted.

With respect to the Does, the Court held that their injury was too speculative to present a case or controversy and therefore dismissed their suit.]

V

The principal thrust of appellant's attack on the Texas statutes is that they improperly invade a right, said to be possessed by the pregnant woman, to choose to terminate her pregnancy. Appellant would discover this right in the concept of personal "liberty" embodied in the Fourteenth Amendment's Due Process Clause; or in personal, marital, familial, and sexual privacy said to be protected by the Bill

pose of saving the life of the mother."

The foregoing Articles, together with Art. 1195, compose Chapter 9 of Title 15 of the Penal Code. Article 1195, not attacked here, reads:

"Art. 1195. Destroying unborn child

"Whoever shall during parturition of the mother destroy the vitality or life in a child in a state of being born and before actual birth, which child would otherwise have been born alive, shall be confined in the penitentiary for life or for not less than five years."

of Rights or its penumbras, see Griswold v. Connecticut, 381 U.S. 479, 85 S.Ct. 1678, 14 L.Ed.2d 510 (1965); Eisenstadt v. Baird, 405 U.S. 438 (1972); id., at 460 (WHITE, J., concurring in result); or among those rights reserved to the people by the Ninth Amendment, Griswold v. Connecticut, 381 U.S., at 486 (GOLDBERG, J., concurring).

[The Court's opinion here includes a long historical account of attitudes toward abortion and of the development of the common law and statutory law on the subject.]

VII

Three reasons have been advanced to explain historically the enactment of criminal abortion laws in the 19th century and to justify their continued existence.

It has been argued occasionally that these laws were the product of a Victorian social concern to discourage illicit sexual conduct. Texas, however, does not advance this justification in the present case, and it appears that no court or commentator has taken the argument seriously. The appellants and *amici* contend, moreover, that this is not a proper state purpose at all and suggest that, if it were, the Texas statutes are overbroad in protecting it since the law fails to distinguish between married and unwed mothers.

A second reason is concerned with abortion as a medical procedure. When most criminal abortion laws were first enacted the procedure was a hazardous one for the woman. This was particularly true prior to the development of antisepsis. Antiseptic techniques, of course, were based on discoveries by Lister, Pasteur, and others first announced in 1867, but were not generally accepted and employed until about the turn of the century. Abortion mortality was high. Even after 1900, and perhaps until as late as the development of antibiotics in the 1940's, standard modern techniques such as dilation and curettage were not nearly so safe as they are today. Thus, it has been argued that a State's real concern in enacting a criminal abortion law was to protect the pregnant woman, that is, to restrain her from submitting to a procedure that placed her life in serious jeopardy.

Modern medical techniques have altered this situation. Appellants and various *amici* refer to medical data indicating that abortion in early pregnancy, that is, prior to the end of the first trimester, although not without its risk, is now relatively safe. Mortality rates for women undergoing early abortions, where the procedure is legal, appear to be as low as or lower than the rates for normal childbirth. Consequently, any interest of the State in protecting the woman from an inherently hazardous procedure, except when it would be equally dangerous for her to forgo it, has largely disappeared. Of course, important state interests in the area of health and medical standards do remain. The State has a legitimate interest in seeing to it that abortion, like any other medical procedure, is performed under circumstances that insure maximum safety for the patient. This interest obviously extends at least to the performing physician and his staff, to the facilities involved, to the availability of after-care, and to adequate provision for any complication or emergency that might arise. The prevalence of high mortality rates at illegal "abortion mills" strengthens, rather than weakens, the State's interest in regulating the conditions under which abortions are performed. Moreover, the risk to the woman increases as her pregnancy continues. Thus, the State retains a definite interest in protecting the woman's own health and safety when an abortion is proposed at a late stage of pregnancy.

The third reason is the State's interest—some phrase it in terms of duty—in protecting prenatal life. Some of the argument for this justification rests on the theory that a new human life is present from the moment of conception. The State's interest and general obligation to protect life then extends, it is argued, to prenatal life. Only when the life of the pregnant mother herself is at stake, balanced against the life she carries within her, should the interest of the embryo or fetus not prevail. Logically, of course, a legitimate state interest in this area need not stand or fall on acceptance of the belief that life begins at conception or at some other point prior to live birth. In assessing the State's interest, recognition may be given to the less rigid claim that as long as at least *potential* life is involved, the State may assert interests beyond the protection of the pregnant woman alone.

Parties challenging state abortion laws have sharply disputed in some courts the contention that a purpose of these laws, when enacted, was to protect prenatal life. Pointing to the absence of legislative history to support the contention, they claim that most state laws were designed solely to protect the woman. Because medical advances have lessened this concern, at least with respect to abortion in early pregnancy, they argue that with respect to such abortions the laws can no longer be justified by any state interest. There is some scholarly support for this view of original purpose. The few state courts called upon to interpret their laws in the late 19th and early 20th centuries did focus on the State's interest in protecting the woman's health rather than in preserving the embryo and fetus. Proponents of this view point out that in many States, including Texas, by statute or judicial interpretation, the pregnant woman herself could not be prosecuted for self-abortion or for cooperating in an abortion performed upon her by another. They claim that adoption of the "quickening" distinction through received common law and state statutes tacitly recognizes the greater health hazards inherent in late abortion and impliedly repudiates the theory that life begins at conception.

It is with these interests, and the weight to be attached to them, that this case is concerned.

VIII

The Constitution does not explicitly mention any right of privacy. In a line of decisions, however, going back perhaps as far as Union Pacific R. Co. v. Botsford, 141 U.S. 250, 251, 11 S.Ct. 1000, 1001, 35 L. Ed. 734 (1891), the Court has recognized that a right of personal privacy, or a guarantee of certain areas or zones of privacy, does exist under the Constitution. In varying contexts, the Court or individual Justices have, indeed, found at least the roots of that right in the First Amendment, * * * in the Fourth and Fifth Amendments, * * * ; in the penumbras of the Bill of Rights, Griswold v. Connecticut, 381 U.S., at 484–485, 85 S.Ct., at 1681–1682; in the Ninth Amendment, id., at 486, 85 S.Ct. at 1682 (GOLDBERG, J., concurring); or in the concept of liberty guaranteed by the first section of the Fourteenth Amendment, * * * These decisions make it clear that only personal rights that can be deemed "fundamental" or "implicit in the concept of ordered liberty," Palko v. Connecticut, 302 U.S. 319, 325, 58 S.Ct. 149, 152, 82 L.Ed. 288 (1937), are included in this guarantee of personal privacy. They also make it clear that the right has some extension to activities relating to marriage, Loving v. Virgina, 388 U.S. 1, 12, 87 S.Ct. 1817, 1823, 18 L.Ed.2d 1010 (1967); procreation, Skinner v. Oklahoma, 316 U.S. 535, 541–542, 62 S.Ct. 1110, 1113–1114, 86 L.Ed. 1655 (1942); contraception, Eisenstadt v. Baird, 405 U.S., at 453–454, 92 S.Ct. at 1038–1039; id., at 460, 463–465 (WHITE, J., concurring in result); family relationships, Prince v. Massachusetts, 321 U.S. 158, 166, 64 S.Ct. 438, 442, 88 L.Ed. 645 (1944); and child rearing and education, Pierce v. Society of Sisters, 268 U.S. 510, 535, 45 S.Ct. 571, 573, 69 L.Ed. 1070 (1925), Meyer v. Nebraska, supra.

This right of privacy, whether it be founded in the Fourteenth Amendment's concept of personal liberty and restrictions upon state action, as we feel it is, or, as the District Court determined, in the Ninth Amendment's reservation of rights to the people, is broad enough to encompass a woman's decision whether or not to terminate her pregnancy. The detriment that the State would impose upon the pregnant woman by denying this choice altogether is apparent. Specific and direct harm medically diagnosable even in early pregnancy may be involved. Maternity, or additional offspring, may force upon the woman a distressful life and future. Psychological harm may be imminent. Mental and physical health may be taxed by child care. There is also the distress, for all concerned, associated with the unwanted child, and there is the problem of bringing a child into a family already unable, psychologically and otherwise, to care for it. In other cases, as in this one, the additional difficulties and continuing stigma of unwed motherhood may be involved. All these are factors the woman and her responsible physician necessarily will consider in consultation.

On the basis of elements such as these, appellant and some *amici* argue that the woman's right is absolute and that she is entitled to terminate her pregnancy at whatever time, in whatever way, and for whatever reason she alone chooses. With this we do not agree. Appellant's arguments that Texas either has no valid interest at all in regulating the abortion decision, or no interest strong enough to support any limitation upon the woman's sole determination, is [sic] unpersuasive. The Court's decisions recognizing a right of privacy also acknowledge that some state regulation in areas protected by that right is appropriate. As noted above, a State may properly assert important interests in safeguarding health, in maintaining medical standards, and in protecting potential life. At some point in pregnancy, these respective interests become sufficiently compelling to sustain regulation of the factors that govern the abortion decision. The privacy right involved, therefore, cannot be said to be absolute. In fact, it is not clear to us that the claim asserted by some *amici* that one has an unlimited right to do with one's body as one pleases bears a close relationship to the right of privacy previously articulated in the Court's decisions. The Court has refused to recognize an unlimited right of this kind in the past. * * *

We, therefore, conclude that the right of personal privacy includes the abortion decision, but that this right is not unqualified and must be considered against important state interests in regulation.

[At this point the Court cited the decisions of state and lower federal courts holding the various abortion statutes constitutional or unconstitutional.]

Although the results are divided, most of these courts have agreed that the right of privacy, however based, is broad enough to cover the abortion decision; that the right, nonetheless, is not absolute and is subject to some limitations; and that at some point the state interests as to protection of health, medical standards, and prenatal life, become dominant. We agree with this approach.

Where certain "fundamental rights" are involved, the Court has held that regulation limiting these rights may be justified only by a "compelling state interest," Kramer v. Union Free School District, 395 U.S. 621, 627, 89 S.Ct. 1886, 1890, 23 L.Ed.2d 583 (1969); Shapiro v. Thompson, 394 U.S. 618, 634, 89 S.Ct. 1322, 1331, 22 L.Ed.2d 600 (1969), Sherbert v. Verner, 374 U.S. 398, 406, 83 S.Ct. 1790, 1795, 10 L.Ed.2d 965 (1963), and that legislative enactments must be narrowly drawn to express only the legitimate state interests at stake. * * * see Eisenstadt v. Baird, 405 U.S., at 460, 463–464, 92 S.Ct., at 1042, 1043–1044 (WHITE, J., concurring in result).

IX

* * *

A. The appellee and certain *amici* argue that the fetus is a "person" within the language and meaning of the Fourteenth Amendment. In support of this, they outline at length and in detail the well-known facts of fetal development. If this suggestion of person-hood is established, the appellant's case, of course, collapses, for the fetus' right to life is then guaranteed specifically by the Amendment. The appellant conceded as much on reargument. On the other hand, the appellee conceded on reargument that no case could be cited that holds that a fetus is a person within the meaning of the Fourteenth Amendment.

The Constitution does not define "person" in so many words. Section 1 of the Fourteenth Amendment contains three references to "person." The first, in defining "citizens," speaks of "persons born or naturalized in the United States." The word also appears both in the Due Process Clause and in the Equal Protection Clause. "Person" is used in other places in the Constitution: in the listing of qualifications for Representatives and Senators, Art. I, § 2, cl. 2, and § 3, cl. 3; in the Apportionment Clause, Art. I, § 2, cl. 3;[53] in the Migration and Importation provision, Art. I, § 9, cl. 1; in the Emolument Clause, Art. I, § 9, cl. 8; in the Electors provisions, Art. II, § 1, cl. 2, and the superseded cl. 3; in the provision outlining qualifications for the office of President, Art. II, § 1, cl. 5; in the Extradition provisions, Art. IV, § 2, cl. 2, and the superseded Fugitive Slave Clause 3; and in the Fifth, Twelfth, and Twenty-second Amendments, as well as in §§ 2 and 3 of the Fourteenth Amendment. But in nearly all these instances, the use of the word is such that it has application only postnatally. None indicates, with any assurance, that it has any possible pre-natal application.[54]

All this, together with our observation, supra, that throughout the major portion of the 19th century prevailing legal abortion practices were far freer than they are today, persuades us that the word "person," as used in the Fourteenth Amendment, does not include the unborn. This is in accord with the results reached in those few cases where the issue has been squarely presented. * * * Indeed, our

---

53. We are not aware that in the taking of any census under this clause, a fetus has ever been counted.

54. When Texas urges that a fetus is entitled to Fourteenth Amendment protection as a person, it faces a dilemma. Neither in Texas nor in any other State are all abortions prohibited. Despite broad proscription, an exception always exists. The exception contained in Art. 1196, for an abortion procured or attempted by medical advice for the purpose of saving the life of the mother, is typical. But if the fetus is a person who is not to be deprived of life without due process of law, and if the mother's condition is the sole determinant, does not the Texas exception appear to be out of line with the Amendment's command?

There are other inconsistencies between Fourteenth Amendment status and the typical abortion statute. It has already been pointed out, supra, that in Texas the woman is not a principal or an accomplice with respect to an abortion upon her. If the fetus is a person, why is the woman not a principal or an accomplice? Further, the penalty for criminal abortion specified by Art. 1195 is significantly less than the maximum penalty for murder prescribed by Art. 1257 of the Texas Penal Code. If the fetus is a person, may the penalties be different?

decision in United States v. Vuitch, 402 U.S. 62, 91 S.Ct. 1294, 28 L. Ed.2d 601 (1971), inferentially is to the same effect, for we there would not have indulged in statutory interpretation favorable to abortion in specified circumstances if the necessary consequence was the termination of life entitled to Fourteenth Amendment protection.

This conclusion, however, does not of itself fully answer the contentions raised by Texas, and we pass on to other considerations.

B. The pregnant woman cannot be isolated in her privacy. She carries an embryo and, later, a fetus, if one accepts the medical definitions of the developing young in the human uterus. See Dorland's Illustrated Medical Dictionary 478–479, 547 (24th ed. 1965). The situation therefore is inherently different from marital intimacy, or bedroom possession of obscene material, or marriage, or procreation, or education, with which *Eisenstadt, Griswold, Stanley, Loving, Skinner, Pierce,* and *Meyer* were respectively concerned. As we have intimated above, it is reasonable and appropriate for a State to decide that at some point in time another interest, that of health of the mother or that of potential human life, becomes significantly involved. The woman's privacy is no longer sole and any right of privacy she possesses must be measured accordingly.

Texas urges that, apart from the Fourteenth Amendment, life begins at conception and is present throughout pregnancy, and that therefore, the State has a compelling interest in protecting that life from and after conception. We need not resolve the difficult question of when life begins. When those trained in the respective disciplines of medicine, philosophy, and theology are unable to arrive at any consensus, the judiciary, at this point in the development of man's knowledge, is not in a position to speculate as to the answer.

[The Court here summarizes the view of various philosophical and religious groups on the question of when life begins, concluding with the modern Roman Catholic position that life begins at the moment of conception.]

Substantial problems for precise definition of this view are posed, however, by new embryological data that purport to indicate that conception is a "process" over time, rather than an event, and by new medical techniques such as menstrual extraction, the "morning-after" pill, implantation of embryos, artificial insemination, and even artificial wombs.[62]

---

62. See Brodie, The New Biology and the Prenatal Child, 9 J. Family L. 391, 397 (1970); Gorney, The New Biology and the Future of Man, 15 U.C.L.A.L.Rev. 273 (1968); Note, Criminal Law—Abortion—The "Morning-After Pill" and Other Pre-Implantation Birth-Control Methods and the Law, 46 Ore.L.Rev. 211 (1967); G. Taylor, The Biological Time Bomb 32 (1968); A. Rosenfeld, The Second Genesis 138–139 (1969); Smith, Through a Test Tube Darkly: Artificial Insemination and the Law, 67 Mich.L.Rev. 127 (1968); Note, Artificial Insemination and the Law, 1968 U.Ill.L.F. 203.

In areas other than criminal abortion, the law has been reluctant to endorse any theory that life, as we recognize it, begins before live birth or to accord legal rights to the unborn except in narrowly defined situations and except when the rights are contingent upon live birth. For example, the traditional rule of tort law denied recovery for prenatal injuries even though the child was born alive. That rule has been changed in almost every jurisdiction. In most States, recovery is said to be permitted only if the fetus was viable, or at least quick, when the injuries were sustained, though few courts have squarely so held. In a recent development, generally opposed by the commentators, some States permit the parents of a stillborn child to maintain an action for wrongful death because of prenatal injuries. Such an action, however, would appear to be one to vindicate the parents' interest and is thus consistent with the view that the fetus, at most, represents only the potentiality of life. Similarly, unborn children have been recognized as acquiring rights or interests by way of inheritance or other devolution of property, and have been represented by guardians *ad litem*. Perfection of the interests involved, again, has generally been contingent upon live birth. In short, the unborn have never been recognized in the law as persons in the whole sense.

X

In view of all this, we do not agree that, by adopting one theory of life, Texas may override the rights of the pregnant woman that are at stake. We repeat, however, that the State does have an important and legitimate interest in preserving and protecting the health of the pregnant woman, whether she be a resident of the State or a nonresident who seeks medical consultation and treatment there, and that it has still *another* important and legitimate interest in protecting the potentiality of human life. These interests are separate and distinct. Each grows in substantiality as the woman approaches term and, at a point during pregnancy, each becomes "compelling."

With respect to the State's important and legitimate interest in the health of the mother, the "compelling" point, in the light of present medical knowledge, is at approximately the end of the first trimester. This is so because of the now-established medical fact, * * * that until the end of the first trimester mortality in abortion may be less than mortality in normal childbirth. It follows that, from and after this point, a State may regulate the abortion procedure to the extent that the regulation reasonably relates to the preservation and protection of maternal health. Examples of permissible state regulation in this area are requirements as to the qualifications of the person who is to perform the abortion; as to the licensure of that person; as to the facility in which the procedure is to be performed, that is, whether it must be a hospital or may be a clinic or some other place of less-than-hospital status; as to the licensing of the facility; and the like.

This means, on the other hand, that, for the period of pregnancy prior to this "compelling" point, the attending physician, in consultation with his patient, is free to determine, without regulation by the State, that, in his medical judgment, the patient's pregnancy should be terminated. If that decision is reached, the judgment may be effectuated by an abortion free of interference by the State.

With respect to the State's important and legitimate interest in potential life, the "compelling" point is at viability. This is so because the fetus then presumably has the capability of meaningful life outside the mother's womb. State regulation protective of fetal life after viability thus has both logical and biological justifications. If the State is interested in protecting fetal life after viability, it may go so far as to proscribe abortion during that period, except when it is necessary to preserve the life or health of the mother.

Measured against these standards, Art. 1196 of the Texas Penal Code, in restricting legal abortions to those "procured or attempted by medical advice for the purpose of saving the life of the mother," sweeps too broadly. The statute makes no distinction between abortions performed early in pregnancy and those performed later, and it limits to a single reason, "saving" the mother's life, the legal justification for the procedure. The statute, therefore, cannot survive the constitutional attack made upon it here.

This conclusion makes it unnecessary for us to consider the additional challenge to the Texas statute asserted on grounds of vagueness. See United States v. Vuitch, 402 U.S., at 67–72, 91 S.Ct., at 1296–1299.

XI

To summarize and to repeat:

1. A state criminal abortion statute of the current Texas type, that excepts from criminality only a *lifesaving* procedure on behalf of the mother, without regard to pregnancy stage and without recognition of the other interests involved, is violative of the Due Process Clause of the Fourteenth Amendment.

(a) For the stage prior to approximately the end of the first trimester, the abortion decision and its effectuation must be left to the medical judgment of the pregnant woman's attending physician.

(b) For the stage subsequent to approximately the end of the first trimester, the State, in promoting its interest in the health of the mother, may, if it chooses, regulate the abortion procedure in ways that are reasonably related to maternal health.

(c) For the stage subsequent to viability, the State in promoting its interest in the potentiality of human life may, if it chooses, regulate, and even proscribe, abortion except where it is necessary, in appropriate medical judgment, for the preservation of the life or health of the mother.

2. The State may define the term "physician," as it has been employed in the preceding numbered paragraphs of this Part XI of this opinion, to mean only a physician currently licensed by the State, and may proscribe any abortion by a person who is not a physician as so defined.

In Doe v. Bolton, post, p. 179, procedural requirements contained in one of the modern abortion statutes are considered. That opinion and this one, of course, are to be read together.[67]

This holding, we feel, is consistent with the relative weights of the respective interests involved, with the lessons and examples of medical and legal history, with the lenity of the common law, and with the demands of the profound problems of the present day. The decision leaves the State free to place increasing restrictions on abortion as the period of pregnancy lengthens, so long as those restrictions are tailored to the recognized state interests. The decision vindicates the right of the physician to administer medical treatment according to his professional judgment up to the points where important state interests provide compelling justifications for intervention. Up to those points, the abortion decision in all its aspects is inherently, and primarily, a medical decision, and basic responsibility for it must rest with the physician. If an individual practitioner abuses the privilege of exercising proper medical judgment, the usual remedies, judicial and intra-professional, are available.

XII

Our conclusion that Art. 1196 is unconstitutional means, of course, that the Texas abortion statutes, as a unit, must fall.
* * *

NOTES AND QUESTIONS

1. Justices White and Rehnquist dissented from the decision of the Court in Roe v. Wade, and in the companion case of Doe v. Bolton, 410 U.S. 179 (1973). Justices Stewart, Burger and Douglas filed separate concurrences in the two cases, Mr. Justice Douglas relying upon his own opinion in Griswold v. Connecticut which deduced a right of privacy from the first

---

67. Neither in this opinion nor in Doe v. Bolton, post, p. 179, do we discuss the father's rights, if any exist in the constitutional context, in the abortion decision. No paternal right has been asserted in either of the cases, and the Texas and the Georgia statutes on their face take no cognizance of the father. We are aware that some statutes recognize the father under certain circumstances. North Carolina, for example, N.C.Gen.Stat. § 14–45.1 (Supp.1971), requires written permission for the abortion from the husband when the woman is a married minor, that is, when she is less than 18 years of age, 41 N.C.A.G. 489 (1971); if the woman is an unmarried minor, written permission from the parents is required. We need not now decide whether provisions of this kind are constitutional.

ten amendments and held it was embodied in the concept of liberty protected by the Fourteenth Amendment.

The companion case, Doe v. Bolton, supra, dealt with the validity of the Georgia abortion statute, a modern act based largely on the American Law Institute's Model Penal Code. The Court held unconstitutional provisions of that act which required that abortions be performed only in hospitals accredited by the Joint Commission on Accreditation of Hospitals (a non-governmental national agency); which required the approval of the abortion by a hospital abortion committee in all cases; which required that the decision of the woman's physician to perform the abortion be concurred in by two other licensed physicians; and which limited the availability of abortions to bona fide legal residents of Georgia.

2. The subject of abortion has been endlessly discussed from all points of view. Some general treatments of the subject include D. Callahan, Abortion: Law, Choice and Morality (1970); G. Hardin, Stalking the Wild Taboo (2d ed. 1978); L. Lader, Abortion (1966); J. Mohr, Abortion in America (1978); J. Noonan, ed., The Morality of Abortion (1970); R. Sloane, ed., Abortion, Changing Views and Practice (1970); D. Smith, ed., Abortion and the Law (1967); Zimring, Of Doctors, Deterrence, and the Dark Figure of Crime: A Note on Abortion in Hawaii, 39 U.Chi.L.Rev. 699 (1972).

3. Which Constitutional provision, in the Supreme Court's view, was violated by the Texas abortion statute? Is the Court just applying the rule of Griswold v. Connecticut, supra, page 73, to abortions, or is the reasoning in Roe v. Wade different from that in Griswold? Cf. question 3, page 81, and Mr. Justice Rehnquist's dissent, 410 U.S. 171, 172–174. If you find the Court's opinion unsatisfactory, could you write a better one, either for or against constitutionality of the statute?

4. Why is it, judging from the Court's opinion, that the state's interest in the protection of the fetus is not sufficiently strong to sustain the Texas statute until the moment when the fetus becomes viable? Does the Court's holding on this point belie its own refusal to take a position on the point at which "life" begins? If, as the Court seems to say, conception is a process over time, why may not the state protect that process from interruption at any point it chooses?

5. Is the question of when "life" begins the same question as whether the fetus is a "person"? Does the answer to the question when life begins or the question whether a fetus is a person control the outcome in Roe v. Wade? Should the answers to these questions control the availability of abortion?

6. A state statute prohibits abortions by anyone other than a physician at any time. Could a woman performing a first trimester abortion upon herself be convicted under such a statute? Rocky Mountain News, August 31, 1978, p. 30, col. 1.

7. Professor Archibald Cox has written: "My criticism of Roe v. Wade is that the Court failed to establish the legitimacy of the decision by not articulating a precept of sufficient abstractness to lift the ruling above the level of a political judgment based upon the evidence currently available from the medical, physical, and social sciences." Cox, The Supreme Court

and Abortion, 2 Human Life Rev. 15, 18 (1976). Do you agree or disagree?

8. How is abortion to be defined? Can it be clearly distinguished from contraception? For example, how should we classify the process of menstrual extraction, by which a woman may induce menstruation herself, perhaps without knowing whether or not she is pregnant? See E. Frankfort, Vaginal Politics 215–242 (1972); Lee and Paxman, Legal Aspects of Menstrual Regulation: Some Preliminary Observations, 14 J. of Fam.L. 181, 183 (1975).

PLANNED PARENTHOOD OF CENTRAL MISSOURI v. DANFORTH

Supreme Court of the United States, 1976.
428 U.S. 52, 96 S.Ct. 2831, 49 L.Ed.2d 788.

Mr. Justice BLACKMUN delivered the opinion of the Court.

This case is a logical and anticipated corollary to Roe v. Wade, 410 U.S. 113, 93 S.Ct. 705, 35 L.Ed.2d 147 (1973), and Doe v. Bolton, 410 U.S. 179, 93 S.Ct. 739, 35 L.Ed.2d 201 (1973), for it raises issues secondary to those that were then before the Court. Indeed, some of the questions now presented were forecast and reserved in Roe and Doe. 410 U.S., at 165 n. 67, 93 S.Ct., at 733.

I

* * *

In June 1974, somewhat more than a year after Roe and Doe had been decided, Missouri's 77th General Assembly, in its Second Regular Session, enacted House Committee Substitute for House Bill No. 1211 (hereinafter Act). * * * The Act is set forth in full as the Appendix to this opinion. It imposes a structure for the control and regulation of abortions in Missouri during all stages of pregnancy.

II

Three days after the Act became effective, the present litigation was instituted in the United States District Court for the Eastern District of Missouri. The plaintiffs are Planned Parenthood of Central Missouri, a not-for-profit Missouri corporation which maintains a facility in Columbia, Mo., for the performance of abortions; David Hall, M.D.; and Michael Freiman, M.D. Doctor Hall is a resident of Columbia, is licensed as a physician in Missouri, is chairman of the Department and Professor of Obstetrics and Gynecology at the University of Missouri Medical School at Columbia, and supervises abortions at the Planned Parenthood facility. * * * Doctor Freiman is a resident of St. Louis, is licensed as a physician in Missouri, is an instructor of Clinical Obstetrics and Gynecology at Washington University Medical School, and performs abortions at two St. Louis hospitals and at a clinic in that city.

The named defendants are the Attorney General of Missouri and the Circuit Attorney of the city of St. Louis "in his representative capacity" and "as the representative of the class of all similar Prosecuting Attorneys of the various counties of the State of Missouri."

The plaintiffs brought the action on their own behalf and, purportedly, "on behalf of the entire class consisting of duly licensed physicians and surgeons presently performing or desiring to perform the termination of pregnancies and on behalf of the entire class consisting of their patients desiring the termination of pregnancy, all within the State of Missouri." Id., at 9. Plaintiffs sought declaratory relief and also sought to enjoin enforcement of the Act on the ground, among others, that certain of its provisions deprived them and their patients of various constitutional rights: "the right to privacy in the physician-patient relationship"; the physicians' "right to practice medicine according to the highest standards of medical practice"; the female patients' right to determine whether to bear children; the patients' "right to life due to the inherent risk involved in childbirth" or in medical procedures alternative to abortion; the physicians' "right to give and plaintiffs' patients' right to receive safe and adequate medical advice and treatment, pertaining to the decision of whether to carry a given pregnancy to term and the method of termination"; the patients' right under the Eighth Amendment to be free from cruel and unusual punishment "by forcing and coercing them to bear each pregnancy they conceive"; and, by being placed "in the position of decision making beset with * * * inherent possibilities of bias and conflict of interest," the physician's right to due process of law guaranteed by the Fourteenth Amendment.

The particular provisions of the Act that remained under specific challenge at the end of trial were § 2(2), defining the term "viability"; § 3(2), requiring from the woman, prior to submitting to abortion during the first 12 weeks of pregnancy, a certification in writing that she consents to the procedure and "that her consent is informed and freely given and is not the result of coercion"; § 3(3), requiring, for the same period, "the written consent of the woman's spouse, unless the abortion is certified by a licensed physician to be necessary in order to preserve the life of the mother"; § 3(4), requiring, for the same period, "the written consent of one parent or person in loco parentis of the woman if the woman is unmarried and under the age of eighteen years, unless the abortion is certified by a licensed physician as necessary in order to preserve the life of the mother"; § 6(1), requiring the physician to exercise professional care "to preserve the life and health of the fetus" and, failing such, deeming him guilty of manslaughter and making him liable in an action for damages; § 7, declaring an infant, who survives "an attempted abortion which was not performed to save the life or health of the mother," to be "an abandoned ward of the state under the jurisdiction of the juvenile court," and depriving the mother, and also the father if he consented to the abortion, of parental rights; § 9, the legislative finding that the method of abortion known as saline amniocentesis "is deleterious to maternal health," and prohibiting that method after the first 12 weeks of pregnancy; and §§ 10 and 11, imposing reporting and maintenance of record requirements for health facilities and for physicians who perform abortions.

The case was presented to a three-judge District Court convened pursuant to the provisions of 28 U.S.C.A. §§ 2281 and 2284. 392 F. Supp. 1362 (1975). The court ruled that the two physician-plaintiffs had standing inasmuch as § 6(1) provides that the physician who fails to exercise the prescribed standard of professional care due the fetus in the abortion procedure shall be guilty of manslaughter, and § 14 provides that any person who performs or aids in the performance of an abortion contrary to the provisions of the Act shall be guilty of a misdemeanor. 392 F. Supp., at 1366–1367. Due to this "obvious standing" of the two physicians, id., at 1367, the court deemed it unnecessary to determine whether Planned Parenthood also had standing.

On the issues as to the constitutionality of the several challenged sections of the Act, the District Court, largely by a divided vote, ruled that all except the first sentence of § 6(1) withstood the attack. That sentence was held to be constitutionally impermissible because it imposed upon the physician the duty to exercise at all stages of pregnancy "that degree of professional skill, care and diligence to preserve the life and health of the fetus" that "would be required * * * to preserve the life and health of any fetus intended to be born." Inasmuch as this failed to exclude the stage of pregnancy prior to viability, the provision was "unconstitutionally overbroad." 392 F.Supp., at 1371.

* * *

In No. 74–1151, the plaintiffs appeal from that part of the District Court's judgment upholding sections of the Act as constitutional and denying injunctive relief against their application and enforcement. In No. 74–1419, the defendant Attorney General cross-appeals from that part of the judgment holding § 6(1) unconstitutional and enjoining enforcement thereof. * * *

For convenience, we shall usually refer to the plaintiffs as "appellants" and to both named defendants as "appellees."

* * *

IV

With the exception specified in n. 2, infra, we agree with the District Court that the physician-appellants clearly have standing. This was established in Doe v. Bolton, 410 U.S., at 188, 93 S.Ct., at 745. Like the Georgia statutes challenged in that case, "[t]he physician is the one against whom [the Missouri Act] directly operate[s] in the event he procures an abortion that does not meet the statutory exceptions and conditions. The physician-appellants, therefore, assert a sufficiently direct threat of personal detriment. They should not be required to await and undergo a criminal prosecution as the sole means of seeking relief."[2] Ibid.

Our primary task, then, is to consider each of the challenged provisions of the new Missouri abortion statute in the particular light of the opinions and decisions in *Roe* and in *Doe*. To this we now turn, with the assistance of helpful briefs from both sides and from some of the *amici*.

A

The definition of viability. Section 2(2) of the Act defines "viability" as "that stage of fetal development when the life of the unborn child may be continued indefinitely outside the womb by natural or artificial life-supportive systems." Appellants claim that this definition violates and conflicts with the discussion of viability in our opinion in *Roe*. 410 U.S., at 160, 163, 93 S.Ct., at 730, 731. In particular, appellants object to the failure of the definition to contain any reference to a gestational time period, to its failure to incorporate and reflect the three stages of pregnancy, to the presence of the word "indefinitely," and to the extra burden of regulation imposed. It is suggested that the definition expands the Court's definition of viability, as expressed in *Roe,* and amounts to a legislative determination of what is properly a matter for medical judgment. It is said that the "mere possibility of momentary survival is not the medical standard of viability."

In *Roe,* we used the term "viable," properly we thought, to signify the point at which the fetus is "potentially able to live outside the mother's womb, albeit with artificial aid," and presumably capable of "meaningful life outside the mother's womb," 410 U.S., at 160, 163, 93 S.Ct. at 730, 732. We noted that this point "is usually placed" at about seven months or 28 weeks, but may occur earlier. Id., at 160.

We agree with the District Court and conclude that the definition of viability in the Act does not conflict with what was said and held

---

2. This is not so, however, with respect to § 7 of the Act pertaining to state wardship of a live-born infant. Section 7 applies "where a live born infant results from an attempted abortion which was not performed to save the life or health of the mother." It then provides that the infant "shall be an abandoned ward of the state" and that the mother—and the father, too, if he consented to the abortion—"shall have no parental rights or obligations whatsoever relating to such infant."

The physician-appellants do not contend that this section of the Act imposes any obligation on them or that its operation otherwise injures them in fact. They do not claim any interest in the question of who receives custody that is "sufficiently concrete" to satisfy the "case or controversy" requirement of a federal court's Art. III jurisdiction. Singleton v. Wulff, post, at 112. Accordingly the physician-appellants do not have standing to challenge § 7 of the Act.

in *Roe*. In fact, we believe that § 2(2), even when read in conjunction with § 5 (proscribing an abortion "not necessary to preserve the life or health of the mother * * * unless the attending physician first certifies with reasonable medical certainty that the fetus is not viable"), the constitutionality of which is not explicitly challenged here, reflects an attempt on the part of the Missouri General Assembly to comply with our observations and discussion in *Roe* relating to viability. Appellant Hall, in his deposition, had no particular difficulty with the statutory definition.[3] As noted above, we recognized in *Roe* that viability was a matter of medical judgment, skill, and technical ability, and we preserved the flexibility of the term. Section 2(2) does the same. Indeed, one might argue, as the appellees do, that the presence of the statute's words "continued indefinitely" favor, rather than disfavor, the appellants, for, arguably, the point when life can be "continued indefinitely outside the womb" may well occur later in pregnancy than the point where the fetus is "potentially able to live outside the mother's womb." Roe v. Wade, 410 U.S., at 160, 93 S.Ct., at 730.

In any event, we agree with the District Court that it is not the proper function of the legislature or the courts to place viability, which essentially is a medical concept, at a specific point in the gestation period. The time when viability is achieved may vary with each pregnancy, and the determination of whether a particular fetus is viable is, and must be, a matter for the judgment of the responsible attending physician. The definition of viability in § 2(2) merely reflects this fact. The appellees do not contend otherwise, for they insist that the determination of viability rests with the physician in the exercise of his professional judgment.

* * *

We conclude that the definition in § 2(2) of the Act does not circumvent the limitations on state regulation outlined in *Roe*. We therefore hold that the Act's definition of "viability" comports with *Roe* and withstands the constitutional attack made upon it in this litigation.

B

The woman's consent. Under § 3(2) of the Act, a woman, prior to submitting to an abortion during the first 12 weeks of pregnancy, must certify in writing her consent to the procedure and "that her consent is informed and freely given and is not the result of coercion." Appellants argue that this requirement is violative of Roe v. Wade, 410 U.S., at 164–165, 93 S.Ct., at 732–733, by imposing an extra layer and burden of regulation on the abortion decision. See Doe v. Bolton, 410 U.S., at 195–200, 93 S.Ct., at 749–751. Appellants also claim that the provision is overbroad and vague.

---

3. "[A]lthough I agree with the definition of 'viability,' I think that it must be understood that viability is a very difficult state to assess." Tr. 369.

The District Court's majority relied on the propositions that the decision to terminate a pregnancy, of course, "is often a stressful one," and that the consent requirement of § 3(2) "insures that the pregnant woman retains control over the discretions of her consulting physician." 392 F.Supp., at 1368, 1369. The majority also felt that the consent requirement "does not single out the abortion procedure, but merely includes it within the category of medical operations for which consent is required." [6] Id., at 1396.   *   *   *

We do not disagree with the result reached by the District Court as to § 3(2). It is true that *Doe* and *Roe* clearly establish that the State may not restrict the decision of the patient and her physician regarding abortion during the first stage of pregnancy. Despite the fact that apparently no other Missouri statute, with the exceptions referred to in n. 6, supra, requires a patient's prior written consent to a surgical procedure, the imposition by § 3(2) of such a requirement for termination of pregnancy even during the first stage, in our view, is not in itself an unconstitutional requirement. The decision to abort, indeed, is an important, and often a stressful one, and it is desirable and imperative that it be made with full knowledge of its nature and consequences. The woman is the one primarily concerned, and her awareness of the decision and its significance may be assured, constitutionally, by the State to the extent of requiring her prior written consent.

We could not say that a requirement imposed by the State that a prior written consent for any surgery would be unconstitutional. As a consequence, we see no constitutional defect in requiring it only for some types of surgery as, for example, an intracardiac procedure, or where the surgical risk is elevated above a specified mortality level, or, for that matter, for abortions.[8]

C

The spouse's consent. Section 3(3) requires the prior written consent of the spouse of the woman seeking an abortion during the first 12 weeks of pregnancy, unless "the abortion is certified by a licensed physician to be necessary in order to preserve the life of the mother."

6. Apparently, however, the only other Missouri statutes concerned with consent for general medical or surgical care relate to persons committed to the Missouri State chest hospital, Mo.Rev.Stat. § 199.240 (Supp.1975), or to mental or correctional institutions, § 105.700 (1969).

8. The appellants' vagueness argument centers on the word "informed." One might well wonder, offhand, just what "informed consent" of a patient is. The three Missouri federal judges who composed the three-judge District Court, however, were not concerned, and we are content to accept, as the meaning, the giving of information to the patient as to just what would be done and as to its consequences. To ascribe more meaning that this might well confine the attending physician in an undesired and uncomfortable straitjacket in the practice of his profession.

*   *   *

In *Roe* and *Doe* we specifically reserved decision on the question whether a requirement for consent by the father of the fetus, by the spouse, or by the parents, or a parent, of an unmarried minor, may be constitutionally imposed. 410 U.S., at 165 n. 67, 93 S.Ct., at 733. We now hold that the State may not constitutionally require the consent of the spouse, as is specified under § 3(3) of the Missouri Act, as a condition for abortion during the first 12 weeks of pregnancy. We thus agree with the dissenting judge in the present case, and with the courts whose decisions are cited above, that the State cannot "delegate to a spouse a veto power which the state itself is absolutely and totally prohibited from exercising during the first trimester of pregnancy." 392 F.Supp., at 1375. Clearly, since the State cannot regulate or proscribe abortion during the first stage, when the physician and his patient make that decision, the State cannot delegate authority to any particular person, even the spouse, to prevent abortion during that same period.

We are not unaware of the deep and proper concern and interest that a devoted and protective husband has in his wife's pregnancy and in the growth and development of the fetus she is carrying. Neither has this Court failed to appreciate the importance of the marital relationship in our society. See, e. g., Griswold v. Connecticut, 381 U.S. 479, 486, 85 S.Ct. 1678, 1682, 14 L.Ed.2d 510 (1965); Maynard v. Hill, 125 U.S. 190, 211, 8 S.Ct. 723, 729, 31 L.Ed. 654 (1888). Moreover, we recognize that the decision whether to undergo or to forgo an abortion may have profound effects on the future of any marriage, effects that are both physical and mental, and possibly deleterious. Nothwithstanding these factors, we cannot hold that the State has the constitutional authority to give the spouse unilaterally the ability to prohibit the wife from terminating her pregnancy, when the State itself lacks that right. See Eisenstadt v. Baird, 405 U.S. 438, 453, 92 S.Ct. 1029, 1038, 31 L.Ed.2d 349 (1972).[11]

11. As the Court recognized in Eisenstadt v. Baird, "the marital couple is not an independent entity with a mind and heart of its own, but an association of two individuals each with a separate intellectual and emotional makeup. If the right of privacy means anything, it is the right of the *individual*, married or single, to be free from unwarranted governmental intrusion into matters so fundamentally affecting a person as the decision whether to bear or beget a child." 405 U.S., at 453, 92 S.Ct., at 1038 (emphasis in original).

The dissenting opinion of our Brother White appears to overlook the implications of this statement upon the issue whether § 3(3) is constitutional. This section does much more than insure that the husband participate in the decision whether his wife should have an abortion. The State, instead, has determined that the husband's interest in continuing the pregnancy of his wife always outweighs any interest on her part in terminating it irrespective of the condition of their marriage. The State, accordingly, has granted him the right to prevent unilaterally, and for whatever reason, the effectuation of his wife's and her physician's decision to terminate her pregnancy. This state determination not only may discourage the consultation that might normally be expected to precede a major decision affecting the marital couple but also, and more importantly, the State has inter-

It seems manifest that, ideally, the decision to terminate a pregnancy should be one concurred in by both the wife and her husband. No marriage may be viewed as harmonious or successful if the marriage partners are fundamentally divided on so important and vital an issue. But it is difficult to believe that the goal of fostering mutuality and trust in a marriage, and of strengthening the marital relationship and the marriage institution, will be achieved by giving the husband a veto power exercisable for any reason whatsoever or for no reason at all. Even if the State had the ability to delegate to the husband a power it itself could not exercise, it is not at all likely that such action would further, as the District Court majority phrased it, the "interest of the state in protecting the mutuality of decisions vital to the marriage relationship." 392 F.Supp., at 1370.

We recognize, of course, that when a woman, with the approval of her physician but without the approval of her husband, decides to terminate her pregnancy, it could be said that she is acting unilaterally. The obvious fact is that when the wife and the husband disagree on this decision, the view of only one of the two marriage partners can prevail. Inasmuch as it is the woman who physically bears the child and who is the more directly and immediately affected by the pregnancy, as between the two, the balance weighs in her favor. Cf. Roe v. Wade, 410 U.S., at 153, 93 S.Ct., at 726.

We conclude that § 3(3) of the Missouri Act is inconsistent with the standards enunciated in Roe v. Wade, 410 U.S., at 164–165, 93 S. Ct., at 732–733, and is unconstitutional. It is therefore unnecessary for us to consider the appellants' additional challenges to § 3(3) based on vagueness and overbreadth.

D

Parental Consent. Section 3(4) requires, with respect to the first 12 weeks of pregnancy, where the woman is unmarried and under the age of 18 years, the written consent of a parent or person *in loco parentis* unless, again, "the abortion is certified by a licensed physician as necessary in order to preserve the life of the mother." It is to be observed that only one parent need consent.

* * *

Of course, much of what has been said above, with respect to § 3(3), applies with equal force to § 3(4). Other courts that have considered the parental-consent issue in the light or *Roe* and *Doe,* have concluded that a statute like § 3(4) does not withstand constitutional scrutiny. See, e. g., Poe v. Gerstein, 517 F.2d, at 792; Wolfe v. Schroering, 388 F.Supp., at 636–637; Doe v. Rampton, 366 F.Supp., at 193, 199; State v. Koome, 84 Wash.2d 901, 530 P.2d 260 (1975).

posed an absolute obstacle to a woman's decision that *Roe* held to be constitutionally protected from such interference.

We agree with appellants and with the courts whose decisions have just been cited that the State may not impose a blanket provision, such as § 3(4), requiring the consent of a parent or person *in loco parentis* as a condition for abortion of an unmarried minor during the first 12 weeks of her pregnancy. Just as with the requirement of consent from the spouse, so here, the State does not have the constitutional authority to give a third party an absolute, and possibly arbitrary, veto over the decision of the physician and his patient to terminate the patient's pregnancy, regardless of the reason for withholding the consent.

Constitutional rights do not mature and come into being magically only when one attains the state-defined age of majority. Minors, as well as adults, are protected by the Constitution and possess constitutional rights. The Court indeed, however, long has recognized that the State has somewhat broader authority to regulate the activities of children than of adults. Prince v. Massachusetts, 321 U. S., at 170, 64 S.Ct., at 444; Ginsberg v. New York, 390 U.S. 629, 88 S.Ct. 1274, 20 L.Ed.2d 195 (1968). It remains, then, to examine whether there is any significant state interest in conditioning an abortion on the consent of a parent or person *in loco parentis* that is not present in the case of an adult.

One suggested interest is the safeguarding of the family unit and of parental authority. It is difficult, however, to conclude that providing a parent with absolute power to overrule a determination, made by the physician and his minor patient, to terminate the patient's pregnancy will serve to strengthen the family unit. Neither is it likely that such veto power will enhance parental authority or control where the minor and the nonconsenting parent are so fundamentally in conflict and the very existence of the pregnancy already has fractured the family structure. Any independent interest the parent may have in the termination of the minor daughter's pregnancy is no more weighty than the right of privacy of the competent minor mature enough to have become pregnant.

We emphasize that our holding that § 3(4) is invalid does not suggest that every minor, regardless of age or maturity, may give effective consent for termination of her pregnancy. The fault with § 3(4) is that it imposes a special-consent provision, exercisable by a person other than the woman and her physician, as a prerequisite to a minor's termination of her pregnancy and does so without a sufficient justification for the restriction. It violates the strictures of *Roe* and *Doe*.

E

Saline amniocentesis. Section 9 of the statute prohibits the use of saline amniocentesis, as a method or technique of abortion, after the first 12 weeks of pregnancy. It describes the method as one whereby the amniotic fluid is withdrawn and "a saline or other fluid" is inserted into the amniotic sac. The statute imposes this proscription on the ground that the technique "is deleterious to maternal health," and places it in the form of a legislative finding. Appellants challenge this provision on the ground that it operates to preclude virtually all abortions after the first trimester. This is so, it is claimed, because a substantial percentage, in the neighborhood of 70% according to the testimony, of all abortions performed in the United States after the first trimester are effected through the procedure of saline amniocentesis. Appellants stress the fact that the alternative methods of hysterotomy and hysterectomy are significantly more dangerous and critical for the woman than the saline technique; they also point out that the mortality rate for normal childbirth exceeds that where saline amniocentesis is employed. Finally, appellants note that the perhaps safer alternative of prostaglandin instillation, suggested and strongly relied upon by the appellees, at least at the time of the trial, is not yet widely used in this country.

We held in *Roe* that after the first stage, "the State, in promoting its interest in the health of the mother, may, if it chooses, regulate the abortion procedure in ways that are reasonably related to maternal health." 410 U.S., at 164, 93 S.Ct., at 732. The question with respect to § 9 therefore is whether the flat prohibition of saline amniocentesis is a restriction which "reasonably relates to the preservation and protection of maternal health." Id., at 163.

The District Court's majority determined, on the basis of the evidence before it, that the maternal mortality rate in childbirth does, indeed, exceed the mortality rate where saline amniocentesis is used. Therefore, the majority acknowledged, § 9 could be upheld only if there were safe alternative methods of inducing abortion after the first 12 weeks. Referring to such methods as hysterotomy, hysterectomy, "mechanical means of inducing abortion," and prostaglandin injection, the majority said that at least the latter two techniques were safer than saline. Consequently, the majority concluded, the restriction in § 9 could be upheld as reasonably related to maternal health.

We feel that the majority in reaching its conclusion, failed to appreciate and to consider several significant facts. First, it did not recognize the prevalence, as the record conclusively demonstrates, of the use of saline amniocentesis as an accepted medical procedure in this country; the procedure, as noted above, is employed in a substantial majority (the testimony from both sides ranges from 68% to 80%) of all post-first-trimester abortions. Second, it failed to recognize that at the time of trial, there were severe limitations on the availability of the prostaglandin technique, which, although promising, was used only on an experimental basis until less than two years before. See Wolfe v. Schroering, 388 F.Supp., at 637, where it was said that at that time (1974), there were "no physicians in Kentucky competent in the technique of prostaglandin amnio infusion." And appellees offered no evidence that prostaglandin abortions were available in Missouri.[12] Third, the statute's reference to the insertion of "a saline or other fluid" appears to include within its proscription the intra-amniotic injection of prostaglandin itself and other methods that may be developed in the future and that may prove highly effective and completely safe. Finally, the majority did not consider the anomaly inherent in § 9 when it proscribes the use of saline but does not prohibit techniques that are many times more likely to result in maternal death.

These unappreciated or overlooked factors place the State's decision to bar use of the saline method in a completely different light. The State, through § 9, would prohibit the use of a method which the record shows is the one most commonly used nationally by physicians after the first trimester and which is safer, with respect to maternal mortality, than even continuation of the pregnancy until normal childbirth. Moreover, as a practical matter, it forces a woman and her physician to terminate her pregnancy by methods more dangerous to her health than the method outlawed.

As so viewed, particularly in the light of the present unavailability—as demonstrated by the record—of the prostaglandin technique, the outright legislative proscription of saline fails as a reasonable regulation for the protection of maternal health. It comes into focus, instead, as an unreasonable or arbitrary regulation designed to inhibit, and having the effect of inhibiting, the vast majority of abortions after the first 12 weeks. As such, it does not withstand constitutional challenge.

---

12. In response to Mr. Justice White's criticism that the prostaglandin method of inducing abortion was available in Missouri, either at the time the Act was passed or at the time of trial, we make the following observations. First, there is no evidence in the record to which our Brother has pointed that demonstrates that the prostaglandin method was or is available in Missouri. Second, the evidence presented to the District Court does not support such a view. Until January 1974 prostaglandin was used only on an experimental basis in a few medical centers. And, at the time the Missouri General Assembly proscribed saline, the sole distributor of prostaglandin "restricted sales to around twenty medical centers from coast to coast." Brief for Appellee Danforth 68.

It is clear, therefore, that at the time the Missouri General Assembly passed the Act, prostaglandin was not available, in any meaningful sense of that term. Because of this undisputed fact, it was incumbent upon appellees to show that at the time of trial in 1974 prostaglandin was available. They failed to do so. Indeed, appellees' expert witness, on whose testimony the dissenting opinion relies, does not fill this void. He was able to state only that prostaglandin was used in a limited way until shortly before trial and that he "would think" that it was more readily available at the time of trial. Tr. 335. Such an experimental and limited use of prostaglandin throughout the country does not make it available or accessible to concerned persons in Missouri.

F

Recordkeeping. Sections 10 and 11 of the Act impose record-keeping requirements for health facilities and physicians concerned with abortions irrespective of the pregnancy stage. Under § 10, each such facility and physician is to be supplied with forms "the purpose and function of which shall be the preservation of maternal health and life by adding to the sum of medical knowledge through the compilation of relevant maternal health and life data and to monitor all abortions performed to assure that they are done only under and in accordance with the provisions of the law." The statute states that the information on the forms "shall be confidential and shall be used only for statistical purposes." The "records, however, may be inspected and health data acquired by local, state, or national public health officers." Under § 11 the records are to be kept for seven years in the permanent files of the health facility where the abortion was performed.

* * *

One may concede that there are important and perhaps conflicting interests affected by recordkeeping requirements. On the one hand, maintenance of records indeed may be helpful in developing information pertinent to the preservation of maternal health. On the other hand, as we stated in *Roe,* during the first stage of pregnancy the State may impose no restrictions or regulations governing the medical judgment of the pregnant woman's attending physician with respect to the termination of her pregnancy. 410 U.S., at 163, 164, 93 S.Ct., at 731, 732. Furthermore, it is readily apparent that one reason for the recordkeeping requirement, namely, to assure that all abortions in Missouri are performed in accordance with the Act, fades somewhat into insignificance in view of our holding above as to spousal and parental consent requirements.

Recordkeeping and reporting requirements that are reasonably directed to the preservation of maternal health and that properly respect a patient's confidentiality and privacy are permissible. This surely is so for the period after the first stage of pregnancy, for then the State may enact substantive as well as recordkeeping regulations that are reasonable means of protecting maternal health. As to the first stage, one may argue forcefully, as the appellants do, that the State should not be able to impose any recordkeeping requirements that significantly differ from those imposed with respect to other, and comparable, medical or surgical procedures. We conclude, however, that the provisions of §§ 10 and 11, while perhaps approaching impermissible limits, are not constitutionally offensive in themselves. Recordkeeping of this kind, if not abused or overdone, can be useful to the State's interest in protecting the health of its female citizens, and may be a resource that is relevant to decisions involving medical experience and judgment. The added requirements for confidentiality, with the sole exception for public health officers, and for retention for seven years, a period not unreasonable in length, assist and persuade us in our determination of the constitutional limits. As so regarded, we see no legally significant impact or consequence on the abortion decision or on the physician-patient relationship. We naturally assume, furthermore, that these recordkeeping and record-maintaining provisions will be interpreted and enforced by Missouri's Division of Health in the light of our decision with respect to the Act's other provisions, and that, of course, they will not be utilized in such a way as to accomplish, through the sheer burden of recordkeeping detail, what we have held to be an otherwise unconstitutional restriction. Obviously, the State may not require execution of spousal and parental consent forms that have been invalidated today.

G

Standard of care. Appellee Danforth in No. 74–1419 appeals from the unanimous decision of the District Court that § 6(1) of the Act is unconstitutional. That section provides:

"No person who performs or induces an abortion shall fail to exercise that degree of professional skill, care and diligence to preserve the life and health of the fetus which such person would be required to exercise in order to preserve the life and health of any fetus intended to be born and not aborted. Any physician or person assisting in the abortion who shall fail to take such measures to encourage or to sustain the life of the child, and the death of the child results, shall be deemed guilty of manslaughter * * *. Further, such physician or other person shall be liable in an action for damages."
* * *

     *   *   *

     *   *   * Section 6(1) requires the physician to exercise the prescribed skill, care, and diligence to preserve the life and health of the *fetus*. It does not specify that such care need be taken only after the stage of viability has been reached. As the provision now reads, it impermissibly requires the physician to preserve the life and health of the fetus, whatever the stage of pregnancy. The fact that the second sentence of § 6(1) refers to a criminal penalty where the physician fails "to take such measures to encourage or to sustain the life of the *child*, and the death of the *child* results" (emphasis supplied), simply does not modify the duty imposed by the previous sentence or limit that duty to pregnancies that have reached the stage of viability.

The appellees finally argue that if the first sentence of § 6(1) does not survive constitutional attack, the second sentence does, and, under the Act's severability provision, § B, is severable from the first.
* * *

We conclude, as did the District Court, that § 6(1) must stand or fall as a unit. Its provisions are inextricably bound together. And a physician's or other person's criminal failure to protect a liveborn infant surely will be subject to prosecution in Missouri under the State's criminal statutes.

The judgment of the District Court is affirmed in part and reversed in part, and the case is remanded for further proceedings consistent with this opinion.

NOTES AND QUESTIONS

(1) Justices Brennan and Marshall joined in Justice Blackmun's opinion. Justices Stewart and Powell concurred specially in that opinion, stating that the question of spousal consent was more difficult than the plurality opinion made it out to be, involving as it did a conflict between the interests of the mother and those of the father, both being constitutionally recognized interests. But they agreed that this conflict should be resolved in favor of the mother's interests. Justices White and Rehnquist and the Chief Justice dissented from the decision that the statute's requirement of spousal consent was unconstitutional, arguing that the state is free to assign as great a value to the father's interest in the child as to the mother's desire for an abortion. They also took the position that the parent consent requirement was a valid exercise of the state's power. The same three justices would have held the prohibition of saline amniocentesis to be constitutional and would also have upheld section 6(1) of the statute on the ground that, properly construed, that section merely meant that if the fetus were capable of surviving outside the womb, the abortion should be conducted in such a way as to preserve that life. Justice Stevens also dissented from the plurality on the parental consent requirement. In his opinion the state's interest in protecting youth and in involving parents in the abortion decision supported its constitutional authority to require the minor to obtain parents' consent.

(2) What do you suppose was the purpose of the statutory provision which defined viability as that stage of fetal development when the life of the unborn child may be continued indefinitely outside the womb? Was this section related to section 5, which provided that no abortion not necessary to preserve the life or health of the mother could be performed unless the physician certified with reasonable medical certainty that the fetus was not viable? In doubtful cases under these sections, who would have the burden of establishing viability or non-viability?

(3) The state of Pennsylvania enacted the following statute:

"(a) Every person who performs or induces an abortion shall prior thereto have made a determination based on his experience, judgment or professional competence that the fetus is not viable, and if the determination is that the fetus is viable or if there is sufficient reason to believe that the fetus may be viable, shall exercise that degree of professional skill, care and diligence to preserve the life and health of the fetus which such person would be required to exercise in order to preserve the life and health of any fetus intended to be born and not aborted and the abortion technique employed shall be that which would provide the best opportunity for the fetus to be aborted alive so long as a different technique would not be necessary in order to preserve the life or health of the mother.

* * *

"(d) Any person who fails to make the determination provided for in subsection (a) of this section, or who fails to exercise the degree of professional skill, care and diligence or to provide the abortion tech· nique as provided for in subsection (a) of this section * * * shall be subject to such civil or criminal liability as would pertain to him had the fetus been a child who was intended to be born and not aborted."

The Supreme Court in Colautti v. Franklin, 439 U.S. 379, 99 S.Ct. 675, 58 L.Ed.2d 596 (1979), held that this provision was "void for vagueness". In so holding the Court reasoned as follows:

(a) It is not clear whether this statute imposed a purely subjective standard of viability or whether it imposed a mixed subjective and objective standard. The statute contained language which suggested that the attending physician should rely upon his own judgment and experience in deciding whether the fetus was viable. At the same time the statute imposed the duty of care when the physician had sufficient reason to believe that the fetus was viable. The effect of the latter provision seemed to be to impose some sort of general community standard of viability inconsistent with the preceding provision.

(b) The use of the terms "is viable" and "may be viable", which in the context could hardly be synonymous, created a second serious ambiguity. The Court said that one or the other of these conditions differed from the definition of viability set out in Roe v. Wade and the Danforth case.

(c) The impact of the statute's vagueness was heightened by the fact that it imposed criminal penalities without regard to fault, and by the fact that viability itself is such an uncertain concept. The result, the Court found, was that the statute had "a profound chilling effect on the willingness of physicians to perform abortions".

(d) The Court also found that the standard of care imposed by the statute was ambiguous in that it did not reveal whether the physician was to have as his paramount duty the preservation of the fetus, or whether he was to balance fetal survival against prejudice to the mother's health in some fashion.

Justice White wrote a dissent in this case which was concurred in by Chief Justice Burger and Justice Rehnquist.

(4) How does the Court in Roe and Danforth define "viability"? In Colautti the Court had this to say about the term:

"As the record in this case indicates, a physician determines whether or not a fetus is viable after considering a number of variables: the gestational age of the fetus, derived from the reported menstrual history of the woman; fetal weight, based on an inexact estimate of the size and condition of the uterus; the woman's general health and nutrition; the quality of the available medical facilities; and other factors."

Is viability the point at which the fetus has a better than even chance to survive? Or is it the point at which the fetus is sure to survive outside the womb? How is this point to be determined by the physician who is asked to do an abortion? For example, a woman seeks an abortion and upon examination by several physicians their estimates of the length of her pregnancy vary between twenty and twenty-four weeks, while the woman herself indicates that she has been pregnant seventeen weeks. The abortion is performed and the evidence is in conflict as to whether the fetus was alive when taken from the woman's body. In any event it did not survive more than a few moments. The attending physician was charged with manslaughter under the applicable state statute. See Commonwealth v. Edelin, 371 Mass. 497, 359 N.E.2d 4 (1976). In another case the physician performed an abortion upon a woman whom he judged to be twenty-five weeks pregnant. The fetus lived for twenty days after being removed from the womb and then died. The physician was charged with illegal abortion under the state statute. Floyd v. Anders, 440 F.Supp. 535 (D.S.C.1977), judgment vacated, 47 L.Wk. 3582 (1979), rehearing denied 47 L.Wk. 3699 (1979). For discussion of viability, see Hoffman, et al., Analysis of Birth Weight, Gestational Age and Fetal Viability, U.S. Births, 1968, 29 Obstetrical and Gynecological Survey 651–681 (1974), indicating a survival rate of 55% where the period of gestation is twenty-five weeks and the fetal weight is two thousand grams.

5. Is the Court correct in Danforth when it asserts that since under Roe v. Wade, the state has no constitutional authority to prohibit a first trimester abortion, it may not constitutionally permit either a spouse or a parent to veto such an abortion when the mother desires one? Does a spouse or a parent have interests in such a situation which differ from the interests of the state?

6. What do you suppose was the purpose of section 6(1) of the Missouri statute which the Court held invalid in Danforth? Is the construction of this section given by the plurality opinion correct, or is Justice White correct in his view that this was only intended to require that where the fetus can survive outside the mother's womb, the abortion must be handled in such a way as to preserve fetal life, notwithstanding the mother's desire that the fetus not be preserved?

7. A state statute provides as follows:

"In every case where a live born infant results from an attempted abortion which was not performed to save the life or health of the mother, such infant shall be an abandoned ward of the State * * * and the mother and father, if he consented to the abortion, of such infant shall have no parental rights or obligations whatsoever relating to such infant."

Is this statute constitutional? Wynn v. Carey, 599 F.2d 193 (7th Cir. 1979); Freiman v. Ashcroft, 584 F.2d 247 (8th Cir. 1978), affirmed per curiam, Ashcroft v. Freiman, 440 U.S. 941, 99 S.Ct. 1416, 59 L.E.2d 630 (1979).

BELLOTTI v. BAIRD

Supreme Court of the United States, 1979.
443 U.S. 622, 99 S.Ct. 3035, 61 L.Ed.2d 797.

Mr. Justice POWELL announced the judgment of the Court and delivered an opinion in which The CHIEF JUSTICE, Mr. Justice STEWART, and Mr. Justice REHNQUIST joined.

These appeals present a challenge to the constitutionality of a state statute regulating the access of minors to abortions. They require us to continue the inquiry we began in Planned Parenthood v. Danforth, 428 U.S. 52, 96 S.Ct. 2831, 49 L.Ed.2d 788 (1976), and Bellotti v. Baird, 428 U.S. 132, 96 S.Ct. 2857, 49 L.Ed.2d 844 (1976).

I

A

On August 2, 1974, the legislature of the Commonwealth of Massachusetts passed, over the Governor's veto, an act pertaining to abortions performed within the State. 1974 Mass. Acts, ch. 706. According to its title, the statute was intended to regulate abortions "within present constitutional limits." Shortly before the act was to go into effect, the class action from which these appeals arise was commenced in the District Court [1] to enjoin, as unconstitutional, the provision of the act now codified as Mass.Gen.Laws Ann., ch. 112, § 12S (West).[2]

Section 12S provides in part:

"If the mother is less than eighteen years of age and has not married, the consent of both the mother and her parents [to an abortion to be performed on the mother] is required. If one or both of the mother's parents refuse such consent, consent may be obtained by order of a judge of the superior court for good cause shown, after such hearing as he deems necessary. Such a hearing will not require appointment of a guardian for the mother. If one of the parents has died or has deserted his or her family, consent by the remaining parent is sufficient. If both parents have died or have deserted their family, consent of the mother's guardian or other person having duties similar to a guardian, or any person who had assumed the care and custody of the mother is sufficient. The commissioner of public health shall prescribe a written form for such consent. Such form shall be signed by the proper person or persons and given to the physician performing the abortion who shall maintain it in his permanent files."

Physicians performing abortions in the absence of the consent required by § 12S are subject to injunctions and criminal penalties. See Mass.Gen.Laws Ann. ch. 112, §§ 12Q, 12T, and 12U (West).

* * *

1. The court promptly issued a restraining order which remained in effect until its decision on the merits. Subsequent stays of enforcement were issued during the complex course of this litigation, with the result that Mass.Gen.Laws Ann., ch. 112, § 12S (West), never has been enforced by Massachusetts.

2. As originally enacted, § 12S was designated as § 12P of chapter 112. In 1977, the provision was renumbered as § 12S, and the numbering of subdivisions within the section was eliminated. No changes of substance were made. We shall refer to the section as § 12S throughout this opinion.

B

[At this point in the opinion the Court described the procedural background of the case in some detail. The plaintiffs were William Baird, director of the Parents Aid Society, the Society, Dr. Zupnick who performed abortions at the Parents Aid Clinic, and Mary Moe, a pregnant minor residing with her parents, who wished an abortion. The defendants were the Attorney General of Massachusetts and the various district attorneys from all the counties in Massachusetts. At the first hearing in the case the district court held the statute unconstitutional. Baird v. Bellotti, 393 F.Supp. 847 (D.Mass.1975), (Baird I). That decision was appealed to the Supreme Court, which vacated the judgment on the ground that the district court should have abstained and certified to the Massachusetts Supreme Judicial Court questions the answers to which would provide an authoritative construction of the statute.]

On remand, the District Court certified nine questions to the Supreme Judicial Court. These were answered in an opinion styled Baird v. Attorney General, 371 Mass. 741, 360 N.E.2d 288 (1977) (Attorney General). Among the more important aspects of § 12S, as authoritatively construed by the Supreme Judicial Court, are the following:

1. In deciding whether to grant consent to their daughter's abortion, parents are required by § 12S to consider exclusively what will serve her best interests. See id., at —— Mass. ——, 360 N.E.2d at 292–293.

2. The provision in § 12S that judicial consent for an abortion shall be granted, parental objections notwithstanding, "for good cause shown" means that such consent shall be granted if found to be in the minor's best interests. The judge "must disregard all parental objections, and other considerations, which are not based exclusively" on that standard. Id., at —— Mass. ——, 360 N.E.2d at 293.

3. Even if the judge in a § 12S proceeding finds "that the minor is capable of making, and has made, an informed and reasonable decision to have an abortion," he is entitled to withhold consent "in circumstances where he determines that the best interests of the minor will not be served by an abortion." Ibid.

4. As a general rule, a minor who desires an abortion may not obtain judicial consent without first seeking both parent's consent. Exceptions to the rule exist when a parent is not available or when the need for the abortion constitutes "an emergency requiring immediate action." Id., at —— Mass. ——, 360 N.E.2d, at 294. Unless a parent is not available, he must be notified of any judicial proceedings brought under § 12S. Id., at ——, 360 N.E.2d, at 297.

5. The resolution of § 12S cases and any appeals that follow can be expected to be prompt. The name of the minor and her parents

may be held in confidence. If need be, the Supreme Judicial Court and the Superior Courts can promulgate rules or issue orders to ensure that such proceedings are handled expeditiously. Id., at ——, 360 N.E.2d at 297–298.

6. Mass.Gen.Laws Ann. ch. 112, § 12F, which provides, inter alia, that certain classes of minors may consent to most kinds of medical care without parental approval, does not apply to abortions, except as to minors who are married, widowed, or divorced. See id., at ——, 360 N.E.2d at 298–300. Nor does the State's common law "mature minor rule" create an exception to § 12S. Id., ——, 360 N.E.2d at 294. See n. 27, infra.

[At this point, in part I C of its opinion, the Supreme Court summarized the action of the district court after receiving the response of the Massachusetts Supreme Judicial Court construing the Massachusetts statute. The district court first issued a stay of the enforcement of the statute, Baird v. Bellotti, 428 F.Supp. 854 (D. Mass.1977) (Baird II). Then after a full hearing the district court held the statute unconstitutional. Baird v. Bellotti, 450 F.Supp. 997 (D.Mass.1978) (Baird III).]

II

A child, merely on account of his minority, is not beyond the protection of the Constitution. As the Court said in *In re Gault,* 387 U.S. 1, 13, 87 S.Ct. 1428, 1436, 18 L.Ed.2d 527 (1967), "whatever may be their precise impact, neither the Fourteenth Amendment nor the Bill of Rights is for adults alone." [12] This observation, of course, is but the beginning of the analysis. The Court long has recognized that the status of minors under the law is unique in many respects. As Mr. Justice Frankfurter aptly put it, "[c]hildren have a very special place in life which law should reflect. Legal theories and their phrasing in other cases readily lead to fallacious reasoning if uncritically transferred to determination of a State's duty towards children." May v. Anderson, 345 U.S. 528, 536, 73 S.Ct. 840, 844, 97 L.Ed. 1221 (1953) (concurring opinion). The unique role in our society of the family, the institution by which "we inculcate and pass down many of our most cherished values, moral and cultural," Moore v. City of East Cleveland, 431 U.S. 494, 503–504, 97 S.Ct. 1932, 1938, 52 L.Ed.2d 531 (1977) (plurality opinion), requires that constitutional principles be applied with sensitivity and flexibility to the special needs of parents and children. We have recognized three reasons justifying the conclusion that the constitutional rights of children can-

12. Similarly, the Court said in Planned Parenthood of Central Missouri v. Danforth, 428 U.S. 52, 74, 96 S.Ct. 2831, 49 L.Ed.2d 788 (1976):

"Constitutional rights do not mature and come into being magically only when one attains the state-defined age of majority. Minors, as well as adults, are protected by the Constitution and possess constitutional rights."

not be equated with those of adults: the peculiar vulnerability of children; their inability to make critical decisions in an informed, mature manner; and the importance of the parental role in child-rearing.

A

The Court's concern for the vulnerability of children is demonstrated in its decisions dealing with minors' claims to constitutional protection against deprivations of liberty or property interests by the State. With respect to many of these claims, we have concluded that the child's right is virtually coextensive with that of an adult. For example, the Court has held that the Fourteenth Amendment's guarantee against the deprivation of liberty without due process of law is applicable to children in juvenile delinquency proceedings. In re Gault, 387 U.S. 1, 87 S.Ct. 1428, 18 L.Ed.2d 527 (1967). In particular, minors involved in such proceedings are entitled to adequate notice, the assistance of counsel, and the opportunity to confront their accusers. They can be found guilty only upon proof beyond a reasonable doubt, and they may assert the privilege against compulsory self-incrimination. In re Winship, 397 U.S. 358, 90 S.Ct. 1068, 25 L. Ed.2d 368 (1970); In re Gault, supra. See also Ingraham v. Wright, 430 U.S. 651, 674, 97 S.Ct. 1401, 1414, 51 L.Ed.2d 711 (1977) (corporal punishment of school children implicates constitutionally protected liberty interest); cf. Breed v. Jones, 421 U.S. 519, 95 S.Ct. 1779, 44 L.Ed.2d 346 (1975) (Double Jeopardy Clause prohibits prosecuting juvenile as an adult after an adjudicatory finding in juvenile court that he had violated a criminal statute). Similarly, in Goss v. Lopez, 419 U.S. 565, 95 S.Ct. 729, 42 L.Ed.2d 725 (1975), the Court held that children may not be deprived of certain property interests without due process.

These rulings have not been made on the uncritical assumption that the constitutional rights of children are indistinguishable from those of adults. Indeed, our acceptance of juvenile courts distinct from the adult criminal justice system assumes that juvenile offenders constitutionally may be treated differently from adults. In order to preserve this separate avenue for dealing with minors, the Court has said that hearings in juvenile delinquency cases need not necessarily "conform with all the requirements of a criminal trial or even of the usual administrative hearing." In re Gault, supra, 387 U.S., at 30, 87 S.Ct., at 1445, quoting Kent v. United States, 383 U.S. 541, 562, 86 S.Ct. 1045, 1057, 16 L.Ed.2d 84 (1966). Thus, juveniles are not constitutionally entitled to trial by jury in delinquency adjudications. McKeiver v. Pennsylvania, 403 U.S. 528, 91 S.Ct. 1976, 29 L.Ed.2d 647 (1978). Viewed together, our cases show that although children generally are protected by the same constitutional guarantees against governmental deprivations as are adults, the State is entitled to adjust its legal system to account for children's vulnerability and their needs for "concern, * * * sympathy, and * * * paternal attention." Id., at 550 (plurality opinion).

B

Second, the Court has held that the States validly may limit the freedom of children to choose for themselves in the making of important, affirmative choices with potentially serious consequences. These rulings have been grounded in the recognition that, during the formative years of childhood and adolescence, minors often lack the experience, perspective, and judgment to recognize and avoid choices that could be detrimental to them.[13]

Ginsberg v. New York, 390 U.S. 629, 88 S.Ct. 1274, 20 L.Ed.2d 195 (1968), illustrates well the Court's concern over the inability of children to make mature choices, as the First Amendment rights involved are clear examples of constitutionally protected freedoms of choice. At issue was a criminal conviction for selling sexually oriented magazines to a minor under the age of 17 in violation of a New York state law. It was conceded that the conviction could not have stood under the First Amendment if based upon a sale of the same material to an adult. Id., at 634, 88 S.Ct., at 1277. Notwithstanding the importance the Court always has attached to First Amendment rights, it concluded that "even where there is an invasion of protected freedoms 'the power of the state to control the conduct of children reaches beyond the scope of its authority over adults * * *,'" id., at 638, 88 S.Ct., at 1280, quoting Prince v. Massachusetts, 321 U.S. 158, 170, 64 S.Ct. 438, 444, 88 L.Ed. 645 (1944).[14] The Court was convinced that the New York Legislature rationally could conclude that the sale to children of the magazines in question presented a danger against which they should be guarded. *Ginsberg,* supra, 390

---

13. As Mr. Justice Sewart wrote of the exercise by minors of the First Amendment rights that "secur[e] * * * the liberty of each man to decide for himself what he will read and to what he will listen," Ginsberg v. New York, 390 U.S. 629, 649, 88 S.Ct. 1274, 1285, 20 L.Ed.2d 195 (1968) (Stewart, J., concurring in the result):

"[A]t least in some precisely delineated areas, a child—like someone in a captive audience—is not possessed of that full capacity for individual choice which is the presupposition of First Amendment guarantees. It is only upon such a premise, I should suppose, that a State may deprive children of other rights—the right to marry, for example, or the right to vote—deprivations that would be constitutionally intolerable for adults." Id., at 649–650, 88 S.Ct., at 1286 (footnotes omitted).

14. In *Prince* an adult had permitted a child in her custody to sell religious literature on a public street in violation of a state child-labor statute. The child had been permitted to engage in this activity upon her own sincere request. 321 U.S., at 162, 64 S.Ct., at 440. In upholding the adult's conviction under the statute, we found that "the interests of society to protect the welfare of children" and to give them opportunities for growth into free and independent well-developed men and citizens," id., at 165, 64 S.Ct., at 442, permitted the State to enforce its statute, which "[c]oncededly * * * would be invalid," id., at 167, 64 S.Ct., at 442, if made applicable to adults.

U.S., at 641, 88 S.Ct., at 1281. It therefore rejected the argument that the New York law violated the constitutional rights of minors.[15]

C

Third, the guiding role of parents in the upbringing of their children justifies limitations on the freedoms of minors. The State commonly protects its youth from adverse governmental action and from their own immaturity by requiring parental consent to or involvement in important decisions by minors.[16] But an additional and more important justification for state deference to parental control over children is that "[t]he child is not the mere creature of the State; those who nurture him and direct his destiny have the right, coupled with the high duty, to recognize and prepare him for additional obligations." Pierce v. Society of Sisters, 268 U.S. 510, 535, 45 S.Ct. 571, 573, 69 L.Ed. 1070 (1925). * * * This affirmative process of teaching, guiding, and inspiring by precept and example is essential to the growth of young people into mature, socially responsible citizens.

We have believed in this country that this process, in large part, is beyond the competence of impersonal political institutions. Indeed, affirmative sponsorship of particular ethical, religious, or political beliefs is something we expect the State *not* to attempt in a society constitutionally committed to the ideal of individual liberty and freedom of choice. Thus, "[i]t is cardinal with us that the custody, care and nurture of the child reside first in the parents, whose primary function and freedom include *preparation for obligations the state can neither supply nor hinder.*" Prince v. Massachusetts, supra, at 166, 64 S.Ct., at 442 (emphasis added).

15. Although the State has considerable latitude in enacting laws affecting minors on the basis of their lesser capacity for mature, affirmative choice, Tinker v. Des Moines Independent Community School District, 393 U.S. 503, 89 S.Ct. 733, 21 L.Ed.2d 731 (1969), illustrates that it may not arbitrarily deprive them of their freedom of action altogether. The Court held in *Tinker* that a school child's First Amendment freedom of expression entitled him, contrary to school policy, to attend school wearing a black armband as a silent protest against American involvement in the hostilities in Viet Nam. The Court acknowledged that the State was permitted to prohibit conduct otherwise shielded by the Constitution that "for any reason—whether it stems from time, place, or type of behavior—materially disrupts classwork or involves substantial disorder or invasion of the rights of others." Id., at 513. It upheld the First Amendment right of the schoolchildren in that case, however, not only because it found no evidence in the record that their wearing of black armbands threatened any substantial interference with the proper objectives of the school district, but also because it appeared that the challenged policy was intended primarily to stifle any debate whatsoever—even nondisruptive discussions—on important political and moral issues. See id., at 510, 89 S.Ct., at 738.

16. See, e., g., Mass.Gen.Laws Ann., ch. 207, §§ 7, 24, 25, 33, 33A (West 1958 & Supp.1979) (parental consent required for marriage of person under 18); Mass.Gen.Laws Ann., ch. 119, § 55A (West Supp.1979) (waiver of counsel by minor in juvenile delinquency proceedings must be made through parent or guardian).

Unquestionably, there are many competing theories about the most effective way for parents to fulfill their central role in assisting their children on the way to responsible adulthood. While we do not pretend any special wisdom on this subject, we cannot ignore that central to many of these theories, and deeply rooted in our nation's history and tradition, is the belief that the parental role implies a substantial measure of authority over one's children. Indeed, "constitutional interpretation has consistently recognized that the parents' claim to authority in their own household to direct the rearing of their children is basic in the structure of our society." Ginsberg v. New York, supra, at 639, 88 S.Ct., at 1280.

Properly understood, then, the tradition of parental authority is not inconsistent with our tradition of individual liberty; rather, the former is one of the basic presuppositions of the latter. Legal restrictions on minors, especially those supportive of the parental role, may be important to the child's chances for the full growth and maturity that make eventual participation in a free society meaningful and rewarding.[17] Under the Constitution, the State can "properly conclude that parents and others, teachers for example, who have [the] primary responsibility for children's well-being are entitled to the support of laws designed to aid discharge of that responsibility." Ginsberg v. New York, supra, at 639, 88 S.Ct., at 1280.[18]

III

With these principles in mind, we consider the specific constitutional questions presented by these appeals. * * * The question before us—in light of what we have said in the prior cases—is whether § 12S, as authoritatively interpreted by the Supreme Judicial Court, provides for parental notice and consent in a manner that does not unduly burden the right to seek an abortion.

Appellees and intervenors contend that even as interpreted by the Supreme Judicial Court of Massachusetts § 12(S) does unduly burden this right. They suggest, for example, that the mere requirement of parental notice constitutes such a burden. As stated in Part

17. See Hafen, Children's Liberation and the New Egalitarianism: Some Reservations About Abandoning Children to their "Rights," 1976 B.Y.U.L. Rev. 605.

18. The Court's opinions discussed in the text above—*Pierce, Yoder, Prince,* and *Ginsberg*—all have contributed to a line of decisions suggesting the existence of a constitutional parental right against undue, adverse interference by the State. See also Smith v. Organization of Foster Families, 431 U.S. 816, 842–844, 97 S.Ct. 2094, 2109, 53 L.Ed.2d 14 (1977); Carey v. Population Services, 431 U.S. 678, 708, 97 S.Ct. 2010, 2028, 52 L.Ed.2d 675 (1977) (opinion of Mr. Justice Powell); Moore v. City of East Cleveland, 431 U.S. 494, 97 S.Ct. 1932, 52 L.Ed.2d 531 (1977) (plurality opinion); Stanley v. Illinois, 405 U.S. 645, 651, 92 S.Ct. 1208, 1212, 31 L. Ed.2d 551 (1972); Meyer v. Nebraska, 252 U.S. 390, 399, 43 S.Ct. 625, 67 L. Ed. 1042 (1923). Cf. Parham v. J. R., 442 U.S. 584, 99 S.Ct. 2493, 61 L.Ed. 2d 101 (1979); id., at 621, 99 S.Ct., at 2513 (opinion of Mr. Justice Stewart, concurring in the result).

II above, however, parental notice and consent are qualifications that typically may be imposed by the State on a minor's right to make important decisions. As immature minors often lack the ability to make fully informed choices that take account of both immediate and long-range consequences, a State reasonably may determine that parental consultation often is desirable and in the best interest of the minor. It may further determine, as a general proposition, that such consultation is particularly desirable with respect to the abortion decision—one that for some people raises profound moral and religious concerns.[20] As Mr. Justice STEWART wrote in concurrence in Planned Parenthood v. Danforth, 428 U.S., at 91, 96 S.Ct., at 2851:

"There can be little doubt that the State furthers a constitutionally permissible end by encouraging an unmarried pregnant minor to seek the help and advice of her parents in making the very important decision whether or not to bear a child. That is a grave decision, and a girl of tender years, under emotional stress, may be ill-equipped to make it without mature advice and emotional support. It seems unlikely that she will obtain counsel and support from the attending physician at an abortion clinic, where abortions for pregnant minors frequently take place." (Footnote omitted.) [21]

20. The expert testimony at the hearings in the District Court uniformly was to the effect that parental involvement in a minor's abortion decision, if compassionate and supportive, was highly desirable. The findings of the court reflect this consensus. See *Baird I*, 393 F.Supp., at 853.

21. Mr. Justice Stewart's concurring opinion in *Danforth* underscored the need for parental involvement in minors' abortion decisions by describing the procedures followed at the clinic operated by the Parents Aid Society and Dr. Gerald Zupnick:

"The counseling * * * occurs entirely on the day the abortion is to be performed * * *. It lasts for two hours and takes place in groups that include both minors and adults who are strangers to one another * * *. The physician takes no part in this counseling process * * *. Counseling is typically limited to a description of abortion procedures, possible complications, and birth control techniques * * *.

"The abortion itself takes five to seven minutes * * *. The physician has no prior contact with the minor, and on the days that abortions are being performed at the [clinic], the physician, * * *

may be performing abortions on many other adults and minors * * *. On busy days patients are scheduled in separate groups, consisting usually of five patients * * *. After the abortion [the physician] spends a brief period with the minor and others in the group in the recovery room * * *." 428 U.S., at 91–92, n. 2, 96 S.Ct., at 2851 n. 2, quoting Brief for Appellants in *Bellotti I*, supra.

In Roe v. Wade, 410 U.S. 113, 93 S.Ct. 705, 35 L.Ed.2d 147 (1973), and Doe v. Bolton, id., 410 U.S. at 179, 93 S. Ct., at 739, we emphasized the importance of the role of the attending physician. Those cases involved adult women presumably capable of selecting and obtaining a competent physician. In this case, however, we are concerned only with minors who, according to the record, may range in age from children of 12 years to 17-year-old teenagers. Even the latter are less likely than adults to know or be able to recognize ethical, qualified physicians, or to have the means to engage such professionals. Many minors who bypass their parents probably will resort to an abortion clinic, without being able to distinguish the competent and ethical from those that are incompetent or unethical.

But we are concerned here with a constitutional right to seek an abortion. The abortion decision differs in important ways from other decisions that may be made during minority. The need to preserve the constitutional right and the unique nature of the abortion decision, especially when made by a minor, require a State to act with particular sensitivity when it legislates to foster parental involvement in this matter.

A

The pregnant minor's options are much different from those facing a minor in other situations, such as deciding whether to marry. A minor not permitted to marry before the age of majority is required simply to postpone her decision. She and her intended spouse may preserve the opportunity for later marriage should they continue to desire it. A pregnant adolescent, however, cannot preserve for long the possibility of aborting, which effectively expires in a matter of weeks from the onset of pregnancy.

Moreover, the potentially severe detriment facing a pregnant woman, see Roe v. Wade, 410 U.S., at 153, 93 S.Ct., at 726, is not mitigated by her minority. Indeed, considering her probable education, employment skills, financial resources, and emotional maturity, unwanted motherhood may be exceptionally burdensome for a minor. In addition, the fact of having a child brings with it adult legal responsibility, for parenthood, like attainment of the age of majority, is one of the traditional criteria for the termination of the legal disabilities of minority. In sum, there are few situations in which denying a minor the right to make an important decision will have consequences so grave and indelible.

Yet, an abortion may not be the best choice for the minor. The circumstances in which this issue arises will vary widely. In a given case, alternatives to abortion, such as marriage to the father of the child, arranging for its adoption, or assuming the responsibilities of motherhood with the assured support of family, may be feasible and relevant to the minor's best interests. Nonetheless, the abortion decision is one that simply cannot be postponed, or it will be made by default with far-reaching consequences.

For these reasons, as we held in Planned Parenthood v. Danforth, supra, at 74, 96 S.Ct., at 2843, "the State may not impose a blanket provision * * * requiring the consent of a parent or person *in loco parentis* as a condition for abortion of an unmarried minor during the first 12 weeks of her pregnancy." Although, as stated in Part II, supra, such deference to parents may be permissible with respect to other choices facing a minor, the unique nature and consequences of the abortion decision make it inappropriate "to give a third party an absolute, and possibly arbitrary, veto over the decision of the physician and his patient to terminate the patient's pregnancy, regardless of the reason for withholding consent." Ibid. We therefore conclude that if the State decides to require a pregnant minor to obtain one or both parents' consent to an abortion, it also must provide an alternative procedure [22] whereby authorization for the abortion can be obtained.

A pregnant minor is entitled in such a proceeding to show either: (1) that she is mature enough and well enough informed to make her abortion decision, in consultation with her physician, independently of her parents' wishes; [23] or (2) that even if she is not able to make this decision independently, the desired abortion would be in her best interests. The proceeding in which this showing is made must assure that a resolution of the issue, and any appeals that may follow, will be completed with anonymity and sufficient expedition to provide an effective opportunity for an abortion to be obtained. In sum, the procedure must ensure that the provision requiring parental consent does not in fact amount to the "absolute, and possibly arbitrary, veto" that was found impermissible in *Danforth*. Ibid.

B

It is against these requirements that § 12S must be tested. We observe initially that as authoritatively construed by the highest court of the State, the statute satisfies some of the concerns that require special treatment of a minor's abortion decision. It provides that if parental consent is refused, authorization may be "obtained by order of a judge of the superior court for good cause shown, after such hearing as he deems necessary." A superior court judge presiding over a § 12S proceeding "must disregard all parental objections, and other considerations, which are not based exclusively on what would serve the minor's best interests." [24] *Attorney General*, 371

---

22. As § 12S provides for involvement of the state superior court in minors' abortion decisions, we discuss the alternative procedure described in the text in terms of judicial proceedings. We do not suggest, however, that a State choosing to require parental consent could not delegate the alternative procedure to a juvenile court or an administrative agency or officer. Indeed, much can be said for employing procedures and a forum less formal than those associated with a court of general jurisdiction.

23. The nature of both the State's interest in fostering parental authority and the problem of determining "maturity" makes clear why the State generally may resort to objective, though inevitably arbitrary, criteria such as age limits, marital status, or membership in the armed forces for lifting some or all of the legal disabilities of minority. Not only is it difficult to define, let alone determine, maturity, but the fact that a minor may be very much an adult in some respects does not mean that his need and opportunity for growth under parental guidance and discipline have ended.

As discussed in the text, however, the peculiar nature of the abortion decision requires the opportunity for case-by-case evaluations of the maturity of pregnant minors.

24. The Supreme Judicial Court held that § 12S imposed this standard on the Superior Court in large part because it construed the statute as containing the same restriction on parents. See pp. 6–7, supra. The court concluded that the judge should not be entitled "to exercise his authority on a standard broader than that to which a parent must adhere." *Attor-*

Mass., at ——, 360 N.E.2d, at 293. The Supreme Judicial Court also stated that "[p]rompt resolution of a [§ 12S] proceedings may be expected * * *. The proceeding need not be brought in the minor's name and steps may be taken, by impoundment or otherwise, to preserve confidentiality as to the minor and her parents. * * * [W]e believe that an early hearing and decision on appeal from a judgment of a Superior Court judge may also be achieved." Id., at ——, 360 N.E.2d, at 298. The court added that if these expectations were not met, either the Superior Court, in the exercise of its rule-making power, or the Supreme Judicial Court would be willing to eliminate any undue burdens by rule or order. Ibid.[25]

Despite these safeguards, which avoid much of what was objectionable in the statute successfully challenged in *Danforth*, § 12S falls short of constitutional standards in certain respects. We now consider these.

(1)

Among the questions certified to the Supreme Judicial Court was whether § 12S permits any minors—mature or immature—to obtain judicial consent to an abortion without any parental consultation whatsoever. See n. 9, supra. The state court answered that, in general, they may not. "[T]he consent required by [§ 12S must] be obtained for every nonemergency abortion where the mother is less than eighteen years of age and unmarried." *Attorney General,* supra, at ——, 360 N.E.2d, at 294. The text of § 12S itself states an exception to this rule, making consent unnecessary from any parent

---

ney General, supra, at ——, 360 N.E.2d, at 293.

Intervenors argue that, assuming state-supported parental involvement in the minor's abortion decision is permissible, the State may not endorse the withholding of parental consent for any reason not believed to be in the minor's best interests. They agree with the District Court that, even though § 12S was construed by the highest state court to impose this restriction, the statute is flawed because the restriction is not apparent on its face. Intervenors thus concur in the District Court's assumption that the statute will encourage parents to withhold consent for impermissible reasons. See *Baird III,* 450 F.Supp., at 1004–1005; *Baird II,* 428 F.Supp., at 855–856.

There is no basis for this assertion. As a general rule, the interpretation of a state statute by the State's highest

court "is as though written into the ordinance itself," *Poulos v. New Hampshire,* 345 U.S. 395, 402, 73 S. Ct. 760, 765, 97 L.Ed. 1105 (1953), and we are obliged to view the restriction on the parental consent requirement "as if [§ 12S] had been so amended by the [Massachusetts] legislature." *Winters v. New York,* 333 U.S. 507, 514, 68 S.Ct. 665, 669, 92 L. Ed. 840 (1948).

25. Intervenors take issue with the Supreme Judicial Court's assurances that judicial proceedings will provide the necessary confidentiality, lack of procedural burden, and speed of resolution. In the absence of any evidence as to the operation of judicial proceedings under § 12S—and there is none, since appellees successfully sought to enjoin Massachusetts from putting it into effect—we must assume that the Supreme Judicial Court's judgment is correct.

who has "died or has deserted his or her family." [26] The Supreme Judicial Court construed the statute as containing an additional exception: Consent need not be obtained "where no parent (or statutory substitute) is available." Ibid. The court also ruled that an available parent must be given notice of any judicial proceedings brought by a minor to obtain consent for an abortion.[27] Id., at ——, 360 N.E. 2d, at 297.

We think that, construed in this manner, § 12S would impose an undue burden upon the exercise by minors of the right to seek an abortion. As the District Court recognized, "there are parents who would obstruct, and perhaps altogether prevent, the minor's right to go to court." *Baird III,* supra, at 1001. There is no reason to believe that this would be so in the majority of cases where consent is withheld. But many parents hold strong views on the subject of abortion, and young pregnant minors, especially those living at home, are particularly vulnerable to their parents' efforts to obstruct both an abortion and their access to court. It would be unrealistic, therefore, to assume that the mere existence of a legal right to seek relief in superior court provides an effective avenue of relief for some of those who need it the most.

We conclude, therefore, that under state regulation such as that undertaken by Massachusetts, every minor must have the opportunity —if she so desires—to go directly to a court without first consulting

---

26. The statute also provides that "[i]f both parents have died, or have deserted their family, consent of the mother's guardian or other person having duties similar to a guardian, or any person who has assumed the care and custody of mother is sufficient."

27. This reading of the statute requires parental consultation and consent more strictly than appellants themselves previously believed was necessary. In their first argument before this Court, and again before the Supreme Judicial Court, appellants argued that § 12S was not intended to abrogate Massachusetts' common-law "mature minor" rule as it applies to abortions. See 428 U.S., at 144, 96 S.Ct., at 2864. They also suggested that, under some circumstances, § 12S might permit even immature minors to obtain judicial approval for an abortion without any parental consultation. See 428 U.S., at 145, 96 S.Ct., at 2865; *Attorney General,* supra, 371 Mass. at ——, 360 N.E.2d, at 294. The Supreme Judicial Court sketched the outlines of the mature minor rule that would apply in the absence of § 12S: "The mature

minor rule calls for an analysis of the nature of the operation, its likely benefit, and the capacity of the particular minor to understand fully what the medical procedure involves. . . . Judicial intervention is not required. If judicial approval is obtained, however, the doctor is protected from a subsequent claim that the circumstances did not warrant his reliance on the mature minor rule, and, of course, the minor is afforded advance protection against a misapplication of the rule." *Attorney General,* supra, at ——, 360 N.E.2d, at 295. "We conclude that, apart from statutory limitations which are constitutional, where the best interests of a minor will be served by not notifying his or her parents of intended medical treatment and where the minor is capable of giving informed consent to that treatment, the mature minor rule applies in this Commonwealth." Id., at ——, 360 N.E.2d, at 296. The Supreme Judicial Court held that the common-law mature minor rule was inapplicable to abortions because it had been legislatively superseded by § 12S.

or notifying her parents. If she satisfies the court that she is mature and well-informed enough to make intelligently the abortion decision on her own, the court must authorize her to act without parental consultation or consent. If she fails to satisfy the court that she is competent to make this decision independently, she must be permitted to show that an abortion nevertheless would be in her best interest. If the court is persuaded that it is, the court must authorize the abortion. If, however, the court is not persuaded by the minor that she is mature or that the abortion would be in her best interest, it may decline to sanction the operation.

There is, however, an important state interest in encouraging a family rather than a judicial resolution of a minor's abortion decision. Also, as we have observed above, parents naturally take an interest in the welfare of their children—an interest that is particularly strong where a normal family relationship exists and where the child is living with one or both parents. These factors properly may be taken into account by a court called upon to determine whether an abortion in fact is in a minor's best interests. If, all things considered, the court determines that an abortion is in the minor's best interests, she is entitled to court authorization without any parental involvement. On the other hand, the court may deny the abortion request of an immature minor in the absence of parental consultation if it concludes that her best interests would be served thereby, or the court may in such a case defer decision until there is parental consultation in which the court may participate. But this is the full extent to which parental involvement may be required.[28] For the reasons stated above, the constitutional right to seek an abortion may not be unduly burdened by state-imposed conditions upon initial access to court.

(2)

Section 12S requires that both parents consent to a minor's abortion. The District Court found it to be "custom" to perform other medical and surgical procedures on minors with the consent of only one parent, and it concluded that "nothing about abortions * * * requires the minor's interest to be treated differently." *Baird I,* supra, at 852. See *Baird III,* supra, at 1004 n. 9.

We are not persuaded that, as a general rule, the requirement of obtaining both parents' consent unconstitutionally burdens a minor's right to seek an abortion. The abortion decision has implications far broader than those associated with most other kinds of medical treatment. At least when the parents are together and the pregnant minor is living at home, both the father and mother have an interest— one normally supportive—in helping to determine the course that is

---

28. Of course, if the minor consults with her parents voluntarily and they withhold consent, she is free to seek judicial authorization for the abortion immediately.

in the best interest of a daughter. Consent and involvement by parents in important decisions by minors long have been recognized as protective of their immaturity. In the case of the abortion decision, for reasons we have stated, the focus of the parents' inquiry should be the best interests of their daughter. As every pregnant minor is entitled in the first instance to go directly to the court for a judicial determination without prior parental notice, consultation or consent, the general rule with respect to parental consent does not unduly burden the constitutional right. Moreover, where the pregnant minor goes to her parents and consent is denied, she still must have recourse to a prompt judicial determination of her maturity or best interests.[29]

(3)

Another of the questions certified by the District Court to the Supreme Judicial Court was the following: "If the superior court finds that the minor is capable [of making], and has, in fact, made and adhered to, an informed and reasonable decision to have an abortion, may the court refuse its consent on a finding that a parent's, or its own, contrary decision is a better one?" *Attorney General,* supra, 371 Mass., at ——, at 293 n. 5. To this the state court answered:

"[W]e do not view the judge's role as limited to a determination that the minor is capable of making, and has made, an informed and reasonable decision to have an abortion. Certainly the judge must make a determination of those circumstances, but, if the statutory role of the judge to determine the best interests of the minor is to be carried out, he must make a finding on the basis of all relevant views presented to him. We suspect that the judge will give great weight to the minor's determination, if informed and reasonable, but in circumstances where he determines that the best interests of the minor will not be served by an abortion, the judge's determination should prevail, assuming that his conclusion is supported by the evidence and adequate findings of fact." Id., at ——, 360 N.E.2d, at 293.

The Supreme Judicial Court's statement reflects the general rule that a State may require a minor to wait until the age of majority before being permitted to exercise legal rights independently. See n. 23, supra. But we are concerned here with the exercise of a constitutional right of unique character. See pp. 18–20, supra. As stated above, if the minor satisfies a court that she has attained sufficient maturity to make a fully informed decision, she then is entitled to make her abortion decision independently. We therefore agree with the District Court that § 12S cannot constitutionally permit judicial disregard of the abortion decision of a minor who has been deter-

---

29. There will be cases where the pregnant minor has received approval of the abortion decision by one parent. In that event, the parent can support the daughter's request for a prompt judicial determination, and the parent's support should be given great, if not dispositive, weight.

mined to be mature and fully competent to assess the implications of the choice she has made.

IV

Although it satisfies constitutional standards in large part, § 12S falls short of them in two respects: First, it permits judicial authorization for an abortion to be withheld from a minor who is found by the superior court to be mature and fully competent to make this decision independently. Second, it requires parental consultation or notification in every instance, without affording the pregnant minor an opportunity to receive an independent judicial determination that she is mature enough to consent or that an abortion would be in her best interests.[31]   Accordingly, we affirm the judgment of the District Court insofar as it invalidates this statute and enjoins its enforcement.[32]

Affirmed.

31. Section 12S evidently applies to all nonemergency abortions performed on minors, without regard to the period in pregnancy during which the procedure occurs. As the court below recognized, most abortions are performed during the early stages of pregnancy, before the end of the first trimester. See *Baird III,* supra, at 1001; see *Baird I,* supra at 853. This coincides approximately with the previability period during which a pregnant woman's right to decide, in consultation with her physician, to have an abortion is most immune to state intervention. See Roe v. Wade, 410 U.S. 113, 164–165, 93 S.Ct. 705, 732, 35 L.Ed.2d 147 (1973).

The propriety of parental involvement in a minor's abortion decision does not diminish as the pregnancy progresses and legitimate concerns for the pregnant minor's health increase. Furthermore, the opportunity for direct access to court which we have described is adequate to safeguard throughout pregnancy the constitutionally protected interests of a minor in the abortion decision. Thus, although a significant number of abortions within the scope of § 12S might be performed during the later stages of pregnancy, we do not believe a different analysis of the statute is required for them.

32. The opinion of Mr. Justice Stevens, concurring in the judgment, joined by three Members of the Court, characterizes this opinion as

"advisory" and the questions it addresses as "hypothetical." Apparently this is criticism of our attempt to provide some guidance as to how a State constitutionally may provide for adult involvement—either by parents or a state official such as a judge—in the abortion decisions of minors. In view of the importance of the issue raised, and the protracted litigation to which these parties already have been subjected, we think it would be irresponsible simply to invalidate § 12S without stating our views as to the controlling principles.

The statute before us today is the same one that was here in *Bellotti I,* supra. The issues it presents were not then deemed "hypothetical." In a unanimous opinion, we remanded the case with directions that appropriate questions be certified to the Supreme Judicial Court of Massachusetts "concerning the meaning of [§ 12S] and the procedure it imposes." Id., 428 U.S., at 151, 96 S.Ct., at 2868. We directed that this be done because, as stated in the opinion, we thought the construction of § 12S urged by appellants would "avoid or substantially modify the federal constitutional challenge to the statute." Id., at 148, 96 S.Ct., at 2866. The central feature of § 12S was its provision that a state court judge could make the ultimate decision, when necessary, as to the exercise by a minor of the right to an abortion. See id., at 145, 96 S. Ct., at 2865. We held that this

Mr. Justice STEVENS, with whom Mr. Justice BRENNAN, Mr. Justice MARSHALL, and Mr. Justice BLACKMUN join, concurring in the judgment.

In Roe v. Wade, 410 U.S. 113, 93 S.Ct. 705, 35 L.Ed.2d 147, the Court held that a woman's right to decide whether to terminate a pregnancy is entitled to constitutional protection. In Planned Parenthood of Missouri v. Danforth, 428 U.S. 52, 72–75, 96 S.Ct. 2831, 2842–2843, 49 L.Ed.2d 788, the Court held that a pregnant minor's right to make the abortion decision may not be conditioned on the consent of one parent. I am persuaded that these decisions require affirmance of the District Court's holding that the Massachusetts statute is unconstitutional.

The Massachusetts statute is, on its face, simple and straightforward. It provides that every woman under 18 who has not married must secure the consent of both her parents before receiving an abortion. "If one or both of the mother's parents refuse such consent, consent may be obtained by order of a judge of the superior court for good cause shown." Mass.Gen.Laws Ann., ch. 112, § 12S (West).

Whatever confusion or uncertainty might have existed as to how this statute was to operate, see Bellotti v. Baird, 428 U.S. 132, 96 S. Ct. 2857, 49 L.Ed.2d 844, has been eliminated by the authoritative construction of its provisions by the Massachusetts Supreme Judicial Court. See Baird v. Attorney General, 371 Mass. 741, 360 N.E.2d 288 (1977). The statute was construed to require that every minor who wishes an abortion must first seek the consent of both parents, unless a parent is not available or unless the need for the abortion constitutes "an emergency requiring immediate action." Id., at ——, 360 N.E.2d, at 294. Both parents, so long as they are available, must also receive notice of judicial proceedings brought under the statute by the minor. In those proceedings, the task of the judge is to determine whether the best interests of the minor will be served by an abortion. The decision is his to make, even if he finds "that the minor is capable of making, and has made, an informed and reasonable decision to have an abortion." Id., at ——, 360 N.E.2d, at 293. Thus, no minor in Massachusetts, no matter how mature and capable of informed decisionmaking, may receive an abortion without the consent of either both her parents or a Superior Court Judge. In every instance, the minor's decision to secure an abortion is subject to an absolute third-party veto.[1]

"would be fundamentally different from a statute that creates a 'parental veto' [of the kind rejected in Danforth.]" Ibid. (footnote omitted). Thus, all Members of the Court agreed that providing for decisionmaking authority in a judge was not the kind of veto power held invalid in Danforth. The basic issues that were before us in Bellotti I remain in the case, sharpened by the construction of § 12S by the Supreme Judicial Court.

1. By affording such a veto, the Massachusetts statute does far more than simply provide for notice to the parents. See post, at 2 (White, J.,

In Planned Parenthood of Missouri v. Danforth, supra, this Court invalidated statutory provisions requiring the consent of the husband of a married woman and of one parent of a pregnant minor to an abortion. As to the spousal consent, the Court concluded that "we cannot hold that the State has the constitutional authority to give the spouse unilaterally the ability to prohibit the wife from terminating her pregnancy, when the State itself lacks that right." 428 U.S., at 70, 96 S.Ct. at 2841. And as to the parental consent, the Court held that "[j]ust as with the requirement of consent from the spouse, so here, the State does not have the constitutional authority to give a third party an absolute, and possibly arbitrary, veto over the decision of the physician and his patient to terminate the patient's pregnancy, regardless of the reason for withholding the consent." Id., at 74, 96 S.Ct., at 2843. These holdings, I think, equally apply to the Massachusetts statute. The differences between the two statutes are few. Unlike the Missouri statute, Massachusetts requires the consent of both of the woman's parents. It does, of course, provide an alternative in the form of a suit initiated by the woman in Superior Court. But in that proceeding, the judge is afforded an absolute veto over the minor's decisions, based on his judgment of her best interests. In Massachusetts, then, as in Missouri, the State has imposed an "absolute limitation on the minor's right to obtain an abortion," id., at 90, 96 S.Ct., at 2851 (Stewart, J., concurring), applicable to every pregnant minor in the State who has not married.

The provision of an absolute veto to a judge—or, potentially, to an appointed administrator [2]—is to me particularly troubling. The constitutional right to make the abortion decision affords protection to both of the privacy interests recognized in this Court's cases: "One is the individual's interest in avoiding disclosure of personal matters, and another is the interest in independence in making certain kinds of important decisions." Whalen v. Roe, 429 U.S. 589, 599–600, 97 S.Ct. 869, 876, 51 L.Ed.2d 64. It is inherent in the right to make the abortion decision that the right may be exercised without public scrutiny and in defiance of the contrary opinion of the sovereign or other third parties. In Massachusetts, however, every minor who cannot secure the consent of both her parents—which under Danforth cannot be an absolute prerequisite to an abortion—is required to secure the consent of the sovereign. As a practical matter, I would suppose that the need to commence judicial proceedings in order to obtain a legal abortion would impose a burden at least as great as, and probably greater than, that imposed on the minor child by the need to obtain the consent of a parent.[3] Moreover, once this

dissenting). Neither *Danforth* nor this case determines the constitutionality of a statute which does no more than require notice to the parents, without affording them or any other third party an absolute veto.

2. See ante, at 20, n. 22.

3. A minor may secure the assistance of counsel in filing and prosecuting her suit, but that is not guaranteed. The Massachusetts Supreme Judicial

burden is met, the only standard provided for the judge's decision is the best interest of the minor. That standard provides little real guidance to the judge, and his decision must necessarily reflect personal and societal values and mores whose enforcement upon the minor—particularly when contrary to her own informed and reasonable decision—is fundamentally at odds with privacy interests underlying the constitutional protection afforded to her decision.

In short, it seems to me that this case is governed by *Danforth;* to the extent this statute differs from that in *Danforth,* it is potentially even more restrictive of the constitutional right to decide whether or not to terminate a pregnancy. Because the statute has been once authoritatively construed by the Massachusetts Supreme Judicial Court, and because it is clear that the statute as written and construed is not constitutional, I agree with Mr. Justice POWELL that the District Court's judgment should be affirmed. Because his opinion goes further, however, and addresses the constitutionality of an abortion statute that Massachusetts has not enacted, I decline to join his opinion.[4]

NOTES AND QUESTIONS

(1) Justice Rehnquist wrote a short paragraph indicating his concurrence with the opinion of the Court. Justice White dissented on the ground that the Massachusetts statute requiring either parental consent or the approval of a court for the abortion of a minor was constitutional.

(2) Is the Court's opinion an advisory one, as Justice Stevens argues? Is the Court therefore violating the constitutional principles governing its own powers by deciding matters which are not "cases or controversies" under Article III of the Constitution? See Muskrat v. United States, 219 U. S. 346 (1911); Poe v. Ullman, 367 U.S. 497 (1961).

(3) Could you draft a statute which would be constitutional in view of the Court's opinion in *Bellotti*? What would it provide?

Court in response to the question whether a minor, upon a showing of indigency, may have court-appointed counsel, "construe[d] the statute of the Commonwealth to authorize the appointment of counsel or a guardian ad litem for an indigent minor at public expense, if necessary, if the judge, *in his discretion,* concludes that the best interests of the minor would be served by such an appointment." Baird v. Attorney General, supra, 371 Mass, at ——, 360 N.E.2d, at 301 (emphasis added).

4. Until and unless Massachusetts or another State enacts a less restrictive statutory scheme, this Court has no occasion to render an advisory opinion on the constitutionality of such a scheme. A real statute—rather than a mere outline of a possible statute

—and a real case or controversy may well present questions that appear quite different from the hypothetical questions Mr. Justice Powell has elected to address. Indeed, there is a certain irony in his suggestion that a statute that is intended to vindicate "the special interests of the State in encouraging an unmarried pregnant minor to seek the advice of her parents in making the important decision whether or not to bear a child," see ante, at 16, need not require notice to the parents of the minor's intended decision. That irony makes me wonder whether any legislature concerned with parental consultation would, in the absence of today's advisory opinion, have enacted a statute comparable to the one my Brethren have discussed.

(4) How would your statute operate in the following situations:

(a) S, a high school girl of fourteen, becomes pregnant as a result of having sexual relations with a boy of sixteen at a party. She tells her parents that she wants an abortion, but they are strongly opposed to abortion on religious or eithical grounds. They will neither consent to an abortion nor pay for one. They are willing, however, to pay her medical and hospital expenses if she has the child, and to make arrangements for placing the baby for adoption. S has heard that a first trimester abortion is safer than childbirth and continues to want an abortion in spite of her parents' opposition.

(b) J, a girl of sixteen, has parents who wish to see her develop her undoubted musical gifts and therefore attempt to enforce quite strict discipline by requiring frequent music lessons, practice periods and by restricting social activities. In order to avoid these restrictions, J begins secretly seeing and sleeping with a man of twenty-two, as a result of which she becomes pregnant. When her parents learn of this, they urge her to have an abortion, offering to pay for it and to make all arrangements. She refuses, saying she wishes to marry the father. Her parents refuse to consent to the marriage, thinking (not without some reason) that this man is irresponsible, immature and a very poor prospect as a husband for their daughter. They also think that marriage so early would be likely to end J's chances of becoming an accomplished musician. Does your statute have anything to say about this sort of conflict? Should it? Cf. In re Smith, 16 Md.App. 209, 295 A.2d 238 (1972).

5. In paragraph 7, supra, page 250, Professor Cox is quoted as stating that Roe v. Wade does not rise above the level of a political judgment. Would the same criticism apply to Bellotti v. Baird? If so, could you write an opinion in the case which would not be open to this criticism?

6. Is the following statute constitutional, in view of Bellotti v. Baird?

"§ 1.   A physician, prior to performing an abortion upon an unemancipated minor under the age of 17, must give actual notice to her parents or guardians no less than 24 hours before performing the abortion. If actual notice cannot be given, the physician must send written notice by certified mail to the parent or guardian's last known address at least 48 hours before performing the abortion. If neither form of notice is possible, the physician must give written notice to the Sears Department of Social Services no less than 24 hours before performing the abortion. If in the physician's judgment the life or health of the minor will be endangered if there is delay, the notice requirements shall not apply, but the physician must then notify the parents or guardians within 24 hours after the abortion is performed, or notify the Department of his inability to give such notice.

"§ 2.   Violation of § 1 hereof shall be a misdemeanor."

MAHER, COMMISSIONER OF SOCIAL SERVICES OF CONNECTICUT v. ROE

Supreme Court of the United States, 1977.
432 U.S. 464, 97 S.Ct. 2376, 53 L.Ed.2d 484.

Mr. Justice POWELL delivered the opinion of the Court.

In Beal v. Doe, ante, p. 438, we hold today that Title XIX of the Social Security Act does not require the funding of nontherapeutic abortions as a condition of participation in the joint federal-state Medicaid program established by that statute. In this case, as a result of our decision in Beal, we must decide whether the Constitution requires a participating State to pay for nontherapeutic abortions when it pays for childbirth.

I

A regulation of the Connecticut Welfare Department limits state Medicaid benefits for first trimester abortions to those that are "medically necessary," a term defined to include psychiatric necessity. Connecticut Welfare Department Public Assistance Program Manual, Vol. 3, c. III, § 275 (1975). Connecticut enforces this limitation through a system of prior authorization from its Department of Social Services. In order to obtain authorization for a first trimester abortion, the hospital or clinic where the abortion is to be performed must submit, among other things, a certificate from the patient's attending physician stating that the abortion is medically necessary.

This attack on the validity of the Connecticut regulation was brought against appellant Maher, the Commissioner of Social Services, by appellees Poe and Roe, two indigent women who were unable to obtain a physician's certificate of medical necessity.[3] In a complaint filed in the United States District Court for the District of Connecticut, they challenged the regulation both as inconsistent with the requirements of Title XIX of the Social Security Act, 79 Stat. 343, as amended, 42 U.S.C.A. § 1396 et seq. (1970 ed. and Supp. V), and as violative of their constitutional rights, including the Fourteenth Amendment's guarantees of due process and equal protection.
* * *

---

3. At the time this action was filed, Mary Poe, a 16-year-old high school junior, had already obtained an abortion at a Connecticut hospital. Apparently because of Poe's inability to obtain a certificate of medical necessity, the hospital was denied reimbursement by the Department of Social Services. As a result, Poe was being pressed to pay the hospital bill of $244. Susan Roe, an unwed mother of three children, was unable to obtain an abortion because of her physician's refusal to certify that the procedure was medically necessary. By consent, a temporary restraining order was entered by the District Court enjoining the Connecticut officials from refusing to pay for Roe's abortion. After the remand from the Court of Appeals, the District Court issued temporary restraining orders covering three additional women. Roe v. Norton, 408 F.Supp. 660, 663 (D.C.Conn.1975).

The District Court enjoined the State from requiring the certificate of medical necessity for Medicaid-funded abortions. The court also struck down the related requirements of prior written request by the pregnant woman and prior authorization by the Department of Social Services, holding that the State could not impose any requirments on Medicaid payments for abortions that are not "equally applicable to medicaid payments for childbirth, if such conditions or requirements tend to discourage a woman from choosing an abortion or to delay the occurrence of an abortion that she has asked her physician to perform." Id., at 665. We noted probable jurisdiction to consider the constitutionality of the Connecticut regulation. 428 U.S. 908, 96 S.Ct. 3219, 49 L.Ed.2d 1216 (1976).

II

The Constitution imposes no obligation on the States to pay the pregnancy-related medical expenses of indigent women, or indeed to pay any of the medical expenses of indigents.[5] But when a State decides to alleviate some of the hardships of poverty by providing medical care, the manner in which it dispenses benefits is subject to constitutional limitations. Appellees' claim is that Connecticut must accord equal treatment to both abortion and childbirth, and may not evidence a policy preference by funding only the medical expenses incident to childbirth. This challenge to the classifications established by the Connecticut regulation presents a question arising under the Equal Protection Clause of the Fourteenth Amendment. The basic framework of analysis of such a claim is well settled:

"We must decide, first, whether [state legislation] operates to the disadvantage of some suspect class or impinges upon a fundamental right explicitly or implicitly protected by the Constitution, thereby requiring strict judicial scrutiny. * * * If not, the [legislative] scheme must still be examined to determine whether it rationally furthers some legitimate, articulated state purpose and therefore does not constitute an invidious discrimination * * *." San An-

---

5. Boddie v. Connecticut, 401 U.S. 371, 91 S.Ct. 780, 28 L.Ed.2d 113 (1971), cited by appellees, is not to the contrary. There the Court invalidated under the Due Process Clause "certain state procedures for the commencement of litigation, including requirements for payment of court fees and costs for service of process," restricting the ability of indigent persons to bring an action for divorce. Id., at 372, 91 S.Ct., at 783. The Court held:

"[G]iven the basic position of the marriage relationship in this society's hierarchy of values and the concomitant state monopolization of the means for legally dissolving this relationship, due process does prohibit a State from denying, solely because of inability to pay, access to its courts to individuals who seek judicial dissolution of their marriages." Id., at 374, 91 S. Ct., at 784. Because Connecticut has made no attempt to monpolize the means for terminating pregnancies through abortion the present case is easily distinguished from Boddie. See also United States v. Kras, 409 U.S. 434, 93 S.Ct. 631, 34 L.Ed.2d 626 (1973); Ortwein v. Schwab, 410 U.S. 656, 93 S.Ct. 1172, 35 L.Ed.2d 572 (1973).

tonio School Dist. v. Rodriguez, 411 U.S. 1, 17, 93 S.Ct. 1278, 1288, 36 L.Ed.2d 16 (1973).

Applying this analysis here, we think the District Court erred in holding that the Connecticut regulation violated the Equal Protection Clause of the Fourteenth Amendment.

A

This case involves no discrimination against a suspect class. An indigent woman desiring an abortion does not come within the limited category of disadvantaged classes so recognized by our cases. Nor does the fact that the impact of the regulation falls upon those who cannot pay lead to a different conclusion. In a sense, every denial of welfare to an indigent creates a wealth classification as compared to nonindigents who are able to pay for the desired goods or services. But this Court has never held that financial need alone identifies a suspect class for purposes of equal protection analysis. Accordingly, the central question in this case is whether the regulation "impinges upon a fundamental right explicitly or implicitly protected by the Constitution." The District Court read our decisions in Roe v. Wade, 410 U.S. 113, 93 S.Ct. 705, 35 L.Ed.2d 147 (1973), and the subsequent cases applying it, as establishing a fundamental right to abortion and therefore concluded that nothing less than a compelling state interest would justify Connecticut's different treatment of abortion and childbirth. We think the District Court misconceived the nature and scope of the fundamental right recognized in *Roe*.

B

At issue in *Roe* was the constitutionality of a Texas law making it a crime to procure or attempt to procure an abortion, except on medical advice for the purpose of saving the life of the mother.   * * *

The Texas statute imposed severe criminal sanctions on the physicians and other medical personnel who performed abortions, thus drastically limiting the availability and safety of the desired service. As Mr. Justice STEWART observed, "it is difficult to imagine a more complete abridgment of a constitutional freedom   * * *." Id., at 170, 93 S.Ct., at 735 (concurring opinion). We held that only a compelling state interest would justify such a sweeping restriction on a constitutionally protected interest, and we found no such state interest during the first trimester. Even when judged against this demanding standard, however, the State's dual interest in the health of the pregnant woman and the potential life of the fetus were deemed sufficient to justify substantial regulation of abortions in the second and third trimesters.   * * *   In the second trimester, the State's interest in the health of the pregnant woman justifies state regulation reasonably related to that concern. At viability, usually in the third trimester, the State's interest in the potential life of the fetus justifies prohibition with criminal penalties, except where the life or health of the mother is threatened.

The Texas law in *Roe* was a stark example of impermissible interference with the pregnant woman's decision to terminate her pregnancy. In subsequent cases, we have invalidated other types of restrictions, different in form but similar in effect, on the woman's freedom of choice. * * * Although a state-created obstacle need not be absolute to be impermissible, see Doe v. Bolton, 410 U.S. 179, 93 S.Ct. 739, 35 L.Ed.2d 201 (1973), Carey v. Population Services International, 431 U.S. 678, 97 S.Ct. 2010, 52 L.Ed.2d 675 (1977), we have held that a requirement for a lawful abortion "is not unconstitutional unless it unduly burdens the right to seek an abortion." Bellotti v. Baird, 428 U.S. 132, 147, 96 S.Ct. 2857, 2866, 49 L.Ed.2d 844 (1976). * * *

These cases recognize a constitutionally protected interest "in making certain kinds of important decisions" free from governmental compulsion. Whalen v. Roe, 429 U.S. 589, 599–600, 97 S.Ct. 869, 876, 51 L.Ed.2d 64, and nn. 24 and 26 (1977). As *Whalen* makes clear, the right in Roe v. Wade can be understood only by considering both the woman's interest and the nature of the State's interference with it. *Roe* did not declare an unqualified "constitutional right to an abortion," as the District Court seemed to think. Rather, the right protects the woman from unduly burdensome interference with her freedom to decide whether to terminate her pregnancy. It implies no limitation on the authority of a State to make a value judgment favoring childbirth over abortion, and to implement that judgment by the allocation of public funds.

The Connecticut regulation before us is different in kind from the laws invalidated in our previous abortion decisions. The Connecticut regulation places no obstacles—absolute or otherwise—in the pregnant woman's path to an abortion. An indigent woman who desires an abortion suffers no disadvantage as a consequence of Connecticut's decision to fund childbirth; she continues as before to be dependent on private sources for the service she desires. The State may have made childbirth a more attractive alternative, thereby influencing the woman's decision, but it has imposed no restriction on access to abortions that was not already there. The indigency that may make it difficult—and in some cases, perhaps, impossible—for some women to have abortions is neither created nor in any way affected by the Connecticut regulation. We conclude that the Connecticut regulation does not impinge upon the fundamental right recognized in *Roe*.[8]

8. Appellees rely on Shapiro v. Thompson, 394 U.S. 618, 89 S.Ct. 1322, 22 L.Ed.2d 600 (1969), and Memorial Hospital v. Maricopa County, 415 U.S. 250, 94 S.Ct. 1076, 39 L.Ed. 2d 306 (1974). In those cases durational residence requirements for the receipt of public benefits were found to be unconstitutional because they "penalized" the exercise of the constitutional right to travel interstate.

C

Our conclusion signals no retreat from *Roe* or the cases applying it. There is a basic difference between direct state interference with a protected activity and state encouragement of an alternative activity consonant with legislative policy. Constitutional concerns are greatest when the State attempts to impose its will by force of law; the State's power to encourage actions deemed to be in the public interest is necessarily far broader.

* * *

[At this point in its opinion the Court stated and relied upon Meyer v. Nebraska, 262 U.S. 390, 43 S.Ct. 625, 67 L.Ed. 1042 (1923) and Pierce v. Society of Sisters, 268 U.S. 510, 45 S.Ct. 571, 69 L.Ed 1070 (1925) as illustrating the principle that the state may not forbid the teaching of certain subjects in the schools or forbid a child's parents to send him to a private school, but that the state might, without offending the Constitution, prescribe certain subjects in the schools, or encourage public schools by providing financial support.]

* * * We think it abundantly clear that a State is not required to show a compelling interest for its policy choice to favor normal childbirth any more than a State must so justify its election to fund public but not private education.[10]

Appellees' reliance on the penalty analysis of *Shapiro* and *Maricopa County* is misplaced. In our view there is only a semantic difference between appellees' assertion that the Connecticut law unduly interferes with a woman's right to terminate her pregnancy and their assertion that it penalizes the exercise of that right. Penalties are most familiar to the criminal law, where criminal sanctions are imposed as a consequence of proscribed conduct. *Shapiro* and *Maricopa County* recognized that denial of welfare to one who had recently exercised the right to travel across state lines was sufficiently analogous to a criminal fine to justify strict judicial scrutiny.

If Connecticut denied general welfare benefits to all women who had obtained abortions and who were otherwise entitled to the benefits, we would have a close analogy to the facts in *Shapiro*, and strict scrutiny might be appropriate under either the penalty analysis or the analysis we have applied in our previous abortion decisions. But the claim here is that the State "penalizes" the woman's decision to have an abortion by refusing to pay for it. *Shapiro* and *Maricopa County* did not hold that States would penalize the right to travel interstate by refusing to pay the bus fares of the indigent travelers. We find no support in the right-to-travel cases for the view that Connecticut must show a compelling interest for its decision not to fund elective abortions.

Sherbert v. Verner, 374 U.S. 398, 83 S. Ct. 1790, 10 L.Ed.2d 965 (1963), similarly is inapplicable here. In addition, that case was decided in the significantly different context of a constitutionally imposed "governmental obligation of neutrality" originating in the Establishment and Freedom of Religion Clauses of the First Amendment. Id., at 409, 83 S.Ct., at 1797.

10. In his dissenting opinion, Mr. Justice Brennan rejects the distinction between direct state interference with a protected activity and state encouragement of an alternative activity and argues that our previous abortion decisions are inconsistent with today's decision. But as stated above, all of those decisions involved laws that placed substantial state-created obstacles in the pregnant woman's path to an abortion. Our recent de-

D

The question remains whether Connecticut's regulation can be sustained under the less demanding test of rationality that applies in the absence of a suspect classification or the impingement of a fundamental right. This test requires that the distinction drawn between childbirth and nontherapeutic abortion by the regulation be "rationally related" to a "constitutionally permissible" purpose. We hold that the Connecticut funding scheme satisfies this standard.

Roe itself explicitly acknowledged the State's strong interest in protecting the potential life of the fetus. That interest exists throughout the pregnancy, "grow[ing] in substantiality as the woman approaches term." 410 U.S., at 162–163, 93 S.Ct., at 731. Because the pregnant woman carries a potential human being, she "cannot be isolated in her privacy. * * * [Her] privacy is no longer sole and any right of privacy she possesses must be measured accordingly." Id., at 159, 93 S.Ct., at 730. The State unquestionably has a "strong and legitimate interest in encouraging normal childbirth," Beal v. Doe, ante, 432 U.S. 438, at 446, 97 S.Ct. 2366 at 2372, 52 L. Ed.2d 464, an interest honored over the centuries.[11] Nor can there be any question that the Connecticut regulation rationally furthers that interest. The medical costs associated with childbirth are substantial, and have increased significantly in recent years. As recognized by the District Court in this case, such costs are significantly greater than those normally associated with elective abortions during the first trimester. The subsidizing of costs incident to childbirth is a rational means of encouraging childbirth.

We certainly are not unsympathetic to the plight of an indigent woman who desires an abortion, but "the Constitution does not provide judicial remedies for every social and economic ill," Lindsey v. Normet, 405 U.S., at 74, 92 S.Ct., at 874. Our cases uniformly have accorded the States a wider latitude in choosing among competing de-

cision in Carey v. Population Services International, 431 U.S. 678, 97 S.Ct. 2010, 52 L.Ed.2d 675 (1977), differs only in that it involved state-created restrictions on access to contraceptives, rather than abortions. Mr. Justice Brennan simply asserts that the Connecticut regulation "is an obvious impairment of the fundamental right established by Roe v. Wade." Post, at 484–485. The only suggested source for this purportedly "obvious" conclusion is a quotation from Singleton v. Wulff, 428 U.S. 106, 96 S. Ct. 2868, 49 L.Ed.2d 826 (1976). Yet, as Mr. Justice Blackmun was careful to note at the beginning of his opinion in Singleton, that case presented "issues [of standing] not going to the merits of this dispute." Id., at 108, 96 S.Ct., at 2871. Significantly, Mr. Justice Brennan makes no effort to distinguish or explain the much more analogous authority of Norwood v. Harrison, 413 U.S. 455, 93 S.Ct. 2804, 37 L.Ed.2d 723 (1973).

11. In addition to the direct interest in protecting the fetus, a State may have legitimate demographic concerns about its rate of population growth. Such concerns are basic to the future of the State and in some circumstances could constitute a substantial reason for departure from a position of neutrality between abortion and childbirth.

292 THE FAMILY Ch. 5

mands for limited public funds. In Dandridge v. Williams, 397 U.S. 471, at 485, 90 S.Ct. 1153, 1162, 25 L.Ed.2d 491, despite recognition that laws and regulations allocating welfare funds involve "the most basic economic needs of impoverished human beings," we held that classifications survive equal protection challenge when a "reasonable basis" for the classification is shown. As the preceding discussion makes clear, the state interest in encouraging normal childbirth exceeds this minimal level.

The decision whether to expend state funds for nontherapeutic abortion is fraught with judgments of policy and value over which opinions are sharply divided. Our conclusion that the Connecticut regulation is constitutional is not based on a weighing of its wisdom or social desirability, for this Court does not strike down state laws "because they may be unwise, improvident, or out of harmony with a particular school of thought." Williamson v. Lee Optical Co., 348 U. S. 483, 488, 75 S.Ct. 461, 464, 99 L.Ed. 563 (1955), quoted in Dandridge v. Williams, supra, at 484, 90 S.Ct., at 116. Indeed, when an issue involves policy choices as sensitive as those implicated by public funding of nontherapeutic abortions, the appropriate forum for their resolution in a democracy is the legislature. *   *   *

In conclusion, we emphasize that our decision today does not proscribe government funding of nontherapeutic abortions. It is open to Congress to require provision of Medicaid benefits for such abortions as a condition of state participation in the Medicaid program. Also, under Title XIX as construed in Beal v. Doe, ante, p. 438, Connecticut is free—through normal democratic processes—to decide that such benefits should be provided. We hold only that the Constitution does not require a judicially imposed resolution of these difficult issues.

III

The District Court also invalidated Connecticut's requirements of prior written request by the pregnant woman and prior authorization by the Department of Social Services. Our analysis above rejects the basic premise that prompted invalidation of these procedural requirements. It is not unreasonable for a State to insist upon a prior showing of medical necessity to insure that its money is being spent only for authorized purposes. The simple answer to the argument that similar requirements are not imposed for other medical procedures is that such procedures do not involve the termination of a potential human life. In Planned Parenthood of Central Missouri v. Danforth, 428 U.S. 52, 96 S.Ct. 2831, 2841–2842, 49 L.Ed.2d 788 (1976), we held that the woman's written consent to an abortion was not an impermissible burden under *Roe*. We think that decision is controlling on the similar issue here.

The judgment of the District Court is reversed, and the case is remanded for further proceedings consistent with this opinion.

Mr. Justice BRENNAN, with whom Mr. Justice MARSHALL and Mr. Justice BLACKMUN join, dissenting.

The District Court held:

"When Connecticut refuses to fund elective abortions while funding therapeutic abortions and prenatal and postnatal care, it weights the choice of the pregnant mother against choosing to exercise her constitutionally protected right to an elective abortion.   *   *   * Her choice is affected not simply by the absence of payment for the abortion, but by the availability of public funds for childbirth if she chooses not to have the abortion.   When the state thus infringes upon a fundamental interest, it must assert a compelling state interest."   Roe v. Norton, 408 F.Supp. 660, 663–664 (1975).

This Court reverses on the ground that "the District Court misconceived the nature and scope of the fundamental right recognized in *Roe* [v. Wade, 410 U.S. 113, 93 S.Ct. 705, 35 L.Ed.2d 147 (1973)]," ante at 471, and therefore that Connecticut was not required to meet the "compelling interest" test to justify its discrimination against elective abortion but only "the less demanding test of rationality that applies in the absence of   *   *   *   the impingement of a fundamental right," ante, at 477, 478.   *   *   *

But a distressing insensitivity to the plight of impoverished pregnant women is inherent in the Court's analysis.   The stark reality for too many, not just "some," indigent pregnant women is that indigency makes access to competent licensed physicians not merely "difficult" but "impossible."   As a practical matter, many indigent women will feel they have no choice but to carry their pregnancies to term because the State will pay for the associated medical services, even though they would have chosen to have abortions if the State had also provided funds for that procedure, or indeed if the State had provided funds for neither procedure.   This disparity in funding by the State clearly operates to coerce indigent pregnant women to bear children they would not otherwise choose to have, and just as clearly, this coercion can only operate upon the poor, who are uniquely the victims of this form of financial pressure.   *   *   *

None can take seriously the Court's assurance that its "conclusion signals no retreat from *Roe* [v. Wade] or the cases applying it," ante, at 475.   *   *   *   Indeed, it cannot be gainsaid that today's decision seriously erodes the principles that *Roe* and *Doe* announced to guide the determination of what constitutes an unconstitutional infringement of the fundamental right of pregnant women to be free to decide whether to have an abortion.

The Court's premise is that only an equal protection claim is presented here.   Claims of interference with enjoyment of fundamental rights have, however, occupied a rather protean position in our constitutional jurisprudence.   Whether or not the Court's analysis may reasonably proceed under the Equal Protection Clause, the Court plainly errs in ignoring, as it does, the unanswerable argument of appellees, and the holding of the District Court, that the regulation unconstitutionally impinges upon their claim of privacy derived from the Due Process Clause.

Roe v. Wade and cases following it hold that an area of privacy invulnerable to the State's intrusion surrounds the decision of a pregnant woman whether or not to carry her pregnancy to term. The Connecticut scheme clearly infringes upon that area of privacy by bringing financial pressures on indigent women that force them to bear children they would not otherwise have. That is an obvious impairment of the fundamental right established by Roe v. Wade. * * *

Most recently, also in a privacy case, the Court squarely reaffirmed that the right of privacy was fundamental, and that an infringement upon that right must be justified by a compelling state interest. Carey v. Population Services International, 431 U.S. 678, 97 S. Ct. 2010, 52 L.Ed.2d 675 (1977). * * *

Finally, cases involving other fundamental rights also make clear that the Court's concept of what constitutes an impermissible infringement upon the fundamental right of a pregnant woman to choose to have an abortion makes new law. We have repeatedly found that infringements of fundamental rights are not limited to outright denials of those rights. First Amendment decisions have consistently held in a wide variety of contexts that the compelling-state-interest test is applicable not only to outright denials but also to restraints that make exercise of those rights more difficult. * * *

Until today, I had not thought the nature of the fundamental right established in Roe was open to question, let alone susceptible of the interpretation advanced by the Court. The fact that the Connecticut scheme may not operate as an absolute bar preventing all indigent women from having abortions is not critical. What is critical is that the State has inhibited their fundamental right to make that choice free from state interference.

Nor does the manner in which Connecticut has burdened the right freely to choose to have an abortion save its Medicaid program. The Connecticut scheme cannot be distinguished from other grants and withholdings of financial benefits that we have held unconstitutionally burdened a fundamental right. Sherbert v. Verner, supra, struck down a South Carolina statute that denied unemployment compensation to a woman who for religious reasons could not work on Saturday, but that would have provided such compensation if her unemployment had stemmed from a number of other nonreligious causes. Even though there was no proof of indigency in that case, Sherbert held that "the pressure upon her to forgo [her religious] practice [was] unmistakable," 374 U.S., at 404, 83 S.Ct., at 1799, and therefore held that the effect was the same as a fine imposed for Saturday worship. Here, though the burden is upon the right to privacy derived from the Due Process Clause and not upon freedom of religion under the Free Exercise Clause of the First Amendment, the governing principle is the same, for Connecticut grants and withholds financial benefits in a manner that discourages significantly the exercise of a fundamental constitutional right. Indeed, the case for application of the principle actually is stronger than in *Verner* since appellees are all indigents and therefore even more vulnerable to the financial pressures imposed by the Connecticut regulations.

Bellotti v. Baird, 428 U.S. 132, 147, 96 S.Ct. 2857, 2866, 49 L.Ed. 2d 844 (1976), held, and the Court today agrees, ante, at 473, that a state requirement is unconstitutional if it "unduly burdens the right to seek an abortion." Connecticut has "unduly" burdened the fundamental right of pregnant women to be free to choose to have an abortion because the State has advanced no compelling state interest to justify its interference in that choice.

Although appellant does not argue it as justification, the Court concludes that the State's interest "in protecting the potential life of the fetus" suffices, ante, at 478.* Since only the first trimester of pregnancy is involved in this case, that justification is totally foreclosed if the Court is not overruling the holding of Roe v. Wade that "[w]ith respect to the State's important and legitimate interest in potential life, the 'compelling' point is at viability," occurring at about the end of the second trimester. 410 U.S., at 163, 93 S.Ct., at 73.
*   *   *

POELKER, MAYOR OF ST. LOUIS v. DOE

Supreme Court of the United States, 1977.
432 U.S. 519, 97 S.Ct. 2391, 53 L.Ed.2d 528, rehearing denied
434 U.S. 880, 98 S.Ct. 241, 54 L.Ed.2d 163 (1977).

PER CURIAM. Respondent Jane Doe, an indigent, sought unsuccessfully to obtain a nontherapeutic abortion at Starkloff Hospital, one of two city-owned public hospitals in St. Louis, Mo. She subsequently brought this class action under 42 U.S.C.A. § 1983 against the Mayor of St. Louis and the Director of Health and Hospitals, alleging that the refusal by Starkloff Hospital to provide the desired abortion violated her constitutional rights. Although the District Court ruled against Doe following a trial, the Court of Appeals for the Eighth Circuit reversed in an opinion that accepted both her factual and legal arguments. 515 F.2d 541 (1975).

---

* The Court also suggests, ante, at 478 n. 11, that a "State may have legitimate demographic concerns about its rate of population growth" which might justify a choice to favor live births over abortions. While it is conceivable that under some circumstances this might be an appropriate factor to be considered as part of a State's "compelling" interest, no one contends that this is the case here, or indeed that Connecticut has any demographic concerns at all about the rate of its population growth.

The Court of Appeals concluded that Doe's inability to obtain an abortion resulted from a combination of a policy directive by the Mayor and a longstanding staffing practice at Starkloff Hospital. The directive, communicated to the Director of Health and Hospitals by the Mayor, prohibited the performance of abortions in the city hospitals except when there was a threat of grave physiological injury or death to the mother. Under the staffing practice, the doctors and medical students at the obstetrics-gynecology clinic at the hospital are drawn from the faculty and students at the St. Louis University School of Medicine, a Jesuit-operated institution opposed to abortion. Relying on our decisions in Roe v. Wade, 410 U.S. 113, 93 S.Ct. 705, 35 L.Ed.2d 147 (1973), and Doe v. Bolton, 410 U.S. 179, 93 S.Ct. 739, 35 L.Ed.2d 201 (1973), the Court of Appeals held that the city's policy and the hospital's staffing practice denied the "constitutional rights of indigent pregnant women * * * long after those rights had been clearly enunciated" in *Roe* and *Doe*. 515 F.2d, at 547. The court cast the issue in an equal protection mold, finding that the provision of publicly financed hospital services for childbirth but not for elective abortions constituted invidious discrimination. In support of its equal protection analysis, the court also emphasized the contrast between nonindigent women who can afford to obtain abortions in private hospitals and indigent women who cannot. * * *

We agree that the constitutional question presented here is identical in principle with that presented by a State's refusal to provide Medicaid benefits for abortions while providing them for childbirth. This was the issue before us in Maher v. Roe, 432 U.S. 464, 97 S.Ct. 2376, 53 L.Ed.2d 484. For the reasons set forth in our opinion in that case, we find no constitutional violation by the city of St. Louis in electing, as a policy choice, to provide publicly financed hospital services for childbirth without providing corresponding services for nontherapeutic abortions.

In the decision of the Court of Appeals and in the briefs supporting that decision, emphasis is placed on Mayor Poelker's personal opposition to abortion, characterized as "a wanton, callous disregard" for the constitutional rights of indigent women. 515 F.2d, at 547. Although the Mayor's personal position on abortion is irrelevant to our decision, we note that he is an elected official responsible to the people of St. Louis. His policy of denying city funds for abortions such as that desired by Doe is subject to public debate and approval or disapproval at the polls. We merely hold, for the reasons stated in *Maher,* that the Constitution does not forbid a State or city, pursuant to democratic processes, from expressing a preference for normal childbirth as St. Louis has done.

The judgment of the Court of Appeals for the Eighth Circuit is reversed, and the case is remanded for further proceedings consistent with this opinion.

NOTES AND QUESTIONS *

1. In a companion case, Beal v. Doe, 432 U.S. 438 (1977), the Supreme Court held that Pennsylvania regulations issued to implement the federal medicaid program did not conflict with the Social Security Act provisions which created the medicaid program. The Pennsylvania regulations limited financial assistance to those abortions which were certified as medically necessary by a physician. "Medically necessary" was defined as meaning that the mother's health would be threatened by the pregnancy; or that there was evidence that the baby would be defective; or there was evidence that the pregnancy resulted from forcible rape or incest and would affect the mother's physical or mental health; and that two other physicians concurred in the finding of necessity. The Social Security Act required that state plans, in order to qualify for federal funding, had to include reasonable standards for determining eligibility. The Court held that the Pennsylvania regulations were "reasonable" and therefore consistent with the Act because the state had "a valid and important interest in encouraging childbirth", and there would be nothing unreasonable in the state's vindication of this interest. The Court also relied upon the fact that when the medicaid portions of the Social Security Act were first passed in 1965 nontherapeutic abortions were unlawful in most states so that Congress could not have intended that such abortions would be funded under the program. Justices Brennan, Marshall and Blackmun dissented from this decision.

2. Justice Marshall wrote a separate dissent from the Beal, Maher and Poelker decisions, in which he said, among other things, the following:

> "It is all too obvious that the governmental actions in these cases, ostensibly taken to 'encourage' women to carry pregnancies to term, are in reality intended to impose a moral viewpoint that no State may constitutionally enforce. * * * Since efforts to overturn those decisions [Roe v. Wade etc.] have been unsuccessful, the opponents of abortion have attempted every imaginable means to circumvent the commands of the Constitution and impose their moral choices upon the rest of society. * * * The present cases involve the most vicious attacks yet devised. The impact of the regulations here falls tragically upon those among us least able to help or defend themselves. As the Court well knows, these regulations inevitably will have the practical effect of preventing nearly all poor women from obtaining safe and legal abortions. * * * I am appalled at the ethical bankruptcy of those who preach a 'right to life' that means, under present social policies, a bare existence in utter misery for so many poor women and their children. * * * Yet I fear that the Court's decisions will be an invitation to public officials, already under extraordinary pressure from well financed and carefully orchestrated lobbying campaigns, to approve more such restrictions. The effect will be to relegate millions of people to lives of poverty and despair. When elected leaders cower before public pressure, this Court, more than ever, must not shirk its duty to enforce the Constitution for the benefit of the poor and powerless." 432 U.S. at 454–462.

* While this book was in press the Supreme Court decided Harris v. McRae, upholding the federal restrictions upon abortion funding imposed by the Hyde Amendment. The opinion in Harris v. McRae (in an abridged form) is an Appendix to the book.

3.   Justices Brennan, Marshall and Blackmun also dissented from the *Poelker* decision.

4.   In recent years Congress has limited medicaid funds available for abortions.   In the bill making appropriations for the Departments of Labor, and Health, Education and Welfare for fiscal year 1978, Congress included the following provision:

> "*Provided,* That none of the funds provided for in this paragraph shall be used to perform abortions except where the life of the mother would be endangered if the fetus were carried to term; or except for such medical procedures necessary for the victims of rape or incest, when such rape or incest has been reported promptly to a law enforcement agency or public health service; or except in those instances where severe and long-lasting physical health damage to the mother would result if the pregnancy were carried to term when so determined by two physicians.

> "Nor are payments prohibited for drugs or devices to prevent implantation of the fertilized ovum, or for medical procedures necessary for the termination of an ectopic pregnancy.

> "The Secretary shall promptly issue regulations and establish procedures to ensure that the provisions of this section are rigorously enforced."

Pub.L. 95–205, 1 U.S.Code Cong. & Admin.News, 95th Cong., 1st Sess., 91 Stat. 1460 (1977), often referred to as the Hyde Amendment.   Implementing regulations have been adopted by the Secretary of the Department of Health, Education and Welfare.   42 C.F.R. §§ 50.301 to 50.310 (1978).   The regulations require, inter alia, that if the rape or incest exception is relied upon, the rape or incest must be reported within sixty days.

Is this statute constitutional under the *Maher* and *Poelker* cases?   See Zbaraz v. Quern, 469 F.Supp. 1212 (N.D.Ill.1979), appeal filed, July 2, 1979, 48 L.Wk. 3126; Zbaraz v. Quern, 596 F.2d 196 (7th Cir. 1979), pet. for cert. filed July 13, 1979, 48 L.Wk. 3127.

5.   The opinion in Maher characterizes the central question as being whether the Pennsylvania regulation "impinges upon a fundamental right explicitly or implicitly protected by the Constitution."   See page 287.   How does the Court answer this central question, in Maher and in Poelker?   Is the right to an abortion a "fundamental right"?   If so, does the Pennsylvania regulation "impinge" upon it?   Does the mayor's directive impinge upon it in Poelker?

6.   Did Roe v. Wade forbid "unduly burdensome" restrictions on abortion during the first trimester, or did it forbid all restrictions?   What does "unduly" mean, judging from the clues provided in the Maher case?

7.   A city council enacts the following ordinance, dealing with abortions performed in the city and with abortion clinics located there:

"Sec. 1.   An unborn child shall conclusively be presumed to be viable after more than 24 weeks of pregnancy.

"Sec. 2.   No abortion may be performed upon any woman under 18 until the expiration of 72 hours' written notice to her parent, or guardian.   If the woman is under 15, no abortion may be performed upon her without the written consent of her parent or guardian.

"Sec. 3.   No abortion may be performed without the informed consent of the woman.   "Informed Consent" for purposes of this section means that the woman must be informed that her unborn child is a human life from the moment of conception; that there have been described in detail to her the anatomical and physiological characteristics of the particular unborn child at the period of development at which the abortion is to be performed, including, but not limited to, its appearance, mobility, tactile sensitivity, including pain, perception or response, brain or heart function, the presence of internal organs and the presence of external members. In addition the woman must be informed that abortion is a major surgical procedure which can result in serious complications; and that abortion may leave essentially unaffected or may worsen any existing psychological problems the woman may have and can result in emotional disturbance. There shall be a 24 hour waiting period between the giving of the woman's consent and the performance of the abortion.

"Sec. 4. All abortion clinics must obtain a license from the city public health officer, the fee for which is $100 per year. Said officer shall inspect such clinics every six months, and shall examine the clinic's medical records. All abortion clinics must have an operating room, or must have access to an operating room within 15 minutes' travel time from the clinic."

What arguments for and against the constitutionality of the various sections of this ordinance would you make? Are the various sections valid or invalid according to the Roe-Poelker line of cases? Cf. Framingham Clinic, Inc. v. Board of Selectman of Southborough, 373 Mass. 279, 367 N. E.2d 606 (1977); Akron Center v. City of Akron, 479 F.Supp. 1172 (N.D. Ohio 1979).

CAREY, GOVERNOR OF NEW YORK, ET AL., v. POPULATION SERVICES INTERNATIONAL ET AL.

Supreme Court of the United States, 1977.
431 U.S. 678, 97 S.Ct. 2010, 52 L.Ed.2d 675.

Mr. Justice BRENNAN delivered the opinion of the Court (Parts I, II, III, and V), together with an opinion (Part IV), in which Mr. Justice STEWART, Mr. Justice MARSHALL, and Mr. Justice BLACKMUN joined.

Under New York Education Law § 6811(8) (McKinney 1972) it is a crime (1) for any person to sell or distribute any contraceptive of any kind to a minor under the age of 16 years; (2) for anyone other than a licensed pharmacist to distribute contraceptives to persons 16 or over; and (3) for anyone, including licensed pharmacists, to advertise or display contraceptives.[1] A three-judge District Court

1. Section 6811(8) provides:
   "It shall be a class A misdemeanor for:
   * * *
   "8. Any person to sell or distribute any instrument or article, or any recipe, drug or medicine for the prevention of contraception to a minor under the age of sixteen years; the sale or distribution of

such to a person other than a minor under the age of sixteen years is authorized only by a licensed pharmacist but the advertisement or display of said articles, within or without the premises of such pharmacy, is hereby prohibited." After some dispute in the District Court the parties apparently now agree that Education Law § 6807(b)

for the Southern District of New York declared § 6811(8) unconstitutional in its entirety under the First and Fourteenth Amendments of the Federal Constitution insofar as it applies to nonprescription contraceptives, and enjoined its enforcement as so applied. 398 F.Supp. 321 (1975). We affirm.

I

We must address a preliminary question of the standing of the various appellees to maintain the action. We conclude that appellee Population Planning Associates, Inc. (PPA) has the requisite standing and therefore have no occasion to decide the standing of the other appellees.

* * *

[Population Planning Associates, Inc. sold contraceptives by mail order from North Carolina to residents of New York. It had been advised by New York officials that its activities violated the New York statute, and the Supreme Court held that this gave it standing to attack the constitutionality of the statute, both on its own behalf and on behalf of its potential customers.]

II

Although "[t]he Constitution does not explicitly mention any right of privacy," the Court has recognized that one aspect of the "liberty" protected by the Due Process Clause of the Fourteenth Amendment is "a right of personal privacy, or a guarantee of certain areas or zones of privacy." Roe v. Wade, 410 U.S. 113, 152, 93 S.Ct. 705, 726, 35 L.Ed.2d 147 (1973). This right of personal privacy includes "the interest in independence in making certain kinds of important decisions." Whalen v. Roe, 429 U.S. 589, 599–600, 97 S.Ct. 869, 876, 51 L.Ed.2d 64 (1977). While the outer limits of this aspect of privacy have not been marked by the Court, it is clear that among the decisions that an individual may make without unjustified government interference are personal decisions "relating to marriage, Loving v. Virginia, 388 U.S. 1, 12, 87 S.Ct. 1817, 1823, 18 L.Ed.2d 1010 (1967); procreation, Skinner v. Oklahoma, 316 U.S. 535, 541–542, 62 S.Ct. 1110, 1113–1114, 86 L.Ed. 1655 (1942); contraception, Eisenstadt v. Baird, 405 U.S., at 453–454, 92 S.Ct. at 1038–1039; id., at 460, 463–465, 92 S.Ct. at 1042, 1043–1044 (White, J., concurring in

---

(1972) constitutes an exception to the distribution prohibitions of § 6811(8). Section 6807(b) provides:
"This article shall not be construed to affect or prevent:
* * *
"(b) Any physician * * * who is not the owner of a pharmacy, or registered store, or who is not in the employ of such owner, from supplying his patients with such drugs as the physician * * * deems proper in connection with his practice * * *."
The definition of "drugs" in Education Law § 6802(7) (1972) apparently includes any contraceptive drug or device. See nn. 7, 13, and 23, and text, infra, at 697–699. See also 398 F.Supp. 321, 329–330, and n. 8.

result); family relationships, Prince v. Massachusetts, 321 U.S. 158, 166, 64 S.Ct. 438, 442, 88 L.Ed. 645 (1944); and child rearing and education, Pierce v. Society of Sisters, 268 U.S. 510, 535 (1925); Meyer v. Nebraska, [262 U.S. 390, 399, 43 S.Ct. 625, 67 L.Ed. 1042 (1923)]." Roe v. Wade, supra, at 152–153, 93 S.Ct., at 726. See also Cleveland Board of Education v. LaFleur, 414 U.S. 632, 639–640, 94 S.Ct. 791, 796–797, 39 L.Ed.2d 52 (1974).

The decision whether or not to beget or bear a child is at the very heart of this cluster of constitutionally protected choices. That decision holds a particularly important place in the history of the right of privacy, a right first explicitly recognized in an opinion holding unconstitutional a statute prohibiting the use of contraceptives, Griswold v. Connecticut, supra, and most prominently vindicated in recent years in the contexts of contraception, Griswold v. Connecticut, supra; Eisenstadt v. Baird, supra; and abortion, Roe v. Wade, supra; Doe v. Bolton, 410 U.S. 179, 93 S.Ct. 739, 35 L.Ed.2d 201 (1973); Planned Parenthood of Central Missouri v. Danforth, 428 U.S. 52, 96 S.Ct. 2831, 49 L.Ed.2d 788 (1976). This is understandable, for in a field that by definition concerns the most intimate of human activities and relationships, decisions whether to accomplish or to prevent conception are among the most private and sensitive. "If the right of privacy means anything, it is the right of the individual, married or single, to be free of unwarranted governmental intrusion into matters so fundamentally affecting a person as the decision whether to bear or beget a child." Eisenstadt v. Baird, supra, at 453. (Emphasis omitted.)

That the constitutionally protected right of privacy extends to an individual's liberty to make choices regarding contraception does not, however, automatically invalidate every state regulation in this area. The business of manufacturing and selling contraceptives may be regulated in ways that do not infringe protected individual choices. And even a burdensome regulation may be validated by a sufficiently compelling state interest. In Roe v. Wade, for example, after determining that the "right of privacy * * * encompass[es] a woman's decision whether or not to terminate her pregnancy," 410 U.S., at 153, 93 S.Ct., at 727 we cautioned that the right is not absolute, and that certain state interests (in that case, "interests in safeguarding health, in maintaining medical standards, and in protecting potential life") may at some point "become sufficiently compelling to sustain regulation of the factors that govern the abortion decision." Id., at 154, 93 S.Ct., at 727. "Compelling" is of course the key word; where a decision as fundamental as that whether to bear or beget a child is involved, regulations imposing a burden on it may be justified only by compelling state interests, and must be narrowly drawn to express only those interests. Id., at 155–156, 93 S.Ct., at 727–728, and cases there cited.

With these principles in mind, we turn to the question whether the District Court was correct in holding invalid the provisions of § 6811(8) as applied to the distribution of nonprescription contraceptives.

III

We consider first the wider restriction on access to contraceptives created by § 6811(8)'s prohibition of the distribution of nonmedical contraceptives to adults except through licensed pharmacists.

Appellants argue that this Court has not accorded a "right of access to contraceptives" the status of a fundamental aspect of personal liberty. They emphasize that Griswold v. Connecticut struck down a state prohibition of the *use* of contraceptives, and so had no occasion to discuss laws "regulating their manufacture or sale." 381 U.S., at 485, 85 S.Ct., at 1682. Eisenstadt v. Baird, was decided under the Equal Protection Clause, holding that "whatever the rights of the individual to access to contraceptives may be, the rights must be the same for the unmarried and the married alike." 405 U.S., at 453, 92 S.Ct., at 1038. Thus appellants argue that neither case should be treated as reflecting upon the State's power to limit or prohibit distribution of contraceptives to any persons, married or unmarried.

The fatal fallacy in this argument is that it overlooks the underlying premise of those decisions that the Constitution protects "the right of the individual * * * to be free from unwarranted governmental intrusion into * * * the decision whether to bear or beget a child." Id., at 453, 92 S.Ct., at 1038 * * * These decisions put *Griswold* in proper perspective. *Griswold* may no longer be read as holding only that a State may not prohibit a married couple's use of contraceptives. Read in light of its progeny, the teaching of *Griswold* is that the Constitution protects individual decisions in matters of childbearing from unjustified intrusion by the State.

Restrictions on the distribution of contraceptives clearly burden the freedom to make such decisions. A total prohibition against sale of contraceptives, for example, would intrude upon individual decisions in matters of procreation and contraception as harshly as a direct ban on their use. Indeed, in practice, a prohibition against all sales, since more easily and less offensively enforced, might have an even more devastating effect upon the freedom to choose contraception.

An instructive analogy is found in decisions after Roe v. Wade, supra, that held unconstitutional statutes that did not prohibit abortions outright but limited in a variety of ways a woman's access to them. Doe v. Bolton, 410 U.S. 179, 93 S.Ct. 739, 35 L.Ed.2d 201 (1973); Planned Parenthood of Central Missouri v. Danforth, 428 U. S. 52, 96 S.Ct. 2831, 49 L.Ed.2d 788 (1976). The significance of these cases is that they establish that the same test must be applied to state regulations that burden an individual's right to decide to prevent conception or terminate pregnancy by substantially limiting access to the means of effectuating that decision as is applied to state statutes that prohibit the decision entirely. Both types of regulation "may be justified only by a 'compelling state interest' * * * and * * * must be narrowly drawn to express only the legitimate state interests at stake." Roe v. Wade, supra, at 155, 93 S.Ct., at 728.[5] This is so not because there is an independent fundamental "right of access to contraceptives," but because such access is essential to exercise of the constitutionally protected right of decision in matters of childbearing that is the underlying foundation of the holdings in *Griswold,* Eisenstadt v. Baird, and Roe v. Wade.

Limiting the distribution of nonprescription contraceptives to licensed pharmacists clearly imposes a signficant burden on the right of the individuals to use contraceptives if they choose to do so. The burden is, of course, not as great as that under a total ban on distribution. Nevertheless, the restriction of distribution channels to a small fraction of the total number of possible retail outlets renders contraceptive devices considerably less accessible to the public, reduces the opportunity for privacy of selection and purchase, and lessens the possibility of price competition. Of particular relevance here is Doe v. Bolton, supra, in which the Court struck down, as unconstitutionally burdening the right of a woman to choose abortion, a statute requiring that abortions be performed only in accredited hospitals, in the absence of proof that the requirement was substantially related to the State's interest in protecting the patient's health. 410 U.S., at 193–195, 93 S.Ct., at 748–749. The same infirmity infuses the limitation in § 6811(8). * * *

There remains the inquiry whether the provision serves a compelling state interest. Clearly "interests * * * in maintaining medical standards, and in protecting potential life," Roe v. Wade, 410 U.S., at 154, 93 S.Ct., at 727, cannot be invoked to justify this statute. Insofar as § 6811(8) applies to nonhazardous contraceptives, it bears no relation to the State's interest in protecting health. Nor is the interest in protecting potential life implicated in state regulation of contraceptives.

---

5. Contrary to the suggestion advanced in Mr. Justice Powell's opinion, we do not hold that state regulation must meet this standard "whenever it implicates sexual freedom," post, at 705, or "affect[s] adult sexual relations," post, at 703, but only when it "burden[s] an individual's right to decide to prevent conception or terminate pregnancy by substantially limiting access to the means of effectuating that decision." Supra, this page. As we observe below, "the Court has not definitively answered the difficult question whether and to what extent the Constitution prohibits state statutes regulating [private consensual sexual] behavior among adults," n. 17, infra, and we do not purport to answer that question now.

Appellants therefore suggest that § 6811(8) furthers other state interests. But none of them is comparable to those the Court has heretofore recognized as compelling. Appellants argue that the limitation of retail sales of nonmedical contraceptives to pharmacists (1) expresses "a proper concern that young people not sell contraceptives"; (2) "allows purchasers to inquire as to the relative qualities of the varying products and prevents anyone from tampering with them"; and (3) facilitates enforcement of the other provisions of the statute. Brief for Appellants 14. The first hardly can justify the statute's incursion into constitutionally protected rights, and in any event the statute is obviously not substantially related to any goal of preventing young people from selling contraceptives.[10] Nor is the statute designed to serve as a quality control device. Nothing in the record suggests that pharmacists are particularly qualified to give advice on the merits of different nonmedical contraceptives, or that such advice is more necessary to the purchaser of contraceptive products than to consumers of other nonprescription items. Why pharmacists are better able or more inclined than other retailers to prevent tampering with prepackaged products, or, if they are, why contraceptives are singled out for this special protection, is also unexplained.[11] As to ease of enforcement, the prospect of additional administrative inconvenience has not been thought to justify invasion of fundamental constitutional rights.

IV[12]

A

The District Court also held unconstitutional, as applied to nonprescription contraceptives, the provision of § 6811(8) prohibiting the distribution of contraceptives to those under 16 years of age.[13] Appellants contend that this provision of the statute is constitutionally permissible as a regulation of the morality of minors, in furtherance of the State's policy against promiscuous sexual intercourse among the young.

10. Nothing in New York law limits the employment of minors who work as sales clerks in pharmacies. To the extent that minors employed in other retail stores selling contraceptive products might be exposed "to undesirable comments and gestures," Brief for Appellants 3–4, or otherwise corrupted by exposure to such products, minors working as sales clerks in pharmacies are exposed to the same hazards.

11. As the District Court pointed out, while these interests are insufficient to justify limiting the distribution of nonhazardous contraceptives to phar-

macists, other restrictions may well be reasonably related to the objective of quality control. We therefore express no opinion on, for example, restrictions on the distribution of contraceptives through vending machines, which are not before us in this case.

12. This part of the opinion expresses the views of Justices Brennan, Stewart, Marshall, and Blackmun.

13. Subject to an apparent exception for distribution by physicians in the course of their practice.

The question of the extent of state power to regulate conduct of minors not constitutionally regulable when committed by adults is a vexing one, perhaps not susceptible of precise answer. We have been reluctant to attempt to define "the totality of the relationship of the juvenile and the state." In re Gault, 387 U.S. 1, 13, 87 S.Ct. 1428, 1436, 18 L.Ed.2d 527 (1967). Certain principles, however, have been recognized. "Minors, as well as adults, are protected by the Constitution and possess constitutional rights." Planned Parenthood of Central Missouri v. Danforth, 428 U.S., at 74, 96 S.Ct., at 2843. * * * On the other hand, we have held in a variety of contexts that "the power of the state to control the conduct of children reaches beyond the scope of its authority over adults." Prince v. Massachusetts, 321 U.S., at 170, 64 S.Ct., at 444.

Of particular significance to the decision of this case, the right to privacy in connection with decisions affecting procreation extends to minors as well as to adults. * * * State restrictions inhibiting privacy rights of minors are valid only if they serve "any significant state interest * * * that is not present in the case of an adult." Id., at 75, 96 S.Ct., at 2844.[15] *Planned Parenthood* found that no such interest justified a state requirement of parental consent.

Since the State may not impose a blanket prohibition, or even a blanket requirement of parental consent, on the choice of a minor to terminate her pregnancy, the constitutionality of a blanket prohibition of the distribution of contraceptives to minors is *a fortiori* foreclosed. The State's interests in protection of the mental and physical health of the pregnant minor, and in protection of potential life are clearly more implicated by the abortion decision than by the decision to use a nonhazardous contraceptive.

Appellants argue, however, that significant state interests are served by restricting minors' access to contraceptives, because free availability to minors of contraceptives would lead to increased sexual activity among the young, in violation of the policy of New York to discourage such behavior.[17] The argument is that minors' sexual

---

15. This test is apparently less rigorous than the "compelling state interest" test applied to restrictions on the privacy rights of adults. See, e. g., n. 16, infra. Such lesser scrutiny is appropriate both because of the States' greater latitude to regulate the conduct of children, and because the right of privacy implicated here is "the interest in independence in making certain kinds of important decisions," Whalen v. Roe, 429 U.S. 589, 599–600, 97 S.Ct., at 876 (1977), and the law has generally regarded minors as having a lesser capability for making important decisions.

17. Appellees argue that the State's policy to discourage sexual activity of minors is itself unconstitutional, for the reason that the right to privacy comprehends a right of minors as well as adults to engage in private consensual sexual behavior. We observe that the Court has not definitively answered the difficult question whether and to what extent the Constitution prohibits state statutes regulating such behavior among adults. But whatever the answer to that question, Ginsberg v. New York, supra, indicates that in the area of sexual mores, as in other areas, the

activity may be deterred by increasing the hazards attendant on it. The same argument, however, would support a ban on abortions for minors, or indeed support a prohibition on abortions, or access to contraceptives, for the unmarried, whose sexual activity is also against the public policy of many States. Yet, in each of these areas, the Court has rejected the argument, noting in Roe v. Wade, that "no court or commentator has taken the argument seriously." 410 U.S., at 148, 93 S.Ct., at 724. The reason for this unanimous rejection was stated in Eisenstadt v. Baird: "It would be plainly unreasonable to assume that [the State] has prescribed pregnancy and the birth of an unwanted child [or the physical and psychological dangers of an abortion] as punishment for fornication." 405 U.S., at 448, 92 S.Ct., at 1036. We remain reluctant to attribute any such "scheme of values" to the State.[18]

Moreover, there is substantial reason for doubt whether limiting access to contraceptives will in fact substantially discourage early sexual behavior. Appellants themselves conceded in the District Court that "there is no evidence that teenage extramarital sexual activity increases in proportion to the availability of contraceptives," 398 F.Supp., at 332, and n. 10, and accordingly offered none, in the District Court or here. Appellees, on the other hand, cite a considerable body of evidence and opinion indicating that there is no such deterrent effect.[19] Although we take judicial notice, as did the District

scope of permissible state regulation is broader as to minors than as to adults. In any event, it is unnecessary to pass upon this contention of appellees, and our decision proceeds on the assumption that the Constitution does not bar state regulation of the sexual behavior of minors.

18. We note, moreover, that other provisions of New York law argue strongly against any conclusion that the deterrence of illegal sexual conduct among minors was an objective of § 6811(8). First, a girl in New York may marry as young as 14, with the consent of her parents and a family court judge. N.Y.Dom.Rel. Law §§ 15–a, 15(2), 15(3) (1964 and Supp.1976–1977). Yet although sexual intercourse by a married woman of that age violates no state law, § 6811(8) prohibits distribution of contraceptives to her. Second, New York requires that birth control information and services be provided to recipients of certain welfare programs, provided only that they are "of childbearing age, including children who can be considered sexually active." N.Y.Soc.Serv.Law § 350(1)

(e) (1976); cf. 42 U.S.C.A. § 602(a)(15) (A). See also N.Y.Soc.Serv.Law § 365–a(3)(c) (1976); cf. 42 U.S.C.A. § 1396d(a)(vii)(4)(C). Although extramarital intercourse is presumably as contrary to state policy among minors covered by those programs as among others, state law requires distribution of contraceptives to them and prohibits their distribution to all others.

19. See, e. g., Settlage, Baroff & Cooper, Sexual Experience of Younger Teenage Girls Seeking Contraceptive Assistance for the First Time, Family Planning Perspectives, Fall 1973, p. 223; Pilpel & Wechsler, Birth Control, Teenagers and the Law: A New Look 1971, Family Planning Perspectives, July 1971, p. 37; Stein, Furnishing Information and Medical Treatment to Minors for Prevention, Termination and Treatment of Pregnancy, Clearinghouse Review, July 1971, p. 131, 132; Reiss, Contraceptive Information and Sexual Morality, Journal of Sex Research, April 1966, p. 51. See also Note, Parental Consent Requirements and Privacy Rights of Minors: The Contraceptive Controversy, 88 Harv.L.Rev. 1001,

Court, id., at 331–333, that with or without access to contraceptives, the incidence of sexual activity among minors is high, and the consequences of such activity are frequently devastating,[21] the studies cited by appellees play no part in our decision. It is enough that we again confirm the principle that when a State, as here, burdens the exercise of a fundamental right, its attempt to justify that burden as a rational means for the accomplishment of some significant state policy requires more than a bare assertion, based on a conceded complete absence of supporting evidence, that the burden is connected to such a policy.

B

Appellants argue that New York does not totally prohibit distribution of contraceptives to minors under 16, and that accordingly § 6811(8) cannot be held unconstitutional. Although § 6811(8) on its face is a flat unqualified prohibition, Education Law § 6807(b) (Supp.1976–1977), see nn. 1, 7, and 13, supra, provides that nothing in Education Law §§ 6800–6826 shall be construed to prevent "[a]ny physician * * * from supplying his patients with such drugs as [he] * * * deems proper in connection with his practice." This narrow exception, however, does not save the statute. As we have held above as to limitations upon distribution to adults, less than total restrictions on access to contraceptives that significantly burden the right to decide whether to bear children must also pass constitutional scrutiny. Appellants assert no medical necessity for imposing a medical limitation on the distribution of nonprescription contraceptives to minors. Rather, they argue that such a restriction serves to emphasize to young people the seriousness with which the State views the decision to engage in sexual intercourse at an early age. But this is only another form of the argument that juvenile sexual conduct will be deterred by making contraceptives more difficult to obtain. Moreover, that argument is particularly poorly suited to the restriction appellants are attempting to justify, which on appellants' construction delegates the State's authority to disapprove of minors'

1010, and n. 67 (1975); Jordan, A Minor's Right to Contraceptives, 7 U. Calif.Davis L.Rev. 270, 272–273 (1974).

21. Although this is not the occasion for a full examination of these problems, the following data sketchily indicate their extent. According to New York City Department of Health statistics, filed with the Court by the American Civil Liberties Union as *amicus curiae*, in New York City alone there were over 6,000 live births to girls under the age of 17 in 1975, as well as nearly 11,000 abortions. Moreover, "[t]eenage motherhood involves a host of problems, including adverse physical and psychological effects upon the minor and her baby, the continuous stigma associated with unwed motherhood, the need to drop out of school with the accompanying impairment of educational opportunities, and other dislocations [including] forced marriage of immature couples and the often acute anxieties involved in deciding whether to secure an abortion." Note, Parental Consent Requirements and Privacy Rights of Minors: The Contraceptive Controversy, 88 Harv.L.Rev. 1001, 1010 (1975) (footnotes omitted). See also Jordan, supra, n. 19, at 273–275.

sexual behavior to physicians, who may exercise it arbitrarily, either to deny contraceptives to young people, or to undermine the State's policy of discouraging illicit early sexual behavior. This the State may not do.

V

The District Court's holding that the prohibition of any "advertisement or display" of contraceptives is unconstitutional was clearly correct. Only last Term Virginia Pharmacy Bd. v. Virginia Consumer Council, 425 U.S. 748, 96 S.Ct. 1817, 48 L.Ed.2d 346 (1976), held that a State may not "completely suppress the dissemination of concededly truthful information about entirely lawful activity," even when that information could be categorized as "commercial speech." Id., at 773, 96 S.Ct., at 1831. Just as in that case, the statute challenged here seeks to suppress completely any information about the availability and price of contraceptives. Nor does the case present any question left open in *Virginia Pharmacy Bd.;* here, as there, there can be no contention that the regulation is "a mere time, place, and manner restriction," id., at 771, 96 S.Ct., at 1830, or that it prohibits only misleading or deceptive advertisements, ibid., or "that the transactions proposed in the forbidden advertisements are themselves illegal in any way. Moreover, in addition to the "substantial individual and societal interests" in the free flow of commercial information enumerated in *Virginia Pharmacy Bd.,* supra, at 763–766, 96 S.Ct., at 1817, the information suppressed by this statute "related to activity with which, at least in some respects, the State could not interfere." 425 U.S., at 760, 96 S.Ct., at 1825. Cf. *Bigelow* v. *Virginia,* 421 U.S. 809, 95 S.Ct. 2222, 44 L.Ed.2d 600 (1975).

Appellants contend that advertisements of contraceptive products would be offensive and embarrassing to those exposed to them, and that permitting them would legitimize sexual activity of young people. But these are classically not justifications validating the suppression of expression protected by the First Amendment. At least where obscenity is not involved, we have consistently held that the fact that protected speech may be offensive to some does not justify its suppression. * * * These arguments therefore do not justify the total suppression of advertising concerning contraceptives.

NOTES AND QUESTIONS

1. Since the views of the justices in Carey were more than usually fragmented, it may be useful to summarize the various concurrences and dissents:

Part I of the opinion, dealing with standing: Justices Brennan, White, Powell, Stevens, Stewart, Marshall, Blackmun.

Part II of the opinion, dealing with the right of privacy: Justices Brennan, Stevens, Marshall, Stewart, Blackmun. Justice White saw no occasion to agree or disagree with this section.

Part III of the opinion, dealing with sale by pharmacists alone: Justices Brennan, White, Powell (concurring in result), Stevens, Marshall, Stewart, Blackmun.

Part IV of the opinion, dealing with sales to minors: Justices Brennan, White (concurring in result), Powell (concurring in result), Marshall, Stewart, Blackmun.

Part V of the opinion, dealing with advertising: Justices Brennan, White, Powell (concurring in result), Stevens, Marshall, Stewart, Blackmun.

Chief Justice Burger and Justice Rehnquist dissented, with Justice Rehnquist alone writing.

2. The Carey case has been noted in 77 Colum.L.Rev. 1216 (1977); 91 Harv.L.Rev. 146 (1977); 16 J.Fam.L. 639 (1978); 126 U.Pa.L.Rev. 1135 (1978) among others.

3. The New York statute in Carey, like the Connecticut statute held unconstitutional in Griswold, were remnants of broader legislation by which many states and the federal government in the Nineteenth Century attempted to prevent the distribution and use of contraceptives. For example, in 1873 Congress passed what was known as the Comstock Law, forbidding the importation into the United States and the transmittal through the mails of articles designed for the prevention of conception and writings describing such articles. 18 U.S.C.A. §§ 1461, 1462. This statute remained in the United States Code until 1971, but was not enforced after the 1920's. But statutes of this kind, and those in such states as Connecticut, New York and Massachusetts undoubtedly reduced the availability of birth control, particularly for those persons who might have relied upon public clinics for advice and contraceptives. See C. Dienes, Law, Politics and Birth Control (1972).

In spite of these statutes, birth control was practiced in this country during the Nineteenth and early Twentieth Centuries. It was not until 1959, however, that medical research on the process of reproduction received the sort of financial support which enabled it to make real progress in the development of contraception. The contraceptive pill was first marketed in 1960 and the intrauterine device (IUD) in 1963. See R. Greep, M. Koblinsky, F. Jaffe, Reproduction and Human Welfare: A Challenge to Research (1976). Both methods of birth control have been questioned on the score of safety and side effects and both have been studied continuously since their introduction. C. Westoff and N. Ryder, The Contraceptive Revolution (1977). Although these modern and effective methods of birth control have had a marked impact on the birth rate, contraception is by no means wholly accepted in American society, as is indicated by the recurring legislative battles over appropriations for contraceptive research and the dissemination of birth control information and devices, and by the continued enforcement of such statutes as the one held invalid in Carey.

4. In Eisenstadt v. Baird, 405 U.S. 438 (1972), cited by the Supreme Court in Roe v. Wade and in Carey, Baird had been convicted in Massachusetts for violation of a statute imposing criminal penalties for selling or giving away contraceptives, the statute containing an exception permitting physicians, or pharmacists on physicians' prescriptions, to furnish contraceptives to married persons for the prevention of pregnancy. Baird had given a lecture on birth control, at the conclusion of which he gave to a young woman a package of vaginal foam, as a sample of one kind of contra-

ceptive. After his conviction in the state court, Baird sought federal habeas corpus, which the Supreme Court granted. The Court first held that
he had standing to raise the constitutionality of the Massachusetts statute,
and then held that the statute violated the Equal Protection Clause of the
Fourteenth Amendment by forbidding access to contraceptives on the part
of unmarried persons while making them available to married persons. The
Court, after a detailed scrutiny of the statute and its possible purposes,
found that the distinction it made between married and unmarried persons
respecting their ability to obtain contraceptives in Massachusetts had no rational relation to any conceivable purposes of the Massachusetts criminal
statute. In the course of its opinion the Court made the following reference to Griswold v. Connecticut: (405 U.S. at 453)

"If under *Griswold* the distribution of contraceptives to married persons cannot be prohibited, a ban on distribution to unmarried persons would
be equally impermissible. It is true that in *Griswold* the right of privacy
in question inhered in the marital relationship. Yet the marital couple is
not an independent entity with a mind and heart of its own, but an association of two individuals each with a separate intellectual and emotional
make-up. If the right of privacy means anything, it is the right of the *individual,* married or single, to be free from unwarranted governmental intrusion into matters so fundamentally affecting a person as the decision
whether to bear or beget a child."

5. Does the Court's opinion in *Carey* apply the fundamental right-
compelling state interest analysis to the New York statute? If so, how is
the fundamental right defined? Justice Powell's opinion asserts that the
earlier cases did not apply the compelling state interest test. Is he correct
in this?

6. How should the following cases be decided, in view of *Carey* and *Eisenstadt*?

(a) The University Health Service of Siwash University provides, as
part of the service available to students, contraceptives in the form of the
"pill" or IUD's. Siwash is a state university. Pursuant to a resolution of
the Board of Regents, however, these may only be dispensed to women students who furnish satisfactory evidence that they are married. An unmarried woman student sues the University, asking the court to order it to furnish her with contraceptives. How should her suit be decided?

(b) A state health clinic has a policy of not providing contraceptives to
minors who are not married unless they have parental consent. An unmarried minor sued to invalidate this policy. How should this suit be decided?
Should the court, as a matter of procedure, give notice of the suit to the
plaintiff's parents? Cf. M. S. v. Wermers, 557 F.2d 170 (8th Cir. 1977),
1978 Wash.U.L.Q. 431. What should be the result if the clinic's policy was
merely that the minor had to give notice to her parents that she was seeking contraceptives? Doe v. Irwin, 615 F.2d 1162 (6th Cir. 1980), 25 Wayne
L.Rev. 1135 (1979).

7. Some states expressly permit minors to obtain contraceptives without parental consent. See Note, A Minor's Right to Contraceptives, 7 U.C.
Davis L.Rev. 270, 279 (1974). Would you advocate such a statute or regulation? The Supreme Court, in footnote 21 to the *Carey* opinion, indicates
some of the physical and psychological harms to mother and child which are

likely to result from teenage pregnancy. The problem of teenage pregnancy is compounded by the increase in sexual activity by teenagers in recent years. Zelnick & Kantner, Sexual and Contraceptive Experience of Young Unmarried Women in the United States, 1976 and 1971, 9 Family Planning Perspectives 55 (1977) found that sexual activity among never-married teenage women increased by 30% between 1971 and 1976. More than one million teenage women became pregnant each year. See Zero Population Growth, Teenage Pregnancy: A Major Problem for Minors (1978). In recognition of the problem some states provide family planning services at state expense. U.S. Dep't of Health, Education and Welfare, Family Planning, Contraception and Voluntary Sterilization: An Analysis of Laws and Policies in the United States, Each State and Jurisdiction 58 (1974).

IN RE STERILIZATION OF MOORE

Supreme Court of North Carolina, 1976.
289 N.C. 95, 221 S.E.2d 307.

On 21 May 1975 a petition was filed in Forsyth County District Court by Gerald M. Thornton, Director, Forsyth County Department of Social Services, requesting that the court enter an order authorizing the sterilization of Joseph Lee Moore, a minor. The petition was accompanied by the consent of the respondent, Joseph Lee Moore, and his mother, Dora I. Moore. A psychological report included in the petition indicated that Joseph is presently functioning at a moderately retarded level of measured intelligence, with a Full Scale I.Q. of under 40 and a Test Age score of 8. The petitioner believed Joseph to be a proper subject for sterilization because it is likely that unless sterilized he would procreate a child or children who would probably have serious physical, mental or nervous diseases or deficiencies. The accompanying statement by the examining physician, Dr. Ruth O'Neal found no known contraindication to the requested surgical procedure.

The respondent, through his guardian ad litem and attorney, in apt time objected to the petition and requested a hearing. This matter was heard on 29 July 1975 before A. Lincoln Sherk, J., in Forsyth District Court, Juvenile Division. The respondent filed a motion to quash and dismiss the petition, alleging that G.S. 35–36, et seq., was unconstitutional. This motion was allowed and notice of appeal was given by the State to Forsyth Superior Court.

The matter was heard *de novo* before McConnell, J., at the 28 July 1975 Civil Session of Forsyth Superior Court. The respondent again made his motions to quash or dismiss the petition. Judge McConnell allowed the motion, finding G.S. 35–36 through G.S. 35–50, inclusive, unconstitutional. The District Attorney for the Twenty-First Judicial District excepted to the judgment and for the State gave notice of appeal to the Court of Appeals. The respondent petitioned the Supreme Court to hear this matter prior to determination by the Court of Appeals. This petition was allowed on 27 August 1975.

MOORE, Justice. The only question before us on this appeal is the constitutionality of G.S. 35–36 through G.S. 35–50, inclusive.

The respondent attacks these statutes on the grounds that they are violative of the Due Process Clause of the Fourteenth Amendment to the United States Constitution and the Law of the Land Clause of Article I, Section 19, of the North Carolina Constitution, both from procedural and substantive standpoints, that they deny the respondent equal protection of the law, are unconstitutionally vague and arbitrary, and provide for cruel and unusual punishment. The term "law of the land" as used in Article I, Section 19, of the Constitution of North Carolina, is synonymous with "due process of law" as used in the Fourteenth Amendment to the Federal Constitution.

The right of a state to sterilize retarded or insane persons was first upheld by the United States Supreme Court in Buck v. Bell, 274 U.S. 200, 47 S.Ct. 584, 71 L.Ed. 1000 (1927). In that case, in upholding a Virginia sterilization law, the Court held that the state may provide for the sterilization of a feebleminded inmate of a state institution where it is found that she is the probable potential parent of socially inadequate offspring likewise afflicted, and that she may be sterilized without detriment to her general health, and that her welfare and that of society will be promoted by her sterilization. Since *Buck,* many states have passed sterilization laws. See Validity of Statutes Authorizing Asexualization or Sterilization of Criminals or Mental Defectives, Annot., 53 A.L.R.3d 960 (1973).

Most of these statutes have been declared constitutional. The grounds for declaring some of the statutes unconstitutional were lack of notice and a hearing, In re Hendrickson, 12 Wash.2d 600, 123 P.2d 322 (1942), In re Opinion of the Justices, 230 Ala. 543, 162 So. 123 (1935), Williams v. Smith, 190 Ind. 526, 131 N.E. 2 (1921); equal protection because limited to those imprisoned or committed, Haynes v. Lapeer, Circuit Judge, 201 Mich. 138, 166 N.W. 938 (1918), Smith v. Board of Examiners of Feeble-Minded, 85 N.J.Law 46, 88 A. 963 (1913), In re Thomson, 103 Misc. 23, 169 N.Y.S. 638, aff'd 185 App. Div. 902, 171 N.Y.S. 1094 (1918), Skinner v. Oklahoma, 316 U.S. 535, 62 S.Ct. 1110, 86 L.Ed. 1655 (1942); or cruel and unusual punishment, Davis v. Berry, 216 F. 413 (S.D.Iowa 1914), rev'd on other grounds, 242 U.S. 468, 37 S.Ct. 208, 61 L.Ed. 441 (1917).

Our research does not disclose any case which holds that a state does not have the right to sterilize an insane or a retarded person if notice and hearing are provided, if it is applied equally to all persons, and if it is not prescribed as a punishment for a crime.

Respondent contends, however, that not all the requirements of procedural due process have been met in this case. A former sterilization statute was held unconstitutional by this Court on procedural grounds, specifically that notice and a hearing were not provided. See Brewer v. Valk, 204 N.C. 186, 167 S.E. 638 (1933). The present statute, effective 1 January 1975, sought to correct the defects found in the former statute. G.S. 35–36 and G.S. 35–37 both provided that "no operation authorized in this section shall be lawful unless and until the provisions of this Article shall first be complied with." G.S. 35–41 provides that at least twenty days prior to a hearing on the petition in the district court, a copy of such petition must be served on the resident of the institution, patient, or noninstitutional individual and on the legal or natural guardian, guardian ad litem, or next of kin of the resident of the institution, patient, or noninstitutional individual. G.S. 35–44 provides for a hearing, if requested, before the judge of the district court. G.S. 35–44 also provides for an appeal from the judgment of the district court to the superior court for a trial *de novo* with the right upon the application of either party to be heard before a jury and the further right of appeal to the appellate courts for judicial review.

G.S. 35–45 provides:

"The person alleged to be subject to the provisions of this section shall have the right to counsel at all stages of the proceedings provided for herein. This person and all others served with the notification provided for in G.S. 35–41 shall be fully informed of the person's entitlement to counsel at the time of this service of notice. This information shall be given in language and in a manner calculated to insure, insofar as such is possible in view of the individual's capability to comprehend it, that the recipient understands the entitlement. Every person subject to be sterilized under this Article after the filing of the petition shall have counsel at every stage of the proceedings. If there is a conflict between the election of the person concerned and that of the other persons being served with notice, determination of the question of representation by counsel shall be made by the court having jurisdiction of the case. The person concerned may, in any instance, be represented by counsel retained by him. In cases of claimed indigency, a request for counsel shall be processed in the manner provided for in Subchapter IX, Chapter 7A, General Statutes of North Carolina."

Despite the above specified safeguards, respondent still asserts that two important procedural rights have been omitted: (1) a provision that the State will provide the funds necessary to obtain a medical expert on behalf of the respondent and (2) the right of cross-examination. It is true that this statute does not require the State to pay a medical expert on behalf of the respondent. However, G.S. 7A–454 allows the court in its discretion to approve a fee for the services of an expert witness who testifies for an indigent person. We know of no constitutional mandate that requires more. See generally "Right of Indigent Defendant in Criminal Case to Aid of State by Appointment of Investigator or Expert," Annot., 34 A.L.R.3d 1256

(1970). As aptly stated by the Supreme Court of Arizona in State v. Crose, 88 Ariz. 389, 357 P.2d 136 (1960):

"* * * [D]efendant contends that the right to have medical experts appointed by the court, at the state's expense, to examine him and assist his defense, is an integral and essential part of his constitutionally-guaranteed right to counsel. He has cited us no authority to support that position, and our own independent investigation has disclosed none. That he has the right to counsel * * * is not in doubt. * * * We know of nothing, however, either by constitution or by statute, requiring the state at its own expense to make available to the defendant, in addition to counsel, the full paraphernalia of defense. * * * We have no doubt that those who make the law could appropriately provide impecunious defendants with such assistance as was sought here, were it deemed practicable and in the public interest to do so. They have not done so. They were under no constitutional compulsion to do so. * * *"

The right of cross-examination is specifically provided by G.S. 35–43: "In the event a hearing is requested, the district attorney * * * shall present the evidence for the petitioner. *The respondent shall be entitled to examine the petitioner's witnesses and shall be entitled to present evidence in his own behalf."* (Emphasis added.) In order to assure this right, the only requirement is that the respondent, his guardian, attorney or other interested party object in writing to the sterilization. Since respondent is represented at every stage of the proceeding, we do not think this requirement is unduly burdensome.

We hold that the provisions of this statute far exceed the minimum requirements of procedural due process.

Respondent further contends that the statutes in question deny him substantive due process. "Due process" has a dual significance, as it pertains to procedure and substantive law. As to procedure, it means notice and an opportunity to be heard and to defend in an orderly proceeding adapted to the nature of the case before a competent and impartial tribunal having jurisdiction of the cause. In substantive law, due process may be characterized as a standard of reasonableness and as such it is a limitation upon the exercise of the police power. "Undoubtedly, the State possesses the police power in its capacity as a sovereign, and in the exercise thereof, the legislature may enact laws, within constitutional limits, to protect or promote the health, morals, order, safety, and general welfare of society. [Citations omitted.]" State v. Ballance, 229 N.C. 764, 769, 51 S.E.2d 731, 734 (1949). "* * * 'If a statute is to be sustained as a legitimate exercise of the police power, it must have a rational, real, or substantial relation to the public health, morals, order, or safety, or the general welfare.' * * *" Surplus Store, Inc. v. Hunter, supra, 25 N. C. at 210, 125 S.E.2d at 767; * * *.

The traditional substantive due process test has been that a statute must have a rational relation to a valid state objective. In a growing series of decisions, the United States Supreme Court has recognized a right of privacy emanating from the Fourteenth Amendment's concept of personal liberty or encompassed within the penumbra of the Bill of Rights that includes the abortion decision, Roe v. Wade, 410 U.S. 113, 93 S.Ct. 705, 35 L.Ed.2d 147 (1973); certain marital activities, Loving v. Virginia, 388 U.S. 1, 87 S.Ct. 1817, 18 L. Ed.2d 1010 (1967), and Griswold v. Connecticut, 381 U.S. 479, 85 S. Ct. 1678, 14 L.Ed.2d 510 (1964); and procreation, Eisenstadt v. Baird, 405 U.S. 438, 92 S.Ct. 1029, 31 L.Ed.2d 349 (1972), and Skinner v. Oklahoma, supra. In Eisenstadt, the Court specifically recognized "* * * the right of the *individual,* married or single, to be free from unwarranted governmental intrusion into matters so fundamentally affecting a person as the decision whether to bear or beget a child.   *   *   *" However, in Roe v. Wade, supra, 410 U.S. at 154–55, 93 S.Ct. at 727, Mr. Justice Blackmun, speaking for the Court, said:

"* * * The Court's decisions recognizing a right of privacy also acknowledge that some state regulation in areas protected by that right is appropriate. As noted above, a State may properly assert important interests in safeguarding health, in maintaining medical standards, and in protecting potential life.   *   *   *

"We therefore, conclude that the right of personal privacy * * * is not unqualified and must be considered against important state interests in regulation.

*   *   *

"Where certain 'fundamental rights' are involved, the Court has held that regulation limiting these rights may be justified only by a 'compelling state interest,' [citations omitted], and that legislative enactments must be narrowly drawn to express only the legitimate state interests at stake. [Citations omitted.]"

The right to procreate is not absolute but is vulnerable to a certain degree of state regulation. Roe v. Wade, supra; Buck v. Bell, supra. The two state interests recognized as paramount to the individual's freedom of choice in Roe v. Wade, supra, at least after the first trimester of pregnancy, were the state's concern with the health of the mother and the potential life of the child. The welfare of the parent and the future life and health of the unborn child are also the chief concerns of the State of North Carolina in authorizing sterilization of individuals under certain circumstances.

The interest of the unborn child is sufficient to warrant sterilization of a retarded individual. "The state's concern for the welfare of its citizenry extends to future generations and when there is overwhelming evidence   *   *   *   that a potential parent will be unable to provide a proper environment for a child because of his own mental illness or mental retardation, the state has sufficient interest to order sterilization." Cook v. State, 9 Or.App. 224, 495 P.2d 768 (1972). The people of North Carolina also have a right to prevent the procreation of children who will become a burden on the State.

"It can hardly be disputed that the right of a woman to bear and the right of a man to beget children is a natural and constitutional right, nor can it be successfully disputed that no citizen has any rights that are superior to the common welfare. Acting for the public good, the state, in the exercise of its police power, may impose reasonable restrictions upon the natural and constitutional rights of its citizens. Measured by its injurious effect upon society, the state may limit a class of citizens in its right to bear or beget children with an inherited tendency to mental deficiency, including feeble-mindedness, idiocy, or imbecility. It is the function of the Legislature, and its duty as well, to enact appropriate legislation to protect the public and preserve the race from the known effects of the procreation of mentally deficient children by the mentally deficient. * * *" In re Cavitt, 182 Neb. 712, 157 N.W.2d 171 (1968).

The United States Supreme Court has also held that the welfare of all citizens should take precedence over the rights of individuals to procreate. In Buck v. Bell, supra, the Court said: "* * * It is better for all the world, if instead of waiting to execute degenerate offspring for crime, or to let them starve for their imbecility, society can prevent those who are manifestly unfit from continuing their kind. The principle that sustains compulsory vaccination is broad enough to cover cutting the Fallopian tubes. Jacobson v. Massachusetts, 197 U.S. 11, 25 S.Ct. 358, 49 L.Ed. 643, 3 Ann.Cas. 765. * * *"

Furthermore, the sterilization of a mentally ill or retarded individual at certain times may be in the best interest of that individual. The mentally ill or retarded individual may not be capable of determining his inability to cope with children. In addition, he may be capable of functioning in society and caring for his own needs but may be unable to handle the additional responsibility of children. This individual also may not be able to practice other forms of birth control and therefore sterilization is the only available remedy. Sterilization itself does not prevent the normal sex drive of the person, it only prevents procreation. Therefore, the State may only be providing for the welfare of the individual when this individual is unable to do so for himself.

We hold that the sterilization of mentally ill or retarded persons under the safeguards as set out in G.S. 35–36 through G.S. 35–50, inclusive, is a valid and reasonable exercise of the police power, and that these state interests rise to the level of a compelling state interest. See Village of Belle Terre v. Boraas, 416 U.S. 1, 94 S.Ct. 1536, 39 L.Ed.2d 797 (1974).

The equal protection clauses of the United States and North Carolina Constitutions impose upon lawmaking bodies the requirement that any legislative classification "be based on differences that are reasonably related to the purposes of the Act in which it is found." Such classifications will be upheld provided the classification is founded upon reasonable distinctions, affects all persons similarly situated or engaged in the same business without discrimination, and has some reasonable relation to the public peace, welfare and safety. "* * * When a special class of persons * * * is singled out by the Legislature for special treatment, there must be a reasonable relation between the classification and the object of the statute. * * *" State v. Mems, 281 N.C. 658, 673, 190 S.E.2d 164, 174 (1972).

The object of G.S. 35–36 through G.S. 35–50, inclusive, is to prevent the procreation of children by a mentally ill or retarded individual who because of physical, mental or nervous disease or deficiency which is not likely to materially improve, would probably be unable to care for a child or children or who would likely, unless sterilized, procreate a child or children who probably would have serious physical, mental or nervous diseases or deficiencies. Considering this object, the classification under these statutes is reasonable.

Sterilization laws in several states have been declared unconstitutional because they affect only a certain class of mentally ill or retarded persons. Skinner v. Oklahoma, supra; Haynes v. Lapeer, Circuit Judge, supra; In Re Thomson, supra; Smith v. Board of Examiners of Feeble-Minded, supra. These cases declared laws unconstitutional when the law provided for a group of the feebleminded to be sterilized, such as those institutionalized, and for another group of feebleminded, such as those not institutionalized, not to be sterilized. G.S. 35–36 and G.S. 35–37 provide for the sterilization of all mentally ill or retarded persons inside or outside an institution who meet the requirments of these statutes. We have found no case that holds that sterilization of all mentally ill or retarded persons denies equal protection. Many cases have held otherwise. Buck v. Bell, supra; Smith v. Command, 231 Mich. 409, 204 N.W. 140 (1925). As said by Mr. Justice Holmes in Buck v. Bell, supra:

"But, it is said, however it might be if this reasoning were applied generally, it fails when it is confined to the small number who are in the institutions named and is not applied to the multitudes outside. It is the usual last resort of constitutional arguments to point out shortcomings of this sort. But the answer is that the law does all that is needed when it does all that it can, indicates a policy, applies it to all within the lines, and seeks to bring within the lines all similarly situated so far and so fast as its means allow. Of course so far as the operations enable those who otherwise must be kept confined to be returned to the world, and thus open the asylum to others, the equality aimed at will be more nearly reached."

Since the North Carolina law applies to all those named in the statute (G.S. 35–43), these statutes, G.S. 35–36 through G.S. 35–50, inclusive, do not violate the equal protection clauses of the United States Constitution or the Constitution of North Carolina.

Respondent next asserts that this legislation provides no adequate judicial standard to guide the court in reaching a decision whether to authorize the sterilization of an individual. Respondent points to the indefiniteness of the terms found in G.S. 35–43:

" * * * If the judge of the district court shall find from the evidence that the person alleged to be subject to this section is subject to it and that because of a physical, mental, or nervous disease or deficiency which is not *likely* to materially improve, the person would *probably* be unable to care for a child or children; or, because the person would be *likely*, unless sterilized, to procreate a child or children which *probably* would have serious physical, mental, or nervous diseases or deficiencies, he shall enter an order and judgment authorizing the physician or surgeon named in the petition to perform the operation." (Emphasis added.)

Defendant contends that these indefinite terms render the statute unconstitutionally vague and arbitrary; that there exists no standard at all, except the subjective determination of an individual judge.

It is true that a statute must be held void if it is so loosely and obscurely drawn as to be incapable of enforcement. But, as stated in Hobbs v. Moore County, 267 N.C. 665, 149 S.E.2d 1 (1966):

"However, as was said in State v. Partlow, supra [91 N.C. 550, 49 Am.Rep. 652 (1884)], 'It is plainly the duty of the court to so construe a statute, ambiguous in its meaning, as to give effect to the legislative intent, if this be practicable.' It is also well established that this Court will not adjudge an act of the General Assembly unconstitutional unless it is clearly so. Where a statute is susceptible of two interpretations, one of which will render it constitutional and the other will render it unconstitutional, the former will be adopted. If possible, the language of a statute will be interpreted so as to avoid an absurd consequence. A statute is never to be construed so as to require an impossibility if that result can be avoided by another fair and reasonable construction of its terms. 'A statute or amendment formally passed is presumed and if permissible should be construed so as to have some meaning.' Mitchell v. R. R., 183 N.C. 162, 110 S.E. 859.

"* * * [I]mpossible standards of statutory clarity are not required by the constitution. When the language of a statute * * * prescribes boundaries sufficiently distinct for judges and juries to interpret and administer it uniformly, constitutional requirements are fully met. United States v. Petrillo, 332 U.S. 1, 67 S.Ct. 1538, 91 L. Ed. 1877." In re Burrus, 275 N.C. 517, 531, 169 S.E.2d 879, 888 (1969).

Several recent United States Supreme Court opinions have spoken to this issue of unconstitutional vagueness or lack of any judicial standard. In Parker v. Levy, 417 U.S. 733, 94 S.Ct. 2547, 41 L.Ed.2d 439 (1974), the Court upheld the statute providing for court-martial of an officer for "conduct unbecoming an officer and a gentleman," against attack that it was too vague and arbitrary, stating, " '[t]he doctrine incorporates notions of fair notice or warning. Moreover, it requires legislatures to set reasonably clear guidelines for law enforcement officials and triers of fact in order to prevent "arbitrary and discriminatory enforcement." * * *' [Citation omitted.]" The same result was reached in Arnett v. Kennedy, 416 U.S. 134, 94 S.Ct. 1633, 40 L.Ed.2d 15 (1974), where the Court sustained a statute providing for removal of nonprobationary federal employees only "for such cause as will promote the efficiency of the service." The Supreme Court has recognized that " * * * words inevitably contain germs of uncertainty and * * * there may be disputes about the meaning of such terms. * * *," but has reiterated that if they can be sufficiently understood and complied with, the statute will be upheld. * * *

In the light of the foregoing principles, we believe that G.S. 35–36 through G.S. 35–50 meet this constitutional standard. The definitions of "mental disease," "mental illness" and "mental defective" are found in G.S. 35–1.1, the same chapter as the sterilization procedure, and are capable of being understood and complied with by the triers of fact with the help of experts in the field. It is conceded that the words "likely" and "probably" necessarily contain germs of uncertainty. However, it is the duty of the court to construe a statute, ambiguous in its meaning, so as to give effect to the legislative intent. Here, it is clear that the General Assembly intended to provide the mentally ill and defective with sufficient safeguards to prevent misuse of this potentially dangerous procedure. The statute does not specify the burden of proof that the petitioner must meet before the order authorizing the sterilization can be entered. In keeping with the intent of the General Assembly, clearly expressed throughout the article, that the rights of the individual must be fully protected, we hold that the evidence must be clear, strong and convincing before such an order may be entered. So construed, we hold that G.S. 35–36 through G.S. 35–50, inclusive, provide a sufficient judicial standard and are not unconstitutionally vague or arbitrary.

The respondent's next contention that sterilization amounts to cruel and unusual punishment is without basis in law in this case. The cruel and unusual punishment clause of the Constitution refers to those persons convicted of a crime. Since this is not a criminal proceeding, there is no basis for the cruel and unusual argument. The two cases cited in the *amicus curiae* brief, Davis v. Berry, supra, and Mickle v. Henrichs, 262 F. 687 (D.Nev.1918), both held that sterilization of criminals as part of a sentence upon conviction was cruel and unusual punishment. That question is not presented in this case and those cases are not pertinent to decision here.

This unfortunate respondent and his mother both consented to the performance of a vasectomy. While we do not attach much importance to the respondent's consent due to his mental condition, his mother unquestionably is in a position to know what is best for the future of her child. Under the provisions of G.S. 35–36 through G.S. 35–50, inclusive, the rights of respondent and the State will be fully protected at hearing.

We hold, therefore, that the trial court erred in declaring these statutes unconstitutional. The judgment so entered is reversed.

NOTES AND QUESTIONS

1. About twenty states presently have statutes authorizing the involuntary sterilization of limited classes of persons. E. g., Ala.Code tit. 45, § 243 (1959); Cal.Welf. & Inst.Code § 7524 (Supp.1978); Minn.Stat.Ann. §§ 252A.11, 252A.13 (Supp.1978); Wis.Stat.Ann. § 46.12 (1957). The origins of these statutes go back to about 1900 and the eugenic movement, whose adherents thought that future generations of man could be improved by preventing the procreation of the "unfit", defining the term in a variety of unscientific ways. In 1927 Mr. Justice Holmes' famous opinion in Buck v. Bell, 274 U.S. 200 (1927), quoted in the Moore case, upheld the Virginia statute which authorized the involuntary sterilization of inmates of institutions "afflicted with hereditary forms of insanity, imbecility etc.". The attack on the statute rested on the claim that it violated substantive due process, a claim which Justice Holmes rejected with the dictum that "Three generations of imbeciles are enough." 274 U.S. at 207. The woman in this case was described as "feeble-minded", as being the daughter of a "feeble-minded" mother, and as having had a "feeble-minded" child. Subsequent investigations have created some doubt whether the facts were as the Supreme Court assumed them, and whether the daughter was retarded at all. O'Hara and Sanks, Eugenic Sterilization, 45 Geo.L.J. 20, 31 (1956).

It is generally held that the courts may not order involuntary sterilization without express statutory authority. Annot., Jurisdiction of Court to Permit Sterilization of Mentally Defective Person in Absence of Specific Statutory Authority, 74 A.L.R.3d 1210 (1976). Contra: Matter of Grady, 170 N.J.Super. 98, 405 A.2d 851 (1979). A judge who ordered the sterilization of a young woman without statutory authority was personally sued for damages by her when she later learned the nature of the operation which had been performed on her, but the Supreme Court of the United States held, in Stump v. Sparkman, 435 U.S. 349 (1978), that judicial immunity applied to protect him from liability, even though the order for sterilization had been entered in an ex parte and completely irregular proceeding. For an illuminating comment on this case see Nagel, Judicial Immunity and Sovereignty, 6 Hast.Const.L.Q. 237 (1978).

2. What interests of the state are being vindicated by the North Carolina statute in the Moore case? Do you agree with the court in that case that these interests are "compelling", so that the statute is constitutional under Roe v. Wade, and Carey v. Population Services International? What

evidence was there in the Moore case that these interests would in fact be vindicated by the sterilization of Moore? Is evidence on this point required in order to establish the constitutionality of the statute? See Ferster, Eliminating the Unfit—Is Sterilization the Answer? 27 Ohio St.L.J. 591 (1966); Murdock, Sterilization of the Retarded: A Problem or a Solution? 62 Cal.L.Rev. 917 (1974); Vukowich, The Dawning of the Brave New World—Legal, Ethical, and Social Issues of Eugenics, 1971 U. of Ill.L. F. 189; Note, Sexual Sterilization—Constitutional Validity of Involuntary Sterilization and Consent Determinative of Voluntariness, 40 Mo.L.Rev. 509 (1975). See also North Carolina Assn. for Retarded Children v. State, 420 F.Supp. 451 (M.D.N.C.1976).

3. A state, perhaps somewhat irritated by the United States Supreme Court's penchant for second-guessing legislatures, enacts the following statute: "If, after hearing all the relevant and material evidence, the court determines that a compelling state interest requires that the petition be granted, it shall enter an order for the sterilization * * * of such person." Assuming that the statute also provided full procedural due process, would it be constitutional? Cf. Utah Code Ann. § 64–10–4 (1978).

4. Assuming that a statute similar to North Carolina's is in force and is constitutional, should the court order sterilization after hearing the following evidence?

D is a girl eleven years old. Her father is dead and her mother makes a precarious living as a part-time cleaning woman, supporting D and two other children. The medical evidence is that D is suffering from Sotos syndrome, a condition which produces an unusual set of congenital abnormalities, including some mental impairment resulting in dull intelligence (I.Q. about 80), accelerated growth during infancy, epilepsy, general clumsiness, unusual facial appearance, behavior problems including emotional instability, and some aggressive tendencies. D has lately been placed in a special school staffed by teachers experienced in working with children who have learning difficulties. As a result she has learned to read and speak reasonably well, and can write but not very well, can dress herself and can ride a bicycle. Her behavior has improved but there are still times when she is aggressive and hard to handle. D reached puberty at the age of ten, and her mother decided she should be sterilized. The mother then brought this proceeding, testifying that she was concerned lest D be seduced and give birth to a child who would be abnormal, or at least whom D would be unable to care for properly. The school authorities testified that in their opinion the operation was not needed, and that predictions about D's ability to care for children would be premature at this stage. D's physician recommended the operation, testifying that it was quite safe and that it would permanently prevent D from having children. He also testified that the operation would be irreversible. See In re D (A Minor), [1976] Fam.Div. 185, [1976] 2 W.L.R. 279.

5. Sterilization for men (vasectomy) consists of a relatively simple procedure in which the surgeon cuts and ties the vas deferens, the tube which carries sperm from the testes to the urinary canal, thereby preventing sperm from being included in the semen when ejaculation occurs. For women the operation is somewhat more complicated and usually requires hospitalization. The abdomen is incised and the fallopian tubes are either tied (tubal ligation) or cut (salpingectomy), thereby preventing the passage

of ova from the ovaries and making union with the sperm impossible. Both operations are relatively safe and both are effective in preventing conception, although there is a slight chance that the severed or tied tubes might grow back together. There is a technique for rejoining the tubes, but the percentage of success with this operation is low enough that sterilization has to be assumed to be an irreversible procedure at the present time. C. Westoff, N. Ryder, The Contraceptive Revolution Ch. V (1977); Overstreet, Female Sterilization, in Manual of Family Planning and Contraceptive Practice 404 (M. Calderone ed. 1970); Tietze, Bongaarts, Schearer, Mortality Associated With the Control of Fertility, 8 Family Planning Perspectives 6 (1976).

In the past there has been some doubt whether voluntary sterilization may be lawfully performed upon a consenting adult for non-therapeutic reasons, that is, as a birth control measure. Miller and Dean, Civil and Criminal Liability of Physicians for Sterilization Operations, 16 A.B.A.J. 158 (1930); G. Williams, The Sanctity of Life and the Criminal Law 74–76, 102–110 (1957). Sterilization for contraceptive purposes is now legal in all or nearly all states when performed upon an adult capable of giving a binding consent. Some states have statutes expressly authorizing contraceptive sterilization, with certain safeguards as to consent. See, e. g., Ga.Code Ann. § 84–932 to 84–936 (1979); N.C.Gen.Stat. § 90–271 (1975); Va.Code Ann. § 32–423 (Supp.1978). And in Jessin v. County of Shasta, 274 Cal. App.2d 737, 79 Cal.Rptr. 359 (1969) the court held that voluntary, non-therapeutic sterilization in California is lawful, suggesting that a contrary rule might violate the constitution, under Griswold v. Connecticut, supra, page 73. See also Greenawalt, Criminal Law and Population Control, 24 Vand.L. Rev. 465, 476 (1971).

6. The matter of voluntary contraceptive sterilization becomes complex where minors are involved. In some states the courts have held that "mature minors" may give consent to surgical operations which can be characterized as not serious. E. g., Baird v. Attorney General, 371 Mass. 741, 360 N.E.2d 288 (1977). Whether sterilization would be so characterized seems doubtful in view of its permanent effect upon the minor's reproductive capacity. Relf v. Weinberger, 372 F.Supp. 1196 (D.D.C.1974) held that certain regulations of the Department of Health, Education and Welfare covering the funding of sterilizations were invalid, on evidence that they had been used to fund the sterilization of minors who either were incapable of giving consent or whose consent had been coerced by threats that welfare benefits or medical treatment would be withheld unless sterilization were consented to. The case seems to assume that minors are incapable of consenting to sterilization under state law, since it took the position that the Department had no authority to fund the sterilization of minors, since they were incompetent to consent to the operation. See also Relf v. Mathews, 403 F.Supp. 1235 (D.D.C.1975), vacated and remanded, Relf v. Weinburger, 565 F.2d 722 (D.C.Cir. 1977). Voe v. Califano, 434 F.Supp. 1058 (D.Conn.1977) held that the ban on medicaid funds for sterilization of minors is constitutional. The present HEW regulations on funding of sterilizations forbid payment for sterilization of persons under twenty-one, notwithstanding that eighteen is the age of majority in most states today. 43 Fed.Reg. 52,146 ff. (1978), to be codified in 42 C.F.R. §§ 50.203, 50.205. These regulations have had an effect beyond the mere question of funding

due to the tendency of medicaid regulations to bcome guides for general medical procedures.

Voe v. Califano, supra, is a good example of the consequences of the bureaucratic bungling one has come to expect from the Department of Health, Education and Welfare, compounded by the uninformed decision in the Relf case. In Voe a twenty-year-old woman who was eligible for medicaid sued to obtain public funding for sterilization. There was no question that she had made a voluntary and informed decision to be sterilized. She had two small children, had had a third child who died within hours of birth, had had one miscarriage and six abortions. For medical reasons oral contraceptives and other forms of birth control were not available to her. The court regretfully held that the HEW regulations were valid and that therefore the young woman had no remedy.

7. The discussion in the preceding paragraph suggests some questions involving the sterilization of minors:

(a) H and W have a thirteen-year-old daughter, Susan. Susan is severely mentally retarded and both blind and deaf. She is enrolled in a special school where she receives the custodial care she requires, but returns to stay with her parents on the weekends. There is no likelihood that she can be admitted to a state institution. Susan began to menstruate at age eleven. Menstruation causes her severe physical and psychological distress and she cannot care for her own needs at those times. She is capable of becoming pregnant, but if she did would be subject to serious risks because of her inability to communicate with her physician. She is unable to use any of the standard contraceptives. H and W have consulted physicians who agree that sterilization is "medically indicated" for Susan, but who refuse to perform the operation on the ground that Susan is incapable of giving a binding consent. The local hospital takes the same position. The state has no statute permitting involuntary sterilization. In a suit by H and W against the physician and hospital seeking a court order for the sterilization, what should be the result? What should be the result in a similar suit brought by both Susan and her parents if Susan were a wholly normal sixteen-year-old girl who insisted she wanted to be sterilized because she never wanted to have any children? See Ruby v. Massey, 452 F.Supp. 361 (D.Conn. 1978).

(b) A state statute provides that no minor may be sterilized without his or her parents' consent. Would such a statute be constitutional under Planned Parenthood v. Danforth, supra, page 251, and Bellotti v. Baird, supra, page 266? Would the statute be constitutional if it merely required consultation with the parents?

(c) June Doe, a girl of seventeen, ran away from home at the age of fourteen and had been living with three other girls and four boys in a slum apartment in a large city. They were supported in a meagre way by pooling the part-time earnings of the boys. At the age of fifteen June had a child but did not know who the father was. The child was removed from her custody by the juvenile court when it was eighteen months old on a finding that the baby was dependent and neglected. June's parental rights with respect to this baby were terminated and the baby successfully placed for adoption. Just recently June has had another baby, and since she had been having sexual relations only with Tom, one of the boys in the group, over the preceding year, she was sure he was the father. Tom is also seventeen years old, and admits with some pride to being the father of at least three other children, although he does not know where these children or their mothers are. The local visiting nurse was given June's name when June was discharged from the hospital after the birth and called upon June two weeks later. The nurse found the baby malnourished and suffering from a skin disease caused by infrequent bathing and lack of care. The nurse notified the juvenile court, and after an investigation of the situation by its staff a petition was filed alleging that the baby was dependent and neglected. Another petition was filed alleging that Tom was delinquent in that he had violated the state statute making fornication a crime and had failed to support the child whose father he was, also a crime. The juvenile court heard both petitions at once, found the baby neglected and placed it in a foster home. The court then ordered June to report to the local clinic of Planned Parenthood to be fitted with an intrauterine contraceptive device (IUD) by the Planned Parenthood physician. The order stated that the IUD was to be retained by June, provided no medical reasons for its removal appeared, until she should reach age twenty-one. The court found Tom to be a delinquent, under the statute which defined a delinquent child to be "any child under the age of eighteen who has violated any state or federal law". The court then sentenced Tom to one year in the state training school, but suspended the sentence on condition that Tom also attend the Planned Parenthood clinic and arrange to be sterilized by the clinic physician.

If you were appointed to represent June and Tom on an appeal from the juvenile court's decision, what arguments would you make and how would you expect the appellate court to rule? Assume that the juvenile court had jurisdiction of the case and that the petition and hearing complied with the statutory procedure. The juvenile code authorizes the court in the case of neglect to require the parent to refrain from acts tending to make the home an improper place for the child, or to terminate parental rights. The code also authorizes the court, in cases of delinquency, to impose fines, or to sentence the child to the state training school for a period ending at the child's age twenty-one, or to assign the child to a state supervised work program. The state has no involuntary sterilization statute, however. See In re Simpson, 180 N.E.2d 206 (Ohio Prob.Ct.1962); Wade v. Bethesda Hospital, 337 F.Supp. 671 (S.D.Ohio 1971). On the issue of the judge's personal liability the latter case is presumably overruled by Stump v. Sparkman, 435 U.S. 349 (1978). See also Note, Constitutional Law-Court-Ordered Contraception: A Reasonable Alternative to Institutionalization for Juvenile Unwed Mothers, 1970 Wis.L.Rev. 899; Young, Alverson and Young, Court-Ordered Contraception, 55 A.B.A.J. 223 (1969). Would this case be affected by the fact that the parents of Tom and June gave their consent to the sterilization and the insertion of an IUD, though Tom and June did not consent?

8. Would a statute which required either the consent of, or a consultation with, the spouse for the sterilization of a married person be constitutional?

9. It is proposed to amend the Internal Revenue Code by adding the following provision:

"(a) In order to reduce the birth rate and to avoid serious overpopulation in the United States, which threatens the exhaustion of the nation's resources and the drastic and permanent impairment of its standard of living, the Congress finds it necessary to create a financial incentive for the limitation of families.

"(b) In the case of an individual the following exemptions shall be allowed as deductions in computing taxable income:

"An exemption of $1,000 for each child of the taxpayer, up to a total of two children, *provided, however,* that if the taxpayer has more than two children, he shall be entitled to no exemptions for any children whatever."

Is this proposed statute constitutional? If it is not, can you draft any population control measure which would be constitutional? See Miller and Davidson, Observations on Population Policy-Making and the Constitution, 40 G.W.L.Rev. 618 (1972); Rabin, Population Control Through Financial Incentives, 23 Hast.L.J. 1353 (1972); Brodie, Privacy: The Family and the State, 1972 U.Ill.L.F. 743, 752; Symposium on Population and the Law, 23 Hastings L.J. 1345 (1972); Sherbert v. Verner, 374 U.S. 398 (1963); Flemming v. Nestor, 363 U.S. 603 (1960); American Communications Ass'n v. Douds, 339 U.S. 382 (1950); Merrill, Unconstitutional Conditions, 77 U. Pa.L.Rev. 829 (1929); Hale, Unconstitutional Conditions and Constitutional Rights, 35 Colum.L.Rev. 321 (1935); Note, 73 Harv.L.Rev. 1595 (1960); French, Unconstitutional Conditions, An Analysis, 50 Geo.L.J. 234 (1961).

10. H and W consult D, an obstetrician and gynecologist, when W becomes pregnant. D performs tests verifying the pregnancy and gives W the usual advice about diet and activities during the pregnancy. D negligently fails, however, to take a complete genealogical history of H and W which would have revealed that there was a serious risk that their child might be born with Tay-Sachs disease, a progressive degenerative illness. In fact the baby is born with the disease and dies two years after birth. H and W sue D for medical malpractice. May they recover? If so, what elements of damages would be recoverable? Could they recover for the auguish and distress of having a child with this disease?

Could the child recover from D?

See Howard v. Lecher, 42 N.Y.2d 109, 397 N.Y.S.2d 363, 366 N.E.2d 64 (1977); Becker v. Schwartz, 46 N.Y.2d 401, 413 N.Y.S.2d 895, 386 N.E.2d 807 (1978); Dumer v. St. Michael's Hosp., 69 Wis.2d 766, 233 N.W.2d 372 (1975); Berman v. Allan, 80 N.J. 421, 404 A.2d 8 (1979).

11. H and W have four children and decide that that is enough. Like many other American couples, they decide upon sterilization as the best method of birth control for them. H then has a vasectomy which is negligently performed by his physician, D. Eighteen months later W becomes pregnant and a fifth child is born. The child is normal and healthy. Assuming that H and W are able to prove that the vasectomy was negligently performed, can they recover from D for malpractice? If so, will their damages include all the expenses of feeding, clothing, educating and caring for the child up to the age of majority? See, e. g., Sherlock v. Stillwater Clinic, 260 N.W.2d 169 (Minn.1977); Berman v. Allan, 80 N.J. 421, 404 A. 2d 8 (1979). For a citation of authorities on this question and that of the preceding paragraph, see Clark, Wrongful Conception: A New Kind of Medical Malpractice, 12 Fam.L.Q. 259 (1979). The direct cost of raising a child in the United States (to age eighteen) in 1977 dollars ranges between $35,000 and $53,000. The opportunity cost of a first child for United

States wives has been stated to be about $34,000 in 1977 dollars. See T. Espenshade, The Value and Cost of Children, 32 Population Bull. 3, 25, 26 (1977). The same author suggests methods for measuring the utility of children, which of course may vary greatly with the number of children in the family. An economic analysis of children as "consumer durables" and their utility may be found in G. Becker, The Economic Approach to Human Behavior ch. 9 (1976).

12. The recent successful birth of a "test-tube baby" raises several possible legal questions which are explored in Flannery, Weisman, Lipsett, Braverman, Test Tube Babies: Legal Issues Raised by *In Vitro* Fertilization, 67 Geo.L.J. 1295 (1979). The process referred to involves the removal of ova from the mother, their fertilization by sperm from the father in a laboratory medium and, after a short period in the laboratory, implantation in the mother's uterus where it is hoped it will develop normally and be born in the usual way.

SECTION 2. LEGITIMACY AND PATERNITY

INTRODUCTORY NOTE

At common law the illegitimate child was considered to be "filius nullius", that is, the child of no one. The chief legal disability that resulted from this status was that the illegitimate child could not inherit from either parent. It is also often asserted that he had no right to support from his father, but recent historical research indicates that there were ecclesiastical remedies by which fathers could be and were ordered to support their illegitimate children. Helmholz, Support Orders, Church Courts, and the Rule of Filius Nullius: A Reassessment of the Common Law, 63 Va.L.Rev. 431 (1977). In any event, the Elizabethan Poor Law gave illegitimate children the right to be supported by their fathers. In addition the illegitimate child had to bear the stigma of being a bastard. H. Krause, Illegitimacy: Law and Social Policy, Introduction (1971), hereinafter cited as Krause.

The legitimate child has been traditionally defined in Anglo-American law as one whose parents were married at the time of his conception, or before his birth, or, as Blackstone put it, one who was "born in lawful wedlock or within a competent time afterwards." 1 Blackstone, Commentaries on the Law of England, 446, 454 (Cooley 4th ed. 1899). All other children were held to be illegitimate. Thus a child conceived before his parents' marriage but born after it was legitimate. And a child born after his parents' divorce was legitimate if the birth was near enough to the divorce so that he would have been conceived during the marriage. But if he was born before his parents married, he remained illegitimate even though they later married. These definitions still apply in our law except to the extent that they have been changed by statutes aimed at improving the illegitimate child's condition. One such statute has already been referred to, supra, page 219 providing that the child of an invalid marriage is deemed to be legitimate. In many states there are statutes providing that a child is legitimated by the marriage of his parents after his birth, or in other ways, such as, for example, by the father's specific acknowledgment of his child. See, e. g., Alaska Stat.Ann. § 25.20.050 (1977) (legitimation by marriage of natural parents); N. J.Stat.Ann. § 9:15–1 (1976) (legitimation by marriage of natural parents); N.Y.Dom.Rel.L. § 24 (1977) (legitimation of natural parents); Wis.Stat.Ann. § 245.25 (Supp.1979–1980) (legitimation by marriage of natural parents). An exhaustive citation of legitimation statutes is contained in Krause 10–15 (1971).

The most comprehensive attempt to alleviate the condition of the illegitimate child and at the same time to deal with the complexities which his condition involves is found in the Uniform Parentage Act, 9 Unif.L.Ann. 516 (Supp.1978), in force in about seven states. Sections of this Act are reproduced in relevant places in the discussion which follows. There is also a Uniform Act on Paternity, 9 Unif.L.Ann. 790 (1973) which has been enacted in a few states.

Statutes in all states now impose a duty of support upon the father of the illegitimate child. And statutes in some states permit the illegitimate child to inherit from his father under certain circumstances. See, e. g., Trimble v. Gordon, infra, page 346.

The United States has seen a marked increase in the rate of illegitimate births following World War II. See Schachter and McCarty, Illegitimate Births: United States, 1938–1957, 47 Vital Statistics (Special Reports) 225 (1960); Krause, 257–267; C. Vincent, Unmarried Mothers, 53, 54 (1961). In New York City, for example, 14.8% of all births in 1966 were out of wedlock. N.Y. Times, October 29, 1967, p. 36, col. 1. The Statistical Abstract of the United States for 1978, 65, states that for 1976 illegitimate live births amounted to 14.-8% of all births. The corresponding figure for 1970 was 10.7%. The highest rates of illegitimacy are found among blacks. As Professor Krause points out, that fact, combined with the fact that black illegitimate children are adopted at only a low rate as compared with white illegitimate children, means that the laws which discriminate against illegitimate children have a wider effect upon black children than upon white children. In addition of course this discrimination falls most heavily upon the poor.

Until very recently, therefore, the illegitimate child had no right to inherit from his father, he may have been without other rights which turn on inheritance (such as the right to sue for the wrongful death of a parent), he was under serious handicaps in suing his father for support even though most states gave him such a claim, he was more often than not black, poor and unlikely to be adopted, and he suffered whatever social stigma was connected with being a bastard. Of course all of the harm did not fall upon the child. The unmarried parents of such a child also suffered material and psychological injury in varying degrees. This list of legal and non-legal handicaps constitutes a description in specific terms of a general social problem whose dimensions are measured by the statistics in the preceding paragraph. It intentionally omits any mention of the moral or religious principles which color our views of illegitimacy and which have had a great influence in the formation of the legal rules, since there now seems to be no general agreement on the continuing validity of those principles. This does not imply that they should be ignored. On the contrary the student should try to make himself aware of his own moral and religious beliefs and consciously to take them into account in thinking about the law of illegitimacy.

One might naturally ask why it is that more and more children are being born out of wedlock. The available studies of the subject suggest that the reasons are infinitely complex and various, ranging from broad social changes to individual psychological reactions. Contemporary attitudes toward marriage, sex and the family are undoubtedly involved in many instances. Individual motivation may include a search for affection not found in the family, or a desire for tangible evidence of manhood or womanhood, or in some cases merely ignorance or carelessness about conception or contraception. For discussion of these issues, see I. Josselyn, The Unmarried Mother, reprinted in R. Slovenko, Sexual Behavior and the Law, 356 (1965); C. Vincent, Unmarried Mothers, Ch. II–VI (1961); L. Young, Out of Wedlock (1954).

The cases in the following pages should be evaluated critically in the light of this background.

LEVY v. LOUISIANA

Supreme Court of the United States, 1968.
391 U.S. 68, 88 S.Ct. 1509, 20 L.Ed.2d 436.

Mr. Justice DOUGLAS delivered the opinion of the Court.

Appellant sued on behalf of five illegitimate children to recover, under a Louisiana statute [1] (La.Civ.Code Ann.Art. 2315 (Supp.1967))

1. Every act whatever of man that causes damage to another obliges him by whose fault it happened to repair it.

"The right to recover damages to property caused by an offense or quasi offense is a property right which, on the death of the obligee, is inherited by his legal, instituted, or irregular heirs, subject to the community rights of the surviving spouse.

"The right to recover all other damages caused by an offense or quasi offense, if the injured person dies, shall survive for a period of one year from the death of the deceased in favor of: (1) the surviving spouse and child or children of the deceased, or either such spouse or such child or children; (2) the surviving father and mother of the deceased, or either of them, if he left no spouse or child surviving; and (3) the surviving brothers and sisters of the deceased, or any of them, if he left no spouse, child, or parent surviving. The survivors in whose favor this right of action survives may also recover the damages which they sustained through the wrongful death of the deceased.

for two kinds of damages as a result of the wrongful death of their mother: (1) the damages to them for the loss of their mother; and (2) those based on the survival of a cause of action which the mother had at the time of her death for pain and suffering. Appellees are the doctor who treated her and the insurance company.

We assume in the present state of the pleadings that the mother, Louise Levy, gave birth to these five illegitimate children and that they lived with her; that she treated them as a parent would treat any other child; that she worked as a domestic servant to support them, taking them to church every Sunday and enrolling them, at her own expense, in a parochial school. The Louisiana District Court dismissed the suit. The Court of Appeal affirmed, holding that "child" in Article 2315 means "legitimate child," the denial to illegitimate children of "the right to recover" being "based on morals and general welfare because it discourages bringing children into the world out of wedlock." 192 So.2d 193, 195. The Supreme Court of Louisiana denied certiorari. 250 La. 25, 193 So.2d 530.

The case is here on appeal (28 U.S.C.A. § 1257(2)); and we noted probable jurisdiction, 389 U.S. 925, 88 S.Ct. 290, 19 L.Ed.2d 276, the statute as construed having been sustained against challenge under both the Due Process and Equal Protection Clauses of the Fourteenth Amendment.

We start from the premise that illegitimate children are not "non-persons." They are humans, live, and have their being. They are clearly "persons" within the meaning of the Equal Protection Clause of the Fourteenth Amendment.[4]

While a State has broad power when it comes to making classifications it may not draw a line which constitutes an invidious discrimination against a particular class. See Skinner v. State of Oklahoma, 316 U.S. 535, 541–542, 62 S.Ct. 1110, 1113–1114, 86 L.Ed. 1655 (1941). Though the test has been variously stated, the end result is whether the line drawn is a rational one.   *   *   *

In applying the Equal Protection Clause to social and economic legislation, we give great latitude to the legislature in making classifications.   *   *   *   Even so, would a corporation, which is a "person," for certain purposes, within the meaning of the Equal Protection Clause be required to forgo recovery for wrongs done its interest because its incorporators were all bastards? However that might be, we have been extremely sensitive when it comes to basic civil rights

A right to recover damages under the provisions of this paragraph is a property right which, on the death of the survivor in whose favor the right of action survived, is inherited by his legal, instituted, or irregular heirs, whether suit has been instituted thereon by the survivor or not.

"As used in this article, the words 'child,' 'brother,' 'sister,' 'father,' and 'mother' include a child, brother, sister, father, and mother, by adoption, respectively."

4. No State shall "deny to any person within its jurisdiction the equal protection of the laws."

and have not hesitated to strike down an invidious classification even though it had history and tradition on its side. The rights asserted here involve the intimate, familial relationship between a child and his own mother. When the child's claim of damage for loss of his mother is in issue, why, in terms of "equal protection," should the tortfeasors go free merely because the child is illegitimate? Why should the illegitimate child be denied rights merely because of his birth out of wedlock? He certainly is subject to all the responsibilities of a citizen, including the payment of taxes and conscription under the Selective Service Act. How under our constitutional regime can he be denied correlative rights which other citizens enjoy?

Legitimacy or illegitimacy of birth has no relation to the nature of the wrong allegedly inflicted on the mother. These children, though illegitimate, were dependent on her; she cared for them and nurtured them; they were indeed hers in the biological and in the spiritual sense; in her death they suffered wrong in the sense that any dependent would.

We conclude that it is invidious to discriminate against them when no action, conduct, or demeanor of theirs is possibly relevant to the harm that was done the mother.

Reversed.

NOTES AND QUESTIONS

1. The *Levy* case and the cases subsequent to it are cited and discussed in Clark, Constitutional Protection for the Illegitimate Child? 12 U.Cal.Davis L.Rev. 383 (1979).

2. The Court in Levy v. Louisiana seems to lay down the general proposition that legislative classifications violate the Equal Protection Clause if they are "invidious", but do not if they are "rational." This suggests some questions:

(a) What do the terms "invidous" and "rational" mean, generally and in this context?

(b) Exactly what was "invidious" about the Louisiana statute which, as construed, permitted legitimate children but not illegitimate children to recover for the wrongful death of their mother? Is it that in this case the illegitimate children were dependent upon and loved by their mother, as much so as legitimate children could be? Is it that illegitimate children bear the same biological relationship to their mother as legitimate children, and that it is "invidious" to distinguish between persons having the same biological relationships? Krause, 69. For example, it is sometimes provided by statute that upon adoption a child loses the right to be supported by his natural parents and gains the right to be supported by his adoptive parents. Does such a statute make an invidious distinction between children who are adopted and those who are not on the basis of a legal rather than a biological relationship? Are such statutes therefore invalid under the Equal Protection Clause? An attempt to answer this question might be postponed to problem 5, page 508, infra, in connection with the discussion of In re B.

To take another example, H and W–2 go through a marriage ceremony, H, however, neglecting to mention that he is already married to, and not divorced from, W–1. H is killed through D's negligence. W–2 sues D for wrongful death under the applicable statute giving such a cause of action to the surviving spouse of the deceased. W–1 intervenes, claiming to be the proper plaintiff under the statute, proving the prior marriage, and that there has been no divorce. W–2 proves that she was dependent upon H and W–1 was not, and that H had great affection for her but none for W–1. The court nevertheless holds that W–1 is the proper plaintiff under the statute. Does this holding violate the Equal Protection Clause on the basis of the *Levy* reasoning? May a statute in this instance make a claim turn upon legal rather than biological relationships, ignoring affection and dependency?

(c) Krause, 67, states that the key to *Levy* is that the illegitimate child was placed at a disadvantage purely by virtue of his status as illegitimate, as to which he had no control. In all cases where one's status is beyond his control, and where his status places him at a disadvantage is the result violative of the Equal Protection Clause? Is any status more crucial to a person than citizenship? Is that within his control? See, e. g., 8 U.S.C.A. § 1401 and Gonzalez de Lara v. United States, 439 F.2d 1316 (5th Cir. 1971). Is the status of an adopted child within the child's control?

(d) Is the statute involved in *Levy* concerned with social and economic rights, and so to be upheld if found to have a "rational basis," or is it concerned with "basic civil rights", as to which only a "compelling state interest" will support the legislative enactment? What criteria exist for answering this question? If basic civil rights are involved under this statute, would the same be true of a statute regulating other aspects of the law of tort, such as, for example, a guest statute? Or is it the existence of motherhood in the case which makes the difference? See Gray and Rudovsky, The Court Acknowledges the Illegitimate: Levy v. Louisiana and Glona v. American Guarantee & Liability Insurance Co., 118 U.Pa.L.Rev. 1, 5 (1969); Gunther, Foreword, 86 Harv.L.Rev. 1, 17 (1972); Dandridge v. Williams, 397 U.S. 471 (1971); Shapiro v. Thompson, 394 U.S. 618 (1969).

Justice Harlan's dissent, reproduced infra, page 333, is concerned with many of these questions. Does he deal with them in a satisfactory way?

3. In Levy the illegitimate children were suing for the wrongful death of their *mother*. Is the *Levy* case authority for the principle that a statute would be unconstitutional if it did not permit the illegitimate child to recover for the wrongful death of his *father?* Cf. Parham v. Hughes, infra, page 336; Cannon v. Transamerican Freight Lines, 37 Mich.App. 313, 194 N.W.2d 736 (1971); Jordan v. Delta Drilling Co., 541 P.2d 39 (Wyo.1975); Annot., 789 A.L.R.3d 1230 (1977).

GLONA v. AMERICAN GUARANTEE CO.

Supreme Court of the United States, 1968.
391 U.S. 73, 88 S.Ct. 1515, 20 L.Ed.2d 441.

Mr. Justice DOUGLAS delivered the opinion of the Court.

This suit was brought in the Federal District Court under the head of diversity jurisdiction to recover for a wrongful death suffered in an automobile accident in Louisiana. The plaintiff, a Texas domiciliary, was the mother of the victim, her illegitimate son. Had the Texas wrongful death statute been applicable, it would, as construed, have authorized the action. But summary judgment was granted on the ground that under Louisiana law [3] the mother had no right of action for the death of her illegitimate son. The Court of Appeals affirmed, rejecting the claim that the discrimination violated the Equal Protection Clause of the Fourteenth Amendment. 379 F.2d 545. We granted the petition for a writ of certiorari, 389 U.S. 969, 88 S.Ct. 477, 19 L.Ed.2d 460, in order to hear the case along with Levy v. Louisiana, 391 U.S. 68, 88 S.Ct. 1509, 20 L.Ed.2d 436 (1968).

Louisiana follows a curious course in its sanctions against illegitimacy. A common-law wife is allowed to sue under the Louisiana wrongful death statute. When a married woman gives birth to an illegitimate child, he is, with a few exceptions, conclusively presumed to be legitimate. Louisiana makes no distinction between legitimate children and illegitimate children where incest is concerned. A mother may inherit from an illegitimate child whom she has acknowledged and vice versa. If the illegitimate son had a horse that was killed by the defendant and then died himself, his mother would have a right to sue for the loss of that property. If the illegitimate son were killed in an industrial accident at his place of employment, the mother would be eligible for recovery under the Louisiana Workmen's Compensation Act, if she were a dependent of his. Yet it is argued that since the legislature is dealing with "sin," it can deal with it selectively and is not compelled to adopt comprehensive or even consistent measures. In this sense the present case is different from the *Levy* case where by mere accident of birth the innocent, although illegitimate, child was made a "nonperson" by the legislature, when it came to recovery of damages for the wrongful death of his mother.

Yet we see no possible rational basis for assuming that if the natural mother is allowed recovery for the wrongful death of her illegitimate child, the cause of illegitimacy will be served. It would, indeed, be farfetched to assume that women have illegitimate children so that they can be compensated in damages for their death. A law which creates an open season on illegitimates in the area of automobile accidents gives a windfall to tortfeasors. But it hardly has a causal connection with the "sin," which is, we are told, the historic

---

3. The applicable statutory provision is set out in Levy v. Louisiana, ante, at 69, n. 1. As the Court of Appeals noted, Article 2315 of the Louisiana Civil Code, providing for wrongful death recovery, gives a cause of action to "the surviving father and mother of the deceased, or either of them. * * *" The statute does not state "legitimate" father or "legitimate" mother, but the Louisiana courts have held that a decedent must be legitimate in order for an ascendant or sibling to recover for his death. Youchican v. Texas & P. R. Co., 147 La. 1080, 86 So. 551 (1920); Buie v. Hester, 147 So.2d 733 (Ct. App.La.1962). See also Green v. New Orleans, S. & G. I. R. Co., 141 La. 120, 74 So. 717 (1917); Jackson v. Lindlom, 84 So.2d 101 (Ct.App.La.1955). See also Vaughan v. Dalton-Lard Lumber Co., 119 La. 61, 43 So. 926 (1907).

reason for the creation of the disability. To say that the test of equal protection should be the "legal" rather than the biological relationship is to avoid the issue. For the Equal Protection Clause necessarily limits the authority of a State to draw such "legal" lines as it chooses.

Opening the courts to suits of this kind may conceivably be a temptation to some to assert motherhood fraudulently. That problem, however, concerns burden of proof. Where the claimant is plainly the mother, the State denies equal protection of the laws to withhold relief merely because the child, wrongfully killed, was born to her out of wedlock.

Reversed.

Mr. Justice HARLAN, whom Mr. Justice BLACK and Mr. Justice STEWART join, dissenting.

These decisions can only be classed as constitutional curiosities.

At common law, no person had a legally cognizable interest in the wrongful death of another person, and no person could inherit the personal right of another to recover for tortious injuries to his body. By statute, Louisiana has created both rights in favor of certain classes of persons. The question in these cases is whether the way in which Louisiana has defined the classes of persons who may recover is constitutionally permissible. The Court has reached a negative answer to this question by a process that can only be described as brute force.

One important reason why recovery for wrongful death had everywhere to await statutory delineation is that the interest one person has in the life of another is inherently intractable. Rather than hear offers of proof of love and affection and economic dependence from every person who might think or claim that the bell had tolled for him, the courts stayed their hands pending legislative action. Legislatures, responding to the same diffuseness of interests, generally defined classes of proper plaintiffs by highly arbitrary lines based on family relationships, excluding issues concerning the actual effect of the death on the plaintiff.

Louisiana has followed the traditional pattern. There the actions lie in favor of the surviving spouse and children of the deceased, if any; if none, then in favor of the surviving parents of the deceased, if any; if none, then in favor of the deceased's brothers and sisters, if any; if none, then no action lies. According to this scheme, a grown man may sue for the wrongful death of parents he did not love, even if the death relieves him of a great economic burden or entitles him to a large inheritance. But an employee who loses a job because of the death of his employer has no cause of action, and a minor child cared for by neighbors or relatives "as if he were their own son" does not therefore have a right to sue for their death. Perhaps most dramatic, a surviving parent, for example, of a Louisiana deceased may sue if and only if there is no surviving spouse or child: it does not matter who loved or depended on whom, or what the economic situation of any survivor may be, or even whether the spouse or child elects to sue. In short, the whole scheme of the Louisiana wrongful death statute, which is similar in this respect to that of most other States, makes everything the Court says about affection and nurture and dependence altogether irrelevant. The only question in any case is whether the plaintiff falls within the classes of persons to whom the State has accorded a right of action for the death of another.

Louisiana has chosen, as have most other States in one respect or another, to define these classes of proper plaintiffs in terms of their legal rather than their biological relation to the deceased. A man may recover for the death of his wife, whether he loved her or not, but may not recover for the death of his paramour.[6] A child may recover for the death of his adopted parents. An illegitimate may recover for the wrongful death of a parent who has taken a few hours to acknowledge him formally, but not for the death of a person who he claims is his parent but who has not acknowledged him.[7] A parent may recover for the death of an illegitimate child he has acknowledged, but not for the death of an illegitimate child whom he did not bother to acknowledge until the possibility of tort recovery arose.

The Court today, for some reason which I am at a loss to understand, rules that the State must base its arbitrary definition of the plaintiff class on biological rather than legal relationships. Exactly how this makes the Louisiana scheme even marginally more "rational" is not clear, for neither a biological relationship nor legal acknowledgment is indicative of the love or economic dependence that may exist between two persons. * * * The rights at issue here stem from the existence of a family relationship, and the State has decided only that it will not recognize the family relationship unless the formalities of marriage, or of the acknowledgment of children by the parent in question, have been complied with.

There is obvious justification for this decision. If it be conceded, as I assume it is, that the State has power to provide that people who choose to live together should go through the formalities of marriage

---

6. Vaughan v. Dalton-Lard Lumber Co., 119 La. 61, 43 So. 926 (1907). At the same time, a wife may recover for the death of a man to whom she is lawfully married, although she is not dependent on him for support and, indeed, is living adulterously with someone else. Jones v. Massachusetts Bonding & Ins. Co., 55 So.2d 88 (1951).

7. In Thompson v. Vestal Lumber & Mfg. Co., 16 So.2d 594, 596, aff'd, 208 La. 83, 22 So.2d 842 (1944), the court stated: "Children referred to in this law [the wrongful death statute] include only those who are the issue of lawful wedlock or who, being illegitimate, have been acknowledged or legitimated pursuant to methods expressly established by law." Article 203 of the Louisiana Civil Code provides that chidren may be acknowledged by a declaration, by either or both parents, executed in the presence of a notary public and two witnesses.

and, in default, that people who bear children should acknowledge them, it is logical to enforce these requirements by declaring that the general class of rights that are dependent upon family relationships shall be accorded only when the formalities as well as the biology of those relationships are present. Moreover, and for many of the same reasons why a State is empowered to require formalities in the first place, a State may choose to simplify a particular proceeding by reliance on formal papers rather than a contest of proof. That suits for wrongful death, actions to determine the heirs of intestates, and the like, must as a constitutional matter deal with every claim of biological paternity or maternity on its merits is an exceedingly odd proposition.

The Equal Protection Clause states a complex and difficult principle. Certain classifications are "inherently suspect," which I take to mean that any reliance upon them in differentiating legal rights requires very strong affirmative justification. The difference between a child who has been formally acknowledged and one who has not is hardly one of these. Other classifications are impermissible because they bear no intelligible proper relation to the consequences that are made to flow from them. This does not mean that any classification this Court thinks could be better drawn is unconstitutional. But even if the power of this Court to improve on the lines that Congress and the States have drawn were very much broader than I consider it to be, I could not understand why a State which bases the right to recover for wrongful death strictly on family relationships could not demand that those relationships be formalized.

I would affirm the decisions of the state court and the Court of Appeals for the Fifth Circuit.

NOTES AND QUESTIONS

1. Does the result in *Glona* follow from the result in *Levy?*

2. So far as you can tell from the opinion in *Glona*, what was the purpose of the statutory scheme which did not permit the mother to recover for the death of her illegitimate child?

3. Under *Glona*, would a statute which provided that the mother of a child could not recover for its wrongful death if the child had been adopted by another violate the Equal Protection Clause? Why or why not? Does *Glona* involve social and economic rights, or basic civil rights?

4. Justice Harlan's dissent, which is a dissent from *Levy* as well as *Glona*, argues that a wrongful death statute must necessarily draw various distinctions which have little or nothing to do with either biology or affection. He therefore would not say such distinctions are irrational or invidious. Is he wrong in this?

PARHAM v. HUGHES

Supreme Court of the United States, 1979.
441 U.S. 347, 99 S.Ct. 1742, 60 L.Ed.2d 269.

Mr. Justice STEWART announced the judgment of the Court and an opinion in which The CHIEF JUSTICE, Mr. Justice REHNQUIST, and Mr. Justice STEVENS join.

Under § 105–1307 of the Georgia Code (hereinafter the "Georgia statute"),[1] the mother of an illegitimate child can sue for the wrongful death of that child. A father who has legitimated a child can also sue for the wrongful death of the child if there is no mother. A father who has not legitimated a child, however, is precluded from maintaining a wrongful death action. The question presented in this case is whether this statutory scheme violates the Equal Protection or Due Process Clauses of the Fourteenth Amendment by denying the father of an illegitimate child who has not legitimated the child the right to sue for the child's wrongful death.

I

The appellant was the biological father of Lemeul Parham, a minor child who was killed in an automobile collision. The child's mother, Cassandria Moreen, was killed in the same collision. The appellant and Moreen were never married to each other, and the appellant did not legitimate the child as he could have done under Georgia law. The appellant did, however, sign the child's birth certificate and contribute to his support. The child took the appellant's name and was visited by the appellant on a regular basis.

After the child was killed in the automobile collision, the appellant brought an action seeking to recover for the allegedly wrongful death. The complaint named the appellee (the driver of the other automobile involved in the collision) as the defendant, and charged that negligence on the part of the appellee had caused the death of the child. The child's maternal grandmother, acting as administratrix of his estate, also brought a lawsuit against the appellee to recover for the child's wrongful death.[4]

---

1. Section 105–1307 provides:
   "A mother, or, if no mother, a father may recover for the homicide of a child, minor or sui juris, unless said child shall leave a wife, husband or child. The mother or father shall be entitled to recover the full value of the life of such child. *In suits by the mother the illegitimacy of the child shall be no bar to a recovery.*" (Emphasis added.)

4. Section 105–1309 of the Georgia Code provides:
   "In cases where there is no person entitled to sue under the foregoing provisions of this Chapter, [the Georgia Wrongful Death Chapter], the administrator or executor of the decedent may sue for and recover and hold the amount recovered for the benefit of the next of kin. In any such case, the amount of the recovery shall be the full value of the life of the decedent."

The appellee filed a motion for summary judgment in the present case, asserting that under the Georgia statute the appellant was precluded from recovering for his illegitimate child's wrongful death. The trial court held that the Georgia statute violated both the Due Process and Equal Protection Clauses of the Fourteenth Amendment and, accordingly, denied a summary judgment in favor of the appellee. On appeal, the Georgia Supreme Court reversed the ruling of the trial court. The appellate court found that the statutory classification was rationally related to three legitimate state interests: (1) the interest in avoiding difficult problems of proving paternity in wrongful death actions; (2) the interest in promoting a legitimate family unit; and (3) the interest in setting a standard of morality by not according to the father of an illegitimate child the statutory right to sue for the child's death. * * *

II

A

State laws are generally entitled to a presumption of validity against attack under the Equal Protection Clause. Legislatures have wide discretion in passing laws that have the inevitable effect of treating some people differently from others, and legislative classifications are valid unless they bear no rational relationship to a permissible state objective.

Not all legislation, however, is entitled to the same presumption of validity. The presumption is not present when a State has enacted legislation whose purpose or effect is to create classes based upon racial criteria, since racial classifications, in a constitutional sense, are inherently "suspect." And the presumption of statutory validity may also be undermined when a State has enacted legislation creating classes based upon certain other immutable human attributes.

In the absence of invidious discrimination, however, a court is not free under the aegis of the Equal Protection Clause to substitute its judgment for the will of the people of a State as expressed in the laws passed by their popularly elected legislatures. * * * The threshold question, therefore, is whether the Georgia statute is invidiously discriminatory. If it is not, it is entitled to a presumption of validity and will be upheld "unless the varying treatment of different groups or persons is so unrelated to the achievement of any combination of legislative purposes that we can only conclude that the legislature's actions were irrational."

III

The appellant relies on decisions of the Court that have invalidated statutory classifications based upon illegitimacy and upon gender to support his claim that the Georgia statute is unconstitutional. Both of these lines of cases have involved laws reflecting invidious discrimination against a particular class. We conclude, however, that neither line of decisions is applicable in the present case.

A

The Court has held on several occasions that state legislative classifications based upon illegitimacy—i. e., that differentiate between illegitimate children and legitimate children—violate the Equal Protection Clause. The basic rationale of these decisions is that it is unjust and ineffective for society to express its condemnation of procreation outside the marital relationship by punishing the illegitimate child who is in no way responsible for his situation and is unable to change it. * * *

It is apparent that this rationale is in no way applicable to the Georgia statute now before us. The statute does not impose differing burdens or award differing benefits to legitimate and illegitimate children. It simply denies a natural father the right to sue for his illegitimate child's wrongful death. The appellant, as the natural father, was responsible for conceiving an illegitimate child and had the opportunity to legitimate the child but failed to do so. Legitimation would have removed the stigma of bastardy and allowed the child to inherit from the father in the same manner as if born in lawful wedlock. Unlike the illegitimate child for whom the status of illegitimacy is involuntary and immutable, the appellant here was responsible for fostering an illegitimate child and for failing to change its status. It is thus neither illogical nor unjust for society to express its "condemnation of irresponsible liaisons beyond the bounds of marriage" by not conferring upon a biological father the statutory right to sue for the wrongful death of his illegitimate child. The justifications for judicial sensitivity to the constitutionality of differing legislative treatment of legitimate and illegitimate children are simply absent when a classification affects only the fathers of deceased illegitimate children.

B

The Court has also held that certain classifications based upon sex are invalid under the Equal Protection Clause. Underlying these decisions is the principle that a State is not free to make overbroad generalizations based on sex which are entirely unrelated to any differences between men and women or which demean the ability or social status of the affected class. * * *

In cases where men and women are not similarly situated, however, and a statutory classification is realistically based upon the differences in their situations, this Court has upheld its validity. * * *

With these principles in mind, it is clear that the Georgia statute does not invidiously discriminate against the appellant simply because he is of the male sex. The fact is that mothers and fathers of illegitimate children are not similarly situated. Under Georgia law, only a father can by voluntary unilateral action make an illegitimate child legitimate. Unlike the mother of an illegitimate child whose identity will rarely be in doubt, the identity of the father will frequently be unknown. Lalli v. Lalli, 439 U.S. 259, 99 S.Ct. 518, 58 L.Ed.2d 503.[7] By coming forward with a motion under § 74-103 of the Georgia Code, however, a father can both estabish his identity and make his illegitimate child legitimate.

Thus the conferral of the right of a natural father to sue for the wrongful death of his child only if he has previously acted to identify himself, undertake his paternal responsibilities, and make his child legitimate, does not reflect any overbroad generalizations about men as a class, but rather the reality that in Georgia only a father can by unilateral action legitimate an illegitimate child. Since fathers who do legitimate their children can sue for wrongful death in precisely the same circumstances as married fathers whose children were legitimate *ab initio*, the statutory classification does not discriminate against fathers as a class but instead distinguishes between fathers who have legitimated their children and those who have not.[9] Such a classification is quite unlike those cases which were premised upon overbroad generalizations and excluded all members of one sex even though they were similarly situated with members of the other sex.

7. As Mr. Justice Powell stated for the plurality in the *Lalli* case:

"That the child is the child of a particular woman is rarely difficult to prove. Proof of paternity, by contrast, frequently is difficult when the father is not part of a formal family unit. The putative father often goes his way unconscious of the birth of a child. Even if conscious, he is very often totally unconcerned because of the absence of any ties to the mother. Indeed the mother may not know who is responsible for her pregnancy." 439 U.S. 268, 99 S.Ct. 525. (Citations omitted.)

In Glona v. American Guaranty Liability Insurance Co., 391 U.S. 73, 88 S. Ct. 1515, 20 L.Ed.2d 441 (1968), the Court held that a Louisiana statute that did not allow a natural mother of an illegitimate child to sue for its wrongful death violated the Equal Protection Clause. That cause was quite different from this one. The invidious discrimination perceived in that case was between married and unmarried mothers. There thus existed no real problem of identity nor of fraudulent claims. See Part IV, infra. Moreover, the statute in *Glona* excluded every mother of an illegitimate child from bringing a wrongful death action while the Georgia statute at issue here excludes only those fathers who have not legitimated their children. Thus the Georgia statute has in effect adopted "a middle ground between the extremes of complete exclusion and case-by-case determination of paternity." Trimble v. Gordon, 430 U.S. 762, 771, 97 S.Ct. 1459, 1465, 52 L.Ed.2d 31 (1976). Cf. Lalli v. Lalli, 439 U.S. 259, 99 S.Ct. 518, 58 L.Ed.2d 503 (1978). We need not decide whether a statute which completely precluded fathers, as opposed to mothers, of illegitimate children from maintaining a wrongful death action would violate the Equal Protection Clause.

9. The ability of a father to make his child legitimate under Georgia law distinguishes this case from Caban v. Mohammed, 441 U.S. 380, 99 S.Ct. 1760, 60 L.Ed.2d 297 (1978), decided today. The Georgia legitimation provision enables the father to change the child's status, and thereby his own for purposes of the wrongful death statute, and at the same time is a rational method for the State to deal with the problem of proving paternity. Lalli v. Lalli, supra; see Part IV, infra. In the *Caban* case, by contrast, the father could neither change his children's status nor his own for purposes of the New York adoption statute.

IV

Having concluded that the Georgia statute does not invidiously discriminate against any class, we still must determine whether the statutory classification is rationally related to a permissible state objective.

This Court has frequently recognized that a State has a legitimate interest in the maintenance of an accurate and efficient system for the disposition of property at death. Of particular concern to the State is the existence of some mechanism for dealing with "the often difficult problem of proving the paternity of illegitimate children and the related danger of spurious claims against intestate estates."

This same state interest in avoiding fraudulent claims of paternity in order to maintain a fair and orderly system of decedent's property disposition is also present in the context of actions for wrongful death. If paternity has not been established before the commencement of a wrongful death action, a defendant may be faced with the possibility of multiple lawsuits by individuals all claiming to be the father of the deceased child. Such uncertainty would make it difficult if not impossible for a defendant to settle a wrongful death action in many cases, since there would always exist the risk of a subsequent suit by another person claiming to be the father.[10] The State of Georgia has chosen to deal with this problem by allowing only fathers who have established their paternity by legitimating their children to sue for wrongful death, and we cannot say that this solution is an irrational one. Cf. Lalli v. Lalli, supra.[11]

The appellant argues, however, that whatever may be the problem with establishing paternity generally, there is no question in this case that he is the father. This argument misconceives the basic principle of the Equal Protection Clause. The function of that provision of the Constitution is to measure the validity of classifications created by state laws.[12] Since we have concluded that the classification created by the Georgia statute is a rational means for dealing with the problem of proving paternity, it is constitutionally irrelevant that the appellant may be able to prove paternity in another manner.

V

The appellant also alleges that the Georgia statute violates the Due Process Clause of the Fourteenth Amendment. * * * The

10. Indeed, this sort of uncertainty is evident in the present case. The appellee has been sued by both the administratrix of the estate and the appellant for the wrongful death of the child.

11. We thus need not decide whether the classification created by the

Georgia statute is rationally related to the State's interests in promoting the traditional family unit or in setting a standard of morality.

12. It cannot seriously be argued that a statutory entitlement to sue for the wrongful death of another is itself a "fundamental" or constitutional right.

only decision of this Court cited by the appellant that is even remotely related to his due process claim is Stanley v. Illinois, 405 U.S. 645, 92 S.Ct. 1208, 31 L.Ed.2d 551. In the *Stanley* case, the Court held that a father of illegitimate children who had raised these children was entitled to a hearing on his fitness as a parent before they could be taken from him by the State of Illinois. The interests which the Court found controlling in *Stanley* were the integrity of the family against state interference and the freedom of a father to raise his own children. The present case is quite a different one, involving as it does only an asserted right to sue for money damages.

For these reasons, the judgment of the Supreme Court of Georgia is affirmed.

NOTES AND QUESTIONS

1. Justice Powell concurred specially in Parham on the ground that the gender-based distinction in the case was substantially related to an important state objective, namely the avoidance of difficulties in proving paternity after the death of the illegitimate child.

Justices White, Brennan, Marshall and Blackmun dissented in this case.

2. The position of the plurality opinion seems to be that the discrimination under the Georgia statute was not "invidious" because the father could have legitimated the child and thereby become eligible to bring a suit for the child's wrongful death. The wrongful death statute was therefore not like that in *Levy*, which imposed a disability upon the child because of a status for which the child was not responsible and which he could not change. The difficulty with this analysis of course is that in *Glona* the mother could have legitimated the child and thereby become eligible to recover for his wrongful death under the Louisiana statute. Justice Harlan so states in his dissent, 391 U.S. at 79, and this is made clear by Scott v. La Fontaine, 148 So.2d 780 (La.App.1963), which denied a mother the right to sue for wrongful death on the ground that she had only legitimated the child after the death had occurred. The *Parham* opinion, in footnote 7, distinguishes *Glona* in part on the ground that it involved a discrimination between married and unmarried mothers. This is incorrect, since an unmarried mother who had legitimated her child could recover. Thus the discrimination in that case was between unmarried mothers who had not legitimated their children and all other mothers.

Does this mean that Parham in fact overrules *Glona*, if the state law in the two cases is properly understood? In other words, does *Parham* mean that in any state whose law permits legitimation of an illegitimate child, there is no constitutional objection to depriving the parent of rights respecting that child, so long as the parent has not legitimated the child?

If the state law, unlike Georgia's, provided that either the mother or the father of an illegitimate child could legitimate the child by a prescribed procedure, would this change the result arrived at in Parham?

3. Having found that the discrimination in the Georgia statute was not "invidious", the Court finds that it is rationally related to the state's legitimate interest in avoiding fraudulent claims of paternity. Presumably the assumption here is that when the child has died, it is impossible to perform

the blood tests which might be helpful, even conclusive, in proving or disproving paternity. See the discussion at page 412, infra. This, the Court decides, justifies the statutory distinction between fathers who have and those who have not legitimated their children.

Could this state interest be classified as merely "administrative convenience" and therefore insufficient to be the basis for a holding of constitutionality? Cf. Stanley v. Illinois, infra, page 432.

LABINE v. VINCENT

Supreme Court of the United States, 1971.
401 U.S. 532, 91 S.Ct. 1017, 28 L.Ed.2d 288, rehearing denied
402 U.S. 990, 91 S.Ct. 1672, 29 L.Ed.2d 156.

Mr. Justice BLACK delivered the opinion of the Court.

In this appeal the guardian (tutrix) of an illegitimate minor child attacks the constitutionality of Louisiana's laws that bar an illegitimate child from sharing equally with legitimates in the estate of their father who had publicly acknowledged the child, but who died without a will. To understand appellant's constitutional arguments and our decision, it is necessary briefly to review the facts giving rise to this dispute. On March 15, 1962, a baby girl, Rita Vincent, was born to Lou Bertha Patterson (now Lou Bertha Labine) in Calcasieu Parish, Louisiana. On May 10, 1962, Lou Bertha Patterson and Ezra Vincent, as authorized by Louisiana law, jointly executed before a notary a Louisiana State Board of Health form acknowledging that Ezra Vincent was the "natural father" of Rita Vincent. This public acknowledgment of parentage did not, under Louisiana law, give the child a legal right to share equally with legitimate children in the parent's estate but it did give her a right to claim support from her parents or their heirs. The acknowledgment also gave the child the capacity under Louisiana law to be a limited beneficiary under her father's will in the event he left a will naming her, which he did not do here.

Ezra Vincent died intestate, that is, without a will, on September 16, 1968, in Rapides Parish, Louisiana, leaving substantial property within the State, but no will to direct its distribution. Appellant, as the guardian of Rita Vincent, petitioned in state court for the appointment of an administrator for the father's estate; for a declaration that Rita Vincent is the sole heir of Ezra Vincent; and for an order directing the administrator to pay support and maintenance for the child. In the alternative, appellant sought a declaration that the child was entitled to support and maintenance of $150 per month under a Louisiana child support law.

The administrator of the succession of Ezra Vincent answered the petition claiming that Vincent's relatives were entitled to the whole estate. He relied for the claim upon two articles of the Louisiana Civil Code of 1870: Art. 206, which provides:

"Illegitimate children, though duly acknowledged, can not claim the rights of legitimate children.   *   *   * "

and Art. 919, which provides:

"Natural children are called to the inheritance of their natural father, who has duly acknowledged them, when he has left no descendants nor ascendants, nor collateral relations, nor surviving wife, and to the exclusion only of the State."

The court ruled that the relatives of the father were his collateral relations and that under Louisiana's laws of intestate succession took his property to the exclusion of acknowledged, but not legitimated, illegitimate children. The court, therefore, dismissed with costs the guardian mother's petition to recognize the child as an heir. The court also ruled that in view of Social Security payments of $60 per month and Veterans Administration payments of $40 per month available for the support of the child, the guardian for the child was not entitled to support or maintenance from the succession of Ezra Vincent. The Louisiana Court of Appeal, Third Circuit, affirmed and the Supreme Court of Louisiana denied a petition for a writ of certiorari. The child's guardian appealed and we noted probable jurisdiction. 400 U.S. 817, 91 S.Ct. 79, 27 L.Ed.2d 44 (1970).

In this Court appellant argues that Louisiana's statutory scheme for intestate succession that bars this illegitimate child from sharing in her father's estate constitutes an invidious discrimination against illegitimate children that cannot stand under the Due Process and Equal Protection Clauses of the Constitution. Much reliance is placed upon the Court's decisions in Levy v. Louisiana, 391 U.S. 68, 88 S.Ct. 1509, 20 L.Ed.2d 436 (1968), and Glona v. American Guarantee & Liability Insurance Co., 391 U.S. 73, 88 S.Ct. 1515, 20 L.Ed.2d 441 (1968). For the reasons set out below, we find appellant's reliance on those cases misplaced, and we decline to extend the rationale of those cases where it does not apply. Accordingly, we affirm the decision below.

In *Levy* the Court held that Louisiana could not consistently with the Equal Protection Clause bar an illegitimate child from recovering for the wrongful death of its mother when such recoveries by legitimate children were authorized. The cause of action alleged in *Levy* was in tort. It was undisputed that Louisiana had created a statutory tort and had provided for the survival of the deceased's cause of action, so that a large class of persons injured by the tort could recover damages in compensation for their injury. Under those circumstances the Court held that the State could not totally exclude from the class of potential plaintiffs illegitimate children who were unquestionably injured by the tort that took their mother's life. *Levy* did not say and cannot fairly be read to say that a State can never treat an illegitimate child differently from legitimate offspring.[6]

The people of Louisiana, through their legislature have carefully regulated many of the property rights incident to family life. Louisiana law prescribes certain formalities requisite to the contracting of marriage. Once marriage is contracted there, husbands have obligations to their wives. Fathers have obligations to their children. Should the children prosper while the parents fall upon hard times, children have a statutory obligation to support their parents. To further strengthen and preserve family ties, Louisiana regulates the disposition of property upon the death of a family man. The surviving spouse is entitled to an interest in the deceased spouse's estate. Legitimate children have a right of forced heirship in their father's estate and can even retrieve property transferred by their father during his lifetime in reduction of their rightful interests.

Louisiana also has a complex set of rules regarding the rights of illegitimate children. Children born out of wedlock and who are never acknowledged by their parents apparently have no right to take property by intestate succession from their father's estate. In some instances, their father may not even bequeath property to them by will. Illegitimate children acknowledged by their fathers are "natural children." Natural children can take from their father by intestate succession "to the exclusion only of the State." They may be bequeathed property by their father only to the extent of either one-third or one-fourth of his estate and then only if their father is not survived by legitimate children or their heirs. Finally, children born out of wedlock can be legitimated or adopted, in which case they may take by intestate succession or by will as any other child.

These rules for intestate succession may or may not reflect the intent of particular parents. Many will think that it is unfortunate that the rules are so rigid. Others will think differently. But the choices reflected by the intestate succession statute are choices which it is within the power of the State to make. The Federal Constitution does not give this Court the power to overturn the State's choice under the guise of constitutional interpretation because the Justices of this Court believe that they can provide better rules. Of course, it may be said that the rules adopted by the Louisiana Legislature "discriminate" against illegitimates. But the rules also discriminate against collateral relations, as opposed to ascendants, and against ascendants, as opposed to descendants. Other rules determining prop-

---

6. Nor is Glona v. American Guarantee & Liability Insurance Co., 391 U.S. 73, 88 S.Ct. 1515, 20 L.Ed.2d 441 (1968), analogous to this case. In *Glona* the majority relied on Louisiana's "curious course" of sanctions against illegitimacy to demonstrate that there was no "rational basis" for prohibiting a mother from recovering for the wrongful death of her son. Id., at 74–75. Even if we were to apply the "rational basis" test to the Louisiana intestate succession statute, that statute clearly has a rational basis in view of Louisiana's interest in promoting family life and of directing the disposition of property left within the State.

erty rights based on family status also "discriminate" in favor of wives and against "concubines." The dissent attempts to distinguish these other "discriminations" on the ground that they have a biological or social basis. There is no biological difference between a wife and a concubine, nor does the Constitution require that there be such a difference before the State may assert its power to protect the wife and her children against the claims of a concubine and her children. The social difference between a wife and a concubine is analogous to the difference between a legitimate and an illegitimate child. One set of relationships is socially sanctioned, legally recognized, and gives rise to various rights and duties. The other set of relationships is illicit and beyond the recognition of the law. Similarly, the State does not need biological or social reasons for distinguishing between ascendants and descendants. Some of these discriminatory choices are perhaps more closely connected to our conceptions of social justice or the ways in which most dying men wish to dispose of their property than the Louisiana rules governing illegitimate children. It may be possible that some of these choices are more "rational" than the choices inherent in Louisiana's categories of illegitimates. But the power to make rules to establish, protect, and strengthen family life as well as to regulate the disposition of property left in Louisiana by a man dying there is committed by the Constitution of the United States and the people of Louisiana to the legislature of that State. Absent a specific constitutional guarantee, it is for that legislature, not the life-tenured judges of this Court, to select from among possible laws. We cannot say that Louisiana's policy provides a perfect or even a desirable solution or the one we would have provided for the problem of the property rights of illegitimate children. Neither can we say that Louisiana does not have the power to make laws for distribution of property left within the State.

We emphasize that this is not a case, like *Levy* where the State has created an insurmountable barrier to this illegitimate child. There is not the slightest suggestion in this case that Louisiana has barred this illegitimate from inheriting from her father. Ezra Vincent could have left one-third of his property to his illegitimate daughter had he bothered to follow the simple formalities of executing a will. He could, of course, have legitimated the child by marrying her mother in which case the child could have inherited his property either by intestate succession or by will as any other legitimate child. Finally, he could have awarded his child the benefit of Louisiana's intestate succession statute on the same terms as legitimate children simply by stating in his acknowledgment of paternity his desire to legitimate the little girl. See Bergeron v. Miller, 230 So.2d 417 (La.App.1970).

In short, we conclude that in the circumstances presented in this case, there is nothing in the vague generalities of the Equal Protection and Due Process Clauses which empowers this Court to nullify the deliberate choices of the elected representatives of the people of Louisiana.

Affirmed.*

NOTES AND QUESTIONS

1. Does this case involve social and economic rights, or basic civil rights? Must the Court find merely a "rational relation" between statute and purpose, or must it find a "compelling state interest"?

2. Is Justice Black's statement accurate, that *Levy* could not fairly be read as saying that a state may never treat an illegitimate child differently from a legitimate child? Cf. Krause, 70, saying that the effect of *Levy* was that a legislative classification based upon illegitimacy is highly vulnerable and may be sustained only where necessary to promote a compelling state interest. After Labine v. Vincent how would you sum up the law on the subject?

3. How does Justice Black distinguish *Labine* from *Levy* and *Glona*? Would you agree with his distinction? Is any other distinction more satisfactory? If the statute involved in *Levy* and *Glona* could not be sustained on the ground that it protected the institution of the family, could the statute in *Labine* be sustained as reasonably calculated to accomplish that purpose?

4. The Court in *Labine* refers to the insurmountable barrier which the *Levy* statute placed in the path of the child's recovery for the mother's wrongful death. But the mother in *Levy* could have legitimated the child by marrying its father, could she not? Is this any more of a barrier than existed in *Labine*? In any event, what possible significance does this assertion have, since in both cases there was nothing the *child* could do to alter its status was there? Is this the same argument that the Court places so much emphasis on in Parham v. Hughes?

TRIMBLE v. GORDON

Supreme Court of the United States, 1977.
430 U.S. 762, 97 S.Ct. 1459, 52 L.Ed.2d 31.

Mr. Justice POWELL delivered the opinion of the Court.

At issue in this case is the constitutionality of § 12 of the Illinois Probate Act [1] which allows illegitimate children to inherit by intestate succession only from their mothers. Under Illinois law, legiti-

[* Mr. Justice Harlan concurred specially in this case. Justices Brennan, Douglas, White and Marshall dissented. The dissenting justices took the position that the Louisiana intestate succession statute violated the Equal Protection Clause of the Fourteenth Amendment.]

1. Ill.Rev.Stat. c. 3, § 12 (1961). Effective January 1, 1976, § 12 and the rest of the Probate Act of which it was a part were repealed and re-placed by the Probate Act of 1975. Public Act 79–328. Section 12 has been replaced by Ill.Rev.Stat. c. 3, § 2–2 (1976–1977 Supp.). Although § 2–2 of the Probate Act of 1975 differs in some respects from the old § 12, that part of § 12 that is at issue here was recodified without material change in § 2–2. As the opinions below and the briefs refer to the disputed statutory provision as § 12, we will continue to refer to it that way.

mate children are allowed to inherit by intestate succession from both their mothers and their fathers.

I

Appellant Deta Mona Trimble is the illegitimate daughter of appellant Jessie Trimble and Sherman Gordon. Trimble and Gordon lived in Chicago with Deta Mona from 1970 until Gordon died in 1974, the victim of a homicide. On January 2, 1973, the Circuit Court of Cook County, Ill., entered a paternity order finding Gordon to be the father of Deta Mona and ordering him to pay $15 per week for her support. Gordon thereafter supported Deta Mona in accordance with the paternity order and openly acknowledged her as his child. He died intestate at the age of 28, leaving an estate consisting only of a 1974 Plymouth automobile worth approximately $2,500.

Shortly after Gordon's death, Trimble as the mother and next friend of Deta Mona, filed a petition for letters of administration, determination of heirship and declaratory relief in the Probate Division of the Circuit Court of Cook County, Ill. That court entered an order determining heirship, identifying as the only heirs of Gordon his father, Joseph Gordon, his mother, Ethel King, and his brother, two sisters, and half-brother. All of these individuals are appellees in this appeal, * * *.

The Circuit Court excluded Deta Mona on the authority of the negative implications of § 12 of the Illinois Probate Act, which provides in relevant part:

"An illegitimate child is heir of its mother and of any maternal ancestor, and of any person from whom its mother might have inherited, if living; and the lawful issue of an illegitimate person shall represent such person and take, by descent, any estate which the parent would have taken, if living. An illegitimate child whose parents inter-marry and who is acknowledged by the father as the father's child shall be considered legitimate."

If Deta Mona had been a legitimate child, she would have inherited her father's entire estate under Illinois law. In rejecting Deta Mona's claim of heirship, the court sustained the constitutionality of § 12.

After a notice of appeal was filed, the Illinois Supreme Court entered an order allowing direct appeal of the decision of the Circuit Court, bypassing the Illinois Appellate Court. * * * On June 2, 1975, the Illinois Supreme Court handed down its opinion in *In re Estate of Karas*, 61 Ill.2d 40, 329 N.E.2d 234 (1975), sustaining § 12 against all constitutional challenges, * * * On September 24, 1975, oral argument was held in the instant case. Chief Justice Underwood orally delivered the opinion of the court from the bench, affirming the decision of the Circuit Court on the authority of *Karas*. * * * We now reverse. As we conclude that the statutory discrimination against illegitimate children is unconstitutional, we do not reach the sex discrimination argument.

II

In *Karas,* the Illinois Supreme Court rejected the equal protection challenge to the discrimination against illegitimate children on the explicit authority of Labine v. Vincent, 401 U.S. 532, 91 S.Ct. 1017, 28 L.Ed.2d 288 (1971). The court found that § 12 is supported by the state interests in encouraging family relationships and in establishing an accurate and efficient method of disposing of property at death. The court also found the Illinois law unobjectionable becase no "insurmountable barrier" prevented illegitimate children from sharing in the estates of their fathers. By leaving a will, Sherman Gordon could have assured Deta Mona a share of his estate.

Appellees endorse the reasoning of the Illinois Supreme Court and suggest additional justifications for the statute. In weighing the constitutional sufficiency of these justifications, we are guided by our previous decisions involving equal protection challenges to laws discriminating on the basis of illegitimacy.[11] "[T]his Court requires, at a minimum, that a statutory classification bear some rational relationship to a legitimate state purpose." Weber v. Aetna Cas. & Surety Co., 406 U.S. 164, 172, 92 S.Ct. 1400, 1405, 31 L.Ed.2d 768 (1972). In this context, the standard just stated is a minimum; the Court sometimes requires more. "Though the latitude given state economic and social regulation is necessarily broad, when state statutory classifications approach sensitive and fundamental personal rights, this Court exercises a stricter scrutiny * * *." Ibid.

Appellants urge us to hold that classifications based on illegitimacy are "suspect," so that any justifications must survive "strict scrutiny." We considered and rejected a similar argument last Term in Mathews v. Lucas, 427 U.S. 495, 96 S.Ct. 2755, 49 L.Ed.2d 651 (1976). As we recognized in *Lucas,* illegitimacy is analogous in many respects to the personal characteristics that have been held to

---

11. This case represents the 12th time since 1968 that we have considered the constitutionality of alleged discrimination on the basis of illegitimacy. The previous decisions are as follows: Mathews v. Lucas, 427 U.S. 495, 96 S.Ct. 2755, 49 L.Ed.2d 651 (1976); Beaty v. Weinberger, 478 F. 2d 300 (CA5 1973), summarily aff'd, 418 U.S. 901, 94 S.Ct. 3190, 41 L.Ed. 2d 1150 (1974); Jimenez v. Weinberger, 417 U.S. 628, 94 S.Ct. 2496, 41 L.Ed.2d 363 (1974); New Jersey Welfare Rights Organization v. Cahill, 411 U.S. 619, 93 S.Ct. 1700, 36 L.Ed. 2d 543 (1973); Griffin v. Richardson, 346 F.Supp. 1226 (Md.), summarily aff'd, 409 U.S. 1069, 93 S.Ct. 689, 34 L.Ed.2d 660 (1972); Davis v. Richardson, 342 F.Supp. 588 (Conn.1972), aff'd, 409 U.S. 1069, 93 S.Ct. 678, 34 L.Ed.2d 659 (1972); Gomez v. Perez, 409 U.S. 535, 93 S.Ct. 872, 35 L.Ed.2d 56 (1973); Weber v. Aetna Casualty & Surety Co., 406 U.S. 164, 92 S.Ct. 1400, 31 L.Ed.2d 768 (1972); Labine v. Vincent, 401 U.S. 532, 91 S.Ct. 1017, 28 L.Ed.2d 288 (1971); Glona v. American Guarantee and Liability Insurance Company, 391 U.S. 73, 88 S. Ct. 1515, 20 L.Ed.2d 441 (1968); Levy v. Louisiana, 391 U.S. 68, 88 S.Ct. 1509, 20 L.Ed.2d 436 (1968).

be suspect when used as the basis of statutory differentiations. Id., at 505, 96 S.Ct., at 2762. We nevertheless concluded that the analogy was not sufficient to require "our most exacting scrutiny." Id., at 506, 96 S.Ct., at 2763. Despite the conclusion that classifications based on illegitimacy fall in a "realm of less than strictest scrutiny," *Lucas* also establishes that the scrutiny "is not a toothless one," id., at 510, 96 S.Ct., at 2764, a proposition clearly demonstrated by our previous decisions in this area.[12]

III

The Illinois Supreme Court prefaced its discussion of the state interests served by § 12 with a general discussion of the purpose of the statute. Quoting from its earlier opinions, the court concluded that the statute was enacted to ameliorate the harsh common-law rule under which an illegitimate child was *filius nullius* and incapable of inheriting from anyone. Although § 12 did not bring illegitimate children into parity with legitimate children, it did improve their position, thus partially achieving the asserted objective. The sufficiency of the justifications advanced for the remaining discrimination against illegitimate children must be considered in light of this motivating purpose.

A

The Illinois Supreme Court relied in part on the State's purported interest in "the promotion of [legitimate] family relationships." Although the court noted that this justification had been accepted in *Labine,* the opinion contains only the most perfunctory analysis. This inattention may not have been an oversight, for § 12 bears only the most attenuated relationship to the asserted goal.[13]

12. See cases cited n. 11, supra. Labine v. Vincent, 401 U.S. 532, 91 S. Ct. 1017, 28 L.Ed.2d 288 (1971), is difficult to place in the pattern of this Court's equal protection decisions, and subsequent cases have limited its force as a precedent. In Weber v. Aetna Casualty & Surety Co., 406 U.S. 164, 92 S.Ct. 1400, 31 L.Ed. 2d 768 (1972), we found in *Labine* a recognition that judicial deference is appropriate when the challenged statute involves the "substantial state interest in providing for 'the stability of * * * land titles and in the prompt and definitive determination of the valid ownership of property left by decedents,' * * * ." 406 U.S., at 170, 92 S.Ct., at 1404, quoting Labine v. Vincent, 229 So.2d 449, 452 (La.App.1969). We reaffirm that view, but there is a point beyond which such deference cannot justify discrimination. Although the proposition is self-evident, Reed v. Reed, 404 U.S. 71, 92 S.Ct. 251, 30 L.Ed.2d 225 (1971), demonstrates that state statutes involving the disposition of property at death are not immunized from equal protection scrutiny. See also Eskra v. Morton, 524 F.2d 9, 13 (CA7 1975) (Stevens, J.). The more specific analysis of *Labine* is discussed throughout the remainder of this opinion.

13. This purpose is not apparent from the statute. Penalizing children as a means of influencing their parents seems inconsistent with the desire of the Illinois Legislature to make the intestate succession law more just to illegitimate children. Moreover, the difference in the rights of illegitimate children in the estates of their mothers and their fathers appears to be unrelated to the purpose of promoting family relationships. In this

In a case like this, the Equal Protection Clause requires more than the mere incantation of a proper state purpose. No one disputes the appropriateness of Illinois' concern with the family unit, perhaps the most fundamental social institution of our society. The flaw in the analysis lies elsewhere. As we said in *Lucas*, the constitutionality of this law "depends upon the character of the discrimination and its relation to legitimate legislative aims." 427 U.S., at 504, 96 S.Ct., at 2761. The court below did not address the relation between § 12 and the promotion of legitimate family relationships, thus leaving the constitutional analysis incomplete. The same observation can be made about this Court's decision in *Labine*, but that case does not stand alone. In subsequent decisions, we have expressly considered and rejected the argument that a State may attempt to influence the actions of men and women by imposing sanctions on the children born of their illegitimate relationships.

* * * The parents have the ability to conform their conduct to societal norms, but their illegitimate children can affect neither their parents' conduct nor their own status.

B

The Illinois Supreme Court relied on *Labine* for another and more substantial justification: the State's interest in "establish[ing] a method of property disposition." 61 Ill.2d, at 48, 329 N.E.2d, at 238. Here the Court's analysis is more complete. Focusing specifically on the difficulty of proving paternity and the related danger of spurious claims, the court concluded that this interest explained and justified the asymmetrical statutory discrimination against the illegitimate children of intestate men. The more favorable treatment of illegitimate children claiming from their mothers' estates was justified because "proof of a lineal relationship is more readily ascertainable when dealing with maternal ancestors." 61 Ill.2d, at 52, 329 N.E. 2d, at 240. Alluding to the possibilities of abuse, the court rejected a case-by-case approach to claims based on alleged paternity.

The more serious problems of proving paternity might justify a more demanding standard for illegitimate children claiming under their fathers' estates than that required either for illegitimate children claiming under their mothers' estates or for legitimate children generally. We think, however, that the Illinois Supreme Court gave inadequate consideration to the relation between § 12 and the State's

respect the Louisiana laws at issue in *Labine* were quite different. Those laws differentiated on the basis of the character of the child's illegitimacy. "Bastard children" were given no inheritance rights. "Natural children," who could be and were acknowledged under state law, were given limited inheritance rights, but still less than those of legitimate children. 401 U.S., at 537, and n. 13, 91 S.Ct., at 2763. The Louisiana categories are consistent with a theory of social opprobrium regarding the parents' relationships and with a measured, if misguided, attempt to deter illegitimate relationships.

proper objective of assuring accuracy and efficiency in the disposition of property at death. The court failed to consider the possibility of a middle ground between the extremes of complete exclusion and case-by-case determination of paternity. For at least some significant categories of illegitimate children of intestate men, inheritance rights can be recognized without jeopardizing the orderly settlement of estates or the dependability of titles to property passing under intestacy laws. Because it excludes those categories of illegitimate children unnecessarily, § 12 is constitutionally flawed.

The orderly disposition of property at death requires an appropriate legal framework, the structuring of which is a matter particularly within the competence of the individual States. In exercising this responsibility, a State necessarily must enact laws governing both the procedure and substance of intestate succession. Absent infringement of a constitutional right, the federal courts have no role here, and, even when constitutional violations are alleged, those courts should accord substantial deference to a State's statutory scheme of inheritance.

The judicial task here is the difficult one of vindicating constitutional rights without interfering unduly with the State's primary responsibility in this area. * * * Our decision last Term in Mathews v. Lucas, supra, provides especially helpful guidance.

       *   *   *

Although the present case arises in a context different from that in *Lucas,* the question whether the statute "is carefully tuned to alternative considerations" is equally applicable here. We conclude that § 12 does not meet this standard. Difficulties of proving paternity in some situations do not justify the total statutory disinheritance of illegitimate children whose fathers die intestate. The facts of this case graphically illustrate the constitutional defect of § 12. Sherman Gordon was found to be the father of Deta Mona in a state court paternity action prior to his death. On the strength of that finding, he was ordered to contribute to the support of his child. That adjudication should be equally sufficient to establish Deta Mona's right to claim a child's share of Gordon's estate, for the State's interest in the accurate and efficient disposition of property at death would not be compromised in any way by allowing her claim in these circumstances.[14] The reach of the statute extends well beyond the asserted purposes.

---

14. Evidence of paternity may take a variety of forms, some creating more significant problems of inaccuracy and inefficiency than others. The states, of course, are free to recognize these differences in fashioning their requirements of proof. Our holding today goes only to those forms of proof which do not compromise the States' interests. This clearly would be the case, for example, where there is a prior adjudication or formal acknowledgment of paternity. Thus, we would have a different case if the state statute were carefully tailored to eliminate imprecise and unduly burdensome methods of establishing paternity.

C

The Illinois Supreme Court also noted that the decedents whose estates were involved in the consolidation appeals could have left substantial parts of their estates to their illegitimate children by writing a will. The court cited *Labine* as authority for the proposition that such a possibility is constitutionally significant. The penultimate paragraph of the opinion in *Labine* distinguishes that case from Levy v. Louisiana, 391 U.S. 68, 88 S.Ct. 1509, 20 L.Ed.2d 436 (1968), because no insurmountable barrier prevented the illegitimate child from sharing in her father's estate. * * * The Court then listed three different steps that would have resulted in some recovery by Labine's illegitimate daughter. Labine could have left a will; he could have legitimated the daughter by marrying her mother; and he could have given the daughter the status of a legitimate child by stating in his acknowledgment of paternity his desire to legitimate her. In *Weber* our distinction of *Labine* was based in part on the fact that no such alternatives existed, as state law prevented the acknowledgment of the children involved.

Despite its appearance in two of our opinions, the focus on the presence or absence of an insurmountable barrier is somewhat of an analytical anomaly. Here, as in *Labine,* the question is the constitutionality of a state intestate succession law that treats illegitimate children differently from legitimate children. Traditional equal protection analysis asks whether this statutory differentiation on the basis of illegitimacy is justified by the promotion of recognized state objectives. If the law cannot be sustained on this analysis, it is not clear how it can be saved by the absence of an insurmountable barrier to inheritance under other and hypothetical circumstances.

By focusing on the steps that an intestate might have taken to assure some inheritance for his illegitimate children, the analysis loses sight of the essential question: the constitutionality of discrimination against illegitimates in a state intestate succession law. If the decedent had written a will devising property to his illegitimate child, the case no longer would involve intestate succession law at all. Similarly, if the decedent had legitimated the child by marrying the child's mother or by complying with the requirements of some other method of legitimation, the case no longer would involve discrimination against illegitimates. Hard questions cannot be avoided by a hypothetical reshuffling of the facts. If Sherman Gordon had devised his estate to Deta Mona this case would not be here. Similarly, in Reed v. Reed, supra, if the decedent had left a will naming an executor, the problem of the statutory preference for male administrators of estates of intestates would not have been presented. The opinion in *Reed* gives no indication that this available alternative had any constitutional significance. We think it has none in this case.

D

Finally, appellees urge us to affirm the decision below on the theory that the Illinois Probate Act, including § 12, mirrors the presumed intentions of the citizens of the State regarding the disposition of their property at death. Individualizing this theory, appellees argue that we must assume that Sherman Gordon knew the disposition of his estate under the Illinois Probate Act and that his failure to make a will shows his approval of that disposition. We need not resolve the question whether presumed intent alone can ever justify discrimination against illegitimates,[16] for we do not think that § 12 was enacted for this purpose. The theory of presumed intent is not relied upon in the careful opinion of the Illinois Supreme Court examining both the history and the text of § 12. This omission is not without significance, as one would expect a state supreme court to identify the state interests served by a statute of its state legislature. Our own examination of § 12 convinces us that the statutory provisions at issue were shaped by forces other than the desire of the legislature to mirror the intentions of the citizens of the State with respect to their illegitimate children.

To the extent that other policies are not considered more important, legislators enacting state intestate succession laws probably are influenced by the desire to reflect the natural affinities of decedents in the allocation of estates among the categories of heirs. A pattern of distribution favoring brothers and sisters over cousins is, for example, best explained on this basis. The difference in § 12 between the rights of illegitimate children in the estates of their fathers and mothers, however, is more convincingly explained by the other factors mentioned by the court below. Accepting in this respect the views of the Illinois Supreme Court, we find in § 12 a primary purpose

---

16. Appellees characterize the Illinois intestate succession law as a "statutory will." Because intent is a central ingredient in the disposition of property by will, the theory that intestate succession laws are "statutory wills" based on the "presumed intent" of the citizens of the State may have some superficial appeal. The theory proceeds from the initial premise that an individual could, if he wished, disinherit his illegitimate children in his will. Because the statute merely reflects the intent of those citizens who failed to make a will, discrimination against illegitimate children in intestate succession laws is said to be equally permissible. The term "statutory will," however, cannot blind us to the fact that intestate succession laws are acts of States, not of individuals. Under the Fourteenth Amendment this is a fundamental difference.

Even if one assumed that a majority of the citizens of the State preferred to discriminate against their illegitimate children, the sentiment hardly would be unanimous. With respect to any individual, the argument of knowledge and approval of the state law is sheer fiction. The issue therefore becomes where the burden of inertia in writing a will is to fall. At least when the disadvantaged group has been a frequent target of discrimination, as illegitimates have, we doubt that a State constitutionally may place the burden on that group by invoking the theory of "presumed intent." See Eskra v. Morton, 524 F.2d 9, 12–14 (CA7 1975) (Stevens, J.).

to provide a system of intestate succession more just to illegitimate
children than the prior law, a purpose tempered by a secondary interest in protecting against spurious claims of paternity. In the absence
of a more convincing demonstration, we will not hypothesize an additional state purpose that has been ignored by the Illinois Supreme
Court.

IV

For the reasons stated above, we conclude that § 12 of the Illinois Probate Act [17] cannot be squared with the command of the Equal
Protection Clause of the Fourteenth Amendment. Accordingly, we
reverse the judgment of the Illinois Supreme Court and remand the
case for further proceedings not inconsistent with this opinion.

* * *

NOTES AND QUESTIONS

1. Chief Justice Burger and Justices Stewart, Blackmun and Rehnquist dissented in the *Trimble* case. Justice Rehnquist wrote a dissenting
opinion which stated that if the Court had, during the period of more than
a century since the adoption of the Fourteenth Amendment, evolved a consistent body of doctrine which expressed the intent of the drafters, or had
evolved a body of doctrine which was consistent and served some useful
purpose, then we might be satisfied with the state of the law on the Equal
Protection Clause of that Amendment. He then went on to say, 430 U.S. at
777:

> "Unfortunately, more than a century of decisions under this Clause
> of the Fourteenth Amendment have produced neither of these results.
> They have instead produced a syndrome wherein this Court seems to
> regard the Equal Protection Clause as a cat-of-nine-tails to be kept in
> the judicial closet as a threat to legislatures which may, in the view of
> the judiciary, get out of hand and pass 'arbitrary', 'illogical', or 'un-
> reasonable' laws. Except in the area of the law in which the Framers
> obviously meant it to apply—classifications based on race or on national
> origin, the first cousin of race, the Court's decisions can fairly be des-
> cribed as an endless tinkering with legislative judgments, a series of
> conclusions unsupported by any central guiding principle."

Justice Rehnquist's dissent then described the difficulties which in general are created by expanding the Equal Protection Clause beyond its obvious prohibitions against classifications based on race or national origin.
When specifically addressing the *Trimble* issues, he asserted that the Court

---

17. The Illinois statute can be distinguished in several respects from the
Louisiana statute in *Labine*. The discrimination in *Labine* took a different
form, suggesting different legislative
objectives. See, e. g., n. 13, supra.
In its impact on the illegitimate children excluded from their parents' estates, the statute was significantly
different. Under Louisiana law, all
illegitimate children, "natural" and

"bastard," were entitled to support
from the estate of the deceased parent. 401 U.S., at 534, n. 2, 91 S.Ct.,
at 1018. Despite these differences, it
is apparent that we have examined
the Illinois statute more critically
than the Court examined the Louisiana statute in *Labine*. To the extent
that our analysis in this case differs
from that in *Labine* the more recent
analysis controls.

was attempting first to divine the motives of the Illinois legislature in passing the intestacy statute, and second to determine whether the statute as passed effectuated the motive or "purpose" attributed to the legislature. In Justice Rehnquist's view the Supreme Court possesses no qualifications enabling them to answer these questions better than the legislature.

In reading the Court's opinions on the illegitimate child, the student might find it useful to reflect on whether Justice Rehnquist's criticisms are applicable to these cases and, if so, what the consequences for the law of illegitimacy would be.

2. In Equal Protection Clause jargon there have evolved two "levels of scrutiny" when the Court judges the constitutionality of a statute. When a "suspect classification" or a "fundamental right" is involved, the scrutiny is said to be "strict". In other cases the scrutiny is "less strict", and it is sufficient if a rational relation between the statutory purpose and the statutory means can be discerned. In *Trimble,* relying upon Mathews v. Lucas, reproduced, infra, page 378, the Court adopts a new kind of "scrutiny", one which is not "toothless". What does this mean? Can you imagine a court saying that in a particular case it will engage in a "toothless scrutiny" of a statute? If not, what can be the meaning of a statement that the "scrutiny" will not be "toothless"? Is the process of legal analysis assisted by the adoption of dental metaphors?

3. (a) How does the opinion in *Trimble* deal with the *Labine* case? Does it distinguish, overrule or limit *Labine*?

(b) If you were asked for an opinion on whether the intestacy statute of State X was constitutional, and you found that the X statute was identical to the Louisiana statute at issue in *Labine,* what would be your opinion?

(c) It is true, is it not, that there was no question about the paternity of the child in either *Labine* or *Trimble*? What effect does that fact have on the relationship between the two decisions?

(d) The Court, in footnote 17, alludes to differences between the Louisiana statute in *Labine* and the Illinois statute in *Trimble.* How were they different? Are the differences, if any, such as to affect the inheritance claims of illegitimate children in a significant way?

4. The Court in *Trimble* seems to do away with the argument made in *Labine* and repeated in *Weber* that in *Labine* there was no insurmountable barrier to the illegitimate child's taking his father's estate, since the father could make a will. Is this apparently defunct argument resurrected in Parham v. Hughes, supra, page 336?

5. The proponents of the Illinois statute in *Trimble* argued that an intestacy statute is really a substitute for a will which the deceased failed to make. It is aimed at achieving the distribution of his estate which he probably would have made if he had executed a will. Since, it is assumed, he could have disinherited his illegitimate child and probably would have in most instances, the state may do the same.

(a) Is the premise correct, that is, does the intestacy statute have as its purpose the making of a substitute for a will? R. Wellman, 1 Uniform Probate Code Practice Manual 59 (1977).

(b) Would any constitutional problems be created if the father of an illegitimate child made a will giving all his property to his legitimate children and giving nothing to his illegitimate child?

(c) How does the Court deal with the "substitute will" argument? Is the Court's treatment of this issue satisfactory?

LALLI v. LALLI

Supreme Court of the United States, 1978.
439 U.S. 259, 99 S.Ct. 518, 58 L.Ed.2d 503.

Mr. Justice POWELL announced the judgment of the Court in an opinion, in which The CHIEF JUSTICE and Mr. Justice STEWART join.

This case presents a challenge to the constitutionality of § 4–1.2 of New York's Estates, Powers, and Trusts Law, which requires illegitimate children who would inherit from their fathers by intestate succession to provide a particular form of proof of paternity. Legitimate children are not subject to the same requirement.

I

Appellant Robert Lalli claims to be the illegitimate son of Mario Lalli who died intestate on January 7, 1973, in the State of New York. Appellant's mother, who died in 1968, never was married to Mario. After Mario's widow, Rosamond Lalli, was appointed administratrix of her husband's estate, appellant petitioned the Surrogate's Court for Westchester County for a compulsory accounting, claiming that he and his sister Maureen Lalli were entitled to inherit from Mario as his children. Rosamond Lalli opposed the petition. She argued that even if Robert and Maureen were Mario's children, they were not lawful distributees of the state because they had failed to comply with § 4–1.2, which provides in part:

"An illegitimate child is the legitimate child of his father so that he and his issue inherit from his father if a court of competent jurisdiction has, during the lifetime of the father, made an order of filiation declaring paternity in a proceeding instituted during of the pregnancy of the mother or within two years from the birth of the child."

Appellant conceded that he had not obtained an order of filiation during his putative father's lifetime. He contended, however, that § 4–1.2, by imposing this requirement, discriminated against him on the basis of his illegitimate birth in violation of the Equal Protection Clause of the Fourteenth Amendment. Appellant tendered certain evidence of his relationship with Mario Lalli, including a notarized document in which Lalli, in consenting to appellant's marriage, referred to him as "my son," and several affidavits by persons who stated that Lalli had acknowledged openly and often that Robert and Maureen were his children.

* * * After reviewing recent decisions of this Court concerning discrimination against illegitimate children, the court ruled that appellant was properly excluded as a distributee of Lalli's estate and therefore lacked status to petition for a compulsory accounting.

On direct appeal the New York Court of Appeals affirmed. In re Lalli, 38 N.Y.2d 77, 378 N.Y.S.2d 351, 340 N.E.2d 721 (1975). * * * After discussing the problems of proof peculiar to establishing paternity, as opposed to maternity, the court concluded that the State was constitutionally entitled to require a judicial decree during the father's lifetime as the exclusive form of proof of paternity.

Appellant appealed the Court of Appeals' decision to this Court. While that case was pending here, we decided Trimble v. Gordon, 430 U.S. 762, 97 S.Ct. 1459, 52 L.Ed.2d 31 (1977). Because the issues in these two cases were similar in some respects, we vacated and remanded to permit further consideration in light of *Trimble*. Lalli v. Lalli, 431 U.S. 911, 97 S.Ct. 2164, 53 L.Ed.2d 220 (1977).

On remand, the New York Court of Appeals, with one judge dissenting, adhered to its former disposition. In re Lalli, 43 N.Y.2d 65, 400 N.Y.S.2d 761, 371 N.E.2d 481 (1977). * * *

Appellant again sought review here, and we noted probable jurisdiction. We now affirm.

II

We begin our analysis with *Trimble*. * * *

We concluded that the Illinois statute discriminated against illegitimate children in a manner prohibited by the Equal Protection Clause. Although classifications based on illegitimacy are not subject to "strict scrutiny," they nevertheless are invalid under the Fourteenth Amendment if they are not substantially related to permissible state interests. Upon examination, we found that the Illinois law failed that test.

* * *

The Illinois statute, was constitutionally flawed because, by insisting upon not only an acknowledgment by the father, but also the marriage of the parents, it excluded "at least some significant categories of illegitimate children of intestate men [whose] inheritance rights can be recognized without jeopardizing the orderly settlement of estates or the dependability of titles to property passing under intestacy laws." We concluded that the Equal Protection Clause required that a statute placing exceptional burdens on illegitimate children in the furtherance of proper State objectives must be more "carefully tuned to alternative considerations," than was true of the broad disqualification in the Illinois law.

III

* * *

A

At the outset we observe that § 4–1.2 is different in important respects from the statutory provision overturned in *Trimble*. The Illinois statute required, in addition to the father's acknowledgment of paternity, the legitimation of the child through the intermarriage of the parents as an absolute precondition to inheritance. This combination of requirements eliminated "the possibility of a middle ground between the extremes of complete exclusion and case-by-case determination of paternity." As illustrated by the facts in *Trimble,* even a judicial declaration of paternity was insufficient to permit inheritance.

Under § 4–1.2, by contrast, the marital status of the parents is irrelevant. The single requirement at issue here is an evidentiary one—that the paternity of the father be declared in a judicial proceeding sometime before his death.[5] The child need not have been legitimated in order to inherit from his father. Had the appellant in *Trimble* been governed by § 4–1.2, she would have been a distributee of her father's estate.

A related difference between the two provisions pertains to the state interests said to be served by them. The Illinois law was defended, in part, as a means of encouraging legitimate family relationships. No such justification has been offered in support of § 4–1.2. The Court of Appeals disclaimed that the purpose of the statute, "even in small part, was to discourage illegitimacy, to mold human conduct or to set societal norms." The absence in § 4–1.2 of any requirement that the parents intermarry or otherwise legitimate a child born out of wedlock and our review of the legislative history of the statute, infra, at 527, confirm this view.

---

5. Section 4–1.2 requires not only that the order of filiation be made during the lifetime of the father, but that the proceeding in which it is sought have been commenced "during the pregnancy of the mother or within two years from the birth of the child." The New York Court of Appeals declined to rule on the constitutionality of the two-year limitation in both of its opinions in this case because appellant concededly had never commenced a paternity proceeding at all. Thus, if the rule that paternity be judicially declared during his father's lifetime were upheld, appellant would lose for failure to comply with that requirement alone. If, on the other hand, appellant prevailed in his argument that his inheritance could not be conditioned on the existence of an order of filiation, the two-year limitation would become irrelevant, since the paternity proceeding itself would be unnecessary. As the New York Court of Appeals has not passed upon the constitutionality of the two-year limitation, that question is not before us. Our decision today therefore sustains § 4–1.2 under the Equal Protection Clause only with respect to its requirement that a judicial order of filiation be issued during the lifetime of the father of an illegitimate child.

Our inquiry, therefore, is focused narrowly. We are asked to decide whether the discrete procedural demands that § 4–1.2 places on illegitimate children bear an evident and substantial relation to the particular state interests this statute is designed to serve.

B

The primary state goal underlying the challenged aspects of § 4–1.2 is to provide for the just and orderly disposition of property at death.[6] We long have recognized that this is an area with which the States have an interest of considerable magnitude.

This interest is directly implicated in paternal inheritance by illegitimate children because of the peculiar problems of proof that are involved. Establishing maternity is seldom difficult. * * * Proof of paternity, by contrast, frequently is difficult when the father is not part of a formal family unit. * * *

Thus, a number of problems arise that counsel against treating illegitimate chlidren identically to all other heirs of an intestate father. These were the subject of a comprehensive study by the Temporary State Commission on the Modernization, Revision and Simplification of the Law of Estates. This group, known as the Bennett Commission,[7] consisted of individuals experienced in the practical problems of estate administration. The Commission issued its report and recommendations to the Legislature in 1965. The statute now codified as § 4–1.2 was included.

Although the overarching purpose of the proposed statute was "to alleviate the plight of the illegitimate child," Commission Report 37, the Bennett Commission considered it necessary to impose the strictures of § 4–1.2 in order to mitigate serious difficulties in the administration of the estates of both testate and intestate decedents. The Commission's perception of some of these difficulties was described by Surrogate Sobel, a member of "the busiest [surrogate's] court in the State measured by the number of intestate estates which traffic daily through this court," In re Flemm, supra, at 857, 381 N.

---

6. The presence in this case of the State's interest in the orderly disposition of a decedent's property at death distinguishes it from others in which that justification for an illegitimacy-based classification was absent. E. g., Jimenez v. Weinberger, 417 U.S. 628, 94 S.Ct. 2496, 41 L.Ed.2d 363 (1974); Gomez v. Perez, 409 U.S. 535, 93 S.Ct. 872, 35 L.Ed.2d 56 (1973); Weber v. Aetna Casualty & Surety Co., 406 U.S. 164, 170, 92 S. Ct. 1400, 1404, 31 L.Ed.2d 768 (1972); Levy v. Louisiana, 391 U.S. 68, 88 S. Ct. 1509, 20 L.Ed.2d 436 (1968).

7. The Bennett Commission was created by the New York Legislature in 1961. It was instructed to recommend needed changes in certain areas of state law, including that pertaining to "the descent and distribution of property and the practice and procedure relating thereto." 1961 N.Y. Laws, ch. 731, § 1.

Y.S.2d at 574 (Sobel S.), and a participant in some of the Commission's deliberations:

"An illegitimate, if made an unconditional distributee in intestacy, must be served with process in the estate of his parent or if he is a distributee in the estate of the kindred of a parent. * * * And, in probating the will of his parent (though not named a beneficiary) or in probating the will of any person who makes a class disposition to 'issue' of such parent, the illegitimate must be served with process. * * * How does one cite and serve an illegitimate of whose existence neither family nor personal representative may be aware? And of greatest concern, how achieve finality of decree in *any* estate when there always exists the possibility however remote of a secret illegitimate lurking in the buried past of a parent or an ancestor of a class of beneficiaries? Finality in decree is essential in the Surrogate's Courts since title to real property passes under such decree. Our procedural statutes and the Due Process Clause mandate notice and opportunity to be heard to all necessary parties. Given the right to intestate succession, *all* illegitimates must be served with process. This would be no real problem with respect to those few estates where there are 'known' illegitimates. But it presents an almost insuperable burden as regards 'unknown' illegitimates. The point made in the [Bennett] commission discussions was that instead of affecting only a few estates, procedural problems would be created for many— some members suggested a majority—of estates."

Even where an individual claiming to be the illegitimate child of a deceased man makes himself known, the difficulties facing an estate are likely to persist. Because of the particular problems of proof, spurious claims may be difficult to expose. The Bennett Commission therefore sought to protect "innocent adults and those rightfully interested in their estates from fraudulent claims of heirship and harassing litigation instituted by those seeking to establish themselves as illegitimate heirs." Commission Report 265.

C

As the State's interests are substantial, we now consider the means adopted by New York to further these interests. In order to avoid the problems described above, the Commission recommended a requirement designed to ensure the accurate resolution of claims of paternity and to minimize the potential for disruption of estate administration. Accuracy is enhanced by placing paternity disputes in a judicial forum during the lifetime of the father. As the New York Court of Appeals observed in its first opinion in this case, the "availability [of the putative father] should be a substantial factor contributing to the reliability of the fact-finding process." In re Lalli, 38 N.Y.2d, at 82, 378 N.Y.S.2d, at 355, 340 N.E.2d, at 724. In addition, requiring that the order be issued during the father's lifetime permits a man to defend his reputation against "unjust accusations in paternity claims," which was a secondary purpose of § 4–1.2. Commission Report 266.

The administration of an estate will be facilitated, and the possibility of delay and uncertainty minimized, where the entitlement of an illegitimate child to notice and participation is a matter of judicial record before the administration commences. Fraudulent assertions of paternity will be much less likely to succeed, or even to arise, where the proof is put before a court of law at a time when the putative father is available to respond, rather than first brought to light when the distribution of the assets of an estate is in the offing.[8]

Appellant contends that § 4–1.2, like the statute at issue in *Trimble,* excludes "significant categories of illegitimate children" who could be allowed to inherit "without jeopardizing the orderly settlement" of their intestate fathers' estates. *Trimble,* supra, 430 U.S. at 771, 97 S.Ct. at 1465. He urges that those in his position—"known" illegitimate children who, despite the absence of an order of filiation obtained during their fathers' lifetimes, can present convincing proof of paternity—cannot rationally be denied inheritance as they pose none of the risks § 4–1.2 was intended to minimize.[9]

We do not question that there will be some illegitimate children who would be able to establish their relationship to their deceased fathers without serious disruption of the administration of estates and that, as applied to such individuals, § 4–1.2 appears to operate unfairly. But few statutory classifications are entirely free from the criticism that they sometimes produce inequitable results. Our inquiry under the Equal Protection Clause does not focus on the abstract "fairness" of a state law, but on whether the statute's relation to the

8. In affirming the judgment below, we do not, of course, restrict a State's freedom to require proof of paternity by means other than a judicial decree. Thus a State may prescribe any *formal* method of proof, whether it be similar to that provided by § 4–1.2 or some other regularized procedure that would assure the authenticity of the acknowledgment. As we noted in *Trimble,* 430 U.S., at 772 n. 14, 97 S.Ct., at 1466 n. 14, such a procedure would be sufficient to satisfy the State's interests. See also n. 11, infra.

9. Appellant claims that in addition to discriminating between illegitimate and legitimate children, § 4–1.2, in conjunction with N.Y.Dom.Rel.Law § 24 (McKinney 1977), impermissibly discriminates between classes of illegitimate children. Section 24 provides that a child conceived out of

wedlock is nevertheless legitimate if, before or after his birth, his parents marry, even if the marriage is void, illegal or judicially annulled. Appellant argues that by classifying as "legitimate" children born out of wedlock whose parents later marry, New York has, with respect to these children, substituted marriage for § 4–1.2's requirement of proof of paternity. Thus, these "illegitimate" children escape the rigors of the rule unlike their unfortunate counterparts whose parents never marry.

Under § 24, one claiming to be the legitimate child of a deceased man would have to prove not only his paternity but also his maternity and the fact of the marriage of his parents. These additional evidentiary requirements make it reasonable to accept less exacting proof of paternity and to treat such children as legitimate for inheritance purposes.

state interests it is intended to promote is so tenuous that it lacks the rationality contemplated by the Fourteenth Amendment.

The Illinois statute in *Trimble* was constitutionally unacceptable because it effected a total statutory disinheritance of children born out of wedlock who were not legitimated by the subsequent marriage of their parents. The reach of the statute was far in excess of its justifiable purposes. Section 4–1.2 does not share this defect. Inheritance is barred only where there has been a failure to secure evidence of paternity during the father's lifetime in the manner prescribed by the State. This is not a requirement that inevitably disqualifies an unnecessarily large number of children born out of wedlock.

The New York courts have interpreted § 4–1.2 liberally and in such a way as to enhance its utility to both father and child without sacrificing its strength as a procedural prophylactic. For example, a father of illegitimate children who is willing to acknowledge paternity can waive his defenses in a paternity proceeding, or even institute such a proceeding himself.[10] In addition, the courts have excused "technical" failures by illegitimate children to comply with the statute in order to prevent unnecessary injustice. E. g., In re Niles, 53 A.D.2d 983, 385 N.Y.S.2d 876 (1976), appeal den., 40 N.Y.2d 809, 392 N.Y.S.2d 1027, 360 N.E.2d 1109 (1977) (filiation order may be signed *nunc pro tunc* to relate back to period prior to father's death when court's factual finding of paternity had been made); In re Kennedy, 89 Misc.2d 551, 554, 392 N.Y.S.2d 365, 367 (Sur.Ct.1977) (judicial support order treated as "tantamount to an order of filiation," even though paternity was not specifically declared therein).

As the history of § 4–1.2 clearly illustrates, the New York Legislature desired to "grant to illegitimates *in so far as practicable* rights of inheritance on a par with those enjoyed by legitimate children," Commission Report 265 (emphasis added), while protecting the important state interests we have described. Section 4–1.2 represents a carefully considered legislative judgment as to how this balance best could be achieved.

Even if, as Mr. Justice BRENNAN believes, § 4–1.2 could have been written somewhat more equitably, it is not the function of a court "to hypothesize independently on the desirability or feasibility of any possible alternative[s]" to the statutory scheme formulated by New York. "These matters of practical judgment and empirical calculation are for [the State]. * * * In the end, the precise accuracy of [the State's] calculations is not a matter of specialized judicial competence; and we have no basis to question their detail be-

10. In addition to making intestate succession possible, of course, a father is always free to provide for his illegitimate child by will.

yond the evident consistency and substantiality." Id., at 515–516, 96 S.Ct. at 2767.[11]

We conclude that the requirement imposed by § 4–1.2 on illegitimate children who would inherit from their fathers is substantially related to the important state interests the statute is intended to promote. We therefore find no violation of the Equal Protection Clause.

The judgment of the New York Court of Appeals is

Affirmed.

NOTES AND QUESTIONS

1. Justice Rehnquist concurred in the judgment in this case for the reasons expressed in his dissent in Trimble v. Gordon. Justice Stewart concurred in the judgment and agreed that there were significant differences between the Illinois and New York intestacy statutes. He therefore indi-

11. The dissent of Mr. Justice Brennan would reduce the opinion in Trimble v. Gordon, 430 U.S. 762, 97 S.Ct. 1459, 52 L.Ed.2d 31 (1977), to a simplistic holding that the Constitution *requires* a State, in a case of this kind, to recognize as sufficient any "formal acknowledgment of paternity." This reading of *Trimble* is based on a single phrase lifted from a footnote. Id., at 772 n. 14, 97 S.Ct. at 1466. It ignores both the broad rationale of the Court's opinion and the context in which the note and the phrase relied upon appear. The principle that the footnote elaborates is that the States are free to recognize the problems arising from different forms of proof and to select those forms "carefully tailored to eliminate imprecise and unduly burdensome methods of establishing paternity." Ibid. The New York Legislature, with the benefit of the Bennett Commission's study, exercised this judgment when it considered and rejected the possibility of accepting evidence of paternity less formal than a judicial order.

The "formal acknowledgment" contemplated by *Trimble* is such as would minimize post-death litigation, i. e., a regularly prescribed, legally recognized method of acknowledging paternity. See n. 8, supra. It is thus plain that footnote 14 in *Trimble* does not sustain the dissenting opinion. Indeed, the document relied upon by the dissent is not an acknowledgment of paternity at all. It is a simple "Certificate of Consent" that apparently was required at the time by New York for the marriage of a minor. It consists of one sentence:

"This is to certify that I, who have hereto subscribed my name, do hereby consent that Robert Lalli who is my son and who is under the age of 21 years, shall be united in marriage to Janice Bivens by an minister of the gospel or other person authorized by law to solemnize marriages." App. A–16.

Mario Lalli's signature to this document was acknowledged by a notary public, but the certificate contains no oath or affirmation as to the truth of its contents. The notary did no more than confirm the identity of Lalli. Because the certificate was executed for the purpose of giving consent to marry, not of proving biological paternity, the meaning of the words "my son" is ambiguous. One can readily imagine that had Robert Lalli's half-brother, who was not Mario's son but who took the surname Lalli and lived as a member of his household, sought permission to marry, Mario might also have referred to him as "my son" on a consent certificate.

The important state interests of safeguarding the accurate and orderly disposition of property at death, emphasized in *Trimble* and reiterated in our opinion today, could be frustrated easily if there were a constitutional rule that any notarized but unsworn statement identifying an individual as a "child" must be accepted as adequate proof of paternity regardless of the context in which the statement was made.

cated his disagreement with Justice Blackmun's view that this decision left *Trimble* a "derelict". Justice Blackmun also concurred in the judgment, but on the ground that the plurality opinion reverted to the principles of Labine, of which he approved. He would have overruled *Trimble*, was not convinced by the plurality's distinguishing of that case, and described it as a "derelict" whose continued existence may create uncertainty about the validity of other statutes on intestacy.

Justice Brennan wrote a dissent, in which Justices White, Marshall and Stevens joined.

2. What degree of "scrutiny" is leveled at the New York statute in this case? Is the statute required merely to pass the "rational relation" test, or some more exacting test?

3. Is Justice Blackmun correct that this decision converts *Trimble* into a "derelict"? "Derelict" is defined by the Oxford English Dictionary as a piece of property abandoned by the owner. Has *Trimble* been abandoned by the Supreme Court?

4. The Court in *Lalli* holds that the New York statute is justified because it accomplishes the "just and orderly disposition of property at death", a state interest of "considerable magnitude". Precisely what does this mean? Would it be impossible or impracticable to draft a statute which permitted the illegitimate child to inherit from his father and at the same time to achieve a just and orderly disposition of decedents' estates?

The Uniform Probate Code § 2–109, 8 Unif.L.Ann. 90 (Supp.1979) contains the following alternative provisions dealing with the illegitimate child's rights of succession to his parents' property:

"**Section 2–109.** [Meaning of Child and Related Terms]

If, for purposes of intestate succession, a relationship of parent and child must be established to determine succession by, through, or from a person,

(1) an adopted person is the child of an adopting parent and not of the natural parents except that adoption of a child by the spouse of a natural parent has no effect on the relationship between the child and either natural parent.

(2) In cases not covered by Paragraph (1), a person is the child of its parents regardless of the marital status of its parents and the parent and child relationship may be established under the [Uniform Parentage Act].

Alternative subsection (2) for states that have not adopted the Uniform Parentage Act.

[(2) In cases not covered by Paragraph (1), a person born out of wedlock is a child of the mother. That person is also a child of the father, if:

(i) the natural parents participated in a marriage ceremony before or after the birth of the child, even though the attempted marriage is void; or

(ii) the paternity is established by an adjudication before the death of the father or is established thereafter by clear and convincing proof, but the paternity established under this subparagraph is ineffective to qualify the father or his kindred to inherit from or through the child unless the father has openly treated the child as his, and has not refused to support the child.]"

Does this statute fail to achieve a just and orderly disposition of estates at death? Are the provisions of the Uniform Probate Code dealing with notice, res judicata and limitation on claims effective in bringing about finality of intestate distributions? Uniform Probate Code §§ 1–401; 1–403; 3–1001; 3–1005. Is there any greater risk to the just and orderly disposition of estates from the existence of illegitimate children as heirs than from any other class of unknown or unborn heirs?

The sections of the Uniform Parentage Act dealing with proof of paternity include the following, 9 Unif.L.Ann. 521 ff.:

"§ 1. [Parent and Child Relationship Defined]

As used in this Act, "parent and child relationship" means the legal relationship existing between a child and his natural or adoptive parents incident to which the law confers or imposes rights, privileges, duties, and obligations. It includes the mother and child relationship and the father and child relationship.

"§ 2. [Relationship Not Dependent on Marriage]

The parent and child relationship extends equally to every child and to every parent, regardless of the marital status of the parents.

"§ 3. [How Parent and Child Relationship Established]

The parent and child relationship between a child and

(1) the natural mother may be established by proof of her having given birth to the child, or under this Act;

(2) the natural father may be established under this Act;

(3) an adoptive parent may be established by proof of adoption or under the [Revised Uniform Adoption Act].

"§ 4. [Presumption of Paternity]

(a) A man is presumed to be the natural father of a child if:

(1) he and the child's natural mother are or have been married to each other and the child is born during the marriage, or within 300 days after the marriage is terminated by death, annulment, declaration of invalidity, or divorce, or after a decree of separation is entered by a court;

(2) before the child's birth, he and the child's natural mother have attempted to marry each other by a marriage solemnized in apparent compliance with law, although the attempted marriage is or could be declared invalid, and,

(i) if the attempted marriage could be declared invalid only by a court, the child is born during the attempted marriage, or within 300 days after its termination by death, annulment, declaration of invalidity, or divorce; or

(ii) if the attempted marriage is invalid without a court order, the child is born within 300 days after the termination of cohabitation;

(3) after the child's birth, he and the child's natural mother have married, or attempted to marry, each other by a marriage solemnized in apparent compliance with law, although the attempted marriage is or could be declared invalid, and

(i) he has acknowledged his paternity of the child in writing filed with the [appropriate court or Vital Statistics Bureau].

(ii) with his consent, he is named as the child's father on the child's birth certificate, or

(iii) he is obligated to support the child under a written voluntary promise or by court order;

(4) while the child is under the age of majority, he receives the child into his home and openly holds out the child as his natural child; or

(5) he acknowledges his paternity of the child in a writing filed with the [appropriate court or Vital Statistics Bureau], which shall promptly inform the mother of the filing of the acknowledgment, and she does not dispute the acknowledgment within a reasonable time after being informed thereof, in a writing filed with the [appropriate court or Vital Statistics Bureau]. If another man is presumed under this section to be the child's father, acknowledgment may be effected only with the written consent of the presumed father or after the presumption has been rebutted.

(b) A presumption under this section may be rebutted in an appropriate action only by clear and convincing evidence. If two or more presumptions arise which conflict with each other, the presumption which on the facts is founded on the weightier considerations of policy and logic controls. The presumption is rebutted by a court decree establishing paternity of the child by another man.

"§ 10. [Pre-Trial Proceedings]

(a) As soon as practicable after an action to declare the existence or nonexistence of the father and child relationship has been brought, an informal hearing shall be held. [The court may order that the hearing be held before a referee.] The public shall be barred from the hearing. A record of the proceeding or any portion thereof shall be kept if any party requests, or the court orders. Rules of evidence need not be observed.

(b) Upon refusal of any witness, including a party, to testify under oath or produce evidence, the court may order him to testify under oath and produce evidence concerning all relevant facts. If the refusal is upon the ground that his testimony or evidence might tend to incriminate him, the court may grant him immunity from all criminal liability on account of the testimony or evidence he is required to produce. An order granting immunity bars prosecution of the witness for any offense shown in whole or in part by testimony or evidence he is required to produce, except for perjury committed in his testimony. The refusal of a witness, who has been granted immunity, to obey an order to testify or produce evidence is a civil contempt of the court.

(c) Testimony of a physician concerning the medical circumstances of the pregnancy and the condition and characteristics of the child upon birth is not privileged.

"§ 11. [Blood Tests]

(a) The court may, and upon request of a party shall, require the child, mother, or alleged father to submit to blood tests. The tests shall be performed by an expert qualified as an examiner of blood types, appointed by the court.

(b) The court, upon reasonable request by a party, shall order that independent tests be performed by other experts qualified as examiner of blood types.

(c) In all cases, the court shall determine the number and qualifications of the experts.

"§ 12. [Evidence Relating to Paternity]

Evidence relating to paternity may include:

(1) evidence of sexual intercourse between the mother and alleged father at any possible time of conception;

(2) an expert's opinion concerning the statistical probability of the alleged father's paternity based upon the duration of the mother's pregnancy;

(3) blood test results, weighted in accordance with evidence, if available, of the statistical probability of the alleged father's paternity;

(4) medical or anthropological evidence relating to the alleged father's paternity of the child based on tests performed by experts. If a man has been identified as a possible father of the child, the court may, and upon request of a party shall, require the child, the mother, the man to submit to appropriate tests; and

(5) all other evidence relevant to the issue of paternity of the child.

"§ 13. [Pre-Trial Recommendations]

(a) On the basis of the information produced at the pre-trial hearing, the judge [or referee] conducting the hearing shall evaluate the probability of determining the existence or non-existence of the father and child relationship in a trial and whether a judicial declaration of the relationship would be in the best interest of the child. On the basis of the evaluation, an appropriate recommendation for settlement shall be made to the parties, which may include any of the following:

(1) that the action be dismissed with or without prejudice;

(2) that the matter be compromised by an agreement among the alleged father, the mother, and the child, in which the father and child relationship is not determined but in which a defined economic obligation is undertaken by the alleged father in favor of

the child and, if appropriate, in favor of the mother, subject to approval by the judge [or referee] conducting the hearing. In reviewing the obligation undertaken by the alleged father in a compromise agreement, the judge [or referee] conducting the hearing shall consider the best interest of the child, in the light of the factors enumerated in Section 15(e), discounted by the improbability, as it appears to him, of establishing the alleged father's paternity or non-paternity of the child in a trial of the action. In the best interest of the child, the court may order that the alleged father's identity be kept confidential. In that case, the court may designate a person or agency to receive from the alleged father and disburse on behalf of the child all amounts paid by the alleged father in fulfillment of obligations imposed on him; and

      (3) that the alleged father voluntarily acknowledge his paternity of the child.

      (b) If the parties accept a recommendation made in accordance with Subsection (a), judgment shall be entered accordingly.

      (c) If a party refuses to accept a recommendation made under Subsection (a) and blood tests have not been taken, the court shall require the parties to submit to blood tests, if practicable. Thereafter the judge [or referee] shall make an appropriate final recommendation. If a party refuses to accept the final recommendation, the action shall be set for trial.

      (d) The guardian ad litem may accept or refuse to accept a recommendation under this Section.

      (e) The informal hearing may be terminated and the action set for trial if the judge [or referee] conducting the hearing finds unlikely that all parties would accept a recommendation he might make under Subsection (a) or (c)."

      5. The Court in *Lalli* holds that the New York statute may discriminate against the illegitimate child in order to avoid difficult problems of proving paternity. But are these problems peculiar to the intestacy context? Were they present in Weber v. Aetna Cas. & Surety Co.? Would they be present in the circumstances of Levy v. Louisiana, if the decedent were the child's father rather than his mother? If so, does that mean that the rule of *Levy* does not apply if the statute bars a suit by the illegitimate child for the wrongful death of his father?

      6. Would a wrongful death statute be constitutional if it provided that those relatives of the deceased could recover for his wrongful death who would take the deceased's property by inheritance, and the intestacy statute of the state were identical with the New York statute involved in Lalli? See Schmoll v. Creecy, 54 N.J. 194, 254 A.2d 525 (1969).

      7. What is the significance to footnote 10 to the Court's opinion? Is the Court returning to the "no insurmountable obstacle" argument which it repudiated in Trimble v. Gordon?

      8. Would the following statutes or judicial principles be constitutional under the *Labine-Trimble-Lalli* cases:

      (a) The New York statute provided that the illegitimate child could only inherit from his father if an order of filiation were entered in a proceeding brought during the mother's pregnancy or within two years after the child's birth. A paternity suit was brought when the child was four years old, and paternity of the defendant was determined. The child's father then died and the New York court held the child could not inherit because the paternity suit had not been brought within the time specified in the statute. See footnote 5 to Lalli v. Lalli.

(b) A state statute provided that the illegitimate child might inherit from a man who in writing, signed in the presence of a competent witness, acknowledged himself to be the child's father. In Re Estate of Burris, 361 So.2d 152 (Fla.1978); White v. Randolph, 59 Ohio St.2d 6, 391 N.E.2d 333 (1979), appeal dism'd., 100 S.Ct. 1000 (1980).

(c) The will of G leaves all of his property to "F for life, with remainder to his children." F has one legitimate and one illegitimate child at the time of his death. The case law of the state is that illegitimate children are not included as "children" in such testamentary dispositions. Does the illegitimate child have a constitutional right to share in this property as one of F's children? Why or why not?

WEBER v. AETNA CASUALTY & SURETY CO.

Supreme Court of the United States, 1972.
406 U.S. 164, 92 S.Ct. 1400, 31 L.Ed.2d 768.

Mr. Justice POWELL delivered the opinion of the Court.

The question before us, on writ of certiorari to the Supreme Court of Louisiana, concerns the right of dependent unacknowledged, illegitimate children to recover under Louisiana workmen's compensation laws benefits for the death of their natural father on an equal footing with his dependent legitimate children. We hold that Louisiana's denial of equal recovery rights to dependent unacknowledged illegitimates violates the Equal Protection Clause of the Fourteenth Amendment. Levy v. Louisiana, 391 U.S. 68, 88 S.Ct. 1509, 20 L.Ed. 2d 436 (1968). Glona v. American Guarantee & Liability Insurance Co., 391 U.S. 73, 88 S.Ct. 1515, 20 L.Ed.2d 441 (1968).

On June 22, 1967, Henry Clyde Stokes died in Louisiana of injuries received during the course of his employment the previous day. At the time of his death Stokes resided and maintained a household with one Willie Mae Weber, to whom he was not married. Living in the household were four legitimate minor children, born of the marriage between Stokes and Adlay Jones Stokes who was at the time committed to a mental hospital. Also living in the home was one unacknowledged illegitimate child born of the relationship between Stokes and Willie Mae Weber. A second illegitimate child of Stokes and Weber was born posthumously.

On June 29, 1967, Stokes' four legitimate children, through their maternal grandmother as guardian, filed a claim for their father's death under Louisiana's workmen's compensation law. The defendant employer and its insurer, impleaded Willie Mae Weber who appeared and claimed compensation benefits for the two illegitimate children.

Meanwhile, the four legitimate children had brought another suit for their father's death against a third-party tortfeasor which was settled for an amount in excess of the maximum benefits allowable under workmen's compensation. The illegitimate children did not share in this settlement. Subsequently, the employer in the initial action requested the extinguishment of all parties' workmen's compensation claims by reason of the tort settlement.

The trial judge awarded the four legitimate children the maximum allowable amount of compensation and declared their entitlement had been satisfied from the tort suit settlement. Consequently, the four legitimate children dismissed their workmen's compensation claim. Judgment was also awarded to Stokes' two illegitimate offspring to the extent that maximum compensation benefits were not exhausted by the four legitimate children. Since such benefits had been entirely exhausted by the amount of the tort settlement, in which only the four dependent legitimate offspring participated, the two dependent illegitimate children received nothing.

I

For purposes of recovery under workmen's compensation, Louisiana law defines children to include "only legitimate children, stepchildren, posthumous children, adopted children, and illegitimate children acknowledged under the provisions of Civil Code Articles 203, 204, and 205." [3] Thus, legitimate children and acknowledged illegitimates may recover on an equal basis. Unacknowledged illegitimate children, however, are relegated to the lesser status of "other dependents" under § 1232(8) of the workmen's compensation statute and may recover *only* if there are not enough surviving dependents in the preceding classifications to exhaust the maximum allowable benefits. Both the Louisiana Court of Appeal and a divided Louisiana Supreme

---

3. La.Rev.Stat. § 23:1021(3). The relevant provisions for acknowledgment of an illegitimate child are as follows:

La.Civ.Code, Art. 202 (1967):
  "Illegitimate children who have been acknowledged by their father, are called natural children; those who have not been acknowledged by their father, or whose father and mother were incapable of contracting marriage at the time of conception, or whose father is unknown, are contra-distinguished by the appellation of bastards."

La.Civ.Code. Art. 203:
  "The acknowledgment of an illegitimate child shall be made by a

declaration executed before a notary public, in presence of two witnesses, by the father and mother or either of them, whenever it shall not have been made in the registering of the birth or baptism of such child."

La.Civ.Code, Art. 204:
  "Such acknowledgment shall not be made in favor of children whose parents were incapable of contracting marriage at the time of conception; however, such acknowledgment may be made if the parents should contract a legal marriage with each other."

Court sustained these statutes over petitioner's constitutional objections, holding that our decision in *Levy,* supra, was not controlling.

We disagree. In *Levy,* the Court held invalid as denying equal protection of the laws, a Louisiana statute which barred an illegitimate child from recovering for the wrongful death of its mother when such recoveries by legitimate children were authorized. The Court there decided that the fact of a child's birth out of wedlock bore no reasonable relation to the purpose of wrongful-death statutes which compensate children for the death of a mother.   *   *   *

The court below sought to distinguish *Levy* as involving a statute which absolutely excluded *all* illegitimates from recovery, whereas in the compensation statute in the instant case acknowledged illegitimates may recover equally with legitimate children and "the unacknowledged illegitimate child is not *denied* a right to recover compensation, he being merely relegated to a less favorable position as are other dependent relatives such as parents   *   *   *." Stokes v. Aetna Casualty & Surety Co., 257 La. 424, 433–434, 242 So.2d 567, 570 (1970). The Louisiana Supreme Court likewise characterized *Levy* as a tort action where the tortfeasor escaped liability on the fortuity of the potential claimant's illegitimacy, whereas in the present action full compensation was rendered, and "no tort feasor goes free because of the law." Id., at 434, 242 So.2d, at 570.

We do not think *Levy* can be disposed of by such finely carved distinctions. The Court in *Levy* was not so much concerned with the tortfeasor going free as with the equality of treatment under the statutory recovery scheme. Here, as in *Levy,* there is impermissible discrimination. An unacknowledged illegitimate child may suffer as much from the loss of a parent as a child born within wedlock or an illegitimate later acknowledged. So far as this record shows, the dependency and natural affinity of the unacknowledged illegitimate child for her father were as great as those of the four legitimate children whom Louisiana law has allowed to recover.[7] The legitimate children and the illegitimate child all lived in the home of the deceased and were equally dependent upon him for maintenance and support. It is inappropriate, therefore, for the court below to talk of relegating the unacknowledged illegitimate "to a less favorable position as are other dependent relatives such as parents." The unacknowledged illegitimate is *not* a parent or some "other dependent relative"; in this case she is a *dependent child,* and as such is entitled to rights granted other *dependent children.*

Respondents contend that our recent ruling in Labine v. Vincent, 401 U.S. 532, 91 S.Ct. 1017, 28 L.Ed.2d 288 (1971), controls this case.

---

7. The affinity and dependency on the father of the posthumously born illegitimate child is, of course, not comparable to that of offspring living at the time of their father's death. This fact, however, does not alter our view of the case. We think a posthumously born illegitimate child should be treated the same as a posthumously born legitimate child, which the Louisiana statutes fail to do.

372 THE FAMILY Ch. 5

In *Labine*, the Court upheld, against constitutional objections, Louisiana intestacy laws which had barred an acknowledged illegitimate child from sharing equally with legitimate children in her father's estate. That decision reflected, in major part, the traditional deference to a State's prerogative to regulate the disposition at death of property within its borders. Id., at 538. The Court has long afforded broad scope to state discretion in this area.[8] Yet the substantial state interest in providing for "the stability of * * * land titles and in the prompt and definitive determination of the valid ownership of property left by decedents," Labine v. Vincent, 229 So.2d 449, 452 (La.App.1969), is absent in the case at hand.

Moreover, in *Labine* the intestate, unlike deceased in the present action, might easily have modified his daughter's disfavored position. As the Court there remarked:

"Ezra Vincent could have left one-third of his property to his illegitimate daughter had he bothered to follow the simple formalities of executing a will. He could, of course, have legitimated the child by marrying her mother in which case the child could have inherited his property either by intestate succession or by will as any other legitimate child." *Labine,* supra, at 539.

Such options, however, were not realistically open to Henry Stokes. Under Louisiana law he could not have acknowledged his illegitimate children even had he desired to do so.[9] The burdens of illegitimacy, already weighty, become doubly so when neither parent nor child can legally lighten them.

Both the statute in *Levy* and the statute in the present case involve state-created compensation schemes, designed to provide close relatives and dependents of a deceased a means of recovery for his often abrupt and accidental death. Both wrongful-death statutes and

8. The Court over a century ago voiced strong support for state powers over inheritance: "Now the law in question is nothing more than an exercise of the power which every state and sovereignty possesses, of regulating the manner and term upon which property real or personal within its dominion may be transmitted by last will and testament, or by inheritance; and of prescribing who shall and who shall not be capable of taking it." Mager v. Grima, 8 How. 490, 493, 12 L.Ed. 1168 (1850). See Lyeth v. Hoey, 305 U.S. 188, 193, 59 S.Ct. 155, 158, 83 L.Ed. 119 (1938).

9. La.Civ.Code, Art. 204, see n. 3, supra, prohibits acknowledgment of children whose parents were incapable of contracting marriage at the time of conception. Acknowledgment may only be made if the parents could contract a legal marriage with each other. Decedent in the instant case remained married to his first wife—the mother of his four legitimate children—until his death. Thus, at all times he was legally barred from marrying Willie Mae Weber, the mother of the two illegitimate children. It therefore was impossible for him to acknowledge legally his illegitimate children and thereby qualify them for protection under the Louisiana Workmen's Compensation Act. See also Williams v. American Emp. Ins. Co., 237 La. 101, 110 So.2d 541 (1959), where the Louisiana Supreme Court held that a posthumously born illegitimate child cannot be classified as a child entitled to workmen's compensation benefits, as defined under La.Rev.Stat. § 23:1021(3).

workmen's compensation codes represent outgrowths and modifications of our basic tort law. The former alleviated the harsh common-law rule under which "no person could inherit the personal right of another to recover for tortious injuries to his body"; the latter removed difficult obstacles to recovery in work-related injuries by offering a more certain, though generally less remunerative compensation. In the instant case, the recovery sought under the workmen's compensation statute was in lieu of an action under the identical death statute which was at issue in *Levy*. Given the similarities in the origins and purposes of these two statutes, and the similarity of Louisiana's pattern of discrimination in recovery rights, it would require a disregard of precedent and the principles of *stare decisis* to hold that *Levy* did not control the facts of the case before us. It makes no difference that illegitimates are not so absolutely or broadly barred here as in *Levy;* the discrimination remains apparent.

II

Having determined that *Levy* is the applicable precedent, we briefly reaffirm here the reasoning which produced that result. The tests to determine the validity of state statutes under the Equal Protection Clause have been variously expressed, but this Court requires, at a minimum, that a statutory classification bear some rational relationship to a legitimate state purpose. * * * Though the latitude given state economic and social regulation is necessarily broad, when state statutory classifications approach sensitive and fundamental personal rights, this Court exercises a stricter scrutiny, * * *. The essential inquiry in all the foregoing cases is, however, inevitably a dual one: What legitimate state interest does the classification promote? What fundamental personal rights might the classification endanger?

The Louisiana Supreme Court emphasized strongly the State's interest in protecting "legitimate family relationships," 257 La., at 433, 242 So.2d, at 570, and the regulation and protection of the family unit has indeed been a venerable state concern. We do not question the importance of that interest; what we do question is how the challenged statute will promote it. * * * Nor can it be thought here that persons will shun illicit relations because the offspring may not one day reap the benefits of workmen's compensation.

It may perhaps be said that statutory distinctions between the legitimate and illegitimate reflect closer family relationships in that the illegitimate is more often not under care in the home of the father nor even supported by him. The illegitimate, so this argument runs, may thus be made less eligible for the statutory recoveries and inheritances reserved for those more likely to be within the ambit of familial care and affection. Whatever the merits elsewhere of this contention, it is not compelling in a statutory compensation scheme where dependency on the deceased is a prerequisite to anyone's recovery, and where the acknowledgment so necessarily to equal recovery rights may be unlikely to occur or legally impossible to effectuate even where the illegitimate child may be nourished and loved.

Finally, we are mindful that States have frequently drawn arbitrary lines in workmen's compensation and wrongful-death statutes to facilitiate potentially difficult problems of proof. Nothing in our decision would impose on state court systems a greater burden in this regard. By limiting recovery to dependents of the deceased, Louisiana substantially lessens the possible problems of locating illegitimate children and of determining uncertain claims of parenthood. Our decision fully respects Louisiana's choice on this matter. It will not expand claimants for workmen's compensation beyond those in a direct blood and dependency relationship with the deceased and avoids altogether diffuse questions of affection and affinity which pose difficult probative problems. Our ruling requires equality of treatment between two classes of persons the genuineness of whose claims the State might in any event be required to determine.

The state interest in legitimate family relationships is not served by the statute; the state interest in minimizing problems of proof is not significantly disturbed by our decision. The inferior classification of dependent unacknowledged illegitimates bears, in this instance, no significant relationship to those recognized purposes of recovery which workmen's compensation statutes commendably serve.

The status of illegitimacy has expressed through the ages society's condemnation of irresponsible liaisons beyond the bonds of marriage. But visiting this condemnation on the head of an infant is illogical and unjust. Moreover, imposing disabilities on the illegitimate child is contrary to the basic concept of our system that legal burdens should bear some relationship to individual responsibility or wrongdoing. Obviously, no child is responsible for his birth and penalizing the illegitimate child is an ineffectual—as well as an unjust—way of deterring the parent. Courts are powerless to prevent the social opprobrium suffered by these hapless children, but the Equal Protection Clause does enable us to strike down discriminatory laws relating to status of birth where—as in this case—the classification is justified by no legitimate state interest, compelling or otherwise.

Reversed and remanded.*

NOTES AND QUESTIONS

1. In 1973 the Supreme Court handed down a short per curiam opinion in which it held that the law of Texas was unconstitutional in permitting a legitimate child to enforce a right to support against his father while denying that right to an illegitimate child. Gomez v. Perez, 409 U.S. 535 (1973). At the time of this decision Texas and Idaho were the only states

[* Mr. Justice Blackmun concurred specially in the result of this case. Mr. Justice Rehnquist dissented from the majority opinion on the ground that Levy and Glona were wrongly decided and should be reexamined.]

which did not permit the illegitimate child to enforce a claim for support against his father, and as a result of the decision this right now exists in all states.

The Court cited *Levy* and *Weber* for the proposition that the Equal Protection Clause of the Fourteenth Amendment forbids this sort of discrimination and then went on to say:

> "Under these decisions, a State may not invidiously discriminate against illegitimate children by denying them substantial benefits accorded children generally. We therefore hold that once a State posits a judicially enforceable right on behalf of children to needed support from their natural fathers there is no constitutionally sufficient justification for denying such an essential right to a child simply because its natural father has not married its mother. For a State to do so is "illogical and unjust." * * * We recognize the lurking problems with respect to proof of paternity. Those problems are not to be lightly brushed aside, but neither can they be made into an impenetrable barrier that works to shield otherwise invidious discrimination. * * *"

2. Do you think that *Weber* overruled Labine v. Vincent?

JIMENEZ v. WEINBERGER

Supreme Court of the United States, 1974.
417 U.S. 628, 94 S.Ct. 2496, 41 L.Ed.2d 363.

Mr. Chief Justice BURGER delivered the opinion of the Court.

A three-judge District Court in the Northern District of Illinois upheld the constitutionality of a provision of the Social Security Act which provides that certain illegitimate children, who cannot qualify for benefits under any other provision of the Act, may obtain benefits if, but only if, the disabled wage-earner parent is shown to have contributed to the child's support or to have lived with him prior to the parent's disability. The District Court held that the statute's classification is rationally related to the legitimate governmental interest of avoiding spurious claims.

The relevant facts are not in dispute. Ramon Jimenez, a wage earner covered under the Social Security Act, became disabled in April 1963, and became entitled to disability benefits in October 1963. Some years prior to that time, the claimant separated from his wife and began living with Elizabeth Hernandez, whom he never married. Three children were born to them, Magdalena, born August 13, 1963, Eugenio, born January 18, 1965, and Alicia, born February 24, 1968. These children have lived in Illinois with claimant all their lives; he has formally acknowledged them to be his children, has supported and cared for them since their birth, and has been their sole caretaker since their mother left the household late in 1968. Since the parents never married, these children are classified as illegitimate under Illinois law and are unable to inherit from their father because they are nonlegitimated illegitimate children.   Ill.Ann.Stat., c. 3, § 12 (Supp.1974).

On August 21, 1968, Ramon Jimenez, as the father, filed an application for child's insurance benefits on behalf of these three children. Magdalena was found to be entitled to child's insurance benefits under the Social Security Act, and no issue is presented with respect to her claim.   The claims of appellants, Eugenio and Alicia, were denied, however, on the ground that they did not meet the requirements of 42 U.S.C.A. § 416(h)(3), since neither child's paternity had been acknowledged or affirmed through evidence of domicile and support before the onset of their father's disability.[2]   In all other respects Eugenio and Alicia are eligible to receive child's insurance benefits, and their applications were denied solely because they are proscribed illegitimate children who were not dependent on Jimenez at the time of the onset of his disability.

[At this point in the opinion the Court quoted from Weber v. Aetna Cas. & Surety Co., and cited Dandridge v. Williams, 397 U.S. 471, 90 S.Ct. 1153, 25 L.Ed.2d 491 (1970), distinguishing the latter case on the ground that it was based upon a recognition of the need to allocate finite resources, while no such need was evident in the purposes of the statute involved in this case.]

As we have noted, the primary purpose of the contested Social Security scheme is to provide support for dependents of a disabled wage earner.   The Secretary maintains that the Act denies benefits to afterborn illegitimates who cannot inherit or whose illegitimacy is not solely because of a formal, nonobvious defect in their parents' wedding ceremony, or who are not legitimated, because it is "likely" that these illegitimates, as a class, will not possess the requisite economic dependency on the wage earner which would entitle them to recovery under the Act and because eligibility for such benefits to those illegitimates would open the door to spurious claims.   Under this view the Act's purpose would be to replace only that support enjoyed prior to the onset of disability; no child would be eligible to receive benefits unless the child had experienced actual support from the wage earner prior to the disability, and no child born after the onset of the wage earner's disability would be allowed to recover. We do not read the statute as supporting that view of its purpose.

2. The contested Social Security scheme provides, in essence, that legitimate or legitimated children (42 U.S.C.A. § 402(d)(3)), illegitimate children who can inherit their parent's personal property under the intestacy laws of the State of the insured's domicile (42 U.S.C.A. § 416(h)(2)(A)), and those children who cannot inherit only because their parents' ceremonial marriage was invalid for nonobvious defects (42 U.S.C.A. § 416(h)(2)(B)), are entitled to receive benefits without any further showing of parental support.   However, illegitimate children such as Eugenio and Alicia who were not living with or being supported by the applicant at the time the claimant's period of disability began, and who do not fall into one of the foregoing categories, are not entitled to receive any benefits.   42 U.S.C.A. § 416(h)(3).

Under the statute it is clear that illegitimate children born after the wage earner becomes disabled qualify for benefits if state law permits them to inherit from the wage earner, § 416(h)(2)(A); or if their illegitimacy results solely from formal, nonobvious defects in their parents' ceremonial marriage, § 416(h)(2)(B); or if they are legitimated in accordance with state law, § 402(d)(3)(A). Similarly, legitimate children born after their wage-earning parent has become disabled and legitimate children born before the onset of disability are entitled to benefits regardless of whether they were living with or being supported by the disabled parent at the onset of the disability, § 402(d)(1) and (3).

In each of the examples just mentioned, the child is by statute "deemed dependent" upon the parent by virtue of his status and no dependency or paternity need be shown for the child to qualify for benefits. However, nonlegitimated illegitimates in appellants' position, who cannot inherit under state law and whose illegitimacy does not derive solely from a defect in their parents' wedding ceremony, are denied a parallel right to the dependency presumption under the Act. Their dilemma is compounded by the fact that the statute denies them any opportunity to prove dependency in order to establish their "claim" to support and, hence, their right to eligibility. § 416(h)(3)(B). The Secretary maintains that this absolute bar to disability benefits is necessary to prevent spurious claims because "[t]o the unscrupulous person, all that prevents him from realizing * * * gain is the mere formality of a spurious acknowledgment of paternity or a collusive paternity suit with the mother of an illegitimate child who is herself desirous or in need of the additional cash." Jimenez v. Richardson, 353 F.Supp., at 1361.

From what has been outlined it emerges that afterborn illegitimate children are divided into two subclassifications under this statute. One subclass is made up of those (a) who can inherit under state intestacy laws, or (b) who are legitimated under state law, or (c) who are illegitimate only because of some formal defect in their parents' ceremonial marriage. These children are deemed entitled to receive benefits under the Act without any showing that they are in fact dependent upon their disabled parent. The second subclassification of afterborn illegitimate children includes those who are conclusively denied benefits because they do not fall within one of the foregoing categories and are not entitled to receive insurance benefits under any other provision of the Act.

We recognize that the prevention of spurious claims is a legitimate governmental interest and that dependency of illegitimates in appellants' subclass, as defined under the federal statute, has not been legally established even though, as here, paternity has been acknowledged. As we have noted, the Secretary maintains that the possibility that evidence of parentage or support may be fabricated is greater when the child is not born until after the wage earner has become entitled to benefits. It does not follow, however, that the blanket and conclusive exclusion of appellants' subclass of illegitimates is reasonably related to the prevention of spurious claims. Assuming that the appellants are in fact dependent on the claimant, it would not serve the purposes of the Act to conclusively deny them an opportunity to establish their dependency and their right to insurance benefits, and it would discriminate between the two subclasses of afterborn illegitimates without any basis for the distinction since the potential for spurious claims is exactly the same as to both subclasses.

The Secretary does not contend that it is necessary or universally true that all illegitimates in appellants' subclass would be unable to establish their dependency and eligibility under the Act if the statute gave them an opportunity to do so. Nor does he suggest a basis for the assumption that all illegitimates who are statutorily deemed entitled to benefits under the Act are in fact dependent upon their disabled parent. Indeed, as we have noted, those illegitimates statutorily deemed dependent are entitled to benefits regardless of whether they were living in, or had ever lived in, a dependent family setting with their disabled parent. Even if children might rationally be classified on the basis of whether they are dependent upon their disabled parent, the Act's definition of these two subclasses of illegitimates is "overinclusive" in that it benefits some children who are legitimated, or entitled to inherit, or illegitimate solely because of a defect in the marriage of their parents, but who are not dependent on their disabled parent. Conversely, the Act is "underinclusive" in that it conclusively excludes some illegitimates in appellants' subclass who are, in fact, dependent upon their disabled parent. Thus, for all that is shown in this record, the two subclasses of illegitimates stand on equal footing, and the potential for spurious claims is the same as to both; hence to conclusively deny one subclass benefits presumptively available to the other denies the former the equal protection of the laws guaranteed by the due process provision of the Fifth Amendment.

*   *   *

Vacated and remanded.*

MATHEWS v. LUCAS

United States Supreme Court, 1976.
427 U.S. 495, 96 S.Ct. 2755, 49 L.Ed.2d 651.

Mr. Justice BLACKMUN delivered the opinion of the Court.

This case presents the issue of the constitutionality, under the Due Process Clause of the Fifth Amendment, of those provisions of the Social Security Act that condition the eligibility of certain illegit-

---

* Justice Rehnquist dissented from the Court's opinion in this case.

imate children for a surviving child's insurance benefits upon a showing that the deceased wage earner was the claimant child's parent and, at the time of his death, was living with the child or was contributing to his support.

I

Robert Cuffee, now deceased, lived with Belmira Lucas during the years 1948 through 1966, but they were never married. Two children were born to them during these years: Ruby M. Lucas, in 1953, and Darin E. Lucas, in 1960. In 1966 Cuffee and Lucas separated. Cuffee died in Providence, R. I., his home, in 1968. He died without ever having acknowledged in writing his paternity of either Ruby or Darin, and it was never determined in any judicial proceeding during his lifetime that he was the father of either child. After Cuffee's death, Mrs. Lucas filed an application on behalf of Ruby and Darin for surviving children's benefits under § 202(d)(1) of the Social Security Act, 70 Stat. 807, as amended, 42 U.S.C.A. § 402(d)(1), based upon Cuffee's earnings record.

II

In operative terms, the Act provides that an unmarried son or daughter of an individual, who died fully or currently insured under the Act, may apply for and be entitled to a survivor's benefit, if the applicant is under 18 years of age at the time of application (or is a full-time student and under 22 years of age) and was dependent, within the meaning of the statute, at the time of the parent's death.[1] A

---

1. Section 202(d)(1) of the Act, as set forth in 42 U.S.C.A. § 402(d)(1), provides in pertinent part:

"Every child (as defined in section 416(e) of this title) * * * of an individual who dies a fully or currently insured individual, if such child—

"(A) has filed application for child's insurance benefits,

"(B) at the time such application was filed was unmarried and (i) either had not attained the age of 18 or was a full-time student and had not attained the age of 22 * * * and

"(C) was dependent upon such individual—

* * *

"(ii) if such individual has died, at the time of such death, * * *

* * *

"shall be entitled to a child's insurance benefit for each month, beginning with the first month after August 1950 in which such child becomes so entitled to such insurance benefits * * *."

Section 216(e), 42 U.S.C.A. § 416(e), includes, under the definition of child, inter alia, "the child * * * of an individual," certain legally adopted children, certain stepchildren, and certain grandchildren and stepgrandchildren. Additionally, § 216(h)(2)(A) of the Act, 42 U.S.C.A. § 416(h)(2)(A), provides:

"In determining whether an applicant is the child * * * of a fully or currently insured individual for purposes of this subchapter, the Secretary shall apply such law as would be applied in determining the devolution of intestate personal property * * * by the courts of the State in which [such insured individual] was domiciled at the time of his death * * *. Applicants who according to such law would have the same status relative to taking intestate personal property as a child * * * shall be deemed such."

child is considered dependent for this purpose if the insured father was living with or contributing to the child's support at the time of death. Certain children, however, are relieved of the burden of such individualized proof of dependency. Unless the child has been adopted by some other individual, a child who is legitimate, or a child who would be entitled to inherit personal property from the insured parent's estate under the applicable state intestacy law, is considered to have been dependent at the time of the parent's death.[2] Even lacking this relationship under state law, a child, unless adopted by some other individual, is entitled to a presumption of dependency if the decedent, before death, (a) had gone through a marriage ceremony with the other parent, resulting in a purported marriage between them which, but for a nonobvious legal defect, would have been valid, or (b) in writing had acknowledged the child to be his, or (c) had been decreed by a court to be the child's father, or (d) had been ordered by a court to support the child because the child was his.[3]

2. Section 202(d)(3) of the Act, 42 U. S.C.A. § 402(d)(3), provides in pertinent part:

"A child shall be deemed dependent upon his father or adopting father or his mother or adopting mother at the time specified in paragraph (1)(C) of this subsection unless, at such time, such individual was not living with or contributing to the support of such child and—

"(A) such child is neither the legitimate nor adopted child of such individual, or

"(B) such child has been adopted by some other individual."

Additionally, any child who qualifies under § 216(h)(2)(A), see n. 1, supra, is considered legitimate for § 202(d)(3) purposes, and thus dependent.

3. Section 202(d)(3), as set forth in 42 U.S.C.A. § 402(d)(3), provides in pertinent part that "a child deemed to be a child of a fully or currently insured individual pursuant to section 416(h)(2)(B) or section 416(h)(3) * * * shall be deemed to be the legitimate child of such individual," and therefore presumptively dependent. Section 216(h)(2)(B), as set forth in 42 U.S.C.A. § 416(h)(2)(B), provides:

"If an applicant is a son or daughter of a fully or currently insured individual but is not (and is not deemed to be) the child of such insured individual under subparagraph (A), such applicant shall nev-

ertheless be deemed to be the child of such insured individual if such insured individual and the mother or father, as the case may be, of such applicant went through a marriage ceremony resulting in a purported marriage between them which, but for a legal impediment described in the last sentence of paragraph (1)(B), would have been a valid marriage."

The specified last sentence of § 216(h)(1)(B), 42 U.S.C.A. § 416(h)(1)(B), in turn, refers only to "an impediment (i) resulting from the lack of dissolution of a previous marriage or otherwise arising out of such previous marriage or its dissolution, or (ii) resulting from a defect in the procedure followed in connection with such purported marriage."

Section 216(h)(3), as set forth in 42 U.S.C.A. § 416(h)(3), provides:

"An applicant who is the son or daughter of a fully or currently insured individual, but who is not (and is not deemed to be) the child of such insured individual under paragraph (2) of this subsection, shall nevertheless be deemed to be the child of such insured individual if:

* * *

"(C) In the case of a deceased individual—

"(i) such insured individual—

"(I) had acknowledged in writing that the applicant is his son or daughter,

An Examiner of the Social Security Administration, after hearings, determined that while Cuffee's paternity was established, the children had failed to demonstrate their dependency by proof that Cuffee either lived with them or was contributing to their support at the time of his death, or by any of the statutory presumptions of dependency, and thus that they were not entitled to survivorship benefits under the Act. * * *

The District Court ultimately affirmed each of the factual findings of the administrative agency: that Robert Cuffee was the children's father; that he never acknowledged his paternity in writing; that his paternity or support obligations had not been the subject of a judicial proceeding during his lifetime; that no common-law marriage had ever been contracted between Cuffee and Lucas, so that the children could not inherit Cuffee's personal property under the intestacy law of Rhode Island; and that, at the time of his death, he was neither living with the children nor contributing to their support. None of these factual matters is at issue here.

* * * It was urged that denial of benefits in this case, where paternity was clear, violated the Fifth Amendment's Due Process Clause, as that provision comprehends the principle of equal protection of the laws, * * *. Addressing this issue, the District Court ruled that the statutory classifications were constitutionally impermissible. * * *

With this conclusion, the District Court reversed the administrative decision and ordered the Secretary to pay benefits for both children. * * *

III

* * *

Although the District Court concluded that close judicial scrutiny of the statute's classifications was not necessary to its conclusion invalidating those classifications, it also concluded that legislation treating legitimate and illegitimate offspring differently is constitutionally suspect,[8] and requires the judicial scrutiny traditionally de-

"(II) had been decreed by a court to be the father of the applicant, or

"(III) had been ordered by a court to contribute to the support of the applicant because the applicant was his son or daughter,

"and such acknowledgment, court decree, or court order was made before the death of such individual, or

"(ii) such insured individual is shown by evidence satisfactory to the Secretary to have been the father of the applicant, and such insured individual was living with or contributing to the support of the applicant at the time such insured individual died."

8. Appellees do not suggest, nor could they successfully, that strict judicial scrutiny of the statutory classifications is required here because, in regulating entitlement to survivorship benefits, the statute discriminatorily interferes with interests of constitutional fundamentality.

The Court, of course, has found the privacy of familial relationships to be entitled to procedural due process protections from disruption by the

voted to cases involving discrimination along lines of race or national origin. Appellees echo this approach. We disagree.

It is true, of course, that the legal status of illegitimacy, however defined, is, like race or national origin, a characteristic determined by causes not within the control of the illegitimate individual, and it bears no relation to the individual's ability to participate in and contribute to society. The Court recognized in *Weber* that visiting condemnation upon the child in order to express society's disapproval of the parents' liaisons "is illogical and unjust. * * *" 406 U.S., at 175, 92 S.Ct., at 1406. (Footnote omitted.)

But where the law is arbitrary in such a way, we have had no difficulty in finding the discrimination impermissible on less demanding standards than those advocated here. And such irrationality in some classifications does not in itself demonstrate that other, possibly rational, distinctions made in part on the basis of legitimacy are inherently untenable. Moreover, while the law has long placed the illegitimate child in an inferior position relative to the legitimate in certain circumstances, particularly in regard to obligations of support or other aspects of family law, perhaps in part because the roots of the discrimination rest in the conduct of the parents rather than the child,[12] and perhaps in part because illegitimacy does not carry an obvious badge, as race or sex do, this discrimination against illegitimates has never approached the severity or pervasiveness of the historic legal and political discriminaton aganst women and Negroes.

We therefore adhere to our earlier view, see Labine v. Vincent, 401 U.S. 532, 91 S.Ct. 1017, 28 L.Ed.2d 288 (1971), that the Act's discrimination between individuals on the basis of their legitimacy does not "command extraordinary protection from the majoritarian political process," San Antonio School Dist. v. Rodriguez, 411 U.S. 1, 28, 93 S.Ct. 1278, 1294, 36 L.Ed.2d 16 (1973), which our most exacting scrutiny would entail.[13]

State, whether or not those relationships were legitimized by marriage under state law. Stanley v. Illinois, 405 U.S. 645, 92 S.Ct. 1208, 31 L.Ed. 2d 551 (1972). But the concerns relevant to that context are only tangential to the analysis here, since the statutory scheme does not interfere in any way with familial relations.

12. The significance of this consideration would seem to be suggested by provisions enabling the parents to legitimatize children born illegitimate. Compare *Weber*, 406 U.S., at 170–171 92 S.Ct., at 1404, with Labine v. Vincent, 401 U.S. 532, 539, 91 S.Ct. 1017,

1021, 28 L.Ed.2d 288 (1971). Of course, the status of "dependency" as recognized by the statute here is wholly within the control of the parent.

13. In *Rodriguez* the court identified a "suspect class' entitled to the protections of strict judicial scrutiny as one "saddled with such disabilities, or subjected to such a history of purposeful unequal treatment, or relegated to such a position of political powerlessness as to command extraordinary protection from the majoritarian political process." 411 U.S., at 28, 93 S.Ct., at 1294.

IV

Relying on *Weber*, the Court, in Gomez v. Perez, 409 U.S. 535, 538, 93 S.Ct. 872, 875, 35 L.Ed.2d 56 (1973), held that "once a State posits a judicially enforceable right on behalf of children to needed support from their natural fathers there is no constitutionally sufficient justification for denying such an essential right to a child simply because its natural father has not married its mother." The same principle, which we adhere to now, applies when the judicially enforceable right to needed support lies against the Government rather than a natural father.

Consistent with our decisions, the Secretary explains the design of the statutory scheme assailed here as a program to provide for all children of deceased insureds who can demonstrate their "need" in terms of dependency at the times of the insureds' deaths. He authenticates this description by reference to the explicit language of the Act specifying that the applicant child's classification as legitimate, or acknowledged, etc., is ultimately relevant only to the determination of dependency, and by reference to legislative history indicating that the statute was not a general welfare provision for legitimate or otherwise "approved" children of deceased insureds, but was intended just "to replace the support lost by a child when his father * * * dies * * *." S.Rep. No. 404, 89th Cong., 1st Sess., 110 (1965).

Taking this explanation at face value, we think it clear that conditioning entitlement upon dependency at the time of death is not impermissibly discriminatory in providing only for those children for whom the loss of the parent is an immediate source of the need.

But appellees contend that the actual design of the statute belies the Secretary's description, and that the statute was intended to provide support for insured decedents' children generally, if they had a "legitimate" claim to support, without regard to actual dependency at death; in any case, they assert, the statute's matrix of classifications bears no adequate relationship to actual dependency at death. Since such dependency does not justify the statute's discriminations, appellees argue, those classifications must fall under Gomez v. Perez, supra. These assertions are in effect one and the same.[14] The basis for

14. We are not bound to agree with the Secretary's description of the legislative design if the legislative history and the structure of the provisions themselves belie it. Appellees are unable, however, to summon any meaningful legislative history to support their position regarding the congressional design. They rely largely upon a section of the House-Senate Conference Committee Report on the 1965 Amendments to the Social Security Act, reproduced at 111 Cong.Rec. 18383 (1965), partially explaining, id., at 18387, the addition of § 216(h)(3), set forth in n. 3, supra, to the Act:

"A child would be paid benefits based on his father's earnings without regard to whether he has the status of a child under State inheritance laws if the father was supporting the child or had a legal obligation to do so."

But the clause's reference to legal obligations to support hardly establishes that the statute was designed to re-

appellees' argument is the obvious fact that each of the presumptions of dependency renders the class of benefit-recipients incrementally overinclusive, in the sense that some children within each class of presumptive dependents are automatically entitled to benefits under the statute although they could not in fact prove their economic dependence upon insured wage earners at the time of death. We conclude that the statutory classifications are permissible, however, because they are reasonably related to the likelihood of dependency at death.

A

Congress' purpose in adopting the statutory presumptions of dependency was obviously to serve administrative convenience. While Congress was unwilling to assume that every child of a deceased insured was dependent at the time of death, by presuming dependency on the basis of relatively readily documented facts, such as legitimate birth, or existence of a support order or paternity decree, which could be relied upon to indicate the likelihood of continued actual dependency, Congress was able to avoid the burden and expense of specific case-by-case determination in the large number of cases where dependency is objectively probable. Such presumptions in aid of administrative functions, though they may approximate, rather than precisely mirror, the results that case-by-case adjudication would show, are permissible under the Fifth Amendment, so long as that lack of precise equivalence does not exceed the bounds of substantiality tolerated by the applicable level of scrutiny.

In cases of strictest scrutiny, such approximations must be supported at least by a showing that the Government's dollar "lost" to overincluded benefit recipients is returned by a dollar "saved" in administrative expense avoided. Under the standard of review appropriate here, however, the materiality of the relation between the statutory classifications and the likelihood of dependency they assertedly reflect need not be " 'scientifically substantiated.' " Nor, in any case, do we believe that Congress is required in this realm of less than strictest scrutiny to weigh the burdens of administrative inquiry solely in terms of dollars ultimately "spent," ignoring the relative amounts devoted to administrative rather than welfare uses. Finally, while the scrutiny by which their showing is to be judged is not a toothless one, the burden remains upon the appellees to demonstrate the insubstantiality of that relation.

place any potential source of lifetime support; in our view the passage appears only to be a partial description of the actual effect of §§ 416(h)(3)(C)(i)(II) and (III), set forth in n. 3, supra, not an enunciation of the general purpose of the Act.

Thus, appellees, in order to make their case, must ultimately rely upon the asserted failure of the legislative product adequately to fit the purported legitimate aim.

B

Applying these principles, we think that the statutory classifications challenged here are justified as reasonable empirical judgments that are consistent with a design to qualify entitlement to benefits upon a child's dependency at the time of the parent's death. To begin with, we note that the statutory scheme is significantly different from the provisions confronted in cases in which the Court has invalidated legislative discriminations among children on the basis of legitimacy. See Gomez v. Perez, 409 U.S. 535, 93 S.Ct. 872, 35 L.Ed.2d 56 (1973); New Jersey Welfare Rights Org. v. Cahill, 411 U.S. 619, 93 S.Ct. 1700, 36 L.Ed.2d 543 (1973); Weber v. Aetna Casualty & Surety Co., 406 U.S. 164, 92 S.Ct. 1400, 31 L.Ed.2d 768 (1972); Levy v. Louisiana, 391 U.S. 68, 88 S.Ct. 1509, 20 L.Ed.2d 436 (1968). These differences render those cases of little assistance to appellees. It could not have been fairly argued, with respect to any of the statutes struck down in those cases, that the legitimacy of the child was simply taken as an indication of dependency, or of some other valid ground of qualification. Under all but one of the statutes, not only was the legitimate child automatically entitled to benefits, but an illegitimate child was denied benefits solely and finally on the basis of illegitimacy, and regardless of any demonstration of dependency or other legitimate factor. In Weber v. Aetna Casualty & Surety Co., supra, the sole partial exception, the statutory scheme provided for a child's equal recovery under a workmen's compensation plan in the event of the death of the father, not only if the child was dependent, but *also* only if the dependent child was legitimate. 406 U.S., at 173–174, and n. 12, 92 S.Ct., at 1405–1406. Jimenez v. Weinberger, supra, invalidating discrimination among afterborn illegitimate children as to entitlement to a child's disability benefits under the Social Security Act, is similarly distinguishable. Under the somewhat related statutory matrix considered there, legitimate children and those capable of inheriting personal property under state intestacy law, and those illegitimate solely on account of a nonobvious defect in their parents' marriage, were eligible for benefits, even if they were born after the onset of the father's disability. Other (illegitimate) afterborn children were conclusively denied any benefits, regardless of any showing of dependency. The Court held the discrimination among illegitimate afterborn children impermissible, rejecting the Secretary's claim that the classification was based upon considerations regarding trustworthy proof of dependency, * * * . But this conclusiveness in denying benefits to some classes of afterborn illegitimate children, which belied the asserted legislative reliance on dependency in *Jimenez,* is absent here, for, as we have noted, any otherwise eligible child may qualify for survivorship benefits by showing contribution to support, or cohabitation, at the time of death.

It is, of course, not enough simply that any child of a deceased insured is eligible for benefits upon *some* showing of dependency. In Frontiero v. Richardson, supra, we found it impermissible to qualify the entitlement to dependent's benefits of a married woman in the uniformed services upon an individualized showing of her husband's actual dependence upon her for more than half his income, when no such showing of actual dependency was required of a married man in the uniformed services to obtain dependent's benefits on account of his wife. The invalidity of that gender-based discrimination rested upon the "overbroad" assumption, Schlesinger v. Ballard, 419 U.S. 498, 508, 95 S.Ct. 572, 578, 42 L.Ed.2d 610 (1975), underlying the discrimination "that male workers' earnings are vital to the support of their families, while the earnings of female wage earners do not significantly contribute to their families' support." Weinberger v. Wiesenfeld, 420 U.S., at 643, 95 S.Ct., at 1231; see *Frontiero*, 411 U.S., at 689 n. 23, 93 S.Ct., at 1771. Here, by contrast, the statute does not broadly discriminate between legitimates and illegitimates without more, but is carefully tuned to alternative considerations. The presumption of dependency is withheld only in the absence of any significant indication of the likelihood of actual dependency. Moreover, we cannot say that the factors that give rise to a presumption of dependency lack any substantial relation to the likelihood of actual dependency. Rather, we agree with the assessment of the three-judge court as it originally ruled in Norton v. Weinberger, 364 F.Supp. 1117, 1128 (Md. 1973): [16]

"[I]t is clearly rational to presume the overwhelming number of legitimate children are actually dependent upon their parents for support. Likewise * * * the children of an invalid marriage * * * would typically live in the wage earner's home or be supported by him. * * * When an order of support is entered by a court, it is reasonable to assume compliance occurred. A paternity decree, while not necessarily ordering support, would almost as strongly suggest support was subsequently obtained. Conceding that a written acknowledgment lacks the imprimatur of a judicial proceeding, it too establishes the basis for a rational presumption. Men do not customarily affirm in writing their responsibility for an illegitimate child unless the child is theirs and a man who has acknowledged a child is more likely to provide it support than one who does not."

Similarly, we think, where state intestacy law provides that a child may take personal property from a father's estate, it may reasonably be thought that the child will more likely be dependent during the parent's life and at his death. For in its embodiment of the popular

---

16. Vacated and remanded for further proceedings in light of *Jimenez*, 418 U.S. 902, 94 S.Ct. 3191, 41 L.Ed.2d 1150 (1974); adhered to on remand, 390 F.Supp. 1084 (1975); aff'd sub nom. Norton v. Mathews, 427 U.S. 524, 96 S.Ct. 2771, 49 L.Ed.2d 672.

view within the jurisdiction of how a parent would have his property devolve among his children in the event of death, without specific directions, such legislation also reflects to some degree the popular conception within the jurisdiction of the felt parental obligation to such an "illegitimate" child in other circumstances, and thus something of the likelihood of actual parental support during, as well as after, life.[18]

To be sure, none of these statutory criteria compels the extension of a presumption of dependency. But the constitutional question is not whether such a presumption is required, but whether it is permitted. Nor, in ratifying these statutory classifications, is our role to hypothesize independently on the desirability or feasibility of any possible alternative basis for presumption. These matters of practical judgment and empirical calculation are for Congress. Drawing upon its own practical experience, Congress has tailored statutory classifications in accord with its calculations of the likelihood of actual support suggested by a narrow set of objective and apparently reasonable indicators. Our role is simply to determine whether Congress' assumptions are so inconsistent or insubstantial as not to be reasonably supportive of its conclusions that individualized factual inquiry in order to isolate each nondependent child in a given class of cases is unwarranted as an administrative exercise. In the end, the precise accuracy of Congress' calculations is not a matter of specialized judicial competence; and we have no basis to question their detail beyond the evident consistency and substantiality. We cannot say that these expectations are unfounded, or so indiscriminate as to render the statute's classifications baseless. We conclude, in short, that, in failing to extend any presumption of dependency to appellees and others like them, the Act does not impermissibly discriminate against them, as compared with legitimate children or those illegitimate children who are statutorily deemed dependent.

NOTES AND QUESTIONS

1. Justice Stevens wrote a dissenting opinion in this case, in which Justices Brennan and Marshall joined.

2. What "level of scrutiny" is employed by the court in *Jimenez*? In *Mathews*? What, if any, significance lies in talking about "levels of scrutiny"? Does it offer an approach to analysis, or merely a pretext for a decision arrived at on other grounds?

3. In footnote 13 the Court quotes from *Rodriguez* language which describes the kinds of "suspect class" in our society which are entitled to "extraordinary protection" under the Constitution. Does the class of illegitimate children fit this description? Is the distinction which the Court

---

18. Appellees do not suggest, and we are unwilling to assume, that discrimination against children in appellees' class in state intestacy laws is constitutionally prohibited, see Labine v. Vincent, 401 U.S. 532, 91 S.Ct. 1017, 28 L.Ed.2d 288 (1971), in which case appellees would be made eligible for benefits under § 216(h)(2)(A).

makes between the discrimination against illegitimates on the one hand and women and blacks on the other persuasive for the view that the Constitution should be construed to give less protection to the illegitimate than to women or blacks? In footnote 12 is the Court justifying this lesser protection to illegitimate children on the basis that there is no "insurmountable barrier" to their receiving the statutory benefits because their father might have legitimated them? But did not the Court in Trimble v. Gordon abandon that argument? See paragraph 4, supra, page 355.

4. The provisions of the Social Security Act quoted in the Court's footnote 1 include in the definition of "child" for purposes of determining death benefits a child of the deceased who would take his property by intestacy under state law. What is the effect of the *Trimble* and *Lalli* cases upon this provision of the Social Security Act? Does the Court's reasoning in *Mathews* support a decision that this provision of the Social Security Act is constitutional?

5. The *Jimenez* and *Mathews* cases were concerned with the constitutionality of the same section of the Social Security Act, namely, 42 U.S.C.A. § 416(h)(3). *Jimenez* was dealing with that section's application to the children of a disabled worker, while *Mathews* was dealing with its application to children of a deceased worker. Does that difference account for the difference in the result of the two cases? In other words, is Congress given greater constitutional latitude when dealing with claims based upon death than when dealing with claims based upon disability?

6. The Social Security Act § 202(g)(1), 42 U.S.C.A. § 402(g)(1) makes certain mother's insurance benefits available to widows and divorced wives of deceased workers covered by the Act. Under this section mothers of illegitimate children whose fathers were deceased workers are not entitled to these benefits. Can these mothers be constitutionally excluded from benefits? Is this situation governed by *Glona*, or *Jimenez*, or *Mathews*, or some other case? For whose benefit do you suppose this section of the Social Security Act was intended, that of mothers, or that of illegitimate children? Califano v. Boles, 99 S.Ct. 2767 (1979).

7. The Supreme Court's decisions on the status of the illegitimate child raise many questions. Some of them are as follows:

(a) Federal statutes authorize life insurance for servicemen and provide that the beneficiaries of these policies are to be the widow, but if there is no widow, any child of the deceased serviceman, and if there is neither widow nor child, parents of the deceased. A serviceman dies leaving no widow but an illegitimate child. The state courts hold that under state law "child" in the federal statute must be construed to exclude illegitimate children. Can this decision be squared with the *Levy-Mathews* line of cases? Prudential Ins. Co. of America v. Willis, 227 Ga. 619, 182 S.E.2d 420 (1971), affirmed by an evenly divided court 405 U.S. 318 (1972).

(b) A state statute provides that there is a five-year statute of limitations upon paternity suits brought to enforce that illegitimate child's claims for support from his father. There is no such limitation in the case of the legitimate child. Is the statute of limitations constitutional? In re People in the Interest of L.B., 179 Colo. 11, 498 P.2d 1157 (1972), dismissed for want of a substantial federal question, 410 U.S. 976 (1973); Cessna v. Montgomery, 63 Ill.2d 71, 344 N.E.2d 447 (1976); Stringer v. Dudoich, 92 N.M. 98, 583 P.2d 462 (1978).

Some states have avoided the constitutional problem by holding that the statute of limitations applies only to suits by the child's mother and not to suits by the child. Huss v. DeMott, 215 Kan. 450, 524 P.2d 743 (1974); Sandifer v. Womack, 230 So.2d 212 (Miss.1970).

(c) The statutes of state A provide that claims for support of an illegitimate child may be compromised by a written contract between the parties. Such a contract is final when approved by the appropriate court as fair and equitable and may not thereafter be modified. Is such a statute constitutional if the law of state A is that any order for the support of a legitimate child may be modified upon proof that the circumstances have changed since the order was entered, so that the child may increase his support, or the father may reduce it, if evidence warranting either kind of a change can be presented? Shan F. v. Francis F., 88 Misc.2d 165, 387 N. Y.S.2d 593 (Fam.Ct.1976); Munn v. Munn, 168 Colo. 76, 450 P.2d 68 (1969); Boyles v. Brown, 69 Mich.App. 480, 245 N.W.2d 100 (1976).

The Uniform Parentage Act § 18, 9 Unif.L.Ann. 536 (Supp.1979), deals with modification as follows:

"§ 18.　[Modification of Judgment or Order]

The court has continuing jurisdiction to modify or revoke a judgment or order

"(1) for future education and support, and

"(2) with respect to matters listed in Subsections (c) and (d) of Section 15 and Section 17(b), except that a court entering a judgment or order for the payment of a lump sum or the purchase of an annuity under Section 15(d) may specify that the judgment or order may not be modified or revoked."

Is this section constitutional in a state which does not permit a parent to make a final, non-modifiable contract for the support of his legitimate child? See also Haag v. Barnes, infra, page 416.

(d) In all states it was formerly held that the wife was entitled to support from her husband. Today the general rule is that the right to support is mutual, so that either spouse is entitled to support from the other, as their respective circumstances may dictate. If a court should hold, as some have and many undoubtedly would, that men and women who live together without being married do not have such rights with respect to support, would this violate the Equal Protection Clause, on the authority of the cases from *Levy* to *Mathews?*

(e) Certain sections of the United States immigration laws grant preferred status to aliens who are either the "children" or "parents" of United States citizens or lawful permanent residents. The statute defines "children" to include legitimate, legitimated, adopted children, stepchildren or illegitimate children seeking a preference because of their relationship with their mothers. 8 U.S.C.A. §§ 1101(b)(1)(D), 1101(b)(2). The effect of this is that an illegitimate child who is an alien and whose father is a citizen does not receive the preferred treatment by virtue of his relationship to his father. Likewise a father whose illegitimate child is a United States citizen does not receive the preferred treatment by virtue of his relationship to his child. Is this statute constitutional under the *Levy-Mathews* line of cases? Fiallo v. Bell, 430 U.S. 787 (1976).

8. Do many of the questions which have been raised concerning the cases in this section strike you as far-fetched? Are they, or questions like them, made mandatory by the fact that judicial decisions rather than statutes are the source of the law under consideration, and by the assumption which lawyers make that judicial decisions should be principled, should bear logical and rational relations to each other and to the statutes or constitution under consideration? Could we avoid these difficulties by frankly conceding that in this line of cases the Supreme Court was engaged in a different sort of law-making, that it was in effect enacting statutes, and that its decisions are no more capable of being reconciled with each other or arranged in a coherent pattern than a body of statute law would be? Should we therefore accept them for what they say on their face, as we would a set of statutes, without troubling ourselves over either their reasoning or their effect on some future imaginable but not yet existing state of facts? If we cannot adopt this course of action, how are we to regard these cases? Can you discern any purpose which the Court is attempting to achieve in these decisions?

SLAWEK v. STROH

Supreme Court of Wisconsin, 1974.
62 Wis.2d 295, 215 N.W.2d 9.

The plaintiff-appellant, Paul Peter Slawek, commenced this action for a declaratory judgment seeking a judicial declaration that he is the father of an illegitimate child born to the defendant-respondent, Crysta Stroh. The illegitimate minor, also named Crysta Stroh, was named a party defendant. The complaint of the plaintiff further prayed for a declaration of his rights and duties with respect to custody, care, visitation, support and maintenance of the minor child.

The respondent-mother answered the complaint and admitted that the plaintiff-appellant was the father of the minor child. By way of an affirmative defense she alleged she was supporting and caring for the minor child, was capable of doing so, that she was a fit and proper person to have the custody of the child and that plaintiff-appellant was not. She further alleged two causes of action by way of counterclaims—one sounding in fraud resulting in assault and battery, breach of promise and seduction—the other an invasion of privacy.

The plaintiff-appellant demurred to the affirmative defense and to both counterclaims. All three demurrers were overruled by the trial court.

The minor child, through her guardian *ad litem,* Jerome P. Tlusty, demurred to the complaint upon the ground the complaint did not state facts sufficient to constitute a cause of action for declaratory relief. This demurrer was sustained and judgment entered dismissing the complaint. The minor child, through her guardian *ad litem,* also alleged two causes of action by way of counterclaim. The first cause of action of the minor child alleged that the plaintiff was her father and that she was not and still is not legitimatized and that as a proximate and direct result of the plaintiff's wilful acts resulting in her illegitimate birth she does suffer and will continue to suffer mental pain, anguish and humiliation and embarrassment and is damaged thereby. The second cause of action alleged that because of the commencement of the action the plaintiff knowingly and intentionally made the fact publicly known that she had an illegitimate birth and that she suffers mental anguish, pain and public humiliation and was thereby damaged.

The plaintiff-appellant demurred to both counterclaims upon the ground the facts alleged failed to state a cause of action. The trial court overruled the demurrer to the first counterclaim and sustained it as to the second.

The plaintiff-appellant appeals from the order sustaining the demurrer of the minor child to his complaint for declaratory relief and the judgment dismissing his complaint and to the order overruling his demurrer to the minor's first counterclaim. He also appeals from the orders overruling his demurrer to the respondent-mother's affirmative defenses and the orders overruling his demurrers to her counterclaims.

BEILFUSS, Justice. The issues presented both as to procedure and substantive law are quite complex. We turn first to the demurrer of the minor-defendant to the plaintiff-appellant's complaint "upon the grounds that the complaint does not state facts sufficient to constitute a cause of action for a declaratory judgment."

The complaint, as paraphrased in the plaintiff-appellant's brief, is as follows:

"It is alleged in the Complaint that the Appellant is a physician actively practicing his profession in the City of Philadelphia, Pennsylvania; that the Appellant is presently married and resides with his wife and three children in the City of Philadelphia; that the Appellant is the father of the Infant Respondent, Crysta Stroh, who was born out of wedlock at Camden, New Jersey, on or about December 29, 1971, that the mother of the Infant Respondent is the Adult Respondent, Crysta Stroh; that they reside together in the City of Medford, Taylor County, Wisconsin; that the Appellant and the Adult Respondent, Crysta Stroh, are not now and never have been married to each other; that no judicial determination of the paternity of the Infant Respondent Crysta Stroh has ever been made; that Appellant requested that the District Attorney of Taylor County, Wisconsin, commence paternity proceedings pursuant to Sec. 52.24, Wisconsin Statutes, but that said District Attorney specifically declined to initiate such proceedings; that the Adult Respondent Crysta Stroh refuses to permit the Appellant to have any contact or visitation with the Infant Respondent; that, on information and belief, the Adult Respondent Crysta Stroh is not able to support the Infant Respondent without assistance; that the Appellant is financially responsible and capable of providing for the care, custody, support, and maintenance of the Infant Respondent and is a fit and proper person to have the care, custody, and control of the Infant Respondent; that it is in the best interests of the Infant Respondent to have a determination of paternity and a determination of the rights and duties of Appellant and of the Adult Respondent Crysta Stroh with respect to the child; that a declaratory judgment action is proper under the circumstances; * * *.

Two recent cases, among others, Stanley v. Illinois (1972), 405 U.S. 645, 92 S.Ct. 1208, 31 L.Ed.2d 551, and State ex. rel. Lewis v. Lutheran Social Services (1973), 59 Wis.2d 1, 207 N.W.2d 826, in effect, recognized that fathers, including putative fathers, do have the right to establish they are a natural parent and, as such, have some parental rights and duties.

* * *

In the second *Lewis* case, in interpreting *Stanley,* we stated at pages 4 and 5, 207 N.W.2d at page 828:

"* * * In *Stanley,* the supreme court decided two things: (1) That the denial of a natural father's parental rights to a child born out of wedlock based on mere illegitimacy violated his constitutional right to equal protection of the laws, and (2) that the termination of a natural father's parental rights to a child born out of wedlock without actual notice to him, if he was known, or constructive notice, if unknown, and without giving him the right to be heard on the termination of his rights denied him due process of law."

In this case, therefore, we conclude that the plaintiff-appellant, as a putative father of an illegitimate child, does have the constitutional right to establish, if he can, his natural parentage, to assert parental rights, and a legal forum with due process procedures to establish these rights.

In Wisconsin, the only specific statutory procedure for establishing the parentage of illegitimate children and making provision for their care, custody and maintenance appears in ch. 52. The chapter deals with the broad problem of the support of dependents and is so titled. Sec. 52.21, and those sections immediately following, provide for the procedures in paternity proceedings. These sections do not contemplate nor provide for procedures for the commencement of a paternity action by the putative father. The action is to be commenced by the complaint of the mother or by the district attorney if he believes the child is or is likely to become a public charge and believes it is in the best interests of the child to do so.

In this case the mother has not and probably will not make a complaint under the paternity statutory provisions. The complaint here alleges that the district attorney has been requested to commence a paternity action under the statute but that he declines to do so. The plaintiff-appellant commenced this action for declaratory relief under sec. 269.56, Stats., and prays for a judgment which declares he is the father of the minor child in question and for a determination of his rights and duties as to the care, custody, maintenance and visitation of the minor child.

* * *

It has been suggested that a proper procedure is by way of a writ of mandamus to require the district attorney to commence a paternity action. Mandamus does not lie to compel a discretionary act. It is apparent from a consideration of all the issues raised in this case that it is primarily a dispute and conflict between the putative father and the mother as to questions of custody and visitation of the minor child. The duty of the district attorney is to prevent the minor child from being or becoming dependent upon the public for its care, support and maintenance. The pleadings here do not compel a belief that there has been a violation or refusal to perform a clear duty on the part of the district attorney so as to warrant a writ of mandamus.

At oral argument, a remedy by way of a writ of habeas corpus was also discussed. Habeas corpus can be utilized to determine questions of right to custody of a minor child, but habeas corpus proceedings, too, are not well designed for continued jurisdiction to meet the changing circumstances in questions of custody, visitation and care of a minor child.

Because the rights asserted by the plaintiff-appellant are of the kind that are constitutionally recognized, some procedures and some forum must be provided for him to assert and litigate these rights.

The Declaratory Judgments Act, sec. 269.56(1), Stats., provides that courts of record have this " * * * power to declare rights, status and other legal relations whether or not further relief is or could be claimed. * * * " Under this broad language certainly the question of whether the plaintiff-appellant is the natural father of the minor child could be determined.

This court has on many occasions stated requisites for a declaratory judgment. They are: (1) A justiciable controversy must exist, (2) it must be ripe for determination, (3) it must be between persons whose interests are adverse, and (4) it must involve a legally protectible interest in the plaintiff. From our examination of the facts as set forth in the complaint we believe all four of these conditions exist.

A common ground for refusing to hear a declaratory judgment action is that the judgment will not terminate the controversy. A declaratory judgment here will terminate the controversy as to whether the plaintiff-appellant is the natural father of the minor. It can also declare the rights as to custody, visitation, care and maintenance as the facts appear at the time of the hearing. It will terminate the controversy as the facts exist at that time and this determination will be final unless there is a subsequent change of the facts and circumstances.

Obviously, we are well aware that the facts and circumstances frequently do change in custody cases and that questions of care, custody and visitation are subject to continuing jurisdiction. In this aspect the controversy is not necessarily terminated. However, the Declaratory Judgments Act provides in sec. 269.56(8), Stats., that: "Further relief based on a declaratory judgment or decree may be granted whenever necessary or proper. * * *"

While declaratory relief in custody matters may be somewhat cumbersome insofar as continuing jurisdiction is concerned, the statutory authority given to the court is adequate and we believe is probably the best remedy available under existing statutory procedures.

* * * We have discussed above the question of termination of the controversy. In any event, the trial court did not sustain the demurrer to the complaint upon an exercise of discretion on this ground. The demurrer was sustained and the complaint dismissed because the trial court was of the opinion that it appeared from the complaint that the plaintiff came into a court of equity with "unclean hands" and asked for affirmative equitable relief, and that under ancient rule he should not be afforded relief because of his own wrongdoing.

The "clean hands" maxim should be applied with some restraint. The adulterous conduct of the plaintiff-appellant may well be relevant evidence in other phases of this litigation, but in view of the recognition of the constitutionally protected rights of a parent as set forth in *Stanley* and *Lewis*, supra, the maxim cannot be invoked to prevent the plaintiff from trying to establish those rights.

It is our opinion that the trial court was in error in sustaining the demurrer to the complaint and in entering judgment dismissing the complaint. The order and judgment are reversed and the matter remanded for trial with the right of the guardian *ad litem* to serve and file an answer within twenty days after remittitur.

Upon remand it would seem, on proper motion, that the trial court could grant judgment on the pleadings as to that phase of the action which requests a determination of parentage. The plaintiff-appellant has alleged he is the natural father of the minor child, the mother, by her answer, has admitted he is, and the minor, by her guardian *ad litem* in her counterclaim, has alleged he is.

The plaintiff-appellant has demurred to the affirmative defense set forth in the answer by the defendant-mother upon the ground the facts stated in the answer do not constitute a defense.

The affirmative defense, in substance, alleges that the minor-defendant is not and is not likely to become a public charge, that the mother is employed, in good health, well educated and capable of caring for herself and the child. Proof of these allegations is very material and relevant to the standard the court must apply, namely, the best interests of the child, and must be considered by the court together with the other evidence. While proof of these allegations does not necessarily bar any right of the plaintiff, they are important and well pleaded.

The demurrer to the affirmative defense was properly overruled and the order should be affirmed.

The first counterclaim of the defendant-mother alleges facts and relationships which sound in (1) fraud, deceit and misrepresentation, (2) breach of promise, (3) seduction, and (4) assault and battery. No motion has been made to separate the causes of action, to make more definite and certain, nor to strike any parts thereof. The plaintiff-appellant's demurrer is basically upon two grounds: (1) That the counterclaim does not state facts sufficient to constitute a counterclaim, and (2) the counterclaim is barred upon the one-year statute of limitations (sec. 893.22(2)) in actions for seduction.

The allegations of the defendant-mother's first counterclaim are in substance as follows: During the first three months of their association plaintiff-appellant told her he was not married, loved her, wanted to marry her and wanted to visit her parents in Marinette, Wisconsin, to discuss marriage. She believed his statements and because of this had sexual relations with him. By accident she found out he was married, living with his wife and had three children. The plaintiff then told her that he was not in love with his wife, that they had separated and divorce was being instituted, and that as soon as he was divorced he would marry her. All of these statements were false and made for the purpose of inducing her to have sexual relations with him. As a result of these relations a son was born in 1969 and has been adopted by third persons. She again became pregnant in 1970, and in August of 1970 suffered a miscarriage "by reason of manipulations and injections given to this defendant by the plaintiff upon false representations that they would not harm the unborn baby when, in fact and truth, they were the direct cause of and induced said miscarriage and abortion." The minor child in this action was born because of the false representations which led to the relationship between them. She also alleges that all the plaintiff's representations to her were false and fraudulent and that he has not and never intended to separate from his wife, and that these representations were made for the purpose of seducing her. She has had two illegitimate children and a miscarriage and abortion, and suffered an assault and battery solely because of his false representations, and suffered pain, both mental and physical, and has been held up to public ridicule and shame. The sexual relations took place in Pennsylvania and New Jersey and she has lived with her parents in Wisconsin since the birth of the minor child in this action.

[In the remainder of its opinion the court held (a) no award for breach of promise could be made, that action having been abolished by statute in Wisconsin; (b) the child's mother had stated a claim for seduction, an action still recognized in Wisconsin, even though the alleged seduction occurred in New Jersey and Pennsylvania where the action had been abolished by statute; (c) the statute of limitations did not begin to run until the last act of seduction; (d) the child's mother also stated claims for assault and battery and for invasion of privacy; (e) the child could not recover for "wrongful birth".]

The order sustaining the minor-defendant's demurrer to the complaint and the judgment dismissing the complaint are reversed; the order overruling the plaintiff's demurrer to the adult defendant's affirmative defense is affirmed; the order overruling the plaintiff's demurrer to the adult-defendant's first and second counterclaims is affirmed; the order overruling the plaintiff's demurrer to minor-defendant's first counterclaim is reversed; judgment should be entered dismissing the minor's counterclaims; and the case is remanded for further proceedings. * * *

* * *

NOTES AND QUESTIONS

1. Stanley v. Illinois is reproduced infra, at page 432 . Assuming that the court is correct about the effect of Stanley in this case, does that foreclose further discussion? Does the mother of this child have any constitutional rights which are relevant here? For example, it seems clear that she does not wish to have anything further to do with the plaintiff-father, nor does she wish him to have any role in the child's life. Does his assertion of a claim to the child invade her privacy, under Griswold v. Connecticut, supra, page 73? And what of the child's interests? Are they prejudiced by having her father bring this suit, thereby publishing the circumstances of the child's conception and birth? See Poulin, Illegitimacy and Family Privacy: A Note on Maternal Cooperation in Paternity Suits, 70 Nw.U.L.Rev. 910 (1976); A—.B—. v. C—.D—., 277 N.E.2d 599 (Ind.App. 1971); Roe v. Roe, 65 Misc.2d 335, 316 N.Y.S.2d 94 (Fam.Ct.1970); Johannesen v. Pfeiffer, 387 A.2d 1113 (Me.1978).

2. The Uniform Parentage Act contains the following provisions dealing with parties to paternity proceedings:

"§ 6. [Determination of Father and Child Relationship; Who May Bring Action; When Action May Be Brought]

"(a) A child, his natural mother, or a man presumed to be his father under Paragraph (1), (2), or (3) of Section 4(a), may bring an action

(1) at any time for the purpose of declaring the existence of the father and child relationship presumed under Paragraph (1), (2), or (3) of Section 4(a); or

(2) for the purpose of declaring the non-existence of the father and child relationship presumed under Paragraph (1), (2), or (3) of Section 4(a) only if the action is brought within a reasonable time after obtaining knowledge of relevant facts, but in no event later than [five] years after the child's birth. After the presump-

tion has been rebutted, paternity of the child by another man may be determined in the same action, if he has been made a party.

"(b) Any interested party may bring an action at any time for the purpose of determining the existence or non-existence of the father and child relationship presumed under Paragraph (4) or (5) of Section 4(a).

"(c) An action to determine the existence of the father and child relationship with respect to a child who has no presumed father under Section 4 may be brought by the child, the mother or personal representative of the child, the [appropriate state agency], the personal representative or a parent of the mother if the mother has died, a man alleged or alleging himself to be the father, or the personal representative or a parent of the alleged father if the alleged father has died or is a minor.

"(d) Regardless of its terms, an agreement, other than an agreement approved by the court in accordance with Section 13(b), between an alleged or presumed father and the mother or child, does not bar an action under this section.

"(e) If an action under this section is brought before the birth of the child, all proceedings shall be stayed until after the birth, except service of process and the taking of depositions to perpetuate testimony.

"§ 9. [Parties]

"The child shall be made a party to the action. If he is a minor he shall be represented by his general guardian or a guardian ad litem appointed by the court. The child's mother or father may not represent the child as guardian or otherwise. The court may appoint the [appropriate state agency] as guardian ad litem for the child. The natural mother, each man presumed to be the father under Section 4, and each man alleged to be the natural father, shall be made parties or, if not subject to the jurisdiction of the court, shall be given notice of the action in a manner prescribed by the court and an opportunity to be heard. The court may align the parties."

The provision creating the presumption of paternity is reproduced supra, at page 365.

(a) Does this statute give a person in the position of the plaintiff in Slawek v. Stroh the right to sue to establish paternity?

(b) If so, would you advocate the adoption of such a statute?

(c) Does this statute permit a man to sue to establish *non-paternity* where he is being threatened with a paternity claim?

3. A state statute provides that mothers of illegitimate children who are receiving welfare assistance for their children are required to reveal to the appropriate state officials the names of the fathers of such children. Failure to disclose the names is punishable by contempt, but does not forfeit the welfare assistance. The evidence shows that a large proportion of mothers of illegitimate children are unwilling to name the fathers of their children. Under these circumstances is such a statute constitutional, or is it an invalid invasion of the mothers' privacy under Griswold v. Connecticut, supra, page 73? Doe v. Norton, 365 F.Supp. 65 (D.Conn.1973), va-

cated and remanded for reconsideration in the light of an amendment to the Social Security Act sub nom. Roe v. Norton, 422 U.S. 391 (1975); Burdick v. Miech, 385 F.Supp. 927 (E.D.Wis.1974), dismissed on the authority of Huffman v. Pursue, 420 U.S. 592 (1975), in Burdick v. Miech, 409 F.Supp. 982 (E.D.Wis.1975).

The Social Security Act was amended in 1974, effective in 1975, so as to require the states to provide that the applicant for aid to families with dependent children (AFDC) cooperate in establishing the paternity of the child and in obtaining support payments from the father. 42 U.S.C.A. § 602(a)(26)(B). This was one section of some broader amendments to the Act, comprising Part D of Title IV, aimed at providing federal assistance to the states in enforcing parental support obligations. The statute authorized financial inducements to the states to set up enforcement agencies, it set up a Parent Locator Service, and it gave the United States District Courts jurisdiction to enforce court orders for support in certain circumstances. These federal remedies apply to the support of both legitimate and illegitimate children.

4. Assuming the facts turned out to be as alleged in the defendant-mother's answer and counterclaim in Slawek, should the father be awarded custody of the child? Visitation rights? Would you wish to have further facts before attempting to answer this question? If so, what would you like to know? Perhaps a full consideration of this question should be postponed to page 441, infra, following Stanley v. Illinois. Should the issue of custody between unmarried mothers and fathers be determined on the same grounds as when it arises between husbands and wives in divorce proceedings?

B. v. O.

Supreme Court of New Jersey, 1967.
50 N.J. 93, 232 A.2d 401.

PROCTOR, J. This case arises under N.J.S.A. 9:16–1 et seq. (Chapter 16) which provides for the support and education of children born out of wedlock. Plaintiff alleged that defendant was the natural father of her infant twin sons. The Hamilton Township Municipal Court dismissed the claim. The Mercer County Court affirmed the dismissal on the ground that plaintiff was a married woman living in Pennsylvania when the children were conceived and born, and under Pennsylvania law a woman could not sue to bastardize children conceived or born during her marriage. * * * We certified plaintiff's appeal on our own motion prior to argument in the Appellate Division.

The parties have stipulated certain facts: 1) that the plaintiff was a resident of Bucks County, Pennsylvania at the time of the conception and birth of the twins and at the time when this action was instituted, 2) that the twins were born in Bucks County, Pennsylvania and lived there with their mother at the time this suit was instituted; 3) that the defendant has at all times been a resident of New Jersey but that his employment took him to Bucks County, Pennsylvania, five days a week; 4) that the twins were born on December 23, 1963; 5) that plaintiff's marriage to one B. was terminated by decree of divorce by the Court of Common Pleas, Bucks County, Pennsylvania on December 24, 1963, one day after the twins were born; and 6) that B. is listed on the Pennsylvania birth certificates of the twins as the father. Also, the parties stipulated that on this state of facts the substantive law of Pennsylvania was controlling.

New Jersey statutory law gives every child the right to be supported and educated by his natural mother and father. Chapter 16 of Title 9 expressly extends his right to children born out of wedlock:

"A child born out of wedlock shall be entitled to support and education from its father and mother to the same extent as if born in lawful wedlock." N.J.S.A. 9:16–2.

An action to enforce this right need not be brought by a governmental agency; rather, one parent can sue the other, or the person having custody of the child may sue one or both parents:

"Proceedings to enforce the obligations imposed by section 9:16–2 of this Title may be maintained by one parent against the other, or by the person having physical custody of the child, or, if the child is or is likely to become a public charge, the proceedings may be instituted by the director of welfare of the municipality or municipalities where the father and mother, or either of them, reside. In such proceedings consideration shall be given to the age of the child and the ability and financial condition of the parent or parents. * * * " N.J.S.A. 9:16–3.

This proceeding, although brought by a parent or one having custody, plainly is for the benefit of the child. * * * If the suit is by the mother against the natural father, she need not have a legal settlement in the county to bring the action. * * * The legitimacy of a child conceived by a married woman, though strongly presumed, may be rebutted. * * * Of course, a proceeding under Chapter 16 would not preclude the rights of the husband who is not a party to it. Cf. In re Adoption of K, 92 N.J.Super. 204, 222 A.2d 552 (Cty.Ct. 1966).

The determinative factual issue in a suit brought under Chapter 16 is whether defendant is the natural father. If so, his duty to support and educate under New Jersey law is the same regardless of legitimacy.

Defendant here claims that, even if plaintiff's allegations are true, the action should still not be allowed because it could bastardize the children contrary to the public policy and law of Pennsylvania. Defendant, the party sought to be charged, at all times was domiciled in New Jersey; and this in itself seems a sufficient basis for adjudicating his duty of support under New Jersey law. See Restatement, Conflict of Laws § 457(b) and Comment (a), pp. 546–547 (1934). However, accepting the stipulation of the parties that the substantive law of Pennsylvania applies, we find no reason to bar the present action. Pennsylvania does not conclusively hold children born to a married woman to be legitimate; rather, it creates a strong rebuttable presumption of legitimacy and forbids either the married woman or her husband to testify directly as to non-access. * * *

In Kowalski v. Wojtkowski, 19 N.J. 247, 116 A.2d 6, 53 A.L.R.2d 556 (1955), a 4–3 decision on which defendant relies, the majority refused to hear the suit under Chapter 16 of a woman against a putative father because she was married and domiciled in Florida when conception occurred, and the majority determined that Florida law denied a woman standing to sue in that state to illegitimize children conceived during her marriage. This still seems to be the law of Florida. See Lorenz v. Jiminez, 163 So.2d 500 (Fla.Dist.Ct.App. 1964), certiorari denied 172 So.2d 597 (Fla.Sup.Ct.1965). However, Pennsylvania law clearly does not deny a married woman standing to prosecute an action for support for illegitimate children born or conceived during wedlock. E. g. Commonwealth v. Ludlow, 206 Pa.Super. 464, 214 A.2d 282 (Super.Ct.1966); Commonwealth v. Fletcher, 202 Pa.Super. 65, 195 A.2d 177 (Super.Ct.1963); Commonwealth v. Jainnini, 198 Pa.Super. 144, 181 A.2d 879 (Super.Ct.1962); Commonwealth v. McMillen, 178 Pa.Super. 581, 115 A.2d 816 (Super.Ct.1955). Our Chapter 16 uses the phrase "born out of wedlock." Pennsylvania has expressly interpreted a like phrase occurring in its statute to include a child born to a married woman and fathered by a man other than her husband. Commonwealth v. Shavinsky, 174 Pa.Super. 273, 101 A.2d 178 (Super.Ct.1953). We note further that Pennsylvania has enacted a civil support law which gives illegitimate children the same rights to support from their parents as legitimate ones. P.L. 431 (July 13, 1953) as amended by P.L. 872, No. 420 (August 14, 1963); 62 P.S. § 2043.31 et seq.; see Commonwealth ex rel. Miller v. Dillworth, 204 Pa.Super. 420, 205 A.2d 111 (Super.Ct.1964). Allowing the mother's suit to be heard in New Jersey would not violate the policy of Pennsylvania. * * *

We hold that plaintiff has standing to prosecute the claim for the support of the twins under Chapter 16, and the trial court had jurisdiction to hear the claim.

It may be questioned whether the plaintiff should be limited in her testimony in the present case. In Pennsylvania a married woman cannot testify to non-access by her husband but is competent to prove

"* * * the fact and time of her marriage, the date and place of birth of her child, the name she gave the child, the fact of access, her separation from her husband, her own adultery, where she and the child have lived, who supported the child, and any other independent facts affecting the question of legitimacy, even though some of those facts may result in establishing illegitimacy." Cairgle, supra, 366 Pa. 249, 77 A.2d at pp. 442–443.

In New Jersey a married woman is competent as to all matters when paternity is at issue including non-access by her husband. * * * Morgan v. Susino Construction Co., 130 N.J.L. 418, 420, 33 A.2d 607 (Sup.Ct.1943); see 7 Wigmore, Evidence (3d ed. 1940), §§ 2063–2064. Competency of witnesses is a matter of procedure as to which the law of the forum applies. Restatement, Conflict of Laws, § 596, p. 713 (1934); * * * On the trial of this case the New Jersey rule of competency will apply.

The *Kowalski* case turned on the majority's conclusion that under Florida law a married woman had no standing to sue on the allegation that a man other than her husband fathered her child, and that she should have no better standing in the courts of New Jersey. We note that under this interpretation the child, whose welfare must be the uppermost consideration, may be wholly deprived of support: the New Jersey putative father is immune from the mother's suit, but the Florida husband can also escape support liability under Florida law by claiming and proving that another man in fact fathered the child. See Eldridge v. Eldridge, 153 Fla. 837, 16 So.2d 163 (Fla.Sup. Ct.1944). This harsh result seems out-of-touch with contemporary views of family law. See Ehrenzweig, "The 'Bastard' in the Conflict of Laws—A National Disgrace," 29 U.Chi.L.Rev. 498 (1962). It is contrary to the statutory objective of Chapter 16 of requiring every father to provide adequate support and education for his children even when born of his adultery with a married woman. The holding of *Kowalski,* insofar as it conflicts with our decision here, is expressly disapproved.

   * * *

Reversed and remanded to the Mercer County Court for trial on the merits.

NOTES AND QUESTIONS

1. Today as a result of the *Gomez* case, supra, page 374, all states must provide a remedy for the support of the illegitimate child, and in fact all states do so. The traditional remedy, adopted from the English law, where it originated in the Elizabethan Poor Law, was the bastardy proceeding, in form a criminal action but having as its major purpose the support of the child, or, more specifically, the shifting of the burden of support from the public to the child's father. Most states like New Jersey in the principal case now enforce the duty to support the illegitimate child by an ordinary civil suit. For a detailed account of the bastardy proceeding and the unnecessary technical difficulties which it involves, see H. Clark, Law of Domestic Relations § 5.3 (1968) and Krause Ch. 4. In New Jersey a court may make a determination of paternity in a delinquency proceeding. In re State in the Interest of O. W., 110 N.J.Super. 465, 266 A.2d 142 (1970). This raises the question whether in such a proceeding the standard of proof should be the criminal one, beyond a reasonable doubt, or the normal civil preponderance of the evidence. In re Gault, 387 U.S. 1 (1967); In re Winship, 397 U.S. 358 (1970); Johnson v. District of Columbia, 271 A.2d 563 (D.C.Ct.App.1970).

Other statutes in the various states may provide remedies for the support of illegitimates, for example, statutes relating generally to the abandonment, neglect or nonsupport of children, and statutes imposing criminal penalties for non-support. Before the *Levy-Gomez* line of cases those statutes were generally construed not to cover illegitimate children unless such children were specifically mentioned. After those cases, would such a construction be constitutional? See Annot., 99 A.L.R.2d 746 (1965).

The Uniform Reciprocal Enforcement of Support Act, now in force in all states, sets up the procedure for a two-state civil suit, in which the claimant for support begins a proceeding in the state of her residence, the file is then sent to the state in which the obligor can be served, he is personally served there, evidence is taken in the second state and that state enters an order for support if that is appropriate. For the full statute, see 9A Unif.L.Ann. 747 (1979). This Act does not specifically refer to illegitimate children, but it has been held, in M. v. W., 352 Mass. 704, 227 N.E.2d 469 (1967), that it may be used for the support of illegitimates. A case contra is Nye v. District Court for the County of Adams, 168 Colo. 272, 450 P.2d 669 (1969). Is it constitutional under *Gomez*, supra, page 374 to provide this convenient procedure for the support of legitimate children, but not for illegitimate children?

2. Traditionally the father of the illegitimate child was primarily responsible for supporting the child. In some states today statutes authorize the courts to impose a duty of support upon the mother as well as the father. See, e. g., Cal.Civ.Code § 4700 (Supp.1979). Oddly enough the Uniform Parentage Act seems to have no such provision. In any event it seems clear that either under state Equal Rights Amendments or under the Equal Protection Clause of the United States Constitution the duty of support lies equally with father and mother. See Crookham v. Smith, 63 Cal.App.3d 773, 137 Cal.Rptr. 428 (1977); Commonwealth v. MacKenzie, 368 Mass. 613, 334 N.E.2d 613 (1975); Kurtz, The State Equal Rights Amendments and Their Impact on Domestic Relations Law, 11 Fam.L.Q. 101, 143 (1977). And see Orr v. Orr, 440 U.S. 268 (1979), reproduced infra, page 868, holding that a state statute imposing upon husbands alone the duty of supporting wives through the payment of alimony was a violation of the Equal Protection Clause.

3. The rebuttable presumption of legitimacy referred to in the principal case is a strong presumption and is found in the law of most states. Its purpose is to protect the status of children by making it difficult to affix the label of illegitimacy. In a few states the presumption may, under some circumstances, be conclusive. See Cal.Evid.Code § 621 (1966). For a discussion of the presumption, see H. Clark, Law of Domestic Relations, 172–173 (1968), and Krause, 15–17.

Would either the rebuttable or the conclusive version of the presumption be constitutional under the *Levy-Mathews* line of cases in that it might prevent the illegitimate child from establishing the identity of his father, and in some cases thereby deprive him of financial advantage? Brown v. Danley, 566 S.W.2d 385 (Ark.1978), cert. den. 439 U.S. 983 (1978).

4. A related rule of evidence also referred to in the principal case prevents the married woman from testifying to non-access by her husband where the effect of such testimony would make the child illegitimate. The rule is named after Lord Mansfield, who invented it. The rule has been

abolished in some states. See Commonwealth ex rel. Leider v. Leider, 434 Pa. 293, 254 A.2d 306 (1969); VII Wigmore, Evidence, §§ 2063, 2064 (3d ed. 1940); Annot., 49 A.L.R.3d 212 (1973). Would the rule remain constitutional under the *Levy-Gomez* line of cases, if it prevented an illegitimate child from establishing the identity of his father?

5. The New Jersey court in the principal case indicates that its inclination would be to follow New Jersey law, so far as substantive matters are concerned. What is the correct solution to this problem, where the conception, birth and domicile of the child are in State A and the residence of the putative father is State B, which is also the forum? Suppose, for example, that the law of State B, the forum, is that there is a conclusive presumption of legitimacy. Should that be employed to defeat the child's claim where the State of his birth and domicile had no such presumption? What arguments can be made on this issue? Should this be characterized as a tort action, and the choice of law rule for torts applied?

6. The leading authority on paternity suits, emphasizing the New York law, is S. Schatkin, Disputed Paternity Proceedings (4th ed. revised 1977).

7. Is the defendant in a paternity suit who, if he loses, will be required to provide support for an illegitimate child, constitutionally entitled to have the state provide counsel for him when he is unable to employ counsel himself? Salas v. Cortez, 24 Cal.3d 22, 593 P.2d 226, 154 Cal.Rptr. 529 (1979), cert. den. 100 S.Ct. 136 (1979); State v. Walker, 87 Wash.2d 443, 553 P.2d 1093 (1976). The Uniform Parentage Act § 19, 9A Unif.L.Ann. 611 (1979) requires the appointment of counsel for any party who is financially unable to obtain counsel.

POINDEXTER v. WILLIS

Appellate Court of Illinois, 1967.
87 Ill.App.2d 213, 231 N.E.2d 1.

GEORGE J. MORAN, Presiding Justice. Defendant appeals from a judgment of the Circuit Court of Madison County, Illinois, rendered pursuant to the Illinois Paternity Act, Chapter 106¾, Sec. 51–66, which found defendant to be the father of plaintiff's child and ordered him to pay for its support and maintenance, and to pay for certain medical expenses incurred in the birth of said child.

Plaintiff filed a complaint against the defendant in the Circuit Court of Madison County, Illinois, alleging that she was a resident of Madison County, Illinois; that she was the mother and defendant the father of a child born out of wedlock on July 22, 1964, as a result of her being seduced by the defendant on several occasions in Champaign, Illinois; that although the defendant was a resident of the State of Ohio, he had subjected himself to the jurisdiction of the courts of Illinois by committing tortious acts within the meaning of Ill.Rev.Stat., Ch. 110, Sec. 17(1)(b) and was therefore subject to personal service outside the State of Illinois pursuant to Ill.Rev.Stat., Ch. 110, Sec. 16.

Personal service was made on the defendant in the State of Ohio pursuant to Ch. 110, Sec. 16. Defendant filed a motion challenging the trial court's jurisdiction over his person on the ground that he was not amenable to service in Ohio since he was not a resident of the State of Illinois and since the complaint did not charge him with committing a tortious act in the State of Illinois within the meaning of Ch. 110, Sec. 17(1)(b). After the denial of his motion he filed an answer denying the allegations of the complaint and also renewing his objection to the trial court's jurisdiction over his person.

Defendant did not appear at the trial. Plaintiff testified to several acts of intercourse between herself and defendant while both were attending school at the University of Illinois; that she became pregnant and went home to Alton, Illinois, where the baby was born; that when she became pregnant she wrote to the defendant, but he offered her no help.

The trial judge found the issues in favor of the plaintiff and ordered the defendant to pay plaintiff the sum of $1460.00 for the reasonable expenses incurred in the birth and also ordered him to pay the sum of $100.00 per month for the support and maintenance of said child.

Appellant does not question the validity of Chapter 110, Secs. 16 and 17 of the Illinois Civil Practice Act, but argues only that a proper construction of said Act precludes a valid service of process on him in Ohio because the violation of a duty under the Paternity Act would constitute a tortious act committed in the State of Illinois within the meaning of Section 17(1)(b).

The Illinois Paternity Act of 1957 places a duty on the father of a child born out of wedlock whose paternity is established under the Act to support the child until the child is 18 or is legally adopted to the same extent and in the same manner as a child born in lawful wedlock. He is also liable for the reasonable expense of the mother during her pregnancy, confinement and recovery which liability is established in the paternity proceeding. The suit must be filed by the mother of the child born out of wedlock or a mother who is pregnant with child. The proceedings under the Act are civil in nature and are governed by the provisions of the Illinois Civil Practice Act. (Ill.Rev.Stat. Ch. 106¾, Sec. 51–66).

Section 16 of the Civil Practice Act provides that summons may be personally served upon any party outside the State; and that as to nonresidents who have submitted to the jurisdiction of our courts, such service has the force and effect of personal service within Illinois. (Ill.Rev.Stat., 1959, Ch. 110, Sec. 16.) Under Section 17(1)(b) a nonresident who, either in person or through an agent, commits a tortious act within this State submits to jurisdiction. (Ill. Rev.Stat., 1959, Ch. 110, Sec. 17.) The question in this case is whether a tortious act was committed here, within the meaning of the statute.

Appellant argues that the statutory action for paternity does not contemplate nor is it based upon the commission of a tortious act; that the sexual intercourse alleged and testified to was consented to by both parties and in such case neither has committed a tort against the other.

Our Supreme Court has not taken so restrictive a view of Sections 16 and 17 of the Civil Practice Act as that urged by the appellant. In Nelson v. Miller, 11 Ill.2d 378, 143 N.E.2d 673 (1957), the court said: "The foundations of jurisdiction include the interest that a State has in providing redress in its own courts against persons who inflict injuries upon, or otherwise incur obligations to, those within the ambit of the State's legitimate protective policy. The limits on the exercise of jurisdiction are not 'mechanical or quantitative'." Id. at 384, 143 N.E.2d at 676. "Sections 16 and 17 of the Civil Practice Act reflect a conscious purpose to assert jurisdiction over nonresident defendants to the extent permitted by the due-process clause." Id. at 389, 143 N.E.2d at 679. "The jurisdictional fact, in the language of section 17(1)(b) is 'the commission of a tortious act within this State.' The word 'tortious' can, of course, be used to describe conduct that subjects the actor to tort liability. For its own purposes the Restatement so uses it. Restatement, Torts, § 6. It does not follow, however, that the word must have that meaning in a statute that is concerned with jurisdictional limits." Id. at 391–392, 143 N.E.2d at 680. "It is unnecessary to interpret section 17(1)(b) as conferring jurisdiction only where the defendant's conduct in the State gives rise to liability to the plaintiff in tort." Id. at 393, 143 N.E.2d at 681. In Gray v. Amer. Radiator & Sanitary Corp., 22 Ill.2d 432, 176 N.E.2d 761 (1961), our Supreme Court in discussing Chapter 110, Sec. 17(1)(b) said: "In determining legislative intention courts will read words in their ordinary and popularly understood sense. (Cases cited.) We think the intent should be determined less from technicalities of definition than from considerations of general purpose and effect." Id. at 436, 176 N.E.2d at 763.

In accordance with the views expressed by our Supreme Court, we interpret Sections 16 and 17 of the Illinois Civil Practice Act to reflect a conscious purpose by the Legislature to assert jurisdiction over nonresidents to the extent permitted by the due process clause and therefore hold that the word "tortious" as used in Section 17(1)(b) of said Act is not restricted to the technical definition of a tort, but includes any act committed in this state which involves a breach of duty to another and makes the one committing the act liable to respondent in damages. Therefore, in our opinion, the failure of the father to support an illegitimate child constitutes a tortious act within the meaning of the statute and subjects him to the jurisdiction of the Illinois courts under Chapter 110, Secs. 16 and 17 of the Illinois Civil Practice Act.

*   *   *

Judgment affirmed.

NOTES AND QUESTIONS

1. The judgment in *Poindexter* was enforced by an Ohio court, on the ground that it was entitled to full faith and credit, in Poindexter v. Willis, 23 Ohio Misc. 199, 256 N.E.2d 254 (1970). The Illinois decision was distinguished in Alsen v. Stoner, 114 Ill.App.2d 216, 252 N.E.2d 488 (1969). See also Backora v. Balkin, 14 Ariz.App. 569, 485 P.2d 292 (1971).

2. Is the decision in *Poindexter* a desirable one? Does the doctrine of *forum non conveniens* have any application here? Is it relevant in answering this question that the leading expert in paternity litigation has characterized the issue of paternity as the "most elusive issue that is placed before any court"? 2 S. Schatkin, Disputed Paternity Proceedings 24–3 (4th ed. revised 1977). The same authority has also suggested that at least 30% of the claims of paternity made by mothers of children are false and that the suit is often a "legal shakedown". Schatkin, Should Paternity Cases Be Tried in a Civil or Criminal Court? 1 Crim.L.Rev. 18, 24 (1954). Is it defensible to characterize this suit as a tort action? Cf. A.R.B. v. G. L.P., 180 Colo. 439, 507 P.2d 468 (1973), in which the court held that sexual intercourse between consenting adults cannot be called a tort and the long-arm statute therefore is not applicable. In response to the argument that the tort is the failure to support, the court said that this is only an ancillary issue in paternity suits, the main issue being, is the defendant the child's father.

3. Does the *Poindexter* decision violate procedural due process? See McGee v. International Life Ins. Co., 355 U.S. 220 (1957); Kulko v. Superior Court of California in and for the City and County of San Francisco, 436 U.S. 84 (1978), reproduced infra, page 851; Restatement, Second Conflict of Laws § 36 (1971). Does it matter, for the purposes of this question, whether the child has a remedy under the Uniform Reciprocal Enforcement of Support Act, or that the defendant is an individual rather than a corporation?

4. The Uniform Parentage Act has the following provision on long-arm jurisdiction, 9 Unif.L.Ann. 527 (Supp.1978):

"§ 8. [Jurisdiction; Venue]

"(a) [Without limiting the jurisdiction of any other court,] [The] [appropriate] court has jurisdiction of an action brought under this Act. [The action may be joined with an action for divorce, annulment, separate maintenance, or support.]

"(b) A person who has sexual intercourse in this State thereby submits to the jurisdiction of the courts of this State as to an action brought under this Act with respect to a child who may have been conceived by that act of intercourse. In addition to any other method provided by [rule or] statute, including [cross reference to 'long arm statute'], personal jurisdiction may be acquired by [personal service of summons outside this State or by registered mail with proof of actual receipt] [service in accordance with (citation to 'long arm statute')].

"(c) The action may be brought in the county in which the child or the alleged father resides or is found or, if the father is deceased, in which proceedings for probate of his estate have been or could be commenced."

Does this section of the Act comply with the requirements of procedural due process? Does it go beyond the *Poindexter* ruling? Notice that in *Poindexter* it was alleged that the mother of the child was "seduced" by the defendant. Does that affect the jurisdictional question? See Levy, Asserting Jurisdiction Over Non-Resident Putative Fathers in Paternity Actions, 45 U.Cin.L.Rev. 207 (1976).

5. A case which enforces a German paternity judgment notwithstanding that the German courts would apparently not grant reciprocity to American judgments is Nicol v. Tanner, 310 Minn. 68, 256 N.W.2d 796 (1976), although the court remanded the case for findings on jurisdictional or other possible grounds for denying enforcement.

HOUGHTON v. HOUGHTON

Supreme Court of Nebraska, 1965.
179 Neb. 275, 137 N.W.2d 861.

BROWER, Justice. Plaintiff and appellee Mary Jane Houghton brought this action on October 10, 1962, for a divorce on the ground of extreme cruelty from the defendant and appellant James Richard Houghton in the district court for Douglas County, Nebraska. The original petition alleged one child, Alice Marie Houghton, was born to this union on May 4, 1961.

After filing the original petition the plaintiff became pregnant and on July 16, 1963, she filed a supplemental petition, alleging that because of defendant's promises the parties had resumed marital relations after the action was begun and were expecting the birth of a second child in the month of October 1963. She again alleged acts of cruelty and sought a divorce, custody of Alice Marie, child support, and alimony.

The defendant thereafter filed an amended answer and cross-petition. It admitted defendant was the father of the first-born child. It alleged that plaintiff enticed the defendant into having sexual relations on February 17, 1963, and on several occasions thereafter but denied having such relations between October 10, 1962, and February 17, 1963. It denied the child the plaintiff alleged to be expecting was the defendant's child. It alleged plaintiff had condoned any alleged acts of cruelty committed against her as a result of enticing him into sexual relations with her. It further alleged the plaintiff had committed adultery and was guilty of extreme cruelty. It prayed for divorce and the custody of the child which was admitted to be his.

The child referred to in the supplemental petition was born October 1, 1963. She was named Sandra Kay and the testimony shows she was fully developed at birth.

After a trial the court found the defendant to be the father of the infant and awarded a decree of absolute divorce to the plaintiff with custody of both minor children in her, subject to visitation rights in the defendant who was ordered to pay $12.50 per week for the support of each child. * * * Defendant's motion for new trial being overruled, defendant has appealed.

* * *

A motion was made previous to the trial by the defendant to require blood tests to be taken of the parties and Sandra Kay for the purpose of determining the parentage of that infant. The motion was never heard but the parties agreed that the tests would be made and agreed that Dr. Earl Greene would make them.

Medical science has established that such tests may determine in some instances that a certain person cannot be a parent of a certain child although they may not affirmatively prove that one is in fact one of the parents.

The doctor was notified of their agreement by the plaintiff's attorney and the parties appeared pursuant to arrangements on December 17, 1963, at the Bishop Clarkson Memorial Hospital, the plaintiff bringing the infant with her. Blood was drawn from each of the three in the presence of the doctor and the samples labeled in his presence. The blood specimens so labeled were taken to the blood bank where blood typing is normally done. The tests on the three specimens were made by qualified medical technologists in the laboratory at Bishop Clarkson Memorial Hospital under the supervision and direction of Dr. Greene. A separate technologist typed each specimen. On the following day the tests were repeated, each by a technologist other than the one who analyzed the particular specimen the day before. The results were identical and thereafter they were recorded and submitted to Dr. Greene for analysis.

Dr. Greene explained the general procedure for blood typing as follows: "* * * blood is typed by what is called an antigen-antibody reaction. The antigen is the red blood cell and the antibodies are derived from the serum or from the portion of the blood that does not have the red cell. These antibodies and cells are incubated together * * * for a period of time and if the antigen that you are seeking with this particular antibody is present you get a clumping of the cell. This is called the positive reaction and this particular type is present and this particular antigen is present. Q. In other words if the antigen is present then you will get the clumping. If it is not present you will not get any clumping, is that right? A. Yes. Q. If there is a clumping you call it positive and if there isn't clumping you call it negative? A. Yes, sir."

Tests were made under two systems of each person's blood, one called the Rh system and one the MN system. In this case Dr. Greene made out a report and copies were sent to counsel for each party, one of which was admitted in evidence, showing the results of the tests as reported to him and his interpretation of them which is therein set out. Although he testified at length in regard to these tests and their significance, his conclusions from that report may be understood better than an attempt to here summarize his evidence. They are as follows:

"(1) Rh system: There are 6 antigens in the Rh system. These are usually written, C, D, and E and c, d, and e. All persons have 6 Rh antigens and these occur in three pairs. There is a pair of 'C's', a pair of 'D's', and a pair of 'E's'. Each pair may be any combination, i. e., CC, cc or Cc. One of the antigens in each of the pairs comes from the father and one from the mother. In the above case, Mary Jane Houghton has e antigen and no E antigen, and her formula for this particular antigen pair must be ee. James Richard Houghton has e antigen and no E antigen, and his formula for this antigen pair must also be ee. Sandra Kay Houghton has e antigen and E antigen. Her formula for this pair, therefore, would have to be eE. Since neither Mary or James have the E antigen, it must have come from another source.

"(2) In the MN system: The MN system is composed of a pair of antigens which occur in the following combinations: MM, NN, or MN. In the above typing, Mary Jane Houghton is positive for M and positive for N. Her formula is MN. James Richard Houghton is negative for M and positive for N. His formula is NN. Sandra Kay Houghton is positive for M and negative for N. Her formula is, therefore, MM. One of the M's in Sandra Kay's formula could have been inherited from the mother, Mary Jane Houghton. However, the other M could not have been inherited from James Richard Houghton since he does not possess this factor. It would, therefore, have to come from another source.

"The above findings would exclude James Richard Houghton as father of the infant, Sandra Kay Houghton."

Irrespective of the weight to be given evidence derived from such blood tests generally, plaintiff contends that the result of the tests and the doctor's conclusions and report therefrom cannot be accepted in the present case. Plaintiff urges she objected to the admission of the doctor's testimony and his conclusions formed therefrom as well as his report because it was without foundation and immaterial because the doctor did not personally perform the tests. The doctor had testified at length as to the procedure regularly followed in making blood tests which he said was followed here. The technologists, he said, were working under his direction. In part he stated: "I might add that as far as supervision or not supervision, this is the blood bank. This is the normal practice for transfusions where the blood is to be given to a patient where incompatible blood if given will cause a reaction, a severe illness, morbidity, even death. These girls do this routinely. The girl in charge of blood banking has been in this blood bank for about five years. This is after her initial training which consists of three years of college, one year of medical technology, four years experience in another hospital, back in our hospital where she has been in the blood bank for five years. * * * The other girls have worked in the blood bank for a period. They are all registered medical technologists except for one but they have been in for periods—I don't believe there is any under one year. This is what they do all year."

Where it is shown that a qualified pathologist made blood grouping tests with the assistance of experienced technicians, and that the technicians recorded the results of their work which were given to the pathologist for interpretation who thereupon in reliance of such records makes a written report, the report and testimony of the pathologist concerning the tests are admissible in evidence without calling the technicians to give foundation testimony under the provision of section 25–12,115, R.R.S.1943.

* * *

We have reviewed the evidence of the doctor carefully and we think the qualifications of his technicians to make the tests have been adequately shown as have his qualifications to interpret them. Although this is the doctor's first test for nonparentage, other tests of that nature have been made by his partner using the same facilities. The plaintiff introduced no medical testimony to refute them. The doctor who performed the tests was agreed upon by both parties and was not working for either one of them. We conclude there is nothing in the record which would indicate any defect in the testing methods, and his testimony and conclusions remain unshaken.

Having determined that no defect in the testing methods appears from the evidence concerning the blood tests in the case before us, the next question presented is what consideration and weight should be given to the results disclosed by them. Various statutes have been passed providing for blood tests in cases where paternity is an issue. Plaintiff contends that in the absence of a statute specifically authorizing such blood tests this court should not consider them in the present case at all. The Supreme Court of New Hampshire, in Groulx v. Groulx, 98 N.H. 481, 103 A.2d 188, 46 A.L.R.2d 994 (1954), a case which had been decided in the trial court before the passage in that state of such a statute, held that judicial recognition should be accorded the accuracy and reliability of blood grouping tests to disprove paternity. See, also, State v. Damm, 62 S.D. 123, 252 N.W. 7, 104 A.L.R. 430 (1934), and particularly the same on rehearing, 64 S. D. 309, 266 N.W. 667, 104 A.L.R 441 (1936), where the court corrected and clarified its original holding of 3 years before, stating: "We therefore say, without further elaboration or discussion, that it is our considered opinion that the reliability of the blood test is definitely, and indeed unanimously, established as a matter of expert scientific opinion entertained by authorities in the field, and we think the time has undoubtedly arrived when the results of such tests, made by competent persons and properly offered in evidence, should be deemed admissible in a court of justice whenever paternity is in issue." Many authorities are thereafter cited. We hold this court should likewise take judicial notice of the scientific accuracy and reliability of such tests.

In cases arising either under such statutes or by courts which have taken judicial notice of the reliability of such tests, the courts are not in harmony as to the weight to be given to such evidence. A review of the cases upon this question is contained in an Annotation in 46 A.L.R.2d, at page 1000. Some cases have held that blood tests indicating nonpaternity are only entitled to the same weight as other evidence. Among them are Arais v. Kalensnikoff, 10 Cal.2d 428, 74 P.2d 1043, 115 A.L.R. 163 (1961); Berry v. Chaplin, 74 Cal.App.2d 652, 169 P.2d 442 (1948); and Ross v. Marx, 24 N.J.Super. 25, 93 A. 2d 597 (1953). The reasoning of the courts holding this view is stated in Arais v. Kalensnikoff, supra, as follows: "Expert testimony 'is to be given the weight to which it appears in each case to be justly entitled.' * * * 'when there is a conflict between scientific testimony and testimony as to the facts, the jury or trial court must determine the relative weight of the evidence.' " This is the view taken by the trial court in the case before us. It admitted into evidence the results of the test but apparently concluded thereafter that the time-honored presumption of legitimacy of a child born in wedlock overweighed the evidence of nonpaternity disclosed by the tests.

The courts of other jurisdictions, while holding the results obtained from tests are not conclusive on the issue of nonpaternity, do hold that such tests should be given great weight. See, Commonwealth v. Gromo, 190 Pa.Super. 519, 154 A.2d 417 (1959); State ex rel. Steiger v. Gray, Ohio Jur., 145 N.E.2d 162 (1957); Beck v. Beck, 153 Colo. 90, 384 P.2d 731 (1963). The last-mentioned case relates to the legitimacy of a child, the court holding the results of the blood test were sufficient to overcome the presumption of legitimacy. The other cases dealt with the paternity of children born out of wedlock.

The defendant contends a third rule followed by some courts is the correct one and should be adopted by this court. It is that, in the absence of evidence of a defect in the testing methods, blood grouping tests are conclusive on the issue of nonpaternity. See, Anonymous v. Anonymous, 1 App.Div.2d 312, 150 N.Y.S.2d 344 (1956); Saks v. Saks, 189 Misc. 667, 71 N.Y.S.2d 797 (1947); Jordan v. Davis, 143 Me. 185, 57 A.2d 209 (1948); Commonwealth v. D'Avella, 339 Mass. 642, 162 N.E.2d 19 (1959); Commonwealth v. Coyle, 190 Pa.Super. 509, 154 A.2d 412 (1959); Retzer v. Retzer, 161 A.2d 469 (D.C.Mun. App.1960).

The case of Anonymous v. Anonymous, supra, was an action for separation brought by the wife as plaintiff based on abandonment, nonsupport, and cruelty. Defendant husband filed a counterclaim for divorce alleging the plaintiff had been living in an adulterous relation with another. He admitted the paternity of the oldest child and denied he was the father of the younger twins. He applied for a blood grouping test of himself, the plaintiff, and the twins. The application was denied. The appellate court modified the judgment of the trial court and ordered the tests to be made. In its opinion the court discussed the question of the weight to be given to such evidence on the new trial, saying: "It is urged that the presumption of legitimacy resulting from the fact that plaintiff and defendant lived together during the period of gestation requires a denial of the motion."

"Reason and logic, as well as a recognition of the modern advances in science, compel a determination that the presumption of legitimacy is not conclusive but rebuttable. The probative value of the results of skillfully conducted blood grouping tests has been widely accepted. The tests of course will be relevant only if they show noncompatibility as between the blood of defendant, the plaintiff, and the twins. If so, such evidence should be deemed conclusive as to nonpaternity." It further stated: "There is no doubt that with the passing of years and the advance of science the age-old concept has gradually given way to the sway of reason, and that the presumption of legitimacy has been withering and shrinking in the face of scientific advances. Hynes v. McDermott, 91 N.Y. 451, 459; Matter of Matthews' Estate, 153 N.Y. 443, 47 N.E. 901 (1897); Matter of Findlay, supra, 253 N.Y. 1, 170 N.E. 471 (1930). Presumptions are looked upon ' " * * * as the bats of the law, flitting in the twilight, but disappearing in the sunshine of actual facts." ' Mockowik v. Kansas City, St. Joseph & Council Bluffs R. Co., 196 Mo. 550, 571, 94 S.W. 256, 262 (1906). It cannot be gainsaid that we have now reached the point where presumptions must yield to modern scientific facts." We agree with the reasoning in the cited case and hold that in the case before us the results of the tests conclusively determine that the defendant is not the father of Sandra Kay.

[The court here held that the divorce would be granted to the husband on the ground of adultery, ordered the custody of the parties' child to be awarded to the wife and ordered the husband to pay child support.]

The judgment of the trial court is reversed and the cause remanded with directions to enter a decree of divorce in accordance with this opinion.

NOTES AND QUESTIONS

1. There are today a dozen or so different methods of classifying human blood, each of which is based upon the isolation of certain substances, which have recently been found to consist of identifiable proteins. The

blood of all persons has been found to contain one or several of these proteins. It has also been found that the type of blood according to the various methods of classification is genetically determined. This means that a child's blood type must be inherited from his parents. By performing careful laboratory tests the blood of each individual involved in a paternity suit can be classified in one or more of the classification systems. If the blood types of mother and child are known, and the alleged father's blood type is also determined, it may turn out that the child's blood is of a class which could not have been inherited from the mother and alleged father together, but must have been the product of the mother's union with some other man. For example, using the simplest of the classifications, the A–B–O system, if the child has type B blood, the mother type O blood, and the allged father type A blood, the alleged father could not be the real father. The combination of type A with type O can only produce a child with type A or type O blood, and cannot produce a child having type B blood. In order to produce a child having type B blood, with the type O mother, the father would have to have either type B or type AB blood. For this reason blood-typing can exclude a particular person as a possible father, with a very high degree of assurance, the margin for error being less than one in ten thousand. The few exceptions are apparently attributable to mutations or "unavoidable errors in technique." Ross, The Value of Blood Tests as Evidence in Paternity Cases, 71 Harv.L.Rev. 466, 467 (1958). On the other hand, the tests cannot show that a particular man is the father. They can only show that a particular man could be the father. It is now the fact, however, that if a number of tests resulting in classification under several systems are performed, a substantial degree of probability that a particular man is the child's father may be arrived at. But courts may still exclude the evidence of a test if they think that test has not yet received general medical acceptance. Huntingdon v. Crowley, 64 Cal.2d 647, 414 P. 2d 382, 51 Cal.Rptr. 254 (1966).

For more detailed descriptions of the technique and use of blood typing, see Krause 123–137, with many citations to additional materials; 1 S. Schatkin, Disputed Paternity Proceedings ch. 5, 6, 7 (4th ed. revised 1977); Polesky and Krause, Blood Typing in Disputed Paternity Cases—Capabilities of American Laboratories, 10 Fam.L.Q. 287 (1976); Krause, Abbott, Miale, Sell, Jennings, Rettberg, Joint AMA–ABA Guidelines: Present Status of Serologic Testing in Problems of Disputed Parentage, 10 Fam.L.Q. 247 (1976), also reprinted in Katz and Inker, Fathers, Husbands and Lovers 15 (1979). There are also other biochemical tests for paternity or non-paternity which can be performed in some laboratories and which are described in 1 S. Schatkin, supra, ch. 8. These authorities indicate that if several of the blood-grouping tests are used in a particular case, a large percentage of men in a given population (perhaps as high as 90%) would be excluded as fathers. See also Lee, Current Status of Paternity Testing, in Katz and Inker, Fathers, Husbands and Lovers 55, 69 (1979). Of course in many cases the cost or the absence of competent laboratories may make multiple tests impracticable.

2. There are three uniform acts which attempt to deal with the use of blood tests in paternity suits. The Uniform Act on Paternity, 9 Unif.L. Ann. 787 (1973), authorizes the court to order blood tests on its own motion or the motion of a party, with the sanction that it may enforce its order, or

resolve the issue against the party refusing the test. The statute contains odd language referring to "experts", raising the question whether the tests must be done by more than one expert in order to be admissible. If the tests indicate exclusion of the alleged father as the father, the statute makes this conclusive of the question. Admission of test evidence showing that the defendant could be the father is in the discretion of the court, depending upon the infrequency of the blood type. The Uniform Act on Blood Tests to Determine Paternity, printed as an Appendix to Harris, Some Observations on the Un-Uniform Act On Blood Tests to Determine Paternity, 9 Vill.L.Rev. 59, 76 (1963), also authorizes the court to order the test, with similar sanctions. It also refers to "experts" and makes the test conclusive if the experts agree and if the test shows that the defendant could not be the father. It permits the court to admit the evidence where it shows the possibility of paternity. Finally, it provides that the presumption of legitimacy is overcome if the evidence of the test excludes paternity of the husband. These statutes are in force in only about seven states, the leading state being California, which has the Uniform Act on Blood Tests. Cal. Evid.Code §§ 890–897 (1966). About half the states have some statutes authorizing the admission of blood-grouping tests without indicating what effect the evidence should have.

The third uniform act is the Uniform Parentage Act, section 11 of which, dealing with blood tests, has been reproduced supra, page 367. Which, if any of these acts would you advocate for adoption in your state? Could you draft a statute on this subject which would be more satisfactory than any of these uniform acts?

The uniform acts do not deal with the question whether an indigent defendant in a paternity suit may have blood tests performed at the state's expense. Should the law provide for this? Franklin v. District Court, —— Colo. ——, 571 P.2d 1072 (1977).

3. In the *Houghton* case, what evidence other than the blood test was there to suggest that the wife had committed adultery? Could the fact that the child's blood type was inconsistent with that of the husband be explained on the ground that the hospital may have confused the wife's child with that of someone else, so that this child was not hers? What is the effect, if any, of that possibility? See the interesting case of King v. Jenkins, [1949] Vict.L.R. 277, aff'd 80 Commw.L.R. 626 (1949).

4. There is a defense to paternity suits known as exceptio plurium concubentium. In plainer terms this means that if the defendant proves that the child's mother had sexual intercourse with a man or men other than the defendant during the relevant time, the defendant cannot be found to be the father. If she denies the intercourse with others, then the issue goes to the jury, who may find paternity in the defendant if they believe the mother. If this defense were made, could the court order the other men to submit to blood-grouping tests? On this defense see H. Clark, Law of Domestic Relations, 167 (1968); Krause, 121–122.

On this defense the Uniform Parentage Act contains this provision:

"§ 14. [Civil Action; Jury]

"(a) An action under this Act is a civil action governed by the rules of civil procedure. The mother of the child and the alleged father are competent to testify and may be compelled to testify. Subsections (b) and (c) of Section 10 and Sections 11 and 12 apply.

"(b) Testimony relating to sexual access to the mother by an unidentified man at any time or by an identified man at a time other than the probable time of conception of the child is inadmissible in evidence, unless offered by the mother.

"(c) In an action against an alleged father, evidence offered by him with respect to a man who is not subject to the jurisdiction of the court concerning his sexual intercourse with the mother at or about the probable time of conception of the child is admissible in evidence only if he has undergone and made available to the court blood tests the results of which do not exclude the possibility of his paternity of the child. A man who is identified and is subject to the jurisdiction of the court shall be made a defendant in the action.

"[(d) The trial shall be by the court without a jury.]"

Do subsections 14(b) and (c) of the Uniform Parentage Act raise any constitutional questions of substance? If so, how should they be resolved? Cf. "HH" v. "II", 31 N.Y.2d 154, 335 N.Y.S.2d 274, 286 N.E.2d 717 (1972), appeal dism'd 409 U.S. 1121, 93 S.Ct. 945, 35 L.Ed.2d 254 (1973).

5. M brings a paternity suit against D, and in the trial produces the baby in court and exhibits it to the trier of fact, arguing that the physical resemblance between the baby and D tends to prove paternity. The baby is three months old. Is it reversible error to permit this to be done? Would it matter for this purpose whether trial was to a jury or to the court? Would it matter that differences in race or color existed between the alleged parents? Would it be preferable to offer the testimony of a qualified physical anthropologist on the resemblances and differences between the child and the alleged father? See Almeida v. Correa, 51 Haw. 594, 465 P. 2d 564 (1970); Glascock v. Anderson, 83 N.M. 725, 497 P.2d 727 (1972); 1973 Wash.U.L.Q. 245; State ex rel. Schlehlein v. Duris, 54 Wis.2d 34, 194 N.W.2d 613 (1972); Annot., Race or Color of Child as Admissible in Evidence On Issue of Legitimacy or Paternity, Or As Basis or Rebuttal or Exception to Presumption of Legitimacy, 32 A.L.R.3d 1303 (1970); Krause, 137–139.

6. Lie detector tests are generally not admissible on the paternity issue. Krause, 144–148; 3A J. Wigmore, Evidence § 999 (rev. ed. Chadbourn 1970); State v. Molina, 117 Ariz. 454, 573 P.2d 528 (App.1977). An argument for the admissibility of such tests is made in 1 S. Schatkin, Disputed Paternity Proceedings ch. 18 (4th ed. revised 1977).

7. Is the decision in the *Houghton* case binding on the child, so that it would bar her from later suing James Houghton for support? Cf. Gonzales v. Pacific Greyhound Lines, 34 Cal.2d 749, 214 P.2d 809 (1950). If the court in the *Houghton* case had found that James Houghton was Sandra's father, could Sandra later rely on that decision in asserting rights against James' estate, or against James directly for additional support? Cf. Note, Res Judicata and Paternity, 37 U.Colo.L.Rev. 479 (1965). Is the judgment of paternity "in rem"? Hartford v. Superior Court In and For Los Angeles County, 47 Cal.2d 447, 304 P.2d 1 (1956); Williams v. Holland, 39 N.C.App. 141, 249 S.E.2d 821 (1978).

8. H and W were married and had five children. For H this was not enough domesticity, and so he began living with X, not troubling to be mar-

ried to her. He and X had three children. W sued H on behalf of their
five children for support. Could the three illegitimate children intervene in
that suit to protect their right to support from H? If in that suit H
should prove that he had three illegitimate children to whom he had obligations, should the court set the support decree at a level allowing H to support the three illegitimate children? Or are there priorities here in favor
of the legitimate children? Do the *Levy-Gomez* cases impose constitutional
limitations on this kind of case? See Mitchell v. Mitchell, 144 U.S.App.
D.C. 246, 445 F.2d 722 (1971).

HAAG v. BARNES

Court of Appeals of New York, 1961.
9 N.Y.2d 554, 216 N.Y.S.2d 65, 175 N.E.2d 441, 87 A.L.R.2d 1301.

FULD, Judge. This appeal is concerned with the effect in New
York of an agreement made in another State for the support of a
child born out of wedlock.

The complainant Dorothy Haag alleges that in 1947 she moved
from Minnesota and took up residence in New York City and that
since then she has been a resident of this State. The defendent Norman Barnes, on the other hand, is now and was, during the period involved in this litigation, a resident of Illinois.

According to the statements contained in the complainant's affidavits, she met the defendant in the spring of 1954 in New York.
She was a law secretary and had been hired by the defendant through
an agency to do work for him while he was in New York on one
of his business trips. The relationship between the man and the girl
soon "ripened into friendship" and, on the basis of representations
that he loved her and planned to divorce his wife and marry her, she
was "importuned" into having sexual relations with him.

The complainant further alleges that she became pregnant as a
result of having sexual relations with the defendant and that, upon
being informed of this, he asked her to move to Illinois to be near
him. She refused and, instead, went to live in California with her
sister to await the birth of her child. Fearing that the defendant
was losing interest in her, however, she returned to Chicago before
the child was born and, upon attempting to communicate with the defendant, was referred to his attorney. The latter told Dorothy to
choose a hospital in Chicago, which she did, and the baby was born
there in December, 1955, the defendant paying the expenses.

Shortly after the birth of the child, her attempts to see the defendant in New York failed and she was advised by his attorney to return to Chicago in order that an agreement might be made for the
support of her and her child. Returning to that city, she procured an
attorney, recommended by a friend in New York, and signed an agree-

ment on January 12, 1956. The agreement provides, in pertinent part, as follows:

1. It recites payment to the complainant by the defendant of $2,000 between September, 1955 and January, 1956 and a willingness on his part to support her child in the future, on condition that such payments "shall not constitute an admission" that he is the child's father;

2. The defendant promises to pay $50 a week and $75 a month, i. e., a total of $275 a month, "continuing while [the child] is alive and until she attains the age of sixteen years";

3. The complainant agrees "to properly support, maintain, educate, and care for [the child]";

4. The complainant agrees to keep the child in Illinois for at least two years, except if she marries within that period;

5. The complainant "remise[s], release[s] and forever discharge[s] Norman Barnes * * * from all manner of actions * * * which [she] now has against [him] or ever had or which she * * * hereafter can, shall or may have, for, upon or by reason of any matter, cause or thing whatsoever * * * including * * * the support of [the child]"; and

6. The parties agree that their agreement "shall in all respects be interpreted, construed and governed by the laws of the State of Illinois".

Shortly after the agreement was signed, the complainant received permission, pursuant to one of its provisions, to live in California where she remained for two years. She then returned to New York where she and her child have ever since been supported by the defendant in full compliance with the terms of his agreement. In fact, he has provided sums far in excess of his agreement; all told, we were informed on oral argument, the defendant has paid the complainant some $30,000.

The present proceeding was instituted in 1959 by the service of a complaint and the defendant was thereafter arrested pursuant to section 64 of the New York City Criminal Courts Act. A motion, made by the defendant, to dismiss the proceeding was granted by the Court of Special Sessions and the resulting order was affirmed by the Appellate Division.

The ground urged for dismissal was that the parties had entered into an agreement providing for the support of the child which has been fully performed; that in this agreement the complainant relinquished the right to bring any action for the support of the child; and that, in any event, the action is precluded by the laws of the State of Illinois which, the parties expressly agreed, would govern their rights under the agreement. In opposition, the complainant contended that New York, not Illinois, law applies; that the agreement in question is not a sufficient basis for a motion to dismiss under either section 63 of the New York City Criminal Courts Act or section 121 of the Domestic Relations Law, since both of these provisions provide that "An agreement or compromise made by the mother * * * shall be binding only when the court shall have determined that adequate provision has been made"; and that, even were the Illinois law to apply, it does not bar the present proceeding.

The motion to dismiss was properly granted; the complainant may not upset a support agreement which is itself perfectly consistent with the public policy of this State, which was entered into in Illinois with the understanding that it would be governed by the laws of that State and which constitutes a bar to a suit for further support under Illinois law.

The complainant is correct in her position that, since the agreement was not court approved, it may not be held to be a bar to her suit under New York internal law. (See New York City Criminal Courts Act, § 63; Domestic Relations Law, § 121.) On the other hand, it is clear that the agreement is a bar under the internal law of Illinois since it provides, in the language of that State's statute, for a "sum not less than eight hundred dollars". (See Ill.Rev.Stat., former ch. 17, § 18, amd. by former ch. 17, § 52 [now ch. 106¾, § 65].) The simple question before us, therefore, is whether the law of New York or of Illinois applies.

The traditional view was that the law governing a contract is to be determined by the intention of the parties. * * * The more modern view is that "the courts, instead of regarding as conclusive the parties' intention or the place of making or performance, lay emphasis rather upon the law of the place 'which has the most significant contacts with the matter in dispute'". * * * Whichever of these views one applies in this case, however, the answer is the same, namely, that Illinois law applies.

The agreement, in so many words, recites that it "shall in all respects be interpreted, construed and governed by the laws of the State of Illinois" and, since it was also drawn and signed by the complainant in Illinois, the traditional conflicts rule would, without doubt, treat these factors as conclusive and result in applying Illinois law. But, even if the parties' intention and the place of the making of the contract are not given decisive effect, they are nevertheless to be given heavy weight in determining which jurisdiction " 'has the most significant contacts with the matter in dispute' ". Auten v. Auten, 308 N.Y. 155, 160, 124 N.E.2d 99, 102 supra (1955). And, when these important factors are taken together with other of the "significant contacts" in the case, they likewise point to Illinois law. Among these other Illinois contacts are the following: (1) both parties are designated in agreement as being "of Chicago, Illinois", and the defendant's place of business is and always has been in Illinois; (2) the child was born in Illinois; (3) the persons designated to act as agents for the principals (except for a third alternate) are Illinois residents, as are the attorneys for both parties who drew the agreement; and (4) all contributions for support always have been, and still are being, made from Chicago.

Contrasted with these Illinois contacts, the New York contacts are of far less weight and significance. Chief among these is the fact that child and mother presently live in New York and that part of the "liaison" took place in New York. When these contacts are measured against the parties' clearly expressed intention to have their agreement governed by Illinois law and the more numerous and more substantial Illinois contacts, it may not be gainsaid that the "center of gravity" of this agreement is Illinois and that, absent compelling public policy to the contrary   *   *   *   Illinois law should apply.

As to the question of public policy, we would emphasize that the issue is *not* whether the New York statute reflects a different public policy from that of the Illinois statute, but rather whether enforcement of the particular agreement before us under Illinois law represents an affront to our public policy.   *   *   *   Restatement 2d, Conflict of Laws, Tentative Draft No. 6, § 332a, comment g.   It is settled that the New York Paternity Law requires something more than the provision of "the bare necessities otherwise required to be supplied by the community", that, "although providing for indemnification of the community, [it] is chiefly concerned with the welfare of the child". See Schaschlo v. Taishoff, 2 N.Y.2d 408, 411, 161 N.Y.S.2d 48, 50, 141 N.E.2d 562, 563 (1957).   In our judgment, enforcement of the support agreement in this case under Illinois law and the refusal to allow its provisions to be reopened in the present proceeding does not do violence to this policy.

As a matter of fact, the agreement before us clearly goes beyond "indemnification of the community" and the provision of "bare necessities".   Whether we read it as a whole, or look only to the financial provisions concerned ($275 a month until the child reaches the age of 16), we must conclude that "the welfare of the child" is fully protected.   *   *   *   The public policy of this State having been satisfied, there is no reason why we should not enforce the provisions of the parties' support agreement under Illinois law and treat the agreement as a bar to the present action for support.

The order of the Appellate Division should be affirmed.

*   *   *

NOTES AND QUESTIONS

1.   The principal case is criticized in Ehrenzweig, The "Bastard" in the Conflict of Laws, 29 U.Chi.L.Rev. 498 (1962).   See also Ester, Illegitimate Children and Conflict of Laws, 36 Ind.L.J. 163 (1961); A. Ehrenzweig, Conflict of Laws, 390–402 (1962) and Stumberg, Principles of Conflict of Laws, 333–337 (3d ed. 1963).

2. What principle does the court in *Haag* announce as a guide for deciding what law is to be applied to the contract in suit? What arguments might be advanced in support of the application of New York law to this case? Cf. Restatement, Second, Conflict of Laws, §§ 187, 188 (1971); Ehrenzweig, The "Bastard" in the Conflict of Laws—A National Disgrace, 29 U.Chi.L.Rev. 498 (1962).

3. You represent a man charged with being the father of an illegitimate child. Your client is wealthy and well known in the community and for obvious reasons does not wish to be a defendant in a paternity suit. He admits that he could be the father of the child, but says he does not believe that he is. He is willing to contribute to the child's support if he can do so without admitting paternity and without a suit and the attendant notoriety.

(a) Is there any way in which such a settlement may be made so as to bind both mother and child in other states as well as where the contract is made? In addition to the law of New York, referred to in *Haag*, see Ill. Ann.Stat. ch. 106¾, § 59a (Supp.1979); Wis.Stat.Ann. § 52.28 (Supp. 1979–1980); State ex rel. Acorman v. Pitner, 42 N.J. 251, 200 A.2d 104 (1964); State v. Bowen, 80 Wash.2d 808, 498 P.2d 877 (1972); Note, The Illegitimate Child Support Contract: A Prophylactic, 1970 Law & Social Order 641; Annot., Validity and Construction of Putative Father's Promise to Support or Provide for Illegitimate Child, 20 A.L.R.3d 500 (1968).

The procedure for settlement under the Uniform Parentage Act is set out in § 13 of that Act, 9 Unif.L.Ann. 532 (1978), which is reproduced supra, at page 367. Apparently such a settlement, if it called for periodic payments of support, would be modifiable under § 18 of the Act.

(b) The question whether the enforcement of a binding and non-modifiable contract of settlement would be unconstitutional under the *Levy-Mathews* line of cases is discusssed supra, at page 389. Such a contract could not be made with respect to the support of a legitimate child.

(c) Assume that M and F have sexual relations and that M later becomes pregnant. When the child is born, F agrees to make payments for its support and for M's expenses. He makes a few payments, but then consults M's phsyician, who conducts blood tests which show that F could not be the father of the child. F thereupon stops making any payments and M brings a paternity suit against him. F wins the paternity suit, the court finding that on the blood test evidence he could not be the child's father. May M now sue and recover from F on the settlement contract? Fiege v. Boehm, 210 Md. 352, 123 A.2d 316 (1956). If she did recover on the contract, could she then bring a paternity suit against X and, if able to prove paternity, recover from X also? How could F's interests be protected in such a situation?

4. Where a child has been legitimated by the law of another state or country, the courts of the forum will generally recognize his status as legitimate, even though the legitimation does not comply with the rules of the forum, if the legitimation occurred at the domicile of the child's parent, and consequently of the child himself. In re Estate of Spano, 49 N.J. 263, 229 A.2d 645 (1967), 20 Stan.L.Rev. 1045 (1968); A. Ehrenzweig, Conflict of Laws, 394 (1962); Restatement, Second, Conflict of Laws, § 287 (1971).

5. Although some of the older authorities limited the support of the illegitimate child in paternity suits to a subsistence level, the modern rule is

that he should receive the same level of support as the legitimate child. The Uniform Parentage Act § 15 contains the following provisions concerning the judgment in a paternity suit:

"§ 15. [Judgment or Order]

"(a) The judgment or order of the court determining the existence or non-existence of the parent and child relationship is determinative for all purposes.

"(b) If the judgment or order of the court is at variance with the child's birth certificate, the court shall order that [an amended birth registration be made] [a new birth certificate be issued] under Section 23.

"(c) The judgment or order may contain any other provision directed against the appropriate party to the proceeding, concerning the duty of support, the custody and guardianship of the child, visitation privileges with the child, the furnishing of bond or other security for the payment of the judgment, or any other matter in the best interest of the child. The judgment or order may direct the father to pay the reasonable expenses of the mother's pregnancy and confinement.

"(d) Support judgments or orders ordinarily shall be for periodic payments which may vary in amount. In the best interest of the child, a lump sum payment or the purchase of an annuity may be ordered in lieu of periodic payments of support. The court may limit the father's liability for past support of the child to the proportion of the expenses already incurred that the court deems just.

"(e) In determining the amount to be paid by a parent for support of the child and the period during which the duty of support is owed, a court enforcing the obligation of support shall consider all relevant facts, including

(1) the needs of the child;

(2) the standard of living and circumstances of the parents;

(3) the relative financial means of the parents;

(4) the earning ability of the parents;

(5) the need and capacity of the child for education, including higher education;

(6) the age of the child;

(7) the financial resources and the earning ability of the child;

(8) the responsibility of the parents for the support of others; and

(9) the value of services contributed by the custodial parent."

PEOPLE v. SORENSEN

Supreme Court of California in Bank, 1968.
68 Cal.2d 280, 437 P.2d 495, 66 Cal.Rptr. 7.

McCOMB, Justice. Defendant appeals from a judgment convicting him of violating section 270 of the Penal Code (willful failure to provide for his minor child), a misdemeanor.

The settled statement of facts recites that seven years after defendant's marriage it was medically determined that he was sterile. His wife desired a child, either by artificial insemination or by adoption, and at first defendant refused to consent. About 15 years after the marriage defendant agreed to the artificial insemination of his wife. Husband and wife, then residents of San Joaquin County, consulted a physician in San Francisco. They signed an agreement, which is on the letterhead of the physician, requesting the physician to inseminate the wife with the sperm of a white male. The semen was to be selected by the physician, and under no circumstances were the parties to demand the name of the donor. The agreement contains a recitation that the physician does not represent that pregnancy will occur. The physician treated Mrs. Sorensen, and she became pregnant. Defendant knew at the time he signed the consent that when his wife took the treatments she could become pregnant and that if a child was born it was to be treated as their child.

A male child was born to defendant's wife in San Joaquin County on October 14, 1960. The information for the birth certificate was given by the mother, who named defendant as the father. Defendant testified that he had not provided the information on the birth certificate and did not recall seeing it before the trial.

For about four years the family had a normal family relationship, defendant having represented to friends that he was the child's father and treated the boy as his son. In 1964, Mrs. Sorensen separated from defendant and moved to Sonoma County with the boy. At separation, Mrs. Sorensen told defendant that she wanted no support for the boy, and she consented that a divorce be granted to defendant. Defendant obtained a decree of divorce, which recites that the court retained "jurisdiction regarding the possible support obligation of plaintiff in regard to a minor child born to defendant."

In the summer of 1966 when Mrs. Sorensen became ill and could not work, she applied for public assistance under the Aid to Needy Children program. The County of Sonoma supplied this aid until Mrs. Sorensen was able to resume work. Defendant paid no support for the child since the separation in 1964, although demand therefor was made by the district attorney. The municipal court found defendant guilty of violating section 270 of the Penal Code and granted him probation for three years on condition that he make payments of $50 per month for support through the district attorney's office.

From the record before us, this case could be disposed of on the ground that defendant has failed to overcome the presumption that "A child of a woman who is or has been married, born during the marriage or within 300 days after the dissolution thereof, is presumed to be a legitimate child of that marriage. This presumption may be disputed only by the people of the State of California in a criminal action brought under Section 270 of the Penal Code or by the husband or wife, or the descendant of one or both of them. In a civil action, this presumption may be rebutted only by clear and convincing proof." (Evid.Code, § 661, former Code Civ.Proc., § 1963, subd. 31.)

The only testimony as to defendant's sterility was that of defendant and his wife that it had been medically determined seven years after the marriage that defendant was sterile. In their written request to the doctor that he artificially inseminate Mrs. Sorensen, dated August 12, 1959, the Sorensens said: "We make this request since we realize that Mr. Sorensen is sterile, adequate laboratory tests having been performed. * * *" There was no medical testimony by a scientific expert in the field of male reproduction that defendant was sterile at the time of conception. However, in view of the settled statement, the only question for our determination is:

Is the husband of a woman, who with his consent was artificially inseminated with semen of a third-party donor, guilty of the crime of failing to support a child who is the product of such insemination, in violation of section 270 of the Penal Code?

The law is that defendant is the lawful father of the child born to his wife, which child was conceived by artificial insemination to which he consented, and his conduct carries with it an obligation of support within the meaning of section 270 of the Penal Code.

Under the facts of this case, the term "father" as used in section 270 cannot be limited to the biologic or natural father as those terms are generally understood. The determinative factor is whether the legal relationship of father and child exists. A child conceived through heterologous artificial insemination does not have a "natural father," as that term is commonly used. The anonymous donor of the sperm cannot be considered the "natural father," as he is no more responsible for the use made of his sperm than is the donor of blood or a kidney. Moreover, he could not dispute the presumption that the child is the legitimate issue of Mr. and Mrs. Sorensen, as that presumption "may be disputed only by the people of the State of California * * * or by the husband or wife, or the descendant of one or both of them." (Evid.Code, § 661, supra.) With the use of frozen semen, the donor may even be dead at the time the semen is used. Since there is no "natural father," we can only look for a lawful father.

It is doubtful that with the enactment of section 270 of the Penal Code and its amendments the Legislature considered the plight of a child conceived through artificial insemination. However, the intent of the Legislature obviously was to include every child, legitimate or illegitimate, born or unborn, and enforce the obligation of support against the person who could be determined to be the lawful parent.

* * *

* * * a reasonable man who, because of his inability to procreate, actively participates and consents to his wife's artificial insemination in the hope that a child will be produced whom they will treat as their own, knows that such behavior carries with it the legal responsibilities of fatherhood and criminal responsibility for nonsupport. One who consents to the production of a child cannot create a temporary relation to be assumed and disclaimed at will, but the arrangement must be of such character as to impose an obligation of supporting those for whose existence he is directly responsible. As noted by the trial court, it is safe to assume that without defendant's active participation and consent the child would not have been procreated.

In a prosecution under section 270 of the Penal Code, paternity is an essential element of the crime of willful failure to support a minor child. * * *

The documentary evidence in this case consisted of the written agreement between husband and wife that the physician inseminate the wife with the sperm of a white male, the birth certificate listing defendant as the father, and a copy of the interlocutory decree of divorce. While defendant testified that he did not know the contents of the birth certificate, this testimony was not sufficient to raise a reasonable doubt that he was the father. Therefore, since, the word "father" is construed to include a husband who, unable to accomplish his objective of creating a child by using his own semen, purchases semen from a donor and uses it to inseminate his wife to achieve his purpose, proof of paternity has been established beyond a reasonable doubt.

It is also essential to a conviction under section 270 that defendant's omission to support his child be willful. * * *

Defendant failed to produce any evidence that his omission to provide for his minor child was not willful. * * * It is immaterial, therefore, that Mrs. Sorensen said that she wanted no support for the child, for she had no authority or power by agreement or release to deprive her child of the legal right to be supported by his father or to relieve defendant of the obligation imposed on him by law. * * *

Rather than punishment of the neglectful parents, the principal statutory objectives are to secure support of the child and to protect the public from the burden of supporting a child who has a parent able to support him. Section 270d of the Penal Code provides that if a fine is imposed on a convicted defendant, the court shall direct its payment in whole or part to the wife of the defendant or guardian of the child, except that if the child is receiving public assistance the fine imposed or funds collected from the defendant shall be paid to the county department either for current support of the child or as reimbursement for past support furnished from public assistance funds.

*   *   *

The question of the liability of the husband for support of a child created through artificial insemination is one of first impression in this state and has been raised in only a few cases outside the state, none of them involving a criminal prosecution for failure to provide. Although other courts considering the question have found some existing legal theory to hold the "father" responsible, results have varied on the question of legitimacy. In Gursky v. Gursky, 39 Misc.2d 1083, 242 N.Y.S.2d 406 (Sup.Ct.1963), the court held that the child was illegitimate but that the husband was liable for the child's support because consent to the insemination implied a promise to support.

In Strnad v. Strnad, 190 Misc. 786, 78 N.Y.S.2d 390 (Sup.Ct. 1948), the court found that a child conceived through artificial insemination was not illegitimate and granted visitation rights to the husband in a custody proceeding.

It is less crucial to determine the status of the child than the status of defendant as the father. Categorizing the child as either legitimate or illegitimate does not resolve the issue of the legal consequences flowing from defendant's participation in the child's existence. Under our statute, both legitimate and illegitimate minors have a right to support from their parents. The primary liability is on the father, and if he is dead or for any reason whatever fails to furnish support, the mother is criminally liable therefor. To permit defendant's parental responsibilities to rest on a voluntary basis would place the entire burden of support on the child's mother, and if she is incapacitated the burden is then on society. Cost to society, of course, is not the only consideration which impels the conclusion that defendant is the lawful father of the offspring of his marriage. The child is the principal party affected, and if he has no father he is forced to bear not only the handicap of social stigma but financial deprivation as well.

The construction thus placed upon the word "father" does not distort the statutory language, and it achieves the statutory objective of providing support for the child and prevents an obvious injustice that would result were a child artificially conceived excluded from the protection of a law intended to benefit all minors, legitimate or illegitimate, born or unborn.

The public policy of this state favors legitimation * * * and no valid public purpose is served by stigmatizing an artificially conceived child as illegitimate. An illegitimate child is "one not recognized by law as lawful offspring; * * * born of parents not married to each other; conceived in fornication or adultery" (Webster's New Internat. Dict. (3d ed. 1961) p. 1126); illegitimacy is defined as "the state or condition of one whose parents were not married at the time of his birth" (Black's Law Dictionary (4th ed. 1951) p. 882); "the status of a child born of parents not legally married at the time of birth" (1 Bouv.Law Dict. (8th ed. 1914) (Rawle's Third Revision, p. 1491).

In the absence of legislation prohibiting artificial insemination the offspring of defendant's valid marriage to the child's mother was lawfully begotten and was not the product of an illicit or adulterous relationship. Adultery is defined as "the voluntary sexual intercourse of a married person with a person other than the offender's husband or wife." (Civ.Code, § 93.) It has been suggested that the doctor and the wife commit adultery by the process of artificial insemination. Since the doctor may be a woman, or the husband himself may administer the insemination by a syringe, this is patently absurd; to consider it an act of adultery with the donor, who at the time of insemination may be a thousand miles away or may even be dead, is equally absurd. Nor are we persuaded that the concept of legitimacy demands that the child be the actual offspring of the husband of the mother and if semen of some other male is utilized the resulting child is illegitimate.

In California, legitimacy is a legal status that may exist despite the fact that the husband is not the natural father of the child. (See Evid.Code, § 621.) The Legislature has provided for legitimation of a child born before wedlock by the subsequent marriage of its parents (Civ.Code, § 215), for legitimation by acknowledgment by the father (Civ.Code, § 230), and for inheritance rights of illegitimates (Prob. Code, § 255), and since the subject of legitimation as well as that of succession of property is properly one for legislative action, we are not required in this case to do more than decide that, within the meaning of section 270 of the Penal Code, defendant is the lawful father of the child conceived through heterologous artificial insemination and born during his marriage to the child's mother.

The judgment is affirmed.

NOTES AND QUESTIONS

1. Two kinds of artificial insemination are known to medical practice, the first artificial insemination with the husband's semen, called homologous artificial insemination (AIH) and the second artificial insemination with the semen of another man, called heterologous artificial insemination (AID). The first of these methods is sometimes recommended where the wife's psychological or physical condition prevents pregnancy and of course

raises no legal problems. A third kind of artificial insemination is really a variation of AID, and occurs when the husband's semen is mingled with that of the donor. This may in some cases make rebuttal of the presumption of legitimacy more difficult and also may have psychological benefits to the husband.

Recent articles dealing with artificial insemination include Dienes, Artificial Donor Insemination: Perspectives on Legal and Social Change, 54 Iowa L.Rev. 253 (1968); Smith, Through a Test Tube Darkly: Artificial Insemination and the Law, 67 Mich.L.Rev. 127 (1968); Wadlington, Artificial Insemination: The Dangers of a Poorly Kept Secret, 64 Nw.U.L.Rev. 777 (1970). See also Finegold, Artificial Insemination (1964).

2. After *Sorensen* was decided California enacted the Uniform Parentage Act, whose provision on artificial insemination is now Cal.Civ.Code § 7005 (Supp.1979). This provision reads as follows:

"§ 5. [Artificial Insemination]

"(a) If, under the supervision of a licensed physician and with the consent of her husband, a wife is inseminated artificially with semen donated by a man not her husband, the husband is treated in law as if he were the natural father of a child thereby conceived. The husband's consent must be in writing and signed by him and his wife. The physician shall certify their signatures and the date of the insemination, and file the husband's consent with the [State Department of Health], where it shall be kept confidential and in a sealed file. However, the physician's failure to do so does not affect the father and child relationship. All papers and records pertaining to the insemination, whether part of the permanent record of a court or of a file held by the supervising physician or elsewhere, are subject to inspection only upon an order of the court for good cause shown.

"(b) The donor of semen provided to a licensed physician for use in artificial insemination of a married woman other than the donor's wife is treated in law as if he were not the natural father of a child thereby conceived."

Georgia, Kansas and Oklahoma also have statutes making such a child legitimate if the artificial insemination is consented to by the husband in writing. Ga. Code Ann. § 74–101.1 (1973); Kan.Stat.Ann. §§ 23–128 to 23–130 (1974); Okl.Stat.Ann. tit. 10, §§ 551–553 (Supp.1978–1979).

Under the Uniform Parentage Act or under the Georgia, Kansas or Oklahoma statutes, what is the status of the child if the statute is not complied with, as for example where the husband's consent is not in writing? Would the presumption of paternity described in § 4 of the Uniform Act, supra, page 365, aid the child of artificial insemination?

3. What is the status of the AID child where the husband gives no consent to the operation?

4. Does the *Sorensen* case mean that if the husband died, the child would be entitled to inherit his property under an intestacy statute authorizing inheritance by children of the deceased?

5. Is the court really relying on the presumption of legitimacy in the *Sorensen* case? If not, how does it reach the conclusion that the husband is liable for the support of the child? On the court's own definition of le-

gitimacy was the child legitimate? What force has the argument that the biological father of the child was unknown? Could you write a better opinion than the court did?

6. Assume for the moment that a blood test would conclusively have proved that the child was not the husband's. It is implicit in the *Sorensen* opinion that the court thought it was acting for the benefit of the child. But Levy v. Louisiana, supra, page 328, seemed to express constitutional doubts about distinctions based upon "legal" rather than biological relationships, saying, in the *Levy* context, that such distinctions are not "rational." In *Sorensen* the husband is singled out and required to support a child not his, while other men are free of any obligation to support children other than their own. This distinction is nonetheless "rational," is it not? Why is that so? What makes this situation different from that in *Levy*? Are those differences enough to make the distinction "rational" in *Sorensen*?

7. How would *Sorensen* apply to the following case? W has an illegitimate child, S, whose father is X. While S is still very young, W and H marry. H is fully aware that W's child is illegitimate and that he (H) is not the father, but nevertheless accepts S in the family. S is known by H's surname and is supported and cared for by H and W. S is listed on H's income tax return as a dependent. After some years the marriage of H and W breaks up and W sues H for divorce, asking for an order in the divorce decree that H continue to support S. Assuming that the court in such a case has authority to order a father to support his child, may the court order H to support S? See Clevenger v. Clevenger, 189 Cal.App.2d 658, 11 Cal.Rptr. 707 (1961); Fuller v. Fuller, 247 A.2d 767 (D.C.Ct.App.1968); Gustin v. Gustin, 108 Ohio App. 171, 161 N.E.2d 68 (1958); Taylor v. Taylor, 58 Wash.2d 510, 364 P.2d 444 (1961); Annot., 90 A.L.R.2d 583 (1963). Cf. the doctrine of equitable adoption, infra, page 570.

8. Does the donor of semen for AID have any rights or obligations with respect to the child so conceived? C.M. v. C.C., 152 N.J.Super. 160, 377 A.2d 821 (Juv. and Dom.Rel.Ct.1977).

9. M, an unmarried woman, wishes to have a child and consults several physicians about artificial insemination. They all refuse to perform the operation on the ground that she is unmarried and that it would not be in the best interests of a child to be raised without a father. Does M have any legal remedy in this situation? Are the physicians on sound ground ethically or professionally in refusing to artificially inseminate an unmarried woman? Should it make a difference that the woman seeking artificial insemination is a lesbian? What would you advise a physician to do in these circumstances?

10. Modern medicine is not only capable of AID, but of storing semen by freezing it and holding it in "sperm banks". This makes possible consciously directed genetic change. The semen of "donors of outstanding ability and vigour, persons whose genuine merits have been indicated in the trials of life" may be collected, held in the sperm bank, and then used by practitioners of AID, not merely in those cases where a husband is sterile, but as a means of producing an especially promising child with a genetic background superior to that of the husband. The quotation is from H. Muller, Genetic Progress by Voluntarily Conducted Germinal Choice, in Man and His Future (G. Wolstenholme ed. 1963), 247, 259. Even now AID is

occasionally being used where the husband has the probability of transmitting a serious genetic defect, or where there is Rh incompatibility with the wife. It is only a limited further step to use artificial insemination for affirmative improvement of the genetic inheritance.

(a) What legal problems are created by the foregoing suggestion?

(b) Could you draft a statute which would at least begin to solve these problems?

(c) Would your statute be constitutional? Can this problem be constitutionally solved at all, in the present state of the law?

11. In 1978 in England the first "test-tube baby" was born. In this case conception occurred in a laboratory, using an ovum removed from a married woman and sperm from her husband. The fertilized embryo was then emplanted in the woman's uterus where it developed normally. This process produced an apparently normal baby. There is also some reason to think that embryos could be frozen for later implantation in a would-be mother. See New York Times, July 26, 1978, p. 1, col. 5; July 27, 1978, p. 1, col. 2. Should statutes be enacted forbidding reproduction by these methods? If not, should such methods be regulated by statute in some way?

12. One hears rumors occasionally about women who are willing to act as "surrogate mothers". This process is apparently resorted to by married couples when the wife rather than the husband is infertile. It involves artificially inseminating another woman with the husband's sperm, on her agreement to turn the child over to the husband and wife when it is born. The surrogate mother is usually paid for this service. Should the law attempt to regulate this process, and if so, how?

13. In Zepeda v. Zepeda, 41 Ill.App.2d 240, 190 N.E.2d 849 (1963), cert. den. 379 U.S. 945 (1964), an illegitimate child sued his father on the theory that by causing him to be born a bastard his father committed a tort against him. The Illinois court held that it was indeed a tort, christening it the tort of wrongful life but refused to permit recovery on the ground that "the social impact could be staggering," that it would be impossible to set limits to the principle which would thereby be announced. In a somewhat similar case, Williams v. State, 18 N.Y.2d 481, 223 N.E.2d 343, 276 N. Y.S.2d 885 (1966) the suit of an illegitimate child against the state of New York was dismissed. The basis for this suit was slightly different. The child's mother had been a patient in a state-operated mental institution and was sexually assaulted, became pregnant and gave birth to the plaintiff. The plaintiff's claim was that the state was negligent in not preventing the assault and that this resulted in harm to the plaintiff, namely, being born out of wedlock with all the deprivations which that involved. The New York Court of Appeals held that being born under one set of circumstances rather than another is not a wrong which is cognizable by a court. These cases are analogous to the cases involving negligent sterilization and negligent genetic counseling, cited supra, page 325. They are all often referred to as involving the tort of "wrongful life". They have been discussed in Note, Compensation for the Harmful Effects of Illegitimacy, 66 Colum.L. Rev. 127 (1966), and Note, 18 Stan.L.Rev. 530 (1966).

Some questions raised by this line of cases might be:

(a) Could and should a statute be drafted which would create and define the tort of "wrongful life"?

(b) What should be the result if an illegitimate child should sue his father in equity, asking the court to order his father to take whatever steps the local law required in order to legitimate the child?

14. The paternity suit is frequently and sharply criticized as being humiliating to the woman involved and more productive of perjury than of support for the child. What changes in the law would you suggest as a remedy for these evils? Would you approve of a statute entitling all illegitimate children to a specified level of support from public funds, with the amounts required being provided by a special additional income tax assessed against all unmarried males over the age of seventeen and under the age of sixty? Would such a statute be constitutional under Stanley v. Illinois, Bell v. Burson and similar cases? Would the inclusion of unmarried females of the same ages make the statute constitutional?

SECTION 3. TERMINATION OF PARENTAL RIGHTS AND ADOPTION

INTRODUCTORY NOTE

The process of adoption occurs when, pursuant to statute, a child's legal rights and responsibilities toward his natural parents are terminated and similar rights and responsibilities toward his adoptive parents are substituted. Both steps, the termination of one set of rights and the creation of the other, may occur in the course of one legal proceeding, or they may be accomplished in two proceedings. In any event it is important to see that there are two steps.

The first step, the termination of the rights and obligations of the natural parent, may be accomplished voluntarily or involuntarily. Voluntary termination occurs when the natural parent initiates a statutory proceeding for the relinquishment of his child, or when he executes a consent to adoption which complies with the statutory requirements. These requirements and the troublesome questions arising when a consent to adoption is revoked are the subject of some of the cases following in this section. Involuntary termination of the natural parent's rights is accomplished by a statutory proceeding, usually called a dependency or neglect proceeding. It may be brought when the natural parent has neglected or mistreated his child to such an extent that, under the applicable statute, termination of his rights is warranted. This sort of proceeding is usually, though not always, brought by a state agency. The construction and validity of statutes authorizing the involuntary termination of parental rights raise fundamental questions about the parent-child relationship in our society and are the subject of several cases in this section of the book.

Adoption statistics in the United States are incomplete, but the figures we do have may be of some interest. According to the Statistical Abstract of the United States, 1972, at page 305, there were a total of 175,000 adoptions in the United States in 1970, as compared with 107,000 in 1960. Of the 1970 adoptions 89,000 were by non-relatives. The corresponding figures for 1975 were about 104,000 adoptions, of which approximately 37,000 were by non-relatives. U.S. Department of Health, Education and Welfare, Social and Rehabilitation Service, Office of Information Systems, National Center for Social Statistics, Adoptions in 1975, DHEW Pub. No. (SRS) 77–03259 (1977). The latter figures reflect reports from only thirty-eight states, the District of Columbia and Puerto Rico, however. Nevertheless they seem to bear out the impression that the number of adoption placements, particularly those made with non-relatives has been declining. See, e. g., Wall Street Journal, September 14, 1971, page 1, col. 4, reporting sharp declines in adoption placements for 1970 in California and Massachusetts, and Bodenheimer, New Trends and Requirements in Adoption Law and Proposals for Legislative Change, 49 So.Cal.L.Rev. 10, 13 (1975). This has been the result, apparently, of more liberal abortion laws, a wider reliance on birth control, and, most important of all, the reduction of the stigma attached to having an illegitimate child, leading unmarried mothers to keep their babies. The decline in placements represents a reduction in the number of white, newborn, healthy babies available for adoption. Unfortunately there is still a substantial number of other children for whom adoption would be beneficial but for whom adoptive parents are not available. These include older children, black children, or children having various kinds of physical or psychological disabilities or illnesses. The New York Times, April 25, 1976, p. 50, col. 3; March 8, 1979, p. 1, col. 4; April 15, 1979, XXIII, p. 16, col. 1. In such an unstable society as exists in the United States these conditions can change rapidly, with corresponding rapid change in the number of children available for adoption. Only twenty years ago the number of adoptions was increasing annually and the number of readily adoptable babies was larger than the number of potential adoptive parents.

One response to the shortage of adoptable babies is the development of a black market, although it is difficult to determine how prevalent this is. The New York Times, April 25, 1976, p. 50, col. 3, reports this market growing and the prices being paid for babies rising. The term black market is usually applied to the placement of children for adoption outside of approved child placement agency channels for fees which greatly exceed the legitimate charges of lawyers for the legal services required to obtain the adoption decree. Such fees are illegal in most states and in fact amount to the purchase price in the sale of a baby.

Since in the adoption process the lawyer and the social worker are both directly involved, it is essential that the lawyer who handles adoption cases be familiar with some of the standards under which the social worker operates and with some of the problems which the social worker faces. The following is a short and partial list of materials which are useful for that purpose:

(a) Child Welfare League of America, Guidelines for Adoption Service (1968). A revised set of standards embodying the latest experience with adoption.

(b) W. Gellhorn, Children and Families in the Courts of New York, Ch. 10 (1954). Still useful although somewhat out of date.

(c) S. Katz, When Parents Fail, The Law's Response to Family Breakdown, especially Ch. 5 (1971). A critical account of the law's approach to the problems of children.

(d) H. Kirk, Shared Fate: A Theory of Adoption and Mental Health (1964). A study of problems created by adoption and the response of some families to those problems.

(e) M. Schapiro, A Study of Adoption Practice (1956). A description of agency practices which is somewhat out of date but still useful.

(f) Huard, The Law of Adoption: Ancient and Modern, 9 Vand. L.Rev. 743 (1956). Good account of the history of the subject.

(g) Katz, Judicial and Statutory Trends in the Law of Adoption, 51 Geo.L.J. 64 (1962). A useful general discussion of modern adoption law.

(h) B. Tizard, Adoption—A Second Chance (1979).

Although we generally think of adoption as involving children, and most adoptions do, it is possible under the statutes of some states to adopt adults. The purpose of such adoptions is to confer rights of inheritance. Adult adoption therefore is really a branch of the law of intestacy and bears no resemblance to the adoption of children. See H. Clark, Law of Domestic Relations, § 18.7 (1968).

A. THE UNITED STATES SUPREME COURT AND THE ADOPTION PROCESS

STANLEY v. ILLINOIS

Supreme Court of the United States, 1972.
405 U.S. 645, 92 S.Ct. 1208, 31 L.Ed.2d 551.

Mr. Justice WHITE delivered the opinion of the Court.

Joan Stanley lived with Peter Stanley intermittently for 18 years, during which time they had three children. When Joan Stanley died, Peter Stanley lost not only her but also his children. Under Illinois law, the children of unwed fathers become wards of the State upon the death of the mother. Accordingly, upon Joan Stanley's death, in a dependency proceeding instituted by the State of Illinois, Stanley's children were declared wards of the State and placed with court-appointed guardians. Stanley appealed, claiming that he had never been shown to be an unfit parent and that since married fathers and unwed mothers could not be deprived of their children without such a showing, he had been deprived of the equal protection of the laws guaranteed him by the Fourteenth Amendment. The Illinois Supreme Court accepted the fact that Stanley's own unfitness had not been established but rejected the equal protection claim, holding that Stanley could properly be separated from his children upon proof of the single fact that he and the dead mother had not been married. Stanley's actual fitness as a father was irrelevant. In re Stanley, 45 Ill.2d 132, 256 N.E.2d 814 (1970).

Stanley presses his equal protection claim here. The State continues to respond that unwed fathers are presumed unfit to raise their children and that it is unnecessary to hold individualized hearings to determine whether particular fathers are in fact unfit parents before they are separated from their children. We granted certiorari, 400 U.S. 1020, 91 S.Ct. 584, 27 L.Ed.2d 631 (1971), to determine whether this method of procedure by presumption could be allowed to stand in light of the fact that Illinois allows married fathers—whether divorced, widowed, or separated—and mothers—even if unwed—the benefit of the presumption that they are fit to raise their children.

[At this point in its opinion the Court held that any defect in the proceedings was not cured by the possibility that Stanley might later have been able to obtain custody of his children or to adopt them. The Court suggested that he would not have been likely to be awarded either custody or a decree of adoption, but that in any event this would not have righted the wrong the state of Illinois had done him.]

We must therefore examine the question that Illinois would have us avoid: Is a presumption that distinguishes and burdens all unwed fathers constitutionally repugnant? We conclude that, as a matter of due process of law, Stanley was entitled to a hearing on his fitness as a parent before his children were taken from him and that, by denying him a hearing and extending it to all other parents whose custody of their children is challenged, the State denied Stanley the equal protection of the laws guaranteed by the Fourteenth Amendment.

II

Illinois has two principal methods of removing non-delinquent children from the homes of their parents. In a dependency proceeding it may demonstrate that the children are wards of the State because they have no surviving parent or guardian. Ill.Rev.Stat., c. 37, §§ 702–1, 702–5. In a neglect proceeding it may show that children should be wards of the State because the present parent(s) or guardian does not provide suitable care. Ill.Rev.Stat., c. 37, §§ 702–1, 702–4.

The State's right—indeed, duty—to protect minor children through a judicial determination of their interests in a neglect proceeding is not challenged here. Rather, we are faced with a dependency statute that empowers state officials to circumvent neglect proceedings on the theory that an unwed father is not a "parent" whose existing relationship with his children must be considered. "Parents," says the State, "means the father and mother of a legitimate child, or the survivor of them, or the natural mother of an illegitimate child, and includes any adoptive parent," Ill.Rev.Stat., c. 37, § 701–14, but the term does not include unwed fathers.

Under Illinois law, therefore, while the children of all parents can be taken from them in neglect proceedings, that is only after notice, hearing, and proof of such unfitness as a parent as amounts to neglect, an unwed father is uniquely subject to the more simplistic dependency proceeding. By use of this proceeding, the State, on showing that the father was not married to the mother, need not prove unfitness in fact, because it is presumed at law. Thus, the unwed father's claim of parental qualification is avoided as "irrelevant."

In considering this procedure under the Due Process Clause, we recognize, as we have in other cases, that due process of law does not require a hearing "in every conceivable case of government impairment of private interest." Cafeteria Workers v. McElroy, 367 U.S. 886, 894, 81 S.Ct. 1743, 1748, 6 L.Ed.2d 1230 (1961). That case explained that "[t]he very nature of due process negates any concept of inflexible procedures universally applicable to every imaginable situation" and firmly established that "what procedures due process may require under any given set of circumstances must begin with a determination of the precise nature of the government function involved as well as of the private interest that has been affected by governmental action." Id., at 895, 81 S.Ct., at 1748.

The private interest here, that of a man in the children he has sired and raised, undeniably warrants deference and, absent a powerful countervailing interest, protection. It is plain that the interest of a parent in the companionship, care, custody, and management of his or her children "come[s] to this Court with a momentum for respect lacking when appeal is made to liberties which derive merely from shifting economic arrangements." Kovacs v. Cooper, 336 U.S. 77, 95, 69 S.Ct. 448, 458, 93 L.Ed. 513 (1949) (Frankfurter, J., concurring).

The Court has frequently emphasized the importance of the family. The rights to conceive and to raise one's children have been deemed "essential," Meyer v. Nebraska, 262 U.S. 390, 399, 43 S.Ct. 625, 626, 67 L.Ed. 1042 (1923), "basic civil rights of man," Skinner v. Oklahoma, 316 U.S. 535, 541, 62 S.Ct. 1110, 1113, 86 L.Ed. 1655 (1942), and "[r]ights far more precious * * * than property rights," May v. Anderson, 345 U.S. 528, 533, 73 S.Ct. 840, 843, 97 L.

Ed. 1221 (1953). "It is cardinal with us that the custody, care and nurture of the child reside first in the parents, whose primary function and freedom include preparation for obligations the state can neither supply nor hinder." Prince v. Massachusetts, 321 U.S. 158, 166, 64 S.Ct. 438, 442, 88 L.Ed. 645 (1944). The integrity of the family unit has found protection in the Due Process Clause of the Fourteenth Amendment, Meyer v. Nebraska, supra, 262 U.S., at 399, 43 S.Ct., at 626, the Equal Protection Clause of the Fourteenth Amendment, Skinner v. Oklahoma, supra, 316 U.S., at 541, 62 S.Ct., at 1113 and the Ninth Amendment, Griswold v. Connecticut, 381 U.S. 479, 496, 85 S.Ct. 1678, 14 L.Ed.2d 510 (1965) (Goldberg, J., concurring).

Nor has the law refused to recognize those family relationships unlegitimized by a marriage ceremony. The Court has declared unconstitutional a state statute denying natural, but illegitimate, children a wrongful-death action for the death of their mother, emphasizing that such children cannot be denied the right of other children because familial bonds in such cases were often as warm, enduring, and important as those arising within a more formally organized family unit. Levy v. Louisiana, 391 U.S. 68, 71–72, 88 S.Ct. 1509, 1511, 20 L.Ed.2d 436 (1968). "To say that the test of equal protection should be the 'legal' rather than the biological relationship is to avoid the issue. For the Equal Protection Clause necessarily limits the authority of a State to draw such 'legal' lines as it chooses." Glona v. American Guarantee Co., 391 U.S. 73, 75–76, 88 S.Ct. 1515, 1516, 20 L.Ed.2d 441 (1968).

These authorities make it clear that, at the least, Stanley's interest in retaining custody of his children is cognizable and substantial.

For its part, the State has made its interest quite plain: Illinois has declared that the aim of the Juvenile Court Act is to protect "the moral, emotional, mental, and physical welfare of the minor and the best interests of the community" and to "strengthen the minor's family ties whenever possible, removing him from the custody of his parents only when his welfare or safety or the protection of the public cannot be adequately safeguarded without removal * * *." Ill. Rev.Stat., c. 37, § 701–2. These are legitimate interests, well within the power of the State to implement. We do not question the assertion that neglectful parents may be separated from their children.

But we are here not asked to evaluate the legitimacy of the state ends, rather, to determine whether the means used to achieve these ends are constitutionally defensible. What is the state interest in separating children from fathers without a hearing designed to determine whether the father is unfit in a particular disputed case? We observe that the State registers no gain towards its declared goals when it separates children from the custody of fit parents. Indeed, if Stanley is a fit father, the State spites its own articulated goals when it needlessly separates him from his family.

In Bell v. Burson, 402 U.S. 535, 91 S.Ct. 1586, 29 L.Ed.2d 90 (1971), we found a scheme repugnant to the Due Process Clause because it deprived a driver of his license without reference to the very factor (there fault in driving, here fitness as a parent) that the State itself deemed fundamental to its statutory scheme. Illinois would avoid the self-contradiction that rendered the Georgia license suspension system invalid by arguing that Stanley and all other unmarried fathers can reasonably be presumed to be unqualified to raise their children.[5]

It may be, as the State insists, that most unmarried fathers are unsuitable and neglectful parents.[6] It may also be that Stanley is such a parent and that his children should be placed in other hands. But all unmarried fathers are not in this category; some are wholly suited to have custody of their children.[7] This much the State readi-

5. Illinois says in its brief, at 21–23
   "[T]he only relevant consideration in determining the propriety of governmental intervention in the raising of children is whether the best interests of the child are served by such intervention.
   "In effect, Illinois has imposed a statutory presumption that the best interests of a particular group of children necessitates some governmental supervision in certain clearly defined situations. The group of children who are illegitimate are distinguishable from legitimate children not so much by their status at birth as by the factual differences in their upbringing. While a legitimate child usually is raised by both parents with the attendant familial relationships and a firm concept of home and identity, the illegitimate child normally knows only one parent—the mother. * * *
   " * * * The petitioner has premised his argument upon particular factual circumstances—a lengthy relationship with the mother * * * a familial relationship with the two children, and a general assumption that this relationship approximates that in which the natural parents are married to each other.
   " * * * Even if this characterization were accurate (the record is insufficient to support it) it would not affect the validity of the statutory definition of parent. * * * The petitioner does not deny that the children are illegitimate. The record reflects their natural mother's death. Given

these two factors, grounds exist for the State's intervention to ensure adequate care and protection for these children. This is true whether or not this particular petitioner assimilates all or none of the normal characteristics common to the classification of fathers who are not married to the mothers of their children."
See also Illinois' Brief 23 ("The comparison of married and putative fathers involves exclusively factual differences. The most significant of these are the presence or absence of the father from the home on a day-to-day basis and the responsibility imposed upon the relationship"), id., at 24 (to the same effect), id., at 31 (quoted below in n. 6), id., at 24–26 (physiological and other studies are cited in support of the proposition that men are not naturally inclined to child-rearing), and Tr. of Oral Arg. 31 ("We submit that both based on history or [sic] culture the very real differences * * * between the married father and the unmarried father, in terms of their interests in children and their legal responsibility for their children, that the statute here fulfills the compelling governmental objective of protecting children * * * ").

6. The State speaks of "the general disinterest of putative fathers in their illegitimate children" (Brief 8) and opines that "[i]n most instances, the natural father is a stranger to his children." Brief 31.

7. See In re Mark T., 8 Mich.App. 122, 154 N.W.2d 27 (1967). There a panel

ly concedes, and nothing in this record indicates that Stanley is or has been a neglectful father who has not cared for his children. Given the opportunity to make his case, Stanley may have been seen to be deserving of custody of his offspring. Had this been so, the State's statutory policy would have been furthered by leaving custody in him.

Carrington v. Rash, 380 U.S. 89, 85 S.Ct. 775, 13 L.Ed.2d 675 (1965), dealt with a similar situation. There we recognized that Texas had a powerful interest in restricting its electorate to bona fide residents. It was not disputed that most servicemen stationed in Texas had no intention of remaining in the State; most therefore could be deprived of a vote in state affairs. But we refused to tolerate a blanket exclusion depriving all servicemen of the vote, when some servicemen clearly were bona fide residents and when "more precise tests," id., at 95, were available to distinguish members of this latter group. * * *

Despite *Bell* and *Carrington,* it may be argued that unmarried fathers are so seldom fit that Illinois need not undergo the administrative inconvenience of inquiry in any case, including Stanley's. The establishment of prompt efficacious procedures to achieve legitimate state ends is a proper state interest worthy of cognizance in constitutional adjudication. But the Constitution recognizes higher values than speed and efficiency.[8] Indeed, one might fairly say of the Bill

of the Michigan Court of Appeals in unanimously affirming a circuit court's determination that the father of an illegitimate son was best suited to raise the boy, said:

"The appellants' presentation in this case proceeds on the assumption that placing Mark for adoption is inherently preferable to rearing by his father, that uprooting him from the family which he knew from birth until he was a year and a half old, secretly institutionalizing him and later transferring him to strangers is so incontrovertibly better that no court has the power even to consider the matter. Hardly anyone would even suggest such a proposition if we were talking about a child born in wedlock.

"We are not aware of any sociological data justifying the assumption that an illegitimate child reared by his natural father is less likely to receive a proper upbringing than one reared by his natural father who was at one time married to his mother, or that the stigma of illegitimacy is so pervasive it requires adoption by strangers and permanent termination of a

subsisting relationship with the child's father." Id., at 146, 154 N. W.2d, at 39.

8. Cf. Reed v. Reed, 404 U.S. 71, 76, 92 S.Ct. 251, 254, 30 L.Ed.2d 225 (1971). "Clearly the objective of reducing the workload on probate courts by eliminating one class of contests is not without some legitimacy. * * * [But to] give a mandatory preference to members of either sex over members of the other, merely to accomplish the elimination of hearings on the merits, is to make the very kind of arbitrary legislative choice forbidden by the Equal Protection Clause of the Fourteenth Amendment." Carrington v. Rash, 380 U.S. 89, 96, 85 S.Ct. 775, 780, 13 L.Ed.2d 675 (1965), teaches the same lesson, " * * * States may not casually deprive a class of individuals of the vote because of some remote administrative benefit to the State. Oyama v. California, 332 U.S. 633. By forbidding a soldier ever to controvert the presumption of nonresidence, the Texas Constitution imposes an invidious discrimination in violation of the Fourteenth Amendment."

of Rights in general, and the Due Process Clause in particular, that they were designed to protect the fragile values of a vulnerable citizenry from the overbearing concern for efficiency and efficacy that may characterize praiseworthy government officials no less, and perhaps more, than mediocre ones.

Procedure by presumption is always cheaper and easier than individualized determination. But when, as here, the procedure forecloses the determinative issues of competence and care, when it explicitly disdains present realities in deference to past formalities, it needlessly risks running roughshod over the important interests of both parent and child. It therefore cannot stand.[9]

Bell v. Burson held that the State could not, while purporting to be concerned with fault in suspending a driver's license, deprive a citizen of his license without a hearing that would assess fault. Absent fault, the State's declared interest was so attenuated that administrative convenience was insufficient to excuse a hearing where evidence of fault could be considered. That drivers involved in accidents, as a statistical matter, might be very likely to have been wholly or partially at fault did not foreclose hearing and proof in specific cases before licenses were suspended.

We think the Due Process Clause mandates a similar result here. The State's interest in caring for Stanley's children is *de minimis* if Stanley is shown to be a fit father. It insists on presuming rather than proving Stanley's unfitness solely because it is more convenient to presume than to prove. Under the Due Process Clause that advantage is insufficient to justify refusing a father a hearing when the issue at stake is the dismemberment of his family.

III

The State of Illinois assumes custody of the children of married parents, divorced parents, and unmarried mothers only after a hearing and proof of neglect. The children of unmarried fathers, however, are declared dependent children without a hearing on parental

---

9. We note in passing that the incremental cost of offering unwed fathers an opportunity for individualized hearings on fitness appears to be minimal. If unwed fathers, in the main, do not care about the disposition of their children, they will not appear to demand hearings. If they do care, under the scheme here held invalid, Illinois would admittedly at some later time have to afford them a properly focused hearing in a custody or adoption proceeding.

Extending opportunity for hearing to unwed fathers who desire and claim competence to care for their children creates no constitutional or procedural obstacle to foreclosing those unwed fathers who are not so inclined. The Illinois law governing procedure in juvenile cases, Ill.Rev. Stat., c. 37, § 704–1 et seq., provides for personal service, notice by certified mail, or for notice by publication when personal or certified mail service cannot be had or when notice is directed to unknown respondents under the style of "All whom it may Concern." Unwed fathers who do not promptly respond cannot complain if their children are declared wards of the State. Those who do respond retain the burden of proving their fatherhood.

fitness and without proof of neglect. Stanley's claim in the state courts and here is that failure to afford him a hearing on his parental qualifications while extending it to other parents denied him equal protection of the laws. We have concluded that all Illinois parents are constitutionally entitled to a hearing on their fitness before their children are removed from their custody. It follows that denying such a hearing to Stanley and those like him while granting it to other Illinois parents is inescapably contrary to the Equal Protection Clause.

The judgment of the Supreme Court of Illinois is reversed and the case is remanded to that court for proceedings not inconsistent with this opinion.

NOTES AND QUESTIONS

1. Chief Justice Burger and Justice Blackmun dissented in *Stanley,* partly on the ground that the due process issue was not raised in the state courts and therefore was not properly before the Supreme Court. They also took the position that the Equal Protection Clause was not violated by Illinois' refusal to recognize the father-child relationship when it did not arise "in the context of family units bound together by legal obligations arising from marriage or from adoption proceedings." 405 U.S. at 663. The dissenters found the purpose of the Illinois rule to be the protection of the welfare of illegitimate children. Stanley's own position in relation to the children they found to be somewhat unclear, since he had turned the children over to the care of a Mr. and Mrs. Ness, did not seek custody or offer to become legally responsible for them, and was concerned with the loss of welfare payments if others were appointed guardians of the children. been placed with adoptive parents and the rights of the mother cut off.

On September 13, 1973, Mr. Stanley was declared to be an "unfit" parent by a Juvenile Court in Chicago and deprived of custody of his two children, who were placed in the permanent custody of the Illinois Department of Children and Family Services. Chicago Daily News, September 14, 1973, page 6, column 3.

2. Two other similar cases were decided at the same time as *Stanley.* In one of them, State ex rel. Lewis v. Lutheran Social Services, 47 Wis.2d 420, 178 N.W.2d 56 (1970), vacated 405 U.S. 1051 (1972), the child had been placed with adoptive parents and the rights of the mother cut off. The Supreme Court vacated the state court judgment and remanded the case for consideration in the light of *Stanley.* As far as appears from the report, the father in this case had not had any relationship with his child, unlike Stanley, but the Wisconsin statute had, like the Illinois statute, provided that the unmarried father had no parental rights. On the remand the Wisconsin Supreme Court held that the father had abandoned the child and on that ground terminated his parental rights. State ex rel. Lewis v. Lutheran Social Services, 68 Wis.2d 36, 227 N.W.2d 643 (1975). The other case is Vanderlaan v. Vanderlaan, 126 Ill.App.2d 410, 262 N.E.2d 717 (1970), vacated 405 U.S. 1051 (1972), on remand, 9 Ill.App.3d 260, 292 N.E.2d 145 (1972), the Illinois court after the remand giving custody of the child to its father. See also Note 70 Mich.L.Rev. 1581 (1972).

At this point the student should read May v. Anderson, reproduced infra, page 1029.

3. Precisely what constitutional provision did the Court rely on in *Stanley*, the Due Process Clause, the Equal Protection Clause, or both of them? What is the relevance of Bell v. Burson, 402 U.S. 535 (1971), cited by the Court, to the *Stanley* case and to the scope of *Stanley?* On Bell v. Burson, see Gunther, Foreword, 86 Harv.L.Rev. 1 (1972).

4. What reasons might there be for the enactment of the Illinois statute which denied the father of an illegitimate child any parental rights in the child? Does the Court's opinion fully discuss those reasons? To what standard of justification does the Court subject those reasons?

5. Apparently one reason for the statute advanced by Illinois was that fathers of illegitimate children are usually not interested in their children and have no desire to have any contact with them. Does the Court have some source of information of its own indicating this is not true or does the Court conclude that the general disinclination of unmarried fathers to support their children is irrelevant? If it is true, for example, that ninety percent of unmarried fathers have no desire ever to see their children, would this validate the Illinois statute, in the Court's view? Why or why not? If this does not validate the statute, what is the impact of the case upon other statutory classifications? For example, what would be the validity of a statute which provided that one could vote at age eighteen? Would the state be required to provide a hearing for a person aged seventeen years and nine months who claimed he was just as mature as any eighteen-year-old? Cf. Lochner v. New York, 198 U.S. 45 (1905); Railroad Retirement Board v. Alton Railroad Co., 295 U.S. 330 (1935).

6. What is the effect of *Stanley* upon the welfare of illegitimate children? Does the Court in its opinion deal adequately with that question? To be more specific, how should the following cases be dealt with in order to comply with *Stanley:*

(a) M, an unmarried girl of fifteen, becomes pregnant. After talking it over with her parents and with a social worker, she decides she would like to place the baby for adoption. She takes the appropriate steps under local law to relinquish the child as soon as it is born. She tells the social worker for the adoption agency that she does not know who the father of the child is. She says she had sexual relations with three boys, none of whose names she knew, at a party and never saw them again. If you represented the adoption agency, what steps would you take to ensure that the child could legally be adopted?

(b) Assume that the girl in the preceding paragraph, when asked about the father of her child, states to the social worker that he is an older married neighbor of her family. The social worker for the adoption agency then writes this man a letter saying that he has been named as the father of the girl's baby and asking him to sign a relinquishment of his rights so that the child may be placed for adoption. The man's wife sees the letter and threatens divorce. The man himself denies emphatically that he is or could be the father of the child, saying that he never had sexual intercourse with the girl, and that the entire matter has done him irreparable harm. What should the adoption agency do at this point?

(c) It is common agency experience that many unmarried mothers refuse to give the names of the fathers of their children, for a variety of reasons. What should the agency do when this occurs? Is the mother's constitutional right of privacy under Griswold v. Connecticut, supra, page 73, involved here?

(d) You represent H and W, a married couple, who wish to adopt a child. They have listed their names with the state welfare department and are notified that a child will soon be born who will be placed with them. They inform you of this and say that since they have heard of cases in which adoptive parents have had their adopted children taken away from them after the children had been in the adoptive homes for some time, they want you to do everything possible to ensure that this does not happen to them. You call the welfare department and are told that their policy is to maintain absolute confidentiality as between natural parents and adoptive parents, and that they therefore cannot reveal to you the names either of the child's mother or father. But they assure you that all the usual legal steps will be taken to make sure that a valid adoption will occur. What do you then advise your clients?

(e) Assume, alternatively, that in the preceding paragraph the agency tells you that they will give you certain information but only upon your strict agreement not to reveal any of it to your clients. They require this pledge in order to maintain the confidentiality which is properly thought necessary for the welfare of all parties in adoptions. You make the promise, and they then give you the name of the baby's mother, and the name of the man the mother gave them as the father of the baby. What do you do at that point? What would you do if you later learned as a result of some independent investigation that some of what the agency had told your clients about the baby's background was untrue?

(f) A baby is left in the vestibule of a local church, with no clues as to the identify of either parent. What does *Stanley* require in the way of notice or service if parental rights are to be terminated so that this baby may be placed for adoption?

7. In some states the courts in deciding custody cases follow the so-called "parental right theory", which is that a parent is entitled to the custody of his child unless he is proven to be unfit. Under *Stanley*, must this theory be applied to the unmarried father in a state which would apply it to married parents? For example, suppose that in the Lewis case, cited supra, page 439, the child had, by the time the case was remanded to the Wisconsin courts, been in the custody of the adoptive parents for two years. Would they only be able to keep the child by proving the unmarried father was unfit to have custody, regardless of what the child's welfare might require? On the remand in *Stanley*, does Mr. Stanley get custody of this children as a matter of right?

8. The Uniform Parentage Act contains the following section, dealing with the rights of fathers of illegitimate children, 9 Unif.L.Ann. 538 (Supp.1978):

"§ 24. [Custodial Proceedings]

"(a) If a mother relinquishes or proposes to relinquish for adoption a child who has (1) a presumed father under Section 4(a), (2) a father whose relationship to the child has been determined by a court, or (3) a father as to whom the child is a legitimate child under prior law of this State or under the law of another jurisdiction, the father shall be given notice of the adoption proceeding and have the rights provided under [the appropriate State statute] [the Revised Uniform Adoption Act], unless the father's relationship to the child has been previously terminated or determined by a court not to exist.

"(b) If a mother relinquishes or proposes to relinquish for adoption a child who does not have (1) a presumed father under Section 4(a), (2) a father whose relationship to the child has been determined by a court, or (3) a father as to whom the child is a legitimate child under prior law of this State or under the law of another jurisdiction, or if a child otherwise becomes the subject of an adoption proceeding, the agency or person to whom the child has been or is to be relinquished, or the mother or the person having custody of the child, shall file a petition in the [   ] court to terminate the parental rights of the father, unless the father's relationship to the child has been previously terminated or determined not to exist by a court.

"(c) In an effort to identify the natural father, the court shall cause inquiry to be made of the mother and any other appropriate person. The inquiry shall include the following: whether the mother was married at the time of conception of the child or at any time thereafter; whether the mother was cohabiting with a man at the time of conception or birth of the child; whether the mother has received support payments or promises of support with respect to the child or in connection with her pregnancy; or whether any man has formally or informally acknowledged or declared his possible paternity of the child.

"(d) If, after the inquiry, the natural father is identified to the satisfaction of the court, or if more than one man is identified as a possible father, each shall be given notice of the proceeding in accordance with Subsection (f). If any of them fails to appear or, if appearing, fails to claim custodial rights, his parental rights with reference to the child shall be terminated. If the natural father or a man representing himself to be the natural father, claims custodial rights, the court shall proceed to determine custodial rights.

"(e) If, after the inquiry, the court is unable to identify the natural father or any possible natural father and no person has appeared claiming to be the natural father and claiming custodial rights, the court shall enter an order terminating the unknown natural father's parental rights with reference to the child. Subject to the disposition of an appeal, upon the expiration of [6 months] after an order terminating parental rights is issued under this subsection, the order cannot be questioned by any person, in any manner, or upon any ground, including fraud, misrepresentation, failure to give any required notice, or lack of jurisdiction of the parties or of the subject matter.

"(f) Notice of the proceeding shall be given to every person identified as the natural father or a possible natural father [in the manner appropriate under rules of civil procedure for the service of process in a civil action in this state, or] in any manner the court directs. Proof of giving the notice shall be filed with the court before the petition is heard. [If no person has been identified as the natural father or a possible father, the court, on the basis of all information available, shall determine whether publication or public posting of notice of the proceeding is likely to lead to identification and, if so, shall order publication or public posting at times and in places and manner it deems appropriate.]"

The Commissioners' Comments to this section state that some parts of it raise constitutional questions. What are those questions and how shuold they be decided, in order to comply with the precepts of Stanley v. Illinois?

9. Does or should *Stanley* apply to claims by fathers whose rights had been terminated and whose children had been adopted before *Stanley* was decided?

10. The traditional legal position was that the mother of an illegitimate child had the primary right to its custody, subject always to what the child's welfare might require. Language to this effect may be found in relatively recent cases. E. g. Anonymous v. Anonymous, 26 N.Y.S.2d 740, 257 N.E.2d 288, 309 N.Y.S.2d 40 (1970); Loretta Z. v. A., 36 A.D.2d 995, 320 N.Y.S.2d 997 (3rd Dep't 1971). But even before *Stanley* some courts were beginning to grant the unmarried father rights of visitation where no prejudice to the child's welfare could be predicted. In re One Minor Child, 295 A.2d 727 (Del.Sup.Ct.1972); Mixon v. Mize, 198 So.2d 373 (Fla.App.1967); R. v. F., 113 N.J.Super. 396, 273 A.2d 808 (1971); M. v. M., 112 N.J.Super. 540, 271 A.2d 1919 (1970); Anonymous v. Anonymous, 34 A.2d 942, 312 N.Y.S.2d 348 (1st Dep't 1970); Commonwealth v. Rozanski, 206 Pa.Super. 397, 213 A.2d 155 (1965), 27 Ohio St.L.J. 738 (1966); Annot., 15 A.L.R.3d 887 (1967). A few cases have gone further and have considered the unmarried father as a candidate for custody, and occasionally have granted him custody. Orezza v. Ramirez, 19 Ariz.App. 405, 507 P.2d 1017 (1973); Creppel v. Thornton, 230 So.2d 644 (La.App.1970); In the Matter of Robert P., 36 Mich.App. 497, 194 N.W.2d 18 (1971); In the Matter of the Guardianship of C., 98 N.J.Super. 474, 237 A.2d 652 (1967); In the Matter of the Guardianships of Morgan et al., 70 Misc.2d 1063, 335 N.Y.S.2d 226 (Surr. Ct.1972); Annot., 45 A.L.R.3d 216 (1972).

Does the *Stanley* case require all courts to consider the unmarried father as a candidate for custody on an equal footing with the mother? See, e. g., Orezza v. Ramirez, 19 Ariz.App. 405, 507 P.2d 1017 (1973); J.M.S. v. H.A., —— W.Va. ——, 242 S.E.2d 696 (1978); In the Matter of Brenda H., 37 Ohio Misc. 123, 305 N.E.2d 815 (Com.Pl.1973); In re Richard M., 122 Cal.Rptr. 531, 14 Cal.3d 783, 537 P.2d 363 (1975); In the Interest of K, 535 S.W.2d 168 (Tex.1976), cert. den. 429 U.S. 907 (1976), reh. den. 429 U.S. 1010 (1976). See also the question raised in paragraph 4, supra, page 440.

QUILLOIN v. WALCOTT

Supreme Court of the United States, 1978.
434 U.S. 246, 98 S.Ct. 549, 54 L.Ed.2d 511, rehearing denied
435 U.S. 918, 98 S.Ct. 1477, 55 L.Ed.2d 511 (1978).

Mr. Justice MARSHALL delivered the opinion of the Court.

The issue in this case is the constitutionality of Georgia's adoption laws as applied to deny an unwed father authority to prevent adoption of his illegitimate child. The child was born in December 1964 and has been in the custody and control of his mother, appellee Ardell Williams Walcott, for his entire life. The mother and the child's natural father, appellant Leon Webster Quilloin, never married each other or established a home together, and in September 1967 the mother married appellee Randall Walcott.[1] In March 1976, she consented to adoption of the child by her husband, who immediately filed a petition for adoption. Appellant attempted to block the adoption and to secure visitation rights, but he did not seek custody or object to the child's continuing to live with appellees. Although appellant was not found to be an unfit parent, the adoption was granted over his objection.

In Stanley v. Illinois, 405 U.S. 645, 92 S.Ct. 1208, 31 L.Ed.2d 551 (1972), this Court held that the State of Illinois was barred, as a matter of both due process and equal protection, from taking custody of the children of an unwed father, absent a hearing and a particularized finding that the father was an unfit parent. The Court concluded, on the one hand, that a father's interest in the "companionship, care, custody, and management" of his children is "cognizable and substantial," id., at 651–652, 92 S.Ct., at 1212–13, and, on the other hand, that the State's interest in caring for the children is "de minimis" if the father is in fact a fit parent, id., at 657–658, 92 S.Ct., at 1215–1216. Stanley left unresolved the degree of protection a State must afford to the rights of an unwed father in a situation, such as that presented here, in which the countervailing interests are more substantial.

I

Generally speaking, under Georgia law a child born in wedlock cannot be adopted without the consent of each living parent who has not voluntarily surrendered rights in the child or been adjudicated an unfit parent.[2] Even where the child's parents are divorced or separated at the time of the adoption proceedings, either parent may veto

1. The child lived with his maternal grandmother for the initial period of the marriage, but moved in with appellees in 1969 and lived with them thereafter.

2. See Ga.Code §§ 74–403(1), (2) (1975). Section 74–403(1) sets forth the general rule that "no adoption shall be permitted except with the written consent of the living parents of a child." Section 74–403(2) provides that consent is not required from a parent who (1) has surrendered rights in the child to a child-placing agency or to the adoption court; (2) is found by the adoption court to have abandoned the child, or to have willfully failed for a year or longer to comply with a court-imposed support order with respect to the child; (3) has had his or her parental rights terminated by court order, see Ga.Code § 24A–3201; (4) is insane or otherwise incapacitated from giving consent; or (5) cannot be found after a diligent search has been made.

the adoption. In contrast, only the consent of the mother is required for adoption of an illegitimate child. Ga. Code § 74–403(3) (1975).[3] To acquire the same veto authority possessed by other parents, the father of a child born out of wedlock must legitimate his offspring, either by marrying the mother and acknowledging the child as his own, § 74–101, or by obtaining a court order declaring the child legitimate and capable of inheriting from the father, § 74–103.[4] But unless and until the child is legitimated, the mother is the only recognized parent and is given exclusive authority to exercise all parental prerogatives, § 74–203,[5] including the power to veto adoption of the child.

Appellant did not petition for legitimation of his child at any time during the 11 years between the child's birth and the filing of Randall Walcott's adoption petition.[6] However, in response to Walcott's petition, appellant filed an application for a writ of habeas corpus seeking visitation rights, a petition for legitimation, and an objection to the adoption.[7] Shortly thereafter, appellant amended his pleadings by adding the claim that §§ 74–203 and 74–403(3) were unconstitutional as applied to his case, insofar as they denied him the rights granted to married parents, and presumed unwed fathers to be unfit as a matter of law.

3. Section 74–403(3), which operates as an exception to the rule stated in § 74–403(1), see n. 2, supra, provides:
  "Illegitimate children.—If the child be illegitimate, the consent of the mother alone shall suffice. Such consent, however, shall not be required if the mother has surrendered all of her rights to said child to a licensed child-placing agency, or to the State Department of Family and Children Services."

Sections of Ga.Code (1975) will hereinafter be referred to merely by their numbers.

4. Section 74–103 provides in full:
  "A father of an illegitimate child may render the same legitimate by petitioning the superior court of the county of his residence, setting forth the name, age, and sex of such child and also the name of the mother, and if he desires the name changed, stating the new name, and praying the legitimation of such child. Of this application the mother, if alive, shall have notice. Upon such application, presented and filed, the court may pass an order declaring said child to be legitimate, and capable of inheriting from the father in the same manner as if born in lawful

wedlock, and the name by which he or she shall be known."

5. Section 74–203 states:
  "The mother of an illegitimate child shall be entitled to the possession of the child, unless the father shall legitimate him as before provided. Being the only recognized parent, she may exercise all the paternal power."

In its opinion in this case, the Georgia Supreme Court indicated that the word "paternal" in the second sentence of this provision is the result of a misprint, and was instead intended to read "parental." See Quilloin v. Walcott, 238 Ga. 230, 231, 232 S.E.2d 246, 247 (1977).

6. It does appear that appellant consented to entry of his name on the child's birth certificate. See § 88–1709(d)(2). The adoption petition gave the name of the child as "Darrell Webster Quilloin," and appellant alleges in his brief that the child has always been known by that name, see Brief for Appellant 11.

7. Appellant had been notified by the State's Department of Human Resources that an adoption petition had been filed.

The petitions for adoption, legitimation, and writ of habeas corpus were consolidated for trial in the Superior Court of Fulton County, Ga. The court expressly stated that these matters were being tried on the basis of a consolidated record to allow "the biological father * * * a right to be heard with respect to any issue or other thing upon which he desire[s] to be heard, including his fitness as a parent * * *." [8] After receiving extensive testimony from the parties and other witnesses, the trial court found that, although the child had never been abandoned or deprived, appellant had provided support only on an irregular basis. [9] Moreover, while the child previously had visited with appellant on "many occasions," and had been given toys and gifts by appellant "from time to time," the mother had recently concluded that these contacts were having a disruptive effect on the child and on appellees' entire family. The child himself expressed a desire to be adopted by Randall Walcott and to take on Walcott's name, and the court found Walcott to be a fit and proper person to adopt the child.

On the basis of these findings, as well as findings relating to appellees' marriage and the mother's custody of the child for all of the child's life, the trial court determined that the proposed adoption was in the "best interests of [the] child." The court concluded, further, that granting either the legitimation or the visitation rights requested by appellant would not be in the "best interests of the child," and that both should consequently be denied. The court then applied §§ 74–203 and 74–403(3) to the situation at hand, and, since appellant had failed to obtain a court order granting legitimation, he was found to lack standing to object to the adoption. Ruling that appellant's constitutional claims were without merit, the court granted the adoption petition and denied the legitimation and visitation petitions.

8. In re: Application of Randall Walcott for Adoption of Child, Adoption Case No. 8466 (Ga.Super.Ct., July 12, 1976), App. 70.

Sections 74–103, 74–203, and 74–403(3) are silent as to the appropriate procedure in the event that a petition for legitimation is filed after an adoption proceeding has already been initiated. Prior to this Court's decision in Stanley v. Illinois, 405 U.S. 645, 92 S.Ct. 1208, 31 L.Ed.2d 551 (1972), and without consideration of potential constitutional problems, the Georgia Supreme Court had concluded that an unwed father could not petition for legitimation after the mother had consented to an adoption. Smith v. Smith, 224 Ga. 442, 445–446, 162 S.E. 2d 379, 383–384 (1968). But cf. Clark v. Buttry, 226 Ga. 687, 177 S.E.2d 89 (1970), aff'g 121 Ga.App. 492, 174 S. E.2d 356. However, the Georgia Supreme Court had not had occasion to reconsider this conclusion in light of Stanley, and, in the face of appellant's constitutional challenge to §§ 74–203, 74–403(3), the trial court evidently concluded that concurrent consideration of the legitimation and adoption petitions was consistent with the statutory provisions. See also Tr. of Hearing before Superior Court, App. 34, 51; n. 12, infra.

9. Under § 74–202, appellant had a duty to support his child, but for reasons not appearing in the record the mother never brought an action to enforce this duty. Since no court ever ordered appellant to support his child, denial of veto authority over the adoption could not have been justified on the ground of willful failure to comply with a support order. See n. 2, supra.

Appellant took an appeal to the Supreme Court of Georgia, claiming that §§ 74–203 and 74–403(3), as applied by the trial court to his case, violated the Equal Protection and Due Process Clauses of the Fourteenth Amendment. In particular, appellant contended that he was entitled to the same power to veto an adoption as is provided under Georgia law to married or divorced parents and to unwed mothers, and, since the trial court did not make a finding of abandonment or other unfitness on the part of appellant, see n. 2, supra, the adoption of his child should not have been allowed.

Over a dissent which urged that § 74–403(3) was invalid under Stanley v. Illinois, the Georgia Supreme Court affirmed the decision of the trial court. 238 Ga. 230, 232 S.E.2d 246 (1977).[12] The majority relied generally on the strong state policy of rearing children in a family setting, a policy which in the court's view might be thwarted if unwed fathers were required to consent to adoptions. The court also emphasized the special force of this policy under the facts of this case, pointing out that the adoption was sought by the child's stepfather, who was part of the family unit in which the child was in fact living, and that the child's natural father had not taken steps to support or legitimate the child over a period of more than 11 years. The court noted in addition that, unlike the father in *Stanley*, appellant had never been a *de facto* member of the child's family unit.

Appellant brought this appeal * * * claiming that he was entitled as a matter of due process and equal protection to an absolute veto over adoption of his child, absent a finding of his unfitness as a parent. In contrast to appellant's somewhat broader statement of the issue in the Georgia Supreme Court, on this appeal he focused his equal protection claim solely on the disparate statutory treatment of his case and that of a married father.[13] * * *

12. The Supreme Court addressed itself only to the constitutionality of the statutes as applied by the trial court and thus, at least for purposes of this case, accepted the trial court's construction of §§ 74–203 and 74–403(3) as allowing concurrent consideration of the adoption and legitimation petitions. See n. 8, supra.

Subsequent to the Supreme Court's decision in this case, the Georgia Legislature enacted a comprehensive revision of the State's adoption laws, which became effective January 1, 1978. 1977 Ga. Laws 201. The new law expressly gives an unwed father the right to petition for legitimation subsequent to the filing of an adoption petition concerning his child. See Ga. Code § 74–406 (1977 Supp.).

The revision also leaves intact §§ 74–103 and 74–203, and carries forward the substance of § 74–403(3), and thus appellant would not have received any greater protection under the new law than he was actually afforded by the trial court.

13. In the last paragraph of his brief, appellant raises the claim that the statutes make gender-based distinctions that violate the Equal Protection Clause. Since this claim was not presented in appellant's jurisdictional statement, we do not consider it. This Court's Rule 15(1)(c); see, e. g., Phillips Chem. Co. v. Dumas School Dist., 361 U.S. 376, 386, and n. 12, 80 S.Ct. 474, 480, 4 L.Ed.2d 384 (1960).

II

At the outset, we observe that appellant does not challenge the sufficiency of the notice he received with respect to the adoption proceeding, see n. 7, supra, nor can he claim that he was deprived of a right to a hearing on his individualized interests in his child, prior to entry of the order of adoption. Although the trial court's ultimate conclusion was that appellant lacked standing to object to the adoption, this conclusion was reached only after appellant had been afforded a full hearing on his legitimation petition, at which he was given the opportunity to offer evidence on any matter he thought relevant, including his fitness as a parent. Had the trial court granted legitimation, appellant would have acquired the veto authority he is now seeking.

The fact that appellant was provided with a hearing on his legitimation petition is not, however, a complete answer to his attack on the constitutionality of §§ 74–203 and 74–403(3). The trial court denied appellant's petition, and thereby precluded him from gaining veto authority, on the ground that legitimation was not in the "best interests of the child"; appellant contends that he was entitled to recognition and preservation of his parental rights absent a showing of his "unfitness." Thus, the underlying issue is whether, in the circumstances of this case and in light of the authority granted by Georgia law to married fathers, appellant's interests were adequately protected by a "best interests of the child" standard. We examine this issue first under the Due Process Clause and then under the Equal Protection Clause.

A

Appellees suggest that due process was not violated, regardless of the standard applied by the trial court, since any constitutionally protected interest appellant might have had was lost by his failure to petition for legitimation during the 11 years prior to filing of Randall Walcott's adoption petition. We would hesitate to rest decision on this ground, in light of the evidence in the record that appellant was not aware of the legitimation procedure until after the adoption petition was filed. But in any event we need not go that far, since under the circumstances of this case appellant's substantive rights were not violated by application of a "best interests of the child" standard.

We have recognized on numerous occasions that the relationship between parent and child is constitutionally protected. See, e. g., Wisconsin v. Yoder, 406 U.S. 205, 231–233, 92 S.Ct. 1526, 1541–42, 32 L.Ed.2d 15 (1972); Stanley v. Illinois, supra; Meyer v. Nebraska, 262 U.S. 390, 399–401, 43 S.Ct. 625, 626–27, 67 L.Ed. 1042 (1923). "It is cardinal with us that the custody, care and nurture of the child reside first in the parents, whose primary function and freedom include preparation for obligations the state can neither supply nor hinder." Prince v. Massachusetts, 321 U.S. 158, 166, 64 S.Ct. 438, 442, 88 L.Ed. 645 (1944). And it is now firmly established that "freedom of personal choice in matters of * * * family life is one of the liberties protected by the Due Process Clause of the Fourteenth Amendment." Cleveland Board of Education v. LaFleur, 414 U.S. 632, 639–640, 94 S.Ct. 791, 796, 39 L.Ed.2d 52 (1974).

We have little doubt that the Due Process Clause would be offended "[i]f a State were to attempt to force the breakup of a natural family, over the objections of the parents and their children, without some showing of unfitness and for the sole reason that to do so was thought to be in the children's best interest." Smith v. Organization of Foster Families, 431 U.S. 816, 862–863, 97 S.Ct. 2094, 2119–2120, 53 L.Ed.2d 14 (1977) (Stewart, J., concurring in judgment). But this is not a case in which the unwed father at any time had, or sought, actual or legal custody of his child. Nor is this a case in which the proposed adoption would place the child with a new set of parents with whom the child had never before lived. Rather, the result of the adoption in this case is to give full recognition to a family unit already in existence, a result desired by all concerned, except appellant. Whatever might be required in other situations, we cannot say that the State was required in this situation to find anything more than that the adoption, and denial of legitimation, was in the "best interests of the child."

B

Appellant contends that even if he is not entitled to prevail as a matter of due process, principles of equal protection require that his authority to veto an adoption be measured by the same standard that would have been applied to a married father. In particular, appellant asserts that his interests are indistinguishable from those of a married father who is separated or divorced from the mother and is no longer living with his child, and therefore the State acted impermissibly in treating his case differently. We think appellant's interests are readily distinguishable from those of a separated or divorced father, and accordingly believe that the State could permissibly give appellant less veto authority than it provides to a married father.

Although appellant was subject, for the years prior to these proceedings, to essentially the same child-support obligation as a married father would have had, compare § 74–202 with § 74–105 and § 30–301, he has never exercised actual or legal custody over his child, and thus has never shouldered any significant responsibility with respect to the daily supervision, education, protection, or care of the child. Appellant does not complain of his exemption from these responsibilities and, indeed, he does not even now seek custody of his child. In contrast, legal custody of children is, of course, a central aspect of the marital relationship, and even a father whose marriage has broken apart will have borne full responsibility for the rearing of his children during the period of the marriage. Under any standard of review, the State was not foreclosed from recognizing this difference in the extent of commitment to the welfare of the child.

For these reasons, we conclude that §§ 74–203 and 74–403(3), as applied in this case, did not deprive appellant of his asserted rights under the Due Process and Equal Protection Clauses. The judgment of the Supreme Court of Georgia is, accordingly,

Affirmed.

NOTES AND QUESTIONS

1. The *Quilloin* case has been noted in 64 A.B.A.J. 435 (1978) and 58 Neb.L.Rev. 610 (1979).

2. The Georgia statute quoted by the Court in footnotes 2 and 3 is similar to statutes in many other states, which first require consent of the parents to the adoption of their child, and then provide for the circumstances in which parental rights may be terminated involuntarily, or, in other words, the circumstances in which consent may be dispensed with. Usually involuntary termination requires proof that the parent abandoned or neglected the child or was guilty of some other serious breach of his parental obligations. See also § 24 of the Uniform Parentage Act, supra, page 441, paragraph 8.

3. How does the Court respond to Mr. Quilloin's argument that he was deprived of due process by the Georgia statute which permitted his child to be adopted without his consent? Was he complaining of a deprivation of procedural due process or substantive due process?

4. How can Mr. Quilloin be heard to complain of this adoption when he had taken no steps to establish his legal claim on the child for eleven years? Could his parental rights have been terminated involuntarily under the Georgia statute?

5. How does the Court respond to the argument that the Georgia statute deprived Mr. Quilloin of equal protection of the laws? Suppose, for example, that a man and woman are married and the woman becomes pregnant. The husband then deserts her and never sees the child. The woman gets a divorce and remarries, after which the second husband files a petition to adopt the child. Under the Georgia statute could the first husband block the adoption by refusing his consent? How does Mr. Quilloin's situation differ from that of the first husband?

6. How does the Court distinguish the *Stanley* case? Is this distinction satisfactory? Or is *Stanley* overruled or limited by *Quilloin*?

7. How should questions 6(a) through (f), supra, page 440, be decided in the light of the Court's opinion in *Quilloin*?

8. Is your view of the constitutionality of section 24 of the Uniform Parentage Act, supra, page 441, affected by the *Quilloin* case?

9. Assume that F and M live together out of wedlock and that M has a child as a result of their relationship. F and M and the child live together and are supported by F for about a year. At the end of that time M takes the child and leaves F, shortly thereafter marrying H. H then files a petition to adopt the child, to which F objects. Would the application of

the Georgia statute to this case, making F's consent to the adoption unnecessary, violate F's constitutional rights? How does this differ from the *Quilloin* case?

10. In footnote 8 of the *Quilloin* opinion the Court indicates that the Georgia law would apparently not permit an unmarried father to legitimate his child after adoption proceedings had been commenced. The cases in the various states are not in agreement on this. Some of them hold that legitimation may not occur after a consent to adoption has been executed by the child's mother, while others would permit legitimation at any time up to the entry of the adoption decree. The latter cases thus provide the father with a means for blocking the adoption and avoiding the impact of the Georgia type of statute. For a discussion of these cases see H. Clark, Law of Domestic Relations 625 (1968). Would the rule that legitimation may not occur after the mother's consent be unconstitutional?

CABAN v. MOHAMMED

Supreme Court of the United States, 1979.
441 U.S. 380, 99 S.Ct. 1760, 60 L.Ed.2d 297.

Mr. Justice POWELL delivered the opinion of the Court.

The appellant, Abdiel Caban, challenges the constitutionality of § 111 of the New York Domestic Relations Law, under which two of his natural children were adopted by their natural mother and stepfather without his consent. We find the statute to be unconstitutional, as the distinction it invariably makes between the rights of unmarried mothers and the rights of unmarried fathers has not been shown to be substantially related to an important state interest.

I

Abdiel Caban and appellee Maria Mohammed lived together in New York City from September of 1968 until the end of 1973. During this time Caban and Mohammed represented themselves as being husband and wife, although they never legally married. Indeed, until 1974 Caban was married to another woman, from whom he was separated. While living with the appellant, Mohammed gave birth to two children: David Andrew Caban, born July 16, 1969, and Denise Caban, born March 12, 1971. Abdiel Caban was identified as the father on each child's birth certificate, and lived with the children as their father through 1973. Together with Mohammad, he contributed to the support of the family.

In December of 1973, Mohammed took the two children and left the appellant to take up residence with appellee Kazim Mohammed, whom she married on January 30, 1974. For the next nine months, she took David and Denise each weekend to visit her mother, Delores Gonzales, who lived one floor above Caban. Because of his friendship with Gonzales, Caban was able to see the children each week when they came to visit their grandmother.

In September of 1974, Gonzales left New York to take up residence in her native Puerto Rico. At the Mohammeds' request, the grandmother took David and Denise with her. According to appellees, they planned to join the children in Puerto Rico as soon as they had saved enough money to start a business there. During the children's stay with their grandmother, Mrs. Mohammed kept in touch with David and Denise by mail; Caban communicated with the children through his parents, who also resided in Puerto Rico. In November of 1975, he went to Puerto Rico, where Gonzales willingly surrendered the children to Caban with the understanding that they would be returned after a few days. Caban, however, returned to New York with the children. When Mrs. Mohammed learned that the children were in Caban's custody, she attempted to retrieve them with the aid of a police officer. After this attempt failed, the appellees instituted custody proceedings in the New York Family Court, which placed the children in the temporary custody of the Mohammeds and gave Caban and his new wife, Nina, visiting rights.

In January 1976, appellees filed a petition under § 110 of the New York Domestic Relations Law to adopt David and Denise.[1] In March, the Cabans cross-petitioned for adoption. After the Family Court stayed the custody suit pending the outcome of the adoption proceedings, a hearing was held on the petition and cross-petition before a Law Assistant to a New York Surrogate in Kings County, N.Y. At this hearing, both the Mohammeds and the Cabans were represented by counsel and were permitted to present and cross-examine witnesses.

The Surrogate granted the Mohammeds' petition to adopt the children, thereby cutting off all of appellant's parental rights and obligations. In his opinion, the Surrogate noted the limited right under New York law of unwed fathers in adoption proceedings: "Although a putative father's consent to such an adoption is not a legal necessity, he is entitled to an opportunity to be heard in opposition to the proposed stepfather adoption." Moreover, the court stated that the appellant was foreclosed from adopting David and Denise, as the natural mother had withheld her consent. Thus, the court considered the evidence presented by the Cabans only insofar as it reflected upon the Mohammeds' qualifications as prospective parents. The Surrogate found them well qualified and granted their adoption petition.

---

1. Section 110 of the New York Domestic Relations Law provides in part that,
    "[a]n adult or minor husband and his adult or minor wife together may adopt a child of either of them born in or out of wedlock and an adult or minor husband or an adult or minor wife may adopt such a child of the other spouse."

Although a natural mother in New York has many parental rights without adopting her child, New York courts have held that § 110 provides for the adoption of an illegitimate child by his mother. See In re Anonymous Adoption, 177 Misc. 683, 31 N.Y.S.2d 595 (App.Div.1941).

The New York Supreme Court, Appellant Division, affirmed. It stated that appellant's constitutional challenge to § 111 was foreclosed by the New York Court of Appeals' decision in In re Malpica-Orsini, 36 N.Y.2d 568, 370 N.Y.S.2d 511, 331 N.E.2d 486, app. dismissed for want of a substantial federal question sub nom. Orsini v. Blasi, 423 U.S. 1042, 96 S.Ct. 765, 46 L.Ed.2d 642 (1977). The New York Court of Appeals similarly affirmed *   *   *.

On appeal to this Court appellant presses two claims. First, he argues that the distinction drawn under New York law between the adoption rights of an unwed father and those of other parents violates the Equal Protection Clause of the Fourteenth Amendment. Second, appellant contends that this Court's decision in Quilloin v. Walcott, 434 U.S. 246, 98 S.Ct. 549, 54 L.Ed.2d 511 (1978), recognized the due process right of natural fathers to maintain a parental relationship with their children absent a finding that they are unfit as parents.[3]

II

Section 111 of the New York Domestic Relations Law provides in part that:

"consent to adoption shall be required as follows: *   *   *   (b) Of the parents or surviving parent, whether adult or infant, of a child born in wedlock; [and] (c) Of the mother, whether adult or infant, of a child born out of wedlock. *   *   *" N.Y.Dom.Rel.Law § 111.

The statute makes parental consent unnecessary, however, in certain cases, including those where the parent has abandoned or relinquished his or her rights in the child or has been adjudicated incompetent to care for the child.[4] Absent one of these circumstances, an

---

3. As the appellant was given due notice and was permitted to participate as a party in the adoption proceedings, he does not contend that he was denied the procedural due process held to be requisite in Stanley v. Illinois, 405 U.S. 645, 92 S.Ct. 1208, 31 L.Ed.2d 551 (1972).

4. At the time of the proceedings before the Surrogate, § 111 as amended by 1975 N.Y. Laws, chs. 246 and 704, provided:

"Subject to the limitations hereinafter set forth consent to adoption shall be required as follows:

"1. Of the adoptive child, if over fourteen years of age, unless the judge or surrogate in his discretion dispenses with such consent;

"2. Of the parents or surviving parent, whether adult or infant, of a child born in wedlock;

"3. Of the mother, whether adult or infant, of a child born out of wedlock;

"4. Of any person or authorized agency having lawful custody of the adoptive child.

"The consent shall not be required of a parent who has abandoned the child or who has surrendered the child to an authorized agency for the purpose of adoption under the provisions of the social services law or of a parent for whose child a guardian has been appointed under the provisions of section three hundred eighty-four of the social services law or who has been deprived of civil rights or who is insane or who has been judicially declared incompetent or who is mentally retarded as defined by the Mental Hygiene Law or who has been adjudged to be an habitual drunkard or who has been

unwed mother has the authority under New York law to block the adoption of her child simply by withholding consent. The unwed father has no similar control over the fate of his child, even when his parental relationship is substantial—as in this case. He may prevent the termination of his parental rights only by showing that the best interests of the child would not permit the child's adoption by the petitioning couple.

* * *

III

Gender-based distinctions "must serve governmental objectives and must be substantially related to achievement of those objectives" in order to withstand judicial scrutiny under the Equal Protection Clause. The question before us, therefore, is whether the distinction in § 111 between unmarried mothers and unmarried fathers bears a substantial relation to some important state interest. Appellees assert that the distinction is justified by a fundamental difference between maternal and paternal relations—that "a natural mother, absent special circumstances, bears a closer relationship with her child * * * than a father does." Tr. of Oral Arg., at 41.

Contrary to appellees' argument and to the apparent presumption underlying § 111, maternal and paternal roles are not invariably different in importance. Even if unwed mothers as a class were closer than unwed fathers to their newborn infants, this generalization concerning parent-child relations would become less acceptable as a basis for legislative distinctions as the age of the child increased.

judicially deprived of the custody of the child on account of cruelty or neglect, or pursuant to a judicial finding that the child is a permanently neglected child as defined in section six hundred eleven of the family court act of the state of New York; except that notice of the proposed adoption shall be given in such manner as the judge or surrogate may direct and an opportunity to be heard thereon may be afforded to a parent who has been deprived of civil rights and to a parent if the judge or surrogate so orders. Notwithstanding any other provision of law, neither the notice of a proposed adoption nor any process in such proceeding shall be required to contain the name of the person or persons seeking to adopt the child. For the purposes of this section, evidence of insubstantial and infrequent contacts by a parent with his or her child shall not, of itself, be sufficient as a matter of law to preclude a finding that such parent has abandoned such child.

"Where the adoptive child is over the age of eighteen years the consents specified in subdivisions two and three of this section shall not be required, and the judge or surrogate in his discretion may direct that the consent specified in subdivision four of this section shall not be required if in his opinion the moral and temporal interests of the adoptive child will be promoted by the adoption and such consent cannot for any reason be obtained.

"An adoptive child who has once been lawfully adopted may be readopted directly from such child's adoptive parents in the same manner as from its natural parents. In such case the consent of such natural parent shall not be required but the judge or surrogate in his discretion may require that notice be given to the natural parents in such manner as he may prescribe."

The present case demonstrates that an unwed father may have a relationship with his children fully comparable to that of the mother. Appellant Caban, appellee Maria Mohammed, and their two children lived together as a natural family for several years. As members of his family, both mother and father participated in the care and support of their children.[7] There is no reason to believe that the Caban children—aged 4 and 6 at the time of the adoption proceedings—had a relationship with their mother unrivaled by the affection and concern of their father. We reject, therefore, the claim that the broad, gender-based distinction of § 111 is required by any universal difference between maternal and paternal relations at every phase of a child's development.

As an alternative justification for § 111, appellees argue that the distinction between unwed fathers and unwed mothers is substantially related to the State's interest in promoting the adoption of illegitimate children. Although the legislative history of § 111 is sparse, in In re Malpica-Orsini, supra, the New York Court of Appeals identified as the legislature's purpose in enacting § 111 the furthering of the interests of illegitimate children, for whom adoption often is the best course.[9] The court concluded that,

"[t]o require the consent of fathers of children born out of wedlock * * *, or even some of them, would have the overall effect of denying homes to the homeless and of depriving innocent children of the other blessings of adoption. The cruel and undeserved out-of-wedlock stigma would continue its visitations. At the very least, the worthy process of adoption would be severely impeded." Id., 36 N.Y. 2d, at 572, 370 N.Y.S.2d, at 516, 331 N.E.2d, at 489.

---

7. In rejecting an unmarried father's constitutional claim in Quilloin v. Walcott, 434 U.S. 246, 98 S.Ct. 549, 54 L.Ed.2d 511 (1978), we emphasized the importance of the appellant's failure to act as a father toward his children, noting that he,

"* * * has never exercised actual or legal custody over his child, and thus has never shouldered any significant responsibility with respect to the daily supervision, education, protection, or care of the child. Appellant does not complain of his exemption from these responsibilities and, indeed, he does not even now seek custody of his child." Id., at 256, 98 S.Ct., at 555.

In *Quilloin* we expressly reserved the question whether the Georgia statute similar to § 111 of the New York Domestic Relations Law unconstitutionally distinguished unwed parents according to their gender, as the claim was not properly presented. See 434 U.S., at 253 n. 13, 98 S.Ct., at 554.

9. In Orsini v. Blasi, supra, the Court dismissed an appeal from the New York Court of Appeals challenging the constitutionality of § 111 as applied to an unmarried father whose child had been ordered adopted by a New York Surrogate. In dismissing the appeal, we indicated that a substantial federal question was lacking. This was a ruling on the merits, and therefore is entitled to precedential weight. At the same time, however, our decision not to review fully the questions presented in Orsini v. Blasi is not entitled to the same deference given a ruling after briefing, argument, and a written opinion. Insofar as our decision today is inconsistent with our dismissal in *Orsini,* we overrule our prior decision.

The court reasoned that people wishing to adopt a child born out of wedlock would be discouraged, if the natural father could prevent the adoption by the mere withholding of his consent. Indeed, the court went so far as to suggest that "[m]arriages would be discouraged because of the reluctance of prospective husbands to involve themselves in a family situation where they might only be a foster parent and could not adopt the mother's offspring." Id., at 573, 370 N.Y.S.2d, at 517, 331 N.E.2d, at 490. Finally, the court noted that if unwed fathers' consent were required before adoption could take place, in many instances the adoption would have to be delayed or eliminated altogether, because of the unavailability of the natural father.

The State's interest in providing for the well-being of illegitimate children is an important one. We do not question that the best interests of such children often may require their adoption into new families who will give them the stability of a normal, two-parent home. Moreover, adoption will remove the stigma under which illegitimate children suffer. But the unquestioned right of the State to further these desirable ends by legislation is not in itself sufficient to justify the gender-based distinction of § 111. Rather, under the relevant cases applying the Equal Protection Clause it must be shown that the distinction is structured reasonably to further these ends. As we repeated in Reed v. Reed, supra, 404 U.S., at 76, 92 S.Ct., at 254, such a statutory "classification 'must be reasonable, not arbitrary, and must rest on some ground of difference having a fair and substantial relation to the object of the legislation, so that all persons similarly circumstanced shall be treated alike.'"

We find that the distinction in § 111 between unmarried mothers and unmarried fathers, as illustrated by this case, does not bear a substantial relation to the State's interest in providing adoptive homes for its illegitimate children. It may be that, given the opportunity, some unwed fathers would prevent the adoption of their illegitimate children. This impediment to adoption usually is a result of a natural parental interest shared by both genders alike; it is not a manifestation of any profound difference between the affection and concern of mothers and fathers for their children. Neither the State nor the appellees have argued that unwed fathers are more likely to object to the adoption of their children than are unwed mothers; nor is there any self-evident reason why as a class they would be.

The New York Court of Appeals in In re Malpica-Orsini, supra, suggested that the requiring of unmarried fathers' consent for adoption would pose a strong impediment for adoption because often it is impossible to locate unwed fathers when adoption proceedings are brought, whereas mothers are more likely to remain with their children. Even if the special difficulties attendant upon locating and identifying unwed fathers at birth would justify a legislative distinction between mothers and fathers of newborns,[11] these difficulties need not persist past infancy. When the adoption of an older child is sought, the State's interest in proceeding with adoption cases can be protected by means that do not draw such an inflexible gender-based distinction as that made in § 111.[12] In those cases where the father never has come forward to participate in the rearing of his child, nothing in the Equal Protection Clause precludes the State from withholding from him the privilege of vetoing the adoption of that child. Indeed, under the statute as it now stands the Surrogate may proceed in the absence of consent when the parent whose consent otherwise would be required never has come forward or has abandoned the child.[13] But in cases such as this, where the father has established a substantial relationship with the child and has admitted his paternity,[14] a State should have no difficulty in identifying the father even of children born out of wedlock.[15] Thus, no showing has been

11. Because the question is not before us, we express no view whether such difficulties would justify a statute addressed particularly to newborn adoptions, setting forth more stringent requirements concerning the acknowledgment of paternity or a stricter definition of abandonment.

12. See Comment, The Emerging Constitutional Protection of the Putative Father's Parental Rights, 70 Mich.L. Rev. 1581, 1590 (1972).

13. If the New York Court of Appeals is correct that unmarried fathers often desert their families (a view we need not question), then allowing those fathers who remain with their families a right to object to the termination of their parental rights will pose little threat to the State's ability to order adoption in most cases. For we do not question a State's right to do what New York has done in this portion of § 111: provide that fathers who have abandoned their children have no right to block adoption of those children.

We do not suggest, of course, that the provision of § 111 making parental consent unnecessary in cases of abandonment is the only constitutional mechanism available to New York for the protection of its interest in allowing the adoption of illegitimate children when their natural fathers are not available to be consulted. In reviewing the constitutionality of statutory classifications, "it is not the function of a court 'to hypothesize independently on the desirability or

feasibility of any possible alternative[s]' to the statutory scheme formulated by [the State]." Lalli v. Lalli, 439 U.S. 259, 274–276, 99 S.Ct. 518, 528, 58 L.Ed.2d 503 (1978) (quoting Mathews v. Lucas, 427 U.S. 495, 515, 96 S.Ct. 2755, 2767, 49 L.Ed.2d 651 (1976)). We note some alternatives to the gender-based distinction of § 111 only to emphasize that the state interests asserted in support of the statutory classification could be protected through numerous other mechanisms more closely attuned to those interests.

14. In Quilloin v. Walcott, supra, we noted the importance in cases of this kind of the relationship that in fact exists between the parent and child. See n. 8, supra.

15. States have a legitimate interest, of course, in providing that an unmarried father's right to object to the adoption of a child will be conditioned upon his showing that it is in fact his child. Cf. Lalli v. Lalli, 439 U.S. 259, 266–268, 99 S.Ct. 518, 524, 58 L.Ed.2d 503 (1978). Such is not, however, the import of the New York statute here. Although New York provides for actions in its Family Courts to establish paternity, see §§ 511 to 571 of the New York Judiciary Court Acts, there is no provision allowing men who have been determined by the court to be the father of a child born out of wedlock to object to the adoption of their children under § 111.

made that the different treatment afforded unmarried fathers and unmarried mothers under § 111 bears a substantial relationship to the proclaimed interest of the State in promoting the adoption of illegitimate children.

In sum, we believe that § 111 is another example of "overbroad generalizations" in gender-based classifications. The effect of New York's classification is to discriminate against unwed fathers even when their identity is known and they have manifested a significant paternal interest in the child. The facts of this case illustrate the harshness of classifying unwed fathers as being invariably less qualified and entitled than mothers to exercise a concerned judgment as to the fate of their children. Section 111 both excludes some loving fathers from full participation in the decision whether their children will be adopted and, at the same time, enables some alienated mothers arbitrarily to cut off the paternal rights of fathers. We conclude that this undifferentiated distinction between unwed mothers and unwed fathers, applicable in all circumstances where adoption of a child of theirs is at issue, does not bear a substantial relationship to the State's asserted interests.[16]

The judgment of the New York Court of Appeals is

Reversed.

*   *   *

Mr. Justice STEVENS, with whom The CHIEF JUSTICE and Mr. Justice REHNQUIST join, dissenting.

Under § 111(1)(c) of the New York Domestic Relations Law, the adoption of a child born out of wedlock usually requires the consent of the natural mother; it does not require that of the natural father unless he has "lawful custody." Appellant, the natural but noncustodial father of two school-aged children born out of wedlock,[1] challenges that provision insofar as it allows the adoption of his natural children by the husband of the natural mother without his consent. Appellant's primary objection is that this unconsented-to termination of his parental rights without proof of unfitness on his part violates the substantive component of the Due Process Clause of the

---

16. Appellant also challenges the constitutionality of the distinction made in § 111 between married and unmarried fathers. As we have resolved that the sex-based distinction of § 111 violates the Equal Protection Clause, we need express no view as to the validity of this additional classification.

Finally, appellant argues that he was denied substantive due process when the New York courts terminated his parental rights without first finding him to be unfit to be a parent. See Stanley v. Illinois, 405 U.S. 645, 92 S.Ct. 1208, 31 L.Ed.2d 551 (1972) (semble). Because we have ruled that the New York statute is unconstitutional under the Equal Protection Clause, we similarly express no view as to whether a State is constitutionally barred from ordering adoption in the absence of a determination that the parent whose rights are being terminated is unfit.

1. The children are presently aged seven and eight years old. At the time of the hearing before the Surrogate Court, they were five and six.

Fourteenth Amendment. Secondarily, he attacks § 111(1)(c)'s disparate treatment of natural mothers and natural fathers as a violation of the Equal Protection Clause of the same Amendment.

* * *

I

This case concerns the validity of rules affecting the status of the thousands of children who are born out of wedlock every day.[2] All of these children have an interest in acquiring the status of legitimacy; a great many of them have an interest in being adopted by parents who can give them opportunities that would otherwise be denied; for some the basic necessities of life are at stake. The state interest in facilitating adoption in appropriate cases is strong—perhaps even "compelling." [3]

Nevertheless, it is also true that § 111(1)(c) gives rights to natural mothers that it withholds from natural fathers. Because it draws this gender-based distinction between two classes of citizens who have an equal right to fair and impartial treatment by their government, it is necessary to determine whether there are differences between the members of the two classes that provide a justification for treating them differently.[5] That determination requires more

2. Illegitimate births accounted for an estimated 14.7% and 15.5% of all births in the United States during the years 1976 and 1977, respectively. See National Center for Health Statistics of the Department of Health, Education, and Welfare, Monthly Vital Statistics Report, February 5, 1979, at 19; id., March 29, 1978, at 17. In total births, this represents 468,100 and 515,700 illegitimate births, respectively. Although statistics for New York State are not available, the problem of illegitimacy appears to be especially severe in urban areas. For example, in 1975, over 50% of all births in the District of Columbia were out of wedlock. National Center for Health Statistics of the Department of Health, Education, and Welfare, I Vital Statistics of the United States (Natality), 1975, at 50.

Adoption is an important solution to the problem of illegitimacy. Thus, about 70% of the adoptions in the 34 States reporting to HEW in 1975 were of children born out of wedlock. The figure for New York State was 78%. National Center for Social Statistics of the Department of Health, Education, and Welfare, Adoptions in 1975, at 11 (hereinafter Adoptions in 1975).

3. The reason I say "perhaps" is that the word "compelling" can be understood in different ways. If it describes an interest that "compels" a conclusion that any statute intended to foster that interest is automatically constitutional, few if any interests would fit that description. On the other hand, if it merely describes an interest that compels a court, before holding a law unconstitutional, to give thoughtful attention to a legislative judgment that the law will serve that interest, then the State's interest in facilitating adoption in appropriate cases, is unquestionably compelling.

5. Section 111 treats illegitimate children somewhat differently from legitimate ones insofar as the former, but not the latter, may be removed from one or both of their natural parents and placed in an adoptive home without the consent of *both* parents. Nonetheless, appellant has not challenged the statute on this basis either on his or his children's behalf, and the difficult questions that might be raised by such a challenge, compare Lalli v. Lalli, 439 U.S. 259, 99 S.Ct. 518, 58 L.Ed.2d 503, with Trimble v. Gordon, 430 U.S. 762, 97 S.Ct. 1459, 52 L.Ed.2d 31, are not now before us.

than merely recognizing that society has traditionally treated the two classes differently. But it also requires analysis that goes beyond a merely reflexive rejection of gender-based distinctions.

Men and women are different, and the difference is relevant to the question whether the mother may be given the exclusive right to consent to the adoption of a child born out of wedlock. Because most adoptions involve newborn infants or very young children,[7] it is appropriate at the outset to focus on the significance of the difference in such cases.

Both parents are equally responsible for the conception of the child out of wedlock. But from that point on through pregnancy and infancy, the differences between the male and the female have an important impact on the child's destiny. Only the mother carries the child; it is she who has the constitutional right to decide whether to bear it or not. In many cases, only the mother knows who sired the child, and it will often be within her power to withhold that fact, and even the fact of her pregnancy, from that person. If during pregnancy the mother should marry a different partner, the child will be legitimate when born, and the natural father may never even know that his "rights" have been affected. On the other hand, only if the natural mother agrees to marry the natural father during that period can the latter's actions have a positive impact on the status of the child; if he instead should marry a different partner during that time, the only effect on the child is negative, for the likelihood of legitimacy will be lessened.

These differences continue at birth and immediately thereafter. During that period, the mother and child are together;[10] the mother's identity is known with certainty. The father, on the other hand, may or may not be present; his identity may be unknown to the world and may even be uncertain to the mother. These natural dif-

---

7. The relevant statistics for New York are not complete. The most comprehensive ones that we have found are for the years 1974 and 1975. Even for those years, however, we could find none that includes a breakdown by age of the adoptive children where one of the adoptive parents is in some way related to the child. (New York adoptions by related parents—including ones by relatives other than a natural parent and step-parent—accounted for just over half of all adoptions in 1974 and just under half in 1975.) Nonetheless, of the children adopted by unrelated parents in New York in 1974 and 1975, respectively, 66% and 62% were under one year old, and 90% and 88% were under six years old. In 1974, moreover, the median age of the child at the time of adoption was five months; no similar figure is available for 1975. New York's figures appear to be fairly close to those obtaining nationally. Adoptions in 1974, supra, at 15–16; Adoptions in 1975, supra, at 15.

10. In fact, there is some sociological and anthropological research indicating that by virtue of the symbiotic relationship between mother and child during pregnancy and the initial contact between mother and child directly after birth a physical and psychological bond immediately develops between the two that is not then present between the infant and the father or any other person. E. g., J. Bowlby, Attachment and Loss, Vols. I, II (19—); M. Mahler, The Psychological Development of the Human Infant (1976).

ferences between married fathers and mothers make it probable that the mother, and not the father or both parents will have custody of the newborn infant.[12]

In short, it is virtually inevitable that from conception through infancy the mother will constantly be faced with decisions about how best to care for the child, whereas it is much less certain that the father will be confronted with comparable problems. There no doubt are cases in which the relationship of the parties at birth makes it appropriate for the State to give the father a voice of some sort in the adoption decision.[13] But as a matter of equal protection analysis,

---

12. Although statistics are hard to find in this area, those I have found bear out the proposition that is developed in text as a logical matter. Thus, in "relinquishment adoptions" in California in 1975, natural mothers signed the "relinquishment" documents—papers that release custody of the child to an adoption agency and that must be signed by the parent(s) with custody, or by a judge in cases involving neglect or abandonment by the parent(s) who previously had custody—in 70% of the cases, while natural fathers did so in only 36% of the cases. On the other hand, fathers took no part in over 27% of the relinquishment adoptions, apparently because they never had custody, while the comparable figure for mothers was 3.5%. California Health and Welfare Agency, Relinquishment Adoptions in California, January-December 1975, at Tables 12 and 13.

13. Cf. Part II, infra. Indeed, New York does give unwed fathers ample opportunity to participate in adoption proceedings. In this case, for example, appellant appeared at the adoption hearing with counsel, presented testimony, and was allowed to cross-examine the witnesses offered by appellees. See N.Y.Dom.Rel.L. § 111–a; App., at 27; ante, at 1763–1764. As a substantive matter, the natural father is free to demonstrate, as appellant unsuccessfully tried to do in this case, that the best interests of the child favor the preservation of existing parental rights and forestall cutting off those rights by way of adoption. Had appellant been able to make that demonstration, the result would have been the same as that mandated by the Court's insistence upon paternal as well as maternal consent in these circumstances: neither parent could adopt the child into

a new family with a stepparent; both would have parental rights (e. g., visitation); and custody would be determined by the child's best interests.

In this case, although the New York courts made no finding of unfitness on appellant's part, there was ample evidence in the record from which they could draw the conclusion that his relationship with the children had been somewhat intermittent, that it fell far short of the relationship existing between the mother and the children (whether measured by the amount of time spent with the children, and responsibility taken for their care and education, or the amount of resources expended on them), and that judging from appellant's treatment of his first wife and his children by that marriage, there was a real possibility that he could not be counted on for the continued support of the two children and might well be a source of friction between them, the mother, and her new husband. E. g., App., at 22, 25; Transcript of Proceedings in Record on Appeal before the New York Court of Appeals, at 74–77, 82–90, 106, 120, 140, 388–393, 414–415, 420–421.

That conclusion, coupled with Surrogate's finding that the mother's marriage to the adoptive father was "solid and permanent" and that the children were "well cared for and healthy" in the new family, App., at 30, surely justify the Surrogate's ultimate conclusion that the legitimacy and stability to be gained by the children from the adoption far outweighed their loss (and even appellant's) due to the termination of appellant's parental rights. See App., at 28: "Whatever the motive for [appellant's] opposition to the adoption, it is perfectly obvious that at the time and immediately after a child is born out of wedlock differences between men and women justify some differential treatment of the mother and father in the adoption process.

Most particularly, these differences justify a rule that gives the mother of the new born infant the exclusive right to consent to its adoption. Such a rule gives the mother, in whose sole charge the infant is often placed anyway, the maximum flexibility in deciding how best to care for the child. It also gives the loving father an incentive to marry the mother,[14] and has no adverse impact on the disinterested father. Finally, it facilitates the interests of the adoptive parents, the child, and the public at large by streamlining the often traumatic adoption process and allowing the prompt, complete and reliable integration of the child into a satisfactory new home at as young an age as is feasible.[15] Put most simply, it permits the maximum participation of interested natural parents without so burdening the adoption process that its attractiveness to potential adoptive parents is destroyed.

This conclusion is borne out by considering the alternative rule proposed by appellant. If the State were to require the consent of both parents, or some kind of hearing to explain why either's consent is unnecessary or unobtainable,[16] it would unquestionably complicate and delay the adoption process. Most importantly, such a rule would remove the mother's freedom of choice in her own and the child's behalf without also relieving her of the unshakable responsibility for the care of the child. Furthermore, questions relating to the adequacy of notice to absent fathers could invade the mother's privacy,[17]

the consequences are the same—harassment of the natural mother in her new relationship and embarrassment to [the children] who though living with and being supported in the new family may not in school and elsewhere bear the family name."

14. Marrying the mother would not only legitimate the child but would also assure the father the right to consent to any adoption. See N.Y. Dom.Rel.L. § 111(1)(b).

15. These are not idle interests. A survey of adoptive parents registered on the New York State Adoption Exchange as of January 1975 showed that over 75% preferred to adopt children under three years old; over half preferred children under one year old. New York Department of Social Services, Adoption in New York State (Program Analysis Report No. 59, July 1975), at 20. Moreover, adoption proceedings, even when judicial in nature,

have traditionally been expeditious in order to accommodate the needs of all concerned. Thus, 61% of all Family Court adoption proceedings in New York during the fiscal year 1972–1973 were disposed of within 90 days. Nineteenth Annual Report of the Judicial Conference to the Governor of the State of New York and the Legislature, at 352.

16. Although the Court is careful to leave the States free to develop alternative approaches, it nonetheless endorses the procedure described in text for adoptions of older children against the wishes of natural fathers who have established substantial relationships with the children. Ante, at 1768–1769, and n. 12.

17. To be effective, any such notice would probably have to name the mother and perhaps even identify her further, for example by address. Moreover, the terms and placement cause the adopting parents to doubt the reliability of the new relationship, and add to the expense and time required to conclude what is now usually a simple and certain process. While it might not be irrational for a State to conclude that these costs should be incurred to protect the interest of natural fathers, it is nevertheless plain that those costs, which are largely the result of differences between the mother and the father, establish an imposing justification for *some* differential treatment of the two sexes in this type of situation.

With this much the Court does not disagree; it confines its holding to cases such as the one at hand involving the adoption of an *older* child against the wishes of a natural father who previously has participated in the rearing of the child and who admits paternity. Ante, at 1768–1769. The Court does conclude, however, that the gender basis for the classification drown [sic] by § 111(1)(c) makes differential treatment so suspect that the State has the burden not only of showing that the rule is generally justified but also that the justification holds equally true for *all* persons disadvantaged by the rule. In its view, since the justification is not as strong for some indeterminately small part of the disadvantaged class as it is for the class as a whole, see id., at 1768, the rule is invalid under the Equal Protection Clause insofar as it applies to that subclass. With this conclusion I disagree.

If we assume, as we surely must, that characteristics possessed by all members of one class and by no members of the other class justify some disparate treatment of mothers and fathers of children born out of wedlock, the mere fact that the statute draws a "gender-based distinction," see id., at 1766, should not, in my opinion, give rise to any presumption that the impartiality principle embodied in the Equal Protection Clause has been violated. Indeed, if we make the further undisputed assumption that the discrimination is justified in those cases in which the rule has its most frequent application—cases involving newborn infants and very young children in the custody of their natural mothers, see [n. 7] supra—we should presume that the law is entirely valid and require the challenger to demonstrate that its unjust applications are sufficiently numerous and serious to render it invalid.

In this case, appellant made no such showing; his demonstration of unfairness, assuming he has made one, extends only to himself and by implication to the unknown number of fathers just like him. Further, while appellant did nothing to inform the New York courts about the size of his subclass and the overall degree of its disadvantage under § 111(1)(c), the New York Court of Appeals has previ-

of the notice in, for example, a newspaper, no matter how discreet and tastefully chosen, would inevitably be taken by the public as an announcement of illegitimate maternity. To avoid the embarrassment of such announcements, the mother might well be forced to identify the father (or potential fathers)—despite her desire to keep that fact a secret.

ously concluded that the subclass is small and its disadvantage insignificant by comparison to the benefits of the rule as it now stands.[20]

20. "To require the consent of fathers of children born out of wedlock * * * or even some of them, would have the overall effect of denying homes to the homeless and of depriving innocent children of the other blessings of adoption. The cruel and undeserved out-of-wedlock stigma would continue its visitations. At the very least, the worthy process of adoption would be severely impeded.

"Great difficulty and expense would be encountered, in many instances, in locating the putative father to ascertain his willingness to consent. Frequently, he is unlocatable or even unknown. Paternity is denied more often than admitted. Some birth certificates set forth the names of the reputed fathers, others do not.

"Couples considering adoptions will be dissuaded out of fear of subsequent annoyance and entanglements. A 1961 study in Florida of 500 independent adoptions showed that 16% of the couples who had direct contact with the natural parents reported subsequent harassment, compared with only 2% of couples who had no contact (Isaac, Adopting a Child Today, pp. 38, 116). The burden on charitable agencies will be oppressive. In independent placements, the baby is usually placed in his adoptive home at four or five days of age, while the majority of agencies do not place children for several months after birth (p. 88). Early private placements are made for a variety of reasons, such as a desire to decrease the trauma of separation and an attempt to conceal the out-of-wedlock birth. It is unlikely that the consent of the natural father could be obtained at such an early time after birth, and married couples, if well advised, would not accept a child, if the father's consent was a legal requisite and not then available. Institutions such as foundling homes which nurture the children for months could not afford to continue their maintenance, in itself not the most desirable, if fathers' consents are unobtainable and the wards therefore unplaceable. These philanthropic agencies would be reluctant to take

infants for no one wants to bargain for trouble in an already tense situation. The drain on the public treasury would also be immeasurably greater in regard to infants placed in foster homes and institutions by public agencies.

"Some of the ugliest disclosures of our time involve black marketing of children for adoption. One need not be a clairvoyant to predict that the grant to unwed fathers of the right to veto adoptions will provide a very fertile field for extortion. The vast majority of instances where paternity has been established arise out of filiation proceedings, compulsory in nature, and persons experienced in the field indicate that these legal steps are instigated for the most part by public authorities, anxious to protect the public purse (see Schaschlo v. Taishoff, 2 N.Y.2d 408, 411 [161 N.Y.S.2d 48, 50, 141 N.E.2d 562, 563 (1957)]). While it may appear, at first blush, that a father might wish to free himself of the burden of support, there will be many who will interpret it as a chance for revenge or an opportunity to recoup their 'losses.'

"Marriages would be discouraged because of the reluctance of prospective husbands to involve themselves in a family situation where they might only be a foster parent and could not adopt the mother's offspring.

"We should be mindful of the jeopardy to which existing adoptions would be subjected and the resulting chaos by an unadulterated declaration of unconstitutionality. Even if there be a holding of nonretroactivity, the welfare of children, placed in homes months ago, or longer, and awaiting the institution or completion of legal proceedings, would be seriously affected. The attendant trauma is unpleasant to envision." In re Malpica-Orsini, supra, 36 N.Y.2d, at 572–574, 370 N.Y.S.2d, at 516–17, 331 N.E.2d, at 489–90.

To the limited extent that the Court takes cognizance of these findings and conclusions, it does not dispute them. Ante, at 1768, n. 12. Instead, the Court merely states that many of

The mere fact that an otherwise valid general classification appears arbitrary in an isolated case is not a sufficient reason for invalidating the entire rule. Nor, indeed, is it a sufficient reason for concluding that the application of a valid rule in a hard case constitutes a violation of equal protection principles. We cannot test the conformance of rules to the principle of equality simply by reference to exceptional cases.

Moreover, I am not at all sure that § 111(1)(c) is arbitrary even if viewed solely in the light of the exceptional circumstances presently before the Court. This case involves a dispute between natural parents over which of the two may adopt the children. If both are given a veto, as the Court requires, neither may adopt and the children will remain illegitimate. If, instead of a gender-based distinction, the veto were given to the parent having custody of the child, the mother would prevail just as she did in the state court.[23] Whether or not it is wise to devise a special rule to protect the natural father who (a) has a substantial relationship with his child, and (b) wants to veto an adoption that a court has been found to be in the best interest of the child, the record in this case does not demonstrate that the Equal Protection Clause requires such a rule.

I have no way of knowing how often disputes between natural parents over adoption of their children arise after the father "has es-

these findings do not reflect appellant's situation and "need not" reflect the situation of any natural father who is seeking to prevent the adoption of his older children. Id., at 1768.

Although I agree that the findings of the New York Court of Appeals are more likely to be true of the strong majority of adoptions that involve infants than they are in the present situation (a conclusion that should be sufficient to justify the classification drawn by § 111(1)(c) in *all* situations), I am compelled to point out that the Court marshals not one bit of evidence to bolster its impirical judgment that most natural fathers facing the adoption of their older children will have appellant's relatively exemplary record with respect to admitting paternity and establishing a relationship with his children. In my mind, it is far more likely that what is true at infancy will be true thereafter—the mother will probably retain custody as well as the primary responsibility for the care and upbringing of the child.

23. In fact, although the Court understands it differently the New York statute apparently *does* turn consent rights on custody. Thus, § 111(1)(d) gives consent rights to "any person * * * having lawful custody of the adoptive child." The New York courts have not had occasion to interpret this section in a situation in which a custodial father is seeking consent rights adverse to the wishes of the mother. Nonetheless, those courts have interpreted "legal custody" in a flexible and practical manner dependent on who actually is acting as the guardian of the child, e. g., In re Ehrhardt, 27 A.D.2d 836, 277 N.Y.S.2d 734 (1967). Moreover, the Uniform Adoption Act, after which the New York statute appears to be patterned, has a similar section that its drafters intended to benefit "a father having custody of his illegitimate minor child." Uniform Adoption Act, § 5(a)(3) Commissioners' Note. In this light, the allegedly improper impact of the gender-based classification in § 111(1)(c) as challenged by appellant is even more attenuated than I have suggested because it only disqualifies those few natural fathers of older children who have established a substantial relationship with the child, have admitted paternity, and who nonetheless do not have custody of the children.

tablished a substantial relationship with the child and [is willing to admit] his paternity," ante, at 1769, but has previously been unwilling to take steps to legitimate his relationship. I am inclined to believe that such cases are relatively rare. But whether or not this assumption is valid, the far surer assumption is that in the more common adoption situations, the mother will be the more, and often the only, responsible parent, and that a paternal consent requirement will constitute a hinderance to the adoption process. Because this general rule is amply justified in its normal application, I would therefore require the party challenging its constitutionality to make some demonstration of unfairness in a significant number of situations before concluding that it violates the Equal Protection Clause. That the Court has found a violation without requiring such a showing can only be attributed to its own "stereotyped reaction" to what is unquestionably, but in this case justifiably, a gender-based distinction.

II

Although the substantive due process issue is more troublesome, I can briefly state the reason why I reject it.

I assume that, if and when one develops, the relationship between a father and his natural child is entitled to protection against arbitrary state action as a matter of due process. See Stanley v. Illinois, 405 U.S. 645, 651, 92 S.Ct. 1208, 1212, 31 L.Ed.2d 551. Although the Court has not decided whether the Due Process Clause provides any greater substantive protection for this relationship than simply against official caprice,[27] it has indicated that an adoption decree that terminates the relationship is constitutionally justified by a finding that the father has abandoned or mistreated the child. In my view, such a decree may also be justified by a finding that the adoption will serve the best interests of the child, at least in a situation such as this in which the natural family unit has already been destroyed, the father has previously taken no steps to legitimate the child and a further requirement such as a showing of unfitness would entirely deprive the child—and the State—of the benefits of adoption and legitimation.[28] As a matter of legislative policy, it can be argued

27. Although some Members of the Court have concluded that greater protection is due the "private realm of *family* life," Prince v. Massachusetts, 321 U.S. 158, 166, 64 S.Ct. 438, 442, 88 L.Ed. 645 (emphasis added), e. g., Moore v. East Cleveland, 431 U.S. 494, 97 S.Ct. 1932, 52 L.Ed.2d 531 (plurality opinion), this appeal does not fall within that realm because whatever family life once surrounded appellant, his children, and appellee Maria Mohammed has long since dissolved through no fault of the State's. In fact, it is the State, rather than appellant, that may rely in this case on the importance of the family insofar as it is the State that is attempting to foster the establishment and privacy of new and legitimate adoptive families.

28. See Parham v. Hughes, 441 U.S. 347, 351–353, 99 S.Ct. 1742, 1746, 60 L. Ed.2d 269. Cf. Quilloin v. Walcott, supra, 434 U.S., at 255, 98 S.Ct., at 555, quoting Smith v. Organization of Foster Families, supra, 431 U.S., at 862–863, 97 S.Ct., at 2119 (STEWART, J., concurring in judgment).

that the latter reason standing alone is insufficient to sever the bonds that have developed between father and child. But that reason surely avoids the conclusion that the order is arbitrary, and is also sufficient to overcome any further protection of those bonds that may exist in the recesses of the Due Process Clause. Although the constitutional principle at least requires a legitimate and relevant reason and, in these circumstances, perhaps even a substantial reason, it does not require the reason to be one that a judge would accept if he were a legislator.

III

There is often the risk that the arguments one advances in dissent may give rise to a broader reading of the Court's opinion than is appropriate. That risk is especially grave when the Court is embarking on a new course that threatens to interfere with social arrangements that have come into use over long periods of time. Because I consider the course on which the Court is currently embarked to be potentially most serious, I shall explain why I regard its holding in this case as quite narrow.

The adoption decrees that have been entered without the consent of the natural father must number in the millions. An untold number of family and financial decisions have been made in reliance on the validity of those decrees. Because the Court has crossed a new constitutional frontier with today's decision, those reliance interests unquestionably foreclose retroactive application of this ruling. See Chevron Oil Co. v. Huson, 404 U.S. 97, 106–107, 92 S.Ct. 349, 355–356, 30 L.Ed.2d 296. Families that include adopted children need have no concern about the probable impact of this case on their familial security.

Nor is there any reason why the decision should affect the processing of most future adoptions. The fact that an unusual application of a state statute has been held unconstitutional on equal protection grounds does not necessarily eliminate the entire statute as a basis for future legitimate state action. The procedure to be followed in cases involving infants who are in the custody of their mothers— whether solely or jointly with the father—or of agencies with authority to consent to adoption, is entirely unaffected by the Court's holding or by its reasoning. In fact, as I read the Court's opinion, the statutes now in effect may be enforced as usual unless "the adoption of older children is sought," and "the father has established a substantial relationship with the child and [is willing to admit] his paternity." State legislatures will no doubt promptly revise their adoption laws to comply with the rule of this case, but as long as state courts are prepared to construe their existing statutes to contain a requirement of paternal consent "in cases such as this," I see no reason why they may not continue to enter valid adoption decrees in the countless routine cases that will arise before the statutes can be amended.[29]

In short, this is an exceptional case that should have no effect on the typical adoption proceeding. Indeed, I suspect that it will affect only a tiny fraction of the cases covered by the statutes that must now be rewritten. Accordingly, although my disagreement with the Court is as profound as that fraction is small, I am confident that the wisdom of judges will forestall any widespread harm.

I respectfully dissent.

NOTES AND QUESTIONS

1. Justice Stewart also wrote a dissenting opinion in *Caban*. He agreed generally with Justice Stevens that the state's interest in promoting the welfare of illegitimate children through adoption justified the statutory distinction between married and unmarried fathers as well as the distinction between unmarried fathers and unmarried mothers. It was his view therefore that neither distinction violated the Equal Protection Clause. Justice Stewart also agreed with Justice Stevens that the Court's decision should not be retroactive in application, and with Part III of Justice Stevens' dissent.

2. What is likely to happen in this case upon its remand to the New York state courts?

3. In view of the treatment of Stanley v. Illinois in both the *Quilloin* and *Caban* cases, for what legal principles, if any, does *Stanley* now stand?

4. What would be the results in questions 6(a) through (f), supra, page 440, when the expressions in *Caban* are taken into account in addition to those in *Stanley* and *Quilloin*? See the Note, The Emerging Constitutional Protection of the Putative Father's Parental Rights, 70 Mich.L.Rev. 1581, 1590 (1972), cited in the Court's footnote 12, in which it is suggested that an adoption could go forward even though the father could not be found or refused to consent, if a hearing were held and a reasonable effort had been made to find the father. Would this be done by publishing a notice of the illegitimate birth in the local paper, giving the mother's name? Cf. footnote 17 to the dissenting opinion.

5. Does footnote 16 to the Court's opinion suggest that *Quilloin* would no longer be followed?

6. Justice Stevens' dissent takes the position that the Court's decision is limited to cases involving the adoption of older children whose fathers have, before the adoption petition, admitted paternity and have participated in the rearing of their children. Do you agree with this characterization of the *Caban* case?

---

29. Cf. Lucas v. Colorado General Assembly, 377 U.S. 713, 739, 84 S.Ct. 1459, 1475, 12 L.Ed.2d 632; Roman v. Sincock, 377 U.S. 695, 711–712, 84 S. Ct. 1449, 1458–1459, 12 L.Ed.2d 620; WMCA, Inc. v. Lomenzo, 377 U.S. 633, 655, 84 S.Ct. 1418, 1429, 12 L. Ed.2d 568; Reynolds v. Sims, 377 U. S. 533, 585, 84 S.Ct. 1362, 1393, 12 L.Ed.2d 506 (valid elections may go forward pursuant to statutes that have been held unconstitutional as violating the one-person, one-vote rule, when an impending election is imminent and the election machinery is already in progress).

7.   Is it also clear that *Caban* is to have only prospective application?

8.   Footnote 5 to Justice Stevens' dissent mentions the distinction between legitimate and illegitimate *children* produced by the New York statute, in that the former may only be adopted after both parents have consented, while the latter need only the mother's consent for adoption. Who would have standing to raise this as a constitutional question? If it were properly raised, how should the question be determined?

9.   In view of your answers to all the foregoing questions, and of the constitutional exegesis in *Stanley, Quilloin* and *Caban*, could you draft a statute which would be constitutional and at the same time would set up a workable and expeditious adoption procedure? Does § 24 of the Uniform Parentage Act, reproduced supra, page 441, reach these goals? Does the Uniform Adoption Act reach them, §§ 5 and 6 of which read as follows, 9 Unif.L.Ann. 23, 26 (1979)?

"§ 5.   [Persons Required to Consent to Adoption]

"(a) Unless consent is not required under section 6, a petition to adopt a minor may be granted only if written consent to a particular adoption has been executed by:

"(1) the mother of the minor;

"(2) the father of the minor if the father was married to the mother at the time the minor was conceived or at any time thereafter, the minor is his child by adoption, or [he has otherwise legitimated the minor according to the laws of the place in which the adoption proceeding is brought] [his consent is required under the Uniform Legitimacy Act];

"(3) any person lawfully entitled to custody of the minor or empowered to consent;

"(4) the court having jurisdiction to determine custody of the minor, if the legal guardian or custodian of the person of the minor is not empowered to consent to the adoption;

"(5) the minor, if more than [10] years of age, unless the Court in the best interest of the minor dispenses with the minor's consent; and

"(6) the spouse of the minor to be adopted.

"(b) A petition to adopt an adult may be granted only if written consent to adoption has been executed by the adult and the adult's spouse."

"§ 6.   [Persons as to Whom Consent and Notice Not Required]

"(a) Consent to adoption is not required of:

"(1) a parent who has [deserted a child without affording means of identification, or who has] abandoned a child;

"(2) a parent of a child in the custody of another, if the parent for a period of at least one year has failed significantly without justifiable cause (i) to communicate with the child or (ii) to provide for the care and support of the child as required by law or judicial decree;

"(3) the father of a minor if the father's consent is not required by section 5(a)(2);

"(4) a parent who has relinquished his right to consent under section 19;

"(5) a parent whose parental rights have been terminated by order of court under section 19;

"(6) a parent judicially declared incompetent or mentally defective if the Court dispenses with the parent's consent;

"(7) any parent of the individual to be adopted, if (i) the individual is a minor [18] or more years of age and the Court dispenses with the consent of the parent or (ii) the individual is an adult;

"(8) any legal guardian or lawful custodian of the individual to be adopted, other than a parent, who has failed to respond in writing to a request for consent for a period of [60] days or who, after examination of his written reasons for withholding consent, is found by the Court to be withholding his consent unreasonably; or

"(9) the spouse of the individual to be adopted, if the failure of the spouse to consent to the adoption is excused by the Court by reason of prolonged unexplained absence, unavailability, incapacity, or circumstances constituting an unreasonable withholding of consent.

"(b) Except as provided in section 11, notice of a hearing on a petition for adoption need not be given to a person whose consent is not required or to a person whose consent or relinquishment has been filed with the petition."

10. In some states there is a parental-preference rule with respect to child custody. What this means is that a child's natural parent, if he or she is not "unfit", has a paramount right to custody as against non-parents. In a particular case M and F, not living together on a regular basis and not married to each other, have a child, C. M consents to the child's adoption, which is all that is required under state law. The child is placed for adoption by a public agency with H and W. They file a petition for adoption, giving notice of the proceeding to F, who appears and objects to the adoption, seeking custody of the child for himself. The trial court finds H and W to be fit parents, and makes the same finding as to F. Is the court required by the Constitution and cases like *Stanley, Quilloin* and *Caban* to apply the parental-preference rule in favor of F, even though the evidence indicates that the child's welfare would be better served by approval of the adoption? In re Lathrop, 2 Kan.App.2d 91, 575 P.2d 894 (1978), 27 Kan. L.Rev. 483 (1979).

11. Pennsylvania has reached a result similar to that in *Caban*, on the basis of the Equal Rights Amendment to the state constitution. See Adoption of Walker, 468 Pa. 165, 360 A.2d 603 (1976), 15 Duq.L.Rev. 757 (1977).

12. M, an unmarried woman, gave birth in State X to a child, C, whose father M thought was F, although she was not entirely sure because she had had sexual relations with two other men at approximately the time when C must have been conceived. The two other men were F–2 and F–3.

When the child was two years old, M decided she could not care for it any longer and consulted Non-Sectarian Services, Inc., a licensed private adoption agency, with a view of placing the child for adoption. After extensive counselling with the agency, M relinquished the child, signing the appropriate consent to adoption. The agency immediately placed the child with H and W, a man and wife who had wanted to adopt a child for some time and who were well qualified prospective adoptive parents in the agency's opinion. An adoption proceeding was brought in State X and notice of the proceeding sent to F at his last known address. The notice was returned with the envelope marked "No such person at this address". No notices were sent to F–2 or F–3. At the final hearing on the adoption F–2 turned up, testified that he had just learned of C's existence, opposed the adoption and asked that he be given custody. In the alternative, he asked that if he were denied custody, he be given rights of visitation. The statute of State X provided: "consent to adoption shall be required of the parents of a child born in wedlock, and of the mother of a child born out of wedlock."

What should be the outcome of this proceeding, under *Caban?*

SMITH v. ORGANIZATION OF FOSTER FAMILIES FOR EQUALITY AND REFORM

Supreme Court of the United States, 1977.
431 U.S. 816, 97 S.Ct. 2094, 53 L.Ed.2d 14.

Mr. Justice BRENNAN delivered the opinion of the Court.

Appellees, individual foster parents and an organization of foster parents, brought this civil rights class action pursuant to 42 U.S.C.A. § 1983 in the United States District Court for the Southern District of New York, on their own behalf and on behalf of children for whom they have provided homes for a year or more. They sought declaratory and injunctive relief against New York State and New York City officials, alleging that the procedures governing the removal of foster children from foster homes provided in New York Social Services Law §§ 383(2) and 400, and in Title 18, New York Codes, Rules and Regulations § 450.14 violated the Due Process and Equal Protection Clauses of the Fourteenth Amendment. * * *

I

A detailed outline of the New York statutory system regulating foster care is a necessary preface to a discussion of the constitutional questions presented.

A

The expressed central policy of the New York system is that "it is generally desirable for the child to remain with or be returned to the natural parent because the child's need for a normal family life will usually best be met in the natural home and * * * parents are entitled to bring up their own children unless the best interests of the child would be thereby endangered," Soc.Serv.L. § 384–

b(1)(a)(ii). But the State has opted for foster care as one response to those situations where the natural parents are unable to provide the "positive, nurturing family relationships" and "normal family life in a permanent home" that "offer the best opportunity for children to develop and thrive." Id., § 384–b(1)(b), (1)(a)(i).

Foster care has been defined as "[a] child welfare service which provides substitute family care for a planned period for a child when his own family cannot care for him for a temporary or extended period and when adoption is neither desirable nor possible." Child Welfare League of America, Standards for Foster Family Care, 5 (1959). Thus, the distinctive features of foster care are first, "that it is care in a *family*, it is noninstitutional substitute care," and second, "that it is for a *planned* period—either temporary or extended. This is unlike adoptive placement, which implies a *permanent* substitution of one home for another." Kadushin, Child Welfare Services, 355 (1967).

Under the New York scheme children may be placed in foster care either by voluntary placement or by court order. Most foster care placements are voluntary. They occur when physical or mental illness, economic problems, or other family crises make it impossible for natural parents, particularly single parents, to provide a stable home life for their children for some limited period. Resort to such placements is almost compelled when it is not possible in such circumstance to place the child with a relative or friend, or to pay for the services of a homemaker or boarding school.

Voluntary placement requires the signing of a written agreement by the natural parent or guardian, transferring the care and custody of the child to an authorized child welfare agency. Soc.Serv.L. § 384–a(1). Although by statute the terms of such agreements are open to negotiation, Soc.Serv.L. § 384–a(2)(a), it is contended that agencies require execution of standardized forms. Brief of Appellants Rodriguez et al., 25 n. 17. See App., at 63a–64a, 65a–67a. The agreement may provide for return of the child to the natural parent at a specified date or upon occurrence of a particular event, and if it does not, the child must be returned by the agency, in the absence of a court order, within 20 days of notice from the parent. Soc.Serv.L. § 384–a(2)(a).

The agency may maintain the child in an institutional setting, Soc.Serv.L. §§ 374–b, 374–c, 374–d, but more commonly acts under its authority to "place out and board out" children in foster homes. Soc.Serv.L. § 374(1). Foster parents, who are licensed by the State or an authorized foster care agency, Soc.Serv.L. §§ 376, 377, provide care under a contractual arrangement with the agency, and are compensated for their services. The typical contract expressly reserves the right of the agency to remove the child on request. Conversely, the foster parent may cancel the agreement at will.

The New York system divides parental functions among agency, foster parents and natural parents, and the definitions of the respective roles are often complex and often unclear.[16]   The law transfers "care and custody" to the agency, Soc.Serv.L. § 384–a; see also Soc.Serv.L. § 383(2), but day-to-day supervision of the child and his activities, and most of the functions ordinarily associated with legal custody, are the responsibility of the foster parent.   Nevertheless, agency supervision of the performance of the foster parents takes forms indicating that the foster parent does not have the full authority of a legal custodian.   Moreover, the natural parent's placement of the child with the agency does not surrender legal guardianship; the parent retains authority to act with respect to the child in certain circumstances.   The natural parent has not only the right but the obligation to visit the foster child and plan for his future; failure of a parent with capacity to fulfill the obligation for more than a year can result in a court order terminating the parent's rights on the ground of neglect.

Children may also enter foster care by court order.   *   *   * The consequences of foster care placement by court order do not differ substantially from those for children voluntarily placed, except that the parent is not entitled to return of the child on demand pursuant to Soc.Serv.L. § 384–a(2)(a); termination of foster care must then be consented to by the court. Soc.Serv.L. § 383(1).

B

The provisions of the scheme specifically at issue in this case come into play when the agency having legal custodianship determines to remove the foster child from the foster home, either because it has determined that it would be in the child's best interests to transfer him to some other foster home, or to return the child to his natural parents in accordance with the statute or placement agreement.   Most children are removed in order to be transferred to another foster home.   The procedures by which foster parents may challenge a removal made for that purpose differ somewhat from those where the removal is made to return the child to his natural parent.

Soc.Serv.L. § 383(2), supra, n. 3, provides that the "authorized agency placing out or boarding [a foster] child   *   *   * may in its discretion remove such child from the home where placed or boarded."   Administrative regulations implement this provision.   The agency is required, except in emergencies, to notify the foster parents in writing 10 days in advance of any removal.   The notice advises the

---

16. The resulting confusion not only produces anomalous legal relationships but also affects the child's emotional status.   The foster child's loyalties, emotional involvements, and responsibilities are often divided among three adult authority figures —the natural parent, the foster parent, and the social worker representing the foster-care agency.

foster parents that if they object to the child's removal they may request a "conference" with the social services department. The department schedules requested conferences within 10 days of the receipt of the request. The foster parent may appear with counsel at the conference, where he will "be advised of the reasons [for the removal of the child], and be afforded an opportunity to submit reasons why the child should not be removed." The official must render a decision in writing within five days after the close of the conference, and send notice of his decision to the foster parents and the agency. The proposed removal is stayed pending the outcome of the conference.

If the child is removed after the conference, the foster parent may appeal to the department of social services for a "fair hearing," that is, a full adversary administrative hearing, under Soc.Serv.L. § 400, the determination of which is subject to judicial review under N.Y.C.P.L.R. Art. 78; however, the removal is not automatically stayed pending the hearing and judicial review.

This statutory and regulatory scheme applies statewide. In addition, regulations promulgated by the New York City Human Resources Administration, Department of Social Services—Special Services for Children (SSC) provide even greater procedural safeguards there. Under SSC Procedure No. 5 (April 5, 1974), in place of or in addition to the conference provided by the state regulations, the foster parents may request a full trial-type hearing *before* the child is removed from their home. This procedure applies, however, only if the child is being transferred to another foster home, and not if the child is being returned to his natural parents.

One further preremoval procedural safeguard is available. Under Soc.Serv.L. § 392, the Family Court has jurisdiction to review, on petition of the foster parent or the agency, the status of any child who has been in foster care for 18 months or longer. The foster parents, the natural parents, and all interested agencies are made parties to the proceeding. Soc.Serv.L. § 392(4). After hearing, the court may order that foster care be continued, or that the child be returned to his natural parents, or that the agency take steps to free the child for adoption. Soc.Serv.L. § 392(7). Moreover, § 392(8) authorizes the court to issue an "order of protection" which "may set forth reasonable conditions of behavior to be observed for a specified time by a person or agency who is before the court." Thus, the court may order not only that foster care be continued, but additionally, "in assistance or as a condition of" that order that the agency leave the child with the present foster parent. In other words, § 392 provides a mechanism whereby a foster parent may obtain preremoval judicial review of an agency's decision to remove a child who has been in foster care for 18 months or more.

[In Part I C of its opinion the Court indulges in a lengthy recapitulation of recent criticisms of foster care systems. These criticisms include:

(a) Since foster care is used more often for the children of the poor than for the children of the rich, it is a "class-based intrusion into the family life of the poor".

(b) Voluntary placements are often not voluntary but coerced by the threat of neglect proceedings.

(c) Children are often left in foster care for quite long periods, longer than the theory of the system would suggest. In such cases the child often develops strong emotional ties with his foster parents.

(d) Notwithstanding such ties, children are often shifted from one set of foster parents to another.

(e) There is rapid turnover of social workers who supervise foster home placements.

(f) Children in foster homes rarely achieve a stable home life by adoption.]

II

A

Our first inquiry is whether appellees have asserted interests within the Fourteenth Amendment's protection of "liberty" and "property."

The appellees have not renewed in this Court their contention, that the realities of the foster-care system in New York gave them a justified expectation amounting to a "property" interest that their status as foster parents would be continued. Our inquiry is therefore narrowed to the question whether their asserted interests are within the "liberty" protected by the Fourteenth Amendment.

The appellees' basic contention is that when a child has lived in a foster home for a year or more, a psychological tie is created between the child and the foster parents which constitutes the foster family the true "psychological family" of the child. See Goldstein, Freud and Solnit, Beyond the Best Interests of the Child (1973). That family, they argue, has a "liberty interest" in its survival as a family protected by the Fourteenth Amendment. Upon this premise they conclude that the foster child cannot be removed without a prior hearing satisfying due process. Appointed counsel for the children, however, disagrees, and has consistently argued that the foster parents have no such liberty interest independent of the interests of the foster children, and that the best interest of the children would not be served by procedural protections beyond those already provided by New York law. The intervening natural parents of children in foster care, also oppose the foster parents, arguing that recognition of the procedural right claimed would undercut both the substantive family law of New York , which favors the return of children to their natural parents as expeditiously as possible, and their constitutionally protected right of family privacy, by forcing them to submit to a hearing and defend their rights to their children before the children could be returned to them.

[At this point in the opinion the Court stated the district court's holding, which was that the New York statutes were unconstitutional because they disrupted the stable family relationships of the foster child in removing him from his foster parents, thereby causing him "grievous loss".]

We therefore turn to appellees' assertion that they have a constitutionally protected liberty interest—in the words of the District Court, a "right to familial privacy," in the integrity of their family unit. This assertion clearly presents difficulties.

B

It is of course true that "freedom of personal choice in matters of * * * family life is one of the liberties protected by the Due Process Clause of the Fourteenth Amendment." There does exist a "private realm of family life which the state cannot enter," that has been afforded both substantive and procedural protection. But is the relation of foster parent to foster child sufficiently akin to the concept of "family" recognized in our precedents to merit similar protection? Although considerable difficulty has attended the task of defining "family" for purposes of the Due Process Clause, we are not without guides to some of the elements that define the concept of "family" and contribute to its place in our society.

First, the usual understanding of "family" implies biological relationships, and most decisions treating the relation between parent and child have stressed this element. Stanley v. Illinois, 405 U.S. 645, 651, 92 S.Ct. 1208, 1212, 31 L.Ed.2d 551 (1972), for example, spoke of "[t]he rights to conceive and raise one's children" as essential rights, citing Meyer v. Nebraska, 262 U.S. 390, 43 S.Ct. 625, 67 L.Ed. 1042 (1923), and Skinner v. Oklahoma, 316 U.S. 535, 62 S.Ct. 1110, 86 L. Ed. 1655 (1942).

A biological relationship is not present in the case of the usual foster family. But biological relationships are not exclusive determination of the existence of a family. The basic foundation of the family in our society, the marriage relationship, is of course not a matter of blood relation. Yet its importance has been strongly emphasized in our cases:

"We deal with a right of privacy older than the Bill of Rights—older than our political parties, older than our school system. Marriage is a coming together for better or for worse, hopefully enduring, and intimate to the degree of being sacred. It is an association that promotes a way of life, not causes; a harmony in living, not political faiths; a bilateral loyalty, not commercial or social projects.

Yet it is an association for as noble a purpose as any involved in our prior decisions." Griswold v. Connecticut, 381 U.S. 479, 486, 85 S.Ct. 1678, 1682, 14 L.Ed.2d 510 (1965).

Thus the importance of the familial relationship, to the individuals involved and to the society, stems from the emotional attachments that derive from the intimacy of daily association, and from the role it plays in "promot[ing] a way of life" through the instruction of children, as well as from the fact of blood relationship. No one would seriously dispute that a deeply loving and interdependent relationship between an adult and a child in his or her care may exist even in the absence of blood relationship. At least where a child has been placed in foster care as an infant, has never known his natural parents, and has remained continuously for several years in the care of the same foster parents, it is natural that the foster family should hold the same place in the emotional life of the foster child, and fulfill the same socializing functions, as a natural family. For this reason, we cannot dismiss the foster family as a mere collection of unrelated individuals.

But there are also important distinctions between the foster family and the natural family. First, unlike the earlier cases recognizing a right to family privacy, the State here seeks to interfere not with a relationship having its origins entirely apart form the power of the State, but rather with a foster family which has its source in state law and contractual arrangements. The individual's freedom to marry and reproduce is "older than the Bill of Rights," Griswold v. Connecticut, supra, 381 U.S., at 486, 85 S.Ct., at 1682. Accordingly, unlike the property interests that are also protected by the Fourteenth Amendment, the liberty interest in family privacy has its source, and its contours are ordinarily to be sought, not in state law, but in intrinsic human rights, as they have been understood in "this Nation's history and tradition." * * * In this case, the limited recognition accorded to the foster family by the New York statutes and the contracts executed by the foster parents argue against any but the most limited constitutional "liberty" in the foster family.

A second consideration related to this is that ordinarily procedural protection may be afforded to a liberty interest of one person without derogating from the substantive liberty of another. Here, however, such a tension is virtually unavoidable. Under New York law, the natural parent of a foster child in voluntary placement has an absolute right to the return of his child in the absence of a court order obtainable only upon compliance with rigorous substantive and procedural standards, which reflect the constitutional protection accorded the natural family. Moreover, the natural parent initially gave up his child to the State only on the express understanding that the child would be returned in those circumstances. These rights are difficult to reconcile with the liberty interest in the foster family relationship claimed by appellees. * * * Whatever liberty interest might otherwise exist in the foster family as an institution, that interest must be substantially attenuated where the proposed removal from the foster family is to return the child to his natural parents. * * * We are persuaded that, even on the assumption that appellees have a protected "liberty interest," the District Court erred in holding that the preremoval procedures presently employed by the State are constitutionally defective.

III

Where procedural due process must be afforded because a "liberty" or "property" interest is within the Fourteenth Amendment's protection, there must be determined "what process is due" in the particular context. * * *

It is true that "[b]efore a person is deprived of a protected interest, he must be afforded opportunity for some kind of hearing, 'except for extraordinary situations where some valid governmental interest is at stake that justifies postponing the hearing until after the event.'" But the hearing required is only one "appropriate to the nature of the case." Mullane v. Central Hanover Bank & Trust Co., 339 U.S. 306, 313, 70 S.Ct. 652, 657, 94 L.Ed. 865 (1950). * * * Only last Term, the Court held that "identification of the specific dictates of due process generally requires consideration of three distinct factors: first, the private interest that will be affected by the official action; second, the risk of an erroneous deprivation of such interest through the procedures used, and the probable value, if any, or additional or substitute procedural safeguards; and finally, the Government's interest, including the function involved and the fiscal and administrative burdens that the additional or substitute procedural requirement would entail." Mathews v. Eldridge, 424 U.S. 319, 335, 96 S.Ct. 893, 903, 47 L.Ed.2d 18 (1976). Consideration of the procedures employed by the City and State of New York in light of these three factors requires the conclusion that those procedures satisfy constitutional standards.

Turning first to the procedure applicable in New York City, SSC Procedure No. 5, see supra, at 2103, and n. 29, provides that before a child is removed from a foster home for transfer to another foster home, the foster parents may request an "independent review." Such a procedure would appear to give a more elaborate trial-type hearing to foster families than this Court has found required in other contexts of administrative determinations. * * *

First, the court held that the "independent review" administrative proceeding was insufficient because it was only available on the request of the foster parents. In the view of the District Court, the proceeding should be provided as a matter of course, because the interests of the foster parents and those of the child would not necessarily be coextensive, and it could not be assumed that the foster parents would invoke the hearing procedure in every case in which it was in the child's interest to have a hearing. Since the child is unable to request a hearing on his own, automatic review in every case is necessary. We disagree. As previously noted, the constitutional liberty, if any, sought to be protected by the New York procedures is a right of *family* privacy or autonomy, and the basis for recognition of any such interest in the foster family must be that close emotional ties analogous to those between parent and child are established when a child resides for a lengthy period with a foster family. If this is so, necessarily we should expect that the foster parents will seek to continue the relationship to preserve the stability of the family; if they do not request a hearing, it is difficult to see what right or interest of the foster child is protected by holding a hearing to determine whether removal would unduly impair his emotional attachments to a foster parent who does not care enough about the child to contest the removal. Thus, consideration of the interest to be protected and the likelihood of erroneous deprivations, the first two factors identified in Mathews v. Eldridge, supra, as appropriate in determining the sufficiency of procedural protections, do not support the District Court's imposition of this additional requirement. Moreover, automatic provision of hearings as required by the District Court would impose a substantial additional administrative burden on the State. According to appellant city officials, during the approximately two years between the institution of SSC Procedure No. 5 in August 1974 and June 1976, there were approximately 2,800 transfers per year in the city, but only 26 foster parents requested hearings. It is not at all clear what would be gained by requiring full hearings in the more than 5,500 cases in which they were not requested.

Second, the District Court faulted the city procedure on the ground that participation is limited to the foster parents and the agency and the natural parent and the child are not made parties to the hearing. This is not fatal in light of the nature of the alleged constitutional interests at stake. When the child's transfer from one foster home to another is pending, the interest arguably requiring protection is that of the foster family, not that of the natural parents. Moreover, the natural parent can generally add little to the accuracy of factfinding concerning the wisdom of such a transfer, since the foster parents and the agency, through its caseworkers, will usually be most knowledgeable about conditions in the foster home. Of course, in those cases where the natural parent does have a special interest in the proposed transfer or particular information that would assist the factfinder, nothing in the city's procedure prevents any party from securing his testimony.

*   *   *

But nothing in the New York City procedure prevents consultation of the child's wishes, directly or through an adult intermediary. We assume, moreover, that some such consultation would be among the first steps that a rational factfinder, inquiring into the child's best interests, would pursue. Such consultation, however, does not require that the child or an appointed representative must be a party with full adversary powers in all preremoval hearings.

The other two defects in the city procedure found by the District Court must also be rejected. One is that the procedure does not extend to the removal of a child from foster care to be returned to his natural parent. But as we have already held, whatever liberty interest may be argued to exist in the foster family is significantly weaker in the case of removals preceding return to the natural parent, and the balance of due process interests must accordingly be different. If the city procedure is adequate where it is applicable, it is no criticism of the procedure that it does not apply in other situations where different interests are at stake. Similarly, the District Court pointed out that the New York City procedure coincided with the informal "conference" and postremoval hearings provided as a matter of state law. This overlap in procedures may be unnecessary or even to some degree unwise, but a State does not violate the Due Process Clause by providing alternative or additional procedures beyond what the Constitution requires.

Outside New York City, where only the statewide procedures apply, foster parents are provided not only with the procedures of a preremoval conference and postremoval hearing provided by 18 N.Y. C.R.R. § 450.10 and Soc.Serv.L. § 400, but also with the preremoval *judicial* hearing available on request to foster parents who have in their care children who have been in foster care for 18 months or more, Soc.Serv.L. § 392. As observed above, a foster parent in such case may obtain an order that the child remain in his care.

The District Court found three defects in this full judicial process. First, a § 392 proceeding is available only to those foster children who have been in foster care for 18 months or more. The class certified by the Court was broader, including children who had been in the care of the same foster parents for more than one year. Thus, not all class members had access to the § 392 remedy. We do not think that the 18-month limitations on § 392 actions renders the New York scheme constitutionally inadequate. The assumed liberty interest to be protected in this case is one rooted in the emotional attachments that develop over time between a child and the adults who care for him. But there is no reason to assume that those attachments ripen at less than 18 months or indeed at any precise point. Indeed, testimony in the record, see App., at 177a, 204a, as well as material in published psychological tests, see, e. g., Goldstein, Freud and Solnit, supra, at 40–42, 49, suggests that the amount of time necessary for the development of the sort of tie appellees seek to protect varies considerably depending on the age and previous attachments of the child. In a matter of such imprecision and delicacy, we see no justification for the District Court's substitution of its view of the appropriate cutoff date for that chosen by the New York Legislature, given that any line is likely to be somewhat arbitrary and fail to protect some families where relationships have developed quickly while protecting others where no such bonds have formed. If New York sees 18 months rather than 12 as the time at which temporary foster care begins to turn into a more permanent and family like setting requiring procedural protection and/or judicial inquiry into the propriety of continuing foster care, it would take far more than this record provides to justify a finding of constitutional infirmity in New York's choice.

The District Court's other two findings of infirmity in the § 392 procedure have already been considered and held to be without merit. The District Court disputed defendants' reading of § 392 as permitting an order requiring the leaving of the foster child in the same foster home. The plain words of the statute and the weight of New York judicial interpretation do not support the court. The District Court also faulted § 392, as it did the New York City procedure, in not providing an automatic hearing in every case even in cases where foster parents chose not to seek one. Our holding sustaining the adequacy of the city procedure, applies in this context as well.

Finally, the § 392 hearing is available to foster parents, both in and outside New York City, even where the removal sought is for the purpose of returning the child to his natural parents. Since this remedy provides a sufficient constitutional preremoval hearing to protect whatever liberty interest might exist in the continued existence of the foster family when the State seeks to transfer the child to another foster home, *a fortiori* the procedure is adequate to protect the lesser interest of the foster family in remaining together at the expense of the disruption of the natural family.

We deal here with issues of unusual delicacy, in an area where professional judgments regarding desirable procedures are constantly and rapidly changing. In such a context, restraint is appropriate on the part of courts called upon to adjudicate whether a particular procedural scheme is adequate under the Constitution. Since we hold that the procedures provided by New York State in § 392 and by New York City's SSC Procedure No. 5 are adequate to protect whatever liberty interest appellees may have, the judgment of the District Court is

Reversed.

NOTES AND QUESTIONS

1. The Chief Justice and Justices Stewart and Rehnquist concurred specially in this case. They took the position that "the interests asserted by the appellees are not of a kind that the Due Process Clause of the Fourteenth Amendment protects." In their view New York's foster case program creates no right in the foster family to remain intact, but rather is

aimed at providing temporary care for the child until he can either be returned to his natural parents or placed in a permanent adoptive home. The concurring opinion seems to concede that if the state should try to break up a natural family solely in order to promote the children's welfare, without proof that the parents were unfit, this would constitute an unconstitutional intrusion upon family life. But here New York was merely intruding upon a temporary status which it had created and therefore is not similar to the breakup of a family.

2. How does the Court define "family" in this case? The Court has had some difficulty with this question in other contexts. For example, in Village of Belle Terre v. Boraas, 416 U.S. 1 (1974), a local zoning ordinance was held constitutional when it defined "family" to include one or more persons related by blood, adoption or marriage, living and cooking together as a single housekeeping unit, or not more than two persons living and cooking together as a single housekeeping unit where not related by blood, adoption or marriage. No invasion of privacy as defined by Griswold was held to be caused by this ordinance, and the legislature was held within its discretion in drawing the line between two unrelated persons and more than two. But in Moore v. City of East Cleveland, 431 U.S. 494 (1977), the Court, in a plurality opinion concurred in by four justices, struck down a housing ordinance which defined "family" so as to include only spouses, unmarried children of the head of household, father or mother of the head of household and certain dependent children of the head of the household. The ordinance in that case forbade a grandmother to live with her son and two grandsons who were first cousins, and the Court held this to be an unconstitutional intrusion upon choices concerning family living arrangements not justified by any legitimate state interest. The case thus might be viewed as a holding that the state may not, consistent with the Due Process Clause, limit the definition of "family" to the traditional nuclear family, at least for housing purposes. It might even be viewed as an endorsement for the extended family.

In view of these cases, what should be the definition of "family" for purposes of the foster care program? Should "family" be defined in the same terms whenever the question of constitutionality of any statute is raised, or should the definition vary when different statutes having different purposes are involved?

The Court cites in its opinion J. Goldstein, A. Freud, A. Solnit, Beyond the Best Interests of the Child (1973). This book, written by authorities in both law and psychology, has been very influential in many cases. It emphasizes, for purposes of decisions on custody and adoption, that the child's interests should be paramount, that placements should provide the least detrimental available alternative for the child's development, and above all that placements should safeguard the child's need for continuity of relationships. It also stresses the idea that the child's psychological parent is more important to the child than his natural parent in those situations where he has been separated from his natural parent.

3. What does Smith v. OFFER have to teach us about the constitutionality of foster care administration? Specifically, what would be its effect in a state in which children are shifted from one foster parent or parents to another without any notice or hearing? Would such shifting violate the Due Process Clause? Would the Due Process Clause be violated if

children were removed from foster parents and transferred to their natural parents without notice to the foster parents and an opportunity to be heard?

These questions have been answered in Drummond v. Fulton County Department of Family and Children's Services, 563 F.2d 1200 (5th Cir. 1977), cert. den. 437 U.S. 910 (1978), albeit with a vigorous dissent. In that case a child of mixed race was placed in the temporary foster care of a white couple and remained with them for about a year, at the end of which time the foster parents indicated to the adoption agency that they wished to adopt the child. At an agency meeting at which the foster parents were not present, it was decided that the child would be placed for adoption with someone other than the foster parents. This was discussed with the foster parents but no hearing was held nor did the foster parents participate in the making of the decision. About six months later the child's natural mother's rights were terminated and he became eligible for adoption. The agency's decision was then reaffirmed and the foster parents brought suit under 42 U.S.C.A. § 1983 to enjoin the agency from removing the child. The racial aspects of this case are discussed infra, at page 565. In holding that the foster parents' constitutional rights were not violated, the Fifth Circuit, en banc, had this to say, 563 F.2d 1206 ff.:

"Plaintiffs maintain that during the period Timmy lived with them mutual feelings of love and dependence developed which are analogous to those found in most biological families. By so characterizing their home situation they seek to come within the protection which courts have afforded to the family unit. They assert that their relationship to Timmy is part of the familial right to privacy which is a protected interest under the Fourteenth Amendment. As the 'psychological parents' of Timmy, they claim entitlement to the parental rights referred to in numerous decisions.

"The argument that foster parents possess such a protected interest was placed squarely before, and discussed by, the Supreme Court in its recent decision in Smith v. Organization of Foster Families for Equality & Reform, 431 U.S. 816, 97 S.Ct. 2094, 53 L.Ed.2d 14 (1977) [hereinafter *OFFER*]. Although the Supreme Court did not find it necessary to resolve whether such an interest exists, Justice Brennan's discussion of that claim is helpful to our analysis. He first considered the elements which have traditionally been thought to define the concept of 'family.' * * * the Court then noted several differences between foster and natural families, particularly the fact that the foster parent relationship has its genesis in state law, unlike the biological relationship, and that with foster parents there is often a natural parent seeking to assert a competing liberty interest.

"We conclude that there is no such constitutionally protected interest in the context of this case. An understanding of the role of the foster parent in a child placement helps make this conclusion plain. In the search for adoptive parents, thorough investigations are made so that long range considerations may be given substantial weight. * * * In short, the goal is to duplicate the relationship that most persons have with their natural parents during their entire lives.

"* * *

"During this process in Georgia, children are placed in foster homes as an alternative to institutional care for what is clearly designed as a transitional phase in the child's life. Foster parents are thus considered only on the basis of the quality of temporary care they can be expected to provide. Therefore, in the eyes of the state, which creates the foster relationship, the relationship is considered temporary at the outset and gives rise to no state created rights in the foster parents.

"Here, the only time potential parents could assert a liberty interest as psychological parents would be when they had developed precisely the relationship which state law warns against [in] foster context. * * * There is no basis in the Georgia law, which creates the foster relationship, for a justifiable expectation that the relationship will be left undisturbed. True liberty rights do not flow from state laws, which can be repealed by action of the legislature. Unlike property rights they have a more stable source in our notions of intrinsic human rights. The very fact that the relationship before us is a creature of state law, as well as the fact that it has never been recognized as equivalent to either the natural family or the adoptive family by any court, demonstrates that it is not a protected liberty interest, but an interest limited by the very laws which create it.

"It needs noting that this conclusion does not necessarily control every 'foster family' situation, but only those in which a child placement agency charged with the custody of a child, places that child for temporary care. Other situations will have to be addressed on a case by case basis.

* * *

"Independent counsel for Timmy claims a liberty right personal to Timmy which he asserts must be dealt with in constitutional due process terms. The interest upon which he bases this claim is one which he has chosen to call the 'right to a stable environment.' He argues that a child has a liberty right not to be moved from home to home, without a prior hearing, particularly in light of the significant literature which indicates a traumatic effect of such moves on young children. Counsel insists this right exists regardless of whether the child is in a natural, adoptive or foster setting and in all other temporary care situations.

"Due to the novelty of this contention, counsel cites no authority in support of such stability interest. * * *

"Here, the state's motive in interrupting Timmy's environment at any point was always to move him to a place which it considered superior, over the long range, for his particular needs at the time. Since Timmy can point to no source for a right in conflict with that state program, we hold that Timmy has no liberty interest as asserted here. This decision by its facts is necessarily applicable only to an infant of tender years placed in a foster home for the length of time and under the circumstances here involved. We cannot by decision here address every conceivable situation, in some of which a child may have acquired some interest, as alluded to in Justice Brennan's opinion in *OFFER*.

* * *

"* * * It cannot be gainsaid that the Georgia mechanism for removing a child from a foster home is much more informal and much less 'judicial' than the New York model. Of course, *OFFER* does not mandate the New York model as constitutionally necessary in every case. Nonetheless we face a scheme which is admittedly less rigorous in its procedural trappings. * * *

"*OFFER* itself, however, by pretermitting the question of the existence of a protected interest, leaves open the possibility that some such an interest might exist. Although no liberty interest of substantial magnitude is present in the instant situation, some might find a lesser interest in these facts deserving of some protection against arbitrary conduct. We thus consider whether the procedures afforded in Georgia were adequate to protect whatever interest might be at stake. * * *

"To the extent there may be some undefined interest in this case that could not be treated by the state arbitrarily, we note that the process afforded by defendants was sufficient to comport with the Fourteenth Amendment mandate in connection with such interest.

    *   *   *

"*   *   * The private interest here is presumably the privacy, reputation, and stability concerns discussed above, the interest flowing from the love, affection and concern developed between the Drummonds and Timmy.

"The agency decision in this case to be made under any procedural format, as all concede, is 'what placement is in the best interest of the child?' The subsidiary inquiries which must be addressed in deciding this question are complex and numerous. The present procedure is designed to maximize information in answering these questions. Several interviews were had with the foster parents. The child was observed and tested mentally and medically. Data was collected about the child's natural mother and father. Persons trained in various skills, including psychology and social work are involved in the process. Informality was used to elicit spontaneous and accurate responses to sensitive inquiries. In sum, the present system seems designed to obtain the most accurate answer possible to the ultimate difficult question and the risk of error is minimized. There has been no indication that additional or more accurate information could be produced at a more structured trial-type hearing that would lead to a superior decision about Timmy's placement. The reason is obvious. In most hearing situations, the question to be resolved is one of fact. Here, however, the ultimate question is essentially one of policy. Child placing is an art, not a science that can be computerized to follow rigid rules. The 'best' home for Timmy is basically a subjective determination. Should intellectual opportunity be stressed over financial or athletic opportunity? Is a rural setting preferable to the city? What age should his adoptive parents be? In what order of the social structure? Should a given child be placed with older siblings, younger siblings or no siblings? The questions could go on for pages. These questions are policy inquiries, not factual disputes. The utility of a hearing in such a situation is doubtful. * * *

"Finally, we consider the Government's interest. The Government desires, of course, to act consistently with the child's best interest. Its additional concern, however, is to move as efficiently as possible. Children in foster care are a state expense, while those in adoptive homes are generally not. Sometimes extreme haste is necessary in an emergency to place a child in foster care. The quicker a child can be placed in a permanent home, the better. The presence of additional procedural safeguards and appeals procedures would naturally slow the placement process down to the detriment of both child and state.

Clark, Cs. on Dom.Rel. 3rd Ed. ACB—12

"Given the nature of the interests at stake, and the inquiry involved, as well as the overwhelming need for flexibility in this situation and the complexity of the decision to be made, this Court holds that whatever process was due was rendered by the state agency in this case."

See also Eason v. Welfare Commissioner, 171 Conn. 630, 370 A.2d 1082 (1976), cert. den. 432 U.S. 907 (1977).

4. If the criticisms of foster care programs paraphrased from Part I C of the Court's opinion in Smith v. OFFER are assumed to be valid, what relevance have they to the constitutional issue?

5. Assuming for present purposes that Drummond is correct in its assessment of Smith v. OFFER and the impact of the constitution on the rights of the foster parent, what should a well drawn statute provide with respect to the removal of a child from his foster parents? Bodenheimer, New Trends and Requirements in Adoption Law and Proposals for Legislative Change, 49 So.Cal.L.Rev. 10, 76–83 (1975).

B. CONSENT TO ADOPTION AND ITS REVOCATION

JOHNSON v. CUPP

Appellate Court of Indiana, Division 1, 1971.
274 N.E.2d 411.

ROBERTSON, Judge. This is an appeal from an adoption proceeding wherein plaintiffs, Robert L. Cupp and Geraldine S. Cupp, petitioned the Howard Circuit Court for adoption of a child born September 26, 1967. Respondents, Jerry L. Johnson and Constance E. Johnson, the natural parents of the infant, filed objections to the adoption alleging the invalidity of consents signed by each of them. The trial court held the consents to be valid and granted the adoption to plaintiffs. Thereafter, respondents timely filed their Motion to Correct Errors which challenged the decision of the trial court as not supported by sufficient evidence, contrary to the evidence, and contrary to law. Said motion was denied, and respondents subsequently perfected this appeal.

A brief recitation of the uncontradicted relevant facts of this case is as follows: respondents are husband and wife; prior to the birth of their child, respondent, Jerry L. Johnson, signed an adoption consent form which was duly notarized; subsequent to the birth of the respondents' child, respondent, Constance E. Johnson, who was at the time a minor, signed a consent form which was also duly notarized; the minor consent form of Constance E. Johnson was approved in writing by Ruth Dawson, a caseworker for the Howard County Welfare Department; the consent forms signed by the respective respondents did not specify the names of the adoptive parents, and were hence "blanket consents"; the Johnson infant was privately placed for adoption in the plaintiffs' home; the fitness of plaintiffs as adoptive parents was not contested.

The paramount issue presented by this appeal is whether or not the respective consents to adoption signed by each of the respondents are valid under Indiana law. The pertinent statute in force at the time the consents were executed was Ind.Ann.Stat. § 3–120 (Burns 1968)[1] which reads:

"3–120. Consent of parent or parents—Abandoned or deserted child—Nonresident parents—Notice—Parents deprived of custody—Child over fourteen—Notice to known kindred—If such child have parent or parents living, he, she or they shall consent in writing to such adoption. The minority of any parent shall not in or of itself be a bar to such consent: Provided, however, That if either parent be a minor, consent of such parent must be accompanied by the written approval of the investigating agency aforesaid if any there be and if none, of the state department of public welfare. Such consent of parent or parents may be dispensed with if such child is adjudged to have been abandoned or deserted for six [6] months or more immediately preceding the date of the filing of the petition. If it appears by indorsement on the petition and by the oath or affirmation of two [2] disinterested persons that such parent or parents or both are nonresidents or that their residence after diligent inquiry is unknown, then such parent or parents shall be notified of the pendency of the action by publication as provided by law in civil cases. If the parent or parents have been legally deprived of their parental rights over such child for reasons other than economic, the written consent of such parent or parents shall not be necessary to such adoption and no notice of the pendency of such adoption proceedings to such parent or parents shall be necessary: Provided, however, That notice of the pendency of such adoption proceedings shall, in such case, be given to such agency or county department of public welfare of which such child may be a ward. In every case where such child shall have been born out of wedlock consent of the mother of such child shall be deemed sufficient, except that where the paternity of such child has been established by law and the father is adequately supporting such child, or where for any reason in the discretion of the court it is deemed advisable that he be heard, he shall have such notice as to the court seems necessary and opportunity to file his objection if any, and oppose such adoption, which objection shall be considered and determined by the court. If such child be fourteen [14] years of age or over, his consent shall be deemed necessary before adoption. In all cases where consent of the parent or parents is required such consent shall be signed in the presence of a duly authorized agent of the state department of public welfare or of such investigating agency as so at-

---

1. Ind.Ann.Stat. § 3–120 (Burns 1968) was completely rewritten and amended by the Acts of 1969 (Chapter 355), IC 1971, 31–3–1–6, Ind.Ann.Stat. § 3–120 (Burns 1970). The consents in the instant case were executed in 1967 prior to the 1969 amendment and this proceeding was tried under the prior law.

tested by such agent; or by notary public: Provided, however, That such attestation shall not be necessary to the consents signed before the taking effect of this act [§§ 3–115—3–125]. Such state department is hereby authorized to furnish to clerks of courts as aforesaid prescribed forms for use by parents or other persons when giving consent. Copies of such consent when same have been signed shall be filed with the investigating agency aforesaid and with the clerk of the court in which the petition for adoption is pending. Such court may cause notice of hearing and opportunity to file objection to be given to the known kindred of the child and any other person or persons deemed entitled to such notice before granting such petition. In all cases where the father of any child or children has failed to pay any support money for a period of one [1] year immediately prior to the filing of adoption proceedings for the adoption of his child or children, the court may in its discretion not require the filing of a consent of the father in such instances." * * *

As respondents correctly assert, the Indiana adoption statute is in derogation of the common law and must be strictly followed in all essential particulars in order to defeat the natural parents' right of custody of their children. * * *

Respondents further contend, and correctly so, that petitioners or persons seeking to adopt a minor child have the burden of proving strict compliance with all particular essentials of the adoption statute. * * *

In the instant case, it was incumbent upon petitioners to prove that the consents obtained from respondents were in strict compliance with the statutory requirements of the Indiana adoption statute, supra. * * * From an examination of the record in this appeal, we fail to find any refutation of the petitioners' proof that the consents satisfied the particular essentials of the statute. * * *

In alleging that the trial court's decision was contrary to law, it would seem upon examination of the arguments set forth in respondents' brief, that respondents challenge the validity of the consents in controversy not for their failure to satisfy the literal requirements of the statute, but rather for their failure to satisfy the statutory requirements as respondents contend they should be interpreted. Their first such contention argues that under the Indiana adoption statute a consent given prior to the birth of the infant to be adopted is not valid. While Burns 3–120 makes no mention of the validity of a consent obtained prior to the birth of a child, respondents contend that the language of the statute is subject only to the interpretation that such a consent is a nullity. Respondents specifically refer to two sentences in the statute which set forth: "If such child have parent or parents living, he, she or they shall consent in writing to such adoption." And, "In every case where such child shall have been born out of wedlock * * *."

It is clear from a careful reading of the statute that it only requires that if the parents are living they must consent in writing to the adoption. We find no direct or indirect reference to the time of the consent in relationship to the birth of the child which would merit the interpretation that the right of custody by consent to adoption can only be given after the birth of the child.

Respondents cite no authority for this interpretation, and while no Indiana court decision directly on point can be found, petitioners have provided us with the case of In re Adoption of Long (1952), Fla., 56 So.2d 450, in support of the contrary interpretation, wherein the Florida Supreme Court stated, at p. 451:

"We cannot agree that the consent agreement, because signed before the birth, was so premature as to be inconsistent with the statutory provision that such a consent be executed by 'the living mother of a child born out of wedlock * * *.' It seems to us that this construction emphasized too much the form and too little the purpose. As we have seen, the welfare of the child has been adequately protected."

*   *   *

Respondents further contend that a "blanket consent" which makes no reference to the adoptive parents in the case of a private placement is not a valid consent. While the controlling statute is silent on the point in issue, and the courts of this state have not been directly confronted with this question, respondents argue that Rhodes et al. v. Shirley et al. (1955), 234 Ind. 587, 129 N.E.2d 60, stands for the proposition that a consent which fails to state the names of the adoptive parents is valid only where the child is placed in the custody of the department of public welfare. We fail to find any language, either expressed or implied, in the *Rhodes,* supra, decision which supports respondents' proposition. In the Rhodes case, it was held that where the natural parents had signed consents to adoption, and had placed their child in the custody of the welfare department for selection of a suitable adoptive home, the validity of the consents would not be defeated for their failure to state the names of the adoptive parents. The question of the effect of a private placement on the validity of a blanket consent was not before the court, and rightfully so that question was not discussed. It was, nonetheless, reasoned in Rhodes that since the welfare department had control over the selection and supervision of a suitable adoptive home, and that since the ultimate responsibility of granting or denying the adoption was with the trial court, that allowing the blanket consents was not inconsistent with adoption procedures as practiced in this state. From such reasoning there may exist the inference that because the welfare department does not exercise the same degree of control over a private placement adoption as it does over a public placement adoption, the use of blanket consents is less desirable in the former than in the latter. However, to hold, as respondents would have us do, that Rhodes stands for the proposition that a consent which fails to state the names of the adoptive parents is only valid where the adoption is by public placement, would be to read into the court's decision something which simply is not there. Furthermore, it should be pointed out that while it is arguably preferable that blanket consents be used only in public placement adoptions, there, nonetheless, exists in private placement adoptions the necessary degree of control by the welfare department, and ultimately by the court, in order to protect the rights of the natural parents, and to reasonably insure that the use of blanket consents does not result in the child being adopted by unsuitable parents. As in the case where a child is placed for adoption in a home by a public agency, in a private placement adoption the ultimate responsibility still rests with the court, aided by the investigation and reports resulting therefrom of the public agency, to upon determination of the facts and issues of the case deny or grant the adoption.

In their brief, respondents state that it is significant that the 1969 Legislature, in enacting the present adoption statute, specifically provided in the section dealing with consents, that:

"A consent which does not name or otherwise identify the adoptive parents is valid if the consent contains a statement by the person whose consent it is, that the person consenting voluntarily executed the consent without disclosure of the name or other identification of the adopting parent." IC 1971, 31–3–1–6, Ind.Ann.Stat. 3–120(c) (Burns 1970).

We cannot agree with respondents' conclusion that prior to the enactment of the present amended statute, that such a consent was not valid unless shown to have been given to the department of public welfare. We find nothing in the cases cited by respondent, or in the statute in effect at the time these consents were executed, which would compel such a conclusion. Since the pertinent section in the statute does not distinguish between adoption cases involving private and public placements, the more reasonable conclusion, we feel, is that a blanket consent in a private placement adoption remains valid in Indiana, but with the recently added safeguard that the natural parents, in addition to consenting in writing to the adoption, must also file a statement that the consent was voluntarily executed without knowledge of the identity of the adoptive parents.

While respondents have not cited any cases in which other jurisdictions have held blanket consents to be invalid in private placement adoptions, they have, nonetheless, referred us to 2 Am.Jur.2d 895, and 24 A.L.R.2d 1138, which indicate that other jurisdictions have so held. The cases cited in the above mentioned annotations have held blanket consents to be invalid for the reasons that: (1) they are against public policy; (2) the consents must be given in or with reference to specific proceedings. The second reason namely that the consent must be given in or with reference to specific proceedings, is not of significance here, since neither our adoption statutes, present or past, nor the courts of the state, have required that consents to be given must be in reference to specific proceedings. In Barwin v. Reidy (1957), 62 N.M. 183, 194, 307 P.2d 175, 182, the Supreme Court of New Mexico, confronted with a factual situation of striking similarity of that of the instant case, dealt with the issue of public policy as follows:

"We are aware of no other statutes or decisions of this Court which may be the basis for the declaration of public policy in this consideration and we are unable to conclude that public policy was violated in the execution of the consents before us.

"We are told that the weight of authority is that blanket consents are void, either by statute, or as violative of public policy, and are referred to an annotation covering the subject in 24 A.L.R.2d at page 1129, where we find analysis of cases from Pennsylvania and North Carolina. In addition, counsel for the natural parents cite to the same effect Sears v. Davis, Tex.Civ.App., 19 S.W.2d 159.

"After examining the cases, we do not think the weight of authority, if such it is, is so formidable as to preclude an independent determination and conclusion to the contrary by this court. Of interest in this connection are the cases: Rhodes v. Shirley, 234 Ind. 587, 129 N.E.2d 60; Lee v. Thomas, 297 Ky. 858, 181 S.W.2d 457; and Adoption of Capparelli, 180 Or. 41, 175 P.2d 153."

As in *Barwin,* supra, this Court is unaware of any statutes or court decisions of this state which have declared blanket consents in private adoptions to be against public policy. To the contrary, the legislature has expressly provided in the present amended statute for blanket consents without distinction between private and public placement.

Of further interest in *Barwin,* supra, is the Court's reasoning, and we feel it to be sound and applicable to the instant case, regarding the legislative intent underlying the adoption statute.

"[6] Since adoption may be refused to petitioners who have the strongest endorsement of the parents, we think it follows that the office of the requirement of consent for adoption is to indicate the willingness of the parents that the natural relationship be swept away and a new one created in its stead. The giving of consent is indicative of the subjective state of mind of the parents—expressive only of the individuals and binding no one unless the court shall choose to act thereon. It is up to the court to perform the objective acts of severing the natural relationship and creating an artificial status by judicial determination. *As it may or may not decree adoption in favor of persons recommended by the natural parents, it seems most unlikely the legislature intended to impose as a condition to the exercise of the court's jurisdiction knowledge of the identity of petitioners in adoption on the part of the natural parents, because even when that circumstance exists, and possibly the further circumstance that the natural parents have investigated the qualifications of the petitioners and given them their unqualified approval, the court may still refuse to decree adoption, the selection of a foster parent being a judicial act and the responsibility being that of the court."* (Emphasis added). 62 N.M. 183, 191, 307 P.2d 175, 181.

It is also significant, respondents' cited annotations notwithstanding, that other jurisdictions besides New Mexico in *Barwin,* supra, have held blanket consents in private adoptions to be valid. Cohen v. Janic (1965), 57 Ill.App.2d 309, 207 N.E.2d 89; McKinney v. Weeks (1961), Fla.App., 130 So.2d 310; In re Adoption of a Minor Child, 127 F.Supp. 256 (D.D.C.1954).

* * *

There being no reversible error, the judgment of the trial court is affirmed.

NOTES AND QUESTIONS

1. The adoption in the *Johnson* case was, as the court indicates, a "private placement". This means that the baby was placed for adoption by someone other than an adoption agency, either by the parents themselves, or more likely by an intermediary such as a lawyer or doctor or both. The other form of adoption is called an agency placement, meaning that the adoption is arranged by a state agency having that authority, such as the state welfare department, or by a licensed private child placement agency. Private agencies are maintained by many religious denominations and operate in many respects like public agencies. Private placements are permitted under the laws of some states but are limited or even prohibited in other states. For an account of the New Jersey procedure for private placements, which may be accomplished only upon a finding that the natural parent has "forsaken parental obligations", see Sees v. Baber, 74 N.J. 201, 377 A.2d 628 (1977).

2. Adoption statutes usually provide specifically for the form and content of the consent to adoption and also specify the persons whose consent is required. Since the consent is of great importance to all parties, it is usually required to be executed before a notary or some other official. For illustrations of consent requirements, see e. g., Cal.Civ.Code §§ 224, 226.1 (Supp.1979); Smith-Hurd Ill.Ann.Stat. ch. 4, §§ 9.1–8, 9.1–9, 9.1–10 (Supp.1979); N.Y.Dom.Rel.L. § 111 (1977); Uniform Adoption Act § 7. The Uniform Parentage Act § 24, 9 Unif.L.Ann. 615 (1979) specifies the consent required for the adoption of an illegitimate child.

Many statutes require that the child himself consent to the adoption when he is over a stated age, usually about fourteen.

3. Where the natural parents' rights have been terminated by their consent to adoption, by a relinquishment proceeding, or by an involuntary proceeding, and their child has been placed in the custody or guardianship of an agency, the agency's consent to the adoption is generally required by

statute. See, e. g., Uniform Adoption Act § 5(a)(3), 9 Unif.L.Ann. 23 (1979). Where the public or private adoption agency refuses to consent to a particular adoption, the courts in many states may override that refusal and approve the adoption, either on a finding that the consent was unreasonably withheld, or that the best interests of the child require approval of the adoption. See, e g, Ritchie v. Children's Home Society of St. Paul, 209 Minn. 149, 216 N.W.2d 900 (1974); State ex rel. Portage County Welfare Dept. v. Summers, 38 Ohio St. 144, 311 N.E.2d 6 (1974), 36 Ohio St.L.J. 451 (1975); Annot., 83 A.L.R.3d 373 (1978); Uniform Adoption Act § 6(a)(8), 9 Unif.L.Ann. 27 (1979). The difficulties created by those statutes which give adoption agencies broad or complete discretion to withhold their consent to adoption are thoroughly discussed in Bodenheimer, New Trends and Requirements in Adoption Law and Proposals for Legislative Change, 49 So.Cal.L.Rev. 10, 76 (1975).

4. What arguments might be made for the natural parents' contention in the *Johnson* case that consents to adoption executed before the birth of the child are invalid? Some statutes, e. g., Smith-Hurd Ill.Ann.Stat. ch. 4, § 9.1–9 (Supp.1979), Uniform Adoption Act § 7(a), 9 Unif.L.Ann. 31 (1979), provide that the consent must occur after the birth of the child. Is that a desirable statutory provision?

5. Why would a "blanket consent" be used in these cases? Why not just fill in the name of the prospective adoptive parent on the consent form? The dissenting judge in *Johnson* argued that the execution of a blanket consent is inconsistent with the duty of the natural parents to select the most suitable foster parents for their child, drew an analogy to deeds and other instruments affecting title to land, and finally argued that blanket consents in private placements aid the black market in babies. Are these arguments persuasive? What should a well drawn adoption statute provide about blanket consents? Cf. Smith-Hurd Ill.Ann.Stat. ch. 4, § 9.-1–10 (Supp.1979), Uniform Adoption Act § 7(b), 9 Unif.L.Ann. 31 (1979); Children's Bureau, Department of Health, Education and Welfare, Legislative Guides for the Termination of Parental Rights and Responsibilities and the Adoption of Children 37 (1961). A case which follows *Johnson* on the question of blanket consents is Matter of Adoption of Jackson, 89 Wash.2d 945, 578 P.2d 33 (1978).

6. You are consulted by H and W who tell you that W has had a child with H's approval through the use of AID. H now wishes to adopt the child in order to avoid any possible questions about the child's status. What consents will be required under the typical adoption statute such as the one in Johnson v. Cupp? Is the typical adoption statute well adapted to the solution of this problem? What should the adoption statute say? If the adoption statute provides that the father of a child must consent to the adoption, would this require the consent of the donor of semen? Cf. In re Adoption of Anonymous, 74 Misc.2d 99, 345 N.Y.S.2d 430 (Surr.Ct.1973), 23 Buff.L.Rev. 548 (1974), in which a child was born to a woman through AID with the consent of her husband. She later was divorced and remarried and her second husband sought to adopt the child. The court held that the "father" of the child was her first husband so that under the applicable statute his consent to the adoption was necessary.

7. Many states have relinquishment statutes which provide a voluntary legal proceeding by which parents may give up their parental rights,

and, of course, also end their parental obligations. The relinquishment proceeding is normally separate from the adoption proceeding, which may occur after the relinquishment decree has been entered. For a carefully drawn statute of this kind, see Colo.Rev.Stat.Ann. §§ 19–4–102, 19–4–103 (1978). See also Uniform Adoption Act § 19, 9 Unif.L.Ann. 51 (1979). Do such statutes present any questions of social policy, as for example when married persons attempt to relinquish their children? Should the court, when passing on a petition for relinquishment, consider the child's welfare as well as the parents' desire to be rid of their child? See Smith v. Welfare Department, 144 Colo. 103, 355 P.2d 317 (1960); MacKay, Today's Controversial Clients: Married Parents Who Place Legitimate Children for Adoption, in I. E. Smith, Readings in Adoption 87 (1963). If the distinctions between legitimate and illegitimate children have been largely eliminated by the Levy v. Louisiana line of cases, why should the relinquishment of a child by married persons be viewed any differently from the relinquishment of a child by unmarried parents?

If the parent relinquishing a child is indigent, should the state be required to furnish such a parent with counsel in the relinquishment proceeding? In re K, 31 Ohio Misc. 218, 282 N.E.2d 370 (Juv.Ct.1969).

8. What should be the effect, under the typical consent statute such as that in *Johnson*, of a consent executed properly in all respects, but containing the condition that the consenting parent be permitted to see and visit the child at reasonable times? Is such a consent valid? What arguments might be made pro and con on this question? See, e. g. In re Adoption of a Minor, 291 N.E.2d 729 (Mass.1973).

9. What should be the result if the parent consented to adoption of her child, but only if the adoptive parents were Mr. and Mrs. Smith? If the court should find that the Smiths were not suitable adoptive parents, could the child be placed with someone else? In re Adoption of Driscoll, 269 Cal.App.2d 735, 75 Cal.Rptr. 382 (1969).

10. Mr. and Mrs. Smith, wishing to adopt a baby, are told by their physician that a patient of his is about to have a baby out of wedlock and that she is willing to consent to its adoption, but that she would like to have her hospital expenses reimbursed, and in addition her wages for time lost from work due to her confinement. The Smiths agree and pay the money to the doctor, who turns over the money to the mother and procures the mother's consent in proper form. Is the consent valid? What are the consequences of saying that it is invalid? (Assume that the father's rights may be properly terminated in a dependency proceeding.)

Many adoption agencies charge fees for their services in arranging adoptions, the amount being based either upon the costs to the agency or upon a more or less arbitrary scale. The income of the adoptive parents may also be relevant in setting the fee. The Child Welfare League of America, Guidelines for Adoption Service, 17–18 (1968) states that adoption service should be financed by the community, but that agencies may properly finance part of their operations by charging fees to those able to pay. The fees, it is said, should be based on the applicants' ability to pay and on the cost of the service. Contributions should not be solicited from applicants.

There are statutes in many states prohibiting the placement of children in adoptive homes for money and imposing criminal penalties for violations. See, e. g., Cal.Penal Code § 273 (1970); Ill.Ann.Stat. ch. 4, §§ 12–1 to 12–5 (1975); N.J.Stat.Ann. § 2A:96–7 (1969). Some of these statutes may contain language broad enough to foreclose the payment of *any* sums in connection with adoption consents. Others may permit the payment of some expenses of the consenting parent. E. g., Colo.Rev.Stat.Ann. § 19–4–115 (1978). A case construing the New Jersey statute and describing the operations of a local black market in babies is State v. Segal, 78 N.J.Super. 273, 188 A.2d 416 (1963), cert. den. 40 N.J. 224, 191 A.2d 63 (1963). People v. Schwartz, 1 Ill.Dec. 8, 64 Ill.2d 275, 356 N.E.2d 8 (1976), cert. den. 429 U.S. 1098 (1977), held the Illinois statute constitutional, rejecting contentions that it was void for vagueness and overbroad. The court held that an attorney performing legal services in adoption proceedings did not violate the statute when he charged a fee for those services, so long as he did not act as an intermediary in the placement of the child.

A news story in the New York Times for April 25, 1976, page 50, col. 3, reports a flourishing black market for adoptions, in which amounts ranging from $5000 to $50,000 were being charged for eligible babies. Although there are many babies who would benefit from adoption, a large proportion of them are either too old, of minority races, suffering from physical or psychological ills or otherwise not attractive to would-be adoptive parents. There is for that reason a shortage of placeable children, according to The Times. The response to the shortage is the development of a commercial market, which of course violates the type of statute described in the preceding paragraph. See also Note, Black—Market Adoptions, 22 Catholic Lawyer 48 (1976); Grove, Independent Adoption: The Case for the Gray Market, 13 Vill.L.Rev. 116 (1967).

It has been proposed as a solution to the problem of the shortage of adoptable babies that the law permit the development of a free market in babies. The suggestion is that if this were done, the price would rise, at least initially, thereby inducing mothers to place their children for adoption rather than to keep them or to have abortions. This would also, they believe, reduce the number of children in foster care. The proposal includes an investigation which would ensure minimal parental competence on the part of the purchasing couple, analogous to the licensing of automobile drivers. As an interim step the authors suggest that fees being presently charged legally by adoption agencies could in part be used for side payments to pregnant women to induce them not to abort, thereby increasing the supply of babies for adoption. Would you favor the creation of such a free market in babies? Landes and Posner, The Economics of the Baby Shortage, 7 J. of Legal Studies 323 (1978).

PEOPLE EX REL. SCARPETTA v. SPENCE–CHAPIN ADOPTION SERVICE

Court of Appeals of New York, 1971.
28 N.Y.2d 185, 269 N.E.2d 787, 321 N.Y.S.2d 65, appeal dismissed and
cert. den. 404 U.S. 805, 92 S.Ct. 54, 30 L.Ed.2d 38 (1971).

JASEN, Judge. This appeal involves the return of an out-of-wedlock infant to its natural mother after she had executed a purported surrender of the child to an authorized adoption agency. The case does not involve the undoing of an adoption or the return of an adopted child to its natural parent. Nor does the case involve the undoing of a surrender by the natural mother on her mere say-so, but rather the undoing is based on a finding of fact that for various reasons, some obvious, the surrender was not made by her with such stability of mind and emotion that the surrender should not be undone for improvidence. On the other hand, there is not the slightest suggestion that the adoption agency was unfair or guilty of any overreaching in obtaining the surrender.

It is or should be obvious that the surrender of a child by its parent, whatever the circumstances or reason, has elements of tragedy in it and that pain, feelings of guilt, and suffering will not be avoided whatever course is taken. And, of course, the foster parents who hope to adopt the child are necessarily touched by the tragedy, guiltless and otherwise uninvolved though they be, if perchance the child is wrested from them on the annulling of a surrender.

A further consideration turns on this court's limited power of review. Where, as here, findings of fact are affirmed by the Appellate Division in a civil matter, the court is bound, by constitutional mandates, to accept those facts. Only questions of law are left for its review. As a consequence, any findings of fact involved in the rendering of the surrender, turning on the mother's then state of mind, or on her fitness to rear her child, are before this court as immutable premises, from which it may only start its review of the applicable questions of law.

The infant child was born on May 18, 1970, to Olga Scarpetta, who was unmarried and 32 years old. She had become pregnant in her native Colombia by a married Colombian in the summer of 1969. Seeking to minimize the shame of an out-of-wedlock child to herself and her family, Miss Scarpetta came to New York for the purpose of having her child. She was well acquainted with this country and its language. She had had her early schooling in New Jersey and her college education in California. Indeed, she had been trained in the social sciences.

Four days after the birth of the child, she placed the infant for boarding care with Spence-Chapin Adoption Service, an agency authorized by statute to receive children for adoption. Ten days later, a surrender document was executed by Miss Scarpetta to the agency, and on June 18, 1970, the baby was placed with a family for adoption. Five days later, on June 23, 1970, the mother repented her actions and requested that the child be returned to her.

After several unsuccessful attempts to regain her child from the agency, the mother commenced this habeas corpus proceeding. Before the surrender, the mother had had a number of interviews with representatives of the adoption agency. On the other hand, shortly before or after the birth of the child, her family in Colombia, well-to-do, and devout in their religion, were shocked that she should put out her child for adoption by strangers. They assured her of their support and backing and urged her to raise her own child.

Special Term, "[a]fter considering all the facts," concluded "that the child should be forthwith returned to petitioner, its natural mother." Following unanimous affirmance by the Appellate Division, 36 A.D.2d 524, 317 N.Y.S.2d 928, we granted leave to appeal, 28 N.Y.2d 658, 320 N.Y.S.2d 527, 269 N.E.2d 196.

The resolution of the issue of whether or not a mother, who has surrendered her child to an authorized adoption agency, may regain the child's custody, has received various treatment by the legislatures and courts in the United States.[1] At one extreme, several jurisdictions adhere to the rule that the parent has an absolute right to regain custody of her child prior to the final adoption decree.[2] On the other hand, some jurisdictions adhere to the rule that the parent's surrender is final, absent fraud or duress.[3] The majority of the jurisdictions, however, place the parent's right to regain custody within the discretion of the court—the position which, of course, our Legislature has taken. The discretionary rule allows the court leeway to approve a revocation of the surrender when the facts of the individual case warrant it and avoids the obvious dangers posed by the rigidity of the extreme positions.

In New York, a surrender executed by a mother, in which she voluntarily consents to a change of guardianship and custody to an authorized agency for the purpose of adoption, is expressly sanctioned by law. (Social Services Law, Consol.Laws, c. 55, § 384.) The statute nowhere endows a surrender with irrevocability foreclosing a mother from applying to the court to restore custody of the child to her. In fact, the legislation is clear that, until there has been

1. See Katz, Law of Adoption, 51 Geo.L.J. 64, 87; Comment, Revocation of Parental Consent to Adoption: Legal Doctrine and Social Policy, 28 U.Chi.L.Rev. 564.

2. See, e. g., In re Baby Girl Larson, 252 Minn. 490, 91 N.W.2d 448; but cf. Minn.Stat. § 259.24, subd. 6, [1969]; S.D.Code, tit. 14, § 14.0406 [1939]. In North Carolina and Tennessee, the right is continuous up until a certain period of time before the issuance of the final decree. (N.C. Gen.Stat., § 48–11 [1966]; Tenn.Code Ann., § 36–117 [1962].)

3. See, e. g., Catholic Charities v. Harper, 161 Tex. 21, 337 S.W.2d 111; Gonzales v. Toma, 330 Mich. 35, 46 N.W.2d 453; La.Rev.Stat.Ann., tit. 9, § 404 (1965).

an actual adoption,[7] or the agency has met the requirements of the Social Services Law (§ 384, subd. 4),[8] the surrender remains under, and subject to, judicial supervision.

Inherent to judicial supervision of surrenders is the recognition that documents of surrender are unilateral, not contracts or deeds, and are almost always executed under circumstances which may cast doubt upon their voluntariness or on understanding of the consequences of their execution. Indeed, no one could reasonably urge that the Legislature enact a statute or that a court decide that the natural mother be prevented from establishing that her surrender was not the voluntary act of a competent person. Of necessity, therefore, there is always an issue about the fact of surrender, document or no document. On the other hand, the courts have the strongest obligation not to permit surrenders to be undone except for the weightiest reasons. * * *

Having the power to direct a change of custody from the agency back to the natural parent, notwithstanding the document of surrender, the court should exercise it only when it determines "that the interest of such child will be promoted thereby and that such parent is fit, competent and able to duly maintain, support and educate such child." (Social Services Law, § 383, subd. 1.) Accordingly, the sole issue before us on this appeal is whether there is any evidence in the record to establish that the interest of the child will be promoted by returning the child to the natural mother.

It has repeatedly been determined, insofar as the best interests of the child are concerned, that "[t]he mother or father has a right to the care and custody of a child, superior to that of all others, unless he or she has abandoned that right or is proved unfit to assume the duties and privileges of parenthood." (People ex rel. Kropp v. Shepsky, 305 N.Y. 465, 468, 113 N.E.2d 801, 803; * * *. It has been well said that "the status of a natural parent" is so important "that in determining the best interests of the child, it may counterbalance, even outweigh, superior material and cultural advantages which may be afforded by adoptive parents * * * For experience

---

7. Domestic Relations Law, Consol. Laws, c. 14 (§ 112, subd. 6) provides: "Where the adoptive child is less than eighteen years of age, no order of adoption shall be made until such child has resided with the adoptive parents for at least six months unless the judge or surrogate in his discretion shall dispense with such period of residence and shall recite in the order the reason for such action."

8. Social Services Law (§ 384): "4. Upon petition by an authorized agen- cy, a surrogate or judge of the family court may approve such surrender, on such notice to such persons as the surrogate or judge may in his discretion prescribe. No person who has received such notice and been afforded an opportunity to be heard may challenge the validity of a surrender approved pursuant to this subdivision in any other proceeding. However, this subdivision shall not be deemed to require approval of a surrender by a surrogate or judge for such surrender to be valid."

teaches that a mother's love is one factor which will endure: possibly endure after other claimed material advantages and emotional attachments may have proven transient." (People ex rel. Grament v. Free Synagogue Child Adoption Committee, supra, 194 Misc. at pp. 337–338, 85 N.Y.S.2d p. 546.) And, indeed, as recently as 1963, the Legislature expressed its approval of this "decisional rule that between parent and non-parent the parent is preferred". (Report of Joint Legislative Committee on Matrimonial and Family Laws, N.Y.Legis. Doc., 1963, No. 34, p. 91.)

The primacy of status thus accorded the natural parent is not materially altered or diminished by the mere fact of surrender under the statute, although it is a factor to be considered by the court. To hold, as the agency suggests—that a surrender to an authorized adoption agency constitutes, as a matter of law, an abandonment—would frustrate the policy underlying our legislation (Social Services Law, § 383, subd. 1), which allows a mother to regain custody of her child, notwithstanding the surrender to the agency, provided, of course, that there is some showing of improvidence in the making of the surrender, that the interest of such child will be promoted and "that such parent is fit, competent and able to duly maintain, support and educate such child." Nor do we perceive any distinction, in principle, between the effect of a surrender to an authorized agency and of a surrender to an individual. "The policy urged that, if surrender may be undone, authorized agencies will be inconvenienced or even frustrated in their placement of children is not a sufficient counterweight. The fact of relationship between a natural parent and child ought not to be subordinated to such considerations, important as they are." (People ex rel. Anonymous v. New York Foundling Hosp., 17 A.D.2d 122, 125, 232 N.Y.S.2d 479, 483, affd. 12 N.Y.2d 863, 237 N.Y.S.2d 339, 187 N.E.2d 791.)

Consequently, to give the fundamental principle meaning and vitality, we have explicitly declared that "[e]xcept where a nonparent has obtained legal and permanent custody of a child by adoption, guardianship or otherwise, he who would take or withhold a child from mother or father must sustain the burden of establishing that the parent is unfit and that the child's welfare compels awarding its custody to the nonparent." (People ex rel. Kropp v. Shepsky, supra, 305 N.Y. at p. 469, 113 N.E.2d at p. 804.)[10] In determining fitness, it

10. And, in our later decision in People ex rel. Anonymous v. Anonymous, supra, 10 N.Y.2d at p. 335, 222 N.Y.S.2d at p. 946, 179 N.E.2d at p. 201, we wrote, in like fashion, that "where the contest for the custody of a child is between parent and nonparent, 'the primacy of parental rights may not be ignored' (People ex rel. Kropp v. Shepsky, 305 N.Y. 465, 469, 113 N.E.2d 801 supra), but it has never been held or suggested that the child's welfare may ever be forgotten or disregarded. In other words, the law presumes that it is in the child's best interests that he be raised by his natural parent, but this presumption fails when it is proved that the parent has abandoned the child or is not fit to rear him. 'The mother or father has a right to the care and custody of a child, superior to that of all

is obvious that a mother who is "a drunkard, an incompetent, a notoriously immoral person, cruel or unkind towards [her] child" (Matter of Gustow, 220 N.Y. 373, 377, 115 N.E. 995, 997), or whose conduct evinces indifference or irresponsibility (Matter of Cleaves, 6 A.D.2d 138, 175 N.Y.S.2d 736) would not be a proper person to assume the duties of motherhood. Another significant factor to be considered is the "motivation of the mother in seeking return of the child. It is recognized that very often there is a substantial risk of improper motivation. In such case the authorized agency and the court must be especially alert not to permit the improper motivation to endanger the interests of the child or lead to any other noxious consequence. As important as this factor is, however, it is also true that the change of mind by a natural mother is not an evil thing. Instead, the change of mind is to be accorded great sympathy, and, in a proper case, encouragement and favorable action." (People ex rel. Anonymous v. New York Foundling Hosp., supra, 17 A.D.2d p. 125, 232 N.Y. S.2d p. 483.)

In no case, however, may a contest between a parent and nonparent resolve itself into a simple factual issue as to which affords the better surroundings, or as to which party is better equipped to raise the child. (People ex rel. Portnoy v. Strasser, 303 N.Y. 539, 104 N. E.2d 895, supra.) It may well be that the prospective adoptive parents would afford a child some material advantages over and beyond what the natural mother may be able to furnish, but these advantages, passing and transient as they are, cannot outweigh a mother's tender care and love unless it is clearly established that she is unfit to assume the duties and privileges of parenthood.

We conclude that the record before us supports the finding by the courts below that the surrender was improvident and that the child's best interests—moral and temporal—will be best served by its return to the natural mother.

Within 23 days after the child had been given over to the agency, and only 5 days after the prospective adoptive parents had gained provisional custody of the child, the mother sought its return. If the matter had been resolved at that time, much heartache and distress would have been avoided. However, since the child was not returned, the mother had no alternative but to commence legal proceedings to regain its custody, and this she did without delay.

In revoking the surrender and directing the return of the child to the mother, the trial court held that the mother was "motivated solely by her concern for the well-being of her child." Moreover, the evidence fully supports the conclusion that the mother "has adequately stabilized her own relationships and has become stable enough in her

others unless', we pointed out in the *Kropp* case (305 N.Y. at p. 468, 113 N.E.2d at p. 803), 'he or she has abandoned that right or is proved unfit to assume the duties and privileges of parenthood.' "

own mind to warrant the return of the child to her." No finding of present or prospective unfitness has been made against the mother. On the contrary, the record discloses that she is well educated, financially secure, and in a position to properly assume the care, training and education of her child.

Concluding as we do that the record supports the determination that the child's interests will be promoted by the award of its custody to the mother, we turn to the remaining issue of whether the prospective adoptive parents were entitled to intervene in this proceeding, as a matter of law, pursuant to CPLR 1012 (subd. [a], par. 2).

It cannot be doubted that the public policy of our State is contrary to the disclosure of the names and identities of the natural parents and prospective adoptive parents to each other. Sections 383 and 384 of the Social Services Law are also reflective of this settled public policy. Since the relationship under section 384 is exclusively between the parent or parents and the adoption agency, and the Legislature has not deemed it appropriate for the prospective adoptive parents to be parties to the proceeding pursuant to section 383, the agency acts as an insulating intermediary, ensuring by the separation of the natural parents and prospective adoptive parents the secrecy necessary to prevent the strife and harassment that could be caused by a parent who institutes a proceeding merely to learn the identity of the prospective adoptive parents.

To allow the prospective adoptive parents to intervene as a matter of right, thereby assuming all the rights of other parties to the action, would necessarily lead to disclosure of the names of the natural parents and prospective adoptive parents to each other. In view of the statutory scheme enacted by the Legislature to guard against such disclosure, and the settled public policy, we are unwilling to hold that the prospective adoptive parents are entitled to intervene.

Similarly, we find no merit to the contention that the failure to allow the prospective adoptive parents to intervene in the instant proceeding deprived them of due process of law so as to render the court's determination awarding custody of the child to the mother, constitutionally invalid. The prospective adoptive parents do not have legal custody of the baby. Spence-Chapin, the adoption agency, by virtue of the mother's surrender, was vested with legal custody. * * * The agency, in turn, had placed the baby with the prospective adoptive parents pursuant to an arrangement reached between them, for the purpose of prospective adoption of the child. This arrangement is, of course, subject to our adoption statutes, and in no way conveys any vested rights in the child to the prospective adoptive parents. (See, e. g., Domestic Relations Law, §§ 112, 114.) It follows, therefore, that, in not being permitted to intervene, they are not deprived of a protected interest, as contemplated by the Constitution.

The order of the Appellate Division should be affirmed, without costs.

* * *

NOTES AND QUESTIONS

1. The New York legislature in 1972 changed the rules governing revocation of consent by enacting extensive new statutes. N.Y.Dom.Rel.L. § 115-b (1977) sets forth the conditions on which consent to private placement adoptions may be revoked, providing among other matters that such consent becomes irrevocable after thirty days. N.Y.Soc.Serv.L. § 384(5) (1976) provides that if the surrender instrument so states, no revocation of the surrender may be had where the child has been placed in the home of adoptive parents and thirty days have elapsed after execution of the surrender, but this does not bar revocation for fraud, duress or coercion. This section governs agency placements. Furthermore, N.Y.Soc.Serv.L. § 383(5) (1976) provides that in a suit for custody of a child placed in an adoptive home, or to revoke a surrender, the parents who surrendered the child shall have no rights superior to that of the adoptive parents, notwithstanding that the surrendering parents are fit and competent. A puzzling case which either refuses to follow Social Services Law § 384 or perhaps holds it unconstitutional is Janet G. v. N.Y. Foundling Hospital, 94 Misc.2d 133, 403 N.Y.S.2d 646 (Fam.Ct.1978), 28 Drake L.J. 211 (1978).

2. The history of this case, which received much newspaper publicity as the case of the "Baby Lenore", is given in Foster, Adoption and Child Custody: Best Interests of the Child? 22 Buff.L.Rev. 1, 7–14 (1972). Before the New York Court of Appeals decision in the case, Mr. and Mrs. Di Martino, the adoptive parents, moved to Florida and claimed from that time to be Florida residents. The child's mother sought habeas corpus in Florida, asking that the New York judgment be enforced, but the Florida court held that the baby should remain with Mr. and Mrs. Di Martino.

3. What is the force of this case as a precedent outside New York, in states having no legislation controlling the revocation of consent, in view of the legislature's evident disapproval of the case and the New York statutes changing the applicable rules? What is the effect of an attempted revocation in New York before thirty days have expired? Notice that Miss Scarpetta apparently revoked her consent before the expiration of thirty days.

4. Should the adoptive parents have been permitted to intervene in the case, under a rule which authorizes intervention as of right when the applicant claims an interest in the transaction which is the subject of the action and he is so situated that the disposition of the action may as a practical matter impair or impede his ability to protect that interest, unless the applicant's interest is adequately represented by existing parties? N.Y.Civ. Prac.L. & R. 1012(a)(2) (1976) permits intervention when representation by a party is or may be inadequate and where the applicant is or may be bound by the judgment.

5. If you had represented Mr. and Mrs. Di Martino, after they had been denied the right to intervene, and the trial court had decided in favor of the natural mother, what would you have advised them to do? Would you have advised them to move to another state, say, Florida? Are there

any ethical problems for the lawyer in this situation? See American Bar Association, Code of Professional Responsibility, Canon 7, DR 7-102, EC 7-22. When the Di Martinos moved to Florida with the child, were they in contempt of the New York court's decision? In this connection you might look at the materials in Chapter 6, section 8, of this book, dealing with somewhat similar questions respecting custody, particularly May v. Anderson, infra, page 1029, and the questions which follow it.

6. Consider the following case: T and P were married and had a baby, D. Eight days after the birth T told P he had lost his job and was going to leave her, whereupon P became hysterical. She talked with a friend, who advised her to place the baby for adoption with Mr. and Mrs. H, people she knew who were responsible and wanted to adopt a child. P did not know that her friend had become "emotionally involved" with T. The friend then told Mr. and Mrs. H about the child, and they had their attorney call P to ask whether she wanted to release the baby for adoption. P talked with T about this, taking the position that she wanted to give up the baby, because she was too troubled by all that was happening to her. At the suggestion of the lawyer, T and P went to the welfare department two days later where they were interviewed by a social worker who explained that any release of the child would be final. The attorney had told them the adoption would not be final for six months. They then executed consents which complied with the local law in form. The applicable statute provided that a properly executed consent would be irrevocable unless obtained by fraud or duress. The same day the baby was turned over to Mr. and Mrs. H, who some time later brought an adoption proceeding. By then P had changed her mind and opposed the adoption. The trial court approved the adoption, but on appeal it was held that the consent of P was obtained by fraud and duress and the decree of adoption, vacated and set aside. The appellate court also was critical of the lawyer for Mr. and Mrs. H on the ground that he had given advice to a person (P) who was not represented by a lawyer. At this point Mr. H took a job in a distant state. If you had represented Mr. and Mrs. H, what would you have advised them to do? See Huebert v. Marshall, 132 Ill.App.2d 793, 270 N.E.2d 464 (1971).

7. The court in Scarpetta seems to say that surrenders, or consents to adoption are generally suspect, as not being voluntary. What evidence has the court for this view? At the same time the court says that surrenders must not be "undone except for the weightiest reasons". Were there weighty reasons in this case? What were they?

8. The court also states that a mother's love endures longer than other attachments. What evidence does the court have for this statement? Is there any evidence in this opinion that Miss Scarpetta had any stronger attachment to this child than Mrs. Di Martino? By the time this case was decided by the Court of Appeals, the child was one year old. Who was her "mother" at that time, Miss Scarpetta whom she had scarcely seen, or Mrs. Di Martino? J. Goldstein, A. Freud, A. Solnit, Beyond The Best Interests of the Child (1973).

9. Should there be any presumption whatever in favor of the biological parent in cases of this kind, or is the better social policy to do as the new New York statute requires and decide the case solely on the basis of the child's welfare? Presumably that welfare will very often dictate leav-

ing the child in the home to which he has become accustomed. See the *Painter* case and discussion following it, infra, page 1091.

10. If the statute permits revocation of consent only for fraud, duress, or coercion, what sorts of circumstances constitute fraud, duress or coercion? Did they exist in the *Huebert* case?

11. Under most statutes, the minority of the parent who is relinquishing the child or consenting to its adoption does not invalidate the relinquishment or consent. See, e. g., Batt v. Nebraska Children's Home Society, 185 Neb. 124, 174 N.W.2d 88 (1970).

12. In the *Scarpetta* case the adoptive parents moved to Florida and subsequent litigation occurred there. This raises the following questions, among others:

(a) In a habeas corpus proceeding brought by Miss Scarpetta in Florida in which she asked that the Florida court enforce the New York judgment, must Florida give full faith and credit to the New York judgment under Article IV, section 1 of the United States Constitution? Cf. May v. Anderson, infra, page 1029 and notes following that case; In re Benfield, 468 S.W.2d 156 (Tex.Civ.App.1971); H. Clark, Law of Domestic Relations, 605 (1968).

(b) If the Florida law were to the effect that a revocation of consent to adoption could not be effected after the child had been placed with the adoptive parents, contrary to the then law of New York, whose law should the Florida court apply in passing on the petition for habeas corpus? See Restatement, Second, Conflict of Laws § 289 (1971).

13. (a) What result should the court reach on the following facts? L, a high school girl of seventeen became pregnant and as a result, several months later married the baby's father. The baby was born two months after the marriage. L and her husband lived together in the home of L's parents for about nine months, after which the husband left and he and L were then divorced. L was able to get a job but her earnings were low and she had many debts, including medical and hospital bills for the birth of the baby and a lawyer's bill for her divorce. Her ex-husband had no job and contributed nothing for the baby's support. L had an infection which was being treated but was not responding to treatment. Her mother and father, with whom she continued to live, then separated and sold the house, so that L had to get an apartment. The new need for rent made her competely unable to meet her expenses, including one hundred dollars per month for baby sitters during working hours. Becoming depressed and quite desperate about her responsibilities for the baby, and about her debts, and without any friends or relatives whom she felt she could turn to for help, L went to Baby Fold, a local adoption agency. She was interviewed there by a social worker, who asked her whether she wanted to place the child in temporary foster care, or with people who would adopt him. L said she wished to place the child for adoption. L made an appointment to return two days later. When she returned with the baby, the same social worker asked whether she still wanted to give the baby up for adoption and L said she did. Thereupon she was given a document containing an agreement to surrender the baby and to give up her parental rights, in form complying with the local law. L signed it after it was explained to her by the social worker, and the baby was left with Baby Fold. Four days later L had a talk

with Mr. and Mrs. A, older acquaintances, and told them she wanted her baby back. They suggested she consult a lawyer, which she did a couple of days later, and three weeks after that the lawyer filed a petition for habeas corpus, seeking the revocation of the consent and the return of the child. In the meantime Baby Fold had placed the baby with Mr. and Mrs. X, a prospective adoptive couple who had been waiting some time to adopt a child and were approved for adoption by Baby Fold's social work staff. Assume that the baby's father's rights have been terminated and that habeas corpus is the proper form of proceeding.

(b) How should this case be decided under the following types of statute dealing with revocation of consent?

i. The New York statute described in paragraph 1, supra.

ii. "A consent to adoption by a parent, including a minor, executed and acknowledged in accordance with the provisions of Section 8 of this Act, or a surrender of a child by a parent, including a minor, to an agency for the purpose of adoption shall be irrevocable unless it shall have been obtained by fraud or duress on the part of the person before whom such consent, surrender, or other document equivalent to a surrender is acknowledged pursuant to the provisions of Section 10 of this Act or on the part of the adopting parents or their agents and a court of competent jurisdiction shall so find." Ill.Ann.Stat. ch. 4, § 9.1–11 (1975).

iii. "A consent to adoption may be withdrawn prior to the entry of a decree of adoption if the Court finds, after notice and an opportunity to be heard is afforded to petitioner, the person seeking the withdrawal, and the agency placing a child for adoption, that the withdrawal is in the best interest of the individual to be adopted and the Court orders the withdrawal." Uniform Adoption Act § 8, 9 Unif.L.Ann. 32 (1979).

iv. Could you draft a statute which would deal more satisfactorily with the problem of revocation of consent?

The facts in this hypothetical case resemble those in Regenold v. Baby Fold, Inc., 12 Ill.Dec. 151, 68 Ill.2d 419, 369 N.E.2d 858 (1977), dismissed for want of a substantial federal question 435 U.S. 963 (1978).

14. Revocation of consent to adoption is a much litigated issue. Many of the cases are collected in Annot., What Constitutes Undue Influence in Obtaining a Parent's Consent to Adoption of a Child, 50 A.L.R.3d 918 (1973); Annot. Right of Natural Parent to Withdraw Valid Consent to Adoption of Child, 74 A.L.R.3d 421 (1976); Annot., Mistake or Want of Understanding As Ground for Revocation of Consent to Adoption or of Agreement Releasing Infant to Adoption Placement Agency, 74 A.L.R.3d 489 (1976); Annot., What Constitutes "Duress" in Obtaining Parent's Consent to Adoption of Child or Surrender of Child to Adoptoin Agency, 74 A.L.R.3d 527 (1976).

15. Considerable publicity was given to Vietnamese parents who gave up their children as the war in Vietnam was coming to an end and who later sought to get them back in the United States. A case which ordered the return of such a child to his natural mother after he was placed for adoption is Doan Thi Hoang Anh v. Nelson, 245 N.W.2d 511 (Iowa 1976).

C. TERMINATING THE RIGHTS OF THE NATURAL PARENT

IN RE B.

Court of Appeals of New York, 1972.
30 N.Y.2d 352, 285 N.E.2d 288, 334 N.Y.S.2d 133.

FULD, Chief Judge. Whether the Family Court is required to advise an indigent parent, charged with child neglect, that he is entitled to be represented by assigned counsel is the question presented by this appeal.[1]

In June of 1969, the Westchester County Commissioner of Social Services, the petitioner-respondent herein, filed a charge of child neglect against the respondent-appellant. The petitioner asserts that the appellant left her three-year-old daughter home alone between one and four o'clock in the morning of June 21 and that, during her absence, the little girl was allegedly kidnapped and raped by a friend of the appellant. The child was represented by a law guardian. When the matter came before the Family Court, the judge presiding, after reading the petition to the appellant, spoke to her as follows:

"You may be represented by an attorney in this proceeding, in which case you must obtain one yourself, and pay for him out of your own funds, or you may waive an attorney and either admit or deny the facts in the petition if you want. Do you want an attorney?

"Mrs. B.: No.

"The Court: Do you admit the facts in the petition?

"Mrs. B.: Yes, I do."

Thereupon, without further ado, the judge stated that he was "going to find that [the appellant's daughter] is a neglected child and will continue the child in custody of the Child Protective Services". An order was entered adjudicating her a neglected child and directing that she be placed in the petitioner's custody.[2]

Very shortly after the adjudication of neglect, which was made in July, 1969, the appellant obtained the assistance of the Legal Aid Society. A notice of appeal was filed and, in September, a Legal Aid attorney instituted a proceeding to terminate the child's placement

---

1. The Family Court Act (§ 1043, subd. [a]; prior to May 1, 1970, § 343, subd. [a]) makes provision for legal representation but is silent with respect to the right of indigent parents to assigned counsel:

"The court shall advise the parent or other person legally responsible for the child's care of a right to be represented by counsel of his own choosing and to have an adjournment to send for counsel and consult with him."

2. Not a word had been said to the appellant that she might lose the custody of the child. Indeed, as the colloquy between the judge and her made clear, she believed that she would be permitted to take the child home and, after the judge indicated that the child was to be taken from her, she made a feeble, and unsuccessful, attempt to set forth circumstances which might have provided a basis for a meritorious defense in the hands of an attorney.

with the petitioner. In February, 1970, while the proceeding was pending, the youngster was informally returned to her mother's home. At the termination hearing some months later—in the fall of 1970—the appellant's attorney, after some preliminary cross-examination of the one witness called, declined to continue the defense because of a "misapprehension" of the nature of the proceeding and moved to strike "all" proceedings previously held and to have a hearing *de novo*. The judge denied the motion, adhered to his original determination and continued the child in the petitioner's custody, noting that she could be taken from the mother's physical custody upon the petitioner's application.

The Appellate Division unanimously affirmed the original order of July, 1969, and the appeal is before us as of right on constitutional grounds (CPLR 5601, subd. [b], par. 1).

The determination must be reversed. In our view, an indigent parent, faced with the loss of a child's society, as well as the possibility of criminal charges   *   *   *   is entitled to the assistance of counsel. A parent's concern for the liberty of the child, as well as for his care and control, involves too fundamental an interest and right (see, e. g., Stanley v. State of Illinois, 405 U.S. 645, 92 S.Ct. 1208, 31 L.Ed. 2d 551, decided April 3, 1972;   *   *   *   to be relinquished to the State without the opportunity for a hearing, with assigned counsel if the parent lacks the means to retain a lawyer. To deny legal assistance under such circumstances would—as the courts of other jurisdictions have already held (see, e. g., Cleaver v. Wilcox, decided March 22, 1972 [40 USLW 2658]; State v. Jamison, 251 Or. 114, 118, 444 P.2d 15, 444 P.2d 1005; see, also, Boddie v. Connecticut, 401 U.S. 371, 91 S.Ct. 780, 28 L.Ed.2d 113; Note, Child Neglect: Due Process for the Parent, 70 Col.L.Rev. 465; but cf. In re Robinson, 8 Cal.App.3d 783, 87 Cal.Rptr. 678, cert. den. *sub nom.* Kaufman v. Carter, 402 U. S. 954, 964, 91 S.Ct. 1624, 29 L.Ed.2d 128)—constitute a violation of his due process rights and, in light of the express statutory provision for legal representation for those who can afford it, a denial of equal protection of the laws as well. As the Federal District Court wrote in the very similar *Cleaver* case,

"whether the proceeding be labelled 'civil' or 'criminal,' it is fundamentally unfair, and a denial of due process of law for the state to seek removal of the child from an indigent parent without according that parent the right to the assistance of court-appointed and compensated counsel.   *   *   *   Since the state is the adversary   *   *   *   there is a gross inherent imbalance of experience and expertise between the parties if the parents are not represented by counsel. The parent's interest in the liberty of the child, in his care and in his control, has long been recognized as a fundamental interest.   *   *   *   Such an interest may not be curtailed by the state without a meaningful opportunity to be heard, which in these circumstances includes the assistance of counsel."

Once the conclusion is reached that one has a right to be represented by assigned counsel—and, as noted, the petitioner does not dispute that the appellant did have such a right—it follows that one is entitled to be so advised. If the rule were otherwise, if the party before the court was not apprised of his right to assigned counsel, there could be no assurance either that he knew he had such a right or that he had waived it. Certainly, the appellant in the present case could not have realized that she would have been provided with a lawyer if she could not afford to retain one. In point of fact, the judge actually told her that, if she desired an attorney, "you must obtain one yourself, and pay for him out of your own funds". This statement completely excluded the availability of assigned counsel or other free legal assistance. Consequently, the appellant's negative answer to the question, "[d]o you want an attorney?" could not possibly be deemed an intelligent or understanding waiver of her right to counsel. * * *

The order appealed from should, therefore, be modified, without costs, and the matter remitted for further proceedings in accordance with this opinion and, as so modified, affirmed.

NOTES AND QUESTIONS

1. Subsequent cases holding that there is a constitutional right to counsel on the part of parents in a proceeding for the termination of their parental rights include Davis v. Page, 442 F.Supp. 258 (S.D.Fla.1977); Smith v. Edmiston, 431 F.Supp. 941 (W.D.Tenn.1977); Department of Public Welfare v. J. K. B., —— Mass. ——, 393 N.E.2d 406 (1979). The assistance of counsel is provided for by statute in some states. E. g., Cal.Civ. Code § 237.5 (Supp.1979), applied in In re Richard E., 21 Cal.3d 349, 146 Cal.Rptr. 604, 579 P.2d 495 (1978), dismissed for want of a substantial federal question, 439 U.S. 1060 (1979).

2. Is it the "possibility of criminal charges" which persuades the New York Court of Appeals that the parent is entitled to have counsel assigned at state expense in this case? Or is it the rule of this case that an indigent person is entitled to counsel in any neglect or dependency proceeding, whether or not criminal charges are a possibility? Cf. In re Gault, 387 U.S. 1 (1967), with Parham v. J. R., 442 U.S. 584, 99 S.Ct. 2493 (1979). See also Kennedy v. Mendoza-Martinez, 372 U.S. 144 (1963) and Heryford v. Parker, 396 F.2d 393 (10th Cir. 1968).

3. Suppose that an unmarried mother consented to the adoption of her child and later changed her mind, seeking to have the consent set aside. If she were indigent, should counsel be provided for her in that case? See paragraph 7, supra, page 493.

4. Under this case must counsel be provided for indigent persons in all cases involving custody of children? Cf. Boddie v. Connecticut, 401 U. S. 371 (1971) with United States v. Kras, 409 U.S. 434 (1973).

5. Under this case does the child have the right to have counsel assigned to represent him in a neglect case where the rights of his parents may be terminated? Bear in mind that the effect of such a decree is to

end any claim the child may have against his natural parents for support or inheritance. N. J. Div. of Youth & Family Services v. Wandell, 155 N.J.Super. 302, 382 A.2d 711 (Juv. and Dom.Rel.Ct.1978); F. v. C., 24 Or.App. 601, 547 P.2d 175 (1976), cert. den. 429 U.S. 907 (1976). Must the child be made a party to such a proceeding? Matter of Shutts, 29 Or.App. 121, 563 P.2d 1221 (1977).

6. There is authority that the requirement of notice in a proceeding to terminate parental rights implies that the notice must specify that parental rights may be terminated as a result of the proceeding. Robinson v. People In Interest of Zollinger, 173 Colo. 113, 476 P.2d 262 (1970). Is this required by the Due Process Clause? Martin v. Superior Court, 3 Wash. App. 405, 476 P.2d 134 (1970).

7. The parents in a termination proceeding must be given a full and fair hearing, at which they are entitled to be present. In the Matter of Houts III, 7 Wash.App. 476, 499 P.2d 1276 (1972). The decree must be based on adequate evidence even though the parents fail to appear or contest the petition. In re M————, 446 S.W.2d 508 (Mo.App.1969).

PETITION OF NEW ENGLAND HOME FOR LITTLE WANDERERS

Supreme Judicial Court of Massachusetts, 1975.
367 Mass. 631, 328 N.E.2d 854.

KAPLAN, Justice. The New England Home for Little Wanderers (Home), which had had custody of the unmarried mother's child from about the time of its birth ten months previously, filed a petition in the Probate Court for Suffolk County on April 23, 1973, to dispense with the need for the mother's consent to a subsequent adoption of the child. The petition was under G.L. c. 210, § 3, as amended through St.1972, c. 800, § 2. Subsections (b) and (c) of § 3 allow a licensed child care agency to commence such a proceeding with regard to any child in its "care or custody"; the court is to approve the petition if it finds that "the best interests of the child" will be served thereby, and in making this determination the court "shall consider the ability, capacity, fitness and readiness of the child's parents * * * to assume parental responsibility, and shall also consider the plan proposed by the * * * agency initiating the petition." In this case, the Home's plan was to sponsor adoption of the child by a specific family. After a hearing at which the mother was represented and the facts were brought out, the probate judge granted the Home's petition. The mother appeals, attacking the court's application of § 3 as well as the constitutionality of that statute.

The mother's major argument is that, since the Home's custody of the child originated in a voluntary consent given by her, and since she later changed her mind and now wishes to keep the child, the court must decide the case, not by applying the standard of "best interests of the child" set out in § 3, but rather by bringing in the parental "unfitness" test used in suits under the guardianship laws to

remove children from the custody of their parents. See G.L. c. 201, §
5. In approaching the mother's contentions, it will be well first to set
out the facts of the case as they appear from the probate judge's report of material facts; the evidence is not reported.

Finding she was pregnant, the mother entered the Crittenton
Hastings House. There a social worker from the Home discussed
with her possible alternatives for caring for the expected child. The
mother said she planned to have the child adopted. Foster care was
explained to her as an alternative which could provide time for her to
make permanent plans for the child. After the birth of the child on
June 28, 1972, the mother returned to the Crittenton for a short time
and while there gave written consent to the Home's assuming care
and custody of the child; she had by that time met the prospective
foster parents with whom the Home was to place the child.

When she gave birth the mother was thirty years old and unmarried. Her mother was dead. She lived with her retired seventy-
year old father and two unmarried brothers; her father was dependent for support on social security benefits and contributions from the
brothers. Her employment since leaving high school after the second
year had mostly been in factories. She returned to work in August,
1972, after the baby was born, but was laid off in April, 1973; at the
time of the Probate Court hearing in January, 1974, she was still unemployed and was receiving unemployment compensation. She had a
bank account of between $500 and $1,000, paid $18 a week toward
the foster care of her child, had a car, and paid for the boarding of a
horse which she owned.

During the period between the birth of the baby and the filing of
the petition by the Home, the mother consulted with the Home's social worker as well as with the family counselor. Her action, however, was vacillating and indecisive; no plan emerged with any defi-
niteness that offered a realistic means by which she could raise and
care for her child. Within a month of the baby's birth, she seemed
to reverse her previous wish and expressed a desire to keep the child.
But she could only suggest vaguely that she would have a friend care
for the child or that she would go on welfare; she had no job at the
time, her father was refusing to allow her to bring the child into his
household, and she had no crib or clothing for the child. About the
same time she failed to show up at a meeting with the foster parents
that was set to allow her to see the child as she requested. In August, by contrast, she made an unannounced visit to the child. The
following month the social worker again met with her to discuss
plans for the child, but although she was employed by this time her
thoughts remained vague and unrealistic. Later in the fall, she had
an attorney write a letter to the Home saying she wished the child
returned, but this was never followed up. In November she again
failed to appear at a meeting arranged with the foster parents so that
she could see the child; again this was followed by an unannounced

visit. She expressed unhappiness with her job to her family counselor and mentioned she would prefer selling, perhaps cars or real estate, or working with animals. She thought of raising and selling Burmese kittens. An appointment was made for her to see a person who raised animals but she failed to keep the appointment. By the time of the hearing on the Home's petition, she had lost her job. Her father now said he was willing to allow the baby into the household. He had thought, however, that his daughter could not cope with a baby. The mother's plan as expressed at the hearing was to get a job and have her father or a babysitter care for the child.

On these facts, the judge concluded that the mother "took an unrealistic approach to her problems and never worked out a practical way to implement her plans for herself or the child." The judge therefore found that it was "in the best interest of * * * t[he child]" to grant the petition to dispense with parental consent to adoption, so that the child could be adopted by the family the Home had selected, a young couple in their early thirties, eight years married, with another adopted child.[3]

In her attack on the application of the "best interests" test to her case, the mother points to the fact that the Home's custody of the child, the basis of the § 3 action, derived from her consent to temporary foster care, and argues that once she withdrew that consent and sought her child's return there was no basis for a § 3 action. She raises the possibility, if the "best interests" test were applied literally in cases of voluntary custody, that a family obliged by temporary adversity such as illness to place its child in foster care might then be deprived of the child against its will if the agency decided that another family could better raise the child. She argues that the Legislature could not so have intended to disregard the ties between the child and the natural parent, and that indeed it would be unconstitutional to do so. Hence she would have us conclude that § 3's "best interests" test can only be applied when the parent has already been deprived of custody of the child by court action, and that in cases where custody is based on voluntary surrender the consent of the parent may be dispensed with only on a showing of parental "unfitness" like that required to deprive a parent of custody under the guardianship statute, G.L. c. 201, § 5. She adds the complaint that she was not fully informed of the possible consequences when she gave consent to foster care and so she denies there was a "custody" to satisfy § 3. Finally, there are arguments that the § 3 "best inter-

---

3. An investigation of the background of that family had furnished convincing evidence that they were suitable as adoptive parents.

The decree itself of course did not consumate the adoption. A fresh petition in the Probate Court for adoption under G.L. c. 210, § 1, remains necessary, see also § 5A (requiring report by Department of Public Welfare or adoption agency on child and adoptive parents), but the § 2 requirement for parental consent was eliminated by the proceedings here in question, thus making the petition for adoption a simple proceeding.

ests" standard is unconstitutionally vague and that it violates the equal protection clause of the Constitution, in that it improperly discriminates against the poor, who are more likely to need foster care for their children.

While we find force in the mother's arguments, we believe they are based essentially on a misunderstanding of the relationship between the notions of "best interests of the child" and parental "unfitness." The mother perceives the two criteria or tests as separate and distinct, with each to be applied in certain clearly defined circumstances. We think that the relationship is more subtle, that elements of parental "unfitness" figure strongly in the "best interests" test, while elements of "best interests of the child" weigh in any consideration of whether a parent is fit to have custody of his child. When the interconnection or overlap is appreciated, the mother's case on the present facts is seen to be unavailing.

To trace the development of the standards: Adoptions by consent of the parents were recognized in the Commonwealth at least by the time of St.1851, c. 324, which described procedures for such adoptions. Promptly afterwards came St.1853, c. 402, which created the first exception to the rule that adoption required the consent of living parents; it dispensed with consent where the parent was "insane." In 1859, by St.1859, c. 61, consent was made unnecessary where the parent had "wilfully deserted and neglected to provide for the proper care and maintenance * * * for one year"; this was eventually codified as part of G.L. c. 210, § 3, which also specified other grounds for dispensing with parental consent, such as current imprisonment of the parent for more than three years.

Chapter 593, § 1, of the Acts of 1953, codified as G.L. c. 210, § 3A, first provided for an independent proceeding, prior to adoption proceedings proper, at which it could be determined whether parental consent was to be necessary for the adoption. Its purpose was to facilitate and expedite the process of adoption of children being held in temporary foster care. See the Department of Public Welfare recommendations, 1953 House Doc. No. 118, accompanying their draft bill 1953 House Doc. No. 124. The proceeding could be brought by the Department of Public Welfare or any appropriate child care agency having custody of the child. But the act was silent as to the standards to be applied in deciding when consent could be dispensed with, and in Consent to Adoption of a Minor, 345 Mass. 706, 189 N.E.2d 505 (1963), this court held that, in the absence of any other indication in the statute, the conditions set out in § 3 for direct adoptions were still to be met; specifically, the court held that a finding of parental "unsuitability," without a finding of wilful desertion or neglect for a year, was not an adequate basis for a decree dispensing with the parental consent.

The department had evidently not intended the § 3 conditions to be read into the independent § 3A proceeding. Therefore the department immediately sponsored St.1964, c. 425, which provided that consent could be dispensed with "if the court finds that the best interests of the child will be served by placement for adoption"; the court was not to be restricted by the § 3 conditions, but was to give "due regard to the ability, capacity and fitness of the child's parents * * * and to the plans proposed by the department or other agency initiating such petition." This statute thus broadened the factors the court could consider in deciding whether to proceed over the parent's objections; unsuitability besides desertion or neglect was now clearly an available ground. In fact this was not a sharp or precipitate departure from the past, for our court had already begun a gradual process of developing a "best interests" approach to § 3 itself.[4]

The last step in the evolution of the adoption laws took place in 1972 with the passage of St.1972, c. 800. The same basic standard was made to apply to direct proceedings for adoption as to the independent proceeding, and the two proceedings were both brought within § 3. To the factors "ability, capacity and fitness" was added "readiness * * * to assume parental responsibility," and a "presumption" was established that "the best interests of the child" would be served by dispensing with the need for parental consent when the child has been in the custody of the department or agency for more than one year (irrespective of incidental parental visits). The revised § 3 in its entirety was made to apply only to petitions by those already having custody of the child.

It will be observed from this brief history that the explicit introduction of the "best interests" standard into the adoption statutes was occasioned by a judicial decision disallowing parental "unsuitability" as the ground for dispensing with consent to adoption. In writing the statute the department and the Legislature were concerned primarily with cases where unfit parents (although not within the categories of old § 3) were blocking the adoption of their children;

---

4. For example, in Adoption of a Minor, 343 Mass. 292, 178 N.E.2d 264 (1961), an aunt who had had custody of a child since a week after birth petitioned to adopt the child despite the objections of the mother. Though the mother was worthy to be a parent, we said expressly that the successive amendments of § 3 disclosed "a clear intent on the part of the Legislature to relax the requirement of parental consent to adoption when the withholding of consent by a neglectful parent would frustrate the furtherance of the best interests of the child." Id. at 298, 178 N.E.2d at 267. We accordingly took into account the bad effect on the child of breaking the bonds of affection between the aunt and the child, and approved the aunt's adoption of the child. See Adoption of a Minor, 357 Mass. 490, 492, 258 N.E.2d 567 (1970); Adoption of a Minor, 362 Mass. 882, 289 N.E.2d 843 (1972). See also Adoption of a Minor, 338 Mass. 635, 156 N.E.2d 801 (1959) (applying "best interests" test to dispute over whether consent to adoption was necessary by unmarried father of child who later married mother); Erickson v. Raspperry, 320 Mass. 333, 69 N.E.2d 474 (1946) (applying "best interests" test to decide whether consent to adoption could be revoked).

we do not think they meant to allow fit parents to be deprived of their children, even if they had temporarily given up custody, unless some factor such as lengthy separation and a corresponding growth in the ties between the child and the prospective adoptive parents indicated that the child would be hurt by being returned to the natural parents. Nor have we found any cases where fit parents who have voluntarily given up temporary custody for appropriate reasons lost their children to adoption by reference to the "best interests" standard simply because another set of parents was found better qualified.

We pass to the second part of our inquiry, a consideration of the law governing the transfer of custody of children under the guardianship law. By G.L. c. 201, § 1, the Probate Court may, "if it appears necessary or convenient" appoint guardians of minors; by § 5 (deriving from St.1873, c. 367), the guardian may have custody of the child, though the parents are alive and do not consent, if the court finds the parents "unfit" to have custody.[7] In Richards v. Forrest, 278 Mass. 547, 553, 180 N.E. 508 (1932), our court held that "the first and paramount duty of courts" in passing on custody cases under that law "is to consult the welfare of the child." Further, it recognized that "certain parents might be fit to bring up one child but unfit to bring up another." In Stinson v. Meegan, 318 Mass. 459, 463, 62 N.E.2d 113, 115 (1945), we added that "the meaning of 'unfit' is not confined to the moral character or personal qualities of the parent," but "embraces other circumstances," particularly those that "involve the welfare of the child himself." The injection of considerations of the child's welfare here thus roughly paralleled that in the adoption situation. Both *Richards* and *Stinson*, however, declined to find "unfitness" sufficient to deprive a parent of custody simply on the basis of a long separation of parent and child, and the growth of close ties between the child and the person seeking custody; the cases held that some negative findings with regard to the actual fitness of the natural parents to raise the child were necessary.

7. Alternatively, G.L. c. 119, § 23(C), as appearing in St.1970, c. 888, § 5, permits the Department of Public Welfare to "seek and * * * accept" on order of the Probate Court "responsibility" for minors "without proper guardianship due to the death, unavailability, incapacity or unfitness of the parent." Such responsibility may, if the court orders, include the right to consent to adoption. Sections 24–26 allow a juvenile court (or the juvenile session of a district court where there is no juvenile court) if it finds after petition by "any person" that a child is "without necessary and proper physical, educational or moral care and discipline, or is growing up under conditions or circumstances damaging to a child's sound character development, or * * * lacks proper attention of parent * * * and whose parents * * * are unwilling, incompetent or unavailable to provide such care," to commit the child to the custody of the department or "make any other appropriate order with reference to the care and custody of the child as may conduce to his best interests, including but not limited to" leaving the child with its parents under supervision, or transferring temporary custody to a qualified individual, agency, or the Department of Public Welfare.

That the language of "best interests" in the cases under the guardianship statute was not rhetoric but had real significance, however, was demonstrated by Wilkins v. Wilkins, 324 Mass. 261, 85 N. E.2d 768 (1949), which weighed heavily the fact that the child loved its guardian and distrusted and had nightmares about its parents. These circumstances, together with the emotional shock to the child were it to be uprooted, and the lack of experience or aptitude of the natural parents in dealing with the child, persuaded the court that the best interests of the child would be served by granting custody to the guardian with whom the child was residing.   Thus by 1970 we could write in Kauch, petitioners, 358 Mass. 327, 329, 264 N.E.2d 371, 373 (1970), that "[n]early all the relevant cases have considered the best interests of the child in determining whether the parents are unfit."

Our result, therefore, is that the tests "best interests of the child" in the adoption statute and "unfitness of the parent" in the guardianship statute reflect different degrees of emphasis on the same factors, that the tests are not separate and distinct but cognate and connected.

It remains to tie the teachings of the historical development to the present case.   In invoking the "best interests of the child" the Legislature did not intend to disregard the ties between the child and its natural parent, or to threaten a satisfactory family with loss of children because by reason of temporary adversity they are placed in foster care.[9]   A parent cannot be deprived unless some affirmative reason is shown for doing so such as a finding of a serious problem with that parent, or of a separation so long as to permit very strong bonds to develop between the child and the prospective adoptive parents.   When such a reason appears, however, it can hardly be argued that the Legislature is powerless to interfere with the parent-child relationship to promote the welfare of the child.   Its power to do so— and this includes the power to act without perfect wisdom—was settled at least by the time of Prince v. Massachusetts, 321 U.S. 158, 64 S.Ct. 438, 88 L.Ed. 645 (1944) (State may prohibit parent's use of child to sell religious pamphlets).   See also Commonwealth v. Brasher, 359 Mass. 550, 270 N.E.2d 389 (1971) (State may try minors for crime of being "stubborn children").

As to the technical argument that once the mother withdrew her consent to custody there was no basis for a § 3 action, we note, first,

9. We are not drawn into the long standing debate among psychiatrists, psychologists, social workers, and lawyers about the precise limits of the claims of "biological" parents or about the precise values of "continuity" in the care of children.   For the current phase, see Goldstein, Freud & Solnit, Beyond the Best Interests of the Child (1973), and reviews by Dembitz, 83 Yale L.J. 1304 (1974); Katkin, Bullington & Levine, 8 Law & Soc.Rev. 669 (1974); Rothman & Rothman, 1 The Civ.Lib.Rev. 110 (1974).   See also Mnookin, Foster Care—In Whose Best Interest? 43 Harv.Educ.Rev. 599 (1973).

that there is nothing in the statute to suggest that custody means anything other than physical custody, whatever the original basis for it. If it be argued that this opens the way to adoptions over the objections of parents from whom custody is being wrongfully withheld, the response is that the present is not such a case. The mother indeed now opposes the petition, but that in itself cannot amount to an effective withdrawal of consent to custody; if it were, most of the field of action of § 3 would disappear, since it would become inapplicable except when the parent had already permanently lost custody by court action finding the parent unfit. Rather, if parental opposition to custody is by itself ever to constitute an effective bar to prosecution of a § 3 proceeding, a question we need not now decide, it must at least be consistently and vigorously pressed before the proceeding is brought. On the record before us, such opposition was not and cannot be found in the vacillating behavior of the mother over the ten-month period between the child's birth and the bringing of this petition, when added to her failure and indeed her inability to take positive action toward creating an environment in which a child could be placed with any substantial hope of future stability or happiness.[10] In the absence of such opposition, the "best interests" standard properly applied.

10. In White v. Minter, 330 F.Supp. 1194 (D.Mass.1971), a three-judge Federal court held that the G.L. c. 248, §§ 35–40, action by which a parent may seek to regain custody of a child was not adequate to protect a mother's rights. The G.L. c. 248 action amounts to a "habeas corpus" proceeding on behalf of a minor by its parent against those wrongfully holding the child. In the White case, the Department of Public Welfare had obtained custody on a voluntary basis during a temporary illness, and the mother had sought to regain the child as soon as she was able to, within three weeks of the placement, and had continued to seek its return. The department, however, neither returned the child nor instituted an action under G.L. c. 119, § 23 (see n. 7 above), letting six months pass. In the circumstances, which are far from those of the present case, the court ruled that the mother's rights had been violated. It held that the department must either return the child or bring suit for custody itself, finding the G.L. c. 248 action an inadequate remedy for the mother because under it, the court said, she had the "burden of proof." Cf. Boyns v. Department of Pub. Wel-fare, 360 Mass. 600, 276 N.E.2d 716 (1971). In Stinson v. Meegan, 318 Mass. 459, 462, 62 N.E.2d 113 (1945), we had held that the issue in a G.L. c. 248 action was exactly that in a guardianship custody proceeding under G.L. c. 201, § 5: was the parent "unfit"? We think the basis of White, therefore, is less one of technical "burden of proof" than of imposition on the mother of the burden of instituting and prosecuting a lawsuit. In any event, White does not apply here. The mother here did not consistently seek the return of the child after she gave it up, and act toward that end. Moreover, it is likely here that the agency refrained from pressing any action against the mother in order to give her time to arrange her affairs and make plans to take the child back if she wished and was able to do so. It may well have felt that an earlier action would be premature because the mother had not yet demonstrated her unfitness, and because the child was still so young that the transfer back to its mother, if she were able and willing to assume responsibility, would not cause a profound shock to it. See pp. —— —— below (Mass.Adv.Sh. [1975] 1393–1394).

As to the claim of lack of comprehension on the mother's part of the possible legal consequences of placing her child in foster care, with possible resulting undermining of the basis of the § 3 proceeding, we of course agree that it is desirable to inform a parent of the full meaning of a decision to place a child in foster care, and, further, to explain the possible alternatives, including, for example, use of day care facilities. But if there was any shortcoming here, it was not critical. In our view, the basis of the decree dispensing with parental consent here was not simply the initial voluntary placement, but the failure, over a ten-month period, to take effective steps to demonstrate either a consistent desire for custody or an ability to care properly for the child if given custody. Had the mother, upon her initial change of heart in July, acted consistently in seeking to regain her child and planning effectively for it, we think she would and should have prevailed in any proceeding brought by the department to dispense with her consent to adoption, despite her signed agreement placing the child in temporary foster care, and regardless of the comparative qualifications of an alternative family.

Our conclusion is that a § 3 proceeding was appropriate in this case, and the result correct. As we have suggested, the "best interests" standard of § 3 is a flexible one; the weight to be accorded the several considerations under it will vary with the circumstances. The decision in the present case was not an easy one. Here parent and child had been separated for only ten months when the proceeding was brought; this period was too short to be a decisive factor, particularly as the record does not state that the foster parents are also to be the adoptive parents. We find most significant, however, the judge's conclusion that the mother "took an unrealistic approach to her problems and never worked out a practical way to implement her plans for herself or the child." The trial judge had the opportunity to observe the parties close up, and her findings are entitled to much respect. In the circumstances we do not think the result would be any different had the analysis been conducted in the language of the "unfitness" standard, as the mother urges it should have been.

In reaching our conclusion to support the judge's finding we wish to point out with emphasis that we do not lend any approval to dispensing with parental consent for other than substantial reasons. The attitude to be taken by the department, the agencies, and the courts as well, was defined by the Legislature in G.L. c. 119, § 1, which declares it "to be the policy of this commonwealth to direct its efforts, first, to the strengthening and encouragement of family life for the protection and care of children; to assist and encourage the use by any family of all available resources to this end; and to provide substitute care of children only when the family itself or the resources available to the family are unable to provide the necessary care and protection." Thus parents should be given ample opportunity to demonstrate an ability to provide proper care for their children before a § 3 proceeding is brought. Precipitate attempts to force adoption over parental objection simply because foster care has occurred are not consistent with the law and must be avoided. It is a condition of dispensing with parental consent that the parents be shown to have grievous shortcomings or handicaps that would put the child's welfare in the family milieu much at hazard.

On the consitutional plane, we see no merit in the argument that the "best interests" standard is overly vague. Section 3 itself sets out factors to be taken into account in deciding if the standard is met. Moreover, as we have indicated in this opinion, the course of the legislative development of the standard and the associated case law provide further definition. Standards of mathematical precision are neither possible nor desirable in this field; much must be left to the trial judge's experience and judgment. Underlying each case are predictions as to the possible future development of a child, and these are beyond truly accurate forecast. In similar situations statutes with unavoidable penumbras of indefiniteness have been upheld, and we think this one, too, is valid. See Commonwealth v. Brasher, 359 Mass. 550, 270 N.E.2d 389 (1974) ("stubborn child"); A Juvenile, petitioner, 364 Mass. 531, 306 N.E.2d 822 (1974) (statute allowing trial of juvenile if "the interests of the public" require it); Guardianship of a Minor, 1 Mass.App. 392, 298 N.E.2d 890 (1973) ("unfitness" in guardianship custody statute).

Nor do we find a violation of the equal protection clause. If the argument be made that under § 3 State interposition in the parent-child relationship will occur more frequently in poor families than in wealthy ones, we can say no more than that the statute's classification is not directly based on wealth, and a differential effect in practice on families with varying incomes occurs also with many valid laws. The overriding constitutional basis for the law is the State's interest in protecting those children found on a reasonable basis to be in need of adoption.

Decree affirmed.

NOTES AND QUESTIONS

1. Justice Hennessey dissented in this case on the ground that the child was not shown to be within the care or custody of the agency, so that the statute requiring evidence of parental "unfitness" was controlling rather than the statute requiring proof of the child's best interests in order to dispense with the parent's consent to adoption.

2. Subsequently the child's mother brought suit in the United States District Court for Massachusetts under both the Civil Rights Act, 42 U.S. C.A. § 1983, and the federal habeas corpus statute, 28 U.S.C.A §§ 2241 and 2254. Her complaint was dismissed by the district court and the dismissal was affirmed by the Court of Appeals for the First Circuit. The latter court held that the civil rights claim was barred by res judicata, the constitutional contention having been fully litigated in the Massachusetts courts.

It held the habeas claim was properly dismissed on the ground that federal habeas corpus is not available to try child custody decisions of the state courts. Sylvander v. New England Home for Little Wanderers, 584 F.2d 1103 (1st Cir. 1978), 13 Ga.L.Rev. 662 (1979).

CUSTODY OF A MINOR

Supreme Judicial Court of Massachusetts, 1979.
—— Mass. ——, 389 N.E.2d 68.

HENNESSEY, Chief Justice.   On January 12, 1976, Elsie Peck, a social worker employed by the Division of Family and Children's Services of the Department of Public Welfare (department), petitioned the Municipal Court of the Dorchester District, pursuant to G. L. c. 119, § 24, for a determination that the respondent-mother's newly-born son was a child in need of care and protection. After a continuance of two and one-half months, and following a hearing, the judge granted the department's petition and awarded it custody of the child. The mother exercised her right to trial de novo, G.L. c. 119, § 27, and her appeal was heard by a judge of the Boston Juvenile Court. Focusing chiefly on the mother's parental fitness as evidenced by her treatment of her other children, the judge entered findings of fact and affirmed the award of custody to the department. The mother appealed to the Appeals Court and we transferred the case to this court on our own motion.

Two arguments are raised on appeal by the child's mother. It is first claimed that the court lacked sufficient basis to justify removal of a child from its natural parent because there were no findings that the welfare of the child was endangered at the time of trial. It is also averred, for the first time ever in this court, that the judge failed to apply the proper standard of proof—"clear and convincing evidence"—in determining the necessity of awarding custody to the department.

We think the judge's findings are more than adequate to support the statutory and constitutional requirements for invading the family unit. We decline to adopt the mother's suggestion that we require "clear and convincing evidence" as the measure of proof in actions where children are removed from their parents. However, we are persuaded that it is constitutionally demanded that a judge exercise the utmost care, as demonstrated through specific and detailed findings of fact, in rendering a judgment which deprives parents of child custody. Although we state this requirement for the first time here, we believe the judge's findings indicate that this standard has been met. Accordingly, we affirm his custody award.

Since there is no dispute as to their accuracy, we accept the findings of the judge. The child involved in these proceedings was born in Boston on January 9, 1976, to a mother having a substantial history of child neglect. Until 1972, the mother was the caretaker of her own three children, who were born between 1960 and 1963, and of two other children, a niece and nephew of her husband, who joined the family between 1964 and 1968. As early as 1965 there were reports that some of the children in the mother's care had been truant from school. These reports continued intermittently, and in May and June, 1970, it was reported that the children were absent from school as much as 50% of the time.

In March, 1972, following reports of chronic truancy regarding the children and of strong odors of urine emanating from the mother's apartment, the department dispatched a social worker, Jeanne Yozell (Yozell), to visit the mother's apartment on Geneva Avenue in Dorchester. See G.L. c. 119, § 51A. On her arrival Yozell found the mother, her children, and eight dogs in a cold, cluttered apartment.[1] The apartment was without heat, electricity, hot water, or gas. It was littered with dog feces and smelling of urine. The children were ill-clothed and dirty, and had difficulty with bowel and bladder control. Two of the children were found locked in a room. The mother explained that the condition of the apartment was attributable, in part, to her being deeply in debt, with past due obligations for rent and utilities. The reason for the children's truancy, she stated, was her inability to provide them sufficient clothing, coupled with the fact that the children simply did not like school.

As a result of Yozell's visit, the mother voluntarily placed the children with the department until she could get reorganized. In turn, the department found foster homes for all the children but one, Leroy, who was allowed to return to his mother because he refused to remain in the foster home provided by the department. Shortly after this event, the mother relocated in Jamaica Plain in an apartment subsequently found to be without heat and littered with glass from broken windows. During the next eight months, attempts to provide financial, housing, and medical care counseling to the mother were frustrated by the mother's failure to keep most of her pre-arranged appointments with Yozell.

In November, 1972, Mary Ann Dougherty (Dougherty), was assigned to replace Yozell as the department's contact with the family. By then, the children had all been placed at St. Vincent's Home in Fall River, where it was found that none of the children was toilet trained and all were behind in schooling. Since Leroy was still at home, but not attending school, Dougherty attempted to establish a relationship with the mother. As before, the home was found to be generally messy and without food or utility service. Attempts to work with the mother became futile because the mother was again inconsistent in keeping the necessary appointments. Meanwhile, Leroy was professionally examined and determined to be suffering from academic neglect and in need of psychiatric counseling.

1. By this time, the mother was separated from her husband.

The mother, since 1972, has changed apartments frequently; on at least one occasion she has been evicted for failure to pay rent. In October, 1974, the father of the child at issue moved in with the mother and Leroy. By the time the child was born, on January 9, 1976, however, the father was no longer living with the family.[2] Three days after the child's birth, the department petitioned for custody of the infant. During the pendency of the petition, until the Dorchester District Court granted custody to the department, the child was allowed to remain with the mother, but under the supervision of a homemaker and a public health nurse supplied by the department.

On the basis of these facts, the judge concluded that the mother "is a deprived, immature, impulsive, inconsistent, disorganized person whose inadequacies as a parent have deprived her children in the past of even basic physical needs of food, clothing and shelter *   *   *. [I]f the Court decided to return the infant to [the mother] even temporarily, she would be in need of massive help, including around-the-clock homemaker service, which homemaker would be invested with the primary responsibility for the children." Believing the mother therefore incompetent to provide proper care for the child, the judge ordered him permanently committed to the department.

1. We turn first to the mother's contention that the judge's findings were inadequate to justify granting custody of the child to the department. The mother maintains that under G.L. c. 119, § 24, and the United States Constitution, the judge is required to make a finding of parental unfitness at the time of trial, a finding she asserts is absent from the record, as a prerequisite to an order depriving a parent of custody of his or her child. We agree that such a finding is required, but we think the judge's findings represent an unequivocal determination of current, as well as past, parental incapacity.

That a finding of current parental unfitness is required in a proceeding which results in a parent's loss of child custody derives from the substantial respect we accord family autonomy. The existence of a "private realm of family life which the state cannot enter," Prince v. Massachusetts, 321 U.S. 158, 166, 64 S.Ct. 438, 442, 88 L.Ed. 645 (1944), is a cardinal precept of our jurisprudence. See Quilloin v. Walcott, 434 U.S. 246, 98 S.Ct. 549, 54 L.Ed.2d 511 (1978); Smith v. Organization of Foster Families for Equality & Reform, 431 U.S. 816, 97 S.Ct. 2094, 53 L.Ed.2d 14 (1977); Griswold v. Connecticut, 381 U. S. 479, 85 S.Ct. 1678, 14 L.Ed.2d 510 (1965); Meyer v. Nebraska, 262 U.S. 390, 43 S.Ct. 625, 67 L.Ed. 1042 (1923).[3] Yet, rights evolving

2. The father of the child, as well as the mother's legal husband, have waived any right to custody in this matter.

3. We have recognized the right of natural parents to raise their children as existing independently of the State. Richards v. Forrest, 278 Mass. 547, 553, 180 N.E. 508 (1932). See J. Locke, Second Treatise of Government (London 1690).

from one's interest in family integrity are not absolute. Indeed, there can be scarce doubt that the State may properly act to protect children of tender years from parental neglect. Stanley v. Illinois, 405 U.S. 645, 652, 92 S.Ct. 1208, 31 L.Ed.2d 551 (1972). Alsager v. District Court of Polk County, Iowa, 406 F.Supp. 10, 16 (S.D.Iowa 1975), aff'd 545 F.2d 1137 (8th Cir. 1976).

The procedure by which this action has been brought, the "care and protection" proceeding, is one legislative response to the problem of child maltreatment. Pursuant to the statutory provision creating the action, G.L. c. 119, § 24, as amended through St.1975, c. 276, § 3, any person concerned for a child's welfare may file a petition in the appropriate court alleging that the child "is without necessary and proper physical, educational or moral care and discipline, or is growing up under conditions or circumstances damaging to a child's sound character development, or who lacks proper attention of parent, guardian with care and custody, or custodian, and whose parents or guardian are unwilling, incompetent or unavailable to provide such care." If the court finds the allegations proved, the judge may commit the child to the department until the minor becomes eighteen years of age or the judge may make any other order deemed appropriate to the child's best interests. G.L. c. 119, § 26. Significantly, parents, among others, retain the right to petition the court every six months for review and redetermination of the current needs of the child. G.L. c. 119, § 26.

While there may have been some question in prior years regarding the kinds of evidence sufficient to prove cases, like those under c. 119, where a parent stands to lose custody of a child, it is now clear that the Commonwealth may not attempt to force the breakup of a natural family without an affirmative showing of parental unfitness. Quilloin v. Walcott, supra, 434 U.S. at 255, 98 S.Ct. 549. Because the interest of the child is thought to be best served in the stable, continuous environment of his own family, see Stanley v. Illinois, supra, 405 U.S. at 651, 92 S.Ct. 1208; Goldstein, Freud & Solnit, Beyond the Best Interests of the Child (1973), State intervention in the parent-child relationship is justified only when parents appear unable to provide for their children's care and protection. Roe v. Conn, 417 F. Supp. 769, 779 (M.D.Ala.1976) (three-judge court); Alsager v. District Court of Polk County, Iowa, supra at 24; Burt, Developing Constitutional Rights of, in, and for Children, 39 L. & Contemp.Prob. 118, 128 (Summer 1975).[5]

5. Fittingly, it is the stated policy of c. 119 to "provide substitute care of children *only* when the family itself or the resources available to the family are unable to provide the necessary care and protection to insure the rights of any child to sound health and normal physical, mental, spiritual and moral development" (emphasis added). G.L. c. 119, § 1, as amended through St.1972, c. 785, § 5.

Notwithstanding this measure of deference that must be accorded parental and family rights, the State interest in protecting neglected children may properly be preventive as well as remedial. The court need not wait until it is presented with the maltreated child before it decides the necessity of "care and protection." Rather, an assessment of prognostic evidence derived from an ongoing pattern of parental neglect or misconduct is appropriate in the determination of future fitness and the likelihood of harm to the child. Such evidence, particularly where unrebutted by more recent proof of parental capacity, provides a satisfactory basis for a finding of current parental unfitness.[6]

We therefore think it plain that the judge was warranted in determining the mother's newborn child to be in need of care and protection at the time of trial. The uncontested facts, as reported by the judge, indicate that the mother is incapable of providing the basic necessities of food and shelter, ignorant of proper child care and supervision, indifferent to her children's education, and apparently unwilling to cooperate with departmental attempts to rearrange her life. To the extent that these findings refer to the mother's past conduct, it is with the understanding that the problems described therein continue unabated through the present. Not unlike the respondent in a prior case of ours, Petition of the Dep't of Pub. Welfare to Dispense with Consent to Adoption, 371 Mass. 651, 358 N.E.2d 794 (1976), the mother here has failed to formulate any realistic plan by which she could care for her two children already in the department's custody. Thus, in these circumstances, court intervention is appropriate in order to protect a child who, although not yet maltreated, is a probable victim of parental neglect.

2. Although it is clear that the judge possessed sufficient grounds to find the child in need of care and protection, a further issue is raised, a question of first impression in this court, concerning the appropriate standard of proof for findings that determine that it is in the child's best interest to be removed from his parent. The mother urges, and the department concedes, that, because of the importance placed on the family, a parent-child relationship should be disturbed only on a showing of "clear and convincing" evidence that a need for such intervention exists. While we agree with the premise that custody of a child should be removed from a parent to the State only on most careful judicial consideration, we decline to adopt the "clear and convincing" standard urged here. We think that the objective to be sought can be better accomplished by a requirement of specific findings than by the injection of a standard of proof which is inter-

---

6. We think this result must have been contemplated by the Legislature, if the purpose of the "care and protection" statute—"to insure that the children of the commonwealth are protected against the harmful ef- fects" of parental abuse or neglect— was to be given full effect. G.L. c. 119, § 1. Report of The Subcommittee on Child Welfare Legislation, 1952 House Doc. No. 2440 at 43.

mediate between the standards ordinarily applied in civil and criminal matters.

Where constitutional rights hang in the balance, a greater level of factual inspection has sometimes been required in civil cases as an additional safeguard against improvident judicial action. Indeed, we believe that important personal rights, such as those involved when the breakup of a family is threatened, warrant an extra measure of evidentiary protection. For some parents, loss of a child may be as onerous a penalty as the deprivation of the parents' freedom. Thus, while it may be observed that a c. 119 custody determination in favor of the department is neither a final nor complete [7] severance of the parent-child relationship, we think that the effect of such an order places a sufficient burden on family integrity to make the determination deserving of added judicial attention.

We think it undesirable, however, to adopt the mother's suggestion that we require "clear and convincing" proof in cases of the kind presented here. "Clear and convincing" evidence standards, as we recently observed in Superintendent of Worcester State Hosp., supra 374 Mass. at —— – ——, 372 N.E.2d 242 often act as the functional equivalent for the more familiar "reasonable doubt" standard. As such, the introduction of this third test of proof may serve no useful purpose and add only confusion. However, if we were, for the sake of simplicity, to adopt a "reasonable doubt" test in cases involving parental neglect, we fear that we might overly jeopardize the welfare of the child. If proof "to a moral certainty," a requirement of our interpretation of "beyond a reasonable doubt," were demanded before a judge could find it necessary to remove a child from his or her parents, preventive intervention by a court, as proposed by the department here, might well be precluded.

We prefer to take the position that the personal rights implicated in proceedings of this character require the judge to exercise the utmost care in promulgating custody awards. Such care, in our view, demands that the judge enter specific and detailed findings demonstrating that close attention has been given the evidence and that the necessity of removing the child from his or her parents has been persuasively shown. Moreover, we do not limit this requirement merely to cases where the ultimate outcome involves the loss of custody by a parent. In all cases of child neglect, including those where a disposition depriving a parent of custody is adjudged unnecessary, we think it well advised that a judge make specific findings of fact.

---

7. Even after a parent has been deprived of child custody under c. 119, the parent retains such residual rights as the right to visit, G.L. c. 119, § 35, to consent to adoption, G. L. c. 210, §§ 2–3, and to determine the child's religious affiliation, G.L. c. 119, § 33. See Campbell, The Neglected Child: His and His Family's Treatment under Massachusetts Law and Practice and their Rights Under the Due Process Clause, 4 Suffolk L. Rev. 631, 656–657 (1970).

In this case the judge's findings, make it manifestly clear that the utmost care was devoted to the determination of the custody award. Accordingly, we hold that the judge's decision and order are to be affirmed.

NOTES AND QUESTIONS

1.   Suppose the facts described in the Home for Little Wanderers case had arisen in a suit brought by an adoption agency or the state as a "care and protection" proceeding under the statute quoted in Custody of a Minor, at page 522. Would the child's situation meet the requirements of that statute? If so, would the application of the statute to a child in those circumstances be constitutional?

2.   Are the opinions in these two cases on the constitutionality of the two statutes inconsistent with each other? If, in other words, parental "unfitness" must be proved before a natural family may be broken up, should not the same requirement be made where the natural parent has placed his or her child in the temporary custody of an agency?

3.   The former Iowa statute provided as follows:

"The court may upon petition terminate the relationship between parent and child:

*   *   *

"2.   If the court finds that one or more of the following conditions exist:

"a.   That the parents have abandoned the child.

"b.   That the parents have substantially and continuously or repeatedly refused to give the child necessary parental care and protection.

"c.   That although financially able, the parents have substantially and continuously neglected to provide the child with necessary subsistence, education, or other care necessary for physical or mental health or morals of the child or have neglected to pay for subsistence, education, or other care of the child when legal custody is lodged with others.

"d.   That the parents are unfit by reason of debauchery, intoxication, habitual use of narcotic drugs, repeated lewd and lascivious behavior, or other conduct found by the court likely to be detrimental to the physical or mental health or morals of the child.

"e.   That following an adjudication of neglect or dependency, reasonable efforts under the direction of the court have failed to correct the conditions leading to the termination."

A suit is brought in the United States District Court to obtain a declaratory judgment that this statute is void for vagueness under the Fourteenth Amendment, and that it permits parents to be deprived of their children without a showing of harm sufficient to support the state's interest in the child's welfare. What should be the result? Would it make a difference if the statute should authorize the court to invoke less drastic remedies than the permanent termination of the parents' rights in their child? Alsager v. District Court of Polk County, Iowa, 406 F.Supp. 10 (S.D.Iowa

1975), aff'd 545 F.2d 1137 (8th Cir. 1976). The Eighth Circuit, in affirming, had this to say, 545 F.2d 1137, 1138:

> "The judgment appealed from is affirmed on the basis that plaintiffs were denied substantive due process, in that the State of Iowa failed to exhibit the threshold harm necessary to give the state a compelling interest sufficient to justify permanent termination of the parent-child relationships, * * * [W]e afford the Iowa courts an additional opportunity to give the statutory provisions a plainly desirable limiting construction."

What do you suppose this language means? Does it mean that each application of the statute to particular states of fact raises an issue of constitutionality in addition to the issue of statutory construction? Would this statute be unconstitutional according to the Eighth Circuit opinion if it were applied to justify termination of parental rights in Custody of a Minor? Cf. In Interest of Ponx, 276 N.W.2d 425 (Iowa 1979).

The Iowa statute has been amended, effective July 1, 1979, to provide for the termination of parental rights on the ground, inter alia, that the parent abandoned the child, or failed without good cause to comply with an order to support the child, or failed to object to the termination after notice and an opportunity to be heard. Iowa Code Ann. § 600A.8 (Supp.1979). Would this form of statute warrant the termination of parental rights in Custody of a Minor?

Are such statutes void for vagueness? See In re William L., 477 Pa. 322, 383 A.2d 1228 (1978), cert. den. sub nom. Beatty v. Lycoming County Children's Services, 439 U.S. 880 (1978); Davis v. Smith, —— Ark. ——, 583 S.W.2d 37 (1979) ("proper home" is too vague); Matter of N. J. W., —— S.D. ——, 273 N.W.2d 134 (1978); Matter of Daniel, Deborah and Leslie H., 591 P.2d 1175 (Okla.1979) ("child who has not the proper parental care or guardianship" is not too vague).

Is the constitutional "void for vagueness" doctrine one which applies only to criminal statutes? If so, how can it be relied upon to attack statutes dealing with the termination of parental rights? Custody of a Minor, —— Mass. ——, 393 N.E.2d 379 (1979).

4. M had a son four years old whose father was white. M and the child's father were not married and were no longer living together. M began living with a black man, whereupon the father complained to the police who then investigated, as did a social worker from the state social services department. The investigation revealed that M was living with a black man to whom she was not married, in a two-bedroom apartment, that their living conditions were adequate, that the child was clean, well fed and in good physical condition. The local juvenile court then issued an order for the immediate removal of the child from M's custody and the child was placed in a foster home. Later the court terminated M's parental rights in the child, under a statute which authorized such action where the child was dependent or neglected, defining a neglected child as "any child, who, while under sixteen years of age * * * has no proper parental care or guardianship or whose home, by reason of neglect, cruelty, or depravity, on the part of his parent * * * is an unfit or improper place for such child." Are any constitutional issues raised by this case? What are they? See, Roe v. Conn, 417 F.Supp. 769 (M.D.Ala. 1976).

5. M, when fifteen years old, gave birth to a child. M's mother refused to help M keep the child and, having little alternative, M consented to place the child with Mrs. J, an older woman and acquaintance of M's mother. Mrs. J thought of adopting the child but never did, and at one point said she would be willing to give the child back to M. Eight years later, when M was twenty-three and a college graduate, she sought the return of the child from Mrs. J. The child in the meantime had been well cared for, was doing well in school and was fond of Mrs. J, who was equally fond of the child and refused to give him up. In a suit by M against Mrs. J for custody of the child, what standards should the court adopt to guide it and other courts in similar cases? Is the outcome governed or affected by constitutional considerations? Assume that no statute exists in this case. Cf. Bennett v. Jeffreys, 40 N.Y.2d 543, 387 N.Y.S.2d 821, 356 N.E.2d 277 (1976).

Who should get custody of this child? Bennett v. Marrow, 59 A.D.2d 492, 399 N.Y.S.2d 697 (2d Dep't 1977). See also J. Goldstein, A. Freud, A. Solnit, Beyond the Best Interests of the Child ch. 4 (1973). If Mrs. J is given custody and she then seeks to adopt the child, what would be the result under a statute requiring proof of abandonment, neglect or unfitness for termination of parental rights? Matter of Sanjivini K., 47 N.Y.2d 374, 391 N.E.2d 1316 (1979).

6. In recent years there has been a flood of criticism of the law's attempts to deal with the circumstances in which the state should intervene to protect children and with the institution of foster care. Some of those criticisms are summarized in Smith v. OFFER, supra page 471, and are referred to in footnote 9 to the opinion in New England Home for Little Wanderers. For other criticisms, see Wald, State Intervention on Behalf of "Neglected" Children: A Search for Realistic Standards, 27 Stan.L.Rev. 985 (1975); Wald, State Intervention on Behalf of Neglected Children: Standards for Removal of Children from Their Homes, Monitoring the Status of Children in Foster Homes and Termination of Parental Rights, 28 Stan.L.Rev. 623 (1976); Mnookin, Child-Custody Adjudication: Judicial Functions in the Face of Indeterminancy, 39 L. & Contemp.Prob. 226 (1975); Note, Children in Limbo: The Illinois Solution, 73 Nw.U.L.Rev. 180 (1978); Ketcham & Babcock, Statutory Standards for the Involuntary Termination of Parental Rights, 29 Rut.L.Rev. 530 (1976); Boskey & McCue, Alternative Standards for the Termination of Parental Rights, 9 Seton Hall L.Rev. 1 (1978); Derdeyn, Rogoff, Williams, Alternatives to Absolute Termination of Parental Rights After Long-Term Foster Care, 31 Vand.L.Rev. 1165 (1978).

As a consequence of this criticism several proposals for model legislation have been made. For example, the Goldstein, Freud, Solnit book suggests a statute which would permit the existing placement to be altered only if it is proved that the child is unwanted where he is, and that his current placement is not the least detrimental alternative. The latter phrase is defined as the placement which maximizes, in accordance with the child's sense of time, his chance to be wanted and to form a continuous and permanent relationship with someone who will become his psychological parent.

The same authors have published another book urging stricter standards for court intervention in the parent-child relationship and proposing a statute which would embody their views. See J. Goldstein, A. Freud, A. Solnit, Before the Best Interests of the Child 193–196 (1979).

Professor Katz has drafted a model act whose crucial provision reads as follows, Katz, Freeing Children for Permanent Placement Through a Model Act, 12 Fam.L.Q. 203, 216 (1978):

"Section 4

*[Grounds for Involuntary Termination of
the Parent-Child Relationship]*

"(a) An order of the court for involuntary termination of the parent-child relationship shall be made on the grounds that the termination is in the child's best interest, in light of the considerations in subsections (b) through (f), where one or more of the following conditions exist:

"(1) the child has been abandoned, as defined by Section 2(a)(4)(iv);

"(2) the child has been adjudicated to have been abused or neglected in a prior proceeding;

"(3) the child has been out of the custody of the parent for the period of one year and the court finds that:

"(i) the conditions which led to the separation still persist, or similar conditions of a potentially harmful nature continue to exist;

"(ii) there is little likelihood that those conditions will be remedied at an early date so that the child can be returned to the parent in the near future; and

"(iii) the continuation of the parent-child relationship greatly diminishes the child's prospects for early integration into a stable and permanent home.

"(b) When a child has been previously adjudicated abused or neglected, the court in determining whether or not to terminate the parent-child relationship shall consider, among other factors, the following continuing or serious conditions or acts of the parents:

"(1) emotional illness, mental illness, mental deficiency, or use of alcohol or controlled substances rendering the parent consistently unable to care for the immediate and ongoing physical or psychological needs of the child for extended periods of time;

"(2) acts of abuse or neglect toward any child in the family; and

"(3) repeated or continuous failure by the parents, although physically and financially able, to provide the child with adequate food, clothing, shelter, and education as defined by law, or other care and control necessary for his physical, mental, or emotional health and development; but a parent or guardian who, legitimately practicing his religious beliefs, does not provide specified medical treatment for a child, is not for that reason alone a negligent parent and the court is not precluded from ordering necessary medical services for the child according to existing state law.

"(c) Whenever a child has been out of physical custody of the parent for more than one year, the court shall consider, pursuant to subsection (a)(3), among other factors, the following:

"(1) the timeliness, nature and extent of services offered or provided by the agency to facilitate reunion of the child with the parent;

"(2) the terms of social service contract agreed to by an authorized agency and the parent and the extent to which all parties have fulfilled their obligations under such contract.

"(d) When considering the parent-child relationship in the context of either subsections (b) or (c), the court shall also evaluate:

"(1) the child's feelings and emotional ties with his birth parents; and

"(2) the effort the parent has made to adjust his circumstances, conduct, or conditions to make it in the child's best interest to return him to his home in the foreseeable future, including:

"(i) the extent to which the parent has maintained regular visitation or other contact with the child as part of a plan to reunite the child with the parent;

"(ii) the payment of a reasonable portion of substitute physical care and maintenance if financially able to do so;

"(iii) the maintenance of regular contact or communication with the legal or other custodian of the child; and

"(iv) whether additional services would be likely to bring about lasting parental adjustment enabling a return of the child to the parent within an ascertainable period of time.

"(e) The court may attach little or no weight to incidental visitations, communications, or contributions. It is irrelevant in a termination proceeding that the maintenance of the parent-child relationship may serve as an inducement for the parent's rehabilitation.

"(f) If the parents are notified pursuant to Section 10(a) and fail to respond thereto, such failure shall constitute consent to termination on the part of the parent involved. The court may also, pursuant to Section 12(c), terminate the unknown father's relationship with the child."

Professor Wald's article, cited above, suggests the following standards which ought to be observed in the drafting of such legislation, 27 Stan.L.Rev. at 1039:

"APPENDIX: PROPOSED STANDARDS FOR COURT INTERVENTION

"General Principles

"1.1 The law should adopt (or maintain) a strong presumption for parental autonomy in childrearing, in structuring a system of coercive state intervention. State intervention, either through active state involvement in child care or through extensive monitoring of each child's development, should only be available as an opportunity provided at the request of, or without objection by, the parent, except when a child is suffering harm, as defined in section 2.1

"1.2. Coercive state intervention should be premised upon specific harms to a child, not on the basis of parental conduct.

"1.3. Coercive state intervention should be authorized only for those categories of harm where

"(a) a child is suffering, or there is substantial likelihood that he will imminently suffer, a serious harm; and

"(b) coercive intervention to alleviate the type of harm will, in general, be the least detrimental way of protecting the child.

"1.4. The grounds for coercive intervention should be defined as specifically as possible. Vague or general laws are both undesirable and unnecessary for protecting children.

"1.5. Fault concepts should not be relevant to determining the need for intervention.

"1.6. The fact that a child is endangered in a manner specified by statute is a necessary but not sufficient reason for a court to declare the minor neglected and make the minor a ward of the court. In every case a court should also find that the child will be placed in a less detrimental position as a result of the proposed intervention.

"Statutory Grounds for Intervention

"2.1. Courts should be authorized to assume jurisdiction, in order to remove a child from his home or to condition custody upon the parent's accepting supervision, only when the child

"(a) has no caring adult available and willing to care for him;

"(b) has suffered or is likely to imminently suffer a physical injury, inflicted upon him by other than accidental means, which causes, or creates a substantial risk of, death, disfigurement, or impairment of bodily functioning;

"(c) has suffered physical injury causing disfigurement or impairment of bodily functioning as a result of conditions created by his parent or the failure of his parent to adequately supervise him or where there is a *substantial* risk that the child imminently will suffer death, disfigurement, or impairment of bodily functions as a result of conditions created by his parent or the failure of his parent to adequately supervise him;

"(d) is suffering serious emotional damage, evidenced by severe anxiety, depression, or withdrawal or untoward aggressive behavior or hostility toward others, and his parents are not willing to provide treatment for him;

"(e) has been sexually abused;

"(f) is in need of medical treatment to cure, alleviate or prevent his suffering serious physical or emotional damage, as defined in sections 2.1(b) & (d) and his parents are unwilling to provide the medical treatment;

> "(g) is committing delinquent acts *as a result of* parental pressure, guidance, or approval."

Would you support these proposals for enactment in your state? Do any of them present any constitutional difficulties?

How would the *Little Wanderers* case, the *Custody of a Minor* case, Bennett v. Jeffreys, supra, paragraph 5, be decided under these proposals?

7. What standard of proof should be required in cases involving the termination of parental rights? Just a preponderance of the evidence, as in Custody of a Minor? Or proof by clear and convincing evidence, or even proof beyond a reasonable doubt? Matter of Welfare of Rosenbloom, 266 N.W.2d 888 (Minn.1978); Matter of J.L.B., infra; State v. Robert H., 393 A.2d 1387 (N.H.1978).

8. In 1978 Congress enacted the Indian Child Welfare Act, 25 U.S.C.A. §§ 1901 ff. 92, Stat. 3069. The Act's findings recite that many Indian families have been broken up by the removal of their children by state agencies, that many such children are placed in non-Indian foster homes, and that the states in exercising their jurisdiction over Indian child custody proceedings have often failed to recognize Indian customs and Indian cultural and social standards. The policy of Congress is declared to be to promote the stability and security of Indian tribes and families. The Act contains a variety of provisions aimed at carrying out this policy. The most significant is perhaps the provision giving Indian tribal courts exclusive jurisdiction over child custody proceedings involving Indian children residing or domiciled on a reservation, and authorizing the tribal court to retain jurisdiction over any Indian child who is a ward of the court irrespective of his residence. 25 U.S.C.A. § 1911. Other provisions grant preference in the placement of Indian children to Indian families, impose safeguards upon consent to the foster care or termination of parental rights to Indian children, and authorize grants to Indian tribes for various forms of family assistance programs. The Act went into effect in May of 1979. Proposed regulations implementing the Act are published in 44 Fed.Reg. 23993 (April 23, 1979) and when adopted will appear as Part 23 of 25 C.F.R.

MATTER OF J. L. B.

Supreme Court of Montana, 1979.
—— Mont. ——, 594 P.2d 1127.

DALY, Justice. A mother brings this appeal from the conclusions and judgment of the District Court, Fourth Judicial District, which declared her daughter a neglected child, and granted permanent custody over the child to the Department of Social and Rehabilitation Services with authority to consent to her adoption. The mother contends first that section 10–1301(2)(a) and (b), R.C.M.1947, now section 41–3–102(2)(a) and (b) MCA, defining "abuse" and "neglect" were unconstitutionally vague as applied to her. Second she contends that the appropriate standard of proof to to applied to the

State in a termination of parental rights proceeding is the "clear and convincing" standard, rather than the "preponderance of evidence" standard. The mother's third contention is that the District Court abused its discretion in removing the child permanently from her mother because that decision was not supported by even a preponderance of the evidence. We affirm the decision of the District Court.

The child was born on May 16, 1975, when her mother was seventeen years old. Her parents were not married at the time of her birth, nor have they ever been married. They did live together on a fairly regular basis from shortly after the child's birth until December 1977.

In her fifth month of pregnancy the mother was referred to a Public Health Service nurse, Mary McCall, by a high school counselor. From that time on the mother and child have been frequently visited by a variety of health and welfare officials offering assistance and instruction in child care.

Mary McCall testified that she met with the mother and arranged to have a social worker assigned to her. She further arranged for the mother to meet with an eligibility technician to provide assistance in receiving Medicaid money for prenatal care and arranged an appointment with a physician to provide her with that care. She also referred the mother to the W.I.C. program, a federal nutritional program for women, infants, and children, for prenatal nutritional assistance. A senior student social worker from the University of Montana, Tricia Williams, made weekly visits to the mother from December 1974 until the child was born.

The mother was later referred to the "At-Risk Program" of the Missoula City-County Health Department, which attempts to identify mothers and children that will be at risk for potential health problems due to prenatal or delivery complications. According to Mary McCall, the mother was referred to the program because she was under eighteen, had not had prenatal care for the first five months of her pregnancy, was unable to read or write, had suffered a kidney infection and anemia during her pregnancy, and was unmarried.

As a result of this referral, Mary McCall regularly visited the mother at her mother's home during the summer of 1975 and learned of the baby's problem of staying awake and crying most of the time. In McCall's judgment, the problem was caused by the infant's diet. Her mother had put cereal in her formula, which McCall concluded was probably constipating the baby because she was too young to handle solid food. McCall also found the mother to be depressed and anxious from lack of sleep. She assisted her with the preparation of formula for her baby, demonstrating each step rather than leaving written instructions because the mother was unable to read.

McCall also helped the mother with an application for a low-income housing project in Missoula when she indicated a desire for independence from her home. The mother obtained the low-income housing and lived in her own apartment in the fall of 1975. Another senior student from the University made a total of 22 visits with the mother that fall to assist with care for her child. During that time, McCall received a referral from the W.I.C. program requesting nutritional counseling for the mother, and visited her once again. The mother had been feeding the child soda pop rather than juice, telling McCall that juice gave the baby diarrhea. McCall testified that the mother's apartment was messy, with empty beer cans lying around, sacks of garbage on the floor and dirty dishes in the sink. She also noted that the mother made no effort to pick up her daughter when she cried, and that the baby appeared irritable. McCall was told by the apartment manager that the baby had been crying all night, but the mother denied that claim when asked by McCall.

McCall also had several visits with the baby's father, who was occasionally with the mother during her visits. He told McCall that he hoped to marry the mother sometime, but never had definite plans. He told her that he had failed one armed services test but was hoping to take another so that he could enter the military and then marry the mother. The marriage always appeared to be contingent upon the father's ability to obtain a stable job and home, but those conditions never materialized.

McCall concluded from her association with the mother that she was not retaining the basic child care information given her:

"When I would visit her, I usually reiterated the same kinds of things about nutritional instructions, the need for a regular physician for [the baby], the need for immunizations to protect [the baby] from preventable childhood diseases and many times when I would visit her, this material seemed to be new as if she had never heard it before. She indicated to me that she was not retaining this information that I had been giving her."

In April 1976, the parents brought the baby to Dr. Kit Johnson, a pediatrician, following their attempts to give the baby a "green dish soap" enema. According to the parents, the baby had suffered constipation for three days prior to the attempted enema. Dr. Johnson testified that the baby appeared "acutely ill" and "screamed of pain." He had her admitted to a hospital where she stayed overnight.

Mary McCall had little formal contact with the mother and child after February 1976 when they moved from her geographical jurisdiction. However, she continued to have some contact. On August 24, 1976, the mother appeared in an alley behind the Missoula County Health and Welfare Building as McCall returned from a home visit. She had the baby with her and told McCall that she was going to have a nervous breakdown; that she and the father had had a fight; that she needed a babysitter for her daughter for two weeks; that she had no money or food for the baby; that the father was drinking heavily; that she was angered by the baby's continuous crying; and that she was afraid she was going to hurt the child. The baby was unwashed and carried a bottle of spoiled, curdled milk.

McCall took them into the Department of Social Services to make care arrangements for mother and daughter. With two social welfare workers there, Gwen Peterson and Arlene Grossman, McCall agreed that the baby should be placed in temporary foster care until her mother was again able to take care of her. The mother went along with this decision, and the child was temporarily placed. The following day, however, the mother reappeared, demanded her child's return and accused the welfare staff of stealing her daughter.

After some discussion with Peterson, Grossman, and McCall, the mother agreed to placement for her child and herself with a family in Clinton, Montana, where the mother herself had once been a foster child. She later signed a stipulation stating the terms of that agreement, which became the basis of a temporary custody order signed by District Court Judge E. Gardner Brownlee on September 3, 1976. The Baker family, with whom mother and daughter were to stay, agreed to serve as parenting models, helping the mother to understand her responsibilities.

In October 1976, the mother and her child returned to Missoula to live with the father. He had obtained a job and a trailer house but soon lost the job due to excessive drinking. Through the fall months the mother missed several W.I.C. appointments at which she was to receive high protein foods. She did, however, receive in-home assistance from Beatrice Fournier, a home attendant for the Missoula County Welfare Department. Fournier helped the mother plan menus and, realizing her inability to read brought her pictures of food groups to aid in her planning. She testified, however, that the mother failed to comprehend the need for a balanced diet and that the instructions were not getting through to her.

In November 1976 Arlene Grossman took the child to Dr. Johnson to examine a stomach rash. Dr. Johnson concluded that the rash was not significant but diagnosed an infection in both of the baby's ears. He prescribed an antibiotic, but Arlene Grossman discovered that the mother failed to give her daughter the prescribed amount at the appropriate times. Nor did the mother return to Dr. Johnson in two weeks for a checkup on the child's ears as she had been instructed.

On January 18, 1977, the child had another appointment with Dr. Johnson. At that time she exhibited physical and emotional signs which Dr. Johnson concluded required foster placement:

"* * * at this time the child was very restless and irritable and she was biting on her mother as her mother put it. She appeared thin, slightly swollen abdomen, her mother stated that she had had inadequate food for the last month because of insufficient amount of money, stated she was not living with [the father], stated [the child] had a cold and not feeding well for the last month * * *. The abdomen was slightly distended, the ears, the right was slightly dull indicating that maybe some residual infection * * * I thought at this time the child was maybe suffering from malnutrition and maternal inadequacy, unable to cope with the child."

Dr. Johnson further testified that his examination showed that the child had lost weight since the previous November.

In February 1977 Dr. Johnson again examined the child when her temporary foster mother, Marlene Donnelly, brought her to him. The ear infection had not yet cleared up but otherwise her physical condition appeared normal. Mrs. Donnelly described to him, however, that the child had a strong tendency to scavenge for food, especially to eat out of household garbage. Dr. Johnson testified that such a tendency bears a high correlation to food deprivation. He reported his findings to the Missoula County Welfare Department and testified later that the child did not receive adequate parental care.

Based upon the mother's and daughter's past record of difficulties, and Dr. Johnson's recommendations, Carol LaCasse, a Missoula County social worker, filed a petition for temporary investigative authority and protective services. The District Court granted the petition on January 19, 1977, authorizing the Department of Social and Rehabilitation Services to take temporary custody of the child. During the next several weeks SRS continued to assist the parents in learning parenting skills, but with results similar to those experienced earlier.

In particular, Carol LaCasse sought parenting training for the mother. She placed the child in the home of an experienced foster mother, Marilyn Fernelius, who served as a parenting model for the mother during January 1977. The mother visited Mrs. Fernelius on weekdays and discussed and planned menus with her. Mrs. Fernelius also instructed the mother in disciplining her daughter but testified that the mother was incapable of controlling the baby, that in effect the child controlled her mother. Mrs. Fernelius testified that she observed the same attraction to garbage which Marlene Donnelly later reported to Dr. Johnson. After several weeks Marilyn Fernelius requested that the child be placed elsewhere because she was already providing foster care for a teenage girl who required a great deal of her time. Within a few weeks the child was placed in the foster care of Mrs. Sadie Milward where she remained until the time of the hearing on the petition to grant permanent custody to SRS. While the child stayed with the Milwards, the parents visited their daughter and took her with them at times but returning her the same day. The record, however, does not reflect that either natural parent was provided with further parental training services during this time.

Following the child's temporary removal the child and parents had psychological examinations by three psychologists, Dr. Richard Ball, Dr. Herman Walters and Dr. William Stratford. Drs. Ball and Walters, who examined the parents, and Dr. Stratford, who examined the child, all concluded that SRS should seek permanent adoptive custody because of the general inadequacy of the parents, the parents' apparent inability to change, and because of the child's special needs. On the other hand, a psychiatrist, Dr. Noel Hoell, who also examined the mother, concluded that he could find no particular characteristics which would absolutely prevent her from being an adequate parent. He testified that many people with relatively low levels of intelligence are adequate parents.

A pediatrician, Dr. Daniel Harper, saw the mother and child on several occasions as Dr. Johnson's successor after the child had been placed in temporary SRS custody. He testified that following the temporary custody order the child while in the presence of her mother seemed more "bonded" to her foster mother than to her natural mother, and that the child did not look to her own mother as an "orientating" or "guiding" force. Dr. Harper also testified that Dr. Johnson's concerns about growth deficiencies were probably not a source of great concern, since it was later clear that the child was of normal short stature.

Following the hearing on the petition for permanent custody, the District Court issued its findings, conclusions and judgment. The court found that the mother's limited education and other learning disabilities and the father's excessive drinking had resulted in "improper parenting" and had "subjected the minor child to physical and emotional neglect as well as other evidence of improper training." It found further that the parents were unable or unwilling to provide the necessary training and guidance for their child; that SRS was required to place the child in foster care primarily because of a lack of and need for emotional development; that foster placement had resulted in "great improvement" in her development; that the best interests of the child would not be served by returning her to one or both parents because the natural mother "appears incompetent to face and handle the problems presented to parents by children in their advancing years"; and that the child's best interests could only be met by her adoption "into a home where the parents have demonstrated their ability" to raise and guide a "child with problems."

The court concluded first that her child was neglected and second that her best interests and future welfare could only be served by granting permanent adoptive custody to the Department of Social and Rehabilitation Services. Based upon these findings and conclusions, the court granted custody to SRS with authority to consent to her adoption.

Constitutionality of the Neglect Statute As Applied

The mother's first contention is that section 10–1301(2)(a) and (b), R.C.M.1947, now section 41–3–102(2)(a) and (b) MCA, was unconstitutionally applied to terminate her parental rights. Her argument is that because section 10–1301(2), which defines "abuse" and "neglect", fails to state any specific harms to a child which might justify termination of parental rights, it is subject to overly-broad interpretation and arbitrary application. She contends that in this case the child is not suffering any particular harm which requires state intervention into family life but that the State merely perceives that the child would be better off in some home other than her natural mother's. This, she asserts, is an inadequate justification for termination of her parental rights.

This Court has recognized that family integrity is a constitutionally protected interest.

[At this point in the opinion the court quoted a section of the opinion in Stanley v. Illinois, supra, page 432, on the importance of the family and on its protection by the Ninth and Fourteenth Amendments.]

The mother contends that section 10–1301(2) will inadequately protect these constitutional interests if it is interpreted to authorize a termination of her rights as a parent in this case. The statute itself merely defines "abuse" or "neglect":

"(2) 'Abuse' or 'neglect' means:

"(a) the commission or omission of any act or acts which materially affect the normal physical or emotional development of a youth. Any excessive physical injury, sexual assault, or failure to thrive, taking into account the age and medical history of the youth, shall be presumed to be nonaccidental and to 'materially affect' the normal development of the youth.

"(b) the commission or omission of any act or acts by any person in the status of parent, guardian, or custodian who thereby and by reason of physical or mental incapacity or other cause refuses or, with state and private aid and assistance is unable, to discharge the duties and responsibilities for proper and necessary subsistence, education, medical, or any other care necessary for the youth's physical, moral, and emotional well-being."

Since a finding of "abuse or neglect" however gives the District Court jurisdiction to terminate parental rights, the meaning applied to it is the parent's only safeguard against unjustified intrusion into the family unit.

To illustrate her contention, the mother contrasts the relatively unspecific terms contained in section 10–1301(2) with the more precise standards proposed by the Institute of Judicial Administration-American Bar Association Joint Commission on Juvenile Justice

Standards in its Standards Relating to Abuse and Neglect (Tentative Draft 1977) (IJA/ABA standards). The IJA/ABA proposals are based upon a "strong presumption for parental autonomy in child rearing," and limit "coercive intervention" to protect children "only where the child is suffering or there is a substantial likelihood that the child will suffer, serious harm." IJA/ABA Standards 1.1 and 1.- 3(A).

The IJA/ABA proposals seek to avoid unnecessary or unjustified instrusions into family integrity by closely defining the grounds for intervention in terms of specific, objective, *serious* harm to the child. For example, a court may order in-home supervision or remove a child from his or her parents if:

"A child has suffered, or there is a substantial risk that the child will imminently suffer, physical harm causing disfigurement, impairment of bodily functioning, or other serious physical injury as a result of conditions created by his/her parents or by the failure of the parents to adequately supervise or protect him/her;

"A child is suffering serious emotional damage, evidenced by severe anxiety, depression, or withdrawal, or untoward aggressive behavior toward self or others, and the child's parents are not willing to provide treatment for him/her." IJA/ABA Standards 2.1(B) and (C).

The rationale behind these standards is particularly important to the mother's position because the District Court's findings focused principally on emotional rather than physical neglect of her daughter:

"*   *   * the Department of Social and Rehabilitation Services was required to place this very young child in foster homes *partially* because of the child's physical needs but *mostly* because the emotional development of the child was so lacking that the only chance for the child to have a reasonable future was to place the child in a home able to provide for its physical and emotional needs." (Emphasis added.)

As the mother points out, vague abuse and neglect statutes often result in arbitrary application when the parents involved in the alleged neglect are poor and uneducated. Katz, Ambrosino, McGrath & Sawitsky, Legal Research on Child Abuse & Neglect: Past and Future, 11 Fam.L.Q. 151, 172–75 (1977); Wald, State Intervention on Behalf of "Neglected" Children: Standards for Removal of Children from Their Homes, Monitoring the Status of Children in Foster Care, and Termination of Parental Rights, 28 Stan.L.Rev. 623 (1976) (Wald II); Wald, State Intervention on Behalf of "Neglected" Children: A Search for Realistic Standards, 27 Stan.L.Rev. 985 (1975) (Wald I); Areen, Intervention Between Parent and Child: A Reappraisal of the State's Role in Child Abuse and Neglect Cases, 63 Geo. L.J. 887, 917–32 (1975) (Areen).

It is likely however that the greatest percentage of child neglect cases involve matters similar to the present one in which the alleged neglect results not from the deliberate design of a parent, but rather from the parent's low mental or emotional capacity and low financial status. Wald I at 1020–21; Areen at 888; Dembitz, Welfare Home Visits: Child versus Parents, 57 A.B.A.J. 871(1971). Parents in this category are sometimes described as "marginal" people: "* * * they are continually at the borderline of being able to sustain themselves—economically, emotionally, and mentally." Wald I at 1021. As Beatrice Fournier described the mother in this case, "Well I think [the mother] is going to have a hard enough time to take care of herself."

A parent's ability to care for himself or herself naturally affects his or her ability to provide a stable, supportive home for a child. "Such parents may provide little emotional support for their children. While the children may not be physically abused, left unattended, dangerously malnourished, or overtly rejected, they may receive little love, attention, stimulation, or emotional involvement." Wald I at 1021.

The United States Supreme Court has recently observed that middle-class social workers tend to favor long term foster placement for children of such families, "thus reflecting a bias that treats the natural parents' poverty and lifestyle as prejudicial to the best interests of the child." Smith v. Organization of Foster Families for Equality & Reform (1977), 431 U.S. 816, 832, 97 S.Ct. 2094, 2105, 53 L.Ed.2d 14, 29 (citing, Rein, Nutt & Weiss, Foster Family Care: Myth and Reality, in Children and Decent People 24, 25–29 (A. Schorr ed. 1974)). Yet, the mother contends poverty and its various attendant lifestyles must not be equated with neglect absent some showing of actual or imminent harm to the child. See Wald I at 1001–02; Wald II at 649–50; Areen at 925–28, 930–32.

This Court has held that the State may not terminate a parent's right to raise his or her own child "merely because a district judge or a state agency might feel that a nonparent has more financial resources or pursues a 'preferable' lifestyle." Beyond that principle, however, it is more difficult to say what is the minimum constitutionally acceptable standard for such an extreme intervention into family integrity. The IJA/ABA standards, which remain in tentative draft form, might provide a policy measure by which to evaluate the adequacy of section 10–1301(2), but they represent only one proposal. Other proposals are equally available for our consideration. Areen for example, has proposed a standard for neglect which is deliberately less specific than the proposed IJA/ABA standards, especially in the area most relevant to this case, "emotional" neglect:

"A 'neglected' child is one whose physical or emotional health is significantly impaired, or is in danger of being significantly impaired, as a result of the action or inaction of his parent, guardian, or primary caretaker." Areen at 933.

While this standard, like the IJA/ABA proposal, focuses the attention of the court on the "condition of the child rather than on parental fault," it deliberately avoids listing specific evidences of emotional damage such as "severe anxiety," "depression," "withdrawal," and "untoward aggressive behavior." The reason, which is of obvious importance here, is a lack of adequate consensus among child behavior experts as to what behavior symptoms indicate emotional deprivation. Areen at 933.

A totally different approach is found in the Model Statute for Termination of Parental Rights (MSTPR), prepared by the Neglected Children Committee of the National Council of Juvenile and Family Court Judges. See, 27 Juv.Just. No. 4, 3, 7 (1976). The MSTPR directs the court to consider the parent's fitness directly rather than look for specific evidence of harm to the child. Section 12(1)(a), for example, requires the court to consider the "emotional illness, mental illness or mental deficiency *of the parent*, of such duration or nature as to *render the parent* unlikely to care for the ongoing physical, mental and emotional needs of the child." (Emphasis added.)

In a preface to the MSTPR, its authors, judges from several states, note that they "have not been isolated from nor unmindful of the cross currents of the behavioral sciences which have preoccupied this nation in recent years." 27 Juv.Just. at 3. Yet as judges, they continue, they have been able to "test these theoretical fermentations against the realities of their day-to-day practice." 27 Juv.Just. at 3–4.

The Council of Juvenile and Family Court Judges has responded more directly to the IJA/ABA proposed standards, concluding that they offer entirely inadequate protection to children:

"This lengthy volume needs drastic revision in that it totally disregards the rights of a child to be protected and safe in his home environment. These standards greatly limit the process by which a neglected or abused child may be protected through the juvenile justice system. There is an attempt by the authors to restrict the interference of society in the upbringing of children. While this is obviously a worthwhile goal, there needs to be a balance so that youngsters can be adequately protected from the physical and mental abuse and neglect of parents." 8 Juvenile and Family Court Newsletter, No. 6 at 9 (1978).

Thus, the IJA/ABA tentative draft proposals which the mother relies on lack not only a consensus of support among child behavior experts, Areen at 933, but are considered inadequate by the National Council of Juvenile and Family Court Judges. While it is not this Court's position to declare whether one proposal or another is a better approach, we can say with some confidence that the IJA/ABA proposal is not the only constitutional approach. The proceedings in this case need not be measured against the IJA/ABA model and rejected on constitutional due process grounds if they fail to meet its strict standards. See *State v. McMaster* (1971), 259 Or. 291, 486 P. 2d 567, 569.

Our past decisions indicate that section 10–1301(2) is not so broadly interpreted as to permit termination of parental rights merely because the courts or the concerned social welfare agency disapprove of the parents' lifestyles. On the other hand, the statute is broad enough to include emotional deprivation, inadequate nutrition, and extreme and prolonged uncleanliness of the child under the definition of neglect.

In the present case the District Court's finding of poor emotional development of the child was based on the testimony of several qualified witnesses. The record does not show that the mother deliberately refused to provide emotional support for her daughter. Rather, the social welfare workers who attempted to help her testified that the mother was simply incapable of caring for her daughter, physically as well as emotionally. Thus, this case involves not so much a legal due process problem of notice to the mother of what behavior was expected of her or what she could do to have her daughter returned to her, but rather a human problem of a mother's inability to understand her child's needs and to realistically provide for them.

We are aware that the mother may have received conflicting instructions, especially regarding discipline of her child. However, an overall reading of the testimony indicates that the mother's problem went beyond these apparent conflicts, for she was not even capable of understanding or retaining simple instructions in the first place.

The mother's condition, which was described to this Court as "borderline mentally retarded," presents a special problem which courts in other states have recently considered. The New York Family Court, in Guardianship of Strausberg (1977), 92 Misc.2d 620, 400 N.Y.S.2d 1013, dealt with the same sort of condition as we face here: * * * The court noted particularly the impending difficulties which would confront parent and child if they were reunited and expressed concern over the time which further attempts at training the mother in child care methods would require:

"The older the child gets the more difficult it will become for the respondent to fulfill the parental role and provide the direction, structure and other emotional needs of the child herein. The infant * * * should not be held in limbo for this indefinite period of time for the purposes of training the respondent in the area of child care." 400 N.Y.S.2d at 1015.

On this basis, the court refused to order the child returned to her mother. However, mental deficiencies alone do not justify termination if there is no evidence that the child is in some way harmed or likely to be harmed because of the parent's condition. In construing its termination statute, the Minnesota Supreme Court made this requirement clear:

"* * * we wish to state unequivocally that mental illness in and of itself shall not be classified as 'other conduct' which will permit termination of parental rights. Rather, in each case, the actual conduct of the parent is to be evaluated to determine his or her fitness to maintain the parental relationship with the child in question so as to not be detrimental to the child." In re Kidd (Minn.1978), 261 N.W.2d 833, 835.

In the present case the District Court found that the child was harmed by her mother's failure to provide adequate emotional support, and concluded that the mother was "incompetent to face and handle the problems presented to parents by children in their advancing years." These considerations are beyond the mere "poverty" or "lifestyle" characterizations which this Court found inadequate in *Fisher* and *Doney*. Here, the District Court's conclusion that the child was harmed by her home environment is supported by the testimony of social workers, physicians, and psychologists. We conclude, therefore, that section 10–1301(2) was constitutionally applied in this case.

[At this point the court held that the appropriate standard of proof for cases of this kind is the "clear and convincing evidence" standard, and that the state had met that standard in this case.]

The District Court did not abuse its discretion in concluding that the mother was an unfit parent; rather, its conclusion is supported by substantial credible evidence. The judgment granting permanent adoptive custody to the Department of Social and Rehabilitation Services is affirmed.

NOTES AND QUESTIONS

1. Somewhat similar decisions include In re David B, 91 Cal.App.3d 184, 154 Cal.Rptr. 63 (1979); State ex rel. Child v. Clouse, 93 Idaho 893, 477 P.2d 834 (1970); In re Love, 9 Ill.Dec. 25, 50 Ill.App.2d 1018, 366 N.E. 2d 139 (1977); In Interest of Kerns, 225 Kan. 746, 594 P.2d 187 (1979); In re L.F.G., —— Mont. ——, 598 P.2d 1125 (1979); In re Rathburn, 128 Vt. 429, 266 A.2d 423 (1970).

2. Does this case, as well as the other cases in this section of the book, leave you with the impression that every petition for termination of parental rights now raises constitutional questions?

3. If the Montana statute in the J.L.B. case had only authorized the termination of parental rights where the parent had abandoned or neglected the child, without defining neglect, would the case have been decided as it was? See Drake v. Drake, 8 Or.App. 57, 491 P.2d 1203 (1971).

4. Where the father of the child has been convicted of a felony and sentenced to prison for five years, during which time he sends the child an occasional card or letter, has he abandoned or neglected the child? See In re Staat, 287 Minn. 501, 178 N.W.2d 709, 713 (1970), defining abandonment

as follows: "We think there is an abandonment when the desertion is accompanied by an intention to entirely foresake the child. There must be an intention to sever the parental relation and wholly throw off all obligations that spring from it." See also Hutson v. Haggard, 475 S.W.2d 330 (Tex. Civ.App.1971), 4 St.M.L.J. 87 (1972); In re Adoption of Jameson, 20 Utah 2d 53, 432 P.2d 881 (1967). Cases on this point are collected in Annot., Parent's Involuntary Confinement, or Failure to Care for Child as a Result there, as Permitting Adoption Without Parental Consent, 78 A.L.R.3d 712 (1977); and Annot., Parent's Involuntary Confinement, or Failure to Care for Child as Result Thereof, as Evincing Neglect, Unfitness, or the Like in Dependency or Divestiture Proceeding, 79 A.L.R.3d 417 (1977).

5. If in the *J.L.B.* case there had been some dispute as to the mother's mental condition, would the court have had authority to order her to submit to a psychiatric examination? In Interest of Kerns, 225 Kan. 746, 594 P. 2d 187 (1979). Would such an order raise any constitutional questions? See In re D, 63 Misc.2d 1012, 314 N.Y.S.2d 230 (Fam.Ct. 1970).

6. How would the *J.L.B.* case have been decided under the standards and suggested statutes quoted in paragraph 6, page 527, supra?

7. M and F have an illegitimate daughter, D. M brings a paternity suit against F and obtains a decree which finds him to be the father of the child and orders him to pay $100 per month for the child's support. F complies with the order for three months, and then stops, due in part to some unforeseen medical expenses of his own. M is unable to support the child by herself, since she works as a waitress, making only $50 per week and cannot afford to pay someone to care for the child while she is at work. M therefore leaves D with her sister and the sister's husband, Mr. and Mrs. X, who have no children of their own. F knows of this disposition of D and consents to it. The arrangement is that Mr. and Mrs. X will care for the child until M is able to resume caring for it. Mr. and Mrs. X have the child for two years, during which time M visits her about once a month, brings her small gifts and on two occasions gives Mr. and Mrs. X small sums to be applied to D's support. F also sends small gifts and visits the child once. At the end of the two years, M marries H, who has a good job. M then asks Mr. and Mrs. X to return her daughter, but they refuse, saying that they have become very fond of the child, and wish to adopt her. Mr. amd Mrs. X then bring an appropriate proceeding for the termination of the parental rights of both M and F, serving them both personally within the jurisdiction. At the hearing of this proceeding both M and F appear and oppose any termination of their parental rights. Mr. and Mrs. X, M, and F are all represented by attorneys and an attorney is appointed to represent D also.

(a) At this hearing should the court be entitled to consider what custody arrangements will be made respecting the child in the course of determining whether parental rights are to be terminated? For example, should the court permit the introduction of evidence concerning the care which D has been receiving from Mr. and Mrs. X, and the circumstances in which D would live if returned to M and her new husband? Or is the case to be decided on the basis of some naked "legal" right?

(b) What should be the decision concerning the parental rights of M and F, under the Montana type of statute? Under a statute referring only to neglect or abandonment? Under the proposed statutes or standards in paragraph 6, supra, page 527? Is the result dependent upon the United States Constitution and Stanley v. Illinois, supra, page 432?

(c) If you were D's assigned counsel in this case, what would you consider your function to be and how would you carry it out?

(d) If the petition of Mr. and Mrs. X should be denied and the parental rights not terminated, does that mean that custody of the child should go to M and H, or to F, or remain with Mr. and Mrs. X?

Some cases dealing with some of these problems include Daugaard v. People, 176 Colo. 38, 488 P.2d 1101 (1971); In re Adoption of Infants Reynard, 252 Ind. 632, 251 N.E.2d 413 (1969); Matter of Sanjivini K., 47 N. Y.2d 374, 391 N.E.2d 1316 (1979); Corey v. Martin L., 45 N.Y.2d 383, 408 N.Y.S.2d 439, 380 N.E.2d 266 (1978), 43 Alb.L.Rev. 189 (1978) (discussing the unhelpful "flicker of interest" test); In re Adoption of Greer, 463 P.2d 677 (Okl.1970); In re Adoption of Rettew, 428 Pa. 430, 239 A.2d 397 (1968); Smith v. Waller, 422 S.W.2d 189 (Tex.Civ.App.1967); Heard v. Bauman, 443 S.W.2d 715 (Tex. 1969).

(e) If the petition for termination of parental rights had been filed by an adoption agency in this case, rather than by individuals, before it could claim abandonment would the agency have to show that it made some effort to assist the parents in order to strengthen their relationship with the child? See Matter of Anonymous, 40 N.Y.2d 96, 351 N.E.2d 707, 386 N.Y. S.2d 59 (1976); Carrieri, Development and Expansion of New York's Permanent Neglect Statute, 5 Ford.Urban L.J. 419 (1977).

8. H and W were married and had one son, S. When S was two years old, they were divorced, custody of S being awarded to W, with H ordered to pay $100 per month in child support. Six months later both H and W had remarried, W to H-2 and H to W-2. A statute of the state provided as follows: "No child shall be adopted without the consent of his parents, except [that] * * * consent shall not be required of a parent who has lost custody of the child through a divorce decree and upon whom notice has been served." H had complied in all respects with the child support order. W and H-2 then filed a petition for adoption, serving H with notice in accordance with the statute. H appeared and at the same time his second wife, W-2 filed a petition for adoption. H opposed the adoption of S by H-2, and supported the adoption by W-2.

(a) Does Stanley v. Illinois, supra, page 432, have any bearing on this case? If so, what effect does it have?

(b) How should the case be decided?

(c) Do you deduce any drafting precepts from this case? Parks v. Torgerson, 267 Minn. 468, 127 N.W.2d 548 (1964). See also In re Adoption of Moriarity, 260 Iowa 279, 152 N.W.2d 218 (1967), 53 Iowa L.Rev. 751 (1967); In re Petition of Wilson v. Barnet, 275 Minn. 32, 144 N.W.2d 700 (1966); Bond v. Carlson, 188 N.W.2d 728 (N.D.1971); In the Matter of the Adoption of Smith, 229 Or. 277, 366 P.2d 875 (1961); Wadlington, The Divorced Parent and the Consent for Adoption, 36 U.Cin.L.Rev. 196 (1967).

9. M had an illegitimate child C. She signed a consent to have C adopted, but the consent did not comply with the local statute. C's father, F, had already given a valid consent to adoption. When it appeared that

M's consent was not valid, she demanded return of the child, but the adoption agency having custody refused, claiming that the child had been abandoned. Should the agency prevail in this contention? See Meyers v. State, 124 Ga.App. 146, 183 S.E.2d 42 (1971); Adoption of Ashton, 374 Pa. 185, 97 A.2d 368 (1953); Hendricks v. Curry, 401 S.W.2d 796 (Tex.1966), 20 S.W.L.Rev. 684 (1966).

10. In view of some of these problems, could you draft a more satisfactory statute defining the circumstances in which parental rights may be terminated?

D. THE ADOPTION PROCESS: ESTABLISHING THE TIES WITH THE ADOPTING PARENTS

BARRY E. (ANONYMOUS) v. INGRAHAM

Court of Appeals of New York, 1977.
43 N.Y.2d 87, 400 N.Y.S.2d 772, 371 N.E.2d 492.

BREITEL, Chief Judge. Petitioners, having secured a Mexican order of adoption for a child now in their possession, bring this proceeding under CPLR article 78 to compel the State Commissioner of Health to issue their "adopted child" a new birth certificate. Special Term granted the relief, the Appellate Division unanimously affirmed, and the commissioner appeals by leave of this court.

The issue is whether section 4138 (subd. 1, par. [c]) of the Public Health Law entitles petitioners to compel issuance of a new birth certificate. Involved is whether the commissioner must act upon an order of a Mexican court relating to the adoption by a New York domiciled couple of a child born in New York to a New York domiciled mother.

The order of the Appellate Division should be reversed, and the petition dismissed. Before issuing a new birth certificate the State Commissioner of Health is required by the statute to ascertain that the adoption order presented issued from a "court of competent jurisdiction". The terms "competence" and "jurisdiction", to be sure, may have as many meanings as there are contexts in which they are used. If the statutory words are to be given any function, however, they must exclude an adoption order of a foreign court from which, on its face, it appears that all of the parties concerned are domiciled, resident, and present in New York. The order of the Mexican court, despite its assertion of power and competence under Mexican statutes, established, therefore, that it lacked any foundation under Anglo-American concepts of jurisdiction to effect a change in the infant's status.

Petitioners, a married couple domiciled in New York, sought to adopt an infant girl born in New York on November 22, 1973. The child's natural mother, who allegedly consented to the adoption, is also a New York domiciliary. The natural father is unknown.

The parties resorted to Mexico. Although the record is unclear whether the would-be adoptive parents were physically before the Mexican court, there is no dispute that neither the child nor her natural mother were in the jurisdiction. The natural mother did, however, purportedly appear by counsel. The ensuing Mexican court order of March 6, 1974 explicitly asserts the competence of the court and recites that petitioners, on whose behalf statements of four character witnesses were filed, are of age and adequate means. It directs that the child be adopted, and that her name be changed in accordance with petitioners' request.

Mexican order in hand, petitioners turned to the State Commissioner of Health for a new birth certificate for the child. Their application was denied. In the commissioner's view, under section 4138 (subd. 1, par. [c]) of the Public Health Law, the Mexican court's lack of competence to order the infant's adoption, apparent from the face of the order, precluded his compliance with their request. This proceeding followed.

None of the facts recited in the Mexican court order establish any basis for the exercise of power by the Mexican court. More important, no further facts were developed in this proceeding establishing any better basis for the Mexican court's arrogation of power. Consequently, the extent of the State Commissioner's authority to accept or reject the Mexican order turns on the recitals in that order and the meaning and purpose of the governing New York statute.

The statute sets forth the circumstances for issuance of a new birth certificate on behalf of an adopted child.

"1. A new certificate of birth shall be made whenever: * * *

"(b) notification is received by, or proper proof is submitted to, the commissioner from or by the clerk of a court of competent jurisdiction or the parents, or their attorneys, or the person himself, of a judgment, order or decree relating to parentage; or,

"(c) notification is received by, or proper proof is submitted to, the commissioner from or by the clerk as aforesaid of a judgment, order or decree relating to the adoption of such person" (Public Health Law, § 4138, subd. 1, pars. [b], [c]).

It is thus not all papers handed him that the commissioner must act upon; only when the papers disclose that a court of "competent jurisdiction" has ordered an adoption is issuance of a new birth certificate required.

That issuance of a new birth certificate may be described, with less than complete accuracy, as a ministerial function does not, nor can it, avoid the principle that even ministerial responsibility depends upon the foundation presented by or with the proffered document. Even officials performing ministerial duties are commonly required to determine at least the facial significance of the documents upon which they are supposed to act. * * *   So, too, a new birth certificate should not be issued unless the judicial order of adoption at least on its face establishes that the order was that of a competent court. The court must be "competent" not only under the law of its own sovereign, but also by virtue of personal and subject matter jurisdiction under the law of the forum in which the New York statute is being applied. (Ehrenzweig, Conflict of Laws, § 26, pp. 85–88.)

On what renders a court competent to adjudicate an adoption there is a wide and diverse range of opinion. Authorities start usually with the requirement of in personam jurisdiction over the adoptive parent and either the adoptive child or his legal custodian (see Restatement, Conflict of Laws 2d, § 78, subd. b; Ehrenzweig, Conflict of Laws, § 26, pp. 85–88; Taintor, Adoption in Conflict of Laws, 15 U. of Pitt.L.Rev. 222, 249–250). Moreover, at least in American jurisdictions, it is often regarded as critical—frequently, because adoption, it is reasoned, works a change in status—that the domicile of one or more of the parties be in the rendering jurisdiction (see Ehrenzweig, Conflict of Laws, § 26, pp. 85–88).

In many instances the domicile of either the adoptive parent or the adoptive child will suffice (see Restatement, Conflict of Laws 2d, § 78, subd. a; Goodrich, Conflict of Laws [4th ed., Scoles, 1974], § 146). Another view is that a court is competent if the adoptive parents or child at least reside in the jurisdiction. It is not unusual in such contexts, however, to treat the term "residence" as "domicile". (See Requirements as to Residence or Domicil, Ann., 33 A.L.R.3d 176, § 12.) Some earlier authorities would even have required that the adoptive parents and child share a common domicile (see, e. g., 2 Beale, Conflict of Laws, § 142.2, pp. 713–714).

What New York requires for its own courts to adjudicate an adoption is not, of course, determinative of the competence of an out-of-State court. The New York procedure does, however, reveal this State's strong concern for, and therefore strong policy with respect to, the adoption of resident children and, in a proper case, children sojourning within its borders. The Domestic Relations Law contemplates the residence in New York of either the adoptive parents or the adoptive child (see §§ 113, 115, subd. 2). Also significant is that the adoptive parents and child must, unless excused by the court, appear before the Judge or Surrogate for an examination (see Domestic Relations Law, § 112, subds. 1, 5; § 115, subds. 3, 7). In addition, an independent investigation into the advisability of the adoption is to be conducted (see Domestic Relations Law, § 112, subd. 7; § 116, subd. 3). (* * * to prevent recognition in New York of out-of-State adoptions not conforming to established standards.)

Matter of Leask v. Hoagland, 197 N.Y. 193, 195–196, 90 N.E. 652, and New York Life Ins. & Trust Co. v. Viele, 161 N.Y. 11, 18, 55 N.E. 311, 312, it is true, treated children of foreign adoptions "as

though they had been duly adopted under the laws of New York".
These cases, however, involved only the adopted child's right to inherit under a will, and the rules there formulated are expressly limited to that purpose. In short, at issue were the consequences of the
adoption, given the unquestioned status of adoption in the foreign
State, not recognition of that status (see, generally, Ehrenzweig, Con-
fict of Laws, § 51, pp. 186–188).

What foundation an out-of-State court must have, in all cases, to
render it competent to order an adoption recognizable in New York
need not now be determined. For purposes of this case and this statute, it is enough that on the submitted documents the Mexican court
was not "competent" to order the adoption of the infant child.

Although there was suggestion in this proceeding that the adoptive parents were physically before the Mexican court, the commissioner disputes this, and the Mexican judicial order does not recite
that they were. In any event it has not been shown that they were
ever residents or domiciliaries of Mexico. Neither the child nor her
natural mother, moreover, was ever domiciled or resident in Mexico.
Nor does it appear that they had ever sojourned in that jurisdiction.
Insofar as any investigation into the advisability of the adoption, the
order recites only that statements of four named but undescribed
character witnesses were filed, and that petitioners are of age with
adequate means of support.

The child's status, situated in New York and not in Mexico, was
no concern of the Mexican court. The Mexican order was a futile effort to produce an extraterritorial result not allowable with respect to
an extraterritorial *res*. And all of this was patent from the face of
the order. As all the authorities agree, however relaxed or strict in
view, it is more than token formalistic submission to personal jurisdiction by the parents concerned, adoptive and natural, that gives a
court power to fix an utterly foreign child's status in a new family.
In sum, New York need not under any authoritative view treat as
"competent" this Mexican court purporting to order the adoption by
a New York couple of a child born in New York to a New York
mother.

General principles governing recognition of foreign judgments
are in harmony with this conclusion. Even assuming the competence
of a given court, comity will not be accorded a foreign judgment if it
violates a strong public policy of the State. Indeed, as observed earlier, the State's vital social interest in the welfare of its children is
one of its strongest public policies. To lend an imprimatur to an
adoption, predicated upon insufficient jurisdictional foundations and a
questionable perfunctory examination into the interests of the child,
would be an inexcusable abdication of the State's role as *parens patriae*. It could also, it is feared, open the door to the mercenary trad-
ing of children. Most troubling, the present record provides no infor-

mation, except for undetailed references in a letter, how the infant child came into possession of petitioners, a placement evidently without the intervention of any public or authorized private agency.

It follows, therefore, that the submitted order of adoption was insufficient on its face, and the commissioner's refusal to issue a new birth certificate under section 4138 should be sustained.

It may be envisaged that it is awkward for the commissioner to determine an issue as potentially abstruse as the competence of a court. But the matter is not ended finally by the commissioner's action. It is precisely in a judicial proceeding such as this, in the nature of mandamus to enforce a legal right, that the commissioner's rejection may be overruled if, but only if, it appears that indeed the adoption order issued from a court of competent jurisdiction. This proceeding, as noted before, did not produce such proof. On the contrary, no more than the naked and inadequate "jurisdictional" facts recited in the Mexican order were produced.

One additional point should be addressed. Because the immediate concern is only the issuance of a new birth certificate, it is true that any decision regarding the Mexican order leaves the purported adoption itself unaffected for better or worse. It is not true, however, that the child is forever left with a New York birth certificate bearing an incomplete name. Petitioners' recourse is a proper adoption proceeding in New York, a proceeding which one would hope would give them the opportunity to establish that the adoption is in the best interests of the child.

Perhaps the most unsettling aspect of this technically narrow proceeding, in which petitioners would studiously avoid any review of the best interests of the child, is that the child herself is unrepresented. At the very least, in this or any other proceeding affecting the child's welfare, a guardian ad litem to participate on behalf of the child should be appointed. The nisi prius court had that power to appoint and should have exercised it (CPLR 1202). The child is the ultimate principal in this proceeding, she is the ward of the court, and no one speaks on her behalf.

Accordingly, the order of the Appellate Division should be reversed, with costs, and the petition dismissed.

NOTES AND QUESTIONS

1. (a) Since adoption is a statutory process, jurisdiction must in the first instance be determined by the applicable statute. Statutes vary widely both with respect to the court and the locality in which adoption petitions may be filed. Very often courts of special jurisdiction, such as juvenile courts or probate courts, have authority to grant adoptions. The statutes also vary widely in their requirements for subject matter jurisdiction. Illinois, for example, authorizes adoption proceedings to be brought in the county of petitioners' residence, or of the adoptive child's residence or birth, or the county of the natural parents' residence, with the proviso that in the

case of an agency placement the adoption may be in any county. Ill.Ann. Stat. ch. 4, § 9.1–4 (1975). In Minnesota the proceeding must be brought in the county of the petitioners' residence and the petitioner must have lived in the state a year. Minn.Stat.Ann. §§ 259.22, 259.23 (1971 & Supp. 1979). In New York agency placements may be heard in the county where the adoptive parents reside, or if they do not reside in the state, in the county where the agency has its principal office. N.Y.Dom.Rel.L. § 113 (1977). The Uniform Adoption Act § 4, 9 Unif.L.Ann. 21 (1979) provides that jurisdiction may be had in the place where the petitioner resides, or the place where the person to be adopted resides, or the place in which the agency is located. The same section contains a forum non conveniens provision. The Act does not reveal whether "resides" means "is domiciled", but presumably it does.

(b) An Interstate Compact on the Placement of Children has been ratified by about three-fourths of the states. It applies to the placement of children in foster care or as a preliminary to adoption. Its provisions require notice to the state receiving a child for such purposes, attempt to promote the child's best interests, and impose penalties for illegal placements. See Ill.Ann.Stat. ch. 23, § 2601 ff. (Supp.1979); Weiland and White, The Law of Interstate Placements of Children, 39 Ohio St.L.J. 327 (1978); Opinion of the Attorney General of California on the Interstate Compact Dealing With the Placement of Children, 5 Fam.L.Rep. 3015 (1978).

(c) H and W, residents of state A, wish to adopt a child but are unable to do so in state A because there are few adoptable babies available and a long list of applicants for the few babies. H and W then go to state B, contact a lawyer there, pay him $5,000 for a baby which he delivers to them, together with a duly notarized consent signed by the baby's mother. The baby's father's identity is unknown as is his present whereabouts. H and W bring the baby back to state A and file a petition for adoption in the appropriate court in A. On inquiry by the judge, they reveal the circumstances in which they obtained the baby, which leads him to point out that they have violated a statute of state A, which forbids private placements and which also forbids payment of money in connection with the placement of children for adoption. What should the court then do with the adoption petition? Would you advise a client to obtain a child in this way? Matter of Adoption of a Child By I.T., 164 N.J.Super. 476, 397 A.2d 341 (1978); Matter of Adoption of a Child By N.P., 165 N.J.Super. 591, 398 A. 2d 937 (1979). See also N.Y.Dom.Rel.L. § 115–a (1977).

2. Why should the law concern itself with subject-matter jurisdiction in adoption at all? What purposes are served, either by the statutes just referred to or by some common law principle of jurisdiction? What does the principal case have to say on this point? Is adoption a proceeding in rem, in personam, or both, or neither? Taintor, Adoption in the Conflict of Laws, 15 Pitt.L.Rev. 222, 228 (1954).

3. What rule of subject-matter jurisdiction does the New York court adopt? Restatement, Second, Conflict of Laws § 78 (1971) provides as follows: "A state has power to exercise judicial jurisdiction to grant an adoption if

(a) it is the state of domicil of either the adopted child or the adoptive parent, and

(b) the adoptive parent and either the adopted child or the person having legal custody of the child are subject to its personal jurisdiction."

Would jurisdiction exist in the principal case under the new Restatement rule? For other views on adoption jurisdiction, see H. Clark, Law of Domestic Relations § 18.2 (1968). For collections of cases see Annot., 33 A. L.R.3d 176 (1970)

Should the state's adoption statute be the sole jurisdictional authority, or should there be additional common law requirements? State ex rel. True v. LaKosky, 301 Minn. 450, 224 N.W.2d 128 (1974).

4. Does the Restatement rule accord with Stanley v. Illinois, supra, page 432? What is the relation between the Restatement rule, Stanley v. Illinois, and May v. Anderson, infra, page 1029? See Hazard, May v. Anderson: Prelude to Family Law Chaos, 45 Va.L.Rev. 379 (1959); Matter of Adoption of a Child By McKinley, 157 N.J.Super. 293, 384 A.2d 920 (1978).

5. Does the result in Barry E. v. Ingraham, or the Restatement rule, serve the purposes which you found to underlie any requirement of subject-matter jurisdiction? Would some different rule be preferable?

6. Why would not the principle of res judicata operate to protect the Mexican decree from attack in Barry E.? Cf. Rosenstiel v. Rosenstiel, 16 N.Y.2d 64, 209 N.E.2d 709, 262 N.Y.S.2d 86 (1965), cert. den. 383 U.S. 943 (1966), 384 U.S. 971 (1966).

7. Under the Restatement rule, § 78(b), how would the adopted child come to be subject to the court's personal jurisdiction? Does this require that if that part of the rule is relied upon, the child must be made a party to the proceeding, have a guardian ad litem appointed, and have his guardian personally served with process? Under In re B, supra, page 506, would the child be entitled to be represented in the adoption hearing in any event?

8. In addition to the mixture of requirements relating to subject-matter jurisdiction and personal jurisdiction described in the Restatement, § 78, what requirements of notice exist? Restatement, Second, Conflict of Laws, § 69 (1971) states, "A state may not exercise judicial jurisdiction over the status of a person unless a reasonable method is employed to give him notice of the action and unless he is afforded a reasonable opportunity to be heard." In Armstrong v. Manzo, 380 U.S. 545 (1965) W and H were divorced, with custody of their daughter to W. W married H-2 and after two years H-2 filed a petition to adopt the daughter. Texas law provided that a stepparent adoption could be granted without the consent of the natural father where he had failed for two years to contribute to the extent of his ability to the support of the child. No notice of the proceeding was given to H and the Court held that this "violated the most rudimentary demands of due process of law," 380 U.S. at 550, and that the defect was not cured by a hearing later given to H on his motion to set aside the decree. Notice, however, that the adoption proceeding in that case encompassed both of the steps referred to at the outset of this section, that is, it terminated the rights of the natural parent and substituted therefor the rights and duties of the adoptive parent. See also Matter of Adoption of Hall, —— Mont. ——, 566 P.2d 401 (1977); Hughes v. Aetna Casualty & Surety Co., 234 Or. 426, 383 P.2d 55 (1963); Annots., 76 A.L.R. 1077 (1932) and 24 A.L.R. 416 (1923).

On the foregoing authority, what notice should be given in the following situations: (a) H and W have a child, custody of which is given to W on their divorce. H fails to make the support payments required by the divorce decree and after a year W brings a dependency and neglect proceeding which results in a decree terminating H's parental rights. H is personally served in this proceeding but does not contest it. W then marries H–2, who files a petition to adopt the child. Need notice of this proceeding be given to H? In Interest of Workman, 14 Ill.Dec. 908, 56 Ill.App.3d 1007, 373 N.E.2d 39 (1978).

(b) M has an illegitimate child, C. In a relinquishment proceeding she gives up the child and the decree places it in the custody of the state welfare department. A dependency decree terminates the parental rights of F, C's father, after personal service upon him. When the welfare department places C with Mr. and Mrs. X for adoption, and an adoption petition is filed, need notice be given either to M or to F?

(c) H and W are divorced, with custody of their child C to W. W then marries H–2, who petitions to adopt C under the state statute which provides that the consent of a divorced parent to adoption of his child is not required where the divorce decree deprives him of custody. Must notice of the adoption be given to H?

(d) M and F have an illegitimate child, C. After counselling they both decide that adoption is the wiser course, and they execute consents to adoption which comply with the local law and place the child in the custody of the welfare department. The department places the child with Mr. and Mrs. X for adoption and the adoption petition is filed. Must notice of the proceeding be given to M and F? In re Adoption of a Minor, 345 Mass. 706, 189 N.E.2d 505 (1963); Matter of Anonymous, 55 A.D.2d 383, 390 N.Y.S.2d 433 (2d Dep't 1977); In re Adoption of a Minor Child, 109 R.I. 443, 287 A.2d 115 (1972).

(e) Must notice be given to anyone other than parents? Barriner v. Stedman, 580 P.2d 514 (Okl.1978) (need not give notice to grandparents who had visitation rights and who had applied for guardianship of the child.) See also Wilson v. Family Services Division, 554 P.2d 227 (Utah 1976) (grandmother entitled to a hearing on her fitness to adopt her grandchild).

9. Jurisdiction over the adoption of Indian children may, under some circumstances, be exclusively vested in the tribal courts. Fisher v. District Court of Sixteenth Judicial District, 424 U.S. 382 (1976), rehearing denied 425 U.S. 926 (1976). See also Indian Child Welfare Act, paragraph 7, supra, page 531, and Matter of Duryea, 115 Ariz. 86, 563 P.2d 885 (1977).

10. Should a child be placed for adoption with a single woman or single man? Is this issue affected by the availability of otherwise eligible adoptive parents? See Adoption of H, 69 Misc.2d 304, 330 N.Y.S.2d 235 (Fam.Ct.1972). State statutes place few restrictions upon those who may adopt a child. Ill.Ann.Stat. ch. 4, § 9.1–2 (1975) authorizes adoption by a reputable person of legal age and either sex, and if such person is married, the spouse must be a party to the petition. If the petitioner is a minor he may adopt by leave of court on good cause shown. In New York adoption may be by any adult unmarried person, or by any adult married person with his adult spouse, except that adult or minor spouses may adopt their own child born out of wedlock. N.Y.Dom.Rel.L. § 110 (1977). Cal.Civ.Code §

222 (Supp.1979) requires that the adopting person be ten years older than the child to be adopted, except where the adoption is by certain relatives and the court finds that it is in the best interests of the parties and the public. The New Jersey statute requires that the adopting person be eighteen and ten years older than the child being adopted, but the court may waive these requirements for good cause. The Uniform Adoption Act § 3, 9 Unif.L. Ann. 20 (1979) permits adoption by husband and wife of any age, by an unmarried adult, and by a married individual in certain specified circumstances.

Child Welfare League of America, Guidelines for Adoption Service, 12 (1969), after recommending that agencies clearly define their qualifications for adoptive parents and also find creative ways to facilitate otherwise impossible adoptions, states, "For example, the agency should select families in which a husband and wife are living together. Yet a single-parent applicant might be considered when no other home is available for a specific child, and when the applicant is part of a family to which the child will have the security of belonging." This seems to represent a slight liberalization of the standard, the earlier similar publication seeming to recommend adoptions only by married persons.

A more rigid approach to the suitability of adoptive parents is outlined in Michaels, Casework Considerations in Rejecting the Adoption Application, reprinted in I. E. Smith, Readings in Adoption, 300–312 (1963). Among other factors leading to disqualification are single status, age, residence outside the area served by the agency, the fact that the couple already have children of their own, or that they have two or more adoptive children.

11. M and F, both brilliant graduate students at a university, were the unmarried parents of D. M and F lived together for a year after D was born, but then they broke up and M placed D in the care of the state welfare department because she was unable to support D, F having left the state. The social worker in charge of the case expected M to consent to the adoption of D very soon, and so placed D in the home of Mr. and Mrs. P, as foster parents. Mr. and Mrs. P had signed a boarding home agreement with the welfare department by which they agreed to accept not more than two children for foster care from the department, to care for any children placed with them, and not to attempt to adopt any child placed with them. On its part the department agreed to pay Mr. and Mrs. P the sum of ten dollars per day per child as reimbursement for the cost of each child's care. Mr. and Mrs. P were each fifty-two years old, childless, had high school educations and lived in a small but comfortable house in a middle class subdivision. Mr. P worked as a barber and had an income of $10,000 per year. Mrs. P did not work outside the home but was an excellent housekeeper and fond of children.

D remained with Mr. and Mrs. P for eighteen months, during which time M was unable to decide whether to consent to D's adoption. During this time D had an attack of meningitis requiring first hospitalization and later constant nursing care at home. The welfare department paid the medical expenses, but Mrs. P cared for and nursed D on her discharge from the hospital for two months. The illness left D with impaired hearing. At the end of the eighteen months M executed a valid consent to the adoption of D, and the welfare department obtained a decree terminating F's parental rights on the ground of abandonment after complying with all jurisdictional requirements for such a decree. The decree gave the department authority to place D for adoption. D was then two and one-half years old and by virtue of this fact and the deafness was considered a "hard-to-place child". Nevertheless the welfare department made efforts to place her with adoptive parents, and at the end of an additional six months succeeded in finding a childless young doctor and his wife possessing substantial wealth who agreed to adopt her. The welfare department then notified Mr. and Mrs. P that D was to be adopted and asked that D be turned over to the department for that purpose. Mr. and Mrs. P refused, immediately filing a petition for adoption themselves. The department opposed the petition, putting in evidence the foregoing facts. Mr. and Mrs. P. gave evidence of their care and affection for D.

The applicable statute provided that in the case of a child who has been committed to the custody of a public or private child placement agency, consent to adoption must be given by the agency, except that if the agency refuses consent the court may in its discretion dispense with such consent. What arguments should be made for either side in such a case? How should the case be decided? What difference would it make if the statute merely required agency consent, without dealing with the question of what effect refusal of that consent would have? See In re Adoption of Runyon, 268 Cal.App.2d 918, 74 Cal.Rptr. 514 (1969); Madsen v. Chasten, 7 Ill.App. 3d 21, 286 N.E.2d 505 (1972); Commonwealth, Department of Child Welfare v. Jarboe, 464 S.W.2d 287 (Ky.1971); Fleming v. Hursh, 271 Minn. 337, 136 N.W.2d 109 (1965); In re Haun, 31 Ohio App.2d 63, 286 N.E. 2d 478 (1972); Adoption of H, 69 Misc.2d 304, 330 N.Y.S.2d 235 (Fam. Ct.1972); Commonwealth ex rel. Children's Aid Society v. Gard, 362 Pa. 85, 66 A.2d 300 (1949); In the Matter of the Adoption of Reinius, 55 Wash.2d 117, 346 P.2d 672 (1959); Wadlington, Minimum Age Difference as a Requisite for Adoption, 1966 Duke L.J. 392; S. Katz, When Parents Fail, Ch. 4 (1971); Note, Adoptions for the Hard-to-Place: The Role of the Court and the Trend Against Matching, 25 U.Miami L.Rev. 749 (1971); J. Goldstein, A. Freud, A. Solnit, Beyond The Best Interests of the Child (1973).

12. For an interesting case approving an adoption by parents who were deaf-mutes, and holding that if their petition to adopt were denied solely on the ground they were deaf-mutes this would violate the Fourteenth Amendment, see Adoption of Richardson, 251 Cal.App.2d 222, 59 Cal.Rptr. 323 (1967).

13. Should the advanced age of a prospective adoptive parent, for example a grandparent who wishes to adopt a grandchild, be the sole reason for denying the adoption? In re Adoption of Michelle Lee T., 44 Cal.App. 3d 699, 117 Cal.Rptr. 856 (1975); In re Niskanen, 301 Minn. 53, 223 N.W. 2d 754 (1974); In re Adoption of Tachick, 60 Wis.2d 540, 210 N.W.2d 865 (1973); Annot., 84 A.L.R.3d 665 (1978).

14. The political upheavals in Viet Nam and other parts of Asia have led to the placement of children from those countries with American parents for adoption. International agencies have been organized to assist in such adoptions and their efforts have benefited the children and the adoptive parents. In a few cases, however, the failure to obtain proper consent from natural parents in foreign countries having different legal systems has led to the adoptions being set aside, with wide publicity. For accounts of some of the difficulties in such placements and of the procedure to be

followed, see Kim and Carroll, Intercountry Adoption of South Korean Orphans: A Lawyer's Guide, 14 J. of Fam.L. 223 (1975); Note, International Adoptions-United States Adoption of Vietnamese Children: Vital Considerations for the Courts, 52 Denver L.J. 771 (1975). See also Huynh Thi Anh v. Levi, 586 F.2d 625 (6th Cir. 1978).

DICKENS v. ERNESTO

Court of Appeals of New York, 1972.
30 N.Y.2d 61, 281 N.E.2d 153, 330 N.Y.S.2d 346.
Appeal dismissed for want of substantial federal question, 407 U.S. 917,
92 S.Ct. 2463, 32 L.Ed.2d 803 (1972).

FULD Chief Judge.   We are here concerned with the validity, under the United States Constitution, of the religious affiliation requirements of certain statutes (Family Ct. Act, § 116; Social Services Law, Consol.Laws, c. 55, § 373; Domestic Relations Law, Consol.Laws, c. 14, § 113), enacted in conformity with article VI (§ 32) of our State Constitution.

On December 22, 1969, the petitioners, Robert and Anne Dickens, sought to file an application as adoptive parents with respondent Erie County Department of Social Services.   Refused permission to do so by respondent department solely on the ground that they did not have a religious affiliation, they brought this article 78 proceeding for a judgment (1) declaring that the challenged constitutional and statutory provisions offend against certain provisions contained in the Federal Constitution and (2) directing the respondent to immediately "process * * * [their] application as adoptive parents."   The courts below decided that there was no violation of petitioners' constitutional rights but directed the respondent to accept and process their application.   From that determination, the petitioners appeal as of right, urging that the provisions in question "create an establishment of religion" and deny them "their freedom of religion" under the First Amendment and also deny them equal protection of the laws under the Fourteenth Amendment.

Religion has always been a relevant and important, though not controlling, consideration in this State in the placement of children for adoption.   Article VI (§ 32) of New York's Constitution requires that a child "shall be committed or remanded or placed [for adoption], *when practicable,* in an institution or agency governed by persons, or in the custody of a person, of the same religious persuasion as the child."   The term, "when practicable", is, we stated in Matter of Maxwell's Adoption, 4 N.Y.2d 429, 434, 176 N.Y.S.2d 281, 151 N.E.2d 848, of "broad content, necessarily designed to accord the trial judge a discretion to approve as adoptive parents persons of a faith different from the child's in exceptional situations." * * *   In 1970, some years after our decision in *Maxwell,* the statutes which required religious conformity of child and adoptive parents "when practicable" were broadened (Family Ct. Act, § 116, subd. [g]; Social Services

Law, § 373, subd. 7; see, also, Domestic Relations Law, § 113) to provide that such religious "matching" in foster care and adoption proceedings be *"consistent with the best interests of the child"* (L. 1970, ch. 494). Because of its significance and scope, we set forth in full one of those new provisions—subdivision (g) of section 116 of the Family Court Act:

"(g) The provisions of subdivisions (a), (b), (c), (d), (e) and (f) of this section [which deal with the placing of a child] shall, *so far as consistent with the best interests of the child, and where practicable,* be applied so as to give effect to the religious wishes of the natural mother, if the child is born out-of-wedlock, or if born in-wedlock, the religious wishes of the parents of the child, or if only one of the parents of an in-wedlock child is then living, the religious wishes of the parent then living. Religious wishes of a parent shall include wishes that the child be placed in the same religion as the parent or in a different religion from the parent or with indifference to religion or with religion a subordinate consideration. Expressed religious wishes of a parent shall mean those which have been set forth in a writing signed by the parent, except that, in a non-agency adoption, such writing shall be an affidavit of the parent. In the absence of expressed religious wishes, as defined in this subdivision, determination of the religious wishes, if any, of the parent, shall be made upon the other facts of the particular case, and, if there is no evidence to the contrary, it shall be presumed that the parent wishes the child to be reared in the religion of the parent." [1] (Emphasis supplied.)

It is thus apparent, first, that religion is but one of many factors in the placement of a child for adoption and, second, that placement in conformity with "the religious wishes of the parents of the child," though desirable, is not mandatory. Indeed, as the Appellate Division observed (37 A.D.2d 102, 106, 322 N.Y.S.2d 581), the above-quoted subdivision (g), as well as subdivision 7 of section 373 of the Social Services Law, "amended the respective statutes * * * to eliminate any requirement that the religious matching provisions be applied mandatorily." Thus, the challenged legislation places primary emphasis on the temporal best interests of the child, although the religious preference of the natural parents remains a relevant consideration.

In dealing with the petitioners' contention that New York, by Constitution and legislation, has created an establishment of religion, we note that "No perfect or absolute separation [of government and religion] is really possible; the very existence of the Religion Clauses

---

1. The quoted subdivision is virtually identical with subdivision 7 of section 373 of the Social Services Law. And section 113 of the Domestic Relations Law, insofar as relevant, provides that "In making orders of adoption the judge * * * when practicable must give custody only to persons of the same religious faith as that of the adoptive child in accordance with article six of the social services law"— which, we note, includes section 373.

is an involvement of sorts". (Walz v. Tax Comm., 397 U.S. 664, 670, 90 S.Ct. 1409, 1412, 25 L.Ed.2d 697.) A number of criteria have been developed, however, to determine when a law is violative of the Establishment Clause. "[T]o withstand the strictures of [that] Clause", the Supreme Court has observed, "there must be a secular legislative purpose and a primary effect that neither advances nor inhibits religion." (School Dist. of Abington Tp., Pa. v. Schempp, 374 U.S. 203, 222, 83 S.Ct. 1560, 1571, 10 L.Ed.2d 844; see, also, Lemon v. Kurtzman, 403 U.S. 602, 612, 91 S.Ct. 2105, 29 L.Ed.2d 745; Board of Educ. of Central School District No. 1 v. Allen, 392 U.S. 236, 243, 88 S.Ct. 1923, 20 L.Ed.2d 1060). More, such legislation "must not foster 'an excessive government entanglement with religion.' *Walz*, supra [397 U.S.] at 674, 90 S.Ct. 1409." (Lemon v. Kurtzman, 403 U.S. 602, 613, 91 S.Ct. 2105, 2111, 29 L.Ed.2d 745, supra; see, also, Tilton v. Richardson, 403 U.S. 672, 687, 91 S.Ct. 2091, 29 L.Ed.2d 790.)

Legislation which provides for the placement of a child with adoptive parents of the same religion "so far as consistent with the best interests of the child, and where practicable" (Family Ct. Act, § 116, subd. [g]), undoubtedly fulfills a "secular legislative purpose" and certainly reflects and preserves a "benevolent neutrality" toward religion. (Walz v. Tax Comm., 397 U.S., at p. 669, 90 S.Ct. 1409.) And, just as clearly, the "matching" provisions neither have the "primary effect" of advancing or inhibiting religion. (School Dist. of Abington Tp., Pa. v. Schempp, 374 U.S., at p. 222, 83 S.Ct. 1560) nor foster an "excessive government entanglement" with church interests. (Walz v. Tax Comm., 397 U.S. at p. 674, 90 S.Ct. 1409.) Religion has never been an exclusive, or, as above indicated, a controlling, factor in adoption proceedings. The standard contained in the new amendments to the religious conformity provisions—namely, "the best interests of the child"—is a flexible one, affording the court a broad discretion in deciding whether a proposed adoption would be best for the child. (See, e. g., In re Adoption of "E", 59 N.J. 36, 46, 279 A.2d 785, 792.)

Certainly subdivision (e) of section 116 of the Family Court Act, relied upon by the petitioners, does not support their claim of unconstitutionality. Insofar as relevant, that statute provides that "The words 'when practicable' * * * shall be interpreted as being without force or effect if there is a proper or suitable person of the same religious faith * * * as that of the child available * * * or * * * if there is a duly authorized * * * society or institution under the control of persons of the same religious faith or persuasion as that of the child, at the time available and willing to assume the responsibility for the custody of or control over any such child." As indicated in the new subdivision (g) of section 116 of the Family Court Act, subdivision (e) must be deemed to require that the "religious wishes" of the natural parent or parents be given effect "so far as consistent with the best interests of the child". And sub-division (g) provides that, in expressing their "religious wishes", the parents themselves may authorize the placement of the child with adoptive parents of a different religion, express their "indifference to religion" as a prerequisite to adoption or make religion a "subordinate consideration." Accordingly, the court, in applying subdivision (e) in the light of the strictures of subdivision (g), still retains discretion to determine whether a particular placement is in the best interests of the child, taking into account both religious and secular considerations.

Nor is the petitioners' First Amendment right to the "free exercise of religion" violated by the religious "matching" requirements. They argue that they are forced to choose between their right to profess no religion and their right to adopt because there are many more prospective parents than adoptive children and because all the natural parents in the Erie County area require their children to be placed with adoptive parents of one of the "predominant" religions. However, there have been instances, as the court below found, in which natural parents have indicated "their indifference to the religious placement of their child." Adoptive parents without religious affiliations would, as the courts below have indicated, be eligible to adopt such a child or a child whose religious background is unknown. Moreover, there is no indication that the petitioners are limited to the Erie County area in their search for an adoptive child. Under these circumstances, religious conformity provisions which serve a valid secular purpose may not be said to discriminate against or penalize the petitioners because they do not have a religious affiliation, nor are they thereby placed under an obligation to assume a religious faith in order to be able to adopt a child. (Cf. e. g., Sherbert v. Verner, 374 U.S. 398, 402, 83 S.Ct. 1790, 10 L.Ed.2d 965.)

Likewise without substance is the petitioners' equal protection argument. They urge that the religious conformity provisions, since they are not reasonably related to the purpose of the adoption laws, create an arbitrary classification which denies them equal protection of the laws. In point of fact, their real quarrel is not with the religious conformity provisions—which quite properly allow surrendering parents to express a religious preference * * * but, rather, with the shortages of adoptive children and surrendering parents without religious affiliation or preference.

The order appealed from should be affirmed, without costs.

NOTES AND QUESTIONS

1. The Court of Appeals cites In re Adoption of "E", 59 N.J. 36, 279 A.2d 785 (1971) without comment. In that case the New Jersey county court denied plaintiffs' application for adoption on the ground that their lack of belief in a Supreme Being made them unfit to be adoptive parents.

They appealed to the New Jersey Supreme Court, which reversed the county court's decision and granted the adoption. There was no question with respect to the eligibility of the petitioners as adoptive parents other than the facts that they were not members of any religious denomination, did not participate in any organized religion and did not believe in a Supreme Being. New Jersey has no statute or constitutional provision like those in New York quoted in Dickens, although the New Jersey case law had held that religion could, in some circumstances, be considered in determining the best interests of the child in custody and adoption proceedings, such as where the natural parents objected to the religion of the adoptive parents, or where the prior religious training of the child could not be pursued due to the environment, or where the child had had some religious training and the shift to parents of a different faith would cause emotional difficulties. After deciding that the trial court's decision was not in accord with state law, the court went on to discuss the constitutional issue. Quotations from its opinion, and from the concurring opinion of Chief Justice Weintraub, follow:

"By basing his decision *solely* on the absence of the Burkes' belief in a Supreme Being and their lack of church affiliation, the trial court relied on a factor which cannot alone be determinative of the 'best interests' of the child 'E'. We do not mean to suggest that a trial court may not probe into the religious background and convictions of prospective adopting parents in the same way as it and the investigating agencies may probe into all aspects of their lives and activities in order to determine fitness. Religion and morality are inextricably interwoven in the lives of most people in this country, and a high moral character of prospective adopting parents is an essential consideration in adoption proceedings. Sincere belief in and adherence to the tenets of a religion may be indicative of moral fitness to adopt in a particular case. Of course, a trial court may not stop the inquiry into moral fitness merely upon assurance that the applicants believe in a Supreme Being and attend church regularly. Such belief may well be inconclusive of the question. Where the applicants do not profess a religion or a belief in a Supreme Being, the court may not stop there and deny an adoption. The question is still whether they are morally fit to adopt and, to answer that question, the court must probe their moral character. The Chief Justice, in his concurring opinion, maintains that in evaluating prospective adoptive parents, a court or an agency can consider only their *conduct* and that neither a court nor an agency may ask questions which bear merely upon beliefs or ethics. This ignores the fact that much of our conduct is determined by our beliefs and ethics. If we were to bar courts and agencies from asking questions in these areas we would hamstring them in their efforts to protect the best interests of the child.

"On the other hand, we do not believe that any reasonable man no matter how devout in his own beliefs, would contend that morality lies in the exclusive province of one or of all religions or of religiosity in general. The present case is proof of this point. No one including the trial judge, has ever questioned the moral character of the Burkes. Indeed, the Society found as fact that they were 'people of high moral and ethical standards.' At the hearing the trial judge himself recognized that morality was not necessarily equatable with religion, and that persons who profess adherence to an established religion may not be 'as good' as the Burkes. Indeed, in staying his judgment pending appeal the trial judge noted that the children (David and 'E') 'are in good hands.'

"Summarizing, while religion when coupled with other considerations may be a factor to be weighed by the court in determining the advisability of granting an adoption of a child, that factor barring special circumstances such as those referred to above, is not and cannot be controlling. Since the trial court denied the adoption solely because of the Burkes' lack of a religious belief, he misused his direction and erred as a matter of law.

"The lower court's decision is also defective in that it runs afoul of the First Amendment of the United States Constitution. * * *

"The First Amendment provides in pertinent part:

Congress shall make no law respecting an establishment of religion, or prohibiting the free exercise thereof. * * *

This freedom of religion provision is appliable to the states through the Fourteenth Amendment. * * * It applies to the judiciary as well as the executive and legislative branches of the government. * * * The provision consists of two separate but related clauses, the Establishment Clause and the Free Exercise Clause. The Establishment Clause bars a state from placing its official support behind a religious belief, while the Free Exercise Clause bars a state from interfering with the practice of religion by its citizens. * * *

"The United States Supreme Court has consistently held that government must maintain a posture of 'wholesome neutrality' on the question of religion. E. g., School District of Abington Twp. v. Schempp, 374 U.S. 203, 83 S.Ct. 1560, 10 L.Ed.2d 844 (1963); * * * The First Amendment not only requires the state to be neutral between various religions, but between religion and non-religion as well: 'That Amendment requires the state to be neutral in its relations with groups of religious believers and non-believers. * * *' Everson v. Board of Education, 330 U.S. 1, 18, 67 S.Ct. 504, 513, 91 L.Ed. 711, 724–725 (1947). * * *

"In Torcaso v. Watkins, supra, the Supreme Court considered a question somewhat analogous to that in the present case. It held that a state could not disqualify atheists from serving as notaries public. The Court stated that neither state nor federal governments can constitutionally compel a person ' "[T]o profess a belief or disbelief in any religion." Neither can constitutionally pass laws or impose requirements which aid all religions as against non-believers, and neither can aid those religions based on a belief in the existence of God as against those religions founded on different beliefs.' 367 U.S. at 495, 81 S.Ct. at 1683, 6 L.Ed.2d at 987.
* * *

"Turning to the trial court's decision first, that court reasoned that the Burkes' First Amendment rights were not violated since adoption is a privilege rather than a right. * * * We cannot accept this distinction. Whatever validity the right—privilege dichotomy has * * * it can have little meaning in First Amendment cases. * * * Whatever the opportunity to adopt is labeled, a court cannot disqualify someone from adopting solely on religious grounds without violating that person's rights to free exercise of his religious beliefs Certainly, the opportunity to hold the office of notary public as in Torcaso is no more valuable than the opportunity to adopt.

"The trial court distinguished *Torcaso* on another ground. It reasoned that 'Torcaso was of age to make his own decision as to his belief or nonbelief in God,' whereas '[i]n the present case E is of tender years' and her decision 'to form a belief or nonbelief in the Supreme Being must await the time when [she] has the maturity, understanding and independent volition to do so * * *. The child should have the freedom to worship as she sees fit and not be influenced by parents or exposed to the views of prospective parents who do not believe in a Supreme Being.' 112 N.J.Super., at 331, 271 A.2d at 30.

"The trial court's reasoning does not confront the fundamental constitutional problem. The issue is not whether an individual has a right to choose religion or non-religion, but whether the government has the power to impose religion or to place a burden on one's beliefs regarding religion. Burdening the opportunity to adopt with religious requirements does both and if, as we believe, the government lacks such a power, religious requirements violate the Establishment Clause and the Free Exercise Clause of the First Amendment. The courts are an arm of the state and, as such, they are required to maintain a neutral posture on the issue of belief and nonbelief. We, as judges, regardless of our own personal beliefs and religious affiliations, cannot take the position that children may be placed only in the homes of believers until they are able to choose for themselves which course to pursue. Under the First Amendment we are incompetent to do so. Should we invade the province of religion in this instance, the religious beliefs of every citizen would be imperiled. We cannot forget that many of our forebears fled to this country to escape religious persecution for professing beliefs which were unpopular in their homeland. It was for this very reason that the Amendment was adopted, and if it is to have any meaning, it must protect minority rights in this area. If judges are to have the power to deny adoptions on the basis of the applicants' lack of religious beliefs, the door is opened to other judicial intrusions into this sensitive field. It is obvious that, in arriving at any decision, a court may not be influenced by its religious predilections. See Note, 'Court Refuses Adoption For Disbelief in a Supreme Being—In re Adoption of E,' 2 Seton Hall L.Rev. 460 (1971), where the author, in criticising the trial court's decision, comments that, '* * * if the right established by the court is to be recognized, it is foreseeable that it portends the right to be raised in the "right" religion.' [5]

5. It may be doubted whether a decision intended to foster belief in a Supreme Being would achieve that goal. See Isaac, Adopting a Child Today, 11–13 (1965) where the author states:
   In applying to the majority of adoption agencies a couple will be considered only if they both belong to the same faith and only if they are practicing members of their church * * * The couples who are active members of their church, and who can readily produce their clergyman's reference, thus start out with a great advantage over couples not affiliated with any church.

The solution for the disadvantaged couple will depend upon their attitudes and beliefs as well as upon the attitude of their local agency * * * The couple who is not affiliated with a church and does not want to become affiliated *or even wish to pretend* to be affiliated may have to abandon hope of adopting through an agency.

* * * Realistically speaking, if they are not served by a liberal agency, couples with no church affiliation have three choices: join a church; *pretend to belong to a church,* perhaps obtaining the ref-

"In *McGowan*, [McGowan v. Maryland, 366 U.S. 420, 81 S.Ct. 1101, 6 L. Ed.2d 393 (1961)] the Court upheld the 'Sunday Closing' laws since it found they served a valid secular purpose. In the present case, no valid secular purpose exists. Since it is uncontradicted that the prospective parents are of high moral character, the only purpose in requiring religious affiliation and belief in a Supreme Being can be religious. Amicus curiae suggests that religiosity serves the secular purpose of reducing the likelihood of juvenile delinquency by an adopted child. But the studies cited by him are inconclusive and, if anything, seem to point in the opposite direction. Similarly, his assertion that divorce and the resulting trauma to children are more likely in non-religious families is not substantiated. In any event, adoptions should be dealt with in a highly individualistic manner rather than on the basis of speculative and sweeping generalizations; they should not be denied because the applicants belong to a class which statistically shows a greater propensity for some unfortunate trait. To deny an adoption, the court must find evidence of that trait or find some other damaging evidence in the individual applicants. Applicants for the adoption of children stand before the judge as individuals and must be judged on their own merits.

"Finally, the court appointed amicus curiae suggests that the likelihood that a child of nonbelievers will be ostracized serves as a valid secular reason for denying adoptions to them. Even assuming that nonbelievers are shunned by some elements of the populace, most minority groups suffer or in the past have suffered the same penalty. Yet, absent special circumstances, no one would contend that members of a minority group should be denied the opportunity to adopt a child on that basis.

"One other point deserves mention. The concurring opinion finds our holding that religion may be a factor in adoption proceedings as objectionable on constitutional grounds as the trial court's holding that it may be the sole factor. That conclusion, of course, rests on the premise that the entire area of ethics and beliefs is irrelevant in adoption proceedings. If it is relevant, as we firmly believe it is, then questions concerning religion as it bears on ethics are not constitutionally forbidden because they serve a valid secular purpose. As stated above, such questions may be evidential of moral fitness to adopt in relation to how the applicants will conduct themselves as adopting parents.

"In view of what we have said above, it is unnecessary for us to consider plaintiffs' further contentions that the trial court's decision denied both them and the child 'E' equal protection and due process of law.
          *   *   *

"WEINTRAUB, C. J. (concurring).

"I concur in the result but cannot join in the opinion of the Court.

"Although the majority opinion concludes the trial court erred in refusing to order the adoption 'solely' on the basis of plaintiffs' lack of belief in a Supreme Being, the opinion does not condemn the trial court's inquiry into the subject. Since satisfaction of a judge's curiosity could hardly war-

erence of a sympathetic clergy-man-friend; *or adopt privately* *   *   *. (emphasis added)

The Burkes, of course, were completely forthright in explaining their humanistic beliefs.

rant that inquiry, I must conclude the majority opinion finds the subject to be relevant and a litigant's views upon it to be capable of constituting a factor in a decision to deny a judgment of adoption. Fortunately for us, the Burkes are not otherwise tainted and hence we are spared the task of deciding how many points should be charged against them because their articles of faith concerning a Supreme Being may deviate from our private views to a degree we severally cannot stand. I think none of this is the proper concern of a terrestrial judge.

"We are not talking about honoring the express stipulation made by a consenting natural parent as to the religious faith of an adoptive parent. Nor are we concerned with the hypothetical case of a child whose prior religious training reached the point where a change of direction might inflict some psychological trauma. Rather the simple question is whether the State may inquire into an individual's religious, spiritual and ethical concepts in order to decide whether that individual is fit to raise a child. I think it is not the State's business to prowl among anyone's thoughts and to label him fit or unfit, in whole or in part, because his views are distasteful to someone in a placement agency or in the judiciary.

"The majority opinion finds the State would violate the demand for neutrality in religious matters embedded in the First Amendment guarantee of freedom of religion if adoption were denied 'solely' because of an applicant's religion or lack of it. With that, I agree, but I cannot understand how the constitutional violation is a whit less because the applicant's religion or lack of it plays some lesser role in the judge's decision. Whether the price of the heresy is the destruction of a man's good character or merely a blot upon it, it is equally true that the State stamps its approval upon some tenets and its disapproval upon others. This is precisely what the First Amendment forbids.

"I can think of nothing more unmanageable than an inquiry into a man's religious, spiritual and ethical creed. There is no catalogue of tolerable beliefs. Nor would the nature of man permit one, for man is inherently intolerant as to matters unknowable, and the intensity of his intolerance is twin with the intensity of his views. I assume the majority would never deny adoption 'solely' because of a belief in that area, but if the belief may be considered as the majority say it may, then how much may be charged against an applicant who is a Jehovah's Witness and therefore opposed to blood transfusions, or a Christian Scientist, who, as I understand his faith, would turn to medical aid only as a last resort? And since a man's religious, spiritual and ethical views may be more evident in his position on specific subjects than in his abstract statement of his faith, will it be all right to inquire of his attitude toward the war in Vietnam, or capital punishment, or divorce, or abortion, or perhaps even public welfare, or income taxation, or caveat emptor, in all of which some people find evidence of moral fiber or lack of it?

"Nor is there anyone competent to pass judgment upon religious, spiritual, and ethical matters. I do not know how a placement agency tests or equips its staff for this demanding task. I do know that neither when they were admitted to the Bar nor when they were appointed to the bench, were judges asked to establish the acceptability of their own tenets or a capacity to appraise the tenets of others. As for me, I disclaim any expertise whatever. I have already interred too many of my eternal truths.

"No matter how it is phrased or explained, an inquiry into religious, spiritual and ethical views can mean no more than this, that a man or a woman is unfit, or a bit unfit, to be a parent, natural or adoptive, if his or her thoughts exceed the tolerance of the mortal who happens to be the judge in a placement bureau or in the judiciary. I find such an inquiry to be as offensive as it is meddlesome and irrelevant to the true issue. Every incursion is sure to repeat the spectacle now before us. I think it strong evidence of good moral character that an applicant wants to rear a child, and that should be quite enough in the absence of positive conduct revealing unfitness for parenthood."

2. In re Adoption of "E" is noted in 76 Dick.L.Rev. 529 (1972), 20 Kan.L.Rev. 187 (1971), 24 Me.L.Rev. 149 (1972), 2 Seton Hall L.Rev. 460 (1971), 17 Vill.L.Rev. 591 (1972).

The Child Welfare League of America, Guidelines for Adoption Service, 13 (1968), has this to say about religion in adoption placements: "The child should have an opportunity for spiritual and ethical development, but religious background alone should not determine whether the family is suitable for the child."

3. Is either the majority opinion or the concurring opinion in In re Adoption of "E" inconsistent with Dickens v. Ernesto? Were the facts in the two cases on all fours? Did the New York statute justify distinguishing the two cases? If the two are not consistent which case is correct? Does the majority in In re Adoption of "E" persuasively respond to Chief Justice Weintraub's position?

4. Might the rationale of the Levy v. Louisiana line of cases, and that of Stanley v. Illinois, be applied to the facts of Dickens v. Ernesto? If it were, how would the argument run and what result would it produce?

5. How should the following cases be decided, under *Dickens*, under In re Adoption of "E" and under your own view of the law and the United States Constitution?

(a) H and W have a son, S, who is twelve years old. H and W were killed in an auto accident and the parents of a close friend of S, Mr. and Mrs. W, seek to adopt S. They are opposed by a maiden aunt, Miss Y, W's sister, who also seeks to adopt. Miss Y is a Catholic, as were H and W, and as is S. Mr. and Mrs. W are atheists and are vocal and aggressive in their opposition to all religion. They are well educated and very fond of S.

(b) M has an illegitimate child, D. Both M and F, the father, are Puerto Ricans and give their religious affiliation as Catholic. The department of welfare files a dependency and neglect petition on the ground that both parents are addicted to drugs and completely unable to care for the child, and the court terminates the parental rights of both. The Catholic adoption agency seeks to have the child's custody, so that she can be placed with a Catholic family for adoption. The Children's Service, a non-sectarian agency, also seeks custody of the child so that it may place the child with eligible adoptive parents, regardless of their religious affiliation. In a conference with the court, the Catholic agency says it presently has no appropriate adoptive home for the child, but expects that one will turn up in five or six weeks. Children's Service says it has a fine home available at once, the parents being without religious affiliation. Cf. In re Efrain C, 63 Misc.2d 1019, 314 N.Y.S.2d 255 (Fam.Ct.1970).

(c) A child is placed for adoption whose parents indicate on their consent form that they are Jewish. The agency making the placement is the state welfare department. They have in their files applications from a childless Protestant couple who have been waiting for a child for two years and who are suitable adoptive parents in all respects. They also have an application from an eligible Jewish couple who applied only a month before, who have two children of their own but who would like to have still another child and are adopting one for reasons having to do with population control. The agency recommends that the child be placed with the Jewish couple because of the desire to match religions, but the Protestant couple intervene in the proceeding and seek to have the child placed with them.

For a thorough analysis of the constitutional question see Note, Religious Matching Statutes and Adoption, 51 N.Y.U.L.Rev. 262 (1976). See also Scott v. Family Ministers, 63 Cal.App.3d 492, 135 Cal.Rptr. 430 (1976); Note, A Reconsideration of the Religious Element in Adoption, 56 Corn.L.Q. 780 (1971); Annot. Religion as a Factor in Adoption Proceedings, 48 A.L.R.3d 383 (1973).

6. In most states there are denominational adoption agencies who are licensed by the state and place children for adoption. Their consent to the adoption of children placed with them is usually required by the adoption statutes, and they are thus an integral part of the statutory adoption process. If they refuse to place children with adoptive parents other than their own, does this raise any constitutional issues, and if so, how should they be resolved? Scott v. Family Ministers, 63 Cal.App.3d 492, 135 Cal. Rptr. 430 (1976).

DRUMMOND v. FULTON COUNTY DEPARTMENT OF FAMILY AND CHILDREN'S SERVICES

United States Court of Appeals, Fifth Circuit, 1977.
563 F.2d 1200, cert. den. 437 U.S. 910 (1978).

RONEY, Circuit Judge: Plaintiffs, Robert and Mildred Drummond, a white couple, acted as state-designated foster parents of a mixed race child for over two years. When the defendant state adoption agency decided to remove the child for permanent placement in another home, plaintiffs commenced this action under 42 U.S.C.A. § 1983. Alleging denial of their rights under both the equal protection and the due process clauses of the Fourteenth Amendment, they sought preliminary and permanent injunctive relief, which was denied by the district court. Although a panel of this Court reversed, Drummond v. Fulton County Department of Family & Children's Services, 547 F.2d 835 (5th Cir. 1977), the full Court finds no deprivation of constitutional rights and affirms the dismissal of plaintiffs' complaint.

Initially, the *en banc* Court adopts the discussion, reasoning and result contained in the dissenting opinion to the panel decision in this matter as the correct statement of the law in this case. That opinion is reported in 547 F.2d at 857–861. We further address the issues here, however, in view of the oral argument before the full Court, a subsequent case decided by the United States Supreme Court, and supplemental briefs filed with this Court.

The factual background of this dispute is set out in full in Judge Tuttle's thorough opinion for the panel which considered this case. 547 F.2d 835–857. A brief recapitulation will suffice to place the following discussion in context.

In December 1973 in an emergency situation, a one-month-old mixed race child named Timmy was placed for temporary care in the home of Mr. and Mrs. Drummond by the Fulton County children's service agency. Lengthy proceedings were commenced to determine whether the child should be permanently removed from his natural mother's custody and placed for adoption.

Within a year, the Drummonds had become sufficiently attached to Timmy to request permission to adopt him. The Drummonds had not signed an agreement that they would not try to adopt their foster child, as is common practice with many placement agencies. Although the level of care provided by them as foster parents had consistently been rated excellent, there was an emerging consensus with the defendant child placement agency charged with Timmy's care that it would be best to look elsewhere for a permanent adoptive home. When this was explained to the Drummonds in March 1975 they appeared to acquiesce. By August of that year, however, they had renewed their request to adopt Timmy.

The child was not legally freed for adoption by the Georgia courts until September 1975. Because this signaled the end of any attempt to return Timmy to his natural mother, the agency began a more focused consideration of what ultimate placement would be best for Timmy. After a number of discussions with the Drummonds, a final decision-making meeting was held in November 1975 with 19 agency employees present. Although the Drummonds were not present at this meeting, caseworkers who had dealt with them during the past two years did attend. As a result of that meeting a final agency decision was made to remove Timmy from the Drummond home and to deny the Drummonds' adoption application. It is clear that the race of the Drummonds and of Timmy and the racial attitudes of the parties were given substantial weight in coming to this conclusion. The agency employees were also aware that as Timmy grew older he would retain the characteristics of his black father. A few months later the plaintiffs filed suit.

* * *

After hearing six witnesses and arguments of counsel the court, by verbal order, dismissed the complaint on the merits. In rendering that decision, the court made the following finding:

It is obvious that race did enter into the decision of the Department. * * * [I]t appears to the Court * * * that the consideration of race was properly directed to the best interest of the child and was not an automatic-type of thing or of placement, that is, that all blacks go to black families, all whites go to white families, and all mixed children go to black families, which would be prohibited.

On appeal counsel was appointed to represent Timmy's separate interest in this litigation.

*   *   *

I.

The Drummonds and counsel for Timmy contend that the state denied them equal protection of the laws because of the extent to which race was considered in making the adoption decision. Although the complaint alleged that race was the sole determining factor, the district court found that this was not the case, and the finding was not clearly erroneous. The argument has thus centered on the question of whether a state agency, charged with the responsibility of placing for adoption a child in its custody, may take into consideration the race of the child and the race of the prospective adoptive parents without violating the equal protection clause of the United States Constitution.

The manner in which race was considered in this case frames the precise issue before us. The district court found that race was not used in an automatic fashion. The Drummonds' application was not automatically rejected on racial grounds. This finding may not be disturbed here because not clearly erroneous. Fed.R.Civ.P. 52(a). But can race be taken into account, perhaps decisively if it is the factor which tips the balance between two potential families, where it is not used automatically? We conclude, as did another court which grappled with the problem, that "the difficulties inherent in interracial adoption" justify the consideration of "race as a relevant factor in adoption, * * * ." Compos v. McKeithen, 341 F.Supp. 264, 266 (E.D.La.1972) (three-judge court).

In this regard, the Supreme Court has recently provided some guidance. It appears that even if government activity has a racially disproportionate impact, the impact alone does not sustain a claim of racial discrimination. "Proof of racially discriminatory intent or purpose is required to show a violation * * * ." Arlington Heights v. Metropolitan Housing Corp., 429 U.S. 252, 265, 97 S.Ct. 555, 563, 50 L.Ed.2d 450 (1977). There has been no suggestion before this Court that the defendants had any purposes other than to act in the best interest of the child when it considered race. Furthermore, the Supreme Court has recently stated in the sensitive area of voting apportionment that the consideration of race is not impermissible. United Jewish Organizations of Williamsburgh, Inc. v. Carey, 430 U.S. 144, 97 S.Ct. 996, 51 L.Ed.2d 229 (1977). As the plurality opinion in that case remarks, where race is considered in a nondiscriminatory fashion and there is "no racial slur or stigma with respect to whites or any other race," there is no discrimination violative of the Fourteenth Amendment.

In concluding that there has been no denial of equal protection in these circumstances, we note the following factors.

First, consideration of race in the child placement process suggests no racial slur or stigma in connection with any race. It is a natural thing for children to be raised by parents of their same ethnic background.

Second, no case has been cited to the Court suggesting that it is impermissible to consider race in adoption placement. The only cases which have addressed this problem indicate that, while the automatic use of race is barred, the use of race as one of the factors in making the ultimate decision is legitimate. In re Adoption of a Minor, 97 U. S.App.D.C. 99, 101, 228 F.2d 446, 448 (1955); Compos v. McKeithen, 341 F.Supp. 264, 266 (E.D.La.1972).

Third, the professional literature on the subject of transracial child placement stresses the importance of considering the racial attitudes of potential parents. The constitutional strictures against racial discrimination are not mandates to ignore the accumulated experience of unbiased professionals. A couple has no right to adopt a child it is not equipped to rear, and according to the professional literature race bears directly on that inquiry. From the child's perspective, the consideration of race is simply another facet of finding him the best possible home. Rather than eliminating certain categories of homes from consideration it avoids the potentially tragic possibility of placing a child in a home with parents who will not be able to cope with the child's problems.

Fourth, in the analogous inquiry over the permissibility of considering the religion of would-be adoptive parents, numerous courts have found no constitutional infirmity. Those cases make the same distinction as this Court makes in the racial context. So long as religion is not an automatic factor, its consideration as one of the number of factors is unobjectionable.

* * *

Finally, adoption agencies quite frequently try to place a child where he can most easily become a normal family member. The duplication of his natural biological environment is a part of that program. Such factors as age, hair color, eye color and facial features of parents and child are considered in reaching a decision. This flows from the belief that a child and adoptive parents can best adjust to a normal family relationship if the child is placed with adoptive parents who could have actually parented him. To permit consideration of physical characteristics necessarily carries with it permission to consider racial characteristics. This Court does not have the professional expertise to assess the wisdom of that type of inquiry, but it is our province to conclude, as we do today, that the use of race as one of those factors is not unconstitutional.

NOTES AND QUESTIONS

1. The portion of the Drummond opinion dealing with the foster parents' right to a hearing is quoted supra, page 483.

2. It has been held on at least two occasions that an absolute prohibition upon interracial adoptions is unconstitutional. Compos v. McKeithen, 341 F.Supp. 264 (E.D.La.1972); In re Gomez, 424 S.W.2d 656 (Tex.Civ. App.1967), 22 S.W.L.J. 696 (1968). It has also been held that a trial court's denial of adoption solely on the ground of racial difference was improper, the constitutional issue not being raised. In re Adoption of a Minor, 97 U.S.App.D.C. 99, 228 F.2d 446 (1955). In this case the applicable statute contained no reference to race. A case in which the welfare of the child was held to outweigh the factor of race is Adoption of Doe, 89 N.M. 606, 555 P.2d 906 (N.M.App.1976). Child v. Beame, 425 F.Supp. 194 (S.D. N.Y.1977) held that racial discrimination was not demonstrated by adoption agencies' failure to place as high a proportion of black children for adoption as white children.

3. Formerly adoption agencies often took race into account in placing children, as an aspect of their attempt to match the child with similar adoptive parents. The Child Welfare League of America Guidelines to Adoption Services 13 (1968) announces a different policy: "In most communities there are families who are able to adopt a child whose race is different from their own. Such couples should be encouraged to consider adopting a minority-group child, or one with a biracial background. The agency should be prepared to help with any difficulties that may arise, and to explain the need to give the child the benefit of close and continuing contact with members of his own race."

4. What relevance, if any, does or should race have in the process of placing children for adoption? If it has relevance, what should adoption statutes provide with respect to it? Note, Race as a Consideration in Adoption and Custody Proceedings, 1969 U.Ill.L.F. 256; Note Racial Matching and the Adoption Dilemma: Alternatives for the Hard to Place, 17 J. of Fam.L. 333 (1979).

5. What remedies, if any, might prospective adoptive parents have if they were refused a child by a placement agency, public or private? Assume that you represent Mr. and Mrs. Smith, a young graduate student and his wife who would like to adopt a child. They consult the local office of the state welfare department, file an application containing information about themselves, and are interviewed twice by a social worker representing the department. For more than a month they hear nothing more from the department, and then in response to their inquiry they are told that their application for adoption has not been approved. When they ask why they have not been approved, the welfare department representative tells them it is the policy of the department not to give reasons for such decisions. What would you advise Mr. and Mrs. Smith to do? See Smith v. OFFER, supra, page 471; Drummond v. Fulton County Department of Family and Children's Services, quoted supra, page 483; C. v. Superior Court, 26 Cal. App.3d 909, 106 Cal.Rptr. 123 (1973), 26 Hast.L.J. 312 (1974); In re Beste, 515 S.W.2d 530 (Mo.1974), 40 Mo.L.Rev. 380 (1975); In re Harshey, 45 Ohio App.2d 97, 341 N.E.2d 616 (1975); Bodenheimer, New Trends and

Requirements in Adoption Law and Proposals for Legislative Change, 49 So.Cal.L.Rev. 10, 76–83 (1975); Note, Judicial Review of Adoption Agency Decisions, 25 Case Wes.Res.L.Rev. 650 (1975); Note, Foster Parents' Emerging Due Process Rights in Pennsylvania, 83 Dick.L.Rev. 123 (1978).

E. EQUITABLE ADOPTION

IN THE MATTER OF THE ESTATE OF SCHULTZ

Supreme Court of Oregon, Department 2, 1959.
220 Or. 350, 348 P.2d 22.

WARNER, Justice. This is one of the two proceedings wherein the same parties, Lester Henry Schultz is plaintiff and the First National Bank of Portland (Oregon), as executor of the last will and testament of Dorothea M. Schultz, deceased, and the heirs and devisees of Mrs. Schultz are defendants. Both cases were consolidated for purpose of argument here.

This first proceeding was initiated in the Probate Department of the circuit court for Multnomah county, in the matter of the estate of Dorothea M. Schultz, deceased, upon the petition of Schultz, seeking a determination of heirship pursuant to ORS 117.510 et seq.

Mrs. Schultz died without issue. The question presented here is whether the plaintiff is entitled to take the estate of Dorothea M. Schultz, as her sole, but pretermitted, heir. His claim to the status of an heir rests upon an alleged agreement to adopt him made by the decedent and her former husband in the state of Nebraska.

The pertinent, and only, allegations of the petition bearing on the adoption agreement read:

"IV.

"* * * That the said Dorothea M. Melcher and Edward T. Schultz were duly married at Wisner, Nebraska, on March 15th, 1911, and thereafter resided at Bonesteel, South Dakota until the parties were duly divorced on or about October 15th, 1938, a period of over 27 years. That subsequent to the said divorce, the deceased, Dorothea M. Schultz, resided in Newport, Nebraska for about a year and a half and then moved to Portland, Oregon, in 1939, where she resided until the time of her death on or about November 29th, 1954.

"V.

"That on or about November, 1923, the deceased, Dorothea M. Schultz and her husband, Edward T. Schultz, made application to the Evangelical Lutheran Orphan's Home in Freemont, Nebraska, for a child to be adopted by them, and said Dorothea M. Schultz and her husband, Edward T. Schultz, were given your petitioner, who was born Lester Stoffer in Norfork, Nebraska, on April 7, 1919, as a child for adoption.

"VI.

"That the deceased, Dorothea M. Schultz, and her husband, Edward T. Schultz, did from the time that they took your petitioner from the said home on the agreement to adopt the said child, they retained your petitioner in their home, gave him their name 'Schultz', and to all intents and purposes considered your petitioner their natural child, and all of the relationship of parents and child were carried out and continued by the deceased, Dorothea M. Schultz, and her husband, Edward T. Schultz, toward your petitioner, the said child, your petitioner, considering himself to be the natural child of the said Dorothea M. Schultz and Edward T. Schultz and gave to his adoptive parents all of the love and affection and privileges that would be accorded to the natural parents, and your petitioner considered himself for all intents and purposes to be the child of said parents since having been taken from the orphan's home."

This is not a suit for breach of contract, nor is it, strictly speaking, one for specific performance. It is a proceeding for the judicial determination whether status as an heir can be said to flow from the alleged agreement. In short, it stands as a petition to the court to apply to the agreement the equitable maxim treating as done that which parties intended should be done, namely, consummation of the adoption of plaintiff as a son and heir of the Schultzes.   *   *   *

Plaintiff appeals from the order of the court dismissing his petition.

*   *   *   The bank's position is that foreign agreements of this character will not be enforced by Oregon courts. The plaintiff argues to the contrary. If the bank found any other alleged elements of insufficiency in the pleading it failed to suggest them.

*   *   *

No matter how sufficient the pleading may be as a pleading of a contract under Oregon law, it must, nevertheless, be declared vulnerable if the foreign contract is invalid or unenforceable in the jurisdiction where executed or, even though a valid contract in the state where made, it would be invalid in Oregon as offensive to our moral standards or here regarded as injurious to the public welfare.

Notwithstanding that the lex loci bearing on the enforcement of this kind of contract is not here pleaded, we will, under the authority of ORS 41.420 and 41.430 (The Uniform Judicial Notice of Foreign Law Act) take notice of the foreign law as far as may be necessary to resolve the question.

Plaintiff argues that the laws of Nebraska, where the contract was made, and the laws of South Dakota, "where the contract was to be performed," allow a person in his position to enforce his alleged right against the estate of a foster parent, and further represents that the laws of either state are equally applicable in solution of the problem presented. But we find nothing in the agreement as pleaded to warrant the conclusion it was in the contemplation of the parties that formal application for adoption was to be made and consummated in the state of South Dakota instead of Nebraska.

We, therefore, content ourselves with examining the applicable law of Nebraska for the determination of the validity and enforceability of the instant agreement in that state, if plaintiff had there sought the relief he seeks here and his foster mother had died leaving an estate in that state.

We observe before going further that the contract as pleaded enjoys two presumptions. The first is in favor of its legality and that the parties made the agreement with relation to the laws governing it. * * *

In Nebraska, we find no controlling statute, but do find a long line of decisions from its highest judicial tribunal which give confirmation to plaintiff's contentions respecting the validity of such contracts in that state and the readiness of its courts to enforce them.

The doctrine relied upon by plaintiff was first promulgated in 1894. Kofka v. Rosicky, 41 Neb. 328, 59 N.W. 788, 25 L.R.A. 207. And as far as our research discloses has been consistently followed ever since without modification or revocation. * * *

This fidelity to the rule in Nebraska does not conclude our inquiry for we must also consider the impact of the enforcement of rights arising under the rule there in relation to the public policy of this state.

Under the strict doctrine established by Furgeson v. Jones, 17 Or. 204, 20 P. 842, 3 L.R.A. 620, and consistently adhered to over the years, an agreement of the character under review would be invalid and unenforceable if made in this jurisdiction. * * *

The invalidity of the agreement had it been made in Oregon does not, however, necessarily relieve the courts of this state from enforcing rights arising under a similar agreement if valid in a sister state unless to do so would clearly be contrary to our stated public policy. In the classic case of Loucks v. Standard Oil Co. of N.Y., 224 N.Y. 99, 120 N.E. 198, Judge Cardozo lays down rules on this subject enabling us to determine when the law of the foreign jurisdiction is so opposed to the public policy of the local forum that it will warrant our courts in refusing to enforce it. One of the persuasive statements in Loucks is found in 120 N.E. at page 202, and reads:

"* * * The courts are not free to refuse to enforce a foreign right at the pleasure of the judges, to suit the individual notion of expediency or fairness. They do not close their doors, unless help would violate some fundamental principle of justice, some prevalent conception of good morals, some deep-rooted tradition of the common weal."

* * *

Can we say that because a contract for adoption would be invalid in Oregon that its enforcement would be so offensive to our deeply-rooted public policy that we should refuse to enforce it here, even though valid under the laws of a sister state? The nub of the Oregon rule emphasizing strictness is that adoption can only be accomplished by compliance with the statutory scheme. The Nebraska rule in conflict recognizes that an *agreement to adopt* in accordance with the statutory procedures of that state may give rise to a de facto adoption status which the courts of that state will ripen into a de jure status when properly presented. As pointed out in McGirl v. Brewer, supra, there must be something more than a statute prohibiting such contracts before our courts will be justified in declining to enforce a foreign agreement. "* * * there must be something which offends by shocking moral standards, or is injurious or pernicious to the public welfare." 132 Or. at page 447, 285 P. at page 213, supra. This is the gist of the rule we take from Loucks, supra, and when applied in test to the instant Nebraska contract, we are forced to conclude that the contract as described in the petition contains nothing which violates any fundamental principle of justice, or prevalent conception of good morals or any deep-rooted tradition of the common weal in this state. Loucks v. Standard Oil Co. of N.Y., supra, 120 N. E. at page 202.

Finding the petition sufficient and invulnerable to defendant's demurrer, the order of the lower court is reversed and the matter remanded for such further proceedings as may be appropriate.

NOTES AND QUESTIONS

1. Although it is frequently stated by the courts that adoption is exclusively the creature of statute, many states do, as a matter of common law, give some effect to contracts to adopt even though the statutory procedure is not followed. For a discussion of the general subject, see H. Clark, Law of Domestic Relations § 18.8 (1968); Note, Equitable Adoption: They Took Him Into Their Home and Called Him Fred, 58 Va.L.Rev. 727 (1972); Annots., 171 A.L.R. 1315 (1947), 142 A.L.R. 84 (1943), and 27 A.L.R. 1325 (1923).

2. What are the arguments for and against the recognition of contracts to adopt? Do they apply to cases in which rights other than the right to inherit are involved? Calista Corp. v. Mann, 564 P.2d 53 (Alaska 1977). Consider the following situations:

(a) H and W took C into their household when he was a young child, agreeing to adopt him. They never did so. H and W died some years later, and much later C died. Plaintiffs were heirs of H and W, and, claiming through H and W, sought to take by inheritance the estate of C. What should be the result? Does adoption by estoppel work backwards as well as forwards? Heien v. Crabtree, 369 S.W.2d 28 (Tex.1963), 15 Baylor L.Rev. 162 (1963); In re Estate of McConnell, 268 F.Supp. 346 (D.D.C.1967).

(b) C, a child, is left by his parents with H and W, who care for him and educate him, in all respects as if he were their own child. H becomes disabled (or is killed), and W files a claim on C's behalf for Social Security benefits. The Act, 42 U.S.C.A. § 402(d)(1) authorizes those benefits for a child of an individual entitled to old-age or insurance benefits, or who dies a fully insured individual, if such child was dependent upon the individual. 42 U.S.C.A. § 416(e) defines "child" as a child or legally adopted child of the insured individual. And 42 U.S.C.A. § 416(h)(2)(A) provides that in determining whether an applicant is the child of the insured individual, the Secretary shall apply that law which controls the devolution of intestate personal property in the state in which the insured individual was domiciled. Is C entitled to these benefits? Annie M. Smith v. Secretary of Health, Education and Welfare, 431 F.2d 1241 (5th Cir. 1970), 2 St.M.L.J. 256 (1970); Stanley v. Secretary of Health, Education and Welfare, 356 F. Supp. 793 (W.D.Mo.1973); Steward v. Richardson, 353 F.Supp. 822 (E.D. Mich.1972); Smith v. Richardson, 347 F.Supp. 265 (S.D.W.Va.1972); Meadows v. Richardson, 347 F.Supp. 154 (S.D.W.Va.1972); Williams v. Richardson, 523 F.2d 999 (2d Cir. 1975).

(c) When H and W were married, W had, as H knew, an illegitimate child fathered by X. H accepted the child in the family, cared for him and treated him in all respects as if he were his own. Later the marriage broke up and W sued for divorce, including a claim against H for the support of the child. Could she argue that the child had been equitably adopted by H, and that H therefore had an obligation to support him? Could she make that argument if H had signed an agreement to adopt the child? Fuller v. Fuller, 247 A.2d 767 (D.C.Ct.App.1968). Cf. problem 7, page 428, supra. And see ten Broek, Impact of Social Welfare Law Upon Family Law, 42 Cal.L.Rev. 458, 478 (1954); Wener v. Wener, 35 A.D.2d 50, 312 N.Y.S.2d 815 (2d Dep't 1970).

(d) M and F had an illegitimate child. M threatened F with a paternity suit. After negotiations, M agreed to drop the suit in return for F's promise to adopt the child and make him the beneficiary under F's will. F died without either adopting the child or making him the beneficiary of his will. Does the child have an enforceable claim against F's estate? Reimche v. First Nat. Bank, 512 F.2d 187 (9th Cir. 1975), 1976 B.Y.U.L. Rev. 583.

(e) C, a child, is left by his mother with H and W, who agree to care for C as if he were their own child. When he reaches the age of sixteen, C brings a suit against H and W, asking that the court order them to adopt him on the theory that he is entitled to specific performance of a contract to adopt. What should be the result? Would the case be different if H and W had expressly agreed with C's mother that they would adopt C? Habecker v. Young, 474 F.2d 1229 (5th Cir. 1973); Korbin v. Ginsberg, 232 So.2d 417 (Fla.App.1970); Maddox v. Maddox, 224 Ga. 313, 161 S.E.2d 870 (1968).

3. What arguments would you make concerning the issue of conflict of laws posed in the *Schultz* case? What should be the result in the converse case, that is, where the contract to adopt was made in a state which does

not recognize such contracts, and where the parent died in a state which does recognize them? In re Lamfrom's Estate, 90 Ariz. 363, 368 P.2d 318 (1962); Deveroex v. Nelson, 529 S.W.2d 510 (Tex.1975).

F. THE CONSEQUENCES OF THE ADOPTION DECREE

NOTE ON INHERITANCE RIGHTS AS AFFECTED BY ADOPTION

The consequences of adoption are based in the first instance upon statute. And most adoption statutes contain a general provision to the effect that adoption terminates the rights of the natural parents and substitutes therefor rights and obligations of the adoptive parents. At first glance one might think that this general statutory provision would be adequate to the solution of most of the questions which might arise, but this would underestimate the ingenuity of courts in the frustration of statutory purposes. With the aid of that silly but ubiquitous maxim that statutes in derogation of the common law are to be strictly construed, courts have in the past managed to prevent the adopted child from receiving the full measure of inheritance rights intended by the statutes. Many legislatures have responded by amending the statutes so as explicitly to cover specific situations, and where that has occurred the adopted child can now be said, for inheritance and testamentary purposes, to be fully integrated into his adoptive family, and no longer a part of his natural family.

The adopted child inherits from his adoptive parents in all states today. The descendants of a deceased adopted child also usually inherit from the adoptive parents. There are cases holding that the adopted child may not inherit from relatives of his adoptive parents, that is, inherit through the adoptive parents, but statutory amendments have overruled many of these, and the legislative trend today is in the direction of making this right explicit. See, e. g., Smith and Fawsett, Florida Adoption and Intestate Succession Laws: A Legal Paralogism, 24 U.Fla.L.Rev. 603 (1972). N.Y.Dom.Rel.L. § 117 (1977) and Uniform Adoption Act § 14, 9 Unif.L.Ann. 44 (1979) exemplify this trend.

Another disability which the adopted child retains in some states is that he is not included in class gifts made by will or inter vivos transfer, where the gift is to "heirs", "issue", "children" etc. of the adoptive parent. Here again legislation aimed at changing this doctrine of the case law has been passed or proposed in several states. See, e. g., Uniform Probate Code § 2–611, 8 Uniform Laws Ann. 362 (1972), which states that adopted persons are included in class gift terminology in accordance with the rules for determining relationships for purposes of intestate succession, and N.Y. Estates, Powers and Trusts L. § 2–1.3 (1967). See also Note, Eligibility of Adopted

Children to Take by Intestate Descent and Under Class Gifts in Missouri, 34 Mo.L.Rev. 68 (1969); Cleveland Trust Co. v. Schumacher, 35 Ohio Misc. 118, 298 N.E.2d 913 (Ohio Com.Pl. 1973); In re Estate of Tower, 463 Pa. 93, 343 A.2d 671 (1975); In re Estate of Tafel, 449 Pa. 442, 296 A.2d 797 (1972), 77 Dick.L.Rev. 415 (1973); Note, Wills: The Effect of the Uniform Adoption Act on the Determination of a Testamentary Class, 29 Okla.L.Rev. 260 (1976); Annot., 96 A.L. R.2d 639 (1964).

The courts have also had some trouble with the issue raised when the adopted child attempts to take by intestacy from his natural parents. Many cases and some statutes permit him to inherit from or through his natural parents, although this is clearly inconsistent with the purpose and theory of adoption. More modern statutes contain express provisions that the child does not inherit from or through his natural parents after he is adopted. See Uniform Probate Code § 2–109, 8 Uniform Laws Ann. 328 (1972); Note, The Adopted Child's Inheritance From Intestate Natural Parents, 55 Iowa L.Rev. 739 (1970); Uniform Adoption Act § 14(a)(1), 9 Unif.L.Ann. 44 (1979); Katz v. Koronchik, 369 Mass. 125, 338 N.E.2d 339 (1975); Annot., Right of Adopted Child to Inherit from Intestate Natural Grandparent, 60 A.L.R.3d 631 (1974).

Since this is essentially a statutory subject, and the statutes are frequently changing, the inheritance rights of an adopted child in any specific jurisdiction can only be determined by a detailed investigation of the local law. The foregoing is only an introduction to such an investigation. For further general discussion see H. Clark, Law of Domestic Relations § 18.9 (1968).

DOULGERIS v. BAMBACUS

Supreme Court of Appeals of Virginia, 1962.
203 Va. 670, 127 S.E.2d 145.

EGGLESTON, Chief Justice. Joseph S. Bambacus, as administrator of the estate of James Odessett, deceased, filed his bill in the court below praying that it determine the heirs at law, next of kin and distributees of the estate of the decedent, a native of Greece, a naturalized citizen of the United States, and a resident of the city of Richmond at the time of his death.

The cause was referred to a commissioner in chancery with direction to report who are the heirs at law and next of kin of the decedent and what persons are entitled to his estate. The commissioner heard the evidence on behalf of a number of claimants, including Dialehti Karavelia Doulgeris, hereinafter referred to as "Doulgeris." She had filed an answer to the bill alleging that she was entitled to the net estate because, she said, she was the sister by adoption of the decedent, having been adopted under the laws of the Kingdom of

Greece as the daughter of decedent's father, and that the decedent had not been survived by any nearer relative.

The commissioner filed a report rejecting the claim of Doulgeris and from a decree overruling her exceptions thereto she has appealed.

The underlying facts are not in dispute. James Odessett, the decedent, died intestate, unmarried, and without issue in the city of Richmond on February 5, 1954, at the age of sixty-nine years, leaving considerable personal estate. He was a native of Greece but had been naturalized under the laws of the United States in 1926. At the time of his death his father and mother were dead and all of his blood brothers and sisters had died without issue.

While the records of the Greek Registry had been destroyed in 1945 by fire resulting from war hostilities in the area, there was evidence on behalf of Doulgeris that she had been adopted by Odessett's father in a court proceeding at Chalkidiki, Greece, in February or March, 1940. At that time she was fourteen years of age and her father consented to the adoption. The adoptive father was eighty-six years of age; the adoptive mother was sixty-eight years old and a bedridden paralytic. According to the statement of the adoptive father, because of his age and his wife's condition, "we have the need of a child for our attendance, consolation and support." The adoptive mother was not present at the adoption proceedings nor was her consent thereto required under the laws of Greece. The child's natural father was present and consented. Her natural mother did not consent.

Doulgeris did not testify in the present case and the record is silent as to whether she ever lived with her adoptive parents. The adoptive mother died in May, 1940, and the adoptive father in September, 1941. The marriage license of Doulgeris, dated 1951, makes no mention of her adoptive parents but gives her natural parents.

According to the opinion of Dr. C .N. Goulimis, an advocate entitled to practice before the Supreme Court of Greece, this proceeding met the requirements of an *adoptio minus plena,* that is, the adoption of a person by one other than an ascendant relative. In that type of adoption no investigation into the propriety of the adoption is required.

Based on this evidence the commissioner and the lower court found that Doulgeris had been adopted by Odessett's father according to the laws of the Kingdom of Greece. While the brief of the appellees questions the correctness of this finding, no cross-assignment of error was filed to it and hence we are not concerned on this appeal with the validity of the adoption. See Rule 5:1, § 4.

However, the commissioner held that the policy of the adoption laws of the Kingdom of Greece "is essentially different and contrary, in practice and concept, to [sic] the public policy of Virginia," in that under the adoption laws of Greece the primary consideration is the best interests of the adoptive father, while under the adoption laws of Virginia the primary consideration is the welfare and best interests of the child, and that because of such difference "in concept and purpose" Doulgeris is not entitled to the status of an adopted sister of the decedent and the right under our adoption laws and the laws of descent and distribution to share in his estate as such. In confirming the report the lower court adopted the same view.

In her appeal Doulgeris makes two contentions: (1) The finding of the commissioner and the lower court that the policy of the adoption laws of the Kingdom of Greece is contrary to the public policy of Virginia is contrary to the law and the evidence; and (2) such finding fails to recognize and give effect to the treaty now in effect between the United States and the Kingdom of Greece.

The appellees concede that under the broad language of Code, §§ 63–357 and 63–358, as amended, and the provisions of §§ 64–1, as amended, and 64–11, Doulgeris would be entitled to share in the distribution of the estate of her adopted brother, Odessett, unless the public policy of this State forbids the recognition of her adoption. In view of that concession and the ultimate conclusion we have reached, it is not necessary that we inquire into that matter.

According to the great weight of authority, "for purposes of determining the descent and distribution of the property of an intestate decedent and the right of an adopted child to share in such estate, a status of adoption acquired under the law of one state will be recognized and given effect in another state where, in the case of real property, the decedent's property is located or, in the case of personal property, where the decedent was domiciled, provided that the foreign court had jurisdiction of the adoption proceedings and also to fix the status of the child with respect to the adoptive parents, and that the recognition of that status as fixed by the foreign decree is not inconsistent with, and will not offend, the laws or the public policy of the forum." * * *

The same principle applies to the recognition of adoption proceedings of a foreign country. * * *

The recognition of such foreign adoption decrees is based upon comity, and not upon the full faith and credit clause of the Federal Constitution. * * *

It is equally well settled that foreign law or rights based thereon will not be given effect or enforced if contrary to the settled public policy of the forum. * * *

In Guarantee Bank & Trust Co. v. Gillies, [8 N.J. 88, 83 A.2d 889], the New Jersey court, in a proceeding to settle the estate of a resident of that State, refused to recognize as an adopted son of the decedent a minor nephew who claimed that he had been adopted by the decedent and his wife under the laws of the Kingdom of Greece, but who had never seen or resided with his adoptive parents either before or after the decree of adoption. It was there held that the recognition of such an adoption would offend the public policy of the State of New Jersey.

On the other hand, in Zanzonico v. Neeld, [17 N.J. 490, 111 A.2d 772], the same court recognized a decree of adoption under the laws of Italy where a small child residing in that country was adopted by her uncle and aunt, residents of New Jersey, and brought to the latter State and lived with her adoptive parents for two and one-half years before the death of the adoptive father. The court there pointed out that while the adoption proceedings in Italy were different from those in New Jersey, such difference did not offend the public policy of the latter State.

In Virginia, as in other jurisdictions in this country, in adoption proceedings the primary consideration is the welfare and best interests of the child. *   *   *

Accordingly, the adoption statutes in this State are designed to that end. In the case of married persons the petition for adoption must be the joint petition of the husband and wife. (Code, § 63–348, as amended.) Both natural parents, if living, must consent to the adoption unless such consent be dispensed with for cause. The child, too, at fourteen years of age or older, must consent thereto in writing. Code, § 63–351, as amended.

Upon the filing of the petition the court directs that an investigation be made as to whether the petitioner is financially able and morally fit to care for and train the child; what the physical and mental condition of the child is and whether it is suitable for adoption by petitioner; why the natural parents, if living, desire to be relieved of the responsibility of the care, custody and maintenance of the child; what their attitude is toward the proposed adoption, and the circumstances under which the child came to live, and is living in the home of the petitioner. The court usually enters an interlocutory order of adoption for a probationary period of one year, during which the child is visited in the new home at least once every three months. (Code, §§ 63–352, 63–354, as amended.) "For good cause shown," and where the best interests of the child so require, the court may revoke the interlocutory order of adoption and dismiss the adoption proceedings. Code, § 63–353, as amended.

Comparing the Greek adoption proceedings, we note that the adoptive mother was not present at the proceedings and did not consent thereto, nor are such presence and consent required. The child's natural father was present and consented. The presence and consent of the natural mother are not required. No investigation was made as to whether the adoption was for the welfare and best interests of the child. Indeed, according to the opinions of Dr. Goulimis, in this type of adoption no such investigation is required under the laws of Greece.

Moreover, there is no evidence that the adoption was ever consummated, that the child severed her relation with her natural parents, went to live with her adoptive parents and became a member of the latter family. As has been said, the record shows that the purpose of the adoption was for the convenience of the adoptive parents, and that because of the adoptive mother's physical condition the child was needed for the couple's attendance, consolation and support. In short, this was merely an arrangement for the convenience of the adoptive parents, consented to by the natural father, and without regard as to how it affected the welfare and interests of the child.

We agree with the commissioner and the lower court that this type of adoption through which Doulgeris claims is so different from the adoption contemplated by our statutes that it would be contrary to the public policy of this State to hold that she is a "legally adopted child" who is entitled to inherit under Code, § 63–358, as amended. As we said in Clarkson v. Bliley, 185 Va. 82, 90, 38 S.E.2d 22, 26, 171 A.L.R. 1308, "the right to inherit as an adopted child cannot in Virginia be created by a private contract."

There is no substance to the appellant's claim that the refusal of the lower court to give her the status of an adopted child within the meaning of our statutes violates the rights guaranteed to her under the existing treaty between the United States of America and the Kingdom of Greece. That treaty guarantees among other things that, "Each Party shall at all times accord equitable treatment to the persons, property, * * * and other interests of nationals * * * of the other Party," that is, "treatment * * * upon terms no less favorable than the treatment accorded therein, in like situations, to nationals * * * of any third country." In short, the contention is that the decree of the lower court denies the appellant the right to inherit the property of her adopted brother under the laws of Virginia, a right which, she says, is guaranteed to her as a "national" of Greece under the terms of the treaty.

The answer to this contention is that the decree does not deny the right of inheritance to the appellant under the laws of Virginia. What it denies to her is the right to inherit by virtue of her status as an alleged adoptive relative of the decedent—a status which we hold has been fixed in a proceeding the purpose and object of which are contrary to the public policy of this State. In refusing to recognize a status thus fixed, the courts of Virginia treat alike the proceedings of all other States and foreign countries. We refuse to recognize the proceedings of any State or foreign country which offend our public policy.

What the appellant asks here is that we afford to her better treatment than we afford to the citizens of other States or nations, that we recognize her status as an adoptive relative of the decedent although it had been fixed in a proceeding whose purpose and object are repugnant to our laws. The treaty upon which she relies guarantees to the nationals of Greece no such preferred right.

In our opinion, the decree of the lower court is right and accordingly it is

Affirmed.

NOTES AND QUESTIONS

1. Recognition of foreign adoption decrees is discussed in Taintor, Adoption in the Conflict of Laws, 222, 225 (1954); Baade, Interstate and Foreign Adoptions in North Carolina, 40 N.C.L.Rev. 691 (1962); Kennedy, Adoption in the Conflict of Laws, 34 Can.Bar Rev. 507 (1956); H. Clark, Law of Domestic Relations, 664–666 (1968). Other cases are cited in Annot., 87 A.L.R.2d 1240 (1963).

The Uniform Adoption Act § 17, 9 Unif.L.Ann. 49 (1979) requires the recognition of adoption decrees of other states and foreign countries.

2. Congress has passed legislation encouraging the immigration of alien orphans who have been or will be adopted by American citizens. 8 U.S. C.A. § 1101(b)(1)(E) and (F); F. Auerbach, Immigration Laws of the United States, 119–120 (2d ed. 1961); C. Gordon and H. Rosenfield, Immigration Law and Procedure, §§ 2.18b(5) and 2.18b(6) (1973). Some of the problems that this has created, especially with respect to Greek children, are discussed in Note, Foreign Adoptions, 28 Bklyn.L.Rev. 324 (1962). Pascual v. O'Shea, 421 F.Supp. 80 (D.Hawaii 1976), held that a child who had been adopted in the Philippines, by a Philippine decree, would be recognized under the immigration laws as an "immediate relative" of his adoptive parents for purpose of entry into the United States.

Recently similar procedures have been used to accomplish the adoption in the United States of Viet Namese children. The Viet Namese goverment has had agreements with three American agencies, one of which is the Friends of Children of Viet Nam. The procedure varies from state to state, but in general an agency investigation of the adoptive parents is made in the United States, that and other information about the adoptive parents are forwarded to Viet Nam, where the American agency institutes an adoption proceeding. The child is brought to the United States by an employee of the agency, and then in most instances a second adoption proceeding is carried through in the state of the adoptive parents' residence, thereby avoiding the sort of difficulty suggested by the result of the *Doulgeris* case. In addition to the formalities of adoption, the immigration authorities must be furnished information establishing that the statutory requirements for the child's entry into the United States have been complied with.

3. What arguments might be made in support of a result contrary to that in the *Doulgeris* case? Corbett v. Stergios, 257 Iowa 1387, 137 N.W. 2d 266 (1965); In re Christoff's Estate, 411 Pa. 419, 192 A.2d 737 (1963), cert. den. 375 U.S. 965 (1964).

4. If the adoption occurs in State A, under circumstances such that State B would consider it contrary to State B's law and policy, as for exam-

ple where the adoption originated in a private placement, State B's law outlawing such placements, is State B nevertheless required to recognize the decree under the Full Faith and Credit Clause? Cf. Delaney v. The First Nat. Bank, 73 N.M. 192, 386 P.2d 711 (1963); Hood v. McGehee, 237 U.S. 611 (1915); Crossley's Estate, 135 Pa.Super. 524, 7 A.2d 539 (1939).

5. H and W were divorced in Illinois and custody of their child, S, was given to W. W later married H–2. H–2 wished to adopt S, but H would only consent on condition that he was given the right to visit S at reasonable times. W and H–2 stipulated their agreement to this arrangement, H gave his consent and the Illinois court granted the adoption, incorporating in the adoption decree the stipulation that H would have rights of visitation at reasonable times and places. All parties then moved to Texas. After a time visitation was denied by H–2 and W, and H brought suit in Texas asking that the Illinois decree be enforced. W and H–2 counterclaimed for a declaratory judgment that the visitation portion of the adoption decree was invalid. If the law of Texas is that such conditions may not be included in adoption decrees, and that adoption terminates all rights of the natural parent, including visitation, what should be the result? Rodgers v. Williamson, 489 S.W.2d 558 (Tex.1973). See also Kattermann v. DiPiazza, 151 N.J.Super. 209, 376 A.2d 955 (1977).

6. By statute or judicial decision in some states grandparents may be given visitation rights with respect to their grandchildren in certain circumstances, as for example after divorce, or when one of the grandchild's parents has died. If a grandparent has been awarded rights of visitation, should such rights be cut off when the grandchild is adopted? Poe v. Case, 263 Ark. 488, 565 S.W.2d 612 (1978); Reeves v. Bailey, 53 Cal.App. 3d 1019, 126 Cal.Rptr. 51 (1975); Browning v. Tarwater, 215 Kan. 501, 524 P.2d 1135 (1974); Smith v. Trosclair, 321 So.2d 514 (La.1975); Bikos v. Nobliski, 88 Mich.App. 157, 276 N.W.2d 541 (1979); Mimkon v. Ford, 66 N.J. 426, 332 A.2d 199 (1975); Acker v. Barnes, 33 N.C.App. 750, 236 S.E. 2d 715 (1977); Graziano v. Davis, 50 Ohio App.2d 83, 361 N.E.2d 525 (1976); Matter of Fox, 567 P.2d 985 (Okl.1977).

7. The Uniform Adoption Act § 16, 9 Unif.L.Ann. 48 (1979), provides, in relevant part, as follows:

§ 16. [Hearings and Records in Adoption Proceedings; Confidential Nature]

"Notwithstanding any other law concerning public hearings and records,

"* * *

"(2) all papers and records pertaining to the adoption whether part of the permanent record of the court or of a file in the [Department of Welfare] or in an agency are subject to inspection only upon consent of the Court and all interested persons; or in exceptional cases, only upon an order of the Court for good cause shown; and

"(3) except as authorized in writing by the adoptive parent, the adopted child, if [14] or more years of age, or upon order of the court for good cause shown in exceptional cases, no person is required to disclose the name or identity of either an adoptive parent or an adopted child."

Similar provisions are found in the adoption statutes of most states. In recent years substantial numbers of adopted children have sought to learn the identity of their natural parents, in some instances their attempts being given wide publicity. Perhaps the best known of the cases has been the subject of a book, Florence Fisher, The Search for Anna Fisher (1973). Adoption agencies, both public and private, seal their records of adoptions and treat them as confidential, even though some state statutes, unlike the Uniform Adoption Act, do not apply to agencies but only to court records of adoptions. M. Jones, The Sealed Adoption Record Controversy: Report of a Survey of Agency Policy, Practice and Opinion, July, 1976, Research Center, Child Welfare League of America. The result of the conflict between agency policies of secrecy and the adopted children's desire to know about their natural parents has been considerable litigation. The cases raise the following kinds of questions with which students of the adoption process should be concerned:

(a) What individual or social interests are served by this sort of statute? Klibanoff, Genealogical Information in Adoption: The Adoptee's Quest and the Law, 11 Fam.L.Q. 185 (1977); In re Adoption of Female Infant, 1 Fam.L. Advocate 25 (D.C.Super.Ct. 1979).

(b) Are statutes like the Uniform Act, so far as they prevent some adopted children from having the information they seek about their own background, constitutional? See Alma Society v. Mellon, 601 F.2d 1225 (2d Cir. 1979), cert. den. —— U.S. ——, 100 S.Ct. 531; Application of Maples, 563 S.W.2d 760 (Mo.1978); Mills v. Atlantic City Department of Vital Statistics, 148 N.J.Super. 302, 372 A.2d 646 (1977); Matter of Linda F. M., 95 Misc.2d 581, 409 N.Y.S.2d 638 (Surr.Ct.1978); Matter of Application of Sage, 21 Wash.App. 803, 586 P.2d 1201 (1978); Note Discovery Rights of the Adoptee-Privacy Rights of the Natural Parent: A Constitutional Dilemma, 4 U. of San Fern.V.L.Rev. 65 (1975); Note, The Adult Adoptee's Constitutional Right to Know His Origins, 48 So.Cal.L.Rev. 1196 (1975).

(c) What kinds of evidence will constitute "good cause" for opening adoption records to the inspection of the adopted child? Just the child's desire to see them? His or her desire to obtain information about possible hereditary diseases? Evidence that the adopted child is in the throes of an "identity crisis" which may be alleviated by learning of his or her origins? How are the interests referred to in a) above to be reconciled in such cases? In addition to the authorities already cited, see In re Anonymous, 92 Misc.2d 224, 399 N.Y.S.2d 857 (Surr.Ct.1977); Application of Anonymous, 89 Misc.2d 132, 390 N.Y.S.2d 779 (Surr.Ct.1976); Massey v. Parker, 369 So.2d 1310 (La.1979); Annot., Restricting Access to Judicial Records of Concluded Adoption Proceedings, 83 A.L.R.3d 800 (1978); J. Triseliotis, In Search of Origins, The Experience of Adopted People (1973); Sorosky, Baran, Pannor, Identity Conflicts in Adoptees, 45 Amer.J. of Orthopsychiatry 18 (1975); Bodenheimer, New Trends and Requirements in Adoption Law and Proposals for Legislative Change, 49 So.Cal.L.Rev. 10, 96–98 (1975).

(d) Could a statute be drafted which would deal with this controversy more satisfactorily than the Uniform Adoption Act? What should such a statute provide?

(e) If the adopted child should be entitled to learn who his natural parents are, should the child conceived through AID have the same right?

G. ATTACK ON ADOPTION DECREES

HUGHES v. AETNA CASUALTY & SURETY CO.

Supreme Court of Oregon, Department 1, 1963.
234 Or. 426, 383 P.2d 55.

LUSK, Justice. Harold J. Hughes, petitioner in the court below, is seeking by this proceeding to be declared the son and lawful heir of Mona LaWanda Nelson, deceased.

The petitioner is the illegitimate son of the deceased. He was born July 16, 1924; was apparently abandoned in infancy by his parents and became an inmate of St. Agnes Baby Home in Portland. On May 10, 1927, by decree of the Court of Domestic Relations for Multnomah County, he was declared to be the child of Mr. and Mrs. J. J. Hughes. He was reared in the home of his adoptive parents and never knew his natural mother. The question is whether the decree of adoption is void because of asserted procedural defects. If that be so, the relationship of mother and son between the petitioner and his natural mother has never been severed and he is her sole heir at law and entitled to take her estate.

The question arose in this way. Mrs. Nelson, nee Oatman, died intestate on February 6, 1957. She was survived by a brother, Ellis F. Oatman, and a sister Bernita O. Taylor. Her estate was probated in the District Court for Washington County and on September 4, 1957, an order of final settlement was entered, including an order of distribution of the estate to the brother and sister (since deceased) as her sole heirs. In March, 1961, the petitioner learned of his natural mother's death and that she had left an estate. After consulting an attorney, on June 26, 1961, he filed a motion to vacate the order of final settlement and allow objections thereto on the ground that the petitioner was the sole surviving heir at law and next of kin of the decedent. The petitioner invoked ORS 18.160 as authority for commencement of the proceeding thus belatedly. As the determination involved the title to real property, the district judge transferred the question to the circuit court. The Aetna Casualty & Surety Company (hereinafter referred to as Aetna), surety on the administrator's bond and respondent here, appeared in opposition to the objections and, after various proceedings unnecessary to be detailed, the court on April 9, 1962, entered an order denying the petitioner's motion to vacate the order of final settlement and overruling his objections thereto. From the order of April 9, 1962, the petitioner has appealed.

The adoption proceedings were commenced by the filing of a petition by Mr. and Mrs. Hughes * * *

As required by statute (Oregon Laws 1921, ch. 215), the petition was served on the Child Welfare Commission of Oregon, which filed a written report with the court recommending that the petition be granted. Included in the report is the following:

"The child was a ward of the St. Agnes Baby Home and was placed by that institution. He has been abandoned for more than one year preceding the filing of the petition. However, since the St. Agnes Baby Home never acquired title, the year's abandonment next preceding the time of filing the petition is the basis upon which this proceeding is instituted:".

On the tenth day of May, 1927, St. Agnes Baby Home filed with the court its "Consent to Adoption", reading as follows:

"Harold Joseph Oatman, minor child, duly and regularly committed by the Court of Domestic Relations of Multnomah County, State of Oregon, to the St. Agnes Baby Home, petition having been filed by J. J. Hughes and M. E. Hughes for the adoption of Harold Joseph Oatman, said minor child having been abandoned by both mother and father; the Child Welfare Commission of Oregon having consented to the adoption and recommended the same;

"It appearing to the said St. Agnes Baby Home that the petitioners for adoption are members of the Catholic Church in Montavilla, and that they are in good standing in the community; now,

"THEREFORE, said St. Agnes Baby Home hereby consents to and recommends that said petition for adopted [sic] be granted."

As previously stated, the court entered a decree of adoption on May 10, 1927. There are no findings other than recitals in the decree to the effect that the petitioners were of sufficient ability to bring up the minor child, Harold Joseph Oatman, properly, and that it was fit and proper that such adoption should take effect and that the child Welfare Commission of Oregon had investigated the condition of the parties and recommended that the petition be granted. The record fails to disclose that notice of the proceeding was given to the minor child's natural mother.

The question for decision is governed by two fundamental principles. One is that the right of adoption "being in derogation of the common law, is a special power conferred by statute, and the rule is that such statutes must be strictly construed." Furgeson v. Jones, 17 Or. 204, 217, 20 P. 842, * * *. The other principle is that the court in adoption proceedings is exercising a special statutory power not according to the course of the common law, and when its decree is called in question, even collaterally, no presumptions in favor of jurisdiction are indulged, but the facts necessary for jurisdiction must appear affirmatively, on the face of the record. * * * It is otherwise with a court of general jurisdiction exercising its customary common law powers, for "it is a rule of general application that every intendment consistent with the record of such courts will be indulged to sustain their proceedings and judgments." Freeman on Judgments (5th ed.) § 383, * * *.

In addition, it is to be observed that the court of domestic relations for Multnomah county was in 1927 a court of special and limited jurisdiction, dealing solely with the problems of dependent, delinquent and neglected children. * * * To such a court apply the same rules respecting the proof of jurisdiction when its judgment is attacked as in the case of a court of record exercising special statutory powers not according to the course of the common law. * * *

* * *

Oregon Laws 1920, section 9809, provided for permanent and temporary commitments by competent courts of dependent or delinquent children to appropriate state and county institutions or suitable private child caring agencies. Temporary commitments were to be made "when the court for good and sufficient reasons decides that final adjudication of the case must be delayed, or that the child or children involved can reasonably be expected to soon return to ordinary home conditions in their own families"; and, in such case, guardianship of the persons of the children, it was provided, "shall remain with the court." Permanent commitments included "guardianship of the persons of such children."

The following sections of Oregon Laws 1920 relating to child caring agencies are pertinent: Such agencies to which dependent or delinquent children were committed by a court of competent jurisdiction through a *permanent* order could consent to the adoption of such children, § 9828. They could receive needy or dependent children from their parents or legal guardians for special, temporary or continued care. The parents or guardians might sign releases or surrenders giving to such agencies guardianship and control of such children, but such releases did not surrender the right of such parents or guardians in respect to the adoption of such children, nor entitle the agency to give consent to the adoption of such children, unless the release or surrender expressly recited that it was given for the purpose of adoption and that any entire severance of family ties by adoption, or otherwise, should be accomplished only by the order of a court of competent jurisdiction, § 9829.

Section 9830 provided:

"In the adoption of a ward of a private agency, society or institution, *to give formal consent to such adoption, it shall be required that such organization shall file with the clerk of the court in which the adoption proceedings are pending, two documents as follows: (1) A certified copy of an order of a court of competent jurisdiction formally and permanently assigning the child to its guardianship or, for the information of the court, a copy of a written surrender from a parent or parents or a guardian;* and written formal consent by the organization to the proposed adoption, which consent shall show that sufficient and satisfactory investigation of the adopting parties has been made, and which consent shall recommend that the petition for adoption be granted." (Italics added.)

The requirements of this section were not complied with. Neither of the documents designated was filed with the clerk of the court, so far as the record discloses. That the defect is jurisdictional there can be no doubt, for the purpose to be accomplished by compliance with the statute was "to give formal consent to such adoption." Consent to an adoption by parents or guardian or other person *in loco parentis* is jurisdictional, except where the statute does not require it. * * * As stated in the case last cited, "consent lies at the foundation of statutes of adoption, and when it is required to be given and submitted to the court, the court cannot take jurisdiction of the subject-matter without it." * * *

We are asked to hold that that was a valid adoption pursuant to section 9768, a part of the original adoption act of this state (Deady, General Laws of Oregon 1845–1864, page 692, § 62), but which was still in effect in 1927. That section read:

"If either parent is insane or imprisoned in the state prison, under a sentence for a term not less than three years, or has *willfully deserted and neglected to provide proper care and maintenance for the child for one year next preceding the time of filing the petition,* the court shall proceed as if such parent were dead, and in its discretion may appoint some suitable person to act in the proceedings as next friend of the child, and give or withhold the consent aforesaid." (Italics added.)

There is internal evidence that, notwithstanding the attempt of St. Agnes Baby Home to give its consent to the adoption, the proceeding was not intended to be governed by the statute relating to adoption of children committed to an institution, but rather by the section just quoted. This conclusion is indicated by the allegation of the petition that the child had been abandoned by his parents for more than one year last past and the statement in the report of the Child Welfare Commission that "since the St. Agnes Baby Home never acquired title, the year's abandonment next preceding the time of filing the petition is the basis upon which this proceeding is instituted." The court had judicial knowledge of the contents of the report. * * *

Although not in the exact language of the statute, it may be assumed that the averment that the parents of the child had "abandoned" him for a period of more than one year last past is the equivalent of a charge that they had "willfully deserted and neglected to provide proper care and maintenance" for him. * * * Where desertion is the issue, consent of a parent is not required; the court is then to "proceed as if such parent were dead." Oregon Laws 1920, § 9768. In this case we are concerned only with the consent of the mother, since the child was illegitimate, § 9767. But notice of the proceeding to the mother was required, for § 9769 provided:

"If a parent does not consent to the adoption of his child, the court shall order a copy of the petition and order thereon to be served on him personally, if found in the state, and if not, to be published once a week for three successive weeks in such newspaper printed in the county as the court directs, the last publication to be at least four weeks before the time appointed for the hearing. *Like notice shall also be published when the child has no parent living,* and no guardian or next of kin in this state. The court may order such further notice as it deems necessary or proper." (Italics added.)

If a notice must be published "when the child has no parent living," it apparently is required when desertion is charged and the court is to "proceed as if such parent were dead." Even though this is not a correct interpretation of the statute, due process required notice to the mother. * * *

It follows that the decree of adoption was void as to the natural mother of the petitioner and she could have attacked the decree collaterally, even though it may have been binding on the parties to the proceeding and their privies. * * * The mother died without having called the adoption decree in question; whether this was because she never learned of it or knew about it and was content, there is no way of telling. The question now is whether the son has the same right which his natural mother had but failed to exercise.

* * *

Two decisions of District Courts of Appeal in California sustain the right of the adopted child to attack the decree—Estate of Hampton, 55 Cal.App.2d 543, 567, 131 P.2d 565; Estate of Martin, 86 Cal. App.2d 474, 195 P.2d 839. In both these cases there was failure to give notice to the parent in proceedings taken prior to the adoption proceedings. The opinion in the Martin case summarizes what was done:

"* * * In the Hampton case the parties used the device of having the child declared abandoned, and given into the custody of an institution so that it could consent to the adoption. The mother was not notified of that proceeding. In the present case the parties used the device of having a guardian appointed so that the guardian could give the required consent. But the father was not notified." 86 Cal. App.2d at 477, 195 P.2d at 841.

The court concluded:

"* * * Under such circumstances there is no escape from the conclusion that the rule of the Hampton case permits the child to attack the validity of such an adoption proceeding." Idem. In the

Hampton case, after holding that failure to give notice to the mother rendered the proceedings void, the court said:

"* * * the respondent [the adopted child], who was the central figure therein and the person whose interests were mainly affected thereby, has the right to attack the decree entered which purports to thus interfere with her right of inheriting from her natural mother." 55 Cal.App.2d at 563, 131 P.2d at 576.

The court applied the rule that strangers to the record may attack a void judgment when, if the judgment were given full effect, some right in them would be affected by its enforcement. See 55 Cal.App.2d at 568, 131 P.2d at 578.

In each of these cases the attack on the decree of adoption came some 37 years after the decree was entered; and in each the decree was held to be void as to the adopted child and, therefore, no obstacle to the child's claim to right of inheritance from the natural parent.

In Dean v. Brown, 216 Ark. 761, 227 S.W.2d 623 (which will be referred to more fully in connection with another phase of the question) the court permitted collateral attack on an adoptoin decree by the adopted person 36 years after the decree was entered. There are two decisions and several dicta to the contrary. In Slattery v. Hartford-Conn. Trust Co., 254 Mich. 671, 236 N.W. 902, as in the two California cases just discussed, the defect in the proceedings was failure to give notice to a parent and, as in those cases and Dean v. Brown, supra, the purpose of the attack was to establish the right of the adopted child to inherit from his natural parent.

It appeared in the Slattery case that the adopted person was 42 years of age at the time he sought to vacate the decree, which had been entered 34 years previously. He had been aware of his adoption for 25 years. The father received no notice of the adoption proceedings, which were commenced by the mother, the parents of the child having been divorced at the time. In its opinion dismissing the suit, the court proceeded upon two grounds; first, that the decree could not be collaterally attacked by anyone, and, second, that the adopted child could not question it. As to the latter point the court said:

"If it be held that the father was entitled to notice, then he alone could complain of want of notice, and, for thirty-four years after the adoption and to the time of his death, he made no such complaint. The father never questioned the validity of the adoption, and, by lapse of time, he was barred from seeking revocation thereof, had he so desired, and plaintiff is equally barred." 254 Mich. at 678, 236 N. W. at 904.

The other case denying the right of the adopted child to attack the decree is a decision of the Surrogate's Court in In re Oddo's Adoption, 186 Misc. 359, 59 N.Y.S.2d 612. The natural mother there consented to the adoption but the father did not consent and was given no notice of the proceeding. His consent was dispensed with on the theory that he had abandoned the child. Upon reaching the age of 16 the adopted child petitioned for an order to set aside the adoption. The court held that the father was entitled to notice, but that, since the child was under the age of 14 when the adoption order was granted and the statute did not require her consent, she could not be a party to a proceeding to vacate the order based on lack of notice to a natural parent or a failure of proof of abandonment by said parent. The court said: "The right of the natural father to challenge the adoption is a personal right which may not be exercised by others." * * * Assuming, without deciding, that delay can operate as an estoppel to attack a void judgment it could be so only if the delay were accompanied by knowledge of the facts. The record in this case discloses that the petitioner had no such knowledge until 1961, although he had been told by his adopting parents at an undisclosed time that he was an adopted child.

 * * *

The petitioner, who was an infant aged three years at the time of the adoption proceedings, was not, and could not have been, a party thereto, but was, as the court said in the Hampton case, "the central figure therein and the person whose interests were mainly affected thereby." We hold that he is entitled to attack the decree in this proceeding.

We come finally to Aetna's contention in support of the order of the court below based upon ORS 109.381 (Oregon Laws 1959, ch. 609, §§ 2–6 inclusive) which reads:

"(1) A decree of a court of this state granting an adoption, and the proceedings in such adoption matter, shall in all respects be entitled to the same presumptions and be as conclusive as if rendered by a court of record acting in all respects as a court of general jurisdiction and not by a court of special or inferior jurisdiction, and jurisdiction over the persons and the cause shall be presumed to exist.

"(2) Except for such right of appeal as may be provided by law, decrees of adoption shall be binding and conclusive upon all parties to the proceeding. No party nor anyone claiming by, through or under a party to an adoption proceeding, may for any reason, either by collateral or direct proceedings, question the validity of a decree of adoption entered by a court of competent jurisdiction of this or any other state.

"(3) After the expiration of one year from the entry of a decree of adoption in this state the validity of the adoption shall be binding on all persons, and it shall be conclusively presumed that the child's natural parents and all other persons who might claim to have any right to, or over the child, have abandoned him and consented to the entry of such decree of adoption, and that the child became the lawful child of the adoptive parents or parent at the time when the decree of adoption was rendered, all irrespective of jurisdictional or other defects in the adoption proceeding; after the expiration of such one-year period no one may question the validity of the adoption for any reason, either through collateral or direct proceedings, and all persons shall be bound thereby; provided, however, the provisions of this subsection shall not affect such right of appeal from a decree of adoption as may be provided by law.

"(4) The provisions of this section shall apply to all adoption proceedings instituted in this state after August 5, 1959. This section shall also apply, after the expiration of one year from August 5, 1959, to all adoption proceedings instituted in this state before August 5, 1959."

This statute has two aspects—in one it is a curative act, in the other a statute of limitations. As to the former, the general rule is that it is not competent for the legislature to validate a judgment void for want of jurisdiction and a statute purporting to have that effect would be unconstitutional, amounting to a denial of due process of law. If, however, the defect in the proceedings is the omission of a requirement that could have validly been dispensed with in the first instance, the judgment may be validated by a retroactive law, subject to the restriction that it could not impair the obligation of a contract or a vested right. * * * The requirement of Oregon Laws 1920, § 9830, that a copy of the order of permanent commitment of a child to an institution must be filed in the adoption proceedings is probably one that could have been validly omitted, but whether so or not, the statute cannot be applied to this case without violating the constitutional rights of the petitioner because in 1957, upon his mother's death, two years prior to the enactment of ORS 109.381, the petitioner's right to inherit his natural mother's estate had vested in him.
* * *

Aetna argues, however, that subsection (1) of ORS 109.381 does no more than provide a presumption of validity of adoption decrees, and since a presumption in this state is a species of evidence, * * * and there is no vested right in a rule of evidence, State v. Randolph, 85 Or. 172, 186, 166 P. 555, no constitutional right of the petitioner would be impaired by applying the statute to this case. More pointedly, it is said, in substance, that the legislature, by enacting subsection (1), has repealed the rule of Furgeson v. Jones. That it has done so validly as to future adoption proceedings there can be no doubt, but as much cannot be said of prior proceedings, for it is not competent for the legislature, by the device of construing a statute, to alter its meaning so as to affect vested rights, * * *. Furgeson v. Jones and the cases that followed it announced the construction of the adoption statute of Oregon. To apply ORS 109.381(1) to this case would be, as Chief Justice Gibson pointed out in the Greenough case, not only a violation of due process, but as well to give effect to an exercise of judical power by the legislature.

By subsections (3) and (4) of ORS 109.381, it is provided, in substance, that actions to question decrees of adoption shall be barred if commenced after the expiration of one year from their entry, but if the adoption proceedings were instituted prior to August 5, 1959, then such an action must be brought within one year from August 5, 1959. That was the effective date of the act and, evidently, the provision as to prior proceedings was adopted in order to avoid the constitutional objection against cutting off remedies simultaneously with the passing of the limitations statute. * * * But a judgment void on its face for want of jurisdiction is a nullity and should be vacated when called to the attention of the court. * * *

The courts therefore hold that a statute of limitations is not applicable to a judgment void upon its face. * * *

In several of the states statutes imposing time limitations for attacking adoption proceedings similar to ORS 109.381 have been enacted. A review of cases construing these statutes may be found in 83 A.L.R.2d 945, an Annotation to Walter v. August, 186 Cal.App.2d 395, 8 Cal.Rptr. 778, 83 A.L.R.2d 941. * * *

In Walter v. August, supra, the adoption decree was based on abandonment of the child and the defect in the proceedings was failure to give notice to the child's natural parents who had not consented to the adoption. Over five years after the decree was entered the natural parents commenced a proceeding to have the decree set aside on grounds of fraud. The court held that the action was barred by a statute of limitation (enacted prior to the adoption proceedings) which provided a limitation of three years for attacking an adoption decree on procedural grounds and five years on any other ground. The court said that as to the natural parents the decree was not void, but voidable. "It would not be void in the sense that it could be treated as a nullity, or even attacked directly, by anyone else except the child himself." It should be observed that in this case there was no question of vested rights and that, as the language just quoted from the opinion shows, the court expressly recognized the right of the child to treat the decree as a nullity. In answering the natural parents' contention that to apply the statute of limitation to the case would deprive them of due process, the court likened the possession of the child by the adoptive parents to constructive notice by adverse possession of land. * * * We think that there might be much reason and justice in the use of this analogy where the natural parents are attacking the adoption proceedings, but it could have no place where the child himself is seeking to have the decree of adoption set aside.

     * * *

We conclude that the petitioner was never legally adopted and, as the sole heir at law of Mona LaWanda Nelson, deceased, is entitled to inherit her estate.

NOTES AND QUESTIONS

1. Another case which seems to have held that the statute of limitations may not cut off jurisdictional objections to the adoption decree, at least where notice is involved, is White v. Davis, 163 Colo. 122, 428 P.2d 909 (1967), 40 U.Colo.L.Rev. 151 (1967). Other cases are cited in Annot., 83 A.L.R.2d 945 (1962).

A case which holds that attack on the adoption decree for fraud is barred by the statute of limitations is In re Kerr, 547 S.W.2d 837 (Mo. App.1977).

The Uniform Adoption Act § 15, 9 Unif.L.Ann. 47 (1979) includes a broad one-year statute of limitations.

2. What arguments might be advanced in favor of validity of the statute of limitations in the principal case? Does it matter whether the defect is one of consent and its requirements, or one of failure to give notice to the natural parent? Compare the following quotation from Walter v. August, cited in the principal case, 186 Cal.App.2d at 400, 8 Cal.Rptr. at 781:

"Respondents assert that to apply section 227d to this case would deprive them of due process. We think there is nothing in the point. Contract rights are protected by the Constitution, but are validly cut off by statutes of limitation, without the giving of any notice to the party whose rights are lost. Property rights are similarly protected, but can likewise be lost by limitation, with no actual notice to the owner; constructive notice by adverse possession is enough. The 'possession' of the child by his adoptive parents is surely analogous. Our courts have held that jurisdictional defects can be cured, in effect, by statutes of limitation."

Which case is correct, the *Hughes* case or Walter v. August? Is there any distinction between ordinary statutes of limitation and the statute in the *Hughes* case?

A case which agrees with *Hughes* on the constitutional issue is Matter of Adoption of Lori Gay W., 589 P.2d 217 (Okl.1979), cert. den. 440 U.S. 978 (1979), which contains the following language:

"* * * it is elementary that [the one-year statute of limitations] is subject to the constitutional limitations of the United States and Oklahoma Constitutions and must not be interpreted so as to bar proceedings beyond the one year period where the question of due process of law is timely presented even though more than one year has expired after the adoption decree was entered."

3. Would or should the *Hughes* case have been differently decided if it had involved an attempt by the child's natural mother to set aside the adoption, rather than an attempt by the adopted child? See Armstrong v. Manzo, supra, paragraph 8, page 551, and Lee v. Superior Court in and for the County of Pima, 25 Ariz.App. 55, 540 P.2d 1274 (1975).

4. Was the attack on the adoption decree in the *Hughes* case a direct or a collateral attack? Does that matter?

5. What arguments might be advanced against the view that the adopted child had standing to attack the decree in the *Hughes* case? If the child is allowed to attack the decree, should the adoptive parents be necessary parties to the proceeding? If the natural parent should attack the

decree, for example on the ground of lack of notice, would the child be a necessary party? If the child were not made a party and not provided with independent representation by counsel, would a decree vacating the adoption be unconstitutional?

6. Assuming that the statute of limitations does not prevent attack on the adoption, what grounds for such attack should be required? Consider these cases: (a) Ann unmarried becomes pregnant, the child's father refuses to help her in any way, financially or emotionally. Ann has a sister, Kathy, who is married but childless and who would like a child. Ann talks with Kathy, and Kathy says she would be very anxious to adopt the child. Kathy and her husband urge Ann to give them the child and promise to give it the best of care in all respects. Ann is naturally lonely and upset and in need of counsel, and when the child is born she executes the proper consent to adoption. The child's father also consents, in order to avoid any responsibility for supporting the child. Kathy and her husband file a petition for adoption, the welfare department makes a statutory investigation and finds them eligible parents, and a decree of adoption is entered. One month after the adoption decree is entered, Ann decides that she would like her baby back. She is encouraged in this by her own parents, who agree to help her care for the child and to provide financial support. Ann then files a suit in equity to set aside the adoption decree on the ground of undue influence. What should be the result? Cf. In re Adoption of Minor Child, 109 R.I. 443, 287 A.2d 115 (1972), and Adoption of Robin, 571 P.2d 850 (Okl.1977).

(b) H and W apply to the state department of welfare to adopt a child. A social worker interviews them and they do not respond truthfully to her questions. They tell her that they are college graduates when in fact they had only high school educations. They also tell her that they are members of the local Congregational church when they are not and never have been. Finally, they tell her that their annual income is $10,000 when in fact it is $7,200. In the course of several months a baby is placed with H and W, the department consents to its adoption by them, and the adoption decree is entered. In the course of another investigation six months later the department learns that H and W did not tell the truth about their circumstances, and brings the appropriate suit to set aside the adoption decree and regain custody of the child. What should be the result?

(c) In either of these cases, if the adoption decree is set aside, what becomes of the child? Is the child's welfare relevant to determining whether the decree should be set aside? If the decree were set aside, might the child nevertheless be left in the custody of the adoptive parents?

ALLEN v. ALLEN

Supreme Court of Oregon, 1958.
214 Or. 664, 330 P.2d 151.

SLOAN, Justice. This is a delicate and difficult case. Plaintiffs-appellants are the adoptive parents of the defendant Debra Jeanne Allen. This is a suit by them attempting to abrogate the adoption proceeding which created that status. The defendant Wav-

erly Baby Home, of Portland, is a licensed child-caring agency, certified as provided by ORS 419.112.

The disposition of the case requires a brief summary of the
chronological facts. At the outset of this case the trial court wisely
entered an order impounding the clerk's file, rendering it secret. Unfortunately, the record on appeal and this opinion impair the effect of
this order. We will, however, eliminate facts not actually required
for decision.

Debra was born in Seattle on May 21, 1950. She was the natural
child of a married couple. It is important to note that although this
case involves only Debra, there was a brother born to the same parents who was equally involved in all the pleadings and process herein
mentioned. We will, for the most part, refer to such proceedings,
however, as though only Debra were mentioned therein. The child's
father and mother were later divorced and the child abandoned. In
July, 1951, she was received into the custody of Waverly Baby Home
for care.

* * *

[At this point in its opinion the court described the following
proceedings which had been taken with respect to Debra:

(a) A dependency petition was filed by a county juvenile officer,
Debra's mother appeared, a hearing was held and the court found Debra to be a dependent child. Debra's father was personally served
but did not appear. He later signed a valid consent to her adoption.
As a result of this proceeding the court made a "temporary commitment" of Debra to the Waverly Baby Home, apparently an adoption
agency.

(b) Later the Waverly Baby Home filed another petition seeking authority to consent to Debra's adoption. The mother's where-a-
bouts could not be determined, after diligent efforts and after registered letters were sent to her last address. The citation in this proceeding was then published. After a hearing Debra was permanently
committed to the Waverly Baby Home, and the Home was authorized
to place her for adoption.]

On December 11, 1953, Waverly placed Debra in the home of
plaintiffs for care. Subsequent to the order of November 24, 1953,
and on February 8, 1954, plaintiffs petitioned the same court for the
adoption of these children. Attached to the petition was a certified
copy of the order of commitment and of the consent of the Waverly
Baby Home to such adoption in the form required by what was then
ORS 109.320. On March 15, 1954, an order of adoption was entered.

During the time the child was committed to Waverly, and since
then, she developed behavior problems culminating in a decree on December 15, 1956, determining the child to be mentally deficient and
committing her to the Fairview Home at Salem. The demands upon

the services of that facility so exceed its capacity that a long waiting list of such committed children exists. Consequently, the plaintiffs are still burdened with the care and problems presented by such a child in their own home. By this proceeding they seek to be relieved of this financial burden as well as to avoid the disturbing influence the child creates in the family life of plaintiffs and other children. Plaintiffs also seek, by this means, to be relieved of the cost imposed by the state upon the parents of a child committed to Fairview, at such time as she is admitted. The court is not unaware of or unsympathetic to the problem confronting plaintiffs.

Plaintiffs allege two separate grounds by which they seek to accomplish this purpose and abrogate this adoption. One, that the adoption decree was void for the reason that the juvenile department did not have jurisdiction of the mother of the child at the time it entered the order authorizing consent to adoption in lieu of the parent. And, two, that the officials of Waverly Baby Home at all times had knowledge of the mental condition or deficiency of the child and fraudulently failed to notify these plaintiffs thereof. That such alleged fraudulent failure was likewise a fraud upon the court awarding the decree of adoption. They also seek monetary damages from Waverly for medical costs incurred in caring for the child. After very extensive hearing and briefs the trial court entered a decree denying the rights sought by plaintiffs. * * *

We have given this case the thorough consideration and attention that a proceeding so vitally affecting the welfare of this and other children requires. We have extended our research well beyond that contained in the briefs of the parties in an endeavor to find every writing that could shed some light on the right of adoptive parents to denounce their obligation to adopted children when unforeseen costs and deficiencies occur.

From the numerous cases considered we adopt the expression of the rule set forth in Coonradt v. Sailors, 186 Tenn. 294, 209 S.W.2d 859, 861, 2 A.L.R.2d 880. It is there held:

"Where one voluntarily assumes the relationship of parent to a child by formal adoption, it cannot be lightly cast aside. The relationship involves duties of care, maintenance and education with rights of custody, control and service of the child. Society has an interest in this relationship, and we think the Legislature alone should supply the procedure to be followed, as well as define the cause, if any, whereby the relationship may be dissolved. In the absence of such a statute the courts will not assume jurisdiction to annul a decree of adoption at the instance of the adopting parent and cast the child adrift to again become a public charge." * * * We have found no case holding to the contrary except as authorized by statute. Some states, notably New York, provide statutory authority permitting adopting parents, in very limited circumstances, to set aside adoptions. It is there held, however, that such a right does not exist in the absence of statute. * * *

It is recognized that a court of general equity jurisdiction may set aside a decree of adoption. At 2 A.L.R.2d 890 are collected all the cases found which have considered this exercise of equity jurisdiction. It is to be carefully noted in the cases there cited that equity will assert this authority only to protect the *best interest and welfare of the child*. In this case there is no allegation that the best interests or welfare of the child Debra is at stake.

The plaintiffs assert that the doctrine of estoppel in pais must be applied to determine their right to prosecute this case. That doctrine is not here involved. The term estoppel is used in some of the cited cases, and in a few references the term estoppel in pais is used. However, the matter is best stated by the New York court in In re Martin's Adoption, supra [269 App.Div. 437, 56 N.Y.S.2d 98], wherein it is stated: "The general rule is that where a person invokes the jurisdiction of a court, he will not be heard to repudiate the judgment which that court entered upon his seeking and in his favor." This is not a matter of estoppel in the strict sense, but rather a rule of law. * * * We conclude the plaintiffs are without right to institute and maintain this proceeding.

Nevertheless, this court has examined with care the allegations and evidence of fraud leveled against the Waverly Baby Home and finds them to be without merit. Certainly there is no evidence of a weight and character sufficient to support a determination that the decree of adoption was void by reason thereof. The record and briefs do support a belief that ill will has magnified inconclusive and inconsequential facts into assertions of gross fraud. We find no good purpose in reviewing this evidence. If there is any criticism to be made of the conduct of that organization it is one of carelessness. Neither can we condone the practice of that organization in urging that its attorney serve as the attorney for adopting parents. An attorney in such a situation should be free to examine the record and conduct of the agency without concern or favor.

Plaintiffs also contend that the adoption proceeding itself was void. To establish this they assert that the allegation of "search and inquiry" in the affidavit, upon which the court entered its order for publication of a citation to the mother in the proceedings by which Waverly was awarded a "permanent" commitment and authority to enter its consent to adoption, was insufficient for that purpose. The averments of the affidavit have been previously set forth. They ask us to hold that for this reason the juvenile department had no jurisdiction over the mother at the time the commitment order was modified and that Waverly's subsequent consent to the adoption was therefore without authority. That without a valid consent the adoption must fail. We believe that upon this ground also this appeal must fail.

* * * When notice has been served upon the parent as directed by ORS 419.506, and particularly when the parent in response to such notice appears in person, as in this case, and the child is likewise before the court, jurisdiction of parent and child is acquired. This jurisdiction continues until dissolved by order of the court or process of law. * * *

We again refer to the original judgment entered in the dependency proceedings. As previously stated, this order included a finding of *dependency*. So long as dependency existed jurisdiction was retained. The order was *res adjudicata* as to all parties upon that one salient determination upon which jurisdiction depends until changed or modified as provided by order of law. * * * Additional notice, order or proceeding could only duplicate that which was already accomplished. It would not detract from existing and effective jurisdiction.

We hope it is thus made clear that the court had the power or jurisdiction to modify or change the authority granted to Waverly to include the authority to enter its consent to adoption. Such exercise of jurisdiction did not infringe upon or alter the status existing between parent and child determined by the original adjudication finding dependency.

Thus the second attempted notice to the mother and the citation issued upon the affidavit were unnecessary to provide continuing jurisdiction of the essential parties, including the mother. When Waverly and the court, acting by its counselors, initiated a second petition and attempted to accomplish a substituted service of citation upon the mother prior to the entry of an order awarding Waverly the right to enter the adoption proceedings the parties, and the court, were undoubtedly motivated by that degree of caution which prompted the court in Stoker v. Gowans, supra, to indicate that the giving of notice prior to a change in the commitment order would have been a matter of better practice, but that its failure to do so was an irregularity and did not deprive the court of jurisdiction. * * *

It must be noted that we have not considered the sufficiency of the affidavit, heretofore mentioned, to sustain the publication of citation to the mother on the occasion of the second hearing. Our disposition of this case renders this unnecessary. The extent, if any, to which the natural mother was by that process deprived of due process is not before us and cannot be determined. Let it be clear, however, that at the time the juvenile department entered the order authorizing Waverly to consent to an adoption proceeding it had jurisdiction of the subject matter and all the necessary parties. If there were any failure of due process it is available only to the mother and not to these plaintiffs. * * *

Plaintiffs rely upon Furgeson v. Jones, 17 Or. 204, 20 P. 842, 3 L.R.A. 620, and subsequent decisions of this court which conform to the rule of that case. These cases hold that in an adoption proceeding the court considering the adoption does not acquire jurisdiction unless some form of notice has been served, directly or substituted, upon the competent, living natural parents. The distinction between that line of cases and this should be clear. We are not here concerned with the jurisdiction obtained by the court in the adoption proceedings. We must and do rely upon the jurisdiction obtained and retained by the juvenile department at the time of the initial dependency proceedings. As heretofore discussed we are satisfied as to that. Having determined that such jurisdiction was acquired, it is decisive of the remaining issues.

Affirmed.

NOTES AND QUESTIONS

1. Another case refusing to permit adoptive parents to attack the adoption decree is In re Adoption of Curtis, 143 Mont. 330, 390 P.2d 209 (1964). See also Annot., 2 A.L.R.2d 887 (1948).

2. Are the natural parents necessary parties to an action of this kind?

3. The court in *Allen* suggests that even if the notice to the natural mother did not meet the requirements of due process, this could not be a reason to set the decree aside at the instance of the adoptive parents. Is this inconsistent with the same court's decision in *Hughes*, supra, page 584? If so, which view is correct?

4. If the plaintiffs had succeeded in this case in having the adoption decree set aside, what would have been the status of the child?

5. H and W wish to adopt a baby, but they find that the local adoption agencies have so few babies available for adoption that they would have to wait more than a year for one, with no assurance that they might receive a baby even then. A friend who knows of their desire introduces them to a local lawyer who arranges independent placements. He agrees to keep them in mind, and a few weeks later calls to tell them he has a baby for them. They inquire about the baby's health and genetic background and the lawyer assures them that the mother, father and baby have been given thorough physical examinations and all three are in good health, with no known genetic defects. H and W take the baby direct from the hospital, file a petition to adopt it and the adoption decree is entered. H and W arrange for regular checkups with a pediatrician, and on the second of these, about six weeks after the baby was born, the pediatrician discovers that the baby is suffering from severe heart disease. H and W then question employees of the hospital where the baby was born and find that the mother had had rubella during her pregnancy, and that this fact had been revealed to the lawyer who placed the baby for adoption.

(a) May H and W have the adoption decree set aside on this ground? What would be the effect of the *Allen* case upon their claim? Cf. In re Welfare of Alle, 304 Minn. 254, 230 N.W.2d 574 (1975).

(b) If the placement had been by an adoption agency which had not known of the rubella, but which in the exercise of proper care, should have known, could H and W have the adoption set aside? If not, could they obtain any other relief from the agency?

(c) If the proceeding suggested in either (a) or (b) above were brought, must the child be made a party and be represented by counsel?

6. A child, L, six years old, was adopted by H and W, the procedure and decree being in all respects regular. Eight years later L went to live with her natural mother and remained with her, writing to H and W that she preferred living with her mother and that she did not want to return to her adoptive home.

(a) Could H and W then have the adoption decree set aside? Cf. In the Matter of the Adoption of L, 56 N.J.Super. 46, 151 A.2d 435 (1959).

(b) Could L have the adoption decree set aside?

7. Cal.Civ.Code § 227b (Supp.1979) provides, in relevant part, as follows:

"If any child heretofore or hereafter adopted under the foregoing provisions of this code shows evidence of a mental deficiency or mental illness as a result of conditions prior to the adoption to such an extent that the child cannot be relinquished to an adoption agency on the grounds that the child is considered unadoptable, and of which conditions the adopting parents or parent had no knowledge or notice prior to the entry of the decree of adoption, a petition setting forth such facts may be filed by the adopting parents or parent with the court which granted the petition for adoption. If such facts are proved to the satisfaction of the court, it may make an order setting aside the decree of adoption.

"The petition must be filed within whichever is the later of the following time limits: (a) within five years after the entering of the decree of adoption, or (b) within one year after the effective date hereof, if such a condition were manifest in the child within five years after the entering of the decree of adoption.

"In every action brought under this section it shall be the duty of the clerk of the superior court of the county wherein the action is brought to immediately notify the State Department of Health of such action. Within 60 days after such notice the State Department of Health shall file a full report with the court and shall appear before the court for the purpose of representing the adopted child."

See Department of Social Welfare v. Superior Court, 1 Cal.3d 1, 459 P. 2d 897, 81 Cal.Rptr. 345 (1969).

(a) Is there any constitutional objection to this or similar statutes permitting attack on adoption decrees? Cf. Levy and Duncan, Constitutional Implications of Adoption Revocation Statutes, 8 Pac.L.J. 611 (1977).

(b) Would you advocate the enactment of similar legislation in your state?

8. Gloria and Dennis were married and lived in State X, and had a son, Jason. A year after Jason's birth they were divorced; custody of Jason being given to Gloria with rights of visitation to Dennis. Shortly after the divorce Gloria married Robert. Some months later Robert filed a petition

to adopt Jason as Jason's stepfather, Gloria consenting. Dennis was served by publication but did not appear in the adoption proceeding since he had moved away from X. Six months after the adoption Robert and Gloria had a conversation about having children which concluded with the following remarks from Gloria: "I'm not going to have any more kids. I've had it, and I'm going to keep using the pill. That's what I've decided and if you don't like it, that's just too bad. You can support the kid." Since Robert had married with the hope and intention of having children of his own, he was much upset and sued to annul his marriage to Gloria on the ground of fraud, in that she had concealed from him her intent never to have children. The court of X granted the annulment, finding that this was fraud going to the essence of the marriage. Robert then sued Gloria and Jason to set aside the adoption decree. An attorney was appointed to represent Jason. At the trial evidence of the foregoing facts was presented, and in addition Jason's attorney presented evidence showing that Dennis had returned to X and wished to have some contact with Jason. Dennis was not a party to the proceeding, however. How should the case be decided? Adoption of Jason R., 88 Cal.App.3d 11, 151 Cal.Rptr. 501 (1979).

SECTION 4. RIGHTS AND DUTIES OF SUPPORT IN THE FAMILY

INTRODUCTORY NOTE

The material in this section is closely related to the cases on alimony, since alimony or maintenance is generally characterized as a substitute for the support claim. It is also related to the cases on child support arising out of divorce. These cases are found in Chapter 6, infra.

The traditional position of English and American law was that the husband had the duty of supporting his wife and children. This remained the guiding principle in our law until just recently, although some inroads upon it were made by statute or judicial decision in a minority of states. About twenty states enacted Family Expense Statutes, which provided that the expenses of the family and the education of the children are chargeable against the property of both husband and wife or that both husband and wife are jointly and severally liable for such expenses. See, e. g., Or.Rev.Stat. § 108.040 (1977); Wash.Rev.Code Ann. § 26–16–205 (Supp.1977). Even in states having these statutes, however, the husband was held to be ultimately liable for these expenses, so that if the wife was forced to pay them, she could obtain reimbursement from him.

Since the late 1960's, under the influence of the women's movement, the law in the various states has changed in the direction of imposing the duty of support upon both spouses. This has been accomplished by statute in some states, e. g., Cal.Civ.Code § 5100 (1970); Conn.Gen.Stat.Ann. § 46–10 (1978); Tex.Fam.Code § 4.02 (1975). In the seventeen states which have state Equal Rights Amendments, it seems clear that the duty of support must constitutionally be imposed upon both spouses. E. g., Rand v. Rand, 280 Md. 508, 374 A.2d 900 (1977). And the Supreme Court of the United States has held, in Orr v. Orr, 440 U.S. 268 (1979), that a state statute imposing the duty to pay alimony upon the husband alone violates the Equal Protection Clause of the Fourteenth Amendment. See page 868, infra. It seems to follow that a state law imposing the duty of support upon husbands alone also violates that Amendment. The result is that today the burden of supporting the family rests equally upon both spouses, with the qualification that in specific cases its impact will depend upon the relative abilities of the two spouses to sustain it. Thus in those cases in which the husband's income or property are sufficient to enable him to support the family and in which the wife has little or no income or property, the obligation to support will continue to be his. Where both parties have income or property, both may have to undertake this obligation in whatever proportions the court finds equitable.

A variety of legal remedies have been created by legislatures and the courts to enforce duties of support within the family. One such remedy was for the wife to buy "necessaries" for herself or the family and thereby make the husband liable to the seller by operation of law. See, e. g. Saks & Co. v. Bennett, 12 N.J.Super. 316, 79 A.2d 479 (1951). "Necessaries" were defined as articles or services reasonably appropriate for the support of the family, taking into account the financial means available to pay for them. If the husband had already supplied the family with such "necessaries", it was held that the tradesman who sold them to the wife could not recover their cost. With such a limitation, the remedy was of little practical value and it is seldom relied upon today.

Other civil remedies for the enforcement of support claims by spouses and children include the suit in equity, a non-statutory remedy, and the statutory actions for separate maintenance or divorce from bed and board. Examples of the equity suit are Heflin v. Heflin, 177 Va. 385, 14 S.E.2d 317 (1941) and McQuade v. McQuade, 145 Colo. 218, 358 P.2d 470 (1960). See also Annot., 13 A.L.R.2d 1142 (1950). For cases on separate maintenance and divorce a mensa et thoro, see H. Clark, Law of Domestic Relations § 6.4 (1968). Although some courts continue to insist that there is some distinction between separate maintenance and legal separation, or divorce a mensa, In re Marriage of E.A.W., 573 S.W.2d 689 (Mo.App.1978), the practical effect of such proceedings is generally the same, that is, to provide support for the spouse.

Since courts are reluctant to interfere in the financial affairs of a going family, these civil remedies for non-support are generally only available when the spouses are separated, an extreme example of this tendency being McGuire v. McGuire, 157 Neb. 226, 59 N.W.2d

336 (1953), 33 Neb.L.Rev. 103 (1953). This rule is sharply criticized in Krauskopf and Thomas, Partnership Marriage: The Solution to an Ineffective and Inequitable Law of Support, 35 Ohio St.L.J. 558, 565 (1974).

Separate maintenance and divorce a mensa et thoro are primarily remedies for non-support, but they also have effects upon the family, by authorizing the parties to live apart and providing for the custody of children of the marriage. From that point of view such proceedings have been much criticized, since they produce a situation in which the parties no longer have the satisfactions of marriage, and yet they cannot form other attachments since they are still married to each other. They have all the disadvantages of being married and none of the advantages. For that reason modern divorce statutes often provide for the conversion of the decree of separate maintenance into a decree of divorce after the passage of time. See, e. g., Uniform Marriage and Divorce Act, §§ 302, 314.

Jurisdiction to award separate maintenance is usually held to rest upon personal jurisdiction over the defendant or quasi in rem jurisdiction over his property. Unlike divorce, the plaintiff need not be domiciled in the state to bring such an action. Goodwine v. Superior Court, 63 Cal.2d 481, 47 Cal.Rptr. 201, 407 P.2d 1 (1965); Nienow v. Nienow, 268 S.C. 161, 232 S.E.2d 504 (1977). On the application of forum non conveniens to such suits, see the *Nienow* case and the cases cited in Annot., 9 A.L.R.3d 545 (1966).

In determining the amount of support to be awarded in such suits, the courts take into account the same factors as in the alimony cases. These include the needs of the spouse or child, the means of the person responsible for support, the spouse's assistance in the accumulation of income or property, the spouse's services in the home, and the extent of the spouse's property or income. For an extensive collection of cases, see Annot., 1 A.L.R.3d 208 (1965). See also Sayland v. Sayland, 267 N.C. 378, 148 S.E.2d 218 (1966), and Uniform Civil Liability for Support Act § 6, 9 Unif.L.Ann. 180 (1979).

If the statute in the particular state authorizes it, the court in separate maintenance may divide the property of the parties. Prentice v. Prentice, 568 P.2d 883 (Wyo.1977); Note, Domestic Relations: Adjudication of Property Rights in Actions for Separate Maintenance, 32 Okl.L.Rev. 210 (1979).

Formerly marital fault on the part of a wife frequently was a defense to her claim to support. Thus if she made cohabitation impossible or prevented it without justification, the husband was no longer required to support her. Martin v. Martin, 134 Conn. 354, 57 A.2d 622 (1948); Noyes v. Noyes, 108 N.H. 462, 237 A.2d 692 (1968). Likewise if the wife were guilty of desertion, adultery or conduct which drove the husband from the home, he would have a defense. See, e. g., Kerner v. Eastern Dispensary and Casualty Hospital, 210

Md. 375, 123 A.2d 333 (1956); Courson v. Courson, 213 Md. 183, 129 A.2d 917 (1957); Larkin v. Larkin, —— Pa.Super. ——, 396 A.2d 761 (1978). Many other cases are collected in Annots., 10 A.L.R.2d 466 (1950) and 60 A.L.R.2d 7 (1958). In some states fault would still be a defense. E. g., Graham v. Graham, 3 Ill.Dec. 141, 44 Ill.App.3d 519, 358 N.E.2d 308 (1976). In other states the statutes have minimized or eliminated fault as a defense to support claims. The Uniform Marriage and Divorce Act § 308, 9 Unif.L.Ann. 160 (1979) provides that marital misconduct is not to be considered in awarding maintenance in either divorce actions or actions for legal separation.

Other defenses to separate maintenance include laches, Streeter v. Streeter, 33 N.C.App. 679, 236 S.E.2d 185 (1977), and a bona fide offer of reconciliation, Annot., 10 A.L.R.2d 466 (1950).

In some states rights to support are lost if the parties separate by agreement. E. g., Cal.Civ.Code § 5131 (Supp.1979); Bruch, The Legal Import of Informal Marital Separations: A Survey of California Law and a Call for Change, 65 Cal.L.Rev. 1015 (1977). In this and many other situations discussed in Professor Bruch's article informal separations may have unforeseen consequences for the parties' legal rights and obligations. For this reason parties who do separate, whether or not they contemplate divorce at the time of separation, should obtain legal advice about the effect of the separation, not only upon rights to support of spouse and child, but also upon other marital rights and obligations. If the parties make a valid agreement providing for payments for spousal support when they separate, compliance with such an agreement is a defense to any further claims for support. Annots., 10 A.L.R.2d 466, 535 (1950), 60 A.L.R.2d 7, 53 (1958). But if the spouse fails to perform the agreement, the other spouse may sue for support and is not limited to the amount specified in the agreement. Cram v. Cram, 116 N.C. 288, 21 S.E. 197 (1895).

Decrees of separate maintenance are enforceable by contempt proceedings, but the defendant may escape a contempt conviction by showing inability to comply with the decree, since the normal contempt proceeding for the enforcement of such decrees is considered to be civil rather than criminal contempt. This rule and the practical difficulties of enforcement enable a determined defendant to frustrate any attempts by his spouse or child to obtain support in many cases. For example, see Barrett v. Barrett, 470 Pa. 253, 368 A.2d 616 (1977), 81 Dick.L.Rev. 851 (1977).

Non-support of dependents was recognized as a national problem by Congress in 1974 in the passage of Public Law 93–647 of that year. This statute became Part D of Title IV and Title XX of the Social Security Act, 42 U.S.C.A. §§ 651 ff. and 1397 ff. and became effective on various dates in 1975. Regulations by the Department of Health, Education and Welfare implementing the statute are contained in 45 C.F.R. Parts 205, 232–235, 301–304 (1976). The general purpose of the legislation was to provide federal remedies for the enforcement of children's support claims against their parents. The act creates a unit in HEW for technical assistance to the states in the collection of child support; sets up a Parent Locator Service to aid the states in tracing parents who fail to support their children; sets standards for state child support plans; provides that debts owed to the states for child support are not dischargeable in bankruptcy and may be collected by the Internal Revenue Service; permits garnishment of wages of United States employees for the payment of child support and alimony; gives jurisdiction to the United States district courts, without regard to amount in controversy, over claims for child support on certain conditions; and provides for financial aid to the states in furtherance of preventing or reducing dependency. Descriptions of the efforts of two states to use the new federal legislation are in Note, 52 Wash.L.Rev. 169 (1976) and Note 30 S.W.L.J. 625 (1976). On the garnishment of the wages of federal employees, see Annot. 44 A.L.R.Fed. 494 (1979) and Overman v. United States, 563 F.2d 1287 (8th Cir. 1977).

One other piece of federal legislation, enacted in 1974 and effective in 1975, is of real though indirect benefit to spouses, particularly wives who need to obtain credit. This is the Equal Credit Opportunity Act, Pub.L. 93–495, 15 U.S.C.A. § 1691 ff. It makes it unlawful for any creditor to discriminate on the basis of sex or marital status with respect to any aspect of a credit transaction. Sanctions include enforcement by the Federal Trade Commission, the federal reserve system where banks are involved, and by suits for civil liability in the federal courts.

Statutes in nearly all states make the wilful failure to support wife or child a crime. In over half the states it is a misdemeanor while in the others it is a felony. The language of these statutes varies widely, but all make the requirement that the failure be wilful, that is, that the defendant must be proved capable of furnishing support before he may be convicted. Burris v. State, —— Ind.App. ——, 382 N.E.2d 963 (1978). In some states the statute may provide that failure to support is prima facie evidence of wilfulness, thereby creating what amounts to a rebuttable presumption of wilfulness. Such statutes have been held constitutional. State v. Shaw, 96 Idaho 897, 539 P.2d 250 (1975); State v. Bauer, 92 Wash.2d 162, 595 P.2d 544 (1979). The Shaw case also held that the defendant could be convicted of a violation even though he was living in another state during the period in which the failure to support occurred.

Criminal non-support statutes have been upheld against contentions that they are unconstitutionally vague in State v. Joyce, 361 So.2d 406 (Fla.1978) and Commonwealth v. Baggs, 258 Pa.Super. 133, 392 A.2d 720 (1978). The latter case also held that where the statute applied to both mothers and fathers, it did not violate the state Equal Rights Amendment. But see People v. Elliott, 186 Colo. 65,

525 P.2d 457 (1974). The *Elliott* case also held that the felony non-support statute does not violate the constitutional prohibition against imprisonment for debt. The fact that the defendant's failure to support his children was caused by his religious beliefs, which enjoined him to engage only in community service without compensation, was held not to be a defense and to involve no violation of constitutional guarantees of religious freedom in State v. Sprague, 25 Ore.App. 621, 550 P.2d 769 (1976).

Extradition for violation of the criminal non-support statute is authorized by the Uniform Reciprocal Enforcement of Support Act §§ 5, 6, 9A Unif.L.Ann. 664 (1979). See also People v. Hinton, 40 N.Y. 2d 345, 386 N.Y.S.2d 703, 353 N.E.2d 617 (1976).

For an argument that incarceration for non-support violates the Equal Protection and Due Process Clauses of the Fourteenth Amendment and also the Eighth Amendment, see Willging and Ellsmore, The "Dual System" in Action: Jail for Nonsupport, 1969 U. Toledo L.Rev. 348. The major point made is that the chief purpose of the statutes imposing criminal sanctions for non-support is the preservation of public funds, and that this purpose is not served by the statutes to a degree sufficient to establish the rational classification required by the Equal Protection Clause. The reference to "dual systems" comes from a long and important analysis of the law's treatment of poor people in California. ten Broek, California's Dual System of Family Law: Its Origin, Development and Present Status, 16 Stan.L.Rev. 257, 900, 17 Stan.L.Rev. 614 (1964, 1965). Comments on this article are Lewis and Levy, Family Law and Welfare Policies: The Case for "Dual Systems", 54 Cal.L.Rev. 748 (1966), and Weyrauch, Dual Systems of Family Law: A Comment, 54 Cal.L.Rev. 781 (1966).

An empirical study of the Michigan friend-of-the-court program, under which a public agency is charged with the enforcement of support claims, indicates that a higher level of compliance with support decrees is achieved if (a) the public agency moves for enforcement on its own initiative, without waiting for the dependent to complain; and (b) if in the particular jurisdiction jail sentences are numerous for non-compliance with such decrees. The study also concluded that greater compliance occurred in Michigan, where the public agency functions, than in Wisconsin, where enforcement is left to the complainants. The study dealt only with contempt enforcement of civil decrees, but presumably its conclusions would apply to criminal enforcement. Chambers, Men Who Know They Are Watched: Some Benefits and Costs of Jailing for Nonpayment of Support, 75 Mich.L. Rev. 900 (1977).

In view of the information and arguments in these law review articles, would you advocate the repeal of criminal non-support statutes? Or should they be enforced by public agencies without waiting for complaints? Or would it be preferable to set up a wage garnishment system as a feature of every non-support decree, as Chambers suggests?

PFUELLER v. PFUELLER

Superior Court of New Jersey, Appellate Division, 1955.
37 N.J.Super. 106, 117 A.2d 30.

CLAPP, S. J. A. D. We are concerned in this case with the operation of the Uniform Reciprocal Enforcement of Support Act, N.J. S.A. 2A:4–30.1 et seq., adopted now in many jurisdictions.

The plaintiff, Kerline Pfueller, instituted these proceedings in the Municipal Court of Philadelphia, Domestic Relations Division, to secure support from the defendant, Adolph Pfueller, her husband. There were no children of the marriage. A statement of information signed by her and a verified complaint were apparently transmitted by the Municipal Court to a Juvenile and Domestic Relations Court in this State. The latter court ordered defendant to pay a stated sum for plaintiff's support. He appeals.

The New Jersey court held that its only responsibility was to ascertain whether plaintiff was the wife of the defendant; that the Philadelphia court had "determined the duty of this man to pay before they sent the complaint to us."

This is an obvious misconception. The statute, N.J.S.A. 2A:4–30.11, in this respect identical with the uniform act, sec. 13, places upon the court in the initiating state the duty merely of finding whether the complaint

"sets forth facts from which it *may* be determined that the defendant owes a duty of support." (Italics inserted.)

Indeed the finding of the Philadelphia court in this case is stated in quite similar terms.

Professor Brockelbank, chairman of the committee which prepared the uniform act for the National Conference of Commissioners on Uniform State Laws, has said of the finding of a court in an initiating state:

"This is not a finding that the defendant owes the duty. The court of the initiating state at that stage could not so find, for the defendant is not before the court." Brockelbank, "Is the Uniform Reciprocal Enforcement of Support Act Constitutional?" 17 Mo.L.Rev. 1, 12 (1952).

In effect it amounts merely to a finding that the allegations of the complaint warrant further proceedings; it is in no way evidentiary as to defendant's liability.

Under the statute it becomes the obligation, not of the initiating court, but of the court in the responding state, to determine whether or not the defendant is under a duty to support the plaintiff. * * * This determination may be made by the latter court only upon the basis of evidence adduced before the court and of depositions taken on notice to defendant after it has secured jurisdiction over him through a summons or warrant.

In the present case the defendant claims he was compelled to testify under penalty of being held in contempt, notwithstanding that he invoked the privilege against self-incrimination. As defendant contends before us, N.J.S.A. 2A:4–30.18 does not affect this privilege; it merely does away with marital disqualifications and the privilege as to confidential communications between husband and wife. * * * In some cases under the uniform act the question may be presented whether the privilege against self-incrimination may be invoked in one jurisdiction with respect to an offense against another jurisdiction. But that controversial question is not presented here. Indeed, we need not deal with any aspect of the privilege against self-incrimination in this case, for it does not appear to us that the trial court here could have understood that this privilege was being invoked. The privilege of course must be claimed, or it is waived. * * *

We turn then to defendant's testimony. In effect he testified that plaintiff deserted him while they were living together in this State. The trial court had before it no proof whatever that he had deserted her. The case will have to be reversed and remanded.

                    * * *

Where, as here, the defendant does not admit the charge of desertion, either expressly or impliedly, the court has open to it two alternative courses of procedure. First, if it is feasible for the wife to appear personally (her residence is fairly near the court in this case), notice can be given to her through the initiating court (perhaps also to her directly by mail) to appear at a specified time, at which time the responding court may take her testimony and such further testimony of the defendant (he having been subpoenaed for the occasion) as may be called for.

Second, if it is not feasible for her to appear personally in court, her deposition may be taken as in a civil action in the Superior Court. Note, 25 Temple L.Q. 336, 342, 343 (1952); Note, 33 Boston Univ.L.Rev. 217, 222 (1953); cf. N.J.S.A. 2A:4–25, repealed, and Comment, 45 Ill.L.Rev. 252, 254 (1950), dealing with a statute similar to N.J.S.A. 2A:4–25; * * * In such a case, the county adjuster should send a copy of the husband's testimony or (since it is usually not available) a summary of it prepared by the adjuster, to the court in the initiating state, suggesting that if the matter is to be pursued further, the wife's deposition be taken before that court or some proper person (R.R. 4:18–2). Due notice (R.R. 4:20–1) of the time and place at which the deposition is to be taken, should be served personally upon the husband, which service could be effected through the adjuster's office. As provided in the rules, the deposition should be taken stenographically and transcribed, R.R. 4:20–3, signed by the wife, R.R. 4:20–5, certified pursuant to R.R. 4:20–6, and returned to the Clerk of the Juvenile and Domestic Relations Court. A copy of the deposition need however not be sent to the defendant under R.R. 4:20–6(c).

The stenographer's charge for such depositions may constitute an expense which may have to be paid for by the wife. The question whether a Juvenile and Domestic Relations Court in this State, where it is a responding state, may compel the husband to reimburse her for this expense, will have to be reserved until the matter is properly presented. * * * In this case it is to be noted that Pennsylvania apparently has adopted section 14 of the uniform act (which was not adopted in this State). 9A U.L.A., 1955, Supp. 109.

When the deposition is returned to the court in this State (the responding state), the defendant should be subpoenaed, the deposition read to him and a further hearing then accorded him, if he wishes it.

Professor Brockelbank has said:

"When the defendant has given his evidence [at the first hearing in the responding state] and has been cross-examined by the agent named in Section 12 [N.J.S.A. 2A:4–30.12], the court *might* then make his order but not necessarily so. The transcript might be sent back to the court of the initiating state to allow the plaintiff to offer evidence denying, qualifying or adding to what is in the record. Such action would usually be taken upon motion by the agent named in Section 12. When the mere complete record is forwarded to the court of the responding state, a further hearing is had when the court may decide to make his order. It will be seen that the procedure outlined here is an imitation, by sending the record back and forth by mail, of the procedure that prevails when both parties are present in court. In the typical trial the plaintiff and his witnesses testify, then comes the turn of the defendant and his witnesses, and finally the plaintiff and his witnesses may reply." Brockelbank, supra, 17 Mo.L.Rev., p. 13.

Here the defendant testifies first, then comes the turn of the plaintiff and finally the defendant may reply.

* * *

Reversed and remanded.

NOTES AND QUESTIONS

1. The Uniform Reciprocal Enforcement of Support Act, in one version or another, is in force in all states and the District of Columbia, so that reciprocal enforcement is available in all states. The discussion in the *Pfueller* case is intended merely as an introduction to its general structure, leaving to a later section a detailed analysis of its operation and effect.

The Act, usually referred to as URESA, is found in 9A Unif.L.Ann. 747 (1979). It was substantially amended in 1968, the amended Act is referred to as Revised Uniform Reciprocal Enforcement of Support Act (RURESA) and is reproduced in 9A Unif.L.Ann. 643 (1979). Not all states have adopted the revised Act. A thorough account of both Acts may be found in Fox, The Uniform Reciprocal Enforcement of Support Act, 12 Fam.L.Q. 113 (1978).

2. URESA has been held constitutional in the few cases in which the question has arisen. See, e. g., Smith v. Smith, 125 Cal.App.2d 154, 270 P.2d 613 (1954); Watson v. Dreadin, 309 A.2d 493 (D.C.App.1973), cert. den. 415 U.S. 959 (1974). Ivey v. Ayers, 301 S.W.2d 790 (Mo.1957); Landes v. Landes, 1 N.Y.2d 358, 153 N.Y.S.2d 14, 135 N.E.2d 562 appeal dism'd 352 U.S. 948, 77 S.Ct. 325, 1 L.Ed.2d 241 (1956).

3. The Revised Act, § 33, 9A Unif.L.Ann. 737 (1979) applies to proceedings to enforce support duties between different counties of a single state. The Act provides new civil remedies for the enforcement of already existing support duties rather than to change the substantive law of support. RURESA §§ 1, 3, 9A Unif.L.Ann. 648, 659 (1979).

4. Blois v. Blois, 138 So.2d 373 (Fla.App.1962) held that in an action brought under URESA the defendant husband may not counterclaim for divorce. This indicates the somewhat limited scope of the Act. Hoover v. Hoover, 271 S.C. 177, 246 S.E.2d 179 (1978), held that issues of visitation could not be adjudicated in a URESA proceeding. See also Mahan v. Read, 240 N.C. 641, 83 S.E.2d 706 (1954) and Martin v. Martin, 58 Misc.2d 459, 296 N.Y.S.2d 453 (Fam.Ct.1968).

HAIGHT v. HAIGHT

Supreme Court of Oregon, 1965, Dept. 1.
241 Or. 532, 405 P.2d 622.

O'CONNELL, Justice. This is a suit brought by plaintiff wife in which she seeks a decree requiring defendant, her husband, to pay a monthly amount for the support of two children of the parties. Defendant appeals from a decree ordering defendant to pay $40 per month for each of the two children.

Plaintiff and defendant have four children. On August 14, 1964, when plaintiff instituted these proceedings, plaintiff and defendant had been separated for approximately two and one-half years. Each had custody of two of their children. The children in plaintiff's custody were 11 and 13; the children in defendant's custody were 10 and 14.

Plaintiff had previously brought a suit for divorce against defendant. Her complaint was dismissed by a decree of the trial court which was affirmed on appeal in Haight v. Haight, 235 Or. 238, 384 P.2d 151 (1963).

Plaintiff relies upon ORS 108.110 as the basis for her petition seeking support money for the children in her custody. ORS 108.110 provides as follows:

"Any married woman may apply to the circuit court of the county in which she resides or in which her husband may be found for an order upon her husband to provide for her support or for the support of her minor children, or both, and, if the woman is pregnant, her unborn child, or both, if he is the natural father of such children or unborn child or if he be the adoptive father of such children. Such woman may apply for the order by filing in such county a petition setting forth the facts and circumstances upon which she relies for such order. If satisfied that a just cause exists, the court shall direct that a citation issue to the husband requiring him to appear at a time set by the court to show cause why an order of support should not be entered in the matter. If it appears to the satisfaction of the court that such woman is without funds to employ counsel and is otherwise unable to obtain counsel, the court may make an order directing the district attorney to prepare such petition and citation."

The sole question on appeal is whether the foregoing statute is applicable to the case before us. We are of the opinion that it is not.

ORS 108.110 does not specify the circumstances under which a wife is entitled to an order of support for herself or for her children. The statute provides that the trial court shall direct that a citation issue to the husband to show cause why an order of support should not be entered if the court is "satisfied that a just cause exists." There is nothing in the record to show that there was a "just cause" for the order requiring defendant to support the children in plaintiff's custody.

The evidence shows that defendant is willing and able to support the children in his own home. Two of the children for whom support is sought are not in defendant's custody simply because plaintiff, without cause, decided not to live with her husband.

We shall assume, arguendo, that under these circumstances defendant would be required to support the children in his wife's custody when the welfare of the children would be better served thereby rather than by returning them to the custody of defendant. But this is not shown. The issue of the right to custody was not raised in the present proceedings. The trial judge stated: "I am not deciding the matter of custody today. All we have is the one issue, I believe, and that is whether or not he should pay any support." There is no evidence that the issue of custody was decided in the previous divorce proceeding or in any other proceeding. Without any evidence on the matter we cannot assume that the welfare of the children is better served by their being in the custody of their mother. Unless the welfare of the children would be jeopardized by returning them to the home of defendant, we can see no "just cause" for imposing upon a husband the obligation of supporting his children in another household simply because his wife, without any legally recognized reason for doing so, decides to take up residence separate from her husband. The cost of supporting children in two households will ordinarily be greater than the cost of supporting them under one roof. Unless the children are better off elsewhere the husband, who we may assume is not legally at fault, should not be required to bear this added expense.

Even in the absence of an added financial burden upon the husband, he should not be required to support the children in his wife's custody if he is not at fault and the welfare of the children would not be jeopardized were the children to be returned to their father. The maintenance of family unity is regarded as an essential element in the preservation of our form of society. That unity would be impaired by an interpretation of the statute urged by plaintiff because, in permitting the wife to obtain support of the children taken from the home without cause, she would feel less constrained to remain at home and make an effort to keep the family united.[1]

We express no view as to the interpretation of ORS 108.110 if the welfare of the children would be better served by their remaining in the custody of the errant wife.

* * *

The decree of the lower court is reversed.

NOTES AND QUESTIONS

1. What effect, if any, would the adoption of the Twenty-Seventh Amendment (the Equal Rights Amendment), or a state Equal Rights Amendment, have on the outcome of this case? What effect would such cases as Reed v. Reed, 404 U.S. 71 (1971), Frontiero v. Richardson, 411 U. S. 677 (1973), or Orr v. Orr, 440 U.S. 268 (1979), invalidating various forms of discrimination against women, have on the outcome of this case?

2. A case which seems to take a contrary position is Santa Clara County v. Hughes, 43 Misc.2d 559, 251 N.Y.S.2d 579 (Fam.Ct.1964), in which the court held that even though the wife took the children and went off to California, leaving the husband in New York in ignorance of where they had gone, the husband was nevertheless required to support the children. This was a case brought by the county in California which had provided support, asking reimbursement, using the procedure provided by the Uniform Reciprocal Enforcement of Support Act. Is this result preferable to that in Haight?

1. "* * * A basic public policy plays a part. The welfare of a child lies in a home with two normal, decent parents. Where there are such parents and a home, public policy dictates that the family unit be maintained. That a price must be paid for it by one or both parents is of no concern from the standpoint of the child. The courts should not, and in our view must not, declare as a matter of law or as a conclusion of fact that circumstances such as those depicted in this record constitute reasonable cause for the destruction of such a home. The welfare of the child dictates otherwise." Bartlett v. Bartlett, 94 U.S.App.D.C. 190, 221 F. 2d 508, 509, 514 (1954) (Concurring Opinion by Prettyman, J.).

3. Most of the states have lowered the age of majority from twenty-one to eighteen. The effect of this is to reduce by three years the period during which parents are responsible for the support of their children. The effect of this change upon outstanding child support decrees is described infra, at page 952. The extent to which and the circumstances in which parents may be required to support their children beyond the age of majority are discussed infra, at page 948. Other issues arising out of the duty to support children are discussed in connection with divorce, in Chapter 6, section 5, infra.

4. A non-legal discussion of the child support problem may be found in J. Cassetty, Child Support and Public Policy (1978).

PARKER v. STAGE

Court of Appeals of New York, 1977.
43 N.Y.2d 128, 400 N.Y.S.2d 794, 371 N.E.2d 513.

WACHTLER, Judge. The question on this appeal is whether the Department of Social Services can compel a father to pay for the support of his 18-year-old daughter after she has left his house, voluntarily and against his wishes, to live with her paramour and have a child. Both the Family Court and the Appellate Division held that, under the circumstances, the father should not be obligated to support his daughter even though she is receiving public assistance. The Commissioner of Social Services has appealed to this court by leave of the Appellate Division.

The facts developed at the Family Court hearing were not disputed. Respondent's daughter was born in September of 1956. Several years later the father and mother were divorced. After the divorce the girl remained in her father's custody. In early 1974 she informed her cousin that she intended to leave home to live with her paramour and have a child. Although neither she nor her boyfriend were employed, she said that she intended to support herself and her child by seeking public assistance. She did not return to school in the fall of 1974. In October, shortly after her 18th birthday, she left home while her father was at work. Nearly two weeks later he was able to locate her with the assistance of the police.

She returned home and for several months resided with her father, but only intermittently. For long periods of time she would "disappear". On each occasion her father accepted her back and continued to support her. He contacted her former guidance counselor and arranged for her to return to school. He informed her of this and continuously urged her to resume her schooling but she refused. She also refused to discuss her goals with him. At one point he helped her to obtain a job, but she quit after four weeks. For a time she was in a job training program but she quit that as well. Finally in the spring of 1975 she took up permanent residence with her paramour who was also unemployed.

In the fall of 1975 respondent's daughter gave birth to a child out of wedlock. She then applied for aid to dependent children and obtained public assistance for her child and for herself, as the mother of an eligible child (Social Services Law, § 349). In February, 1976 the Commissioner of Social Services of Orange County commenced this proceeding in the Family Court to compel the respondent to contribute toward his daughter's support. The proceeding was brought pursuant to subdivision 3 of section 101-a of the Social Services Law which authorizes a social services official to institute a support proceeding against a parent or other responsible relative if the applicant or recipient of public assistance "fails" to do so.

At the conclusion of the hearing the Family Court Judge dismissed the petition on the ground that respondent's daughter, by leaving home to live with her paramour and have his child, had "emancipated herself from her father and his household * * * and * * * as a result of that emancipation, the respondent is relieved of any obligation to support" her.

The Appellate Division unanimously affirmed. * * *

On appeal to our court the commissioner admits that respondent's daughter "willfully abandoned her home with her father" and thus would be unable to compel him to support her if she had brought the suit on her own behalf. The commissioner argues however that when the suit is brought by a social welfare official pursuant to section 101 of the Social Services Law the duty to support "is absolute upon a showing of sufficient ability on the part of the parent. There is no other qualification or exception in the statute."

Initially it should be noted that even in a case like Matter of Roe v. Doe when the suit is brought directly on the child's behalf pursuant to section 413 of the Family Court Act, the father's obligation to support is stated in mandatory terms. Our determination in that case, that a child who voluntarily and without good cause abandons the parent's home "forfeits her right to demand support" is not based on any express statutory exception. It rests on the State policy of fostering "the integrity of the family" by precluding the courts from interfering in the special relationship between parent and child, absent "a showing of misconduct, neglect or abuse" (Matter of Roe v. Doe, supra, 29 N.Y.2d pp. 191, 194, 324 N.Y.S.2d pp. 73, 75, 272 N.E. 2d pp. 568, 570). It recognizes that the father's obligation to support includes the right to exercise parental control and guidance even though the child may be old enough "to elect not to comply" (Matter of Roe v. Roe, supra, p. 194, 324 N.Y.S.2d p. 75, 272 N.E.2d p. 570).

The question then is whether a different policy applies when the suit is brought by a public welfare official to compel a father to support a child who would otherwise become a public charge.

It was once the policy of this State to place the financial burden of supporting needy individuals upon designated relatives, rather than the public, in order to reduce the amount of welfare expenditures (see, e. g., Foster, Freed & Midonick, Child Support: The Quick and the Dead, 26 Syracuse L.Rev. 1157, 1162). Thus the common-law obligation to support wife and minor children was expanded by statute to include adult children, grandchildren and parents when they would otherwise become public charges (see, e. g., former Domestic Relations Ct. Act, § 101, subds. 1, 4, 5; former Children's Ct. Act, § 31, subds. 4, 5; Family Ct. Act, former § 415).

In recent years however the Legislature relented. The laws were amended to relieve individuals of the obligation to support grandchildren (L.1965, ch. 674, § 1), adult children and parents (L.1966, ch. 256) who were unemployed and destitute. Thereafter the burden passed to the public. In a message accompanying the 1966 bill the Governor noted that this was in part prompted by the need to comply with Federal law in order to qualify for Federal financial assistance. But he also noted that "Experience has shown that the financial responsibility of a broad class of relatives, imposed by statute, is more often a destructive, rather than cohesive, factor in family unity" (McKinney's Session Laws of N.Y., 1966, pp. 2989, 2990). Thus the legislative history shows that the current statutory scheme recognizes the need to preserve family unity even though the consequence is to place needy relatives on the public welfare rolls.

In addition the Legislature has expressly granted the courts discretionary powers in these cases. A father, of course, is still generally obligated to support his children until they are 21 years of age (Family Ct. Act, §§ 413, 415; Social Services Law, § 101, subd. 1; cf. Domestic Relations Law, § 32, subd. 2). And public welfare officials may seek to enforce the obligation if the child is an applicant for or recipient of public assistance (Social Services Law, § 102, subd. 1; § 101-a, subd. 3; Family Ct. Act, § 422, subd. [a]). But in such cases the obligation is not absolute. Section 415 of the Family Court Act states: "The spouse or parent of a recipient of public assistance or care or of a person liable to become in need thereof or of a patient in an institution in the department of mental hygiene, if of sufficient ability, is responsible for the support of such person or patient, provided that a parent shall be responsible only for the support of his child or children who have not attained the age of twenty-one years. *In its discretion*, the court may require any such person to contribute a fair and reasonable sum for the support of such relative and may apportion the costs of such support among such persons as may be just and appropriate in view of the needs of the petitioner and the other circumstances of the case and their respective means". (Emphasis added.) The committee which drafted the Family Court Act noted in its report that section 415 consolidated certain sections from prior laws "but substitutes for the current mandatory language a discretionary provision." The change was designed to permit the courts to refuse to compel support when it might lead to an injustice in a particular case (see Committee Comment to Family Ct. Act, § 415, McKinney's Cons. Laws of N.Y., Book 29A, p. 259).

In sum we cannot agree with the commissioner that whenever an older child chooses to leave home, for any reason, the parents must pay for the child's separate maintenance, or contribute support, if the child applies for public assistance. The courts must still consider the impact on the family relationship and the possibility of injustice in the particular case. Of course the fact that the child is eligible for public assistance may, as is evident her, [sic] permit her to avoid her father's authority and demands however reasonable they may be. But it does not follow that the parent must then finish what has been begun by underwriting the lifestyle which his daughter chose against his reasonable wishes and repeated counsel.

It should be emphasized that this is not a case of an abandoned child, but of an abandoned parent. There is nothing to indicate that the respondent abused his daughter or placed unreasonable demands upon her. There is no showing that he actively drove her from her home or encouraged her to leave in order to have the public assume his obligation of support. Indeed the contrary appears to be true. The undisputed proof in this record establishes that the father continuously supported his daughter from birth; that he urged her to remain at home and continue her schooling; that he was a forgiving parent who always accepted her back after her absences and that he made efforts to obtain employment for her. We simply hold that under these circumstances the courts below could properly refuse to compel him to pay for her support when she chose to leave home to live with her paramour.

Accordingly, the order of the Appellate Division should be affirmed.

NOTES AND QUESTIONS

1. The earlier New York case of Roe v. Doe, cited in the *Parker* case, is noted in 46 St.J.L.Rev. 139 (1971). New York is one of the states in which children still have the right to be supported until age twenty-one. N.Y.Dom.Rel.L. § 32 (1977). The same statute places primary responsibility for child support on the father, which would seem to be unconstitutional under Orr v. Orr, 440 U.S. 268 (1979). For a discussion of the New York law on child support, see Foster, Freed, Midonick, Child Support: The Quick and the Dead, 26 Syr.L.Rev. 1157 (1975).

2. Is the age of the child in *Parker* relevant? For example, would the father have a defense when sued either by his daughter or the state for support of the daughter if she were fourteen years old and a persistent runaway? Or if she were sixteen and married? Earlier cases are cited in Annot., 32 A.L.R.3d 1055 (1970). See Suire v. Miller, 363 So.2d 945 (La. App.1978).

3. Does the *Parker* case give rise to the inference that if the child had remained at home but thought that her father was not supporting her ade-

quately, she could sue him and thereby obtain a higher level of support, assuming of course that he was capable of paying it? The closely related question of the parent's liability for private school or college expenses of his children is dealt with in Chapter 6, section 5, infra, in connection with child support orders in divorce decrees.

4. Would it be preferable in a case like *Parker* to order the father to support his child on condition that father and child participate in some family counseling sessions as a way of resolving their disagreement about where and how the daughter would live? If the counseling produced no resolution of the conflict, the court could then excuse further duty of support by the father.

5. The Supreme Court has held that a statute which establishes different ages for the support of males and females is unconstitutional. Stanton v. Stanton, 421 U.S. 7 (1975). The comical but undignified response of the Utah Supreme Court to the United States Supreme Court's mandate is found in Stanton v. Stanton, 552 P.2d 112 (Utah 1976), which in turn called forth another United States Supreme Court opinion in Stanton v. Stanton, 429 U.S. 501 (1977), followed by still another Utah opinion in Stanton v. Stanton, 564 P.2d 303 (Utah 1977). Public disrespect for courts and lawyers is hardly surprising in the face of this kind of behavior.

6. In many, probably most, American states the age of majority is now eighteen for all purposes including the right of support. The somewhat unusual cases in which support may be decreed for a son or daughter over the age of majority are discussed in Chapter 6, section 5, infra. The cases dealing with the question whether the reduction in the age of majority from twenty-one to eighteen affects rights under preexisting decrees are not in agreement, partly due to differences in the wording of the statute or of the decree or of an underlying separation agreement. See, e. g., Annot., 75 A.L.R.3d 228 (1977); Note, 8 Akron L.Rev. 338 (1975); Note, 23 Kan. L.Rev. 181 (1974); Note, 11 Willamette L.J. 70 (1974) collecting the cases.

IN RE H

Supreme Court of California, In Bank, 1970.
2 Cal.3d 513, 86 Cal.Rptr. 76, 468 P.2d 204.

BURKE, Justice. Petitioner is a 17-year-old juvenile committed to the custody of the California Youth Authority and presently detained at the O. H. Close School for Boys, having participated in a burglary. Prior to and during the proceedings in juvenile court which led to his commitment, petitioner was correctly advised that he had the right to be represented by counsel at all stages of the proceedings, and that if he could not afford to retain his own counsel, or if his parents failed to provide counsel for him, the court would appoint counsel to represent him. However, petitioner was also advised that since his father was employed, the county would be entitled to reimbursement from him for the cost of appointed counsel.[1]

1. Welfare and Institutions Code section 903.1 provides: "The father, mother, spouse, or other person liable for the support of a minor person, * * * shall be liable for the cost to the county of legal services ren-

Petitioner, whose father was already indebted to the county for the cost of petitioner's prior detentions,[2] elected to waive his right to appointed counsel rather than cause his father to incur additional obligations to the county. Consequently, at the hearing on the petition to declare petitioner a ward of the court, petitioner formally waived counsel, admitted the truth of the petition's allegations, and was thereupon committed to the custody of the Youth Authority in accordance with the recommendations of the probation department.

Petitioner now challenges the validity of section 903.1 of the Welfare and Institutions Code, which makes parents and other responsible relatives liable to the county for the cost of legal services rendered to the minor in juvenile court proceedings. We have concluded that section 903.1 must be upheld as reasonably necessary and proper to carry out the goals which underlie the juvenile court program. However, we have also concluded that petitioner should not have been permitted to waive counsel to avoid the operation of section 903.1, as a purported waiver made by a minor under such circumstances is neither voluntary nor intelligent, and is therefore ineffective.

Petitioner first contends that section 903.1 unreasonably and arbitrarily discriminates against the parents of indigent juveniles, thereby denying petitioner and his parents equal protection of the laws. (U.S.Const., 14th Amend., § 1; Cal.Const., art. I, §§ 11, 21.) Petitioner relies on Department of Mental Hygiene v. Hawley, 59 Cal.2d 247, 28 Cal.Rptr. 718, 379 P.2d 22, and Dept. of Mental Hygiene v. Kirchner, 60 Cal.2d 716, 36 Cal.Rptr. 488, 388 P.2d 720, remanded 380 U.S. 194, 85 S.Ct. 871, 13 L.Ed.2d 753, subsequent opin-

dered to the minor by the public defender pursuant to the order of the juvenile court, or for the cost to the county for legal services rendered to the minor by private attorney appointed pursuant to the order of the juvenile court. The liability of such persons (in this article called relatives) and estates shall be a joint and several liability."

Section 903.1 contemplates that reimbursement will be sought only from parents or other relatives having the ability to pay for counsel. (See § 700, supra, fn. 2.) Thus, section 907 authorizes an investigation to determine whether the minor's relatives are financially able to pay the charges provided for in section 903.1, et al., and section 905 authorizes the county to reduce or cancel these charges upon proof that the minor's relatives are unable to pay them.

In the instant case, petitioner was allegedly told that the public defender would charge $35 to represent him. Petitioner was also advised of a "possibility" that the court might appoint private counsel at no cost to himself or his parents. Although petitioner failed to request the court to appoint private counsel at no charge, his neglect was excusable, since the applicable statutory provisions and especially section 903.1, expressly require reimbursement of counsel fees charged by both the public defender and private counsel.

2. Section 903 of the Welfare and Institutions Code imposes liability upon the minor's parents and other responsible relatives for the cost of care and support of the minor while he is confined in any county institution pursuant to order of the juvenile court.

ion 62 Cal.2d 586, 43 Cal.Rptr. 329, 400 P.2d 321, which invalidated certain "responsible relatives" legislation on similar grounds.

In considering petitioner's challenge we must keep in mind that section 903.1 was enacted subsequent to our decisions in *Hawley* and *Kirchner*. Consequently, "Such deliberate acts of the Legislature come before us clothed with a presumption of constitutionality. 'All presumptions and intendments favor the validity of a statute and mere doubt does not afford sufficient reason for a judicial declaration of invalidity. Statutes must be upheld unless their unconstitutionality clearly, positively and unmistakably appears. [Citations].' "
* * *

This court invalidated the legislation involved in the *Hawley* and *Kirchner* cases primarily because of our conviction that the state, rather than any arbitrarily selected group of private citizens, should bear the cost of such state functions as supporting persons committed to state institutions for the benefit and protection of the general public. As stated in *Kirchner*, "Whether the commitment is incidental to an alleged violation of a penal statute, as in *Hawley*, or is essentially a civil commitment as in the instant case, the purposes of confinement and treatment or care in either case encompass the protection of society from the confined person, and his own protection and possible reclamation as a productive member of the body politic. Hence the cost of maintaining the state institution, including provision of adequate care for its inmates, cannot be *arbitrarily* charged to one class in the society; such assessment violates the equal protection clause." (Italics added; 60 Cal.2d at p. 720, 36 Cal.Rptr., at p. 490, 388 P.2d at p. 722.)

In the instant case, the statutory provisions entitling an indigent juvenile to be represented by appointed counsel in juvenile court proceedings were enacted for the protection and preservation of the minor's constitutional rights (see In re Gault, 387 U.S. 1, 34–42, 87 S.Ct. 1428, 18 L.Ed.2d 527), rather than for the protection of society generally. As stated in In re Dennis M., supra, 70 Cal.2d 444, 456, 75 Cal.Rptr. 1, 8, 450 P.2d 296, 303, "[I]n adult criminal prosecutions * * * a major goal is corrective confinement of the defendant for the protection of society. But even after *Gault* as we have seen, juvenile proceedings retain a *sui generis* character: although certain basic rules of due process must be observed, the proceedings are nevertheless conducted for the protection and benefit of the youth in question." Thus, the rationale of *Hawley* and *Kirchner,* prohibiting the state from recouping the cost of social welfare programs from private sources, is less compelling when applied to section 903.1.
* * *

Moreover, *Hawley* involved the liability of a father for the care of his insane adult son, who had been charged with the murder of his mother, and *Kirchner* involved the liability of a daughter for the care of her mentally ill mother. Neither case concerned the discharge of common-law support obligations, since "At common law there was no liability on a child to support parents, or on parents to support an adult child. [Citations.]" (Dept. of Mental Hygiene v. Kirchner, supra, 60 Cal.2d 716, 718, fn. 4, 36 Cal.Rptr. 488, 489, 388 P.2d 720, 721.)

The instant case, on the other hand, presents questions regarding the extent of the parents' obligation to support their minor children, an obligation which did exist at common law. * * *

Several recent cases have distinguished *Hawley* and *Kirchner* on the ground that those cases did not involve common-law support obligations. (In re Shaieb, 250 Cal.App.2d 553, 557–558, 58 Cal.Rptr. 631 [parent-minor child]; Department of Mental Hygiene v. Kolts, 247 Cal.App.2d 154, 157, 163, 55 Cal.Rptr. 437 [husband-wife]; Dept. of Mental Hygiene v. O'Connor, 246 Cal.App.2d 24, 27–29, 54 Cal. Rptr. 432 [husband-wife]; County of Alameda v. Espinoza, supra, 243 Cal.App.2d 534, 541–544, 52 Cal.Rptr. 480 [parent-minor child]; In re Dudley, 239 Cal.App.2d 401, 408–409, 48 Cal.Rptr. 790 [parent-minor child]; County of Alameda v. Kaiser, supra, 238 Cal.App.2d 815, 818, 48 Cal.Rptr. 343 [parent-minor child]). The *Espinoza* and *Shaieb* cases, supra, upheld the validity of section 903 of the Welfare and Institutions Code, which obligates the parents, spouse, or other person liable for the minor's support, to reimburse the county for the cost of supporting the minor in county facilities pursuant to juvenile court law.

Therefore, if the expenses incurred in procuring counsel to represent the minor in juvenile court proceedings are properly chargeable to the parents as an element of their preexisting support obligation, the reasoning of the foregoing cases should apply, and section 903.1 should be upheld.

Speaking generally of the necessity of representation in criminal proceedings, the United States Supreme Court has stated that "lawyers in criminal courts are necessities, not luxuries." (Gideon v. Wainwright, 372 U.S. 335, 344, 83 S.Ct. 792, 796, 9 L.Ed.2d 799.) The court made the same observation in the context of juvenile proceedings which could involve a loss of liberty: "The child 'requires the guiding hand of counsel at every step in the proceedings against him.'" (In re Gault, supra, 387 U.S. 1, 36, 87 S.Ct. 1428, 1448.) Consequently, it would be anamolous [sic] to suggest that the parental support obligation extends to furnishing food, clothing, shelter and medical care, but not legal assistance essential to protect and preserve the minor's constitutional rights.

There exists substantial authority holding that counsel fees incurred on behalf of a minor child are in the nature of "necessaries" for which the parents are liable. * * *

Moreover, a parent's support obligation does not end with furnishing mere necessaries, for the minor is entitled to be maintained in a style and condition consonant with his parent's financial ability and position in society.   *   *   *

The foregoing authorities are especially persuasive as applied to the instant case wherein, in the words of petitioner's counsel, "the minor has been previously incarcerated and the threat of long-term detention is present." We conclude that section 903.1 is merely declarative of the parents' preexisting obligation to provide reasonable and necessary support to their minor children, and to reimburse third persons providing that support upon the parents' failure to do so. (See Civ.Code, §§ 207, 248.) Consequently, the imposition of liability for counsel fees under section 903.1 cannot be characterized as arbitrary or a denial of equal protection of the laws.

Petitioner points out that presently there exist no statutory provisions imposing upon indigent adults, or their parents, any obligation to reimburse the county for the cost of appointed counsel in criminal proceedings. However, the fact that the Legislature has not acted in other areas is not necessarily dispositive, for "The Legislature is not bound, in order to adopt a constitutionally valid statute, to extend it to all cases which might possibly be reached, but is free to recognize degrees of harm and to confine its regulation to those classes of cases in which the need is deemed to be the most evident." (Board of Education, etc. v. Watson, 63 Cal.2d 829, 833, 48 Cal.Rptr. 481, 484, 409 P. 2d 481, 484;   *   *   *. The Legislature could well have determined that legislation requiring reimbursement of costs in juvenile court proceedings had a greater priority or urgency than comparable legislation in other areas, or that the likelihood of ultimately obtaining reimbursement from indigent adults was too minimal to justify the cost of administering such legislation.

Although statutes which affect a particular class must be based upon rational distinctions or classifications   *   *   *   there is no constitutional requirement of uniform treatment   *   *   *   Class legislation is not arbitrary if it is based upon some difference or distinction having a substantial relation to the purpose of the statute   *   *   *   This court must presume that section 903.1 is based upon a valid classification.   *   *   *

Moreover, it is apparent that the reimbursement provision is reasonably necessary to accomplish valid legislative purposes. First, reimbursement obviously assists the various counties in meeting the increasing cost of providing appointed counsel for indigent juveniles. *   *   *   To invalidate the reimbursement provision could endanger the entire juvenile court program.

Secondly, section 903.1 helps promote the substantive aims underlying that program by encouraging parents and children alike to avoid further acts of delinquency. As stated in County of Alameda v.

Espinoza, supra, 243 Cal.App.2d 534, 547, 52 Cal.Rptr. 480, 489, which upheld Welfare and Institutions Code section 903, requiring parents and other responsible relatives to reimburse the county for the cost of supporting juveniles committed to county facilities, "It is not facetious to state that making a parent aware of his obligation to support his child commensurate with his ability may affect his desire to make a change in conditions which will enable the child to accomplish a better adjustment under the parental roof." The court noted that the alternative of relieving the parent of all responsibility is hardly conducive of future parental cooperation in any corrective program with which it is expected that the parents will assist.

Thus, we conclude that there is no merit to petitioner's contention that section 903.1 unreasonably or arbitrarily denies him or his parents equal protection of the laws.

Petitioner also contends that section 903.1 impermissibly restrains or "chills" the free exercise of the constitutional right to counsel. Of course, petitioner does not contend that the reimbursement condition itself constitutes a denial of that right. Just as a nonindigent adult has no constitutional right to appointed counsel in a criminal case * * * neither does a minor have a constitutional right to appointed counsel without reference to the financial status of his parents. As stated in In re Gault, supra, 387 U.S. 1, 41, 87 S.Ct. 1428, 1451, which established the right to counsel in juvenile proceedings: "We conclude that the Due Process Clause of the Fourteenth Amendment requires that in respect of proceedings to determine delinquency which may result in commitment to an institution in which the juvenile's freedom is curtailed, the child and his parents must be notified of the child's right to be represented by counsel retained by them, or if *they* are unable to afford counsel, that counsel will be appointed to represent the child." (Italics added.)

Petitioner relies upon In re Allen, supra, 71 A.C. 409, 78 Cal. Rptr. 207, 455 P.2d 143, wherein this court declared invalid the condition in a grant of probation requiring the probationer to reimburse the county for the cost of appointed counsel. We reasoned that the widespread use of such a condition in grants of probation could unnecessarily discourage the free exercise of the constitutional right to appointed counsel by indigent defendants. As we stated in *Allen* (pp. 411–412, 78 Cal.Rptr. p. 208, 455 P.2d p. 144), "The government is without constitutional authority to impose a predetermined condition on the exercise of a constitutional right or penalize in some manner its use. [Citations.] Thus, in finding unconstitutional the statute involved in *Jackson,* supra [United States v. Jackson, 390 U.S. 570, 88 S.Ct. 1209, 20 L.Ed.2d 138], the court declared that 'Whatever might be said of Congress' objectives, they cannot be pursued by means that needlessly chill the exercise of basic constitutional rights. * * * The question is not whether the chilling effect is "incidental" rather than international; the question is whether the effect is unnecessary and therefore excessive.' "

In *Allen,* the chilling effect of the probation condition was unnecessary and excessive. Although the county may have had a legitimate interest in obtaining reimbursement from persons with an ability to repay counsel costs, that interest could have been promoted without duress, without threatening to withhold or suspend valuable probation privileges. The court in United States v. Jackson, supra, 390 U.S. 570, 582–583, 88 S.Ct. 1209, cited as controlling in *Allen,* suggested that the existence of reasonable alternative procedures for accomplishing valid state purposes is a significant factor in determining whether statutory provisions needlessly chill the exercise of constitutional rights.

Moreover, we pointed out in *Allen* that there is a basic inconsistency and unfairness in advising an indigent defendant of his right to the free services of an attorney, and subsequently requiring reimbursement, in an amount concerning which defendant had no voice. (71 A.C. at pp. 413–414, 78 Cal.Rptr. 207, 455 P.2d 143.)

The considerations which impelled us to strike down the probation condition in *Allen* do not require us to invalidate section 903.1. Unlike the petitioner in *Allen,* petitioner herein was advised in advance that his father could be charged with the cost of appointed counsel, and petitioner does not claim that the fee involved was unreasonable or excessive. Moreover, in the instant case no unfair or unnecessary threat was made to withhold probation or other privileges unless counsel fees were reimbursed.

Nevertheless, it is conceivable that the reimbursement requirement of section 903.1 could, under certain circumstances, cast an undesirable chill upon the minor's free exercise of the right to appointed counsel. However, rather than invalidate that section and thereby defeat the worthy legislative purposes which underlie it, we have concluded that the juvenile court should not permit minors to waive their right to appointed counsel for the purpose of avoiding the operation of the reimbursement requirement.

Sections 634 and 700 of the Welfare and Institutions Code require the appointment of counsel "unless there is an *intelligent* waiver of the right of counsel by the minor." (Italics added.) Moreover, this court has adopted a policy of reviewing the "totality of circumstances" in each particular case, to determine whether or not the minor has knowingly, intelligently and voluntarily waived his constitutional rights including right to counsel. *   *   *

There are numerous authorities holding that a purported waiver of constitutional rights which is induced by fear, coercion or threats is wholly ineffective. *   *   *

As stated in *Gault,* supra, involving waiver of the privilege against self-incrimination by a minor: "We appreciate that special problems may arise with respect to waiver of the privilege by or on behalf of children   *   *   *   If counsel was not present for some permissible reason when an admission was obtained, the greatest care must be taken to assure that the admission was voluntary, in the sense not only that it was not coerced or suggested, but also that it was not the product of ignorance of rights or of adolescent fantasy, fright, or despair."   (387 U.S. at p. 55, 87 S.Ct. at p. 1458.)

It is apparent that a waiver of appointed counsel made to avoid or reduce parental pressure or displeasure can be characterized as neither intelligent nor voluntary, being in essence the product of coercion or fear. Therefore, in any case where, having been fully advised of his rights thereto, a minor of nonindigent parents purports to waive appointed counsel, the juvenile court should refuse to permit the waiver if the circumstances indicate to the court that such extraneous and improper factors are substantially influencing the minor's decision.

     *   *   *

The order to show cause is discharged and a writ of habeas corpus is granted. The order of commitment of August 6, 1969, is vacated and petitioner is discharged from the custody of the California Youth Authority.

NOTES AND QUESTIONS

1. The *Kirchner* case, cited in the principal case, was a suit by the California Department of Mental Hygiene to recover from the estate of a daughter the expense of caring for the daughter's mentally ill mother in a state hospital for the mentally ill. A statute provided that the husband, wife, father, mother or children of a mentally ill person should be liable for the support of such person in a state institution. The court denied recovery, holding that the statute violated the equal protection clause of the state constitution. The reasoning was that "*   *   *   the purposes of confinement and treatment or care in either case encompass the protection of society from the confined person, and his own protection and possible reclamation as a productive member of the body politic. Hence the cost of maintaining the state institution, including provision of adequate care for its inmates, cannot be arbitrarily charged to one class in the society; such assessment violates the equal protection clause." At a later point in the opinion the court suggested that the statute violated the equal protection clause by selecting a particular class of persons for a species of taxation without rational basis for the classification.

The *Kirchner* case was widely commented upon. See, e. g., Note, 49 Corn.L.Q. 516 (1964); Note, 77 Harv.L.Rev. 1523 (1964); Note, 16 Hast. L.J. 129 (1964); Note, 13 Kan.L.Rev. 298 (1964); Note, 12 U.C.L.A.L.Rev. 605 (1965). Professor tenBroek called *Kirchner* a landmark decision and stated that "The principle enunciated applies with equal force to the relatives of other public aid recipients." tenBroek, California's Dual System of Family Law: Its Origin, Development, and Present Status, 17 Stan.L.Rev. 614, 638, 639 (1965). Many cases contrary to *Kirchner* are collected in Annot., 20 A.L.R.3d 363 (1968).

The New York Court of Appeals has held that a statute did not deny equal protection in requiring the parent of a child committed to a state institution as a juvenile delinquent to reimburse the state for his support. In re Jesmer v. Dundon, 29 N.Y.2d 5, 323 N.Y.S.2d 417, 271 N.E.2d 905 (1971), appeal dismissed, 404 U.S. 953 (1971).

2. How does the court in In re H distinguish the *Kirchner* case? Is the distinction persuasive?

3. As the court in In re H points out, several California cases subsequent to *Kirchner* have purported to distinguish it. Some of them made the distinction turn on the difference in relationship, some on the fact that there was a common law duty of support rather than solely a statutory duty, some on the purpose of the commitment, that is, that it was made for the purpose of benefiting the person committed rather than to protect the public. Are these distinctions valid? See Note, Relatives' Support Liability: Two Years After *Kirchner*, 18 Hast.L.J. 720 (1967). Or do these cases and In re H suggest that Kirchner is no longer law in California?

4. Statutes like that in In re H and in *Kirchner* are quite common in the various states. In addition many states have statutes imposing a general duty of supporting indigent persons upon named relatives, with the right to enforce that duty being given either to the indigent person or to the state where the state has been furnishing support, or to both. See H. Clark, Law of Domestic Relations, 213 (1968), and Mandelker, Family Responsibility Under the American Poor Laws, 54 Mich.L.Rev. 497, 607 (1956). The relatives upon whom the support obligations are imposed vary, some states limiting them to spouses and children, others including grandparents and grandchildren and a few including brothers and sisters.

Some questions raised by these statutes are:

(a) Are they unconstitutional under the *Kirchner* case or on any other theory, such as the Equal Protection Clause? See tenBroek, California's Dual System of Family Law: Its Origin, Development, and Present Status, 17 Stan.L.Rev. 614, 640–646 (1965); Lopes, Filial Support and Family Solidarity, 6 Pac.L.J. 508 (1975); Levy and Gross, Constitutional Implications of Parental Support Laws, 13 U.Rich.L.Rev. 517 (1979).

(b) Most such statutes impose the duty of support only where the obligor has sufficient means to provide it. How should this limitation be construed? For example, would the obligor be required to restrict his own scale of living or that of his immediate family in order to provide for an aged parent? See Mandelker, Family Responsibility Under the American Poor Laws, 54 Mich.L.Rev. 497, 522 (1956).

(c) What should be the obligor's responsibility where he is required to support more than one indigent relative? Must he contribute equally to the support of each?

(d) What should be the result if several children are responsible for the support of a single indigent parent? If one of the children is substantially better off financially than the others, should he be required to bear a greater share of the burden of support? Mandelker, 54 Mich.L.Rev. 607, 618.

(e) D lives in Texas. He has an aged mother living in California who has been receiving public assistance from the state of California. A California statute makes children civilly liable for the support of indigent parents, but Texas has no such statute. The state of California sues D in Texas to recover the support so furnished. What should be the result? State of California v. Copus, 158 Tex. 196, 309 S.W.2d 227, 67 A.L.R.2d 758 (1958), cert. den. 356 U.S. 967 (1958), 57 Mich.L.Rev. 116 (1958); Commonwealth of Pa. ex rel. Dept., etc. v. Mong, 160 Ohio St. 455, 117 N.E.2d 32 (1954).

(f) Would the result in the preceding problem be different if D had investigated in advance, found that California had an especially good program of care for the aged, and had sent his mother there for that reason?

(g) Would the result in problem (e) be different if the state of California had had a "long-arm" statute providing for service by mail on a non-resident obligor where his indigent relative lives in California, and the suit were brought in California, serving D by mail in Texas?

(h) Would the result in problem (e) be different if the suit were brought by California in California under the Uniform Reciprocal Enforcement of Support Act, and then forwarded in accordance with that Act to Texas?

(i) Would the result in problem (e) be different if California had managed to get a California judgment against D, and then sued him in Texas on the California judgment? Bjorgo v. Bjorgo, 402 S.W.2d 143 (Tex. 1966).

(j) D, living in New York, has a mentally ill mother living in a California mental hospital. The state of California sues D in New York for reimbursement of the expenses of caring for D's mother. The *Kirchner* case held the California statute under which reimbursement is due unconstitutional, but the law of New York is that such statutes are valid. Should the New York court give judgment for California for these expenses?

SECTION 5. THE CARE AND SUPERVISION OF CHILDREN: THE RESPONSIBILITIES OF THE PARENT AND THE POWER OF THE STATE

INTRODUCTORY NOTE

The subject of children's "rights" is one of the most, if not the most, litigated and debated subjects in the entire field of domestic relations. The debate straddles analytical lines and concerns the conflicts between the interests of parents and those of the state; between the interests of children and those of the parents; and between the interests of children and those of the state. A particular case may involve all three kinds of conflict. The cases which follow have been separated into various classifications merely in order to make the class discussion of them a bit more manageable than it might otherwise be. All of them may be considered in one way or another as involving broad issues of the definition and functions of the contemporary family and the extent to which the state has invaded those functions or should invade them. Some of these issues have already been raised in connection with the cases on the involuntary termination of parental rights in section 3C of Chapter 5, and students should refresh their recollections of those cases at this point.

Some law review discussions of this broad subject, reflecting a variety of points of view include Skolnick, The Limits of Childhood: Conceptions of Child Development and Social Context, 38 L. & Contemp.Prob. 38 (No. 3, 1975); Burt, Developing Constitutional Rights of, in, and for Children, 39 L. & Contemp.Prob. 118 (No. 3, 1975); Hafen, Children's Liberation and the New Egalitarianism: Some Reservations About Abandoning Youth to Their "Rights", 1976 B.Y.U.L. Rev. 605; Levy, The Rights of Parents, 1976 B.Y.U.L.Rev. 693; Goode, State Intervention and the Family: Problems of Policy, 1976 B.Y.U.L.Rev. 715; Solnit, Child-Rearing and Child Advocacy, 1976 B.Y.U.L.Rev. 723; Note, State Intrusion Into Family Affairs: Justifications and Limitations, 26 Stan.L.Rev. 1383 (1974).

A. STATE REGULATION OF THE CHILD'S EDUCATION

WISCONSIN v. YODER

Supreme Court of the United States, 1972.
406 U.S. 205, 92 S.Ct. 1526, 32 L.Ed.2d 15.

Mr. Chief Justice BURGER delivered the opinion of the Court.

On petition of the State of Wisconsin, we granted the writ of certiorari in this case to review a decision of the Wisconsin Supreme Court holding that respondents' convictions of violating the State's compulsory school-attendance law were invalid under the Free Exercise Clause of the First Amendment to the United States Constitution made applicable to the States by the Fourteenth Amendment. For the reasons hereafter stated we affirm the judgment of the Supreme Court of Wisconsin.

Respondents Jonas Yoder and Wallace Miller are members of the Old Order Amish religion, and respondent Adin Yutzy is a member of the Conservative Amish Mennonite Church. They and their families are residents of Green County, Wisconsin. Wisconsin's compulsory school-attendance law required them to cause their children to attend public or private school until reaching age 16, but the respondents declined to send their children, ages 14 and 15, to public school after completing the eighth grade.[1] The children were not enrolled in any private school, or within any recognized exception to the compulso-

---

1. The children, Frieda Yoder, aged 15, Barbara Miller, aged 15, and Vernon Yutzy, aged 14, were all graduates of the eighth grade of public school.

ry-attendance law,[2] and they are conceded to be subject to the Wisconsin statute.

On complaint of the school district administrator for the public schools, respondents were charged, tried, and convicted of violating the compulsory-attendance law in Green County Court and were fined the sum of $5 each.[3] Respondents defended on the ground that the application of the compulsory-attendance law violated their rights under the First and Fourteenth Amendments.[4] The trial testimony

2. Wis.Stat. § 118.15 (1969) provides in pertinent part:

"**118.15 Compulsory school attendance**

"(1)(a) Unless the child has a legal excuse or has graduated from high school, any person having under his control a child who is between the ages of 7 and 16 years shall cause such child to attend school regularly during the full period and hours, religious holidays excepted, that the public or private school in which such child should be enrolled is in session until the end of the school term, quarter or semester of the school year in which he becomes 16 years of age.

* * *

"(3) This section does not apply to any child who is not in proper physical or mental condition to attend school, to any child exempted for good cause by the school board of the district in which the child resides or to any child who has completed the full 4-year high school course. The certificate of a reputable physician in general practice shall be sufficient proof that a child is unable to attend school.

"(4) Instruction during the required period elsewhere than at school may be substituted for school attendance. Such instruction must be approved by the state superintendent as substantially equivalent to instruction given to children of like ages in the public or private schools where such children reside.

"(5) Whoever violates this section * * * may be fined not less than $5 nor more than $50 or imprisoned not more than 3 months or both."

Section 118.15(1)(b) requires attendance to age 18 in a school district containing a "vocational, technical and adult education school," but this section is concededly inapplicable in this case, for there is no such school in the district involved.

3. Prior to trial, the attorney for respondents wrote the State Superintendent of Public Instruction in an effort to explore the possibilities for a compromise settlement. Among other possibilities, he suggested that perhaps the State Superintendent could administratively determine that the Amish could satisfy the compulsory-attendance law by establishing their own vocational training plan similar to one that has been established in Pennsylvania. Supp.App. 6. Under the Pennsylvania plan, Amish children of high school age are required to attend an Amish vocational school for three hours a week, during which time they are taught such subjects as English, mathematics, health, and social studies by an Amish teacher. For the balance of the week, the children perform farm and household duties under parental supervision, and keep a journal of their daily activities. The major portion of the curriculum is home projects in agriculture and homemaking. See generally J. Hostetler & G. Huntington, Children in Amish Society (1971); Socialization and Community Education, c. 5 (1971). A similar program has been instituted in Indiana. Ibid. See also Iowa Code § 299.24 (1971); Kan.Stat.Ann. § 72–1111 (Supp.1971).

The Superintendent rejected this proposal on the ground that it would not afford Amish children "substantially equivalent education" to that offered in the schools of the area. Supp. App. 6.

4. The First Amendment provides: "Congress shall make no law respecting an establishment of religion, or prohibiting the free exercise thereof * * *."

showed that respondents believed, in accordance with the tenets of Old Order Amish communities generally, that their children's attendance at high school, public or private, was contrary to the Amish religion and way of life. They believed that by sending their children to high school, they would not only expose themselves to the danger of the censure of the church community, but, as found by the county court, also endanger their own salvation and that of their children. The State stipulated that respondents' religious beliefs were sincere.

In support of their position, respondents presented as expert witnesses scholars on religion and education whose testimony is uncontradicted. They expressed their opinions on the relationship of the Amish belief concerning school attendance to the more general tenets of their religion, and described the impact that compulsory high school attendance could have on the continued survival of Amish communities as they exist in the United States today. The history of the Amish sect was given in some detail, beginning with the Swiss Anabaptists of the 16th century who rejected institutionalized churches and sought to return to the early, simple, Christian life deemphasizing material success, rejecting the competitive spirit, and seeking to insulate themselves from the modern world. As a result of their common heritage, Old Order Amish communities today are characterized by a fundamental belief that salvation requires life in a church community separate and apart from the world and worldly influence. This concept of life aloof from the world and its values is central to their faith.

A related feature of Old Order Amish communities is their devotion to a life in harmony with nature and the soil, as exemplified by the simple life of the early Christian era that continued in America during much of our early national life. Amish beliefs require members of the community to make their living by farming or closely related activities. Broadly speaking, the Old Order Amish religion pervades and determines the entire mode of life of its adherents. Their conduct is regulated in great detail by the *Ordnung,* or rules, of the church community. Adult baptism, which occurs in late adolescence, is the time at which Amish young people voluntarily undertake heavy obligations, not unlike the Bar Mitzvah of the Jews, to abide by the rules of the church community.

Amish objection to formal education beyond the eighth grade is firmly grounded in these central religious concepts. They object to the high school and higher education generally because the values it teaches are in marked variance with Amish values and the Amish way of life; they view secondary school education as an impermissible exposure of their children to a "worldly" influence in conflict with their beliefs. The high school tends to emphasize intellectual and scientific accomplishments, self-distinction, competitiveness, worldly success, and social life with other students. Amish society emphasizes informal learning-through-doing, a life of "goodness," rather than a life of intellect, wisdom, rather than technical knowledge, community welfare rather than competition, and separation, rather than integration with contemporary worldly society.

Formal high school education beyond the eighth grade is contrary to Amish beliefs not only because it places Amish children in an environment hostile to Amish beliefs with increasing emphasis on competition in class work and sports and with pressure to conform to the styles, manners, and ways of the peer group, but because it takes them away from their community, physically and emotionally, during the crucial and formative adolescent period of life. During this period, the children must acquire Amish attitudes favoring manual work and self-reliance and the specific skills needed to perform the adult role of an Amish farmer or housewife. They must learn to enjoy physical labor. Once a child has learned basic reading, writing, and elementary mathematics, these traits, skills, and attitudes admittedly fall within the category of those best learned through example and "doing" rather than in a classroom. And, at this time in life, the Amish child must also grow in his faith and his relationship to the Amish community if he is to be prepared to accept the heavy obligations imposed by adult baptism. In short, high school attendance with teachers who are not of the Amish faith—and may even be hostile to it—interposes a serious barrier to the integration of the Amish child into the Amish religious community. Dr. John Hostetler, one of the experts on Amish society, testified that the modern high school is not equipped, in curriculum or social environment, to impart the values promoted by Amish society.

The Amish do not object to elementary education through the first eight grades as a general proposition because they agree that their children must have basic skills in the "three R's" in order to read the Bible, to be good farmers and citizens, and to be able to deal with non-Amish people when necessary in the course of daily affairs. They view such a basic education as acceptable because it does not significantly expose their children to worldly values or interfere with their development in the Amish community during the crucial adolescent period. While Amish accept compulsory elementary education generally, wherever possible they have established their own elementary schools in many respects like the small local schools of the past. In the Amish belief higher learning tends to develop values they reject as influences that alienate man from God.

On the basis of such considerations, Dr. Hostetler testified that compulsory high school attendance could not only result in great psychological harm to Amish children, because of the conflicts it would produce, but would also, in his opinion, ultimately result in the destruction of the Old Order Amish church community as it exists in the United States today. The testimony of Dr. Donald A. Erickson, an expert witness on education, also showed that the Amish succeed in preparing their high school age children to be productive members of the Amish community. He described their system of learning-through-doing the skills directly relevant to their adult roles in the Amish community as "ideal" and perhaps superior to ordinary high school education. The evidence also showed that the Amish have an excellent record as law-abiding and generally self-sufficient members of society.

Although the trial court in its careful findings determined that the Wisconsin compulsory school-attendance law "does interfere with the freedom of the Defendants to act in accordance with their sincere religious belief" it also concluded that the requirement of high school attendance until age 16 was a "reasonable and constitutional" exercise of governmental power, and therefore denied the motion to dismiss the charges. The Wisconsin Circuit Court affirmed the convictions. The Wisconsin Supreme Court, however, sustained respondents' claim under the Free Exercise Clause of the First Amendment and reversed the convictions. A majority of the court was of the opinion that the State had failed to make an adequate showing that its interest in "establishing and maintaining an educational system overrides the defendants' right to the free exercise of their religion." 49 Wis.2d 430, 447, 182 N.W.2d 539, 547 (1971).

I

There is no doubt as to the power of a State, having a high responsibility for education of its citizens to impose reasonable regulations for the control and duration of basic education. See, e. g. Pierce v. Society of Sisters, 268 U.S. 510, 534, 45 S.Ct. 571, 573, 69 L.Ed. 1070 (1925). Providing public schools ranks at the very apex of the function of a State. Yet even this paramount responsibility was, in *Pierce* made to yield to the right of parents to provide an equivalent education in a privately operated system. There the Court held that Oregon's statute compelling attendance in a public school from age eight to age 16 unreasonably interfered with the interest of parents in directing the rearing of their offspring including their education in church-operated schools. As that case suggests, the values of parental direction of the religious upbringing and education of their children in their early and formative years have a high place in our society. See also * * * Meyer v. Nebraska, 262 U.S. 390, 43 S.Ct. 625, 67 L.Ed. 1042 (1923); * * * Thus, a State's interest in universal education, however highly we rank it, is not totally free from a balancing process when it impinges on other fundamental rights and interests, such as those specifically protected by the Free Exercise Clause of the First Amendment and the traditional interest of parents with respect to the religious upbringing of their children so long as they, in the words of *Pierce,* "prepare [them] for additional obligations." 268 U.S., at 535, 45 S.Ct., at 573.

It follows that in order for Wisconsin to compel school attendance beyond the eighth grade against a claim that such attendance interferes with the practice of a legitimate religious belief, it must appear either that the State does not deny the free exercise of religious belief by its requirement, or that there is a state interest of sufficient magnitude to override the interest claiming protection under the Free Exercise Clause. Long before there was general acknowledgment of the need for universal formal education, the Religion Clauses had specifically and firmly fixed the right to free exercise of religious beliefs, and buttressing this fundamental right was an equally firm, even if less explicit, prohibition against the establishment of any religion by government. * * *

The essence of all that has been said and written on the subject is that only those interests of the highest order and those not otherwise served can overbalance legitimate claims to the free exercise of religion. * * *

II

We come then to the quality of the claims of the respondents concerning the alleged encroachment of Wisconsin's compulsory school-attendance statute on their rights and the rights of their children to the free exercise of the religious beliefs they and their forebears have adhered to for almost three centuries. In evaluating those claims we must be careful to determine whether the Amish religious faith and their mode of life are, as they claim, inseparable and interdependent. A way of life, however virtuous and admirable, may not be interposed as a barrier to reasonable state regulation of education if it is based on purely secular considerations; to have the protection of the Religion Clauses, the claims must be rooted in religious belief. Although a determination of what is a "religious" belief or practice entitled to constitutional protection may present a most delicate question, the very concept of ordered liberty precludes allowing every person to make his own standards on matters of conduct in which society as a whole has important interests. Thus, if the Amish asserted their claims because of their subjective evaluation and rejection of the contemporary secular values accepted by the majority, much as Thoreau rejected the social values of his time and isolated himself at Walden Pond, their claim would not rest on a religious basis. Thoreau's choice was philosophical and personal rather than religious, and such belief does not rise to the demands of the Religion Clauses.

Giving no weight to such secular considerations, however, we see that the record in this case abundantly supports the claim that the traditional way of life of the Amish is not merely a matter of personal preference, but one of deep religious conviction, shared by an organized group, and intimately related to daily living. That the Old

Order Amish daily life and religious practice stems from their faith is shown by the fact that it is in response to their literal interpretation of the Biblical injunction from the Epistle of Paul to the Romans, "be not conformed to this world * * *." This command is fundamental to the Amish faith. Moreover, for the Old Order Amish, religion is not simply a matter of theocratic belief. As the expert witnesses explained, the Old Order Amish religion pervades and determines virtually their entire way of life, regulating it with the detail of the Talmudic diet through the strictly enforced rules of the church community.

The record shows that the respondents' religious beliefs and attitude toward life, family, and home have remained constant—perhaps some would say static—in a period of unparalleled progress in human knowledge generally and great changes in education. The respondents freely concede, and indeed assert as an article of faith, that their religious beliefs and what we would today call "life style" have not altered in fundamentals for centuries. Their way of life in a church-oriented community, separated from the outside world and "worldly" influences, their attachment to nature and the soil, is a way inherently simple and uncomplicated, albeit difficult to preserve against the pressure to conform. Their rejection of telephones, automobiles, radios, and television, their mode of dress, of speech, their habits of manual work do indeed set them apart from much of contemporary society; these customs are both symbolic and practical.

As the society around the Amish has become more populous, urban, industrialized, and complex, particularly in this century, government regulation of human affairs has correspondingly become more detailed and pervasive. The Amish mode of life has thus come into conflict increasingly with requirements of contemporary society exerting a hydraulic insistence on conformity to majoritarian standards. So long as compulsory education laws were confined to eight grades of elementary basic education imparted in a nearby rural schoolhouse, with a large proportion of students of the Amish faith, the Old Order Amish had little basis to fear that school attendance would expose their children to the worldly influence they reject. But modern compulsory secondary education in rural areas is now largely carried on in a consolidated school, often remote from the student's home and alien to his daily home life. As the record so strongly shows, the values and programs of the modern secondary school are in sharp conflict with the fundamental mode of life mandated by the Amish religion; modern laws requiring compulsory secondary education have accordingly engendered great concern and conflict. The conclusion is inescapable that secondary schooling, by exposing Amish children to worldly influences in terms of attitudes, goals, and values contrary to beliefs, and by substantially interfering with the religious development of the Amish child and his integration into the way of life of the Amish faith community at the crucial adolescent stage of development, contravenes the basic religious tenets and practice of the Amish faith, both as to the parent and the child.

* * * As the record shows, compulsory school attendance to age 16 for Amish children carries with it a very real threat of undermining the Amish community and religious practice as they exist today; they must either abandon belief and be assimilated into society at large, or be forced to migrate to some other and more tolerant region.[9]

In sum, the unchallenged testimony of acknowledged experts in education and religious history, almost 300 years of consistent practice, and strong evidence of a sustained faith pervading and regulating respondents' entire mode of life support the claim that enforcement of the State's requirement of compulsory formal education after the eighth grade would gravely endanger if not destroy the free exercise of respondents' religious beliefs.

III

Neither the findings of the trial court nor the Amish claims as to the nature of their faith are challenged in this Court by the State of Wisconsin. Its position is that the State's interest in universal compulsory formal secondary education to age 16 is so great that it is paramount to the undisputed claims of respondents that their mode of preparing their youth for Amish life, after the traditional elementary education, is an essential part of their religious belief and practice. Nor does the State undertake to meet the claim that the Amish mode of life and education is inseparable from and a part of the basic tenets of their religion—indeed, as much a part of their religious belief and practices as baptism, the confessional, or a sabbath may be for others.

Wisconsin concedes that under the Religion Clauses religious beliefs are absolutely free from the State's control, but it argues that "actions," even though religiously grounded, are outside the protection of the First Amendment.[10] But our decisions have rejected the

9. Some States have developed working arrangements with the Amish regarding high school attendance. See n. 3, supra. However, the danger to the continued existence of an ancient religious faith cannot be ignored simply because of the assumption that its adherents will continue to be able, at considerable sacrifice, to relocate in some more tolerant State or country or work out accommodations under threat of criminal prosecution. Forced migration of religious minorities was an evil that lay at the heart of the Religion Clauses. See, e. g., Everson v. Board of Education, 330 U.S. 1, 9–10 (1947); Madison, Memorial and Remonstrance Against Religious Assessments, 2 Writings of James Madison 183 (G. Hunt ed. 1901).

10. That has been the apparent ground for decision in several previous state cases rejecting claims for exemption similar to that here. See, e. g., State v. Garber, 197 Kan. 567, 419 P.2d 896 (1966), cert. denied 389 U.S. 51 (1967); State v. Hershberger, 103 Ohio App. 188, 144 N.E.2d 693 (1955); Commonwealth v. Beiler, 168 Pa.Super. 462, 79 A.2d 134 (1951).

idea that religiously grounded conduct is always outside the protection of the Free Exercise Clause. It is true that activities of individuals, even when religiously based, are often subject to regulation by the States in the exercise of their undoubted power to promote the health, safety, and general welfare, or the Federal Government in the exercise of its delegated powers. * * * But to agree that religiously grounded conduct must often be subject to the broad police power of the State is not to deny that there are areas of conduct protected by the Free Exercise Clause of the First Amendment and thus beyond the power of the State to control, even under regulations of general applicability. * * * This case, therefore, does not become easier because respondents were convicted for their "actions" in refusing to send their children to the public high school; in this context belief and action cannot be neatly confined in logic-tight compartments. * * *

Nor can this case be disposed of on the grounds that Wisconsin's requirement for school attendance to age 16 applies uniformly to all citizens of the State and does not, on its face, discriminate against religions or a particular religion, or that it is motivated by legitimate secular concerns. A regulation neutral on its face may, in its application, nonetheless offend the constitutional requirement for governmental neutrality if it unduly burdens the free exercise of religion. * * * The Court must not ignore the danger that an exception from a general obligation of citizenship on religious grounds may run afoul of the Establishment Clause, but that danger cannot be allowed to prevent any exception no matter how vital it may be to the protection of values promoted by the right of free exercise. * * *

We turn, then to the State's broader contention that its interest in its system of compulsory education is so compelling that even the established religious practices of the Amish must give way. Where fundamental claims of religious freedom are at stake, however, we cannot accept such a sweeping claim; despite its admitted validity in the generality of cases, we must searchingly examine the interests that the State seeks to promote by its requirement for compulsory education to age 16, and the impediment to those objectives that would flow from recognizing the claimed Amish exemption. * * *

The State advances two primary arguments in support of its system of compulsory education. It notes, as Thomas Jefferson pointed out early in our history, that some degree of education is necessary to prepare citizens to participate effectively and intelligently in our open political system if we are to preserve freedom and independence. Further, education prepares individuals to be self-reliant and self-sufficient participants in society. We accept these propositions.

However, the evidence adduced by the Amish in this case is persuasively to the effect that an additional one or two years of formal high school for Amish children in place of their long-established pro-

gram of informal vocational education would do little to serve those interests. Respondents' experts testified at trial, without challenge, that the value of all education must be assessed in terms of its capacity to prepare the child for life. It is one thing to say that compulsory education for a year or two beyond the eighth grade may be necessary when its goal is the preparation of the child for life in modern society as the majority live, but it is quite another if the goal of education be viewed as the preparation of the child for life in the separated agrarian community that is the keystone of the Amish faith.
* * *

The State attacks respondents' position as one fostering "ignorance" from which the child must be protected by the State. No one can question the State's duty to protect children from ignorance but this argument does not square with the facts disclosed in the record. Whatever their idiosyncrasies as seen by the majority, this record strongly shows that the Amish community has been a highly successful social unit within our society even if apart from the conventional "mainstream." Its members are productive and very law-abiding members of society; they reject public welfare in any of its usual modern forms. * * *

It is neither fair nor correct to suggest that the Amish are opposed to education beyond the eighth grade level. What this record shows is that they are opposed to conventional formal education of the type provided by a certified high school because it comes at the child's crucial adolescent period of religious development. Dr. Donald Erickson, for example, testified that their system of learning-by-doing was an "ideal system" of education in terms of preparing Amish children for life as adults in the Amish community, and that "I would be inclined to say they do a better job in this than most of the rest of us do." As he put it, "These people aren't purporting to be learned people, and it seems to me the self-sufficiency of the community is the best evidence I can point to—whatever is being done seems to function well."

We must not forget that in the Middle Ages important values of the civilization of the Western World were preserved by members of religious orders who isolated themselves from all worldly influences against great obstacles. There can be no assumption that today's majority is "right" and the Amish and others like them are "wrong." A way of life that is odd or even erratic but interferes with no rights or interests of others is not to be condemned because it is different.

The State, however, supports its interest in providing an additional one or two years of compulsory high school education to Amish children because of the possibility that some such children will choose to leave the Amish community, and that if this occurs they will be ill-equipped for life. The State argues that if Amish children leave their church they should not be in the position of making their way in the world without the education available in the one or two additional years the State requires. However, on this record, that argument is highly speculative. There is no specific evidence of the loss of Amish adherents by attrition, nor is there any showing that upon leaving the Amish community Amish children, with their practical agricultural training and habits of industry and self-reliance, would become burdens on society because of educational shortcomings. Indeed, this argument of the State appears to rest primarily on the State's mistaken assumption, already noted, that the Amish do not provide any education for their children beyond the eighth grade, but allow them to grow in "ignorance." To the contrary, not only do the Amish accept the necessity for formal schooling through the eighth grade level, but continue to provide what has been characterized by the undisputed testimony of expert educators as an "ideal" vocational education for their children in the adolescent years.

There is nothing in this record to suggest that the Amish qualities of reliability, self-reliance, and dedication to work would fail to find ready markets in today's society. Absent some contrary evidence supporting the State's position, we are unwilling to assume that persons possessing such valuable vocational skills and habits are doomed to become burdens on society should they determine to leave the Amish faith, nor is there any basis in the record to warrant a finding that an additional one or two years of formal school education beyond the eighth grade would serve to eliminate any such problem that might exist.

Insofar as the State's claim rests on the view that a brief additional period of formal education is imperative to enable the Amish to participate effectively and intelligently in our democratic process, it must fall. The Amish alternative to formal secondary school education has enabled them to function effectively in their day-to-day life under self-imposed limitations on relations with the world, and to survive and prosper in contemporary society as a separate, sharply identifiable and highly self-sufficient community for more than 200 years in this country. * * * The independence and successful social functioning of the Amish community for a period approaching almost three centuries and more than 200 years in this country are strong evidence that there is at best a speculative gain, in terms of meeting the duties of citizenship, from an additional one or two years of compulsory formal education. * * *

We should also note that compulsory education and child labor laws find their historical origin in common humanitarian instincts, and that the age limits of both laws have been coordinated to achieve their related objectives. * * * It is true, then, that the 16-year child labor age limit may to some degree derive from a contemporary impression that children should be in school until that age. But at the same time, it cannot be denied that, conversely, the 16-year education limit reflects, in substantial measure, the concern that children under that age not be employed under conditions hazardous to their health, or in work that should be performed by adults.

    * * * The two kinds of statutes—compulsory school attendance and child labor laws—tend to keep children of certain ages off the labor market and in school; this in turn provides opportunity to prepare for a livelihood of a higher order than that children could pursue without education and protects their health in adolescence.

    In these terms, Wisconsin's interest in compelling the school attendance of Amish children to age 16 emerges as somewhat less substantial than requiring such attendance for children generally. For, while agricultural employment is not totally outside the legitimate concerns of the child labor laws, employment of children under parental guidance and on the family farm from age 14 to age 16 is an ancient tradition that lies at the periphery of the objectives of such laws. There is no intimation that the Amish employment of their children or family farms is in any way deleterious to their health or that Amish parents exploit children at tender years. Any such inference would be contrary to the record before us. Moreover, employment of Amish children on the family farm does not present the undesirable economic aspects of eliminating jobs that might otherwise be held by adults.

IV

    Finally, the State, on authority of Prince v. Massachusetts, argues that a decision exempting Amish children from the State's requirement fails to recognize the substantive right of the Amish child to a secondary education, and fails to give due regard to the power of the State as *parens patriae* to extend the benefit of secondary education to children regardless of the wishes of their parents. Taken at its broadest sweep, the Court's language in *Prince,* might be read to give support to the State's position. However, the Court was not confronted in *Prince* with a situation comparable to that of the Amish as revealed in this record; this is shown by the Court's severe characterization of the evils that it thought the legislature could legitimately associate with child labor, even when performed in the company of an adult. 321 U.S., at 169–170, 64 S.Ct., at 443–444. The Court later took great care to confine *Prince* to a narrow scope in Sherbert v. Verner, when it stated:

    "On the other hand, the Court has rejected challenges under the Free Exercise Clause to governmental regulation of certain overt acts prompted by religious beliefs or principles, for 'even when the action is in accord with one's religious convictions, [it] is not totally free from legislative restrictions.' Braunfeld v. Brown, 366 U.S. 599, 603, 81 S.Ct. 1144, 1146, 6 L.Ed.2d 563. The conduct or actions so regulated have invariably posed some substantial threat to public safety, peace or order. See, e. g., Reynolds v. United States, 98 U.S. 145, 25 L.Ed. 244; Jacobson v. Massachusetts, 197 U.S. 11, 25 S.Ct. 358, 49 L.Ed. 643; Prince v. Massachusetts, 321 U.S. 158, 64 S.Ct. 438, 88 L. Ed. 645 * * *.'' 374 U.S., at 402–403, 83 S.Ct., at 1793.

This case, of course, is not one in which any harm to the physical or mental health of the child or to the public safety, peace, order, or welfare has been demonstrated or may be properly inferred. The record is to the contrary, and any reliance on that theory would find no support in the evidence.

Contrary to the suggestion of the dissenting opinion of Mr. Justice DOUGLAS, our holding today in no degree depends on the assertion of the religious interest of the child as contrasted with that of the parents. It is the parents who are subject to prosecution here for failing to cause their children to attend school, and it is their right of free exercise, not that of their children, that must determine Wisconsin's power to impose criminal penalties on the parent. The dissent argues that a child who expresses a desire to attend public high school in conflict with the wishes of his parents should not be prevented from doing so. There is no reason for the Court to consider that point since it is not an issue in the case. The children are not parties to this litigation. The State has at no point tried this case on the theory that respondents were preventing their children from attending school against their expressed desires, and indeed the record is to the contrary. The State's position from the outset has been that it is empowered to apply its compulsory-attendance law to Amish parents in the same manner as to other parents—that is, without regard to the wishes of the child. That is the claim we reject today.

Our holding in no way determines the proper resolution of possible competing interests of parents, children, and the State in an appropriate state court proceeding in which the power of the State is asserted on the theory that Amish parents are preventing their minor children from attending high school despite their expressed desires to the contrary. Recognition of the claim of the State in such a proceeding would, of course, call into question traditional concepts of parental control over the religious upbringing and education of their minor children recognized in this Court's past decisions. It is clear that such an intrusion by a State into family decisions in the area of religious training would give rise to grave questions of religious freedom comparable to those raised here and those presented in Pierce v. Society of Sisters, 268 U.S. 510, 45 S.Ct. 571, 69 L.Ed. 1070 (1925). On this record we neither reach nor decide those issues.

The State's argument proceeds without reliance on any actual conflict between the wishes of parents and children. It appears to rest on the potential that exemption of Amish parents from the requirements of the compulsory-education law might allow some parents to act contrary to the best interests of their children by foreclosing their opportunity to make an intelligent choice between the Amish way of life and that of the outside world. The same argument could, of course, be made with respect to all church schools short of college. There is nothing in the record or in the ordinary course of human experience to suggest that non-Amish parents generally consult with children of ages 14–16 if they are placed in a church school of the parents' faith.

Indeed it seems clear that if the State is empowered, as *parens patriae*, to "save" a child from himself or his Amish parents by requiring an additional two years of compulsory formal high school education, the State will in large measure influence, if not determine, the religious future of the child. Even more markedly than in *Prince*, therefore, this case involves the fundamental interest of parents, as contrasted with that of the State, to guide the religious future and education of their children. The history and culture of Western civilization reflect a strong tradition of parental concern for the nurture and upbringing of their children. This primary role of the parents in the upbringing of their children is now established beyond debate as an enduring American tradition. If not the first, perhaps the most significant statements of the Court in this area are found in Pierce v. Society of Sisters, in which the Court observed:

"Under the doctrine of Meyer v. Nebraska, 262 U.S. 390, 43 S.Ct. 625, 67 L.Ed. 1042, we think it entirely plain that the Act of 1922 unreasonably interferes with the liberty of parents and guardians to direct the upbringing and education of children under their control. As often heretofore pointed out, rights guaranteed by the Constitution may not be abridged by legislation which has no reasonable relation to some purpose within the competency of the State. The fundamental theory of liberty upon which all governments in this Union repose excludes any general power of the State to standardize its children by forcing them to accept instruction from public teachers only. The child is not the mere creature of the State; those who nurture him and direct his destiny have the right, coupled with the high duty, to recognize and prepare him for additional obligations." 268 U.S., at 534–535, 45 S.Ct., at 573.

The duty to prepare the child for "additional obligations," referred to by the Court, must be read to include the inculcation of moral standards, religious beliefs, and elements of good citizenship. *Pierce,* of course, recognized that where nothing more than the general interest of the parent in the nurture and education of his children is involved, it is beyond dispute that the State acts "reasonably" and constitutionally in requiring education to age 16 in some public or private school meeting the standards prescribed by the State.

However read, the Court's holding in *Pierce* stands as a charter of the rights of parents to direct the religious upbringing of their children. And, when the interests of parenthood are combined with a free exercise claim of the nature revealed by this record, more than merely a "reasonable relation to some purpose within the competency of the State" is required to sustain the validity of the State's requirement under the First Amendment. To be sure, the power of the parent, even when linked to a free exercise claim, may be subject to limitation under *Prince* if it appears that parental decisions will jeopardize the health or safety of the child, or have a potential for significant social burdens. But in this case, the Amish have introduced persuasive evidence undermining the arguments the State has advanced to support its claims in terms of the welfare of the child and society as a whole. *   *   *

V

For the reasons stated we hold, with the Supreme Court of Wisconsin, that the First and Fourteenth Amendments prevent the State from compelling respondents to cause their children to attend formal high school to age 16.[22] Our disposition of this case, however, in no way alters our recognition of the obvious fact that courts are not school boards or legislatures, and are ill-equipped to determine the "necessity" of discrete aspects of a State's program of compulsory education. This should suggest that courts must move with great circumspection in performing the sensitive and delicate task of weighing a State's legitimate social concern when faced with religious claims for exemption from generally applicable educational requirements. It cannot be overemphasized that we are not dealing with a way of life and mode of education by a group claiming to have recently discovered some "progressive" or more enlightened process for rearing children for modern life.

Aided by a history of three centuries as an identifiable religious sect and a long history as a successful and self-sufficient segment of American society, the Amish in this case have convincingly demon-

---

22. What we have said should meet the suggestion that the decision of the Wisconsin Supreme Court recognizing an exemption for the Amish from the State's system of compulsory education constituted an impermissible establishment of religion. In *Walz v. Tax Commission,* the Court saw the three main concerns against which the Establishment Clause sought to protect as "sponsorship, financial support, and active involvement of the sovereign in religious activity." 397 U.S. 664, 668, 90 S.Ct. 1409, 1411, 25 L.Ed.2d 697 (1970). Accommodating the religious beliefs of the Amish can hardly be characterized as sponsorship or active involvement. The purpose and effect of such an exemption are not to support, favor, advance, or assist the Amish, but to allow their centuries-old religious society, here long before the advent of any compulsory education, to survive free from the heavy impediment compliance with the Wisconsin compulsory education law would impose. Such an accommodation "reflects nothing more than the governmental obligation of neutrality in the face of religious differences, and does not represent that involvement of religious with secular institutions which it is the object of the Establishment Clause to forestall." *Sherbert v. Verner,* 374 U.S. 398, 409, 83 S.Ct. 1790, 1797, 10 L.Ed.2d 965 (1963).

strated the sincerity of their religious beliefs, the interrelationship of belief with their mode of life, the vital role that belief and daily conduct play in the continued survival of Old Order Amish communities and their religious organization, and the hazards presented by the State's enforcement of a statute generally valid as to others. Beyond this, they have carried the even more difficult burden of demonstrating the adequacy of their alternative mode of continuing informal vocational education in terms of precisely those overall interests that the State advances in support of its program of compulsory high school education. * * *

NOTES AND QUESTIONS

1. Mr. Justice White concurred specially in this case, taking the position that the relatively slight deviation from the school attendance laws was not sufficient to outweigh the importance of the Amish religious customs, but expressing doubt whether the Amish would be entitled under the Constitution to keep their children out of school entirely. Mr. Justice Douglas dissented in part from the majority opinion, on the ground that the children themselves should have been heard on their religious preference and their desire to continue in school. He suggests that if the children should wish to continue public school perhaps the state would be entitled to override their parents' religious preferences.

2. The *Yoder* case has been noted in 61 Geo.L.J. 236 (1972); 51 N.C. L.Rev. 302 (1972); and 34 U.Pitt.L.Rev. 274 (1972) among other reviews, and is criticized in Burt, Developing Constitutional Rights Of, In and For Children, 38 L. & Contemp.Prob. No. 3, 118 (1975).

3. What is the relevance of the majority opinion's generally laudatory account of Amish virtues, such as industry, self-reliance, reliability, dedication to work and (in a footnote not reproduced here) the statement that they had never been known to commit crimes or receive public assistance and were not unemployed? Cf. dissenting opinion, 406 U.S. at 246.

4. The majority opinion states that there is no specific evidence of the loss of Amish adherents by attrition. Mr. Justice Douglas' opinion states, however, that the loss of members of the Amish communities is very little in some places and considerable in others, with rates up to 30% and 50% in some instances, quoting from authorities on the subject. If defections from the religion should be that large, what relevance does that have to the positions taken in the majority opinion?

5. What clues can you get from the majority opinion concerning what the result would be if the Amish or a similar sect should seek to keep their children out of the public schools entirely, giving as their reason that a public school education would destroy their religion?

6. What effect, if any, does the *Yoder* case have in the following situations: (a) M, divorced, has two children, aged four and five. She has a primary school teaching certificate, and perhaps for that reason she also has a horror of public school education. She also has a profound, sincere, philosophical belief in individual freedom, which in her view is threatened by the forced conformity of public school. She therefore determines to teach her children at home and does so. When questioned about compli-

ance with the school attendance laws, she responds that her children will be willing and ready to stand examinations in any of the subjects being taught at their age levels in the public schools and if they should not pass, she will not object to their attending public school. Would this be violating the compulsory school attendance statute quoted in footnote 2 to the *Yoder* case? Cf. State ex rel. Shoreline School District v. Superior Court, 55 Wash.2d 177, 346 P.2d 999 (1959); J Baker, Children in Chancery (1964). If educating children in this way would violate the statute, is that unconstitutional under the *Yoder* case? Would the case be different if M and the children were members of the Seventh Elect Church in Spiritual Israel, whose tenets forbade the eating of fish, fowl or meat, listening to music and dancing, and also forbade being present where those things were done?

(b) H and W, members of a fundamentalist religious sect, have a daughter D, who is in seventh grade in the public schools. In the social studies curriculum in that grade there is a unit on Darwin and the theory of evolution. H and W tell D to disregard that unit, that it is all wrong and contrary to the Bible. They inform D's teacher of this, who consults the principal. D fails in that unit of the course and is made to feel humiliated and isolated by the teacher's comments on what D has been told at home. How should this situation be resolved? By a petition in the juvenile court alleging that D is a neglected child?

(c) A program of sex education is proposed for the public schools. H and W, parents of D, a girl in the ninth grade object to many features of the program which they feel depart from the strict moral teachings about sex which they and their religion hold. They therefore insist that their daughter shall not attend any of the classes in this program. The school board has ruled, however, that the program is to be part of the regular class instruction and that no students shall be excused except for illness or similar reason. How should this conflict be handled? Cf. Cornwell v. State Board of Education, 314 F.Supp. 340 (D.Md.1969), aff'd 428 F.2d 471 (4th Cir. 1970), cert. den. 400 U.S. 942 (1970).

(d) H is a Catholic and W a protestant. They have a son, S, six years old who is about to enter school. H wishes him to attend parochial school and W wishes him to attend public school. Each is adamant. As the opening of school approaches, H files a suit in equity asking an injunction requiring S to be entered in parochial school. What should be the result? Cf. Kilgrow v. Kilgrow, 268 Ala. 475, 107 So.2d 885 (1958).

7. How does the Court in *Yoder* define "religion" for the purposes of this case?

8. What is the relevance of the Court's argument in footnote 22 of the opinion?

9. In Prince v. Massachusetts, 321 U.S. 158 (1944) a woman who was a Jehovah's Witness was accustomed to take her children with her and permit them to participate when she distributed the "Watchtower" on the public streets. She was convicted for violation of the state child labor statute prohibiting a boy under twelve or a girl under eighteen from selling newspapers or magazines on the public streets. The Court held that the statute as applied to this situation was constitutional, rejecting contentions based upon the First Amendment and upon the Fourteenth Amendment. The Court saw the case as involving a conflict between the parent's claim to

raise her children and control their religious training on the one hand and the state's interest in protecting the welfare of children on the other. The parent's claim was regarded as particularly important in this case because it related to freedom of conscience and of religion.

Although the Court recognized that "it is cardinal with us that the custody, care and nurture of the child reside first in the parents", it also said that "the state has a wide range of power for limiting parental freedom and authority in things affecting the child's welfare", and that "the state's authority over children's activities is broader than over like actions of adults". The Court found that the statute would clearly be constitutional as applied to sales by an unaccompanied child, and reasoned that the mother's presence with the child did not forestall all the evils that the statute was aimed at preventing. For that reason it upheld the conviction under the statute.

Does the *Yoder* case announce principles which are inconsistent either with the holding or the language of *Prince?* Does *Yoder* in effect overrule Prince?

10. In the *Yoder* case what should be the result if the Amish children had sought to intervene, alleging that they wished to go to school beyond the eighth grade and that their parents would not let them? Would the children have a constitutional right to intervene in this case in any event, on the ground that important interests of theirs were at stake, even though in form the proceeding was merely a misdemeanor prosecution against their parents? Or would the children have to bring an independent suit of some kind in order to be heard? Cf. Buckholz v. Leveille, 37 Mich.App. 166, 194 N.W.2d 427 (1971).

11. If the children were permitted to intervene, or even if not but they wished to be heard, would they have a constitutional right to require the state to furnish them with counsel?

12. The parents' failure to send a child to school may be the basis for a charge of truancy against the child under a statute providing that a truant child is a Person In Need of Supervision (PINS) and within the jurisdiction of the juvenile court. Their failure may also be the basis for the state's charge of child neglect. Should the parents have a defense to these charges if they give the child instruction at home? Should they have a defense that the education in the public schools is inadequate or unsuitable for their child? See People v. Y. D. M., —— Colo. ——, 593 P.2d 1356 (1979); In re Davis, 114 N.H. 242, 318 A.2d 151 (1974); In re Gregory B, 88 Misc. 2d 313, 387 N.Y.S.2d 380 (Fam.Ct.1976); Rosenberg and Rosenberg, Truancy, School Phobia and Minimal Brain Dysfunction, 61 Minn.L.Rev. 543 (1977).

If this is not a defense, is there any other legal process by which the parents can assert a claim that their child is not receiving an adequate public school education? Elson, A Common Law Remedy for the Educational Harms Caused by Incompetent or Careless Teaching, 73 Nw.U.L.Rev. 641 (1978). See also Sugarman and Kirp, Rethinking Collective Responsibility for Education, 39 L. & Contemp.Prob. 144 (No. 3, 1975).

13. The courts have from time to time been presented with questions of discipline in the public schools which explicitly or implicitly involve the rights of parents to control their children. For example Goss v. Lopez, 419 U.S. 565 (1975) held that before a student may be temporarily suspended

from school the Due Process Clause requires that he be given a hearing, with notice of the charges against him and an opportunity to present his version of the facts, before the suspension unless immediate suspension is dictated by the circumstances, in which case notice and hearing must be given later. In Ingraham v. Wright, 430 U.S. 651 (1977) the Court held that corporal punishment in the public schools did not violate the Eighth Amendment's prohibition of cruel and unusual punishment. It also held that the common law remedies are sufficient to provide due process for the student punished, so that he is not entitled to a hearing in advance of the punishment. And in Carey v. Piphus, 435 U.S. 247 (1978) the Court held that a suspension from school without procedural due process could only be the basis for a damage award if actual damages were proved. The Second Circuit, in Trachtman v. Anker, 563 F.2d 512 (2d Cir. 1977), cert. den. 435 U.S. 925 (1978), held that school officials could, without violating the First Amendment, forbid a high school student from distributing a sex questionnaire to other students at a New York City high school. The basis for this decision was that there was substantial evidence for the school officials' belief "that distribution of the questionnaire would result in significant emotional harm to a number" of the school's students.

B. MEDICAL AND PSYCHIATRIC CARE FOR THE CHILD

IN RE GREEN

Supreme Court of Pennsylvania, 1972.
448 Pa. 338, 292 A.2d 387.

JONES, Chief Justice. The Director of the State Hospital for Crippled Children at Elizabethtown, Pennsylvania, filed a "petition to initiate juvenile proceedings" under The Juvenile Court Law, Act of June 2, 1933, P.L. 1433, § 1 et seq., as amended, 11 P.S. § 243 et seq., which sought a judicial declaration that Ricky Ricardo Green (hereinafter "Ricky") was a "neglected child" within the meaning of the Act and the appointment of a guardian. After an evidentiary hearing, the Court of Common Pleas, Family Division, Juvenile Branch, of Philadelphia dismissed the petition. On appeal, the Superior Court unanimously reversed and remanded the matter for the appointment of a guardian. Green Case, 220 Pa.Super.Ct. 191, 286 A.2d 681 (1971). We granted allocatur.

Ricky was born on September 10, 1955, to Nathaniel and Ruth Green. He lives with his mother as his parents are separated and the father pays support pursuant to a court order. Ricky has had two attacks of poliomyelitis which have generated problems of obesity and, in addition, Ricky now suffers from paralytic scoliosis (94% curvature of the spine).*

---

* Scoliosis is defined as a lateral curvature of the spine. Stedman's Medical Dictionary, 1338 (1961). A "94%" curvature is quite severe, the actual severity depending upon which of two methods of measurement is used. [Editor's Note]

Due to this curvature of the spine, Ricky is presently a "sitter," unable to stand or ambulate due to the collapse of his spine; if nothing is done, Ricky could become a bed patient. Doctors have recommended a "spinal fusion" to relieve Ricky's bent position, which would involved [sic] moving bone from Ricky's pelvis to his spine. Although an orthopedic specialist testified, "there is no question that there is danger in this type of operation," the mother did consent conditionally to the surgery. The condition is that, since the mother is a Jehovah's Witness who believes that the Bible proscribes any blood transfusions which would be necessary for this surgery,[1] she would not consent to any blood transfusions. Initially, we must recognize that, while the operation would be beneficial, there is no evidence that Ricky's life is in danger or that the operation must be performed immediately. Accordingly, we are faced with the situation of a parent who will not consent to a dangerous operation on her minor son requiring blood transfusions solely because of her religious beliefs.

By statute, a "neglected child"—"a child whose parent * * * neglects or refuses to provide proper or necessary * * * medical or surgical care"—may be committed "to the care, guidance and control of some respectable citizen of good moral character * * *" appointed by the court. The guardian appointed by the court may, with the court's approval, commit the child to a "crippled children's home or orthopaedic hospital or other institution" for treatment. Thus, it has been held that a child whose parent views smallpox vaccination as "harmful and injurious" may be considered a "neglected child." * * * On the other hand, In re Tuttendario, 21 Pa.Dist. 561 (Q.S.Phila.1912), held that surgery on a seven-year-old male to cure rachitis would not be ordered over the parents' refusal due to fear of the operation. While these statutes could be construed to cover the facts of this appeal, we cannot accept the Commonwealth's construction if it abridges the Free Exercise clause of the First Amendment.

Almost a century ago, the United States Supreme Court enunciated the twofold concept of the Free Exercise clause: "Laws are made for the government of actions, and while they cannot interfere with mere religious belief and opinions, they may with practices." Reynolds v. United States, 98 U.S. 145, 166, 25 L.Ed. 244 (1878). [At this point in the opinion the court quoted from Prince v. Massachusetts, 321 U.S. 158 (1944).]

On the other hand, the United States Supreme Court recently stated, "to agree that religiously grounded conduct must often be subject to the broad police power of the State is not to deny that there are areas of conduct protected by the Free Exercise Clause of the First

1. The mother also rejected the suggestion that Ricky's own blood, obtained by periodic bleeding, might be employed.

Amendment and thus beyond the power of the State to control, even under regulations of general applicability." Wisconsin v. Yoder, 406 U.S. 205, 92 S.Ct. 1526, 32 L.Ed.2d 15 (1972). "The conduct or actions so regulated have invariably posed some substantial threat to public safety, peace or order." Sherbert v. Verner, 374 U.S. 398, 403, 83 S.Ct. 1790, 1793, 10 L.Ed.2d 965 (1963). Without appearing callous, Ricky's unfortunate condition, unlike polygamy, vaccination, child labor and the like, does not pose a substantial threat to society; in this fashion, *Pierce* [sic] and its progeny are readily distinguishable.

When dealing with *adults* requiring medical attention who voice religious objections, other jurisdictions have come to varying conclusions depending, in large measure, upon the facts of each case. See, generally, Annot., 9 A.L.R.3d 1391 (1966). Some courts have found medical treatment to be properly ordered by the public authority despite the adult's religious beliefs when his or her life hangs in the balance. Thus, it was held in Application of President & Directors of Georgetown College, Inc., 331 F.2d 1000 (C.A.D.C.1964), rehearing denied 331 F.2d 1010, cert. denied 377 U.S. 978, 84 S.Ct. 1883, 12 L. Ed.2d 746 (1964), that a blood transfusion could be ordered for an adult Jehovah's Witness whose life was immediately endangered. While a similar result was reached in United States v. George, 239 F. Supp. 752 (D.C.Conn.1965), that court dissolved the order several days later when the patient was no longer *in extremis* and could decide whether to allow further necessary transfusions. The Supreme Court of New Jersey likewise ordered blood transfusions for a pregnant Jehovah's Witness in order to save the life of the mother and unborn child. Raleigh Fitkin-Paul Morgan Memorial Hospital v. Anderson, 42 N.J. 421, 201 A.2d 537, cert. denied 377 U.S. 985, 84 S.Ct. 1894, 12 L.Ed.2d 1032 (1964). Cf., Collins v. Davis, 44 Misc.2d 622, 254 N.Y.S.2d 666 (1964). On the other hand, the Illinois Supreme Court reversed an ordered blood transfusion where the emergency patient had no children and notified the doctor beforehand that blood transfusions violated her religious beliefs. In re Brooks' Estate, 32 Ill.2d 361, 205 N.E.2d 435 (1965). See, also, Nemser Petition, 51 Misc.2d 616, 273 N.Y.S.2d 624 (1966); Erickson v. Dilgard, 44 Misc. 2d 27, 252 N.Y.S.2d 705 (1962).

Turning to the situation where an adult refuses to consent to blood transfusions necessary to save the life of his infant son or daughter, other jurisdictions have uniformly held that the state can order such blood transfusions over the parents' religious objections. People ex rel. Wallace v. Labrenz, 411 Ill. 618, 104 N.E.2d 769 (1952); Morrison v. State, 252 S.W.2d 97 (C.A.Kansas City, Mo., 1952); State v. Perricone, 37 N.J. 463, 181 A.2d 751 (1962); Hoener v. Bertinato, 67 N.J.Super. 517, 171 A.2d 140 (1961); In re Santos, 16 A.D.2d 755, 227 N.Y.S.2d 450, appeal dismissed 232 N.Y.S.2d 1026 (1962); Application of Brooklyn Hospital, 45 Misc.2d 914, 258 N.Y.

S.2d 621 (1965); In re Clark, 21 Ohio Op.2d 86, 185 N.E.2d 128 (C. P.Lucas 1962). Cf., Mitchell v. Davis, 205 S.W.2d 812 (Texas C.C.A. 1947). See, generally, Annot., 30 A.L.R.2d 1138 (1953). The fact that the child was over twenty-one made no difference to the New Jersey Supreme Court in John F. Kennedy Memorial Hospital v. Heston, 58 N.J. 576, 279 A.2d 670 (1971), which ignored the mother's religious objections.

In a somewhat different posture, the United States District Court for the Western District of Washington entertained a class action brought on behalf of all Jehovah's Witnesses in the State against certain physicians and hospitals in that State. The relief requested was a declaration that a "dependent child" statute similar to our own was unconstitutionally applied to sustain blood transfusions for children of Jehovah's Witnesses where the blood transfusion "was or would be vital to save the life of the patient." Jehovah's Witnesses in State of Washington v. King County Hospital, 278 F.Supp. 488, 503 n. 10 (W. D.Wash.1967). Relying on Prince v. Massachusetts, 321 U.S. 158, 64 S.Ct. 438, 88 L.Ed. 645 (1944), that court held that the statute in question was constitutionally valid. On appeal, the United States Supreme Court, citing the *Prince* opinion, affirmed per curiam, 390 U.S. 598, 88 S.Ct. 1260, 20 L.Ed.2d 158 (1968). Because the Washington case directly contested the constitutional application of the state statute in the situation *where the children's lives were in imminent danger,* we do not consider this Court to be bound by the Supreme Court's per curiam affirmance under the factual posture in the case at bar.

In our view, the penultimate question presented by this appeal is whether the state may interfere with a parent's control over his or her child in order to enhance the child's physical well-being when the child's life is in no immediate danger and when the state's intrusion conflicts with the parent's religious beliefs. Stated differently, does the State have an interest of sufficient magnitude to warrant the abridgment of a parent's right to freely practice his or her religion when those beliefs preclude medical treatment of a son or daughter whose life is not in immediate danger? We are not confronted with a life or death situation as in the cases cited earlier in this opinion. Nor is there any question in the case at bar of a parent's omission or neglect for non-religious reasons. *   *   *

In the very recent *Yoder* decision, the United States Supreme Court ruled that the Free Exercise clause barred the application of a compulsory education statute to members of the Amish sect. While skirting the precise issue before this Court, the Supreme Court did state, "[t]o be sure, the power of the parent, even when linked to a free exercise claim, *may* be subject to limitation under *Prince* if it appears that parental decisions will jeopardize the health or safety of the child, or have a potential for significant social burdens." 406 U.

S. at 233–234, 92 S.Ct. at 1542 (emphasis added). Although the use of the word "may" arguably supports the Commonwealth's position in this case, the only analogous case cited by both Mr. Chief Justice Burger, 406 U.S. at 230, n. 20, 92 S.Ct. at 1540, and Mr. Justice Stewart, 406 U.S. at 239, n. 1, 92 S.Ct. at 1545 (concurring opinion), in support of this proposition is the *Georgetown College* case,[5] which is readily distinguished as a life or death situation involving an adult. For this reason, the Commonwealth is not aided by the *Yoder* opinion. Indeed, the broad holding of *Yoder* that the state's interest in the education of its children must fall before a parent's religious beliefs lends support to the mother's position.

Our research disclosed only two opinions on point; both are from the New York Court of Appeals but the results differ. In Matter of Seiferth, 309 N.Y. 80, 127 N.E.2d 820 (1955), the State of New York sought the appointment of a guardian for a "neglected child," a fourteen-year-old boy with a cleft palate and harelip. The father's purely personal philosophy, "not classified as religion," precluded any and all surgery as he believed in mental healing; moreover, the father had "inculcated a distrust and dread of surgery in the boy since childhood." 309 N.Y. at 84, 127 N.E.2d at 822. The boy was medically advised and the Children's Court judge interviewed both the boy and his father in chambers. The trial judge concluded that the operation should not be performed until the boy agreed. After reversal by the Appellate Division, Fourth Department, the Court of Appeals, by a four-to-three vote, reinstated the order of the Children's Court. The primary thrust of the opinion was the child's antagonism to the operation and the need for the boy's cooperation for treatment; since the Children's Court judge saw and heard the parties involved and was aware of this aspect, the Court of Appeals decided that the discretion of the Children's Court judge should be affirmed.

On facts virtually identical to this appeal, the Family Court of Ulster County ordered a blood transfusion in In re Sampson, 65 Misc. 2d 658, 317 N.Y.S.2d 641 (1970). Kevin Sampson, fifteen years old, suffered from Von Recklinghausen's disease which caused a massive disfigurement of the right side of his face and neck. While the incurable disease posed no immediate threat to his life, the dangerous surgery requiring blood transfusions would improve "not only the function but the appearance" of his face and neck. It should also be noted that all physicians involved counselled delay until the boy was old enough to decide since the surgical risk would decrease as the boy

---

5. The other cited opinions clearly involved substantial threats to society: Cleveland v. United States, 329 U.S. 14, 67 S.Ct. 13, 91 L.Ed. 12 (1946) (polygamy); Prince v. Massachusetts, 321 U.S. 158, 64 S.Ct. 438, 88 L.Ed. 645 (1944) (child labor laws); Jacobson v. Massachusetts, 197 U.S. 11, 25 S.Ct. 358, 49 L.Ed. 643 (1905) (compulsory vaccination); Wright v. DeWitt School District, 238 Ark. 906, 385 S.W.2d 644 (1965) (compulsory vaccination).

grew older. The Family Court judge ruled in an extensive opinion that the State's interest in the child's health was paramount to the mother's religious beliefs. That court further decided not to place this difficult decision on the boy and to order an immediate operation, thereby preventing psychological problems. On appeal, the Appellate Division, Third Department, unanimously affirmed the order in a memorandum decision. In re Sampson, 37 A.D.2d 668, 323 N.Y. S.2d 253 (1971). That court rejected the argument that "State intervention is permitted only where the life of the child is in danger by a failure to act * * * [as] a much too restricted approach." 37 A.D.2d at 669, 323 N.Y.S.2d at 255. When the matter reached the Court of Appeals, In re Sampson, 29 N.Y.2d 900, 328 N.Y.S.2d 686, 278 N.E.2d 918 (1972), that Court affirmed per curiam the opinion of the Family Court but added two observations: (1) the *Seiferth* opinion turned upon the question of a court's discretion and not the existence of its power to order surgery in a non-fatal case, and (2) religious objections to blood transfusions do not "present a bar at least where the transfusion is necessary to the success of the required surgery," 29 N.Y.2d at 901, 328 N.Y.S.2d at 687, 278 N.E.2d at 919.

With all deference to the New York Court of Appeals, we disagree with the second observation in a non-fatal situation and express no view of the propriety of that statement in a life or death situation. If we were to describe this surgery as "required," like the Court of Appeals, our decision would conflict with the mother's religious beliefs. Aside from religious considerations, one can also question the use of that adjective on medical grounds since an orthopedic specialist testified that the operation itself was dangerous. Indeed, one can question who, other than the Creator, has the right to term certain surgery as "required." This fatal/non-fatal distinction also steers the courts of this Commonwealth away from a medical and philosophical morass: if spinal surgery can be ordered, what about a hernia or gall bladder operation or a hysterectomy? The problems created by *Sampson* are endless. We are of the opinion that as between a parent and the state, the state does not have an interest of sufficient magnitude outweighing a parent's religious beliefs when the child's life is *not immediately imperiled* by his physical condition.

Unlike *Yoder* and *Sampson,* our inquiry does not end at this point since we believe the wishes of this sixteen-year old boy should be ascertained; the ultimate question, in our view, is whether a parent's religious beliefs are paramount to the possibly adverse decision of the child. In *Yoder,* Mr. Justice Douglas, dissenting in part, wanted to remand the matter in order to determine whether the Amish children wished to continue their education in spite of their parents' beliefs: "if an Amish child desires to attend high school, and is mature enough to have that desire respected, the State may well be able to override the parents' religiously motivated objections," 406 U.S. at 242, 92 S.Ct. at 1546. The majority opinion as well as the concurring opinion of Mr. Justice Stewart did not think it wise to reach this point for two principal reasons: (1) it was the parents, not the children, who were criminally prosecuted for their religious beliefs; and (2) the record did not indicate a parent-child conflict as the testimony of the lone child witness coincided with her parents' religious beliefs. While the record before us gives no indication of Ricky's thinking, it is the child rather than the parent in this appeal who is directly involved which thereby distinguishes *Yoder's* decision not to discuss the beliefs of the parents vis-a-vis the children. In *Sampson,* the Family Court judge decided not to "evade the responsibility for a decision now by the simple expedient of foisting upon this boy the responsibility for making a decision at some later day. * * *" 65 Misc.2d 658, 317 N.Y.S.2d at 655. While we are cognizant of the realistic problems of this approach enunciated by Judge (now Chief Judge) Fuld in his *Seiferth* dissent, we believe that Ricky should be heard.

It would be most anomalous to ignore Ricky in this situation when we consider the preference of an intelligent child of sufficient maturity in determining custody. * * * Moreover, we have held that a child of the same age can waive constitutional rights and receive a life sentence. * * * Indeed, minors can now bring a personal injury action in Pennsylvania against their parents. * * * We need not extend this litany of the rights of children any further to support the proposition that Ricky should be heard. The record before us does not even note whether Ricky is a Jehovah's Witness or plans to become one. We shall, therefore, reserve any decision regarding a possible parent-child conflict and remand the matter for an evidentiary hearing similar to the one conducted in *Seiferth* in order to determine Ricky's wishes.

The order of the Superior Court is reversed and the matter remanded to the Court of Common Pleas of Philadelphia, Family Division, Juvenile Branch, for proceedings consistent with the views expressed in this opinion. In the meantime, awaiting the evidentiary hearing and result thereof, we will retain our jurisdiction in this matter.

EAGEN, Justice (dissenting). With all due deference to the majority of this Court, I am compelled to dissent. I would affirm the order of the Superior Court.

The Court's analysis presumes there are two primary interests at stake, that of the state to protect its citizens, and that of the mother to follow her religious convictions. The difficulty, and what I believe to be the fatal flaw in this reasoning, is that too little consideration and attention is given to the interests of the health and well-being of this young boy. Although the mother's religious beliefs must be given the fullest protection and respect, I do not believe the mother's religious convictions should be our primary consideration. * * *

The reasoning of Judge Spaulding, who delivered the opinion of the Superior Court, more than adequately expresses what I believe to be the correct and salutory [sic] approach to this situation and I take the liberty of quoting from his opinion:

"This case places before the appellate courts of Pennsylvania another of the many conflicts between the exercise of First Amendment rights by Jehovah's Witnesses and the Commonwealth's police power to safeguard the welfare of its citizens. The First Amendment of the United States Constitution, as applied to the States by the Fourteenth Amendment, provides that the States shall not limit the free exercise of religion. However, the free exercise clause does not guarantee parents complete control, free of all State authority, merely because the parent asserts that his control is based on religion. * * * The court below determined that the mother's exercise of control here would undoubtedly expose the child to progressively worsening ill health, but it still refused to assert the State's power by finding the child neglected.

"Under the Juvenile Court Law, the courts of this Commonwealth can order the appointment of a guardian for a child where the natural parnets [sic] refuse to provide necessary medical care. * * * Further, several jurisdictions have recognized that the courts have the power and duty to authorize the use of blood transfusions necessary for the immediate preservation of the life of a child, despite the religious objections of the parents. Jehovah's Witnesses in the State of Washington v. * * * The question here, however, is whether the State's interest in the health and welfare of this child is sufficient to overcome the religious objections of the parents where no immediate threat to life exists.

"In re Sampson, 65 Misc.2d 658, 317 N.Y.S.2d 641 (Fam.Ct. 1970), recently answered this question in the affirmative in an almost identical situation. The case involved a 15 year old boy who required an admittedly dangerous operation for the partial correction of a facial deformity. His mother was a Jehovah's Witness and opposed the necessary blood transfusions. The court held that despite the fact that there was no immediate threat to the child's life, the operation would be less risky and of more benefit if performed immediately. Therefore, it found the boy neglected within the meaning of the New York Family Court Act, which is very similar to our statute. After reviewing the decisions involving emergency situations, the court concluded that: '[A]lthough the mother's religious objections to the administration of a blood transfusion * * * is founded upon the scriptures and is sincerely held, it must give way before the state's paramount duty to insure his right to live and grow up without disfigurement—the right to live and grow up with a sound mind and body. * * * The same is true here especially in view of the fact that the proposed operation is not categorized as peculiarly 'danger-ous.' "

220 Pa.Super.Ct. 191, 195–97, 286 A.2d 681, 683–84 (1971). With the approach of the Superior Court and the *Sampson* court, I wholeheart-edly agree.

The majority takes the approach that the broad holding of Yoder v. Wisconsin, 406 U.S. 205, 92 S.Ct. 1526, 32 L.Ed.2d 15 (1972), sup-ports the position of the mother. However, I do not read *Yoder* as having any bearing on this case, and if it has any, it would support the position the boy should have the operation. *   *   *

Moreover, the following language supports the position that the boy should have the operation:

"To be sure, the power of the parent, even when linked to a free exercise, may be subject to limitation under *Prince* if it appears *that the parental decisions will jeopardize the health* or safety of the child, or have a potential for significant social burdens." [Emphasis sup-plied.]   Id. at 233, 92 S.Ct. 1542.

Furthermore, I believe one of the prime considerations in *Yoder* was the effect of compulsory education on the religious beliefs of the children, this is absent in the present case. Our sole consideration with respect to the child should be his health, a consideration not present in *Yoder*.

I also do not agree with the emphasis the majority places on the fact this is not a life or death situation. The statute with which we are dealing (Juvenile Court Law, Act of June 2, 1933, P.L. 1433 § 1, as amended, 11 P.S. § 243 et seq.) does not contain any such lan-guage, nor do I find support for this position in the case law (note the use of the word health in the *Yoder* and *Prince* opinions). The statute in pertinent part states:

"A child whose parent *   *   * neglects or refuses to provide *proper or necessary* subsistence, education, *medical or surgical care, or other care necessary for his or her health* *   *   *." [Emphasis supplied.]   11 P.S. § 243(5)(c)

The statute only speaks in terms of "health", not life or death. If there is a substantial threat to health, then I believe the courts can and should intervene to protect Ricky. By the decision of this Court today, this boy may never enjoy any semblance of a normal life which the vast majority of our society has come to enjoy and cherish.

Lastly, I must take issue with the manner in which the majority finally disposes of the case. I do not believe that sending the case back to allow Ricky to be heard is an adequate solution. We are herein dealing with a young boy who has been crippled most of his life, consequently, he has been under the direct control and guidance of his parents for that time. To now presume that he could make an independent decision as to what is best for his welfare and health is not reasonable. * * * Moreover, the mandate of the Court presents this youth with a most painful choice between the wishes of his parents and their religious convictions on the one hand, and his chance for a normal, healthy life on the other hand. We should not confront him with this dilemma.

On the basis of the foregoing, I would affirm the Order of the Superior Court.

NOTES AND QUESTIONS

1. Upon remand to the trial court, Ricky Green testified that he did not wish to have the operation, his unwillingness apparently not being based solely on religious grounds. The trial judge then refused to order the operation and his refusal was upheld by the Pennsylvania Supreme Court, three judges dissenting. In re Green, 452 Pa. 373, 307 A.2d 279 (1973). On the general subject, see Guides to the Judge in Medical Orders Affecting Child, April 1968, Crime and Delinquency 109, by The Council of Judges, National Council on Crime and Delinquency; Note, Minors' Rights to Medical Care, 14 J. of Fam.L. 581 (1976).

2. Lowering the age of majority from twenty-one to eighteen has obviously increased the capacity of youth to consent to their own medical treatment, without the intervention of parents. In addition there are statutes in many states permitting minors to consent to specific types of medical treatment. Emergency treatment may be consented to by the minor, as well as treatment for pregnancy, for venereal disease, and for drug related illnesses. Some states have the common law "mature minor" rule, also occasionally found in statutes, which permits the mature minor to consent to treatment for minor illnesses. In addition to the Note cited in the preceding paragraph, see Wadlington, Minors and Health Care: The Age Consent, 11 Osgoode Hall L.J. 115 (1973); Note, Consent to the Medical Treatment of a Minor Under the Family Code, 27 Baylor L.Rev. 319 (1975).

Would you favor a statute which provided that all minors have capacity to consent to medical or surgical treatment, without parental consent? Wilkins, Children's Rights: Removing the Parental Consent Barrier to Medical Treatment of Minors, 1975 Ariz.St.L.J. 31.

3. Is the majority in *Green* correct in saying that *Yoder* supports its position? Or does *Yoder* support the dissent?

4. In the *Yoder* case the Court, with some expert testimony to support its view, seemed to think that insistence upon the attendance of Amish children at public school beyond the eighth grade would ultimately destroy the Amish sect. Is a similarly crucial issue at stake in the *Green* case?

5. Is the majority correct in distinguishing Prince v. Massachusetts on the ground that it involved a condition posing "a substantial threat to society", while Ricky Green's condition did not? This is on the assumption that in referring to "Pierce and its progeny" the Court means "Prince and its progeny".

6. In the unlikely event that Ricky should desire the operation in opposition to his mother's views, what result do you think this court would reach? Since the operation is serious and success by no means sure, should the court obtain other medical opinions before ordering it? In any

event does Ricky have a constitutional right to have counsel furnished him under In re Gault infra, page 666.

7. What relevance has the court's citation of cases refusing to order medical treatment for adults?

8. Does *Green* seem to be supported by the other cases which it cites and by the cases discussed in the dissent?

9. H and W had a son B, ten years old. In the winter he developed a severe sore throat, which was accompanied by coughing and difficulty in breathing. He missed school for a week. During the same winter this condition recurred four times, causing him to miss more than a month of school. After one of these illnesses he was examined by the school nurse, who asked that he be examined by the school physician. The physician examined him, and found markedly enlarged and inflamed tonsils. He prescribed medication, which was ineffective, and at a later examination the physician strongly urged that the tonsils be removed. H informed the school physician that he objected to surgery out of "religious conviction", without explaining what the conviction involved. After the fourth episode of illness the school principal filed a petition in the juvenile court asking the court to order the operation, under the authority of a statute like that in the *Green* case. Cf. In re Karwath, 199 N.W.2d 147 (Iowa 1972).

(a) How should the petition be disposed of?

(b) Would it matter that H objected merely because he had a general reluctance to have surgery except as an absolute last resort?

(c) Would it matter that B was in the temporary custody of the state welfare department and living in a foster home, because H and W were for the time unable to care for him?

(d) Would B be entitled to state-furnished counsel in this case?

10. A girl was born with a congenital deformity of the left arm, consisting of a greatly enlarged arm, much larger than the right arm. When she was twelve years old, on the urging of an adult sister, her mother had her examined by a physician, who recommended amputation of the arm. The medical testimony was that the greatly enlarged arm caused the child to be frail, that she would be susceptible to infections due to her weakened condition, and that her heart was overburdened by having to pump blood through the enlarged arm. It appeared that no treatment other than amputation was possible. The amputation was recommended by the examining physicians, although they conceded that there was a fair degree of risk of death involved in such an operation. The parents of the child refused to have the operation performed and a juvenile proceeding was brought to obtain court approval for the operation. The child's father expressed no opinion on the matter, leaving the decision to the court. The child's mother had no religious scruples, but opposed the operation on the ground of the risk involved, saying the child herself could decide when she became older. Should the court order the operation? Would the *Green* case be authority for not ordering the operation? See In re Hudson, 13 Wash.2d 673, 126 P.2d 765 (1942).

11. H and W had a son, S, who one night began to run a very high fever. They took S at once to their family doctor, who diagnosed acute lymphocytic leukemia, a blood disease causing death if not treated. The treat-

ment consists of a three-year course of chemotherapy, using a variety of drugs in series. After one year of treatment the statistics indicate that 90% of children are free of the disease. After two years the figure is 70%, after three years it is 65% and in the fourth year and thereafter there is a survival pattern of about 50% H and W consented to the treatments, but after about a three month period, at which time the disease was in remission, they discontinued administering the drugs. Three months later S exhibited symptoms of the disease again, H and W admitted to their doctor they had not been giving the medication, and refused to give it further. The reason for the parents' refusal was that S had suffered stomach cramps, constipation and some psychological side effects from the drugs, and that the parents wished to attempt treatment by diet and prayer. The expert testimony was that diet had no effect in such cases. S's physician filed a petition with the appropriate court asking that continuation of drug therapy be authorized over the parents' objection. What should be the result? Custody of a Minor, —— Mass. ——, 379 N.E.2d 1053 (1978), —— Mass. ——, 393 N.E.2d 836 (1979).

Would the result be different if there were some medical testimony to the effect that diet or some other kind of therapy might benefit the child, although all physicians agreed that chemotherapy was still the "conventional" treatment? Matter of Hofbauer, 47 N.Y.2d 648, 419 N.Y.S.2d 936, 393 N.E.2d 1009 (1979) (parents arranged for laetrile treatments).

12. Should a parent refusing to permit medical treatment for a child in a situation like that in the *Green* case be guilty of violating the criminal statute punishing parents who contribute to the neglect of their children? Or would the parent refusing to permit the operation in paragraph 9 be guilty of murder or manslaughter if the child contracted an infection and died by reason of the enlarged arm? Would the parent be guilty of murder or manslaughter if, out of religious scruples, he refused to permit a blood transfusion for the child and this cost the child's life? See Trescher and O'Neil, Medical Care for Dependent Children: Manslaughter Liability of the Christian Scientist, 109 U.Pa.L.Rev. 203 (1960); Perkins, Negative Acts in Criminal Law, 22 Iowa L.Rev. 659 (1937); Annot., Failure to Provide Medical or Surgical Attention, 10 A.L.R. 137 (1921) and 12 A.L.R.2d 1047 (1950). And see B. DeMott, The Body's Cage (1959).

What action should a court take in the converse situation, in which a child is seriously injured, to such an extent that the medical testimony is that he cannot recover, but in which he can be kept alive by the use of artificial respirators or other complex life support systems in the hospital, and in which the parent or guardian wishes to have the life support system removed? Are religious or ethical teachings relevant to the court's decision in such a case? Matter of Quinlan, 70 N.J. 10, 355 A.2d 647, cert. den. 429 U.S. 922 (1976). Karen Quinlan remained alive on her twenty-fifth birthday, three years after the life support system was disconnected, New York Times, March 29, 1979, section III, p. 14, col. 5, and remains alive at present writing. New York Times, Sept. 27, 1979, sec. B, p. 17, col. 4. Comments on the *Quinlan* case include Cantor, Quinlan, Privacy, and the Handling of Incompetent Dying Patients, 30 Rut.L.Rev. 243 (1977); Hirsch and Donovan, The Right to Die: Medico-Legal Implications of In re Quinlan, 30 Rut.L.Rev. 267 (1977); Collester, Death, Dying and the Law: A Prosecutorial View of the Quinlan Case, 30 Rut.L.Rev. 304 (1977).

13. Somewhat different issues are raised where the operation to be done on the minor is a kidney transplant, and where the donor of the kidney is an identical twin of the donee. In such a case the donor is not ill and the operation does not benefit him physically, although one case found a benefit to the donor in preserving the life of the donee, where the donor was mentally incompetent. Strunk v. Strunk, 445 S.W.2d 145 (Ky.1969). The operation was approved, where the parents consented, in Hart v. Brown, 29 Conn.Supp. 368, 289 A.2d 386 (1972), and Little v. Little, 576 S.W.2d 493 (Tex.Civ.App.1979). See also Note, Spare Parts from Incompetents: A Problem of Consent, 9 J.Fam.L. 309 (1970).

14. Could you draft a statute which would satisfactorily define the circumstances in which the courts would be permitted to order operations on children over the opposition of their parents? For suggested legal approaches to these problems, see Goldstein, Medical Care for the Child at Risk: On State Supervention of Parental Authority, 86 Yale L.J. 645 (1977); Bennett, Allocation of Child Medical Care Decision-Making Authority: A Suggested Interest Analysis, 62 Va.L.Rev. 285 (1976).

PARHAM v. J. R.*

Supreme Court of the United States, 1979.
442 U.S. 584, 99 S.Ct. 2493, 61 L.Ed.2d 101.

Mr. Chief Justice BURGER delivered the opinion of the Court.

The question presented in this appeal is what process is constitutionally due a minor child whose parents or guardian seek state administered institutional mental health care for the child and specifically whether an adversary proceeding is required prior to or after the commitment.

[The Court's opinion described this as a class suit brought by two young males who had been placed in state hospitals after their behavior had proved uncontrollable both in school and at home. The class was defined as all persons under eighteen currently undergoing diagnosis or treatment in Georgia mental hospitals. The defendants were state officials responsible for direction of Georgia's mental hospitals. The plaintiffs sought a declaratory judgment that the state's voluntary commitment of children under eighteen to mental hospitals was in violation of the Due Process Clause. They also asked for injunctive relief.

The Georgia statute provided that a parent or guardian could apply for the admission of his child or ward to the state's mental hospitals, and if the child were found to be suitable for treatment as having a mental illness, he could be admitted. Discharge could be obtained after five days at the request of the parent or guardian, or

* Due to its inordinate length the opinion in this case had to be drastically abridged, to an extent greater than usual in this book. Students may therefore wish to consult the original report of the case, although in the editor's view the sections included here give a fair and adequate sample of the Court's reasoning.

when the hospital superintendent could determine that hospitalization
was not longer desirable. No state-wide regulations governing admission procedures existed, and the procedures at the different hospitals
varied. The Court's opinion described the procedures and admissions
criteria for each hospital in detail. In general admission was subject
to approval by members of the hospital staff, and the child's need for
continued hospitalization was usually reviewed periodically by members of the staff. In some instances admission was through referral
from local mental health centers.

The three-judge district court from whose judgment this appeal
was taken held that these admission procedures violated the Due
Process Clause of the Fourteenth Amendment by failing to provide
for notice to the child and a hearing before an impartial tribunal.
The district court also held that Georgia was appropriating too little
for nonhospital care and ordered the state to appropriate such funds
as would be necessary to provide such care for those children who
needed it.

After two introductory sections the Court's opinion addressed
the legal issues.]

III

In an earlier day, the problems inherent in coping with children
afflicted with mental or emotional abnormalities were dealt with
largely within the family. * * * While some parents no doubt
were able to deal with their disturbed children without specialized assistance, others especially those of limited means and education, were
not. Increasingly, they turned for assistance to local, public sources
or private charities. Until recently most of the states did little more
than provide custodial institutions for the confinement of persons
who were considered dangerous. Slovenko, Criminal Justice Procedures in Civil Commitment, 24 Wayne L.Rev. 1, 3 (1977) (hereinafter Slovenko).

As medical knowledge about the mentally ill and public concern
for their condition expanded, the states, aided substantially by federal
grants, have sought to ameliorate the human tragedies of seriously
disturbed children. * * *

The parties agree that our prior holdings have set out a general
approach for testing challenged state procedures under a due process
claim. Assuming the existence of a protectible property or liberty interest, the Court has required a balancing of a number of factors:

"First, the private interest that will be affected by the official
action; second, the risk of an erroneous deprivation of such interest
through the procedures used, and the probable value, if any, of additional or substitute procedural safeguards; and finally, the Government's interest, including the function involved and the fiscal and administrative burdens that the additional or substitute procedural re-

quirement would entail." Mathews v. Eldridge, 424 U.S. 319, 335, 96 S.Ct. 893, 903, 47 L.Ed.2d 18 (1976); Smith v. OFFER, 431 U.S. 816, 847–848, 97 S.Ct. 2094, 2111–2112, 53 L.Ed.2d 14 (1977).

* * *

(a) It is not disputed that a child, in common with adults, has a substantial liberty interest in not being confined unnecessarily for medical treatment and that the State's involvement in the commitment decision constitutes state action under the Fourteenth Amendment. In re Gault, 387 U.S. 1, 27, 87 S.Ct. 1428, 1443, 18 L.Ed.2d 527 (1967). We also recognize that commitment sometimes produces adverse social consequences for the child because of the reaction of some to the discovery that the child has received psychiatric care.

This reaction, however, need not be equated with the community response resulting from being labeled by the state as delinquent, criminal, or mentally ill and possibly dangerous. The state through its voluntary commitment procedures does not "label" the child; it provides a diagnosis and treatment that medical specialists conclude the child requires. In terms of public reaction, the child who exhibits abnormal behavior may be seriously injured by an erroneous decision not to commit. Appellees overlook a significant source of the public reaction to the mentally ill, for what is truly "stigmatizing" is the symptomatology of a mental or emotional illness. See also Schwartz, Myers & Astrachan, Psychiatric Labeling and the Rehabilitation of the Mental Patient, 31 Archives of General Psychiatry 329 (1974). The pattern of untreated, abnormal behavior—even if nondangerous —arouses at least as much negative reaction as treatment that becomes public knowledge. A person needing, but not receiving, appropriate medical care may well face even greater social ostracism resulting from the observable symptoms of an untreated disorder.

However, we need not decide what effect these factors might have in a different case. For purposes of this decision, we assume that a child has a protectible interest not only in being free of unnecessary bodily restraints but also in not being labeled erroneously by some because of an improper decision by the state hospital superintendent.

(b) We next deal with the interests of the parents who have decided, on the basis of their observations and independent professional recommendations, that their child needs institutional care. * * *

Our jurisprudence historically has reflected Western Civilization concepts of the family as a unit with broad parental authority over minor children. Our cases have consistently followed that course; our constitutional system long ago rejected any notion that a child is "the mere creature of the State" and, on the contrary, asserted that parents generally "have the right, coupled with the high duty, to recognize and prepare [their children] for additional obligations." Pierce v. Society of Sisters, 268 U.S. 510, 535, 45 S.Ct. 571, 573, 69

L.Ed. 1070 (1924). Surely, this includes a "high duty" to recognize symptoms of illness and to seek and follow medical advice. The law's concept of the family rests on a presumption that parents possess what a child lacks in maturity, experience, and capacity for judgment required for making life's difficult decisions. More important, historically it has recognized that natural bonds of affection lead parents to act in the best interests of their children.

* * * That some parents "may at times be acting against the interests of their child" as was stated in Bartley v. Kremens, 402 F. Supp. 1039, 1047–1048 (ED Pa.1975), vacated 431 U.S. 119, 97 S.Ct. 1709, 52 L.Ed.2d 184 (1977), creates a basis for caution, but is hardly a reason to discard wholesale those pages of human experience that teach that parents generally do act in the child's best interests. The statist notice that governmental power should supersede parental authority in *all* cases because *some* parents abuse and neglect children is repugnant to American tradition.

Nonetheless, we have recognized that a state is not without constitutional control over parental discretion in dealing with children when their physical or mental health is jeopardized. Moreover, the Court recently declared unconstitutional a state statute that granted parents an absolute veto over a minor child's decision to have an abortion. Planned Parenthood of Missouri v. Danforth, 428 U.S. 52, 96 S.Ct. 2831, 49 L.Ed.2d 788 (1976). * * *

* * * Simply because the decision of a parent is not agreeable to the child or because it involves risks does not automatically transfer the power to make that decision from the parents to some agency or officer of the state. * * * Most children, even in adolescence, simply are not able to make sound judgments concerning many decisions, including their need for medical care or treatment. Parents can and must make those judgments. * * * Neither state officials nor federal courts are equipped to review such parental decisions. * * *

In defining the respective rights and prerogatives of the child and parent in the voluntary commitment setting, we conclude that our precedents permit the parents to retain a substantial, if not the dominant, role in the decision, absent a finding of neglect or abuse, and that the traditional presumption that the parents act in the best interests of their child should apply. We also conclude, however, that the child's rights and the nature of the commitment decision are such that parents cannot always have absolute and unreviewable discretion to decide whether to have a child institutionalized. They, of course, retain plenary authority to seek such care for their children, subject to a physician's independent examination and medical judgment.

(c) The State obviously has a significant interest in confining the use of its costly mental health facilities to cases of genuine need.

The Georgia program seeks first to determine whether the patient seeking admission has an illness that calls for in-patient treatment. To accomplish this purpose, the State has charged the superintendents of each regional hospital with the responsibility for determining, before authorizing an admission, whether a prospective patient is mentally ill and whether the patient will likely benefit from hospital care. In addition, the State has imposed a continuing duty on hospital superintendents to release any patient who has recovered to the point where hospitalization is no longer needed.

The State in performing its voluntarily assumed mission also has a significant interest in not imposing unnecessary procedural obstacles that may discourage the mentally ill or their families from seeking needed psychiatric assistance. * * *

The State also has a genuine interest in allocating priority to the diagnosis and treatment of patients as soon as they are admitted to a hospital rather than to time-consuming procedural minuets before the admission. * * *

(d) We now turn to consideration of what process protects adequately the child's constitutional rights by reducing risks of error without unduly trenching on traditional parental authority and without undercutting "efforts to further the legitimate interests of both the state and the patient that are served by" voluntary commitments. We conclude that the risk of error inherent in the parental decision to have a child institutionalized for mental health care is sufficiently great that some kind of inquiry should be made by a "neutral factfinder" to determine whether the statutory requirements for admission are satisfied. That inquiry must carefully probe the child's background using all available sources, including, but not limited to, parents, schools and other social agencies. Of course, the review must also include an interview with the child. It is necessary that the decisionmaker have the authority to refuse to admit any child who does not satisfy the medical standards for admission. Finally, it is necessary that the child's continuing need for commitment be reviewed periodically by a similarly independent procedure.

* * *

Due process has never been thought to require that the neutral and detached trier of fact be law-trained or a judicial or administrative officer. * * * Thus, a staff physician will suffice, so long as he or she is free to evaluate independently the child's mental and emotional condition and need for treatment.

It is not necessary that the deciding physician conduct a formal or quasi-formal hearing. * * * What is best for a child is an individual medical decision that must be left to the judgment of physicians in each case. We do no more than emphasize that the decision should represent an independent judgment of what the child requires and that all sources of information that are traditionally relied on by physicians and behavioral specialists should be consulted.

    *   *   *

Here the questions are essentially medical in character: whether the child is mentally or emotionally ill and whether he can benefit from the treatment that is provided by the state. While facts are plainly necessary for a proper resolution of those questions, they are only a first step in the process. * * *

Although we acknowledge the fallibility of medical and psychiatric diagnosis, we do not accept the notion that the shortcomings of specialists can always be avoided by shifting the decision from a trained specialist using the traditional tools of medical science to an untrained judge or adminstrative hearing officer after a judicial-type hearing. * * *

Another problem with requiring a formalized, factfinding hearing lies in the danger it poses for significant intrusion into the parent-child relationship. Pitting the parents and child as adversaries often will be at odds with the presumption that parents act in the best interests of their child. * * *

Moreover, it is appropriate to inquire into how such a hearing would contribute to the long range successful treatment of the patient. Surely, there is a risk that it would exacerbate whatever tensions already existed between the child and the parents. Since the parents can and usually do play a significant role in the treatment while the child is hospitalized and even more so after release, there is a serious risk that an adversary confrontation will adversely affect the ability of the parents to assist the child while in the hospital. Moreover, it will make his subsequent return home more difficult. These unfortunate results are especially critical with an emotionally disturbed child; they seem likely to occur in the context of an adversary hearing in which the parents testify. A confrontation over such intimate family relationships would distress the normal adult parents and the impact on a disturbed child almost certainly would be significantly greater.

It has been suggested that a hearing conducted by someone other than the admitting physician is necessary in order to detect instances where parents are "guilty of railroading their children into asylums" or are using "voluntary commitment procedures in order to sanction behavior of which they disapprove." Ellis, Volunteering Children: Parental Commitment of Minors to Mental Institutions, 62 Calif.L. Rev. 840, 850–851 (1974). Curiously it seems to be taken for granted that parents who seek to "dump" their children on the state will inevitably be able to conceal their motives and thus deceive the admitting psychiatrists and the other mental health professionals who make and review the admission decision. * * * It is unrealistic to believe that trained psychiatrists, skilled in eliciting responses, sorting medically relevant facts and sensitive to motivational nuances will often be deceived about the family situation surrounding a child's emotional disturbance. Surely a lay, or even law-trained factfinder, would be no more skilled in this process than the professional.

By expressing some confidence in the medical decisionmaking process, we are by no means suggesting it is error free. On occasion parents may initially mislead an admitting physician or a physician may erroneously diagnose the child as needing institutional care either because of negligence or an overabundance of caution. That there may be risks of error in the process affords no rational predicate for holding unconstitutional an entire statutory and administrative scheme that is generally followed in more than 30 states. * * * In general, we are satisfied that an independent medical decisionmaking process, which includes the thorough psychiatric investigation described earlier followed by additional periodic review of a child's condition, will protect children who should not be admitted; we do not believe the risks of error in that process would be significantly reduced by a more formal, judicial-type hearing. The issue remains whether the Georgia practices, as described in the record before us, comport with these minimum due process requirements.

(e) Georgia's statute envisions a careful diagnostic medical inquiry to be conducted by the admitting physician at each regional hospital. * * *

In the typical case the parents of a child initially conclude from the child's behavior that there is some emotional problem—in short, that "something is wrong." They may respond to the problem in various ways, but generally the first contact with the State occurs when they bring the child to be examined by a psychologist or psychiatrist at a community mental health clinic.

Most often, the examination is followed by outpatient treatment at the community clinic. In addition, the child's parents are encouraged, and sometimes required, to participate in a family therapy program to obtain a better insight into the problem. In most instances, this is all the care a child requires. However, if, after a period of outpatient care, the child's abnormal emotional condition persists, he may be referred by the local clinic staff to an affiliated regional mental hospital.

At the regional hospital an admissions team composed of a psychiatrist and at least one other mental health professional examines and interviews the child—privately in most instances. This team then examines the medical records provided by the clinic staff and interviews the parents. Based on this information, and any additional background that can be obtained, the admissions team makes a diagnosis and determines whether the child will likely benefit from institutionalized care. If the team finds either condition not met, admission is refused.

If the team admits a child as suited for hospitalization, the child's condition and continuing need for hospital care are reviewed periodically by at least one independent, medical review group. For the most part, the reviews are as frequent as weekly but none are less often than once every two months. Moreover, as we noted earlier the superintendent of each hospital is charged with an affirmative statutory duty to discharge any child who is no longer mentally ill or in need of therapy.

      *   *   *

Although our review of the record in this case satisfies us that Georgia's general administrative and statutory scheme for the voluntary commitment of children is not *per se* unconstitutional, we cannot decide on this record, whether every child in appellees' class received an adequate, independent diagnosis of his emotional condition and need for confinement under the standards announced earlier in this opinion. On remand, the District Court is free to and should consider any individual claims that intitial admissions did not meet the standards we have described in this opinion.

      *   *   *

IV

(a) Our discussion in Part III was directed at the situation where a child's natural parents request his admission to a state mental hospital. Some members of appellees' class, including J. R., were wards of the State of Georgia at the time of their admission. Obviously their situation differs from those members of the class who have natural parents. While the determination of what process is due varies somewhat when the state, rather than a natural parent, makes the request for commitment, we conclude that the differences in the two situations do not justify requiring different procedures at the time of the child's initial admission to the hospital.

For a ward of the State, there may well be no adult who knows him thoroughly and who cares for him deeply. Unlike with natural parents where there is a presumed natural affection to guide their action, the presumption that the state will protect a child's general welfare stems from a specific state statute. Ga.Code Ann. § 24A–101. * * * As Mr. Justice Stewart's concurring opinion points out, no one has questioned the validity of the statutory presumption that the State acts in the child's best interest. Nor could such a challenge be mounted on the record before us. There is no evidence that the State, acting as guardian, attempted to admit any child for reasons unrelated to the child's need for treatment. * * *

Once we accept that the State's application of a child for admission to a hospital is made in good faith, then the question is whether the medical decisionmaking approach of the admitting physician is adequate to satisfy due process. We have already recognized that an independent medical judgment made from the perspective of the best interests of the child after a careful investigation is an acceptable means of justifying a voluntary commitment. We do not believe that the soundness of this decisionmaking is any the less reasonable in this setting.

Indeed, if anything, the decision with regard to wards of the State may well be even more reasonable in light of the extensive written records that are compiled about each child while in the State's custody. In J. R.'s case, the admitting physician had a complete social and medical history of the child before even beginning the diagnosis. After carefully interviewing him and reviewing his extensive files, three physicians independently concluded that institutional care was in his best interests.

Since the state agency having custody and control of the child *in loco parentis* has a duty to consider the best interests of the child with respect to a decision on commitment to a mental hospital, the State may constitutionally allow that custodial agency to speak for the child, subject, of course, to the restrictions governing natural parents. On this record we cannot declare unconstitutional Georgia's admission procedures for wards of the State.

* * *

The absence of an adult who cares deeply for a child has little effect on the reliability of the initial admission decision, but it may have some effect on how long a child will remain in the hospital. * * * For a child without natural parents, we must acknowledge the risk of being "lost in the shuffle." Moreover, there is at least some indication that J. R.'s commitment was prolonged because the Department of Family and Children Services had difficulty finding a foster home for him. Whether wards of the State generally have received less protection than children with natural parents, and, if so, what should be done about it, however, are matters that must be decided in the first instance by the District Court on remand, if the Court concludes the issue is still alive.

V

* * *

On this record we are satisfied that Georgia's medical factfinding processes are reasonable and consistent with constitutional guarantees. Accordingly, it was error to hold unconstitutional the State's procedures for admitting a child for treatment to a state mental hospital. The judgment is therefore reversed and the case is remanded to the District Court for further proceedings consistent with this opinion.

* * *

NOTES AND QUESTIONS

1. Justices Brennan, Marshall and Stevens dissented in this case. The basis for their disagreement was that the Constitution requires at least one post-admission hearing for children hospitalized by their parents, and that it requires pre-confinement hearings for juveniles who are committed to mental hospitals by the state acting *in loco parentis*. They relied upon earlier cases holding that adults are entitled to full adversarial hearings before being committed to mental institutions and upon factors which convinced them that children need even greater protection in this respect than adults. The dissent also asserted that this case is governed by Planned Parenthood v. Danforth, supra, page 251. The hearings which the dissent would require seem to be full scale trial-type hearings, with the child having the right to counsel, the right to confront witnesses, the right to cross-examine and the right to offer evidence opposing the commitment.

In a companion case, Secretary of Public Welfare v. Institutionalized Juveniles, 442 U.S. 640, 99 S.Ct. 2523, 61 L.Ed.2d 142 (1979), the Court upheld Pennsylvania's procedures for commitment of mentally ill or retarded juveniles.

2. In re Roger S. (People v. Gainer), 19 Cal.3d 835, 566 P.2d 997, 139 Cal.Rptr. 861 (1977) held that under both the United States and the California Constitutions due process required a pre-commitment, trial-type hearing for juveniles over fourteen being committed to state mental hospitals. The California Supreme Court did not require a trial before a jury or judge, but did say that the child must have counsel, the right to present evidence and to cross-examine witnesses, adequate written notice of the basis for the commitment, and findings by a preponderance of the evidence, to be made by a neutral fact-finder. The court expressly refrained from deciding what due process requires for children under fourteen. For a further discussion of the application of the Due Process Clause to the commitment of children, with an argument for requiring a full hearing, see Note, The Mental Hospitalization of Children and the Limits of Parental Authority, 88 Yale L.J. 186 (1978).

3. Precisely what is the rationale of Parham v. J.R.?

4. Which case is correct, Parham v. J.R., or In re Roger S.? Does the Due Process Clause make different requirements for the commitment of the adolescent child than for the pre-adolescent child? Does Planned Parenthood v. Danforth control the answer to these questions? What effect on them does Bellotti v. Baird, supra, page 266, have?

5. The opinion in Parham v. J. R. cites In re Gault, 387 U.S. 1 (1967). In that case, which arose in Arizona, a fifteen-year-old boy was picked up by the police on the complaint of a neighbor that he had made an obscene telephone call to her. He was held in the detention home for about four days, during which time a "hearing" was held before the juvenile judge in chambers, the boy's parents being present, but neither they nor the boy was represented by counsel. No one was sworn, the woman who complained of receiving the call did not appear, no record was made, but the boy was asked about his part in the obscene call and seems to have admitted some participation. Later another similar hearing was held, still without counsel for the boy and without the presence of the complainant as a result of which

the boy was committed to the State Industrial School until he should reach age twenty-one, unless sooner discharged. A petition for habeas corpus was then filed in the Arizona courts, and upon denial of the writ the case came to the Supreme Court of the United States. Granting the writ and reversing the Supreme Court of Arizona, the Court held that in a proceeding in which a juvenile is charged with being a "delinquent", as a result of which he may be committed to a state institution, the Due Process Clause entitles him (a) to adequate notice of the charges, (b) to be advised of his right to counsel either of his own choosing or to be furnished by the state, (c) to confront the witnesses against him, to cross-examine them, and (d) to the privilege against self-incrimination.

Justice Fortas in the *Gault* case reviewed the history of the juvenile court movement in the United States, the basic theory of which was that in juvenile delinquency proceedings the state acted as *parens patriae* for the child's benefit, rather than as the child's accuser. He found that the result of this approach was too often arbitrary action lacking in due process, and unfairness to the child. He also found that the juvenile court approach had failed to reduce crime or rehabilitate juvenile offenders. The *Gault* case has generally been assumed to stand for the proposition that the fundamental guarantees of the Due Process Clause apply to children as well as to adults, and that they apply in proceedings which may result in a deprivation of liberty notwithstanding that the proceedings are labeled civil rather than criminal.

A subsequent case, In re Winship, 397 U.S. 358 (1970), held that in the adjudicatory stage of a juvenile delinquency proceeding in which the child is charged with an offense which would be a crime if committed by an adult, the Due Process Clause requires that the standard of proof be the criminal standard, of proof beyond a reasonable doubt. But in McKeiver v. Pennsylvania, 403 U.S. 528 (1971), the Court held that the Due Process Clause does not require the preservation of the right to trial by jury in the adjudicatory phase of a juvenile delinquency proceeding. Beginning with the acknowledged proposition that the Court had refrained in past cases from holding that all the adult criminal's due process rights are applicable to juvenile delinquency proceedings, the Court refused to label such proceedings either "civil" or "criminal" and said that the standard is one of fundamental fairness. The jury was then held not to be a necessary element of fundamental fairness.

C. THE BATTERED CHILD

STATE v. LOSS

Supreme Court of Minnesota, 1973.
204 N.W.2d 404.

TODD, Justice. Defendant appeals from the judgment and from the denial of his motion for a judgment of acquittal notwithstanding the verdict, or, alternatively, for a new trial following his conviction for manslaughter in the first degree, Minn.St. 609.20. Defendant contends that the circumstantial evidence in this case, including the use of medical testimony regarding the "battered child syndrome" and the "battering parent syndrome," does not form a complete chain leading directly to his guilt beyond a reasonable doubt and that it was improper to receive evidence regarding the syndromes. We affirm.

Defendant was the father of Lance Running, the deceased minor child of the age of 6 months. The mother was Lynn Marie Running. The parents had dated for several years and had broken up in the late fall of 1969, subsequent to which the mother discovered she was pregnant and bore the infant victim. Defendant was adjudicated the father, began seeing the mother again, and moved into her apartment in February of 1971, the parties contemplating being married the ensuing summer.

Defendant was employed part time, and on the morning of Saturday, March 13, 1971, arose early and left for his place of employment, returning to the apartment shortly before noon. The mother was contemplating doing the laundry and in preparation had stripped the baby's crib. Normally, the couple took the child with them to a laundromat to do the laundry, but the child had been suffering from a serious cold for about a week, so the mother decided to leave him at home and the defendant was to care for the child. The deceased had been treated by Dr. William Watson, the family doctor, on Wednesday of that week for the cold and also for a foot infection caused by a bite by a puppy belonging to the parties. The doctor testified that when he examined the child on Wednesday, other than suffering from the cold and the apparent infection, the child was in good health and there was no indication of any trauma.

On the day of the tragedy the mother had left the apartment about noon, having placed the child in a twin bed of Hollywood-type construction. She had placed a blanket over it and had propped the mattress up with pillows so that the baby could not roll off the bed. The bed was approximately 2 feet high from the floor. Defendant testifies that the baby was sleeping on the bed when the mother left and that he turned on the TV for a while and then proceeded to straighten up the apartment and stack the dishes in the kitchen. He testified he shut off the TV and then stopped to check the baby. He noticed that the baby was not on the bed but was on the floor at the end of the bed. It looked as if the baby had "crawled off the end or squirmed or something." He testified that the baby was on the floor and there was a rug near the bed and a red blanket with the corner hanging down and a brown blanket on the floor just directly beneath the bed. He further testified that he picked the baby up and that the baby seemed tense and started to cry softly for a few minutes; that he gave him a pacifier; and that he put him to sleep in the crib.

Following this incident, defendant continued straightening the apartment when he claimed the mother called and asked how the baby was. He testified he told her about the baby falling off the bed and going back to sleep. The call from the mother was followed by a telephone call in which the caller did not indicate who was calling. The mother had been receiving similar calls apparently from a former boy friend, and she testified that these had angered the defendant. Defendant testified that after the second phone call the dog started barking, whereupon the baby awoke and began to cry. Defendant allegedly attempted to give the baby a bottle but it did not seem to want it. The baby then went back to sleep, so defendant proceeded to do the dishes. Defendant testified that he did not hear the baby breathing, and when he went in to check, the baby was lying there with his hand up in the air and that he, defendant, became scared and grabbed the baby and could barely hear his heartbeat. Defendant then proceeded to give the baby mouth-to-mouth resuscitation and splashed cold water on its face with his fingers. He called the telephone operator and asked for emergency help. The baby was taken by the emergency vehicle to St. Paul Ramsey Hospital and was admitted to the emergency room, and defendant called the mother at her parents' home and met her at the hospital.

At the hospital, defendant related the story to the mother, except the mother indicated in her testimony that defendant told her that, when he found the baby on the floor, it was lying on a blanket. The hospital report simply indicated that the child may have fallen out of bed.

Later in the evening, X-rays were taken which disclosed a skull fracture and a broken leg, and a doctor contacted both parents and advised them that the medical history did not correspond with the objective findings of the X-rays. At this time, Dr. Homer D. Venters, a pediatrician, was contacted by telephone and advised as to the circumstances. A spinal cut was authorized, disclosing blood and indicating hemorrhaging. On the following morning, Dr. Venters examined the child and noted that a bruise on the baby's forehead had increased in size from the time of the admission of the child, indicating it was of recent origin. The child was pronounced dead at noon on Sunday, March 14.

The mother and father had returned to the apartment just prior to the death of the infant, where the father showed the mother what he claimed had happened. On the day following the death, defendant was contacted at the apartment by Carolen F. Bailey, a police officer, who advised defendant of his rights and indicated that she was investigating the death of the child. Officer Bailey testified that defendant told her that when he found the baby on the floor, he was wrapped in a blanket and was lying on another blanket on the floor and was playing with the blankets. Defendant denied that he ever told this to the police officer.

Defendant also told the police officer that about a week before, while shopping at Har Mar Shopping Center, he had been left in charge of the baby and had had a coke at a drug store with a friend of his. He told the officer that at that time the baby had gotten something in its eyes. He took the baby out to the car on that occasion, wrapped it in a blanket, and placed it in the back seat, and when he returned home he explained to the mother that the baby's eyes were red because it had gotten some pepper in them. He subsequently indicated to the mother that the baby had bumped its head on the steering wheel, and on cross-examination he claimed that the bumping of the head on the steering wheel and the pepper incident were two separate incidents. Regarding this incident, the mother testified that she had noticed the reddening of the eyes when she arrived home and that a small bruise by the eye appeared the next day but disappeared quickly.

The mother testified that defendant had a temper; that the crying of the baby annoyed him; that the telephone calls had caused him to lose his temper; and that on one occasion he had thrown her about the apartment when he had lost his temper.

On Thursday, following the death of the baby, defendant was to see Officer Bailey again, but did not keep the appointment. Instead, he went to Owatonna where he contacted a relative and called the mother, saying that he had written a note explaining many things and that he was contemplating suicide. Defendant was arrested in Owatonna, and a grand jury returned an indictment containing counts of third-degree murder, Minn.St. 609.195, and first-degree manslaughter, Minn.St. 609.20, against defendant. Following the trial, the conviction of first-degree manslaughter was returned by the jury.

The prosecution introduced through Dr. Wayne H. Schrader, a pathologist, the results of an autopsy performed on the decedent. Dr. Schrader testified that the examination consisted of an external examination of the body, as well as a pathological examination of the organs of the abdomen, thoracic cavity, and skull. He testified that there were bruises over the head and neck area; there was a tannish-colored bruise measuring about a half inch in the midline center of the forehead; there was a purplish-tan bruise measuring nearly $1\frac{1}{2}$ by 3 inches on the left frontal parietal area, which would be just above the ear; a small linear or long rod-shaped bruise about 1 by $2\frac{1}{2}$ inches along the angle of the right jawbone. There were other marks on the body indicating the medical treatment rendered the child.

Dr. Schrader testified that the color of the bruises indicated that they were probably not more than 1 to 2 days in age. Examination of the skull area revealed blood beneath the skin, especially in the area of the previously mentioned bruise on the left side of the head; a fracture on the left side of the skull which was somewhat V-shaped, the long arm being approximately $2\frac{1}{2}$ inches long and the short arm about 1 inch in length. He further testified that there had been extensive hemorrhaging under the skull and the brain was swollen. Examination of the tissue disclosed that the hemorrhaging was of recent origin and had occurred approximately 24 hours before death. He further testified that the bruises he had described were larger than when measured at the time of the admittance of the child to the hospital. Dr. Schrader testified that the cause of death was direct trauma to the head.

The prosecution presented as a witness Dr. Venters, who, as has been indicated, had examined the deceased child immediately before its demise. Dr. Venters is a specialist in the field of pediatrics, is head of the Department of Pediatrics at St. Paul Ramsey Hospital, and professor of pediatrics at the University of Minnesota. He testified that he had worked in the field of injuries to small children and had examined between 90 and 100 such cases in the past 2 years at St. Paul Ramsey Hospital. He had attended a national conference on the problem in 1970 and was preparing to give a report on his studies in the field at an international seminar in Vienna, Austria.

Dr. Venters testified that the term "battered child syndrome" had been introduced into medical terminology to describe the conditions which manifested themselves in this field in which he had become interested. He defined battered child syndrome as "a term that is now widely recognized as a condition by which children are injured other than by accident." That is to say, by some adult or some other child, by causes which are not accidental.

Dr. Venters further testified that there is associated with the term "battered child syndrome" the term "battering person." This type of person fits into various patterns. One pattern is that of an individual simply repeating the type of discipline or child management to which he was subjected as a child. A child who is frequently beaten while growing up may develop the same pattern of discipline for his or her own children in later life. A second pattern is frequently seen in an individual who, as a child, has been shunted from foster home to foster home and feels rejected. A third pattern involves a role reversal in which the individual exhibits an even more significant lack of identity and poor self-concept or self-image, and when a child is born, it usually is seen as a love object who returns love and provides love for the needy parent. The fourth category of patterns involves parents who are hostile, abusive, impetuous, and who lash out at insignificant things frequently and react in a hair-triggered manner. Another category of child-abusing individuals is in the field of sexual molestation, but that usually occurs with older children.

Dr. Venters also testified that the battered child syndrome usually appears among children under 3 or 4 years of age. The statistics to which he testified show that various types of skeletal injuries are frequently seen and that the most frequently encountered are skull trauma and trauma to the so-called long bones of the body, the arms and the legs. He further testified that the fracture to the deceased infant's leg was a spiral, twisting-type fracture and that this fracture is more frequently encountered in battered-child syndrome cases than are straight-across fractures.

Dr. Venters further testified that, based upon his experience, he regarded the history of the child given by the parents as incompatible with what was found clinically and by X-rays and that injuries sustained by the child could not have happened by accident. He testified that the cause of death was brain injury secondary to battered child syndrome. Dr. Venters had not talked with the defendant directly and did not testify that defendant was a battering parent.

1. This case presents to our court for the first time the use of the medical terminology "battered child syndrome" and "battering parent syndrome" in a case involving substantial injuries and resulting death to a minor child. Medical authorities have recently expanded their investigation into this field, which has developed from a series of conferences beginning in the late 1950's and early 1960's to the present state of medical research and analysis of the phenomena peculiar to the field. As a result of this investigation, legislation has been proposed in numerous states. Minnesota adopted such legislation in 1965 regarding the reporting of maltreatment of minors. This section appears as Minn.St. 626.554. Subd. 1 thereof declares the purpose of the statute as follows:

"The purpose of this section is to provide for the protection of minor children who have had physical injury inflicted upon them, by other than accidental means, where the injury appears to have been caused as a result of physical abuse or neglect."

The previously quoted definition by Dr. Venters of the battered child syndrome fits with our statutory scheme of reporting such injuries.

2. Counsel for defendant in oral argument admitted that the deceased in this case was a battered child. However, defendant strenuously argues that the state must not only establish the battered child syndrome, but must have evidence identifying defendant as a battering parent, which was not done directly in this case. Here, the medical evidence established the various categories into which a battering parent would fall. Adequate evidence was introduced regarding defendant's temperament and past experiences with the child to raise questions regarding his conduct, and the evidence was sufficient to enable the jury to find that defendant was a battering parent of the type described in the fourth category presented by Dr. Venters.

We hold that the establishment of the existence of a battered child, together with the reasonable inference of a battering parent, is sufficient to convict defendant herein in light of the other circumstantial evidence presented by the prosecution. It is very difficult in these prosecutions for injuries and death to minor children to establish the guilt of a defendant other than by circumstantial evidence.

Normally, as was the case here, there are no eyewitnesses. The establishment of the fact that the deceased child was a battered child was proper, and adequate foundation was laid for the introduction of the evidence which conclusively established a battered child syndrome. The prosecution properly presented to the jury the psychological framework which constitutes a battering parent. It did not attempt to point the finger of accusation at defendant as a battering parent by its medical testimony. Rather, it presented sufficient evidence from which the jury could reasonably conclude that defendant fit one of the psychological patterns of a battering parent.

3.   Further, considering the facts as totally presented, particularly the fact that defendant was in exclusive control and custody of the minor child immediately prior to the report of injury, the evidence as a whole sustained a finding of his guilt beyond a reasonable doubt. In this respect, it should be noted that, other than the cold from which the child was suffering, the swelling from the apparent infection of the leg caused by the dog incident, and a small bruise on his forehead possibly caused from bumping the crib, the child was apparently in good health. The mother testified that none of the extreme bruises which were subsequently discovered on the child was apparent at the time she left the child in the custody of the defendant.

4.   Defendant further claims that the circumstantial evidence in this case was insufficient to establish his guilt beyond a reasonable doubt.

The applicable rule to determine the sufficiency of circumstantial evidence was set forth originally in State v. DeZeler, 230 Minn. 39, 52, 41 N.W.2d 313, 322 (1950), which held that circumstantial evidence will support a conviction only where the facts described by it—

"* * * form a complete chain which, in the light of the evidence as a whole, leads so directly to the guilt of the accused as to exclude, beyond a reasonable doubt, any reasonable inference other than that of guilt * * *."

* * * In other words, circumstantial evidence "must do more than create a suspicion of guilt. It must point unerringly to the accused's guilt." * * * However, in determining whether there is sufficient evidence to support the jury's conclusion the facts must be reviewed in the light most favorable to a finding of guilt. * * *

In State v. Kotka, 277 Minn. 331, 334, 152 N.W.2d 445, 448 (1967), it was stated:

"* * * [A] conviction upon circumstantial evidence cannot be sustained, against the presumption of innocence, unless the reasonable inferences from such evidence are consistent only with defendant's guilt and inconsistent with any rational hypothesis except that of his guilt."

We are of the opinion that the circumstantial evidence at trial established defendant's guilt beyond a reasonable doubt. Defendant's conduct with the decedent prior to the incident in question, his prior displays of temper, his exclusive control over the baby at or near the time the death-causing injuries were sustained, the improbability that decedent could have sustained such multiple injuries as a result of a fall from a height of 2 feet, and competent medical testimony to the effect that death had not been caused by accident are elements which "form a complete chain" leading "directly to the guilt of the accused." No reasonable inference other than guilt exists.

FABRITZ v. TRAURIG

United States Court of Appeals, Fourth Circuit, 1978.
583 F.2d 697.

BRYAN, Senior Circuit Judge: Habeas corpus was refused by the District Court to Virginia Fabritz, a 20-year old mother, who was imprisoned under a conviction and five-year sentence in a Maryland court for abuse—delayed medical attention—touching the death of her daughter, Windy, three years of age. Md. Code Ann. Art. 27, § 35A(a) (Cum.Supp.1975).[1] The Court of Special Appeals of Maryland reversed, but the Court of Appeals affirmed.[2]

While fully recognizing the lettered study and explication of both the statute and the evidence by the Maryland Judges as well as by the District Judge, we are forced to the view that the conviction is void for denial of Fourteenth Amendment due process. This is because the "conviction [is] based on a record lacking any relevant evidence as to a crucial element of the offense charged," i. e., that the mother had knowledge of the critical gravity of her daughter's condition when she deferred resort to medical advice for the little girl.

True, she saw the multiple severe bruises (later counted as 70) on the child, apparently caused by body blows, but the testimony indisputably establishes, and the State conceded, that she was totally

1. § 35A. Causing abuse to child under eighteen.
* * *

(a) *Penalty.*—Any parent, adoptive parent or other person who has the permanent or temporary care or custody or responsibility for the supervision of a minor child under the age of eighteen years *who causes abuse* to such minor child shall be guilty of a felony and upon conviction shall be sentenced to not more than fifteen years in the penitentiary. (Accent added.)
* * *

(b) 7. *"Abuse"* shall mean any: (A) *physical injury or injuries* sustained by a child as a result of *cruel or inhumane treatment* or as a result of malicious act or acts by any parent, adoptive parent or other person who has the permanent or temporary care or custody or responsibility for supervision of a minor child, (B) any sexual abuse of a child, whether physical injuries are sustained or not. (Accent added.)
* * *

2. 276 Md. 416, 348 A.2d 275 (1975), rev'g 24 Md.App. 708, 332 A.2d 324, cert. denied 425 U.S. 942, 96 S.Ct. 1680, 48 L.Ed.2d 185 (1976).

ignorant of when or how they had been inflicted. Indeed, she had been away from home the two or three days previous. Furthermore, mother and daughter loved each other deeply, and the mother set about at once to learn of the child's ailments and to give relief. The narration, in a moment, of the evidence will not reveal a modicum of it as manifesting to the mother the precarious state of Windy's life. Only after watching her for almost eight hours, and then with the assistance of a woman neighbor, did the two of them realize the child's peril. It was then they sought medical advice, but the child died in the ambulance en route to the hospital about one-half hour later.

Appellant, Virginia Fabritz, was indicted in two counts, child abuse and assault and battery. At trial acquittal was ordered on the latter for absence of proof, but the jury found her guilty of child abuse.

The evidence follows. Fabritz resided with her daughter, Windy, in the home of Thomas L. Crockett and his wife, Ann. The child was three years old when, on October 1, 1973, she was left with the Crocketts while her mother went to her grandfather's funeral in another county. She did not again see Windy until her return at one o'clock on the afternoon of October 3d. She was met by Crockett with his motorcycle and with Windy riding in the side car. To the mother the child looked unwell. Crockett attributed this appearance to the bumpiness of the motorcycle ride.

On arrival home about 2:30 that afternoon, Windy began to suffer with cramps and to her mother seemed feverish with the flu. At this time she noted the bruises on her body. After bathing her, Fabritz put her to bed or on a couch. Soon afterwards, Windy was seen to have gotten up and curled herself in a blanket on the floor. At 5:00 the child was semi-conscious and improved, sitting up for a brief interval after receiving some liquid nourishment. Near 6:00 that afternoon, Windy vomited and showed she was not feeling well. At 7:00 she was put back to bed. Believing the child to have a temperature, her mother sent for a thermometer. The little girl was given soda to settle her stomach, as well as more liquid nourishment, and placed in bed again around 7:30 or 8:00.

Fabritz twice telephoned Connie Schaeffer, a neighbor for assistance, telling her of the child's flu and of her worsening condition. On arrival Schaeffer, too, saw that Windy had a fever. Asked about the bruises on Windy, the mother replied, "Tommy hits hard." They bathed her in alcohol and put her to bed. At this point the child appeared to Schaeffer to be half asleep, neither moaning nor crying.

Schaeffer testified at trial that she did not know what was the matter with Windy, and had left the Crockett house without suggesting medical assistance. Further testimony related that at this moment Ann Crockett arrived home and discussed with Fabritz the procurement of medical attention and Fabritz asked Ann to keep an eye on Windy. The two concluded it was necessary to seek help. Ann called the County Hospital, and was advised by the doctor that the women should bring the child to the hospital.

It was then that Ann, on entering the child's bedroom, perceived she was not breathing. Thereupon she sought an ambulance while Fabritz applied mouth-to-mouth resuscitation. The rescue ambulance took Windy, accompanied by Ann, to the hospital. Meanwhile, Schaeffer saw Fabritz in a hysterical condition, endeavored to calm her and drove her to the hospital, where they were informed the child had been declared dead on arrival at 10:35. In this state she told Schaeffer, "It is my fault, I killed her."

The medical opinion was that 18 to 24 hours before death—during Fabritz' absence from home—the child had been struck in the abdomen by a blunt instrument, possibly a fist, rupturing the duodenum and leading to death from peritonitis. No evidence intimated that Fabritz had knowledge that the person in whose custody Windy was left would abuse her.

At one juncture Fabritz remarked that she had not taken Windy to the hospital because Fabritz "was too ashamed of the bruises" on her body. On his trial Crockett was acquitted of any connection with the death. At her trial the prosecution conceded that Fabritz had not struck the child.

The Maryland Court of Appeals' conclusion was that Fabritz' "inaction amounted to child abuse;" that her "failure to obtain medical attention" constituted "cruel or inhumane treatment;" and that this treatment was a cause of the child's "physical injury." In determining to grant Fabritz habeas corpus, we accept the statute as valid, as did the Court of Appeals of Maryland and the District Court, and accept, too, their clear exposition of the critical words of the law. The statute simply was unconstitutionally applied.

Our conclusion does not affront the conclusion of the Maryland Court, nor that of the District Court. The three steps of the State Court's reasoning do not preclude a finding that the evidence is wholly wanting in proof of an indispensable factor: that during the three stages of the syllogism Fabritz had knowledge that she was risking the life of her child. That is the decisive issue here.

The evidence is utterly bare of proof of a consciousness of criminality during her bedside vigil. This may have been an error of judgment, however dreadfully dear, but there was no awareness of wrongdoing on her part. The jury's contrary verdict on that question finds no warrant in the testimony. Fabritz' error amounted to a failure to procure medical attention in less than eight hours after her arrival at home. Without expert medical knowledge to place her on notice of the fatal nature of the child's illness, she treated her as best she knew. The misjudgment was only to the significance of the symptoms and of the immediacy of demand for professional care. In these circumstances the conviction cannot stand—without even so much as a murmur of evidential justification.

As the Court said in Thompson v. Louisville, 362 U.S. 199, 80 S. Ct. 624, 4 L.Ed.2d 654 (1960):

The ultimate question presented to us is whether the charges against petitioner were so totally devoid of evidentiary support as to render his conviction unconstitutional under the Due Process Clause of the Fourteenth Amendment. Decision of this question turns not on the sufficiency of the evidence, but on whether this conviction rests upon any evidence at all. Id. at 199, 80 S.Ct. at 625.

* * *

[S]o is it a violation of due process to convict and punish a man without evidence of his guilt. Id., at 206, 80 S.Ct. at 629 (footnote omitted).

It would be a radical overthrow of the universal understanding of motherly devotion, as well as the confidence gained by experience to be accorded the judgment of two women having the responsibility of a sick 3-year old, to hold the conduct of the mother or of her friend suspect. Especially is this true when it is remembered that although the child would have survived "had an operation been performed within at least twelve hours prior to death," Fabritz had not even then returned from her grandfather's funeral. The callings of nursing and baby-sitting ought not impose so frightening a trusteeship.

The judgment on appeal will be vacated and the case remanded to the District Court to grant the writ.

HAYNSWORTH, Chief Judge, dissenting:

I have a great deal of sympathy for this young woman who has spent a time in prison on a conviction of child abuse arising out of the death of her three-year old daughter, though generally the mother had been a loving and considerate one. My sympathy for the mother is enhanced by the fact that the person who inflicted the fatal injury upon the child has remained unpunished. I think, however, that the proof at trial did not permit a conclusion on our part that there was no evidence to support a finding of a violation of the statute by the mother.

Of course, a parent should not go to prison for an erroneous diagnosis of a child's illness, but the Court of Appeals of Maryland has clearly held that the statute is violated if a custodian of a child knowingly withholds medical assistance and if the child's condition is aggravated or if death ensues as a result of want of medical attention.

Indeed, Maryland has long embraced the common law doctrine that one who, through gross negligence, fails to perform a legal duty owing to another as a result of which the other dies is guilty of involuntary manslaughter.

There can be no doubt here that the multiple bruises were not symptomatic of influenza. When the neighbor saw the child, she was moaning in pain. That and her comatose condition should have signalled a more serious condition than the flu. That the mother recognized that there may have been internal injuries is supported by the testimony that she explained the child's bruised condition to the neighbor by saying, "Tommy hits hard."

One may suppose that this three-year old child had told her mother who had beaten her, and the record clearly indicates that Tommy Crockett was the lover of both of the women who shared the house with him. Thus, she explained to the neighbor that she had not sought a physician's help because she was ashamed of the bruised condition of the child's body and that if the child were seen by a physician she would have to explain the origin of the bruises.

I put no great weight on her exclamation after being informed that the child was dead, "I killed her", but her statements to the neighbor before the child was dead of her reasons for not having sooner sought medical help furnished support for a finding that for some hours the mother consciously refrained from seeking medical help to protect Crockett from possible criminal charges and to support her own ego. Though the mother was generally loving and protective of her daughter, a conscious indulgence of such a preference is in violation of Maryland's Child Abuse Law when earlier medical attention might have saved the child's life.

I cannot agree that this conviction was devoid of evidentiary support.

IN RE J. Z.

Supreme Court of North Dakota, 1971.
190 N.W.2d 27.

DOUGLAS B. HEEN, District Judge. John Z. and his wife, Susan Z., have appealed, asking trial de novo, from a district court judgment terminating their parental rights to their son, J. Z., born to their marriage on February 24, 1970. We affirm the judgment.

On August 14, 1970, Lynn Aas, manager of a Minot medical clinic, reported to Cal Asendorf, a Ward County Juvenile Supervisor, that there was reasonable cause to believe that J. Z., a five-month-old baby being attended by the clinic staff, had suffered serious injury or was suffering physical neglect not explained by available medical history as being accidental in nature. This report is required by N.D.C. C. Sec. 50–25–01. Immediate temporary placement in a foster home was ordered, and the child has been in a foster home since his release from the hospital.

On August 28, 1970, a petition signed by William H. Blore, Juvenile Supervisor, was filed in the Juvenile Division of District Court for Ward County, alleging that J. Z. was a deprived child, which condition was likely to continue, and asking that parental rights of John Z. and Susan Z. be terminated. At the appellants' request, the proceedings were continued and came on for hearing on October 29, 1970, with a concluding hearing on November 12, 1970.

The trial court terminated the appellants' parental rights, finding beyond a reasonable doubt that J. Z. suffered serious physical injuries because of mistreatment by his father, John Z., as follows: that on or about August 13, 1970, the father by force inserted a toy telephone into the mouth of the child, nearly causing his death by suffocation; that shortly before the above occasion, the father forced or induced a boiling liquid or very hot substance into J. Z.'s mouth, causing serious burns to his throat; and that previously J. Z. received numerous bruises on different parts of his body and five fractured ribs which were the result of striking, slapping, dropping, or other rough treatment by his father; that the mother, Susan Z., acquiesced in his treatment; that J. Z. thereby was a deprived child; and that such treatment by the parents was likely to continue and would probably cause J. Z. serious physical, mental, moral, or emotional harm.

An appeal taken under the Uniform Juvenile Court Act, N.D.C.C. 27–20, is triable anew in this Court. * * *

The trial court judgment is attacked on the ground that the appellants made incriminating statements to a juvenile supervisor in the absence of counsel; that there was error in the admission of expert medical testimony; that the statutory definition of deprived child is unconstitutional for vagueness and uncertainty; that the appellant parents were denied their constitutional rights by this termination; and that the evidence does not support the judgment.

The fundamental natural right of a parent to the custody and society of his child and to provide for his moral, mental, and physical welfare has been recognized to be of constitutional dimension. This, however, is not an absolute right. * * *

The North Dakota Juvenile Court Act likewise acknowledges the inherent right of parents to their child's custody and to care for his welfare, the act providing that its interpretation and construction shall be:

To achieve the foregoing purposes in a family environment whenever possible, separating the child from his parents only when necessary for his welfare or in the interest of public safety.

North Dakota Century Code, Sec. 27–20–01(3).

Accordingly, any judicial disposition of J. Z. may be made only if the child is brought within the jurisdiction of the trial court as a "deprived child."

The Juvenile Court Act, N.D.C.C. Sec. 27–20–02(5), defines a "deprived child" as a child who:

a. Is without proper parental care or control, subsistence, education as required by law, or other care or control necessary for his physical, mental, or emotional health, or morals, and the deprivation is not due primarily to the lack of financial means of his parents * * * ;

and our law requires that the court's finding that a juvenile is a "deprived child" be by clear and convincing evidence. N.D.C.C. Sec. 27–20–29(3).

This proceeding is based upon N.D.C.C. Sec. 27–20–44, which in part provides:

1. The court by order may terminate the parental rights of a parent with respect to his child if:

* * *

b. The child is a deprived child and the court finds that the conditions and causes of the deprivation are likely to continue or will not be remedied and that by reason thereof the child is suffering or will probably suffer serious physical, mental, moral, or emotional harm;

* * *

Not only must the trial court find that a child is deprived by clear and convincing evidence, but the probability of continuance of deprivation must be by the same degree of proof before there may be a termination of parental rights under this section of our law.

On trial, the evidence developed that early on the evening of August 13, 1970, half of a toy telephone, the broken part first, lodged in J. Z.'s throat. His parents rushed him to a Minot Hospital, where the broken toy was extracted by Dr. Fred Erenfeld, who fortunately happened to be at the hospital. At the time, Dr. Erenfeld thought the baby was dead. Following extraction and resuscitation procedures, the baby's own doctor, Dr. Gunay Raghib, having arrived at the hospital, assumed care of the child. Upon examination, Dr. Raghib found the child to be bruised below his umbilicus, to have a half-inch laceration at the soft palate, to be bleeding from his nose and mouth, and to be in shock and exhibiting evidence of pneumonia.

It was Dr. Erenfeld's opinion that lodgment of the toy rattle in the baby's throat was not accidental but required outside force. Dr. Raghib was of the opinion that J. Z., a baby of five months, did not insert the rattle into his own throat nor did he have the strength to break the toy.

During his subsequent hospitalization, the baby would not swallow and did not eat. Again the child was examined by Dr. Raghib, who concluded that this complication was caused by burns, probably chemical in nature, to the child's mouth and throat tract, the esophagus, to the stomach. This, in his opinion, occurred one day, and not more than two days, prior to J. Z.'s admission to the hospital. Dr.

Raghib could find no rational cause or explanation for these internal burns, stating that because of the age of the baby, the liquid or substance causing the burns, of necessity, had to appear in the baby's bottle; that, while the liquid causing the burns may have been given accidentally, yet the baby would not take the substance accidentally, because he would reject the burning substance or liquid. From this, the inference arises, in the opinion of Dr. Raghib, that the baby was prevented from so rejecting the liquid or substance causing the burn.

Dr. Dionisio Libi, a throat specialist, examined the baby on August 18, 1970, in consultation with Dr. Raghib and concurred in finding severe chemical burns to the mouth and throat of the child. Although unable to account for the cause of the burns, Dr. Libi did state that the burns had to be forced.

X-rays taken of J. Z. during his August period of hospitalization to aid in the treatment of his pneumonia, revealed five healing rib fractures to his left side. These fractures, according to Dr. Raghib, could only have been caused by application of strong force and probably had occurred some weeks before.

Some two months earlier, June 1970, J. Z. was briefly admitted to the hospital for treatment of an infected nose and throat by Dr. Raghib. On admission, the child had four or five bruises on his left chest, a bruised right cheek and pelvis. The youngster was x-rayed but apparently not extensively enough to disclose the fractures, if such existed at the time.

Four days after J. Z. was hospitalized, on August 17, 1971, the Juvenile Supervisor, Mr. Asendorf, interviewed both parents at his office relative to the events surrounding lodgment of the toy rattle in J. Z.'s throat. At the time, the parents were not represented by counsel. During trial, on direct examination, and without objection, Mr. Asendorf related portions of the interview. On cross-examination, the appellant parents' counsel developed that Mr. Asendorf did not, either before or during the interview, advise the parents of a right to counsel before discussion of these events with the Juvenile Supervisor. Appellants' attorney then, for the first time, objected to Mr. Asendorf's "prior" testimony. The overruling by the trial court of this objection is assigned as error on this appeal, the appellant parents claiming their statements were privileged because made at an informal adjustment conference.

A party is entitled to counsel at all stages of any proceeding under the North Dakota Juvenile Court Act. N.D.C.C. Sec. 27–20–26. Parental termination procedures are a part of the Juvenile Court Act, and the right to counsel extends to parties involved in such proceedings.

In appropriate instances, before a petition under the Juvenile Court Act is filed, there may be an informal adjustment of differences—that is, court-sponsored counselling, advice, and imposition of

"conditions for the conduct and control of the child" if there is jurisdiction, if in the best interest of the public and the child, and if
"[t]he child and his parents * * * consent thereto with knowledge that consent is not obligatory." N.D.C.C. Sec. 27–20–10. This
section further provides that incriminating statements made during
"informal adjustment" are privileged.

Consideration of the statute in question, N.D.C.C. Sec. 27–20–10,
leads to the conclusion that "informal adjustment" has application
only to a child—that is, an individual under eighteen years of age,
unmarried, and not a member of the armed services [N.D.C.C. Sec.
27–20–02]—who is alleged to be delinquent, unruly, or deprived.
Being so excluded by the implicit language of the statute, parents involved in parental termination proceedings are not entitled to the
benefits of informal adjustment.

During this initial interview with the parents, the juvenile supervisor was proceeding under N.D.C.C. Sec. 27–20–06, which empowers
him in that capacity to make investigations, to receive and examine
complaints and "charges of * * * deprivation of a child for the
purpose of considering the commencement of proceedings * * *."
He was not simply screening a complaint to determine if there was
jurisdiction or if there was no evidence substantiating the complaint.
Rather, he was functioning as a law enforcement officer gathering
evidence, on the one hand, and, on the other, determining whether
there would be court proceedings to terminate parental rights. At
the outset of the initial interview which was a critical stage in these
proceedings * * * the parents, although not entitled to informal
adjustment, should have been advised of their right to counsel and
should have been afforded the opportunity of consulting a lawyer before proceeding with the initial interview. N.D.C.C. Sec. 27–20–26.

In the case at hand, however, as noted, the appellants did not object to Mr. Asendorf's direct testimony detailing his conversation
with the appellant parents at the initial interview; and, as stated, it
was not until commencement of cross-examination that there was
such an objection. Timely objection not having been made, and there
being no motion to strike such evidence from the record coupled with
a showing of surprise, Mr. Asendorf's direct testimony was properly
received. * * *

Juvenile Supervisor Asendorf's direct testimony was identical,
save in some small detail, to that given by the appellant parents, John
Z. and Susan Z., as such is hereafter summarized.

Both of the baby's parents, the father, John Z., and the mother,
Susan Z., testified at the trial. Neither their testimony, whether for
or against the other spouse, nor that of the doctors in any particular,
is privileged under North Dakota law. * * *

A summary of the testimony of the child's mother, Susan Z., follows:

She testified that the father, John Z., was bottle-feeding the baby in the front room while she was on the telephone in the kitchen. The father appeared in the kitchen, with the child, who was bleeding from the mouth, in his arms, and said, "Get something out of his throat." Unsuccessful in their efforts to remove the foreign object from the baby's throat and sensing the extremity of the situation, the parents rushed J. Z. to the hospital.

She could offer no explanation of the baby's body and facial bruises and contusions, other than that the father at times played roughly with the child. From time to time, she did question her husband about the baby's injuries, of which he denied all knowledge. She did remark that his rough play with the child should stop. At times, the father physically abused the mother. On one occasion the mother called her pastor to the home. In the course of his ministering, the pastor observed that the baby was bruised and counseled that J. Z. be taken to a doctor. The mother, however, did nothing.

The mother disclaimed any knowledge of how the baby's ribs came to be fractured. She never at any time saw the baby mistreated, and she stated that the only punishment ever administered by her husband was to put the child to bed when he cried.

Neither could the mother account for her child's throat burns, except that a couple of days before the baby's admission to the hospital for emergency extraction of the rattle, the father may have given him boiling water.

Just before the rattle incident, the mother saw the toy, then in one piece, in the crib. She could not explain how the rattle came to be broken or how half of the damaged toy lodged in the baby's throat, but she did suspect that her husband had something to do with it.

For his part the father testified that while the mother was answering the phone in the kitchen, he put the baby "in his crib, braced his bottle up with his blanket and gave him his rattle," which was then in one piece, and left to get a pacifier. When John Z. returned, the child had the rattle up to his lips, and then events moved swiftly, in the words of the father:

Yes, I just returned with his pacifier, and I don't know, it happened so fast. I remember vaguely, remember trying to get a portion of the rattle out of his mouth, and I tried to get his mouth open, and I don't know, the more I tried, the farther down it went, so I held him upside down, and I hit him on the back, hard, a couple of times. He started bleeding. That is when I ran in and got my wife.

Upon being asked if he remembered the rattle breaking—which, as noted earlier in this decision, Dr. Raghib described as being too substantial to have been broken by this baby—John Z. replied:

No, I don't, not actually how it broke or anything. I can't remember. I don't know if it was broke off before it went in the mouth, or it snapped off prior to being—me coming into the room or anything. When I come into the room, he had it up to his lips. Everything happened so fast: * * *

He further testified he had no memory of placing the rattle in the baby's mouth.

Several members of the families of the parents testified as to the bruises appearing from time to time on the baby's body, of their apprehension for the child, and of the fact that such concern had been expressed to these parents. The father and the mother described how the father would blow with some force upon the child's neck and body and said they thought this could be a possible source of the bruises.

The father admitted that he had a quick temper, that he had physically abused his wife on occasion, and that he was institutionalized for alcoholism in April 1970 until the first part of the following June.

It is significant that some of the bruises, the fractured ribs, the burned mouth and throat tract, and the rattle lodgment sustained by this baby all occurred after completion of the father's alcoholism treatment and while the father was alone, or had been alone, with the child.

After commencement of these proceedings, the father was interviewed by a clinical psychologist, Dr. Robert Edmunds, who at the trial testified that the father, among other things, was a danger to himself and others and that his life style would remain relatively unchanged.

In addition, the parents undertook marriage counseling during pendency of this proceeding. A family therapist, Mrs. Mary Ekberg, a consultant with a medical clinic, believed that while John Z. and Susan Z. at the time of trial were not fit and proper parents, yet was of the opinion that in a year they could become so with proper counseling. This conclusion was supported by testimony of the clinic psychiatrist, Dr. R. O. Saxvik, who worked in conjunction with the family therapist and who testified on behalf of the appellants. He was of the opinion that the father, John Z., was not neurotic or psychotic but was immature, antisocial, and possessed a character disorder. This expert witness could give no idea of the length of time required to overcome these difficulties.

Testifying for the State, Dr. Raghib on direct examination, over objection, termed J. Z. a battered child. The appellants contend that the term *battered child* is synonymous with *deprived child* and that the expression of this opinion by the doctor prejudiced their case. The term *battered child* is directly related to N.D.C.C. Sec. 50–25–01, which in part provides:

Any physician * * * having reasonable cause to believe that a child under the age of eighteen years coming before him for medical examination, attendance, care, or treatment has suffered serious injury or physical neglect not explained by the available medical history as being accidental in nature, shall make written report of such fact * * * to the appropriate juvenile commissioner.

* * *

This section further requires disclosure by the doctor of "any other information which may be helpful in establishing the cause of injury or neglect and identity of the perpetrator."

Accordingly, the doctor by statute is required to express his opinion based upon reasonable cause if he believes a patient is a battered child. The terms *deprived child* and *battered child* do not constitute an opinion on the ultimate issue of this case and were admissible testimony to be considered with all other evidence in the case.

* * *

The appellants next argue that the evidence produced at the trial does not support the findings of fact made by the Juvenile Court in this case.

On appeal, although the findings of fact by the trial court are accorded appreciable weight, the Supreme Court is not bound thereby but has the duty to review all evidence, to find the facts anew independently of the trial court's findings, and to apply the law to the facts as found by the appellate court. * * *

After independent appraisal of the facts in this case, this Court finds that J. Z., the child here involved, is a deprived child within the meaning of N.D.C.C. Sec. 27–20–02(5). The baby's fractured ribs, the broken rattle forced into his throat, the child's burned mouth and throat tract, the various bruises on his face and body, under the circumstances as detailed by the doctors and other witnesses, are clear and convincing evidence that there was an absence of proper parental care. It is significant, as earlier stated, that these badges of abuse are unexplained and that all appeared, excepting possibly the fractured ribs, only after the father, John Z., had been alone with the baby. So much of the abuse of the baby as was known or suspected by her was accepted by the mother, Susan Z., who thereby failed to protect, nurture, and care for the child. Such passive acceptance by the mother amounted to acquiescence and likewise is clear and convincing evidence of omission of proper parental care.

The appellants' counsel contends that the evidence in this case lacks probative force because it is largely, if not entirely, circumstantial. But that is not the law in this State. Proof of the elements of an action or proceeding may consist entirely of circumstantial evidence. In this case, the facts and circumstances proved were consistent with the theory of absence of proper parental care and inconsistent with any other rational theory.

It is further found by this Court by clear and convincing evidence that the conditions and causes of the deprivation are likely to continue, and that by reason thereof the baby is suffering and will probably suffer serious physical, mental, moral, or emotional harm; and that clear and convincing evidence supports the trial court's judgment terminating the appellants' parental rights to J. Z., their child.

Finally, the appellants attack the district court judgment terminating their parental rights on the ground that the North Dakota statutory definition of "deprived child", N.D.C.C. Sec. 27–20–02(5), is unconstitutional for vagueness and uncertainty. It is their claim that the trial court decree of termination deprives them of their constitutional right of due process guaranteed them by the Constitutions of the United States and of the State of North Dakota.

In State v. Henderson, 156 N.W.2d 700, 706 (N.D.1968), this Court, citing United States v. National Dairy Products Corp., 372 U. S. 29, 32 83 S.Ct. 594, 598, 9 L.Ed.2d 561 (1963) stated the test for determining whether a statute is void for vagueness and uncertainty as follows:

Void for vagueness simply means that criminal responsibility should not attach where one could not reasonably understand that his contemplated conduct is proscribed.

The North Dakota statute providing for termination of parental rights, which defines a deprived child as one "without proper parental care or control," afforded the appellants a commonly understood and well known standard to which their conduct and responsibility must conform. * * * The meaning of the questioned statutes is plain and not subject to varying impressions of those attempting to comply with the statutes and those attempting to enforce those laws. The appellants were accorded due process under the statutes here involved.

The judgment is affirmed.

NOTES AND QUESTIONS

1. In the *Loss* case was the evidence sufficient to go to the jury, under the standards prevailing in criminal cases? If you had been on the *Loss* jury, would you have voted for conviction?

2. In the *Fabritz* case was the majority correct in granting the writ, or should it have been denied as the dissent thought? If the child had not died, but had been found to be seriously injured, would the civil remedy of termination of the mother's parental rights have been appropriate, as was

done in the *J. Z.* case? If not, what other possible remedy might be useful?

3. In the *J. Z.* case, if you had been the trier of fact would you have found that there was clear and convincing evidence that the father had injured the child? In another civil case, not involving children, would this quantity and quality of evidence be sufficient to support findings of fact?

4. If you had been consulted by John Z. and Susan Z. after the juvenile proceeding had been brought to terminate their parental rights, and you had heard their version of the facts, what would you have done? Would your obligations and functions as a lawyer be any different in this kind of a case from what they would be in any other civil or criminal litigation? If, in the *Loss* case, the baby had not died, so that the criminal charge had been assault or something like it, what would you have done in representing the parents? Cf. R. E. Helfer and C. H. Kempe, ed., The Battered Child, 200 (1967): "In our experience more satisfactory dispositions are made when attorneys, parents, welfare personnel and physicians meet together in the judge's chambers and, using proper legal formality, discuss all aspects of the case in question. The judge is then in a much better position to make an intelligent decision resulting in a more satisfactory disposition for all concerned."

5. The court in the *Fabritz* case assumes the constitutionality of the Maryland statute, while in the other two cases the issue was not raised. What, if any, constitutional objections might be raised against these statutes? If the constitutional objections are valid in your opinion, how should the statutes define child abuse? Could the constitutional difficulties which you see with such statutes be mitigated by any procedural devices? See e. g., People v. Hoehl, 193 Colo. 557, 568 P.2d 484 (1977) (placing the child in a situation which "may endanger" his life or health is not unconstitutionally vague); State v. Meinert, 225 Kan. 816, 594 P.2d 232 (1979) (causing the child "to suffer unjustifiable physical pain or mental distress" is unconstitutionally vague); Bowers v. State, 283 Md. 115, 389 A.2d 341 (1978) (Maryland statute is constitutional); State v. Coe, 92 N. M. 320, 587 P.2d 973 (App.1978) (statute held constitutional); State v. Sammons, 58 Ohio St. 460, 391 N.E.2d 713 (1979).

6. Suppose, in either of these two cases, that there had been a second baby in the family who had not been injured or abused. If a proceeding were brought to terminate parental rights with respect to the second baby as well as the first, what should be the result? See In re S, 66 Misc.2d 683, 322 N.Y.S.2d 170 (Fam.Ct.1971); In re Edwards, 70 Misc.2d 858, 335 N.Y.S.2d 575 (Fam.Ct.1972); Matter of T.Y.K., —— Mont. ——, 598 P.2d 593 (1979).

7. These two cases exemplify the most drastic remedies the law has for child abuse, the criminal conviction and the termination of parental rights. Would you expect them to be effective? Are they too drastic? Are there any other legal remedies which might be more effective? Before dealing with these questions, you might read the following brief account of work which has been done on the battered child syndrome.

8. Child abuse and neglect are not new in history and certainly not peculiar to the United States. Brutality towards children and the killing of children have been practiced in nearly all civilizations, in earlier times with

the more or less tacit approval of the authorities. In the English legal system where much of our law originated the father was entitled to the custody of his children and the law gave him the right also to exercise complete control over them. His right to discipline his children was subject to few limitations and harsh punishments were by no means unusual. In the United States in the Eighteenth and Nineteenth Centuries the accepted ways of providing for poor, abandoned or orphaned children included apprenticeship or commitment to an institution. Children were not unlikely to be abused or neglected either as apprentices or as inmates of institutions. The remedies afforded by the criminal law were of course available to deter or punish cruelty to children but they were not often used, and were often ineffective because the crimes were hard to prove. An extensive review of the history of child abuse and early attempts at controlling it may be found in Thomas, Child Abuse and Neglect, Part I: Historical Overview, Legal Matrix and Social Perspectives, 50 N.C.L.Rev. 293 (1972), which includes citation to much of the legal and non-legal writing on the subject.

After World War II many people in the medical profession became concerned about child abuse and began to classify and identify its symptoms. The results of their investigations and publications were that physicians in general became more sensitive to the existence and indications of child abuse, the public became more aware of the problem, and legislation aimed at providing a procedure for the detection and prevention of child abuse was enacted. The graphic phrases "battered child" and "battered child syndrome" were coined as labels for the condition. There were in existence statutes of some significance to the battered child problem before these developments occurred, including legislation providing various protective services for children, and legislation setting up juvenile courts, giving them jurisdiction in child neglect cases and authorizing various criminal and civil remedies.

The most important statutory protection for the battered child came from the child abuse reporting laws which are now found in every state. These statutes in general require the physician or hospital official where a child is treated who is suspected of having been abused or neglected to report the facts to a public official, usually either the police or the welfare department or the juvenile authorities. Such a report is referred to in the J. Z. case. Many of the statutes extend the duty to report to a much larger group, including nurses, school employees or social workers, and in some instances to all persons who learn of the abuse. The reports so made are required to be investigated and appropriate legal action must then be taken. The statutes specifically exempt from liability any physician or other person making such a report and also provide that the physician-patient privilege or any other evidentiary privilege shall not be a ground for excluding evidence of the child's condition in any legal proceeding. The statute may also be construed to abrogate the husband-wife privilege. State v. Suttles, 287 Or. 3, 597 P.2d 786 (1979). For a general review of the statutes, see Paulsen, The Legal Framework for Child Protection, 66 Colum.L.Rev. 679 (1966); Paulsen, Child Abuse Reporting Laws: The Shape of the Legislation, 67 Colum.L.Rev. 1 (1967); Note, The California Approach to Wilful Child Abuse, 54 Cal.L.Rev. 1805 (1966). Many of the reporting acts have been modified and refined so as to be more effective in assuring that the reports are made at a time and in a way to be properly acted upon, in assuring that the courts receive sufficient evidence to evaluate the case accurately, and so as to provide a range of remedies in the juvenile court appropriate to the various contexts in which child abuse occurs.

In 1974 Congress took a hand in the child abuse campaign by passing The Child Abuse Prevention and Treatment Act of that year, 42 U.S.C.A. §§ 5101–5106 which has since been amended several times. This statute established a National Center on Child Abuse and Neglect in the Department of Health, Education and Welfare, whose function is to study child abuse, conduct research into its causes, make grants to public or private agencies for the study, prevention or treatment of child abuse and make grants to the states for assistance in developing child abuse prevention and treatment programs.

One such program which has been set up in many states is the establishment of multidisciplinary teams having a variety of functions in the prevention and treatment of child abuse. The teams are made up of individuals who have been trained in the professions concerned with child abuse, such as physicians, psychiatrists, social workers, lawyers or psychologists. The broad purpose of setting up such teams is to facilitate inter-professional and inter-agency cooperation in dealing with child abuse. Statutes in the various states differ somewhat, but they often provide that the multidisciplinary team will work together in the diagnosis, prevention, or treatment of child abuse, and in educating the public about the problem and about the community's resources. For a description of the operation of such teams, see National Center on Child Abuse and Neglect, Multidisciplinary Teams in Child Abuse and Neglect Programs (August 1978). Some states have also come to use volunteers in the treatment of child abuse, as indicated in the discussion of the work of Drs. Helfer and Kempe below. National Center on Child Abuse and Neglect, Volunteers in Child Abuse and Neglect Programs (August 1978).

Two leaders of the medical profession's attack on the battered child problem, Dr. Ray E. Helfer and Dr. C. Henry Kempe, have edited three books, The Battered Child (1968), Helping the Battered Child and His Family (1972), and Child Abuse and Neglect: The Family and the Community (1976). Another extensive treatment on child abuse is R. Bourne and E. Newberger, eds., Critical Perspectives on Child Abuse (1979). See also Violence Toward Youth in Families, 35 Journal of Social Issues No. 2 (1979). All of these works contain extensive bibliographies. All of them contain chapters written by physicians, psychiatrists, social workers, lawyers and others whose expertise might be applied to child abuse cases. They indicate the scope of the problem by statistics which suggest that there are from 250 to 300 cases of battered children per million of the population each year. A small portion of the battering parents, perhaps ten percent or less, are said to be so emotionally disturbed or psychotic that they would not be able to care for their children. The remainder are characterized as having emotional problems sufficiently severe to be accepted for treatment by a psychiatrist or clinic. They come from all social and economic classes, but they do have in common an extremely strong determination that the child perform in such a way as to gratify them, the habit of using physical punishment to obtain that performance and a generally low self-esteem. Many of the battering parents were battered children themselves. Often the particular battering is precipitated by a family crisis.

Drs. Helfer and Kempe in Helping the Battered Child and His Family, Ch. 3, and 12 (1972) describe a program of therapy for the battering parents and their children. The program enlists the cooperation of hospital personnel, the juvenile courts and their staff, protective services in the community and a group of lay persons called parents' aides. Needless to say this requires an absence of professional jealousies and a willingness to work together which are qualities often lacking as between the various professions. In brief summary, the program calls for an immediate preliminary diagnosis of the child when he is brought to the hospital by a welfare worker or policeman. The diagnosis is reported to the juvenile authorities, or welfare department or other child protective service at once, and they begin an evaluation of the child's home. The next step is a conference of all parties involved in the case to decide what should be done. If this conference thinks it desirable, the case is brought to the juvenile court, a decision which is influenced by the closeness of the working relationship in the particular community between hospital and welfare workers and the juvenile courts. The authors express the view that more cases should be brought to the courts than is now done. The treatment to be followed then is outlined and begun. It may or may not involve removal of the child from the home. It does require the cooperation of a hospital social worker, a welfare department social worker and the parent aide, who is a lay person functioning as a friend of the parent. The parent aides are used where the diagnosis indicates that the child has had insufficient mothering from its parents. The aides, over a period of from eight to twelve months visit the parents' home once or twice a week and are available on call at other times. Their function is that of a sympathetic, understanding friend, who provides companionship, an interested listener and moral support, both in the daily routine and in moments of crisis. They must be patient, and uncritical of the parents even in circumstances which might be expected to arouse their anger. They are untrained but of course must be selected with care, since many persons would be unable to meet the very heavy demands made on them for empathy, gentleness and kindness. The parent aides are rather closely supervised by professional social workers and others on the hospital staff. Other services for the home in which an abused child has lived may be offered, such as that of the visiting nurse, or a "homemaker", whose function it is to help with the housework and care of the child. The goal of all this activity is to enable the battered child to be returned to his home with assurance that he will not again be injured, and to enable his parents to enjoy him and to function as mature members of the community.

This and similar programs have not been universally accepted as beneficial. In a review of The Battered Child in the October, 1968, Atlantic Monthly, Dr. Thomas S. Szasz sharply attacked what he saw as central assumptions of the book, that the parents are mentally ill, require psychiatric care, and are to be given that care whether they want it or not. He characterizes as "utter nonsense" another assumption which he finds underlying the authors' views, namely, that the conflicts in life, including the conflicts demonstrated by the parents who batter their children, could be resolved if everyone exhibited a little goodwill.

9. Are Dr. Szasz's criticisms justified, so far as you can tell, either by the work of those physicians who attempt to treat child-battering parents or by the law? See Newberger and Bourne, The Medicalization and Legaliza-

tion of Child Abuse, in R. Bourne and E. Newberger, Critical Perspectives on Child Abuse 139 (1979). Is there a substantial risk of infringement on family privacy in these attempts to combat child abuse? Biederman, Child Abuse and the Right to Privacy, 1 Fam.L.Rep. 4029 (1975).

If his criticisms are justified, what, if anything, is the law to do about battered children? Should the law in that event content itself with imposing criminal penalties or terminating parental rights? Burt, Forcing Protection on Children and Their Parents: The Impact of Wyman v. James, 69 Mich.L.Rev. 1259, 1278–1279 (1971). Wyman v. James 400 U.S. 309 (1971) held that a recipient of aid to families with dependent children must, under the applicable state statute, submit to a home inspection by a caseworker on pain of losing her benefits, and that the statute as so applied did not violate the federal constitution's Fourth Amendment prohibiting unreasonable searches and seizures.

10. Under many modern juvenile court acts proceedings involving child abuse are separated into two stages (as are other proceedings for protection of children). The first, the adjudicatory stage, is concerned with whether the child was abused or neglected as defined by the statute. The second stage is called the dispositional stage. This takes place after the court has determined that the child has been abused and is concerned only with the remedy. Here again modern juvenile statutes are comprehensive and authorize the court to select in its discretion from a broad range of remedies that one which best fits the circumstances. The available remedies include releasing the child to the custody of his parents, with or without a protective order or some form of supervision, placing the child in the custody of other persons, in a foster home, in the custody of a child care agency, or in an institution, or terminating parental rights, or any combination of these remedies.

The New York statute defining child abuse is extensive and relatively specific, reading in relevant part as follows:

N.Y.Fam.Ct. Act § 1012 (1975 and Supp. 1978–1979):

"(e) 'Abused child' means a child less than eighteen years of age whose parent or other person legally responsible for his care

"(i) inflicts or allows to be inflicted upon such child physical injury by other than accidental means which causes or creates a substantial risk of death, or serious or protracted disfigurement, or protracted impairment of physical or emotional health or protracted loss or impairment of the function of any bodily organ, or

"(ii) creates or allows to be created a substantial risk of physical injury to such child by other than accidental means which would be likely to cause death or serious or protracted disfigurement, or protracted impairment of physical or emotional health or protracted loss or impairment of the function of any bodily organ, or

"(iii) commits, or allows to be committed, a sex offense against such child, as defined in the penal law, provided, however, that the corroboration requirements contained therein shall not apply to proceedings under this article.

"(f) 'Neglected child' means a child less than eighteen years of age

"(i) whose physical, mental or emotional condition has been impaired or is in imminent danger of becoming impaired as a result of the failure of his parent or other person legally responsible for his care to exercise a minimum degree of care

"(A) in supplying the child with adequate food, clothing, shelter or education in accordance with the provisions of part one of article sixty-five of the education law, or medical, dental, optometrical or surgical care, though financially able to do so or offered financial or other reasonable means to do so; or

"(B) in providing the child with proper supervision or guardianship, by unreasonably inflicting or allowing to be inflicted harm, or a substantial risk thereof, including the infliction of excessive corporal punishment; or by using a drug or drugs; or by using alcoholic beverages to the extent that he loses self-control of his actions; or by any other acts of a similarly serious nature requiring the aid of the court; or

"(ii) who has been abandoned, in accordance with the definition and other criteria set forth in subdivision five of section three hundred eighty-four-b of the social services law, by his parents or other person legally responsible for his care.

"(g) 'Person legally responsible' includes the child's custodian, guardian, any other person responsible for the child's care at the relevant time. Custodian may include any person continually or at regular intervals found in the same household as the child when the conduct of such person causes or contributes to the abuse or neglect of the child.

"(h) 'Impairment of emotional health' and 'impairment of mental or emotional condition' includes a state of substantially diminished psychological or intellectual functioning in relation to, but not limited to, such factors as failure to thrive, control of aggressive or self-destructive impulses, ability to think and reason, or acting out or misbehavior, including incorrigibility, ungovernability or habitual truancy; provided, however, that such impairment must be clearly attributable to the unwillingness or inability of the respondent to exercise a minimum degree of care toward the child."

The *J. Z.* case contains the North Dakota definition, less specific but equally comprehensive, as is the Maryland statute in the *Fabritz* case.

In 1971 the Institute of Judicial Administration, a private, nonprofit research organization with headquarters at New York University Law School, undertook the drafting of standards to guide the administration of juvenile justice. In 1973 the American Bar Association became a co-sponsor of the project. The standards have been published in twenty-four volumes, one of which contains the standards on child abuse and neglect, together with extensive commentary and citation of authorities. The standards have been subjected to considerable criticism, a sample of which is Bourne and Newberger, "Family Autonomy" or "Coercive Intervention"? Ambiguity and Conflict in the Proposed Standards for Child Abuse and Neglect, in R. Bourne and E. Newberger, Critical Perspectives on Child Abuse

97 (1979). The criticism is responded to in McCathren, Accountability in the Child Protection System; A Defense of the Proposed Standards Relating to Abuse and Neglect, 57 B.U.L.Rev. 707 (1977). The standards' proposed definition of child abuse is as follows:

"2.1 Statutory grounds for intervention.

"Courts should be authorized to assume jurisdiction in order to condition continued parental custody upon the parents' accepting supervision or to remove a child from his/her home only when a child is endangered in a manner specified in subsections A.–F.:

"A. a child has suffered, or there is a substantial risk that a child will imminently suffer, a physical harm, inflicted nonaccidentally upon him/her by his/her parents, which causes, or creates a substantial risk of causing disfigurement, impairment of bodily functioning, or other serious physical injury;

"B. a child has suffered, or there is a substantial risk that the child will imminently suffer, physical harm causing disfigurement, impairment of bodily functioning, or other serious physical injury as a result of conditions created by his/her parents or by the failure of the parents to adequately supervise or protect him/her;

"C. a child is suffering serious emotional damage, evidenced by severe anxiety, depression, or withdrawal, or untoward aggressive behavior towards self or others, and the child's parents are not willing to provide treatment for him/her;

"D. a child has been sexually abused by his/her parent or a member of his/her household (alternative: a child has been sexually abused by his/her parent or a member of his/her household, and is seriously harmed physically or emotionally thereby);

"E. a child is in need of medical treatment to cure, alleviate, or prevent him/her from suffering serious physical harm which may result in death, disfigurement, or substantial impairment of bodily functions, and his/her parents are unwilling to provide or consent to the medical treatment;

"F. a child is committing delinquent acts as a result of parental encouragement, guidance, or approval.

"2.2 Need for intervention in specific case.

"The fact that a child is endangered in a manner specified in Standard 2.1 A.–F. should be a necessary but not sufficient condition for a court to intervene. In order to assume jurisdiction, a court should also have to find that intervention is necessary to protect the child from being endangered in the future. This decision should be made in accordance with the standards proposed in Part VI."

11. (a) How should the *Fabritz* and *J. Z.* cases be decided under either the New York statute, or the IJA-ABA Standards for child abuse?

(b) DT was a fourteen-year-old girl who one day took twenty-three adult migraine aspirin tablets after which she called a doctor who got her to the hospital where she remained for a week. The doctor and a social worker at the hospital requested DT's parents to let her be tested at a local mental health center in order to evaluate DT's emotional stability, but the parents refused and then later consented only as a result of threats of juvenile court action. DT was tested and evaluated as having "normal intelligence" but displaying "signs of depression, hostility, and impulsiveness." Placement in a foster home and individual therapy were recommended. The parents refused to carry out the recommendations. Was DT abused or neglected under any of the foregoing statutes or the IJA-ABA Standards? Bjerke v. D.T., 248 N.W.2d 808 (N.D.1976).

(c) M was pregnant but continued to take heroin, as she had done in the past. She was warned by a nurse that the health of her child was thereby being endangered. When the child was born it was addicted to heroin and suffered withdrawal symptoms. Was the child abused or neglected under the foregoing statutes or the IJA-ABA Standards? Reyes v. Superior Court, 75 Cal.App.3d 214, 141 Cal.Rptr. 912 (1977).

(d) R is a boy of seven who was a truant from school on several occasions. His father learned about the boy's absences from a neighbor and asked R about it. R then lied to his father, saying he had been in school on the days in question. The father took this very seriously and beat R with a leather strap hard enough to leave marks on the backs of R's legs. R's gym teacher noticed the marks and reported them to the police, in accordance with the state child abuse reporting statute. Did this amount to child abuse under the foregoing statutes and the IJA-ABA Standards? In Matter of Rodney C., 91 Misc.2d 677, 398 N.Y.S.2d 511 (Fam.Ct.1977).

(e) A fifth grade school teacher noticed that a girl in his class was often depressed, fatigued, and unable to concentrate on her school work. The teacher talked to the child sympathetically and learned that the child's parents regularly said they did not love her, that she was a burden to them, that they wished she had never been born, that she was dumb and clumsy, and that they wished they could get rid of her some way. At the same time they made her do most of the house cleaning and dish washing so that the child was too tired to do her homework or to pay attention in school. Should the teacher report the child as an abused child under the foregoing statutes or the Standards? Cf. Note, Emotional Neglect in Connecticut, 5 Conn.L.Rev. 100 (1972).

(f) A girl of fifteen reports to her aunt that her father has been having sexual relations with her. Is this child abuse under the foregoing statutes and the Standards?

(g) M had a daughter, N, out of wedlock when M was seventeen. She was unable to care for N for about two years and N was in the custody of foster parents. At the end of that time M took custody of N. Social workers following the case later testified to the following facts. For a time M and N lived in a three-room apartment with five other adults and three other children. They then moved into another small apartment where they lived with H, who later married M, along with another child and two teenage girls. The second apartment was described as filthy and disorganized and infested with cockroaches. Here N slept on a couch with the two girls and was thin, sickly, dirty and used obscene language. On psychiatric examination N was found to show signs of emotional disturbance evidenced by nightmares and nail-biting, and M was found to be immature, of inadequate personality and poor ego strength. On visits with the foster parents, which occurred occasionally, N appeared to have a warm relationship with them.

Was N an abused or neglected child under the foregoing statutes or the Standards? Is this determination to be affected by the fact that the foster parents would like to keep N with them? Doe v. D. G., 146 N.J.Super. 419, 370 A.2d 27 (1976), aff'd 74 N.J. 196, 377 A.2d 626 (1977).

If the state took custody of N without compliance with the applicable statute, would state employees be risking personal liability? Cf. Duchesne v. Sugarman, 566 F.2d 817 (2d Cir. 1978).

(h) Which of these statutes, if any, do you think best deals with the problem of child abuse? Are the IJA-ABA Standards preferable to the statutes? Could you draft a statute which would be superior to any of the others and to the Standards?

12. (a) In a proceeding such as that in the *J. Z.* case, are parents entitled to be represented by counsel, at the state's expense if they are unable to afford counsel? See In re B, supra, page 506; Note, Child Neglect, Due Process for the Parent, 70 Colum.L.Rev. 465 (1970). Is the child entitled to counsel? Note, Domestic Relations—Appointment of Counsel for Abused Child—Statutory Scheme and the New York Approach, 58 Corn.L.Q. 177 (1972).

(b) In such a proceeding what should be the rule as to the standard of proof, the usual civil one of preponderance of the evidence, or the criminal standard that the offense must be proved beyond a reasonable doubt? Is this a constitutional issue? See In re Henderson, 199 N.W.2d 111 (Iowa 1972).

(c) May the court in such a case order the parent to submit to psychiatric examination, the psychiatrist's report to be delivered to the court and considered with other evidence to determine whether parental rights should be terminated or some other remedy selected? Cf. Aronson, Should the Privilege Against Self-Incrimination Apply to Compelled Psychiatric Examinations, 26 Stan.L.Rev. 55 (1973); Note, Requiring a Criminal Defendant to Submit to a Government Psychiatric Examination: An Invasion of the Privilege Against Self-Incrimination, 83 Harv.L.Rev. 648 (1970).

13. Dr. X, a pediatrician, sees a child in the hospital for treatment of a fractured arm. X-rays of this arm reveal old fractures, and x-rays of the other arm also show an old, healed fracture. The child's mother is unable to explain in any convincing way how it is that the child has broken his arms so many times. Nevertheless Dr. X does not report the injuries although the local statute requires that incidents of suspected child abuse coming to the attention of physicians must be reported. A year later the child returns to the hospital with a skull fracture which is proved to have been inflicted by his father. Would Dr. X be liable in tort to the child? If there were another child in the family who was also abused by the father after Dr. X had failed to report the arm fracture, would Dr. X be liable to him in tort? Landeros v. Flood, 17 Cal.3d 399, 131 Cal.Rptr. 69, 551 P.2d 389 (1976). Should the child abuse statute specifically provide for this form of tort liability?

14. It has been proposed that the state offer a training course for parents, to be devised by a board of educators, doctors, psychologists, sociologists and successful parents. The course would not be required, but resumably would become appealing because it would lead to a "Parent Certificate" signifying qualification as a parent. The basic purpose of the course

would be to enlighten and sensitize adults to how children feel and think. Shlensky, Proposed: A Parent Certificate, 18 Fam.Law Newsletter p. 9, col. 3 (1978). Would you favor such a course? Should it be made compulsory?

D. THE CHILD IN NEED OF SUPERVISION

MARTARELLA v. KELLEY

United States District Court, Southern District of New York, 1972.
349 F.Supp. 575.

LASKER, District Judge. The rapid urbanization of the United States in this century and the heavy influx of the poor to the cities in the last two decades have produced a numerous class of children whose conduct, although not criminal in character or legal designation, results in their incarceration.

Robert Martarella and his fellow plaintiffs [1] are members of that group—alleged or adjudicated to be "Persons In Need of Supervision" (PINS) pursuant to § 732 of the Family Court Act of New York (The Act). They bring this civil rights action for a declaration that their temporary detention in the "maximum security" facilities,—Spofford, Manida and Zerega, juvenile centers operated by the City of New York—deprives them of due process and equal protection and constitutes cruel and unusual punishment under the conditions prevailing at those institutions.

The plaintiffs moved for preliminary injunctive relief. Pursuant to Rule 65(a)(2), Fed.R.Civ.Pr., the trial of the action was consolidated with the hearing of the application.

* * *

1. At the time the complaint was filed, Martarella had been confined at Spofford because he had run away from home on seven occasions for periods up to ten days in the prior nine months and refused to go to school. At first, he was paroled for investigation. His mother, however, reported that he ran away again and a warrant was issued. On the return of the warrant, he was remanded for full study and report so that a placement other than a training school could be explored. However, his mother refused to take him home and remand was continued for several weeks. He was again placed on probation but a week later ran away from home and was found unconscious in a school hallway. His probation was revoked and he was remanded for about six weeks with weekend parole privileges. A full study and psychiatric report were ordered. He was paroled again and ran away. On his return, on a warrant, the court ordered placement at Lincoln Hall, a privately operated institution. Martarella's case is not unique. Although no precise facts are in evidence as to the rate of recidivism among children in the centers, the witnesses agreed that recidivism was significant. A case like Martarella's presents difficult problems of final disposition and these difficulties may explain in part the number of cases of long stays at the centers. The details of the cases of the other plaintiffs are set forth in the pleadings (Complaint Par. IV, Answer Pars. V through VIII inclusive). None of the other plaintiffs testified at the trial and the particular facts of their cases have no determining influence in regard to the issues before us.

The boys at Spofford range in age from 7 through 15; the girls at Manida and Zerega from 7 through 17.

The Family Court Judges are authorized, by § 739 of the Act, to direct that a PINS be detained if "(a) there is a substantial probability that he will not appear in court on the return date; or (b) there is a serious risk that he may before the return date do an act which if committed by an adult would constitute a crime."

The Presiding Justices of the Appellate Division are responsible for the designation of appropriate detention centers for PINS.

*   *   *

The injunctive relief sought by the plaintiffs is to prevent the Family Court Judges from remanding PINS to the centers, to order the Presiding Justices of the Appellate Division to designate non-secure facilities which comply with New York law and the Federal Constitution as to the care and treatment of children in custody, and to order the administrator of the centers to close Manida and Zerega permanently, and Spofford until it is made "safe, sanitary and decent for its inmates."

They also move for determination of the case as a class action.

[The court's opinion goes on to describe the juvenile detention centers (the centers) as institutions at which both PINS and juvenile delinquents are held in temporary custody pending permanent disposition of their cases. Most of the PINS are either truants or runaways, while juvenile delinquents are persons under sixteen who have committed acts which would be crimes if committed by adults. The plaintiffs' claims were that placing the two classifications of juveniles in the centers violated the Eighth and Fourteenth Amendments to the United States Constitution.

The centers were three in number, named Spofford, Manida and Zerega. The latter had been closed by the time of the opinion, so the case as to it became moot. The other two were not well designed as detention centers and in some respects were in poor repair. Both were locked institutions and operated much like a jail. The evidence indicated that punishment rather than treatment or helping the children was the function of these centers. The opinion describes in detail the numbers and training of center staffs, and the relationship between the staffs and the children.

The evidence concerning the effect upon the children of placing PINS and delinquents in the same center was in conflict, some witnesses testifying that this was damaging to PINS by teaching them to engage in criminal acts, while others testified that this sort of mingling was common in juvenile institutions. Furthermore, it was testified that the distinction between PINS and juvenile delinquents is often not clearcut, since a criminal charge is often reduced to a PINS charge for purposes of treatment.]

Presently no distinction is made between PINS and JDs with respect to treatment afforded, sleeping arrangements, recreation or schooling. However, the Bureau is "just now" developing a system of classification based on the nature of the child's problem rather than his status as a PINS or JD. A team of social worker, counsellor, teacher, psychiatrist and physician will observe and evaluate each child for placement. Thereafter, the child will be housed on the basis of age, maturity, emotional development, emotional and psychiatric history (when available), the charge against him or her, and evidence, if any, of drug use, but without regard to whether the child is charged as a PINS or JD * * * Children who are charged with committing rape or murder will be separated from other children "whenever necessary", the criteria for such separation again including, in addition to the charge itself, age, maturity and psychiatric history and evaluation. * * * A separate dormitory and program for treatment has been set up for drug users for boys at Spofford, although entry into the dormitory is on a voluntary basis. * * *

In sum the evidence establishes that PINS and JDs are not separately treated or housed on the basis of their "labels", but on a set of criteria which relate to the problems, offense and personality of each child.

Questions of Law

[At this point in the opinion the court held (a) that it had jurisdiction of the case under 42 U.S.C.A. § 1983; (b) that the suit could be brought against the Justices of the Appellate Division sued as individuals; and (c) that although the judges would be immune from a suit for damages, they were not immune where the remedy sought was declaratory and injunctive. The court also held that the case was properly brought as a class action under Rule 23(a), (b)(2).]

At the end of a long journey we come to the legal questions raised on the merits of the case.

    3. *The Constitutionality of Common Custody of PINS and JDs:*
* * *

The question before us is whether the distinction between PINS and neglected children which allows the former, but not the latter, to be held in common custody with JDs has some relevance to the purpose for which the classification is made. We believe that it does.

It is true, of course, that a PINS and a neglected child—as distinct from a JD—have in common that neither is charged with acts of a criminal nature; but this fact alone does not require the state to treat PINS and neglected children identically if a rational basis exists for some other mode of action. The rationality demanded by the Equal Protection clause is not to be found in legal designations or labels, but must derive from the facts.

From the evidence before us we conclude that the distinction made in the custody and treatment of PINS and neglected children bears a reasonable relation to the purpose for which the classification is made.

A neglected child is defined by § 312 of The Family Court Act:

"A 'neglected child' means a male less than sixteen years of age or a female less than eighteen years of age.

(a) whose parents or other person legally responsible for his care does not adequately supply the child with food, clothing, shelter, education, or medical or surgical care, though financially able or offered financial means to do so; or

(b) who suffers or is likely to suffer serious harm from the improper guardianship, including lack of moral supervision or guidance, of his parents or other person legally responsible for his care and requires the aid of the court; or

(c) who has been abandoned or deserted by his parents or other person legally responsible for his care."

A person in need of supervision is defined by § 712 of the Act:

" 'Person in need of supervision' means a male less than sixteen years of age and a female less than eighteen years of age who is an habitual truant or who is incorrigible, ungovernable or habitually disobedient and beyond the lawful control of parent or other lawful authority."

The distinction drawn by the definitions, and the consequent factual difference in the membership of the two classes of children is evident, and forms a clearly rational basis for differences in their conditions of custody. Judge Kelley articulated the distinction clearly: a PINS is himself charged with misbehavior; in the case of a neglected child, the parent is the "defendant". Neglected children are victims, PINS are (non-criminal) offenders, or at least socially maladjusted. The neglected child is sinned against rather than sinning. On the other hand, a PINS' personal behavior is the cause of his subjection to legal authority.

While realism compels acknowledgement that the lines are often blurred, and that the PINS' maladjustment is frequently caused by misguidance or mistreatment by parents or other authority (as may be equally true of JDs) the acknowledgement does not vitiate the rationality of the distinction. For these reasons we find no violation of the equal protection clause.

We also find the purposes and criteria of the classification system at the centers to be rational and justifiable. While even defense witnesses agreed that it would be "desirable" to establish separate facilities for PINS and JDs, the conflict among experts as to whether joint custody is damaging to PINS is too sharp to sustain a finding of unconstitutionality either as a matter of due process or cruel and unusual punishment. Clearly the system of classification in effect at the time of trial, and its improved sequel, do not violate professional standards for the care of PINS and JDs. Of course, there is considerable debate within the child care profession as to whether PINS should be held in secure detention under *any* circumstances, and clearly they may not be so detained unless treatment is provided, but those questions are separate.

It is significant that among the otherwise divided experts there was virtual unanimity that no child—PINS or otherwise—should be treated according to his label, but rather according to his personal need. As Dr. Rothman, defendants' key witness and the witness most knowledgeable about the actualities at the centers, stated: "There are no significant personality differences between people who are adjudged PINS and people who are adjudged JDs".

The system in effect which classifies the child according to his age, maturity, emotional development, emotional and psychiatric history, the charge against him or her, and evidence if any, of drug use * * *, assuming that each factor is given a professionally acceptable weight, is rationally calculated to accomplish the objective approved by all the experts: treatment of the child according to his need rather than his label.

The rationality of the system assures its constitutionality. However, even were this not so and even though we may find more persuasive the view of the experts who strongly favor separation of PINS and JDs, we are bound by the rule, most recently explicated in Sostre v. McGinnis, 442 F.2d 178, 191 (2d Cir.1971), that:

"Even a lifetime of study in prison administration and several advanced degrees in the field would not qualify us *as a federal court* to command state officials to shun a policy that they have decided is suitable because to us the choice may seem unsound or *personally* repugnant. As judges we are obliged to school ourselves in such objective sources as historical usage, see Wilkerson v. Utah, 99 U.S. 130, 25 L.Ed. 345 (1870), practices in other jurisdictions, see Weems v. United States, 217 U.S. 349, 30 S.Ct. 544, 54 L.Ed. 793 (1910), and public opinion, see Robinson v. California, 370 U.S. 660, 666, 82 S.Ct. 1417, 8 L.Ed.2d 758 (1962), before we may responsibly exercise the power of judicial review to declare a punishment unconstitutional under the Eighth Amendment." (Emphasis in original.)

Nor do we find that common custody of PINS and JDs is unconstitutional on the analogy of those cases such as White v. Reid, 125 F.Supp. 647 (D.D.C.1954), Kautter v. Reid, 183 F.Supp. 352 (D.D.C. 1960) and United States ex rel. Stinnett v. Hegstrom, 178 F.Supp. 17 (D.Conn.1959), which hold common custody of juvenile offenders and adult criminals to be impermissible. While the analogy is relevant, it is not compelling. *All* experts agree that common custody of juveniles and those who are usually described—whether accurately or not

—as "hardened" criminals is damaging to the juvenile, whereas here the schools are sharply divided. Beyond that, however, the *legal* rationale as to the impermissibility of common custody of juveniles and adults is normally that the young offender is not classified as a criminal, and, therefore, may not be held in a penal institution jointly with criminals. In the case before us, however, neither a JD (though he has committed an offense which would be criminal if committed by an adult) nor, of course, a PINS is so classified.

Indeed the Court of Appeals of this Circuit appears recently, at least by implication, to have found that custody of juvenile offenders together with adult criminals does not offend the constitution. United States ex rel. Murray v. Owens, et al., 2d Cir., 465 F.2d 289, 1972.

For the reasons stated, we hold that common custody of PINS and JDs does not violate the equal protection clause, due process or the Eighth Amendment.

4. *The Constitutionality of Physical Conditions at the Center:* Plaintiffs contend that the physical conditions at the centers are so hazardous and unhealthy that holding them in custody there constitutes cruel and unusual punishment.

There is no doubt that the Eighth Amendment's prohibition of cruel and unusual punishment is not restricted to instances of particular punishment inflicted on a given individual but also applies to mere confinement to an institution which is "characterized by conditions and practices so bad as to be shocking to the conscience of reasonably civilized people". Holt v. Sarver, 309 F.Supp. 362, 373 (E.D. Ark.1970). See also Jones v. Wittenberg, 323 F.Supp. 93 (N.D.Ohio W.D.1971) and Rhem v. McGrath, 326 F.Supp. 681 (S.D.N.Y.1971). Plaintiffs argue that conditions at the centers fall within the parameters of those decisions and violate the Eighth Amendment.

*   *   * a HEW expert consultant in 1963, submitted a report to the Director of the Centers in which he concluded that Manida was unsuitable for the detention of children, and that the condition had not been improved. Indeed the defendants have stipulated that Manida is an inappropriate facility for child detention *   *   *

The word "unsuitable" is a euphemism for conditions that in their totality violate the Eighth Amendment rights of the young girls who are held in custody at Manida although not even charged with crime.

The situation is different at Spofford. With all its drawbacks including its architectural resemblance to a small prison of modern construction, Spofford is a relatively contemporary building (built in 1958) whose physical conditions, although they should be improved, are acceptable and, at the least, correctable. None of the deficiencies at Spofford can reasonably be classified as hazardous. The Stone Report stated (p. 31) that Spofford "does not appear to be in such condition as to represent a physical danger to its occupants and thereby require immediate replacement—" and it includes positive advantages, such as school rooms, game rooms, room for religious services, gymnasium, swimming pool and an outdoor playing yard.

While we do not adhere to the view that the Eighth Amendment comes into play only if the facility in question is a chambers of horrors, we do not find that the physical conditions alone at Spofford are such that confinement there constitutes cruel and unusual punishment.

5. *Does the Program at the Centers Provide Treatment which Constitutionally Justifies Holding PINS in Secure Detention:* We come to the final and most difficult legal issue in this case, which has poignantly presented questions of the rights of children in urban American society: The right to treatment.

  *   *   *

Although the concept of the right to "effective treatment" was first articulated not much more than a decade ago, it has come into nearly full flower in the intervening period, and has been applied to the mentally ill, sexual psychopaths, defective delinquents, persons committed following acquittal by reason of insanity, drug addicts and children, whether delinquent or merely in need of supervision.

Even before the development of the doctrine of the right to treatment for all persons held in noncriminal custody, the courts asserted an analogous right for children derived from due process concepts and statutes. See, e. g., White v. Reid, 125 F.Supp. 647 (D.D.C. 1954), which held that a juvenile not convicted of a crime could not be held with criminals in a federal jail; and Kautter v. Reid, 183 F. Supp. 352 (D.D.C.1960) ruling that a juvenile who had violated parole could not be held in a jail which lacked particular and adequate facilities for children.

There can be no doubt that the right to treatment, generally, for those held in non-criminal custody (whether based on due process, equal protection or the Eighth Amendment, or a combination of them) has by now been recognized by the Supreme Court, the lower federal courts and the courts of New York.

Robinson v. California, 370 U.S. 660, 82 S.Ct. 1417, 8 L.Ed.2d 758 (1962) dealt with the rights of a drug addict plaintiff. The court held California's statute, which declared addiction a crime, unconstitutional in the absence of rehabilitative treatment. This was punishment for a *status*, rather than a crime; and although the State might legally detain non-criminals for compulsory treatment or other legitimate purposes which protected society or the person in custody, detention for mere illness—without a curative program—would be impermissible. "Even one day in prison would be a cruel and unusual punishment for the 'crime' of having a common cold"—Robinson, supra at 667, 82 S.Ct. at 1421.   *   *   *

Judge Bazelon's seminal opinion in Rouse v. Cameron, 125 U.S. App.D.C. 366, 373 F.2d 451, 1966, dealt more directly with the issue of the right to treatment, and is generally regarded as the leading case. *Rouse* was involuntarily hospitalized in a mental hospital after having been acquitted of a misdemeanor by reason of insanity. He petitioned for a writ of habeas corpus, claiming the right to be discharged in the absence of receiving treatment. The court sustained his argument on statutory grounds but with considerable emphasis on the consitutional questions raised, observing that:

"absent treatment, the hospital is transform[ed]   *   *   *   into a penitentiary where one could be held indefinitely for no convicted offense, *   *   *   ". (at 453)

*   *   *

Prior to *Rouse*, in Sas v. State of Maryland, 334 F.2d 506, 4th Cir., 1964, the court had recognized analogous rights under Maryland's defective delinquent statute, observing (at 517) that "[d]eficiencies in staff, facilities, and finances would undermine *   *   *   the justification for the law, and ultimately the constitutionality of its application".

Haziel v. United States, 131 U.S.App.D.C. 298, 404 F.2d 1275, 1968, emphasized the points made by earlier cases, and stressed the particular obligation of the community to provide treatment for detainees who cannot afford it. As the court observed (at 1280):

" *   *   *   we also cannot ignore the mockery of a benevolent statute unbacked by adequate facilities. And to the extent that a juvenile with more affluent parents might avoid waiver [i. e. custody] because of the availability of privately-financed treatment and rehabilitation, constitutional issues may lurk in the problem."

In Wyatt v. Stickney, 325 F.Supp. 781 (N.D.Ala.1971), Chief Judge Johnson strongly affirmed the right of treatment for persons in noncriminal custody and held that hospital programs for the mentally ill in the case before him were *constitutionally* inadequate. In following Rouse v. Cameron, supra, he declared:

"To deprive any citizen of his or her liberty upon the altruistic theory that the confinement is for humane therapeutic reasons and then fail to provide adequate treatment violates the very fundamentals of due process." (at 785)

New York judges (including defendants here) have been equally alert to sustain the right to treatment, as indicated in "Anonymous" v. (People) Fish (v. Horn), 20 A.D.2d 395, 247 N.Y.S.2d 323 (1st Dept.1964) (PINS are entitled to rehabilitory treatment and not to be committed to penal institutions); People ex rel. Kaganovitch v. Wilkins, 23 A.D.2d 178, 259 N.Y.S.2d 462 (4th Dept. 1965) (Retaining sex offender in custody in spite of absolute failure to provide treatment is cruel and unusual punishment); People ex rel. Meltsner

v. Follette, 32 A.D.2d 389, 302 N.Y.S.2d 624 (2nd Dept. 1969) (youthful offender confined beyond maximum term to which he would have been sentenced as an adult must be furnished rehabilitory treatment); In re I, 64 Misc.2d 878, 316 N.Y.S.2d 356, 1970, (facility's refusal or inability to provide psychiatric care for a 15 year old girl PINS required the court to terminate her placement and release her on probation), and Matter of Lloyd, 33 A.D.2d 385, 308 N.Y.S.2d 419 (1st Dept. 1970) (declaring the Legislature's obligation to make available the facilities necessary to provide treatment for the noncriminally detained).

* * *

We move on, then, to determining the criteria by which the court should measure the centers' programs to determine whether they furnish "regenerative" or "effective" treatment. * * *

We start with the observations of Judge Bazelon in *Rouse* that: (1) The institution need not demonstrate that its treatment program will cure or improve, but only that there is "a bona fide effort to do so", (2) the effort must be to provide treatment adequate in light of present knowledge, (3) the fact that science has not reached finality of judgment as the most effective therapy cannot relieve the court of its duty to render an informed decision and (4) continued failure to provide suitable adequate treatment cannot be justified by lack of staff or facilities, since, as the Supreme Court stated in Watson v. City of Memphis, 373 U.S. 526, 533, 83 S.Ct. 1314, 1318, 10 L.Ed.2d 529 (1963), "The rights here asserted are, like all such rights, *present* rights; * * * and, unless there is an overwhelmingly compelling reason, they are to be promptly fulfilled."

Some suggestions of the American Psychiatric Association's "Position Statement on the Question of Adequacy of Treatment" (123 Am.J.Psychiatry 1458, (1967), considered and criticized in Civil Restraint, Mental Illness and The Right to Treatment, 77 Yale Law Journal 87 at 110ff) are relevant and useful. They include (1) the purpose of institutionalization, and reference to the length of custody, (2) the importance of interrupting the "disease process" as in separating the addict from his drugs or the psychotic from his family stress situation, (3) efforts to change the emotional climate around the "patient" and (4) the availability of conventional psychological therapies.

The Commentator in "Mental Illness," supra, at pp. 112ff, concurs with Judge Bazelon that courts should not determine adequacy of treatment by "forcing the psychiatric professional toward an ideal but unrealizable system, but that bona fide treatment be made available."

We accept this view as sound. Measured by this limiting standard we find that the treatment of children who stay at the centers for a truly temporary period may be minimally acceptable. However, in the light of the solemn meaning which the phrase "bona fide" has acquired through the ages we find that there has not been a bona fide effort to treat the child who is a long termer at the centers, nor is the treatment of such a child adequate in the light of present knowledge. Even those defense witnesses who approved the secure detention of PINS, described as the justification for such detention, treatment programs and facilities vastly superior to those which prevail at the centers. Without attempting to delineate in detail the differences between those institutions and the centers, we emphasize the substantial differences in ratio of professional personnel to children and in the training of counsellors, case-workers and other supporting personnel. The conclusion is inescapable that the shortage of key staff members at the centers, their lack of training, the poor communication among them, the shortage of information available about the child to those who treat him, and the other deficiencies noted in the discussion of facts above, results in a failure to provide adequate treatment for the long term detainee.

The distinction in measuring the adequacy of treatment for true temporary detainees, on one hand, and long termers on the other, is justified by the facts and the law. It is a reasonable inference that factually a treatment program for a temporary detainee need not provide in depth what is necessary for adequate treatment of the long termer, or, put another way, the child who is truly temporarily detained does not suffer deprivation of constitutional proportions, while the long termers do. * * *

There is legal support for the dichotomy detween the rights of short and long termers. The relevance of time as a factor in measuring constitutional rights has been very recently recognized in another context by the Supreme Court. In Jackson v. Indiana, 406 U.S. 715, 92 S.Ct. 1845, 32 L.Ed.2d 435 (1972), the court held that an untried defendant who had been committed as incompetent to stand trial could only be held for a reasonable period to determine whether he might attain competency within the foreseeable future, and that it was a violation of due process to hold him indefinitely. The court observed at 738, 92 S.Ct. at 1858, in words relevant here, that

"At the least, due process requires that the *nature* and duration of commitment bear some reasonable relation to the purpose for which the individual is committed." (Emphasis added)

In McNeil v. Director Patuxent Institution, 407 U.S. 245, 92 S.Ct. 2083, 32 L.Ed.2d 719 (1972), the petitioner was held for an indefinite period for "observation". Rejecting the state's argument that the custody was constitutional, the court stated, that: (in Jackson, supra)

"We held that because the commitment was permanent in its *practical effect*, it required safeguards commensurate with a long-term commitment." (At 249, 92 S.Ct. at 2087; emphasis added)

The decision continued:

"If the commitment is properly regarded as a short-term confinement with a limited purpose, as the State suggests, then lesser safeguards may be appropriate, but by the same token, the duration of the confinement must be strictly limited."

The Court of Appeals for the District of Columbia has applied a similar rationale to the subject at hand, holding in Creek v. Stone, 126 U.S.App.D.C. 329, 379 F.2d 106, 111 (1967), that while interim custody may not necessitate the extensive therapeutic program involved in a final disposition, some attempt must be made to relate the detention to the needs of the juvenile.

We recognize the danger that in deciding these issues the court may be "tempted to act as super-legislature and super-executive" * * * but that risk lies in the realm of remedy rather than analysis. In any event, we agree with the *Rouse* court that the difficulties of decision " * * * cannot relieve the court of its duty to render an informed decision".

*   *   *

*   *   *

REMEDY

We conclude that plaintiffs are entitled to a declaration that the conditions existing at Manida violate the Eighth Amendment, and that the program at the centers does not furnish adequate treatment for children who are not true temporary detainees, and thereby violated their right to due process. There remains for determination the sensitive and complex matter of the scope of injunctive relief.

*   *   *

*   *   *   The parties are instructed to prepare for a conference to determine the scope and contents of injunctive relief.

NOTES AND QUESTIONS

1. The New York Court of Appeals has held that the provision of the New York PINS statute which imposes an age limit for males of sixteen and for females of eighteen is unconstitutional in that there is no reasonable ground for differentiating between males and females in this respect. A. v. City of New York, 31 N.Y.2d 83, 335 N.Y.S.2d 33, 286 N.E.2d 432 (1972). Presumably the court was relying upon the Equal Protection Clause. The same case held that the PINS statute is not void for vagueness and that it is sufficiently definite to meet constitutional requirements. S**** S**** and L**** B**** v. State, 299 A.2d 560 (Me.1973) upheld the Maine statute as not unconstitutionally vague, when it authorized the juvenile courts to treat as a juvenile offender a juvenile "living in circumstances of manifest danger of falling into habits of vice or immorality".

In C. v. Redlich, 32 N.Y.2d 588, 300 N.E.2d 424, 347 N.Y.S.2d 51 (1973) the court held that confinement of PINS in the state training school along with juvenile delinquents violated the Family Court Act § 255 (Supp. 1978–1979). It further held that such confinement could not be justified on the ground that this was the only facility which could help the PINS. See also Ola Mae Vann v. Scott, 467 F.2d 1235 (7th Cir. 1972).

2.   Precisely what is the line of reasoning which leads the court in *Martarella* to hold that the PINS has a "right to treatment"? Is this a statutory right or a constitutional right? If the latter, what constitutional provision confers the right? See Note, A Right to Treatment For Juveniles: 1973 Wash.U.L.Q. 157. See also Note, Persons in Need of Supervision: Is There a Constitutional Right to Treatment? 39 Bklyn.L.Rev. 624 (1973); Gough, The Beyond-Control Child and the Right to Treatment: An Exercise in the Synthesis of Paradox, 16 St.L.U.L.J. 182 (1971). On the right to treatment in general, see Symposium, The Right to Treatment, 57 Geo.L.J. 673 ff. (1969); Symposium, The Right to Treatment, 36 U.Chi.L.Rev. 742 ff. (1969); Note, Civil Restraint, Mental Illness and the Right to Treatment, 77 Yale L.J. 87 (1967); Note, The Nascent Right to Treatment, 53 Va.L.Rev. 1134 (1967); Birnbaum, The Right to Treatment, 46 A.B.A.J. 499 (1960). In Morales v. Turman, 562 F.2d 993, 997 (5th Cir. 1977) the court said that "A right to treatment for juvenile offenders has not yet been firmly established." In O'Connor v. Donaldson, 422 U.S. 563 (1975) the Supreme Court found it unnecessary to determine whether there was a constitutional right to treatment on the part of a patient confined to a state mental hospital, although Chief Justice Burger in a separate concurrence stated his view to be that there is no such constitutional right. But see State ex rel. Harris v. Calendine, —— W.Va. ——, 233 S.E.2d 318 (1977).

3.   If there is a right to treatment, is it violated by including in the "treatment" some forms of corporal punishment? Cf. Nelson v. Heyne, 491 F.2d 352 (7th Cir. 1974), cert. den. 417 U.S. 976 (1974).

4.   Does the right to treatment which the court announces mean that the individual PINS is entitled to treatment for his specific difficulty and condition, or does it mean that the general conditions prevailing in the institution to which he is committed must meet some standard of adequacy? If the latter, whose standard of adequacy? Cf. Patton v. Dumpson, 425 F.Supp. 621 (S.D.N.Y.1977).

5.   In the case described in the preceding paragraph, what alternatives to commitment to an institution does the juvenile court have? See, e. g., N.Y.Fam.Ct. Act §§ 754, 755, 756 (Supp.1978–1979), authorizing the court to suspend judgment, with or without conditions as established by rule of court, conditions which may include restitution; or to continue the proceeding with provision for placement of the child in his own home, or with a suitable relative or other private person, or with an agency.

6.   Is there a right to treatment which applies outside of institutions? Is the PINS who is not committed by the juvenile court entitled to demand some standard of adequacy in the disposition which the court makes of his case?

7.   Can you outline the provisions of an appropriate injunction in the *Martarella* case? What problems of enforcement would your injunction create? Martarella v. Kelley, 359 F.Supp. 478 (S.D.N.Y.1973).

8. Should a juvenile with respect to whom a PINS petition has been filed have a constitutional right to counsel? Does the *Martarella* case shed any light on this question? Cf. In re Walker, 282 N.C. 28, 191 S.E.2d 702 (1972).

IN RE WELFARE OF SNYDER

Supreme Court of Washington, En Banc, 1975.
85 Wash.2d 182, 532 P.2d 278.

HUNTER, Associate Justice. Paul Snyder and Nell Snyder, petitioners, seek review of the King County Juvenile Court's finding that their daughter, Cynthia Nell Snyder, respondent, was an incorrigible child as defined under RCW 13.04.010(7). The issue before this court is whether the juvenile court's determination is supported by substantial evidence.

Cynthia Nell Snyder is 16 years old, attends high school, and has consistently received above average grades. Prior to the occurrences which led to this action, she resided with her parents in their North Seattle home. The record shows that as Cynthia entered her teen years, a hostility began to develop between herself and her parents. This environment within the family home worsened due to a total breakdown in the lines of communication between Cynthia and her parents. Cynthia's parents being strict disciplinarians, placed numerous limitations on their daughter's activities, such as restricting her choice of friends, and refusing to let her smoke, date, or participate in certain extracurricular activities within the school, all of which caused Cynthia to rebel against their authority. These hostilities culminated in a total collapse of the parent-child relationship. This atmosphere resulted in extreme mental abuse to all parties concerned.

On June 18, 1973, Mr. Snyder, having concluded that the juvenile court might be able to assist him in controlling his daughter, removed Cynthia from the family home and delivered her to the Youth Service Center. As a result, Cynthia was placed in a receiving home. On July 19, 1973, in an attempt to avoid returning home, Cynthia filed a petition in the Juvenile Department of the Superior Court for King County, alleging that she was a dependent child as defined by RCW 13.04.010(2) and (3), which provided:

This chapter shall be known as the "Juvenile Court Law" and shall apply to all minor children under the age of eighteen years who are delinquent or dependent; and to any person or persons who are responsible for or contribute to, the delinquency or dependency of such children.

For the purpose of this chapter the words "dependent child" shall mean any child under the age of eighteen years:

* * *

(2) Who has no parent, guardian or other responsible person; or who has no parent or guardian willing to exercise, or capable of exercising, proper parental control; or

(3) Whose home by reason of neglect, cruelty or depravity of his parents or either of them, or on the part of his guardian, or on the part of the person in whose custody or care he may be, or for any other reason, is an unfit place for such child; * * *

On July 23, 1973, Cynthia was placed in the temporary custody of the Department of Social and Health Services and an attorney was appointed to be her guardian ad litem. On October 12, 1973, the juvenile court held that the allegations attacking the fitness of Cynthia's parents were incorrect, at least to the extent that they alleged dependency, and that Cynthia should be returned to the custody of her parents. Cynthia did return to the family residence, where she remained until November 16, 1973. At that time, following additional confrontations in her home, Cynthia went to Youth Advocates, a group which assists troubled juveniles, who in turn directed her to the Youth Service Center. On November 21, 1973, Margaret Rozmyn, who was in charge of the intake program at the center, filed a petition alleging that Cynthia was incorrigible as defined under RCW 13.04.010(7), which provides:

For the purpose of this chapter the words "dependent child" shall mean any child under the age of eighteen years:

(7) Who is incorrigible; that is, who is beyond the control and power of his parents, guardian, or custodian by reason of the conduct or nature of said child;

A hearing was held on December 3, 1973, to determine temporary custody. The court limited the proceedings to arguments of opposing counsel and ultimately decided that Cynthia should be placed in a foster home pending the outcome of the fact-finding hearing. This hearing was held on December 10 and 11, 1973. At that time, Commissioner Quinn found that Cynthia was incorrigible and continued the matter for one week in order for the entire family to meet with a counselor. Originally, the commissioner indicated that he was inclined to have Cynthia return home, while at the same time being placed under supervised probation. However, on December 18, 1973, Commissioner Quinn, upon hearing the comments and conclusions of the counseling psychiatrists chosen by the parents, decided that Cynthia was to be placed in a foster home, under the supervision of the probation department of the juvenile court, and that she and her parents were to continue counseling, subject to subsequent review by the court. The parents immediately filed a motion for revision of the commissioner's decision, which was denied by the Superior Court for King County in August of 1974.

This court assumed jurisdiction of the case upon our issuance of the requested writ of certiorari.

The sole issue presented by these facts is whether there is substantial evidence in the record, taken as a whole, to support the juvenile court's determination that Cynthia Nell Snyder is incorrigible. Her parents contend that Cynthia is not incorrigible, as a matter of law, since the only evidence to support such a finding is their daughter's own statements. We disagree.

A child is incorrigible when she is beyond the power and control of her parents by reason of her own conduct. RCW 13.04.010(7). In reviewing the record in search of substantial evidence, we must find "evidence in sufficient quantum to persuade a fair-minded, rational person of the truth of a declared premise." Helman v. Sacred Heart Hospital, 62 Wash.2d 136, 147, 381 P.2d 605, 612 (1963). In applying this criteria for review, we are mindful that our paramount consideration, irrespective of the natural emotions in cases of this nature, must be the welfare of the child. In re Todd, 68 Wash.2d 587, 414 P. 2d 605 (1966); In re Russell, 70 Wash.2d 451, 423 P.2d 640 (1967). When the questions of dependency and incorrigibility arise, "we have often noted what we think is a realistic and rational appellate policy of placing *very strong* reliance on trial court determinations of what course of action will be in the best interests of the child." In reviewing the record, we find no evidence which would indicate that Commissioner Quinn acted unfairly, irrationally, or in a prejudicial manner in reaching his conclusion. Therefore, we must give "very strong" credence to his determinations. We feel it is imperative to recognize that the issue of who is actually responsible for the breakdown in the parent-child relationship is irrelevant to our disposition of this case. The issue is whether there is substantial evidence to support a finding that the parent-child relationship has dissipated to the point where parental control is lost and, therefore, Cynthia is incorrigible. It is for this reason that Cynthia's conduct, her state of mind, and the opinion of Doctor Gallagher, the psychiatrist chosen by Mr. and Mrs. Snyder, are of such paramount importance. This child has established a pattern of refusing to obey her parents and, on two occasions, has, in effect, fled her home by filing petitions in the juvenile court in order that she might be made a ward of the court. Cynthia's adamant state of mind can be best understood by considering her *clear* and *unambiguous* testimony in response to her attorney's direct examination.

Q. Your petition alleges that you absolutely refuse to go home and obey your parents, is that correct? A. Yes. Q. You are under oath today, of course, and is that the statement you would make to the Court today? A. Yes. Q. Cindy, do you understand the consequences of filing a petition of this nature? A. Yes. Q. Did we discuss this matter?

A. Yes. Q. Have we discussed this on several occasions? A. Yes. Q. What is your understanding of what might be the consequences of this type of petition? A. I could be put in the Youth Center or I could be put into another institution of some kind or I could go into the custody of the Department of Social and Health Services. Q. So you understand it is conceivable that you might not be able to go back home even if you want to go back home, is that correct?

A. Yes. Q. In spite of all that, is it still your statement today that at the time of the petition anyway you refused to go back home? A. Yes. Q. Is that your position right now? A. Yes. Q. The position then, why don't you state that for the Court? A. I refuse to go back there. I just won't do it. MR. SANDERS [Attorney for parents]: I object to the whole line of testimony. I think it is irrelevant whether she refuses to go back home. That is not an issue in the case. THE COURT: Overruled. A. *I just absolutely refuse to go back there. I can't live with them.*

(Italics ours.)

In addition, the parents and the older sister, by their testimony, admitted that a difficult situation existed in the home. The court also considered the testimony of the intake officer from the Youth Service Center as to the attitude of Cynthia. Finally, the court considered the opinion of Dr. Gallagher, who met with Cynthia and her parents, and reported that counseling would not be beneficial until all of the individuals concerned backed away from the hard and fast positions they now held in regard to this matter which, in his opinion, was the cause of the tension which resulted in overt hostility. In other words, the finding of incorrigibility is not supported solely by Cynthia's testimony and her refusal to return home. But in addition thereto, the commissioner's opinion finds support in the testimony of other individuals who are familiar with the situation, either from a personal or a professional standpoint. The fact that the commissioner gave serious consideration to the testimony of Cynthia, an interested party, is inconsequential since it only goes to the weight to be given to her statements as a witness. Furthermore, we have not deviated from the rule that when an interested party testifies the rate at which that evidence is discounted, if at all, should be determined by the trial judge, who is far better qualified to make that judgment than we. Hanford v. Goehry, 24 Wash.2d 859, 167 P.2d 678 (1946).

* * *

The parents also contend that RCW 13.04.010(7), is unconstitutionally vague. Our recent upholding of this statute in Blondheim v. State, 84 Wash.2d 874, 529 P.2d 1096 (1974), is dispositive of this issue and no further discussion is warranted.

It is implicit in the record that the petitioner parents believe the juvenile court has given sympathy and support to Cynthia's problems in disregard of their rights as parents, and that the juvenile court has failed to assume its responsibility to assist in the resolution of the parents' problems with their minor child. We find this presumption of the petitioners to be unsupported by the evidence.

The record clearly shows that numerous attempts were made by the juvenile court commissioner to reconcile the family differences, as evidenced by its unsuccessful attempt at sending Cynthia home subsequent to the disposition of the first petition, the attempt to gain assistance through professional counseling, and the numerous and extensive exchanges between Commissioner Quinn and the Snyder family during the proceeding. The avenues for counseling were to remain open and counseling of both parties was to continue, which was interrupted by the interposition of the application by the parents for our review. In view of our disposition of this case, we are satisfied that the juvenile court, in exercising its continuing jurisdiction, will continue to review the progress of the parties to the end of a hoped for reconciliation.

The decision of the juvenile court for King County is affirmed.

NOTES AND QUESTIONS

1. The *Snyder* case is the subject of a law review comment in Note, Status Offenses and the Status of Children's Rights: Do Children have the Legal Right to be Incorrigible? 1976 B.Y.U.L.Rev. 659. Some questions presented by the case and this comment include the following:

(a) What is the definition of "incorrigible" which the opinion adopts? What should be the definition of "incorrigible"?

(b) What is the purpose of the statute which creates the so-called "status offenses", such as incorrigibility, truancy, running away from home, all of which share the characteristic that they are not offenses which would be crimes if committed by an adult? Is the purpose to protect the child from unreasonable parental control? Or to aid the parent in controlling the child? Or some other purpose? See L.A.M. v. State, 547 P.2d 827 (Alaska 1976).

(c) If the state of Washington's legislation had included running away from home in its CHINS or PINS statute, would that have affected the outcome of the *Snyder* case? For such a statute see Colo.Rev.Stat.Ann. § 19-1-103(5)(b) (1973). Is the normal remedy for runaway children cases the return of the child to his or her parents?

(d) What assumptions about parent-child relations are reflected by the Washington Supreme Court's disposition of this case?

(e) Would any other disposition of this case be more satisfactory for all parties? For example, would it be preferable to require parents and child to undergo a further course of counselling?

(f) In this case, assume that instead of invoking the juvenile court's jurisdiction the parents employ a private individual who finds Cynthia, returns her to her home and, with the consent of Mr. and Mrs. Snyder, subjects her to a long and intense series of counselling sessions in an effort to convince her of the error of her ways and of the necessity of obeying her parents. A sympathetic aunt and uncle hear of this and consult you, asking what can be done about this family disharmony. What would you advise? Would you bring a juvenile court proceeding on Cynthia's behalf? Is she an abused or neglected child? Cf. In re Katz, 73 Cal.App.3d 952, 141 Cal. Rptr. 234 (1977).

(g) Would the disposition of this case have been different if Cynthia had been thirteen years old instead of sixteen?

(h) Is there, or should there be a statutory or constitutional right to *individual* treatment on the part of Cynthia in the *Snyder* situation? In other words, does she have some claim to have her individual problem dealt with outside of an institutional setting, by a psychiatrist or other appropriate professional, at public expense, on the authority of cases like *Martarella*?

(i) Do Cynthia's parents have a statutory or constitutional right to treatment respecting their difficulties with Cynthia, as an alternative to losing the custody of their daughter? See In re Susan M., 125 Cal.Rptr. 707, 53 Cal.App.3d 300 (1976); In re David B., 91 Cal.App.3d 184, 154 Cal. Rptr. 63 (1979). Cf. Colo.Rev.Stat.Ann. § 19–11–105(b)(I) (1978), requiring an "appropriate treatment plan" before parental rights may be terminated. Does this sort of statute require treatment for parents?

2. Snyder held that the Washington PINS statute on incorrigibility was constitutional, relying upon the earlier case of Blondheim v. State, 84 Wash.2d 874, 529 P.2d 1096 (1974). What arguments might be advanced against the constitutionality of the status offense statutes? Should these arguments prevail? See D.T.H. v. State, 348 So.2d 1155 (Fla.1977); In Interest of Hutchins, 345 So.2d 703 (Fla.1977); In re Napier, 532 P.2d 423 (Okl.1975); Gregory, Juvenile Court Jurisdiction Over Noncriminal Misbehavior: The Argument Against Abolition, 39 Ohio St.L.J. 242 (1978); Roybal, Void for Vagueness: State Statutes Proscribing Conduct Only For a Juvenile, 1 Pepperdine L.Rev. 1 (1973); Katz and Teitelbaum, PINS Jurisdiction, the Vagueness Doctrine, and the Rule of Law, in L. Teitelbaum, A. Gough, Beyond Control Status Offenders in the Juvenile Court 201 (1977); Robinson v. California, 370 U.S. 660 (1962); Powell v. Texas, 392 U.S. 514 (1968).

3. Does the result in the *Snyder* case constitute an infringement of the parents' constitutional rights or of the right of family privacy, under Wisconsin v. Yoder, supra, page 627, Prince v. Massachusetts, supra, page 643, Stanley v. Illinois, supra, page 432, or Griswold v. Connecticut, supra, page 73? Would a decree ordering Cynthia to return to her parents' home violate her constitutional rights under In re Gault, supra, page 666?

4. Consider the following points of view:

(a) P. Wald, Making Sense Out of the Rights of Youth, 4 Human Rights 13, 25 (1974): "In sum, contemporary concepts of fairness strongly support adoption of a general presumption that children should be allowed the same rights and freedoms as adults unless there is a significant risk of irreversible damage to them—physical, psychological, emotional—from exercising such rights or a general consensus backed by empirical data that at particular ages children do not have sufficiently developed skills to exercise those rights."

(b) Foster and Freed, A Bill of Rights for Children, 6 Fam.L.Q. 343, 347 (1972) propose a "bill of rights for children" which would give the child a legal right to parental affection; to maintenance and education; to be regarded as a person; to receive fair treatment; to be heard; to keep his earnings; to obtain medical care; to emancipation when the relationship with his parents has broken down and he has left home due to abuse or neglect or serious family conflict or other sufficient cause; to be free of legal disabilities except where necessary for his protection; and to receive special care and protection in the administration of the law.

See also Rosenberg & Rosenberg, The Legacy of the Stubborn and Rebellious Son, 74 Mich.L.Rev. 1097 (1976).

(c) Hafen, Children's Liberation and the New Egalitarianism: Some Reservations About Abandoning Youth to Their "Rights", 1976 B.Y.U.L. Rev. 605, 607: "This article suggests that serious risks are involved in an uncritical transfer of egalitarian concepts from the contexts in which they developed to the unique context of family life and children. The family life context has a history all its own—a history replete with psychological, economic, sociological, and political implications. The use of 'children's rights' language in this day of rights movements offers a way to leap over that history and its implications into the realm of abstract ideology. Whether that leap is the result of strategy or ignorance, its consequences are the same. The most harmful of the potential consequences is that the long-range interests of children themselves may be irreparably damaged as the state and parents abandon children to their 'rights'."

And at 1976 B.Y.U.L.Rev. 654: "Ironically, limiting parental authority is likely to require some kind of state intervention on behalf of children, perhaps in the form of more far-reaching recognitions of children's rights in contexts where their actual needs for protection are not at stake. It is not possible for the state to remain truly neutral, particularly when parents begin with a position of authority over their children within the inherent status quo. Denying a portion of parental authority necessarily adds to the authority of children. Such an addition may be appropriate when the circumstances make it clear in an individual case that children have some special need. But, as long as the limited capacities of children make it either impossible, unrealistic, or unfair to them to let them assume full responsibility for their own lives, ultimate control over their conduct must and will necessarily rest either with their parents or with the state. Thus, reducing parental authority simply creates increased state involvement. That, it is submitted, would be the worse of two potential evils."

(d) Levy, The Rights of Parents, 1976 B.Y.U.L.Rev. 693:

"My topic today transcends doctrinal confines. My concern is perpetuation of the family as the most important relationship in our society—as the unit which provides, and should continue to provide, the basic emotional and socializing experiences for our children. Those functions can be served effectively, I believe, only if the family is considered to be and is treated as an autonomous unit, and if families are protected from untoward governmental interference with their operations. Yet the current 'children's rights' campaign, by increasing government intrusion into family decisionmaking, has at least the potential to upset the traditional social compact that undergirds these family-centered values. To eliminate the threat, we must strive to maintain a stance of 'family privacy'—a policy that families may not be supervised by judicial or other agents of the state. I choose to call that stance 'Respect for Family Autonomy;' the people I call the 'new child savers' claim that I am simply an old-fashioned supporter of 'parental rights.' "

Professor Gregory likewise argues for "family autonomy" in Juvenile Court Jurisdiction Over Noncriminal Misbehavior: The Argument Against Abolition, 39 Ohio St.L.J. 242, 263 (1978).

(e) The foregoing quotations are necessarily only brief extracts from more complete analyses. They nevertheless provide some bases for answering such questions as the following:

 i. How should the *Snyder* case have been decided, in order to be consistent with the views of these several commentators?

 ii. What answer would these commentators give to the question (which is often raised) whether the statutes creating "status offenses" should be repealed or drastically amended? What answer would you give?

 iii. Which, if any, of these quotations would you agree with?

 iv. How would you express in statutory form your view of the correct legal approach to family autonomy, children's rights and state intervention in decisions affecting the family?

5. H and W are poor and uneducated people who have a son, S, who is sixteen. He does not do well in school and stays out of school as much as two or three days a week. He often stays away from home for a week or two at a time, drinks when he can get liquor and smokes marijuana regularly. His high school teachers and principal file a PINS petition alleging these facts, the PINS age limit being eighteen. The compulsory school attendance laws apply only up to age sixteen. H and W appear at the PINS proceeding and tell the court their son is a good boy, kind to his parents, and that they have no objection to the way he lives. How should the juvenile court dispose of the petition? Cf. In re Burr, 119 Ill.App.2d 134, 255 N.E.2d 57 (1970). Is the answer to this question affected by Wisconsin v. Yoder, supra, page 627?

6. One way of dealing with juvenile misconduct, at least in some limited circumstances is the juvenile curfew. Would a statute authorizing such a curfew be constitutional? Would the imposition of a curfew be constitutional without statutory authority? Are the answers to these questions affected by the considerations discussed in paragraph 4, supra? Could you draft a satisfactory curfew statute or ordinance? See Note, Juvenile Curfew Ordinances and the Constitution, 76 Mich.L.Rev. 109 (1977); People v. Chambers, 66 Ill.2d 36, 4 Ill.Dec. 308, 360 N.E.2d 55 (1976).

NOTE ON THE VICARIOUS RESPONSIBILITY OF PARENTS

Many states have statutes which in one form or another impose upon parents civil liability for the torts, usually the willful torts, of their children. The Illinois statute, Smith-Hurd Ill.Ann.Stat. ch. 70, §§ 51–56 (Supp.1979) is more or less typical:

§ 51. Short Title and citation

This Act shall be known and may be cited as the Parental Responsibility Law.

§ 52. Definitions

As used in this Act, unless the context otherwise requires, the terms specified have the meanings ascribed to them:

(1) "Legal guardian" means a person appointed guardian, or given custody, of a minor by a circuit court of the State, but does not include a person appointed guardian, or given custody, of a minor under the "Juvenile Court Act", approved August 5, 1965, as now or hereafter amended.

(2) "Minor" means a person who is above the age of 11 years, but not yet 19 years of age.

§ 53. Parent or legal guardian—Liability—Wilful or malicious acts of minor

The parent or legal guardian of an unemancipated minor who resides with such parent or legal guardian is liable for actual damages for the wilful or malicious acts of such minor which cause injury to a person or property.

§ 54. Persons or entities entitled to enforce Act

Any municipal corporation, county, township, village or any other political subdivision or department of the State of Illinois, or any person, partnership, corporation, association or any incorporated or unincorporated religious, educational or charitable organization is entitled to enforce the liability imposed by this Act.

§ 55. Limitation on damages—Damages allowable

No recovery under this Act may exceed $500 actual damages for each person, or legal entity as provided in Section 4 of this Act, for each occurrence of such wilful or malicious acts by the minor causing injury, in addition to taxable court costs. In determining the damages to be allowed in an action under this Act for personal injury, only medical, dental and hospital expenses may be considered.

§ 56. Common law damages

This Act shall not affect the recovery of damages in any other cause of action where the liability of the parent or legal guardian is predicated on a common law basis.

A majority of the cases in which the issue has come up have held civil liability statutes of this type constitutional. See, e. g., Watson v. Gradzik, 34 Conn.Sup. 7, 373 A.2d 191 (1977); In re Sorrell, 20 Md.App. 179, 315 A.2d 110 (1974); General Ins. Co. of America v. Faulkner, 259 N.C. 317, 130 S.E.2d 645 (1963). Cases holding the statute unconstitutional are Corley v. Lewless, 227 Ga. 745, 182 S.E. 2d 766 (1971); Board of Education of Piscataway Tp. v. Caffiero, 159 N.J.Super. 347, 387 A.2d 1263 (1978). See also Note, A Constitutional Caveat on the Vicarious Liability of Parents, 47 N.Dame L. 1321 (1972).

The parental responsibility laws raise a number of questions, both as to their policy and as to their application to specific cases. Many of them are not answered by the statutes or the cases, but some are discussed in Note, Criminal Liability of Parents for Failure to Control Their Children, 67 Val.U.L.Rev. 332 (1972). Some of these questions are:

(a) What is the rationale of these statutes, to provide a source of compensation for the harms of children, a kind of "deep pocket" theory, or is it to force parents to supervise their children more closely, or both? Vanthournout v. Burge, 69 Ill.App.3d 193, 25 Ill.Dec. 685, 387 N.E.2d 341 (1979).

(b) Are the statutes effective in causing parents to prevent misconduct by their children?

(c) If the statutory purpose is deterrence, can the parents obtain insurance against liability and if so, what effect does insurance have? Liberty Mut. Ins. Co. v. Davis, 52 Ohio Misc. 26, 368 N.E.2d 336, 6 O.O.3d 108 (1977).

(d) May the parent be held liable for damage done by an emancipated minor child? Albert v. Ellis, 59 Ohio App.2d 152, 392 N.E.2d 1309 (1978).

(e) Why should there be a $500 limit on the damages in such cases? If the statute rests on either of the rationales suggested, why should the parent not be held liable for the entire damage?

(f) If damage is done by several children, is there contribution among the various parents? Cf. Liberty Mut. Ins. Co. v. Davis, 52 Ohio Misc. 26, 368 N.E.2d 336, 6 O.O.3d 108 (1977).

For further discussion of such statutes, see Note, The Iowa Parental Responsibility Act, 55 Iowa L.Rev. 1037 (1970); Note, The Pennsylvania Parental Liability Statute, 29 U.Pitt.L.Rev. 578 (1968); Annot., Parents' Liability for Injury or Damage Intentionally Inflicted by Minor Child, 54 A.L.R.3d 974 (1974).

In the absence of a parental responsibility statute, at common law the parent was liable for the torts of his children only if he participated in them or was negligent himself in some way causing the harm, as by failing properly to control his child, or by permitting him to use some dangerous device without supervision. Note, Parental Liability for a Child's Tortious Acts, 81 Dick.L.Rev. 755 (1977); W. Prosser, Torts 871–873 (4th ed. 1971).

There are also statutes in many states which impose vicarious criminal liability upon parents for the crimes of their children. Such statutes are generally known as "contributing to delinquency" laws, and they vary in their provisions. The more limited ones make it a misdemeanor for the parent actively to encourage or participate in his child's criminal activity. Thus the Colorado statute provides that it is a misdemeanor for an adult to induce, aid or encourage a child to violate a state or federal law. Colo.Rev.Stat.Ann. § 19–3–119 (1973). But some states go beyond this, and, as in New York, make it a crime for the parent to fail to exercise reasonable diligence in the control of the child thereby failing to prevent the child from becoming a juvenile delinquent. N.Y. Penal L. § 260.10 (Supp.1979–1980). The broad version of the contributing statute has been held to be unconstitutional as too vague. State v. Hodges, 254 Or. 21, 457 P.2d 491 (1969), 15 Vill.L.Rev. 767 (1970). And in Doe v. City of Trenton, 143 N.J.Super. 128, 362 A.2d 1200 (1976), aff'd p.c. 75 N.J. 137, 380 A.2d 703 (1977) a city ordinance was held unconstitutional when it provided that a parent was presumed responsible for the misconduct of his child where the child was convicted twice in one year for violations of the peace. The narrower type of statute, requiring active conduct on the adult's part, has been held valid in Brockmueller v. State, 86 Ariz. 82, 340 P.2d 992 (1959), cert. den. 361 U.S. 913 (1959).

SECTION 6.   THE CHILD'S LEGAL CAPACITY

NOTE ON THE CHILD'S LEGAL CAPACITY

Until recently the age of majority in the United States was twenty-one for both males and females. Twenty-one was apparently the age at which men of the Middle Ages were thought to be strong enough to bear arms and give military service, and that age remained the legal measure of maturity long after the responsibilities of maturity changed. See James, The Age of Majority, 4 Am.J. of Legal Hist. 22 (1960). Oddly enough, the recent reduction in the age of majority which has occurred for voting purposes in all states, and for all purposes in some states, has undoubtedly been influenced by the fact that in the modern age men of eighteen were considered sufficiently mature to bear arms and so were drafted. The change for voting purposes made by the Twenty-Sixth Amendment to the United States Constitution is discussed in the *Jolicoeur* case, supra, page 63.

Under the influence of that Amendment most states have reduced the age of majority for both men and women to eighteen. See, e. g., Cal.Civ.Code §§ 25, 25.1 (Supp.1979); Ill.Ann.Stat. ch. 3, § 131 (1978); Mich.Stat.Ann. § 25.244(52) (1974); N.Y.Dom.Rel.L. § 2 (1977). Colorado has taken the odd position that the age of majority is eighteen for such purposes as legal capacity to make contracts, own property, sue or be sued, but that the child is entitled to be supported by his parents until age twenty-one, thereby giving children the best of both worlds. Colo.Rev.Stat.Ann. § 13–22–101 (1973); In re Weaver, 39 Colo.App. 523, 571 P.2d 307 (1977).

Special statutes in many states permit minors to make specific kinds of contracts or engage in specific transactions. See Uniform Minor Student Capacity to Borrow Act, 9 Unif.L.Ann. 223 (1979). By statute banks are protected when they receive and pay out the deposits of persons under the age of majority. See H. Clark, Law of Domestic Relations, 235 (1968). These developments are causing the minor's incapacity to be of less practical importance.

A person under the age of majority may make contracts and enforce them, but he has the right to disaffirm them when asserted against him at any time before reaching majority and for a reasonable time thereafter. Warwick Municipal Employees Credit Union v. McAllister, 293 A.2d 516 (R.I.1972). If both parties to a contract are under age, either may disaffirm. If the person is under age when he makes the contract, he may disaffirm even though his guardian approves of it. Likewise a person under age may own property, but he may disaffirm his conveyance of property just as he may disaffirm his contracts. He may disaffirm his conveyance even as against a subsequent purchaser of the property for value without notice of the infancy. Under the Uniform Commercial Code, § 3–207, however, a minor who transfers a negotiable instrument may not disaffirm as against a holder in due course.

The purpose of these legal rules is of course to protect children against the consequences of their own improvidence. See Edge, Voidability of Minors' Contracts: A Feudal Doctrine in a Modern Economy, 1 Ga.L.Rev. 205 (1967). As is common in the law, however, other social interests conflict with this, the obvious one being the interests of persons contracting with minors. One qualification on the right of disaffirmance has been created for the benefit of both minors and others. This is the rule which says that a minor's contract for the purchase of "necessaries" may not be disaffirmed, if the minor is not living with a parent or guardian, and if his parent or guardian is unable or unwilling to furnish him with necessaries. International Text-Book Co. v. Connelly, 206 N.Y. 188, 99 N.E. 722 (1912); Cal. Civ.Code § 36 (Supp.1973). The definition of "necessaries" in this context is much like that in cases where the support of a spouse is involved. It includes not only the bare essentials of food, shelter, clothing, medical care and education, but perhaps other articles or services, depending upon the scale of living enjoyed by the minor. As a recent case put it, necessaries include "such articles of property and such services as are reasonably necessary to enable the infant to earn the money required to provide the necessities of life for himself and those who are legally dependent upon him." This may include, for example, the services of an employment agency. Gastonia Personnel Corp. v. Rogers, 276 N.C. 279, 172 S.E.2d 19 (1970). And it may include an automobile. Rose v. Sheehan Buick, Inc., 204 So.2d 903 (Fla.App.1967). The services of a lawyer may also be necessaries, at least where related to the minor's person rather than his property. See cases collected in Annot., 13 A.L.R.3d 1251 (1967). The burden of proving that the claim is for necessaries rests upon the person asserting it.

Where the child misrepresents his age, there is obvious hardship to the person dealing with him. Some courts, though not all, have held that when a child seeks to disaffirm the contract he is liable for the damages caused to the other party by his misrepresentation, or that he is estopped to disaffirm. See Keser v. Chagnon, 159 Colo. 209, 410 P.2d 637 (1966); H. Clark, Law of Domestic Relations, 237 (1968).

Most cases hold that when the minor disaffirms a contract, he must return to the other party the consideration he received if he still has it. If he does not have it, or it has been destroyed, the minor may disaffirm without being required to return the consideration. H. Clark, Law of Domestic Relations, 238 (1968), citing cases. But see Hamrick v. Hospital Service Corp., 296 A.2d 15 (R.I.1972). Where the consideration for the contract has depreciated in value, the cases are in disagreement as to whether and under what circumstances the minor will be charged with the depreciation. Cases are collected in Annot., 12 A.L.R.3d 1174 (1967).

In one special situation it is essential that the minor make a contract, that is, where he has a claim for tortious injury which the other party is willing to settle. In order to induce the defendant to settle, the child must be able to give a binding release of the claim. The statutes or practice of most states have developed a procedure for making the infant's release binding, thereby encouraging the settlement of suits. This generally requires the appointment of a guardian for the child and the approval of the settlement by the court. If this procedure is followed, the release will not usually be set aside, even though the settlement later appears to have been unfair to the child. Hudson v. Thies, 35 Ill.App.2d 189, 182 N.E.2d 760 (1962), aff'd 27 Ill.2d 548, 190 N.E.2d 343 (1963); Handley v. Mortland, 54 Wash.2d 489, 342 P.2d 612 (1959). A case the other way is Spaulding v. Zimmerman, 263 Minn. 346, 116 N.W.2d 704 (1962). See also Bucklin, Settlement of Personal Injury Claims of Children, 44 N.D.L.Rev. 52

(1967), and Note, Settling the Personal Injury Claim of a Minor, 38 U.Colo.L.Rev. 377 (1966).

The breakdown of custom and tradition in America has been reflected in numerous controversies over names, particularly the names of married women and of children. A comprehensive treatment of these issues by the Massachusetts Supreme Judicial Court is found in Secretary of the Commonwealth v. City Clerk of Lowell, 373 Mass. 178, 366 N.E.2d 717 (1977). The court held, inter alia, that parents were entitled to choose surnames for their children, that they might choose a surname other than that of the father, either a hyphenated combination of the mother's and father's name or an entirely different surname, and that the keeper of birth records was required to register the name so chosen. The mother of an illegitimate child was held to be entitled to name the child, at least in absence of objection from the father. Doe v. Dunning, 87 Wash.2d 50, 549 P.2d 1 (1976) agrees that the mother of an illegitimate child may give the child her name.

NOTE ON EMANCIPATION

Emancipation should be a relatively simple concept, but the courts have made it unnecessarily confusing. In general emancipation consists of the legal process by which a minor is released from the control and authority of his parents. The traditional way for courts to define emancipation is to say that "Emancipation is a renunciation by a parent of the latter's legal duties whereby he surrenders all his parental rights to the child or others. * * * In determining whether a child has been emancipated it is the intention of the *parent* which governs and, further, it is the intention of a parent who has control and/or custody of the child involved. * * * Whether or not a parent emancipates his minor child, however, rests with the parent and not with the child." Bates v. Bates, 62 Misc.2d 498, 310 N.Y.S.2d 26 (Fam.Ct.1970). This sort of talk sounds as though emancipation has the same effect as the reaching of majority, that is, of releasing a child from all his disabilities. In fact it does not have this effect. Emancipation may be partial and limited rather than general, releasing the minor from some disabilities and not others. Fevig v. Fevig, 90 N.M. 51, 559 P.2d 839 (1977). Nearly every emancipation is partial. Thus where a parent permits a child to live away from home and keep his own earnings, the child is probably emancipated for purposes of acquiring his own domicile, and retaining his earnings, but if he should become ill and unable to work, he would probably be entitled to obtain support from his parent. And at least some cases would hold that his emancipation does not effect his right to disaffirm contracts and conveyances. Kiefer v. Fred Howe Motors, Inc., 39 Wis.2d 20, 158 N.W.2d 288 (1968). Other courts seem to hold that emancipation does cut off the right to disaffirm. In re Greer, 184 So.2d 104 (La.App.1966); H. Clark, Law of Domestic

Relations, 244 (1968). And even if emancipation occurs, it may be revoked and the child may resume his dependent status. Cf. Vaupel v. Bellach, 261 Iowa 376, 154 N.W.2d 149 (1967).

Thus whether emancipation has occurred depends in large part on the context in which the question arises. It would be absurd, to take an extreme case, if the law should permit the father of a twelve-year-old child to say, "I hereby emancipate you", and thereby free himself from any duty of support. It is more accurate to say that emancipation occurs when parent and child consent that it occur, and that it has the effect which the parties intend under the circumstances. The courts have developed various rules of thumb, holding that marriage emancipates, as does enlistment in the army and departure from the parental home to set up a residence elsewhere. But all such holdings must be understood as limited to the context in which they appear, and to the effect on the minor's legal capacity which is involved in the case.

The doctrine of emancipation was originally a product of judicial decision. Today in some states a statutory procedure by which a child may be emancipated is available. For example, the Oregon statute authorizes a child over sixteen to file a petition for emancipation in the juvenile court, which that court may grant after taking into account such circumstances as whether the parent consents, whether the minor lives away from home and is self-supporting and whether he is sufficiently mature to manage his own affairs. Or. Rev.Stat. §§ 109.555, 109.565, 419.476, 482.270 (1977). The statute is analyzed in Note, Juvenile Law-Emancipation: New Legislation for Oregon's Children, 57 Or.L.Rev. 573 (1978).

For further analysis of the concept of emancipation, see H. Clark, Law of Domestic Relations § 8.3 (1968); Katz, Schroeder, Sidman, Emancipating Our Children—Coming of Legal Age in America, 7 Fam.L.Q. 211 (1973); Marks, Detours on the Road to Maturity: A View of the Legal Concept of Growing Up and Letting Go. 38 L. & Contemp.Prob.No. 3, 78 (1975).

NOTE ON GUARDIANSHIP

A guardian is one who is appointed to protect various interests of another, called the ward, who may be a child, a mentally incompetent, or other person under a disability. In English law there were a great many varieties of guardians, but for our purposes today we need talk about only four. The parent of a child is normally referred to as the natural guardian of the child, and by statute in many states the parent is made the natural guardian of the child. Another kind of guardian is the guardian of the person of a child. This guardian, when he is someone other than a parent, has custody of the child and is responsible for the child's care, education, and training. The guardian of the person is normally not under a duty to support the child. A third type of guardian is the guardian of the child's estate or property. Like the guardian of the person, the guardian of the estate must be appointed by a court, but his function is quite different from that of the guardian of the person. The guardian of the estate is responsible for managing property belonging to the child under the supervision of the court which appointed him. In carrying out this duty the guardian of the estate is a fiduciary whose activities and obligations very closely resemble those of a trustee. The fourth type of guardian is the guardian ad litem, who is appointed to represent and protect the interests of the child in particular litigation. See Fed.R.Civ.Proc. 17(c) and Annot., 68 A.L.R.2d 752 (1959).

Jurisdiction to appoint a guardian of the person of a child depends upon the same factors as does jurisdiction to enter an order with respect to the child's custody, since this is essentially the function of a guardian of the person. For cases dealing with this and with other custody issues, see chapter 6, section 3.

Guardianships of the estate are generally regulated by statute in the various states. Unfortunately the statutes are fragmentary and ill organized so that it is impossible in many instances to get a comprehensive picture of the appointment, duties, and powers of guardians of the estate solely from state statutes. In general guardians of the estate are appointed whenever the ward has property. Normally the parent of the child will be appointed the guardian of the estate but the mere relationship of parent and child does not give the parent the right to administer the estate of the child. Unlike other fiduciaries, the guardian does not take legal title to the property of the child. He does ordinarily have the power to take possession of the property, both real and personal, to manage it and protect it from injury or loss. Where necessary he may bring actions to vindicate the rights of the child in the property, and he may also defend actions brought against the child unless a guardian ad litem has been appointed in the particular case.

The guardian of the estate has a duty to collect the rent, profit or income from the property of the ward and must invest the money so collected. Individual state law varies with respect to the type of investment which is considered valid for guardians of the estate. The authorized investments may or may not differ from those authorized for trustees.

The guardian is personally liable on contracts made in the course of the management of the ward's estate, although he is entitled to reimbursement out of that estate for contracts properly made. This rule has been changed in some jurisdictions by statutes which authorize collection directly from the ward's estate.

Since the guardian is a fiduciary he is bound by the usual rules applying to fiduciaries not to engage in self dealing nor to profit from his position as guardian.

The usual guardianship, both in procedure and substantive rules, is so cumbersome, expensive and generally unsatisfactory as to call forth widespread criticism. One method of avoiding the expense and inconvenience of guardianship is the Uniform Gifts to Minors Act, enacted in many states and establishing a simple and inexpensive way of making gifts of securities to children without either a guardianship or a trust. See Uniform Gifts to Minors Act, 8 Uniform Laws Annotated 181 (1979). Gifts to minors under this statute are made by delivery of the security to a custodian for the minor. Such a gift conveys full legal title to the minor but enables the custodian to manage, invest and reinvest the property. If the child has a guardian the guardian does not receive any rights with respect to the property given under the act. The act gives to the custodian broad powers of management, provides that the custodian is a fiduciary and provides convenient and inexpensive methods for the administration of the custodial property.

For discussions of the various contemporary forms of guardianship, with references to statute and case law, see Symposium on Guardianship, 45 Iowa L.Rev. 209–413 (1960), and H. Clark, Law of Domestic Relations § 8.4 (1968).

SECTION 7. THE MARRIED WOMAN'S LEGAL STATUS

INTRODUCTORY NOTE

In many other places throughout this book questions relating to the contemporary position of the married woman have been raised and discussed, such as, for example, alimony and property on divorce, the right to support, age requirements for marriage, contracts restraining marriage, and the action for loss of consortium. In this section are included materials which do not fit readily into other parts of the book and which may be of more or less relevance to the rapidly changing position of married women. These materials reveal only a small part of the much broader changes now occurring in the condition of all women in the United States, changes which are reflected and influenced by such legal reforms as the Civil Rights Act of 1964, forbidding discrimination in employment on account of sex, quoted, supra, page 21, and the many Supreme Court cases such as Reed v. Reed, 404 U.S. 71 (1971); Frontiero v. Richardson, 411 U.S. 677 (1973); Schlesinger v. Ballard, 419 U.S. 498 (1975); Weinberger v. Wiesenfeld, 420 U.S. 636 (1975); Califano v. Goldfarb, 430 U.S. 199 (1977). The proposed Twenty-Seventh Amendment prohibiting the abridgment of rights on account of sex is quoted supra, page 21. Similar provisions are found in the constitutions of about seventeen states. The present section must necessarily be limited to problems arising directly out of marriage and the family, leaving the wider issues of sex equality to be treated elsewhere.

Although the unmarried woman at common law had full legal capacity (except the right to vote), the married woman's position was quite different. The married woman was subject to many disabilities. The personal property which she possessed became her husband's absolutely, to do with as he liked, except such articles of wearing apparel or ornament as were characterized as her paraphernalia. These became his also, but if not disposed of by him during his life they became hers on his death. The wife's choses in action could be reduced to possession by the husband, and if they were, they also became his. Her chattels real, i. e., leases, could be enjoyed by the husband during his life, but passed to the wife on his death.

The economic importance of land made it particularly significant that the husband was given broad powers with respect to his wife's land. He was entitled during the marriage to the rents and profits from any lands in which she held an estate of inheritance and if issue was born alive, he acquired a tenancy by the curtesy which gave him the rents and profits during his life. On his death the wife or her heirs took the land. If the land was sold by the wife and her husband, the money received as the price became his absolutely, like the rest of her personalty. The husband also became seised of any lands in which the wife held a life estate, and was entitled to the rents and profits for the duration of the life estate.

Equity was able to mitigate the harshness of the common law property rules by the use of the trust device. Thus land or personal property could be conveyed to a trustee, in trust for a married woman, and would remain free of her husband's control. It gradually came to be the law that property conveyed to the wife herself, with a clearly expressed intention that the wife should take and the husband should not, would be treated by equity as her separate property, not subjected to his common law rights. This was known as the wife's separate estate in equity. In most jurisdictions she could dispose of her separate estate. The married woman's position with respect to property was therefore not as abject as the common law by itself would have made it.

At common law, the married woman had no capacity to make contracts. She could, however, make contracts which bound her equitable separate estate though they did not bind her personally.

A parallel development occurred in the married woman's right of access to the courts. By the common law she could sue or be sued only jointly with her husband. But she could sue or be sued alone in cases relating to her equitable separate estate.

In some ways the relations between husbands and wives at common law reflected the maxim that husband and wife are one person in law. The domicile of both was the domicile of the husband. The wife could not be guilty of larceny of the husband's goods. No action between them for tort could be brought. Husband and wife could not be guilty of conspiring with one another. Yet it is clear that the maxim, originating with the Bible and repeated uncritically by legal authorities, is a fiction and does not begin to account for the common law position of women. In fact it cannot really be taken seriously other than as a rationalization of the traditional subjugation of married women in the law.

Other common law features of the relation of husband to wife have some vitality today. The husband was obliged to support his wife, and if he failed to do so, she could pledge his credit in order to buy the necessaries of life. Conversely, the husband was entitled to his wife's services, and to her earnings if she worked outside the home. He was also entitled to her society and to sexual relations with her, although for the most part these rights could only be recognized in collateral ways, as in suits for divorce or actions against strangers for making the exercise of the rights impossible.

Today all states have statutes, generally known as Married Women's Property Acts, aimed at removing the legal disabilities of married women. Comprehensive citation of such statutes may be found in H. Clark, Law of Domestic Relations, 222 (1968). In general such statutes provide that property acquired by a married woman before or after marriage is to be her sole and separate property, and may be used and disposed of by her just as if she were unmarried. They also provide that she may make contracts, sue and be sued, and that she is fully responsible for her own torts and crimes. Finally, the statutes generally provide that the wages or earnings of a married woman are her separate property, as if she were unmarried.

The statistics indicate that in 1978 53.5% of all married women were in the labor force. New York Times, December 21, 1978, page 20, col. 2. The corresponding figure for 1971 was 40.8% and for 1950 was 23.8%. Statistical Abstract of the United States, 1972, page 220. The striking increase in these figures is graphic evidence of the change in the role of women which has occurred in the last three decades.

SECRETARY OF THE COMMONWEALTH v. CITY CLERK OF LOWELL

Supreme Judicial Court of Massachusetts, 1977.
373 Mass. 178, 366 N.E.2d 717.

BRAUCHER, Justice. In 1974 the Attorney General issued three opinions with respect to the recording and use of names. Those opinions asserted and elaborated a common law principle that people may select or change their names freely if there is no fraudulent intent. The defendants, city and town clerks, refused to follow those opinions and that principle in recording births and marriages, asserting a power to determine people's surnames according to customary rules, regardless of the desires of the people concerned. The responsible State officials, particularly the Registrar of Vital Records and Statistics (Registrar), brought this action to settle the controversy. We hold that the Attorney General is right and the city and town clerks are wrong, and order that the rights of the parties be declared accordingly.

We summarize the stipulated facts, omitting statements of law. Only initials of surnames are given.

[At this point in the opinion the court stated the facts relating to children's names. These facts have been omitted, as has that section of the opinion dealing with the parents' freedom of choice respecting the names of their children.]

(5) Ms. L was divorced from Mr. L and resumed her maiden name McC. Two of the defendants refused to issue a marriage license to her in the name McC, and she received and used a marriage license in the name L, the name on her divorce decree. She and her husband both took the name McC– M, and a third defendant refused to register the legitimation of their daughter unless the child's name was changed from McC to M. City and town clerks customarily do not change a name on a birth or marriage record except by court order or pursuant to specific statutory provisions. City and town clerks are requested, on a continuing and regular basis, and are required to furnish certified copies of birth and marriage certificates to citizens so that they may use them in obtaining passports, public assistance, inheritance claims, social security, drivers' licenses, insurance and other benefits, registering a child for school and registering to vote, enforcing support obligations, establishing identification and family relationships, and for many other purposes. If a birth or marriage is not recorded, such certified copies cannot be furnished.

In marriage records, the facts to be recorded include "names and places of birth of the parties married," "the names of their parents, and the maiden names of the mothers. If the woman is a widow or divorced, her maiden name shall also be given." G.L. c. 46, § 1.

2. *Surnames at common law.* "It is well settled that at common law a person may change his name at will, without resort to legal proceedings, by merely adopting another name, provided that this is done for an honest purpose." Merolevitz, petitioner, 320 Mass. 448, 450, 70 N.E.2d 249, 250 (1946), and cases cited. This principle was recognized by this court very early: "* * * we know not why corporations may not be known by several names as well as individuals." Minot v. Curtis, 7 Mass. 441, 444 (1811). "Where a person is in fact known by two names, either one can be used. This principle has been applied in about every connection." Young v. Jewell, 201 Mass. 385, 386, 87 N.E. 604 (1909), and cases cited. Numerous authorities in other jurisdictions are in accord. See Smith v. United

States Cas. Co., 197 N.Y. 420, 423–429, 90 N.E. 947 (1910), and cases cited.

3. *Statutes affecting surnames.* Statute 1849, c. 141, empowered the judge granting a divorce decree to a married woman "to allow said woman to resume her maiden name." See G.L. c. 208, § 23, as appearing in St.1973, c. 379, which permits a woman to resume her maiden name or the name of a former husband, regardless of who obtained the divorce. "The first statute enacted in this Commonwealth allowing a change of name by judicial decree was St.1851, c. 256, § 1." Merolevitz, petitioner, 320 Mass. 448, 449, 70 N.E.2d 249, 250 (1946). Cf. G.L. c. 210, § 12. By St.1871, c. 310, § 7, a court making a decree of adoption might "also decree such change of name as the petitioner may pray for." Cf. G.L. c. 210, § 6. See Curran, petitioner, 314 Mass. 91, 95–96, 49 N.E.2d 432 (1943).

Those statutes might have been read to limit the common law principle of free choice in the matter of name. Indeed, in Bacon v. Boston Elevated Ry., 256 Mass. 30, 32, 152 N.E. 35 (1926), we relied on G.L. c. 208, § 23, for the proposition that after Alice W. Willard married Walter O. Bacon her "legal name," as matter of law, was Alice W. Bacon. The result was that her automobile was improperly registered and was a trespasser on the highway; it also appeared that she was generally known as Alice W. Bacon. Later cases made it clear that registration in the name Mrs. Walter O. Bacon or in another name by which she was generally known would have been proper. Koley v. Williams, 265 Mass. 601, 603, 164 N.E. 444 (1929) (Mrs. John P. Williams). Bridges v. Hart, 302 Mass. 239, 245, 18 N.E.2d 1020 (1939) (Theophilus Doucette, generally known as Thomas Douey). Korsun v. McManus, 318 Mass. 642, 645, 63 N.E.2d 457 (1945) (unmarried woman generally known by surname of supposed husband). In any event, the doctrine of trespass by improper registration was later abolished. G.L. c. 90, § 9. See Green v. Commissioner of Corps. & Taxation, 364 Mass. 389, 393, 305 N.E.2d 92 (1973).

In Merolevitz, petitioner, 320 Mass. 448, 450, 70 N.E.2d 249, 250 (1946), we said, "In jurisdictions where this subject has been regulated by statute, it has generally been held that such legislation is merely in aid of the common law and does not abrogate it. [Citations omitted.] We assume, in view of the wording of our statute (G.L. [Ter.Ed.] c. 210, § 12), that it provides the only method by which one can change his name with legal effect. But it does not follow that one may not assume or use another name without resort to the statute if such use is for an honest purpose." We have since adhered to this view. Buyarsky, petitioner, 322 Mass. 335, 338, 77 N.E.2d 216, 218 (1948): "The common law recognizes his freedom of choice to assume a name which he deems more appropriate and advantageous to him than his family name in his present circumstances, if the change is not motivated by fraudulent intent." Mark v. Kahn, 333 Mass. 517, 520–521, 131 N.E.2d 758 (1956). So far as our cases suggest that a person has a "legal name" or a name "with legal effect," different from the name he has lawfully chosen, those suggestions were not necessary to decision.

Under G.L. c. 46, § 1, the city or town clerk is to record in the record of births and marriages the "names" of various persons. No rule is laid down by which to determine any "name." In these circumstances we are remitted to the common law or to governing statutes to determine what is a "name." No tradition of city and town clerks can override the law or the rights of the people.

4. *Recent developments.* In applying the common law to an unprecedented situation, we may properly inquire whether the traditional rule is suited to present conditions. We therefore take note of a number of recent legal developments which, though not directly controlling, contribute to the setting in which the questions now before us arise. We have been authoritatively advised that freedom of personal choice in matters of family life is one of the liberties protected by the due process clause of the Fourteenth Amendment, and that there is a private realm of family life which the State cannot enter. Smith v. Organization of Foster Families for Equality and Reform, 431 U.S. 816, 842, 97 S.Ct. 2094, 52 L.Ed.2d 14 (1977), and cases cited. Important changes in popular and legal thinking suggest that ancient canards about the proper role of woman have no place in the law. As amended by art. 106 of the Amendments, adopted in November, 1976, art. 1 of the Massachusetts Declaration of Rights provides, "Equality under the law shall not be denied or abridged because of sex."

More directly relevant is the enactment of G.L. c. 151B, § 4, cl. 15, by St.1975, c. 84, and c. 367, § 3, under which it is "an unlawful practice: . . . 15. For any person responsible for recording the name of or establishing the personal identification of an individual for any purpose, including that of extending credit, to require such individual to use, because of such individual's sex or marital status, any surname other than the one by which such individual is generally known." We have no doubt that a city or town clerk recording a birth or marriage is a "person responsible for recording the name of * * * an individual" within the meaning of that statute. It is stipulated that one of the defendants required that Ms. G use on an affidavit of paternity, because of her sex and marital status, the name L, a name other than the one by which she was generally known. Similarly, two of the defendants required Ms. McC to use on her marriage license, because of her sex and marital status, the name L, a name other than the one by which she was generally known. But the present action has not followed the statutory procedure. G. L. c. 151B, §§ 1–9. We therefore do not decide the case under the statute. But we think we may take into account the policy embodied in the statute.

All these recent developments seem to us to indicate strongly that the common law principle of freedom of choice in the matter of names is not out of harmony with modern conditions.

5. *Names of married and divorced women.* It follows from what we have said that a woman, like a man, may change her name at will, without resorting to legal proceedings, provided that this is done for an honest purpose. We illustrate with situations presented in the present case. When Jane Doe marries Richard Roe she may, but need not, assume the name Jane Roe and at the same time the name Mrs. Richard Roe. She is also free to retain the name Jane Doe or to assume some other name chosen by her, such as Jane Roe-Doe or Jane Doe-Roe. It has been held that such freedom of choice is not compelled by the United States Constitution. Forbush v. Wallace, 341 F.Supp. 217, 222 (M.D.Ala.1971), aff'd on appeal, 405 U.S. 970, 92 S.Ct. 1197, 31 L.Ed.2d 246 (1972) (driver's license). But the results indicated accord with the overwhelming weight of recent authority in other States. Davis v. Roos, 326 So.2d 226, 229 (Fla.Dist. Ct.App.1976) (maiden name on driver's license). In re Natale, 527 S.W.2d 402, 404–405 (Mo.App.1975) (court order for change to name of choice). In re Lawrence, 133 N.J.Super. 408, 412–414, 337 A.2d 49 (App.Div.1975) (court order for change to maiden name). Dunn v. Palermo, 522 S.W.2d 679, 688 (Tenn.1975) (registration in maiden name). In re Strikwerda, 216 Va. 470, 472, 220 S.E.2d 245 (1975) (court order for change to maiden name). Doe v. Dunning, 87 Wash.2d 50, 52, 549 P.2d 1, 3 (1976) (right to use maiden name). Kruzel v. Podell, 67 Wis.2d 138, 152, 226 N.W.2d 458 (1975) (same). See Annot., 67 A.L.R.3d 1266 (1975). But cf. In re Mohlman, 26 N. C.App. 220, 228, 216 S.E.2d 147 (1975) (no sufficient reason for ordering change to maiden name). We note that the husband may retain the name Roe or may assume the name Doe or some other name, whether or not his wife assumes the same name.

Similarly, on divorce from Richard Roe, with or without a court order as to her name, Jane Roe may retain that name or resume the name Jane Doe as her maiden name or the name of a previous husband or she may assume a new name. Like G.L. c. 210, § 12, so also G.L. c. 208, § 23, does not restrict her choice but aids her to secure an official record that definitely and specifically establishes her change of name. It seems unlikely that after divorce she would desire to retain the name Mrs. Richard Roe; no such case is presented to us, and we do not pass on such a case.

When a woman's "name" is to be recorded on a birth or marriage record, the name to be recorded is the name chosen by her. See Custer v. Bonadies, 30 Conn.Supp. 385, 318 A.2d 639, 644 (Super.Ct.1974) (voting); Stuart v. Board of Supervisors, 266 Md. 440,

449, 295 A.2d 223 (1972) (same). When her "maiden name" is to be recorded, it is the name used by her before her first marriage. Inevitably the city or town clerk must rely on information supplied by her. If a certificate of divorce submitted under G.L. c. 207, § 21, shows a different name from that shown in a notice of intention of marriage, G.L. c. 207, § 35, authorizes the clerk to require a deposition under oath to prove the facts.

The defendants argue that under present practice "it is possible to trace ancestral chains because all changes in names are noted on the official record," and that the use of names of choice will make it "impossible or at best practically impossible to trace ancestral chains, even with the best of index." Similar arguments have been rejected elsewhere. In re Halligan, 46 A.D.2d 170, 172, 361 N.Y.S.2d 458 (N. Y.1974). Dunn v. Palermo, 522 S.W.2d 679, 688 (Tenn.1975). Not all changes in men's names are noted on any public record. The birth certificates in the record before us show the father's name, birthplace and age, but not the date or place of his marriage; there is no cross-reference to his birth or marriage record, and no assurance that he bore the same name at birth or on his marriage, either or both of which may have taken place outside Massachusetts. In practice the supposed ease of tracing ancestral chains is often a chimera.

We recognize that a foolish choice of name may have undesired consequences. "But freedom to choose is freedom to choose foolishly." City and town clerks are not empowered to prevent such folly. In argument the defendants disclaimed any right to review first or middle names. Neither the common law nor our statutes give them any greater right to review surnames.

* * *

9. *Disposition.* A judgment is to be entered in the county court declaring the rights of the parties in accordance with this opinion. Injunctive relief is to be denied because we assume that the declaratory judgment will be sufficient to accomplish compliance by the defendants and others similarly situated. * * *

* * *

NOTES AND QUESTIONS

1. Forbush v. Wallace, 341 F.Supp. 217 (M.D.Ala.1971), aff'd p.c. 405 U.S. 970 (1972), cited in the principal case, held that a state's requirement that for driver's license purposes a woman must take her husband's name did not violate the United States Constitution. Whitlow v. Hodges, 539 F.2d 582 (6th Cir. 1976), cert. den. 429 U.S. 1029 (1976), 38 Ohio St.L.J. 157 (1977), involving Kentucky's driver's license rule, reached a similar result, relying on Forbush. Would the constitutional issue be differently decided if the proposed Twenty-Seventh Amendment, supra, page 21, were adopted? Brown, Emerson, Falk, Freedman, The Equal Rights Amendment, 80 Yale L.J. 871, 940 (1971).

2. Several other cases recognize the married woman's right to choose her name, usually in the context of permitting her to retain her maiden name after marriage. See, e. g., Application of Halligan, 46 A.D.2d 170, 361 N.Y.S.2d 458 (4th Dep't 1974); In re Erickson, 547 S.W.2d 357 (Tex. Civ.App.1977); In re Miller, 218 Va. 939, 243 S.E.2d 464 (1978); Kruzel v. Podell, 67 Wis.2d 138, 226 N.W.2d 458 (1975), 50 Tul.L.Rev. 967 (1976), 59 Mar.L.Rev. 876 (1976). In general these cases take the position that a change of name by a married woman is to be granted upon the same basis as any other change of name, that is, to be granted unless for an illegal, fraudulent or immoral purpose.

3. For early cases on the married woman's name, see Annot., 35 A.L. R. 417 (1925). For cases on change of name, see Annot., 110 A.L.R. 219 (1937), 79 A.L.R.3d 562 (1977). Much law review commentary has been devoted to the married woman's choice of name, most of it arguing for her freedom in this respect. See, e. g., Note, Married Woman's Right to Her Maiden Name: The Possibilities for Change, 23 Buff.L.Rev. 243 (1973); Note, Pre-Marriage Name Change, Resumption and Reregistration Statutes, 74 Colum.L.Rev. 1508 (1974); Note, Married Women and the Name Game, 11 U.Rich.L.Rev. 121 (1976); Note, A Women's Right to Her Name, 21 U. C.L.A.L.Rev. 665 (1973); Note, Domestic Relations—The Right of a Married Woman to Retain Her Maiden Name, 79 W.Va.L.Rev. 108 (1976).

LADDEN v. LADDEN

Superior Court of New Jersey, Appellate Division, 1960.
59 N.J.Super. 502, 158 A.2d 189.

SULLIVAN, J. A. D. This is an appeal in a matrimonial action in which plaintiff, the wife of defendant Matthew L. Ladden, sued her husband and three business corporations which he owned. The first count of the complaint asked for separate maintenance from the husband, for the support of plaintiff and two children then living with her. The second count, against the corporate defendants, sought the recovery of salary earned by plaintiff as an employee but never paid to her. The third count charged defendant husband with taking the aforesaid salary due plaintiff and using the funds for his own purposes. In the fourth count it was alleged that defendant husband fraudulently induced plaintiff to turn over to him her twenty-five per cent stock interest in one of defendant corporations. The return of the stock was sought.

The trial was lengthy and bitterly contested. At the conclusion thereof the court awarded plaintiff separate maintenance for the support of herself and a daughter living with her, the other daughter having decided to live with her father after the commencement of the suit. On the second and third counts, involving the salary claim, the court found for plaintiff and entered a judgment of $25,000 in her favor against all defendants. *   *   *

Plaintiff has not appealed from any part of the court's ruling. All of the defendants have appealed from that part of the judgment awarding plaintiff $25,000 on the second and third counts. * * *

The parties were married in 1931. The union seems to have been happy enough in the beginning and produced three children. The oldest, a son, is married and has his own home. He works for his father. The two daughters attend school.

Plaintiff as well as her husband was employed for the first few years of the marriage. During that period of time their income was pooled to pay living expenses. She gave up her employment prior to the birth of her first child in 1935, and thereafter her husband was the sole support of the family. About 1944 Mr. Ladden decided to go in business for himself, and organized Ladden Asbestos Corporation with borrowed money. Plaintiff came to work in the corporation office in 1946 and stayed until May 1955. In the beginning it was a "one-girl office" with plaintiff attending to numerous duties. As the business expanded an office staff was added and plaintiff's work became supervisory or executive in character. Her salary reflected the situation. In the beginning it was modest but was increased from time to time until her earnings reached $200 or more weekly. It was stipulated that over the period of time involved, 1946 to May 1955, plaintiff's earnings were approximately $75,000.

Plaintiff claims that none of the salary was ever paid to her, and that her husband appropriated all of it. Mr. Ladden denies this. The trial court made no finding thereon but it is unnecessary to resolve the precise issue because, no matter how the money came to Mr. Ladden, it is obvious that it was with plaintiff's knowledge and consent. From 1946 to 1952 her salary went into a joint bank account on which she could, and did, draw checks. If she had any objection to the receipt of her salary by her husband she could have taken or used the money as she saw fit. She also could have terminated her employment if she did not approve of the situation. On the contrary she continued to work, acquiesced in Mr. Ladden's course of conduct and, together with her husband, signed yearly joint federal income tax returns acknowledging receipt of the salary.

The crux of this appeal is whether or not plaintiff can compel her husband to account to her for this money. This in turn depends on the nature of the arrangement between the parties. Was it a gift or a loan? Was her salary made available to her husband under some agreement that he was to use it for specified purposes only, or was it just turned over to him or taken by him without any agreement at all as to its use or disposition?

It is settled law in this State that when a wife turns her income over to her husband who spends it with her knowledge and without objection on her part, a gift will be presumed. * * * In Jones v.

Davenport, 44 N.J.Eq. 33, 47, 13 A. 652, 659 (Ch.1888), the court commented on this type of situation as follows:

"A wife, by permitting her husband to take her income and make such use of it as he sees fit, induces him to live in a style much more expensive than he otherwise would. He spends more for her, and gives her more to spend than he would if she required him to pay her income over to her. And she gets just as much benefit, as a general rule, from his increased expenditures as he does. It would, in many cases, not only be extremely unjust, but ruinous, if the wife could, after years of silence, call upon her husband to return to her everything he had received for [sic] her. A rule which permitted her to do so would very greatly multiply the hazards of business, and serve as a new encouragement to fraud."

In order to avoid the application of this presumptive rule, it was incumbent on plaintiff to establish that the arrangement was otherwise.

* * *

In the present case the court did not make any finding as to what agreement, if any, the parties had as to plaintiff's salary.

* * *

* * * the trial judge * * * held that Mr. Ladden did not have to account for any of the moneys spent for household expenses and maintenance of the family, but was accountable for all other money. The court then determined that plaintiff should be reimbursed in the amount of $25,000, but did not indicate how it arrived at that figure. * * *."

We do not agree with this ruling. * * * As to the husband, there is not the slightest evidence indicating that plaintiff made her salary available to him under an agreement that he would return it to plaintiff or be accountable for it, or that it was to be used for limited purposes only. Indeed, the indication is that there was no particular understanding with reference to this money other than that the husband simply combined it with his own funds and used it as he saw fit. The parties had done the same thing when they were first married and plaintiff had never claimed that her husband was accountable for her salary spent at that time.

Mr. Ladden testified that the joint moneys were used for household expenses, education of the children and similar living costs. It is unquestioned that the parties lived on a luxurious scale. At the time of the separation they occupied an 18-room home on a seven-acre estate in Morris County. This property, by the way, had been purchased in the name of one of the corporations and leased to Mr. Ladden. The furnishings of the house, which were paid for by the corporation, were selected by plaintiff at a cost of $90,000. A staff of two full-time and two part-time servants took care of the household.

The grounds required gardening and maintenance. The children attended private schools and colleges.

It appears that not all of the money was spent in living expenses. Mr. Ladden also used available funds to broaden and improve his business interests. Plaintiff stated that on two or three occasions she asked for the money "when huge expenditures were being made" by her husband for business purposes, but he said "no." This assertion is hard to reconcile with her continuing to work several years thereafter under the same arrangement.

Plaintiff also urges that the presumption of a gift does not apply to her situation because the evidence shows that certain essential elements of a gift, to wit, freedom of will, donative intent and irrevocable delivery to the donee, were not present. She claims that her husband unrelentingly and tyrannically dominated and completely controlled and influenced her. The proof, however, is otherwise. Mr. Ladden may have been the head of the household, as most husbands are. There is no indication though that he was taking and using her money without her free consent. Mrs. Ladden, by her own admission, was a "top level executive." The entire record indicates that she was anything but passively subject to her husband. As a matter of fact, when their personal differences reached the point of a separation, it was Mr. Ladden who was obliged to yield and move out of the family home. Except for her uncorroborated statement that she had asked for the money on two or three occasions, the evidence shows that she willingly went along with and enjoyed the fruits of her husband's handling of the finances. There is nothing to show that she ever had or claimed to have a separate estate of her own.

Plaintiff also sees a lack of donative intent and irrevocable delivery on her part, because up until 1952 her salary was deposited in a joint bank account on which she had the power to and did draw checks. This proves nothing. The fact is that plaintiff's husband did use the money and the joint account was closed in December 1952. Thereafter, plaintiff's salary was deposited in the husband's personal bank account.

It can be argued that while plaintiff may have had no specific arrangement with her husband over the use to which her earnings were to be put, the reason was that they were then a happily married couple and plaintiff had no reason to expect that a time would come when the legal consequences of her donation to her husband would have to be considered. There is some hardship on the wife in this type of situation, but in the nature of things, her disappointment cannot be given legal status.   *   *   *

In the present case it seems clear that, if the unfortunate matrimonial dispute had not come into being, plaintiff would never have asserted her present claim for an accounting from her husband. Her situation, moreover, is not without some advantage. While she may not have the security of a separate estate of her own, she is entitled to adequate support and maintenance from her husband and can look to his resources for satisfaction thereof. * * *

Our conclusion that over the years plaintiff made an irrevocable donation of her salary to her husband is dispositive of the entire question and makes it unnecessary to consider how the money was spent. * * * In the absence of any agreement or understanding that the money is to be used for specific purposes only, the presumption of gift applies no matter how the husband expends the money so long as he does so with his wife's knowledge and acquiescence.

* * *

The judgment for $25,000 against the defendants must be set aside and a judgment entered in their favor on the second and third counts.

* * *

NOTES AND QUESTIONS

1. The New Jersey statutes on the property and contracts of married women, which are more or less typical of the Married Women's Property Acts found in other states, read, in relevant part, as follows: N.J.Stat.Ann. (1968):

§ 37:2–12. Property owned at time of marriage and property acquired thereafter

The real and personal property of a woman which she owns at the time of her marriage, and the real and personal property, and the rents, issues and profits thereof, of a married woman, which she receives or obtains in any manner whatever after her marriage, shall be her separate property as if she were a feme sole.

§ 37:2–13. Wages and earnings

The wages and earnings of a married woman acquired or gained by her in any employment, occupation or trade since July fourth, one thousand eight hundred and fifty-two, or acquired or gained by her prior thereto in any employment, occupation or trade carried on separately from her husband, and all investments of such wages, earnings, money or property shall be her separate property as if she were a feme sole. All work and labor performed by a married woman, from and after April third, one thousand nine hundred and twenty-eight, for third persons shall, unless there is an agreement on her part to the contrary, be deemed to be performed on her separate account.

§ 37:2–16. Contracts of married woman without joinder or consent of husband

Any married woman shall have the right to bind herself by contract in the same manner and to the same extent as though she were unmarried, which contract shall be legal and obligatory, and may be enforced by and against such married woman in her own name and apart from her husband. Any contract relating to or affecting her estate, interest or right in her real property or that of her husband shall be valid without the joinder therein or consent thereto of her husband, but shall not affect any estate, interest or right of her husband in such real estate.

2. Is the outcome of the principal case consonant with the New Jersey statutes? If the salary in question had been that of the husband rather than the wife, do you think the court would have held that he had made a gift to his wife?

3. Would the teachings of Reed v. Reed, Frontiero v. Richardson, Schlesinger v. Ballard, Weinberger v. Wiesenfeld, and Califano v. Goldfarb, cited supra, page 724, which held unconstitutional various types of discrimination against women, invalidate the presumption upon which the court bases its opinion in the principal case? Would the proposed Twenty-Seventh Amendment to the United States Constitution?

4. If the presumption were eliminated from the case, how should it be decided? Should the court make some effort to determine what would be the normal expectations of husbands and wives in similar situations? If so, how would the case come out? Cf. Krasner v. Krasner, 285 N.E.2d 398 (Mass.1972).

5. Compare the following case: H and W were married in 1929. H was in the process of building up a popcorn business, which he had started some years before and W helped in this business. Shortly after the marriage the business was incorporated and H gave W all the stock as a wedding present. They went on as before, both working in the business, but with H in control and in many ways disregarding the corporate form. W received no salary, but money for the household expenses was taken from the cash receipts of the business. In 1946 marital troubles arose. W then elected herself and her son to the corporate offices, taking control of the business by virtue of her stock ownership, and excluding H from any influence in the conduct of the business. H then sued W, claiming to be the equitable owner of the stock and asking that she be required to turn it over to him and enjoined from interfering with his management of the business. The trial judge found that a completed gift had been made to W and gave judgment for her. On appeal this was affirmed, the court saying that this was merely a question of fact as to H's intent, and that there was ample evidence that he intended to make a gift of the stock to W. Franke v. Franke, 140 Conn. 133, 98 A.2d 804 (1953). See also Ross v. Ross, 2 Mass.App. 502, 314 N.E.2d 888 (1974), cert. den. 420 U.S. 947 (1975), rehearing den. 421 U.S. 1017 (1975); Leatherman v. Leatherman, 297 N.C. 618, 256 S.E.2d 793 (1979). Would the Reed, Frontiero, Schlesinger cases or the Twenty-Seventh Amendment have any bearing on the outcome of this case? Would the situation of H and W in this case be an appropriate one for an antenuptial or post-nuptial contract governing their property rights? If so, what should such a contract provide?

6. Suppose, in the *Ladden* case that the husband and wife had, at the outset of their marriage, signed a written contract by which the husband agreed to pay the wife a stated salary for her work in the family business. Is there any reason why the wife could not recover on such a contract? See, e. g., Bendler v. Bendler, 3 N.J. 161, 69 A.2d 302 (1949); "But a con-

tract of hire between spouses is utterly void and unenforceable at law. * * * It would seem that on principle a contract void at law for mutual disability is likewise without contractual force in equity, for otherwise the legislative policy could be set at naught by the exercise of the equitable function. It is not the province of equity to invade this fundamental policy of the law. * * * Contracts between husband and wife have been deemed objectionable, not only because they are inconsistent with the common-law doctrine of unity of person and interest, 'but because they introduce the disturbing influence of bargain and sale into the marriage relation, and induce a separation rather than a unity of interests.' "

Is there any substantial reason why, in the latter half of the Twentieth Century, husband and wife should not be permitted to make such a contract? What effect would a statute have when it provided that husband and wife may not alter their legal relations by contract? What is the purpose of such a statute? Ohio Rev. Code § 3013.06 (1972). See Krauskopf and Thomas, Partnership Marriage: The Solution to An Ineffective and Inequitable Law of Support, 35 Ohio St.L.J. 558 (1974).

Does the Reed, Frontiero, Schlesinger line of cases have any bearing on this question? Does Griswold v. Connecticut, supra, page 73? Does the proposed Twenty-Seventh Amendment? Weitzman, Legal Regulation of Marriage: Tradition and Change, 62 Cal.L.Rev. 1169 (1974).

7. Should the wife who works in the home as a housewife, caring for her children and doing the other household tasks, be entitled to wages for her work, either by virtue of a contract with her husband, or by operation of law? Do the authorities cited in the preceding paragraph have any bearing on this question? Could you draft a statute which would effectuate what you consider to be good policy respecting this question? What would be the federal income tax consequences of paying the wife for her work in the home? I.R.C. §§ 61 (a), 212, 44A.

8. Should the wife who works for her husband, or the husband who works for his wife, receive workmen's compensation when injured in the course of such work, whether in the home or in an outside business? Cf. 1A A. Larson, The Law of Workmen's Compensation, § 47.20 (1967).

9. H and W both work, earning roughly the same amounts per year. The earnings of both go into their joint checking account. In order to have a systematic way of saving, however, they agree that the wife's earnings will be used to pay for the support of the family while the husband's will be invested in various kinds of income-producing assets, such as corporate securities and income real estate. Title to this property was taken in H's name for convenience in buying, selling, and managing it and in reinvesting income from the property. Under *Ladden* and the Married Women's Property Acts, who owns the investment property? Fischer v. Wirth, 38 A.D. 2d 611, 326 N.Y.S.2d 308 (3d Dep't 1971). Should spouses wishing to do this have a written contract dealing with ownership and management of the property? If so, what should it provide?

SANDITEN v. SANDITEN

Supreme Court of Oklahoma, 1972.
496 P.2d 365.

HODGES, Justice.   This appeal was filed following issuance of an order of the district court sustaining a demurrer to plaintiff's first amended petition and an order dismissing non-resident defendants for reason of no in personam jurisdiction.

Plaintiff filed a verified petition in which she alleges her husband, who is not a party to this suit, made gratuitous transfers to the defendants over a period of time of property acquired by joint efforts of plaintiff and her husband during coverture; that she had no knowledge of the transfers made by her husband, that her husband made the transfers with the intent to defraud her of her marital and vested rights; and that she is entitled to judgment against the beneficiaries for one half of the gifts together with accretions and earnings from the property.

While we do not agree with plaintiff's argument that a wife has a vested interest in jointly acquired property, we do find, by this opinion, that a married man cannot make gifts of jointly acquired property during his lifetime without the consent or knowledge of his wife where the transfer is in fraud of the wife's marital rights.

In Oklahoma the property of married persons generally falls into two classes: the separate property of each of the parties; and jointly acquired property which has been accumulated by the business side of the marriage. * * *

In regard to the separate property of a married man, it appears to be well settled in this jurisdiction that a husband may give his separate property away, during his lifetime, if the gift is bona fide and complete and neither the wife nor children have any claim to the property of the husband or father, except so far as he is liable for their support. * * * The property in this case though involves property acquired during coverture and our attention will be directed to this issue.

Plaintiff argues she has a vested interest in property acquired during coverture and for that reason the gratuitous gifts were in and of itself a fraud on her marital rights. In support of her conclusion she cites two cases. Collins v. Oklahoma Tax Commission, Okl., 446 P.2d 290; Thompson v. Thompson, 70 Okl. 207, 173 P. 1037 (1918). We disagree. Both of these cases involve an interpretation of jointly acquired property under our divorce statutes. They do not purport to construe the vested interest of a wife in jointly acquired property beyond the statutory disposition of property in a divorce action. When a divorce action is pending her right to the jointly acquired property is vested. But the vesting takes place by reason of the divorce pendency under our statute and not by the marriage relationship which existed between the parties.

A wife does not have joint ownership in jointly acquired property as we held in Catron v. Catron, Okl., 434 P.2d 263 (1967), for if she did that would return this jurisdiction to a community property state which was repealed by the legislature in 1949.

The interest of a wife in property acquired during coverture depends upon the occurrence of a statutorily enacted contingency such as divorce, separation, inability to support, homestead and death, all of which emanate from the marriage relationship. A wife then has no vested interest in property acquired during coverture, but a contingent interest which the law protects. For instance, it is well established a husband cannot make a gift which is incomplete in that he retains some interest in the gift during his lifetime thereby depriving his wife of her rights in the property at his death, as provided in 84 O.S.1961, Section 213; nor can he make a disposition of the property anticipatory to a divorce proceeding to defeat a division of jointly acquired property under 12 O.S.1961, Section 1278; * * * nor can he transfer funds or property where his estate is so depleted that he cannot afford to support his wife as he is required by 32 O.S. § 3; nor can he dispose of their homestead which is restrictive under 16 O.S. § 4. When a husband has violated these rights his actions constitute a fraud upon the marital rights of the wife. We see no difference in this case. If plaintiff's husband gave away their jointly acquired property with an intent to defraud her of her marital rights to this property upon his death then the law should be just as responsive in protecting her interest as in instances above stated where the gift is made anticipatory to a divorce, or where it is given incomplete [sic] with an attempt to defeat her interest upon his death. In all of these instances the principle criteria is the fraudulent intent of the husband to deprive the wife of her marital rights as provided by statute.

Of course, we do not intend to diminish the authority of a husband as head of the family or interfere with his duty to support himself and his wife. By statute he has the right to use his separate property and property acquired during coverture to fulfil his marital obligations and to conduct the affairs of his business in a manner which he deems proper and necessary. Title 32 O.S.1961, Section 3. Nor do we intend to prohibit either spouse from making gifts of their jointly acquired property. A wife cannot complain of reasonable gifts by a husband to his children by a former marriage. In York v. Trigg, 87 Okl. 214, 209 P. 417 (1922), we held specifically that a husband may give away property acquired during coverture unless it is shown the gift was made in fraud of the marital rights and that Title 84 O.S.1961, Section 44, which prohibits a married man from bequeathing more than two thirds of his property away from his wife, does not in any way limit or restrict him in making such gifts. It is only when the gift has sinister elements of fraud of the marital rights that the law protects the wife. The burden of proof though rests strongly upon the wife. In determining the good faith of the charitable transfers the court must look to the condition and relationship of the parties, the amount of the gifts in relation to the husband's estate and income and all other attending circumstances.

* * *

Plaintiff's petition alleges the gifts of jointly acquired property were made without consideration with intent to defraud plaintiff of her marital rights. She alleges the gifts were in excess of $8,000,000.00 and that she had no knowledge of the gratuitous transfers and their magnitude with relation to the total amount of their jointly acquired property. She does not allege in particular which marital right has been violated, but the only meaning that can be attributed to her allegation is that her husband fraudulently gave the property away so she would not inherit it at his death as provided in 84 O.S.1961, § 213. The petition is not as precise and definitive as it should be, but perhaps it is excusable in view of the unexplored area of law that is involved. In any event, we can determine from it that if the facts alleged are true then she is entitled to relief in a court of law.

* * *

Judgment reversed and remanded.

NOTES AND QUESTIONS

1. What do you suppose is meant by "jointly acquired property" in the *Sanditen* case? The answer to this question is revealed in a series of income tax cases which arose in Oklahoma. Collins v. Commissioner, 388 F.2d 353 (10th Cir. 1968) held that for tax purposes the division of jointly held property on divorce did not constitute a division of property between co-owners but rather was a taxable transfer made in satisfaction of a marital obligation. The Supreme Court granted certiorari and vacated this judgment, remanding the case for further consideration in the light of the opinion in Collins v. Oklahoma Tax Commission, cited in the *Sanditen* case. Collins v. Commissioner, 393 U.S. 215 (1968). On the remand the Tenth Circuit held that such a division under Oklahoma law was a division of property between co-owners and therefore non-taxable.

Collins v. Oklahoma Tax Commission, 446 P.2d 290, 295 (Okl.1968), contains this language describing the wife's interest in jointly acquired property: "Property acquired during married life as the result of industry, economy and business ability is the jointly acquired property subject to the equitable division required under the statute. * * * If property has been acquired by joint effort during marriage the wife has a vested interest therein which is not forfeited even though she may be at fault. * * * The nature of the wife's interest is similar in conception to community property of community property states, and is regarded as held by a species of common ownership." The Oklahoma Supreme Court then held that the division of this property on divorce was not subject to the state income tax on the ground that the wife has a vested interest in jointly acquired property.

2. Is the *Sanditen* case inconsistent with the *Collins* case? When a court says that a person has a vested interest in property, does that ordinarily imply that he can prevent someone else from conveying that property? And of what value to the wife is the statute giving her a "just and reasonable" division of jointly held property on divorce if the husband is permitted to do as he likes with the property before the "divorce pendency"?

3. This raises another question. Just what does *Sanditen* hold concerning the limitations on the husband's right to give away jointly acquired property? The majority opinion merely tells us that the plaintiff's petition alleged that the husband "fraudulently" gave the jointly acquired property away so that the wife could not inherit it. What conceivable meaning would "fraudulent" have in this context? Does it refer to the husband's subjective intent? Or does it refer to the usual meaning of fraudulent conveyance, i. e., a transfer for less than fair consideration made when a person believes he will incur debts beyond his ability to pay as they mature? See, e. g., Uniform Fraudulent Conveyance Act § 6, 9B Uniform Laws Ann. 137 (1966). Or does it refer to a sham transfer, one after which the husband remains in substantial control of the property? See Newman v. Dore, 275 N.Y. 371, 9 N.E.2d 966 (1937).

4. Most states today have abolished dower and substituted for it a statutory right by the surviving spouse to take a stated proportion of the deceased spouse's estate, usually one-half, in disregard of the deceased's will, if he or she so desires. These statutes raise essentially the question raised in *Sanditen*, that is, what if any inter vivos transfers by a deceased will be effective to reduce his estate and correspondingly reduce the share to which the surviving spouse is entitled under the statute? The case law is confused and uncertain on the point. The *Newman* case cited in the preceding paragraph held that "illusory" transfers would not be effective to bar the statutory forced share, but "illusory" was not defined. The most extensive discussion of this problem is in W. MacDonald, Fraud on the Widow's Share (1960).

Modern intestacy statutes now attempt to define some kinds of inter vivos transfers which will be ineffective against the surviving spouse's statutory forced share. See, e. g., N.Y.Est., Powers & Trusts L. § 5–1.1(b) (1967 and Supp.1979–1980). The Uniform Probate Code has a long and complex section on this. Section 2–201 of the Code, 8 Unif.L.Ann. 332 (1972), gives the surviving spouse the right to elect one-third of the deceased's "augmented estate". Section 2–202, 8 Unif.L.Ann. 92 (Supp. 1979), defines the "augmented estate" to include inter vivos transfers by the deceased as to which he retained the right of possession or enjoyment, or the right to revoke or to invade the principal, or any transfer after which property is held by the decedent and another with right of survivorship, and any transfer at all made within two years of death in excess of $3,000 to any single donee. In addition section 2–202 includes in the "augmented estate" certain inter vivos gifts, insurance proceeds and other provisions made by the deceased to or for the surviving spouse. The comment on these sections states their purpose to be, on the one hand to prevent the deceased from making transfers deliberately to defeat the prospects of the surviving spouse, and on the other hand to prevent the surviving spouse from electing a share of the estate when he or she has already received a fair share of the deceased's estate either during his life or at death by life insurance or other non-probate arrangements.

5.   When the marriage ends in divorce rather than death, many contemporary statutes authorize the divorce court to make a fair and equitable division of the property of the spouses, as in Oklahoma.   The Uniform Marriage and Divorce Act § 307 (Alternative A), 9A Unif.L.Ann. 142 (1979), in its current version, authorizes the court to "equitably apportion between the parties the property and assets belonging to either or both however and whenever acquired, and whether the title thereto is in the name of the husband or wife or both."   Some states have enacted statutes which create two classes of property for divorce purposes.   "Marital property" is that property acquired during the marriage by either spouse, other than through gift or devise.   "Separate property" is property acquired before marriage or through gift or devise after marriage.   The effect of such statutes is to give each spouse his separate property on divorce, and to divide the marital property between them on some equitable basis.   See, e. g., Colo.Rev.Stat. Ann. § 14–10–113 (1973), which includes in the definition of "marital property" any appreciation which occurs in separate property after the marriage or after its acquisition.

6.   The effect of these rules concerning the property of spouses, and of the Married Women's Property Acts, has been that before death or divorce the property of each spouse has been subject to the control and disposition of the spouse having title to the property.   There are some qualifications to be made to this generalization.   The *Sanditen* case represents one such qualification limiting the owner's right of conveyance.   Another such qualification is imposed by those cases which hold that although where one spouse acquires property, but takes title in the name of the other spouse a gift is presumed, the presumption is rebuttable and the acquiring spouse may assert his own title.   See, e. g., Blanchette v. Blanchette, 362 Mass. 518, 287 N.E.2d 459 (1972).   In other words, aside from these limitations, the statutes and decisions have aimed at achieving equality between husband and wife in their property relations, each being considered the owner of that property which he or she has acquired, until the marriage ends in death or divorce.   When the marriage does end, the property of the spouses is shared between them in some fashion, equality as the guiding principle being abandoned at that point.   Equality seems to work reasonably well for those marriages in which both spouses work outside the home and receive roughly comparable wages or salaries.   It does not work very well for those marriages of the traditional kind in which the husband alone earns the money which supports the family while the wife keeps house, raises the children and performs all the other tasks involved in being a housewife, but receives no compensation.   In those cases the principle of equality leaves control over the family property during the marriage to the husband if he takes title in his own name.

The hardships of the housewife may be mitigated to some extent by the practice in many families of taking title to the family home, the family automobile and the family bank accounts in joint tenancy.   Where this is done, the housewife does have some control over the real property and the tangible personalty, and either party may draw on the bank account under the usual bank rules. But where joint tenancy is not used, for example in order to avoid the adverse impact of gift or estate taxes on affluent spouses, the housewife has no effective control over the family property during the existence of the marriage. For an illuminating discussion of these matters, see M. Glendon, State, Law and Family ch. 4, especially pages 148–149, 154–158 (1977). See also Prager, Sharing Principles and the Future of Marital Property Law, 25 U.C.L.A.L.Rev. 1 (1977), and Kulzer, Law and the Housewife: Property, Divorce and Death, 28 U.Fla.L.Rev. 1 (1975).

Another partial protection for the housewife is provided by the homestead laws which are in force in most states. These provide that the family home, with some limitations on amount, may not be sold without the concurrence of husband and wife, and may not be subject to creditors' claims. See 1 R. Powell, Real Property § 117; 2A Id. § 263 (Rev. ed. 1977).

Of course the spouses themselves may create difficulties over the ownership or control of property during marriage by taking title in joint tenancy or in other ways which make it difficult to trace the actual beneficial ownership. One solution to these difficulties is the antenuptial agreement discussed in chapter 1 of this work.

7. In eight states the description of the property rights of spouses outlined in the preceding paragraph is not applicable. These states, Arizona, California, Idaho, Louisiana, Nevada, New Mexico, Texas and Washington, are the community property states. Although all eight states have statutes providing for the division of community property on divorce, in that respect resembling the Oklahoma statute cited in *Sanditen,* these statutes differ as to the relative proportions in which the division must be made. In California the division must be equal, indicating that the wife actually does have a vested interest in the community property. Cal.Civ.Code § 4800 (Supp.1979). In Texas the division must be made in such proportions as may be "just and right". Tex.Fam.Code § 3.63 (1975).

The community property states also regulate by statute the manner in which the community property is to be managed, controlled and transferred. In California either spouse has the authority to manage and control community personal property, with power of disposition, but neither may give such property away without the written consent of the other. The spouse who is operating a business which is community property has the sole management and control of the business. Each is required to act in good faith with respect to the other in the management or control of the community property. Cal.Civ.Code § 5125 (Supp.1979). With respect to community real estate, either spouse may exercise management and control, but both must join in conveyances. Cal.Civ.Code § 5127 (Supp.1979). In Texas each spouse has the sole right to manage, control and dispose of the community property he would have owned if single. Tex.Fam.Code § 5.22 (1975). The same statute provides for joint management of community property other than that which each would have owned if single, and of community property subject to the control of one spouse if mixed with community property subject to the control of the other. New Mexico has an elaborate system for allocating the control and management and disposition of community property, the rights depending upon the type of property and the manner in which it was conveyed to the spouses. N.M.Stat.Ann. §§ 40–3–13, 40–3–14, 40–3–16 (1978). For discussion of these matters see Rappeport, The Husband's

Management of Community Real Property, 1 Ariz.L.Rev. 13 (1959); M. Glendon, State Law and Family 143–148 (1977). See also Bodenheimer, The Community Without Community Property: The Need for Legislative Attention to Separate-Property Marriages Under Community Property Laws, 8 Cal.Western L.Rev. 381 (1972); Kirchberg v. Feenstra, 609 F.2d 727 (5th Cir. 1979).

8.   (a) The broad question suggested by the *Sanditen* case, the cases and statutes ensuring the surviving spouse an effective forced share, and the cases and statutes authorizing division of property on divorce is this: Do all these doctrines, when looked at as a whole, create interests in each spouse in the property of the other which ought to be recognized fully before, as well as after, death or divorce ends the marriage? Have the common law property states gone so far toward establishing the rights and obligations of community property that in fairness to both spouses they should go the rest of the way?

(b) To be more specific, could the court in *Sanditen* have held, on the basis of its statute and the *Collins* case, that the wife had a present interest in jointly acquired property which could not be defeated by the husband's conveyance made without her concurrence? Should it have so held? Or is that a matter on which the legislature must act? If so, should the legislature act?

(c) If you think that a satisfactory result in cases like *Sanditen*, or in cases involving the control or management of property belonging to married persons cannot be reached by judicial decision in common law states, what form should a statute take which would produce a satisfactory result? Would you favor a community property type of statute like that in California or Texas?

(d) What effect would the Equal Protection Clause and the *Reed, Frontiero, Schlesinger* line of cases have upon your statute?

(e) What effect would the proposed Twenty-Seventh Amendment have upon your statute? See Ryman, A Comment on Family Property Rights and the Proposed Twenty-Seventh Amendment, 22 Drake L.Rev. 505 (1973); Annot., Construction and Application of State Equal Rights Amendments Forbidding Determination of Rights Based on Sex, 90 A.L.R. 3d 158, 196 (1979).

9.   One obvious corollary of the married woman's right to own and control her property is that the husband can be guilty of larceny when he steals his wife's property. Stewart v. Commonwealth, 219 Va. 887, 252 S. E.2d 329 (1979).

NOTE ON INTERSPOUSAL VIOLENCE

Public attention has recently been drawn to the widespread occurrence of violence between husbands and wives. The term "battered wife" has been coined, from analogy to the battered child, to refer to women who have been subjected to physical violence by their husbands. Separate statistics on these crimes are not available, partly because the violence often is not reported, but there are indications that incidents of assault, battery and even homicide between husband and wife have become disturbingly numerous in our society. Buzawa & Buzawa, Legislative Responses to the Problem of Domestic Violence in Michigan, 25 Wayne L.Rev. 859 (1979).

Although violence between spouses is obviously criminal, the law's treatment of it has not been satisfactory for several reasons. The police have often been slow to respond to calls involving domestic violence, they have often been reluctant to make arrests, and when arrests are made, prosecutors have often failed to prosecute the defendants very vigorously. Legal authorities, both police and prosecutors, understandably have not had very well defined ideas about what remedies would be most effective in preventing repetitions of family violence. Parnas, Prosecutorial and Judicial Handling of Family Violence, 9 Crim.L.Bull. 733 (1973). And much family violence remains unreported since many wives who are subjected to such violence are wholly dependent on their husbands and fear to take legal action which would break up the family. If the incident is reported to the police, the wife often changes her mind later and asks that the proceeding be dismissed.

One particular kind of violence, rape of wives by their husbands, has been entirely immune from prosecution because of the common law rule that a husband cannot be guilty of raping his wife. The basis for this rule is the historical notion that when she marries the wife consents to sexual relations with her husband. A majority of American states still retain this rule notwithstanding its outdated basis and vigorous criticism from most commentators. State v. Smith, 148 N.J.Super. 219, 372 A.2d 386 (1977), 82 Dick.L.Rev. 608 (1978); Note, The Marital Rape Exemption, 52 N.Y.U.L. Rev. 306 (1977). Some states have eliminated this immunity by statute, however. See, e. g., Del.Code Ann. tit. 11, § 763 (Supp.1978).

Many states have begun to take action designed to reduce or mitigate the effects of interspousal violence. In some localities shelters have been set up in which battered wives may take refuge and be housed pending some final disposition of their relationships with their husbands. Police training programs are attempting to instruct officers in the handling of domestic disputes. Statutes have created new civil remedies for spouses who have been subjected to abuse, providing for temporary and permanent protective orders, as in Penn.Stat.Ann. tit. 35 §§ 10181–10190 (1977) and N. Y.Fam.Ct. Act §§ 811, 812, 821, 828, 838, 841. The various remedies being proposed or tried are described in Note, The Battered Wife—The Legal System Attempts to Help, 48 U.Cin.L.Rev. 419 (1979); Buzawa & Buzawa, Legislative Responses to the Problem of Domestic Violence in Michigan, 25 Wayne L.Rev. 859 (1979); Note, Relief for Victims of Intra-Family Assault—The Pennsylvania Protection From Abuse Act, 81 Dick.L.Rev. 815 (1977); Progress of State Domestic Violence Legislation, 5 Fam.L.Reporter 4043 (1979).

SECTION 8.   INTENTIONAL AND NEGLIGENT INTERFERENCE WITH FAMILY RELATIONSHIPS

NOTE ON ALIENATION OF AFFECTIONS AND CRIMINAL CONVERSATION

Lawyers used to sum up the intangible aspects of the relationship between husband and wife in the word consortium, and in many cases even today the word is still used. A hundred years ago it denoted some definite marital duties and rights, such as the husband's right to his wife's services, society, companionship and sexual relations, and the wife's right to her husband's society, companionship, affection, sexual relations, and perhaps financial support, although the latter right was often considered separately from consortium. Under the influence of the women's rights movement the rights and duties which the law used to attribute to marriage have fallen into disrepute and are mentioned today only with disdain or embarrassment. But the term consortium perhaps still has some utility as a label for whatever relationships may exist between husband and wife. It is also used, though less commonly, to refer to the relationships between parents and child.

The actions for alienation of affections and criminal conversation are the remedies provided by the law for intentional invasion of the marital relationship and interference with consortium. They are available to both husbands and wives. The elements of the action for alienation are generally said to be a) some wrongful conduct by the defendant with the plaintiff's spouse; b) the loss of affection or consortium; and c) a causal relation between the defendant's conduct and the loss of consortium. Alaimo v. Schwanz, 56 Wis.2d 198, 201 N.W.2d 604 (1972). The real basis for the suit is not merely the plaintiff's loss of the affections of his spouse, but the loss of consortium. Fischer v. Mahlke, 18 Wis.2d 429, 118 N.W.2d 935 (1963). An action for alienation will lie even though the alienation occurred after the spouses had separated, the reasoning being that there is always some chance of reconciliation which the defendant may have frustrated. McNelis v. Bruce, 90 Ariz. 261, 367 P.2d 625 (1961). It is generally held that some active conduct by the defendant calculated to alienate the spouse's affections must be proved before the plaintiff may recover. Dube v. Rochette, 110 N.H. 129, 262 A.2d 288 (1970). The elements of damage in such a case include mental distress, humiliation, loss of affection and society. If the wife is plaintiff, she may also recover for the loss of financial support caused by the alienation, unless of course either the Equal Protection Clause or the Twenty-Seventh Amendment are construed to alter support obligations.

One of the common types of alienation of affections occurs when a relative of one of the spouses breaks up the marriage by giving advice. The cases hold that if the advice is given honestly, reasonably and in good faith, the defendant is not liable. On the other hand if the relative acts maliciously, out of ill will, or fraudulently, or if his activity amounts to officious meddling in the marriage, then he will be liable for alienation. A curious Ohio case has held that a man who had been divorced and married again could not recover from a church and a minister who had advised his second wife that her relation to her husband was adulterous, thereby causing her to leave him. Bradesku v. Antion, 21 Ohio App.2d 67, 255 N.E.2d 265 (1969).

For general discussions of alienation of affections, see Payne, Tortious Invasion of the Right of Marital Consortium, 8 J.Fam.L. 41 (1968); Note, Piracy on the Matrimonial Seas—The Law and the Marital Interloper, 25 S.W.L.J. 594 (1971); Note, Alienation of Affections: Flourishing Anachronism, 13 Wake Forest L.Rev. 585 (1977); H. Clark, Law of Domestic Relations § 10.2 (1968). For a review of the justification for the action for alienation, see Bearbower v. Merry, 266 N.W.2d 128 (Iowa 1978), which refused to abolish the proceeding, but did abolish the suit for criminal conversation.

The action for criminal conversation requires only proof that the defendant had intercourse with the plaintiff's spouse. It is thus a recovery for adultery. The elements of damage are the same as for alienation of affections. Impotency on the plaintiff's part, if caused by the tort, may be an element of damage in either action. Keye v. Newhall, 277 N.E.2d 697 (Mass.1972). The two actions are closely related, but not identical, so that a judgment of no alienation would not bar a suit for criminal conversation. Schneider v. Mistele, 39 Wis.2d 137, 158 N.W.2d 383 (1968). For additional authorities on criminal conversation, see H. Clark, Law of Domestic Relations, § 10.3 (1968).

"Heart Balm" legislation in sixteen states has abolished suits for alienation of affections and criminal conversation. Legislation in about seven other states has abolished suits for alienation of affections but not for criminal conversation. See Doe v. Doe, —— Mass. ——, 390 N.E.2d 730 (1979). The statutes generally have been held constitutional. Wallace v. Wallace, 155 W.Va. 569, 184 S.E.2d 327 (1971); Goldberg v. Musim, 162 Colo. 461, 427 P.2d 698 (1967). Arguments against the passage of such statutes are made in Note, The Case for Retention of Causes of Action for Intentional Interference With the Marital Relationship, 48 Notre Dame Law. 426 (1972). On the conflicts issues created by such statutes, see Albert v. McGrath, 107 U.S.App.D.C. 336, 278 F.2d 16 (1960). In addition to the Bearbower case cited supra, Fadgen v. Lenkner, 469 Pa. 272, 365 A.2d 147 (1976) abolished criminal conversation by judicial decision. But Kremer v. Black, 201 Neb. 467, 268 N.W.2d 582 (1978) refused to abolish the action.

NOTE ON INTENTIONAL INTERFERENCE WITH THE PARENT-CHILD RELATIONSHIP

The parent is given two remedies against strangers who invade his interest in the custody, society and services of his child, one for abduction or enticement and the other for seduction. A person who forcibly abducts a child, or who entices the child away from the parent, is liable in damages to the parent. Today this tort may sometimes be characterized as alienation of the child's affections. See, e. g., Hinton v. Hinton, 141 U.S.App.D.C. 57, 436 F.2d 211 (1970). The parent's claim was held to have been abolished by the enactment of "heart balm" legislation in Bock v. Lindquist, 278 N.W.2d 326 (Minn. 1979). The basis for the suit and the damages are the same in any event. But the action does not lie against a parent who removes the child from the custody of the other parent. McGrady v. Rosenbaum, 62 Misc.2d 182, 308 N.Y.S.2d 181 (Sup.Ct.1970), aff'd 37 A.D.2d 917, 324 N.Y.S.2d 876 (1st Dep't.1971). On the parent's claim generally, see W. Prosser, Torts, 882–884 (4th ed. 1971).

The parent also has a cause of action for the seduction of a daughter. At common law the father alone could sue, and the tort was viewed as an interference with his right to his daughter's services. Presumably the Equal Protection Clause or the proposed Twenty-Seventh Amendment will be held to entitle the mother to sue also. And the courts have already recognized that the interference with the right to services is essentially fictional, the damages being awarded to compensate for the parent's distress and loss of the daughter's society. For a more complete discussion of this tort, see W. Prosser, Torts, 884–886 (4th ed. 1971), and H. Clark, Law of Domestic Relations, 270–271 (1968). See also Annot., 20 A.L.R.3d 1441 (1968).

It is generally held that the child has no remedy for the alienation of the affections of his parent, although four courts have recognized such claims. There seems to be no good reason for denial of the right, the courts seeming to rely on the fictional argument that the child has no right to the services of his parent. See Kane v. Quigley, 1 Ohio St.2d 1, 203 N.E.2d 338 (1964), 45 B.U.L.Rev. 416 (1965); W. Prosser, Torts, 886 (4th ed. 1971).

DIAZ v. ELI LILLY & CO.

Supreme Judicial Court of Massachusetts, 1973.

364 Mass. 153, 302 N.E.2d 555.

KAPLAN, Justice.   A spouse suffers bodily injuries through the negligence of a third party. Does the other spouse have a claim against the tortfeasor for a loss of consortium that results from the injuries? The present appeal provides us with an opportunity to reconsider this question upon which the common law has spoken in recent years with exceptional vigor.

The case arises on the pleadings. Milagros Diaz alleges in her declaration in one count that she is the wife of Jose Santos Diaz; that the defendant Eli Lilly and Company is the manufacturer and merchant of a fungicide called "Parnon"; that Jose made use of "Parnon" in the course of his work on various dates from August, 1968, to September, 1970; that as a result of his exposure to "Parnon," Jose sustained severe bodily injuries; that in consequence of these injuries to Jose, the plaintiff Milagros has suffered a loss of the consortium of Jose, including his "services, society, affection, companionship, [and] relations," all to her damage; that the defendant is responsible therefor because it manufactured the product negligently in that it failed to give adequate warning of the dangers involved to the user. To this declaration the defendant demurred on the ground that it stated no cause of action. A judge of the Superior Court sustained the demurrer, refusing leave to amend. From this ruling the plaintiff takes her appeal.   *   *   *

Some perspective is needed. In olden days, when married women were under legal disabilities corresponding to their inferior social status, any action for personal or other injuries to the wife was brought in the names of the husband and wife, and the husband was ordinarily entitled to the avails of the action as of his own property. The husband had, in addition, his own recourse by action without even nominal joinder of the wife against those who invaded the conjugal relationship, for example, by criminal conversation with or abduction of his wife. At one time the gravamen of the latter claims for loss of consortium was the deprivation of the wife's services conceived to be owing by the wife to the husband; the action was similar to that of a master for enticement of his servant. Later the grounds of the consortium action included loss of the society of the wife and impairment of relations with her as a sexual partner, and emphasis shifted away from loss of her services or earning capacity. The defendant, moreover, need not have infringed upon the marital relation by an act of adultery or the like, for he could inflict similar injuries upon the husband in the way of loss of consortium by an assault upon the wife or even a negligent injury. Meanwhile, what of the wife's rights? She had none analogous to the husband's. The husband was of course perfectly competent to sue without joinder of the wife for injuries to himself, and there was no thought that the wife had any legal claim to the husband's services or his sexual or other companionship—any claim, at any rate, in the form of a cause of action for third-party damage to the relationship.

With the coming in of the married women's acts in the mid-nineteenth century, the wife became competent to sue in her own name for injuries to herself and could retain the proceeds of those actions. Her injuries for which she could recover judgment included loss of her capacity to render services in the home as well as to earn money on the outside; the husband, in Massachusetts at least, no longer had a claim even for household help required because of his wife's disablement. The question naturally arose whether after the married women's acts the husband's actions above described for loss of consortium should be ruled obsolete or whether, on the contrary, they should be held to survive in substantial dimension and be complemented by analogous remedies extended to the wife. To be sure, loss of the wife's services or earnings could no longer figure in a right of consortium on the part of the husband, but the other components of the right—the wife's society or companionship or assistance and her sexual availability—could remain. It was held very widely that husbands still retained their consortium rights, the element of loss of wives' services and earnings, however, being excluded from the husbands' recoveries as belonging to the wives themselves. And it was generally held that the new status of married women implied at least some rights of consortium on their part. If adultery with or alienation of the affections of a wife was a wrong to the husband, similar traffic of another woman with the husband should be actionable by the wife. Wives were readily accorded these rights of action.

However, there was difficulty about wives' recovery for acts of third parties not so plainly attacking the marriage relation, say acts of negligence toward the husband injuring him in such a way as to deprive the wife of his society and sexual comfort. The difficulty was perhaps traceable in the end to the reluctance of judges to accept the women's emancipation acts as introducing a broad general premise for fresh decision. This court had peculiar trouble with the problem and was finally led to deny the cause of action to the wife—and then to go on to reverse previous decisions and withdraw the parallel cause of action from the husband.

* * * Feneff v. New York Cent. & Hudson River R.R., 203 Mass. 278, 89 N.E. 436 (1909), changed the direction of the law. That was an action by the wife for loss of consortium of her husband who had been injured by negligence of the defendant railroad. The husband had sued the railroad previously and had had judgment. The court now held that the wife could not maintain her action, and the reasons assigned were such as to call logically for abrogation of the husband's right as well * * * saving only the husband's right to reimbursement for expenditures for care and cure. * * * In Lombardo v. D. F. Frangioso & Co. Inc., Mass., 269 N.E.2d 641, the majority of the court considered it to be the law of the Commonwealth that a spouse had no enforceable right for loss of consortium resulting from personal injury negligently inflicted on the other spouse. * * *

To revert to the lines of reasoning used or intimated in the *Feneff* opinion. The opinion conceded that for "intentional" invasions of the wife's right of consortium—as by adultery with or alienation of affections of the husband—the wife could now recover. This was explained on a technical ground as following from the fact that by statute the wife had become entitled to sue in her own name; formerly the husband would have had to institute such an action joining his wife, but his own misconduct would be taken to bar him. In fact the wife's right for the "intentional" invasions had been earlier established in Massachusetts on broader grounds of policy.

There is an incongruity in allowing either spouse a consortium right for an "intentional" invasion but denying the right when the conjugal relationship suffers as much or more disturbance and injury through third-party negligence. It is true that in the "intentional" cases of criminal conversation or alienation of affections the third person would often escape all civil liability if a consortium right was not recognized, while in the negligence cases that person remains in all events subject to a conventional action by the spouse physically injured. But to make a consortium claim hang on this difference seems to overplay the motive of punishment and hardly explains why actual injury to the other spouse should go uncompensated. In fact, the "intentional" characterization is not always quite deserved, for a defendant charged with criminal conversation or alienation of affections can be liable although harboring no malicious design, being in truth the seduced rather than the seducer, and at least in the case of criminal conversation, unaware even that a marital relation existed.[18] The institution of marriage may be thought to suffer more shock from "intentional" than from negligent acts. But with respect to the reality of the injuries to the persons involved, we have to compare the hurt feelings, which may be temporary, of the wife whose husband's affections have been diverted, with the wife's loss of companionship and affection, of sexual enjoyment, and of prospects of motherhood, when her husband has been reduced to a husk of manhood by physical and psychological injury caused by negligent fault of the defendant, when she has been changed "from a loving wife into a lonely nurse."[19] It was merely obfuscating for the *Feneff* court to call the "intentional" type of injury "direct" and the negligent "indirect" or "remote" (203 Mass. at 280, 281, 89 N.E. 436), and erroneous to suppose that the damages are more speculative in the latter case than in the former. A consortium action resulting from physical injury of the spouse through negligence, moreover, carries no potentiality for blackmail such as notoriously attaches to the "heart balm" actions of criminal conversation and alienation of affections; the danger of ex-

18. See McGrath v. Sullivan, 303 Mass. 327, 331, 21 N.E.2d 53 (1939); Prosser, supra, § 124, at pp. 877–878.

19. Ekalo v. Constructive Serv. Corp. of America, 46 N.J. 82, 84, 215 A.2d 1, 2 (1965). See Montgomery v. Stephan, 359 Mich. 33, 35, 101 N.W.2d 227 (1960).

It has been noted that for adultery or desertion the wife can seek a divorce and with it a chance to remarry, whereas in case of serious disability of the husband due to negligent injury she may be left with a permanent burden and lose all possibility of rearing children. See Igneri v. Cie. de Transports Oceaniques, 323 F.2d 257, 262, n. 13 (2d Cir. 1963).

tortion has indeed led to the abolition of those actions by statute in a number of States.   It is noteworthy that the consortium action by either spouse for negligence of a third party has been affirmed by courts despite the legislative abolition in those States of the "intentional," "heart balm" actions.[22]

A spouse physically injured through the negligence of a stranger has an action against him, and the *Feneff* court evidently thought it was supererogative and dangerously productive of double recovery to add an action by the other spouse for loss of consortium, especially as the benefits of a favorable judgment in the negligence action tend as a practical matter to be shared by both spouses.   The recovery in that action, it was suggested, is a "full" one.   Where the husband is plaintiff, his recovery includes compensation for impairment of his capacity to support his wife, and where the wife is plaintiff, she recovers for impairment of her earning capacity including her ability to render household services.   The *Feneff* opinion appears to suggest that these recoveries themselves cover and thereby exhaust any right of consortium.   But the mistake here lies in failing to recall that consortium had long since comprised the right to society and sexual relations, and had in fact been emptied of the element of services or earning capacity; that was entirely clear in the actions for criminal conversation or the like.   Indeed, no recovery allowed to the plaintiff spouse in the negligence action can properly extend to the loss of consortium suffered by the other spouse.   This proposition holds when there is recovery in the negligence action for impairment of the plaintiff's ability to perform sexually or to procreate; the corresponding and additional injury to the other spouse is not entitled to figure in the award of damages to the plaintiff.

To say all this is not to deny the real, as opposed to the theoretical possibilities of double recovery when a consortium action is maintained in addition to the negligence action.   The danger arises when the judge in the negligence action instructs loosely and the jury quite naturally, but improperly, considers all the damage to the marriage entity rather than just the damage to the spouse who is the plaintiff in the action.   But the danger can be obviated, as courts elsewhere have clearly recognized.   As a practical matter, the consortium claim, when asserted at all, will usually be presented together with the negligence claim for the physical injuries, husband and wife joining in the same action.   Such joinder is of course permitted and invited by the procedural rules.   When, perchance, separate actions have been brought, the defendant (or plaintiffs in the actions) would normally

---

22.   This is the case in New York, New Jersey, and Michigan which are among the many jurisdictions that have now allowed the consortium action by either spouse.   Millington v. Southeastern Elev. Co. Inc., 22 N.Y.2d 498, 293 N.Y.S.2d 305, 239 N.E.2d 897 (1968).   Ekalo v. Constructive Serv. Corp. of America, 46 N.J. 82, 215 A. 2d 1 (1965).   Montgomery v. Stephan, 359 Mich. 33, 101 N.W.2d 227 (1960).

be entitled to have them consolidated for trial. Further, we think the defendant could ordinarily insist, if he considered it to his advantage, that the other spouse be joined in the main negligence action so that a possible claim for loss of consortium should not be outstanding when the negligence claim was disposed of, leaving a possibility of duplicating recoveries. Further to avoid redundant recovery, there should in all events be plain instructions to the jury describing and distinguishing the different elements of compensable damage. The key to the present problem can thus be seen as procedural. * * *

We conclude that the reasoning of the *Feneff* case is vulnerable, and its result unsound, and we are strengthened in this view by the movement of opinion in this country since 1950 toward recognizing a right of action in either spouse for loss of consortium due to negligent injury of the other. We should be mindful of the trend although our decision is not reached by a process of following the crowd. Without attempting a count of the decisions, we may summarize the position roughly as follows. The right of the husband has long been acknowledged in a very substantial majority of the jurisdictions. The right of the wife, first confirmed in Hitaffer v. Argonne Co. Inc., 87 U.S.App.D.C. 57, 183 F.2d 811, cert. den. sub nom., Argonne Co. Inc. v. Hitaffer, 340 U.S. 852, 71 S.Ct. 80, 95 L.Ed. 624 (1950), and most recently in Glendale v. Bradshaw, 108 Ariz. 582, 503 P.2d 803 (1972), has now been established in perhaps half the American jurisdictions; the result has been achieved in some States by overruling relatively recent precedent in point.[33] In certain jurisdictions the wife's right has been denied although the husband's right is still affirmed—a regrettable solecism.[34] A few jurisdictions have followed our *Feneff* case or another route to a conclusion denying the right both to husband and wife.[35] Having in the first Restatement of Torts published in 1938 affirmed the husband's right and denied the wife's in accordance with the then weight of authority, the American Law Institute in Restatement Second will state that husband and wife have the right on equal terms, adding the requirement—in recognition of the significant procedural point—that where possible the consortium claim must be joined with the claim for bodily injury.[37] This resolution of the problem conforms to the prevailing ideas of the commentators.

33. As in New York, Millington v. Southeastern Elev. Co. Inc., 22 N.Y.2d 498, 293 N.Y.S.2d 305, 239 N.E.2d 897 (1968); Arizona, Glendale v. Bradshaw, 108 Ariz. 582, 503 P.2d 803 (1972); Maryland, Deems v. Western Md. Ry., 247 Md. 95, 231 A.2d 514 (1966).

34. The argument has been made that this condition of the law infringes constitutional guaranties of equal protection of the laws. See cases cited, annotation, 36 A.L.R.3d at 924–926.

35. See Marri v. Stamford St. R.R., 84 Conn. 9, 78 A. 582 (1911).

37. The relevant sections have not yet been published in final form, but the substance with argumentation is given in Tent. draft No. 14, *supra*, n. 32, at pp. 13–21, and Am.Law Inst., Proceedings of the Forty-Sixth Annual Meeting (1969), pp. 148–158, 162–163.

To a few critics the idea of a right of consortium seems no more than an anachronism harking back to the days when a married woman was a chattel slave, and in a formulation such as that of the new Restatement they would find a potential for indefinite expansion of a questionable liability. But that formulation, reflecting a strong current of recent decisions, is a natural expression of a dominant (and commonplace) theme of our modern law of torts, namely, that presumptively there should be recourse for a definite injury to a legitimate interest due to a lack of the prudence or care appropriate to the occasion. That it would be very difficult to put bounds on an interest and value it is a possible reason for leaving it without protection at least in the form of an action for money damages. But the law is moderately confident about the ability of the trier (subject to the usual checks at the trial and appellate levels) to apply common sense to the question. The marital interest is quite recognizable and its impairment may be definite, serious, and enduring, more so than the pain and suffering or mental or psychic distress for which recovery is now almost routinely allowed in various tort actions. The valuation problem here may be difficult but is not less manageable. Nor does it follow that if the husband-wife relationship is protected as here envisaged, identical protection must be afforded by analogy to other relationships from that of parent-child in a lengthy regress to that of master-servant; courts will rather proceed from case to case with discerning caution. In the same spirit we should accept that courts may have an interpretive task ahead in spelling out the consortium right in harmony with existing statutes.

The majority opinion in the *Lombardo* case suggested that if the *Feneff* doctrine were to be overruled, it should be by legislation rather than judicial decision. But it is worth recalling that the *Feneff* case itself overruled doctrine reiterated by the court only three years before. In a field long left to the common law, change may well come about by the same medium of development. Sensible reform can here be achieved without the articulation of detail or the creation of administrative mechanisms that customarily comes about by legislative enactment. Indeed the Legislature may rationally prefer to act, if it acts at all, after rather than before the common law has fulfilled itself in its own way. In the end the Legislature may say that we have mistaken the present public understanding of the nature of the marital relation, but that we cannot now divine or anticipate.

The reform is not a drastic or radical incursion upon existing law. In no serious way will an existing interest be impaired or an expectation be disappointed or a reliance be defeated. Accordingly there is no occasion to take full precautions to confine our decision to prospective operation. As a matter of sound administration and fairness, however, we declare that where the claim for the physical injuries has been concluded by judgment or settlement or the running of limitations prior to the coming down of this opinion, no action for loss of consortium thereafter instituted arising from the same incident will be allowed, even if that action would not be otherwise barred by limitations. In this we follow the declarations made in similar circumstances by the courts of New York, New Jersey and Maryland.[48]

Overruling the *Lombardo* decision, and holding that either spouse has a claim for loss of consortium shown to arise from personal injury of the other spouse caused by negligence of a third person, we reverse the order sustaining the demurrer to the present declaration. The parties will then be at liberty to take appropriate steps to consolidate or otherwise combine the two pending actions.

NOTES AND QUESTIONS

1. As the principal case indicates, the number of states which recognize the action for negligent impairment of consortium has grown dramatically. About forty American jurisdictions now permit both husband and wife to recover on such claims. See Note, Loss of Consortium in Admiralty: A Yet Unsettled Question, 1977 B.Y.U.L.Rev. 133, 135. For example California has now taken that position, overruling an earlier case the other way, in Rodriguez v. Bethlehem Steel Corp., 12 Cal.3d 382, 115 Cal.Rptr. 765, 525 P.2d 669 (1974), as has Connecticut, in Hopson v. St. Mary's Hospital, 176 Conn. 485, 408 A.2d 260 (1979).

2. In those states which permit the husband to sue, and which have an equal rights provision in their state constitutions, the wife is also entitled to sue. Hopkins v. Blanco, 457 Pa. 90, 320 A.2d 139 (1974).

3. Would the Equal Protection Clause of the Fourteenth Amendment require that wives be given the same right to sue for negligent impairment of consortium as husbands, under the *Reed, Frontiero, Schlesinger* line of cases? Duncan v. General Motors Corp., 499 F.2d 835 (10th Cir. 1974).

4. Would you agree with the court in *Diaz* that it is "incongruous" to allow a consortium right for intentional invasion but not for negligent invasion? Is the converse true, i. e., is it incongruous to allow the claim for negligent impairment of consortium, but not for intentional impairment?

5. What is the effect on the claim for loss of consortium of the enactment of a "no-fault" insurance statute in the jurisdiction which often provides that all tort liability for noneconomic loss in the operation of a motor vehicle is abolished except where the injured person has suffered death or certain specified forms of serious injury? See Cotton v. Minter, 469 F. Supp. 199 (E.D.Mich. 1979).

6. In view of Marvin v. Marvin, supra, page 38, and the assumption by some courts that "Marvinizing" is replacing conventional marriage in the United States, should rights of consortium be recognized between a man

---

48. See the *Millington, Ekalo,* and *Deems* cases, 22 N.Y.2d at 507–508, 293 N.Y.S.2d 305, 239 N.E.2d 897; 46 N.J. at 95–96, 215 A.2d 1; 247 Md. at 115, 231 A.2d 514.

It is also to be understood that any consortium claim which, independent-

ly considered, has been barred by limitations, will not be revived by attempted joinder in an action by the other spouse for the physical injuries which may itself have been timely instituted.

and woman who are living together although not married? Should a person living in such a relationship have actions for alienation of affections, criminal conversation or negligent impairment of consortium?

7. What conflict of laws rules should govern the grant or denial of the wife's claim? Consider the following cases:

(a) Husband and wife live in a state which does not recognize the wife's claim, but the husband is negligently injured in a state which does allow the wife to sue, and suit is brought in the latter state.

(b) Husband and wife live in a state which permits the wife to sue, the negligent injury to the husband occurs in a state which does not recognize the wife's claim, and suit is brought in the latter state.

On these questions see Folk v. York-Shipley, 239 A.2d 236 (Del.1968); Annot., 46 A.L.R.3d 880 (1972); Restatement, Second, Conflict of Laws, §§ 145, 146, 154 (1971).

8. The damages in a suit by either husband or wife are given to compensate for impairment of the plaintiff's interest in the society, companionship and sexual relations of the spouse. A recent case has added as an unusual element of damages the fact that the injury to the wife caused the parties to have marital difficulties finally resulting in a separation. Maxworthy v. Horn Electric Service, Inc., 452 F.2d 1141 (4th Cir. 1972). Punitive damages are usually not granted in such cases. Annot., 25 A.L.R.3d 1416 (1969); Annot., Measure and Elements of Damages in Wife's Action for Loss of Consortium, 74 A.L.R.3d 805 (1976).

9. Should the husband's contributory negligence be a defense against the wife's claim? Is it correct to characterize her claim as derivative? And can the wife's claim be barred by an adverse judgment against the husband in his own suit for damages, if the wife is not a party to his suit? If the wife should sue first and lose, would the husband's claim for compensation for his own injuries be barred? W. Prosser, Torts, 892 (4th ed. 1971); H. Clark, Law of Domestic Relations, 272–273 (1968); Snodgrass v. General Tel. Co. of Northwest, Inc., 275 Or. 79, 549 P.2d 1120 (1976); Laws v. Fisher, 513 P.2d 876 (Okl.1973), 27 Okl.L.Rev. 267 (1974).

10. H and W are riding in their car, driven by H. He negligently drives off the highway, the car turns over several times, and H is seriously and permanently injured. May W sue H for impairment of her consortium? Cf. Plain v. Plain, 307 Minn. 399, 240 N.W.2d 330 (1976).

11. Where a child is negligently injured, the parents may have an independent claim for the harm they suffer. At common law that harm was the loss of the child's services. Today it seems clear that in most instances the claim for lost services is fictional and that the interests of the parent are similar to those underlying the husband's or wife's claim for loss of consortium, that is, the deprivation of the society and companionship of the child and the distress caused by the child's injury. Cases which permit this recovery are Wright v. Standard Oil Co., 470 F.2d 1280 (5th Cir. 1973), and Shockley v. Prier, 66 Wis.2d 394, 225 N.W.2d 495 (1975), 1976 Wis.L.Rev. 641. Several states continue to hold that the parent may not recover for loss of society and companionship of his child, however. Annot., 69 A.L.R.3d 553 (1976). See also H. Clark, Law of Domestic Relations § 10.6 (1968).

Would the child's contributory negligence bar the parent's claim? Handeland v. Brown, 216 N.W.2d 574 (Iowa 1974).

12. What arguments might be made for and against giving a child a claim for loss of consortium when one of his parents receives a serious and incapacitating injury through the negligence of a third person? Cf. Borer v. American Airlines, Inc., 19 Cal.3d 441, 138 Cal.Rptr. 302, 563 P.2d 858 (1977) with Berger v. Weber, 82 Mich.App. 199, 267 N.W.2d 124 (1978). See also Annot., 69 A.L.R.3d 528 (1976); H. Clark, Law of Domestic Relations § 10.6 (1968).

13. Do the cases permitting or denying recovery for emotional distress caused when a parent witnesses the negligent injury of his child provide a useful analogy for the consortium cases? See, e. g., Justus v. Atchison, 19 Cal.3d 564, 139 Cal.Rptr. 97, 565 P.2d 122 (1977), 66 Cal.L.Rev. 410 (1978); Tobin v. Grossman, 24 N.Y.2d 609, 301 N.Y.S.2d 554, 249 N.E.2d 419 (1969).

SECTION 9.   INTRA–FAMILY TORTS

MERENOFF v. MERENOFF

Supreme Court of New Jersey, 1978.
76 N.J. 535, 388 A.2d 951.

HANDLER, J.   These two cases present the issue of whether the claim of a husband or wife for damages for personal injuries arising from a domestic or household accident attributable to the negligence of the other spouse is barred by the doctrine of interspousal tort immunity.   Resolution of this important question requires a decision whether to extend our holding in Immer v. Risko, 56 N.J. 482, 267 A.2d 481 (1970) which abrogated interpousal immunity in automobile negligence suits.

For purposes of the appeals, no essential facts are disputed.   In the *Merenoff* case, Barbara and Allen *Merenoff* were trimming the bushes in the walkway in front of their house on September 2, 1974. Allen noticed that his wife seemed to be having trouble with a low bush she was trying to trim and he walked over to her, picked up the hedge trimmer and clipped the bush.   In so doing, Allen cut off his wife's left index finger at the first phalanx.   Barbara commenced a tort action against her husband on April 17, 1975 for the injuries he inflicted.   In his answer Allen alleged that plaintiff's injuries were caused by her own negligence and that plaintiff's claim is barred by the doctrine of interspousal immunity.   In response to interrogatories, however, he stated that he clipped the bush without giving notice to his wife and before "checking" with her and that his negligence was the sole cause of the accident.

Both Merenoffs are insured under a homeowner's insurance policy which provides for personal liability coverage of "all sums which the Insured shall become legally obligated to pay as damages because of bodily injury * * * caused by an occurrence." The insurance company is defending in this action. Each party filed a motion for summary judgment and defendant's motion based on interspousal tort immunity was granted. * * *

In the companion *Mercado* litigation, according to depositions, on or about October 20, 1972, Santos Mercado bought two one gallon cans of Canolite Contact Cement for the purpose of attaching formica in the kitchen of his apartment. He had never used this cement at any time prior to this accident. A Canolite Contact Cement can has the word "flammable" written on it. Santos was unable to read English; nevertheless, he had had experience as a painter and was accustomed to seeing the word on paint cans and understood its meaning. The next day Santos was using the cement when Bienvenida, his wife, entered the kitchen and stood with her back to a gas stove. Her husband was in front of her spreading glue from the can which was about one and one-half feet from the stove. A flame leapt from the pilot light in the stove, igniting the cement can, a brush and the piece of formica which Santos was holding. Bienvenida, who was in the path of the fire as it shot from the oven toward the glue, was set aflame and burned, severely in some respects, on the left side of her face, left elbow and both legs.

On June 11, 1973 Bienvenida filed a complaint against her husband Santos for her injuries. She later added as defendants Two Guys From Harrison, Inc., Woodall Industries, Inc. and Staley Chemical, respectively, the retailer, manufacturer and distributor of the cement. Santos denied negligence and posed as defenses the negligence of plaintiff and the doctrine of interspousal immunity. A number of cross-claims were filed by defendants. The Mercados have a homeowner's insurance policy in both their names which provides the same personal liability coverage as the Merenoff policy. The insurance company is defending the action.

Summary judgment was granted in favor of defendant Santos against plaintiff and defendants who cross-claimed against him on the ground that the interspousal immunity doctrine barred such actions. Plaintiff then appealed to the Appellate Division. The trial court's judgment was affirmed on the ground that interspousal immunity continues to apply to a tort action based on "simple domestic negligence." * * *

I

To set a perspective to the legal issue we address, it is helpful to recapitulate briefly the history and nature of the doctrine of interspousal immunity. That doctrine originated at common law and had its roots in the historical, legal identity of husband and wife as a single, juridical entity. The rigidity and tenacity of the traditional immunity arising from this legal conception of marriage are exemplified by Phillips v. Barnet, 1 Q.B.D. 436 (1876), first followed in this country by Abbott v. Abbott, 67 Me. 304 (Sup.Jud.Ct.1877), which ruled categorically that "the legal character of an act of violence by husband upon wife and of the consequences that flow from it, is fixed by the [marital] condition of the parties at the time the act is done." Abbott v. Abbott, supra, 67 Me. at 305. The legal incidents and characteristics of marriage at common law, "some substantive, some procedural, some conceptual" were in effect hybridized into an absolute bar "* * * for one spouse ever to be held civilly liable as a tortfeasor, in any situation and without exception, to the other for any act, antenuptial or during marriage, causing personal injury which would have been a tort but for the marriage." McCurdy, "Personal Injury Torts Between Spouses", 4 Vill.L.Rev. 303, 307 (1959).

For more than a century, starting about 1844, Married Women's Acts so-called were enacted in every American jurisdiction. The intended effect of these statutes was to give married women a separate legal identity. They purported to confer upon women separate ownership and control of their own property, including choses in action. Women became separately responsible for their torts and were given the capacity to sue or be sued without joinder of the husband. These statutes, however, rarely addressed with any preciseness the question of whether a cause of action for tort between married persons could be brought. Consequently, the impact of these statutory laws upon the doctrine of interspousal immunity has been uneven throughout common law jurisdictions. As a result, it is difficult to categorize and characterize the status of the doctrine of interspousal immunity at the present time.

It is generally believed that a majority of jurisdictions favor marital immunity. Upon close analysis, however, one finds that currently only a handful of states unqualifiedly retain the doctrine in its pristine formulation. See, e. g., Paiewonsky v. Paiewonsky, 446 F.2d 178 (3 Cir. 1971), cert. den. 405 U.S. 919, 92 S.Ct. 944, 30 L.Ed.2d 788 (1972) (applying Virgin Islands law); Monk v. Ramsey, 223 Tenn. 247, 443 S.W.2d 653 (Sup.Ct.1969); Donsbach v. Offield, 488 S.W.2d 494 (Tex.Ct.Civ.App.1972). Most courts have abrogated the concept in varying degrees. For example, many permit suit where the marriage has been terminated by death or divorce. See, e. g., Jones v. Pledger, 124 U.S.App.D.C. 254, 363 F.2d 986 (1966) (applying District of Columbia law); Apitz v. Dames, 205 Or. 242, 287 P.2d 585 (Sup.Ct.1955). Several allow recovery for antenuptial torts. See, e. g., Moulton v. Moulton, 309 A.2d 224 (Me.Sup.Jud.Ct.1973); O'Grady v. Potts, 193 Kan. 644, 396 P.2d 285 (Sup.Ct.1964). A few have invalidated the immunity in the broad field of automobile negligence. See, e. g., Rupert v. Stienne, 90 Nev. 397, 528 P.2d 1013 (Sup.Ct.1974); Richard v. Richard, 131 Vt. 98, 300 A.2d 637 (Sup. Ct.1973); Surratt v. Thompson, 212 Va. 191, 183 S.E.2d 200 (Sup.Ct. 1971). Some have sanctioned recovery between spouses for intentional personal injury. See, e. g., Flores v. Flores, 84 N.M. 601, 506

P.2d 345 (Ct.App.), cert. den. 84 N.M. 592, 506 P.2d 336 (Sup.Ct. 1973). Others indicate that if the action can be brought against a third party, the action can be maintained even though it assumes a cause of action between spouses. See, e. g., Fields v. Synthetic Ropes, Inc., 59 Del. 135, 9 Storey 135, 215 A.2d 427 (Del.Supr.1965) (wife's suit against husband's employer for injuries negligently inflicted by husband in course of his employment sustainable).

Some jurisdictions have oscillated. Compare Taylor v. Patten, 2 Utah 2d 404, 275 P.2d 696 (Sup.Ct.1954) (abrogating immunity) with Rubalcava v. Gisseman, 14 Utah 2d 344, 384 P.2d 389 (Sup.Ct. 1963) (reinstating immunity). In several states, the legislature has reacted to judicial initiatives and has passed legislation to overcome or otherwise modify court decisions. E. g., Ill.Rev.Stat. ch. 68, § 1 (1953) (Ill.Ann.Stat. ch. 40, § 1001 (Smith-Hurd 1977)) (reinstating interspousal immunity) supplanting Brandt v. Keller, 413 Ill. 503, 109 N.E.2d 729 (Sup.Ct.1953) (abrogating interspousal immunity); N. Y.Dom.Rel.Law § 57 (1937) (N.Y.Gen.Oblig.Law § 3–313 (McKinney 1964)) (granting either spouse a right of action against the other for tortious injury to person or property) and N.Y.Ins.Law § 109(3–a) (N.Y.Ins.Law § 167(3) (McKinney 1939)) (no insurance policy shall be deemed to insure against an injury to an insured's spouse, unless expressly provided for in the policy) superseding Allen v. Allen, 246 N.Y. 571, 159 N.E. 656 (Ct.App.1927) (disallowing tort suits between spouses); Wis.Stat. § 246.075 (1951) and N.C.Gen.Stat. § 52–5 (1951) (each authorizing interspousal suits by both spouses) overruling respectively Fehr v. General Accident Fire & Life Assurance Corp., 246 Wis. 228, 16 N.W.2d 787 (Sup.Ct.1944) and Scholtens v. Scholtens, 230 N.C. 149, 52 S.E.2d 350 (Sup.Ct.1949) (each holding that Married Women's Acts authorized suits only by wives against their husbands but not the converse). In fact if any one dominant position can be said to have emerged from this variegated experience, it is that expressed by a plurality of at least twenty jurisdictions which have completely abrogated interspousal immunity. See, e. g., Klein v. Klein, 58 Cal.2d 692, 26 Cal.Rptr. 102, 376 P.2d 70 (Sup.Ct. 1962); Freehe v. Freehe, 81 Wash.2d 183, 500 P.2d 771 (Sup.Ct. 1972). See generally American Law Institute, Restatement (Second) Torts (Tentative Draft No. 18) § 895(G) at 72–78 (April 26, 1972); Annot., "Right of one spouse to maintain action against other for personal injury", 43 A.L.R.2d 632 (1955) and Later Case Service.

What thus unfolds from a canvass of the doctrine of interspousal immunity across the country is that its application is far from consistent or uniform; its efficacy as a legal principle has divided jurisdictions; and its utility as a social tool or instrument of justice has confounded courts, legislators and commentators. It is clear, nonetheless, that despite its survival in varying forms, interspousal immunity is no longer the doctrinal monolith it was in olden times.

II

The experience of our State with the doctrine of interspousal immunity in many ways typifies the unstable interaction between a common law tradition whose potency has waned in modern times and statutory laws of uncertain import.

[At this point in its opinion the court discussed the New Jersey experience under the state's Married Women's Property Acts. It described earlier cases in which a wife was permitted to sue a partnership in which her husband was a member, in which she was permitted to sue her husband's employer and in which she was permitted to sue her husband's estate for personal torts.]

It was not until Immer v. Risko, supra, that there was a sharp and clean, albeit narrow, break from the quintessence of the traditional interspousal immunity doctrine. The Court there characterized the common law marital unity of husband and wife as "fictitious * * *, [a] metaphysical concept [which] cannot be seriously defended today." Id., 56 N.J. at 485, 488, 267 A.2d at 484. It concluded that the foundations for the common law doctrine of interspousal tort immunity had been thoroughly eroded. Having satisfied itself that the immunity doctrine could no longer be sustained by its common law underpinnings, the Court's inquiry shifted to an examination of other reasons and considerations of public policy which had been advanced to warrant the continuation of the doctrine. These were identified as "(1) 'the disruptive effect upon the harmony of the family' and (2) 'the possibility of fraudulent and collusive litigation against the frequent real party in interest—the insurance carrier.' " Id. at 488, 267 A.2d at 484. Finding these modern day rationales wanting, the Court lifted the bar to interspousal tort actions but, as noted, only high enough to allow automobile negligence actions. The Court eschewed very pointedly any broader abrogation of the doctrine.

Defendants underscore this express disclaimer in *Immer* and argue, accurately enough, that the Court there went no further than to remove the bar of interspousal immunity in automobile negligence cases. In Small v. Rockfeld, 66 N.J. 231, 330 A.2d 335 (1974), however, the Court took a more expansive view of *Immer*. It ruled that there is no interspousal or intrafamilial immunity in an action brought on behalf of the estate and surviving child as next of kin for the wrongful death of a deceased spouse, the complaint having charged the defendant husband with killing his wife or causing her death through gross negligence. * * *

III

At the outset of our analysis we accept as fundamental the notion that the essence of our civil laws is to achieve justice and, in so doing, provide redress for wrongful injury. * * *

In the tort field, immunities, which furnish "absolution from liability", stand as conflicting exceptions to the general principle that there should be reparation for wrongful injury. Consistent with this conception of justice and fairness many immunities in the evolution of the law have withered or perished as legal relics not fit for survival in contemporary times. Marital and family immunities, like other protective enclaves in the law, have also atrophied over the years.

In Immer v. Risko, supra, *   *   *   Court undertook the judicial exercise, in the manner of the common law as it were, to determine whether there existed any reasons which still justly undergird the doctrine of interspousal tort immunity.

The Court first turned its attention to domestic harmony as one important reason for preserving the immunity. It had been pointed out earlier by Justice Jacobs in his *Koplik* dissent that there have been a great many cases where our courts permitted wives to maintain, in equity, contract and property actions against their husbands. He made the trenchant observation that "*   *   *   it is difficult to see how a personal injury action would disrupt tranquillity more than a property or contract action which is admittedly maintainable." 27 N.J. at 14–15, 141 A.2d at 42;   *   *   *. The truism expressed by Justice Jacobs that "[i]n the rare instance where the wife will sue her husband despite his objection there is probably not much tranquillity to preserve   *   *   *", Koplik v. C. P. Trucking Corp., supra, 27 N.J. at 14–15, 141 A.2d at 42, was reiterated in *Immer*: "[W]e are doubtful that the marital relationship will be any more disturbed by allowing a cause of action than by denying it.   *   *   *   A person would not sue his spouse if there were perfect harmony, and it is unlikely that adjudication of the rights will worsen the relationship." 56 N.J. at 488, 267 A.2d at 484.

Another salient factor in the Court's rejection in *Immer* of domestic harmony as a valid reason for the immunity doctrine was the prevalence of automobile insurance. As Justice Jacobs had mentioned in *Koplik*: " '*   *   *   there is no danger of domestic tranquillity being disturbed by an action for negligence by a wife against her husband who carries indemnity insurance   *   *   *.' " 27 N.J. at 15, 141 A.2d at 42 n. 1. "[R]ealistically", the Court echoed in *Immer,* "[t]he presence of insurance militates against the possibility that the interspousal relationship will be disrupted since a recovery will in most cases be paid by the insurance carrier rather than by the defendant spouse.   *   *   *   Domestic harmony may be more threatened by denying a cause of action than by permitting one where there is insurance coverage." 56 N.J. at 489, 267 A.2d at 484.

The danger of marital disruption becomes almost academic where liability insurance is available. While this Court in *Immer* was strongly influenced by the prevalence of automobile insurance, we do not believe that, because general liability insurance covering household and non-automobile accidents is not as widespread as automobile insurance, this should leave claims for tortious injury arising from domestic negligence barred and unredressed. It is probable that general homeowner liability insurance is held by a substantial number of householders and is otherwise readily available. Moreover, in a given case, if there is homeowners' insurance, there is no reason impacting upon marital peace to preclude damages for personal injuries sustained by one spouse at the negligent hands of the other. The fact that some married couples may not have household insurance, should not defeat the claims of others who do have such insurance and whose marital stability is cushioned by that insurance.

There is, in addition to all else, a certain mischief in the unspoken assumption at the heart of the domestic harmony rationale for the immunity doctrine, namely, that in this context courts are somehow fit to monitor marital morality. Courts can claim no penetrating insight by which to fathom the impact of an interspousal law suit or gauge its effect upon the strength or fragility of a marriage. The threat to domestic harmony posed by a legal action between spouses is an imponderable; the cohesiveness of a marriage may be jeopardized as much by barring a cause of action as by allowing it.

Furthermore, "* * * the marital couple is not an independent entity with a mind and heart of its own, but an association of two individuals each with a separate intellectual and emotional makeup." Eisenstadt v. Baird, 405 U.S. 438, 453, 92 S.Ct. 1029, 1038, 31 L.Ed.2d 349, 362 (1972). Happiness in marriage belongs to the married persons and the pursuit of that happiness is personal to them. * * * Cf. Loving v. Virginia, 388 U.S. 1, 87 S.Ct. 1817, 18 L.Ed.2d 1010 (1967) (right to make decisions relating to marriage is personal and private). This thought was caught in Freehe v. Freehe, supra, 81 Wash.2d at 189, 500 P.2d at 774:

> If a state of peace and tranquility exists between the spouses, then the situation is such that either no action will be commenced or that the spouses—*who are, after all, the best guardians of their own peace and tranquility*—will allow the action to continue only so long as their personal harmony is not jeopardized. (Emphasis added).

In the final analysis, the choice to sue, or not to sue, should be that of the parties to the marriage, who as individuals are entitled to seek their personal happiness according to their own lights.

We, therefore, conclude that the potential danger to marital tranquility posed by the availability of a legal action for personal injuries based on negligence between spouses cannot be grounds for denying relief.

The second major objection to eliminating interspousal tort immunity is the risk of fraudulent and collusive actions against insurance companies, * * *.

In the cases now before us, and we assume in a great many cases involving household accidents, liability insurance is available. Hence, we cannot dismiss out of hand the argument that the threat of fraud upon an insurance carrier is a real one which cannot easily be overcome in the context of interspousal domestic negligence.

This Court has repeatedly expressed confidence that our judicial system is well-equipped to sift out fraud. * * * Moreover, in other similar situations where fraud might well have been considered a troublesome factor due to the familial or close personal relationship of the parties, courts have not even tarried on the point but proceeded directly to resolve the merits of the liability claim. Other jurisdictions have agreed that in our adversary system courts are equal to the task of screening out fraudulent claims. * * *

We entertain no doubt that our courts have at their command ample means to cope with the real or asserted spectre of fraud in the context of marital tort claims. For example, the courts could, if necessary, fashion a high standard of care to compensate for the risk of collusion between the parties. Or this danger could be addressed by imposing a burden of proof commensurate with the dimensions of fraud perceived in the particular case or situation. Moreover, the full glare of truth may be the best antidote for fraud. Insurance companies might in appropriate circumstances reveal their status in the case, treating the covered defendant-spouse as a hostile witness in order to attack credibility and show that the husband and wife may be scheming to gain a recovery against the insurance company. And if allegations of fraud reach proportions where insurance coverage itself is questioned or jeopardized, a declaratory judgment action following disclaimer could be brought to air and resolve the claims.

Closely akin to the problems posed by fraud and collusion, and amenable to similar solutions, are those presented by the threat of frivolous, picayune or inflated claims of marital, personal injury. Here also, courts have the capacity to scotch such overreaching on the part of married couples. The danger from this quarter is met most efficaciously by defining and delineating marital conduct which cannot and should not be the basis for tort litigation.

There is a range of activity arising in the course of a marriage relationship beyond the reach of the law of torts. Special matters of privacy and familiarity may be encompassed by a marital or nuptial privilege and fall outside the bounds of a definable and enforceable duty of care. Certain conduct may also be regarded as "consensual", involving the "give-and-take" and subtle ebb and flow of married life. In these areas courts and juries cannot be expected to grasp sensibly and consistently the acceptable norm of married living or chart the parameters of reasonable marital behavior as a predicate for affixing liability in tort.

Similarly, certain kinds of claimed injuries between married persons will be based on simple domestic carelessness arising from activities which partake of the everyday exigencies of regular household existence and, for that reason, may not readily be controlled or influenced by the law of torts through the judicial imposition of a duty of care and the corresponding obligation to respond in damages for its breach. Thus, absent the immunity bar, the fear that trivial, exaggerated or unrealistic claims for personal injury will be brought by married persons is counterpoised by the realization that such claims for the most part will not be cognizable by courts or rewarded by juries.

* * *

We add, on a closing note as to the existence of reasons asserted for the continuation of the doctrine of interspousal immunity, that no court in this day and age subscribes seriously to the view that the abrogation of marital immunity for tortious injury is "unnecessary" because redress for the wrong can be obtained through other means. This additional, "alternative remedy" theory was advanced generations ago as a justification for retaining interspousal tort immunity and was even then the subject of dissent. The criminal law may vindicate society's interest in punishing a wrongdoer but it cannot compensate an injured spouse for her or his suffering and damages. Divorce or separation provide escape from tortious abuse but can hardly be equated with a civil right to redress and compensation for personal injuries. Equally arcane and unworthy is the notion that a wronged spouse, who has been injured at the hands of her or his mate, can and should resort to an arsenal of "private sanctions". Regardless of the ways a person can "get back" at one's spouse, they do not add up to an enforceable civil right of recovery for damages.

We thus reach the conviction that where personal injuries are tortiously inflicted by one spouse upon another, it is just and fair that compensation in appropriate circumstances be afforded the wronged and injured party and, to this end, a suit be allowed to effectuate such recovery. * * * Recognition of the right in an injured spouse to seek redress for tortious injury against the offending spouse in a suitable case constitutes judicial neutrality toward married persons. It is an attitude based upon the circumspect and modest belief that courts are not the keepers of the marital conscience and are not omniscient or inspired to intuit the mysterious and complex ways marriages rise and fall. It adopts as a premise that it is given, not to judges, but to the married individuals, to make the difficult choices in the search for their personal happiness and well-being. And the right to bring a lawsuit for compensation for wrongful injury is an option or choice that ought not be denied a person solely because of marriage.

In conclusion, we recognize that there still remain situations wherein, as a matter of law or fact, claims for personal injuries between married persons will not justify a recovery of damages. We hold that, subject to these excepted areas which are best left to be defined and developed on a case-by-case basis, there presently exists no cogent or logical reason why the doctrine of interspousal tort immunity should be continued and it is hereby abrogated as a bar to a civil suit between married persons for damages for personal injuries.

IV

In view of our ruling, the cases before us on appeal will have to be remanded for trial. It is appropriate, therefore, for the guidance of the trial courts, to comment further upon the application of the general principles herein discussed to the present cases.

On the records before us the conduct charged to the offending spouse in each case does not in the slightest indicate that a trier of fact or trial court would have to deal with marital privilege or other circumstances suggesting consent or the acceptance of jointly shared risks special to the particular marriage, factors which might otherwise constitute matters of defense and serve to excuse the injurious behavior of the defendant spouse and avoid liability in tort. The asserted tortious behavior in these cases does not trench remotely upon the privileged or consensual aspects of married life.

Moreover, the activity giving rise to the injuries in each case, according to the facts in the records on appeal, could not be characterized as simple domestic negligence. The activity in each case involved a distinct element of special danger and an unusual risk of injury or harm if not performed with reasonable care and ordinary caution. Thus, in the *Merenoff* case, the hedge clipper in the hands of Allen became a dangerous instrumentality and his careless handling of its resulted in the traumatic, partial amputation of his wife's finger; and in the *Mercado* case, it appears that the solvent was applied without proper precautions by Santos in circumstances which created a substantial risk of injury from fire, which in fact occurred.

We would also point out that, in view of the traumatic nature of the injuries suffered, and the undoubted need for immediate help and medical assistance for the injured parties, it is to be expected that the accidents were investigated and in some measure subject to corroboration by the insurance carrier. This is a circumstance which would mitigate somewhat the risk of a fraudulent scheme between the spouses.

We do not discern against this background a need to adopt a special standard of care different from the ordinary duty of reasonable care under all the circumstances. In effect the ordinary standard of care as between married people, correctly and fairly applied, will reflect the root fact and realities of married life. It is because spouses

768   THE FAMILY   Ch. 5

enjoy mutual liberties with one another and share jointly certain risks in their own lives together, that the ordinary standard of care applied in the marital context should enable a trier of fact to differentiate qualitatively between the conduct of married and unmarried persons and to recognize that certain behavior as between a married couple is acceptable and reasonable, even though such conduct might well be considered unreasonable and result in liability if engaged in by unmarried persons.

Similarly, we perceive no necessity for departing from the accepted burden of proof applicable to negligence actions in general, namely, a preponderance of the evidence. In other situations where the potential for fraud is strong because of the relationship of the parties, we have not seen fit to tamper with the ordinary duty of care or burden of proof. Nor have we done so with respect to the abrogation of the marital and family immunities undertaken thus far. If time reveals flaws in this approach, we will not hesitate to select a burden of proof, as well as a standard of care, adequate to meet the problem.

* * *

Accordingly, the judgments below are reversed and the matters remanded. It is to be understood, in view of the significant change in the law represented by the decision in these cases, that the effect and application of our holding, except as to the cases now adjudicated, shall be prospective only.

NOTES AND QUESTIONS

1. As is indicated in *Merenoff,* ever since the enactment of Married Women's Property Acts the courts have held that the spouses might sue each other for torts committed against their property. But following the authority of Thompson v. Thompson, 218 U.S. 611 (1910) the rule was established that they could not sue each other for torts resulting in personal injury. *Merenoff* cites many cases which have either abolished the rule or have restricted its operation in various ways. Other recent cases which limit the rule include Lusby v. Lusby, 283 Md. 334, 390 A.2d 77 (1978), allowing suit for an outrageous intentional tort; Imig v. March, 203 Neb. 537, 279 N.W.2d 382 (1979), abrogating interspousal immunity; Maestas v. Overton, 87 N.M. 213, 531 P.2d 947 (1975), abrogating the immunity; Bounds v. Caudle, 560 S.W.2d 925 (Tex.1978), abrogating the immunity. The immunity was retained in Varholla v. Varholla, 56 Ohio St.2d 269, 383 N.E.2d 888, 10 O.O.3d 403 (1978); Coffindaffer v. Coffindaffer, —— W.Va. ——, 244 S.E.2d 338 (1978). For citation of other cases see Annot., 92 A. L.R.3d 901 (1979).

2. In states where the interspousal immunity is retained, courts sometimes permit the wife to sue her husband's employer for the negligent conduct of the husband in the scope of his employment, notwithstanding that a recovery by her would entitle the employer to recover over against the husband. Schubert v. August Schubert Wagon Co., 249 N.Y. 253, 164 N.E. 42 (1928). In Eule v. Eule Motor Sales, 34 N.J. 537, 170 A.2d 241 (1961) the

wife was permitted to sue a partnership of which her husband was a member, even though the partnership could thereafter sue the husband for contribution if necessary to pay the judgment.

3.   Do you think the *Merenoff* case would have been decided differently if the injuries involved had not been covered by insurance?

4.   The court in *Merenoff* says "that there still remain situations wherein, as a matter of law or fact, claims for personal injuries between married persons will not justify a recovery of damages". What do you suppose the court meant by that language? Can you state a hypothetical set of facts which would come within that language and therefore not permit a husband to sue his wife or vice versa for personal injuries?

5.   Would a husband who attached a recording device to his wife's telephone and recorded her conversations (as a means of obtaining evidence for a divorce action) be liable to her under the federal wiretap statute, which provides that any person whose wire communication is intercepted shall have a civil action against the person intercepting it? 18 U.S.C.A. § 2520. See United States v. Jones, 542 F.2d 661 (6th Cir. 1976); Simpson v. Simpson, 490 F.2d 803 (5th Cir. 1974).

GIBSON v. GIBSON

Supreme Court of California, In Bank, 1971.
3 Cal.3d 914, 92 Cal.Rptr. 288, 479 P.2d 648.

SULLIVAN, Justice.   We are asked to reexamine our holding in Trudell v. Leatherby (1931) 212 Cal. 678, 300 P. 7 that an unemancipated minor child may not maintain an action against his parent for negligence. That decision, announced 40 years ago, was grounded on the policy that an action by a child against his parent would "bring discord into the family and disrupt the peace and harmony which should exist between members of the same household." (Id. at p. 680, 300 P. 9). If this rationale ever had any validity, it has none today. We have concluded that parental immunity has become a legal anachronism, riddled with exceptions and seriously undermined by recent decisions of this court. Lacking the support of authority and reason, the rule must fall.

James A. Gibson, plaintiff herein, is the minor son of defendant, Robert Gibson. James' complaint alleges in substance as follows. In January 1966 he was riding at night in a car which was being driven by his father and which was towing a jeep. His father negligently stopped the car on the highway and negligently instructed James to go out on the roadway to correct the position of the jeep's wheels. While following these directions, James was injured when another vehicle struck him.

Defendant filed a general demurrer on the theory that a minor child has no right of action against his parent for simple negligence.[1]

---

1.   We assume that James, whose age is not alleged, was unemancipated. Otherwise, his right to sue his father for personal injuries would be unques- tionable under Martinez v. Southern Pacific Co. (1955) 45 Cal.2d 244, 253– 254, 288 P.2d 868.

Judgment of dismissal was entered on an order sustaining the demurrer without leave to amend. This appeal followed.

The doctrine of parental immunity for personal torts is only 80 years old, an invention of the American courts. Although the oft-compared rule of interspousal immunity reached back to the early common law, English law books record no case involving a personal tort suit between parent and child. * * * Since children have long been allowed to sue their parents in matters involving property, however, some scholars have concluded that "there is no good reason to think that the English law would not permit actions for personal torts as well. * * *." (Prosser, op. cit. supra, § 116, p. 886 (citing Reeve, Domestic Relations (1816) p. 287; Eversley, Domestic Relations (3d ed. 1906) p. 578); Dunlap v. Dunlap, supra, 84 N.H. 352, 356, 150 A. 905). Modern decisions in Scotland and Canada have recognized such personal injury suits. * * *

In 1891, however, the Mississippi Supreme Court laid the egg from which parental immunity was hatched. Citing no authorities,[2] in Hewlett v. George (1891) 68 Miss. 703, 9 So. 885, the Mississippi court barred a minor daughter's false imprisonment action against her mother who had wrongfully committed her to an insane asylum. The court declared that the "peace of society, and of the families composing society, and a sound public policy, designed to subserve the repose of families and the best interests of society" would be disturbed by such an action and concluded that a child's only protection against parental abuse was to be found in the criminal law. (Id. at p. 711, 9 So. at p. 887.) This "compelling" logic soon led the Washington Supreme Court to conclude that family peace and harmony would be irreparably destroyed if a 15-year-old girl were allowed to sue her father for rape. (Roller v. Roller (1905) 37 Wash. 242, 79 P. 788; see also McKelvey v. McKelvey (1903) 111 Tenn. 388, 77 S.W. 664, upholding a demurrer to a minor's complaint seeking damages for "cruel and inhuman treatment" by her father and stepmother.)

2. Three earlier nineteenth century American cases had suggested that parental liability in tort might exist, at least in exceptional cases. In the earliest, Gould v. Christianson (S.D. N.Y.1836) 10 Fed.Cas. 857 (No. 5636), a sea captain claimed immunity in an action for battery on the ground that he stood *in loco parentis* toward the 18-year-old seaman plaintiff. The court rejected the captain's defense, but went on to declare, in dictum, that a parent enjoyed immunity except for punishments which "are cruel and injurious to the life or health of the child or are a public offense." (Id. at p. 864.) In Lander v. Seaver (1859) 32 Vt. 114, a battery suit by a student against his teacher, it was stated, again in dictum, that a parent would be liable "in extreme cases of cruelty and injustice" for "malice or wicked motives or an evil heart in punishing his child." (Id. at p. 122.) Nelson v. Johansen (1885) 18 Neb. 180, 24 N.W. 730 held, without discussion of the issue, that a guardian *in loco parentis* to the 10-year-old plaintiff was liable for injuries resulting from negligence in failing to properly clothe her for the bitter winter weather. (See McCurdy, supra, 43 Harv.L.Rev. at pp. 1061–1063.)

Other states quickly adopted the rule of *Hewlett* and *Roller,* applying it to actions for negligence as well as for intentional torts, occasionally with more emotion than reason. * * *

Trudell v. Leatherby, supra, 212 Cal. 678, 300 P. 7, decided in 1931, involved an action by a minor plaintiff for damages for personal injuries sustained while a passenger in a car driven by his stepmother. After a discussion of barely one page on the issue of parental immunity, it was there concluded, "That a minor child, unemancipated by its parents, cannot sustain an action against its parents seems to be well settled by the authorities." (Id. at p. 680, 300 P. at p. 8.) In support were cited "well considered" cases from eight states, and even a passage from Hewlett (as quoted in 20 R.C.L. 631). Trudell's only rationale was the threat of family discord.

No sooner had American courts, including our own, embraced the parental immunity doctrine than they began to fashion a number of qualifications and exceptions to it. In Martinez v. Southern Pacific Co., supra, 45 Cal.2d 244, 288 P.2d 868, we allowed an *emancipated* minor to sue her parent for simple negligence; in Emery v. Emery (1955) 45 Cal.2d 421, 289 P.2d 218, we held that wilful or malicious torts were not within the scope of the immunity. Courts in other states compounded the doctrine's idiosyncrasies in decisions permitting tort actions by minors against the estate of a deceased parent * * * against the parent in his business capacity * * * and against the parent's employer under *respondeat superior* for the tort of the parent within the scope of his employment.[5] * * * Although purporting to distinguish the situation of a negligence action directly against a living parent, such cases probably rested as much on growing judicial distaste for a rule of law which in one sweep disqualified an entire class of injured minors.

Apart from this general trend to restrict parental immunity, however, we believe that a trilogy of recent California cases in the area of intra-family tort immunity has weakened, if not eroded, the doctrinal underpinnings of the rule. In Emery v. Emery, supra, 45 Cal.2d 421, 289 P.2d 218, we recognized the right of an injured minor to sue her father for wilful or malicious tort and to sue her brother for negligence. In Self v. Self (1962) 58 Cal.2d 683, 26 Cal.Rptr. 97, 376 P.2d 65 and Klein v. Klein (1962) 58 Cal.2d 692, 26 Cal.Rptr. 102, 376 P.2d 70, we abrogated *interspousal* immunity for intentional and negligent torts. We think that the reasoning of those decisions has totally destroyed two of the three grounds traditionally advanced in support of parental immunity: (1) disruption of family harmony and (2) fraud or collusion between family "adversaries." The third

---

5. California has avoided this inconsistency by denying an action in this situation, on the ground that the employer would have an indemnity right against the negligent parent, thus allowing the child to sue his parent indirectly. (Myers v. Tranquility Irr. Dist. (1938) 26 Cal.App.2d 385, 389–390, 79 P.2d 419.)

ground, the threat to parental authority and discipline, although of legitimate concern, cannot sustain a total bar to parent-child negligence suits. We shall examine these arguments one by one.

The danger to family harmony was the only rationale for immunity mentioned in *Trudell.* In *Self,* however, we termed this argument "illogical and unsound." Observing that spouses commonly sue each other over property matters, we concluded that "It would not appear that such assumed conjugal harmony is any more endangered by tort actions than by property actions * * *." (58 Cal.2d 683, 690, 26 Cal.Rptr. 97, 101, 376 P.2d 65, 67.) Indeed, as we shall discuss, infra, the risk of family discord is much less in negligence actions, where an adverse judgment will normally be satisfied by the defendant family member's insurance carrier, than in property actions, where it will generally be paid out of the defendant's pocket. Since the law has long allowed a child to sue his parent over property matters (King v. Sells (1938) 193 Wash. 294, 75 P.2d 130; Lamb v. Lamb (1895) 146 N.Y. 317, 41 N.E. 26), the rationale of *self* [sic] is equally applicable to parent-child tort suits.

We found the family argument similarly unpersuasive in *Emery* when advanced to bar a suit between a minor sister and her minor brother. We said: "Exceptions to the general principle of liability, Civ.Code, § 3523 ['For every wrong there is a remedy.'] * * * are not to be lightly created, and we decline to create such an exception on the basis of the speculative assumption that to do so would preserve family harmony. An uncompensated tort is no more apt to promote or preserve peace in the family than is an action between minor brother and sister to recover damages for that tort." (45 Cal. 2d 421, 430–431, 289 P.2d 218, 224.)

Arguments based on the fear of fraudulent actions are also adequately answered by reference to *Emery, Self,* and *Klein.* While some danger of collusion cannot be denied, the peril is no greater when a minor child sues his parent than in actions between husbands and wives, brothers and sisters, or adult children and parents, all of which are permitted in California. In short, as we stated in *Klein:* "The possibility of fraud or perjury exists to some degree in all cases. But we do not deny a cause of action to a party because of such a danger. * * * It would be a sad commentary on the law if we were to admit that the judicial processes are so ineffective that we must deny relief to a person otherwise entitled because in some future case a litigant may be guilty of fraud or collusion. Once that concept were accepted, then all causes of action should be abolished. Our legal system is not that ineffectual." (58 Cal.2d 692, 695–696, 26 Cal.Rptr. 102, 104, 105, 376 P.2d 70, 72, 73.)

Moreover, we pointed out in *Emery* that concern with collusion is entirely inconsistent with the dire predictions of familial discord. The collusion argument assumes that the suit is in reality aimed not at the defendant family member but at his insurance carrier. In such case, the tort action poses no threat whatever to family tranquility; in fact, "domestic harmony will not be disrupted so much by allowing the action as by denying it." (Prosser, op cit. supra, § 116, p. 889.) As we concluded in *Emery*, "The interest of the child in freedom from personal injury caused by the tortious conduct of others is sufficient to outweigh any danger of fraud or collusion." (45 Cal.2d 421, 431, 289 P.2d 218, 224.)

The threat to parental authority and discipline is the only one of the traditional arguments for immunity which was not fully answered by *Self, Klein,* and *Emery.* "Preservation of the parent's right to discipline his minor children has been the basic policy behind the rule of parental immunity from tort liability." (Emery v. Emery, supra, 45 Cal.2d 421, 429, 289 P.2d 218, 223.) Since *Self* and *Klein* dealt with suits between spouses, who are equals, we were not called upon to consider this issue. Nor does *Emery* adequately deal with this contention, for it involved parental misconduct which, because of its wilful or malicious character, forfeited all claim to immunity under the cloak of parental authority.

However, the absence of precedent on this point is not decisive. In our view, the possibility that some cases may involve the exercise of parental authority does not justify continuation of a blanket rule of immunity. In many actions, no question of parental control will arise. Thus, the parent who negligently backs his automobile into his child or who carelessly maintains a lawnmower, which injures the child, cannot claim that his parental role will be threatened if the infant is permitted to sue for negligence. To preserve the rule of immunity in such cases, where the reason for it fails, appears indefensible.

We do recognize, however, that issues of parental discretion and supervision will occasionally be raised when children sue their parents in tort. In such situations, some jurisdictions, although abrogating a broad doctrine of immunity * * * have nevertheless retained a limited one where basic parental functions are involved. For example, in Goller v. White, supra, 20 Wis.2d 402, 122 N.W.2d 193, the Wisconsin Supreme Court, while ending parental immunity in general, delineated two areas where immunity should remain: "(1) [w]here the alleged negligent act involves an exercise of parental authority over the child; and (2) where the alleged negligent act involves an exercise of ordinary parental discretion with respect to the provision of food, clothing, housing, medical and dental services, and other care." (Id. at p. 413, 122 N.W.2d at p. 198.)

We agree with this approach in its recognition of the undeniable fact that the parent-child relationship is unique in some aspects, and that traditional concepts of negligence cannot be blindly applied to it. Obviously, a parent may exercise certain authority over a minor child which would be tortious if directed toward someone else. For example, a parent may spank a child who has misbehaved without being liable for battery, or he may temporarily order the child to stay in his room as punishment, yet not be held responsible for false imprisonment.

However, we reject the implication of *Goller* that within certain aspects of the parent-child relationship, the parent has carte blanche to act negligently toward his child. As we noted in *Emery,* "Since the law imposes on the parent a duty to rear and discipline his child and confers the right to prescribe a course of reasonable conduct for its development, the parent has a wide discretion in the performance of his parental functions, but that discretion does not include the right wilfully to inflict personal injuries *beyond the limits of reasonable parental discipline."* (45 Cal.2d 421, 430, 289 P.2d 218, 224.) (Italics added.) Although *Emery* involved *wilful* parental misconduct, we think this reasoning is applicable to a parent's *negligent* exercise of his familial duties and powers. In short, although a parent has the prerogative and the duty to exercise authority over his minor child, this prerogative must be exercised within reasonable limits. The standard to be applied is the traditional one of reasonableness, but viewed in light of the parental role. Thus, we think the proper test of a parent's conduct is this: what would an ordinarily reasonable and prudent *parent* have done in similar circumstances?

We choose this approach over the *Goller*-type formula for several reasons. First, we think that the *Goller* view will inevitably result in the drawing of arbitrary distinctions about when particular parental conduct falls within or without the immunity guidelines. Second, we find intolerable the notion that if a parent can succeed in bringing himself within the "safety" of parental immunity, he may act negligently with impunity.

In deciding to abrogate parental immunity, we are also persuaded by several policy factors. One is the obvious but important legal principle that "when there is negligence, the rule is liability, immunity is the exception." * * * As we stated in *Klein,* this fundamental doctrine of compensation for injury proximately caused by the act of another governs "in the absence of statute or compelling reasons of public policy." (58 Cal.2d 692, 695, 26 Cal.Rptr. 102, 104, 376 P.2d 70, 72.) Of course, no statute requires parental immunity, and as we have already explained, public policy compels liability, not immunity.

Secondly, we feel that we cannot overlook the widespread prevalence of liability insurance and its practical effect on intra-family suits. Although it is obvious that insurance does not create liability where none otherwise exists * * * it is unrealistic to ignore this factor in making an informed policy decision on whether to abolish parental negligence immunity. * * * We can no longer consider child-parent actions on the outmoded assumption that parents may be required to pay damages to their children. As Professor James has observed: "Recovery by the unemancipated minor child against his parent is almost uniformly denied for a variety of reasons which involve the integrity of the family unit and the family exchequer and the importance of parental discipline. But in truth, virtually no such suits are brought except where there is insurance. And where there is, none of the threats to the family exists at all." (James, Accident Liability Reconsidered: The Impact of Liability Insurance (1948) 57 Yale L.J. 549, 553.)

By our decision today we join 10 other states which have already abolished parental tort immunity. We think it is significant that since 1963, when the Wisconsin Supreme Court drove the first wedge (Goller v. White, supra, 20 Wis.2d 402, 122 N.W.2d 193), other jurisdictions have steadily hacked away at this legal deadwood. Of particular interest from our viewpoint is Hebel v. Hebel (Alaska 1967) 435 P.2d 8, where the Alaska Supreme Court relied in part on our decisions in *Self* and *Klein*. Other states which now allow children to sue their parents in tort include Kentucky (Rigdon v. Rigdon (Ky. 1970) 465 S.W.2d 921); New Jersey (France v. A.P.A. Transport Corp. (1970) 56 N.J. 500, 267 A.2d 490); Arizona (Streenz v. Streenz (1970) 106 Ariz. 86, 471 P.2d 282); New York (Gelbman v. Gelbman (1969) 23 N.Y.2d 434, 297 N.Y.S.2d 529, 245 N.E.2d 192); Illinois (Schenk v. Schenk (1968) 100 Ill.App.2d 199, 241 N.E.2d 12); Minnesota (Silesky v. Kelman (1968) 281 Minn. 431, 161 N.W.2d 631); North Dakota (Nuelle v. Wells (N.D.1967) 154 N.W.2d 364); and New Hampshire (Briere v. Briere (1966) 107 N.H. 432, 224 A.2d 588).

Applying what we have said above to the case at bench, we hold that the trial court erred in sustaining the defendant's demurrer in reliance on Trudell v. Leatherby. We overrule *Trudell,* and hold that an unemancipated minor child may maintain an action for negligence against his parent. Consequently, plaintiff's complaint stated a cause of action and was not vulnerable to demurrer.

The judgment is reversed and the cause is remanded to the trial court with directions to overrule the demurrer and to allow the defendant a reasonable time within which to answer.

NOTES AND QUESTIONS

1. The courts of the various states have generally held that an unemancipated child may sue his parent for breach of contract, and for torts to the child's property. Likewise the emancipated child may sue his parent for torts to his person. H. Clark, Law of Domestic Relations § 9.2 (1968).

2. Many states permit suits by an unemancipated child against his parents for intentional torts. Note, The "Reasonable Parent" Standard: An Alternative to Parent-Child Tort Immunity, 47 U. of Colo.L.Rev. 795, 802 (1976), citing cases. And some states permit the child to sue his parent for personal injuries caused by negligence arising out of the parent's

business or occupation. Trevarton v. Trevarton, 151 Colo. 418, 378 P.2d 640 (1963). A substantial number of states permit the child to sue his parent for the negligent operation of an automobile where insurance coverage is available, apparently on the theory that family harmony will not thereby be impaired if the insurance company pays for the injury. Sorensen v. Sorensen, 369 Mass. 350, 339 N.E.2d 907 (1975), citing many cases; Lee v. Comer, —— W.Va. ——, 224 S.E.2d 721 (1976). See also S.C.Code § 15–5–210 (1976).

3. H and W, formerly married and living in the State of Holmes, were divorced, with custody of their son S, given to W. H had the right under the decree to have S visit him on weekends. S is now twelve years old. On one of the weekends while S was staying with H, S became involved with a gang of older boys who engaged in acts of vandalism, breaking into a vacant house and destroying the interior. When S came home, H learned of this exploit and became so angry that he beat S severely with a leather belt. When S returned to W at the end of the weekend, he told W of the beating and was still very bruised and sore. W took S to a doctor, who administered first aid. Soon after, W brought suit on S's behalf against H for assault and battery.

What should be the result of such a suit? Is this tort intentional or negligent? Does the fact that the parents were divorced have any effect on the case? Cf. Fugate v. Fugate, 582 S.W.2d 663 (Mo.1979).

4. C, a four-year-old child walking on the sidewalk in the company of his mother, suddenly darted out into the street between two parked cars and was struck and injured by an automobile driven by the defendant.

(a) Should C be permitted to sue his mother for her negligence in failing to control him, thereby causing his injury?

(b) If C should sue the defendant for his negligent operation of the automobile which struck C, could the defendant file a third-party complaint against C's mother for indemnification or apportionment, under state procedure which permits indemnification or apportionment in tort actions?

(c) If indemnification or apportionment of the loss is permissible under the local practice, is that a reason (in addition to the usual arguments about disrupting family harmony and defrauding insurance companies) for adhering to the parent-child immunity? Holodook v. Spencer, 36 N.Y.2d 35, 364 N.Y.S.2d 859, 324 N.E.2d 338 (1974) made the argument that the potentiality of indemnification would make uninsured parents reluctant to sue third parties for injuries to their children, if the parents knew that the third party could recover indemnification from them for negligent supervision of the child. The court advanced this as an additional reason for preserving the parent-child immunity in cases involving parents' negligent failure to supervise their child. See also Schneider v. Coe, 405 A.2d 682 (Del. 1979).

(d) How should these questions be answered in a state which followed *Gibson*?

(e) In a jurisdiction following *Holodook*, how should this case be decided? Walter had a son, Scott, who was sixteen years old. Scott was blind in one eye, had impaired vision in the other and his long distance vision was not correctable by glasses. Walter gave Scott a motocycle, for which Scott had no operator's license. While riding the bike, Scott ran into a barrier allegedly negligently placed across a road by G & S Construction Company, and was seriously injured. Walter brought suit for negligence on behalf of Scott against G & S. G & S counterclaimed against Walter for his negligence in providing Scott with a motorcycle which he was not competent to operate. Walter moved to dismiss the counterclaim. Nolechek v. Gesuale, 46 N.Y.2d 332, 413 N.Y.S.2d 340, 385 N.E.2d 1268 (1978); Romanik v. Toro Co., 277 N.W.2d 515 (Minn.1979).

(f) How would the California court, following *Gibson*, decide the case outlined in paragraph (e), supra?

5. H and W were married and had a five-year-old daughter, D. In the living-room of their house H and W had only two electrical outlets, and in order to place a table lamp where they wished, they used a long, extension cord. The cord was old and at one place its insulation had worn through, as both H and W knew. In fact one day H had said, "we really should get a new extension cord for that lamp." Shortly thereafter D was playing on the floor with some metal toys, and ran one across the extension cord, causing a short circuit, and severely burning herself. Could D sue her parents for their negligence? Cosmopolitan Nat. Bank of Chicago v. Heap, 128 Ill.App.2d 165, 262 N.E.2d 826 (1970); Cherry v. Cherry, 203 N.W.2d 352 (Minn.1972). Would it matter that such an injury was covered by liability insurance?

6. A ten-year-old child, C, files a complaint against her mother, alleging that her mother neglected her, failed to give her proper parental care or affection, left her unattended on occasion, and in general failed to perform the parental duties which the mother owed to C. The complaint further alleged that this caused C serious emotional and psychological injury. The complaint finally characterized the mother as having been guilty of "malpractice of parenting", and asked for substantial money damages. C's mother moved to dismiss the complaint as not stating a claim upon which relief could be granted.

(a) How should this motion be disposed of? Burnette v. Wahl, 284 Or. 705, 588 P.2d 1105 (1978), 48 U.Cin.L.Rev. 940 (1979).

(b) Would your answer be different if C should seek an injunction or other non-pecuniary relief?

(c) What would be the result if C waited until she reached majority and then brought the suit?

7. The cases generally apply the same immunity principles to persons standing *in loco parentis* to child plaintiffs as are applied in the particular state to parents. See, e. g. Mathis v. Ammons, 453 F.Supp. 1033 (E.D. Tenn.1978); Thomas v. Chicago Bd. of Ed., 77 Ill.2d 65, 32 Ill.Dec. 308, 395 N.E.2d 538 (1979) (school teachers by statute are in loco parentis); Busillo v. Hetzel, 58 Ill.App.3d 682, 16 Ill.Dec. 315, 374 N.E.2d 1090 (1978); Hush v. Devilbiss Co., 77 Mich.App. 639, 259 N.W.2d 170 (1977); Van Wart v. Cook, 557 P.2d 1161 (Okl.App.1976).

8. Difficult questions of the conflict of laws may arise in connection with either spousal or parent-child immunity. For example, an accident occurs in State A in which H negligently causes injury to W. H and W are domiciled in State B. By the law of State A, W would be permitted to sue H for this injury. By the law of State B she would not. She sues in State A.

(a) Would a motion to dismiss her suit be granted?

(b) If the accident occurred in State B, the parties were domiciled in State A and suit were brought in State B, what should be the result?

(c) If the parent-child immunity were involved, as, for example, where a child was injured in the accident and suit was brought against the parent in either State A or State B, would the result be different?

For authorities dealing with these situations, see Zurzola v. General Motors Corp., 503 F.2d 403 (3d Cir. 1974); Krick v. Carter, 477 F.Supp. 152 (M.D.Penn.1979); Sweeney v. Sweeney, 402 Mich. 234, 262 N.W.2d 625 (1978); Huff v. LaSieur, 571 S.W.2d 654 (Mo.App.1978); Gordon v. Gordon, 118 N.H. 356, 387 A.2d 339 (1978); Henry v. Henry, 291 N.C. 156, 229 S.E.2d 158 (1976); Zelinger v. State Sand and Gravel Co., 38 Wis.2d 98, 156 N.W.2d 466 (1968); Mager v. Mager, 197 N.W.2d 626 (N.D.1972); Restatement, Second, Conflict of Laws §§ 169, 145 (1971).

9. H and W were married and had a sixteen-year-old son S who had just obtained his driver's license. In backing the family car out of the garage one day S negligently struck and injured his father, H. May H recover for the tort from S? Are the arguments for and against liability in this situation the same as when the child sues the parent? Cf. Balts v. Balts, 273 Minn. 419, 142 N.W.2d 66 (1966), 71 Dick.L.Rev. 145 (1966); H. Clark, Law of Domestic Relations 260 (1968).

10. What should be the result if, in the case described in the preceding paragraph, S had negligently run over his ten-year-old sister, D? Could D recover from S? See Emery v. Emery, 45 Cal.2d 421, 289 P.2d 218 (1955).

11. Could you draft a statute which would deal successfully with the problems created by the husband-wife and the parent-child immunities?

Chapter 6

DIVORCE *

INTRODUCTION

BODDIE ET AL. v. CONNECTICUT ET AL.

Supreme Court of the United States, 1971.
401 U.S. 371, 91 S.Ct. 780, 28 L.Ed.2d 113.

Mr. Justice HARLAN delivered the opinion of the Court.

Appellants, welfare recipients residing in the State of Connecticut, brought this action in the Federal District Court for the District of Connecticut on behalf of themselves and others similarly situated, challenging, as applied to them, certain state procedures for the commencement of litigation, including requirements for payment of court fees and costs for service of process, that restrict their access to the courts in their effort to bring an action for divorce.

It appears from the briefs and oral argument that the average cost to a litigant for bringing an action for divorce is $60. Section 52–259 of the Connecticut General Statutes provides: "There shall be paid to the clerks of the supreme court or the superior court, for entering each civil cause, forty-five dollars * * *." An additional $15 is usually required for the service of process by the sheriff, although as much as $40 or $50 may be necessary where notice must be accomplished by publication.

There is no dispute as to the inability of the named appellants in the present case to pay either the court fees required by statute or the cost incurred for the service of process. The affidavits in the record establish that appellants' welfare income in each instance barely suffices to meet the costs of the daily essentials of life and includes no allotment that could be budgeted for the expense to gain access to the courts in order to obtain a divorce. Also undisputed is appellants' "good faith" in seeking a divorce.

Assuming, as we must on this motion to dismiss the complaint, the truth of the *undisputed* allegations made by the appellants, it appears that they were unsuccessful in their attempt to bring their divorce actions in the Connecticut courts, simply by reason of their indigency. The clerk of the Superior Court returned their papers "on

---

* In some states the statutes have replaced "divorce" with the term "dissolution of marriage". The Uniform Marriage and Divorce Act, notwithstanding the "divorce" in its title, also refers to "dissolution of marriage", in section 302. Since no virtue is evident in the new terminology and since it requires three words where one more precise one was formerly sufficient, in this work divorce will continue to be called "divorce".

the ground that he could not accept them until an entry fee had been paid." Subsequent efforts to obtain a judicial waiver of the fee requirement and to have the court effect service of process were to no avail.

Appellants thereafter commenced this action in the Federal District Court seeking a judgment declaring that Connecticut's statute and service of process provisions, "requiring payment of court fees and expenses as a condition precedent to obtaining court relief [are] unconstitutional [as] applied to these indigent [appellants] and all other members of the class which they represent." As further relief, appellants requested the entry of an injunction ordering the appropriate officials to permit them "to proceed with their divorce actions without payment of fees and costs." A three-judge court was convened pursuant to 28 U.S.C.A. § 2281, and on July 16, 1968, that court concluded that "a state [may] limit access to its civil courts and particularly in this instance, to its divorce courts, by the requirement of a filing fee or other fees which effectively bar persons on relief from commencing actions therein." 286 F.Supp. 968, 972. * * * We now reverse. Our conclusion is that, given the basic position of the marriage relationship in this society's hierarchy of values and the concomitant state monopolization of the means for legally dissolving this relationship, due process does prohibit a State from denying, solely because of inability to pay, access to its courts to individuals who seek judicial dissolution of their marriages.

I

At its core, the right to due process reflects a fundamental value in our American constitutional system. Our understanding of that value is the basis upon which we have resolved this case.

Perhaps no characteristic of an organized and cohesive society is more fundamental than its erection and enforcement of a system of rules defining the various rights and duties of its members, enabling them to govern their affairs and definitively settle their differences in an orderly, predictable manner. Without such a "legal system," social organization and cohesion are virtually impossible; with the ability to seek regularized resolution of conflicts individuals are capable of interdependent action that enables them to strive for achievements without the anxieties that would beset them in a disorganized society. Put more succinctly, it is this injection of the rule of law that allows society to reap the benefits of rejecting what political theorists call the "state of nature."

American society, of course, bottoms its systematic definition of individual rights and duties, as well as its machinery for dispute settlement, not on custom or the will of strategically placed individuals, but on the common-law model. It is to courts, or other quasi-judicial official bodies, that we ultimately look for the implementation of a regularized, orderly process of dispute settlement. Within this framework, those who wrote our original Constitution, in the Fifth Amendment, and later those who drafted the Fourteenth Amendment, recognized the centrality of the concept of due process in the operation of this system. Without this guarantee that one may not be deprived of his rights, neither liberty nor property, without due process of law, the State's monopoly over techniques for binding conflict resolution could hardly be said to be acceptable under our scheme of things. Only by providing that the social enforcement mechanism must function strictly within these bounds can we hope to maintain an ordered society that is also just. It is upon this premise that this Court has through years of adjudication put flesh upon the due process principle.

Such litigation has, however, typically involved rights of defendants—not, as here, persons seeking access to the judicial process in the first instance. This is because our society has been so structured that resort to the courts is not usually the only available, legitimate means of resolving private disputes. Indeed, private structuring of individual relationships and repair of their breach is largely encouraged in American life, subject only to the caveat that the formal judicial process, if resorted to, is paramount. Thus, this Court has seldom been asked to view access to the courts as an element of due process. The legitimacy of the State's monopoly over techniques of final dispute settlement, even where some are denied access to its use, stands unimpaired where recognized, effective alternatives for the adjustment of differences remain. But the successful invocation of this governmental power by plaintiffs has often created serious problems for defendants' rights. For at that point, the judicial proceeding becomes the only effective means of resolving the dispute at hand and denial of a defendant's full access to that process raises grave problems for its legitimacy.

Recognition of this theoretical framework illuminates the precise issue presented in this case. As this Court on more than one occasion has recognized, marriage involves interests of basic importance in our society. * * * It is not surprising, then, that the States have seen fit to oversee many aspects of that institution. Without a prior judicial imprimatur, individuals may freely enter into and rescind commercial contracts, for example, but we are unaware of any jurisdiction where private citizens may covenant for or dissolve marriages without state approval. Even where all substantive requirements are concededly met, we know of no instance where two consenting adults may divorce and mutually liberate themselves from the constraints of legal obligations that go with marriage, and more fundamentally the prohibition against remarriage, without invoking the State's judicial machinery.

Thus, although they assert here due process rights as would-be plaintiffs, we think appellants' plight, because resort to the state courts is the only avenue to dissolution of their marriages, is akin to that of defendants faced with exclusion from the only forum effectively empowered to settle their disputes. Resort to the judicial process by these plaintiffs is no more voluntary in a realistic sense than that of the defendant called upon to defend his interests in court. For both groups this process is not only the paramount dispute-settlement technique, but, in fact, the only available one. In this posture we think that this appeal is properly to be resolved in light of the principles enunciated in our due process decisions that delimit rights of defendants compelled to litigate their differences in the judicial forum.

II

These due process decisions, representing over a hundred years of effort by this Court to give concrete embodiment to this concept, provide, we think, complete vindication for appellants' contentions. In particular, precedent has firmly embedded in our due process jurisprudence two important principles upon whose application we rest our decision in the case before us.

A

Prior cases establish, first, that due process requires, at a minimum, that absent a countervailing state interest of overriding significance, persons forced to settle their claims of right and duty through the judicial process must be given a meaningful opportunity to be heard. Early in our jurisprudence, this Court voiced the doctrine that "[w]herever one is assailed in his person or his property, there he may defend," Windsor v. McVeigh, 93 U.S. 274, 277, 23 L.Ed. 914 (1876). * * * Although "[m]any controversies have raged about the cryptic and abstract words of the Due Process Clause," as Mr. Justice Jackson wrote for the Court in Mullane v. Central Hanover Tr. Co., 339 U.S. 306, 70 S.Ct. 652, 94 L.Ed. 865 (1950), "there can be no doubt that at a minimum they require that deprivation of life, liberty or property by adjudication be preceded by notice and opportunity for hearing appropriate to the nature of the case." Id., at 313.

Due process does not, of course, require that the defendant in every civil case actually have a hearing on the merits. A State, can, for example, enter a default judgment against a defendant who, after adequate notice, fails to make a timely appearance, see *Windsor,* supra, at 278, or who, without justifiable excuse, violates a procedural rule requiring the production of evidence necessary for orderly adjudication, Hammond Packing Co. v. Arkansas, 212 U.S. 322, 351, 29 S. Ct. 370, 380, 53 L.Ed. 530 (1909). What the Constitution does require is "an *opportunity* * * * granted at a meaningful time and in a meaningful manner," Armstrong v. Manzo, 380 U.S. 545, 552

(1965) (emphasis added), "for [a] hearing appropriate to the nature of the case," Mullane v. Central Hanover Tr. Co., supra, at 313. The formality and procedural requisites for the hearing can vary, depending upon the importance of the interests involved and the nature of the subsequent proceedings. That the hearing required by due process is subject to waiver, and is not fixed in form does not affect its root requirement that an individual be given an opportunity for a hearing *before* he is deprived of any significant property interest, except for extraordinary situations where some valid governmental interest is at stake that justifies postponing the hearing until after the event. In short, "within the limits of practicability," id., at 318, a State must afford to all individuals a meaningful opportunity to be heard if it is to fulfill the promise of the Due Process Clause.

B

Our cases further establish that a statute or a rule may be held constitutionally invalid as applied when it operates to deprive an individual of a protected right although its general validity as a measure enacted in the legitimate exercise of state power is beyond question. Thus, in cases involving religious freedom, free speech or assembly, this Court has often held that a valid statute was unconstitutionally applied in particular circumstances because it interfered with an individual's exercise of those rights.

No less than these rights, the right to a meaningful opportunity to be heard within the limits of practicality, must be protected against denial by particular laws that operate to jeopardize it for particular individuals. See Mullane v. Central Hanover Tr. Co., supra; Covey v. Town of Somers, 351 U.S. 141, 76 S.Ct. 724, 100 L.Ed. 1021 (1956).

In Mullane this Court held that the statutory provision for notice by publication in a local newspaper, although sufficient as to beneficiaries of a trust whose interests or addresses were unknown to the trustee, was not sufficient notice under the Due Process Clause for known beneficiaries. Similarly, Covey held that notice by publication in a foreclosure action, even though sufficient to provide a normal person with an opportunity for a hearing, was not sufficient where the defendant was a known incompetent. The Court expressly rejected an argument that "the Fourteenth Amendment does not require the State to take measures in giving notice to an incompetent beyond those deemed sufficient in the case of the ordinary taxpayer." Id., at 146.

Just as a generally valid notice procedure may fail to satisfy due process because of the circumstances of the defendant, so too a cost requirement, valid on its face, may offend due process because it operates to foreclose a particular party's opportunity to be heard. The State's obligations under the Fourteenth Amendment are not simply generalized ones; rather, the State owes to each individual that process which, in light of the values of a free society, can be characterized as due.

III

Drawing upon the principles established by the cases just canvassed, we conclude that the State's refusal to admit these appellants to its courts, the sole means in Connecticut for obtaining a divorce, must be regarded as the equivalent of denying them an opportunity to be heard upon their claimed right to a dissolution of their marriages, and, in the absence of a sufficient countervailing justification for the State's action, a denial of due process.[8]

The arguments for this kind of fee and cost requirement are that the State's interest in the prevention of frivolous litigation is substantial, its use of court fees and process costs to allocate scarce resources is rational, and its balance between the defendant's right to notice and the plaintiff's right to access is reasonable.

In our opinion, none of these considerations is suficient to override the interest of these plaintiff-appellants in having access to the only avenue open for dissolving their allegedly untenable marriages. Not only is there no necessary connection between a litigant's assets and the seriousness of his motives in bringing suit,[9] but it is here beyond present dispute that appellants bring these actions in good faith. Moreover, other alternatives exist to fees and cost requirements as a means for conserving the time of courts and protecting parties from frivolous litigation, such as penalties for false pleadings or affidavits, and actions for malicious prosecution or abuse of process, to mention only a few. In the same vein we think that reliable alternatives exist to service of process by a state-paid sheriff if the State is unwilling to assume the cost of official service. This is perforce true of service by publication which is the method of notice least calculated to bring to a potential defendant's attention the pendency of judicial proceedings.

8. At least one court has already recognized the special nature of the divorce action. Justice Sobel in a case like that before us took note of the State's involvement in the marital relationship:

"Marriage is clearly marked with the public interest. In this State, a marriage cannot be dissolved except by 'due judicial proceedings. * * *' We have erected by statute a money hurdle to such dissolution by requiring in many circumstances the service of a summons by publication * * *. This hurdle is an effective barrier to [plaintiff's] access to the courts. The loss of access to the courts in an action for divorce is a right of substantial magnitude when only

through the courts may redress or relief be obtained." Jeffreys v. Jeffreys, 58 Misc.2d 1045, 1056, 296 N.Y.S.2d 74, 87 (1968).

See also Brown v. Chastain, 416 F.2d 1012, 1014 (C.A.5 1969) (Rives, J., dissenting).

9. We think Cohen v. Beneficial Loan Corp., 337 U.S. 541, 69 S.Ct. 1221, 93 L.Ed. 1528 (1949), has no bearing on this case. Differences between divorce actions and derivative actions aside, unlike Cohen, where we considered merely a statute on its face, the application of this statute here operates to cut off entirely access to the courts.

See Mullane v. Central Hanover Tr. Co., supra. We think in this case service at defendant's last known address by mail and posted notice is equally effective as publication in a newspaper.

We are thus left to evaluate the State's asserted interest in its fee and cost requirements as a mechanism of resource allocation or cost recoupment. Such a justification was offered and rejected in Griffin v. Illinois, 351 U.S. 12, 76 S.Ct. 585, 100 L.Ed. 891 (1956). In *Griffin* it was the requirement of a transcript beyond the means of the indigent that blocked access to the judicial process. While in *Griffin* the transcript could be waived as a convenient but not necessary predicate to court access, here the State invariably imposes the costs as a measure of allocating its judicial resources. Surely, then, the rationale of *Griffin* covers this case.

IV

In concluding that the Due Process Clause of the Fourteenth Amendment requires that these appellants be afforded an opportunity to go into court to obtain a divorce, we wish to re-emphasize that we go no further than necessary to dispose of the case before us, a case where the *bona fides* of both appellants' indigency and desire for divorce are here beyond dispute. We do not decide that access for all individuals to the courts is a right that is, in all circumstances, guaranteed by the Due Process Clause of the Fourteenth Amendment so that its exercise may not be placed beyond the reach of any individual, for, as we have already noted, in the case before us this right is the exclusive precondition to the adjustment of a fundamental human relationship. The requirement that these appellants resort to the judicial process is entirely a state-created matter. Thus we hold only that a State may not, consistent with the obligations imposed on it by the Due Process Clause of the Fourteenth Amendment, preempt the right to dissolve this legal relationship without affording all citizens access to the means it has prescribed for doing so.

Reversed.

Mr. Justice DOUGLAS, concurring in the result.

I believe this case should be decided upon the principles developed in the line of cases marked by Griffin v. Illinois, 351 U.S. 12. There we considered a state law which denied persons convicted of a crime full appellate review if they were unable to pay for a transcript of the trial. Mr. Justice BLACK's opinion announcing the judgment of the Court stated:

"Such a denial is a misfit in a country dedicated to affording equal justice to all and special privileges to none in the administration of its criminal law. There can be no equal justice where the kind of a trial a man gets depends on the amount of money he has. Destitute defendants must be afforded as adequate appellate review as defendants who have money enough to buy transcripts." Id., at 19.

Griffin has had a sturdy growth. "Our decisions for more than a decade now have made clear that differences in access to the instruments needed to vindicate legal rights, when based upon the financial situation of the defendant, are repugnant to the Constitution." Roberts v. LaVallee, 389 U.S. 40, 42, 88 S.Ct. 194, 196, 19 L.Ed.2d 41. * * * But *Griffin* has not been limited to securing a record for indigents who appeal their convictions. If the more affluent have counsel on appeal, then counsel for indigents must be provided on appeal of a criminal conviction. Douglas v. California, 372 U.S. 353, 83 S.Ct. 814, 9 L.Ed.2d 811. The tie to *Griffin* was explicit. "In either case [*Griffin* or *Douglas*] the evil is the same: discrimination against the indigent." Id., at 355.

* * *

The reach of the Equal Protection Clause is not definable with mathematical precision. But in spite of doubts by some, as it has been construed, rather definite guidelines have been developed: *race* is one (Strauder v. West Virginia, 100 U.S. 303, 25 L.Ed. 664; McLaughlin v. Florida, 379 U.S. 184); *alienage* is another (Takahashi v. Fish & Game Comm'n, 334 U.S. 410, 68 S.Ct. 1138, 92 L.Ed. 1478); *religion* is another (Sherbert v. Verner, 374 U.S. 398); *poverty* is still another (Griffin v. Illinois, supra); and *class* or *caste* yet another (Skinner v. Oklahoma, 316 U.S. 535, 62 S.Ct. 1110, 86 L.Ed. 1655.

The power of the States over marriage and divorce is, of course, complete except as limited by specific constitutional provisions. * * *

Here the invidious discrimination is based on one of the guidelines: *poverty*.

An invidious discrimination based on poverty is adequate for this case. While Connecticut has provided a procedure for severing the bonds of marriage, a person can meet every requirement save court fees or the cost of service of process and be denied a divorce. Connecticut says in its brief that this is justified because "the State does not favor divorces; and only permits a divorce to be granted when those conditions are found to exist, in respect to one or the other of the named parties, which seem to the legislature to make it probable that the interests of society will be better served and that parties will be happier, and so the better citizens, separate, than if compelled to remain together."

Thus, under Connecticut law divorces may be denied or granted solely on the basis of wealth. Just as denying further judicial review in *Burns* and *Smith*, appellate counsel in *Douglas*, and a transcript in *Griffin* created an invidious distinction based on wealth, so, too, does making the grant or denial of a divorce to turn on the wealth of the parties. Affluence does not pass muster under the Equal Protection Clause for determining who must remain married and who shall be allowed to separate.

NOTES AND QUESTIONS

1. Mr. Justice Brennan in a separate concurrence agreed that procedural due process required the result reached by the majority but rejected the argument that divorce is a special case because of the state's monopoly over one's exit from marriage. In his view all cases should be treated alike in this respect, so that no suit could be put outside the indigent's reach because of the fees imposed. In addition he agreed with the argument based upon the Equal Protection Clause.

Mr. Justice Black dissented, characterizing this as "a strange case and a strange holding". He argued that this civil case should not be controlled by precedents from the criminal law, that this result was inconsistent with Cohen v. Beneficial Industrial Loan Co., cited in footnote 9 of the Court's opinion, and that by this and other decisions both the Due Process and Equal Protection Clauses were given little more content than the judges' sense of fairness.

2. On the remand the State of Connecticut was ordered to permit the plaintiffs to prosecute their divorce action without payment of fees. Boddie v. Connecticut, 329 F.Supp. 844 (D.Conn.1971).

3. What does "indigency" mean, for purposes of applying the *Boddie* rule? Coonce v. Coonce, 356 Mass. 690, 255 N.E.2d 330 (1970); Wilson v. Wilson, 218 Pa.Super. 344, 280 A.2d 665 (1971). Cf. Harris v. Harris, 424 F.2d 806 (D.C.Cir.1970).

4. How is indigency to be determined under this case? Earls v. Superior Court, 6 Cal.3d 109, 490 P.2d 814, 98 Cal.Rptr. 302 (1971); Miserak v. Terrill, 130 Vt. 7, 285 A.2d 753 (1971).

5. In cases where the whereabouts of the defendant is unknown, many state rules of court provide that service shall be by publication in a newspaper. This may involve substantial expense, in many instances a greater expense than the filing fees. Does the *Boddie* case require the state to bear this expense also where the plaintiff is indigent? Hart v. Superior Court, 16 Ariz.App. 184, 492 P.2d 433 (1972); Cohen v. Board of Supervisors for County of Alameda, 20 Cal.App.3d 236, 97 Cal.Rptr. 550 (1971); Ashley v. Superior Court, 82 Wash.2d 188, 509 P.2d 751 (1973). If the state or county is required to bear this expense, the burden may be heavy. Can you see any way of minimizing it?

6. Does it follow from the *Boddie* case that the attorney fees of indigent plaintiffs and defendants in divorce actions must be paid by the state? Would it be a valid response to a claim for attorney fees that the parties could obtain their divorce without relying on an attorney, particularly in a state like California where divorces are granted for marriage breakdown? See In re Smiley, 36 N.Y.2d 433, 369 N.Y.S.2d 87, 330 N.E.2d 53 (1975).

7. Does it follow from the *Boddie* case that filing and other court fees for indigent parties in habeas corpus or other proceedings concerning custody of children must be paid by the state? Attorney fees in such proceedings? Filing fees and attorney fees in proceedings for the collection of maintenance or child support? Cf. United States v. Kras, 409 U.S. 434 (1973), 48 Ind.L.Rev. 452 (1973).

8. Does the distinction made in the *Boddie* case between divorce actions and other civil suits impress you? If the *Boddie* case is right, does the Due Process Clause require the state to waive filing fees in all civil suits? Would you agree with Mr. Justice Black that *Boddie* is inconsistent with Cohen v. Beneficial Industrial Loan Co., in footnote 2 of the court's opinion?

9. Does the reasoning in the *Boddie* case raise any questions about the constitutionality of the choices made by state legislatures concerning the grounds for divorce or procedural limitations upon obtaining a divorce?

SECTION 1. JURISDICTION TO TERMINATE THE MARRIAGE

Statutory Requirements for Divorce Jurisdiction

There are statutes in all states governing jurisdiction to grant divorces. The first inquiry in any divorce action must therefore be, what jurisdictional requirement does the state's legislation make? There is no inherent equity power to grant divorces, so that the courts' authority must be found in the statutes. Chrastka v. Chrastka, 2 Ill.App.3d 722, 277 N.E.2d 729 (1971). Most such statutes provide that the plaintiff in the divorce action must have been a resident of the state for a specified period before bringing the suit. "Residence" in this context is generally construed to mean domicile. Smith v. Smith, 45 Cal.2d 235, 288 P.2d 497 (1955); Annot., 106 A. L.R. 6 (1937) and Annot., 159 A.L.R. 496 (1945). In Illinois, however, the term "residence" in the statute has been construed not to mean "domicile", but the courts define residence in a way not easily distinguishable from domicile. Garrison v. Garrison, 107 Ill.App.2d 311, 246 N.E.2d 9 (1969). But in a few states the period of residence, as distinguished from residence or domicile itself, may not be a jurisdictional requirement. E. g. Lacks v. Lacks, 41 N.Y.2d 71, 390 N.Y.S.2d 875, 359 N.E.2d 384 (1976); Schreiner v. Schreiner, 502 S. W.2d 840 (Tex.Civ.App.1973); Hammond v. Hammond, 45 Wash.2d 855, 278 P.2d 387 (1954) (Idaho law).

Even in Nevada, the most notorious of the divorce mill states, the official position taken in reported cases is that its statute, which requires six weeks' residence for divorce jurisdiction, is to be construed as requiring six weeks' domicile. Nev.Rev.Stat. § 125.020 (1975); Barber v. Barber, 47 Nev. 377, 222 P. 284 (1924); Plunkett v. Plunkett, 71 Nev. 159, 283 P.2d 225 (1955). Nevada's divorce decrees apparently contain findings of domicile, no matter how phony such findings may be. See, e. g., Coe v. Coe, 334 U.S. 378 (1948). Idaho, which also authorizes divorce on six weeks' residence, Idaho Code Ann. § 32–701 (1963), similarly defines residence to mean domicile. Milbourn v. Milbourn, 86 Idaho 213, 384 P.2d 476 (1963); Smestad v. Smestad, 94 Idaho 181, 484 P.2d 730 (1971).

The period of residence required varies from state to state. Perhaps under the influence of the Uniform Marriage and Divorce Act, section 302 of which requires that one of the parties shall have been domiciled in the state only ninety days, the required period of residence has been shortened in many states. See, e. g., Conn.Gen.Stat. § 46b–44 (Supp.1979), reducing the residence requirement from three years to one year, with some qualifications; Cal.Civ.Code § 4530 (1970), reducing it from one year six months. In New York the period is one year where the marriage occurred in the state; or where both parties have resided in the state as husband and wife; or where the grounds for divorce arose in the state. There is no durational requirement at all when the ground for divorce occurred in the state and both parties were residents of the state when the suit was brought. Conversely, if either party has resided in the state for *two* years before the commencement of the action, this by itself is sufficient for jurisdiction under the New York statute. N.Y.Dom.Rel.L. § 230 (1977).

In some states the plaintiff must meet the durational residence requirements. In others it is sufficient if either party to the divorce action has been a resident for the prescribed period.

SOSNA v. IOWA

Supreme Court of the United States, 1975.
419 U.S. 393, 95 S.Ct. 553, 42 L.Ed.2d 532.

Mr. Justice REHNQUIST delivered the opinion of the Court.

[The question before the Court in this case was whether Iowa's statute was constitutional in requiring that a petitioner for divorce be a resident of the state for one year preceding the filing of her petition.]

II

The durational residency requirement under attack in this case is a part of Iowa's comprehensive statutory regulation of domestic relations, an area that has long been regarded as a virtually exclusive province of the States. * * *

The statutory scheme in Iowa, like those in other States, sets forth in considerable detail the grounds upon which a marriage may be dissolved and the circumstances in which a divorce may be obtained. Jurisdiction over a petition for dissolution is established by statute in "the county where either party resides," Iowa Code § 598.2 (1973), and the Iowa courts have construed the term "resident" to have much the same meaning as is ordinarily associated with the concept of domicile. Iowa has recently revised its divorce statutes,

incorporating the no-fault concept, but it retained the one-year durational residency requirement.

* * *

Appellant contends that the Iowa requirement of one year's residence is unconstitutional for two separate reasons: *first,* because it
establishes two classes of persons and discriminates against those
who have recently exercised their right to travel to Iowa, thereby
contravening the Court's holdings in Shapiro v. Thompson, 394 U.S.
618, 89 S.Ct. 1322, 22 L.Ed.2d 600 (1969); Dunn v. Blumstein, 405
U.S. 330, 92 S.Ct. 995, 31 L.Ed.2d 274 (1972); and Memorial Hospital
v. Maricopa County, 415 U.S. 250, 94 S.Ct. 1076, 39 L.Ed.2d 306
(1974); and, *second,* because it denies a litigant the opportunity to
make an individualized showing of bona fide residence and therefore
denies such residents access to the only method of legally dissolving
their marriage. Boddie v. Connecticut, 401 U.S. 371, 91 S.Ct. 780
(1971).

State statutes imposing durational residency requirements were,
of course, invalidated when imposed by States as a qualification for
welfare payments, *Shapiro,* supra; for voting, *Dunn,* supra; and for
medical care, *Maricopa County,* supra. But none of those cases intimated that the States might never impose durational residency requirements, and such a proposition was in fact expressly disclaimed.
What those cases had in common was that the durational residency
requirements they struck down were justified on the basis of budgetary or recordkeeping considerations which were held insufficient to
outweigh the constitutional claims of the individuals. But Iowa's divorce residency requirement is of a different stripe. Appellant was
not irretrievably foreclosed from obtaining some part of what she
sought, as was the case with the welfare recipients in *Shapiro,* the
voters in *Dunn,* or the indigent patient in *Maricopa County.* She
would eventually qualify for the same sort of adjudication which she
demanded virtually upon her arrival in the State. Iowa's requirement delayed her access to the courts, but, by fulfilling it, she could
ultimately have obtained the same opportunity for adjudication which
she asserts ought to have been hers at an earlier point in time.

Iowa's residency requirement may reasonably be justified on
grounds other than purely budgetary considerations or administrative
convenience. A decree of divorce is not a matter in which the only
interested parties are the State as a sort of "grantor," and a divorce
petitioner such as appellant in the role of "grantee." Both spouses
are obviously interested in the proceedings, since it will affect their
marital status and very likely their property rights. Where a married couple has minor children, a decree of divorce would usually include provisions for their custody and support. With consequences of
such moment riding on a divorce decree issued by its courts, Iowa
may insist that one seeking to initiate such a proceeding have the
modicum of attachment to the State required here.

Such a requirement additionally furthers the State's parallel interests both in avoiding officious intermeddling in matters in which another State has a paramount interest, and in minimizing the susceptibility of its own divorce decrees to collateral attack. A State such as Iowa may quite reasonably decide that it does not wish to become a divorce mill for unhappy spouses who have lived there as short a time as appellant had when she commenced her action in the state court after having long resided elsewhere. Until such time as Iowa is convinced that appellant intends to remain in the State, it lacks the "nexus between person and place of such permanence as to control the creation of legal relations and responsibilities of the utmost significance." Williams v. North Carolina, 325 U.S. 226, 229, 65 S.Ct. 1092, 1095, 89 L.Ed. 1577 (1945). Perhaps even more important, Iowa's interests extend beyond its borders and include the recognition of its divorce decrees by other States under the Full Faith and Credit Clause of the Constitution, Art. IV, § 1. For that purpose, this Court has often stated that "judicial power to grant a divorce—jurisdiction, strictly speaking—is founded on domicil." Williams, supra. Where a divorce decree is entered after a finding of domicile in ex parte proceedings, this Court has held that the finding of domicile is not binding upon another State and may be disregarded in the face of "cogent evidence" to the contrary. Williams, supra, 325 U.S. at 236, 65 S.Ct. at 1098. For that reason, the State asked to enter such a decree is entitled to insist that the putative divorce petitioner satisfy something more than the bare minimum of constitutional requirements before a divorce may be granted. The State's decision to exact a one-year residency requirement as a matter of policy is therefore buttressed by a quite permissible inference that this requirement not only effectuates state substantive policy but likewise provides a greater safeguard against successful collateral attack than would a requirement of bona fide residence alone. This is precisely the sort of determination that a State in the exercise of its domestic relations jurisdiction is entitled to make.

We therefore hold that the state interest in requiring that those who seek a divorce from its courts be genuinely attached to the State, as well as a desire to insulate divorce decrees from the likelihood of collateral attack, requires a different resolution of the constitutional issue presented than was the case in Shapiro, supra, Dunn, supra, and Maricopa County, supra.

Nor are we of the view that the failure to provide an individualized determination of residency violates the Due Process Clause of the Fourteenth Amendment. * * * An individualized determination of physical presence plus the intent to remain, which appellant apparently seeks, would not entitle her to a divorce even if she could have made such a showing.[22] For Iowa requires not merely "domicile" in that sense, but residence in the State for a year in order for its courts to exercise their divorce jurisdiction.

In Boddie v. Connecticut, supra, this Court held that Connecticut might not deny access to divorce courts to those persons who could not afford to pay the required fee. Because of the exclusive role played by the State in the termination of marriages, it was held that indigents could not be denied an opportunity to be heard "absent a countervailing state interest of overriding significance." 401 U.S., at 377, 91 S.Ct., at 785. But the gravamen of appellant Sosna's claim is not total deprivation, as in *Boddie,* but only delay. The operation of the filing fee in *Boddie* served to exclude forever a certain segment of the population from obtaining a divorce in the courts of Connecticut. No similar total deprivation is present in appellant's case, and the delay which attends the enforcement of the one-year durational residency requirement is, for the reasons previously stated, consistent with the provisions of the United States Constitution.

Affirmed.

* * *

NOTES & QUESTIONS

1. Justices White, Marshall and Brennan dissented in this case.

2. If the right to marry is a "fundamental right", as seems to be the purport of Griswold v. Connecticut, supra, page 73, and Zablocki v. Redhail, supra, page 83, is the right not to be married, i. e. the right to a divorce, likewise a "fundamental right"? Does Sosna throw any light on this question?

3. Does this case validate durational residency requirements longer than one year? Would it validate the elaborate distinctions made by the New York statute which is summarized, supra, page 789?

NOTE ON FEDERAL JURISDICTION
IN DOMESTIC RELATIONS CASES

On the face of the Constitution and the statutes, it would appear that if the parties were citizens of different states, and if the prescribed amount were in controversy, the federal courts should have jurisdiction to grant divorces. U.S.Const. art. III, § 2, cl. 1; 28 U.S. C.A. § 1332. As a result of dicta in a number of Supreme Court opinions, however, it is settled that the federal courts do not have jurisdiction to grant divorces or alimony. Barber v. Barber, 62 U.S.

22. In addition to a showing of residence within the State for a year, Iowa Code § 598.6 (1973) requires any petition for dissolution to state "that the maintenance of the residence has been in good faith and not for the purpose of obtaining a marriage dissolution only." In dismissing appellant's petition in state court, Judge Keck observed that appellant had failed to allege good-faith residence. (Jurisdictional Statement App.B. 2).

(21 How.) 582 (1859); Simms v. Simms, 175 U.S. 162 (1899); De La Rama v. De La Rama, 201 U.S. 303 (1906); State of Ohio ex rel. Popovici v. Agler, 280 U.S. 379 (1930). See also In re Burrus, 136 U.S. 586 (1890).

But the Supreme Court does hear appeals in divorce actions from the territorial courts and from the Court of Appeals for the District of Columbia. Simms v. Simms, supra, and Bottomley v. Bottomley, 104 U.S.App.D.C. 311, 262 F.2d 23 (1958), so that such cases apparently fall within the federal judicial power.

The reasons for the view that there is no federal jurisdiction to grant divorces or award alimony are not clear. The dissent in Barber v. Barber, supra, suggested it is because the federal courts' jurisdiction extends to all cases in law and equity, and divorce and alimony are neither law nor equity, being branches of the English ecclesiastical courts' powers historically. The same reason probably underlies the familiar doctrine that the state courts have no divorce jurisdiction without specific statutory authority. Other reasons for refusing federal jurisdiction in these cases which are relied upon by contemporary cases include the state courts' expertise in domestic relations and the federal courts' lack of expertise, the increase in docket congestion which would result if the federal courts entered the field, and the danger of conflict between state and federal courts. Crouch v. Crouch, 566 F.2d 486 (5th Cir. 1978).

The problem which this creates is how the scope of the exception to federal jurisdiction is to be determined in specific cases. In Spindel v. Spindel, 283 F.Supp. 797 (E.D.N.Y.1968), 44 N.Y.U.L.Rev. 631 (1969), 55 Va.L.Rev. 361 (1969), the court denied a motion to dismiss a suit by a wife to recover damages from her husband on the ground that he had fraudulently induced her to marry him. In the same suit she asked for a declaratory judgment that a Mexican divorce obtained by her husband was invalid. Diversity of citizenship and amount in controversy were present. The court said that any broad disclaimer of federal jurisdiction over domestic relations cases was unwarranted.

Cases since Spindel have for the most part refused to expand federal jurisdiction over what might be called domestic relations cases. Thus Huynh Thi Anh v. Levi, 586 F.2d 625 (6th Cir. 1978) dismissed a petition for habeas corpus seeking custody of Viet Namese children placed for adoption in the United States. Bossom v. Bossom, 551 F. 2d 474 (2d Cir. 1976) refused federal jurisdiction in a suit by a husband against his wife attacking a stipulation incorporated in a divorce decree. The stipulation involved both child support and visitation rights. The court disclaimed jurisdiction of cases which it characterized as "on the verge" of matrimonial actions. And in Phillips, Nizer, Benjamin, Krim & Ballon v. Rosenstiel, 490 F.2d 509 (2d Cir. 1973), after an extensive discussion by Judge Friendly, the court found that there was jurisdiction of a lawyer's claim against a husband for legal fees pursuant to the doctrine of necessaries, but indicated that a motion to stay the case pending state court proceedings would have been granted if it had been made at the proper time. See also Solomon v. Solomon, 516 F.2d 1018 (3d Cir. 1975), relying on the *Phillips, Nizer* case.

Federal courts will occasionally hear cases touching on domestic relations issues, however. For example, Zimmermann v. Zimmermann, 395 F.Supp. 719 (E.D.Pa.1975) took jurisdiction of a suit by a wife against her husband for breach of an agreement for support which had been incorporated in a divorce decree. The court emphasized that in this case no issues of custody were involved, the parties had been separated for nine years and there was no pending state court proceeding. And Bergstrom v. Bergstrom, 478 F.Supp. 434 (D.N.D.1979) asserted federal jurisdiction under 28 U.S.C.A. § 1331(a) and the Fifth Amendment to enter a decree which had the effect of granting custody of a child to her father after custody had been granted to her mother by a court of the District of Columbia.

One particular aspect of divorce jurisdiction involves both state and federal law. This is the question of what courts have jurisdiction to grant divorces to American Indians. Under some circumstances at least a marriage of Indians may be dissolved by an Indian divorce. Voorhees v. Spencer, 89 Nev. 1, 504 P.2d 1321 (1972). Whether the state courts may grant divorces to Indians depends upon the existence of treaties dealing with the question, upon federal statutes and upon enactments of the various tribes. See, e. g., Bad Horse v. Bad Horse, 163 Mont. 445, 517 P.2d 893 (1974), cert. den. 419 U.S. 847 (1974), 51 N.D.L.Rev. 217 (1974) (state court had jurisdiction where the marriage of Indians took place off the reservation); State ex rel. Iron Bear v. District Court, 162 Mont. 335, 512 P.2d 1292 (1973) (state court has jurisdiction where the federal treaties and statutes have not preempted jurisdiction, where the state's exercise of jurisdiction would not interfere with reservation self-government, and where the Tribal Court is not exercising jurisdiction in such a manner as to preempt state jurisdiction). Cf. Fisher v. District Court, 424 U.S. 382 (1976), holding that a Tribal Court had exclusive jurisdiction in an adoption proceeding arising on the reservation in which all parties were tribal members residing on the reservation.

NOTE ON THE EFFECT OF THE FULL FAITH AND CREDIT CLAUSE ON JURISDICTION TO DISSOLVE MARRIAGES

The common law principles governing jurisdiction to grant divorces largely developed in the days when migratory divorce was an important feature of divorce practice. When the laws of most states permitted divorce only upon proof of such grounds as adultery, desertion or cruelty, or (in the case of New York) on proof of adultery alone, many residents of those states yielded to the temptation produced by the offer of a quickie divorce on trivial grounds made in such places as Nevada, Idaho, Florida, Alabama or the Virgin Islands. Avoidance of waiting periods or long interlocutory periods, or of local notoriety was also a reason for getting a divorce away from home, as was the desire of some husbands to evade financial responsibility to their wives.   This not uncommon practice of seeking the benefits of migratory divorce led to much litigation over the validity of divorces so obtained and ultimately to a line of decisions in the United States Supreme Court which laid down some rules concerning the interstate recognition of divorce decrees.   These decisions had the effect of establishing the bases on which the courts in the various states could terminate the marital status of litigants coming before them.

Although some people still seek the benefits (such as they are) of migratory divorce, the enactment in many states of statutes authorizing divorce for marriage breakdown or other non-fault and liberal grounds has sharply reduced its incidence and thus its importance in the lives of the unhappily married.   For this reason the reproduction of these Supreme Court cases has been omitted from these materials.   Instead the attempt is made in this note to state the essential doctrines of the cases, following which some of their implications are explored by means of questions and problems.

The development of modern doctrines began with the *Williams* cases, Williams v. State of North Carolina, 317 U.S. 287 (1942) (Williams I), and Williams v. State of North Carolina, 325 U.S. 226 (1945) (Williams II).   Both cases arose out of the same circumstances.   Two married residents of North Carolina, Mr. Williams and Mrs. Hendrix, went to Las Vegas and obtained Nevada divorces from their respective spouses.   Neither of the spouses was personally served in Nevada, nor did either spouse enter an appearance in the divorce actions.   Service was by publication in a Las Vegas paper, by mailing copies of the summons and complaint to a defendant in North Carolina, and by delivery of copies of the summons and complaint to a defendant in North Carolina.   In granting the divorces the Nevada court made findings that the plaintiffs were bona fide residents of Nevada and had been residents of the state for six weeks prior to the commencement of the suits.   Mr. Williams and Mrs. Hendrix married each other in Nevada as soon as the divorces were granted and returned to North Carolina where they lived together until they were both indicted for bigamous cohabitation.   They were convicted and the conviction was affirmed by the North Carolina Supreme Court. The case come to the United States Supreme Court on certiorari, where the convictions were reversed in Williams I.

The Supreme Court held that domicile of the plaintiff is the basis for jurisdiction over the subject matter of divorce at least for purposes of entitling the divorce decree to recognition in other states.

Since the record in the North Carolina proceeding contained no evidence that Mr. Williams and Mrs. Hendrix were not domiciled in Nevada, and since the Nevada decree contained a finding that they were domiciled there, the Supreme Court felt itself required to assume that they did have a Nevada domicile. Therefore the Court held that Nevada did have jurisdiction to grant the divorce. That being so, North Carolina was required to recognize the divorce under Article IV, section 1 of the United States Constitution, the Full Faith and Credit Clause, which provides: "Full Faith and Credit shall be given in each State to the public Acts, Records, and Judicial Proceedings of every other State * * *." The statute implementing this Clause, 28 U. S.C.A. § 687, now 28 U.S.C.A. § 1738 has been amended somewhat since Williams I was decided, but its essential meaning remains about the same. It now provides, in relevant part:

> "Such Acts, records and judicial proceedings * * * shall have the same full faith and credit in every court within the United States and its Territories and Possessions as they have by law or usage in the courts of such State, Territory or Possession from which they are taken."

In the course of holding that the state of the plaintiff's domicile may grant a divorce which must be recognized in all other states, the Court overruled Haddock v. Haddock, 201 U.S. 562 (1906) which had held that only the state of the "matrimonial domicile" could enter a divorce decree which would be entitled to full faith and credit in other states. The Supreme Court also, in its Williams I opinion, referred to the traditional notion that a divorce suit is a proceeding in rem, but suggested that placing the in rem label on the case does not aid in determining what the rules for subject matter jurisdiction should be. The Restatement, Second, Conflict of Laws § 71 (1971) has adopted the rule of Williams I, with a slight change, providing that "A state has power to exercise judicial jurisdiction to dissolve the marriage of spouses one of whom is domiciled in the state." Thus the Restatement takes the view, which many cases would doubtless agree with, that the domicile of *either* the plaintiff or the defendant has jurisdiction to grant a divorce. In fact some expressions in Williams I indicate that the domicile of either spouse has jurisdiction to grant a divorce which must be recognized elsewhere. The policy reason for this rule, according to the Supreme Court, is that domicile constitutes a relationship between person and state sufficient to give the state an interest in controlling the person's marital status.

Williams I, in the course of deciding when a divorce decree is entitled to full faith and credit in states other than the forum, announced that domicile is required for subject matter jurisdiction over divorce proceedings. There is of course the further requirement, common to all proceedings, that reasonable notice of the suit be given to the defendant. Mullane v. Central Hanover Bank & Trust Co., 339

U.S. 306 (1950); Dillon v. Dillon, 46 Wis.2d 659, 176 N.W.2d 362 (1970). That notice was present in Williams I. The opinion implies also that if domicile and adequate notice are present, personal service within the divorcing jurisdiction, or its equivalent, need not be had. In other words, some form of substituted service, if reasonable under the circumstances, is sufficient for divorce. In personam jurisdiction was not present in Nevada when Mr. Williams and Mrs. Hendrix obtained their divorces, but notice was given to the absent spouses by mail and by service in North Carolina.

One further point, not involved in Williams I explicitly, but underlying the attraction of migratory divorce, relates to the applicable law in divorce suits. It is well established, but for reasons which remain obscure, that the law governing the grounds for divorce in divorce proceedings is the law of the forum, even though the suit involves conduct of the parties occurring entirely in some other state. This meant in Williams I, for example, that Nevada would rely upon its law in determining whether grounds for divorce existed notwithstanding that the events leading to the divorce took place exclusively in North Carolina. Restatement, Second, Conflict of Laws § 285 (1971).

As a result of Williams I, the case was remanded to the North Carolina courts. After a second trial at which the State argued that the defendants had never acquired a bona fide domicile in Nevada and that therefore their divorces were invalid, the jury entered another verdict of guilty, which was affirmed by the North Carolina Supreme Court. The United States Supreme Court affirmed the conviction in Williams v. North Carolina, 325 U.S. 226 (1945) (Williams II). The Court's opinion reiterated the proposition that jurisdiction to grant a divorce is founded upon domicile. Although the Nevada court's finding of Nevada domicile was "entitled to respect and more", North Carolina could reexamine that finding. In doing so, the North Carolina court gave appropriate weight to the Nevada finding of domicile and the jury could properly decide that the defendants never acquired a Nevada domicile.

The effect of Williams II was that an ex parte divorce need not be given full faith and credit if not based on domicile of one of the parties. A state in which such a divorce is attacked must give weight to the finding of domicile by the divorcing court, but if, after doing so, it finds that the evidence proves that neither spouse was domiciled in the divorcing state, it may refuse to recognize the divorce.

Two subsequent cases, Sherrer v. Sherrer, 334 U.S. 343 (1948) and Johnson v. Muelberger, 340 U.S. 581 (1951) added important qualifications to the doctrines of *Williams* I and II. *Sherrer* involved a Florida divorce obtained by a wife who had been domiciled in Massachusetts. The husband appeared in the Florida suit and participated in it but did not attempt to rebut the wife's assertion of a Florida domicile. The Florida court found that the wife was domiciled in Florida. The Supreme Court held that the husband could not later, in a proceeding in Massachusetts, attack Florida's jurisdiction. The reason given was that he had participated in the Florida proceeding, he could have litigated the question of the wife's domicile, and not having done so, he was barred from attacking Florida's finding of domicile by doctrines of res judicata. Thus Massachusetts had to give full faith and credit to the Florida divorce.

Johnson v. Muelberger extended the doctrine of the *Sherrer* case by applying it to persons not parties to the divorce under attack. Bruce Johnson had a daughter, Eleanor, by his first marriage. When his first wife died, Bruce married Madoline and lived with her in New York. Madoline then got a Florida divorce from Bruce without acquiring a Florida domicile. Bruce appeared in the Florida proceeding through an attorney, but he did not raise the question of domicile and the Florida court made a finding of domicile. Following the divorce Bruce married Genevieve and then died, leaving all his property to Eleanor. Genevieve elected to take her statutory forced share under New York law. The election was contested by Eleanor, who claimed Bruce's divorce from Madoline was invalid, and that therefore his third marriage to Genevieve was invalid. The Supreme Court held that under *Sherrer*, Bruce could not have attacked Florida's finding of domicile since he had participated in the Florida proceedings. It also found that Florida would not permit a third party such as Eleanor to attack the decree under these circumstances. That being so, New York could not permit the attack either, under the Full Faith and Credit Clause.

Restatement, Second, Conflict of Laws § 73 (1971) follows the *Sherrer* and *Johnson* cases. As that section of the Restatement says, the rule of those cases has been applied by the Supreme Court to cover all situations in which the defendant spouse in the divorce proceeding was personally subject to the divorce court's jurisdiction. Cook v. Cook, 342 U.S. 126 (1951).

In addition to the migratory divorces offered by American states, the years after World War II saw Mexico making such divorces available, up until March 7, 1971. The unhappily married could, until that date, get a Mexican divorce by mail order without ever going to Mexico; they could get one ex parte when the plaintiff alone went to Mexico; and they could get a divorce on the *Sherrer* model, with the plaintiff going to Mexico and the defendant entering an appearance in the suit either by going there in person or by having an attorney represent him. Since the Full Faith and Credit Clause had no application to such divorces, the only question they raised was whether American states would recognize them as a matter of comity. Mail order divorces were generally not recognized at all, although as will later appear, under some circumstances and in some states the parties might be estopped to attack them. Rosenbaum v. Rosenbaum, 309 N.Y. 371, 130 N.E.2d 902 (1955). Likewise Mexican divorces in which only one spouse went to Mexico generally were not recognized. Caldwell v. Caldwell, 298 N.Y. 146, 81 N.E.2d 60 (1948). But New York did recognize a Mexican divorce in which the husband went to Mexico, signed the book of residents of Juarez, which by Mexican law established Mexican residence, and in which the wife then filed a general appearance in the Mexican court through an attorney, filed an answer and submitted to the Mexican court's jurisdiction. Rosenstiel v. Rosenstiel, 16 N.Y.2d 64, 262 N.Y S.2d 86, 209 N.E.2d 709 (1965), cert. den. 383 U.S. 943 (1966). The New York court reasoned that the Mexican proceeding had the character of a judicial action, the husband acquired Mexico's version of residence, carrying the legal incidents of the marriage with him, the wife submitted to the Mexican jurisdiction, and the public interest of New York was no more greatly prejudiced by the formality of a one day "residence" in Mexico than it would be by a six weeks "residence" in Nevada. Other state courts would not recognize this type of Mexican divorce, however. E. g., Steffke v. Steffke, 65 Wis.2d 199, 222 N.W.2d 628 (1974).

Since Mexico in effect abolished migratory divorce as of March 7, 1971 by making it much more difficult to establish a Mexican residence, the migratory divorce traffic has moved to the Dominican Republic where divorces are now available without any period of residence if both spouses submit to the jurisdiction, on grounds of "incompatibility of temperaments". Whether these divorces are to be recognized by the various states is governed by the authorities dealing with Mexican divorces. A case which did recognize a Dominican divorce is Hyde v. Hyde, 562 S.W.2d 194 (Tenn.1978). Cases refusing recognition include Everett v. Everett, 345 So.2d 586 (La.App.1977); Weber v. Weber, 200 Neb. 659, 265 N.W.2d 436 (1978). For general discussion of comity for foreign judgments, see Chaudry v. Chaudry, 159 N.J.Super. 566, 388 A.2d 1000 (1978), cert. den. 78 N.J. 335, 395 A.2d 204 (1978) (recognizing a Pakistani divorce); Peterson, Foreign Country Judgments and the Second Restatement of Conflict of Laws, 72 Colum.L.Rev. 220 (1972); Restatement, Second, Conflict of Laws § 98 (1971).

Although the Supreme Court, in *Williams I* and *II*, emphasized that jurisdiction for divorce is based upon the domicile of one spouse within the state, it was writing in a context in which the question was interstate recognition of divorce under the Full Faith and Credit Clause. The question which remains to be answered is whether a state may, consistent with the United States Constitution, grant a divorce where neither spouse is domiciled within its borders. In other words, even if such a divorce would not be entitled to interstate recognition under the Full Faith and Credit Clause, would the state be violating the Constitution merely by authorizing it to be granted when neither spouse is a domiciliary? One well known decision, Alton v. Alton, 207 F.2d 667 (3d Cir. 1953), held that a Virgin Islands statute authorizing a divorce without domicile where both spouses were personally subject to the court's jurisdiction violated the Due Process Clause of the Fourteenth Amendment. The *Alton* opinion is unsatisfactory for its failure to explain in what respect such a statute could be said to deprive either party of due process. The court also relied for its result on the desirability of removing the evils of migratory divorce and on the argument that since *Williams* I and II would deny full faith and credit to the divorces authorized by the statute, such decrees should not be entered in the first place.

The Uniform Marriage and Divorce Act § 302, 9A Unif.L.Ann. 121 (1971) raises the same question as that in *Alton*. It authorizes divorces for service men who have been stationed in the state for ninety days next preceding the date of the court's findings in the suit. Most of the cases in which these service men's statutes have come have held them constitutional. See In re Marriage of Ways, 85 Wash.2d 693, 538 P.2d 1225 (1976), 52 Wash.L.Rev. 369 (1977) (dictum) and cases collected in Annot., 73 A.L.R.3d 431 (1976). These cases seem inconsistent with *Alton* although they are distinguishable in that the contact with the state required by the service men's statutes is greater than in *Alton* and in that the service men's statutes do not encourage forum-shopping or migratory divorce. The Restatement, Second, Conflict of Laws § 72 (1971) evades the issue by stating that a state may exercise judicial jurisdiction to dissolve the marriage of spouses neither of whom is domiciled in the state if either spouse has such a relationship to the state as to make such a dissolution "reasonable", but the Reporter's Note to the section seems to approve of the service men's statutes and other non-domicile bases for jurisdiction over divorce.

If the cases upholding the service men's statutes are correct, they will be in the position of granting divorce decrees which, under *Williams I* and *II*, are not entitled to full faith and credit in other states. For this reason one case, Viernes v. District Court, 181 Colo. 284, 509 P.2d 306 (1973), in order to avoid constitutional questions, construed the Uniform Act to require that the service man be domiciled within the state before he could be granted a divorce. Even if full faith and credit were not required for divorces granted under the Uniform Act provision or similar statutes adopting jurisdictional bases other than domicile, such divorces could be recognized in other states as a matter of comity without violation of any constitutional principle. For that reason the objection to such statutes and decrees pursuant to them may not have as much practical significance as might otherwise appear.

NOTES AND QUESTIONS

1. Who has standing to attack a divorce decree on jurisdictional grounds? H marries W–1 in New York, where they live. He then obtains a Nevada divorce from her, spending only the required six weeks in Nevada. He returns to New York and marries W–2, who dies shortly thereafter. H then marries W–3 in New York. After some years W–3 consults an attorney who tells her H's Nevada divorce was invalid. W–3 then sues H in New York, asking a declaratory judgment that his divorce from W–1 was invalid, so that his marriage to W–3 is also invalid, W–1 being still alive. Does W–3 have standing to make this claim? Or, if H died, W–1 already having died, could H's brother attack the divorce from W–1, in order to make good his claim to inherit from H, in opposition to W–3? Could children of the second marriage attack the divorce in order to inherit from H? Rappel v. Rappel, 39 Misc.2d 222, 240 N.Y.S.2d 692 (Sup.Ct.1963), aff'd p. c., 20 A.D.2d 850, 247 N.Y.S.2d 995 (1st Dep't 1964); Porter v. Hawkins, 240 So.2d 912 (La.App.1970); Old Colony Trust Co. v. Porter, 324 Mass. 581, 88 N.E.2d 135 (1949); Bair v. Bair, 91 Idaho 30, 415 P.2d 673 (1966); Annot., 12 A.L.R.2d 717, 723, 733 (1950); Note, 50 Colum.L.Rev. 833 (1950). What reasons dictate granting or denying standing to sue in this situation?

Would it matter, in the preceding situation that the attack on the divorce is made in a third state, say New Jersey? Meeker v. Meeker, 52 N. J. 59, 243 A.2d 801 (1968).

2. H obtains a divorce in Nevada, ex parte, W being served by registered mail at her home in New York. W does not appear or participate in the Nevada proceeding. Immediately thereafter W sues H in New York and obtains, on the authority of *Williams II*, a declaratory judgment that the Nevada decree was void for lack of jurisdiction, the New York court finding that H was at all times domiciled in New York. In this proceeding service is on H under N.Y.Civ.Prac.L. & R. § 313 by delivery of process to him in Nevada by a deputy sheriff, a service which under the New York rule cited gives personal jurisdiction over a domiciliary. W then sues H in Nevada asking for a declaratory judgment on the same terms as the New York judgment, to the effect that she and H are still married. Assuming that such relief is procedurally available in Nevada, what result? See Sutton v. Leib, 342 U.S. 402 (1952); Southard v. Southard, 305 F.2d 730 (2d Cir. 1962); Rocker v. Celebrezze, 358 F.2d 119 (2d Cir. 1966); Porter v. Porter, 101 Ariz. 131, 416 P.2d 564 (1966), cert. den. 386 U.S. 957 (1967), reh. den. 386 U.S. 1027 (1967); Colby v. Colby, 78 Nev. 150, 369 P.2d 1019 (1962), cert. den. 371 U.S. 888 (1962), 63 Colum.L.Rev. 560 (1963); Kram v. Kram, 52 N.J. 545, 247 A.2d 316 (1968); Kessler v. Fauquier Nat. Bank, 195 Va. 1095, 81 S.E.2d 440 (1954), cert. den. 348 U.S. 834 (1954), 68 Harv.L.Rev. 719 (1955); Layton v. Layton, 538 S.W.2d 642 (Tex.Civ.App. 1976), 55 Tex.L.Rev. 127 (1976); Note, 82 Harv.L.Rev. 798 (1969).

3. W brought an action for divorce in Oklahoma, the state of her domicile, serving H personally in the state. Before the action came to trial H moved to Texas and acquired a domicile there. He then sued for divorce in Texas, serving W by registered mail, and was granted a divorce by the Texas court. H did not inform the Texas court of the pending action in Oklahoma. H then filed a motion to dismiss in the Oklahoma case, attaching a

copy of the Texas decree and arguing that Oklahoma must recognize that decree. What should be the outcome? Meeks v. Meeks, 384 P.2d 902 (Okl.1963), 49 Iowa L.Rev. 915 (1964). Cf. Friedland v. Friedland, 295 F. Supp. 237 (D.Virgin Is.1968).

4. H and W were married and lived in Pennsylvania. As a result of a marital quarrel one day H packed up his clothes and angrily left the house, shouting that he was going to Nevada to get a divorce. Next day W consulted a lawyer who advised her, first, that if H got a Nevada divorce ex parte which was recognized as valid in Pennsylvania, this would terminate any claim for support which W might have against him, and, second, that they could obtain an injunction which would prevent H from getting the Nevada divorce. Assume that the advice concerning the effect of the Nevada divorce on W's right to support in Pennsylvania is correct, as it seems to be. (Esenwein v. Commonwealth, 325 U.S. 279, 280 (1945); Commonwealth ex rel. McCormack v. McCormack, 164 Pa.Super. 553, 67 A.2d 603 (1949)).

(a) Could W persuade a court to enjoin H from obtaining a Nevada divorce? What general rationale for equity's authority to grant injunctions applies here, if any? What evidence would W have to produce to get such an injunction? Would H's angry statement be sufficient, or would something more be required? See, e. g., Baumann v. Baumann, 250 N.Y. 382, 165 N.E. 819 (1929), 43 Harv.L.Rev. 477 (1930); Garvin v. Garvin, 302 N. Y. 96, 96 N.E.2d 721 (1951); Martin v. Martin, 62 Misc.2d 703, 309 N.Y.S. 2d 477 (Sup.Ct.1970); Monihan v. Monihan, 438 Pa. 380, 264 A.2d 653 (1970), 32 U.Pitts.L.Rev. 92 (1970). Would a federal court grant such an injunction? Rosenstiel v. Rosenstiel, 278 F.Supp. 794 (S.D.N.Y.1967); 28 U.S.C.A. § 2283.

(b) Should the court issue the injunction even though H testifies that he intends to make a bona fide change of domicile to Nevada? Monihan v. Monihan, 438 Pa. 380, 385, 264 A.2d 653, 655 (1970) (concurring opinion).

(c) Should such an injunction be granted when H's intention is to get a divorce in Haiti or the Dominican Republic rather than Nevada? Rosenbaum v. Rosenbaum, 309 N.Y. 371, 130 N.E.2d 902 (1955), 69 Harv.L.Rev. 1327 (1956); Arpels v. Arpels, 8 N.Y.2d 339, 207 N.Y.S.2d 663, 170 N.E.2d 670 (1960). If it were granted and H consulted you on the eve of his departure from home for Reno, how would you advise him?

(d) Would the grant of such an injunction violate the constitutional right of freedom to travel? Monihan v. Monihan, 438 Pa. 380, 385, 264 A.2d 653, 655 (1970) (concurring opinion).

(e) How must H be served with process in such an injunction suit? Foris v. Foris, 103 N.J.Super. 316, 247 A.2d 156 (1968).

(f) If the Pennsylvania court should grant an injunction, would Nevada be required to enforce it by refusing to hear H's suit for divorce? Would it be entitled to Full Faith and Credit? Rapoport v. Rapoport, 273 F.Supp. 482 (D.Nev.1967), rev'd for lack of amount in controversy, 416 F. 2d 41 (9th Cir. 1969); R. Leflar, Conflict of Laws §§ 53, 73 (1959); G. Stumberg, Principles of Conflict of Laws 120–127 (3d ed. 1963). Would Nevada be likely to honor the Pennsylvania injunction as a matter of comity? Corbin v. Corbin, 26 Conn.Supp. 443, 226 A.2d 799 (1967), various motions denied 155 Conn. 714, 229 A.2d 701 (1967), 155 Conn. 716, 230 A.

2d 438 (1967), 156 Conn. 642, 237 A.2d 371 (1968), 156 Conn. 660, 241 A.2d 878 (1968); Cunningham v. Cunningham, 25 Conn.Supp. 221, 200 A.2d 734 (1964); Seabrook v. Seabrook, 264 A.2d 311 (D.C.Ct.App.1970); Abney v. Abney, —— Ind.App. ——, 374 N.E.2d 264 (1978), cert. den. 439 U.S. 1069 (1979), 17 J.Fam.L. 387 (1978).

(g) If W should attempt to persuade the Nevada court to honor the Pennsylvania injunction, would she be running a risk that the rule of Sherrer v. Sherrer, would be applied against her in subsequent Pennsylvania litigation?

(h) If W fails or is unable to have Nevada recognize the Pennsylvania injunction, what effect does the injunction have in Pennsylvania, for example if H should return to Pennsylvania with his Nevada decree? Lawler v. Lawler, 2 N.J. 527, 66 A.2d 855 (1949); Dominick v. Dominick, 26 Misc.2d 344, 205 N.Y.S.2d 503 (Sup.Ct.1960); Annot., 74 A.L.R.2d 828 (1960); Stambaugh v. Stambaugh, 458 Pa. 147, 329 A.2d 483 (1974).

(i) In view of your response to the foregoing issues, would you advise W in this case to sue for an injunction in Pennsylvania as her lawyer did? If not, what should she do?

5. What is the prevailing rule of res judicata in general, as to jurisdictional questions which the party had "full opportunity" to litigate in the first suit but did not: May they be litigated in the second suit? Does this depend upon the importance which we attribute to matters of jurisdiction as compared with the importance of leaving at rest controversies which have been finally decided? Which is more important to our legal system, leaving such controversies at rest, or upsetting a decision made by a court which did not have authority to make it? The case commonly cited as stating the general rule on this issue of res judicata is Chicot County Drainage District v. Baxter State Bank, 308 U.S. 371 (1940). See also Note, 49 Yale L.J. 959 (1940). Assuming that the *Chicot County* case is correct and applies between states as well as between federal courts, should the rule be the same for matrimonial litigation?

6. In general, what meaning should be given to the presumed rationale of *Sherrer* and *Johnson*, that is, that subsequent attack is foreclosed because the party attacking had a full opportunity to raise the jurisdictional issue in the divorce case and failed to do so? In this connection, consider the following:

(a) H and W are married and live in New Jersey. H desires a divorce but has no grounds in New Jersey. W has no objection to his getting a divorce, and she agrees to cooperate in his obtaining a Nevada decree. H goes to Nevada and employs an attorney. The attorney draws up a document entitled "Waiver of Service, Entry of Appearance and Consent to Decree", which recites that W waives any service of process, enters her personal appearance in the action and consents to entry of the divorce decree at once. The attorney mails this document to W, accompanied by a summons and copy of the divorce complaint. She signs it and has it acknowledged, returns it and the attorney files it in the divorce action. Promptly on the expiration of six weeks, H receives his decree and takes the first plane back to New Jersey, on his arrival marrying his secretary. May W then attack the divorce in New Jersey, or must New Jersey give full faith and credit to the Nevada decree? Does the reliance upon the document which W signed

to establish personal jurisdiction meet the requirements of the Due Process
Clause?   Cf. D. H. Overmyer, Inc., of Ohio v. Frick Co., 405 U.S. 174
(1972); National Equipment Rental Ltd. v. Szukhent, 375 U.S. 311 (1964);
Somportex Ltd. v. Philadelphia Chewing Gum Corp., 453 F.2d 435 (3d Cir.
1971).   Does it make much sense to talk of an opportunity to litigate jurisdiction when both parties wanted the decree and cooperated to get it?   Eaton v. Eaton, 227 La. 992, 81 So.2d 371 (1955); Day v. Day, 237 Md. 229,
205 A.2d 798 (1965), 65 Colum.L.Rev. 924 (1965); Zenker v. Zenker, 161
Neb. 200, 72 N.W.2d 809 (1955), 69 Harv.L.Rev. 1325 (1956); Schlemm v.
Schlemm, 31 N.J. 557, 158 A.2d 508 (1960); Staedler v. Staedler, 6 N.J.
380, 78 A.2d 896 (1951), 31 B.U.L.Rev. 422 (1952); Davis v. Davis, 259
Wis. 1, 47 N.W.2d 338 (1951); Note, 34 Ind.L.J. 592 (1959).   Whose law
should govern i) whether such a procedure subjects W to the court's personal jurisdiction, and ii) whether this is sufficient to constitute the participation required by *Sherrer* and *Johnson,* assuming that the procedure followed
met the requirements of due process?

(b) What should be the result if W happened to be passing through
Nevada when H sued, was personally served within Nevada, but did not appear or in any way participate in the action?   Did she have an opportunity
to litigate the issue of jurisdiction, when the suit was being brought two
thousand miles from her home?   Cook v. Cook, 342 U.S. 126 (1951).

7.   What should be the result if H should obtain a Nevada divorce after a personal appearance in the suit by W, and a finding of domicile by the
Nevada court, and then should return to his home in New Jersey and be
prosecuted by the state for bigamy or bigamous cohabitation?   Would New
Jersey be required in such a case to recognize the Nevada divorce as valid
even though the evidence clearly showed lack of a Nevada domicile?   A
Ehrenzweig, Conflict of Laws, 253 (1962); H. Goodrich, Conflict of Laws
259 (4th ed. Scoles 1964); Cavers, Book Review, 47 Cal.L.Rev. 414, 417
(1959).

8.   Could a wife whose husband obtains an invalid Mexican divorce and
marries another woman recover for mental distress caused thereby, in a
state which permits tort actions between husband and wife?   Weicker v.
Weicker, 53 Misc.2d 570, 279 N.Y.S.2d 852 (Sup.Ct.1967), rev'd 28 A.D.2d
138, 283 N.Y.S.2d 385 (1st Dep't 1967), aff'd p.c. 22 N.Y.2d 8, 290 N.Y.S.
2d 732, 237 N.E.2d 876 (1968).   Cf. Morris v. MacNab, 25 N.J. 271, 135 A.
2d 657 (1957).

9.   H and W were married and lived in New York.   After some marital disagreements, they determined to get a divorce.   H flew to Mexico, employed a Mexican attorney to represent him and obtained a divorce.   W did
not go to Mexico but she did employ Mexican counsel who entered an appearance for her in the divorce proceeding.   Three years later W moved to
New Mexico and married T, who knew she had been divorced but knew
nothing of the circumstances.   This marriage also proved unhappy.   After
a year had gone by, T learned the facts concerning the Mexican divorce and
sued W for annulment in New Mexico.   W filed a motion for summary judgment, the foregoing facts not being disputed, and being fully set forth in
appropriate affidavits.   What arguments should be made for and against
this motion?   Note, New York Approved Mexican Divorces: Are They
Valid in Other States?   114 U.Pa.L.Rev. 771 (1966).

10.   H–1 and W–1 are married and live in the State of Holmes.   W–1 goes to the Dominican Republic and in one day obtains a divorce from H–1, without notice to him.   H–1 and W–1 have one child.   A year later H–1 marries W–2 and W–1 marries H–2.   H–1 and W–2 have one child and H–2 and W–1 have one child.   At this point W–1 learns that there may be something defective about her divorce from H–1 and she consults a lawyer.

(a)   What advice should W–1 be given about her marital status and the status of the child of her second "marriage"?

(b)   Could W–1 get a divorce from H–1?   Would this require proof that the Dominican divorce was invalid?

(c)   What are the consequences for such potential legal questions as inheritance, income tax, estate tax, or social security, which may turn on her status?

SPELLENS v. SPELLENS

Supreme Court of California, In Bank, 1957.
49 Cal.2d 210, 317 P.2d 613.

CARTER, Justice.   Plaintiff, married to Robert Seymon, had marital difficulties because of Robert's conduct; there were two children of the marriage.   While this condition existed and she was considering divorce, defendant, Sol Spellens, told her he was in love with her and wanted to marry her.   He was an old family friend of substantial wealth with extensive business experience and represented that he had had wide legal experience.   He said he was aware of plaintiff's marital problems and that she was entitled to a divorce.   He promised that when she divorced Robert he would marry her, take care of her and her children and make her a partner in all of his property.   She still tried to save her marriage with Robert but was unsuccessful.   In January, 1951, she decided to divorce Robert and defendant arranged for an attorney to represent her and provided funds therefor.   She commenced an action for divorce the next month, based on extreme cruelty.   After the commencement of the action, defendant conferred with Robert about a property settlement and advised plaintiff to waive her rights to any community property and all but a nominal $1.00 per month alimony.   This she did, and defendant again made the same promises he had made before.   Plaintiff obtained an interlocutory divorce decree on March 13, 1951, and defendant represented that upon the granting of the interlocutory decree he and plaintiff could be legally married in Mexico and the marriage would be valid anywhere.   He took her to Mexico where he obtained an attorney who gave the same advice.   Four days after the interlocutory decree, plaintiff and defendant returned to Mexico and saw the same attorney who was shown the decree and confirmed his former advice.   As a result of this advice plaintiff and defendant were married in Mexico by the attorney, and they began living together as husband and wife with plaintiff's children as part of the family.

* * * During the time they lived together defendant was extremely cruel to plaintiff, and in March, 1952, defendant suggested they separate, to which plaintiff objected, but defendant said he had been advised they were not legally married. Plaintiff consulted an attorney and was advised that the validity of her marriage lay in the field of unsettled law, but he thought defendant would be estopped to assert its invalidity. Plaintiff thereupon commenced her action (hereinafter called main action) on March 24, 1952. * * *

In an amended complaint plaintiff asked that her marriage be declared valid, that defendant be estopped to question its validity, and for separate maintenance, or, in the alternative, if the marriage was found invalid, damages because of defendant's fraudulent representations and promises and an award of the "community property" (that property accumulated while they were purportedly married). Plaintiff filed amendments and supplements to her complaint, adding other causes of action, and after an adverse determination by the court as to some of them, a second amended complaint for damages for fraud was filed. She sought a division of the community property and to be appointed guardian ad litem for her children and an allowance for their support on the theory of putative spouse. Defendant made general denials and asserted as an affirmative defense that the marriage was void as being after the entry of an interlocutory decree but before the entry of a final decree of divorce and asked that it be declared invalid.

* * *

Accordingly judgment was entered determining the marriage to be invalid; that no estoppel existed and no damages were recoverable [2] for defendant's fraud; that plaintiff was the putative wife of defendant from March 17, 1951, to September 22, 1952; that by reason of the latter fact and defendant's cruelty, plaintiff was entitled to all the "community" property (that earned during the mentioned period), plus $10,052, the balance of the "quasi-community property after deduction of quasi-community expense"; that plaintiff may not recover her attorney's fees incurred in the action; that plaintiff should not recover on the other issues disposed of on stipulation and objection to her evidence. Both plaintiff and defendant appealed from the portions of the judgment unfavorable to each of them.

* * *

2. "A subsequent marriage contracted by any person during the life of a former husband or wife of such person, with any person other than such former husband or wife, is illegal and void from the beginning, unless:
"1. The former marriage has been annulled or dissolved. In no case can a marriage of either of the parties during the life of the other, be valid in this state, if contracted within one year after the entry of an interlocutory decree in a proceeding for divorce." Cal. Civ.Code, § 61, subd. 1.

[This statute is now Cal.Civ.Code § 4401 (1970). Ed. note.]

Plaintiff contends that the defendant was estopped to deny the validity of the Mexican marriage or, stated another way, that he was estopped to deny that the California interlocutory decree of divorce from Robert terminated that marriage and made the Mexican marriage valid as far as he was concerned; that thus the parties, as far as defendant and this litigation is concerned, must be treated as husband and wife. Defendant contends that the strong policy of this state forbids the establishing of an estoppel; that no marriage contrary to statute may be created by estoppel.

The rule on estoppel is stated in Watson v. Watson, 39 Cal.2d 305, 307, 246 P.2d 19, 20, "To maintain his action it is necessary for the plaintiff to deny the validity of the Nevada divorce decree which he secured from his first wife. * * * In Rediker v. Rediker, 35 Cal.2d 796, 805, 221 P.2d 1, 20 A.L.R.2d 1152, the court stated that '*the validity of a divorce decree cannot be contested by a party who has procured the decree or a party who has remarried in reliance thereon, or by one who has aided another to procure the decree so that the latter will be free to remarry.*' The decisions in this state and in other states are ample authority for the statement in the Rediker case.

"The fact that in the present case it had been determined in a prior action that no marriage existed at the time of the alleged tort does not benefit the plaintiff's position. Such an eventuality was taken into consideration in Harlan v. Harlan, 70 Cal.App.2d 657, 161 P.2d 490. Before their marriage the plaintiff husband in that case had been instrumental in securing a Mexican divorce for the defendant from her first husband. Thereafter the plaintiff sought an annulment of their marriage as bigamous, asserting that the Mexican divorce was invalid for want of jurisdiction of the court. That situation is analogous to the present case in that in bringing his action it is necessary for the plaintiff to assert the invalidity of a previous divorce obtained by him. In the Harlan case the trial court found that the Mexican divorce decree was invalid, as was the Nevada divorce in the present case, and granted the annulment. In reversing the judgment the court held that notwithstanding the fact that the Mexican decree was invalid, the plaintiff was estopped from asserting its invalidity because he had aided and counseled the defendant in procuring it. In the present case the plaintiff is likewise estopped from asserting the invalidity of the Nevada divorce obtained through his own machination. The fact that he obtained that divorce as the party participant states a stronger case against him than operated as an estoppel in the Harlan case.

" * * * It is said in Dietrich v. Dietrich, 41 Cal.2d 497, 505, 261 P.2d 269, 273, 'On this record it is immediately obvious that the very evidence offered to show the *invalidity of the ceremonial marriage* was properly excluded because that same evidence shows that

Noah is estopped to assert the claimed invalidity of the Nevada divorce [obtained by Carol from another man]. With full knowledge of the circumstances under which that divorce was obtained, and in reliance on such divorce, Noah went through a marriage ceremony and lived with Carol as her husband for many years. The *public policy* of this state, in the circumstances of this case, as in those considered in Rediker v. Rediker (1950) 35 Cal.2d 796, 808, 221 P.2d 1, 20 A.L.R.2d 1152, requires recognition of the second marriage rather than the "dubious attempt to resurrect the original" marriage.' (Emphasis added.) * * * Roberts v. Roberts, 81 Cal.App.2d 871, 185 P.2d 381, insofar as it is to the contrary must be deemed as disapproved. The theory is that the marriage is not made valid by reason of the estoppel but that the estopped person may not take a position that the divorce or latter marriage was invalid. * * * And as to the public policy it is said: ' "To hold otherwise protects neither the welfare nor morals of society but, on the contrary, such holding is a flagrant invitation to others to attempt to circumvent the law, cohabit in unlawful state, and when tired of such situation, apply to the courts for a release from the indicia of the marriage status.' '" Harlan v. Harlan, 70 Cal.App.2d 657, 663–664, 161 P.2d 490, 494. * * *

"Defendant contends, however, that the public policy of the state requires the annulment of bigamous marriages whenever their bigamous character is discovered. We find no basis for such a sweeping application of public policy. * * * Defendant does not indicate how any public purpose is served by the annulment of his marriage. * * *

" 'It can no longer be said that public policy requires non-recognition of all irregular foreign divorces. We have recognized that the interest of the state in many situations may lie with recognition of such divorces and preservation of remarriages rather than a dubious attempt to resurrect the original. From a pragmatic viewpoint, judicial invalidation of irregular foreign divorces and attendant remarriages, years after both events, is a less than effective sanction against an institution whose charm lies in its immediate respectability. We think it may now be stated that the *general* public policy in this jurisdiction, as judicially interpreted, no longer prevents application in annulment actions of the laches and estoppel doctrines in determining the effect to be given such divorce decrees.' Vinson, J., in Goodloe v. Hawk, 72 App.D.C. 287, 113 F.2d 753, 757; * * *. We conclude that the public policy of this state requires the preservation of the second marriage and the protection of the rights of the second spouse 'rather than a dubious attempt to resurrect the original' marriage." * * *

The foregoing authorities involved an estoppel to deny the validity of a decree invalid because of lack of jurisdiction of the court which purported to grant it but we think the same policy requires the same result in the instant case where there was a marriage before a year after the entry of an interlocutory decree. The policy applies equally in one case as the other. The policy against a bigamous marriage expressed in the first sentence of section 61 of the Civil Code, supra, involved in the cited cases, is no stronger nor more compelling than that involved here which is that there may not be a valid marriage if contracted within less than a year after the entry of an interlocutory decree of divorce. * * * We fail to see any difference in this case and one where defendant had participated in the obtaining of an invalid Nevada or Mexican divorce rather than a California interlocutory decree. It is not the marriage which is found valid as indicated by the above authorities and thus the policy of section 61, subd. 1, is not thwarted. Rather it is that defendant by reason of his conduct will not be permitted to question its validity or the divorce; so far as he is concerned, he and plaintiff are husband and wife. The interlocutory decree declared that the parties were entitled to a divorce and it was not unreasonable for plaintiff to have been led to believe that a marriage in Mexico would be valid. The circumstances here clearly show fraud and estoppel as far as the defendant is concerned; it would be difficult to imagine a stronger case in this field of law.

* * * the judgment in the main action is reversed in the respects heretofore indicated.

GIBSON, C. J., and TRAYNOR and SPENCE, JJ., concur.

SCHAUER, Justice (concurring and dissenting). *Estoppel to Deny the Validity of the Mexican Marriage.* I agree that the extension of the doctrine of estoppel to the facts of this case is appropriate, but I would make it unmistakably clear that here the marriage in respect to which the doctrine is being applied is absolutely void *ab initio.*

The conclusion in this respect is reached through reasoning as follows: Where the parties go through a marriage ceremony in reliance upon a void decree of divorce their marriage is no more "valid" than the marriage of the parties here where there was no judgment of divorce.[1] Therefore, as the opinion of Justice Carter indicates, public policy against bigamous marriage is no more disserved by a holding that defendant is estopped to deny the "validity" of the marriage here than it is by the more familiar holding that "The validity

---

1. Here there was an interlocutory decree but it is indisputable that, in this state, the interlocutory decree entered in a divorce action is in no sense a judgment of divorce. It neither purports to nor can affect the legal status of the parties as husband and wife. It is merely a determination, in so far as status is concerned, that a divorce "ought to be granted" and that one party or the other or both, after the expiration of a year from entry of the interlocutory decree, shall be "entitled to a divorce." (Civ.Code, §§ 131, 132; De Burgh v. De Burgh (1952), 39 Cal.2d 858, 250 P.2d 598.)

of a divorce decree cannot be contested by a party who has procured the decree or a party who has remarried in reliance thereon, or by one who has aided another to procure the decree so that the latter will be free to remarry." * * *

Broad statements to the effect that public policy favors the declaration of nullity of a bigamous marriage, even at the suit of the guilty party * * * made without reference to the question of estoppel, should here yield to the apposite policy, stated as a conclusive presumption in the Code of Civil Procedure (§ 1962, subd. 3) that "Whenever a party has, by his own declaration, act, or omission, intentionally and deliberately led another to believe a particular thing true, and to act upon such belief, he cannot, in any litigation arising out of such declaration, act, or omission, be permitted to falsify it." Defendant with full knowledge of the facts led plaintiff to believe that by going through a bigamous marriage ceremony she was acquiring the status and incident rights of a lawful wife. He should not now be permitted to rely, to her injury, upon her innocent bigamy.

It appears pertinent to observe that caution should be exercised in applying the doctrine of estoppel in favor of one spouse who goes through a bigamous marriage ceremony during the interlocutory period, i. e. after entry of the interlocutory decree determining *rights* but before granting or entry of the judgment of *divorce,* which alone affects the marital status. Plaintiff's ignorance of the invalidity in California of the Mexican marriage is conceivable in the circumstances of her lack of experience, defendant's representations as to his wide experience, and the facts that she relied upon defendant to and defendant did arrange for her procuring the interlocutory decree establishing her right to obtain a judgment of divorce after the one year waiting period and the advice of the Mexican attorney as to the validity of a Mexican marriage. Although it is obvious that a court should scrutinize with caution a claimed belief that an interlocutory decree which is incompetent to affect status permitted a remarriage in another jurisdiction before expiration of the waiting period, until which time neither party was even entitled to apply for the judgment of divorce in California, a plaintiff's knowledge of the facts concerning the invalidity of the void marriage will not always preclude invocation of the doctrine of estoppel against defendant. * * * Recognizing that here there can be no successful attempt to give validity to the absolutely void Mexican "marriage," we hold that defendant is estopped to assert its unquestionable invalidity.

* * *

NOTES AND QUESTIONS

1. The estoppel doctrine is discussed in H. Clark, Law of Domestic Relations § 11.3 (1968). See also Note, 36 St. John's L.Rev. 126 (1961), Note, 24 U.Chi.L.Rev. 376 (1957). Phillips, Equitable Preclusion of Jurisdictional Attacks on Void Divorces, 37 Ford.L.Rev. 355 (1969) collects and discuss-

es the New York cases, and Annot., 81 A.L.R.3d 110 (1977) cites many cases.

2.   In the *Spellens* case did Sol Spellens make misrepresentations to the plaintiff on which she relied to her detriment? Is that the rationale of the case, that is, is this a case of equitable estoppel in the usual sense of the term?

3.   If you were asked by a woman client in Mrs. Spellens' situation whether she is married to her second "husband" or not, what would you respond? Would you say that her marital status is uncertain? If the *Spellens* case had come out the other way, and if the California court had rejected any claim of estoppel, would you say that your hypothetical client's status was not uncertain? What do your answers to these questions suggest as to the soundness or unsoundness of the *Spellens* result?

4.   How could the California court reach the result it did in the face of the statute quoted in footnote 2 of the opinion? How does the court deal with that problem?

5.   How should the following cases be decided?

(a) H, married to W–1, got an ex parte Nevada divorce, without troubling to obtain a Nevada domicile. H's home was in New York and he returned there and married W–2. Some time later W–2 sued him for separate maintenance and he defended on the ground that the Nevada divorce was invalid (as it was) and that therefore he was never married to W–2.

(i) Assume that W–2 knew nothing of the Nevada divorce.

(ii) Assume that W–2 knew all about the Nevada divorce and in fact was the inducing cause of H's obtaining that divorce. Krause v. Krause, 282 N.Y. 355, 26 N.E.2d 290 (1940); Marc v. Marc, 68 Misc.2d 340, 326 N. Y.S.2d 489 (Fam.Ct.1971); Gardner v. Gardner, 144 W.Va. 630, 110 S.E.2d 495 (1959).

(b) H, married to W–1, tired of her and obtained a Mexican mail-order divorce, without ever going to Mexico. H then married W–2. After ten years of marriage he also tired of W–2 and sued her for annulment, alleging that his Mexican divorce was void and that he was therefore never married to W–2.

(i) Assume that W–2 knew nothing about the Mexican divorce.

(ii) Assume that W–2 knew all about the Mexican divorce. See Sears v. Sears, 110 U.S.App.D.C. 407, 293 F.2d 884 (1961), 110 U.Pa.L.Rev. 747 (1962); Magner v. Hobby, 215 F.2d 190 (2d Cir. 1954); Cross v. Cross, 94 Ariz. 28, 381 P.2d 573 (1963); Rediker v. Rediker, 35 Cal.2d 796, 221 P.2d 1 (1950); Mattos v. Correia, 274 Cal.App.2d 413, 79 Cal.Rptr. 229 (1969); Oakley v. Oakley, 30 Colo.App. 292, 493 P.2d 381 (1972); Warrender v. Warrender, 79 N.J.Super. 114, 190 A.2d 684 (1963); Caldwell v. Caldwell, 298 N.Y. 146, 81 N.E.2d 60 (1948), 47 Mich.L.Rev. 574 (1949); Lorenzo v. Lorenzo, 85 N.M. 305, 512 P.2d 65 (1973); Smoak v. Smoak, 269 S.C. 313, 237 S.E.2d 372 (1977) (Haitian divorce); Kazin v. Kazin, 81 N.J. 85, 405 A.2d 360 (1979).

(iii) Would it matter whether the suit for annulment was brought in a state like New York, whose statute authorized alimony in annulment suits? See Landsman v. Landsman, 302 N.Y. 45, 96 N.E.2d 81 (1950), 51 Colum.L. Rev. 388 (1951).

(c) H obtained an ex parte Alabama quickie divorce from W–1, without obtaining an Alabama domicile. W–1 remarried shortly thereafter. H married W–2. Some years later H died and W–1 claimed an intestate share of his estate, being opposed of course by W–2.

(i) Assume that W–2 did not know of the Alabama divorce.

(ii) Assume that W–2 did know of the Alabama divorce. See Marvin v. Foster, 61 Minn. 154, 63 N.W. 484 (1895); Sorrentino v. Mierzwa, 25 N. Y.2d 59, 250 N.E.2d 58, 302 N.Y.S.2d 565 (1969), 36 Bklyn.L.Rev. 493 (1970).

(d) W obtained an ex parte Nevada divorce from H–1 without ever being domiciled in Nevada. W then married H–2. Three years later H–1 sued for a declaratory judgment that the divorce was void and that he was still married to W. Krieger v. Krieger, 25 N.Y.2d 364, 254 N.E.2d 750, 306 N.Y.S.2d 441 (1969); Heckathorn v. Heckathorn, 77 N.M. 369, 423 P.2d 410 (1967). Is H–2 an essential party defendant in H–1's suit?

(e) W obtained a divorce from H in a court of the state of their domicile, the decree being regular and valid in all respects. Shortly after the divorce they became reconciled, H falsely telling W that he had had the divorce decree set aside. They lived together as husband and wife for several years and then had another falling out, whereupon W brought suit again for divorce. H defended on the ground that they were not married, their marriage having been validly dissolved by the earlier divorce. Fox v. Fox, 247 Ark. 188, 444 S.W.2d 865 (1969).

(f) H–1 and W were married. H–1 deserted W and after about five years W, not having heard from H–1, married H–2 who knew of the prior marriage. Later H–2 sued for annulment. Anderson v. Anderson, 27 Conn.Supp. 342, 238 A.2d 45 (1967); Townsend v. Morgan, 192 Md. 168, 63 A.2d 743 (1949); Danes v. Smith, 30 N.J.Super. 292, 104 A.2d 455 (1954). Cf. the Enoch Arden statute discussed supra, page 127.

(g) H obtained an ex parte Nevada divorce from W, without obtaining a domicile in Nevada. A year or two later, in discussing his personal affairs with his lawyer, he learned that his divorce was invalid. He then brought suit for divorce from W at his domicile. Assume he has grounds for divorce.

(h) H obtained an ex parte Alabama quickie from W, being present in Alabama only one day. Neither H nor W remarried. Twenty years later H died and W filed a claim for social security benefits as H's widow, the statute requiring that she be married to the deceased for a period of not less than nine months immediately before his death. Mott v. Secretary of Health, Education and Welfare, 407 F.2d 59 (3d Cir. 1969); Perry v. Richardson, 336 F.Supp. 451 (E.D.Pa.1972). Would your analysis be different if H had remarried and the question was whether W–1 or W–2 should receive social security benefits? Cf. Rosenberg v. Richardson, 538 F.2d 487 (2d Cir. 1976), construing 42 U.S.C.A. § 416(h)(1)(A) and (B).

(i) H and W–1 were married and lived in State X, a state which had abolished common law marriage. After some years they quarrelled and H went to Nevada, stayed the required six weeks, got a divorce and immediately returned to X. W–1 did not go to Nevada, nor did she employ an attorney to represent her there. She did, however, write a letter to the Nevada court which said: "I do not wish to contest my husband's divorce. I waive any objections I may have to his getting the divorce, and I ask that the divorce be granted." This letter was included in the file of the case. On his return to X, H married W–2. Shortly thereafter H was prosecuted for the crime of bigamy in accordance with the applicable statute of X, and convicted. He was sentenced to prison for six months, served three months and then was released. After the bigamy conviction he never again lived with W–2. On his release from prison he resumed living with W–1 and continued to live with her until her death some years later. W–1 died without a will, leaving a substantial estate.

On the death of W–1 H filed a claim in her estate for the statutory share of a surviving spouse, all of the estate under the applicable statute of X. He was opposed by a sister of W–1, her nearest collateral relative, who would be entitled to W–1's entire estate if H's claim should be denied.

What arguments should be made on behalf of either party here?

In re Estate of Shufelt, 125 Vt. 131, 211 A.2d 173 (1965).

6. On the basis of your solutions to the foregoing cases, how would you define the doctrine of estoppel? What is its rationale? Could you draft a statute which would correctly define and limit the doctrine?

7. Do you perceive any relation between estoppel and common law marriage, between estoppel and the presumption that the later of successive marriages is valid, or between estoppel and Taczanowska v. Taczanowski, supra, page 95? Is there any relation between estoppel and the doctrine of Marvin v. Marvin, supra, page 38? In re Estate of Atherley, 44 Cal. App.3d 758, 119 Cal.Rptr. 41 (1975).

SECTION 2.   DIVORCE GROUNDS AND DEFENSES

A.   GROUNDS FOR DIVORCE IN GENERAL

INTRODUCTORY NOTE ON GROUNDS FOR DIVORCE

Up until quite recently the layman generally assumed that the grounds for divorce were at the heart of the divorce action. To some extent this was true, since the statute books said that divorce could only be granted upon proof of such serious marital fault as adultery, cruelty or desertion. The seriousness of the cruelty which had to be proved was often emphasized by the addition of such adjectives as "extreme and repeated" or "intolerable". The official doctrine thus was that a divorce could only be obtained by a spouse who was innocent of any fault, and then only from a spouse who had been proved to be guilty of the prescribed forms of serious misconduct. The emphasis on fault was an inheritance from the English ecclesiastical law which was the source of much of our law of divorce grounds. This then was the law in the books.

Any statement about the former state of the law on divorce grounds had to be qualified by what Professor Max Rheinstein has called the dualism of American divorce law. M. Rheinstein, Marriage Stability, Divorce and the Law, Ch. 10 (1972). See also Silva v. Silva, 28 Conn.Sup. 336, 260 A.2d 408 (1969). The dualism which Professor Rheinstein referred to was produced by another system of divorce law, one not found in the books but in the practices of trial courts all over the United States. Before the advent of non-fault grounds for divorce, it was customary for the parties or their lawyers to engage in negotiation and counseling leading to the choice of the least inconvenient ground for divorce, the one causing the least scandal and delay. This was usually cruelty. At this point the law in action diverged sharply from the law on the books. In uncontested cases the sort of cruelty which would persuade a trial court to grant a divorce was generally no more serious than the sort of marital unkindness which occurs at times in nearly every marriage. There was not the slightest pretence of meeting the strict requirements of the reported cases. The result was that even before non-fault divorce appeared, divorce by consent was generally available in the United States. The statistics indicated that between 75% and 95% of all divorces were not contested.

The fact that most divorces were uncontested and that the ground of cruelty in effect produced divorce by consent did not mean that the grounds for divorce were wholly without significance. In the negotiations leading to agreements about alimony, property and the custody and support of children, the existence or non-existence of grounds gave bargaining leverage to one party or the other. In addition, the parties' awareness of the importance of grounds so far as the law in the books was concerned may have increased the hostility with which they entered the divorce process, correspondingly increasing the emotional and psychological harm which they and their children suffered.

The fault grounds for divorce and the whole idea that divorce was a legal remedy to be granted only to one who was innocent and against one who was guilty of marital misconduct were subjected to sharp and continuous criticism for forty or fifty years before any significant reform was undertaken. This criticism finally began to take effect in the late 1960's and early 1970's. In 1970 the Uniform Marriage and Divorce Act was approved by the National Conference of Commissioners on Uniform State Laws. It was amended in 1971 and 1973. As now written, that Act provides, in §§ 302, 305, that marriages may be dissolved if they are found to be "irretrievably broken". This phrase is defined as occurring where the parties have lived apart for 180 days before commencement of the suit, or where there is serious marital discord adversely affecting their attitude toward the marriage. 9A Unif.L.Ann. 121, 132 (1979).

Influenced by this Act and by the extensive public discussion which preceded and followed it, about thirty states have enacted some version of marriage breakdown as a ground for divorce, variously labeled "irretrievable breakdown" or "irremediable breakdown", or "irreconcilable differences" or the like. This group of states includes Alabama, Arizona, California, Colorado, Connecticut, Delaware, Florida, Georgia, Hawaii, Idaho, Indiana, Iowa, Kentucky, Maine, Massachusetts, Michigan, Minnesota, Mississippi, Missouri, Montana, Nebraska, New Hampshire, North Dakota, Oregon, Rhode Island, Tennessee, Texas, Washington, Wisconsin, and Wyoming. Of these, Delaware, Mississippi and Missouri preserve some remnants of the fault requirement. In addition five states have enacted incompatibility as a ground for divorce. These states are Alaska, Kansas, Nevada, New Mexico and Oklahoma. Twenty-five states have adopted the non-fault ground of living separate and apart, for periods ranging from six months to three years, as a basis for divorce. This ground is of somewhat less practical importance than marriage breakdown or incompatibility because of the delay which its use involves. Nevertheless this indicates that fault has very generally been abandoned by the states as a ground for divorce, Illinois, Pennsylvania and South Dakota being apparently the only states which continue to insist exclusively upon proof of the old fault grounds. Cf. Freed and Foster, Divorce in the Fifty States: An Overview as of 1978, 13 Fam.L.Q. 105 (1979).

Several technical rules concerning divorce grounds must be mentioned. In the first place grounds are exclusively statutory. If the conduct alleged does not fit into one of the statutory categories of grounds, the divorce may not be granted. State v. Brown, 213 Ind. 118, 11 N.E.2d 679 (1937). Secondly, generally speaking the law of the forum is that which will be applied in determining whether the divorce will be granted. This is true even though the conduct relied upon as grounds for divorce occurred in another state. Torlonia v. Torlonia, 108 Conn. 292, 142 A. 843 (1928); D. S. v. J. S., 247 A.2d 125 (Del.1968). Cf. N.J.Stat.Ann. § 2A:34–10 (Supp.1979–1980). Finally, when the statutes governing grounds for divorce are amended, most, but not all, courts hold that the new statute may be retroactively applied to conduct occurring before the amendment. See the cases collected in Annot., 23 A.L.R.3d 626 (1969). Such retroactive application is generally held to be constitutional.

B. ADULTERY

Adultery is a ground for divorce in most states, but for obvious reasons it accounts for only a small proportion of the divorces granted. It is defined as the voluntary sexual intercourse of a married person with a person other than the spouse. When a married woman is raped, that is not adultery, since not voluntary. Likewise, when the spouse is insane, intercourse with someone other than the marital partner is usually held not to be adultery, although a few cases take the contrary position. Homosexual contacts have been held not to be adultery. Cohen v. Cohen, 200 Misc. 19, 103 N.Y.S.2d 426 (Sup.Ct. 1951). But see N.Y.Dom.Rel.L. § 170(4) (1977).

A few cases and authorities have maintained that artificial insemination by a donor other than the husband (AID) constitutes adultery on the wife's part, but this view seems mistaken. See Annot., 25 A.L.R.3d 1103, 1107 (1969); Note, The Legal Status of Artificial Insemination: A Need for Policy Formulation, 19 Drake L. Rev. 409, 418 (1970). What is needed is comprehensive statutory regulation of artificial insemination.

Adultery has also been made a crime in many states. Recent revision of thinking about sex crimes has resulted in the removal of adultery from the list of such crimes. The Model Penal Code exemplified and influenced this change. See Model Penal Code, Art. 207, Comment to § 207.1 (Tent.Draft No. 4 (1955)), and Art. 213 (Proposed Official Draft 1962). Colorado is entitled to an award for ineptitude in statute-drafting, by virtue of its statute which provides that adultery is a crime but sets no penalty. Colo.Rev.Stat.Ann. § 18–6–501 (1973). On the constitutionality of such statutes, see Annot., 41 A.L.R.3d 1338 (1972). That the purpose of the adultery prosecution is vengeance is made explicit by the law of some states which provides that only the spouse may initiate a prosecution for adultery. See Dale v. State, 449 P.2d 921 (Okl.Crim.App.1969).

The major problem with the ground of adultery is that of proving the occurrence. Circumstantial evidence must necessarily be relied upon in most cases. Illustrating the courts' reactions to such proof are the following cases: Anonymous v. Anonymous, 283 Ala. 374, 217 So.2d 240 (1968); Husband v. Wife, 253 A.2d 63 (Del.1968); Havens v. Havens, 236 So.2d 260 (La.App.1970); Breault v. Breault, 250 Md. 173, 242 A.2d 116 (1968); Covault v. Covault, 182 Neb. 119, 153 N.W.2d 292 (1967). At least one case has held that the invocation of the Fifth Amendment may be considered as creating an inference of adultery in a divorce case. Molloy v. Molloy, 46 Wis.2d 682, 176 N.W.2d 292 (1970).

For further citation of authority on adultery, see H. Clark, Law of Domestic Relations § 12.2 (1968).

C. DESERTION

Desertion as a ground for divorce is more important statistically than adultery. It is a ground for divorce in most states, under some statutes being called abandonment. It is defined as being (a) the voluntary separation by one spouse from the other, (b) with the intent not to resume marital cohabitation, (c) without the consent of the other spouse and (d) without justification.

Most of the desertion statutes impose the additional requirement that some specified period of time must elapse after the desertion occurs before the desertion may ripen into a ground for divorce. This period is most commonly a year but can be as long as five years under a few statutes. The period must be uninterrupted, runs from the moment of desertion, and usually, but not always, must exclude time spent in prior marital litigation between the parties, and the time during which they lived apart under a prior separation decree. Van Dolman v. Van Dolman, 378 Ill. 98, 37 N.E.2d 850 (1941); Koolish v. Koolish, 214 Pa.Super. 304, 257 A.2d 680 (1969); Annot., 80 A.L.R. 2d 855 (1961); 25 A.L.R. 1047 (1923), 61 A.L.R. 1268 (1929). If the defendant leaves the home under circumstances not amounting to desertion, as where he intends to return, the period begins to run when the intent not to return is formed. A reconciliation will interrupt the running of the period. Annot., 155 A.L.R. 132 (1945). If an offer of reconciliation is made in good faith by the deserter, it has the effect of stopping the running of the period, and if it is unjustifiably refused, constitutes desertion by the other spouse. Hite v. Hite, 210 Md. 576, 124 A.2d 581 (1956); Jacobs v. Jacobs, 109 N.J.Super. 287, 263 A.2d 155 (1970). This rule has the obvious effect of tempting the parties and their counsel to make dubious offers of reconciliation to gain litigation advantages. If the court finds the offer of reconciliation was not made in good faith, the offer will be disregarded. Zimmerman v. Zimmerman, 428 Pa. 118, 236 A.2d 785 (1968).

Where the separation is acquiesced in or agreed to by the spouses, this does not constitute desertion. Wilner v. Wilner, 251 Md. 13, 246 A.2d 273 (1968); Smith v. Smith, 202 Va. 104, 116 S.E.2d 110 (1960). But if, after the desertion occurs, the deserted spouse makes an agreement concerning alimony or property which does not amount to consent to the desertion, this does not affect his right of action for the divorce.

One New Jersey case has held that a husband was guilty of desertion when he was imprisoned for the statutory period as a result of a criminal conviction. Brady v. Brady, 98 N.J.Super. 600, 238 A. 2d 201 (1968), 23 Rut.L.Rev. 389 (1969).

Many cases have had to define the term "separation" as used in the context of desertion. When one of the spouses does not leave the marital home, but withdraws from association with the other, is that desertion? Or when one spouse refuses to engage in sexual relations with the other, is that desertion? As might be expected, the cases are not in agreement on these matters. The leading case of Diemer v. Diemer, 8 N.Y.2d 206, 168 N.E.2d 654, 203 N.Y.S.2d 829 (1960) held that the refusal of sexual relations on the wife's part, maintained for religious reasons, constituted abandonment entitling the husband to a decree of separation. Desertion or abandonment was defined by that case as being the refusal to fulfill a basic obligation of the marriage. A similar holding is found in Jacobs v. Jacobs, 109 N.J.Super. 287, 263 A.2d 155 (1970). Cases refusing to grant the divorce for this reason are Howison v. Howison, 128 Ill.App.2d 377, 262

N.E.2d 1 (1970) (semble), and Vickers v. Vickers, 255 S.C. 25, 176 S.E.2d 561 (1970).

As has been indicated, one element in the offense of desertion is the absence of justification for departure from the marital home. If the departure is found to be justified, this finding has a double consequence. It causes the departure not to be characterized as desertion, and secondly in those states which recognize "constructive" desertion it gives the departing spouse a claim for divorce. Thus when the conduct of one spouse is so intolerable that the other is forced to leave the home, this conduct is called constructive desertion and is made a ground for divorce. The cases are not in agreement on the question of how serious such conduct must be before it can qualify as constructive desertion. One group of states holds that only conduct which would be an independent ground for divorce may constitute constructive desertion. Thus if the husband's cruelty causes the wife to leave the home, the divorce could be granted for either cruelty or constructive desertion. Lemon v. Lemon, 14 Ill.2d 15, 150 N.E.2d 608 (1958); Carneal v. Carneal, 211 Va. 162, 176 S.E.2d 305 (1970); Annot., 19 A.L.R.2d 1428 (1951); Note, 51 Iowa L.Rev. 108 (1965).

Some courts have taken a broader view of constructive desertion, holding that it may occur when a spouse leaves home in response to conduct which is not independently a ground for divorce. This enabled these courts to construct a new, nonstatutory ground for divorce which might be based upon individual notions of how married persons ought to behave. See, e. g. Soles v. Soles, 248 Md. 723, 238 A.2d 235 (1968); Lindquist v. Lindquist, 137 Conn. 165, 75 A.2d 397 (1950).

For other authorities on desertion, see H. Clark, Law of Domestic Relations § 12.3 (1968).

D. CRUELTY

This brief discussion of cruelty is intended to summarize only the law on the books, the law as announced by statute and reported case. As the introduction to this section has stated, there is another law of cruelty, the law which applies in uncontested cases. The quantum of proof required in those cases varies from state to state and from judge to judge within states, but it may be fairly characterized in general as relatively slight. In most states it amounts to little more than the granting of divorces at the request of the parties.

Cruelty is still a ground for divorce in several states and is still relied upon. The statutes make it plain that they require severe conduct, by adding such adjectives as "intolerable", "inhuman", "extreme", "grievous" or "barbarous". See, e. g., N.J.Stat.Ann. § 2A:34–2 (Supp.1979–1980); N.Y.Dom.Rel.L. § 170(1) (1977). At least one state limits the offense to physical cruelty. S.C.Code § 20–3–10 (1977). A few states also have the ground of indignities, which seems to be substantially similar to cruelty. E. g., Pa.Stat.Ann. tit. 23, § 10 (1955).

Taking the diversity of statutory language as a starting point, the case law occasionally attempts to define cruelty in general terms, although usually the definitions are not very satisfactory as aids in the decision of specific cases, and they too differ somewhat from state to state. An example of the older, strict definition of cruelty: "* * * the cruelty we demand is more than display of temper, more than exasperating habits of conduct or expression. We must get into the realm of the evil and the wicked, of brutality, of malignancy, of indignities endangering mental or physical health". Williams v. Williams, 351 Mich. 210, 213, 88 N.W.2d 483, 484 (1958). A more typical definition in a Connecticut case, quoting from an earlier case: "[T]here are trials causing much weariness and suffering, which parties to the marriage contract must bear * * *. It is only when the cumulative effect * * * upon the suffering victim has become such that the public and personal objects of matrimony have been destroyed beyond rehabilitation, that the condition of fact contemplated by the intolerable cruelty clause of the statute * * * should be found to exist." Sarafin v. Sarafin, 28 Conn.Supp. 24, 247 A.2d 500 (1968). A similar definition from a Nebraska case: "A continuing course of conduct which so grievously wounds the mental feelings or so utterly destroys the peace of mind so as to nullify or destroy the legitimate objects and ends of matrimony constitutes 'mental cruelty' within the meaning of the statute." Sims v. Sims, 185 Neb. 479, 176 N.W.2d 683 (1970). These statements demonstrate a change in the purpose for which cruelty is made a ground for divorce. Originally that purpose was merely to protect the spouse from harm. The contemporary cases suggest that the purpose now is to authorize the courts to dissolve marriages which have deteriorated so far as not to serve the interests either of the parties or of society.

Although the cases do not offer very helpful general definitions, some clear elements of the charge of cruelty can be deduced from them. They are: (a) Cruelty generally must consist of a course of conduct over a period. The cases often say that a single act of cruelty is not sufficient to constitute grounds for divorce, except in the rare cases in which the act is outrageous or shocking or very brutal. Richardson v. Richardson, 258 S.C. 135, 187 S.E.2d 528 (1972); Stephenson v. Stephenson, 111 N.H. 189, 278 A.2d 351 (1971) (course of conduct, though not long continued); Ellzey v. Ellzey, 253 So.2d 249 (Miss.1971) (single act sufficient when it consisted of husband's attempt to shoot his wife); Gray v. Gray, 220 Pa.Super. 143, 286 A.2d 684 (1971) (single act of shooting is cruelty); Merten v. National Manufacturer's Bank of Neenah, 26 Wis.2d 181, 131 N.W.2d 868 (1965), 49 Marq.L.Rev. 449 (1965) (single blow was sufficient for cruelty). Many other cases are collected in Annot., 7 A.L.R.3d 761 (1966).

(b) The plaintiff must prove that the cruelty had some effect upon his or her health before it will be held to be a ground for divorce. Garrison v. Garrison, 179 N.W.2d 466 (Iowa 1970); Rios v. Rios, 34 A.D.2d 325, 311 N.Y.S.2d 664 (1st Dep't 1970), aff'd 29 N.Y. 2d 840, 327 N.Y.S.2d 853, 277 N.E.2d 786 (1971); Cary v. Cary, 47 Wis.2d 689, 177 N.W.2d 924 (1970); McMurtrie v. McMurtrie, 52 Wis.2d 577, 191 N.W.2d 43 (1971).

(c) The cases are not in agreement on whether the defendant's state of mind is relevant to whether he has been guilty of cruelty. Some hold that it is, and that the defendant's insanity or mental incompetence would be a defense. Vaughan v. Vaughan, 223 Ga. 298, 154 S.E.2d 592 (1967). Others hold that insanity is not a defense. Nunes v. Nunes, 62 Cal.2d 33, 396 P.2d 37, 41 Cal.Rptr. 5 (1964), 38 So.Cal.L.Rev. 713 (1965); Dankers v. Dankers, 285 Minn. 120, 172 N.W.2d 318 (1969); Wadlington, A Case of Insanity and Divorce, 56 Va.L.Rev. 12 (1970).

(d) To some degree at least, the cruelty is to be judged by its effect upon the individual plaintiff, with his or her sensibilities and weaknesses, not upon some mythical reasonable person. Surratt v. Surratt, 12 Ill.2d 21, 145 N.E.2d 594 (1957).

Some specific examples of conduct which amounts to cruelty follow. In considering them, however, it must be kept in mind that in most such cases a considerable range and variety of conduct is involved. For this reason no two cases are likely to be very similar on their facts and the value of precedents is correspondingly diminished. The plaintiff has the burden of proof. Walber v. Walber, 40 Wis.2d 313, 161 N.W.2d 898 (1968).

Physical beatings and assaults clearly constitute cruelty. Brown v. Brown, 250 S.C. 114, 156 S.E.2d 641 (1967). The withdrawal of a spouse from marital companionship may also be cruelty, at least under circumstances showing an effect on the health of the plaintiff. Nelken v. Nelken, 176 N.W.2d 195 (Iowa 1970); Peter v. Peter, 208 Pa.Super. 221, 222 A.2d 511 (1966). Even though the withdrawal results from preoccupation with religious observances, it may constitute cruelty. Sinclair v. Sinclair, 204 Kan. 240, 461 P.2d 750 (1969); Rogers v. Rogers, 430 S.W.2d 305 (Mo.App.1968).

Perhaps the most common form of cruelty consists of what might be characterized as general marital unkindness. This includes abuse, quarrelling, harassment, ridicule, refusal to speak to the spouse, accusations of infidelity or other misconduct, abuse of the children, attempts to alienate the children from the spouse and similar conduct. Cases granting divorces for this sort of cruelty include Breazeale v. Breazeale, 248 Ark. 437, 451 S.W.2d 865 (1970); McGehee v. McGehee, 448 S.W.2d 300 (Mo.App.1969); Sims v. Sims, 185

Neb. 479, 176 N.W.2d 683 (1970); Schipper v. Schipper, 46 Wis.2d 303, 174 N.W.2d 474 (1970), overruled on another point, O'Connor v. O'Connor, 48 Wis.2d 535, 180 N.W.2d 735 (1970); Jackowick v. Jackowick, 39 Wis.2d 249, 159 N.W.2d 54 (1968); Mecha v. Mecha, 36 Wis.2d 29, 152 N.W.2d 923 (1967); Garot v. Garot, 24 Wis.2d 88, 128 N.W.2d 393 (1964). An unusual Kansas case held that it constituted cruelty that the husband married the wife for her money and failed to provide her with support. Haynes v. Haynes, 202 Kan. 83, 446 P. 2d 749 (1968).

Drug addiction and heavy drinking may also support a finding of cruelty, although they are usually associated with other forms of cruel conduct. Lawler v. Lawler, 175 N.W.2d 103 (Iowa 1970); DeMeo v. DeMeo, 110 N.J.Super. 179, 264 A.2d 751 (1970). See cases cited in Annot., 76 A.L.R.2d 419 (1961).

Various conduct relating to the sexual relations of the parties has been held to be cruelty by some courts. Examples are refusal of intercourse, Jizmejian v. Jizmejian, 16 Ariz.App. 270, 492 P.2d 1208 (1972); and "excessive" or "abnormal" sexual demands, Annot., 88 A.L.R.2d 553 (1963). In Goldstein v. Goldstein, 97 N.J.Super. 534, 235 A.2d 498 (1967) the court held that the husband's insistence that the wife take the "pill" as a condition on sexual relations did not constitute cruelty.

The question which the latter cases raise is, to what extent can such decisions survive Griswold v. Connecticut, supra, page 73? Can the courts in these divorce actions be permitted to "search the sacred precincts of marital bedrooms"? The same question arises in connection with those desertion cases which hold that refusal of intercourse constitutes desertion. See Cotner v. Henry, 394 F.2d 873 (7th Cir. 1968), cert. den. 393 U.S. 847 (1968), and Buchanan v. Batchelor, 308 F.Supp. 729 (N.D.Tex.1970), vacated and remanded 401 U.S. 989 (1971).

For additional authorities on cruelty, see H. Clark, Law of Domestic Relations § 12.4 (1968).

E. LIVING SEPARATE AND APART

This is a ground for divorce in about half of the states. It is to be distinguished from desertion, in that it does not require evidence that one party departed from the marital domicile without justification, but only that the parties lived apart for a prescribed period, with certain qualifications depending upon the statutory language. The period specified by the various statutes ranges from six months to three years.

There are three types of statute authorizing divorce for separation, the proof required varying with the different language of the statute. The first type, exemplified by the New York statute, authorizes divorce when the parties have lived apart for the specified time pursuant to a separation decree. N.Y.Dom.Rel.L. § 170 (1977). New York also authorizes the divorce when the parties have lived apart pursuant to a written agreement of separation for the prescribed year.

The second type of statute authorizes the divorce when the parties have, for the statutory period lived apart "voluntarily" or "willingly". The cases construe this type of statute to require that the parties lived apart by express or implied mutual agreement with intent not to resume the relationship; that they lived apart for the period without cohabitation; and that there is no reasonable chance of reconciliation.

The third class of statute merely provides that the divorce may be granted when the parties have lived apart for the prescribed time. Under this form of statute either party may normally obtain the divorce, no matter how the separation came about.

In two cases a divorce sought on this ground has been denied where the defendant was mentally incompetent. Shaw v. Shaw, 256 S.C. 453, 182 S.E.2d 865 (1971); Crittenden v. Crittenden, 210 Va. 76, 168 S.E.2d 115 (1969), 4 U.Rich.L.Rev. 347 (1970), 11 W. & M.L. Rev. 554 (1969). See also the ingenious discussion of this problem in Wadlington, A Case of Insanity and Divorce, 56 Va.L.Rev. 12 (1970).

For other authorities on living separate and apart, see Annot., 35 A.L.R.3d 1238 (1970); H. Clark, Law of Domestic Relations § 12.6 (1968); Waddington, Divorce Without Fault Without Perjury, 52 Va.L.Rev. 32 (1966).

F. INCOMPATIBILITY

Five states now recognize incompatibility as a ground for divorce. They are Alaska, Kansas, Nevada, New Mexico and Oklahoma. The Virgin Islands, whose law introduced incompatibility into the United States, now has shifted to marriage breakdown as a ground for divorce.

The leading judicial definition of incompatibility is from Burch v. Burch, 195 F.2d 799, 806–807 (3d Cir. 1952):

> We conclude that while incompatibility of temperament in the Virgin Islands Divorce Law does not refer to those petty quarrels and minor bickerings which are but the evidence of that frailty which all humanity is heir to, it unquestionably does refer to conflicts in personalities and dispositions so deep as to be irreconcilable and to render it impossible for the parties to continue a normal marital relationship with each other. To use the ancient Danish phrase, the disharmony of the spouses in their common life must be so deep and intense as to be irremediable. It is the legal recognition of the proposition long established in the earlier Danish law of the Islands that if the parties are so

mismated that their marriage has in fact ended as the result of their hopeless disagreement and discord the courts should be empowered to terminate it as a matter of law.

The dictionary definition of incompatibility is the state of being mutually intolerant, incapable of existing together in the same subject, contrary or opposed in character, discordant, incongruous or inconsistent. V Oxford English Dictionary 165 (1961).

All of the definitions suggest that a marital relationship is incompatible when the parties can no longer live in harmony, when their interests and desires are seriously and irreconcilably at odds. All definitions also plainly imply that it does not matter how the state of disharmony came about, and that no assessment of fault between the parties need be made. See North v. North, 217 Kan. 213, 535 P.2d 914 (1975); Gordon v. Gordon, 218 Kan. 686, 545 P.2d 328 (1976). Unfortunately some courts are so firmly commited to restricting divorce and are so concerned about fault that they sometimes refuse to find incompatibility where the party alleging it and seeking the divorce have been at fault. For example, two extraordinary cases from the Third Circuit deny divorces where the facts as stated seem clearly to reveal incompatibility of temperament. Shearer v. Shearer, 356 F.2d 391 (3d Cir. 1965), cert. den. 384 U.S. 940 (1966); Schlesinger v. Schlesinger, 399 F.2d 7 (3d Cir. 1968).

In Oklahoma one case states flatly that incompatibility involves fault, for the purpose of granting the wife alimony under a statute which requires a finding of fault as a prerequisite to alimony awards. Dowdell v. Dowdell, 463 P.2d 948 (Okl.1970). To the same effect is Buonassisi v. Buonassisi, 267 A.2d 888 (Del.1970), which states that some degree and element of fault are contained in the gravamen of the incompatibility ground for divorce. To the same effect is T. v. T., 314 A.2d 176 (Del.1973).

In New Mexico the court has indicated that the infamous doctrine of recrimination has no application to the ground of incompatibility, recriminatory acts being admissible only as proof on the issue of incompatibility. See Garner v. Garner, 512 P.2d 84 (N.M.1973), overruling Clark v. Clark, 54 N.M. 364, 225 P.2d 147 (1950). See also Cooper v. Cooper, 57 Ala.App. 674, 331 So.2d 689 (1976).

Some examples of cases in which incompatibility has been held to be proved include Colby v. Colby, 283 F.Supp. 150 (D.V.I.1968); Husband v. Wife, 280 A.2d 705 (Del.1971); H. v. H., 253 A.2d 500 (Del.1969).

Further authorities on incompatibility may be found in Annot., 58 A.L.R.2d 1218 (1958) and H. Clark, Law of Domestic Relations § 12.5 (1968).

G. MISCELLANEOUS GROUNDS FOR DIVORCE

There are several other grounds for divorce scattered through the statutes of the various states, none of them statistically important. Although the statutory language relating to these grounds is not uniform, the variations in construction from state to state are not great.

The first such grounds relate to the validity of marriage. Their inclusion among the grounds for divorce is illogical, since divorce normally is granted only where there is a valid marriage. None the less their inclusion makes sense, since it enables the courts to grant alimony and other incidental relief in annulment suits. Instead of directly authorizing alimony in annulment suits, which some states have done, these states have merely changed the label on the suit from annulment to divorce, thereby making available all the normal incidents of divorce including alimony. For this reason we find as grounds for divorce in some states prior subsisting marriage, impotence, fraud of certain kinds, duress and incest.

A fault ground for divorce found in a few states is gross neglect of duty. This seems to include elements of desertion and cruelty, overlapping to a great extent with cruelty. Talman v. Talman, 203 Kan. 601, 455 P.2d 574 (1969). In a few states non-support or the failure of a husband to provide for his wife and family are grounds for divorce.

Some statutes make conviction of a felony, or of an "infamous" crime a ground for divorce. Imprisonment for a stated time after conviction may also be required as a condition on the grant of a divorce.

Drunkenness, usually described in the statute as habitual drunkenness, and drug addiction are also often found among the grounds for divorce. These are construed to mean a serious addiction to alcohol and a fixed habit of drug use.

Finally insanity is not an uncommon ground for divorce. It is usually qualified in several ways, as by requiring that it be proved to be incurable, or that there be evidence that the defendant has been confined in an institution for a stated period, or that the defendant has been adjudicated or certified as insane by a specified number of doctors. The plaintiff's assumption of the responsibility for supporting the defendant may be made a condition on the grant of the divorce, provided the plaintiff is able to do so.

For additional discussion of these grounds, see H. Clark, Law of Domestic Relations § 12.7 (1968).

H. MARRIAGE BREAKDOWN

DESROCHERS v. DESROCHERS

Supreme Court of New Hampshire, 1975.
115 N.H. 591, 347 A.2d 150.

KENISON, Chief Justice. The parties married in September 1970. Their only child, a daughter, was born in January 1973. The parties separated in May of that year and the wife brought this libel for divorce the following September. A month later the parties agreed to and the court approved arrangements for custody, visitation and support. The defendant did not support his wife and child from the time of separation until the temporary decree. He made the payments called for by the decree from its entry until June 1975. In July 1974, the Hillsborough County Superior Court, Loughlin, J., held a hearing and made certain findings of fact. The critical portion of these findings is: "[T]he action was originally brought because the defendant did not work steadily and stated that he, when he learned that the plaintiff was pregnant, wanted a boy instead of a girl; if the plaintiff bore a girl he would like to put the child up for adoption. After the birth of the child [a daughter] the defendant became very attached to the child, has visited the child weekly except on two occasions, and has been faithfully making support payments under the temporary order of $25.00 a week. The defendant claims that he loves his wife, does not want a divorce. The wife claims that she no longer loves her husband, but since the filing of the divorce he has been an industrious worker and is very attached to the child." The superior court transferred without ruling the question "whether, on all the findings of fact, cause exists for granting a divorce under the provisions of RSA 458:7–a." This appeal was argued in September 1975. At the argument counsel informed the court that the defendant had stopped making support payments and had gone to Nevada in June 1975. At that time he had written to his attorney expressing his desire to remain married.

RSA 458:7–a (Supp.1973) provides: "A divorce from the bonds of matrimony shall be decreed, irrespective of the fault of either party, on the ground of irreconcilable differences which have caused the irremediable breakdown of the marriage. In any pleading or hearing of a libel for divorce under this section, allegations or evidence of specific acts of misconduct shall be improper and inadmissible, except where child custody is in issue and such evidence is relevant to establish that parental custody would be detrimental to the child or at a hearing where it is determined by the court to be necessary to establish the existence of irreconcilable differences. If, upon hearing of an action for divorce under this section, both parties are found to have committed an act or acts which justify a finding of irreconcilable differences, a divorce shall be decreed and the acts of one party shall not negate the acts of the other nor bar the divorce decree." This section must be applied in conjunction with RSA 458:7–b (Supp.1973) which precludes divorce when "there is a likelihood for rehabilitation of the marriage relationship" or when "there is a reasonable possibility of reconciliation."

RSA 458:7–a (Supp.1973) is the product of a national discussion regarding the proper grounds for divorce. It follows in important respects the California Family Law Act of 1969. That statute, and others following it, have been criticized for vagueness, but have been held to be sufficiently definite to afford due process of law. Ryan v. Ryan, 277 So.2d 266 (Fla.1973); In re Marriage of Walton, 28 Cal. App.3d 108, 104 Cal.Rptr. 472 (1972). A consensus has emerged that a period of separation due to marital difficulties is strong evidence of the irremediable breakdown of a marriage. These developments can be traced in the following commentaries: Bodenheimer, Reflections on the Future of Grounds for Divorce, 8 J.Fam.L. 179, 198–207 (1968); Foster and Freed, Divorce Reform: Brakes on Breakdown?, 13 J.Fam.L. 443, 448–453 (1973); Zuckman, The ABA Family Law Section v. The NCCUSL: Alienation, Separation and Forced Reconciliation over the Uniform Marriage and Divorce Act, 24 Cath. U.L.Rev. 61 (1974); and Annot., 55 A.L.R.3d 581 (1974). When asked to interpret a statute similar to RSA 458:7–a the Florida Court of Appeal stated: "The Legislature has not seen fit to promulgate guidelines as to what constitutes an 'irretrievably broken' marriage. It is suggested that this lack of definitive direction was deliberate and is desirable in an area as volatile as a proceeding for termination of the marital status. Consideration should be given to each case individually and predetermined policy should not be circumscribed by the appellate courts of this State.

"Thus, we are hesitant to set forth specific circumstances which trial courts could utilize as permissible indices of an irretrievable breakdown of the marital status. Were we to attempt to do so, we feel that the basic purpose of the new dissolution of marriage law would be frustrated. Such proceedings would either again become primarily adversary in nature or persons would again fit themselves into tailor-made categories or circumstances to fit judicially defined breakdown situations. It is our opinion that these two problems are the very ones which the Legislature intended to eliminate." Riley v. Riley, 271 So.2d 181, 183 (Fla.App.1972).

The existence of irreconcilable differences which have caused the irremediable breakdown of the marriage is determined by reference to the subjective state of mind of the parties. While the desire of one spouse to continue the marriage is evidence of "a reasonable possibility of reconciliation," it is not a bar to divorce. If one spouse resolutely refuses to continue and it is clear from the passage of time or other circumstances that there is no reasonable possibility of a change of heart, there is an irremediable breakdown of the marriage.

H. Clark, Jr., Domestic Relations, § 12.5, at 351 (1968). Comment, Irreconcilable Differences: California Courts Respond to No-fault Dissolutions, 7 Loyola of L.A.L.Rev. 453, 459–60, 466, 485 et seq. (1974). The defendant may attempt to impeach the plaintiff's evidence of his or her state of mind regarding the relationship. If the trial court doubts plaintiff's evidence that the marriage has irremediably broken down, the court may continue the action to determine if reconciliation is possible. However, if the parties do not reconcile, dissolution should be granted.

Knowledge of the sources of marital discord is helpful in determining whether a breakdown is irremediable or whether there is a reasonable possibility of reconciliation. Yet the statutory test is the existing state of the marriage. The statute authorizes the trial court to receive evidence of specific acts of misconduct where it is determined by the court to be necessary to establish the existence of irreconcilable differences. This authority is an exception to the general rule of the statute excluding such evidence, and the intent of the statute to minimize the acrimony attending divorce proceedings.

The question whether a breakdown of a marriage is irremediable is a question to be determined by the trial court. RSA 458:7–a contemplates the introduction of factual testimony sufficient to permit a finding of irreconcilable differences which have caused the irremediable breakdown of the marriage. Nevertheless there are limits to the inquiry. "In the first place, there is the natural tendency to withhold information of a personal nature from anyone but a trusted and discreet adviser; secondly, any probing into personal matters against the wishes of the party examined would be objectionable * * * ; and thirdly, the parties have come to court for a purpose. Their answers, which may be perfectly honest ones, will inevitably be slanted in the direction of their ultimate goal, which is divorce." *Bodenheimer*, supra at 200 (1968). Within these limits the trial court must be adequately informed before acting in matters of such importance. But the statute does not contemplate a complete biopsy of the marriage relationship from the beginning to the end in every case. This is a difficult task, but judges face similar problems in other cases.

The separation of the parties for two and one-half years and the plaintiff's persistence in seeking a divorce during that period is evidence from which the trial court could find that this marriage has irremediably broken down.

HAGERTY v. HAGERTY

Supreme Court of Minnesota, 1979.
281 N.W.2d 386.

STEPHEN L. MAXWELL, Justice. Appellant, the respondent below, in a marriage dissolution action appeals from a judgment granting the petition for dissolution and from the order denying her alternative motion for a new trial. We affirm.

Claire and William Hagerty were married in Chicago in 1947 and moved to Minnesota in 1965. They were parents of five children whose ages ranged from 17 to 28 years at the time of the 1978 dissolution proceedings. William had employment problems but was working at time of trial, and Claire, also employed, had started working about 1973. The three youngest children developed serious drug and behavior problems during the last few years of the marriage, and difficulties with communication and discipline precipitated the family's involvement with counseling and treatment programs by 1975, at which time William's alcoholism became apparent. All of those problems were sources of marital discord.

Claire, after unsuccessfully urging William to seek treatment for alcoholism, asked him in the summer of 1976 to leave the home. William moved out in August and filed for divorce in September. He made several unsuccessful attempts at reconciliation, but testified that no hope of reconciliation remained at the time of the proceedings. Claire claimed the marriage could be saved if William were treated for alcoholism, but she had not otherwise been willing to take him back.

Prior to the hearing on the dissolution petition, Claire had unsuccessfully sought a court order dismissing the petition unless her husband completed treatment for his alcoholism within 6 months and agreed to a one-year after-care program; if thereafter he wanted the dissolution she would not resist.

On April 6, 1978, the trial court dissolved the marriage after finding, among other things, that William suffered from alcoholism, a treatable disease; that it was a principal cause of marital discord which adversely affected his attitude towards the marriage; and that the marriage was irretrievably broken.

The pithy statement in appellant's brief that she "simply suggests that the alcoholism is the culprit and that Petitioner's assessment of the marriage is deluded," sets the scene. She then asks (1) how lucid are the perceptions of an alcoholic about the marriage; (2) whether the same perception would exist after recovery from alcoholism; and (3) whether the petitioner proved that the marriage was irretrievably broken.

The record amply supports the finding of serious marital discord, and Minn.St.1976, § 518.06, subd. 2, expressly permits a finding of irretrievable breakdown upon such evidence.[1]

Since the record also amply supports the findings of alcoholism as a principal cause of the discord and as a treatable disease, the issue is whether the petitioner's unlitigated alcoholism can or should defeat findings of discord and breakdown. The "can" issue is one of statutory construction; the "should" issue is one of public policy.

1. *Statutory Construction:* Although irretrievable breakdown was the only ground for dissolution in the 1976 statute, several former grounds were retained in altered form in Minn.St.1976, § 518.06, subd. 2, as evidentiary guidelines for establishing that ground, and the guideline of serious marital discord was added. There was no requirement for reconciliation attempts or stay of dissolution for any specified, limited period. Without requirements indicating a legislative policy of affirmatively encouraging a possibility of reconciliation, the statute contemplates that the likelihood of reconciliation be considered in the determination of irretrievable breakdown along with the evidentiary guidelines.[2]

Commentators and cases in other jurisdictions which have interpreted the grounds in no-fault dissolution statutes generally agree that the underlying concern is whether a meaningful marriage exists or can be rehabilitated.[3] With that concern as the central issue, irre-

1. Minn.St.1976, § 518.06, applies to this action since the appeal was pending prior to the effective date of the 1978 amendment. It provided in pertinent part:

"Subdivision 1. A dissolution of a marriage may be granted by a court of competent jurisdiction upon a showing to the satisfaction of the court that there has been an irretrievable breakdown of the marriage relationship.

"Subd. 2. A court may make a finding that there has been an irretrievable breakdown of the marriage relationship if the finding is supported by evidence of any of the following:
* * *
"(6) Serious marital discord adversely affecting the attitude of one or both of the parties toward the marriage."

The statute was amended by L. 1978, c. 722, §§ 22, 23, 63, effective March 1, 1979. Section 63 repealed subd. 2, and the repeal applies to actions pending prior to the effective date unless an appeal

was pending or a new trial had been ordered. In that event the law in effect at the time of the order sustaining the appeal of the new trial governs. L.1978, c. 772, § 61(b)(d).

2. Compare Minn.St.1976, § 518.06, with N.H.Rev.Stat.Ann. §§ 458:7-a, 458:7-b (Supp.1977) where irremediable breakdown is based upon irreconcilable differences, but divorce is precluded when "there is a likelihood for rehabilitation" or "reasonable possibility of reconciliation."

3. See, Foster, Divorce Reform and the Uniform Act, 7 Fam.L.Q. 179, 184, 194, 198 and note 74 (1973); Zuckman and Fox, The Ferment in Divorce Legislation, 12 J.Fam.L. 515, 601 (1972–1973); Note, 16 N.Y.L.F. 119, 164 (1970); Comment, 17 U.C.L. A.L.Rev. 1306, 1319 (1970); Annot. 55 A.L.R.3d 581, 595 § 5 (1974); New Topic Service Am.Jur.2d, No-Fault Divorce, §§ 9, 17, 23 (1977).

trievable breakdown is a fact which can be shown where both parties acknowledge that a breakdown exists at the time of the proceedings and one sees no reconciliation possibility. See, Flora v. Flora, 337 N.E.2d 846, 851 (Ind.App.1975); Kretzschmar v. Kretzschmar, 48 Mich.App. 279, 210 N.W.2d 352 (1973). It can also be shown by evidence of only one party's belief that it is the existing state, particularly where the parties have been living apart. See, In re Marriage of Franks, 542 P.2d 845, 852 (Colo.1975); Smith v. Smith, 322 So.2d 580 (Fla.App.1975); Desrochers v. Desrochers, 115 N.H. 591, 594, 347 A.2d 150, 152 (1975).

Where one party urged that the marriage situation was remediable but the other refused to pursue counseling or reconciliation, the subjective factor proving irretrievable breakdown was established and dissolution was granted. See, In re Marriage of Baier, 561 P.2d 20 (Colo.App.1977); Kretzschmar v. Kretzschmar, 48 Mich.App. 279, 210 N.W.2d 352 (1973). In situations where statutes authorize counseling or continuance and the testimony of the party alleging breakdown might be impeachable or doubtful, a continuance is favored over a denial, with dissolution following in the event reconciliation is not accomplished. See, Riley v. Riley, 271 So.2d 181, 184 (Fla.App.1972); Desrochers v. Desrochers, supra; Comment, 17 U.C.L.A.L.Rev. 1306, 1324–25 and note 135 (1970).

Because the courts look at the existing subjective attitude, evidence of cause is no more determinative than evidence of fault. Similarly, the Supreme Court of Florida declared in Ryan v. Ryan, 277 So.2d 266, 271 (Fla.1973):

"* * * The new statutory test for determining if a marriage is irretrievably broken is simply whether for whatever reason or cause (no matter whose 'fault') the marriage relationship is for all intents and purposes ended, no longer viable, a hollow sham beyond hope of reconciliation or repair."

Since, here, the issue of breakdown calls for a factual determination and since § 518.06 does not provide for a separate determination of the likelihood of reconciliation, the court could properly consider the impact of treatment upon both the husband's attitude and the existence of serious marital discord. If the evidence established, which it does not, that rehabilitation of this marriage was likely, the court would have been acting within its discretion in continuing the action.

Upon the evidence introduced, however, and under the prevailing view of the single ground for dissolution in no-fault statutes, the husband's untreated alcoholism cannot defeat findings of serious marital discord and irretrievable breakdown.

2. *Public Policy:* Appellant presents compelling arguments for requiring treatment before an alcoholic can obtain a marriage dissolution. The arguments are based upon social considerations regarding both divorce and alcoholism, two major public problems, and urge

a significant "judicially carved" exception to the statute's liberal policy and broad language.

Both the Florida and New Hampshire courts were faced with similar requests to look beyond findings of irretrievable breakdown, and both espoused the view stated by the Florida court that "predetermined policy should not be circumscribed by the appellate courts * * *." Riley v. Riley, 271 So.2d 181, 183 (Fla.App.1972).

 * * *

This court recently expressed its rejection of judicial carving with regard to consideration of fault in property distribution decisions and said that the forum for excluding that factor was the legislature. See, Elliott v. Elliott, 274 N.W.2d 75, 77 (Minn.1978).[4] Our position is consistent with the settled rule that extensions of statutory provisions are to be made by the legislature rather than the courts.

Based upon that judicial policy, we will not apply the requested alcoholism exception to the findings of discord and breakdown.

Affirmed.

 * * *

NOTES AND QUESTIONS

1. As indicated in the introductory note to this section, some thirty states have adopted some form of marriage breakdown as the only ground for divorce, or as one ground along with others. The New Hampshire and Minnesota statutes are more or less typical of the language used in other states. The California statute, one of the earliest to be enacted, provides that there are only two grounds for divorce, "irreconcilable differences, which have caused the irremediable breakdown of the marriage", and "incurable insanity". Cal.Civ.Code § 4506 (1970). Cal.Civ.Code § 4507 (1970) defines irreconcilable differences as follows: "Irreconcilable differences are those grounds which are determined by the court to be substantial reasons for not continuing the marriage and which make it appear that the marriage should be dissolved."

2. The Uniform Marriage and Divorce Act, §§ 302, 305, 9A Unif.L. Ann. 121, 132 (1979) deals with grounds for divorce in the following manner:

"§ 302.   [Dissolution of Marriage; Legal Separation]

    "(a) The [_____] court shall enter a decree of dissolution of marriage if:

        '* * *

        '(2) the court finds that the marriage is irretrievably broken, if the finding is supported by evidence that (i) the parties have

---

4. The court acknowledged in a footnote that the legislature had subsequently made marital fault an improper consideration in the property distribution decision in L.1978, c. 772, § 53, effective March 1979. Elliott v. Elliott, 274 N.W.2d 77, note 7.

lived separate and apart for a period of more than 180 days next preceding the commencement of the proceeding, or (ii) there is serious marital discord adversely affecting the attitude of one or both of the parties toward the marriage;

'(3) the court finds that the conciliation provisions of Section 305 either do not apply or have been met; '

"(b) If a party requests a decree of legal separation rather than a decree of dissolution of marriage, the court shall grant the decree in that form unless the other party objects."

"§ 305. [Irretrievable Breakdown]

"(a) If both of the parties by petition or otherwise have stated under oath or affirmation that the marriage is irretrievably broken, or one of the parties has so stated and the other has not denied it, the court, after hearing, shall make a finding whether the marriage is irretrievably broken.

"(b) If one of the parties has denied under oath or affirmation that the marriage is irretrievably broken, the court shall consider all relevant factors, including the circumstances that gave rise to filing the petition and the prospect of reconciliation, and shall:

'(1) make a finding whether the marriage is irretrievably broken; or

'(2) continue the matter for further hearing not fewer than 30 nor more than 60 days later, or as soon thereafter as the matter may be reached on the court's calendar, and may suggest to the parties that they seek counseling. The court, at the request of either party shall, or on its own motion may, order a conciliation conference. At the adjourned hearing the court shall make a finding whether the marriage is irretrievably broken.'

"(c) A finding of irretrievable breakdown is a determination that there is no reasonable prospect of reconciliation."

3. The Uniform Marriage and Divorce Act § 305(b)(2) provides an opportunity for counseling or conciliation. Some state statutes contain similar provisions. For example Cal.Civ.Code § 4509 (Supp.1979) provides that if there is a reasonable possibility of reconciliation, the court shall continue the proceeding for up to thirty days. Iowa Code Ann. § 598.16 (Supp.1979–1980) contains the following provision:

"§ 598.16 Conciliation

"A majority of the judges in any judicial district, with the co-operation of any county board of social welfare in such district, may establish a domestic relations division of the district court of the county where such board is located. Said division shall offer counseling and related services to persons before such court.

"Upon the application of the petitioner in the petition or by the respondent in the responsive pleading thereto or, within twenty days of appointment, of an attorney appointed under section 598.12, the court shall require the parties to participate in conciliation efforts for a period of sixty days from the issuance of an order setting forth the conciliation procedure and the conciliator.

"At any time upon its own motion or upon the application of a party the court may require the parties to participate in conciliation efforts for sixty days or less following the issuance of such an order.

"Every order for conciliation shall require the conciliator to file a written report by a date certain which shall state the conciliation procedures undertaken and such other matters as may have been required by the court. The report shall be a part of the record unless otherwise ordered by the court. Such conciliation procedure may include, but is not limited to, referrals to the domestic relations division of the court, if established, public or private marriage counselors, family service agencies, community health centers, physicians and clergymen.

"The costs of any such conciliation procedures shall be paid in full or in part by the parties and taxed as court costs; however, if the court determines that such parties will be unable to pay the costs without prejudicing their financial ability to provide themselves and any minor children with economic necessities, such costs may be paid in full or in part from the court expense fund."

Colo.Rev.Stat.Ann. § 14–10–110 (1973) provides that where one party denies that the marriage is irretrievably broken, the court may continue the case for from thirty to sixty days and may suggest that the parties seek counseling.

The purpose of these provisions is presumably to attempt to reduce the numbers of divorces thereby counteracting the supposed effect of the marriage breakdown ground, which, it was widely assumed, would lead to increased divorce rates. Although the American divorce rate has increased markedly in the 1970's, at least one study has concluded that this increase cannot be attributed to the enactment of a marriage breakdown statute. Frank, Berman, Mazur-Hart, No Fault Divorce and the Divorce Rate: The Nebraska Experience—An Interrupted Time Series Analysis and Commentary, 58 Neb.L.Rev. 1, 18 (1979).

"Counseling" in the divorce setting can involve a number of techniques, many of which are discussed in Bodenheimer, New Approaches of Psychiatry: Implications for Divorce Reform, 1970 Utah L.Rev. 191. Some of the problems involved in a court counseling program are discussed in Bodenheimer, The Utah Marriage Counseling Experiment: An Account of Changes in Divorce Law and Procedure, 7 Utah L.Rev. 443 (1961).

Should all states couple the marriage breakdown ground for divorce with provisions like those in Iowa? Or should the counseling provisions be stronger, requiring counseling in all cases, or in certain classes of cases, before a divorce may be granted? Is a period of thirty days, or sixty days, sufficient for effective counseling?

4. Would the divorce have been granted in *Desrochers* if the parties had not been separated for any considerable period?

5. Would the *Desrochers* and *Hagerty* cases have been decided as they were under the Uniform Marriage and Divorce Act?

6. Is the statutory language involved in these two cases, and in California, Iowa, or the Uniform Act, sufficiently similar so that cases decided under one statute are authorities in the construction of another statute?

7. Can you imagine a case in which both spouses ask for a divorce in a state having a marriage breakdown statute and in which a court would refuse the divorce? If you can think of a case in which this might occur, outline the facts as fully as your imagination permits. If you cannot think of such a case, would you then characterize the statute as one which authorizes divorce at the request of both parties?

8. In a divorce action by H against W, the following was the only testimony:

Q. Have irreconcilable differences developed in your marriage?

A. (By H) Yes.

Q. Have those differences brought about a breakdown of your marriage?

A. Yes.

Q. Is there any chance of reconciliation?

A. No.

Should the court grant the divorce, where a marriage breakdown statute exists? See Cal.Civ.Code § 4509 (Supp.1978–1980); Note, 17 U.C. L.A.L.Rev. 1306, 1322 (1970). Should the Court admit in evidence a letter from a marriage counsellor stating that the marriage had broken down? In re Marriage of Boyd, 200 N.W.2d 845 (Iowa 1972). If so, would that alone support a finding that the marriage had broken down?

See the following language in In re Marriage of Morgan, 218 N.W.2d 552, 560 (Iowa 1974): "Marriage is a relationship between two people, and if one of those people has determined it shall not continue, this would seem to be plain evidence the relationship has broken down."

9. What should be the result in cases like *Desrochers* or *Hagerty* if the trial court refused to hear any evidence on the part of the respondents other than statements that they wished to undergo marriage counseling or conciliation in order to achieve a reconciliation with their spouses? Should such a decision be reversed on appeal? Should the trial court be required to investigate all the circumstances in the lives of the parties leading to the suit for divorce? See Note, 17 U.C.L.A.L.Rev. 1306, 1322 (1970); Cal.Civ.Code § 4509 (Supp.1979–1980), which excludes from evidence testimony concerning specific acts of misconduct.

10. What should be the result under the marriage breakdown type of statute in the following circumstances? H sues for divorce from W, alleging and proving that they had been married ten years, that two years previously W had begun to suffer from acute episodes of anger, that she then began seeing a psychiatrist and was hospitalized for about six months with a diagnosis of paranoid schizophrenia. On her release from the hospital she returned to live with H. Her condition was then improved but occasionally she still had periods of anger, moodiness and acute unhappiness. She testified that she did not wish to be divorced, that the very thought of it caused her great distress. Her psychiatrist testified that further improvement in her condition was quite possible, but that he was unable to make any firmer prediction than that. Cf. Crittenden v. Crittenden, 210 Va. 76, 168 S.E.2d 115 (1969); Wadlington, A Case of Insanity and Divorce, 56 Va.L.Rev. 12 (1970); Cal.Civ.Code § 4506 (Supp.1979–1980), making incurable insanity the only ground for divorce in addition to marital breakdown.

11. H and W, happily married, went on vacation together and, due to H's negligence, had a serious auto accident. W was so severely injured that she became permanently paralyzed from the waist down and had to look forward to the remainder of her life in a wheel chair. Sexual relations were impossible for her. Two years later H sued for divorce on the ground of marriage breakdown. The evidence showed that he was spending much time with another woman. What should be the result?

12. The marriage breakdown type of divorce statute has survived the relatively few and unfocused constitutional attacks which have been made upon it. In re Marriage of Franks, 189 Colo. 499, 542 P.2d 845 (1975); Dickson v. Dickson, 238 Ga. 672, 235 S.E.2d 479 (1977).

13. Where both parties wish the divorce, and where no property, support or custody of children are involved, it is possible for the parties to obtain a divorce without being represented by counsel. In many states these "pro se" divorces are not uncommon, under marriage breakdown statutes.

The question then arises, in such cases, where there is no controversy either over the grounds, or property, or children, why should a hearing of any sort be required? One Georgia case, Manning v. Manning, 237 Ga. 746, 229 S.E.2d 611 (1976) held that a husband could be granted a summary judgment of divorce on the basis of his affidavit that the marriage was broken but the case was overruled almost at once by Dickson v. Dickson, 238 Ga. 672, 235 S.E.2d 479 (1977). The latter case seems to have left open some possibility of summary judgment of divorce, however, in cases in which there is no genuine issue of material fact. In England, where both parties wish the divorce, have lived apart for two years, and there are no children under sixteen, they may obtain a divorce by mail. Matrimonial Causes Rules 1973, Stat.Inst. 1973 No. 2016 rr. 33(3), 48, and Practice Direction, (1973) 3 All E.R. 1182.

14. Assume that you are a member of the Senate Judiciary Committee of your state legislature. As such a member, how would you react to the following proposed statute?

"(a) Any man and women applying for a marriage license under the provisions of sections _____, may file with their application a written contract, signed by both and duly acknowledged. Such contract may contain such provisions as the parties desire for the regulation of their marital rights and responsibilities, including, but not limited to, a provision establishing a limit on the duration of their marriage of not less than one year. Such contracts so filed shall be matters of public record and open to inspection.

"(b) On or after the date set by any contract filed under subsection (a) hereof for the termination of any marriage, the parties or either of them may file with the county clerk a written, signed and acknowledged statement that their marriage has terminated in accordance with the terms of the contract.

"(c) Either party to such contract may, at any time after such termination, bring suit in a court of competent jurisdiction to have adjudicated any financial, property, custody or other disputes arising out of the marriage or the marriage contract filed under subsection (a) hereof. Such disputes shall be decided by reference to the parties' contract filed under subsection (a) hereof if possible, but if not possible, in accordance with the applicable statutes and common law.

"(d) If no action under subsection (b) hereof is taken, contracts filed under subsection (a) hereof shall be deemed to be renewed for subsequent periods equal in length to the period of duration prescribed in the contract as originally filed. At any time the parties may file written, signed and acknowledged amendments to the contracts authorized by subsection (a)."

I. DEFENSES TO DIVORCE

There are four traditional affirmative defenses to divorce actions. All of them are related in one way or another to fault, and all of them were inherited from the English ecclesiastical law. They are collusion, connivance, condonation and recrimination. In many states some or all of these defenses are established by statute. In others they have been adopted by judicial decision. The statutes of individual states must be examined in any case since sometimes the defense as defined in the statute differs from the defense as defined by the common law.

In addition to the traditional defenses mentioned, delay in bringing suit for divorce may be a defense under the law of some states, either by virtue of the application of a statute of limitations or of the doctrine of laches.

Since the defenses are related to fault, it would seem logical that those states which have adopted marriage breakdown as a ground or the ground for dissolution of marriage would abolish the defenses as being no longer relevant. Some of those states and the Uniform Marriage and Divorce Act § 303(e), 9A Unif.L.Ann. 126 (1979), have done this. Cal.Civ.Code § 4509 (Supp.1979) (excludes evidence of specific acts of misconduct); Colo.Rev.Stat.Ann. § 14–10–107(5) (1973); Fla.Stat.Ann. § 61.044 (Supp.1979) (condonation, collusion, recrimination and laches abolished); Iowa Code Ann. § 598.18 (Supp.1979–1980) (recrimination abolished); Or.Rev.Stat. § 107.055 (1977); Tex.Fam.Code § 3.08 (1975) (recrimination abolished, condonation recognized as a defense only if there is a reasonable expectation of reconciliation.) But even if not abolished by statute, these defenses are so clearly inconsistent with marriage breakdown that they no longer have any practical effect in those states which have adopted marriage breakdown as a ground for divorce.

Although of little current practical importance, the defenses may be worth defining very briefly. Collusion is defined in general as an agreement between the parties that one of them will not defend the case or will appear to have committed adultery or other marital offense in order to obtain the divorce. Thus when drafting a separation agreement, the parties should be careful not to include a provision that one of them will sue and the other will not defend the case. Such an agreement has been held collusive in the past and may invalidate the entire agreement.

Connivance is generally defined as occurring when the plaintiff consents to the defendant's commission of the marital offense. It is sometimes confused with collusion, but the two are quite different. Collusion occurs when the parties collaborate to impose on the court by fabricating a ground for divorce, while connivance is merely consent to an offense which actually is committed.

Condonation occurs when there is a resumption or continuance of marital cohabitation with knowledge of the marital misconduct, so as to imply forgiveness on the part of the innocent spouse. It is generally held to require voluntary forgiveness and to be conditional on the defendant's future good behavior.

Recrimination, like other divorce defenses came to the United States from the English ecclesiastical practice. The doctrine in its broad common law form states that when both spouses have been guilty of marital misconduct which would be grounds for divorce, neither may obtain the divorce. In other words, when both parties have given the clearest indication that their marriage is dead, that is precisely the point at which the law said that no divorce could be granted. The doctrine was so silly and so pernicious that many courts had begun to restrict or abolish it even before the enactment of no-fault grounds for divorce. Of course, it, and the other affirmative defenses, have no place in a suit based upon marriage breakdown.

In a few states delay in bringing suit may be a defense to divorce, either because there is a specific statute of limitations or because the courts have held divorce to be within general omnibus statutes of limitations. In other states a very few cases have held the suit barred on the ground of laches. This defense, although it does not turn on fault, likewise has no place where the ground for divorce is marriage breakdown or other non-fault grounds.

For a more complete discussion of the affirmative defenses to divorce see H. Clark, Law of Domestic Relations §§ 12.8 to 12.12 (1968).

SECTION 3. JURISDICTION OVER THE ALIMONY, PROPERTY AND CHILD SUPPORT ASPECTS OF DIVORCE

ESTIN v. ESTIN

Supreme Court of the United States, 1948.
334 U.S. 541, 68 S.Ct. 1213, 92 L.Ed. 1561.

Mr. Justice DOUGLAS delivered the opinion of the Court.

This case, here on certiorari to the Court of Appeals of New York, presents an important question under the Full Faith and Credit Clause of the Constitution. Article IV, § 1. It is whether a New York decree awarding respondent $180 per month for her maintenance and support in a separation proceeding survived a Nevada divorce decree which subsequently was granted petitioner.

The parties were married in 1937 and lived together in New York until 1942 when the husband left the wife. There was no issue of the marriage. In 1943 she brought an action against him for a separation. He entered a general appearance. The court, finding that he had abandoned her, granted her a decree of separation and awarded her $180 per month as permanent alimony. In January 1944 he went to Nevada where in 1945 he instituted an action for divorce. She was notified of the action by constructive service but entered no appearance in it. In May, 1945, the Nevada court, finding that petitioner had been a bona fide resident of Nevada since January 30, 1944, granted him an absolute divorce "on the ground of three years continual separation, without cohabitation." The Nevada decree made no provision for alimony, though the Nevada court had been advised of the New York decree.

Prior to that time petitioner had made payments of alimony under the New York decree. After entry of the Nevada decree he ceased paying. Thereupon respondent sued in New York for a supplementary judgment for the amount of the arrears. Petitioner appeared in the action and moved to eliminate the alimony provisions of the separation decree by reason of the Nevada decree. The Supreme Court denied the motion and granted respondent judgment for the arrears. * * * The judgment was affirmed by the Appellate Division, * * *, and then by the Court of Appeals. * * *

We held in Williams v. North Carolina, 317 U.S. 287, 63 S.Ct. 207, 87 L.Ed. 279, * * *, (1) that a divorce decree granted by a State to one of its domiciliaries is entitled to full faith and credit in a bigamy prosecution brought in another State, even though the other spouse was given notice of the divorce proceeding only through constructive service; and (2) that while the finding of domicile by the court that granted the decree is entitled to prima facie weight, it is not conclusive in a sister State but might be relitigated there.
  * * The latter course was followed in this case, as a consequence of which the Supreme Court of New York found, in accord with the Nevada court, that petitioner "is now and since January 1944, has been a bona fide resident of the State of Nevada." * * *

Petitioner's argument therefore is that the tail must go with the hide—that since by the Nevada decree, recognized in New York, he and respondent are no longer husband and wife, no legal incidence of the marriage remains. We are given a detailed analysis of New York law to show that the New York courts have no power either by statute or by common law to compel a man to support his ex-wife, that alimony is payable only so long as the relation of husband and wife exists, and that in New York, as in some other states, * * *, a support order does not survive divorce.

The difficulty with that argument is that the highest court in New York has held in this case that a support order can survive divorce and that this one has survived petitioner's divorce. That conclusion is binding on us, except as it conflicts with the Full Faith and Credit Clause. It is not for us to say whether that ruling squares with what the New York courts said on earlier occasions. It is enough that New York today says that such is her policy. The only question for us is whether New York is powerless to make such a ruling in view of the Nevada decree.

We can put to one side the case where the wife was personally served or where she appears in divorce proceedings. * * * The only service on her in this case was by publication and she made no appearance in the Nevada proceeding. The requirements of procedural due process were satisfied and the domicile of the husband in Nevada was foundation for a decree effecting a change in the marital capacity of both parties in all the other States of the Union, as well as in Nevada. * * * But the fact that marital capacity was changed does not mean that every other legal incidence of the marriage was necessarily affected.

Although the point was not adjudicated in Barber v. Barber, 21 How. 582, 588, 16 L.Ed. 226, the Court in that case recognized that while a divorce decree obtained in Wisconsin by a husband from his absent wife might dissolve the vinculum of the marriage, it did not mean that he was freed from payment of alimony under an earlier separation decree granted by New York. An absolutist might quarrel with the result and demand a rule that once a divorce is granted, the whole of the marriage relation is dissolved, leaving no roots or tendrils of any kind. But there are few areas of the law in black and white. The grays are dominant and even among them the shades are innumerable. For the eternal problem of the law is one of making accommodations between conflicting interests. This is why most legal problems end as questions of degree. That is true of the present problem under the Full Faith and Credit Clause. The question involves important considerations both of law and of policy which it is essential to state.

The situations where a judgment of one State has been denied full faith and credit in another State, because its enforcement would contravene the latter's policy, have been few and far between. * * * The Full Faith and Credit Clause is not to be applied, accordion-like, to accommodate our personal predilections. It substituted a command for the earlier principles of comity and thus basically altered the status of the States as independent sovereigns. * * * It ordered submission by one State even to hostile policies reflected in the judgment of another State, because the practical operation of the federal system, which the Constitution designed, demanded it. The fact that the requirements of full faith and credit, so far as judgments are concerned, are exacting, if not inexorable (Sherrer v. Sher-

rer, supra), does not mean, however, that the State of the domicile of one spouse may, through the use of constructive service, enter a decree that changes every legal incidence of the marriage relationship.

Marital status involves the regularity and integrity of the marriage relation. It affects the legitimacy of the offspring of marriage. It is the basis of criminal laws, as the bigamy prosecution in Williams v. North Carolina dramatically illustrates. The State has a considerable interest in preventing bigamous marriages and in protecting the offspring of marriages from being bastardized. The interest of the State extends to its domiciliaries. The State should have the power to guard its interest in them by changing or altering their marital status and by protecting them in that changed status throughout the farthest reaches of the nation. For a person domiciled in one State should not be allowed to suffer the penalties of bigamy for living outside the State with the only one which the State of his domicile recognizes as his lawful wife. And children born of the only marriage which is lawful in the State of his domicile should not carry the stigma of bastardy when they move elsewhere. These are matters of legitimate concern to the State of the domicile. They entitle the State of the domicile to bring in the absent spouse through constructive service. In no other way could the State of the domicile have and maintain effective control of the marital status of its domiciliaries.

Those are the considerations that have long permitted the State of the matrimonial domicile to change the marital status of the parties by an ex parte divorce proceeding, * * *, considerations which in the Williams cases we thought were equally applicable to any State in which one spouse had established a bona fide domicile. * * * But those considerations have little relevancy here. In this case New York evinced a concern with this broken marriage when both parties were domiciled in New York and before Nevada had any concern with it. New York was rightly concerned lest the abandoned spouse be left impoverished and perhaps become a public charge. The problem of her livelihood and support is plainly a matter in which her community had a legitimate interest. The New York court, having jurisdiction over both parties, undertook to protect her by granting her a judgment of permanent alimony. Nevada, however, apparently follows the rule that dissolution of the marriage puts an end to a support order. * * * But the question is whether Nevada could under any circumstances adjudicate rights of respondent under the New York judgment when she was not personally served or did not appear in the proceeding.

Bassett v. Bassett, 9 Cir., 141 F.2d 954, held, that Nevada could not. We agree with that view.

The New York judgment is a property interest of respondent, created by New York in a proceeding in which both parties were present. It imposed obligations on petitioner and granted rights to respondent. The property interest which it created was an intangible, jurisdiction over which cannot be exerted through control over a physical thing. Jurisdiction over an intangible can indeed only arise from control or power over the persons whose relationships are the source of the rights and obligations. * * *

Jurisdiction over a debtor is sufficient to give the State of his domicile some control over the debt which he owes. It can, for example, levy a tax on its transfer by will * * * appropriate it through garnishment or attachment * * * collect it and administer it for the benefit of creditors. * * * But we are aware of no power which the State of domicile of the debtor has to determine the personal rights of the creditor in the intangible unless the creditor has been personally served or appears in the proceeding. The existence of any such power has been repeatedly denied. * * *

We know of no source of power which would take the present case out of that category. The Nevada decree that is said to wipe out respondent's claim for alimony under the New York judgment is nothing less than an attempt by Nevada to restrain respondent from asserting her claim under that judgment. That is an attempt to exercise an in personam jurisdiction over a person not before the court. That may not be done. Since Nevada had no power to adjudicate respondent's rights in the New York judgment, New York need not give full faith and credit to that phase of Nevada's judgment. A judgment of a court having no jurisdiction to render it is not entitled to the full faith and credit which the Constitution and statute of the United States demand. * * *

The result in this situation is to make the divorce divisible—to give effect to the Nevada decree insofar as it affects marital status and to make it ineffective on the issue of alimony. It accommodates the interests of both Nevada and New York in this broken marriage by restricting each State to the matters of her dominant concern.

Since Nevada had no jurisdiction to alter respondent's rights in the New York judgment, we do not reach the further question whether in any event that judgment would be entitled to full faith and credit in Nevada. * * *

Affirmed.

* * *

Mr. Justice JACKSON, dissenting. If there is one thing that the people are entitled to expect from their lawmakers, it is rules of law that will enable individuals to tell whether they are married and, if so, to whom. Today many people who have simply lived in more than one state do not know, and the most learned lawyer cannot advise them with any confidence. The uncertainties that result are not merely technical, nor are they trivial; they affect fundamental rights and relations such as the lawfulness of their cohabitation, their children's legitimacy, their title to property, and even whether they are law-abiding persons or criminals. In a society as mobile and nomadic as ours, such uncertainties affect large numbers of people and create a social problem of some magnitude. It is therefore important that, whatever we do, we shall not add to the confusion. I think that this decision does just that.

* * *

Now the question is whether the New York judgment of separation or the Nevada judgment of divorce controls the present obligation to pay alimony. The New York judgment of separation is based on the premise that the parties remain husband and wife, though estranged, and hence the obligation of support, incident to marriage, continues. The Nevada decree is based on the contrary premise that the marriage no longer exists and so obligations dependent on it have ceased.

premises differ

The Court reaches the Solomon-like conclusion that the Nevada decree is half good and half bad under the full faith and credit clause. It is good to free the husband from the marriage; it is not good to free him from its incidental obligations. Assuming the judgment to be one which the Constitution requires to be recognized at all, I do not see how we can square this decision with the command that it be given full faith and credit. * * * But if we are to hold this divorce good, I do not see how it can be less good than a divorce would be if rendered by the courts of New York.

As I understand New York law, if, after a decree of separation and alimony, the husband had obtained a New York divorce against his wife, it would terminate her right to alimony. If the Nevada judgment is to have full faith and credit, I think it must have the same effect that a similar New York decree would have. I do not see how we can hold that it must be accepted for some purposes and not for others, that he is free of his former marriage but still may be jailed, as he may in New York, for not paying the maintenance of a woman whom the Court is compelled to consider as no longer his wife.

NOTES AND QUESTIONS

1. *Estin* is noted in 48 Colum.L.Rev. 1083 (1948); 49 Colum.L.Rev. 153 (1949); 61 Harv.L.Rev. 1454 (1948); 33 Minn.L.Rev. 307 (1949); 1 Stan.L.Rev. 137 (1948). A companion case is Kreiger v. Kreiger, 334 U.S. 555 (1948). For a general discussion of the problem of the case see Krauskopf, Divisible Divorce and Rights to Support, Property and Custody, 24 Ohio St.L.J. 346 (1963).

2. Mr. Justice Frankfurter's dissent in *Estin* asserts that the case rests on three independent grounds: (a) New York may, without violating full faith and credit, hold that its prior separate maintenance decree survives a decree of divorce granted either by New York or some other state. (b) New York may hold that its separate maintenance decree survives a sister-state divorce without violation of full faith and credit, because of its in-

terest in assuring support for its citizens. (c) A separate maintenance decree creates an obligation which may not be cut off without personal jurisdiction of the wife, under the Due Process Clause.

Do you agree with his analysis of the majority opinion? Is it the interest of New York or of the parties to the divorce which is crucial in this case?

3. But the statute, 28 U.S.C.A. § 1738, implementing the Full Faith and Credit Clause, provides, "Such * * * judicial proceedings * * * shall have the same full faith and credit in every court within the United States * * * as they have by law or usage in the courts of such State * * * from which they are taken." Isn't the plain meaning of this statute that New York must give that effect to the Nevada divorce which Nevada would give it, provided of course there is jurisdiction in Nevada to grant the divorce under *Williams I*? And if Nevada law is that its divorces terminate obligations under outstanding separate maintenance decrees, must New York give the divorce that effect?

4. If Mrs. Estin had been personally served in the Nevada proceeding, or had entered a general appearance there, would the result of this case have been different? What does the answer to that question indicate as to the rationale of *Estin*?

5. What would have been the result in *Estin* if the New York court had found, under *Williams II*, that the husband had never been domiciled in Nevada? Would this fact alone justify a holding that the New York separation decree was not affected by the divorce? Esenwein v. Commonwealth, 325 U.S. 279 (1945).

6. What should be the result in an *Estin*-type case if the husband remained in Nevada, and the wife sued him there to collect unpaid arrears due under the New York separate maintenance decree? Perry v. Perry, 51 Wash.2d 358, 318 P.2d 986 (1958), 10 Stan.L.Rev. 758 (1958).

7. What should be the result under *Estin* if the wife had first brought a suit for separate maintenance in New York, and the husband then moved his domicile to another state, sued there for divorce and managed to obtain a decree before the wife could get a decree in her own suit, the wife making a general appearance in the divorce suit and contesting it on the merits? Would this prevent her from obtaining the decree of separate maintenance at her domicile? Nowell v. Nowell, 157 Conn. 470, 254 A.2d 889 (1969), cert. den. 396 U.S. 844 (1969).

8. What would be the result if the law of the wife's domicile (say Pennsylvania) were that obligations under separation decrees are cut off by ex parte sister-state divorces? Would this offend the due process clause?

VANDERBILT v. VANDERBILT

Supreme Court of the United States, 1957.
354 U.S. 416, 77 S.Ct. 1360, 1 L.Ed.2d 1456.

1948-52

Mr. Justice BLACK delivered the opinion of the Court.

Cornelius Vanderbilt, Jr., petitioner, and Patricia Vanderbilt, respondent, were married in 1948. They separated in 1952 while living in California. The wife moved to New York where she has resided since February 1953. In March of that year the husband filed suit for divorce in Nevada. This proceeding culminated, in June 1953, with a decree of final divorce which provided that both husband and wife were "freed and released from the bonds of matrimony and all the duties and obligations thereof. * * * "[1] The wife was not served with process in Nevada and did not appear before the divorce court.

In April 1954, Mrs. Vanderbilt instituted an action in a New York court praying for separation from petitioner and for alimony. The New York court did not have personal jurisdiction over him, but in order to satisfy his obligations, if any, to Mrs. Vanderbilt, it sequestered his property within the State. He appeared specially and, among other defenses to the action, contended that the Full Faith and Credit Clause of the United States Constitution compelled the New York court to treat the Nevada divorce as having ended the marriage and as having destroyed any duty of support which he owed the respondent. While the New York court found the Nevada decree valid and held that it had effectively dissolved the marriage, it nevertheless entered an order, under § 1170–b of the New York Civil Practice Act,[4] directing petitioner to make designated support payments to respondent. 207 Misc. 294, 138 N.Y.S.2d 222. The New York Court of Appeals upheld the support order. 1 N.Y.2d 342, 135 N.E.2d 553. Petitioner then applied to this Court for certiorari contending that § 1170–b, as applied, is unconstitutional because it contravenes the Full Faith and Credit Clause.

In Estin v. Estin, 334 U.S. 541, 68 S.Ct. 1213, 92 L.Ed. 1561, this Court decided that a Nevada divorce court, which had no personal jurisdiction over the wife, had no power to terminate a husband's obligation to provide her support as required in a pre-existing New York separation decree. The factor which distinguishes the present case from Estin is that here the wife's right to support had not been reduced to judgment prior to the husband's *ex parte* divorce. In our opinion this difference is not material on the question before us. Since the wife was not subject to its jurisdiction, the Nevada divorce

---

1. It seems clear that in Nevada the effect of this decree was to put an end to the husband's duty to support the wife—provided, of course, that the Nevada courts had power to do this. Sweeney v. Sweeney, 42 Nev. 431, 438–439, 179 P. 638, 639–640; Herrick v. Herrick, 55 Nev. 59, 68, 25 P.2d 378, 380. See Estin v. Estin, 334 U.S. 541, 547, 68 S.Ct. 1213, 1217, 92 L.Ed. 1561.

4. "In an action for divorce, separation or annulment, * * * where the court refuses to grant such relief by reason of a finding by the court that a divorce * * * declaring the marriage a nullity had previously been granted to the husband in an action in which jurisdiction over the person of the wife was not obtained, the court may, nevertheless, render in the same action such judgment as justice may require for the maintenance of the wife." Gilbert-Bliss' N. Y.Civ.Prac., Vol. 6A, 1956 Cum.Supp. § 1170–b.

[This provision is now incorporated in N.Y.Dom.Rel.L. § 236 (Supp.1971–72). Ed. Note.]

court had no power to extinguish any right which she had under the law of New York to financial support from her husband. It has long been the constitutional rule that a court cannot adjudicate a personal claim or obligation unless it has jurisdiction over the person of the defendant.[6] Here, the Nevada divorce court was as powerless to cut off the wife's support right as it would have been to order the husband to pay alimony if the wife had brought the divorce action and he had not been subject to the divorce court's jurisdiction. Therefore, the Nevada decree, to the extent it purported to affect the wife's right to support, was void and the Full Faith and Credit Clause did not obligate New York to give it recognition.[7]

* * *

Affirmed.

NOTES AND QUESTIONS

1. Mr. Justice Frankfurter's dissent argued that *Vanderbilt* was clearly distinguishable from *Estin* since the crucial fact in *Estin* was the existence of a prior New York decree of separation, to which Nevada was required to give full faith and credit. He also asserted that the property or alimony aspect of the divorce is not to be treated differently from the dissolution of the status of marriage, since both are "personal", and that Nevada had jurisdiction to cut off a right to alimony as well as to end the marriage. Would you agree with this line of argument?

2. *Vanderbilt* is noted in 43 Corn.L.Q. 265 (1958); 69 Harv.L.Rev. 1497 (1956); 43 Iowa L.Rev. 645 (1958); 30 Rocky Mt.L.Rev. 89 (1957). See also Ritz, Migratory Alimony: A Constitutional Dilemma in the Existence of In Personam Jurisdiction, 29 Ford.L.Rev. 83 (1960).

3. The majority opinion states that since the wife was not subject to Nevada's jurisdiction, the Nevada divorce court had no power to extinguish any right which she had under New York law to support from her husband. Does such a right remain inchoate until it is enforced by a court decree?

4. The majority opinion also states that it is a constitutional rule that a court cannot adjudicate a personal claim unless it has jurisdiction over the person of the defendant, citing Pennoyer v. Neff. What does that suggest as to the rationale of *Vanderbilt*?

In some states the local rule is that an ex parte divorce granted in another state cuts off rights under an existing separate maintenance decree, or

---

6. Pennoyer v. Neff, 95 U.S. 714, 726–727, 24 L.Ed. 565. If a defendant has property in a State it can adjudicate his obligations, but only to the extent of his interest in that property. Pennington v. Fourth Nat. Bank of Cincinnati, 243 U.S. 269, 37 S.Ct. 282, 61 L.Ed. 713; Harris v. Balk, 198 U.S. 215, 25 S.Ct. 625, 49 L.Ed. 1023.

7. A concurring opinion in Armstrong v. Armstrong, 350 U.S. 568, 575, 76 S.Ct. 629, 633, 100 L.Ed. 705, and the authorities collected there, set forth

in greater detail the reasons underlying this holding. Cf. Meredith v. Meredith, 96 U.S.App.D.C. 355, 226 F.2d 257, 69 Harv.L.Rev. 1497.

"A state lacks judicial jurisdiction to absolve a spouse from any duty of support which, under the law of a second state, he may owe the other spouse in the absence of personal jurisdiction over the latter." Restatement, Conflict of Laws, § 116(2) (Tent.Draft No. 1, 1953), and see Comment f to § 116.

rights to alimony which a spouse might normally be able to assert on divorce. For examples, see Esenwein v. Commonwealth, 325 U.S. 279 (1945) (Pennsylvania law); Stambaugh v. Stambaugh, 458 Pa. 147, 329 A.2d 483 (1974); Brown v. Brown, 249 Or. 274, 437 P.2d 845 (1968); Burton v. Burton, 52 Tenn.App. 484, 376 S.W.2d 504 (1963), 16 Syra.L.Rev. 150 (1964); Loeb v. Loeb, 118 Vt. 472, 114 A.2d 518 (1955); Brady v. Brady, 151 W.Va. 900, 158 S.E.2d 359 (1967), and cases cited in Annots., 1 A.L.R. 2d 1423 (1948) and 28 A.L.R.2d 1346 (1953).

Restatement, Second, Conflict of Laws § 77, comment f (1971) makes this statement: "Although full faith and credit does not bar a wife from seeking support from a husband who has previously obtained an *ex parte* divorce, she may nevertheless be unable to obtain such relief. This is because a valid divorce decree severs the marital relationship and the local law of some States makes no provision for requiring an ex-husband to support an ex-wife."

Do *Estin* and *Vanderbilt* hold that such a rule is unconstitutional? In Lewis v. Lewis, 49 Cal.2d 389, 317 P.2d 987 (1957) there is language suggesting that the *Vanderbilt* and *Estin* cases go no further than to leave the issue open to the law of the wife's domicile. And in Hudson v. Hudson, 52 Cal.2d 735, 344 P.2d 295 (1959) the same distinguished judge, Mr. Justice Traynor, amplifies his view of the effect of *Estin* and *Vanderbilt,* saying that those cases held that the wife could not, without being personally subject to the Nevada court's jurisdiction, be deprived of whatever rights of support she may have had under the law of the domicile at the time of the divorce, without a violation of due process. But if the wife, before the divorce, has a right to be supported by her husband, as she does in nearly all states, and if she could enforce that right against him in a variety of ways, civil and criminal, as she may in nearly all states, how can any state after *Estin* and *Vanderbilt* say that that right may be terminated by a legal proceeding to which she is not a party? In other words, if the New York court in *Vanderbilt* had held that the wife's claim to support was cut off by the ex parte Nevada divorce, would that have violated the Due Process Clause by depriving her of a personal claim for money without in personam jurisdiction over her?

5. What should be the result of *Vanderbilt* if Nevada's law was that a valid ex parte divorce cuts off any right to support or alimony, but New York law was that it does not?

6. What would be the result if the wife were domiciled in New York at the time the husband obtained his ex parte Nevada divorce, but later she moved to Pennsylvania, whose law apparently is that such a divorce cuts off any claim to alimony that the wife might have, and she then sued her husband there for support? Cf. Lewis v. Lewis, cited supra, paragraph 4; Herczog v. Herczog, 186 Cal.App.2d 318, 9 Cal.Rptr. 5 (1960); Worthley v. Worthley, infra, page 933.

7. California is a community property state. Upon divorce it is customary to divide the community property, and in fact even in states which do not have community property, this is often done under statutory authority. Suppose that H obtains an ex parte divorce in Nevada, W remaining in California, and suppose it is assumed that H acquired a valid Nevada domicile so that the divorce is valid under *Williams I.* H then returns to California.

(a) Can W then assert a claim for her share of the community property in existence at the time of the Nevada divorce, on the theory that this claim is a personal right which under the rationale of *Vanderbilt* survives the ex parte divorce?

(b) Suppose that H returns to California and continues to work and accumulate property. Can W assert a claim to a share of the property which H acquires after the Nevada divorce, on the theory that for property and financial purposes they are still married under *Vanderbilt?*

(c) Suppose that H returns to California and continues to work and accumulate property, and also marries W–2. Can W assert a claim against H and W–2 for her share of the community property accumulated by H after the Nevada divorce and remarriage to W–2? For community property purposes, to whom is H married? It is clear, is it not, that he has obligations to support both W and W–2?

SIMONS v. MIAMI BEACH FIRST NAT. BANK, EXECUTOR

Supreme Court of the United States, 1965.
381 U.S. 81, 85 S.Ct. 1315, 14 L.Ed.2d 232.

Mr. Justice BRENNAN delivered the opinion of the Court.

The question to be decided in this case is whether a husband's valid Florida divorce, obtained in a proceeding wherein his nonresident wife was served by publication only and did not make a personal appearance, unconstitutionally extinguished her dower right in his Florida estate.

The petitioner and Sol Simons were domiciled in New York when, in 1946, she obtained a New York separation decree that included an award of monthly alimony. Sol Simons moved to Florida in 1951 and, a year later, obtained there a divorce in an action of which petitioner had valid constructive notice but in which she did not enter a personal appearance.[1] After Sol Simons' death in Florida in 1960, respondent, the executor of his estate, offered his will for probate in the Probate Court of Dade County, Florida. Petitioner appeared in the proceeding and filed an election to take dower under Florida law, rather than have her rights in the estate governed by the terms of the will, which made no provision for her.[2] The respon-

---

1. Petitioner was served by publication while still living in New York and received copies of the order for publication and the divorce complaint. She did not enter an appearance in the Florida proceeding on advice of counsel.

2. 21 Fla.Stat.Ann.1964, § 731.34 provides as follows:

"Whenever the widow of any decedent shall not be satisfied with the portion of the estate of her husband to which she is entitled under the law of descent and dis-

tribution or under the will of her husband, or both, she may elect in the manner provided by law to take dower, which dower shall be one third in fee simple of the real property which was owned by her husband at the time of his death or which he had before conveyed, whereof she had not relinquished her right of dower as provided by law, and one third part absolutely of the personal property owned by her husband at the time of his death * * *."

dent opposed the dower claim, asserting that since Sol Simons had divorced petitioner she had <u>not been his wife</u> at his death, and consequently was <u>not entitled</u> to dower under Florida law. Petitioner thereupon brought the instant action in the Circuit Court for Dade County in order to set aside the divorce decree and to obtain a declaration that the divorce, even if valid to alter her marital status, did not destroy or impair her claim to dower. The action was dismissed after trial, and the Florida District Court of Appeal for the Third District affirmed. 157 So.2d 199. The Supreme Court of Florida declined to review the case, 166 So.2d 151. We granted certiorari, 379 U.S. 877, 85 S.Ct. 150, 13 L.Ed.2d 85. We affirm.

Petitioner's counsel advised us during oral argument that he no longer challenged the judgment below insofar as it embodied a holding that the <u>1952 Florida divorce was valid and terminated the marital status of the parties.</u> We therefore proceed to the decision of the question <u>whether the Florida courts unconstitutionally denied petitioner's dower claim.</u>

Petitioner argues that since she had <u>not appeared</u> in the Florida divorce action the Florida divorce court had no power to extinguish any right which she had acquired under the New York decree. She invokes the principle of Estin v. Estin, 334 U.S. 541, 68 S.Ct. 1213, 92 L.Ed. 1561, where this Court decided that a Nevada divorce court, which had no personal jurisdiction over the wife, had no power to terminate a husband's obligation to provide the wife support as required by a pre-existing New York separation decree. As this was so, we there ruled that New York, in giving continued effect to the maintenance provisions of its separation decree, did not deny full faith and credit to the Nevada decree. See U.S. Const., Art. IV, § 1.[5] The application of the *Estin* principle to the instant case, petitioner contends, dictates that we hold the Florida courts to their constitutional duty to give effect to the New York decree, inherent in which is a preservation of her dower right.

The short answer to this contention is that the only obligation imposed on Sol Simons by the New York decree, and the <u>only rights granted</u> petitioner under it, concerned monthly alimony for <u>petitioner's support.</u> Unlike the ex-husband in *Estin,* Sol Simons made the support payments called for by the separate maintenance decree notwithstanding his *ex parte* divorce. In making these payments until his death he complied with the full measure of the New York decree; <u>when he died</u> there was consequently nothing left of the New York decree for Florida to dishonor.

This conclusion embodies our judgment that <u>there is nothing in the New York decree</u> itself that can be construed as creating or preserving any interest in the nature of or in lieu of dower in any prop-

5. "Full Faith and Credit shall be given in each State to the public Acts,   Records, and judicial Proceedings of every other State. * * *"

erty of the decedent, wherever located. Petitioner refers us to no New York law that treats such a decree as having that effect, or, for that matter, to any New York law that has such an effect irrespective of the existence of the decree. We think it clear that the burden of showing this rested upon petitioner. Cf. State Farm Ins. Co. v. Duel, 324 U.S. 154, 160, 65 S.Ct. 573, 89 L.Ed.2d 812; Alaska Packers Ass'n v. Industrial Accident Comm'n, 294 U.S. 532, 547–548, 55 S.Ct. 518, 523–524, 79 L.Ed. 1044. It follows that insofar as petitioner's argument rests on rights created by the New York decree or by New York law, the denial of her dower by the Florida courts was not a violation of the Full Faith and Credit Clause. Cf. Armstrong v. Armstrong, 350 U.S. 568, 76 S.Ct. 629, 100 L.Ed. 705.

Insofar as petitioner argues that since she was not subject to the jurisdiction of the Florida divorce court its decree could not extinguish any dower right existing under Florida law, Vanderbilt v. Vanderbilt, 354 U.S. 416, 418, 77 S.Ct. 1360, 1 L.Ed.2d 1456, the answer is that under Florida law no dower right survived the decree. The Supreme Court of Florida has said that dower rights in Florida property, being inchoate, are extinguished by a divorce decree predicated upon substituted or constructive service. Pawley v. Pawley, 46 So.2d 464.[6]

It follows that the Florida courts transgressed no constitutional bounds in denying petitioner dower in her ex-husband's Florida estate.

Affirmed.

---

6. In *Pawley* the Supreme Court of Florida distinguished the dower right from the right to support, saying at 46 So.2d 464, 472–473, n. 2:

"In this, if not in every jurisdiction, right of dower can never be made the subject of a wholly independent issue in any divorce suit. It stands or falls as a result of the decree which denies or grants divorce. It arises upon marriage, as an institution of the law. The inchoate right of dower has some of the incidents of property. It partakes of the nature of a lien or encumbrance. It is not a right which is originated by or is derived from the husband; nor is it a personal obligation to be met or fulfilled by him, but it is a creature of the law, is born at the marriage altar, cradled in the bosom of the marital status as an integral and component part thereof, survives during the life of the wife as such and finds its sepulcher in divorce. Alimony too is an institution of the law but it is a personal obligation of the husband which is based upon the duty imposed upon him by the common law to support his wife and gives rise to a personal right of the wife to insist upon, if she be entitled to, it. It has none of the incidents of, and is in no sense a lien upon or interest in, property. Consequently, the right of the wife to be heard on the question of alimony should not, indeed lawfully it cannot, be destroyed by a divorce decree sought and secured by the husband in an action wherein only constructive service of process was effected."

A petition for writ of certiorari to this Court alleged, "Petitioner is thus permitted to file another suit for alimony, but her contract of marriage is annulled and her inchoate dower rights destroyed without due process of law." Brief for petitioner, p. 9, Pawley v. Pawley, No. 325, October Term, 1950. The petition was denied 340 U.S. 866, 71 S.Ct. 90, 95 L.Ed. 632.

NOTES AND QUESTIONS

1. *Simons* is noted in 33 U.Chi.L.Rev. 837 (1966).

2. Mr. Justice Harlan, concurring in *Simons,* said that two rules were announced by *Vanderbilt:* a) an ex parte divorce can have no effect on property rights; b) a state in which a wife subsequently acquires a domicile can grant support to her regardless of her connection with that state at the time of the ex parte divorce and regardless of the law in her former state of domicile. He then goes on to say that *Simons* abolishes the first of these rules, and thereby makes a partial retreat from *Vanderbilt.* On the other hand Mr. Justice Douglas, concurring in *Simons,* says that Mrs. Simons' Florida dower was not terminated by the ex parte divorce. "It simply never came into existence." Therefore she had no property rights cut off by the divorce, and *Simons* does not amount to a retreat from *Vanderbilt.* Which of the justices was correct? If dower rights are inchoate, as the majority opinion says, does that make them different from rights to support? Are rights to support inchoate? For a discussion of the nature of property rights of spouses, see Sanditen v. Sanditen, 496 P.2d 365 (Okl.1972), supra, page 739.

3. The *Simons* case seems to rest in part on the court's finding that by Florida law dower does not survive divorce. Is that inconsistent with the *Vanderbilt* decision, which seems to make the effect of the divorce turn on the law of the wife's domicile rather than the law of the divorcing state?

4. Does *Simons* impair the *Vanderbilt* case as a precedent on its own facts, that is, on the effect of an ex parte divorce upon the wife's right to support under the law of her domicile? See Spadea v. Spadea, 225 Ga. 80, 165 S.E.2d 836 (1969); Dackman v. Dackman, 252 Md. 331, 250 A.2d 60 (1969), 30 Md.L.Rev. 73 (1970); Kram v. Kram, 52 N.J. 545, 247 A.2d 316 (1968); Rymanowski v. Rymanowski, 105 R.I. 89, 249 A.2d 407 (1969), all decided since *Simons* and all purporting to follow the holdings of *Estin* and *Vanderbilt.* At least two states have, after *Simons* was decided, enacted statutes adopting the *Estin-Vanderbilt* rule. Ga.Code Ann. §§ 30–226, 30–227, 30–228 (1969); N.J.Stat.Ann. § 2A:34–24.1 (Supp.1979–1980).

5. W and H were married and lived in the State of X. After ten years of marriage and two children they began to have marital disagreements and finally H went to Reno, where he got a motel room and after being there five weeks obtained a divorce. An attorney contacted by H with W's consent, but who never met W, appeared for her, but did not contest either the merits or the jurisdiction of the court. No provision was made in the divorce decree either for alimony, a property division or child support. H then returned to X, where he had a prosperous business, and owned substantial real estate. He refused to give W or the children any money. She was therefore forced to collect state welfare payments for herself and children, under a statute which authorized such relief for indigent persons, and which also provided that the state might obtain reimbursement for payments so made from any person legally obligated to furnish support to the indigent person. After a year of such payments the state initiated a suit against H for reimbursement for the sums paid to W for herself and the children. H moved to dismiss. What arguments would you make for and against this motion?

KULKO v. SUPERIOR COURT OF CALIFORNIA IN AND FOR THE CITY AND COUNTY OF SAN FRANCISCO

Supreme Court of the United States, 1978.
436 U.S. 84, 98 S.Ct. 1690, 56 L.Ed.2d 132.

Mr. Justice MARSHALL delivered the opinion of the Court.

The issue before us is whether, in this action for child support, the California state courts may exercise *in personam* jurisdiction over a nonresident, nondomiciliary parent of minor children domiciled within the State. For reasons set forth below, we hold that the exercise of such jurisdiction would violate the Due Process Clause of the Fourteenth Amendment.

I

Appellant Ezra Kulko married appellee Sharon Kulko Horn in 1959, during appellant's three-day stopover in California en route from a military base in Texas to a tour of duty in Korea. At the time of this marriage, both parties were domiciled in and residents of New York State. Immediately following the marriage, Sharon Kulko returned to New York as did appellant after his tour of duty. Their first child, Darwin, was born to the Kulkos in New York in 1961, and a year later their second child, Ilsa, was born, also in New York. The Kulkos and their two children resided together as a family in New York City continuously until March 1972, when the Kulkos separated.

Following the separation, Sharon Kulko moved to San Francisco, California. A written separation agreement was drawn up in New York; in September 1972, Sharon Kulko flew to New York City in order to sign this agreement. The agreement provided, *inter alia,* that the children would remain with their father during the school year but would spend their Christmas, Easter and summer vacations with their mother. While Sharon Kulko waived any claim for her own support or maintenance, Ezra Kulko agreed to pay his wife $3,000 per year in child support for the periods when the children were in her care, custody and control. Immediately after execution of the separation agreement, Sharon Kulko flew to Haiti and procured a divorce there;[1] the divorce decree incorporated the terms of the agreement. She then returned to California, where she remarried and took the name Horn.

The children resided with appellant during the school year and with their mother on vacations, as provided by the separation agree-

---

1. While the Jurisdictional Statement at 5 asserts that "the parties" flew to Haiti, appellant's affidavit submitted in the Superior Court stated that Sharon Kulko flew to Haiti with a power of attorney signed by appel- lant. App. 29. The Haitian decree states that Sharon Kulko appeared "in person" and that appellant filed a "Power of Attorney and submission to jurisdiction." App. 14.

ment, until December 1973. At this time, just before Ilsa was to leave New York to spend Christmas vacation with her mother, she told her father that she wanted to remain in California after her vacation. Appellant bought his daughter a one-way plane ticket, and Ilsa left, taking her clothing with her. Ilsa then commenced living in California with her mother during the school year and spending vacations with her father. In January 1976, appellant's other child, Darwin, called his mother from New York and advised her that he wanted to live with her in California. Unbeknownst to appellant, appellee Horn sent a plane ticket to her son, which he used to fly to California where he took up residence with his mother and sister.

Less than one month after Darwin's arrival in California, appellee Horn commenced this action against appellant in the California Superior Court. She sought to establish the Haitian divorce decree as a California judgment; to modify the judgment so as to award her full custody of the children; and to increase appellant's child support obligations.[2] Appellant appeared specially and moved to quash service of the summons on the ground that he was not a resident of California and lacked sufficient "minimum contacts" with the State under International Shoe Co. v. Washington, 326 U.S. 310, 316, 66 S.Ct. 154, 158, 90 L.Ed. 95 (1945), to warrant the State's assertion of personal jurisdiction over him.

The trial court summarily denied the motion to quash, and appellant sought review in the California Court of Appeal by petition for a writ of mandate. Appellant did not contest the court's jurisdiction for purposes of the custody determination, but, with respect to the claim for increased support, he renewed his argument that the California courts lacked personal jurisdiction over him. The appellate court affirmed the denial of appellant's motion to quash, reasoning that, by consenting to his children's living in California, appellant had "caused an effect in th[e] state" warranting the exercise of jurisdiction over him. 133 Cal.Rptr. 627, 628 (1976).

The California Supreme Court granted appellant's petition for review, and in a 4–2 decision sustained the rulings of the lower state courts. 19 Cal.3d 514, 138 Cal.Rptr. 586, 564 P.2d 353 (1977). It noted first that the California Code of Civil Procedure demonstrated an intent that the courts of California utilize all bases of *in personam* jurisdiction "not inconsistent with the Constitution."[3] Agreeing with

---

2. Appellee Horn's complaint also sought an order restraining appellant from removing his children from the State. The trial court immediately granted appellee temporary custody of the children and restrained both her and appellant from removing the children from the State of California. See 19 Cal.3d, at 520, 138 Cal.Rptr. at 588, 564 P.2d, at 355. The record does not reflect whether appellant is still enjoined from removing his children from the State.

3. Section 410.10 of the California Code of Civil Procedure provides:

"A court of this state may exercise jurisdiction on any basis not inconsistent with the Constitution of this state or of the United States." The opinion below does not appear to distinguish between

the court below, the Supreme Court stated that, where a nonresident defendant has caused an effect in the State by an act or omission outside the State, personal jurisdiction over the defendant in causes arising from that effect may be exercised whenever "reasonable." Id., at 521, 138 Cal.Rptr., at 588, 564 P.2d, at 356. * * *

On Ezra Kulko's appeal to this Court, probable jurisdiction was postponed. We have concluded that jurisdiction by appeal does not lie, but, treating the papers as a petition for a writ of certiorari, we hereby grant the petition and reverse the judgment below.

II

The Due Process Clause of the Fourteenth Amendment operates as a limitation on the jurisdiction of state courts to enter judgments affecting rights or interests of nonresident defendants. See Shaffer v. Heitner, 433 U.S. 186, 198–200, 97 S.Ct. 2569, 2577, 53 L.Ed.2d 683 (1977). It has long been the rule that a valid judgment imposing a personal obligation or duty in favor of the plaintiff may be entered only by a court having jurisdiction over the person of the defendant. Pennoyer v. Neff, 95 U.S. 714, 732–733, 24 L.Ed. 565, 572 (1878); International Shoe Co. v. Washington, supra, 326 U.S., at 316, 66 S.Ct., at 158. The existence of personal jurisdiction, in turn, depends upon the presence of reasonable notice to the defendant that an action has been brought. Mullane v. Central Hanover Trust Co., 339 U.S. 306, 313–314, 70 S.Ct. 652, 656–657, 94 L.Ed. 865 (1950), and a sufficient connection between the defendant and the forum State as to make it fair to require defense of the action in the forum. Milliken v. Meyer, 311 U.S. 457, 463–464, 61 S.Ct. 339, 342–343, 85 L.Ed. 278 (1940). In this case, appellant does not dispute the adequacy of the notice that he received, but contends that his connection with the State of California is too attenuated, under the standards implicit in the Due Process Clause of the Constitution, to justify imposing upon him the burden and inconvenience of defense in California.

The parties are in agreement that the constitutional standard for determining whether the State may enter a binding judgment against appellant here is that set forth in this Court's opinion in International Shoe Co. v. Washington, supra: that a defendant "have certain minimum contacts with [the forum state] such that the maintenance of the suit does not offend 'traditional notions of fair play and substantial justice.' " 326 U.S., at 316, 66 S.Ct., at 158, quoting Milliken v. Meyer, supra, 311 U.S. at 463, 61 S.Ct., at 342. While the interests of the forum State and of the plaintiff in proceeding with the cause in the plaintiff's forum of choice are of course to be considered, see McGee v. International Life Insurance Co., 355 U.S. 220, 223, 78 S.Ct. 199, 201, 2 L.Ed.2d 223 (1957), an essential criterion in all cases is

the requirements of the Federal and State Constitutions. See 19 Cal.3d, at 521–522, 138 Cal.Rptr., at 588–589, 564 P.2d, at 356.

whether the "quality and nature" of the defendant's activity is such that it is "reasonable" and "fair" to require him to conduct his defense in that State. International Shoe Co. v. Washington, supra, 326 U.S., at 316–317, 319, 66 S.Ct., at 158, 159.

Like any standard that requires a determination of "reasonableness," the "minimum contacts" test of *International Shoe* is not susceptible of mechanical application; rather, the facts of each case must be weighed to determine whether the requisite "affiliating circumstances" are present. We recognize that this determination is one in which few answers will be written "in black and white. The greys are dominant and even among them the shades are innumerable." Estin v. Estin, 334 U.S. 541, 545, 68 S.Ct. 1213, 1216, 92 L.Ed. 1561 (1948). But we believe that the California Supreme Court's application of the minimum contacts test in this case represents an anwarranted extension of *International Shoe* and would, if sustained, sanction a result that is neither fair, just nor reasonable.

A

In reaching its result, the California Supreme Court did not rely on appellant's glancing presence in the State some 13 years before the events that led to this controversy, nor could it have. Appellant has been in California on only two occasions, once in 1959 for a three-day military stopover on his way to Korea, see p. 1694, supra, and again in 1960 for a 24-hour stopover on his return from Korean service. To hold such temporary visits to a State a basis for the assertion of *in personam* jurisdiction over unrelated actions arising in the future would make a mockery of the limitations on state jurisdiction imposed by the Fourteenth Amendment. Nor did the California court rely on the fact that appellant was actually married in California on one of his two brief visits. We agree that where two New York domiciliaries, for reasons of convenience, marry in the State of California and thereafter spend their entire married life in New York, the fact of their California marriage by itself cannot support a California court's exercise of jurisdiction over a spouse who remains a New York resident in an action relating to child support.

Finally, in holding that personal jurisdiction existed, the court below carefully disclaimed reliance on the fact that appellant had agreed at the time of separation to allow his children to live with their mother three months a year and that he had sent them to California each year pursuant to this agreement. As was noted below, 19 Cal.3d, at 523–524, 138 Cal.Rptr., at 590, 564 P.2d, at 357, to find personal jurisdiction in a State on this basis, merely because the mother was residing there, would discourage parents from entering into reasonable visitation agreements. Moreover, it could arbitrarily subject one parent to suit in any State of the Union where the other parent chose to spend time while having custody of their offspring pursuant to a separation agreement.[6] As we have emphasized,

"The unilateral activity of those who claim some relationship with a nonresident defendant cannot satisfy the requirement of contact with the forum State. * * * [I]t is essential in each case that there be some act by which the defendant purposefully avails [him]self of the privilege of conducting activities within the forum State * * *." Hanson v. Denckla, supra, 357 U.S., at 253, 78 S. Ct., at 1240.

The "purposeful act" that the California Supreme Court believed did warrant the exercise of personal jurisdiction over appellant in California was his "actively and fully consent[ing] to Ilsa living in California for the school year * * * and * * * sen[ding] her to California for that purpose." 19 Cal.3d, at 524, 138 Cal.Rptr., at 591, 564 P.2d, at 358. We cannot accept the proposition that appellant's acquiescence in Ilsa's desire to live with her mother conferred jurisdiction over appellant in the California courts in this action. A father who agrees, in the interests of family harmony and his children's preferences, to allow them to spend more time in California than was required under a separation agreement can hardly be said to have "purposefully availed himself" of the "benefits and protection" of California's laws. See Shaffer v. Heitner, supra, 433 U.S., at 216, 97 S.Ct., at 2586.[7]

Nor can we agree with the assertion of the court below that the exercise of *in personam* jurisdiction here was warranted by the financial benefit appellant derived from his daughter's presence in California for nine months of the year. 19 Cal.3d at 524–525, 138 Cal.Rptr., at 590–591, 564 P.2d, at 358. This argument rests on the premise that, while appellant's liability for support payments remained unchanged, his yearly expenses for supporting the child in New York decreased. But this circumstance, even if true, does not support California's assertion of jurisdiction here. Any diminution in appellant's household costs resulted, not from the child's presence in California, but rather from her absence from appellant's home. Moreover, an action by appellee Horn to increase support payments could now be

---

6. Although the separation agreement stated that appellee Horn resided in California and provided that child-support payments would be mailed to her California address, it also specifically contemplated that appellee might move to a different State. The agreement directed appellant to mail the support payments to appellee's San Francisco address or "any other address which the Wife may designate from time to time in writing." App. 10.

7. The court below stated that the presence in California of appellant's daughter gave appellant the benefit of California's "police and fire protection, its school system, its hospital services, its recreational facilities, its libraries and museums * * *." 19 Cal.3d, at 522, 138 Cal.Rptr., at 589, 564 P.2d at 356. But, in the circumstances presented here, these services provided by the State were essentially benefits to the child, not the father, and in any event were not benefits that appellant purposefully sought for himself.

brought, and could have been brought when Ilsa first moved to California, in the State of New York; [8] a New York court would clearly have personal jurisdiction over appellant and, if a judgment were entered by a New York court increasing appellant's child support obligations, it could properly be enforced against him in both New York and California.[9] Any ultimate financial advantage to appellant thus results not from the child's presence in California but from appellee's failure earlier to seek an increase in payments under the separation agreement.[10] The argument below to the contrary, in our view, confuses the question of appellant's liability with that of the proper forum in which to determine that liability.

B

In light of our conclusion that appellant did not purposefully derive benefit from any activities relating to the State of California, it is apparent that the California Supreme Court's reliance on appellant's having caused an "effect" in California was misplaced. See p. 1965, supra. This "effects" test is derived from the American Law Institute's Restatement (Second) of Conflicts § 37 (1971), which provides:

"A state has power to exercise judicial jurisdiction over an individual who causes effects in the state by an act done elsewhere with respect to any cause of action arising from these effects unless the nature of the effects and of the individual's relationship to the state make the exercise of such jurisdiction unreasonable." [11]

While this provision is not binding on this Court, it does not in any event support the decision below. As is apparent from the examples

---

8. Under the separation agreement, appellant is bound to "indemnify and hold [his] Wife harmless from any and all attorney fees, costs and expenses which she may incur by reason of the default of [appellant] in the performance of any of the obligations required to be performed by him pursuant to the terms and conditions of this agreement." App. 11. To the extent that appellee Horn seeks arrearages, her litigation expenses, presumably including any additional costs incurred by appellee as a result of having to prosecute the action in New York, would thus be borne by appellant.

9. A final judgment entered by a New York court having jurisdiction over the defendant's person and over the subject matter of the lawsuit would be entitled to Full Faith and Credit in any State. See New York ex rel.

Halvey v. Halvey, 330 U.S. 610, 614, 67 S.Ct. 903, 905, 91 L.Ed. 1133 (1947). See also Sosna v. Iowa, 419 U.S. 393, 407, 95 S.Ct. 553, 561, 42 L. Ed.2d 532 (1975).

10. It may well be that, as a matter of state law, appellee Horn could still obtain through New York proceedings additional payments from appellant for Ilsa's support from January 1974, when a de facto modification of the custody provisions of the separation agreement took place, until the present. See H. Clark, Domestic Relations § 15.2, at 500 (1968); cf. County of Santa Clara v. Hughes, 43 Misc.2d 559, 251 N.Y.S.2d 579 (1964).

11. Section 37 of the Restatement has effectively been incorporated into California law. See Judicial Council Comment (9) to California Code Civ. Proc. § 410.10.

accompanying § 37 in the Restatement, this section was intended to reach wrongful activity outside of the State causing injury within the State, see, e. g., Comment a, p. 157 (shooting bullet from one State into another), or commercial activity affecting state residents, *ibid.* Even in such situations, moreover, the Restatement recognizes that there might be circumstances that would render "unreasonable" the assertion of jurisdiction over the nonresident defendant.

The circumstances in this case clearly render "unreasonable" California's assertion of personal jurisdiction. There is no claim that appellant has visited physical injury on either property or persons within the State of California. Compare Hess v. Pawloski, 274 U.S. 352, 47 S.Ct. 632, 71 L.Ed. 1091 (1927). The cause of action herein asserted arises, not from the defendant's commercial transactions in interstate commerce, but rather from his personal, domestic relations. It thus cannot be said that appellant has sought a commercial benefit from solicitation of business from a resident of California that could reasonably render him liable to suit in state court; appellant's activities cannot fairly be analogized to an insurer's sending an insurance contract and premium notices into the State to an insured resident of the State. Compare McGee v. International Life Ins. Co., supra. Furthermore, the controversy between the parties arises from a separation that occurred in the State of New York; appellee Horn seeks modification of a contract that was negotiated in New York and that she flew to New York to sign. As in Hanson v. Denckla, supra, 357 U.S., at 252, 78 S.Ct., at 1239, the instant action involves an agreement that was entered into with virtually no connection with the forum State. See also n. 6, supra.

Finally, basic considerations of fairness point decisively in favor of appellant's State of domicile as the proper forum for adjudication of this case, whatever the merits of appellee's underlying claim. It is appellant who has remained in the State of the marital domicile, whereas it is appellee who has moved across the continent. Cf. May v. Anderson, 345 U.S. 528, 534–535, n. 8, 73 S.Ct. 840, 843–844, 97 L. Ed. 1221 (1953). Appellant has at all times resided in New York State, and, until the separation and appellee's move to California, his entire family resided there as well. As noted above, appellant did no more than acquiesce in the stated preference of one of his children to live with her mother in California. This single act is surely not one that a reasonable parent would expect to result in the substantial financial burden and personal strain of litigating a child-support suit in a forum 3,000 miles away, and we therefore see no basis on which it can be said that appellant could reasonably have anticipated being "haled before a [California] court," Shaffer v. Heitner, supra, 433 U. S., at 216, 97 S.Ct., at 2586. To make jurisdiction in a case such as this turn on whether appellant bought his daughter her ticket or instead unsuccessfully sought to prevent her departure would impose an unreasonable burden on family relations, and one wholly unjustified by the "quality and nature" of appellant's activities in or relating to the State of California. International Shoe Co. v. Washington, supra, 326 U.S., at 319, 66 S.Ct., at 159.

III

In seeking to justify the burden that would be imposed on appellant were the exercise of *in personam* jurisdiction in California sustained, appellee argues that California has substantial interests in protecting the welfare of its minor residents and in promoting to the fullest extent possible a healthy and supportive family environment in which the children of the State are to be raised. These interests are unquestionably important. But while the presence of the children and one parent in California arguably might favor application of California law in a lawsuit in New York, the fact that California may be the " 'center of gravity' " for choice of law purposes does not mean that California has personal jurisdiction over the defendant. And California has not attempted to assert any particularized interest in trying such cases in its courts by, e. g., enacting a special jurisdictional statute.

California's legitimate interest in ensuring the support of children resident in California without unduly disrupting the children's lives, moreover, is already being served by the State's participation in the Uniform Reciprocal Enforcement of Support Act of 1968. This statute provides a mechanism for communication between court systems in different States, in order to facilitate the procurement and enforcement of child-support decrees where the dependent children reside in a State that cannot obtain personal jurisdiction over the defendant. California's version of the Act essentially permits a California resident claiming support from a nonresident to file a petition in California and have its merits adjudicated in the State of the alleged obligor's residence, without either party having to leave his or her own State. Cal.Code Civ.Proc. § 1650 et seq.[13] New York State is a

13. In addition to California, 25 other States are signatories to this Act. 9 Uniform Laws Ann. 473 (Supp. Pamph.1977). Under the Act, an "obligee" may file a petition in a court of his or her State (the "initiating court") to obtain support. §§ 11, 14. If the court "finds that the [petition] sets forth facts from which it may be determined that the obligor owes a duty of support and that a court of the responding state may obtain jurisdiction of the obligor or his property," it may send a copy of the petition to the "responding state." § 14. This has the effect of requesting the responding State "to obtain jurisdiction over the obligor." § 18(b). If jurisdiction is obtained, then a hearing is set in a court in the responding State at which the obligor may, if he chooses, contest the claim. Ibid. The claim may be litigated in that court, with deposition testimony submitted through the initiating court by the initiating spouse or other party. § 20. If the responding state court finds that the obligor owes a duty of support pursuant to the laws of the State where he or she was present during the time when support was sought, § 7, judgment for the petitioner is entered. § 24. If the money is collected from the spouse in the responding State, it is then sent to the court in the initiating State for distribution to the initiating party. § 28.

signatory to a similar act.[14] Thus, not only may plaintiff-appellee here vindicate her claimed right to additional child support from her former husband in a New York court, see pp. 1698–1699, supra, but the uniform acts will facilitate both her prosecution of a claim for additional support and collection of any support payments found to be owed by appellant.[15]

It cannot be disputed that California has substantial interests in protecting resident children and in facilitating child-support actions on behalf of those children. But these interests simply do not make California a "fair forum," Shaffer v. Heitner, supra, 433 U.S., at 215, 97 S.Ct., at 2586, in which to require appellant, who derives no personal or commercial benefit from his child's presence in California and who lacks any other relevant contact with the State, either to defend a child-support suit or to suffer liability by default.

IV

We therefore believe that the state courts in the instant case failed to heed our admonition that "the flexible standard of *International Shoe*" does not "herald[ ] the eventual demise of all restrictions on the personal jurisdiction of state courts." Hanson v. Denckla, supra, 357 U.S., at 251, 78 S.Ct., at 1238. In McGee v. Interna-

---

14. While not a signatory to the Uniform Reciprocal Enforcement of Support Act of 1968, New York is a party to the Uniform Reciprocal Enforcement of Support Act of 1950, as amended. N.Y. Domestic Relations Law § 30 et seq. (Uniform Support of Dependents Law). By 1957 this Act, or its substantial equivalent, had been enacted in all States, organized territories and the District of Columbia. 9 Uniform Laws Annotated 885 (1973). The "two-state" procedure in the 1950 Act for obtaining and enforcing support obligations owed by a spouse in one State to a spouse in another is similar to that provided in the 1968 Act. See n. 14, supra. See generally Note, 48 Cornell L.Q. 541 (1963).

In Landes v. Landes, 1 N.Y.2d 358, 153 N.Y.S.2d 14, 135 N.E.2d 562, appeal dismissed, 352 U.S. 948, 77 S.Ct. 325, 1 L.Ed.2d 241 (1956), the court upheld a support decree entered against a divorced husband living in New York, on a petition filed by his former wife in California pursuant to the Uniform Act. No prior support agreement or decree existed between the parties; the California spouse sought support from the New York husband for the couple's minor child, who was residing with her mother in California. The New York Court of Appeals concluded that the procedures followed—filing of a petition in California, followed by its certification to New York's Family Court, the obtaining of jurisdiction over the husband, a hearing in New York on the merits of the petition, and entry of an award—were proper under the laws of both States and were constitutional. The constitutionality of these procedures has also been upheld in other jurisdictions. See, e. g., Watson v. Dreadin, 309 A.2d 493 (D. C.App.1973), cert. denied, 415 U.S. 959, 94 S.Ct. 1488, 39 L.Ed.2d 574 (1974); State ex rel. Terry v. Terry, 80 N.M. 185, 453 P.2d 206 (1969); Harmon v. Harmon, 184 Cal.App.2d 245, 7 Cal.Rptr. 279 (1960), appeal dismissed, cert. denied 366 U.S. 270, 81 S.Ct. 1100, 6 L.Ed.2d 382 (1961).

15. Thus, it cannot here be concluded, as it was in McGee v. International Life Insurance Co., supra, 355 U.S., at 223–224, 78 S.Ct. at 201, with respect to actions on insurance contracts, that resident plaintiffs would be at a "severe disadvantage" if *in personam* jurisdiction over out-of-state defendants were sometimes unavailable.

tional Life Insurance Co., supra we commented on the extension of *in personam* jurisdiction under evolving standards of due process, explaining that this trend was in large part "attributable to the * * * increasing nationalization of commerce * * * [accompanied by] modern transportation and communication [that] have made it much less burdensome for a party sued to defend himself in a State where he engages in economic activity." 355 U.S., at 222–223, 78 S.Ct., at 201. But the mere act of sending a child to California to live with her mother is not a commercial act and connotes no intent to obtain nor expectancy of receiving a corresponding benefit in the State that would make fair the assertion of that State's judicial jurisdiction.

Accordingly, we conclude that the appellant's motion to quash service, on the ground of lack of personal jurisdiction, was erroneously denied by the California courts. The judgment of the California Supreme Court is, therefore,

Reversed.

NOTES AND QUESTIONS

1. Justices Brennan, White and Powell dissented in *Kulko* on the ground that in their opinion "appellant's connection with the State of California was not too attenuated, under the standards of reasonableness and fairness implicit in the Due Process Clause, to require him to conduct his defense in the California courts."

2. Where a divorce decree, in addition to dissolving the marital status, makes awards of alimony, support for the wife or children, or divides the property of the parties, it has generally been characterized by the courts as an in personam judgment. The effect of this is to require that the defendant against whom such a judgment is sought be personally subjected to the court's jurisdiction. This may be done in a variety of ways. The most common is by personal service upon him within the state. Under local rules the same result may be reached by prescribed forms of substituted service within or without the state if the defendant is domiciled in the state. Milliken v. Meyer, 311 U.S. 457 (1940), held such service meets the requirements of due process, provided adequate provision for notice is made. Recent cases resting in personam jurisdiction upon domicile include Cannon v. Cannon, 242 So.2d 291 (La.App.1970); Stucky v. Stucky, 186 Neb. 636, 185 N.W.2d 656 (1971), 51 Neb.L.Rev. 159 (1971); Gross v. Gross, 56 Misc.2d 286, 288 N.Y.S.2d 674 (Sup.Ct.1968). Locating the domicile of the defendant may be as difficult here as in other contexts. Renaudin v. Renaudin, 37 A.D.2d 183, 323 N.Y.S.2d 145 (1st Dep't 1971).

A general personal appearance by the defendant also enables the court to enter against him a decree for alimony, property or child support. Kai Sing Lam v. Neng Yee Lam, 86 Nev. 908, 478 P.2d 146 (1970); Sundlun v. Sundlun, 103 R.I. 25, 234 A.2d 358 (1967).

Without personal jurisdiction over the defendant, the judgment for alimony, child support or a division of property cannot be granted, or, if it is granted, may be attacked as a violation of the Due Process Clause. See, e. g., Meredith v. Meredith, 96 U.S.App.D.C. 355, 226 F.2d 257 (1955); Baldwin v. Baldwin, 28 Cal.2d 406, 170 P.2d 670 (1946); Carnie v. Carnie, 252 S.C. 471, 167 S.E.2d 297 (1969); Overby v. Overby, 224 Tenn. 523, 457 S.W.2d 851 (1970).

3. How are the courts to determine what is "reasonable and fair" or whether "traditional notions of fair play and substantial justice" are not offended? What standards exist for determining these issues?

4. Does this case stand for the proposition that stricter standards of personal jurisdiction are required for family law matters than for suits arising out of commercial transactions?

5. If California had a statute which provided specifically that visits of children in the state would constitute a basis for jurisdiction to award child support, would that be constitutional under this case?

6. If there were no such statute as the Uniform Reciprocal Enforcement of Support Act, would the Supreme Court find jurisdiction on the facts in this case?

7. What would be the result, under *Kulko* and a long-arm statute similar to California's, in the following case? The parties were married and lived in State X. They then moved to State Y, later returned to State X for about a year, and then moved to State Z. At H's insistence W returned to her parents' home in State X. When H wrote that she was not to come back, and that he was in love with someone else, W sued for divorce in State X, asking for support. Does State X have jurisdiction to order H to support her? Hines v. Clendenning, 465 P.2d 460 (Okl.1970).

8. What would have been the result in *Kulko* if H had failed to make the child support payments provided for in the divorce decree, covering periods when the children were with W, if

(a) the California long-arm statute were in force; or

(b) the forum state had a long-arm statute providing that in personam jurisdiction may be based upon the commission of a tortious act in the state? Boyer v. Boyer, 73 Ill.2d 331, 383 N.E.2d 223 (1978). Cf. Poindexter v. Willis, supra, page 403.

9. A state's long-arm statute authorizes in personam jurisdiction over a defendant who is transacting business in the state. Would this statute give a court jurisdiction over a husband who had executed a separation agreement in the state, but who was not a resident of the state and had no other contacts with it? If so, would the result be constitutional under *Kulko*? Ross v. Ross, 371 Mass. 439, 358 N.E.2d 437 (1976).

10. Would the result in *Kulko* have been different if the husband had lived in Nevada, rather than New York? Or if the wife had lived in New Jersey and the husband in New York, with suit brought in New Jersey?

11. What would be the result if the husband and wife had been married in California, lived there ten years, then moved to Washington where they were divorced, and then the wife moved back to California where she sued for child support? Hoerler v. Superior Court, 85 Cal.App.3d 533, 149 Cal.Rptr. 569 (1978).

12. The reliance of the courts upon "long-arm" statutes to obtain jurisdiction over defendants for alimony and support purposes is a relatively recent development. Kansas and Illinois have enacted statutes which expressly apply to divorce, and authorize personal judgments for alimony, child support and property against absent defendants where certain contacts with the state exist. The Illinois statute rests on the maintenance of the matrimonial domicile in the state at the time the cause of action arose, or the commission in Illinois of any act giving rise to the cause of action. Ill.Ann.Stat. ch. 110, § 17(1)(e) (Supp.1979). The Kansas statute permits the court to assume personal jurisdiction where the parties lived in the marital relationship within the state, notwithstanding the departure of one of them, provided that the other continues to reside in the state. Kan.Stat. Ann. § 60–308(b)(8) (1976). Wisconsin has a somewhat similar statute. Dillon v. Dillon, 46 Wis.2d 659, 176 N.W.2d 362 (1970). Are these statutes constitutional, under *Kulko?*

13. If there is no statute which expressly covers service on absent defendants in divorce or non-support actions, the question is whether the general long-arm statute in the jurisdiction covers such suits. The strongly felt need to hold wandering spouses to their financial responsibilities has led several courts to grant and to recognize judgments for alimony or child support based upon more or less general long-arm statutes. A leading case is Mizner v. Mizner, 84 Nev. 268, 439 P.2d 679 (1968), cert. den. 393 U.S. 847, 972 (1968), 20 Hast.L.J. 361 (1968), 1969 Utah L.Rev. 606, 22 Vand.L. Rev. 199 (1968). In that case the wife had obtained an alimony decree in California, serving the husband outside California under the California long-arm statute which at that time authorized personal judgments based upon such service when the defendant was a resident of California at the time the cause of action arose. Residence under that statute is construed to mean domicile. The wife then appeared in a Nevada divorce action which had been brought by the husband, asking that the Nevada court enforce the California alimony decree. The court held that the California decree was valid, was entitled to full faith and credit, and would be enforced in Nevada where the husband was then living. Another case, Stucky v. Stucky, 186 Neb. 636, 185 N.W.2d 656 (1971), 51 Neb.L.Rev. 159 (1971), held that a judgment for alimony and child support in Nebraska could be based upon service on the husband in Pennsylvania. The court did not rely upon any specific clause of the Nebraska long-arm statute, but upon the doctrine that minimum contacts between the defendant and the state existed. The contacts in this case were that Nebraska was the last marital domicile, that the defendant maintained his family there after he left them, and that his conduct had its effect in Nebraska, where the cause of action arose. There was an alternative basis for the decision that the husband was still domiciled in the state, weakening the case as an authority. See also Wright v. Wright, 114 N.J.Super. 439, 276 A.2d 878 (1971), upholding jurisdiction against a nonresident in a separate maintenance suit where he was served outside the state on the basis of "doing business" in the state, the business consisting of writing a weekly column in a New Jersey newspaper.

A case refusing to apply the long-arm statute to a suit for divorce is Stanley v. Stanley, 271 A.2d 636 (Me.1970).

14. Formerly, under local statutes and rules of procedure, it was possible to assert claims for alimony or support against property of the obligor located in the state by attaching the property, without personal jurisdiction over the obligor himself. This was referred to as "quasi in rem" jurisdiction and produced a judgment valid only to the extent of the property attached. Such judgments were held entitled to full faith and credit by Harris v. Balk, 198 U.S. 215 (1905).

The Supreme Court in Shaffer v. Heitner, 433 U.S. 186 (1978), has now overruled Harris v. Balk. The opinion in *Shaffer* says that "in order to justify an exercise of jurisdiction *in rem,* [or presumably quasi in rem] the basis for the jurisdiction must be sufficient to justify exercising 'jurisdiction over the interests of persons in a thing' ". The precise holding of *Shaffer* was that the presence of the defendant's property in the state, of itself and without other "contacts" with the state, was not sufficient to confer jurisdiction on the state's courts to enter a judgment against the owner of the property, even a judgment limited to the property. The state's attempt to do this was characterized as a violation of the Due Process Clause. In other words, jurisdiction for in rem and quasi in rem proceedings must be based upon the same sort of contacts with the state as jurisdiction for in personam actions.

What *Shaffer* does, in suits for alimony or support, is to make it plain that the attachment of property within a state, by itself, is not sufficient to be the basis for a judgment. Other contacts between the defendant and the state must exist. The standard is that of *Kulko,* i. e. what is "reasonable and fair", or whether "traditional notions of fair play and substantial justice" are observed. The Court does say, in *Shaffer,* that when claims to the property itself are the source of the lawsuit, it would be "unusual" for the state not to have jurisdiction. What this seems to suggest is that if claims to marital property within the state were being asserted, the presence of the property alone might be sufficient to confer jurisdiction. In the *Shaffer* case itself the plaintiffs' claim had nothing to do with the property which was seized.

In a cryptic footnote (footnote 30) the Court in *Shaffer* said: "We do not suggest that jurisdictional doctrines other than those discussed in text, such as the particularized rules governing adjudications of status, are inconsistent with the standard of fairness." This seems to mean that *Shaffer* does not alter the jurisdictional rules applicable to divorce. Whether it affects custody jurisdiction is discussed infra, section 8. The New York Court of Appeals has dealt with the relation between *Shaffer* and divorce jurisdiction in Carr v. Carr, 46 N.Y.2d 270, 413 N.Y.S.2d 305, 385 N.E.2d 1234 (1978). In that case wife #2, domiciled in New York, brought suit against wife #2, domiciled in California, to establish the rights of wife #1 to foreign service survivor's benefits after the death of the hsuband. Wife #1's claim was that her husband's Honduran divorce was invalid and that consequently the first marriage was still in existence and the marriage to wife #2 was void. The court, while indicating that the "classical concepts of divorce jurisdiction" survived *Shaffer,* held that only property rights were at stake in this case, and that New York had no jurisdiction because there were no contacts between that state and wife #2 which could confer personal jurisdiction.

Another qualification in *Shaffer* (in footnote 36) indicates that a judgment already obtained could be enforced against the defendant's property in the state, whether or not the state's court would have had jurisdiction to adjudicate the original claim. This would seem to permit quasi in rem jurisdiction as a technique for the enforcement of alimony or support judgments.

Finally, *Shaffer*'s footnote 37 states, "This case does not raise, and we therefore do not consider, the question whether the presence of a defendant's property in a State is a sufficient basis for jurisdiction when no other forum is available to the plaintiff." Perhaps this is another "exception" to the rule of *Shaffer* though a less positive statement could hardly be imagined. One case has relied upon this language, however, to enter a judgment for child support on the basis of quasi in rem jurisdiction, where the defendant husband was in France and therefore not suable anywhere in the United States. This case also involved enforcement of a judgment, so two "exceptions" to *Shaffer* were involved. Rich v. Rich, 93 Misc.2d 409, 402 N.Y.S.2d 767 (Sup.Ct.1978).

For extensive discussion of *Shaffer* and its implications, see the Symposium, 45 Bklyn.L.Rev. 493 (1979).

15. The cases in the foregoing two sections demonstrate the ways in which the courts have attempted to solve the problems created by the fact that different states are concerned with the marital relations of citizens who move from state to state. A phrase which has been coined to describe some of the solutions is "divisible divorce". One might about as well refer to "divisible marriage". What this phrase means is that two persons may be married for one purpose or in one state, but not for other purposes or in other states. This condition of affairs strikes many people as bizarre, or at least highly undesirable. You might give some thought to the following questions, the answers to which test your reactions to divisible divorce.

(a) What interests of the spouses are protected by the existing rules and principles as to jurisdiction?

(b) What interests of the various states are protected by these rules?

(c) Do the interests of the spouses and of the states sometimes collide? In that event which set of interests should prevail?

(d) What interests of spouses or of the states are not being protected by these rules?

(e) Do the jurisdictional principles of *Kulko* and *Shaffer* strike you as wise or workable for a legal system which seems to be seriously overburdened and subject to long delays in some localities? See, e. g., Younger, Quasi In Rem Defaults After Shaffer v. Heitner: Some Unanswered Questions, 45 Bklyn.L.Rev. 675 (1979).

(f) Could you devise a set of rules in the form of a statute which would provide greater protection for the interests of spouses or states, would satisfactorily resolve conflicts between those interests and which would meet Due Process Clause requirements?

SECTION 4. ALIMONY (OR MAINTENANCE), TEMPORARY AND PERMANENT, AND DIVISION OF PROPERTY ON DIVORCE *

NOTE ON TEMPORARY ALIMONY (OR MAINTENANCE) AND COUNSEL FEES

The statutes of the various states have generally authorized the courts to grant alimony or maintenance during the pendency of the suit (called temporary alimony or alimony pendente lite) and attorney fees to wives who are parties to divorce actions. E. g., N.Y. Dom.Rel.L. §§ 236, 237 (1977). After the decision in Orr v. Orr, infra, page 868, however, the right to such payments may not be given exclusively to wives, but must run both ways. Many states have already amended their statutes so as to authorize temporary alimony and attorney fees to be awarded to either husbands or wives and to be charged against either wives or husbands. See, e. g., Cal.Civ. Code §§ 4357, 4370 (Supp.1979); Colo.Rev.Stat.Ann. §§ 14–10–108, 14–10–119 (1973); Fla.Stat.Ann. § 61.071 (Supp.1979); N.J.Stat. Ann. § 2A:34–23 (Supp.1979–1980); Wis.Stat.Ann. § 247.23 (Supp. 1979–1980). Those states which have not amended their statutes, such as New York, will have to give their statutes this bilateral effect. Stitt v. Stitt, 243 Ga. 301, 253 S.E.2d 764 (1979). The Uniform Marriage and Divorce Act §§ 304, 313, 9 Unif.L.Ann. 128, 177 (1979) likewise imposes the obligation upon either party to the divorce.

The purpose of temporary alimony and attorney fees is to provide support during the pendency of the suit for the spouse who needs it. Temporary alimony and attorney fees substitute for the normal obligation prevailing in the going marriage a sum established by the divorce court. Such orders, being in personam, must be based upon personal service or its equivalent. Adequate notice and an opportunity for a hearing must be given. See cases in Annot., 10 A.L. R.3d 280 (1966). Such orders may be made even when the divorce is denied or when the jurisdiction of the court over the subject matter is questioned, in order to enable the spouse to present his or her side of the issues. Chlupacek v. Chlupacek, 226 Ga. 520, 175 S.E.2d 834 (1970); Prewitt v. Prewitt, 459 S.W.2d 720 (Tex.Civ.App.1970). But no further orders may be made after it has been found that subject matter jurisdiction is lacking. Morgan v. Morgan, 103 Conn. 189, 130 A. 254 (1926).

---

* The older term, "alimony", meaning payments to the divorced spouse in substitution for the right to support existing during marriage, has to some extent been replaced by the term "maintenance", which apparently means the same thing. See, e. g., Uniform Marriage and Divorce Act §§ 304, 308, 9A Unif.L.Ann. 128, 160 (1979). The two terms will therefore be used interchangeably here.

Where the validity of the marriage is questioned, the spouse seeking temporary alimony may obtain it only upon presenting prima facie evidence that the marriage is valid. In effect she must show that there was a ceremony or a common law marriage and that she lived with the defendant as husband and wife. Dietrich v. Dietrich, 41 Cal.2d 497, 261 P.2d 269 (1953), cert. den. 346 U.S. 938 (1954); Harris v. Harris, 171 Colo. 233, 466 P.2d 70 (1970). The same rule applies when the applicant for temporary alimony is accused of marital faults which would bar her claim for support. She is then required merely to show that she is suing or making her defense in good faith and with reasonable cause. The merits of the case are not tried out on the application for temporary alimony. Berbiglia v. Berbiglia, 442 S.W.2d 949 (Mo.App.1969); Hanson v. Hanson, 177 Pa.Super. 384, 110 A.2d 750 (1955); Annot., 2 A.L.R.2d 307 (1948).

The level of temporary alimony is established by reference to the needs of the applicant and the obligor's ability to pay. More precisely, such factors as the age, health, occupation and earning ability of the parties, their style of living and expenses, the property they own, the debts they owe and the taxes they are required to pay are all considered in determining how much temporary alimony is to be granted. Wechsler v. Wechsler, 242 Pa.Super. 356, 363 A.2d 1307 (1976). Normally the wife's possession of independent means would foreclose her from receiving temporary alimony. Annot., 60 A.L.R.3d 728 (1974). The decision on the amount of temporary alimony is held to be within the trial court's discretion, reviewable on appeal only for abuse of that discretion. See cases cited in Annot., 1 A.L.R.3d 280 (1965). In some states at least the order for temporary alimony is appealable, is enforceable as a judgment, as to the accrued sums, even after the death of one of the parties, and dismissal of the main action does not affect liability for the accrued amounts. See In re Marriage of Skelley, 18 Cal.3d 365, 134 Cal.Rptr. 197, 556 P.2d 297 (1976). But Colom v. Colom, 58 Ohio St.2d 245, 389 N.E.2d 856, 12 O.O.3d 242 (1979) holds that arrears of temporary alimony may not be enforced after the final decree is entered unless previously reduced to judgment or mentioned in the final decree. And the Uniform Marriage and Divorce Act § 304(f)(3), 9 Unif.L.Ann. 130 (1979) provides that temporary orders terminate when a final decree is entered or the proceeding is voluntarily dismissed. See also Hill v. District Court, 189 Colo. 356, 540 P.2d 1079 (1975). In a proper case temporary alimony may be given in the form of the use of a dwelling, Little v. Little, 9 N.C.App. 361, 176 S.E.2d 521 (1970), or may include expenses incurred in travelling to the place of trial, McMillion v. McMillion, 497 P.2d 331 (Colo.App.1972); Greaney v. Greaney, 109 N.H. 305, 250 A.2d 502 (1969), or even the expense of hiring a private detective to discover the spouse's transgressions. Annot., 99 A.L.R.2d 264 (1965).

The obligation of a spouse for temporary alimony is not discharged by the bankruptcy of the obligor, under section 523(a)(5) of the Bankruptcy Code, 11 U.S.C.A. § 523(a)(5).

Attorney fees are granted on substantially the same reasoning as temporary alimony, that is, that the applicant requires legal advice in order to make good his claim or defense in the divorce suit, and the other spouse is able to bear the expense of the attorneys' services. When litigation is in prospect, the services of a lawyer are as necessary an element of support as the services of a physician when one is ill. See In re Marriage of Pallesi, 73 Cal.App.3d 424, 140 Cal.Rptr. 842 (1977). The procedure differs among the states, some ordering payment to the wife and leaving it to her to pay her attorney, others permitting payment direct to the attorney and even permitting the attorney to enforce the order for payment of fees. In most states attorney fees may be awarded to a spouse notwithstanding that she was the losing party in the divorce action itself. See cases collected in Annot., 32 A.L.R.3d 1227 (1970). And Lockard v. Lockard, 193 Neb. 400, 227 N.W.2d 581 (1975) held that under a no-fault divorce statute the adulterous wife could be awarded attorney fees.

Like temporary alimony, attorney fees may be awarded even though it later turns out that the marriage was invalid. Weitz v. Weitz, 24 N.Y.2d 930, 249 N.E.2d 768, 301 N.Y.S.2d 991 (1969). Attorney fees also are within the discretion of the trial court, who should, in granting or denying them, be guided by such factors as the needs of the applicant, the ability of the other spouse to pay, and, according to some courts at least, the spouse's good faith in bringing or defending the action. Mayer v. Mayer, 150 N.J.Super. 556, 376 A.2d 214 (1977). In arriving at the amount of attorney fees the courts take into account the number of hours spent on the case, the complexity of the case, the results achieved by the attorney, and the ability of the spouse to pay. See, e. g., Green v. Green, 41 Ill.App.3d 154, 354 N.E.2d 661 (1976); Burkhart v. Burkhart, — Ind.App. —, 349 N.E.2d 707 (1976); Hennen v. Hennen, 53 Wis.2d 600, 193 N.W.2d 717 (1972). Other cases are collected in Annot., 59 A.L.R.3d 152 (1974). In Matter of a Proceeding for Support, 87 Misc.2d 547, 385 N.Y.S.2d 740 (Fam.Ct.1976) it was held that attorney fees in a child support proceeding could be ordered even though the obligee spouse had means of her own, since the services of the lawyer were for the child's benefit rather than the spouse's.

It has been held that an order for attorney fees may not be entered after the spouses have been reconciled and the divorce case dismissed. McNutt v. Beaty, 370 So.2d 998 (Ala.1979). But a California court has held that an order for the payment of fees is enforceable notwithstanding that the parties were reconciled after entry of the order. In re Marriage of Pallesi, 73 Cal.App.3d 424, 140 Cal.Rptr. 842 (1977). But it would seem that the attorney should have a claim against his client's spouse under the doctrine of necessaries, even if a reconciliation did occur before any order for fees could be entered. See Matter of Steingesser, 602 F.2d 36 (2d Cir. 1979).

Attorney fees may also be granted in connection with some proceedings after the entry of the divorce decree, as, for example, where there is an appeal, or a motion for the modification of alimony or custody. The extent to which this may be done is largely a matter for the trial court's discretion, the exercise of that discretion being governed by the language of the state's statute, the type of proceeding, and whether the proceeding offers reasonable prospects for success. There are both logical and policy difficulties with the award of fees in such cases, since after the divorce has been granted any obligation to support the spouse has ended. Nevertheless in some cases awards are made. See H. Clark, Law of Domestic Relations 430–431 (1968); Note, Counsel Fees in Matrimonial Actions, 38 Neb.L.Rev. 761 (1959); Annot., 15 A.L.R.2d 1270 (1951); Fitts v. Fitts, 284 Ala. 109, 222 So.2d 696 (1969) (no attorney fees to a wife in a contempt proceeding against her); Waltrip v. Waltrip, 3 Ill.App.3d 892, 279 N. E.2d 405 (1972) (attorney fees allowed on appeal from a proceeding to increase alimony and child support); Horwitz v. Horwitz, 130 Ill. App.2d 424, 264 N.E.2d 723 (1970) (attorney fees may be allowed in proceedings to modify the divorce decree where the need of the children rather than convenience of the spouses is involved, after consideration of which party precipitated the necessity for the proceeding); Peterman v. Peterman, 14 Md.App. 310, 286 A.2d 812 (1972) (no attorney fees in a proceeding to increase alimony); Klipstein v. Klipstein, 47 Wis.2d 314, 177 N.W.2d 57 (1970) (attorney fees allowed in a proceeding to increase child support).

The cases are in general agreement that the obligation to pay attorney fees is not dischargeable in bankruptcy, the theory being that it is an an aspect of the spouse's duty of support which both the former Bankruptcy Act and the new Bankruptcy Code provide is not dischargeable. Matter of Steingesser, 602 F.2d 36 (2d Cir. 1979); In re Birdseye, 548 F.2d 321 (10th Cir. 1977); Jones v. Tyson, 518 F.2d 678 (9th Cir. 1975); Goldman v. Roderiques, 370 Mass. 435, 349 N. E.2d 335 (1976).

ORR v. ORR

Supreme Court of the United States, 1979.
440 U.S. 268, 99 S.Ct. 1102, 59 L.Ed.2d 306.

Mr. Justice BRENNAN delivered the opinion of the Court.

The question presented is the constitutionality of Alabama alimony statutes which provide that husbands, but not wives, may be required to pay alimony upon divorce.[1]

1. The statutes, Ala.Code, Tit. 30, provide that:
    "§ 30–2–51. If the wife has no separate estate or if it be insuffi-

cient for her maintenance, the judge, upon granting a divorce, at his discretion, may order to the wife an allowance out of the estate

On February 26, 1974, a final decree of divorce was entered, dissolving the marriage of William and Lillian Orr. That decree directed appellant, Mr. Orr, to pay appellee, Mrs. Orr, $1,240 per month in alimony. On July 28, 1976, Mrs. Orr initiated a contempt proceeding in the Circuit Court of Lee County, Ala., alleging that Mr. Orr was in arrears in his alimony payments. On August 19, 1976, at the hearing on Mrs. Orr's petition, Mr. Orr submitted in his defense a motion requesting that Alabama's alimony statutes be declared unconstitutional because they authorize courts to place an obligation of alimony upon husbands but never upon wives. The Circuit Court denied Mr. Orr's motion and entered judgment against him for $5,524, covering back alimony and attorney fees. Relying solely upon his federal constitutional claim, Mr. Orr appealed the judgment. On March 16, 1977, the Court of Civil Appeals of Alabama sustained the constitutionality of the Alabama statutes, 351 So.2d 904 (1977). On May 24, the Supreme Court of Alabama granted Mr. Orr's petition for a writ of certiorari, but on November 10, without court opinion, quashed the writ as improvidently granted. 351 So.2d 906 (1977). We noted probable jurisdiction, 436 U.S. 924, 98 S.Ct. 2817, 56 L.Ed.2d 767 (1978). We now hold the challenged Alabama statutes unconstitutional and reverse.

I

We first address three preliminary questions not raised by the parties or the Alabama courts below, but which nevertheless may be jurisdictional and therefore are considered of our own motion.

[At this point in the opinion the Court discussed Mr. Orr's standing to raise the constitutional issue. It concluded that he did have standing because there was no way to predict how Alabama would respond to a holding that the statute was unconstitutional and therefore he could conceivably benefit from a holding that the statute was invalid, in the event that the state should deny the benefits of the statute to both men and women. Further, the Court suggested that

of the husband, taking into consideration the value thereof and the condition[s] of his family.

"§ 30–2–52. If the divorce is in favor of the wife for the misconduct of the husband, the judge trying the case shall have the right to make an allowance to the wife out of the husband's estate, or not make her an allowance as the circumstances of the case may justify, and if an allowance is made, it must be as liberal as the estate of the husband will permit, regard being had to the condition of his family and to all the circumstances of the case.

"§ 30–2–53. If the divorce is in favor of the husband for the misconduct of the wife and if the judge in his discretion deems the wife entitled to an allowance, the allowance must be regulated by the ability of the husband and the nature of the misconduct of the wife."

The Alabama Supreme Court has held that "there is no authority in this state for awarding alimony against the wife in favor of the husband. * * * The statutory scheme is to provide alimony only in favor of the wife." Davis v. Davis, 279 Ala. 643, 644, 189 So.2d 158, 160 (1966).

Clark, Cs. on Dom.Rel. 3rd Ed. ACB—20

Mr. Orr would benefit from lower payments if the statute were held unconstitutional, even if it were to remain in force in a gender-neutral form.

The Court also held that Mr. Orr's challenge to the statute was not untimely since the Alabama courts had considered the issue properly presented and had considered it on the merits.

Finally, the Court held that there was no independent and adequate state ground on which to uphold the Alabama judgment. The argument was made that the stipulation between Mr. and Mrs. Orr would support the alimony obligation even if the statute were held unconstitutional, and that therefore there was an adequate state ground for the judgment below. The Court rejected this argument on the ground that the state court had not decided the case on the state ground, but had clearly decided the constitutional issue. It held it could not decline to decide the case merely because the state court might have been based its decision on the state ground.]

II

In authorizing the imposition of alimony obligations on husbands, but not on wives, the Alabama statutory scheme "provides that different treatment be accorded * * * on the basis of * * * sex; it thus establishes a classification subject to scrutiny under the Equal Protection Clause," Reed v. Reed, 404 U.S. 71, 75, 92 S.Ct. 251, 253, 30 L.Ed.2d 225 (1971). The fact that the classification expressly discriminates against men rather than women does not protect it from scrutiny. Craig v. Boren, 429 U.S. 190, 97 S.Ct. 451, 50 L.Ed.2d 397 (1976). "To withstand scrutiny" under the equal protection clause, " 'classifications by gender must serve important governmental objectives and must be substantially related to achievement of those objectives.' " Califano v. Webster, 430 U.S. 313, 316–317, 97 S.Ct. 1192, 1194, 51 L.Ed.2d 360 (1977). We shall, therefore, examine the three governmental objectives that might arguably be served by Alabama's statutory scheme.

Appellant views the Alabama alimony statutes as effectively announcing the State's preference for an allocation of family responsibilities under which the wife plays a dependent role, and as seeking for their objective the reinforcement of that model among the State's citizens. We agree, as he urges, that prior cases settle that this purpose cannot sustain the statutes.[9] Stanton v. Stanton, 421 U.S. 7, 10,

9. Appellee attempts to buttress the importance of this objective by arguing that while "[t]he common law stripped the married woman of many of her rights and most of her property, * * * it attempted to partially compensate by giving her the assurance that she would be supported by her husband." Br. for Appellee

11–12. This argument, that the "support obligation was imposed by the common law to compensate the wife for the discrimination she suffered at the hands of the common law," id., at 11, reveals its own weakness. At most it establishes that the alimony statutes were part and parcel of a larger statutory scheme which invidi-

95 S.Ct. 1373, 1376, 43 L.Ed.2d 688 (1975), held that the "old notion" that "generally it is the man's primary responsibility to provide a home and its essentials," can no longer justify a statute that discriminates on the basis of gender. "No longer is the female destined solely for the home and the rearing of the family, and only the male for the marketplace and the world of ideas," id., at 14 15, 95 S.Ct., at 1378. If the statute is to survive constitutional attack, therefore, it must be validated on some other basis.

The opinion of the Alabama Court of Civil Appeals suggests other purposes that the statute may serve. Its opinion states that the Alabama statutes were "designed" for "the wife of a broken marriage who needs financial assistance," 351 So.2d, at 905. This may be read as asserting either of two legislative objectives. One is a legislative purpose to provide help for needy spouses, using sex as a proxy for need. The other is a goal of compensating women for past discrimination during marriage, which assertedly has left them unprepared to fend for themselves in the working world following divorce. We concede, of course, that assisting needy spouses is a legitimate and important governmental objective. We have also recognized "[r]eduction of the disparity in economic condition between men and women caused by the long history of discrimination against women * * * as * * * an important governmental objective," Califano v. Webster, 430 U.S., at 317, 97 S.Ct., at 1194. It only remains, therefore, to determine whether the classification at issue here is "substantially related to achievement of those objectives."

Ordinarily, we would begin the analysis of the "needy spouse" objective by considering whether sex is a sufficiently "accurate proxy," Craig v. Boren, 429 U.S., at 204, 97 S.Ct., at 460, for dependency to establish that the gender classification rests " 'upon some ground of difference having a fair and substantial relation to the objective of the legislation,' " Reed v. Reed, 404 U.S., at 76, 92 S.Ct., at 254. Similarly, we would initially approach the "compensation" rationale by asking whether women had in fact been significantly discriminated against in the sphere to which the statute applied a sex-based classification, leaving the sexes "not similarly situated with respect to opportunities" in that sphere, Schlesinger v. Ballard, 419 U.S. 498, 508, 95 S.Ct. 572, 577, 42 L.Ed.2d 610 (1975). Compare Califano v. Webster, 430 U.S., at 318, 97 S.Ct., at 1195, and Kahn v. Shevin, 416 U.S. 351, 353, 94 S.Ct. 1734, 1736, 40 L.Ed.2d 189 (1974), with

ously discriminated against women, removing them from the world of work and property and "compensating" them by making their designated place "secure." This would be reason to invalidate the entire discriminatory scheme—not a reason to uphold its separate invidious parts. But appellee's argument is even weaker when applied to the facts of this case, as Alabama has long ago removed, by statute, the elements of the common law appellee points to as justifying further discrimination. See Ala.Const., Art. 10, § 209 (married women's property rights).

Weinberger v. Wiesenfeld, 420 U.S. 636, 648, 95 S.Ct. 1225, 1233, 43 L.Ed.2d 514 (1975).[11]

But in this case, even if sex were a reliable proxy for need, and even if the institution of marriage did discriminate against women, these factors still would "not adequately justify the salient features of" Alabama's statutory scheme, Craig v. Boren, 429 U.S., at 202, 97 S.Ct., at 459–460. Under the statute, individualized hearings at which the parties' relative financial circumstances are considered *already* occur. There is no reason, therefore, to use sex as a proxy for need. Needy males could be helped along with needy females with little if any additional burden on the State. In such circumstances, not even an administrative convenience rationale exists to justify operating by generalization or proxy.[12] Similarly, since individualized hearings can determine which women were in fact discriminated against vis à vis their husbands, as well as which family units defied the stereotype and left the husband dependent on the wife, Alabama's alleged compensatory purpose may be effectuated without placing burdens solely on husbands. Progress toward fulfilling such a purpose would not be hampered, and it would cost the State nothing more, if it were to treat men and women equally by making alimony burdens independent of sex. "Thus, the gender-based distinction is gratuitous; without it the statutory scheme would only provide benefits to those men who are in fact similarly situated to the women the statute aids," Weinberger v. Wiesenfeld, 420 U.S., at 653, 95 S.Ct., at 1236, and the effort to help those women would not in any way be compromised.

Moreover, use of a gender classification actually produces perverse results in this case. As compared to a gender-neutral law placing alimony obligations on the spouse able to pay, the present Alabama statutes give an advantage only to the financially secure wife whose husband is in need. Although such a wife might have to pay

11. We would also consider whether the purportedly compensatory "classifications in fact penalized women," and whether "the statutory structure and its legislative history revealed that the classification was not enacted as compensation for past discrimination." Califano v. Webster, 430 U.S. 313, 317, 97 S.Ct. 1192, 1194, 51 L.Ed.2d 360 (1977).

12. It might be argued that Alabama's rule at least relieves the State of the administrative burden of actions by husbands against their wives for alimony. However, when the wife is also seeking alimony, no savings will occur, as a hearing will be required in any event. But even when the wife is willing to forego alimony, it appears that under Alabama law savings will still not accrue, as Alabama courts review the financial circumstances of the parties to a divorce despite the parties' own views—even when settlement is reached. See Russell v. Russell, 247 Ala. 284, 24 So.2d 124, 126 (1946). Even were this not true, and some administrative time and effort were conserved, "[t]o give a mandatory preference to members of either sex * * * merely to accomplish the elimination of hearings on the merits, is to make the very kind of arbitrary legislative choice forbidden by the Equal Protection Clause," Reed v. Reed, 404 U.S. 71, 76, 92 S.Ct. 251, 254, 30 L.Ed.2d 225 (1971).

alimony under a gender-neutral statute, the present statutes exempt her from that obligation. Thus, "[t]he [wives] who benefit from the disparate treatment are those who were * * * nondependent on their husbands," Califano v. Goldfarb, 430 U.S. 199, 221, 97 S.Ct. 1021, 1034, 51 L.Ed.2d 270 (1977) (Stevens J., concurring). They are precisely those who are not "needy spouses" and who are "least likely to have been victims of * * * discrimination," ibid., by the institution of marriage. A gender-based classification which, as compared to a gender-neutral one, generates additional benefits only for those it has no reason to prefer cannot survive equal protection scrutiny.

Legislative classifications which distribute benefits and burdens on the basis of gender carry the inherent risk of reinforcing the stereotypes about the "proper place" of women and their need for special protection. Thus, even statutes purportedly designed to compensate for and ameliorate the effects of past discrimination must be carefully tailored. Where, as here, the State's compensatory and ameliorative purposes are as well served by a gender-neutral classification as one that gender-classifies and therefore carries with it the baggage of sexual stereotypes, the State cannot be permitted to classify on the basis of sex. And this is doubly so where the choice made by the State appears to redound—if only indirectly—to the benefit of those without need for special solicitude.

III

Having found Alabama's alimony statutes unconstitutional, we reverse the judgment below and remand the cause for further proceedings not inconsistent with this opinion. That disposition, of course, leaves the state courts free to decide any questions of substantive state law not yet passed upon in this litigation. Therefore, it is open to the Alabama courts on remand to consider whether Mr. Orr's stipulated agreement to pay alimony, or other grounds of gender-neutral state law, bind him to continue his alimony payments.

NOTES AND QUESTIONS

1. Justices Blackmun and Stevens concurred specially in this case, each writing brief opinions which did not disagree with the merits as decided by the Court's opinion. Justice Powell dissented on the ground that the Court should have abstained until the state law questions of timeliness and the stipulation's effect could be decided. Justice Rehnquist wrote a dissent in which Chief Justice Burger joined, urging that Mr. Orr did not have standing to raise the constitutional issue since he could not show that he would benefit if the Alabama alimony statute were held to be unconstitutional.

On the remand from the Supreme Court the Alabama court held that as between abolishing alimony or making it available to husbands, it would choose the latter alternative. Orr v. Orr, 374 So.2d 895 (Ala.App.1979).

KOVER v. KOVER

Court of Appeals of New York, 1972.
29 N.Y.2d 408, 328 N.Y.S.2d 641, 278 N.E.2d 886.

FULD, Chief Judge. The husband and wife in each of these three childless marriage cases had lived apart for more than two years following a decree of separation which contained a provision for alimony. In subsequent actions for divorce, brought pursuant to section 170 (subd. [5]) of the Domestic Relations Law, Consol.Laws, c. 14, each husband opposed the continuation of any alimony, in large part on the ground that his wife was self-supporting. The present appeals deal principally with (1) the effect of a provision for alimony in the prior separation decree and (2) with factors to be considered by the court in fixing alimony in the suit for divorce.

The cases before us—in which a wife, who was awarded alimony in the separation decree, seeks alimony in the later divorce action— differ from those in which the wife or husband seeks modification of an alimony provision contained in an earlier matrimonial decree. In the latter instance, despite the broad language of section 236 of the Domestic Relations Law the courts have ruled that a party seeking a reduction or increase must show a "substantial change of circumstances". * * * This accords with the fundamental principle that litigation must have an end and that a court, having performed its function, may not lightly be asked to do it all over again.

In a case, however, where divorce follows separation—whether under the recently enacted provision of the Domestic Relations Law (§ 170, subd. [5] [L.1966, ch. 254]) or under prior law on the ground of adultery—the parties are before the court in a new and different proceeding, in which different relief is sought. Under such circumstances, the court is privileged to consider the question of alimony *de novo*. * * * Thus, it has been expressly held that "the alimony provision in the separation decree is not conclusive with respect to the fixation of alimony in the divorce action and does not require plaintiff to bear the burden of showing change of circumstances". (Goshin v. Goshin, 281 App.Div. 979, 120 N.Y.S.2d 596, supra.) And, in the *Bishop* case (15 A.D.2d 494, 495, 222 N.Y.S.2d 232, 233, supra), the court declared, "[t]he stipulation and the separation decree do not deprive the Trial Judge in the divorce action of the power to award amounts for support which are different from the amounts specified in the separation decree".

Concluding, therefore, that the courts are not bound by the prior alimony awards, we must now determine the relevant elements or factors to be considered in fixing alimony in suits instituted under subdivision (5) of section 170.

Formerly, various provisions of the Civil Practice Act (e. g., §§ 1155, 1169, 1170) directed a husband to provide for the wife "as justice requires" and "having regard to the circumstances of the respective parties". This was originally interpreted as mandating the measure of alimony to be simply "commensurate with the manner in which the parties have lived and a consideration of the ability of the husband to furnish means of support." (Tirrell v. Tirrell, 232 N.Y. 224, 230, 133 N.E. 569, 570; * * *.) But, as the Appellate Division noted in 1956 in Phillips v. Phillips (1 A.D.2d 393, 395, 150 N.Y.S.2d 646, 649, affd. 2 N.Y.2d 742, 157 N.Y.S.2d 378, 138 N.E.2d 738), the times have changed, owing not alone to the coequal status which a married woman today shares with her husband but also to the increase in the number of married women working in gainful occupations. * * *

In fixing the amount of alimony to be awarded, the courts look, in the first instance, to the provisions of section 236 of the Domestic Relations Law (L.1962, ch. 313, as amd., L.1968, ch. 699). This provision * * * vests the courts with an exceedingly wide latitude in determining the right to alimony and its amount. The Orenstein statute recites, in part, that

"In any action or proceeding brought * * * for a separation, or * * * for a divorce, the court may direct the husband to provide suitably for the support of the wife as, in the court's discretion, justice requires, having regard to the *length of time of the marriage, the ability of the wife to be self supporting, the circumstances of the case and of the respective parties*." (Emphasis supplied.)   *Factors*

In addition to "the length of time of the marriage [and] the ability of the wife to be self supporting"—factors expressly added to section 236 in 1968 (L.1968, ch. 699)—the courts have indicated a number of other circumstances to be taken into account in fixing alimony. These include the husband's financial resources and the established standard of living of the parties * * * the age and health of the parties and, to a limited extent, their conduct. * * * As stated in the *Phillips* case, "The ultimate determination in each case must depend upon a balancing of several factors—the financial status of the respective parties, their age, health, necessities and obligations, their station in life, the duration and nature of the marriage, and the conduct of the parties" (1 A.D.2d 393, 398, 150 N.Y.S.2d 646, 651, affd. 2 N.Y.2d 742, 157 N.Y.S.2d 378, 138 N.E.2d 738, supra.) [3]

3. A study by the Special Committee on Divorce of the National Conference of Commissioners on Uniform State Laws, entitled, "Uniform Marriage and Divorce Legislation: A Preliminary Analysis," lists the same factors as those mentioned above:

"The maintenance order shall be in such amounts and for such periods of time as the court may deem just, without regard to marital misconduct, and after consideration of the following factors:

"(a) the financial resources of the party seeking maintenance and his or her ability to meet his or her financial needs independently, including the extent to which a provision for support of any child living with the party includes a sum for that party;

When it amended section 236 to specify that the court should consider the wife's "ability * * * to be self supporting," the Legislature gave explicit statutory recognition to a circumstance which the courts, even absent legislative specification, had increasingly considered in making alimony awards in recent years. * * * In the *Phillips* case, for instance, the Appellate Division declared that regard was to be had "not only [for] the standard of living the parties enjoyed jointly during marriage, but [for] the financial resources of each, considered separately * * * There must be a nice but realistic balancing of the wife's needs and her independent means for meeting them with the husband's abilities to pay" (1 A.D.2d 393, 396, 150 N.Y.S.2d 646, 650, affd. 2 N.Y.2d 742, 157 N.Y.S.2d 378, 138 N.E. 2d 738, supra). Then, pointing out that the courts of other States, where the divorce results from the husband's wrongdoing, "usually take the realistic view that the amount of [alimony] should be fixed with an eye to the ex-wife's resources or abilities for self-support" (p. 397, 150 N.Y.S.2d 651), the Appellate Division concluded that "the financial circumstances of the wife, while not controlling, are relevant as one of the factors that must guide the court's discretion in determining the amount of maintenance which justice requires" (pp. 397–398, 150 N.Y.S.2d p. 651).

With these principles in mind, we turn to the cases on appeal. It should be noted that, in reaching a decision, this court will not review the propriety of the Appellate Division's award, even when it differs from the trial court's, unless the reduction or increase is so gross and excessive as to show an abuse of judicial discretion or unless an underlying question of law arises. * * *

Kover v. Kover

Married in 1959, plaintiff wife obtained a separation decree from defendant husband in 1967, on the ground of abandonment. At that time she was earning $9,450 a year, and the defendant was preparing to give up an annual salary of $20,000 and accept a $15,000 a year fellowship to study for two years. The court fixed alimony at $225 a month. When this divorce action was brought three years later, the husband was earning $14,000 a year, the wife, the sum of $10,785; however, in consequence of the husband's debts, the net income of each was about equal. The court at Trial Term denied alimony to the wife, and the Appellate Division affirmed that determination.

"(b) the time necessary to acquire sufficient education or training to enable the party seeking maintenance to find suitable employment;

"(c) the standard of living established during the marriage;

"(d) the duration of the marriage and the physical or emotional conditions of the spouse seeking maintenance; and

"(e) the ability of the spouse from whom maintenance is sought to meet his or her own financial needs while meeting those of the spouse seeking maintenance."

Both before and since the enactment of section 236 in 1962 (L. 1962, ch. 313), the courts have held that they possess the power to refuse a wife's application for alimony. (See, e. g., Phillips v. Phillips, 1 A.D.2d 393, 396, 150 N.Y.S.2d 646, 650 affd. 2 N.Y.2d 742, 157 N.Y.S.2d 378, 138 N.E.2d 738, supra; * * *) In the *Phillips* case, the court after noting that times have changed and that women have " 'practically unlimited opportunities * * * in the business world of today' ", (p. 395, 150 N.Y.S.2d p. 650), went on to state that, " 'in an era where the opportunities for self-support by the wife are so abundant, the fact that the marriage has been brought to an end because of the fault of the husband does not necessarily entitle the wife to be forever supported by a former husband who has little, if any, more economic advantages than she has.' * * * The abiding interest of the State is in the preservation of the family, and in maintaining it as a self-sufficient, independent unit. Even when the familial entity has been destroyed, however, the State has a continuing interest in allocating the economic burdens fairly, so that members of the former family group, including the husband, are not individually destroyed by crushing economic and psychological pressures. Alimony must therefore be measured largely by the need for support rather than the desire for vengeance" (1 A.D.2d at pp. 396–397, 150 N.Y.S. 2d at pp. 650–651).

Since, then, a court in a divorce proceeding is not bound by a provision for support in an earlier separation decree and possesses discretionary power to deny alimony to the wife, we conclude that the courts below did not, in light of the record presented, abuse their discretion in refusing to grant alimony. The couple was childless, the wife was still in her thirties and capable of supporting herself, the marriage was of moderately short duration and the income of the spouses almost equal.

This does not, however, mean that the plaintiff is forever barred from obtaining support. As indicated, one of the factors to be considered in determining alimony is "the standard of living the parties enjoyed jointly during marriage". Here, the husband had been making $20,000 a year while living with his wife but the courts below found this to be outweighed by his reduced circumstances. Nevertheless, upon a "substantial change" in his financial position for the better, or the wife's for the worse, the courts—upon a future application for modification of the decree—would be warranted in giving added significance to the husband's income during marriage, since the "preseparation mode and style of living" of the parties would then become a more significant factor in determining the question of alimony. * * *

Miraldi v. Miraldi

Having lived with defendant husband for only two years—from 1958 to 1960—the wife, in 1962, obtained a separation decree on the ground of abandonment. The husband, a physician making $16,000 a year, was required to pay alimony of $60 a week. When this divorce action was brought in 1969, the husband was earning about $33,000 annually, the wife approximately $2,646. She is a licensed real estate saleswoman, owns an automobile and is owner in common with her parents of a two-family house. She estimates that her expenses are about $100 a week. The husband not only objected to an award of alimony but counterclaimed to have the marital home—where he has his medical practice and which is now owned by the parties as tenants by the entirety—returned to him "as sole owner".

The Supreme Court denied the wife alimony and enjoined her from interfering with the husband's "use" of their residence. The Appellate Division modified the resulting judgment by directing the latter to pay $60 a week, by dismissing his counterclaim and by providing that title to the house "be deemed held by [the parties] as tenants in common". On the husband's appeal to our court, we perceive no basis for stamping as an abuse of discretion the Appellate Division's grant of alimony of $60 a week or for upsetting its dismissal of the defendant's counterclaim, based upon his assertion that his wife had fraudulently induced him to place the marital home in both their names as tenants by the entirety. His act of taking title in that fashion gives rise to a presumption that he intended to make a gift to his wife * * * and we need but say that the record supports the Appellate Division's conclusion that that presumption was not rebutted. It follows, therefore, that, upon the termination of the marriage, the parties became tenants in common of the premises in question.

Dulber v. Dulber

Plaintiff husband and defendant wife, each previously wed, were married in 1958. The wife obtained a decree of separation in 1967, based on the husband's abandonment, and the husband was required to pay $42.50 a week for her support out of a salary of about $10,000 a year. When he commenced this action for divorce in 1969, he was earning some $14,000 annually. In the prior year, the wife, who had worked intermittently during the marriage, had earned about $8,800. The court at Special Term refused her alimony but the Appellate Division, finding such denial an "improvident exercise of discretion", modified the judgment and awarded alimony of $42.50 a week. The husband appeals and seeks reinstatement of Special Term's judgment. In view of the difference in the earnings of each of the parties, it may not be said that the Appellate Division abused its discretion when it granted this relatively modest sum to the wife.

In each case, the order appealed from should be affirmed.

IN THE MATTER OF THE MARRIAGE OF GROVE

Supreme Court of Oregon, 1977.
280 Or. 341, 571 P.2d 477, modified 280 Or. 769, 572 P.2d 1320.

LENT, Justice. This is a dissolution of marriage case in which the issue on appeal was the amount and duration of spousal support for the wife. The Court of Appeals increased the amount of the monthly support payment and held that it should not terminate after five years, as the trial court's decree had provided, but should continue until death or the wife's remarriage. The husband, in his petition for review, contends that the Court of Appeals, in this and similar cases, has not given proper effect to the statutory criteria for determining spousal support, and has been deciding the cases before it on an *ad hoc* basis. We granted review to consider generally the proper approach to determining the amount and duration of spousal support. In particular, we asked the parties to address the following questions in argument:

1. ORS 107.105(1)(c) defines certain factors which a court shall consider in determining the amount and duration of spousal support. Has the Court of Appeals erred by emphasizing some of these factors at the expense of others? Can this court provide a guideline for consistent application of the statutory criteria? If so, what might that guideline be?

2. In this case, the Court of Appeals held that spousal support would terminate upon the wife's remarriage. Should spousal support automatically terminate upon the remarriage of the party receiving support? What is the rationale for termination of support upon remarriage?

We will discuss these and other general questions involving the award of spousal support before considering the specific facts of this case.

At the time of the proceedings and decree in this case, ORS 107.-105(1)(c) empowered the court, in a dissolution case, to provide:

"For the support of a party in gross or in instalments, or both, such amount of money for such period of time as it may be just and equitable for the other party to contribute. * * * In making such support order, the court shall consider the following matters:

(A) The duration of the marriage;

(B) The ages of the parties;

(C) Their health and conditions;

(D) Their work experience and earning capacities;

(E) Their financial conditions, resources and property rights;

(F) The provisions of the decree relating to custody of the minor children of the parties;

(G) The ages, health and dependency conditions of the children of the parties, or either of them; and

(H) Such other matters as the court shall deem relevant."

Our discussion of the application of this provision begins with some general observations. In the first place, although the issue with which we are here concerned is spousal support, that issue cannot adequately be considered except in light of the provisions in the dissolution decree for division of property and child support. Legislative recognition of this interrelationship is found in paragraphs (E), (F) and (G) of ORS 107.105(1)(c). In practice, the financial portions of a dissolution decree are worked out together, and none can be considered in isolation. For example, one spouse may be awarded specific assets as part of the property division in order to provide that spouse with income. Where minor children are involved, the custodial spouse will necessarily derive some benefit from child support payments, insofar as they are applied to the maintenance of the household. It is proper to consider such matters in determining the appropriate level of spousal support.

In the second place, the cases in which the Court of Appeals considers matters of spousal support are not, for the most part, representative of marriage dissolution cases generally. The cases which are appealed are, with an occasional exception, those in which the parties' assets or projected incomes, or both, are sufficient to permit some flexibility of disposition without depriving either party of the basic necessities. Many of these cases involve parties in their middle forties or older. Frequently the marriage being dissolved is of long duration.

The present case is fairly typical of those which the Court of Appeals often considers. The parties had been married for 23 years, and their total net income, at the time of the decree, exceeded $20,000 a year. Much of what we say in this opinion will be said with this type of case in mind, and will not necessarily be directly applicable to other situations.

Legislative policy governing spousal support

The legislature in ORS 107.105(1)(c) made certain policy choices by indicating that the factors listed shall be considered in awarding spousal support and by providing that the courts may consider other matters. The legislature has not, however, indicated how the various factors are to be weighed or given the courts any specific directions for determining what kind of spousal support is "just and equitable." For example, the statute directs the court to consider the duration of the marriage. It does not indicate, however, the significance to be given that factor. The courts must determine, because the legislature has not, whether support payments should be higher or lower upon the dissolution of a lengthy marriage than upon the dissolution of a relatively brief marriage (assuming that all other factors are the same).

We find limited additional guidance to legislative policy in ORS 107.407 [2] which indicates that efforts by the supported spouse to become self-supporting and independent of the former spouse are favored. We also note that the 1977 legislature has amended the marriage dissolution statutes in several particulars which are helpful in determining the applicable policy, although they were not in force at the time of the decree which we are considering in this case.

One such change is the addition to ORS 107.105(1)(c) of a provision that the court, in determining spousal support, is to consider:

"The need for maintenance, retraining or education to enable the spouse to become employable at suitable work or to enable the spouse to pursue career objectives; * * *" 1977 Or.Laws ch. 847 § 2.

Although "suitable work" is not defined, we interpret the term, in light of the further provision for enabling the supported spouse to pursue career objectives, as not necessarily limited to work which will provide the supported spouse with an income adequate for minimal self-support.

In addition, the courts have been directed, when dividing the parties' property, to:

"* * * view the contribution of a spouse as a homemaker in the contribution of marital assets. There is a rebuttable presumption that both spouses have contributed equally to the acquisition of property during the marriage. * * *" 1977 Or.Laws ch. 847 § 2.

Although this provision is not directly applicable to spousal support awards, it indicates a legislative intent that the homemaker spouse, who is most likely to seek spousal support, be recognized as an economic contributor to the marriage rather than as a passive recipient of economic benefits provided by the breadwinner.

Refinement of spousal support policy by the Court of Appeals

An award of spousal support involves two determinations—the appropriate duration of support and the amount to be awarded. In its leading case on the principles governing the duration of spousal support, the Court of Appeals reviewed the statutory standards and its prior decisions and made the following general statement:

"While each case must be decided on its own facts and no formula can be stated, certain principles emerge from an examination of the above cases. The most significant factor usually is whether the wife is employable at an income not overly disproportionate from the

2. "If an individual has paid an amount of money in instalments for more than 10 years for the support of a former spouse under a court decree of annulment or dissolution of marriage that ordered such payment, and when the former spouse has not made a reasonable effort during that period of time to become financially self-supporting and independent of the support provided under the decree, the individual paying the support may petition the court that issued the decree to set aside so much of the decree as may provide for the support of the former spouse."

standard of living she enjoyed during the marriage. The wife's employability includes consideration of her education, training, experience, age, health, capacity, whether she has custody of small children, etc. Length of the marriage is germane because the longer the marriage, the more likely it is that the wife has foregone employment experiences, the absence of which will make it more difficult for her to achieve employment and self-sufficiency. If the wife is employable at an income not overly disproportionate from the standard of living she enjoyed during marriage, then, generally speaking, if support is appropriate it should be for a limited period of, for example, one to three years. In such a situation, it is not the policy of the law to give the wife an annuity for life or, stated differently, a perpetual lien against her former husband's future income. Conversely, if the wife is not employable or only employable at a low income compared to her standard of living during marriage then, generally speaking, permanent support is appropriate." Kitson and Kitson, 17 Or.App. 648, 655–56, 523 P.2d 575, 578 rev. denied (1974).[4]

In *Kitson* there were few assets besides the encumbered family home. The husband's taxable income was approximately $21,000. The wife was given custody of the parties' one minor child. She had not worked since the early days of the 28-year marriage, and had no employment skills. Under those circumstances, the Court of Appeals held that spousal support should not be terminated after three years, as the trial court's decree had provided, but should continue until death or remarriage of the wife.

The passage quoted from *Kitson* focuses on the wife's employability. Under the facts of that case the wife had no source of income other than her own earnings. A more generalized statement of the principle announced there would be: the most significant factor is usually whether the wife's property and potential income, including what she can earn or can become capable of earning, will provide her with a standard of living which is not overly disproportionate to the one she enjoyed during the marriage.

Permanent [5] awards of spousal support were ordered or approved in a number of other cases involving similar factual patterns and on

4. The language employed in *Kitson* assumes that it is the wife who will receive spousal support, if any is allowed. In this opinion we will also speak of the wife as the party whose support is in issue. We do so for the sake of clarity and ease of expression, in light of the fact that the reported cases virtually all conform to that pattern. We are mindful, however, that the statute authorizes support awards to either party to a dissolution proceeding and directs that the same considerations be taken into account, regardless of which party is seeking support.

5. "Permanent" is a relative term in this context. Spousal support may be modified or terminated at any time upon a showing of a sufficient change of circumstances. We speak of "permanent" support as that which continues indefinitely if no such change is shown as distinct from support awards which, by the terms of the decree, terminate after a specified period unless grounds for extention are shown.

similar reasoning. In some of these cases the wife was not entirely without employment skills, although in all of them there was a significant discrepancy between the wife's probable future income and an income which would provide the standard of living she had enjoyed during the marriage.

* * * In addition to the general principle adopted in *Kitson*, we note that the Court of Appeals has stated and applied a number of general guidelines.

The court has said, in the dissolution of a marriage of substantial duration, that it attempts in such cases to see that the parties separate on as equal a basis as possible. It has noted, on the other hand, that where the parties are relatively young and their circumstances are modest, permanent support will not generally be awarded. In such cases, the purpose of the support award is to give the wife time for readjustment and to prepare herself for employment.

Special circumstances have been taken into account in a principled fashion. For example, the court has given consideration, in setting the amount and duration of spousal support, to the fact that the wife has made a direct contribution to the husband's education or to his professional or occupational success. And where the wife suffers from health problems that reduce her earning capacity or increase the cost of her support, the court has rejected the argument that the burden of such continuing problems should be borne by society rather than by the former spouse.

The husband has argued, in the present case, that the Court of Appeals acted improperly in *Kitson*, and the cases which follow it, in comparing the wife's probable income with the standard of living she enjoyed during the marriage, and that the court has been attempting, in those cases, to provide the wife with that standard at the husband's expense and without proper consideration of his financial situation and other factors specified in the statute. These arguments are not well taken.

We find no evidence in the Court of Appeals' opinions that it has required the husband to provide his former wife with support sufficient to enable her to maintain an unchanged standard of living. On the contrary, the court has observed that the same standard of living usually cannot be maintained. The principle of *Kitson* that the most significant factor usually is whether the wife's income can provide a standard of living not overly disproportionate to that she enjoyed during the marriage is addressed not to the amount of spousal support but to its duration.

In Maley and Maley, 28 Or.App. 597, 600–601, 560 P.2d 309 (1977), reducing the amount of permanent spousal support, the court observed that the supporting spouse, where children are not involved, ought generally to be allowed to retain more than half of his net income. In fact, in reviewing the Court of Appeals' opinions, we have found only two cases in which child support and spousal support combined appear to exceed half of the husband's net income. Most often, as nearly as we can determine from the figures in the reported cases, permanent spousal support operates to lessen, but not to eliminate, substantial financial inequality between the spouses, taking into account their needs and those of their dependents and their probable incomes from all sources.

Summary of applicable policy

In response to our request for a guideline which this court could furnish for the resolution of support disputes, the husband, on oral argument, suggested the following:

"If the dependent spouse is awarded the family home, and the minor children in his or her custody are being supported at a reasonable level by the supporting spouse, and the dependent spouse is employed at a job commensurate with his or her skills and abilities, then a reasonable standard of living is made available to that dependent spouse and if spousal support is appropriate at all, it should be limited to a short adjustment period of one to two years."

We cannot approve this general statement as a guideline to be applied to marriages of long duration. We will not ignore the fact that, at least until recent years, young women entering marriage were led to believe—if not expressly by their husbands-to-be, certainly implicitly by the entire culture in which they had come to maturity—that they need not develop any special skills or abilities beyond those necessary to homemaking and child care, because their husbands, if they married would provide their financial support and security. We cannot hold that women who relied on that assurance, regardless of whether they sacrificed any specific career plans of their own when they married, must as a matter of principle be limited to the standard of living they can provide for themselves if "employed at a job commensurate with [their] skills and abilities." The marriage itself may well have prevented the development of those skills and abilities.

The statutory standards do not require such an approach. The legislature has directed the courts to consider, among other things, the wife's earning capacity and financial condition. For those factors to be meaningfully considered, they must be compared to something. The Court of Appeals has chosen to compare them to the standard of living during the marriage and to the husband's income potential. Nothing in the statutory scheme forbids that approach or directs that the comparison be made instead to the minimum amount necessary to provide food, shelter, and other basic necessities.

The legislature has given the courts only limited guidance in this area. The expressed legislative policy is that spousal support may be awarded in an amount, and for a period of time, that is "just and equitable," and that in making this determination the factors listed in

ORS 107.105(1)(c) are relevant. It is significant that the legislature chose to express the standard in terms of what is just and equitable rather than solely in terms of need. We conclude, in light of this choice and in light of the statutory direction to consider such matters as the duration of the marriage and the parties' "conditions," as well as purely financial matters, that the purpose of spousal support is not solely to prevent the supported spouse from becoming a public charge. The courts must attempt to do justice between the parties as well as provide the supported spouse with a minimally adequate living. The legislature has also indicated, however, its disapproval of sole reliance on spousal support by providing for its termination if the supported spouse has not, during a period of ten years, made reasonable attempts to become self-supporting. We conclude from this provision that the legislature has not deemed it just and equitable for one former spouse to look to the other for indefinite support if self-support at a reasonable level is possible. The 1977 amendment to ORS 107.105(1)(c), listing the need for training for suitable work or career objectives as a consideration in determining support matters, is additional evidence of that policy.

What the courts must attempt, then, is to award spousal support, if it is appropriate, on terms that are equitable between the parties that take into account need and ability to pay and that further the goal of ending the support-dependency relationship within a reasonable time if that can be accomplished without injustice or undue hardship.

We further conclude that, although each case must be considered on its own facts, it is proper to develop general principles, in addition to and consistent with those provided by the legislature, to the end that similar cases will be treated similarly. We approve the Court of Appeals' attempts to do so. In particular, we approve the general approach adopted in *Kitson* to determine the duration of spousal support, and the attempt, in determining the amount of that support, to reduce substantial financial inequality between the parties to marriages of long duration.

It is proper and desirable, however, where the circumstances permit, to tailor the financial provisions of a dissolution decree in a way which will provide the wife an opportunity to increase her earning capacity and thus to eliminate the need for permanent support or to reduce the amount required. This approach may require a higher level of support payments at first while the wife acquires training or experience, even though she already has or is capable of earning an income minimally adequate for her support.

Effect of remarriage on spousal support

We turn now to the second question upon which we requested argument: whether spousal support awards should routinely provide that the support payments will terminate upon the remarriage of the supported spouse. We hold that they should not.

The only statute which is relevant is that which gives the court the authority to "set aside, alter, or modify" the support portion of the decree upon motion of either party. ORS 107.135(1)(a). That authority may be exercised when a substantial change in circumstances since the original decree has been shown. There is no statutory provision for automatic termination of spousal support under any circumstances.

In other jurisdictions where the matter is not governed by statute, there is a division of authority over whether remarriage of the supported spouse automatically terminates the support obligation or is simply a change in circumstances which may justify such a termination upon proper application to the court. See Annot., Alimony as Affected by Wife's Remarriage, In Absence of Controlling Specific Statute, 48 ALR2d 270 (1956). We have consistently taken the latter position.

Although this court has expressed the opinion that it was against public policy to permit a woman to look for her support to two different men, that policy has never been held in this state to operate automatically without regard to the particular circumstances. The cases announcing the position that it does not were decided at a time when the husband was considered to have an absolute unilateral obligation to support his wife. We would not now hold otherwise, when legal duties of spousal support are mutual. Public policy does not require that a woman whose first marriage has been dissolved be free to remarry only if her new husband is able to support her.

If remarriage by the supported spouse is not, as a matter of law, grounds for automatic termination of spousal support, we cannot approve the general practice of inserting provisions to that effect in support decrees as a matter of routine. Unless there is reason, at the time the decree is entered, to predict a remarriage which will substantially change the circumstances relevant to the support award, the question of the effect of remarriage upon a support decree should await the event and proper application for modification of the decree. As we said, in another context, in Picker v. Vollenhover, 206 Or. 45, 72, 290 P.2d 789, 801 (1955):

"* * * At the time of divorce the court should not lay down rules for the future whose propriety would depend on circumstances materially different from those shown by the evidence and which can not reasonably be predicted from the evidence. In particular, it should not in the original decree provide for future changes in the quantum of support based on the single criterion of the change in the amount of earnings of the defendant. The original decree retains its vitality unless and until the court on proper showing finds that on all of the evidence presented a change in support is required. A provision [for changes in the amount of child support based on a sliding scale tied to defendant's future earnings] is not only based on speculation as to future events,—it is also based on the assumption that a change in one only of the many circumstances which may be relevant to the issue shall be conclusive."

These considerations, stated above with reference to child support decrees, apply with equal force to awards of spousal support.

We hold, then, that it is improper for the dissolution decree to provide in advance for automatic termination of spousal support upon remarriage of the supported spouse unless there is some reason disclosed by the evidence for such a provision in the specific case.[12a]

Spousal support in the present case

We now turn to the application of what we have said above to the specific facts of this case.

The parties to this proceeding were married for 23 years and were both in their mid-forties at the time of the dissolution. Both were in good health. Custody of their two children, ages 13 and 16 at the time of the decree, was awarded to the wife. The husband holds a doctorate in economics and is a full professor at the University of Oregon. His net monthly income averages about $1500 a month if he teaches summer school and about $1200 a month if he does not. He is not guaranteed the opportunity to teach summer school and, in fact, he prefers not to do so. He testified that it is important to his career to have his summers free for research and writing.

The wife worked full time during the early years of the marriage while the husband obtained his education. For most of the past 15 years she has devoted herself primarily to homemaking activities although she has taken a variety of part-time and temporary jobs during that period. At the time of the decree she was employed full time in a clerical position. Her net monthly income was approximately $320. A vocational expert called by the husband testified that her skills and experience qualified her for employment as an executive secretary at a gross salary of $600 to $800 a month. She testified, however, that her actual experience as a secretary to executives was more than 15 years old and that she had been unable to find a better position than that she held at the time of the decree. She also testified that she does not wish to work as a secretary indefinitely. She outlined to the trial court her plan to obtain a master's degree in business administration, which will require a total of four

12a. This holding, of course, does not apply to a case in which there is either a valid property settlement contract or a valid prenuptial contract which provides for automatic termination of spousal support upon remarriage of the supported spouse. In any decree which provides for spousal support, the decree should enjoin upon the supported spouse a duty forthwith to advise the other party if and when the supported spouse remarries.

years of college work and which would enable her, according to her testimony, to earn something over $10,000 a year.

The parties, during their marriage, accumulated few assets besides their home, in which they had an equity valued at $12,670 to $15,100 and the husband's equity in his retirement plan, amounting to approximately $13,400. The trial court awarded the home to the wife and the retirement equity to the husband, thus accomplishing an approximately equal division of the accumulated assets in an appropriate manner. The wife was also awarded child support in the amount of $250 a month for each child and spousal support of $150 a month for five years.

Upon appeal by the wife, the spousal support award was modified to provide for payments of $200 until death or her remarriage. Judge Johnson dissented on the grounds that the spousal support would be inadequate after the child support payments ended and that the decree should not provide for automatic termination of support payments upon the wife's remarriage. We granted the husband's petition for review.

The wife has urged us to adopt the approach suggested by the dissent in the Court of Appeals. In effect, that approach would treat the dissolution of a marriage like the dissolution of a business partnership and would also, in cases like this one, consider the husband's earning capacity to the development of which both parties contributed, as a joint asset to be allocated between them. The principles we have approved in this opinion will support similar results in many cases. We do not, however, approve the allocation of future earnings on principles applicable to property rights. It is proper to recognize each party's contribution, whether financial or in the form of services, to the economic aspects of the marriage. But it is also important to retain flexibility to deal with the parties as the court finds them at the time of the dissolution. The marital history should not be allowed to overshadow present circumstances.

In light of the great disparity between the parties' earning capacities in this case, there are two general approaches by which we might arrive at a spousal support award which would be just and equitable between the parties. The first possibility is to structure the award in such a way that the spousal support payments, together with child support and the wife's present earning capacity, would enable her to enjoy a standard of living not overly disproportionate to that which the husband can maintain for himself. This approach would call for relatively lower spousal support payments during the years when the wife is receiving substantial child support payments and a somewhat higher permanent award in later years after the child support has terminated.

The second approach is to award proportionately higher spousal support at the outset so that the wife will not have to work full time to support herself and the children. This will permit her to complete the educational program which she has planned and will permit a somewhat lower level of permanent support later. The wife outlined a four-year plan of schooling which should significantly increase her earning capacity.

Under the circumstances of this case, taking into account the expressed legislative policy that favors efforts to reduce the dependence of one spouse on the other over the long run, we hold that the second approach is the preferable one here.

While the support payments for both children last, the husband's total support obligation of $700 a month, the level set by the Court of Appeals, is a heavy one. He may well find it necessary to obtain summer employment in order to meet it and still provide comfortably for himself. On the other hand, $700 a month is probably not enough to enable the wife to support herself and two teenage children and to pursue a college education. She will likely find it necessary to work part time in order to carry out her plans. Spousal support during this period in the amount set by the Court of Appeals, $200 a month, presents some hardships for both parties, but we are unable to arrive at a more satisfactory figure.

[The original opinion in this case was modified by deleting language which occurred at this point in the opinion and by substituting therefore the following language.]

"* * * We approve the award of spousal support in the amount of $200 a month to and including the payment due in January 1981, provided that support payments for both children continue until that time. If support payments for either child terminate before that time, spousal support should be temporarily increased to $300, in order to permit the wife to complete her training.

"In any event, spousal support should be reduced after said January 1981 payment. By that time, the wife will have had time to complete her contemplated schooling and to find a position in her field."

[The original opinion then concludes with the following language.] Taking into account the wife's predictions of her eventual earning capacity and the fact that she has been awarded the family home (upon which the payments are quite low compared to today's normal housing costs), we believe that permanent spousal support payments of $125 a month will be appropriate. This will not put the parties on an equal footing financially, but will permit both of them some flexibility in their personal financial arrangements.

The decree of the circuit court should be modified in accordance with this opinion.

NOTES AND QUESTIONS

1. The *Grove* case was criticized in 57 Or.L.Rev. 566 (1978).

2. The Uniform Marriage and Divorce Act § 308, 9A Unif.L.Ann. 160 (1979) provides as follows with respect to maintenance awards in divorce:

"§ 308. [Maintenance]

"(a) In a proceeding for dissolution of marriage, legal separation, or maintenance following a decree of dissolution of the marriage by a court which lacked personal jurisdiction over the absent spouse, the court may grant a maintenance order for either spouse only if it finds that the spouse seeking maintenance:

"(1) lacks sufficient property to provide for his reasonable needs; and

"(2) is unable to support himself through appropriate employment or is the custodian of a child whose condition or circumstances make it appropriate that the custodian not be required to seek employment outside the home.

"(b) The maintenance order shall be in amounts and for periods of time the court deems just, without regard to marital misconduct, and after considering all relevant factors including:

"(1) the financial resources of the party seeking maintenance, including marital property apportioned to him, his ability to meet his needs independently, and the extent to which a provision for support of a child living with the party includes a sum for that party as custodian;

"(2) the time necessary to acquire sufficient education or training to enable the party seeking maintenance to find appropriate employment;

"(3) the standard of living established during the marriage;

"(4) the duration of the marriage;

"(5) the age and the physical and emotional condition of the spouse seeking maintenance; and

"(6) the ability of the spouse from whom maintenance is sought to meet his needs while meeting those of the spouse seeking maintenance."

3. Judge Fuld in the *Kover* case refers at two points in his opinion to the employment opportunities of women in today's world, characterizing them as "practically unlimited". Under Title VII of the Civil Rights Act of 1964, 42 U.S.C.A. § 2000e–2, discrimination in employment by reason of sex, on the part of employers covered by the Act, is forbidden. Does this justify Judge Fuld's remarks? Or is there continuing de facto discrimination against women in employment? If there is, should a court's decisions respecting the award of alimony be made with reference to the statutory requirements, or with reference to the situation which the particular spouse faces in the labor market, taking into account any de facto discrimination which might exist or any other difficulties which the individual spouse might encounter?

4. What do you suppose Judge Fuld meant when he said that among the factors to be taken into account in the alimony decision is, "to a limited extent" the conduct of the parties? Should "marital fault" be considered at all in awarding or denying alimony? Notice that the Uniform Act expressly excludes "marital misconduct" in determining the amount of alimony. Notice also that there is no mention of marital misconduct in the *Grove* case or the Oregon statute under which it was decided. In some states, however, some consideration of marital misconduct still enters into the decision whether to award alimony and the calculation of its amount. See, e. g., Williamson v. Williamson, 367 So.2d 1016 (Fla.1979); Bryan v. Bryan, 242 Ga. 826, 251 S.E.2d 566 (1979); Bender v. Bender, 282 Md. 525, 386 A.2d 772 (1978); Dyer v. Tsapis, —— W.Va. ——, 249 S.E.2d 509 (1978). A case which held fault might be considered but which seems to give it less effect than formerly is Lynn v. Lynn, 165 N.J.Super. 328, 398 A.2d 141 (1979), cert. den. 81 N.J. 52, 404 A.2d 1152 (1979). Other cases are cited in Annots., 86 A.L.R.3d 97 (1978) and 86 A.L.R.3d 1116 (1978).

5. In your opinion should the same result be reached in the three New York cases (*Kover, Miraldi, Dulber*) if they were decided (a) under the standards described in *Grove;* or (b) under the Uniform Act?

6. Is the *Grove* opinion internally inconsistent in saying that the decree should not provide in advance for the future possibility of the wife's remarriage, but that it should provide in advance for her future needs after the children are grown up and she supposedly is able to obtain a master's degree? If the decree can take account of the latter highly uncertain event, why may it not take account of possible remarriage? Cf. Stanton-Abbott v. Stanton-Abbott, 372 Mass. 814, 363 N.E.2d 1311 (1977).

7. Assume that you are a trial court to whom the evidence outlined in the following cases is presented. The marriages involved are childless. How would you dispose of the alimony claims under (a) the *Kover* case; (b) the *Grove* case; (c) the Uniform Act?

(a) H and W have been married for fifteen years, H being forty-five years old and W forty-three. H is the vice-president of a chemical manufacturing firm, not a large company, but one which has been successful and consistently profitable. H's salary is $25,000 per year. The marriage has not been harmonious for the past three years, but the divorce was precipitated by H's affection for a young woman working for his company, whom he intends to marry, a divorcee thirty years old with two small children. H and W have always lived up to the full extent of his income, and their only property is a $50,000 house, in which their equity is $25,000, with an equal amount due on a mortgage held by a local bank, two automobiles, a joint checking account in the local bank containing about $2,000, a savings account with $3,000 in it, and a life insurance policy on H's life having a face value at his death of $50,000 and a present cash value of $3,500. H's company has a retirement plan under which H can retire at age sixty-five with an income of $15,000 per year for his life, or, if he should so elect, an income of $12,000 per year for the lives of himself and his spouse. Before the divorce action was brought H moved out of the house and into the apartment of the young woman and has been living with her and supporting her and the children. Since he provided for W only inadequately and under protest before she sued for divorce, she was forced to find work and did so, getting a job as an assistant in the local public library at $100 per week.

She will be able to keep this job as long as she wants it. Would your assessment of the alimony claim be different if there were two children of the marriage, aged seventeen and sixteen? On the question of the treatment of pension benefits, see, In re Karlin, 24 Cal.App.3d 25, 101 Cal.Rptr. 240 (1972); Robbins v. Robbins, 463 S.W.2d 876 (Mo.App.1971); Miser v. Miser, 475 S.W.2d 597 (Tex.Civ.App.1971); DeRevere v. DeRevere, 5 Wash.2d 741, 491 P.2d 249 (1971).

(b) The circumstances surrounding the marriage are those of problem 6, page 168, supra. W sues H for divorce, rather than annulment, after three years of marriage, and H asks the court to award him alimony. W has an income from investments of $90,000 per year, her property being worth about two million dollars. H has no income and no property. At the time of the divorce action he has not been able to find a job, although he has made some efforts in that direction. He drinks heavily, occasionally still uses various kinds of pills to the point of being disabled for useful work, and often taunts W with having no affection for her and having married her solely for her money. During the marriage H and W lived in a luxurious fashion, with all expenses being paid out of W's income.

(c) H and W were married when H was 48 and W 45. H was a rich man, with a net worth in excess of three million dollars. His annual salary was $100,000 from a construction firm which he owned and ran. For tax reasons the firm paid no dividends, although it was highly profitable. It was the second marriage for both H and W, W being a widow and H divorced from his first wife. H was required to pay his first wife $20,000 per year in alimony.

The construction firm was incorporated, H owning all but a few shares of the stock. Due to his policy of not withdrawing profits, the corporation had retained earnings of $2.5 million. H was a self-made man, with some of the virtues and many of the vices of that sort of person. W testified that before they were married H seemed to be a kind and affectionate person, but that after about two years of married life he became harsh, cruel, abusive and tyrannical. He refused to engage in any social life with her and spent most of his evenings playing poker or drinking in his favorite bar with male friends or business associates. On two occasions he hit W hard enough to leave marks on her face and arms. W's response to this conduct was to try to persuade H to change, and to return to his earlier kinder ways. When this failed, she suggested they both visit a psychiatrist or counselor, which so angered H that he left the house and did not return for three days. H always gave W plenty of money, however, and they lived on a scale corresponding to his wealth. W before marriage had been a professor of sociology at a state university, with a gross income of $15,000 per year. She stopped teaching on her marriage, and did not work at all, largely because H insisted that she not work, that he had plenty of money to care for her. W sued for divorce after four years of marriage. By that time her old teaching position was no longer available to her and teaching positions everywhere had become very hard to find, particularly for a woman of her age. She finally did manage to find a job as a saleswoman in a department store, earning about $500 per month. See, e. g., Ingram v. Ingram, 217 Va. 27, 225 S.E.2d 362 (1976).

(d) H and W had been married for eighteen years, both being forty-four years old. H was a successful physician, earning an income of about

$75,000 per year. One day he informed W that he had fallen in love with a nurse on the staff of a local hospital and that he wanted a divorce. He also told W he was tired of the rat race of ordinary practice and intended to take a position teaching half time in medical school. His income from the teaching position would be $20,000. Are H's earnings for purposes of determining how much maintenance W should receive to be judged on the basis of his former practice or on the basis of his medical school salary? Would it be different if the husband were older and decided to take voluntary early retirement from his job, thereby reducing his earnings? If the husband decided to "drop out" altogether, living on savings, could he avoid paying any alimony to an otherwise deserving wife? See, e. g., In re Marriage of McCarthy, 533 P.2d 928 (Colo.App.1975); Olsen v. Olsen, 98 Idaho 10, 557 P.2d 604 (1976); In re Marriage of Smith, 77 Ill.App.3d 858, 33 Ill.Dec. 332, 396 N.E.2d 859 (1979); Hickland v. Hickland, 39 N.Y.2d 1, 382 N.Y.S.2d 475, 346 N.E.2d 243 (1976), cert. den. 429 U.S. 941 (1976); Commonwealth ex rel. Burns v. Burns, 232 Pa.Super. 295, 331 A.2d 768 (1974); Butler v. Butler, 217 Va. 195, 227 S.E.2d 688 (1976).

8. Looking back at the *Kover* and *Grove* cases and the alimony problems, what would you say the purpose or purposes of alimony are? Why is it that divorce ends all obligations of one spouse toward the other except for the financial one? What are the statutes and cases aiming to accomplish by providing for alimony? Do the purposes you discern have social utility? Should the availability of alimony be expanded, curtailed, or left about as these statutes provide?

9. Obviously precedent is of relatively little value in determining the number of dollars of alimony which are to be awarded in a given case, since the facts of the cases are capable of infinite variation. For useful illustration of the way in which some courts have approached the alimony decision, however, see the excellent study, Hopson, Economics of Divorce: A Pilot Empirical Study at the Trial Court Level, 11 Kan.L.Rev. 107 (1962), and the extensive collections of cases in Annot., Excessiveness of Amount of Money Awarded as Permanent Alimony Where Divorce is or Has Been Granted, 1 A.L.R.3d 6 (1965), and Annot., Adequacy of Amount of Money Awarded as Permanent Alimony Where Divorce is or Has Been Granted, 1 A.L.R.3d 123 (1965). As the court in *Kover* indicated, it is well established that the award of alimony rests in the discretion of the trial court, whose determination is to be reversed only where abuse of that discretion can be found.

10. The most serious aspect of the alimony question is that in the overwhelming majority of divorces there is not sufficient money or property to provide adequate alimony. The breakup of the family increases the living expenses of the members who must then support two establishments rather than one. Even with both husband and wife working, this cannot ordinarily be done at the same level at which the family lived before the divorce. A graphic demonstration of this can be found in a study of alimony by W. Goode, After Divorce, 228ff. (1956). Although the figures in that study are now out of date, the current inflation has undoubtedly made the financial plight of divorced persons more severe rather than less so. For this reason the attorney consulted by divorce clients should advise them early in the game that the divorce will probably involve financial hardship for both spouses, and that they should not go ahead with plans to obtain a di-

vorce without making concurrent, definite plans for coping with the financial situation which they can expect to face after the divorce. In some instances this sort of advice may induce second thoughts about the advisability of the divorce itself.

WILBERSCHEID v. WILBERSCHEID

Supreme Court of Wisconsin, 1977.
77 Wis.2d 40, 252 N.W.2d 76.

ABRAHAMSON, Justice. The issues presented for our consideration relate to the property division set forth in the judgment of divorce.

The appellant, Dorothy Wilberscheid, and the respondent, Cyril Joseph Wilberscheid, were married on January 14, 1956. She was at home while he worked as a laborer for the Kohler Company. In February of 1957 he quit his job and bought a tavern in Kiel, Wisconsin, with funds Mrs. Wilberscheid had saved prior to the wedding. A daughter, Carol, was born. Despite the efforts of both parties the business lost money for two and one-half years so they sold out and returned to Sheboygan, where they purchased a home for $13,500 with money Mrs. Wilberscheid had inherited from her mother. With the exception of about $500 worth of appliances, the household furnishings were also paid for with her money. In Sheboygan Mr. Wilberscheid's earnings from various jobs, primarily washing and polishing cars for automobile dealers, were insufficient to cover the family's living expenses. Initially Mrs. Wilberscheid used her savings to cover the shortfall. For the last thirteen years of the marriage, her income as a beautician which averaged $100 net earnings per week provided the main source of family revenue. Mr. Wilberscheid's average annual wages in this period ranged from $2,800 to $3,400.

The extent of the husband's contribution to the maintenance and support of the family during the last thirteen years was disputed. His income usually covered the gas, electric and telephone bills but little else. Mrs. Wilberscheid's earnings paid the taxes and bought the food and other essentials. While his wife was working Mr. Wilberscheid claims to have done all the housework; washing, cleaning, cooking, vacuuming and scrubbing, with some help from his daughter in recent years. Mrs. Wilberscheid disputed this assertion, claiming to have done most of this work herself, except for Carol's recent help and some minimal assistance with the cooking chores from her husband.

The family's assets included the house, whose value was assessed at $17,000 (the fair market value of which was estimated at $22,000–$23,000 by Mr. Wilberscheid), and its furnishings which had a value estimated at $6,000 by Mrs. Wilberscheid. In addition, each party owned an automobile and each had a savings account. The wife's car, a 1973 Pontiac, had a blue book value of $3,250 and her savings account had a balance of $7,000. The husband's car, a 1968 Pontiac, was valued by Mr. Wilberscheid at $500 and his savings account balance was $2,000. Mrs. Wilberscheid also had a checking account with $1,000 in it. The trial court found the divisible assets and their respective values to be as follows:

Home	$22,000.00
Furnishings	6,000.00
1973 Pontiac	3,250.00
1968 Pontiac	500.00
His Savings Account	2,000.00
Her Savings Account	7,000.00
Her Checking Account	1,000.00
	$41,750.00

On the basis of undisputed testimony, alleging the husband's misconduct, the court granted the wife an absolute divorce upon the grounds of cruel and inhuman treatment. The court awarded custody of Carol Wilberscheid to her mother, together with $75 per month for child support to be paid by the father.

The court stated that after reviewing the testimony it was satisfied that the wife was entitled to a more substantial division of the assets than the husband. In lieu of alimony to either party the court ordered a final division of assets wherein the wife received two-thirds of the assets and the husband received one-third of the assets, and the court assigned to the wife the home, its furnishings, her two bank accounts and her car. The husband was assigned his bank account, his car and a lien on the home in the amount of $11,416. The lien bore interest at 6 percent per annum. The sum was due and payable when Carol reached majority but it was chargeable for child support payments any time prior to maturity. The wife is alleging that the property division was excessive in favor of the husband and hence constitutes an abuse of discretion on the part of the trial court. She wishes this court to eliminate the husband's lien.

This court has long held that the division of property is within the sound discretion of the trial court and that the division will not be disturbed unless an abuse of discretion is shown. An abuse of discretion arises when the trial court has failed to consider proper factors, has made a mistake or error with respect to the facts upon which the division was made, or when the division itself was, under the circumstances, either excessive or inadequate.

Prior to Lacey v. Lacey, 45 Wis.2d 378, 173 N.W.2d 142 (1970), one of the guidelines of this court was that a property division awarding one-third of the net marital estate to the wife was considered a liberal allowance to the wife subject to increase or decrease according to special circumstances. We have specifically rejected a "rule of thumb" or a strict mathematical formula for the division of the marital estate in a divorce action, and we emphasized that each case must be decided upon the material facts and factors present therein.

We do not believe that the trial court has applied an arbitrary one-third, two-thirds mathematical formula. The decision and the findings of fact and conclusions of law show that the court considered the factors which this court in *Lacey,* supra at p. 383, 173 N.W.2d at p. 145, set forth as the factors to be considered in the division of the marital estate:

"* * * Whatever is material and relevant in establishing a fair and equitable basis for division of the property of the parties may be considered. Such relevant factors certainly include the length of the marriage, the age and health of the parties, their ability to support themselves, liability for debts or support of children, general circumstances, including grievous misconduct, although a division is not a penalty imposed for fault. Whether the property award is in lieu of or in addition to alimony payments is a material factor. Whether the property was acquired during the marriage or brought to the marriage makes a difference. * * * "

The substance of the above quote from the *Lacey* opinion is now codified in sec. 247.26, Stats.[5]

It is not necessary that the trial court consider and discuss each and every one of the factors set forth in the statute or cases. Also it is for the trial judge to determine the weight and effect of the various considerations.

Mrs. Wilberscheid argues that her husband's meager contributions to his family's welfare and his misconduct which precipitated this divorce action warrant his receipt of less than one-third of the marital estate. She points out that her efforts and individual resources provided the bulk of the divisible assets. However, under *Lacey,* supra, and under sec. 247.26, Stats., the ownership of assets prior to the marriage is only one of many factors determinative of the final property division.[7] The record indicates that the husband provided

---

5. Sec. 247.26, Stats., provides in part:
   "* * * The court may also finally divide and distribute the estate, both real and personal, of either party between the parties and divest and transfer the title of any thereof accordingly, after having given due regard to the legal and equitable rights of each party, the length of the marriage, the age and health of the parties, the liability of either party for debts of support of children, their respective abilities and estates, whether the property award is in lieu of or in addition to alimony, the character and situation of the parties and all the circumstances of the case. * * *"

7. The legislative history of the 1971 amendment to sec. 247.26 supports the interpretation that the estate of both husband and wife are subject to division and award to either party. In its initial report the Board of Directors of the State Bar of Wisconsin Family Law Section recommended "that the court shall have the right to divide the estate of either or both of the parties in its discretion after considering their relative estates, health, age, income, length of mar-

financial support in the early years of the marriage. The court also had testimony (though disputed) of the husband's efforts as homemaker househusband. This court recognizes the value of the uncompensated work of housewives or househusbands. In Bussewitz v. Bussewitz supra at p. 86, 248 N.W.2d 417, we noted that in dividing property upon divorce, the contribution of a full time homemaker may be considered greater than, or at least as great as, that of a working spouse. The fact that one party to the marriage worked outside the home while the other cared for the home and children has little bearing on the outcome of the property division if marriage is to be viewed as a "partnership" wherein both parties contribute of their respective abilities to the acquisition and preservation of marital assets.

The trial court heard testimony concerning the length of the marriage, the relative efforts of each party in contributing to the marriage, each party's age, health, income, and liabilities, and the sources of the funds used to acquire the marital estate. The court stated that it based its decision upon a review of all the testimony, and the court considered the defendant's misconduct, the burden of child support imposed upon him and the fact that the division was made in lieu of alimony either party might otherwise pay.

Certain factors are particularly relevant in determining whether a property division is inadequate or excessive. As the trial court noted, the parties were married for eighteen years. Such length implies some balance of contributions between the parties. The husband's capability for self-support is arguably below that of the wife; he was assessed (we think properly) for child support. While the husband's misconduct is undisputed and may be considered in the property division, the division should not be utilized to punish misconduct. Neither party received alimony, a circumstance the trial court properly considered as relevant to the property division. The trial court clearly exercised its discretion considering proper factors, and on this record we cannot conclude that there was an abuse of discretion.

* * *

Relying upon our decision in Horel v. Horel, 260 Wis. 336, 50 N. W.2d 673 (1952), Mrs. Wilberscheid contends that the manner in which the property division is to be executed is improper, since *Horel* mandates an actual division. The court said in *Horel* (p. 339, 50 N. W.2d p. 675) that "there should be an actual division wherever possible." In the present case an award of similar amounts which did not

riage, method of acquisition of the estate, etc." Legislative Reference Bureau, Drafting File, Chapter 220 (1971). In its analysis of the proposed law, the Legislative Reference Bureau concluded that:

"The estate of either or both parties may be divided by the court after considering all appropriate factors. The wife's separate estate is no longer shielded from distribution in actions affecting marriage." Id. (1971 Senate Bill 241, March 3, 1971).

encumber the house would have required a sale of the house or the award to the husband of all cash assets and automobiles. These alternatives would cause great hardship, and we find that the trial court acted within its discretionary authority in ordering this division.

Finding no error or abuse of discretion, we conclude that this decision and award must be affirmed.

NOTES AND QUESTIONS

1. The Uniform Marriage and Divorce Act § 307, 9A Unif.L.Ann. 142 (1979), proposes two alternative provisions covering the disposition of property on divorce. Alternative B is designed for community property states and merely authorizes the division of the community property "in just proportions". Alternative A is the provision generally recommended and reads as follows:

"Alternative A of § 307

"§ 307. [Disposition of Property]

"(a) In a proceeding for dissolution of a marriage, legal separation, or disposition of property following a decree of dissolution of marriage or legal separation by a court which lacked personal jurisdiction over the absent spouse or lacked jurisdiction to dispose of the property, the court, without regard to marital misconduct, shall, and in a proceeding for legal separation may, finally equitably apportion between the parties the property and assets belonging to either or both however and whenever acquired, and whether the title thereto is in the name of the husband or wife or both. In making apportionment the court shall consider the duration of the marriage, and prior marriage of either party, antenuptial agreement of the parties, the age, health, station, occupation, amount and sources of income, vocational skills, employability, estate, liabilities, and needs of each of the parties, custodial provisions, whether the apportionment is in lieu of or in addition to maintenance, and the opportunity of each for future acquisition of capital assets and income. The court shall also consider the contribution or dissipation of each party in the acquisition, preservation, depreciation, or appreciation in value of the respective estates, and the contribution of a spouse as a homemaker or to the family unit.

"(b) In a proceeding, the court may protect and promote the best interests of the children by setting aside a portion of the jointly and separately held estates of the parties in a separate fund or trust for the support, maintenance, education, and general welfare of any minor, dependent, or incompetent children of the parties."

An earlier version of the Uniform Act provision was held constitutional in Kujawinski v. Kujawinski, 71 Ill.2d 563, 17 Ill.Dec. 801, 376 N.E.2d 1382 (1978).

2. Judging from the criteria listed in the *Wilberscheid* case and in the Uniform Act, what purpose or purposes are served by the division of property on divorce? Is the idea to give to each spouse that property which belongs to him or her, but title to which had become obscured or confused

during the vicissitudes of marriage? Or does the distribution have other purposes? What is the relationship between the division of property and the award of alimony? Do they serve the same purposes or different ones? What is the relationship between them and child support awards? The present Wisconsin statute is Wis.Stat.Ann. § 247.255 (Supp.1979).

3. Would you have divided the property in the *Wilberscheid* case as the trial court did? Was that division "fair and equitable"? How can you tell whether it was or was not? Should "marital misconduct" be considered in making the property disposition, and if so, in what way or to what extent?

4. In some states, doubtless influenced by the concept of community property, the parties' property is classified as either separate or marital property. Marital property is defined as any property acquired by either spouse during the marriage other than by gift or devise, and separate property is all other property. These statutes provide that the separate property be assigned to the spouse who owns it, and that the marital property then be divided between them on an equitable basis. Cf., e. g., Colo.Rev. Stat.Ann. § 14–10–113 (1973). Is this a better technique for dividing the property than that in the Wisconsin statute or the Uniform Act?

5. Unfortunately for legal symmetry, it is necessary for several reasons to draw a distinction between a division of property and an award of alimony. For example, under the law of many states alimony is modifiable subsequently on proof of a change in relevant circumstances, while a division of property is not modifiable. See, e. g., Uniform Marriage and Divorce Act § 316(a), 9A Unif.L.Ann. 183 (1979). But see LeBreton v. Le- Breton, 604 P.2d 469 (Utah 1979). Likewise alimony orders are enforceable by contempt, property orders are usually not. Alimony terminates automatically in many states upon the wife's remarriage, while property orders do not. Property obligations are dischargeable in bankruptcy, while alimony obligations are not. And alimony receives a different federal income tax treatment from that accorded to a division of property.

Since the distinction between orders requiring the payment of alimony and those calling for the division of property must be made, what principles should be relied upon in making it? Does the form of the order control? Do the statutes quoted above help? Does the purpose of the award control? Or does the label placed on the award by the trial court determine its character? For a discussion of this problem see Daggett, Division of Property Upon Dissolution of Marriage, 6 Law & Contemp.Prob. 225 (1939). Could you draft a statute solving this problem?

Alimony, although it is usually payable in installments, need not always be so payable. Alimony in gross or lump sum alimony is permitted by the law of many states and occasionally is awarded in that form. See, e. g., Whitfield v. Whitfield, 283 Ala. 433, 218 So.2d 146 (1969); Judy v. Warner, 474 P.2d 233 (Colo.App.1970); Chester v. Chester, 241 So.2d 190 (Fla. App.1970); Reed v. Reed, 457 S.W.2d 4 (Ky.1970); Shomaker v. Shomaker, 183 Neb. 609, 163 N.W.2d 102 (1968). There is authority that alimony in gross cannot be modified. Ball v. Ball, 183 Neb. 216, 159 N.W.2d 297 (1968).

To test the principles underlying this distinction, consider the following examples: (a) The trial court finds that the wife has, during the marriage, assisted the husband in his business by acting as his bookkeeper. The business has been profitable. For this reason the court awards her $10,000 payable in installments over ten years. Is this alimony or a distribution of property?

(b) Early in the marriage the wife received a small inheritance and put $5,000 of it in the husband's business which later turned out to be successful. For this reason the trial court awards the wife ten percent of the present net worth of the business, payable in a single sum. Is this a distribution of property?

(c) The evidence indicated that the wife had been a diligent housekeeper and mother, had cared well for the children, had entertained her husband's business acquaintances, and helped him in many non-pecuniary ways during the days when they had little money. At the time of the divorce the husband had become wealthy and the court awarded the wife alimony in gross of $100,000, payable in five equal annual installments. Is this alimony?

(d) The trial court found that the parties owned, as joint tenants, a home worth $30,000, in which their equity was $15,000, the remainder being due on a mortgage. The equity had been built up by payments out of the husband's wages. The court stated that since the wife was being given custody of the two children and would need a place to live, rather than require the husband to pay an amount in cash sufficient to provide housing, the court would order the husband to convey the family home to the wife and to make the mortgage payments. Is this a distribution of property?

6. In eight states, Arizona, California, Idaho, Louisiana, Nevada, New Mexico, Texas and Washington there is the civil law institution of community property. The rationale of community property is that the property resulted from the efforts of both spouses during the marriage and should belong to both. In general community property consists of that property acquired by husband and wife during the marriage other than by gift, devise or inheritance. Some of the statutes define it by first defining separate property as that property of husband or wife either owned before marriage or acquired after marriage by gift, devise or inheritance, and then stating that community property includes other real property within the state and all other personal property acquired during the marriage. See, e. g., Cal.Civ.Code §§ 5107, 5108, 5110 (1970 and Supp.1979). California also has a class of property called quasi-community property, consisting of property, wherever situated, acquired by either spouse while domiciled outside California, which would have been community property if the spouse had been domiciled in California. Cal.Civ.Code § 4803 (Supp.1979).

Obviously many difficulties may arise in determining whether specific property is separate or community property. For a discussion of these problems see 4A R. Powell, Real Property § 624.4 (Rohan ed. 1979). Examples of the difficulty in distinguishing between community and separate property are Beam v. Bank of America, 6 Cal.3d 12, 98 Cal.Rptr. 137, 490 P.2d 257 (1971), where earnings produced by the husband's devotion of more than a minimal time and effort to handling his separate property were held to be community property; In re Marriage of Mason, 93 Cal.App.3d 215, 155 Cal.Rptr. 350 (1979), where an award of damages to the husband for his personal injury was held to be separate property; and Fite v. Fite, 3

Wash.App. 726, 479 P.2d 560 (1970), where the source of the funds producing the property was in issue.

In the community property states the statutes authorize the courts to divide the community property on divorce. The proportions in which the division must be made vary from state to state. California now takes the logical position that the community property (and the quasi-community property) must be divided equally on divorce. Cal.Civ.Code § 4800 (Supp.1979). Other states, such as Texas, Washington and Nevada, require only that the division be made in a manner which is just and equitable, or just and right. Tex.Fam.Code § 3.63 (1975); Wash.Rev.Code Ann. § 26.08.110 (1961); Nev.Rev.Stat. § 125.150 (1977). The factors which enter into the decision of what is just and right are similar to those discussed in the *Wilberschied* case, Waggener v. Waggener, 460 S.W.2d 251 (Tex.Civ.App.1970) and may include in some cases the relative fault of the parties, Belmondo v. Belmondo, 3 Wash.App. 958, 480 P.2d 786 (1970). In Texas the parties' separate property may be divided as well as the community property, under some circumstances. Muns v. Muns, 567 S.W.2d 563 (Tex.Civ.App.1978).

For a thorough discussion of community property, see W. de Funiak, M. Vaughan, Principles of Community Property (2d ed. 1971); I. Baxter, Marital Property, ch. 6 to 24 (1973); 4A R. Powell, Real Property ch. 53 (Rohan ed. 1979).

The situation in community property states with respect to the division of property on divorce is thus not very different from that in common law property states, at least those common law states where a distinction is made between marital and separate property. In most community property states the property is to be divided on similar terms and there is similar difficulty in determining what is a division of property and what an award of alimony, with the same necessity for making that distinction.

7. A man and woman, M and W, live together for three years without being married. They have no agreement or understanding concerning their financial affairs. During this time W keeps house and M supports them out of his earnings, and out of those earnings buys a house in which they live. At the end of the three years M says he is tired of the arrangement and asks W to move out of "his" house. By this time the value of the house has trebled. W sues M for a portion of the value of the house.

(a) Should she recover in a state which has the Wisconsin type of statute dealing with division of property on divorce? Or the Uniform Act? Or does the statute have nothing to do with this question? Cf. Marvin v. Marvin, supra, page 38.

(b) Would it matter whether common law marriage was or was not recognized in the state?

BLOOMER v. BLOOMER

Supreme Court of Wisconsin, 1978.
84 Wis.2d 124, 267 N.W.2d 235.

HEFFERNAN, Justice. This case arises out of the divorce of the parties and relates to the proper valuation, for the purpose of the division of the marital estate, of Herbert Bloomer's interest in his Wisconsin employee's pension plan.

Herbert and Janet Bloomer were married on April 4, 1953, and at the time of the trial were ages forty-two and thirty-nine, respectively. Trial was held to the court on September 22, 1975. The trial court found that Herbert's retirement fund account with the Wisconsin Department of Employee Trust Funds was an asset of the marital estate subject to consideration in dividing the marital property.

Herbert is a municipal employee, and he has participated in the Wisconsin Retirement Fund continuously from December 1, 1954, through the date of trial. During a part of that time, he made direct employee contributions to the Fund. At the end of the calendar quarter nearest to the commencement of this action, his total contribution to the fund, plus interest was $8,047.61, exclusive of any employer contributions. This sum would be available immediately to Herbert upon termination of employment but is not available to him as long as he continues his employment.[1]

In the event Herbert terminates his employment before age fifty-five, he could elect the immediate receipt of the balance of employee contributions plus interest. Alternatively, upon termination of employment before age fifty-five, he could elect to leave this amount invested in the Fund and receive a retirement annuity commencing, at the earliest, at age fifty-five.

If, on the other hand, Herbert continues as an employee and retires at age fifty-five or older, the Fund provides for the payment of a retirement annuity.

The trial court found the present value of Herbert's account to be $2,600, despite the current balance of $8,047.61. The trial court expressed some doubt as to the correctness of the method of computation, but it concluded that this result was required under this court's decision in Parsons v. Parsons, 68 Wis.2d 744, 229 N.W.2d 629 (1975). Judgment was entered on November 10, 1975, and it is from the part of the judgment valuing Herbert's interest in the pension fund that Janet appeals.

Janet also petitioned the trial court for an allowance of attorneys' fees and costs on appeal. The trial court denied this petition in an order entered on May 7, 1976. * * *

1. As far as the record indicates, Herbert remained a municipal employee after the divorce. It is clear, however, that any contributions to the retirement fund after the divorce, whether made by employer or employee, would not be assets of the marital estate subject to division. Therefore, for the purpose of dividing the marital estate, only that part of the fund or the benefits under it which are attributable to the marriage should be considered. Because of the likelihood of future contributions to the fund, therefore, the fund should be treated as if it were two funds, with only that part of the fund attributable to the marriage being considered and divided.

It is Janet's contention on this appeal that the method of valuation used in *Parsons,* and in the trial court decision in this case, is improper in that it, in effect, results in "double discounting" of the value of the interest in the fund. We agree and therefore reverse.

In many divorce situations, the pension rights of one or both employee spouses are the most significant marital assets owned by the couple. Dickinson, Role of Retirement Plans, 10 Real Prop., Prob. & Tr.J. 644 (1975). The climate for recognition of the rights of the non-employee spouse in the pension plan of the employee spouse seems to be more salubrious in the community-property states. I. Baxter, Marital Property, sec. 11.2 (Cum.Supp.1977). Wisconsin, however, is in the forefront of common-law-property states recognizing the rights of the non-employee spouse. Schafer v. Schafer, 3 Wis.2d 166, 87 N.W. 2d 803 (1958), determined that pension rights earned during marriage are properly included as a marital asset in dividing the property of the spouses.

Although it is settled that pension rights must be considered, trial courts are presented with a complex task in properly valuing the rights in those plans. Herbert's rights in the pension plan can properly be described as vested, but non-matured. His interest is vested, in the sense that were he to retire immediately, he would not lose all rights under the plan.[3] His interest is non-matured, in that his right to receive payments in the form of a pension based in part on employee contributions will not accrue, at the earliest, until he reaches age fifty-five. See generally, In re Marriage of Bruegl, 47 Cal.App.3d 201, 120 Cal.Rptr. 597 (1975), overruled on other grounds, In re Marriage of Brown, 15 Cal.3d 838, 126 Cal.Rptr. 633, 544 P.2d 561 (1976).

The problem of valuing prospective benefits under a pension plan is frequently exacerbated by the fact that unmatured rights may be terminated by death, discharge, or other contingencies. Hughes, Community-Property Aspects of Profit-Sharing and Pension Plans in Texas—Recent Developments and Proposed Guidelines for the Future, 44 Tex.L.Rev. 860, 879 (1966). Valuation is further complicated by the dual nature of most pension plans. If the employee continues to work until retirement, the payments to the employee, to the extent derived from employer's contributions, are in the nature of deferred compensation. If, however, the employee terminates work before retirement age, the usual plan provides at least for the return of employee contributions.

None of the Wisconsin cases have explicitly faced the question presented on this appeal. A variety of methods of valuation have been approved in the individual cases, without any analysis of the

---

3. Although Herbert's rights in the plan are vested, we note that even non-vested rights must be considered in dividing the marital property. Leighton v. Leighton, 81 Wis.2d 620, 261 N.W.2d 457 (1978).

proper theory for valuing the asset. In Schafer v. Schafer, supra, this court noted that the employee contributions (apparently exclusive of interest) amounted to $4,065.08. The husband was eligible to retire then and would have received $2,880 per year as a pension. We said that this pension, for the husband's life expectancy, discounted at 5 percent, would have a present value of $29,000. It was said that this figure might be too high, since the husband had no intention of retiring at that time. We said, however, that the intrinsic value of the pension rights was probably as great as the value of the homestead (which was valued at $17,800). After remand, this same case was again appealed to this court in Schafer v. Schafer, 9 Wis.2d 502, 101 N.W.2d 780 (1960) (*Schafer II*). In *Schafer II*, we stated that the husband's contributions plus interest amounted to $6,234.04. He could have retired at the time of trial and received a pension of $237 per month. If he retired at age sixty, he would receive $281 per month. If he were to die immediately, his estate would collect $6,263.04. The evidence was that a private, single-premium annuity equivalent to the husband's rights would cost $49,000. The trial court valued the pension at $6,263.04, and we affirmed. This sum equalled the death benefit currently and also closely approximated the total of employee contributions plus interest.

In Schneider v. Schneider, 15 Wis.2d 245, 112 N.W.2d 584 (1961), the husband had $5,000 in the fund, which he would receive if he were to quit, retire, or be fired. Because the husband apparently had no intent to retire at the time, the money would not be immediately available. This court indicated that the proper value should probably be a little less than $5,000, since the funds were not currently available.

In Kronforst v. Kronforst, 21 Wis.2d 54, 123 N.W.2d 528 (1963), the husband had $9,749 in the fund, which he was entitled to receive as a lump sum or in annuity form on retirement. The valuation at $9,749 was upheld, and this court analogized the interest in the fund to the interest in a savings account. However, the husband was disabled, and it appeared that he would not return to work, so that for practical purposes the husband was immediately entitled to receive this sum.[4]

Parsons v. Parsons, supra, was the case relied on by the trial court in reducing the value of the account to the "present value." In *Parsons,* the husband was seventeen years from retirement, and he had $39,495 in his retirement account. The husband argued that this

---

4. Unlike the situation in the *Kronforst* case, there is no indication in the present record that Herbert has any intention of retiring early. In Pinkowski v. Pinkowski, 67 Wis.2d 176, 226 N.W.2d 518 (1975), we stated that the husband should not be forced to retire early in order to realize the lump-sum retirement benefits. Nevertheless, the present value of the interest must be ascertained and divided by the court. There are a number of ways in which this can properly be done, as we discuss infra.

sum had to be discounted to present value, since it was not available until retirement. We have reexamined the briefs in *Parsons,* and they disclose that the wife's argument in that case was simply that full face value should be used, rather than "so called present values." With the arguments presented in this posture, we held that present values must be used in dividing the marital assets, and we now reaffirm that much of the holding in *Parsons.* Since the wife in *Parsons* did not really dispute the husband's methodology for calculating present value, we did not question the basic methodology utilized in discounting the value of the account for seventeen years at 5 percent, yielding a value of $17,246.72. In this case, Janet has clearly defined the issue which was not posed in the *Parsons* case—not whether present values should be used but how present value should be calculated.

Janet argues that were the interest in the fund to be determined with reference to the current balance in the account, that balance should not be discounted, because it already equals (or at least approximates) the present value. This case involves a marital asset consisting of $8,047.61 at the time of trial, which will not be available until retirement, since Herbert is not to be forced to retire early, under the *Pinkowski* rule. Assume, for the sake of illustration, that Herbert retires at age sixty-five, twenty-three years after the trial in this case. If the value of Herbert's interest in the fund would be $8,047.61 *when distributed* in twenty-three years, then the trial court would undoubtedly be right in discounting the $8,047.61 for twenty-three years at 5 percent. The error in this method is that the $8,047.61 will continue to accrue interest over the next twenty-three years. Assuming a 5 percent rate of growth, the value of the fund will approximately triple over that period. If we were to take the approximately tripled figure, twenty-three years in the future, and then discount *that* figure at 5 percent, we would end up where we started, with a present value of approximately $8,047.61. To take, however, the uninflated current balance and discount that sum *as if* it were a future sum, as was done in *Parsons* and in the trial court here, is to "double discount" the sum to a figure well below present value. The problem presented by this type of marital asset is that it cannot be reached until some time in the future. Therefore, before it is discounted from its future value to present value, a court must first calculate what it will be worth at a designated time in the future. Were we to adopt Herbert's theory of proper valuation, the effect would be that all future growth of this marital asset would be credited to him, and none to Janet.

Cases involving the discounting of pension benefits to present value typically discuss discounting sums to be paid in the future, at the future rate of payment. For example, in Ramsey v. Ramsey, 96 Idaho 672, 535 P.2d 53 (1975), the husband was receiving and would continue to receive $341 per month for life. In this context, where the future payments are known, it is widely recognized that the future payments should be reduced to present value through discounting. Thiede, The Community Property Interest of the Non-Employee Spouse in Private Employee Retirement Benefits, 9 U.San Fran.L. Rev. 635, 662 (1975); Dickinson, supra, 10 Real Prop., Prob. & Tr.J. at 646; Projector, Valuation of Retirement Benefits in Marriage Dissolutions, 50 L.A.Bar Bull. 229, 231 (1975). In the present case, however, it was inappropriate to discount the present sum as if it were a future sum, without first accounting for future growth in the asset up to the time of distribution.

None of what we have said detracts from the fact that the trial court retains broad discretion in valuing pension rights and in dividing them between the parties. These rights are subject to several different general methods of valuation, and the actual calculations may change radically depending on different actuarial assumptions in respect to particular factors. We do, however, disapprove the method of valuation accepted by the parties in *Parsons,* because it involves double discounting, and find that the trial court's use of this method in the present case amounted to an abuse of discretion, albeit an understandable one, since it was based on the method relied upon by the parties in *Parsons* and not rejected by this court.

We remand this case to the trial court for a determination of value and for a revision of the order apportioning marital assets. Since the pension rights are substantially more valuable than heretofore determined by the trial court, it may be necessary to make a new overall division of the assets. For example, the increased value of the interest in the pension may make it inequitable to require Herbert to satisfy Janet's interest in a lump-sum payment. Other equitable adjustments may be made in the discretion of the trial court.

Because of the substantial element of trial court discretion in valuing pension rights, we can do no more than make some general observations as to appropriate methods of valuation. There are at least three ways in which the value can be determined. Whether any one of these methods is an appropriate exercise of discretion depends upon the circumstances of the case, the status of the parties, and whether the result is a reasonable valuation of the marital asset.

First, the trial court could consider the amount of Herbert's contributions to the fund, plus interest, and award Janet an appropriate share. W. De Funiak & M. Vaughn, Principles of Community Property, sec. 233 (2d ed. 1971). Under this approach, Janet, in the trial court's discretion, would be awarded some portion of the $8,047.61. Second, the trial court could attempt to calculate the present value of Herbert's retirement benefits when they vest under the plan. Id. Under this approach, the benefits payable in the future would have to be discounted for interest in the future, for mortality (the probability that Herbert will die before qualifying for the benefits), and for vesting (since Herbert will have to continue to work at least until age fifty-five before qualifying for fully vested pension rights). Projector, supra. The benefits would then have to be calculated with respect to Herbert's life expectancy as a retiree. This calculation involves considerable uncertainty, and the amount yielded changes as different assumptions are used with respect to mortality, job turn-over, etc. In the instant case, the testimony at trial indicated that the present value of the plan calculated in this manner would be in the range of $8,500 to $17,000. The trial court rejected this evidence as being too speculative, and it was its prerogative to do so, as long as it adopted a reasonable manner of calculating the present value. It has been recognized that this kind of calculation can be very difficult and that, where it becomes too speculative, the trial court should use a different method of valuation.

Under either of the above two methods, the trial court would have the discretion to order the payment to Janet of her share in either a lump sum or in installments, depending primarily on the other assets and relative financial positions of the parties. The third method, which has been used widely in other states and is referred to as an alternative in *Pinkowski,* supra 67 Wis.2d at 184, 226 N.W.2d 518, is to determine a fixed percentage for Janet of any future payments Herbert receives under the plan, payable to her as, if, and when paid to Herbert. Under this approach, of course, it is unnecessary to determine the value of the pension fund at all. The court need do no more than determine the appropriate percentage to which the non-employee spouse is entitled. In community-property states, the non-employee spouse's share is set at 50 percent of the benefits attributable to earnings during marriage. In Wisconsin, however, the trial court has the discretion to determine the appropriate percentage.

Janet, by motion after judgment, requested an allowance for attorneys' fees and costs on this appeal, which request was denied. In her petition, she requested allowance of the entire estimated cost of appeal, or $2,800 plus costs and disbursements.

Allowance of attorneys' fees and costs on appeal is governed by secs. 257.39 and 251.72, Stats. Janet followed these statutory procedures by petitioning for the allowance in the trial court. Whether to grant the allowance is in the sound discretion of the trial court.

Where trial attorneys' fees are involved, the trial court should consider the need of the wife for the allowance and the ability of the husband to pay. When appellant attorneys' fees are at issue, the trial court must consider an additional factor, whether reasonable grounds exist to support a belief that the appeal will be successful. Nothing in the trial court's decision indicates that it considered the likelihood that the appeal would be successful. Therefore, the trial court's denial of the allowance constitutes an abuse of discretion, because it failed to consider all the relevant factors and principles of law.

* * *

Judgment and order reversed, and cause remanded for proceedings consistent with this opinion.

NOTES AND QUESTIONS

1. Further discussion of the valuation of pensions occurs in Selchert v. Selchert, 90 Wis.2d 1, 280 N.W.2d 293 (1979). One practitioner suggests that the valuation problems may be complex enough in some instances to require the services of both an accountant and an actuary. See the report of a discussion of pensions in 4 Fam.L.Rep. 2128 (1978). See also 2 Family Advocate No. 1 (1979) which contains several articles on valuation.

2. What is the rationale for holding that a spouse's pension or retirement claims constitute property available for division on divorce? Does this rationale provide any clues for the method of valuation to be used? What method of valuation should be used in the *Bloomer* case on remand to the trial court?

3. As the *Bloomer* opinion indicates, California has been a leader in holding that pension rights constitute community property to be divided on divorce, an important case being *In re Marriage of Brown,* cited in *Bloomer.* In re Marriage of Stenquist, 21 Cal.2d 779, 148 Cal.Rptr. 9, 582 P.2d 96 (1978) cites other cases and holds that a husband's military retirement pay is divisible, while disability pay would not be. Other community property states have held pensions or retirement pay to be divisible on divorce. See Annot., 94 A.L.R.3d 176 (1979); Taggart v. Taggart, 552 S.W.2d 422 (Tex.1977) (military retirement benefits).

Is there any reason why the common law property states should not follow the California cases with respect to pension rights, or is *Bloomer* correct in its result? A case holding that military retirement pay is not property because it does not have a cash surrender value, a loan value, a redemption value, a lump sum value, or a value realizable after death, is Ellis v. Ellis, 191 Colo. 317, 552 P.2d 506 (1976). Should the courts make distinction for property division purposes between vested and unvested or matured and unmatured pension claims?

4. Where the pension or retirement claims sought to be divided on divorce are payable under various federal statutes, their availability for division depends upon the Supreme Court's decision in Hisquierdo v. Hisquierdo, 439 U.S. 572 (1979). In that case the husband was employed by a railway and a passenger terminal so that he was covered by the Railroad Retirement Act. He sued for divorce in California and his wife claimed a share of his retirement benefits under that Act as community property. The Act contains a provision to the effect that "no annuity * * * shall be assignable or be subject * * * to garnishment, attachment, or other legal process under any circumstances whatsoever, nor shall the payment thereof be anticipated * * *." 45 U.S.C.A. § 231m. The Court held that this provision preempts state community property law and prevents retirement benefits authorized by the Act from being divided on divorce. The Court found that the wife's claim here conflicted with the express

terms of the Act in such a way as to frustrate the objectives of the federal program. Congress' objective in passing the Act was to provide "finite funds" considered appropriate to support the employee's old age in order to encourage him to retire. The wife's claim would reduce his benefits and discourage the employee from retiring. This the Court held would impair the incentives created by Congress. Justices Stewart and Rehnquist dissented in this case.

The question which *Hisquierdo* raises is whether its reasoning applies to other federal retirement and pension programs. Umber v. Umber, 591 P.2d 299 (Okl.1979) holds that it applies to Social Security Act benefits. That Act contains a provision to the effect that money due from the United States to individuals, including members of the armed forces, is subject to legal process for the enforcement of child support and alimony claims. It then goes on to provide specifically that "alimony" does not include a division of property on divorce. 42 U.S.C.A. §§ 659(a), 662(c). The *Umber* case relied upon this statute and *Hisquierdo* to hold that social security benefits are the separate property of the husband and not subject to division on divorce.

The cases are in conflict on whether military retirement pay may be divided on divorce. Cose v. Cose, 592 P.2d 1230 (Alaska 1979) holds that it may not be, relying upon *Hisquierdo*. In re Marriage of Musser, 70 Ill. App.3d 706, 27 Ill.Dec. 240, 388 N.E.2d 1289 (1979), distinguishing *Hisquierdo* on the ground that there is no similar statute governing the military retirement, held that military retirement pay is marital property. Czarnecki v. Czarnecki, 123 Ariz. 466, 600 P.2d 1098 (1979) agrees with *Musser*. Of course if *Cose* is correct many earlier cases will have to be overruled, including *Stenquist*, cited supra, paragraph 3.

5. Another federal statute, the Employee Retirement Income Security Act of 1974 (ERISA) raises questions about the power of state courts to divide private pension claims on divorce where those pensions are subject to the Act. The Act, 29 U.S.C.A. § 1003, applies to any employee benefit plan maintained by an employer engaged in commerce or in any industry affecting commerce. In 29 U.S.C.A. § 1144 the Act provides that the Act supersedes all state laws insofar as they may relate to employee benefit plans. Finally, the Act provides, in 29 U.S.C.A. § 1056(d)(1): "Each pension plan shall provide that benefits provided under the plan may not be assigned or alienated." See also I.R.C. § 401(a)(13).

The question then is, in view of these statutory provisions forbidding assignment or alienation and applying to many private corporate pension plans, may a spouse's rights under such a plan be allocated to the other spouse on divorce by the state court having jurisdiction over the divorce? Footnote 24 of the *Hisquierdo* opinion states that the Court there is expressing no view concerning the application of community property principles to benefits payable under private plans regulated by federal statute. Two Second Circuit cases have held that ERISA does not prevent a wife from reaching her husband's pension benefits in order to enforce alimony and child support judgments. Cody v. Riecker, 594 F.2d 314 (2d Cir. 1979); American Tel. & Tel. Co. v. Merry, 592 F.2d 118 (2d Cir. 1979). But the *Cody* case seems to draw a distinction between alimony and a division of property. The cases which have directly dealt with the issue of

property division are divided. The most comprehensive discussion of the
problem is Stone v. Stone, 450 F.Supp. 919 (N.D.Cal.1978), 1979 Wis.L.Rev.
277, holding that ERISA does not prevent a wife from reaching her community property interest in her husband's pension. To the same effect is In
re Marriage of Pilatti, 96 Cal.App.3d 63, 157 Cal.Rptr. 594 (1979). A case
holding that ERISA preempts the community property laws is Francis v.
United Technologies Corp., 458 F.Supp. 84 (N.D.Cal.1978). An extensive
discussion of this and other issues is Reppy, Community and Separate Interests in Pensions and Social Security Benefits After Marriage of Brown
and ERISA, 25 U.C.L.A.L.Rev. 417, 519–522 (1978).

(a) What do you suppose was the Congressional purpose in enacting
the cited sections of ERISA, forbidding assignment and preempting state
law?

(b) In view of that purpose, should ERISA prevent a spouse in a community property state from being awarded her share of the pension on divorce?

(c) If a spouse in a community property state may reach the other
spouse's pension notwithstanding ERISA, should the result be the same in a
common law property state? Are the spousal interests in the pension sufficiently different to warrant a different result in the common law state?

(d) If, as the Second Circuit has held, pensions may be reached for the
enforcement of alimony judgments notwithstanding ERISA, should they
likewise be taken into account in dividing the spouses' property?

6. H and W are in the process of getting a divorce. H is a successful
lawyer with a remunerative practice. W has been a housewife during the
marriage, caring for their house and children, entertaining H's clients and
associates and in other respects assisting in H's career. Should the divorce
court award to W, in dividing the parties' property, a portion of the goodwill represented by H's practice? If so, how should it be valued? In re
Marriage of Fonstein, 17 Cal.3d 738, 131 Cal.Rptr. 873, 552 P.2d 1169
(1976); Stern v. Stern, 66 N.J. 340, 331 A.2d 257 (1975); Matter of Marriage of Fleege, 91 Wash.2d 324, 588 P.2d 1136 (1979); Annots., 52 A.L.R.
3d 1344 (1973), 74 A.L.R.3d 621 (1976).

7. H and W were married while H was in medical school. W worked
as an airline stewardess for four years while H was going through medical
school, her earnings being used to support both of them, to pay for H's tuition, books, and supplies. After his graduation and periods of internship
and residency, H took a position with a large medical clinic at a salary of
$35,000 per year. At this time W continued to work. As soon as he start-
ed work, H brought suit for divorce, telling W he had fallen in love with a
nurse. In the divorce proceeding W sought a division of jointly owned
property, the property she claimed being the value of the medical education
and training which her earnings had provided for H. How should the court
rule on W's claim? If W's claim is upheld, how should the education be
valued? In re Marriage of Aufmuth, 89 Cal.App.3d 446, 152 Cal.Rptr. 668
(1979); In re Marriage of Graham, 194 Colo. 29, 574 P.2d 75 (1978); In
re Marriage of McManama, —— Ind.App. ——, 386 N.E.2d 953 (1979); In
re Marriage of Horstmann, 263 N.W.2d 885 (Iowa 1978), 64 Iowa L.Rev.
705 (1979); Inman v. Inman, 578 S.W.2d 266 (Ky.App.1979); Hubbard v.
Hubbard, 603 P.2d 747 (Okl.1979); Erickson, Spousal Support Toward the

Realization of Educational Goals: How the Law Can Ensure Reciprocity, 1978 Wis.L.Rev. 943.

8. (a) H and W are married and live in State A. They own land in State B. W sues for divorce in A and seeks a division of H's property. A's law is that on divorce all property belonging to either spouse may be divided between them in such a way as to be just and equitable. B's law is that only marital property may be so divided. H's land in B is his separate property, not marital property. Should it be held available for division by the court in A?

(b) H and W live together in California. While there they accumulate community property. They then move to a common law property state where they seek a divorce. How should the property be divided, as community property in accordance with California law, or as common law property in accordance with the law of their new domicile?

See, e. g., In re Marriage of Furimsky, 122 Ariz. 430, 595 P.2d 662 (1979); Ladd v. Ladd, —— Ark. ——, 580 S.W.2d 696 (1979); Schubot v. Schubot, 363 So.2d 841 (Fla.App.1978); Stephens v. Stephens, 93 N.M. 1, 595 P.2d 1196 (1979); Hughes v. Hughes, 91 N.M. 339, 573 P.2d 1194 (1978); Annot., 14 A.L.R.3d 404 (1967); Restatement, Second, Conflict of Laws §§ 222, 233, 234 (1971).

LEVITT v. LEVITT

Supreme Court of California, In Bank, 1965.
62 Cal.2d 477, 42 Cal.Rptr. 577, 399 P.2d 33.

PEEK, Justice. Plaintiff Irmgard Dawson Levitt appeals from that portion of an order which reduces from $500 per month to a token amount the allowance for her support by defendant husband Gene Levitt awarded by a previous decree of divorce. Since we conclude that the provisions for support of plaintiff Irmgard were severable from an agreement signed by the parties respecting the division of property and other marital rights, and since the parties may not by stipulation deprive the court of jurisdiction to modify alimony payments provided for by judicial decree, we affirm the trial court's order.

Irmgard and Gene were married in June 1949 and separated in July 1954. One child, Christopher, was born to the parties during their marriage. James Francis Levitt, Irmgard's child by a prior marriage, also resided with them.

A complaint for divorce was filed by Irmgard in December 1954. The following month Irmgard and Gene signed a property settlement agreement, which at one point recited that "The parties desire to settle their respective property rights and interests as of the date of this agreement and to arrange by agreement for the making of periodical payments by Husband to Wife in discharge of his legal obligation to support and maintain Wife because of their marital and family relationship. * * *" The parties also stated therein that "each does hereby declare that the consideration for the execution of this agreement is such resolution between themselves as to the disposition of their property rights and interests and the settlement of support and maintenance rights of one to the other. *   *   * ''

In a separate article the agreement provided for payments by Gene to Irmgard and the children. The contracting parties expressly stated in that portion of the agreement that "Husband and Wife, *in discharge of Husband's obligation to support and maintain Wife because of their marital and family relationship,* hereby agree that Husband, *by way of alimony and not as a part of a property settlement* shall pay to Wife for *alimony, support, and maintenance* so long as Husband is alive and so long as Wife is living and remains unmarried, * * * '' $400 per month "for the support and maintenance of Wife," and $225 per month "for the support and maintenance of each of the minor children," Christopher and James. (Italics added.)

An interlocutory judgment of divorce was entered in February 1955, which incorporated to the extent not inconsistent with the decree the provisions of the property settlement agreement and ordered compliance with the terms of that agreement. Final judgment of divorce was entered March 1956.

In November 1956 the parties stipulated that the final decree be modified so that $500 was payable by defendant each month "for the support and maintenance of Plaintiff," and $250 was payable each month for Christopher's support. All of defendant's financial obligations to James were terminated. The stipulation for modification further recited: "It is understood and agreed that Defendant reserves any rights he may presently have or may obtain in the future to seek further modification in the Property Settlement Agreement, Interlocutory Decree and Final Decree hereunder *but Defendant covenants and agrees not to seek any modification or make any collateral attack concerning alimony or child support except in the event of a substantial decrease from Defendant's 1956 income.''* (Italics added.) The final judgment of divorce entered March 1956 was ordered modified to incorporate those portions of the stipulation for modification pertaining to alimony, child custody, and child support. The parties concede that the above portions of the stipulation were merged in the final judgment. (See Flynn v. Flynn, 42 Cal.2d 55, 58–59, 265 P.2d 865.)

In May 1962 defendant Gene sought modification of the prior orders, including the cessation of his payments to Irmgard or their reduction to a nominal amount. He stated in a certified declaration that he had remarried and had one child by his present wife, in addition to the care of Christopher for a substantial portion of the year. He also alleged that to his best information Irmgard, who was born in Germany and was a naturalized United States citizen, had established residence in Germany and had resided in the United States for only 28 months of the previous seven years. Gene further stated that he was at present a free-lance television writer and had no other employment, although it was admitted that up to the present his yearly income had not fallen below his income in 1956.

Defendant declared that he had not defaulted in his payments to Irmgard, having paid over $40,000 for her support and maintenance in the previous seven years. He stated that "Plaintiff is able-bodied and capable of being self-supporting and the continuance of support and maintenance by defendant places an undue burden on defendant and puts a premium on plaintiff's remaining unmarried." It further appears, * * * that at the time of hearing Irmgard was not employed. Ten years previously she worked as a motion picture extra. Her sole source of income was defendant's alimony payments, and she leased a house in Germany relying upon the continuation of those payments. The settled statement also recited that defendant resided with his present wife and their child, along with two of his wife's children by a prior marriage.

The order now challenged by plaintiff was entered in June 1962. It provides that defendant continue his payments of $500 per month to Irmgard only until January 1, 1963, whereupon alimony payments are reduced to one dollar per year "to continue until further order of the Court." Defendant was awarded custody of Christopher for the nine-month school year, plaintiff to have custody during the three-month school vacation period. Under the present order defendant must pay to plaintiff the support and maintenance for Christopher only during the three-month period the boy resides with his mother.

Appellant urges that the support and maintenance provisions are part of an integrated property settlement agreement and cannot be modified without consent of the parties except in the event defendant's income falls below the level attained in 1956, thereby satisfying the condition specified in the stipulation of November of that year (see Flynn v. Flynn, supra, 42 Cal.2d 55, 60–61, 265 P.2d 865). Several portions of the agreement are cited in an attempt to uphold it as an integrated bargain, including the portion quoted above wherein the parties stated that the consideration for the execution of the agreement was the resolution of property claims and the settlement of rights to support and maintenance.

However, regardless of the latter general statement of intent and other indicia of an integrated agreement, the parties clearly expressed their specific intention that the support and maintenance to be provided Irmgard was "by way of alimony and not as a part of a property settlement." In the face of that declaration it must be held that the support provisions were in the nature of alimony and severable from the division of property rights. * * * Hence the payments are subject to modification by the court upon a showing of changed circumstances. * * *

Appellant next points to defendant husband's statement in the stipulation for modification of November 1956, where he agreed not to seek any modification in alimony "except in the event of a substantial decrease" from his 1956 income, an event which has not occurred. She urges that the court had no jurisdiction to modify that agreement unless the above condition was satisfied, * * *

The nonintegrated agreement before us provides for severable payments of support or alimony, and such payments are modifiable "subject to the discretion of the court as justice may require" Rule * * * It was further held in Hough that the provision of section 139 of the Civil Code authorizing the modification of support allowances becomes an implied part of any such agreement whenever, as herein, the agreement is merged in the decree. * * * Thus in contracting concerning alimony payments when incorporation in the decree is contemplated the parties are presumed to be aware that the trial court has the power to modify or revoke such agreements in accordance with changed circumstances. * * *

From the foregoing it is clear that the parties' stipulation that the alimony payments would not be modified unless defendant's income decreased below the level in 1956 did not preclude the court from ordering the present modification of its decree based on that stipulation. * * *

Appellant argues in the alternative that even if the court had jurisdiction to order the instant modification of alimony payments, the order was an abuse of discretion because it plainly effected an injustice in depriving her of all support from her former husband. However, under all of the present circumstances we cannot say that the trial court abused its discretion in reducing to a token amount the support payments to Irmgard.

The trial court has jurisdiction to modify orders for support where the conditions of the parties have changed subsequent to entry of the prior order. * * * Each application for modification must be determined on its own facts, and the exercise of the trial court's discretion in this regard * * * will not be disturbed unless abuse of that power is shown. * * * Also, the evidence presented must be considered in the light favorable to support rather than to defeat the order determining the application for modification. * * *

In opposing Gene's application on the grounds of injustice, Irmgard merely stated that the parties had made an earlier oral agreement whereby their child, Christopher, would until he attained the age of 12 years spend six months of each year in Germany with her and the remainder of the year in this country. She declared that in reliance on that arrangement which had continued for three years she had leased a house in Germany and purchased an automobile, household goods and appliances, "all of which cannot be sold or discontinued on such short notice without serious financial losses to the plaintiff." She did not controvert Gene's statement that she is able to work and be self-supporting. We note that the trial court met her objection of short notice by ordering Gene to continue the alimony payments of $500 per month for an additional seven months, apparently to allow Irmgard to make adjustments in her financial commitments and to seek employment if necessary.

The court was entitled to consider as a changed circumstance Irmgard's apparent ability to produce her own income now that her child was older and would be under her care for only the three-month school vacation period. * * * Christopher was born in February 1952, so he was less than five years old and could well have required Irmgard's constant care at the time the final judgment of divorce was modified in November 1956 to provide for alimony payments to her of $500 each month. But the boy was nearly 11 years old and presumably more self-sufficient when Irmgard's payments were reduced to a token amount. Her earning potential was thus increased during summer months as well as for the balance of the year. * * *

Although Gene's increased family obligations would not, alone, have justified modification if Irmgard's situation had not changed * * * it was a factor which the court could also consider. * * * Finally, by the terms of its order reducing alimony payments the court retained jurisdiction to order Gene to increase his payments to Irmgard in the event that in the future she is unable to earn her own livelihood, or requires additional funds for any other valid purpose. * * *

The order modifying the final judgment of divorce is affirmed.

PETERS, Justice (dissenting).

I dissent.

* * * it is my view that the trial court abused its discretion in making the challenged modification.

The power to modify is dependent, of course, upon a showing of change of circumstances. In other words, without a real change in the circumstances as to one or both of the parties the court is without jurisdiction to modify * * * .

Here, as the majority opinion shows on its face, the condition of the wife, so far as her need for support is concerned, has not become less than it was in 1956 when she was awarded the $500 monthly. The husband averred that in 1962, when the challenged modification was made, his former wife was "able-bodied and capable of being self-supporting." So she was in 1956. There is no showing of a change of circumstance here. At the time of hearing in 1962 the former wife was unemployed, but in 1952 she was employed as a movie extra. Whether she was employed in 1956 does not appear. Certainly, under the showing made, the former wife had a greater not a lesser need in 1962 than she had 10 years previous. Her sole source of income was the alimony. She had removed her residence to Germany. That, of course, does not show less need in 1962. She had leased a house in Germany relying on the continuation of the alimony payments. This shows no less need in 1962 than in 1956. As to the former wife, therefore, it is quite clear that there was a total failure to show less need in 1962 than in 1956.

As to the claimed change of circumstances of the husband as to his ability to pay, he showed that he had remarried, had a child by his present wife, and that it was difficult to support his first wife and his present family. This is not a change of circumstances that, alone, would justify a modification. * * * It is true that the husband made a showing that his method of working had changed since 1956, but it was also shown that his income was not below what it was in 1956. There was no showing that his needs, except for the remarriage, had increased. In this connection it must be remembered that in 1956, as part of the modification then ordered, he stipulated that he would not seek further modification unless his income diminished. While that stipulation is not binding on the trial court, it is a factor to be considered in determining whether a further modification should be permitted. This is an equitable proceeding, and the fact that the husband secured one modification predicated on his promise, is certainly a factor that should be considered by a court when determining whether to grant the husband a further modification in direct violation of his promise.

The 1956 award gave the wife $250 for Christopher's support. The 1962 award gave the husband custody of Christopher for the nine months of the school year. This did not impose a greater financial responsibility on the husband, because during those nine months he was relieved of any payment to his former wife for Christopher's support. The $250 is apparently the amount necessary for Christopher's support. Thus the 1962 order did not increase the financial obligations of the husband.

* * * To justify a modification there must be evidence of a change of circumstances in one or the other or both respects mentioned. Here there was no such showing. It follows that there was an abuse of discretion in making the modification. The order should be reversed.

NOTES AND QUESTIONS

1. As in the principal case, alimony decrees are generally modifiable upon proof of such a change in circumstances after the entry of the original decree as makes the modification equitable. Many states confer the power to modify by statute. See, e. g., Cal.Civ.Code § 4801 (Supp.1979); Conn. Gen.Stat. § 46b–86 (Supp.1979); Ill.Ann.Stat. ch. 40, § 510 (Supp.1979); N.Y.Dom.Rel.L. § 236 (1977). Without such statutory authority the court may still have the power to modify its decree if such a power is reserved in the divorce decree itself. If the power is neither given by statute nor re-

served in the decree, the decree may not be modified. Cases are collected in Annots., 127 A.L.R. 741 (1940) and 71 A.L.R. 723 (1931).

The statutes authorizing modification take two different forms. The first, exemplified by the California statute cited supra, authorizes the modification only of future installments of alimony, that is, installments which have not become due before the motion to modify is made. See also Kan. Stat.Ann. § 60–1610(d) (Supp.1979) and Uniform Marriage and Divorce Act § 316, 9A Unif.L.Ann. 183 (1979). Even where the statute does not expressly state whether future installments are alone modifiable, the majority of decisions limit the right to modification to such installments. Sanchione v. Sanchione, 173 Conn. 397, 378 A.2d 522 (1977). See Annot., Retrospective Increase in Allowance for Alimony, Separate Maintenance or Support, 52 A.L.R.3d 156 (1973). The corollary of this is that the accrued installments, being immune to change, are held to be final judgments. See Engleman v. Engleman, 145 Colo. 299, 358 P.2d 864 (1961). Thus where alimony is awarded in installments, the decree is modifiable for the future, but as each installment falls due, it automatically is transformed into a final judgment, enforceable like other judgments for money.

The normal procedure for obtaining a modification of alimony is by filing a petition in the original suit, the modification proceeding being considered a continuation of the divorce action. It follows that no new personal service need be had on the defendant, but of course he must be given notice and an opportunity to be heard.

The second type of statute is exemplified by N.Y.Dom.Rel.L. § 236 (1977), authorizing the modification of both accrued installments of alimony and installments coming due later. The procedure for obtaining retroactive modification varies from state to state, but one state's procedure is described by Zelek v. Brosseau, 47 N.J.Super. 521, 136 A.2d 416 (1957). In most such states there is also a procedure for obtaining a final, nonmodifiable judgment, by giving notice to the obligor and having a judgment in the amount of the arrears docketed. N.Y.Dom.Rel.L. § 244 (1977); Griffin v. Griffin, 327 U.S. 220 (1946).

2. It is usually held that both lump sum alimony and orders dividing or distributing the property of the parties are not modifiable. See, e. g., In re Marriage of Gallegos, 41 Colo.App. 116, 580 P.2d 838 (1978); Duncan v. Duncan, 239 Ga. 789, 238 S.E.2d 902 (1977); Walters v. Walters, 409 Ill. 298, 99 N.E.2d 342 (1951); Cummings v. Lockwood, 84 Ariz. 335, 327 P.2d 1012 (1958).

3. The court in *Levitt* speaks of changes in circumstances as being the basis for modification of alimony. What sort of changes should the court be looking for? Had those changes occurred in *Levitt*? Does the husband's remarriage of itself justify modifying his alimony obligation? Does the birth of children of his second marriage justify it?

4. The Uniform Marriage and Divorce Act § 316 authorizes modification of future installments only upon a showing of changed circumstances so substantial and continuing as to make the terms of the decree "unconscionable". What does "unconscionable" mean in this context? Under this provision should the *Levitt* case be decided differently?

5. Would the following events entitle either spouse to a modification of alimony?

(a) The wife, receiving alimony from her first husband, married a second husband who was much less wealthy than her first. Her first husband moved to terminate alimony payments, arguing that this should follow automatically from her remarriage. See Cal.Civ.Code § 4801(b) (Supp.1979); Ill.Ann.Stat. ch. 40, § 510 (Supp.1979); Nugent v. Nugent, 152 N.W.2d 323 (N.D.1967); In the Matter of the Marriage of Grove, 280 Or. 341, 571 P.2d 477 (1977). Cf. the *Gaines* and *Sefton* cases, supra, pages 220, 226.

(b) The wife, receiving alimony, met and fell in love with another man, but her attorney advised her that if she married him, she would risk losing her alimony. She and her new mate thereupon began living together without marrying, although they represented themselves as being married. The husband moved to terminate alimony. See Cal.Civ.Code § 4801.5 (Supp.1979), providing that there will be a rebuttable presumption, affecting the burden of proof, of decreased need for support if the supported party is cohabiting with a person of the opposite sex. Holding oneself out as a husband or wife of the person is not necessary to constitute cohabitation. The court may reduce alimony on the basis of such changed circumstances. The N.Y.Dom.Rel.L. § 248 (1977) authorizes the termination of alimony if the wife is living with and holding herself out as the wife of another man. See also Ill.Ann.Stat. ch. 40, § 510 (Supp.1979); In re Marriage of Leib, 80 Cal.App.3d 629, 145 Cal.Rptr. 763 (1978); Fleming v. Fleming, 221 Kan. 290, 559 P.2d 329 (1977); Abbott v. Abbott, 282 N.W.2d 561 (Minn.1979); Northrup v. Northrup, 43 N.Y.2d 566, 402 N.Y.S.2d 997, 373 N.E.2d 1221 (1978); Taake v. Taake, 70 Wis.2d 115, 233 N.W.2d 449 (1975). What should be the result if the parties made no representations about being married? Why should "holding oneself out" as married be relevant? What effect on this issue has the *Marvin* case, supra, page 38?

(c) The wife obtained a job which gave her a substantial income and the husband moved to terminate alimony. Hornbaker v. Hornbaker, 25 Ariz.App. 577, 545 P.2d 425 (1976); Carter v. Carter, 584 P.2d 904 (Utah 1978).

(d) At the time of the divorce the husband's income was $18,000 per year, and the court awarded alimony in the amount of $500 per month. Two years later the husband invented a valuable electronic device and his income from patent royalties, together with his salary, became $60,000 per year. The wife moved for an increase in alimony, giving evidence also that inflation had produced an increase in her living expenses. Lott v. Lott, 17 Md.App. 440, 302 A.2d 666 (1973); Kaiser v. Kaiser, 290 Minn. 173, 186 N.W.2d 678 (1971); Ward v. Ward, 41 Or.App. 477, 599 P.2d 1150 (1979).

(e) The alimony order read that the wife was to receive $500 per month "until further order of this court". The husband died some years later leaving a substantial estate. His executor refused to make any further payments of alimony. Six months after the husband died, the executor moved to terminate the alimony. Does the divorce court have the authority to order periodic alimony which is to continue beyond the husband's death, particularly since, if they had remained married, the wife would have had no right to be supported beyond his death? Is the construction of the decree the crucial issue? See Uniform Marriage and Divorce Act § 316; Cal.Civ.Code § 4801 (Supp.1979); Ill.Ann.Stat. ch. 40, § 510 (Supp.1979); Estate of Kuhns v. Kuhns, 550 P.2d 816 (Alaska 1976); McDonnell v. McDonnell, 166 Conn. 146, 348 A.2d 575 (1974) (decree based on a separation agreement); First National Bank in St. Petersburg v. Ford, 283 So.2d 342 (Fla.1973); Kendall v. Kendall, 218 Kan. 713, 545 P.2d 346 (1976); Funnell v. Funnell, 584 P.2d 1319 (Okl.1978). Could the decree order the husband to buy or maintain life insurance or an annuity payable to the wife?

(f) At the time of the divorce the husband was a prosperous business man with an annual income of $75,000. The wife was awarded alimony in the amount of $2,000 per month. Five years later, at the age of fifty-five, the husband decided to retire, thereby reducing his income to $30,000 per year. He moves to reduce the alimony payments proportionately. Olsen v. Olsen, 98 Idaho 10, 557 P.2d 604 (1976); Ellis v. Ellis, 262 N.W.2d 265 (Iowa 1978).

(g) H and W were divorced, with alimony awarded to W. Some time later H remarried, his second wife being a successful writer with a substantial income. In a later proceeding for modification of the alimony award, should the second wife's income be considered in determining H's ability to pay? Gammell v. Gammell, 90 Cal.App.3d 90, 153 Cal.Rptr. 169 (1979).

(h) The alimony order gave the wife $500 per month. Two years later the parties made an agreement by which she agreed to accept $300 per month in full satisfaction of her claims for the future. The husband then moved for a modification of the original award to $300 per month. Must the court grant his motion? Alternatively, assume that the husband made no such motion, but thenceforth paid at the rate of $300 per month. Three years later the wife brought a proceeding for enforcement of the original order of $500 per month. Would she prevail in this proceeding? See Hoops v. Hoops, 292 N.Y. 428, 55 N.E.2d 488 (1944); Feves v. Feves, 198 Or. 151, 254 P.2d 694 (1953).

(i) The wife sued her husband for divorce and served him personally within the jurisdiction. She asked for alimony in her complaint, but the divorce decree which she obtained was wholly silent respecting alimony. A year later she suffered an illness and her need for alimony became exigent.

(i) She then filed a petition in the divorce action asking that the decree be modified so as to award her alimony, proving her need without question. What should the court do? Would it matter if in the original divorce decree the court had awarded a nominal alimony of $1 per month? See Bickford v. Bickford, 229 Ga. 229, 190 S.E.2d 70 (1972); Baird v. Baird, 311 Mass. 329, 41 N.E.2d 5 (1942); McCarthy v. McCarthy, 293 Minn. 61, 196 N.W.2d 305 (1972); Annot., 43 A.L.R.2d 1387, 1396 (1955). Cf. Ill.Ann.Stat. ch. 40, § 19 (Supp.1972).

(ii) What should be the result if, instead of moving for alimony in the original suit, the wife brought an entirely new action, either in the same or a different state, for alimony? Would it matter that in the original suit she had not been able to obtain personal service or its equivalent on her husband? H. Clark, Law of Domestic Relations, § 14.4 (1968).

6. The *Levitt* case also involves the question whether an order for alimony is modifiable when the decree is based upon a separation agreement made by the spouses, the agreement here having been "incorporated" into the divorce decree. This question is discussed infra at page 1010.

7. In a state which permits modification of future installments of alimony, but not of accrued installments, what should be the result if the wife

remarries but the husband does not learn about it and many months go by, during which installments accrue? May the wife get a writ of execution for the installments which accrued after her remarriage? Bean v. Bean, 86 R.I. 334, 134 A.2d 146 (1957), and Annot., 48 A.L.R.2d 270, 292 (1956). What should be the result if the husband goes on paying for many months after the wife's remarriage, in ignorance of that marriage? Would he be entitled to recover back the installments which accrued after the remarriage? Schneider v. Schneider, 204 Misc. 918, 125 N.Y.S.2d 739 (1953) (applying Missouri law). What precepts do these questions suggest for the lawyer advising divorce clients?

DECKER v. DECKER

Supreme Court of Washington, En Banc, 1958.
52 Wash.2d 456, 326 P.2d 332.

FINLEY, Justice. This is a contempt proceeding by an exwife to compel her exhusband to comply with a provision of a divorce decree which required him to pay certain community debts incurred prior to the divorce.

The basic question presented is whether the constitutional prohibition against imprisonment for debt (Art. I, § 17) bars the trial court from using contempt powers and imprisonment to enforce compliance with the aforementioned provision of the divorce decree.

The trial court emphasized the fact that the provision for payment of the community debts was a part of a *property settlement, agreed upon orally by the parties.* In his memorandum opinion, the trial judge relied upon dictum in Robinson v. Robinson, infra, for the proposition that property settlement agreements are not enforceable by contempt; he refused to grant the requested relief to the exwife. She has appealed.

The problem presented involves considerably more than the mere fact of noncompliance with a court order. It prompts considerations other than the matter of an affront to the dignity of the court— which in itself is serious enough. Society has a vital interest in marital disputes and their adjustment by the courts. The enforceability of provisions of divorce decrees as to support and custody, particularly, involves serious problems of public policy, which should not be resolved through the simple expedient of referring somewhat automatically to previous decisions of this or other courts. Precedents must be weighed and evaluated. They are not merely to be noted or tallied numerically, as noses, for or against a particular proposition.

We believe the constitutional prohibition against imprisonment for debt relates to run-of-the-mill debtor-creditor relationships arising, to some extent, out of tort claim, but principally, out of matters basically contractual in nature. In such cases the judgment of the court is merely a declaration of an amount owing and is not an order to pay. Problems of domestic relations involving alimony, support payments, property settlements, together with court orders in connection therewith, do not normally fall into the debtor-creditor category.

* * *

It has been clear in this state for over fifty years that arrearages in alimony and support payments do not constitute a debt within the meaning of the constitutional prohibition. Art. I, § 17. Provisions as to support contained in a divorce decree simply make specific the husband's legal duty to support his wife or children. * * * However, in cases wherein such provisions were not clearly spelled out or were not characterized as alimony or support, our decisions are in conflict.

[At this point the court summarized some of the earlier Washington cases dealing with the problem.]

* * *

The landmark case of In re Cave, 1901, 26 Wash. 213, 66 P. 425, 427, briefly mentioned above, warrants further discussion. Two questions were presented: (1) Whether the courts of Washington had authority to order the payment of alimony in divorce decrees; and (2) Whether, assuming such authority, the court had the constitutional power to enforce payment of alimony through contempt and imprisonment. The court answered both questions in the affirmative. With respect to the second question, the court merely said that it is well settled in this country that alimony is not a debt within the meaning of constitutional prohibitions against imprisonment for debt. With respect to the first question, the court recognized that there was no express statutory authorization for granting alimony in divorce decrees, but noted that the legislature had given express authorization to divide the property of the parties. The court continued:

"There are no restrictions upon the court as to the manner of such disposition. It may be disposed of in a lump sum, or by installments monthly or otherwise, and subsequently reduced to a lump sum, * * * This method of disposing of the property of the parties, call it alimony or whatever name you will, has been recognized by this court in a number of cases:

* * * In all these cases the rule was distinctly recognized that the court should make such disposition of the property as might appear just, and, *whether it was denominated alimony or division of the property, the effect was the same.* * * * " (Emphasis supplied.)

* * *

The inherent similarity between alimony and property settlements is emphasized by the foregoing decisions. Fundamentally, most decisions relative to marriage problems recognize that the trial court has a duty to protect the interests of the public in such matters, as well as the welfare of the parties—and usually this means the duty to see that the wife or children are adequately supported. This duty is made specific by the following statutory language requiring the courts to make:

"* * * such disposition of the property of the parties, either community or separate, as shall appear just and equitable, having regard to the respective merits of the parties, to the condition in which they will be left by such divorce or annulment, to the party through whom the property was acquired, and to the burdens imposed upon it for the benefit of the children, and shall make provision for costs, and for the custody, support and education of the minor children of such marriage." RCW 26.08.110.

Certain language in some marital-relations decisions of this and other courts appears to emphasize unduly the contractual rights of the parties in the settlement of their marital difficulties by agreement or contract. We should be slow to conclude that a trial court waives or abdicates its duty to the public when it embodies or incorporates by reference in its decree of divorce the parties' agreed settlement. By and large, a trial court does not accept a settlement agreement of the parties simply because of their contractual rights, but because its provisions seem just and equitable and in furtherance of sound public policy, *all* factors being considered. Insofar as courts refuse to examine critically the technical language or nomenclature involved in the provisions of a settlement agreement to determine whether the particular provisions are in fact *support* provisions, dictated by the husband's duty to support, such courts falter in their duty to the public by according undue homage to freedom of contract.

* * *

It is clear that the parties to a divorce action cannot foreclose the public interest in their marital responsibilities by a contract or an agreement of settlement. Marital problems involve something more fundamental than nomenclature and technical contract rights. There is no sound reason for allowing a husband to contract away his duty to support his wife and children under the guise of a "property settlement agreement."

We hold that contempt proceedings are a proper remedy to enforce the court's order with respect to property settlements—whether or not the settlement was previously agreed to by the parties, so long as it is embodied or incorporated by reference in the divorce decree. The husband may be imprisoned until he complies with the court's order, unless: (1) he can show that he does not have the means to comply with the order, or (2) he can show that the particular provision sought to be enforced has no reasonable relation to his duty to support his wife and/or children.

* * *

There should be no question as to the power or authority of the divorce court to incorporate in its decree a provision like the one which the ex-wife seeks to enforce through contempt proceedings in the case at bar. * * *

In the superior court hearing, the trial court made no finding as to whether there is a reasonable relation between the provision here sought to be enforced through contempt proceedings and the duty of respondent to support appellant. This is a question of fact, all things considered, including the factor of possible defenses to the debts by the husband and wife. Respondent did not question the validity of any of the debts; and there is nothing in the record to indicate that he and appellant have any *bona fide* defenses to any or all of the debts. If, on remand, respondent can show that he and appellant have valid defenses to any of the debts, then he will have established *pro tanto* that the provision relative to the payment of community debts bears no reasonable relation to his duty to support appellant.

* * *

The order of the trial court should be reversed, and the case remanded for further proceedings in accord with views expressed herein. * * *

NOTES AND QUESTIONS

1. The principal case is noted in 6 U.C.L.A.L.Rev. 328 (1959) and in 34 Wash.L.Rev. 192 (1959).

2. An order of the divorce court directing the division of community property was held enforceable by contempt in Ex Parte Preston, 162 Tex. 379, 347 S.W.2d 938 (1961), 41 Tex.L.Rev. 141 (1962). Many courts would hold such orders not enforceable by contempt, however. See, e. g., Proffit v. Proffit, 105 Ariz. 222, 426 P.2d 391 (1969); Bradley v. Superior Court, 48 Cal.2d 509, 310 P.2d 634 (1957); Thomas v. Thomas, 337 Mich. 510, 60 N.W.2d 331 (1953).

3. Contempt is a common method of enforcing alimony and maintenance awards, either under specific statutory authority or by virtue of the courts' inherent equity powers. Contempt of this type is generally considered civil rather than criminal, since its purpose is to coerce the husband to pay his alimony, rather than to punish him for a violation of a court decree. Johansen v. State, 491 P.2d 759 (Alaska 1971); People ex rel. Kazubowski v. Ray, 48 Ill.2d 413, 272 N.E.2d 225 (1971). Since the contempt proceeding is a part of the original action, and may be instituted by a motion filed in that proceeding, the in personam jurisdiction over the defendant obtained in the original suit is sufficient to support the contempt proceeding, without new personal service. Application of Jess, 11 Cal.App.3d 819, 91 Cal. Rptr. 72 (1970); State ex rel. Brubaker v. Pritchard, 236 Ind. 222, 138 N. E.2d 233 (1956); Annot., 60 A.L.R.2d 1239 (1958). Contra: Strauss v. Strauss, 231 Ga. 248, 200 S.E.2d 878 (1973). But notice of the contempt proceeding and an opportunity to be heard before commitment must be given to the defendant. Lubbehusen v. Lubbehusen, 16 Ariz.App. 45, 490 P.2d 1173 (1971); Yoder v. Cumberland County, 278 A.2d 379 (Me.1971); Mills v. Howard, 109 R.I. 25, 280 A.2d 101 (1971).

Is the defendant in a contempt proceeding for the enforcement of alimony entitled to have counsel furnished for him by the state? Duval v. Duval, 114 N.H. 422, 322 A.2d 1 (1974).

The defendant's inability to pay is a defense to contempt proceedings. Clausen v. Clausen, 250 Minn. 293, 84 N.W.2d 675 (1957); Katz v. Katz, 113 N.J.Eq. 75, 166 A. 176 (1933); Nelson v. Nelson, 82 N.M. 324, 481 P.2d 403 (1971). According to some cases, the burden of proving inability to pay rests upon the defendant. Hopp v. Hopp, 279 Minn. 170, 156 N.W.2d 212 (1968). If the divorce decree ordered payment of $500 per month, and the evidence showed that the defendant could have paid $200 but in fact paid nothing, should the defendant be held in contempt? State ex rel. Wolf v. Wolf, 503 P.2d 1255 (Or.App.1972).

Commitment for civil contempt should be for an indefinite term, until the defendant complies with the divorce decree, commitment for a fixed term being generally held improper. This follows from the purpose of civil contempt, which is coercion rather than punishment. See, e. g., McDaniel v. McDaniel, 256 Md. 684, 262 A.2d 52 (1970).

Why is it that enforcement of alimony decrees by contempt does not violate state constitutional provisions forbidding imprisonment for debt? Compare State ex rel. Schutz v. Marion Superior Court, Room No. 7, 261 Ind. 535, 307 N.E.2d 53 (1974) with State ex rel. Stanhope v. Pratt, 533 S. W.2d 567 (Mo.1976), 42 Mo.L.Rev. 325 (1977).

For a general discussion of civil contempt, see Note, The Coercive Function of Civil Contempt 33 U.Chi.L.Rev. 120 (1965).

4. The statute of limitations applicable to judgments may bar enforcement of alimony decrees. In those states in which each succeeding installment becomes a final judgment as it accrues, the statute would begin to run on each installment when it accrued. See H. Clark, Law of Domestic Relations 469 (1968).

5. There is also dictum in many cases to the effect that laches may bar the contempt enforcement of alimony decrees. The doctrine of laches, based upon the passage of time and a change of position by the obligor, is actually applied only rarely, however. Brandt v. Brandt, 107 U.S.App.D.C. 242, 276 F.2d 488 (1960); Frick v. Frick, 500 P.2d 373 (Colo.App.1972); Annot., 70 A.L.R.2d 1250 (1960).

6. There is authority that an alimony decree operates as a lien to the extent of the due and unpaid installments, but not as to future installments. H. Clark, Law of Domestic Relations 473–474 (1968).

7. Alimony decrees may also be enforced by execution and, depending upon the local practice, by garnishment. Apparently notice and an opportunity to be heard are not constitutionally required before property may be seized on execution or before debts may be garnished, Brown v. Liberty Loan Corp. of Duval, 539 F.2d 1355 (5th Cir. 1976), cert. den. 430 U.S. 949 (1977), notwithstanding Sniadach v. Family Finance Corp. of Bay View, 395 U.S. 337 (1969) and Fuentes v. Shevin, 407 U.S. 67 (1972).

8. Claims for alimony are provable but not dischargeable in bankruptcy. Bankruptcy Code § 523(a)(5), 11 U.S.C.A. § 523(a)(5). The cases under the former bankruptcy act distinguished between awards of alimony which were not dischargeable, and awards of property which were, and pre-

sumably the same distinction must be made under the Bankruptcy Code. Matter of Albin, 591 F.2d 94 (9th Cir. 1979); Nitz v. Nitz, 568 F.2d 148 (10th Cir. 1977); Cox v. Cox, 543 F.2d 1277 (10th Cir. 1976); Nichols v. Hensler, 528 F.2d 304 (7th Cir. 1976). According to the *Albin* and *Nitz* cases the characterization of the obligation as alimony or property is to be determined in accordance with state law. Goldman v. Roderiques, 370 Mass. 435, 349 N.E.2d 335 (1976) held that the husband's obligation to pay the wife's attorney fees was not dischargeable by the husband's bankruptcy. Other cases on the effect of bankruptcy on these obligations are collected in Annot., 74 A.L.R.2d 758 (1960); Note, 12 Ind.L.Rev. 379 (1979); Swann, Dischargeability of Domestic Obligations in Bankruptcy, 43 Tenn.L.Rev. 231 (1976).

Conversely, the wife's claim for alimony usually does not pass to the trustee in bankruptcy when she becomes bankrupt, since it is by the law of most states considered exempt property. But a property claim would pass to the trustee. Adler v. Nicholas, 381 F.2d 168 (5th Cir. 1967). Other cases are cited in Annot., 10 A.L.R.Fed. 881 (1972).

9. Should it follow from the *Decker* case that the property settlement provisions of the decree are modifiable as well as enforceable by contempt? Should modification and the contempt power be coextensive?

10. Jane obtained a valid divorce in the State of Lincoln from Tom and was awarded custody of their two children. Tom was a brilliant but eccentric electronics engineer who had a small and not very profitable consulting business. He made about $14,000 per year at the time of the divorce. Tom had title to the family home and the decree ordered him "to convey said residence to Jane, to be hers absolutely". They had a twenty-year mortgage on the house which then had ten years to run. Tom was ordered by the divorce decree to pay the monthly installments of $165 as they came due. Jane was a joint signer with Tom of the note underlying the mortgage. The decree also ordered payment of $50 per month alimony and $100 per month child support.

Tom conveyed the house as ordered and for about one year made all the payments required under the decree. After the divorce he commenced drinking heavily and his business deteriorated. Three years after the divorce he filed a petition in voluntary bankruptcy, was adjudicated a bankrupt and the obligation to make the mortgage payments was discharged along with his other debts. Jane received notice of the bankruptcy proceeding but did not appear. Tom's general creditors received 5¢ on the dollar for their claims. After this Tom joined Alcoholics Anonymous, stopped drinking, got a good job with a large electronics firm, making $18,000 per year. He has kept up the alimony and child support payments but has made no payments on the mortgage since his bankruptcy. Jane filed a petition in the divorce action alleging the foregoing facts and asking that Tom be held in contempt for undergoing voluntary bankruptcy, that he be ordered to reimburse Jane for the mortgage payments she had paid, and to pay future mortgage installments in accordance with the decree, and that if the discharge of the mortgage should be held valid the alimony be increased to $215 per month on the ground of changed circumstances. Tom moved for summary judgment, admitting all the facts alleged in the petition. What arguments should be made for and against Tom's motion? The Bankruptcy Code § 523(a)(5) provides that a bankruptcy discharge does not discharge the debtor from any debt "to a spouse, former spouse, or child of the debtor, for alimony to, maintenance for, or support of both spouse or child * * *", but that this exception to non-dischargeability does not apply if "such debt is assigned to another entity, voluntarily, by operation of law, or otherwise" or "unless such liability is actually in the nature of alimony, maintenance, or support".

SISTARE v. SISTARE

Supreme Court of the United States, 1910.
218 U.S. 1, 30 S.Ct. 682, 54 L.Ed. 905.

Mr. Justice WHITE delivered the opinion of the court:

In 1899, by a judgment of the supreme court of the state of New York, the plaintiff in error was granted a separation from bed and board from her husband, the defendant in error, and he was ordered to pay her weekly the sum of $22.50 for the support of herself and the maintenance and education of a minor child. * * *

In July, 1904, at which time none of the instalments of alimony had been paid, the wife commenced this action in the superior court of New London county, Connecticut, to recover the amount then in arrears of the decreed alimony. * * *

The court, * * * adjudged in favor of the plaintiff, and awarded her the sum of $5,805, the arrears of alimony at the commencement of the action.

On appeal, the supreme court of errors * * * reversed the judgment and remanded the cause "for the rendition of judgment in favor of the defendant;" and such a judgment, the record discloses, was subsequently entered by the trial court. This writ of error was prosecuted.

The supreme court of errors of Connecticut reached the conclusion that the power conferred upon a New York court to modify a decree for alimony by it rendered extended to overdue and unsatisfied instalments as well as those to accrue in the future; that hence decrees for future alimony, even as to instalments, after they had become past due, did not constitute debts of record, and were not subject to be collected by execution, but could only be enforced by the special remedies provided in the law, and were not susceptible of being made the basis of judgments in the state of New York in another court than the one in which the decree for alimony had been made. Guided by the interpretation thus given to the New York law, and the character of the decree for future alimony which was based thereon, it was decided that the New York judgment for alimony which was sought to be enforced even although the instalments sued for were all past due, was not a final judgment, which it was the duty of the courts of Connecticut to enforce in and by virtue of the full faith and credit clause of the Constitution of the United States. While the ruling of the court was, of course, primarily based upon the interpretation of the New York law, the ultimate ruling as to the inapplicability of the full faith and credit clause of the Constitution was expressly rested upon the decision of this court in Lynde v. Lynde, 181 U.S. 187, 21 S.Ct. 555, 45 L.Ed. 814 (1901).

* * *

First. *The application, as a general rule, of the full faith and credit clause to judgments for alimony as to past-due instalments.*

[At this point in its opinion the Court discussed the decisions in Lynde v. Lynde, 181 U.S. 183 (1901) and Barber v. Barber, 62 U.S. (21 How.) 582 (1858). As a result of its discussion the Court concluded that the two cases were not in conflict, but that if they were, some language in *Lynde* should be qualified so as not to overrule *Barber*. The Court then went on as follows:]

* * * we think the conclusion is inevitable that the *Lynde* Case cannot be held to have overruled the *Barber* Case, and therefore that the two cases must be interpreted in harmony, one with the other, and that on so doing it results: First, that, generally speaking, where a decree is rendered for alimony and is made payable in future instalments, the right to such instalments becomes absolute and vested upon becoming due, and is therefore protected by the full faith and credit clause, provided no modification of the decree has been made prior to the maturity of the instalments, since, as declared in the *Barber* Case, "alimony decreed to a wife in a divorce or separation from bed and board is as much a debt of record, until the decree has been recalled, as any other judgment for money is." Second, that this general rule, however, does not obtain where, by the law of the state in which a judgment for future alimony is rendered, the right to demand and receive such future alimony is discretionary with the court which rendered the decree, to such an extent that no absolute or vested right attaches to receive the instalments ordered by the decree to be paid, even although no application to annul or modify the decree in respect to alimony had been made prior to the instalments becoming due.

It follows, therefore, from the statement which we have made of the case, that the New York judgment which was relied upon came within the general rule, and, therefore, that the action of the supreme court of errors of Connecticut in refusing to enforce it was in conflict with the full faith and credit clause, unless it be, as a result of the law of the state of New York, the judgment for future alimony in that state, even as to past-due instalments, was so completely within the discretion of the courts of that state as to bring it within the exceptional rule embodied in the second proposition. A consideration of this subject brings us to an investigation of the second question, which we have previously stated.

Second. *The finality of the New York judgment as to past-due instalments, for future alimony under the law of the state of New York.*

[At this point the Court considered the finality of the New York decree and concluded that it was final and not open to modification, so far as the accrued and unpaid instalments of alimony were concerned].

* * *

Contenting ourselves in conclusion with saying that, as pointed out in Lynde v. Lynde, although mere modes of execution provided by the laws of a state in which a judgment is rendered are not, by operation of the full faith and credit clause, obligatory upon the courts of another state in which the judgment is sought to be enforced, nevertheless, if the judgment be an enforceable judgment in the state where rendered, the duty to give effect to it in another state clearly results from the full faith and credit clause, although the modes of procedure to enforce the collection may not be the same in both states.

It follows that the judgment of the Supreme Court of Errors of Connecticut must be reversed, and the case remanded to that court for further proceedings not inconsistent with this opinion.

* * *

NOTES AND QUESTIONS

1. The Full Faith and Credit Clause and implementing legislation read as follows: United States Constitution, Art. IV, section 1:

"Section 1. Full Faith and Credit shall be given in each State to the public Acts, Records, and judicial Proceedings of every other State. And the Congress may by general Laws prescribe the Manner in which such Acts, Records and Proceedings shall be proved, and the Effect thereof."

28 U.S.C.A. § 1738: The first two paragraphs of this section prescribe the method of authentication and proof of legislative acts and of the records and judicial proceedings of the courts of states or territories. The third paragraph then reads as follows:

"Such Acts, records and judicial proceedings or copies thereof, so authenticated, shall have the same full faith and credit in every court within the United States and its Territories and Possessions as they have by law or usage in the courts of such State, Territory or Possession from which they are taken."

Are they in terms limited to "final" judgments? If not, what is the basis for the result in *Sistare,* other than precedent?

A case following *Sistare* is Corliss v. Corliss, 89 N.M. 235, 549 P.2d 1070 (1976).

2. Are there any arguments in favor of according full faith and credit to the non-final aspects of alimony decrees? What arguments are there

against granting full faith and credit to modifiable decrees? See Light v. Light, 12 Ill.2d 502, 147 N.E.2d 34 (1957), 26 U.Chi.L.Rev. 136 (1958); Jackson, J., concurring in Barber v. Barber, 323 U.S. 77, 87 (1944); Hill v. Hill, 153 W.Va. 392, 168 S.E.2d 803 (1969).

3. The Uniform Enforcement of Foreign Judgments Act, 13 Unif.L. Ann. 171 (1979), in force in about sixteen states, provides a simplified method for registering and enforcing the judgments, including alimony judgments, of other states. The procedure is described in the *Light* case, supra, paragraph 2. See also Ehrenzweig v. Ehrenzweig, 86 Misc.2d 656, 383 N.Y.S.2d 487 (Sup.Ct.1976), aff'd 61 A.D.2d 1003, 402 N.Y.S.2d 638 (2d Dep't 1978).

4. If the foreign alimony decree is not final, and may be modified either as to future or past installments, so that under *Sistare* no full faith and credit is due it, does that mean that the court may not, if it wishes to, enforce such a decree? Shulman v. Miller, 191 F.Supp. 418 (E.D.Wis. 1961); Restatement, Second, Conflict of Laws § 109 (1971).

GRIFFIN v. GRIFFIN

Supreme Court of the United States, 1946.
327 U.S. 220, 66 S.Ct. 556, 90 L.Ed. 635.

Mr. Chief Justice STONE delivered the opinion of the Court.

This is a suit brought in the District Court of the District of Columbia, in which respondent sought to recover the amount of a judgment which she had secured against petitioner in 1938 in the Supreme Court of New York for arrears of alimony. The question for decision is the extent to which due process permits the New York adjudication to be made the basis for recovery in another jurisdiction.

[The court's statement of facts may fairly be summarized as follows:

1. In 1926, after an earlier divorce decree, the husand was ordered to pay alimony in the amount of $3,000 per year, in equal monthly installments, the decree being apparently based on personal jurisdiction.

2. In 1929 the husband moved away from New York.

3. In 1936 the New York Supreme Court, after a motion by the wife, and a hearing before a referee, entered an order declaring that there was due to the wife from the husband the sum of $18,493.64, representing installments of alimony and accrued interest for the period ending October 25, 1935.

4. Some time later the wife made another motion for a judgment for the arrears of alimony due and unpaid, and on February 23, 1938 her motion was granted and a judgment in her favor in the amount of $25,382.75 was entered against her husband. This judgment was entered ex parte, without notice to the husband.

5. The wife then sued in the District of Columbia for the amount of the 1938 judgment, to which the husband responded that that judgment was void because entered without notice to him.

6. The District Court for the District of Columbia granted the wife's motion for summary judgment, entering a judgment for her in the amount of $25,382.75, with interest from February 23, 1938. The Court of Appeals for the District of Columbia affirmed.]

We have examined the New York law, and conclude that the 1926 New York alimony decree was, under the New York practice, subject to some power of modification nunc pro tunc as to alimony accrued but unpaid up to the time of modification. See New York Civil Practice Act, Sec. 1170, Laws 1925, Ch. 240. Under the local practice, alimony which was accrued under a decree of divorce may not be collected by execution unless and until a judgment for the amount of alimony accrued but unpaid is docketed by order of the court which issued the decree. * * * And upon a motion to docket as a judgment, arrears of alimony awarded under a prior decree, the husband may defend on the grounds that the alimony or some part of it is not due because of the death or remarriage of the wife, * * * or that the obligation has been discharged by payment or otherwise, * * * or that circumstances have so changed as to justify a reduction of alimony already accrued by modification of the alimony decree * * *.

Concededly the 1938 judgment was entered without actual notice to or appearance by petitioner, and without any form of service of process calculated to give him notice of the proceedings. * * * Because of the omission, and to the extent that petitioner was thus deprived of an opportunity to raise defenses otherwise open to him under the law of New York against the docketing of judgment for accrued alimony, there was a want of judicial due process, and hence want of that jurisdiction over the person of petitioner prerequisite to the rendition of a judgment *in personam* against him. * * * It is plain in any case that a judgment *in personam* directing execution to issue against petitioner, and thus purporting to cut off all available defenses, could not be rendered on any theory of the state's power over him, without some form of notice by personal or substituted service. * * * Such notice cannot be dispensed with even in the case of judgments *in rem* with respect to property within the jurisdiction of the court rendering the judgment. * * *

A judgment obtained in violation of procedural due process is not entitled to full faith and credit when sued upon in another jurisdiction. * * * Moreover, due process requires that no other jurisdiction shall give effect, even as a matter of comity, to a judgment elsewhere acquired without due process. Restatement of Judgments, § 11, Comment (c).

While it is undoubtedly true that the 1926 decree, taken with the New York practice on the subject, gave petitioner notice at the time of its entry that further proceedings might be taken to docket in judgment form the obligation to pay installments accruing under the decree, we find in this no ground for saying that due process does not require further notice of the time and place of such further proceedings, inasmuch as they undertook substantially to affect his rights in ways in which the 1926 decree did not. By § 1170 of the New York Civil Practice Act, petitioner was afforded the opportunity to move to modify the alimony decree *nunc pro tunc*. The right afforded by that section is a substantial one, and may, under the law of New York, be exercised by him, in effect by way of defense, in addition to the defense of payment, in a proceeding begun by his wife to docket a judgment for accrued alimony. * * * As we read the 1938 judgment, which recited that the alimony was "due and unpaid," and directed the issuance of execution for its collection, it purported to cut off any defense of payment or claim under Section 1170, which petitioner might have been prompted to assert, and which he had the right to assert in the very proceeding which culminated in the judgment sued upon. That right could not be rendered nugatory by failure to give him notice of that proceeding.

                    * * *

Due process forbids any exercise of judicial power which, but for the constitutional infirmity, would substantially affect a defendant's rights. To the suggestion that under the presumed New York practice the power asserted by the judgment does not include the final adjudication of any of the defenses which petitioner might have had, and that notice is therefore not required, the answer must be that the judgment authorized the immediate issuance of execution. We are unable to reconcile the direction that petitioner's property be seized on execution to satisfy an obligation for the first time found by the judgment to be "due and unpaid" with the theory that the obligation is, for constitutional purposes, thus only tentatively adjudicated. There can be no doubt that a levy upon any property petitioner might have in New York would substantially, and in at least some instances, permanently affect his rights. We cannot say that this could be done without notice of the proceeding said to justify the levy. Even though petitioner could, if he knew of the judgment before execution is actually levied, move to set the judgment aside, that could not save the judgment from its due process infirmity, since it and the New York practice purport to authorize the levy of execution before petitioner is notified of the proceeding or the judgment.

Since by virtue of the due process clause the judgment is ineffective in New York to adjudicate petitioner's rights for enforcement purposes, it cannot be made the instrument for enforcing elsewhere the obligation purportedly adjudicated by it. And even if we were to say that by virtue of the New York practice, and without reference to due process, the 1938 judgment is not an assertion of judicial power to bind petitioner's property for the obligation which the judgment purports to establish, such a judgment would obviously add nothing to the 1926 decree as a basis for enforcing the obligation in another jurisdiction. Neither the judgment nor the earlier decree would do more than establish the original obligation to pay alimony subject to defenses which the supposed New York practice would preserve if due process did not.

It follows that to the extent that the 1938 judgment purports to adjudge as due and owing arrears of alimony accrued since October 25, 1935, the end of the period covered by the 1936 order, it is ineffective to establish petitioner's personal liability, or to deprive him of defenses to his asserted liability for those arrears.

But the 1938 judgment, so far as it confirmed the adjudication of the amount of alimony and interest due as of October 25, 1935, stands on a different footing. It has not been suggested, and we have not found any New York authority holding that any of the questions with respect to payment, or to the modification of the alimony decree *nunc pro tunc* which petitioner raised or might have raised in the 1936 proceedings were thereafter open to him as to the accrued installments which were the subject of his motion to modify the decree. The 1936 order became final upon the dismissal of petitioner's appeal from it, and was an adjudication between the parties that arrears of alimony were then due and owing by petitioner to respondent in the specified amount. As we said in Barber v. Barber, 323 U.S. 77, 82, 65 S.Ct. 137, 139, 157 A.L.R. 163, paraphrasing Sistare v. Sistare, 218 U.S. 1, 30 S.Ct. 682, 54 L.Ed. 905, * * * where a decree for alimony is made the basis of an action in another jurisdiction, " 'every reasonable implication must be resorted to against the existence of' a power to modify or revoke installments of alimony already accrued 'in the absence of clear language manifesting an intention to confer it.' "

Defenses which might otherwise have been open to petitioner in the 1938 proceeding with respect to alimony accrued to October 25, 1935 must thus be taken as having been foreclosed by the 1936 proceedings, of which petitioner had actual notice, and in which he actively participated. The 1938 judgment, so far as it confirmed the 1936 order by which petitioner was already bound, impaired no rights of petitioner, and foreclosed no defense which he had not had opportunity to offer. Due process does not require that notice be given before confirmation of rights theretofore established in a proceeding of which adequate notice was given.

Upon the facts shown, respondent was therefore entitled to maintain the present suit on the 1938 judgment for the amount, with interest, thus adjudicated to be due by the order of 1936, and as so adjudicated, confirmed by the judgment of 1938. For in Sistare v. Sistare, supra, we held that the full faith and credit clause of the Constitution required a Connecticut court to render judgment for past due installments of alimony which had accrued under a New York decree for future alimony, the right to which we held had become vested under the then existing New York law, even though the decree might be subject to modification prospectively as to future installments by further orders of the New York court.

We have said that the failure to give petitioner notice of the 1938 proceeding did not prejudice him as to any of the defenses which he might have raised in the 1936 proceeding. But although it purported to do so the 1938 judgment, because rendered without notice, could not foreclose defenses going to the discharge of the obligation established by the order of 1936, and arising since its date. It follows that upon further proceedings upon the remand of this cause to the district court, respondent will be taken as having established the amount of alimony accrued to October 25, 1935 remaining due and unpaid as of February 25, 1936, subject to any subsequent defense going to the discharge of the obligation so established, which petitioner should be permitted to raise, if any he has.

* * *

The judgment will be reversed and the case remanded for further proceedings in conformity to this opinion. So ordered.

* * *

NOTES AND QUESTIONS

1. The *Griffin* case was noted in 34 Cal.L.Rev. 760 (1946); 46 Colum.L.Rev. 634 (1946); 32 Iowa L.Rev. 119 (1946); 41 Ill.L.Rev. 571 (1946); 31 Minn.L.Rev. 95 (1946); 19 Rocky Mt.L.Rev. 101 (1946).

2. Does the *Griffin* case have any application to those states in which the alimony is only modifiable for the future? Suppose, for example that in such a state alimony is ordered in the amount of $200 per month. The husband pays nothing and after installments amounting to $5000 have accrued, the wife gets a writ of execution from the clerk of the court without notice to the husband and seizes his property. Does this violate due process, either under *Griffin* or under Sniadach v. Family Finance Corp. of Bay View, 395 U.S. 337 (1969)? Why or why not? See Brown v. Liberty Loan Corp. of Duval, 539 F.2d 1355 (5th Cir. 1976), cert. den. 430 U.S. 939 (1977); Haas v. Haas, 282 Minn. 420, 165 N.W.2d 240 (1969).

WORTHLEY v. WORTHLEY

Supreme Court of California, In Bank, 1955.
44 Cal.2d 465, 283 P.2d 19.

TRAYNOR Justice. Plaintiff appeals from a judgment barring further prosecution of this action. The judgment was entered after a trial of defendant's special defense, * * * to plaintiff's complaint for prospective and retroactive enforcement of defendant's obligations under a separate maintenance decree entered in the New Jersey Court of Chancery on May 19, 1947. Plaintiff and defendant were married in New Jersey in March 1943, and separated in November 1946. In the action for separate maintenance defendant appeared personally and by counsel, and the decree ordered him to pay $9 a week for plaintiff's support. About ten months after the decree was entered, defendant left New Jersey for Nevada, and in March 1948 he commenced an action for divorce in that state. Although plaintiff was served in New Jersey with summons and a copy of the complaint in the Nevada action, she did not appear therein. On July 7, 1948, the Nevada Second Judicial District Court granted defendant a divorce.

Defendant had paid all of the sums due under the New Jersey decree at the time the divorce was granted by the Nevada court but made no further payments thereafter. The Nevada decree contained no provision for alimony. On November 16, 1951, plaintiff commenced this action in the Superior Court of Los Angeles County, the county of defendant's present residence. She alleged that the New Jersey decree "has become final and has never been vacated, modified, or set aside" and that defendant is delinquent in his payments thereunder in the amount of $1,089. She seeks a judgment for the accrued arrearages and asks that the New Jersey decree be established as a California decree and that defendant be ordered to pay her $9 a week until further order of the court. Defendant answered the complaint by a general denial and by alleging, as an affirmative defense, that the Nevada divorce decree had terminated his obligations under the earlier New Jersey separate maintenance decree. On defendant's motion, the affirmative defense was tried first under the procedure established by section 597 of the Code of Civil Procedure. The trial court concluded that the Nevada decree dissolved the marriage and was therefore a bar to the maintenance of an action to enforce defendant's obligations under the New Jersey decree.

Since plaintiff does not question the validity of the divorce granted by the Nevada court, that decree, being regular on its face, must be accorded full faith and credit in this state. * * * The controlling questions on this appeal are, therefore, (1) whether the dissolution of the marriage terminated defendant's obligations under the New Jersey decree and, if not, (2) whether and to what extent those obligations are enforceable in this state.

Since the full faith and credit clause compels recognition of the Nevada decree only as an adjudication of the marital status of plaintiff and defendant and not of any property rights that may be incident to that status, Estin v. Estin, 334 U.S. 541, 548–549, 68 S.Ct. 1213, 92 L.Ed. 1561, the effect of the dissolution of the marriage on defendant's pre-existing obligations under the New Jersey maintenance decree must be determined by the law of New Jersey. * * *

The Supreme Court of that state has recently held that a New Jersey "decree for maintenance [is not] superseded by a judgment of the foreign state where jurisdiction has only been obtained by publication entered in an *ex parte* proceeding in which *in personam* jurisdiction over the wife to whom the maintenance decree runs was not obtained." Isserman v. Isserman, 11 N.J. 106, 93 A.2d 571, 575. We must therefore conclude that defendant's obligations under the New Jersey decree were not terminated by the dissolution of the marriage effected by the Nevada court in a proceeding in which personal jurisdiction over plaintiff was not obtained.

The second question is more difficult. Since the New Jersey decree is both prospectively and retroactively modifiable, N.J.S.A. § 2A:34–23, we are not constitutionally bound to enforce defendant's obligations under it. * * * Nor are we bound *not* to enforce them. People of State of New York ex rel. Halvey v. Halvey, 330 U. S. 610, 615, 67 S.Ct. 903, 91 L.Ed. 1133; Cummings v. Cummings, 97 Cal.App. 144, 151, 275 P. 245. The United States Supreme Court has held, however, that if such obligations are enforced in this state, at least as to accrued arrearages, due process requires that the defendant be afforded an opportunity to litigate the question of modification. Griffin v. Griffin, 327 U.S. 220, 233–234, 66 S.Ct. 556, 90 L.Ed. 635; * * * It has also clearly indicated that as to either prospective or retroactive enforcement of such obligations, this state "has at least as much leeway to disregard the judgment, to qualify it, or to depart from it as does the State where it was rendered." People of State of New York ex rel. Halvey v. Halvey, supra, 330 U.S. 610, 615, 67 S.Ct. 903, 906.

In Biewend v. Biewend, 17 Cal.2d 108, 113–114, 109 P.2d 701, 704, 132 A.L.R. 1264, it was held that the California courts will recognize and give prospective enforcement to a foreign alimony decree, even though it is subject to modification under the law of the state where it was originally rendered, by establishing it "as the decree of the California court with the same force and effect as if it had been entered in this state, including punishment for contempt if the defendant fails to comply. [Citations.]" * * * It was stated in the *Biewend* case, however, that the Missouri decree would be established as a decree of the California courts "until such time as the Missouri court modifies its decree." 17 Cal.2d 108, 114, 109 P.2d 701, 705. On reconsideration we have concluded, for reasons that appear below, that this statement was erroneous insofar as it implied that the California courts will not try the issue of modification on its merits, and that the courts of this state should undertake to try such issues.

* * *

Although the question of retroactive modification has been seldom litigated, the United States Supreme Court has expressed its approval of the proposition that actions to enforce retroactively modifiable decrees should be tried in a forum that has personal jurisdiction over both parties, and that in the trial of such actions the defendant must be afforded an opportunity to set up any mitigating defenses that would be available to him if the suit were brought in the state where the alimony or support decree was originally rendered. Griffin v. Griffin, 327 U.S. 220, 233–234, 66 S.Ct. 556, 90 L.Ed. 635; * * * The same rule has been expressed by the Supreme Court of New Jersey, O'Loughlin v. O'Loughlin, 6 N.J. 170, 78 A.2d 64, 68–69; * * * and its adoption has been commended by scholars that have recently studied the problem. See, Scoles, "Enforcement of Foreign 'Non-Final' Alimony and Support Orders," 53 Col.L.Rev. 817, 823–825; Ehrenzweig, "Interstate Recognition of Support Duties," 42 Cal.L.Rev. 382, 393–394.

* * *

It is suggested that even if there are no binding California authorities on the question, we should follow certain sister-state decisions holding that alimony and support obligations created by a prospectively and retroactively modifiable decree are enforceable only in the state in which the decree was rendered. The policy implicit in those decisions is that a modifiable duty of support in one state "is of no special interest to other states and * * * is not enforceable elsewhere under principles of Conflict of Laws." Restatement, Conflict of Laws, § 458, comment a. This policy was rejected by this court in the Biewend case, see also Hiner v. Hiner, 153 Cal. 254, 257, 94 P. 1044, and by the Legislature of this state in enacting the Uniform Reciprocal Enforcement of Support Act. Code Civ.Proc. §§ 1650–1690. In proceedings commenced pursuant to the provisions of that act, the California courts must recognize and enforce foreign alimony and support decrees whether modifiable or not, Code Civ.Proc. § 1670, and must afford the defendant an opportunity to litigate the issue of modification. Code Civ.Proc. § 1682; Griffin v. Griffin, supra, 327 U.S. 220, 233–234, 66 S.Ct. 556. If we should now refuse to follow the policy expressed by the Legislature in the Uniform Act, and by this court and the United States Supreme Court in the Sampsell and Griffin cases, and should hold that even though the courts of this state have personal jurisdiction over the defendant his obligations under a prospectively and retroactively modifiable sister-state support decree cannot be enforced in this state, the result would be anomalous. There would then be two rules in California, one for proceedings commenced under the Uniform Act, and a contrary one for all other proceedings to enforce foreign-created alimony and support obligations.

Moreover, there is no valid reason, in a case in which both parties are before the court, why the California courts should refuse to hear a plaintiff's prayer for enforcement of a modifiable sister-state decree and the defendant's plea for modification of his obligations thereunder. If the accrued installments are modified retroactively, the judgment for a liquidated sum entered after such modification will be final and thus will be entitled to full faith and credit in all other states. * * * If the installments are modified prospectively, the issues thus determined will be res judicata so long as the circumstances of the parties remain unchanged. * * * Moreover, the interests of neither party would be served by requiring the plaintiff to return to the state of rendition and reduce her claim for accrued installments to a money judgment. In the present case, for example, defendant, a domiciliary of this state, would have to travel 3,000 miles from his home, family, and job to secure a modification of plaintiff's allegedly stale claim and to protect his interests in any proceeding for the enforcement of his support obligation that she might institute in New Jersey. If defendant is unable to afford the time or money to travel to New Jersey to make an effective appearance in plaintiff's proceedings in that state, his substantive defenses to plaintiff's claims will be foreclosed. By the same token, unless plaintiff elected to proceed under the Uniform Reciprocal Enforcement of Support Act, which has been adopted in New Jersey, N.J.S.A. §§ 2A:4–30.1 to 30.22, defendant's failure to pay the installments as they came due would force her constantly to relitigate his obligation to support. Repeated suits for arrearages would have to be brought in New Jersey as installments accrued, to be followed by repeated actions in California to enforce the New Jersey judgments for accrued installments, with the net result that the costs of litigation and the dilatoriness of the recovery would substantially reduce the value of the support to which plaintiff is entitled.

Furthermore, there is no merit to the contention that as a matter of practical convenience the issue of modification should be tried in the courts of the state where the support decree was originally rendered. Proof of changed circumstances in support cases is no more difficult than in custody cases and, as noted above, a California court that has jurisdiction of the subject matter must undertake to adjudicate a plea for modification of custody rights established by a sister-state decree. Sampsell v. Superior Court, 32 Cal.2d 763, 197 P.2d 739. Moreover, in most states the problem of modification is dealt with according to general equitable principles, and the law of the state in which the support obligation originated can be judicially noticed, Code Civ.Proc. § 1875, and applied by the California courts.

Accordingly, we hold that foreign-created alimony and support obligations are enforceable in this state. In an action to enforce a modifiable support obligation, either party may tender and litigate any plea for modification that could be presented to the courts of the state where the alimony or support decree was originally rendered.

The judgment is reversed.

* * *

NOTES AND QUESTIONS

1. The principal case is discussed in 31 N.Y.U.L.Rev. 397 (1956), 3 U.C.L.A.L.Rev. 247 (1956); 1956 Wash.U.L.Q. 246 (1956). See also Hopkins v. Hopkins, 46 Cal.2d 313, 294 P.2d 1 (1956).

2. According to the *Worthley* case, what law determines the effect of the Nevada divorce upon the separate maintenance decree? Why?

3. According to the *Worthley* case, what law governs the question whether the alimony decree is modifiable? Why? Lumpkins v. Lumpkins, 83 N.M. 591, 495 P.2d 371 (1972); Gorvin v. Stegmann, 74 Wash.2d 177, 443 P.2d 821 (1968).

4. Why should there have been any question whether the New Jersey decree should be enforced for the future, that is, by the entry of a California judgment ordering the husband to make the weekly payments thereafter? Are there any substantial objections to the entry of such a decree in California? For an example of the older view that the foreign decree may only be enforced by entry of a judgment and issue of execution for past due installments, see Henderson v. Henderson, 86 Ga.App. 812, 72 S.E.2d 731 (1952); Overman v. Overman, 514 S.W.2d 625 (Mo.App.1974), 40 Mo.L. Rev. 335 (1975). Cases following *Worthley* include Walzer v. Walzer, 173 Conn. 62, 376 A.2d 414 (1977); Alig v. Alig, —— Va. ——, 255 S.E.2d 494 (1979); Salmeri v. Salmeri, 554 P.2d 1244 (Wyo.1976). On the general question see Foster and Freed, Modification, Recognition and Enforcement of Foreign Alimony Orders, 11 Cal.West.L.Rev. 280 (1975).

5. What law governs the method of enforcement of the decree of another state? For example, assume that a Washington decree dividing the property of the parties was sued upon in California. Under the *Decker* case, supra, page 920, Washington law would apparently hold that such a decree could be enforced by contempt proceedings. However, the California law seems to be that contempt is not available to enforce a property division. In the event that suit is brought in California upon the Washington decree, with personal service on the defendant in California, and the court finds that the plaintiff is entitled to have the decree enforced, may it be enforced by contempt, or only by legal means?

6. H and W were married and lived in Massachusetts. W sued for and obtained a decree of separate maintenance in Massachusetts, after personal service on H in the state. The decree ordered H to pay W $300 per month in alimony. H then moved to the state of Washington where he acquired a domicile. He sued W in Washington for divorce, serving her by registered mail sent to her home in Massachusetts. A decree of divorce was entered in H's favor, W not appearing or contesting, although she had notice of the suit. Later W sued H in Washington on the Massachusetts decree, asking for a judgment and execution for the unpaid arrears, and for an order directing H to make the $300 payments in the future. H was personally served in Washington. What should be the result? Should the result be different if it appeared that under Massachusetts law a valid ex parte divorce cuts off obligations under a prior separate maintenance decree? Lewis v. Lewis, 49 Cal.2d 389, 317 P.2d 987 (1957); Perry v. Perry, 51 Wash.2d 358, 318 P.2d 968 (1957), 33 N.Y.U.L.Rev. 746 (1958).

7. W sued for and obtained a divorce and alimony in Ohio, the decree ordering H to pay her $400 per month until her death or remarriage. H moved to Virginia where he acquired a domicile, W remaining domiciled in Ohio.

(a) May W sue H in the federal courts in Virginia to enforce the Ohio alimony decree? See the Note on Federal Jurisdiction in Domestic Relations Cases, supra, page 792.

(b) If it appears that the Virginia state courts would enter an equity decree on the same terms as the Ohio decree, enforcing alimony for the future, should the federal court do the same? Does Erie R. R. v. Tompkins, 304 U.S. 64 (1938) govern this question? Harrison v. Harrison, 214 F.2d 571 (4th Cir. 1954), cert. den. 348 U.S. 896 (1955); Maner v. Maner, 401 F.2d 616 (5th Cir. 1968).

8. Judge Traynor in *Worthley* indicated that either party might move to have the alimony obligation modified. This suggests several questions:

(a) How can California modify a New Jersey judgment? See Lopez v. Avery; 66 So.2d 689 (Fla.1953).

(b) If modification is sought in California, what law governs on the kinds of change in circumstances which will justify modification? Thus if the state in which the original decree was entered had the Uniform Marriage and Divorce Act, § 316 of which seems to impose a stricter standard for modification than that of the common law, would that prevail, or would California apply its own standard?

(c) Assume that W obtained a divorce from H in Nebraska, the decree giving her alimony in the amount of $200 per month. Assume further that in Nebraska alimony decrees are modifiable, upon proof of changed circumstances, but only with respect to future installments. Accrued installments become final judgments as they accrue. W then moved to California. She succeeded in serving H personally when he visited California, thereby commencing a suit in California to enforce and modify the Nebraska alimony. The California court entered a decree enforcing the accrued installments, and finding that W's circumstances had changed, ordered that for the future H should pay $300 per month. H returned to Nebraska where he was still domiciled, and made the payments of accrued alimony ordered by the California court, but he only paid $200 each month thereafter. After a year, W brought a proceeding in Nebraska to enforce the California judgment, claiming that H owed her $100 per month for 12 months. H defended on the ground that he had complied with the Nebraska decree. What should the Nebraska court do? Connell v. Connell, 119 Ga.App. 485, 167 S.E.2d 686 (1969), 21 Mercer L.Rev. 675 (1970) (child support).

(d) Assume that as in the preceding question, W had a Nebraska divorce and alimony of $200 per month. H then moved to California, and W sued him there both for accrued installments and for an order that H make payments in the future of $200 per month. H then moved for a reduction of alimony and the California court ordered that in the future he need only pay $150 per month. He paid the arrears and each month thereafter paid the $150 to W. W waited two years and then sued in California to enforce the Nebraska judgment, claiming that *Sistare* required California to give full faith and credit to the Nebraska decree, and that H therefore owed her

$50 per month for each of 24 months. What should be the result? Cf. Oglesby v. Oglesby, 29 Utah 2d 419, 510 P.2d 1106 (1973).

10. The courts of American states will on occasion apply doctrines of comity to enforce the alimony judgments of foreign countries. Wolff v. Wolff, 40 Md.App. 168, 389 A.2d 413 (1978), aff'd 285 Md. 185, 401 A.2d 479 (1979); Nicol v. Tanner, 310 Minn. 68, 256 N.W.2d 796 (1976).

WEESNER v. WEESNER

Supreme Court of Nebraska, 1959.
168 Neb. 346, 95 N.W.2d 682.

CHAPPELL, Justice. Plaintiff, Kenneth O. Weesner, brought this action in the district court for Lincoln County against defendants, Ruth Weesner, plaintiff's former wife, and three-named minor children of the parties, seeking to have declared void a divorce decree rendered by the district court for Goshen County, Wyoming, on September 22, 1954, insofar as same purported to directly affect and determine the title to described real property located in North Platte, Lincoln County, Nebraska, which property was allegedly owned by plaintiff and Ruth Weesner as joint tenants with right of survivorship. Plaintiff prayed for an order cancelling such portion of said decree of record in Lincoln County, quieting the title to his interest in the property, and enjoining defendants from asserting any right, title, or interest therein as against plaintiff by virtue of said Wyoming decree.

Plaintiff's amended petition alleged in substance that plaintiff and Ruth Weesner, hereinafter called defendant, were married at Stapleton, Nebraska, on April 24, 1936; that the three minor defendants were born of said marriage; that on February 23, 1943, during their marriage, the title to the property involved was conveyed to plaintiff and defendant as joint tenants with right of survivorship by warranty deed recorded March 2, 1943, in Lincoln County; and that on September 22, 1954, the Wyoming court rendered a divorce decree in an action wherein plaintiff herein was plaintiff and defendant herein was defendant and cross-petitioner. * * *

However, an admittedly true copy of said Wyoming decree, as far as important here, disclosed the following: That on September 22, 1954, plaintiff appeared in the Wyoming court in person with his attorney, and defendant as cross-petitioner also appeared in person with her attorney, after having been regularly served with process. * * * Thereupon the court found and adjudged the issues generally in favor of defendant on her cross-petition and against plaintiff; * * * and that defendant was entitled to and was granted an absolute divorce from plaintiff, together with the custody and control of their three-named minor children with right of reasonable visitation by plaintiff. The decree then ordered plaintiff to pay to the clerk of the district court of Goshen County, Wyoming, designated monthly amounts payable semi-monthly for support and care of the children, and ordered plaintiff to pay the costs, including $200 as fees for defendant's attorney. Defendant was then *"awarded the dwelling house of the parties located in North Platte, Nebraska"* particularly describing same, which is admittedly the property here involved, *"provided that the Defendant * * * cannot, for a period of five years from date hereof sell or mortgage said property without Court order and provided, further, that in the event of the"* defendant's *"death during said five year period, said real estate shall then become the property of the children hereinabove named in equal portions * * * that the Plaintiff * * * shall make, execute, and deliver to the Defendant * * * a Quitclaim Deed of his interest in and to the above described real estate * * * and in the event of his failure to do so this Decree shall act as a conveyance of his interest in and to said real estate to the Defendant * * *."* (Italics supplied.)

      *   *   *

After a hearing on the merits, the trial court's decree found and adjudged that plaintiff was without equity; that he was not entitled to quiet title to his interest in the property as against the Wyoming decree; and dismissed his petition. On the other hand, it found and adjudged that defendant's cross-petition should be and was dismissed for the reason that the Wyoming court was without jurisdiction to directly affect title to the property and that the award of the property to defendant as made was not res judicata and binding on the Nebraska court. * * *

In that connection, plaintiff did not make, execute, and deliver a quitclaim deed to defendant of his interest in the property as ordered by the decree of the Wyoming court, despite the fact that in his petitions in said action plaintiff had described the real property here involved and as an inducement for granting of the decree had prayed that said property should be equitably divided between plaintiff and defendant. Thereafter, plaintiff admittedly permitted said decree to become final, then left the jurisdiction of the Wyoming court and returned to the situs of the property and the jurisdiction of the district court for Lincoln County, Nebraska. * * *

Concededly, a court of one state cannot directly affect or determine the title to real property located in another state. Thus, that part of the Wyoming decree which awarded and attempted to convey the described dwelling house real property in North Platte, Nebraska, to defendant with limitations on the ownership thereof, was void and of no force and effect as claimed by plaintiff. However, plaintiff concedes here that the parties were residents of Goshen County, Wyoming, and were present with counsel in court there which had jurisdiction of the parties and subject matter of the divorce proceeding. Also, plaintiff concedes that the Wyoming decree became final and that the Wyoming court had jurisdiction, power, and authority to determine such part thereof as granted defendant an absolute divorce together with custody of their minor children, allowances for their support, and other equitable relief. Further plaintiff concedes that so much of said decree as ordered plaintiff to "make, execute, and deliver to the Defendant * * * a Quitclaim Deed of his interest in" the described dwelling house real property in North Platte, Nebraska, was an order in personam and not in rem, which order the Wyoming court had jurisdiction, power, and authority to make.

However, plaintiff argued, citing and relying upon Fall v. Fall, 75 Neb. 120, 113 N.W. 175, 121 Am.St.Rep. 767, and Fall v. Eastin, 215 U.S. 1, 30 S.Ct. 3, 54 L.Ed. 65, 23 L.R.A.,N.S., 924, that only the Wyoming court could compel performance of such personam order to convey, although plaintiff had admittedly failed and refused to make the conveyance and had returned to Nebraska and the situs of the real property involved, and was before the district court for Lincoln County, Nebraska, in this action. We do not agree.

A careful study of Fall v. Fall, supra, and Fall v. Eastin, supra, discloses that they are the same case and clearly distinguishable from the case at bar upon at least two basic grounds. First, Fall v. Fall, supra, decided on rehearing by this court on July 12, 1907, and affirmed in Fall v. Eastin, supra, stressed the point that the courts of this state did not at that time have any statutory power and authority to award the real estate of a husband as alimony in a divorce case, and that the courts of this state would not be compelled under the full faith and credit clause of the Consititution of the United States to recognize an award or order such as that at bar contained in the decree of another state which the equity courts of this state could not themselves lawfully render. However, in 1907, that rule of law relied upon by the court was changed by the enactment of what is now section 42–321, R.R.S.1943. * * *

Another distinguishable ground is that E. W. Fall, a defendant in Fall v. Fall, supra, who had been ordered by a court in the State of Washington in a divorce decree to convey the Nebraska land involved to his wife, Sarah F. Fall, which he had neglected and refused to do, was not served personally and made no appearance in the suit to quiet title to the land brought by his wife in the district court for Hamilton County, Nebraska, but had even left the State of Washington and was a resident of California. In the case at bar, plaintiff, who was ordered by the Wyoming court to convey his interest in the North Platte home real estate to defendant, had also left the State of Wyoming and had neglected and refused to obey the personam order of the Wyoming court to convey to his wife, but plaintiff herein had not only returned to the situs of the real estate in Nebraska but also was and is before the Nebraska court, having brought this action himself to quiet the title to his interest in the real estate.

In that connection, it is universally held that a court of one state cannot directly affect or determine the title to land in another state.

However, it is also now well established that a court of competent jurisdiction in one state with all necessary parties properly before it in an action for divorce, generally has the power and authority to render a decree ordering the execution and delivery of a deed to property in another state in lieu of alimony for the wife. Such an order is personam in character, and when final it is generally res judicata, bringing into operation the doctrine of collateral estoppel. Thus, where all necessary parties are before a competent court in the land situs state, such an order will be given force and effect under the full faith and credit clause of the Constitution of the United States, and same may in a proper case be pleaded as a defense, or as a cause of action to enforce the obligation of the order, if the related public policy of the situs state is in substantial accord with that of the other state. In that connection, the court of this state will presume that the public policy of the other state with regard to division of the real property in a divorce action is the same as our own, in the absence of a showing to the contrary.

* * *

We conclude that the judgment of the trial court denying plaintiff any relief except as aforesaid, should be and hereby is affirmed. On the other hand, the judgment of the trial court dismissing defendant's cross-petition and thereby refusing to recognize and enforce the personam obligations imposed upon plaintiff by the Wyoming decree which required him to execute and deliver a quitclaim deed of his interest in the described dwelling house real property in North Platte, Nebraska, to defendant, should be and hereby is reversed and the cause is remanded with directions to render a judgment either enforcing such order of the Wyoming court or in the alternative by quieting the title in defendant to plaintiff's interest in the property.

* * *

Affirmed in part, and in part reversed and remanded with directions.

NOTES AND QUESTIONS

1. The leading articles on the subject of the *Weesner* case include B. Currie, Full Faith and Credit to Foreign Land Decrees, 21 U.Chi.L.Rev. 620 (1954); Barbour, The Extra-Territorial Effect of the Equitable Decree, 17 Mich.L.Rev. 527 (1919); and Lorenzen, Application of Full Faith and Credit Clause to Equitable Decrees for the Conveyance of Foreign Land, 34 Yale L.J. 591 (1925).

2. Cases reaching the same result as *Weesner* are McElreath v. McElreath, 162 Tex. 190, 345 S.W.2d 722 (1961), 50 Geo.L.J. 157 (1961), 47 Iowa L.Rev. 712 (1962) and perhaps Owen v. Stewart, 283 A.2d 492 (N.H. 1971). See also Allis v. Allis, 378 F.2d 721 (5th Cir. 1967), cert. den. 389 U.S. 953 (1967), and Annot., Power of Divorce Court to Deal With Real Property Located in Another State, 34 A.L.R.3d 962 (1970) and Annot., Res

Judicata or Collateral Estoppel Effect, in State Where Real Property is Located, of Foreign Decree Dealing With Such Property, 32 A.L.R.3d 1330 (1970).

3. It is a frequently repeated dogma that a divorce court in one state has no power directly to affect the title to real property situated in another state. Annot., 34 A.L.R.3d 962, 968 (1970), citing many cases. Why is this so? How is real property to be distinguished from personal property for this purpose? Does the *Weesner* case contradict this dogma or run counter to it?

4. Is there any qualification in the Full Faith and Credit Clause, supra page 928, suggesting that it is not applicable to decrees affecting land located outside the state of the forum? If not, why should there be any question as to the duty of respecting and enforcing such decrees?

ALDRICH v. ALDRICH

Supreme Court of the United States, 1964.
378 U.S. 540, 84 S.Ct. 1687, 12 L.Ed.2d 1020.

PER CURIAM. Petitioner, Marguerite Loretta Aldrich, was granted a divorce from M. S. Aldrich by the Circuit Court of Dade County, Florida, in 1945. The jurisdiction of that court to award the divorce was not contested then, nor is it contested in this action. M. S. Aldrich was ordered by the Court to pay petitioner $250 a month as permanent alimony, and the decree provided that "said monthly sum of $250.00 shall, upon the death of said defendant [husband], become a charge upon his estate during her [petitioner's] lifetime * * *." There was no prior express agreement between the parties that the estate would be bound. Subsequently, the husband petitioned the Florida court for a rehearing, which was denied, but the court reduced alimony from $250 to $215 per month. No appeal was taken by either party.

M. S. Aldrich died testate, a resident of Putnam County, West Virginia, on May 29, 1958. His will was duly probated in Putnam County and petitioner filed a claim against the estate for alimony which had accrued after the death of her former husband. The appraisal of the estate showed assets of $7,283.50. Petitioner commenced this action in the Circuit Court of Putnam County, West Virginia, in order to have her rights in the estate determined. She also demanded that certain allegedly fraudulent transfers of real and personal property made by M. S. Aldrich be set aside and the properties which were the subject of such transfers administered as a part of the estate, so as to be subject to her claim for alimony under the Florida divorce decree.

On motion for summary judgment by the defendants, the Circuit Court of Putnam County held that the decree of the Florida divorce court was invalid and unenforceable insofar as it purported to impose upon the estate of M. S. Aldrich an obligation to pay alimony accruing after his death. The Supreme Court of West Virginia affirmed the judgment, 147 W.Va. 269, 127 S.E.2d 385. It characterized the controlling question in the case as "whether the judgment * * * to the extent that it awards alimony to accrue after the death of M. S. Aldrich and makes the alimony so accruing a charge upon his estate, is a valid judgment which is entitled to full faith and credit in the courts of this state; for if such judgment is not entitled to such full faith and credit the question of its enforceability against the property and assets formerly owned by M. S. Aldrich becomes unimportant and need not be considered or discussed." 147 W.Va., at 274, 127 S.E.2d, at 388.

Recognizing that, as required by the Full Faith and Credit Clause, Art. IV, § 1, of the Federal Constitution, "a judgment of a court of another state has the same force and effect in this state as it has in the state in which it was pronounced," 147 W.Va., at 275, 127 S.E.2d, at 388, the court also noted that "no greater effect is to be given to it than it would have in the state where it was rendered." 47 W.Va., at 275, 127 S.E.2d, at 389. Although apparently not questioning the power of Florida to impose a charge upon the estate, the court concluded that such a charge was, absent express agreement by the parties to the divorce, improper under Florida law and that "the judgment awarding such alimony was void and of no force and effect under the law of the State of Florida, in which such judgment was rendered and will not be given full faith and credit in the courts of this state." 147 W.Va., at 283, 127 S.E.2d, at 393. We granted certiorari, 372 U.S. 963, 83 S.Ct. 1088, 10 L.Ed.2d 128, to decide whether West Virginia had complied with the mandate of the Full Faith and Credit Clause.

Being uncertain regarding the relevant law of Florida and believing that law to be determinative of the effect to be given the Florida judgment, we certified (375 U.S. 75, 84 S.Ct. 184, 11 L.Ed.2d 141, 375 U.S. 249, 251–252, 84 S.Ct. 305, 11 L.Ed.2d 304) the following questions of state law to the Florida Supreme Court, pursuant to Rule 4.-61 of the Florida Appellate Rules, 31 F.S.A.:

1. Is a decree of alimony that purports to bind the estate of a deceased husband permissible, in the absence of an express prior agreement between the two spouses authorizing or contemplating such decree?

2. If such a decree is not permissible, does the error of the court entering it render that court without subject matter jurisdiction with regard to that aspect of the cause?

3. If subject matter jurisdiction is thus lacking, may that defect be challenged in Florida, after the time for appellate review has expired, (i) by the representatives of the estate of the deceased husband or (ii) by persons to whom the deceased husband has allegedly transferred part of his property without consideration?

4. If the decree is impermissible but not subject to such attack in Florida for lack of subject matter jurisdiction by those mentioned in subparagraph 3, may an attack be successfully based on this error of law in the rendition of the decree?

The Florida court, in answer to our certification, has determined that although the award of alimony purporting to bind the estate was not proper under Florida law, the court rendering the decree did not thereby lose its jurisdiction over that part of the case. It further decided that "when the husband failed to take an appeal and give a reviewing court the opportunity to correct the error, the decree of the Circuit Court on such question passed into verity, became final, and is not now subject to collateral attack." Fla., 163 So.2d 276, 284. Having given a negative answer to both the first two questions, the court believed it unnecessary to consider the latter two questions. We accordingly take the passage quoted above as meaning that collateral attack on any ground would not have been sustained.

Given the answers of the Florida court, it becomes plain that the judgment of the Supreme Court of West Virginia, based as it was on a misapprehension regarding the law of a sister State, cannot stand. The Florida alimony decree must be treated as if it were perfectly correct under substantive principles of Florida law. It cannot be argued that a rule of law imposing a burden on the estate of a divorced man who has had his day in court violates due process, and if the judgment is binding upon him, it is also binding on those whom Florida law considers to be in privity with him, so long as Florida does not seek to bind those who cannot be bound consistent with due process. That West Virginia must give the decree of alimony as broad a scope as that it has in Florida is clear, see Johnson v. Muelberger, 340 U.S. 581, 71 S.Ct. 474, 95 L.Ed. 552, and is questioned neither by the Supreme Court of West Virginia nor by respondents.

The judgment below is reversed, and the case remanded for proceedings not inconsistent with this opinion. It is so ordered.

* * *

NOTES AND QUESTIONS

1. The *Aldrich* case seems to have involved only arrears of alimony due and unpaid. Does the case also stand for the proposition that the West Virginia court must enter a decree ordering future alimony to be paid out of the husband's estate until the wife's death? Picker v. Vollenhover, 206 Or. 45, 290 P.2d 789 (1955). If the view of full faith and credit taken in the *Light* case, supra, page 929 should prevail, would this be the effect?

2. Assume that the husband in the *Aldrich* case had remarried following the Florida divorce and had two children by his second marriage at the time he died domiciled in West Virginia. Assume that the first wife had also moved to West Virginia and was domiciled there at the time of the husband's death. If the law of West Virginia were that alimony may not

be awarded so as to continue beyond the husband's death, does the *Aldrich* case nevertheless require West Virginia to continue to enforce the Florida decree beyond the husband's death? Compare the language of Mr. Justice Stone's dissent in Yarborough v. Yarborough, 290 U.S. 202, 219 (1933): "* * * full faith and credit does not command that the obligations attached to a status, because once appropriately imposed by one state, shall be forever placed beyond the control of every other state, without regard to the interest in it and the power of control which the other may later acquire."

Is this an accurate view of the Full Faith and Credit Clause?

See also Restatement, Second, Conflict of Laws § 103 (1971).

SECTION 5. CHILD SUPPORT ORDERS IN DIVORCE PROCEEDINGS

NOTES AND QUESTIONS

1. In many ways the child support order in a divorce decree resembles the order for alimony or maintenance to the wife. Thus it is an order which must rest on personal jurisdiction over the obligor, it requires installment payments, it is enforceable by both legal and equitable sanctions (that is, by execution and contempt), and it is generally modifiable for the future in those jurisdictions where future installments of alimony are so modifiable, and in some states may be modifiable with respect to past installments if alimony is so modifiable. In addition the parties and their counsel, when negotiating the financial aspects of divorce, and the court in making money and property orders, generally treat alimony, property and child support as all parts of a single financial award, as the *Grove* case, supra, page 879, pointed out. Nevertheless there are also differences between child support and alimony, the differences may often be crucial to the decision of cases, and counsel and courts should be aware of those differences at all times. There is a regrettable failure to distinguish between the two forms of financial provision in divorce decrees on the part of judges when approving them which may often cause hardship and unfairness to the parties. For general discussions of child support, see Teass, Support Orders for Infants in Divorce Proceedings, 26 Va.L.Rev. 401 (1940); Whitmire, Maintenance On Appeal, 10 Law & Contemp.Prob. 757 (1944); and H. Clark, Law of Domestic Relations Ch. 15 (1968).

2. In the past the general rule was that the father was primarily responsible for support of the children. Today, as a result of Orr v. Orr, supra, page 868, the support obligation may not be constitutionally allocated on the basis of sex. The result is that both mother and father are responsible for the support of their children, to the extent of their abilities and resources. See the discussion, supra, page 601.

3. The Uniform Marriage and Divorce Act § 309, 9A Unif.L.Ann. 167 (1979) provides as follows concerning child support:

"**§ 309. [Child Support]**

"In a proceeding for dissolution of marriage, legal separation, maintenance, or child support, the court may order either or both parents owing a duty of support to a child to pay an amount reasonable or necessary for his support, without regard to marital misconduct, after considering all relevant factors including:

'(1) the financial resources of the child;

'(2) the financial resources of the custodial parent;

'(3) the standard of living the child would have enjoyed had the marriage not been dissolved;

'(4) the physical and emotional condition of the child and his educational needs; and

'(5) the financial resources and needs of the noncustodial parent.' "

Many cases have held that there is inherent equity jurisdiction to order the support of children and the courts may therefore enter the order even when they deny the divorce either on the merits or for lack of jurisdiction. Chopp v. Chopp, 257 Minn. 526, 102 N.W.2d 318 (1960); Hampshire v. Hampshire, 70 Idaho 522, 223 P.2d 950 (1950). But see Cobb v. Cobb, 145 Va. 107, 113 S.E.2d 193 (1960). Cases are in conflict as to whether child support may be adjudicated in a habeas corpus proceeding brought to determine rights to custody. White v. Baughman, 490 P.2d 347 (Wyo.1971); Annot., 17 A.L.R.3d 764 (1968).

4. Unlike the Uniform Act, the statutes in many states provide no standards for determining how much support is to be awarded, and in any event no precise measure can be devised. The cases generally emphasize the child's needs and the obligor's ability to pay, taking into account his property, income and other responsibilities. For a very comprehensive citation of authorities see Annot., Adequacy of Amount of Money Awarded as Child Support, 1 A.L.R.3d 324 (1965) and Annot., Excessiveness of Amount of Money Awarded as Child Support, 1 A.L.R.3d 382 (1965).

One much litigated issue is whether a parent may be required to pay for the expenses of private school and college for his children. The courts do not agree on this, but many of the more recent cases seem to be imposing the liability where the parent can afford the expenses and the child's qualifications enable him to benefit from it. E. g., Cleveland v. Cleveland, 161 Conn. 452, 289 A.2d 909 (1971) (private school); Khalaf v. Khalaf, 58 N.J. 63, 275 A.2d 132 (1971); Spingola v. Spingola, 91 N.M. 737, 580 P.2d 958 (1978) (private school); Manacher v. Manacher, 35 A.D.2d 705, 314 N.Y.S. 2d 955 (1st Dep't 1970) (private school). Contra: Genoe v. Genoe, 373 So. 2d 940 (Fla.App.1979) holding that the courts have no authority to compel parents to provide a college education where that requires support beyond age eighteen. Recent statutes, perhaps reflecting the lowering of the age of majority to eighteen, have authorized the courts to enter child support orders in divorce actions which require the support of children beyond age eighteen. The Illinois statute was held constitutional in Kujawinski v. Kujawinski, 71 Ill.2d 563, 17 Ill.Dec. 801, 376 N.E.2d 1382 (1978). The recently enacted Washington statute authorizes the court to order either parent to support a child of the marriage "dependent upon either". The Washington Supreme Court has held that this permits a trial court in its discretion to order a father to pay the costs of a college education for his son beyond eighteen, the age of majority. Childers v. Childers, 89 Wash.2d 592, 575 P.2d 201 (1978), 54 Wash.L.Rev. 459 (1978). Would the Uniform Marriage and Divorce Act § 309 empower the court to do this? Should it? See Note, College Education as a Legal Necessary, 18 Vand.L.Rev. 1400 (1965); Note, The College Support Doctrine, 1969 Wash.U.L.Q. 425.

A novel trial court order directing the husband to pay for an abortion of a child with which the wife was pregnant at the time of the divorce, but absolving him from support liability if the wife chose not to have the abortion, was held error in Matter of Marriage of Godwin, 30 Or.App. 425, 567 P.2d 144 (1977).

5. It should be plain that child support payments are made for the benefit of the child, even though they are payable to the custodial parent, usually the mother. In extreme cases the mother may be held accountable for such payments as a fiduciary. Rosenblatt v. Birnbaum, 16 N.Y.2d 212, 212 N.E.2d 37, 264 N.Y.S.2d 521 (1965). See also Gallagher v. Houston, 24 Mich.App. 558, 180 N.W.2d 477 (1970).

The Uniform Marriage and Divorce Act § 308(b)(1), 9A Unif.L.Ann. 160 (1979) listed among the factors deemed relevant in determining the amount of maintenance for a spouse "* * * the extent to which a provision for support of a child living with the party includes a sum for that party as custodian". Is it either appropriate or desirable to enter a child support order which includes an amount intended to support the child's custodian? Why or why not? Cf. Gebhardt v. Gebhardt, —— Colo. ——, 595 P.2d 1048 (1979).

6. Child support orders are modifiable upon proof of change in the relevant circumstances as are maintenance orders, by express statutory provision in some states or pursuant to the common law in others. Since the original support order would have to be based upon in personam jurisdiction of the parent, and since the motion to modify is considered to be a continuation of the original suit, no new personal service is required, although of course notice and an opportunity to be heard must be given. Garlitz v. Garlitz, 18 Ariz.App. 94, 500 P.2d 354 (1972); Atwood v. Atwood, 253 Minn. 185, 91 N.W.2d 728 (1958); Kinsella v. Kinsella, 181 N.W.2d 764 (N.D.1970). This is true even though the respondent has left the state in which the original decree was entered. McClellan v. McClellan, 125 Ill.App. 2d 477, 261 N.E.2d 216 (1970); Carpenter v. Carpenter, 240 So.2d 13 (La. App.1970); Davi v. Davi, 456 S.W.2d 238 (Tex.Civ.App.1970). In most states only the future installments of child support may be modified. Rhodes v. Gilpin, 264 A.2d 497 (D.C.Ct.App.1970); Kinsella v. Kinsella, supra; Albright v. Albright, 454 S.W.2d 957 (Mo.App.1970). In some, both accrued and future installments may be modified. Zieman v. Zieman, 265 Minn. 190, 121 N.W.2d 77 (1963).

The Uniform Marriage and Divorce Act § 316(a), 9A Unif.L.Ann. 183 (1979) provides that "* * * the provisions of any decree respecting maintenance * * * may be modified only as to installments accruing subsequent to the motion for modification and only upon a showing of changed circumstances so substantial and continuing as to make the terms unconscionable."

Even though no child support is awarded by the original divorce decree, that decree may later be modified to include child support, assuming personal jurisdiction and the appropriate change in circumstances, in the view of some courts. Mund v. Mund, 252 Minn. 442, 90 N.W.2d 309 (1958);

Annot., 71 A.L.R.2d 1370, 1378 (1960). This is contrary to the rule which prevents modification of divorce decrees to insert an alimony provision, discussed, supra, page 919. Similarly, if the wife obtains a divorce, with or without personal jurisdiction over the husband, she may later bring an independent suit against him for child support. Annot., 69 A.L.R.2d 203, 240 (1960). The judgment in such a suit, according to many cases, could also order the husband to reimburse her for past expenditures made for the benefit of the child. Annot., 69 A.L.R.2d 203 (1960).

The kinds of change in circumstance which justify modifying a child support order are in general those which would be relevant in the original determination of the level of support, that is, circumstances relating to the child's need and the parent's ability to pay. Annot., 89 A.L.R.2d 7 (1963). The child's emancipation is one such obvious change, although if the child is incapable of supporting himself, the parent may be required to continue supporting him. Sayne v. Sayne, 39 Tenn.App. 422, 284 S.W.2d 309 (1955); Van Tinker v. Van Tinker, 38 Wash.2d 390, 229 P.2d 333 (1951). Some cases on which courts do not agree follow:

(a) H is ordered to pay $200 per month for the support of two children of the marriage. H then remarries and has two more children. Is his remarriage and/or the birth of children of the second marriage a ground for reducing his original child support obligation? Lewis v. Lewis, 73 Idaho 165, 248 P.2d 1061 (1952); Annot., 89 A.L.R.2d 106 (1963).

(b) If, after H has been ordered to pay child support, he remarries and his second wife is working, may that fact be considered by the court in a proceeding by the first wife to get an increase in child support? Morace v. Morace, 220 So.2d 775 (La.App.1969), 44 Tulane L.Rev. 203 (1970) (community property state); Renaud v. Renaud, —— R.I. ——, 373 A.2d 1198 (1977).

(c) H was ordered to pay $200 per month for the support of his two children. W later remarried, so that H's two children then lived with H-2. Is this a ground for the reduction of the child support or its elimination?

(d) The divorce decree provided that H pay $500 per month to W, "for the support of W and the two children of the marriage", as authorized by the Uniform Marriage and Divorce Act, § 308(b)(1). Two years later W remarried and H moved for a termination of his obligation under the decree. What should the court do with this motion? Roth v. Roth, 10 N.J. Super. 406, 76 A.2d 818 (1950); Gebhardt v. Gebhardt, —— Colo. ——, 595 P.2d 1048 (1979).

(e) The divorce decree entered in State A gave W custody of the child and ordered H to pay $200 per month for the child's support, also giving H the right to visit the child at reasonable times on weekends and school holidays. W then moved to State B with the child, making it impossible for H to see the child except during his own vacations.

i. If H moves in State A to terminate child support payments, so long as his visitation rights remain ineffective, should the motion be granted? Comiskey v. Comiskey, 48 Ill.App.3d 17, 8 Ill.Dec. 925, 366 N.E.2d 87 (1977); Ryan v. Ryan, 300 Minn. 244, 219 N.W.2d 912 (1974); Kinsella v. Kinsella, 181 N.W.2d 764 (N.D.1970); Annot., 95 A.L.R.2d 118 (1964). Would the case be different if W just deliberately prevented H from visiting the child in an attempt to alienate father and child? Cooper v. Cooper, 59 Ill.App.3d 457, 16 Ill.Dec. 818, 375 N.E.2d 925 (1978).

ii. If H just stops making the payments when W removes the child, and W then files a Uniform Reciprocal Enforcement of Support Act suit in State B, seeking enforcement of the child support decree, should she prevail? Does the fact that she has made visitation impossible give H a defense? Clark v. Clark, 46 Ala.App. 432, 243 So.2d 517 (1970); Baures v. Baures, 13 Ariz.App. 515, 478 P.2d 130 (1970); Atwell v. Hill, 226 Ga. 560, 176 S.E.2d 60 (1970); von Trotha v. Hansen, 171 N.W.2d 744 (N.E.1969); Hester v. Hester, 59 Tenn.App. 613, 443 S.W.2d 28 (1969); Annot., 95 A. L.R.2d 118 (1964). Would the case be different if, without removing the child from the state, W just prevented H from seeing him, out of hostility and a desire for revenge? White v. Baughman, 490 P.2d 347 (Wyo.1971).

(f) The divorce decree gave custody of daughter, D, to W, and ordered H to pay $100 per month in child support, to continue until D should reach 21 or be emancipated. H remarried and had two children by his second wife. He was then killed in an auto accident, D being then 12, leaving a substantial estate. His executor moved to terminate the child support payments. What should be the result? Bailey v. Bailey, 86 Nev. 483, 471 P. 2d 220 (1970); Guggenheimer v. Guggenheimer, 99 N.H. 399, 112 A.2d 61 (1955); Hill v. Matthews, 76 N.M. 474, 416 P.2d 144 (1966), 7 Nat.Res.J. 129 (1967); Colombo v. Walker Bank and Trust Co., 26 Utah 2d 350, 489 P.2d 998 (1971). The Uniform Marriage and Divorce Act § 316(c), 9A Unif.L.Ann. 183 (1979) provides that child support terminates on emancipation of the child, but not on the death of a parent. Could the court order H to keep in force life insurance policies on his own life with D as the beneficiary? Annot., 59 A.L.R.3d 9 (1974). Or does this question have no relation to the preceding one? Would the answer to these questions be different if the court's decree were based upon a separation agreement executed by the parties? Hill v. Matthews, 76 N.M. 474, 416 P.2d 144 (1966), 7 Nat.Res.J. 129 (1967).

(g) The divorce decree ordered H to pay $100 per month for child support. At the time of the divorce H's income was $10,000 per year. Two years later his income had increased to $20,000 per year. Would that fact alone justify an increase in child support? Lane v. Lane, 4 Wash.App. 632, 483 P.2d 644 (1971).

(h) Three years after the divorce decree and child support order, H decided to drop out of the rat race, thereby reducing his income to zero, intending to live on his savings and when they ran out, to pick up enough to live on by doing odd jobs. Would this reduction in income be the basis for H's obtaining a reduction or elimination of his child support obligation? Moncada v. Moncada, 81 Mich.App. 26, 264 N.W.2d 104 (1978), 25 Wayne L.Rev. 951 (1979); Giacalone, Guidelines for Child Support After Voluntary Reduction in Income, 2 Fam.L.Rep. 4061 (1976).

(i) The divorce decree ordered H to pay $200 per month for the support of the two children of the marriage. He married again and began having difficulty making the payments. He and W then agreed that she would accept $150 per month for the children. Would the court reduce the payments if this agreement were presented to it, without scrutinizing the situations of the parties, including the children? Ruby v. Shouse, 476 S.W.2d

823 (Ky.1972); Weaver v. Garrett, 13 Md.App. 283, 282 A.2d 509 (1971). What would be the result if H just reduced his payments in reliance on the agreement, without obtaining a modification of the decree, and later W sought, either by contempt proceedings or by execution, to collect the $50 per month difference between the payments ordered and the agreed payments? Would the child be bound by such an agreement? Pappas v. Pappas, 247 Iowa 638, 75 N.W.2d 264 (1956). Does this problem suggest the desirability of any preventive action by counsel representing divorce clients?

7. The statutory change in the age of majority from twenty-one to eighteen which occurred in nearly all states in the 1970's caused much litigation concerning the effect of the change upon outstanding child support orders. As might be expected, the results were not uniform, some cases holding that the child support obligation under existing decrees continued until age twenty-one, others holding that it terminated at age eighteen. See, e. g., Wodicka v. Wodicka, 17 Cal.3d 181, 130 Cal.Rptr. 515, 550 P.2d 1051 (1976) and Orlandella v. Orlandella, 370 Mass. 225, 347 N.E.2d 665 (1976), holding that the support decree was not affected, and Stanley v. Stanley, 112 Ariz. 282, 541 P.2d 382 (1975), and Eaton v. Eaton, 215 Va. 824, 213 S.E.2d 789 (1975), holding that the obligation terminated at age eighteen. See also Annot., 75 A.L.R.3d 228 (1977) citing other cases.

8. For the most part child support orders are enforceable by the same means as alimony decrees, that is, by contempt or by legal means such as execution. In some jurisdictions, as in the case of alimony, the unpaid arrears of child support automatically become judgments and may be enforced as such. In other states the wife must file a motion for the entry of a judgment for the arrears before legal means of enforcement become available, and until this is done, the arrears may be modified. But some courts have held that the power to enforce child support orders by contempt is lost when the child reaches maturity, as to installments accruing before that time. Corbridge v. Corbridge, 230 Ind. 201, 102 N.E.2d 764 (1952); Annot., 32 A.L.R.3d 888 (1970).

Various defenses to the enforcement of the support order may arise. The most obvious is the obligor's inability to pay. Ex Parte Howe, 457 S. W.2d 642 (Tex.Civ.App.1970). But inability may not be a defense if the defendant has not made a reasonable effort to work and thereby carry out the order. Weinand v. Weinand, 286 Minn. 303, 175 N.W.2d 506 (1970); Rapson v. Rapson, 165 Colo. 188, 437 P.2d 780 (1968). Laches or the statute of limitations may apply. Larsen v. Larsen, 5 Utah 2d 224, 300 P.2d 596 (1956).

The parent may also attempt to base a defense upon the fact that he made payments direct to the child, perhaps in the form of presents. The courts generally refuse to accept this, primarily because it would condone an interference with the control over the children given to the custodian by the custody provisions of the divorce decree. It is the custodian's right and responsibility to determine how the support money for the children is to be spent. E. g., Ediger v. Ediger, 206 Kan. 447, 479 P.2d 823 (1971); Annot., 2 A.L.R.2d 831 (1948). But where the differences from the payments required by the decree are not great, they may be tolerated, substantial compliance being generally sufficient. For a large collection of cases, see

Annot., Right to Credit on Accrued Support Payments for Time Child is in Father's Custody or for Other Voluntary Expenditures, 47 A.L.R.3d 1031 (1973).

ELKIND v. BYCK

Supreme Court of California, In Bank, 1968.
68 Cal.2d 453, 67 Cal.Rptr. 404, 439 P.2d 316.

TRAYNOR, Chief Justice. Plaintiff appeals from an order denying her application for child support filed under the Uniform Reciprocal Enforcement of Support Act (hereafter URESA; Code Civ.Proc. § 1670 et seq.).

Plaintiff and defendant were married in New York on May 4, 1956, and divorced in Georgia on July 31, 1957. Their daugher, Kim Ivy, was born on April 19, 1957. "In lieu of permanent alimony," the judgment of divorce "incorporated in its entirety" the agreement made between the parties on July 3, 1957, "with reference to the support and maintenance" of the plaintiff and her minor child.

The agreement recited the parties' wish to have a "complete and final settlement" of their rights and obligations. Plaintiff received custody of the child. Defendant agreed to deposit with a designated Georgia bank, as trustee, the sum of $11,500 to form the corpus of a trust for the support of the child until she reached the age of 18 years, "in lieu of any claim which said child or the legal representative of said child now has or may hereafter be entitled to from her father or his estate for past, present and future support and maintenance, alimony or a year's support." The profits of the trust were to be applied by the trustee for the payment of $60 per month for the support of the child, and the corpus could be invaded under certain circumstances. In addition, defendant agreed to establish a trust of $2,500 for the sole purpose of providing a college education for the child. The parties agreed that "No changes in the financial condition or circumstances of the parties or of said minor shall authorize either of said parties and/or court to change or modify the terms or provisions of said agreement or any judgment or decree that might be rendered in any regard to any of the matters set out in said agreement; the parties to this agreement having taken into consideration said changes of conditions or circumstances and also the possibility that an act or statute might be passed in the future authorizing the modification of any judgment or decree with reference to alimony. Said parties waive and renounce any rights which might accrue to them by virtue of any change or condition, or by virtue of any statute or law being passed that might grant to them rights that are not set out at the present time."

In 1965 plaintiff, residing in New York with the child, initiated proceedings pursuant to the URESA provisions of that state for an order directing defendant to provide "fair and reasonable" support of the dependent child. She did not allege any failure by defendant to comply with the divorce decree, but testified that she now required $750 per month for the support of the child. The New York court ordered the petition transmitted to the Superior Court of Los Angeles, where defendant resides, for proceedings under California's URESA provisions. That court denied the application for support "by reason of the lump sum settlement under the Georgia statute."

A 1955 Georgia statute provides that a judgment for alimony may not be revised if it awards payment from the corpus of the husband's estate in lieu of weekly, monthly, annual or other periodic payments to the wife or child. (Ga.Code Ann. § 30–222; Daniel v. Daniel (1961) 216 Ga. 567, 118 S.E.2d 369.)

At the time the divorce decree incorporating the lump-sum settlement was rendered, however, the parties' duties were subject also to Georgia's URESA provisions enacted in 1956, superseded by substantially similar provisions in 1958. Under the 1956 statute, a duty to support dependent children is imposed upon a father "notwithstanding the fact" that he "has obtained in any State or county a final decree of divorce or separation from the other spouse," and he "shall be deemed legally liable for the support under this Act of any dependent child of such marriage, whether or not there has been an award of alimony or support for said child * * *." (Ga.Laws 1956, URESA § 2(6)(a); see Ga.Code Ann. § 99–903a(6)(a).)

The act further provides that "Duties of support applicable under this Act are those imposed or imposable under the laws of any State where the obligor was present during the period for which support is sought." (Ga.Laws 1956, URESA § 6; see Ga.Code Ann. § 99–907a.) Thus, if defendant were present in Georgia during the period for which support is sought, a Georgia court would deny plaintiff's petition on the ground that under Georgia law a lump-sum settlement is conclusive upon the parties.[1] Clearly, however, the Georgia decree does not purport to deprive the courts of the obligor's residence of the power to impose a duty of support in accordance with their law. (See Ehrenzweig, Interstate Recognition of Support Duties (1954) 42 Cal.L.Rev. 382, 394.)[2]

---

1. But see Barfield v. Harrison (1960) 101 Ga.App. 497, 114 S.E.2d 302 requiring a father residing in Georgia to provide support under URESA notwithstanding a divorce decree providing for no support, on the ground that URESA affords an independent remedy. (There is no indication whether the decree was nonmodifiable as a lump-sum settlement under Ga.Code Ann. § 30–222. The result may be explained on the ground that Georgia law permits a wife to obtain support for the child when the divorce decree fails to provide for any support. Thomas v. Thomas (1959) 215 Ga. 383, 110 S.E.2d 657.)

2. It is of no consequence that under URESA Georgia may continue to measure defendant's obligations within its borders under the decree, notwithstanding a subsequent order of support. ("Any order of support" under URESA "shall not supersede any previous order of support issued in a divorce or separate maintenance action, but the amounts for a particular period paid pursuant to either order shall be credited against amounts

Whether defendant is subject to a duty of support imposed apart from, and notwithstanding the lump-sum settlement must therefore be determined in accordance with the law of California, his residence during the period for which such support is sought. Civil Code, section 139 provides that "The provisions of any agreement for child support shall be deemed to be separate and severable from all other provisions of such agreement relating to property and support of the wife or husband. * * * All * * * orders for child support, even when there has been an agreement between the parties on the subject of child support, may be modified or revoked at any time at the discretion of the court except as to any amount that may have accrued prior to the order of modification * * *." Although this provision was added in 1967 and applies prospectively only it codifies the law existing in 1957—when the parties' agreement was made—insofar as it permits the upward modification of child support orders. In 1957 Civil Code, section 139 provided: "That portion of the decree or judgment making any such allowance or allowances [for the support or maintenance of a spouse or child] may be modified or revoked at any time at the discretion of the court * * *." Cases construing the effect of the statute upon integrated property agreements designed, as was the parties' agreement herein, to settle all rights and duties as to support as well, make it clear that "No such contract may, insofar as the children are concerned, abridge the power of the court * * * to provide for the support of the children." (Puckett v. Puckett (1943) 21 Cal.2d 833, 839, 136 P.2d 1, 5;) * * *

Moreover, Civil Code, section 138, providing that in divorce or separate maintenance actions the court may "make such order for the custody of such minor children as may seem necessary or proper and may at any time modify or vacate the same," has been construed to govern orders for child support as well. * * * Thus, it has long been the law of this state that parents cannot abridge the right of their minor child to proper support by any agreement.[3] * * * That right has been enforced under uniform reciprocal support legislation notwithstanding the parents' divorce and any support provisions in the decree. * * *

Defendant contends, however, that under Yarborough v. Yarborough (1933) 290 U.S. 202, 54 S.Ct. 181, 78 L.Ed. 269, California cannot impose, consistent with the full faith and credit clause of the

accruing or accrued for the same period under both." Ga.Laws 1956, URESA § 26; Ga.Code Ann. § 99–927a.) Under this provision it is possible that Georgia need not enforce a subsequent URESA order of another state (see Howard v. Howard (Miss. 1966) 191 So.2d 528; Despain v. Despain (1956) 78 Idaho 185, 300 P.2d

500), nor entertain an application for support based upon the law of the father's residence elsewhere, but no restraint would thereby be imposed upon the courts of that residence.

3. Georgia's contrary local law is apparently unique. (See Ehrenzweig, Conflict of Laws (1962) p. 280.)

United States Constitution (Art. IV, § 1; 28 U.S.C.A. § 1738), any support obligation in excess of defendant's duty under the Georgia decree incorporating the parties' agreement. In *Yarborough,* a Georgia decree incorporating a lump-sum settlement for child support was final and nonmodifiable in that state. The child subsequently resided in South Carolina, where personal jurisdiction was acquired over the father, a Georgia resident, for the purpose of requiring him to support the child in accordance with South Carolina law. Over a vigorous dissent by Justice Stone, the Supreme Court concluded that "the mere fact of [the child's] residence in South Carolina does not give that state the power to impose such a duty upon the father who is not a resident and who long has been domiciled in Georgia. He has fulfilled the duty which he owes her by the law of his domicile and the judgment of its court. Upon that judgment he is entitled to rely." (Yarborough v. Yarborough, supra, 290 U.S. at p. 212, 54 S.Ct. at p. 185.)

The *Yarborough* case is inapposite here. That decision was based upon the father's continued domicile and residence in Georgia. The court expressly reserved the question "whether South Carolina would have power to require the father, if he were domiciled there, to make further provision for the support, maintenance, or education of his daughter." (Yarborough v. Yarborough, supra, 290 U.S. at p. 213, 54 S.Ct. at p. 185.) The South Carolina court obtained jurisdiction by attachment of Yarborough's property, and only later was he served personally within that state. By contrast, defendant appears to have made California his home and place of business. Although the record does not indicate whether he has become a domiciliary of this state, clearly his substantial relationship with it justifies the application of its law of support.

Moreover, at the time of the *Yarborough* decision Georgia had not adopted the URESA provisions. The decree defendant invokes, however, was subject to that statute, which expressly reserves to the state of the obligor's residence the power to apply its law of support notwithstanding the decree. The decree therefore does not purport to govern defendant's obligations when he does not reside in Georgia. Thus, to hold that the decree bars the imposition of support duties in the circumstances of this case would give it greater credit than it claims for itself. The Constitution requires no such result.   *   *   *

The purpose of the full faith and credit clause is to "establish throughout the federal system the salutary principle of the common law that a litigation once pursued to judgment shall be as conclusive of the rights of the parties in every other court as in that where the judgment was rendered,   *   *   *." (Magnolia Petroleum Co. v. Hunt, supra, 320 U.S. at p. 439, 64 S.Ct. at p. 214.) Thus the Constitution requires that judgments for alimony to a divorced wife that cannot be modified under the law of the rendering state, cannot be modified elsewhere. (Sistare v. Sistare (1910) 218 U.S. 1, 30 S.Ct. 682, 54 L.

Ed. 905; Barber v. Barber (1944) 323 U.S. 77, 65 S.Ct. 137, 89 L.Ed. 82.) A divorce decree incorporating child support provisions, however, does not terminate the relationship of parent and child as it terminates the relationship of husband and wife. This case demonstrates why the divorce state should not be permitted to determine the welfare of the child for all time and in all states: More than ten years following the divorce, none of the parties appears to have any connection at all with Georgia: the mother and child reside in New York, and the father resides in California.[4]

Indeed, by the adoption of the reciprocal support legislation in almost all states (see 9C Unif.Laws Ann. 1 (1957)), the federal system now espouses the principle that no state may freeze the obligations flowing from the continuing relationship of parent and child. * * * The states now share the power over that relationship to the extent of the obligor's presence in each—a modified version of the exception suggested by *Yarborough* in favor of the power of the obligor's domicile.[5] * * * In deference to the clearly articulated national policy of preserving the flexibility of support obligations, Georgia has expressly refrained from demanding that its judgment be conclusive elsewhere. The parties were therefore entitled to rely upon that judgment in Georgia alone.

Plaintiff should be allowed to prove that defendant has failed to provide fair and reasonable support for his child. The judgment is reversed.

NOTES AND QUESTIONS

1. Another case which modified the child support order of a sister state is Hall v. Hall, 585 S.W.2d 384 (Ky.1979).

In the *Yarborough* case, stated by Mr. Justice Traynor in *Elkind*, the Supreme Court held that the child, Sadie Yarborough, was bound by the child support order in the Georgia divorce decree cutting off any further right to support from her father, even though she was not a party to the divorce suit. Mr. Justice Brandeis in that case based his holding upon the assertion that (a) the child support order does not vest a property right in the child; (b) jurisdiction over the parent confers jurisdiction over the child's support; and (c) child support in Georgia is a legal incident of the divorce proceeding. Are these reasons persuasive? How can a claim, re-

---

4. The *Yarborough* decision has been widely criticized. See, e. g., Reese and Johnson, The Scope of Full Faith and Credit to Judgments (1949) 49 Colum.L.Rev. 152, 175; Ehrenzweig, op. cit. supra, Conflict of Laws pp. 205, 279–280; Stumberg, Conflict of Laws (2d ed. 1951) p. 345; Note (1934) 47 Harv.L.Rev. 712.

5. The "provider's domicile" rule has been criticized as permitting deserters to flock to no-duty havens. See

Ehrenzweig, Interstate Recognition of Support Duties (1954) 42 Cal.L.Rev. 382, 386. California's URESA version avoids that possibility by providing that "Duties of support * * * are those imposed or imposable under the laws of any state where the alleged obligor was present during the period for which support is sought or where the obligee was present when the failure to support commenced, at the election of the obligee." (Code Civ.Proc. § 1670.)

gardless of the method of enforcement, be cut off without making the claimant a party to the suit, under the Due Process Clause? Cf. 2 Freeman, Judgments, § 911 (5th ed. 1925); Restatement, Judgments § 85 (1942). Or is the case merely saying Mrs. Yarborough's claim is cut off, but Sadie still might sue in her own right?

2. What distinction or distinctions does the *Elkind* case rely upon to justify its refusal to follow *Yarborough?* If there are more than one, which is the crucial one? Since the Uniform Reciprocal Enforcement of Support Act or similar legislation is in force in every state, is this question academic? Or is the Full Faith and Credit Clause being violated in *Elkind?*

3. Is the *Elkind* result consistent or inconsistent with Aldrich v. Aldrich, supra, page 944?

4. Does the *Elkind* opinion suggest that if the father of the children were still domiciled in Georgia, but had been sued and served in California, no further child support could be granted?

5. W obtained a divorce in State A, the decree ordering H to pay $75 per month for the support of C, their son, aged fifteen. According to the law of State A, child support orders terminate automatically when the child reaches age eighteen. A year later W and C moved to State B, and H moved to State X. Under the law of B and X fathers are primarily responsible for the support of their children up to the age of twenty-one. State B also has cases which hold that fathers who are able to afford the expense must send qualified children to college. The law of States A and X is that a father has no duty to pay the educational expenses of his children beyond high school. When C reached eighteen, H having ceased further payments, W brought a suit in State B under the Uniform Reciprocal Enforcement of Support Act seeking an additional $150 (or a total of $225) per month for C's support until C should reach twenty-one, and alleging a) that the increase was needed for college expenses, and b) that H's income was sufficient to enable him to pay the increase. W also filed affidavits supporting her allegations. By order of the court in State B, W's petition and affidavits were transmitted to the appropriate court in State X, H was properly served in X, and he then filed a motion to dismiss the suit. What arguments might be made supporting and opposing this motion?

6. What would be the result in the preceding problem if the divorce had been granted in State B, if W, C and H had all moved to State A after the divorce, and if H had then refused to support C beyond age eighteen? If W should sue H in State A to enforce the order of State B, and to increase the support to cover C's college expenses, should the court of State A grant her the decree she seeks? Cf. D. R. T. v. O. M., 244 So.2d 752 (Fla. App.1971), 25 Ark.L.Rev. 322 (1971).

7. The following problem reviews some of the issues raised earlier in this work concerning both marriage and divorce:

H and W met in the state of Lincoln in 19—, were much attracted to each other and after living together for a time decided to marry. H had formerly been married to X, and he and W therefore talked a good deal about marriage and its difficulties. H's first marriage, as he told W, had ended when X had obtained an ex parte Dominican quickie divorce about two years before. These conversations led them to conclude that they would like to have a contract controlling some aspects of their relationship. They worked out more or less what they wished to agree on, and then went to a lawyer friend, Charlie Clerk, who at their request drew up a contract which provided, among other matters not relevant here, as follows:

(a) They agree to marry and live together as husband and wife so long as mutual affection exists.

(b) Both agree to work and to contribute to the expenses of the household equally.

(c) They agree that they will not have children unless both later decide to change their minds and have children, that W will practice contraception by means of the pill, and will have an abortion in the unlikely event that she should become pregnant.

(d) In the event of divorce W will not claim alimony or any part of H's property and H will not claim alimony or any part of W's property.

At this time neither H nor W had substantial property but both had good jobs, H earning about $22,000 per year as a real estate salesman and W earning about an equal amount as a buyer for a large department store. They were married and lived in an apartment in Lincoln.

In the course of time H and W set up a joint bank account for the household expenses and a joint savings account also. After they had been married for five years, W became pregnant, having, as she told H, "forgotten" to take the pill for a week or so. He became very angry at this and insisted that she had violated their agreement, and that she should get an abortion and pay for it out of her own funds. She refused, saying she could not bear the thought of an abortion and wanted a child. He then moved out of the house and moved to the state of Holmes, where he got a new job similar to his old one and settled down, a confirmed cynic about marriage. Before the baby was born W went back to her parents in the state of Jefferson. She had the baby there and got an apartment. When she was settled with the help of her parents, she sued H in Jefferson for divorce, serving him by registered mail in accordance with the Jefferson statutes, asking also for custody, alimony and child support. Since H had also taken the trouble to clean out both joint accounts, amounting to $2,000 in the checking account, and $20,000 in the savings account, W also sought these amounts in her suit.

(a) H entered a special appearance in the suit, moving to dismiss it for lack of jurisdiction. What should be the ruling on this motion?

(b) Assuming that H's motion is denied, and that he files an answer denying all claims, what should be the result? H in the trial puts in evidence the Dominican divorce decree, and counterclaims for annulment. He also proves that W is quite capable of working in Jefferson at a job and salary like those she held in Lincoln, and that the amounts in the joint bank accounts came from his earnings, so they were his. W's evidence concedes that the bank accounts came from his earnings, but was uncontradicted to the effect that W's earnings had all been spent on household expenses such as food, rent, clothing, recreation, etc.

The Uniform Marriage and Divorce Act is in force in all states.

SECTION 6. FEDERAL TAX TREATMENT OF SEPARATION AND DIVORCE

WRIGHT v. COMMISSIONER OF INTERNAL REVENUE

United States Court of Appeals, Seventh Circuit, 1976.
543 F.2d 593.

WILLIAM J. CAMPBELL, Senior District Judge.

These appeals are taken from a single decision of the United State Tax Court rendered in four consolidated cases wherein petitioners challenged certain federal income tax deficiency determinations made by the Commissioner of Internal Revenue.[2] The issues on appeal are those which were before the Tax Court:

"(1) Whether the cash payments made by William C. Wright during the calendar years 1968, 1969, and 1970 to his former wife, Jean W. Wright, are includable in her gross income for such years as alimony under the provisions of section 71, I.R.C.1954, and consequently deductible for such years by William C. and Ellen W. Wright under the provisions of section 215; and

"(2) Whether annual premiums paid by William C. Wright during the calendar years 1968, 1969, and 1970 on a term life insurance policy owned by his former wife, Jean W. Wright, are includable in her gross income for such years as alimony under the provisions of section 71 and consequently deductible for such years by William C. and Ellen W. Wright under the provisions of section 215."

In the Tax Court, the parties stipulated to all facts relevant to a determination of the foregoing issues. Those facts have been set forth in the Tax Court's opinion, and may be summarized as follows:

William C. Wright (William) and Jean W. Wright (Jean) were married in Milwaukee, Wisconsin on January 31, 1948. In 1967, William filed for divorce and for custody of their minor children. Jean

---

2. The Commissioner took inconsistent positions in his deficiency determinations against petitioners, thus insuring the recovery of back taxes from whichever taxpayer was determined by the Court to be liable. Thus, he determined deficiencies against William C. and Ellen W. Wright for the years 1968, 1969 and 1970 in the amounts of $8,603.13, $14,963.76 and $14,367.14, respectively, while also determining deficiencies against Jean W. Wright, for the same years, in the amounts of $6,667.59, $7,330.41 and $7,093.34, respectively. The inconsistency arises from the fact that, in each instance, the correctness of the Commissioner's ruling rests on whether or not certain payments made by William were income to Jean under section 71(a) and therefore deductible by William under section 215. To the extent that they are, the deficiency against Jean is correct and that against William is incorrect. On the other hand, to the extent that such payments are not income to Jean, neither are they deductible by William, in which event the Commissioner's deficiency determination is correct as to William and incorrect with respect to Jean.

As the Commissioner's brief indicates, his cross-appeals to this Court "are for protective purposes only."

filed a counterclaim seeking a divorce, alimony, a division of property, attorneys' fees, costs, and custody of the children. On October 4, 1967, the action for divorce came to trial, the parties having elected to proceed on Jean's counterclaim. The parties entered into a stipulation in open court with regard to the disposition of property owned by each of them, custody of their children, alimony, attorneys' fees and court costs. In all pertinent respects, the stipulation of the parties was accepted and adopted by Judge L. J. Foley, Jr. of the Circuit Court for Milwaukee County, Wisconsin in his findings of fact, conclusions of law and judgment orally made at the hearing and included as part of the transcript thereof. The court found, on the basis of her counterclaim, that Jean was "entitled to an absolute divorce."

The parties stipulated that their combined net worth was $1,065,122.00. Of this amount, assets worth $227,752.00, consisting of property which was either inherited from her mother or purchased with the proceeds of that inheritance, were owned by Jean. The remaining assets, valued at $837,370.00, had been purchased and were owned by William.

At the divorce hearing, Jean acknowledged under oath that she understood alimony was to be denied; William acknowledged that he understood there was to be a full and complete division of estate in lieu of any claim upon him by Jean for alimony.

Subsequent to the hearing, Jean's attorney submitted proposed findings of fact and conclusions of law, including the following:

"Twenty-first. That alimony be and hereby is denied.

"*　*　*

"Twenty-fifth. (a) That as and for a complete division of estate and to complete the division of property of the parties, the plaintiff shall pay to the defendant the sum of $228,000.00 within ten and one-half (10½) years of October 4, 1967, *　*　*".

William subsequently objected to these proposed findings of fact and conclusions of law, contending that they did not conform with his understanding of the parties' stipulation. His attorney submitted an alternate conclusion of law which stated:

"25a That alimony be and hereby is denied and in lieu of said alimony and in full satisfaction of any claim therefore, and as a complete division of estate and to complete the division of property of the parties, the plaintiff shall pay to the defendant the sum of $228,000.-00 in 10½ years of entry of judgment, said sum to be paid at the rate of $2,000.00 each month for a period of six months and $1,800.00 each month thereafter for a period of 10 years."

Jean's attorney argued that the lump sum payment of $228,000.-00 constituted a division of the estate, not alimony, and that at the time the 10½ year period was agreed upon, she did not consider the payment as alimony and would not report it as such. William's attorney argued that the 10½ year period provided for in the stipulation was designed to permit William an income tax deduction for the payments made over that period of time.

On January 29, 1968, the court entered its findings of fact and conclusions of law including the following:

"Twenty-second.   That alimony be and hereby is denied.

"Twent-third.   [sic] That the plaintiff, William C. Wright, shall maintain the present $200,000.00 of life insurance, being with the Northwestern Mutual Life Insurance Company.   Policy No. 5 553 595, date of issuance, August 22, 1963 [sic], of which the defendant is owner in full force and effect and shall maintain the defendant as beneficiary thereon for as long as said policy shall provide and at least to age 65 and shall keep the defendant as beneficiary of all the proceeds of said policy until she dies or remarries;   that if there are any proceeds of this insurance that the defendant collects, whatever is not used by the defendant in her lifetime shall be left at the time of her death to the children of the parties, either by her will or by trust or by separate trusts in her will.

          "*   *   *

"Twenty-sixth.   (a) That as and for a complete division of estate and to complete the division of property of the parties, the plaintiff *   *   *   shall pay the defendant the sum of $228,000.00 within ten and one-half (10½) years of October 4, 1967;   *   *   *".

The decree then set forth the terms under which the $228,000.00 was to be paid, requiring that William make payments of not less than $2,000.00 per month for the first six months, and no less than $1800.-00 per month over a 10½ year period, until the full $228,000 has been paid.   The divorce decree further provided that payment of this sum was to be secured by sufficient marketable securities in the investment portfolio awarded to William, and that said securities were to be placed in escrow under terms and conditions suitable to secure the payment of the money awarded to Jean.   In the event of William's death prior to full payment of the $228,000.00, Jean was to be paid promptly the balance due, either from the estate of William C. Wright or from the escrow account, unless the estate "is not liquid or is insolvent, or impaired in any manner," in which event the balance due was to be paid from the escrow account.

The value of the assets awarded to Jean under the divorce decree, including the present value of the $228,000.00 lump sum payment, was determined to be $459,018.00.   The value of the assets awarded to William was determined to be $606,104.00.   In May of 1968, the parties executed a mutual release which, in part, stated: "WHEREAS, said judgment of divorce which was entered February 2, 1968 provided for, among other things, a property settlement between the parties in lieu of alimony;   *   *   *".

During the calendar years of 1968, 1969, and 1970, William paid Jean $22,200.00, $21,600.00, $21,600.00, respectively, as installments on the principal sum of $228,000.00. He also paid in those years, respectively, $1,505.50, $1,459.50, and $1,415.50 to Northwestern Mutual Life Insurance Company as premiums on the $200,000.00 term life insurance policy referred to in the twenty-third paragraph of the decree.

The Tax Court determined that the installment payments made by William to Jean should have been included in Jean's gross income for the years 1968, 1969, and 1970, pursuant to Section 71, and that William was entitled to deduct the amounts of said payments for those years pursuant to Section 215(a). The court further held "that Jean did not constructively receive an economic benefit under the [insurance] policy and no amount is includable in her income because of the payments of the premium on this policy by William." Accordingly, the premiums paid were held not to be income to Jean, and not deductible by William.

On appeal, Jean contends that the Tax Court erred in construing the installment payments as "periodic payments" within the meaning of Section 71(a), and therefore taxable income to her. William contends that the court erred in holding that no part of the insurance premiums constituted income to Jean, thus disallowing his claim to deductions under Section 215.

Section 71 provides that where "periodic payments" are received by a divorced wife from her former husband subsequent and pursuant to a decree of divorce "in discharge * * * of a legal obligation which, because of the marital or family relationship, is imposed on or incurred by the husband under the decree * * *", such payments are included in the wife's gross income.

Under Section 71(c), installment payments discharging an obligation to pay a principal sum specified in the decree are not to be treated as "periodic payments" within the meaning of Section 71(a) unless the decree provides that the principal sum "is to be paid or may be paid over a period ending more than 10 years from the date of such decree * * *", in which event the amount received constitutes a "periodic payment" within the meaning of Section 71(a) "to the extent of 10 percent of the principal sum." Under Section 215, the husband may deduct "amounts includable under Section 71 in the gross income of his wife * * *."

Thus, to be includable under Section 71 in the gross income of the wife, the principal sum must be payable in installments over a period in excess of ten years (Section 71(c)(2)) and must be in discharge of an obligation imposed under the decree because of the marital relationship (Section 71(a)). This latter requirement "contemplates a payment made in pursuance of the husband's obligation of support and not in satisfaction of some property rights of the former spouse." Van Orman v. Commissioner, 418 F.2d 170 (7th Cir. 1969).

The Tax Court held that the principal sum ($228,000.00) could be paid in installments over a period of 10½ years and that these installments therefore constituted "periodic payments" for the purposes of Section 71(a). The Court further held that William's obligation to so compensate Jean was due to "their marital and family relationship", i. e. pursuant to William's obligation of support rather than in satisfaction of Jean's property rights.

On appeal, Jean challenges both of these findings. She argues that the record is silent as to her need for support, that she had substantial property of her own and that the divorce court's decree reflects an intention that the payments be part of a property settlement, not contributions toward her support. She also notes that the payments were not subject to the contingencies of death or remarriage, and were secured. The Tax Court's decision, she contends, also ignores two decisions of this Court, Van Orman v. Commissioner, supra, and Houston v. Commissioner, 442 F.2d 40 (7th Cir. 1970).

In holding that the payments "were intended by the parties to be payments in discharge of a legal obligation which was imposed on her former husband, William because of the marital relationship", the Tax Court correctly observed that the question of whether payments are made in recognition of the general obligation to support or in settlement of a wife's property rights depends upon the facts and circumstances of each case. The use of a particular label in the divorce decree or settlement agreement is not conclusive; nor is any other factor irrebuttable proof of the parties' intentions. While we consider this a close and difficult case, we have concluded that the Tax Court's determination should be upheld.

Among the factors which we believe supportive of this conclusion is the fact that the $228,000.00 awarded to Jean was obviously not paid in exchange for tangible property owned by her at the time of divorce. That property, valued at $227,752.00, was separately awarded to her under the decree. In addition, she received property owned by William consisting of furnishings valued at $20,000.00, two automobiles and the discharge of her liabilities in the amount of $41,266.-00.

In response to Jean's contention that the $228,000.00 was paid in exchange for her inchoate rights to her husband's property, the Tax Court held that such rights do not establish co-ownership of the property held in the husband's name, and from this premise seems to have concluded that the loss of inchoate rights through divorce cannot support a division of property. Thus, the Court concluded that "Jean did not surrender any property interests or give up anything that is recognized as supporting a division of property in exchange for the disputed payments other than her right of alimony."

To the extent that the court held that surrender of inchoate rights cannot support a division of property, we disagree. Where the record clearly shows that the parties so intended the payments for this purpose, surrender of a wife's inchoate rights in exchange for a lump sum payment, to be made in installments over a number of years, might well preclude a finding that the payments were made in pursuance of the husband's obligation of support. The intention of the parties is the principal determinant. But here, the record is not clear and, in fact, is silent respecting the surrender of inchoate rights and the payment of a lump sum in exchange therefor. It appears, rather, that the parties contemplated a division of property on the basis of their respective ownership at the time of divorce, plus payments for Jean's support to be made over a period of 10½ years.

Further supportive of this finding is the use of a 10½ year payment period. Had the parties intended these to be installment payments under Section 71(c)(1), rather than periodic payments under Section 71(a), they could easily have provided that the principal sum of $228,000.00 must be paid within ten years. In addition, we note that the release signed by the parties following issuance of the decree referred to "a property settlement between the parties in lieu of alimony", which Jean had sought in her counterclaim for divorce.

As Jean contends, the fact that the payments were for a fixed sum, were secured and were not contingent upon death or remarriage is indicative of a division of property rather than payment of support. So also is the divorce court's adoption, and inclusion in the divorce decree, of the findings and conclusions submitted by Jean's attorney. We find, however, that these conclusions are more than counterbalanced by those factors indicating that the payments were intended for the purpose of support rather than as a division of property. As the Tax Court noted, a payment of a fixed and secured sum over a definite period of time may nevertheless be intended to discharge the general obligation of support. It is not uncommon for the parties to provide for such payments, in lieu of alimony, where they wish to insure that the decree of divorce will not be subject to later modification by the Court.

Contrary to Jean's contention, we do not consider the result in this case to be inconsistent with our previous decision in *Van Orman* and *Houston,* supra. In *Van Orman,* the "Property Settlement Agreement" obliged the taxpayer to purchase a home for his former wife. The home was to be selected by her and was to cost not more than $40,000.00. The taxpayer was required to deliver free and clear title to the home to his former wife within ten years.

In early 1962, he paid $7700.00 down on the purchase price of a home and borrowed the remainder of the $37,500.00 purchase price, secured by a mortgage. For the years 1962 and 1963, he attempted to deduct the mortgage and home insurance payments under Section

215(a). The Tax Court's decision upholding the Commissioner's disallowance of these deductions was affirmed by this Court. As Jean argues, we held that Section 71(a)(1) "contemplates a payment made in pursuance of the husband's obligation of support and not in satisfaction of some property rights of the former spouse." While we identified certain factors which are also present in this case as indicating the satisfaction of a property right rather than the payment of periodic support,[4] we also pointed out that title to the home was to be delivered within the ten year limitation period of Section 71(c). More important, unlike the instant case, the Agreement provided for support payments, requiring "alimony of [$1300.00] to [$900.00] per month for a period of ten years and one month, the specific amount depending on taxpayer's income during that period." 418 F.2d at 171. No such separate provision for the payment of support was included in the Wright divorce decree.

Contrary to Jean's contention, we find *Houston* supportive of the Tax Court's decision. In that case, Houston (husband) was obliged under the settlement agreement to transfer assets worth $505,699.44 to Schwab (wife). He was to convey non-cash assets worth $90,699.-14 and $415,000.00 in cash, the latter to be paid through the immediate transfer of $115,000.00 and the annual payment of $25,000.00 per year for the next twelve years.

In 1959, Houston deducted $50,569.94 as "ten percent of the total of thirteen periodic payments payable over a period of thirteen years to former spouse * * *". The Commissioner disallowed the deduction and the Tax Court upheld the Commissioner's ruling. We affirmed, holding that the $90,699.14 in non-cash assets and the $115,000.00 in cash represented a division of property. We reasoned that "[w]here there is a substantial payment, such as this, which comes soon after the entry of the divorce decree, we think it is not unreasonable to conclude that a property settlement was intended." 442 F.2d at 42.

In the instant case however the question at issue concerns whether the annual payments—not a lump sum transferred immediately after the divorce—were intended as support or as a division of assets. These payments are more closely akin to the $25,000.00 annual payment in *Houston,* which this Court impliedly considered deductible by Houston and income to Schwab. Our opinion states: "[w]e think that the Tax Court correctly noted that the 1959 payment *was distinguished from the later* [$25,000.00] *amounts* both by its size and by the time of payment." 442 F.2d at 42. It is clear that both the Tax Court and this Court considered the fixed annual payments to have been intended as support.

---

4. "[T]he payments made by reason of the absolute obligation to purchase the new home would not be affected by such factors as remarriage or change in economic status." 418 F. 2d at 171.

Jean also challenges the Tax Court's finding that the payments were "periodic payments" within the meaning of Section 71(a) and Section 71(c). She contends that the decree of divorce, entered October 4, 1967, did not become final under Wisconsin law until October 4, 1968. Since the last payment will be due April 4, 1978, she argues that full payment of the principal sum will be paid over a period ending less than ten years from the date of the decree, and that, therefore, the payments received constitute "installment payments" under Section 71(c)(1), rather than "periodic payments" under Section 71(a).

Under Wisconsin law, the parties to a divorce may not remarry for a period of one year subsequent to issuance of the decree. On this basis, Jean characterizes the decree as "interlocutory" until one year following its issuance, at which point it becomes "final". During the period of one year following the issuance of the decree, either party may appeal, and the court may vacate or modify the judgment as it affects the marital status of the parties.

For the purposes of Section 71, we find that the decree is final at the time of its issuance. The fact that either party may appeal is indicative of its finality, as is the fact that the court may vacate the judgment within that one year period and "restore the parties to the marital relation that existed before the granting of such judgment." Wis.Stats. of 1967, Sec. 247.37(2). Moreover, obligations imposed upon the parties under the decree become effective at the time it is granted.

For the foregoing reasons, we hold that the Tax Court correctly construed the payments as "periodic payments received * * * in discharge of * * * a legal obligation which, because of the marital or family relationship, is imposed on or incurred by the husband under the decree * * *". Accordingly, they constitute gross income to Jean and are deductible under Section 215(a) by William.

We further agree with the Tax Court's finding that the premiums paid by William on the term life insurance policy should not be included in Jean's gross income and therefore are not deductible by William. That the premium payments satisfy the requirements of Section 71(a) is undisputed in all but one respect: whether the payments were constructively received by Jean, i. e. whether she received in any of the years under consideration an ascertainable economic benefit through the payment by William of premiums.

The divorce decree requires William to purchase term insurance which, unlike whole insurance, entitles the owner-beneficiary, Jean, to no ascertainable benefits other than the proceeds of the policy upon William's death. Furthermore, her entitlement to the proceeds is defeasible by her remarriage, death or attainment of age 65 prior to William's death.

We find that the benefits derived by Jean through the payment of premiums by William are no greater than the benefits received by the wife in Seligmann v. Commissioner, 207 F.2d 489 (7th Cir. 1953). Under *Seligmann,* and for the reasons set forth in the opinion of the Tax Court herein, 62 T.C. 377, 395–400, we find that the premiums paid by William on the term life insurance policy are not includable in the gross income of Jean and are not deductible by William.

For the foregoing reasons, the decision of the Tax Court is affirmed.

NOTES AND QUESTIONS

1. The sections of the Internal Revenue Code with which the *Wright* case was concerned are the following: Int.Rev.Code of 1954 § 71:

"§ 71. **Alimony and separate maintenance payments**
"(a) **General rule.—**

"(1) **Decree of divorce or separate maintenance.**—If a wife is divorced or legally separated from her husband under a decree of divorce or of separate maintenance, the wife's gross income includes periodic payments (whether or not made at regular intervals) received after such decree in discharge of (or attributable to property transferred, in trust or otherwise, in discharge of) a legal obligation which, because of the marital or family relationship, is imposed on or incurred by the husband under the decree or under a written instrument incident to such divorce or separation.

"(2) **Written separation agreement.**—If a wife is separated from her husband and there is a written separation agreement executed after the date of the enactment of this title, the wife's gross income includes periodic payments (whether or not made at regular intervals) received after such agreement is executed which are made under such agreement and because of the marital or family relationship (or which are attributable to property transferred, in trust or otherwise, under such agreement and because of such relationship). This paragraph shall not apply if the husband and wife make a single return jointly.

"(3) **Decree for support.**—If a wife is separated from her husband, the wife's gross income includes periodic payments (whether or not made at regular intervals) received by her after the date of the enactment of this title from her husband under a decree entered after March 1, 1954, requiring the husband to make the payments for her support or maintenance. This paragraph shall not apply if the husband and wife make a single return jointly.

"(b) **Payments to support minor children.**—Subsection (a) shall not apply to that part of any payment which the terms of the decree, instrument, or agreement fix, in terms of an amount of money or a part of the payment, as a sum which is payable for the support of minor children of the husband. For purposes of the preceding sentence, if any payment is less than the amount specified in the decree, instrument, or agreement, then so much of such payment as does not exceed the sum payable for support shall be considered a payment for such support.

"**(c) Principal sum paid in installments.—**

"**(1) General rule.**—For purposes of subsection (a), installment payments discharging a part of an obligation the principal sum of which is, either in terms of money or property, specified in the decree, instrument, or agreement shall not be treated as periodic payments.

"**(2) Where period for payment is more than 10 years.**—If, by the terms of the decree, instrument, or agreement, the principal sum referred to in paragraph (1) is to be paid or may be paid over a period ending more than 10 years from the date of such decree, instrument, or agreement, then (notwithstanding paragraph (1)) the installment payments shall be treated as periodic payments for purposes of subsection (a), but (in the case of any one taxable year of the wife) only to the extent of 10 percent of the principal sum. For purposes of the preceding sentence, the part of any principal sum which is allocable to a period after the taxable year of the wife in which it is received shall be treated as an installment payment for the taxable year in which it is received.

"**(d) Rule for husband in case of transferred property.**—The husband's gross income does not include amounts received which, under subsection (a), are (1) includible in the gross income of the wife, and (2) attributable to the transferred property.

"Int.Rev.Code of 1954 § 215:

"§ 215.   Alimony, etc., payments

"**(a) General rule.**—In the case of a husband described in section 71, there shall be allowed as a deduction amounts includible under section 71 in the gross income of his wife, payment of which is made within the husband's taxable year. No deduction shall be allowed under the preceding sentence with respect to any payment if, by reason of section 71(d) or 682, the amount thereof is not includible in the husband's gross income.

"Int.Rev.Code of 1954 § 682:

"§ 682.   Income of an estate or trust in case of divorce, etc.

"**(a) Inclusion in gross income of wife.**—There shall be included in the gross income of a wife who is divorced or legally separated under a decree of divorce or of separate maintenance (or who is separated from her husband under a written separation agreement) the amount of the income of any trust which such wife is entitled to receive and which, except for this section, would be includible in the gross income of her husband, and such amount shall not, despite any other provision of this subtitle, be includible in the gross income of such husband. This subsection shall not apply to that part of any such income of the trust which the terms of the decree, written separation agreement, or trust instrument fix, in terms of an amount of money or a portion of such income, as a sum which is payable for the support of minor children of such husband. In case such income is less than the amount specified in the decree, agreement, or instrument, for the purpose of applying the preceding sentence, such income, to the extent of such sum payable for such support, shall be considered a payment for such support.

"(b) Wife considered a beneficiary.—For purposes of computing the taxable income of the estate or trust and the taxable income of a wife to whom subsection (a) or section 71 applies, such wife shall be considered as the beneficiary specified in this part. A periodic payment under section 71 to any portion of which this part applies shall be included in the gross income of the beneficiary in the taxable year in which under this part such portion is required to be included.

2. One of the crucial distinctions made by the Code, in §§ 71(a)(1) and 71(c)(1) and (2) is between "periodic" payments to a spouse and "installment" payments, the first being taxable to the payee and deductible by the payer, while the second type of payment is not so treated unless it is spread over a period of more than ten years. The reason for the distinction seems to be that sums paid to a spouse at regular intervals for her support look more like income to her than lump sum payments unless the latter are spread over a long time.

"Periodic" payments are those which are indefinite in total amount because contingent in some way. Thus if the sums to be paid are fixed in amount but are payable for a period whose duration is contingent upon an uncertain event, they are periodic. This covers the usual form of alimony decree which orders payments of $200 per month to the wife until her death or remarriage. Likewise, if the amount of the payment is contingent but the period is fixed, the payments are contingent, as where the separation agreement provides that the husband will pay the wife 30% of his income for five years. Of course if both the amount and the period over which payments are to be made are contingent, the payments qualify as periodic. Where the contingency of the payments is caused by state law, as where that law terminates alimony upon the remarriage of the payee, or where state law authorizes modification of alimony decrees, the payments are considered periodic. Treas.Reg. § 1.71–1(d)(3) (1972); Note, Alimony, Income Taxation of Installment Payments, 24 U.Fla.L.Rev. 499 (1972).

A case which held the payments not to be "periodic" where they were not contingent on any future events, either under the decree or under state law, and where they were not to continue more than ten years, is Stock v. Commissioner, 551 F.2d 614 (5th Cir. 1977).

Where the alimony is payable pursuant to an annulment decree and meets the other requirements of the Internal Revenue Code, it is taxable to the payee and deductible by the payer. Newburger v. Commissioner, 61 T. C. 457 (1974).

Likewise payments made pursuant to a decree for temporary alimony are taxable to the payee and deductible by the payer, under § 71(a)(3). Sydnes v. Commissioner, 577 F.2d 60 (8th Cir. 1978). This case held that the spouses had "separated" for purposes of this section even though they continued to live under the same roof, where they lived in separate parts of the house and avoided seeing each other. But see Dunn v. Commissioner, 70 T.C. 361 (1978).

The statute also makes it clear that in order to have the payments treated as alimony the parties must file separate returns. But since the crucial date for determining whether a joint return may be filed is the last day of the year, the Internal Revenue Service has ruled that a joint return may be filed when, as in Wisconsin in the *Wright* case, an interlocutory decree of divorce is entered in the fall but does not become final until six months later, after the first of the next year. Thus if the parties find it advantageous to file jointly in such a situation, they may, but then they may not rely on sections 71 and 215 of the Code. See Rev.Rul. 75–536, 1975–2 C.B. 462.

Where the attempt is made to take advantage of § 71(c)(2) by spreading payments of a specified total sum over more than ten years, care must be taken that the final payment is to be made at a time more than ten years after the obligation to begin the payments accrues. See, e. g., Joslin v. Commissioner, 424 F.2d 1223 (7th Cir. 1970). Was the *Wright* case correct in holding that the ten year period began to run at the date of the interlocutory decree rather than at the date of the final decree?

The statute imposes the further limitation that the deduction to the payer in any one year may not exceed 10% of the total sum.

3. The *Wright* case deals with a second requirement of § 71(a)(1) and (2), that is that the payments must be "* * * in discharge of * * * a legal obligation which, because of the marital or family relationship * * *" is imposed upon the payer (the husband as the statute puts it). Treasury Reg. § 1.71–1(b)(4) (1972) amplifies this by limiting § 71(a) to payments made "* * * because of the family or marital relationship in recognition of the general obligation to support which is made specific by the instrument or agreement." For a discussion of this requirement see Harris, The Federal Income Tax Treatment of Alimony Payments —The "Support" Requirement of the Regulations, 22 Hast.L.J. 53 (1970); Derickson v. Commissioner, 35 T.C.M. (C.C.H.) 1325 (1976); Hjorth, Tax Consequences of Post-Dissolution Support Payment Arrangements, 51 Wash.L.Rev. 233 (1976).

(a) What standards does the *Wright* case adopt for determining whether payments are made because of the marital or family relationship?

(b) What circumstances surrounding the divorce decree in the case indicated that these payments were alimony? What circumstances suggested they were not alimony?

(c) Would the language of the Wisconsin statute pursuant to which the divorce decree was entered be relevant on whether the payments should be characterized as alimony or property? The statute in force at the time the divorce was granted to the Wrights read: "The court may also finally divide and distribute the estate * * * of the husband, and so much of the estate of the wife as has been derived from the husband, between the parties * * * after having given due regard to the legal and equitable rights of each party, the ability of the husband, the special estate of the wife, the character and situation of the parties and all the circumstances of the case. * * *" Wis.L.1961, ch. 406. What, if anything, does this indicate about the nature of the payments?

(d) Would the result be different under the statute in force in Wisconsin at the time of the *Wilberscheid* case, as indicated by footnote 5 in that opinion, supra, page 896? Would it be different under the Uniform Marriage and Divorce Act provision, supra, page 898? cf. Hayutin v. Commissioner, 508 F.2d 462 (10th Cir. 1974).

(e) What lessons for the draftsmen of separation agreements can be learned from the *Wright* case?

(f) In view of the provisions in the various state statutes authorizing the division of property on divorce, what conceivable purpose is served by the distinction made in § 71(a) and the *Wright* case, between payments made because of the family relationship and payments not so made?

(g) H and W were divorced, the decree providing that H should pay to W the sum of $24,200, at the rate of $200 per month for 121 months. The court in its findings states that in arriving at this figure it had taken into account the factors listed in *Wilberscheid*, supra, page 894, especially that W had been a good wife during the years of marriage and had helped H in his business, all of which factors were authorized in the divorce statute. The payments were to be made in all events and were not to end on the death of either H or W or W's remarriage. In the event of W's death they were to be made to her estate or as her will should appoint. How should these payments be characterized for tax purposes? Cf. West v. United States, 332 F.Supp. 1102 (S.D.Tex.1971).

(h) In a community property state, H and W made a separation agreement in which H agreed to pay to W $200 per month until her death or remarriage "in full satisfaction of W's claims to alimony, support and community property", the agreement reciting that it was intended as an integrated property settlement and alimony agreement. How should these payments be treated for federal income tax purposes? Riddell v. Guggenheim, 281 F.2d 836 (9th Cir. 1960); Campbell v. Lake, 220 F.2d 341 (5th Cir. 1955); Clyda T. Jones, 20 CCH Tax Ct.Mem. 1385 (1961); Ann H. Ryker, 33 T.C. 924 (1960); McCombs v. Commissioner, 397 F.2d 4 (10th Cir. 1968); Mauk v. Phinney, 280 F.Supp. 167 (S.D.Tex.1967), reversed 411 F.2d 1196 (5th Cir. 1969); Warnack v. Commissioner, 71 T.C. 541 (1979).

4. If payments are made by the husband for the benefit of the wife, although not directly to her, they may be taxable to her, assuming the other requirements of § 71 are met, the rationale being that they are "constructively received" by her. For example, where under the separation agreement or divorce decree the husband is required to pay the premiums on a whole life policy of insurance on his own life, he may deduct the payments and the wife must pay the tax on them, provided that she is the sole owner and irrevocable beneficiary of the policy, and the husband retains no incidents of ownership. If the proceeds of the insurance policy may ultimately go to someone other than the wife, the premiums are not considered constructively received by her and therefore are not taxable to her. See, e. g., Piel v. Commissioner, 340 F.2d 887 (2d Cir. 1965).

In the *Wright* case, however, only term life insurance was involved. The premiums for such insurance, as the court says, are not considered to be constructively received by the spouse because she receives no present interest from them, but only "peace of mind", as the court said in Brodersen v. Commissioner, 57 T.C. 412 (1971).

A less troublesome way of handling the insurance problem on divorce might be to divide the cash value of existing policies between husband and wife, and then have each take out a policy on the husband's life, at the same time including in the alimony a sum sufficient to enable the wife to pay the premiums on her policy. Under this arrangement she would not be taxed on the proceeds of the policy when they are paid to her. See Bell, Tax Planning in Divorce Cases—With Emphasis on Community Property States, 1 Fam.L.Q. No. 2, 41, 51 (1967).

Similarly, when the wife has the entire ownership in the family home, the husband's obligation to make mortgage payments on the property confers a benefit upon her so as to justify the application of the doctrine of constructive receipt, and if the payments otherwise qualify, she should pay the tax on them. For a discussion of these problems with a citation of cases, see Note, Alimony Taxation of Indirect Benefits: A Critique and a Proposal, 66 Colum.L.Rev. 1118 (1966).

5. For discussions of the taxation of alimony trusts under Int.Rev. Code §§ 71(a)(1), 215, 682, see Note, Tax Aspects of Alimony Trusts, 66 Yale L.J. 881 (1957); Gunn, Douglas v. Willcuts Today: The Income Tax Problems of Using Alimony Trusts, 63 Corn.L.Q. 1022 (1978); Del Cotto, The Alimony Trust: Its Relationship With Subchapter J; The Right to Amortize Basis, 33 Tax.L.Rev. 577 (1978).

6. Obviously there are many situations in which the impact of federal taxes turns on the question whether parties are "husband" and "wife", e. g. I.R.C.1954 § 6011 (joint returns), or § 151 (dependents). Apart from the formal provisions of § 7701(a)(17), which merely provides that "husband" or "wife" may be read as "ex-husband" or "ex-wife" and that "wife" may be read as "husband" or vice versa, where the context demands, there is no definition in the Code of the terms "husband" or "wife" or "marriage". In one section, 143(b), a married person living apart from his spouse and maintaining a household of which his spouse is not a member, may be considered unmarried for purposes of taking certain deductions. But this does not provide a general definition of what marriage means for tax purposes.

A line of cases has dealt with this question in the context of the migratory divorce. The first of these, Estate of Borax v. Commissioner, 349 F.2d 666 (2d Cir. 1965), cert. den. 383 U.S. 935 (1966), held that where H obtained a Mexican divorce from W-1, and then married W-2, the second marriage would be recognized as valid even though W-1 had obtained a New York state court decree declaring the divorce to be invalid and the second marriage of no force and effect. The Second Circuit's recognition of the second marriage meant that in this case H could deduct the alimony payments made to his first wife, and that he could file joint income tax returns with his second wife. This was an example of what might be called the doctrine of de facto marriage, but was not wholly without precedent in the domestic relations law, as evidenced by the *Taczanowska* case, supra, page 95, and the *Spellens* case, supra, page 805. The *Borax* case was heavily criticized in the law reviews. D. Currie, Suitcase Divorce in the Conflict of Laws: Simons, Rosenstiel, and Borax, 34 U.Chi.L.Rev. 26, 64 (1966); Spolter, Invalid Divorce Decrees, 24 Tax.L.Rev. 163 (1969). The Internal Revenue Service refused to acquiesce in it. Rev.Rul. 67–442, 1967–2 C.B. 65.

Borax has subsequently had a mixed treatment in the courts. In Estate of Spalding v. Commissioner, 537 F.2d 666 (2d Cir. 1976) the Second Circuit held that the estate of W-2 was entitled to the marital deduction when W-2 left property to H, even though H's earlier Nevada divorce from W-1 had been held invalid by a New York state court, the New York decree also holding that H continued to be married to W-1. *Spalding* relied at least in part on *Borax*. But Estate of Goldwater v. Commissioner, 539 F.2d 878 (2d Cir. 1976) held that H's estate was not entitled to the marital estate tax deduction with respect to property devised to W-2 where a New York state court had held that H's Mexican divorce from W-1 was invalid and that H had remained married to W-1. *Goldwater* distinguished *Spalding* on the ground that there the invalidity of the second marriage had not been declared by the state in which the estate was being administered, while in *Goldwater* the estate was administered in New York, where the divorce had been invalidated. *Goldwater* distinguished *Borax* on the ground that there the income tax was involved, whereas in *Goldwater* it was the estate tax which was in issue. The Tax Court has refused to follow *Borax* on the ground that state law is the basis for determining whether parties are married for tax purposes. Lee v. Commissioner, 64 T.C. 552 (1975), aff'd p.c. 550 F.2d 1201 (9th Cir. 1977).

It thus appears that *Borax* is of limited value although not actually overruled, and that state law will be looked to for the determination whether individuals are married or divorced for federal tax purposes. See also Rev.Rul. 67–442, 1967–2 C.B. 65, in which the Internal Revenue Service indicates that it will generally not question the validity of any divorce decree until a court of competent jurisdiction declares it to be invalid.

This state of the law raises some interesting questions:

(a) Would Mr. and Mrs. Spellens be considered married for federal tax purposes? See the *Spellens* case, supra, page 805. When the California court said that they were not married, but that Mr. Spellens was estopped to assert that they were not, would the resulting support award be deductible as alimony?

(b) Would payments made by a man to a woman with whom he was living, under Marvin v. Marvin, supra, page 38, be alimony for federal tax purposes? See Peacock v. Commissioner, T.C.M. 1978–30; Jones v. Commissioner, T.C.M. 1977–329. Would Marvin be entitled to claim a dependency exemption for Michelle while they lived together? Esminger v. Commissioner, 610 F.2d 189 (4th Cir. 1979).

7. Another federal tax issue may depend upon the technicalities of the state law of separation decrees. In Capodanno v. Commissioner, 602 F.2d 64 (3d Cir. 1979) the wife had a New Jersey separate maintenance decree, under which the husband was required to make payments of support to her. The court held that such a decree under New Jersey law does not effect a "legal separation" under 26 U.S.C.A. § 143(a)(2) and 6013(d)(2), so that the wife could not file a return as an unmarried individual. The same case held that when the husband was required to make a large payment of arrears in his support obligation, the total amount was deductible by him and taxable to the wife in the year in which it was made, the 10% limitation under § 71(c)(2) not applying to this situation. But see Dunn v. Commissioner, 70 T.C. 361 (1978).

8. The federal income tax rates are currently so arranged that where a man and woman have roughly equal taxable incomes, they will pay a lower total tax if they are unmarried than they will pay if married. I.R.C. § 1 (1979). If that is the case, there may be a temptation to obtain a divorce shortly before, and remarry shortly after, December thirty-first each year, that being the day on which calendar year taxpayers' marital status is determined for federal tax purposes. I.R.C. § 6013(d)(1) (1979). The Internal Revenue Service has issued a ruling to the effect that this sort of divorce will not be recognized, however, their position being that it is a sham. Would you agree? See Rev.Rul. 76–225, 1976–2 C.B. 40; Note, The Haitian Vacation: The Applicability of Sham Doctrine to Year-End Divorces, 77 Mich.L.Rev. 1332 (1979).

The difference in rates between married and unmarried persons was held not to be unconstitutional in Mapes v. U. S., 576 F.2d 896 (Ct.Cl. 1978), cert. den. 439 U.S. 1046 (1978).

9. Normally where spouses file a joint return, and where the return fails to report the full income or is incorrect in some other particular, both spouses are liable for the full amount of the tax properly due, plus interest and penalties. This may cause hardship in some cases. For example, if the husband failed to report his full income and his wife signed the joint return without knowing this, she would still be liable for the additional tax ultimately computed to be due, and for interest and penalties. This liability might be asserted against her at a later and inconvenient time. The hardship might be especially acute if the parties were living apart, since the wife might then be quite unfamiliar with the husband's affairs and have no opportunity to check the accuracy of the joint return so far as his income and deductions were involved. In 1971 § 6013(e) of the Internal Revenue Code was enacted to relieve such an innocent spouse of liability in certain cases of this kind. The requirements for such relief are: (a) that a joint return was filed omitting from gross income a sum properly includable, attributable to one spouse and amounting to more than 25% of the gross income reported in the return; (b) that the other spouse did not know or have reason to know of the omission; and (c) that it is inequitable to hold such other spouse liable for the deficiency, taking into account the circumstances, including whether the other spouse benefited from the items omitted from gross income. Note, 5 Valparaiso L.Rev. 616 (1971); Annot., 31 A.L.R.Fed. 14 (1977).

10. It is apparent from the statute that periodic payments made to a wife by her husband under a written separation agreement executed after the effective date of the 1954 Internal Revenue Code are deductible by the husband and taxable to the wife. Likewise such payments made pursuant to a decree of divorce or separation, or pursuant to a written instrument incident to such a decree are similarly treated. As the *Borax* case suggests, "incident" in this context is given a broad construction, so that where the payments are made pursuant to an agreement which is followed by a divorce decree which makes no mention of the agreement, the payments are nevertheless deductible by the husband and taxable to the wife. See, e. g., Holt v. Commissioner, 226 F.2d 757 (2d Cir. 1955), cert. den. 350 U.S. 982 (1955). The theory is that the agreement is incident to the "status" of divorce. Internal Revenue Code of 1954, § 7701(a)(17) defines "husband" and "wife" in such a way as to make it clear that where alimony is paid by

the wife rather than by the husband, the tax consequences will be as outlined above.

Conversely, when by the state law the obligation to make the payments ends, the husband's right to the deduction and the wife's duty to pay the tax also end. Hoffman v. Commissioner, 455 F.2d 161 (7th Cir. 1972).

11. The Tax Reform Act of 1976, in a provision which is now I.R.C. § 62(13) (1979), authorized alimony deductions allowed by § 215 to be deducted from gross income in order to arrive at adjusted gross income. This provides a tax saving for those wishing to use the optional standard deduction. It may also enable the alimony-paying taxpayer to increase the tax benefits from his medical expenses, but it reduces the benefits of the charitable deduction.

BROCK v. COMMISSIONER OF INTERNAL REVENUE

United States Court of Appeals, Fifth Circuit, 1978.
566 F.2d 947.

RONEY, Circuit Judge: In this case Sarah Brock appeals from a judgment of the Tax Court requiring her to include in her taxable income the entire amount of payments made by her former husband under a divorce decree. The Tax Court determined that the support agreement incorporated in the divorce decree did not "fix" a certain portion of the total payment exclusively for the support of their four children. We affirm.

The facts in this case are not in dispute. On November 29, 1971, Sarah and W. Kenneth Brock were divorced by a decree entered in Superior Court of DeKalb County, Georgia. Incorporated in this decree was the following provision from an earlier separation agreement between the parties:

> Husband agrees to pay to the Wife during her life the sum of Six Hundred ($600.00) Dollars per week as alimony and child support until she remarries, with said amount to be reduced by One Hundred ($100.00) Dollars per week as each child becomes self-supporting, marries, dies or becomes twenty-one (21) years of age. Said payments to start November 26, 1971. In the event she remarries, he shall pay her for the support of each minor child, unmarried and under the age of 21, the sum of $100.00 per week, until each child becomes self-supporting, marries, dies or becomes twenty-one (21) years of age.

Pursuant to this provision Mr. Brock paid Ms. Brock $4,800 in 1971 and $29,400 in 1972. Ms. Brock filed no tax return for 1971 and reported only $9,600 in alimony income on her 1972 return. The Commissioner determined that she had received alimony income in the amounts of $4,800 in 1971 and $29,400 in 1972 and notified her of the deficiency. Ms. Brock contends that the amount of the deficiency is attributable to child support and was therefore properly excluded from her income under § 71(b) of the Internal Revenue Code of 1954, 26 U.S.C.A. § 71(b). Relying upon Commissioner of Internal Revenue v. Lester, 366 U.S. 299, 81 S.Ct. 343, 6 L.Ed.2d 306 (1961), the Tax Court held that the quoted provision did not "fix" any part of the payments as child support. Thus, the payments in question were held to be taxable in their entirety as alimony income. From this decision Ms. Brock appeals.

Section 71(a) includes in a divorced wife's gross income all periodic payments received in discharge of a legal obligation which, because of the marital or family relationship, is imposed on or incurred by the husband under the decree or a written instrument incident to the divorce. 26 U.S.C.A. § 71(a). Section 71(b), however, excepts from her gross income "that part of any payment which the terms of the decree, instrument, or agreement fix, in terms of an amount of money or a part of the payment, as a sum which is payable for the support of minor children of the husband."

In *Lester* the Supreme Court strictly interpreted this language:

> The agreement must expressly specify or "fix" a sum certain or percentage of the payment for child support before any of the payment is excluded from the wife's income. The statutory requirement is strict and carefully worded. It does not say that "a sufficiently clear purpose" on the part of the parties is sufficient to shift the tax. It says that the "written instrument" must "fix" that "portion of the payment" which is to go to the support of the children. Otherwise, the wife must pay the tax on the whole payment.

366 U.S. at 303, 81 S.Ct. at 1346. The support agreement in *Lester* made no specific allocation of payments between alimony and child support, but contained a reduction clause providing that one-sixth of the payments would cease upon the marriage, death, or emancipation of each of the couples' three children. The agreement further provided that on the wife's remarriage all payments would cease. The Court found this agreement insufficient to "fix" a portion of the payment as child support. The Brock's support agreement differs from the agreement in *Lester* only in that the remarriage of Ms. Brock would operate to convert the alimony payments into child support payments of $100 per month [sic] for each child. This provision, however, is expressly contingent on Ms. Brock's remarriage. It cannot transform alimony payments into child support payments until it becomes operative. See Weil v. Commissioner of Internal Revenue, 240 F.2d 584, 588 (2d Cir. 1957), quoted in Commissioner of Internal Revenue v. Lester, 366 U.S. 299, 306 n.6, 81 S.Ct. 1343, 6 L.Ed.2d 306 (1961). During the period here in question, Ms. Brock remained unmarried. In Fryer v. Commissioner of Internal Revenue, 434 F.2d 67 (2d Cir. 1970), the Second Circuit held a substantially identical support agreement to lack the specificity required by § 71(b) and *Lester*.

Ms. Brock argues that Commissioner of Internal Revenue v. Gotthelf, 407 F.2d 491 (2d Cir. 1969), cert. denied, 396 U.S. 828, 90 S.Ct. 78, 24 L.Ed.2d 79 (1969), and West v. United States, 413 F.2d 294 (4th Cir. 1969), compel a contrary result. The divorce decrees in both cases contained clauses providing for a reduction in the payment if the wife remarried or a child reached the age of 21. Unlike the instant case, however, the agreements at issue in both *Gotthelf* and *West* contained additional language found sufficient to fix the amount of child support payments. Indeed, both courts intimated that had the support agreement contained only the reduction clauses, as in this case, the specificity requirements of *Lester* would not be satisfied.

Affirmed.

NOTES AND QUESTIONS

1. The facts in Commissioner v. Lester, cited in the *Brock* case, were as follows. A husband and wife executed a separation agreement providing for periodic payments to the wife by the husband. There were three children of the marriage. The agreement also contained the following language: "* * * [i]n the event that any of the [three] children of the parties hereto shall marry, become emancipated, or die, then the payments herein specified shall * * * be reduced in a sum equal to one-sixth of the payments which would otherwise accrue * * *". The Commissioner argued that under this agreement one-half of the payments were made for the support of the children and therefore not deductible by the husband under § 215 of the Internal Revenue Code. The Supreme Court rejected this contention, saying, "We have concluded that the Congress intended that, to come within the exception portion of § 22(k), [now § 71(b)] the agreement providing for the periodic payments must specifically state the amounts or parts thereof allocable to the support of the children." See also Treas.Reg. § 1.71–1(e) (1972).

The *Gotthelf* case, also cited in *Brock*, was concerned with a separation agreement incorporated in a divorce decree which provided for payments of $12,000 per year (at the rate of $1,000 per month) to the wife for her support and the support of the children. It also provided that on the wife's remarriage the payments would be reduced to $7,000 per year, and that on the emancipation or majority of either of the two children, the payments would be reduced in the amount of $3,500 per child per year. A final provision stated that the agreement would be binding on the husband's estate to the extent of $7,000 "for the benefit of the two children, as in this agreement provided for". The Second Circuit held that this agreement and decree did "fix" an amount for the support of the children, relying on the final provision just quoted.

(a) Are the *Lester*, *Gotthelf* and *Brock* cases consistent in their approach and results?

(b) A separation agreement provided that H would pay to W $35 per week as alimony and for the support of the three children of the marriage. When any child should be emancipated, the agreement provided, the weekly sum was to be reduced by $10, and if W should remarry it was to be reduced by $5. May H deduct the $35 per week as alimony? Would it matter that the agreement went on to provide that "W promises to expend at least $30 per week of the payments for the use and benefit of the children?" West v. United States, 413 F.2d 294 (4th Cir. 1969).

(c) In arriving at a sum for alimony and child support, or in dividing the property of the parties, should the divorce court take into account the tax consequences of the various allocations which might be made? Cf. Drucker v. Drucker, 239 So.2d 117 (Fla.App.1970); Young v. Young, 200 Neb. 787, 265 N.W.2d 666 (1978); Knigge v. Knigge, 204 Neb. 421, 282 N. W.2d 581 (1979); Seiler v. Seiler, 48 Wis.2d 400, 180 N.W.2d 627 (1970); Annot., 51 A.L.R.3d 461 (1973).

2. H and W were on the verge of divorce. W was 25 and H 30. W had worked as a school teacher in the past, receiving salaries only slightly less than H's, although at the time of the divorce she was not working. They had one child, eighteen months old. In the course of the negotiations over alimony W's lawyer told her that under the new divorce statute (the Uniform Marriage and Divorce Act) she would not be likely to be awarded any alimony because she could resume work as a teacher. W therefore agreed to accept $200 per month for the support of the child, who was to be placed in her custody. W asked her lawyer whether she might spend part of this on her own support, and he told her she might. H agreed to this sum, but insisted that in the separation agreement and divorce decree the payments be labeled alimony in order to entitle him to an income tax deduction. The agreement was so drafted. When presented to the court for approval, the court questioned the alimony provision, saying it was not disposed to approve alimony for a wife capable of working. H's lawyer explained that the $200 per month was really child support, but that it was labeled alimony merely for tax purposes. The court then said it was satisfied and approved the agreement.

(a) Is H entitled to the alimony deduction and is W liable for income tax on the $200 per month? Is your answer to this question affected by the fact that W gets the $1000 dependency exemption if the payments are considered alimony? Cf. Talberth v. Commissioner, 47 T.C. 326 (1966), 39 Univ. of Colo.L.Rev. 602 (1966); Emmons v. Commissioner, 36 T.C. 728 (1961), aff'd 311 F.2d 223 (6th Cir. 1962).

(b) A year later H found that W had begun living with another man, X, and was spending the $200 per month for the support of herself and X, rather than on the child. Does H have any remedy for this situation? If he does have a remedy, what effect does it have on his income tax obligations? Cf. Rosenblatt v. Birnbaum, 16 N.Y.2d 212, 264 N.Y.S.2d 521, 212 N.E.2d 37 (1965).

(c) Does state or federal law control on the question whether an amount is "fixed" for support of the children?

(d) What, if any, general principles govern the definition of "fixed" as the term is used in § 71(b) of the Code?

3. When § 71(b) excludes from alimony treatment amounts fixed as a sum payable for support of the minor children of the payer, federal law determines what the age of majority is, and that is apparently still twenty-one even though state law ends minority at age eighteen. Borbonus v. Commissioner, 42 T.C. 983 (1964). The minor children must be those of the payer to come within § 71(b). If they are the children of the payee, but

not of the payer, i. e. are stepchildren of the paying husband, the payments may qualify as alimony since they are relieving the wife of her obligation to support her child. Faber v. Commissioner, 264 F.2d 127 (3d Cir. 1959).

4. Where the parents are divorced, the question necessarily arises as to which of them may take the personal exemption for their child or children authorized by I.R.C. § 151 (1979), under the current provision the exemption being $1,000 per child. Section 151(e) defines "child" as a son, stepson, daughter or stepdaughter of the taxpayer under age nineteen at the close of the year or a student. The rules by which it is to be determined which of the divorced parents are entitled to the personal exemption are complex and are set out in § 152(e) of the Code, as follows:

"(e) **Support test in case of child of divorced parents, etc.—**
"(1) **General rule.**—If—

"(A) a child (as defined in section 151(e)(3)) receives over half of his support during the calendar year from his parents who are divorced or legally separated under a decree of divorce or separate maintenance, or who are separated under a written separation agreement, and

"(B) such child is in the custody of one or both of his parents for more than one-half of the calendar year,

such child shall be treated, for purposes of subsection (a), as receiving over half of his support during the calendar year from the parent having custody for a greater portion of the calendar year unless he is treated, under the provisions of paragraph (2), as having received over half of his support for such year from the other parent (referred to in this subsection as the parent not having custody).

"(2) **Special rule.**—The child of parents described in paragraph (1) shall be treated as having received over half of his support during the calendar year from the parent not having custody if—

"(A)(i) the decree of divorce or of separate maintenance, or a written agreement between the parents applicable to the taxable year beginning in such calendar year, provides that the parent not having custody shall be entitled to any deduction allowable under section 151 for such child, and

"(ii) such parent not having custody provides at least $600 for the support of such child during the calendar year, or

"(B)(i) the parent not having custody provides $1,200 or more for the support of such child (or if there is more than one such child, $1,200 or more for each of such children) for the calendar year, and

"(ii) the parent having custody of such child does not clearly establish that he provided more for the support of such child during the calendar year than the parent not having custody.

For the purposes of this paragraph, amounts expended for the support of a child or children shall be treated as received from the parent not having custody to the extent that such parent provided amounts for such support.

"(3) **Itemized statement required.**—If a taxpayer claims that paragraph (2)(B) applies with respect to a child for a calendar year and the other parent claims that paragraph (2)(B)(i) is not satisfied or claims to have provided more for the support of such child during such calendar year than the taxpayer, each parent shall be entitled to receive, under regulations to be prescribed by the Secretary, an itemized statement of the expenditures upon which the other parent's claim of support is based.

"**(4) Exception for multiple-support agreement.**—The provisions of this subsection shall not apply in any case where over half of the support of the child is treated as having been received from a taxpayer under the provisions of subsection (c).

"**(5) Regulations.**—The Secretary shall prescribe such regulations as may be necessary to carry out the purposes of this subsection."

A case construing the exception under § 152(e)(2)(A) as not applying where the separation agreement failed specifically to say that the husband was to get the exemption is Yancey v. Commissioner, 72 T.C. 37 (1979).

If the parent having custody remarries and the new spouse makes contributions to the support of the child, it has been held by the Tax Court, and the Internal Revenue Service agrees, that the new spouse's contributions may be included in determining whether the custodial parent provided over half the child's support. Rev.Rul. 73–175, I.R.B. 1973–16, p. 6; Colton v. Commissioner, 56 T.C. 471 (1971).

For a case construing "clearly establish" for purposes of the § 152(e)(2)(B) exception, see LaBay v. Commissioner, 55 T.C. 6 (1971), aff'd p.c. 450 F.2d 280 (5th Cir. 1971), 37 Mo.L.Rev. 718 (1972). See also Sander, The New Amendment to the Internal Revenue Code Relating to Dependency Exemptions for Children of Divorced or Separated Spouses, 1 Fam.L.Q. 114 (1967).

5.   What precepts for the drafting of separation agreements do you deduce from *Brock* and the other cases and rulings cited, supra? See DuCanto, Tax Aspects of Separation and Divorce, 16 Fam.L. Newsletter, No. 2, 15, 26 (1975); F. Sander, H. Gutman, Tax Aspects of Divorce and Separation A-21 (Bureau of National Affairs 1975).

6.   Under I.R.C. § 44A a divorced spouse may take as a credit against his or her tax twenty percent of the employment-related expenses for the care of children under fifteen if he or she has custody of such a child. This credit is independent of the dependency exemption. It may be taken when the child receives over half of his support from divorced parents, he is in the custody of one or the other for more than half of the year, and the taxpayer has custody for a longer time during the year than the other parent. I.R.C. § 44A(f)(5)(1979).

UNITED STATES v. DAVIS

Supreme Court of the United States, 1962.
370 U.S. 65, 82 S.Ct. 1190, 8 L.Ed.2d 335.

Mr. Justice CLARK delivered the opinion of the Court.

These cases involve the tax consequences of a transfer of appreciated property by Thomas Crawley Davis to his former wife pursuant to a property settlement agreement executed prior to divorce, as well as the deductibility of his payment of her legal expenses in connection therewith. The Court of Claims upset the Commissioner's determination that there was taxable gain on the transfer but upheld his ruling that the fees paid the wife's attorney were not deductible. * * * We granted certiorari on a conflict in the Court of Appeals and the Court of Claims on the taxability of such transfers. * * * We have decided that the taxpayer did have a taxable gain on the transfer and that the wife's attorney's fees were not deductible.

In 1954 the taxpayer and his then wife made a voluntary property settlement and separation agreement calling for support payments to the wife and minor child in addition to the transfer of certain personal property to the wife. Under Delaware law all the property transferred was that of the taxpayer, subject to certain statutory marital rights of the wife including a right of intestate succession and a right upon divorce to a share of the husband's property. Specifically as a "division in settlement of their property" the taxpayer agreed to transfer to his wife, *inter alia*, 1,000 shares of stock in the E. I. du Pont de Nemours & Co. The then Mrs. Davis agreed to accept this division "in full settlement and satisfaction of any and all claims and rights against the husband whatsoever (including but not by way of limitation, dower and all rights under the laws of testacy and intestacy) * * *." Pursuant to the above agreement which had been incorporated into the divorce decree, one-half of this stock was delivered in the tax year involved, 1955, and the balance thereafter. Davis' cost basis for the 1955 transfer was $74,775.37, and the fair market value of the 500 shares there transferred was $82,250. The taxpayer also agreed orally to pay the wife's legal expenses, and in 1955 he made payments to the wife's attorney, including $2,500 for services concerning tax matters relative to the property settlement.

I.

The determination of the income tax consequences of the stock transfer described above is basically a two-step analysis: (1) Was the transaction a taxable event? (2) If so, how much taxable gain resulted therefrom? Originally the Tax Court (at that time the Board of Tax Appeals) held that the accretion to property transferred pursuant to a divorce settlement could not be taxed as capital gain to the transferor because the amount realized by the satisfaction of the husband's marital obligations was indeterminable and because, even if such benefit were ascertainable, the transaction was a nontaxable division of property. Mesta v. Commissioner, 42 B.T.A. 933 (1940); Halliwell v. Commissioner, 44 B.T.A. 740 (1941). However, upon being reversed in quick succession by the Courts of Appeals of the Third and Second Circuits, Commissioner v. Mesta, 123 F.2d 986 (3d Cir. 1941); Commissioner v. Halliwell, 131 F.2d 642 (2d Cir. 1942), the Tax Court accepted the position of these courts and has continued to apply these views in appropriate cases since that time, Hall v. Commissioner, 9 T.C. 53 (1947); Patino v. Commissioner, 13 T.C. 816 (1949); Estate of Stouffer v. Commissioner, 30 T.C. 1244 (1958); King v. Commissioner, 31 T.C. 108 (1958); Marshman v. Commissioner, 31 T.C. 269 (1958). In *Mesta* and *Halliwell* the Courts of Appeals reasoned that the accretion to the property was "realized" by the transfer and that this gain could be measured on the assumption that the relinquished marital rights were equal in value to the property transferred. The matter was considered settled until the Court of Appeals for the Sixth Circuit, in reversing the Tax Court, ruled that, although such a transfer might be a taxable event, the gain realized thereby could not be determined because of the impossibility of evaluating the fair market value of the wife's marital rights. Commissioner v. Marshman, 279 F.2d 27 (6th Cir. 1960). In so holding that court specifically rejected the argument that these rights could be presumed to be equal in value to the property transferred for their release. This is essentially the position taken by the Court of Claims in the instant case.

II.

We now turn to the threshold question of whether the transfer in issue was an appropriate occasion for taxing the accretion to the stock. There can be no doubt that Congress, as evidenced by its inclusive definition of income subject to taxation, i. e., "all income from whatever source derived including   *   *   *   [g]ains derived from dealings in property," [4] intended that the economic growth of this stock be taxed. The problem confronting us is simply when is such accretion to be taxed. Should the economic gain be presently assessed against taxpayer, or should this assessment await a subsequent transfer of the property by the wife? The controlling statutory language, which provides that gains from dealings in property are to be taxed upon "sale or other disposition," [5] is too general to include or exclude conclusively the transaction presently in issue. Recognizing this, the Government and the taxpayer argue by analogy with transactions more easily classified as within or without the ambient of taxable events. The taxpayer asserts that the present disposition is comparable to a nontaxable division of property between two co-owners,[6] while the Government contends it more resembles a taxable

---

4. Internal Revenue Code of 1954 § 61(a).

5. Internal Revenue Code of 1954 §§ 1001, 1002.

6. Any suggestion that the transaction in question was a gift is completely unrealistic. Property transferred pursuant to a negotiated settlement in return for the release of admittedly valuable rights is not a gift in any sense of the term. To intimate that there was a gift to the extent the value of the property exceeded that of the rights released not only invokes the erroneous premise that every exchange not precisely equal involves a gift but merely raises the measurement problem discussed in Part III, infra, p. 71. Cases in which this Court has held transfers of prop-

transfer of property in exchange for the release of an independent legal obligation. Neither disputes the validity of the other's starting point.

In support of his analogy the taxpayer argues that to draw a distinction between a wife's interest in the property of her husband in a common-law jurisdiction such as Delaware and the property interest of a wife in a typical community property jurisdiction would commit a double sin; for such differentiation would depend upon "elusive and subtle casuistries which   *   *   *   possess no relevance for tax purposes," Helvering v. Hallock, 309 U.S. 106, 118, 60 S.Ct. 444, 450, 84 L.Ed. 604 (1940), and would create disparities between common-law and community property jurisdictions in contradiction to Congress' general policy of equality between the two. The taxpayer's analogy, however, stumbles on its own premise, for the inchoate rights granted a wife in her husband's property by the Delaware law do not even remotely reach the dignity of co-ownership. The wife has no interest —passive or active—over the management or disposition of her husband's personal property. Her rights are not descendable, and she must survive him to share in his intestate estate. Upon dissolution of the marriage she shares in the property only to such extent as the court deems "reasonable." 13 Del.Code Ann. § 1531(a). What is "reasonable" might be ascertained independently of the extent of the husband's property by such criteria as the wife's financial condition, her needs in relation to her accustomed station in life, her age and health, the number of children and their ages, and the earning capacity of the husband.   *   *   *

This is not to say it would be completely illogical to consider the shearing off of the wife's rights in her husband's property as a division of that property, but we believe the contrary to be the more reasonable construction. Regardless of the tags, Delaware seems only to place a burden on the husband's property rather than to make the wife a part owner thereof. In the present context the rights of succession and reasonable share do not differ significantly from the husband's obligations of support and alimony. They all partake more of a personal liability of the husband than a property interest of the wife. The effectuation of these marital rights may ultimately result in the ownership of some of the husband's property as it did here, but certainly this happenstance does not equate the transaction with a division of property by co-owners. Although admittedly such a view

erty in exchange for the release of marital rights subject to gift taxes are based not on the premise that such transactions are inherently gifts but on the concept that in the contemplation of the gift tax statute they are to be taxed as gifts. Merrill v. Fahs, 324 U.S. 308 (1945); Commissioner v. Wemyss, 324 U.S. 303 (1945); see Harris v. Commissioner, 340 U.S. 106 (1950). In interpreting the particular income tax provisions here involved, we find ourselves unfettered by the language and considerations ingrained in the gift and estate tax statutes. See Farid-Es-Sultaneh v. Commissioner, 160 F.2d 812 (2d Cir. 1947).

may permit different tax treatment among the several States, this Court in the past has not ignored the differing effects on the federal taxing scheme of substantive differences between community property and common-law systems. * * *

Our interpretation of the general statutory language is fortified by the long-standing administrative practice as sounded and formalized by the settled state of law in the lower courts. * * *

III.

Having determined that the transaction was a taxable event, we now turn to the point on which the Court of Claims balked, viz., the measurement of the taxable gain realized by the taxpayer. The Code defines the taxable gain from the sale or disposition of property as being the "excess of the amount realized therefrom over the adjusted basis * * *." I.R.C. (1954) § 1001(a). The "amount realized" is further defined as "the sum of any money received plus the fair market value of the property (other than money) received." I.R.C. (1954) § 1001(b). In the instant case the "property received" was the release of the wife's inchoate marital rights. The Court of Claims, following the Court of Appeals for the Sixth Circuit, found that there was no way to compute the fair market value of these marital rights and that it was thus impossible to determine the taxable gain realized by the taxpayer. We believe this conclusion was erroneous.

It must be assumed, we think, that the parties acted at arm's length and that they judged the marital rights to be equal in value to the property for which they were exchanged. There was no evidence to the contrary here. Absent a readily ascertainable value it is accepted practice where property is exchanged to hold, * * * that the values "of the two properties exchanged in an arms-length transaction are either equal in fact, or are presumed to be equal." * * * To be sure there is much to be said of the argument that such an assumption is weakened by the emotion, tension and practical necessities involved in divorce negotiations and the property settlements arising therefrom. However, once it is recognized that the transfer was a taxable event, it is more consistent with the general purpose and scheme of the taxing statutes to make a rough approximation of the gain realized thereby than to ignore altogether its tax consequences. * * *

Moreover, if the transaction is to be considered a taxable event as to the husband, the Court of Claims' position leaves up in the air the wife's basis for the property received. In the context of a taxable transfer by the husband [7] all indicia point to a "cost" basis for this

---

7. Under the present administrative practice, the release of marital rights in exchange for property or other consideration is not considered a taxable event as to the wife. For a discussion of the difficulties confronting a wife under a contrary approach, see Taylor and Schwartz, Tax As-

property in the hands of the wife.[8] Yet under the Court of Claims' position her cost for this property, i. e., the value of the marital rights relinquished therefor, would be indeterminable, and on subsequent disposition of the property she might suffer inordinately over the Commissioner's assessment which she would have the burden of proving erroneous, * * * Our present holding that the value of these rights is ascertainable eliminates this problem; for the same calculation that determines the amount received by the husband fixes the amount given up by the wife, and this figure, i. e., the market value of the property transferred by the husband, will be taken by her as her tax basis for the property received.

Finally, it must be noted that here, as well as in relation to the question of whether the event is taxable, we draw support from the prior administrative practice and judicial approval of that practice. * * * We therefore conclude that the Commissioner's assessment of a taxable gain based upon the value of the stock at the date of its transfer has not been shown erroneous.

IV.

The attorney-fee question is much simpler. It is the customary practice in Delaware for the husband to pay both his own and his wife's legal expenses incurred in the divorce and the property settlement. Here petitioner paid $5,000 of such fees in the taxable year 1955 earmarked for tax advice in relation to the property settlement. One-half of this sum went to the wife's attorney. The taxpayer claimed that under § 212(3) of the 1954 Code, which allows a deduction for the "ordinary and necessary expenses paid * * * in connection with the determination, collection, or refund of any tax," he was entitled to deduct the entire $5,000. The Court of Claims allowed the $2,500 paid taxpayer's own attorney but denied the like amount paid the wife's attorney. The sole question here is the deductibility of the latter fee; the Government did not seek review of the amount taxpayer paid his own attorney, and we intimate no decision on that point. As to the deduction of the wife's fees, we read the statute, if applicable to this type of tax expense, to include only the expenses of the taxpayer himself and not those of his wife. Here the fees paid her attorney do not appear to be "in connection with the determination, collection, or refund" of any tax of the taxpayer. As the Court of Claims found, the wife's attorney "considered the problems from the standpoint of his client alone. Certainly then it

pects of Marital Property Agreements, 7 Tax L.Rev. 19, 30 (1951); Comment, The Lump Sum Divorce Settlement as a Taxable Exchange, 8 U.C.L.A.L.Rev. 593, 601–602 (1961).

8. Section 1012 of the Internal Revenue Code of 1954 provides that: "The basis of property shall be the cost of such property, except as otherwise provided in this subchapter and subchapters C (relating to corporate distributions and adjustments), K (relating to partners and partnerships), and P (relating to capital gains and losses) * * *."

cannot be said that * * * [his] advice was directed to plaintiff's tax problems * * *." 152 Ct.Cl., at 805, 287 F.2d, at 171. We therefore conclude, as did the Court of Claims, that those fees were not a deductible item to the taxpayer.

Reversed in part and affirmed in part.

NOTES AND QUESTIONS

1.   The *Davis* case was noted in Solomon, Property Transfer Pursuant to Divorce-Taxable Event? 17 Stan.L.Rev. 478 (1965); Schwartz, Divorce and Taxes: New Aspects of the Davis Denouement, 15 U.C.L.A.L.Rev. 176 (1967); 1963 Duke L.J. 365; 61 Mich.L.Rev. 612 (1963); and 10 U.C.L.A. Rev. 425 (1963), among other reviews.

2.   Would the transfer of property from husband to wife be a taxable event under *Davis* if it occurred by virtue of the divorce decree alone, without a prior agreement between the spouses? Wallace v. United States, 439 F.2d 757 (8th Cir. 1971), cert. den. 404 U.S. 831 (1971); Pulliam v. Commissioner, 329 F.2d 97 (10th Cir. 1964), cert. den. 379 U.S. 836 (1964).

3.   *Davis* makes a distinction between common law property states and community property states, recognizing as a taxable event the division of property in the former states but not in the latter states. The reason seems to be that community property is considered a kind of co-ownership, and the division of this property between husband and wife is not a sale but merely assignment to each of what he or she already owns. The same would be true if, in a common law state, the property were owned by husband and wife in joint tenancy, tenancy by the entireties or in tenancy in common, a division of such property not being a taxable event. Rev.Rul. 74–347, 1974–2 C.B. 26; Rev.Rul. 56–437, 1956–2 C.B. 507.

The foregoing rule concerning "co-owned" property applies where there is an equal division between the spouses. Wren v. Commissioner, 24 T.C.M. 290 (1965). But where "one spouse receives property having an aggregate value equal to substantially more than half the value of the entire community property, the transaction is a taxable one * * *. Similarly, where one spouse gives his note or other separate property for a substantial portion of the other spouse's community property set aside to him, the transaction may be a taxable one * * *." Siewert v. Commissioner, 72 T.C. 326, 333 (1979). See also Showalter v. Commissioner, 33 T.C.M. 192 (1974); Schacht v. Commissioner, 47 T.C. 552 (1967), acq. 1968–2 C.B. 2. Presumably this same distinction between a "division" and a "sale" would have to be made when property held in joint tenancy or tenancy in common is disposed of on divorce.

4.   The *Davis* case seems to say that although the property division is a taxable event for the husband, it is not for the wife. Why should there be this distinction, in view of Int.Rev.Code of 1954, § 61(a), which provides that "gross income means all income from whatever source derived"? See Solomon, Property Transfer Pursuant to Divorce-Taxable Event?, 17 Stan. L.Rev. 478, 480–481 (1965), urging that the property division should be a taxable event for neither husband nor wife. See also Mulloch, Divorce and Taxes: Rev.Rul. 67–221, 23 U.Miami L.Rev. 736 (1969). If the transfer were taxable to the wife, how would her gain be computed?

5. Although any taxpayer is naturally distressed at being required to pay a tax on a particular transaction, in most instances at least the transaction produces the funds with which to pay the tax. What makes the *Davis* rule an especial hardship is that the transaction does not produce the funds with which to pay the tax. All the transferor of the property receives is his spouse's release of her marital rights, so that the tax must be paid out of other assets which may or may not be available. With that in mind some state courts in common law property states have created a new type of marital property which, when divided on divorce, does not result in a taxable event, thereby relieving the spouse of this hardship. The first such state was Oklahoma. Collins v. Oklahoma Tax Commission, 446 P.2d 290 (Okl. 1968) held that property acquired during marriage by the joint efforts of both spouses is jointly acquired property in which the wife has a vested interest similar to the wife's interest in community property in community property states. When this property is divided on divorce, the court said, the purpose is to sever the common title. Therefore the division was held not to result in a taxable event for Oklahoma income tax purposes. This analysis of Oklahoma property law was held controlling with respect to the federal income tax in Collins v. Commissioner, 412 F.2d 211 (10th Cir. 1969), so that no tax was due when jointly acquired property was divided upon an Oklahoma divorce.

In Colorado the same question arose in the United States District Court, and that court certified to the State Supreme Court the question whether a transfer of property on divorce, made in acknowledgment of the spouse's contribution to the accumulation of the marital estate, was a taxable event. The Colorado Supreme Court responded, relying in part on *Collins,* and in large part on the Colorado statute authorizing the division of marital property on divorce, by holding that the transfer was "a recognition of a 'species of common ownership' of the marital estate by the wife resembling a division of property between co-owners." The transfer was held not to be a conveyance by the husband in exchange for a release of an independent obligation owed by him. This interest vested in the wife, the court said, when the action for dissolution of the marriage was filed. In re Questions Submitted by United States District Court, 184 Colo. 1, 8, 517 P.2d 1331, 1334 (1974). Upon receipt of this information, the federal courts, to no one's surprise, held that the transfer by the husband was a division by co-owners of jointly held property which resulted in no capital gain taxable to the husband. Imel v. United States, 523 F.2d 853 (10th Cir. 1975).

The Kansas Supreme Court has recently followed Colorado, after an earlier Tenth Circuit case had applied the *Davis* rule to Kansas transfers. Compare Cady v. Cady, 224 Kan. 339, 581 P.2d 358 (1978) and Wiles v. Commissioner, 499 F.2d 255 (10th Cir. 1974), cert. den. 419 U.S. 996 (1974). It has been argued that other states having similar statutes authorizing the division of marital property on divorce should do the same. See Note, 44 Mo.L.Rev. 92 (1979); Note 53 Or.L.Rev. 544 (1974); Note 57 Or.L.Rev. 365 (1978).

For useful general discussion of the consequences of the *Davis* case see Del Cotto, Sales and Other Dispositions of Property Under Section 1001: The Taxable Event, Amount Realized and Related Problems of Basis, 26 Buff.L.Rev. 219 (1975); Lawson, Tax Implications of Using Appreciated Property in a Property Settlement, 42 J. of Tax. 58 (1975); Note, Should

Federal Income Tax Consequences of Divorce Depend on State Property Law, 49 So.Cal.L.Rev. 1401 (1976).

6. If the husband in the *Davis* case had transferred to his wife securities which had depreciated rather than appreciated in value, he would have been permitted to deduct the loss if the asset had been one which, in an ordinary sale transaction, would have produced a deductible loss. McKinney v. Commissioner, 64 T.C. 263 (1975). But if the transfer had occurred when the parties were still married to each other, the loss would be disallowed under I.R.C. § 267, which disallows the recognition of losses on sales between family members, including husband and wife. Siewert v. Commissioner, 72 T.C. 326 (1979) held that a transaction was subject to § 267 when it occurred pursuant to a separation agreement signed when the parties were still married to each other but which was contingent upon the subsequent granting of a divorce. The property transfer, the court said, took effect simultaneously with, not after, the entry of the divorce decree.

If the transfer is of depreciable property and occurs when the parties are still married to each other, it falls within I.R.C. § 1239, which means that any gain recognized to the transferor would constitute ordinary income rather than a capital gain. Deyoe v. Commissioner, 66 T.C. 904 (1976).

7. The holding of the *Davis* case that the attorney fees paid by the husband to the wife's attorney were not deductible under Int.Rev.Code of 1954, § 212(3) on the ground that the fees were not paid in connection with the determination of any tax of the husband has been extended by the later case of United States v. Gilmore, 372 U.S. 39 (1963). This case held that under Int.Rev.Code of 1954, § 212(2) a husband was not entitled to deduct that portion of his legal fees attributable to his successful resistance against his wife's claims to community property in a divorce action. That section of the Code authorizes the deduction of ordinary and necessary expenses incurred for the management, conservation or maintenance of property held for the production of income. The Court in *Gilmore* reasoned that §§ 212 and 262 have as their purpose making a distinction between those expenses originating in business transactions, and those attributable to personal, living or family necessities. The former are deductible under § 212, the latter are not, under § 262. The Court then said that legal expenses incurred in resisting the wife's community property claims in the divorce suit were personal or family expenses, rather than business expenses. The test was said to be whether "the claim arises in connection with the taxpayer's profit-seeking activities", and not whether the claim might have consequences for the taxpayer's income-producing property. The Supreme Court applied the same test in the companion case of United States v. Patrick, 372 U.S. 53 (1963) to hold that the taxpayer could not deduct legal fees incurred in the negotiation of a property settlement with his wife before divorce, even though the purpose of the settlement was to ensure that the taxpayer retained control of a corporation in which he and his wife had held a large block of stock. Notwithstanding these cases, the attorney fees incurred by a taxpayer for tax advice in connection with a property settlement would be deductible, under § 212(3).

The expenditures made in the *Gilmore* case were later added to the basis of the property when it was subsequently sold, so that the taxpayer was not left totally without tax benefits from his legal fees. Gilmore v. United States, 245 F.Supp. 383 (N.D.Cal.1965).

8. Int.Rev.Code of 1954, § 101(a)(1) provides that the proceeds of life insurance policies paid on the death of the insured are not included in the recipient's gross income. But if the owner of the policy transfers it for value, the transferee, on the death of the insured and payment of the proceeds, may exclude from his gross income only his basis, that is, the consideration which he gave for the policy plus any premiums which he paid. If an insurance policy is transferred by the husband to the wife, would the *Davis* rule apply so as to require the husband to pay a tax on the difference between his basis and the fair market value at the time of the transfer? Wenig, Use of Life Insurance in Divorce and Separation Agreements, N.Y. U. 28th Inst. on Fed.Tax 837 (1970); Walzer, The Disposition of Life Insurance in Divorce Settlements, 46 Taxes 248 (1968). If the husband then dies, may the wife be required to include part or all of the insurance proceeds in her gross income? I.R.C. §§ 101(a)(2)(B), 101(e). Would the wife's release of her marital property rights be considered "a valuable consideration" under §§ 101(a)(2)(B)?

9. Gift tax liability for transfers made in connection with property settlements or divorce actions may be avoided by ensuring that the transfers take either of two forms. In the first place, if the transfer is ordered by the divorce decree, it is not considered a gift, even though the decree is based upon an agreement of the parties. Harris v. Commissioner, 340 U.S. 106 (1950). A second method of avoiding the gift tax is by making the transfer pursuant to a property settlement agreement, "in settlement of his or her marital or property rights", or to "provide a reasonable allowance for the support of issue of the marriage during minority". The quoted language is from I.R.C. § 2516, which provides that transfers made in this manner are deemed made for a full and adequate consideration in money or money's worth and consequently not subject to the gift tax. But in order to get the benefit of this section the parties must obtain a divorce within two years of the execution of the agreement.

By negative implication from § 2516 transfers made in consideration for the relinquishment of dower, curtesy or of a statutory estate created in lieu of dower or curtesy, of other marital rights in the spouse's property or estate, are not deemed to be made for an adequate and full consideration in money or money's worth, and are therefore subject to the gift tax. Treas. Reg. § 25.2512–8 (1958); I.R.C. § 2512(b); Commissioner v. Wemyss, 324 U.S. 303 (1945).

10. The crucial provision affecting the impact on marital property settlements of the estate tax is Int.Rev.Code of 1954, § 2043(b). This section provides that for estate tax purposes a relinquishment or promised relinquishment of dower, curtesy, or of a statutory estate in lieu thereof, or of other marital rights in the decedent's property shall not be deemed a consideration in money or money's worth. The effect of this section is that if the decedent, in connection with his divorce, made transfers in consideration for the release of these rights, and if he made them in contemplation of death (I.R.C. § 2035), or made them retaining a life estate (I.R.C. § 2036), or made them so as to take effect at death (I.R.C. § 2037), or if they were revocable (I.R.C. § 2038), such transfers will be included in his gross estate on his death. Transfers in consideration of money or money's worth are not included in the gross estate under sections 2035–2038, but section 2043(b) excludes transfers in exchange for the above described marital

claims or in satisfaction of those claims from the category of transfers for money. There is no estate tax provision analogous to I.R.C. § 2516 which exempts transfers pursuant to separation agreements. Property subject to a general power of appointment by the decedent may also be includible in his gross estate if certain complex circumstances exist, under I.R.C. § 2041.

On the death of an ex-spouse claims for alimony or for a division of property may, depending upon state law and the terms of a separation agreement or divorce decree, be a charge on the decedent's estate. If the claim is based upon the divorce decree, it is deductible from the decedent's gross estate for estate tax purposes. I.R.C. § 2053(a)(3) or (4); Robinson's Estate v. Commissioner, 63 T.C. 717 (1975). Where the claim against the estate arises out of a separation agreement, and not the divorce decree, it must be based upon consideration in money or money's worth. As indicated, I.R.C. § 2043(b) provides that the release of marital rights in the decedent's property or estate is not deemed to be such consideration. But where the separation agreement provides for release of a spouse's right to support, this is a consideration in money or money's worth and the spouse's claim is therefore deductible from the decedent's gross estate. I.R.C. § 2053(c)(1)(A); Estate of Iversen v. Commissioner, 552 F.2d 977 (3d Cir. 1977); Gray v. United States, 541 F.2d 228 (9th Cir. 1976).

11. The *Davis* case and its progeny create some complex and difficult questions, such as, for example:

(a) H and W, shortly after their marriage, buy a home for $20,000, taking title in joint tenancy with right of survivorship. Ten years later the home is paid for in full and has a fair market value of $60,000. At this point H and W decide to obtain a divorce. Since there are two young children to be in W's custody, and since there is not enough cash available to buy a similarly suitable home, H agrees to transfer his interest in the house to W. What are the tax consequences? DuCanto, Federal Tax Law: Where You Divorce Does Make a Difference, 9 Loyola-Chicago L.Rev. 397 (1978).

(b) In the above case, H transferred his interest in the property to W, in return for her note in the amount of $30,000 payable in five years. What are the tax consequences? Hornback v. United States, 298 F.Supp. 977 (W.D.Mo.1969); I.R.C. § 453.

(c) H and W, at the time they decide to be divorced, own two pieces of real estate in joint tenancy, a large piece of mountain property and a home in the city. The fair market value of each property is $80,000. In their separation agreement they agree that H will take the mountain property and W will keep the city home. The appropriate deeds are executed. What are the tax consequences? Beth W. Corp. v. United States, 350 F.Supp. 1190 (S.D.Fla.1972), aff'd p.c. 481 F.2d 140 (5th Cir. 1973), cert. den. 415 U.S. 916 (1974); Del Cotto, Sales and Other Dispositions of Property Under Section 1001: The Taxable Event, Amount Realized and Related Problems of Basis, 26 Buff.L.Rev. 219, 261(1977).

(d) What are the tax consequences when upon divorce H pays to W $30,000 representing a one-third interest in his vested but not matured pension rights? Would the tax consequences vary depending upon what methods of valuation are used? If so, what would be the effects of the methods suggested in the *Bloomer* case, supra, page 901?

12. *Bibliography*: Obviously the foregoing pages on the tax aspects of divorce can only be limited and somewhat superficial. For discussions in more detail, see F. Sander & H. Gutman, Tax Aspects of Divorce and Separation (Bureau of National Affairs 1975); H. Rudick, Tax Consequences of Marriage and Its Termination (1964); Wren, Tax Problems Incident to Divorce and Property Settlement, 49 Cal.L.Rev. 665 (1961); Note, Divorce, Separation and the Federal Income Tax: The ABC's of Alimony Child Support and Attorney's Fees, 39 U.Colo.L.Rev. 544 (1967); Bell, Tax Planning in Divorce Cases—With Emphasis on Community Property States, 1 Fam. L.Q. No. 2, 41 (1967); Note, Selected Tax Aspects of Divorce and Property Settlements, 41 Ind.L.Rev. 732 (1966); Daniels, Divorce and Separation: An Analysis of a Wide Range of Related Problems, 30 J.Tax. 254 (1969); Mills, Tax Checklist for Negotiating Divorce and Separation Agreements, 22 J.Tax. 368 (1965); Kapp, Tax Aspects of Alimony Agreements and Divorce Decrees: The Effect of Conflicting Decrees, N.Y.U. 27th Inst. on Fed.Tax. 1231 (1969); Wegher, Federal Tax Considerations in Divorce and Separation, 3 Tulsa L.J. 113 (1966); Graves, Federal Taxation in Separation and Divorce, 29 W. & L.L.Rev. 1 (1972).

For a thoughtful, critical and thorough treatment of a somewhat broader subject, see Bittker, Federal Income Taxation and the Family, 27 Stan.L. Rev. 1389 (1975).

SECTION 7. SEPARATION AGREEMENTS AND PROPERTY SETTLEMENTS

WIFE, B. T. L. v. HUSBAND, H. A. L.

Court of Chancery of Delaware, 1972.
287 A.2d 413.

SHORT, Vice Chancellor. This is an action by a wife against her former husband for the specific performance of certain provisions of a separation agreement pertaining to child support and maintenance of the parties' marital domicile. The wife brings this action individually and as guardian ad litem for the couple's two children, ages 10 and 13. The husband has counterclaimed for mitigation of the strict terms of the agreement alternatively through a decree of partial specific performance, reformation, or separate maintenance, averring that the agreement presently operates oppressively and in a manner not originally contemplated by the parties.

The parties executed the separation agreement while living apart on February 4, 1969. The controversy out of which this proceeding arises concerns the obligations incurred by the husband under paragraphs II and IX(b) of the agreement.

Paragraph II provides:

"Commencing July 1st, 1970, so long as wife has not remarried or either of said children reside in the house, husband shall pay one-half of the cost of necessary replacement, repair, and maintenance of the house, fixtures, and appliances therein, and half the monthly mortgage payments."

Paragraph IX provides:

"(b) July 1, 1970, Husband will pay to Wife for the support and maintenance of the children of the parties, whichever of the following two sums is greater:

$800.00 or 40 per cent of net income, until the youngest child reaches its 21st birthday; thereafter if Wife be not remarried—a flat 20% of net income for support and maintenance of Wife."

* * * The parties further stipulated that the husband was in arrears with respect to his share of payments for maintenance of the marital domicile, and that he had not raised his support payments to $800 monthly as specified in the agreement. * * * It thus being clear that the husband is in substantial default, consideration will be limited to the merits of the defenses raised by him.

The facts are these: The parties were married in August of 1948. Subsequently, the husband acquired a medical license and engaged in the general practice of medicine in suburban New Castle County for 10 years. On July 1, 1967, after some discussion, the husband gave up general practice for psychiatric training at a significant reduction in earnings. The parties separated on September 30 of the same year. At various times during 1968 the husband consulted an attorney for the purpose of obtaining a divorce. Initially, the husband was advised that he had no grounds to bring a divorce action. When it became apparent that due to a favorable change in the law that the husband could prevail in obtaining a divorce from the plaintiff he filed an action in January 1969. The husband testified that his motivation for a divorce at this particular time was an existing relationship with another woman. The possibility of reconciliation from the husband's point of view was extremely remote if not non-existent. The wife's attitude toward a divorce may be characterized as indifferent, her prime consideration being that she and the children be provided for in the event of divorce. In contemplation of this divorce the separation agreement was executed. Thereafter the husband was granted an uncontested divorce on the grounds of incompatibility.

The record indicates that in the drafting of the agreement the husband's assumption of the support obligations therein was premised on his anticipation that after a short transitional period his institutional earnings would equal his income from private practice. This expectation has been largely realized as the husband's current salary of $24,500 from the University of Delaware (plus the small supplementary income from his limited private practice) compares favorably with $18,608.25 net profit earned in his last full year of practice. It thus appears that the financial strain that the husband now bears under the agreement results not from a miscalculation of future available resources, but rather from the accrual of obligations which might have been provided for at the time of contracting. It is observed in this connection that a short time after the divorce decree became final the husband remarried and is now responsible for the support of his new wife and one year old child of this remarriage. In addition, the husband's financial condition has been depleted because of an adverse tax ruling denying him an anticipated deduction on the payments made for the support of the children.

The first defense raised by the husband is that the agreement is void on grounds of illegality because premised on a divorce consideration and violative of a public policy encouraging the stability of the family. Specifically, he alleges an oral understanding between the spouses whereby the husband assumed the terms of the settlement as a condition precedent to the wife's agreement not to contest the divorce. As evidentiary support for this contention, the husband notes that execution of the agreement was "on the eve" of the divorce hearing. Finally, the husband states that at the time he signed the agreement, he had an "ideation" that the wife was prepared to contest the divorce and this presumably had a coercive effect upon him. On the other hand, it appears that the husband was advised by an attorney and was aware that under the amended Delaware law the wife could not effectively defend an action brought on the grounds of incompatibility. Moreover, both the wife and her attorney deny that the divorce was the bargained for consideration for the agreement.

Generally stated, agreements between husband and wife relating to support or the adjustment of property rights will be upheld, though in contemplation of divorce, if not directly conducive to the procurement of a divorce and free of collusion. * * * The law thus manifests a preference for the private settlement of marital obligations at the time of separation. Of course, where one spouse agrees not to contest a divorce action irrespective of the availability of any defense, the contract is unenforceable. Clark, Law of Domestic Relations, Sec. 16.4; Staedler v. Staedler, 6 N.J. 380, 78 A.2d 896 (1951); Zlotziver v. Zlotziver, 355 Pa. 299, 49 A.2d 779 (1946). But the evidence here adduced is wholly insufficient to bring the case within that principle. In line with the policy favoring family settlements, even where made in contemplation of divorce, in order to render an agreement unenforceable some overt manifestation of mutual assent with respect to bargained for divorce must appear. The substance of husband's complaint is that by a combination of his wife's indifference and his own anxiety to expedite the divorce he entered into a bad bargain. Such an allegation does not contain the requisite mutual assent to constitute a bargained for divorce.

The husband places heavy reliance upon Viles v. Viles, 14 N.Y.2d 365, 251 N.Y.S.2d 672, 200 N.E.2d 567 (1965), wherein a separation agreement was held invalid as having a direct tendency to dissolve the marriage in light of a collateral oral agreement by which defendant reimbursed his wife for expenses incurred in making a general appearance in a Virgin Islands divorce proceeding. The *Viles* decision was over a strong dissent and has received unfavorable comment. 10 Villanova L.Rev. 171. The better reasoned cases hold that where the continuation of the marital status is no longer a viable alternative, public policy is not subserved by refusing to enforce the private contractual arrangements of the spouses. * * * Hill v. Hill, 23 Cal. 2d 82, 142 P.2d 417 (1943). In the instant action defendant's own persistence and determination suggest the inevitability of divorce and total marital breakup. Under these circumstances, the *Viles* rationale is not pertinent. Accordingly, in the absence of any overriding domestic considerations, collusion, or duress, there is no merit in husband's defense.

Next, husband argues that the agreement never contemplated the actual situation and enforcement would work great injury on the defendant and prejudice innocent parties. Husband's reference in this connection is obviously to the obligations assumed by his subsequent remarriage and the increased burden placed upon him by an unforeseen adverse tax ruling, rather than any mutual mistakes as to the husband's estimated future income. Though a financial strain may now confront the husband, it is well settled that an unfavorable change in economic circumstance is not a valid defense to an action for the specific performance of a separation agreement, unless so provided in the agreement. Dumel v. Dumel, 42 Del.Ch. 465, 213 A.2d 859 (1965); Kaiser v. Kaiser, 290 Minn. 173, 186 N.W.2d 678 (1971). The husband's obligations under the agreement here are not made subject to changed circumstances. If such a rule seems on first impression unduly harsh, it should be noted that neither of the changed circumstances relied upon were unforeseeable or unavoidable. Since husband's first family is no more than adequately provided for I do not see how enforcement of this agreement prejudices husband's second family; rather it merely illustrates that a given quantum of resources will go further in support of one family than two.

The husband challenges the fairness of the settlement. He argues that the agreement lacks mutuality of obligation in that the child support payments may be increased at any time as the best interests of the children dictate. The Supreme Court has held in a proceeding to modify child support obligations under a separation agreement that where the separation agreement is consistent with the best interests of the child it is controlling, and that in any event it cannot be ignored. G.W.F. v. G.P.F., 271 A.2d 38 (Del.Supr.1970). In light of this limitation on the modifiability of child support in a separation agreement the husband's contention that there exists no mutuality of obligation is without merit. Nor is there unfairness in the agreement judged by factors existing at the time of its execution. Pomerance v. Pomerance, Sup., 68 N.Y.S.2d 182 (1946). It is, of course, true that Chancery will not enforce a contract that is obviously unfair or oppressive. Gray Co. v. Alemite Corp., 20 Del.Ch. 244, 174 A. 136 (1934). Here, however, the husband committed himself (in addition to certain educational and medical expenses of the children) to payments of $800 plus the assumption of one-half the mortgage payments as to which he retains an equity. He thus retained approximately 40% of his net income for his own support, with the remainder distributed among his three dependents. While the husband's financial situation may have deteriorated it cannot be said that the settlement was unreasonable at its inception.

* * *

An order may be submitted requiring defendant to specifically perform the agreement of February 4, 1969 according to its terms.

NOTES AND QUESTIONS

1. For an extended discussion of separation agreements, see H. Clark, Law of Domestic Relations Ch. 16 (1968); and A. Lindey, Separation Agreements and Antenuptial Contracts (1967).

2. The *Viles* case, relied upon by the husband in the principal case, held that a separation agreement was invalid because made as an inducement to divorce. The evidence indicated that at the time the separation agreement was made a collateral agreement was negotiated whereby the wife was to get a divorce and the husband to pay her travel expenses to the Virgin Islands for that purpose, the husband's attorney stating that her going to the Virgin Islands for a divorce was a condition upon the execution of the agreement. In addition there was a New York statute invalidating a "contract to alter or dissolve the marriage * * *". N.Y.Gen.Oblig.L. § 5–311 (1978). The *Viles* case received very extensive comment in 31 Bklyn.L. Rev. 404 (1965); 14 Buff.L.Rev. 318 (1964); 51 Corn.L.Q. 135 (1965); 63 Mich.L.Rev. 735 (1965); 50 Va.L.Rev. 1448 (1964); 10 Vill.L.Rev. 171 (1964). It may have been overruled by an amendment to N.Y.Gen.Oblig.L. § 5–311 (1978) stating: "An agreement * * * shall not be considered a contract to alter or dissolve the marriage unless it contains an express provision requiring the dissolution of the marriage or provides for procurement of grounds for divorce." See also Note, 33 Bklyn.L.Rev. 308 (1967). For similar cases see Rifkin v. Rifkin, 155 Conn. 7, 229 A.2d 358 (1967); Culhane v. Culhane, —— N.H. ——, 402 A.2d 490 (1979).

3. How is the principal case to be read? For example, is it a holding that a separation agreement is valid even though there is a contemporaneous oral agreement or understanding that one of the parties will obtain a divorce? Does it matter that it is understood that the divorce is to be obtained at the domicile of both parties rather than in some migratory divorce state, as in *Viles*? Does it matter that incompatibility was a ground for divorce in Delaware, but was not such a ground in New York, where *Viles* was decided? Is the parol evidence rule involved in this situation? Groves v. Alexander, 255 Md. 715, 259 A.2d 285 (1969); 3 A. Corbin, Contracts § 580 (1960). Under the principal case what would be the result if the parties inserted in their written separation agreement a clause stating that "this agreement shall not become effective until or unless the party of the second part may have obtained a divorce"? Cf. Hill v. Hill, cited in

the principal case; and Stern v. Stern, 430 Pa. 605, 243 A.2d 319 (1968); Lurie v. Lurie, 246 Pa.Super. 307, 370 A.2d 739 (1976).

4. What would be the result under the principal case if the parties should insert in their written separation agreement a provision that "Within ninty days after the execution of this agreement, the wife agrees to file a complaint for divorce in the district court of _____, and to use reasonable efforts to obtain a divorce as soon thereafter as possible, and the husband agrees that he will make no defense to such a suit"? Would it matter in answering this question whether the parties lived in a state in which marriage breakdown was a ground for divorce and in which the usual divorce defenses had been abolished?

5. Does the Uniform Marriage and Divorce Act § 306(a), which provides that the parties may make a written separation agreement covering maintenance, disposition of property, and the custody, support and visitation of children, in order "to promote amicable settlement of disputes between parties to a marriage attendant upon their separation or the dissolution of their marriage", 9A Unif.L.Ann. 135 (1979), permit the sort of provision suggested in paragraph 4, supra? Is there any public purpose to be served, when divorce may be had on the breakdown of the marriage and the legislature has said it wants to promote amicable settlements, in refusing to permit the parties to agree that they will procure a divorce? Or does the list of matters which the statute provides may be included in a separation agreement impliedly exclude other matters not on the list?

6. What would be the result under the principal case if the separation agreement included the following provision? "The wife hereby agrees that she will take all necessary steps to submit to the in personam jurisdiction of any court in which the husband should bring suit for divorce. The husband hereby agrees to pay all counsel fees incurred by the wife in the course of any divorce proceedings." Hudson v. Hudson, 36 N.J. 549, 178 A.2d 202 (1962). Why would the parties wish to include such a provision?

7. In the principal case the wife was suing for specific performance. May a separation agreement be specifically enforced? Silvestri v. Slatowski, 423 Pa. 498, 224 A.2d 212 (1966); Annot., 154 A.L.R. 323 (1945).

8. Many courts have imposed as other requirements for the validity of separation agreements that there must be no fraud or duress in the negotiations leading to the agreement, that the husband (and presumably the wife also) must make a full disclosure of the extent of his property and that both parties must sign the agreement freely and with full understanding of its terms. These are requirements similar in purpose and scope to those for valid antenuptial agreements described supra, Chapter 1, section 3. See In re Estate of Ratony, 443 Pa. 454, 277 A.2d 791 (1971); De Bry v. De Bry, 27 Utah 2d 337, 496 P.2d 92 (1972). Whether the parties who are negotiating a separation agreement are deemed to be in a confidential relationship with each other is a matter on which courts no longer agree. Francois v. Francois, 599 F.2d 1286 (3d Cir. 1979) takes the position that this depends upon the circumstances in each marriage, and that a presumption of such a relationship in all marriages is not warranted. Eckstein v. Eckstein, 38 Md.App. 506, 379 A.2d 757 (1978) seems to say that the state Equal Rights Amendment eliminates any rule of confidential relationship, a view which is certainly not self-evident, though the Amendment might make

it mandatory that the wife would have the same obligations in such a relationship as the husband, and would make obsolete any presumption that the husband is the dominant figure in the marriage. Bell v. Bell, 38 Md.App. 10, 379 A.2d 419 (1977).

The earlier requirement that the parties receive independent legal advice as a condition on the validity of the separation agreement seems to be weakening. In re Marriage of Hadley, 88 Wash.2d 649, 565 P.2d 790 (1977), 53 Wash.L.Rev. 763 (1978); Whitney v. Seattle-First Nat. Bank, 90 Wash.2d 105, 579 P.2d 937 (1978).

The Uniform Marriage and Divorce Act § 306(b), (c), (d), 9A Unif.L. Ann. 135, 136 (1979) provides that the divorce court must approve the parties' separation agreement, except with respect to the provisions dealing with custody and support of children, "unless it finds, after considering the economic circumstances of the parties and any other relevant evidence * * * that the separation agreement is unconscionable." What do you suppose "unconscionability" means in this context? Does it mean what it means in the Uniform Commercial Code § 2–302, 1 Unif.L.Ann. 252 (1976)? Should the court's inquiry be directed at the relative experience, understanding and bargaining power of the parties? Or at the agreement itself and the provision it makes for the parties? Marriage of Wigner, 40 Colo.App. 253, 572 P.2d 495 (1977); Christian v. Christian, 42 N.Y.2d 63, 396 N.Y.S.2d 817, 365 N.E.2d 849 (1977). Should an agreement ·be set aside as produced by duress, or as unconscionable, where it results from heavy pressure by a trial judge to force the parties to settle their differences without a trial? In re Marriage of Hitchcock, 265 N.W.2d 599 (Iowa 1978).

9. The requirement is made by many cases that the parties must have actually separated, or at least be on the point of separating, before they may make a valid separation agreement. See Hill v. Hill, cited in the principal case; Stenson v. Stenson, 45 Ill.App.3d 249, 3 Ill.Dec. 928, 359 N.E.2d 787 (1977); H. Clark, Law of Domestic Relations § 16.1 (1968). Why should this requirement continue to be made in states which follow Posner v. Posner, supra, page 66?

10. In the Husband-Wife Agreement used in the Los Angeles Conciliation Court (reprinted in Pfaff, The Conciliation Court of Los Angeles County, p. 16 (1960)) the following provisions are proposed for the purpose of reducing marital friction and reducing the incidence of divorce:

"_____ agrees to pay to the other party $_____ per _____ out of which the latter will provide for the necessary food and clothing for the family and for the following items: _____, _____, _____, _____."

Alternative provision:

"Parties agree that the _____ shall be the treasurer of the family partnership and that all pay checks shall be properly endorsed promptly upon receipt and delivered to said party. Said party shall apply the funds from such checks in payment of the regular monthly bills and installment payments when due and provide necessary food, clothing and other necessities for the family. Any remaining balance shall be applied by said party only as agreed upon by husband and wife. Said party, as the family treasurer, shall maintain an accurate account of all receipts and payments in a permanent notebook which shall be available for inspection by the other party and by the court upon demand."

Is either of these provisions valid and enforceable? Cf. Whalen v. Whalen, 581 S.W.2d 578 (Ky.1979); Snyder v. Snyder, 196 Neb. 383, 243 N.W.2d 159 (1976); Lacks v. Lacks, 12 N.Y.2d 268, 238 N.Y.S.2d 949, 189 N.E.2d 487 (1963), 30 Bklyn.L.Rev. 133 (1963); Towles v. Towles, 256 S.C. 307, 182 S.E.2d 53 (1971). Would you advise a client having marital difficulties to execute this or a similar contract as a way of achieving marital harmony?

11. What would you say about the validity of a separation agreement which provided for payments of $100 per week in alimony, commencing with the execution of the agreement, and for payment of a lump sum of $10,000 by the husband to the wife in the event that the wife should obtain a divorce? Is such an agreement different from a promise by one party to obtain the divorce? Niman v. Niman, 15 Misc.2d 1095, 181 N.Y.S.2d 260 (Sup.Ct.1958), aff'd 8 A.D.2d 793, 188 N.Y.S.2d 948 (1st Dep't 1959).

12. Would an agreement be valid which provided that the wife should have custody of the children, but that in the event she should remarry, custody should revert to the first husband, the children's father? Holder v. Holder, 226 Ga. 254, 174 S.E.2d 408 (1970).

13. What should be the effect upon the separation agreement as a whole of the invalidity of one or more of the foregoing kinds of provision? Cf. Hummel v. Hummel, 62 Misc.2d 595, 309 N.Y.S.2d 429 (Sup.Ct.1970); Smith v. Smith, 358 Mass. 551, 265 N.E.2d 858 (1971); Trecker v. Trecker, 107 Ill.App.2d 94, 246 N.E.2d 56 (1969).

14. Should or can the law do anything, beyond the sort of vague encouragement of the Uniform Act § 306(a) referred to in paragraph 5, supra, to induce spouses to settle their financial and custody conflicts in divorce through separation agreements rather than through litigation? Can you think of changes in either the substantive rules or the procedural rules governing divorce which might have this effect? As you read the cases in this section you might bear this in mind and ask what effect, if any, the particular cases might have on the parties' willingness to negotiate rather than litigate. For an argument that the law could and should take action of this kind, see Mnookin, Kornhauser, Bargaining in the Shadow of the Law: The Case of Divorce, 88 Yale L.J. 950 (1979).

BORAX v. BORAX

Court of Appeals of New York, 1958.
4 N.Y.2d 113, 149 N.E.2d 326.

VAN VOORHIS, Judge. This appeal is from an order dismissing the complaint in a separation action on motion upon the ground that it is barred by a previous separation agreement between the parties. A valid and subsisting provision for support and maintenance in a separation agreement bars the maintenance of a separation action. * * * The complaint anticipates and endeavors to avoid this basis for dismissal, by alleging that the separation agreement was broken by defendant husband by violating the covenant against molestation of plaintiff. He has paid all of the installments for her support. It is alleged that he molested her by obtaining a Mexican divorce without jurisdiction, purporting to marry another woman whom he held out publicly as his wife, and giving his name to her child. It is also alleged that he sent to her malicious written communications.

Special Term held that no molestation of plaintiff by defendant was alleged in the complaint or established by affidavits. The Appellate Division affirmed upon the ground that regardless of whether this husband molested his wife, a promise not to molest is an independent covenant in a separation agreement under the English case of Fearon v. Aylesford (14 Q.B.D. 792). In our view that determination was correct.

The usual form taken by molestation between separated spouses consists in an endeavor to compel the restoration of conjugal rights. The law favors resumption of marital relations even if the parties to the marriage are living in a state of separation, and clauses in separation agreements and decrees which provide for living separate and apart in the future are of doubtful validity. * * * The tendency to treat promises to live separately as independent covenants has arisen from the circumstance that otherwise their invalidity might impair the maintenance provisions in separation agreements. Insofar as a covenant against molestation merely purports to prohibit importunities to resume the marital relationship, such a covenant may well be void, in which event it would have to be construed as an independent covenant unless it were to vitiate the entire separation agreement. Even assuming molestation to be a broader term covering other behavior between separated spouses, consistency requires that a covenant against all kinds of molestation should be treated as independent. Even where valid, covenants against molestation are similar historically to covenants to live separate and apart, and resemble them in structure and design in separation agreements. Lindey on Separation Agreements and Ante-Nuptial Contracts recognizes that covenants against molestation other than to compel restitution of conjugal rights may be valid, but treats such covenants as independent (Rev. ed., 1953, pp. 108–109). * * *

Inasmuch as it is the continuance in effect of support and maintenance provisions in separation agreements that precludes the maintenance of separation actions, it would be impossible to distinguish between the dependence or independence of covenants of molestation according to whether the action is brought by the husband or by the wife. In either event the issue of the contract as a bar would turn upon the existence in force of the covenant to support and maintain as the decisive factor. It is wiser in neither instance to hold that separation agreements are terminated under the name of molestation, by the acrimonious interchanges which are so often an aftermath of matrimonial disputes.   If we were to assume freely that conduct of this kind constitutes molestation, which is not decided, it would frequently be unjust to allow a husband to escape payment of promised support for the reason that the wife has at some time engaged in bitter invectives or humiliating behavior.   The same rule holds good for both sides.   These agreements survive divorce for adultery   *   *   *, and it seems wiser to follow the rule treating molestation as an independent covenant rather than to have it constantly brought into court as a litigious basis for ending these agreements, the chief merit and object of which is to bring some stability and continuity into what is at best a troublesome relationship.

Covenants of this kind are different from those providing for visitation rights for children which are held to be dependent   *   *   *. There installments of money are to be paid, at least in part, for the support of the persons whom the defendant has a right to see and visit under the terms of a separation agreement.   The father's right to see his children is tied into his covenant to provide agreed sums of money for their support.   Neither are visitation rights subject to the factors which have led to the independent status of covenants of separation and nonmolestation.

The judgment of the Appellate Division is affirmed, without costs.

*   *   *

NOTES AND QUESTIONS

1.   The *Borax* case is noted in 25 Bklyn.L.Rev. 130 (1958).   Other cases are collected in Annot., 160 A.L.R. 471 (1946).

2.   What do you suppose the court meant by the statement that agreements to live separate and apart in the future are of "doubtful validity"? Does that mean that all separation agreements which so provide are suspect, since most of them recite that the parties have agreed to separate?   The form books recommend the inclusion of an agreement to live apart.   1 A. Lindey, Separation Agreements and Antenuptial Contracts, pp. 8-1 ff. (1967).   Does this case throw doubt on the validity of such agreements?

3.   What reason is there for treating the non-molestation clause and the agreements concerning support as independent?   What is the usual rule with respect to clauses in contracts?   Are they considered dependent or independent in the absence of an express intention?   3A A. Corbin, Contracts § 656 (1960).

4.   H and W, being unhappily married, decide to separate.   They sign an agreement by which H agrees to pay $100 per week to W for her support.   There is also a covenant in the agreement by which each promises to live apart and not to molest the other.   H makes the payments as promised. W, however, takes to harassing him by calling him on the telephone, calling his employer and making such a nuisance of herself that she finally causes H to lose his job.   He stops the support payments and W sues him for violation of the agreement.   Under the *Borax* case has H any defense on the ground of W's violation of the non-molestation clause?

5. If H has no defense, has he any other remedy? Aspinwall v. Aspinwall, 49 N.J.Eq. 302, 24 A. 926 (Ch. 1892); Snedaker v. King, 111 Ohio St. 225, 145 N.E. 15 (1924). If no other remedy exists, what point is there in including the non-molestation clause in a separation agreement? 1 A. Lindey, Separation Agreements and Antenuptial Contracts, p. 9–6 (1967).

6. Would the husband be entitled to terminate support payments under the contract upon the wife's violation of the non-molestation clause if the separation agreement expressly provided that the two covenants were dependent? Shedler v. Shedler, 32 Misc.2d 290, 223 N.Y.S.2d 363 (1961), aff'd 15 A.D.2d 810, 225 N.Y.S.2d 495 (2d Dep't 1962), aff'd 12 N.Y.2d 828, 187 N.E.2d 361, 236 N.Y.S.2d 348 (1963), 13 Buff.L.Rev. 223 (1963).

7. What should be the result if the separation agreement provided for custody of the parties' child to the wife, with the husband to have the right of visitation, and for support payments by the husband to the wife in the amount of $100 per week, and the wife deliberately prevented the husband from exercising the rights of visitation? Would that excuse him from making the payments? Hammond v. Hammond, 76 U.S.App.D.C. 357, 131 F.2d 351 (1942), cert. den. 318 U.S. 770 (1943); Annot., 105 A.L. R. 901 (1936).

8. Would the wife's adultery, committed after the separation, entitle the husband to discontinue support payments to her under the agreement? Wilson v. Atwood, 63 App.D.C. 80, 69 F.2d 398 (1934), 19 Minn.L.Rev. 218 (1935).

9. Suppose the separation agreement provided that the wife was to have custody of the children and the husband would pay $2,500 per month for her support and the support of the children. Some months after the separation the husband took over custody of the children. The wife then brought habeas corpus to regain custody and lost, the court finding that the children's interests would best be served by leaving them with the husband. The husband then stopped paying the support money and the wife sued on the agreement. The husband's defense was that he was furnishing support to the children in kind and that he should not have to furnish it in cash also. What result? Nichols v. Nichols, 306 N.Y. 490, 119 N.E.2d 351 (1954); Coffman v. Hayes, 259 Md. 708, 270 A.2d 808 (1970).

FENCE v. FENCE

Family Court, City of New York, New York County, 1970.
64 Misc.2d 480, 314 N.Y.S.2d 1016.

Justine Wise POLIER, Judge. The petitioner filed a petition for support for herself and three children in which she alleged a separation agreement had been entered into on July 21, 1965 providing for $15 a week for her support and $60 a week for the three children. She further alleged that the respondent had refused and neglected to provide reasonable support according to his means since November 1969. After an adjournment for possible settlement outside court, during which time respondent undertook to pay the petitioner $300 monthly, the case came on for hearing on October 8, 1970.

At the hearing, counsel for the respondent offered in evidence (Resp.Exh.A), a separation agreement which provided that:

"Any controversy or claim arising out of or relating to this contract, or the breach thereof, shall be settled by arbitration in accordance with the Rules of the American Arbitration Association, and judgment upon the award rendered by the arbitrators may be entered in any court having jurisdiction thereof." (Par. 16)

On the basis of this provision, counsel for respondent moved that this Court should refer all questions including questions of support and custody to the American Arbitration Association. Counsel for the petitioner opposed the motion on the ground that the children were not bound by the agreement for arbitration and that the questions of support and custody were properly before the Family Court. Counsel further moved to amend the petition to seek enforcement of the separation agreement and for an upward modification based on alleged change in circumstances. Petition was so amended.

The separation agreement, dated July 21, 1965, provides that the wife shall have custody and control of the children subject to visitation rights of the father. It provides that the wife may elect to live in Europe and that her residence whether temporary or permanent shall not affect her custody. It further provides that during such periods as the wife may reside in Europe, she may leave one or more children with her mother and that this also will not affect custody. The intention of the wife to reside in Europe for an indefinite period commencing in September or October 1965 was included in the separation agreement (Par. 6). Counsel agree that petitioner has been residing abroad for some time with the youngest child, now seven years of age, and that the two older children have been living for a considerable time with the respondent and not with either the mother or maternal grandmother, as comtemplated in the separation agreement. There is now a contest both as to where the two older children, 13 and 10 years of age, should reside and what support the respondent shall pay to the petitioner. Clearly, a decision on support will depend in part on whether the father has or has not custody of the two older children.

Motion of counsel for the father that all questions raised in the present dispute be referred to the American Arbitration Association raises several questions.

First: Has this Court the power to issue a stay or refer the disputes between the parties to the American Arbitration Association? The answer is in the negative without prejudice to the right of respondent to move in the appropriate court to secure a stay against further proceedings in this Court. The existence of an arbitration clause in a separation agreement does not constitute ground for dismissal in an action for support of a child. It is rather the basis for a motion, in the proper court, to compel arbitration. Matter of Banks

v. Banks, 54 Misc.2d 186, 282 N.Y.S.2d 298 (1967) citing, Sperling v. Sperling, 26 A.D.2d 827, 274 N.Y.S.2d 107 (1966).

Second: Is a provision in a separation agreement for arbitration of questions of support for a wife or children enforceable in this State? The law is settled in this State that such a provision is enforceable. Schneider v. Schneider, 17 N.Y.2d 123, 269 N.Y.S.2d 107, 216 N.E.2d 218 (1966); See Sheets v. Sheets, 22 A.D.2d 176, 254 N. Y.S.2d 320 (1964); Matter of Lasek, 13 A.D.2d 242, 215 N.Y.S.2d 983 (1961). The courts have, however, required that when such a provision is part of a separation agreement, an application for a stay pending arbitration will be granted only on condition that the party seeking such a stay initiates the arbitration within a stated time. See, Schneider, supra; See also, Matter of Adams v. Rhoades, 56 Misc.2d 249, 288 N.Y.S.2d 710 (1968).

Third: Does a comprehensive provision in a separation agreement that all matters arising out of or relating to the agreement shall be referred for arbitration oust the courts of jurisdiction to consider questions of custody and visitation. The answer is in the negative. In Sheets v. Sheets, supra, the Appellate Division (First Department) affirmed an order staying arbitration on questions of visitation, secular and religious education of children, and the alleged alienation of affection of children. In doing so the court held that the demands of the appellant husband for arbitration of these issues did not fall within the provisions for arbitration of the separation agreement. The appellate court reiterated that it was settled law in New York that provisions for arbitration of disputes regarding the amount of support included in separation agreements were enforceable. The court also noted that the courts in New York have held disputes between parents as to rights of custody and visitation are to be determined by the courts and are not a proper subject for arbitration. The court cited Matter of Michelson, 5 Misc.2d 570, 135 N.Y.S.2d 608 (1954) and Matter of Hill, 199 Misc. 1035, 104 N.Y.S.2d 755 (1951). After noting these decisions, the opinion engaged in a general discussion of the need for clarification and restatement of the proper position to be taken by courts as to arbitration provisions in separation agreements which affect matters of custody and visitation. With many *caveats* in regard to the best interests of a child and the right of judicial review of arbitration decisions, the court states "submissions of disputes in custody and visitation matters to voluntary arbitration need no longer receive general interdiction * * *" (22 A.D.2d at p. 179, 254 N.Y.S.2d at p. 325). This part of the opinion, as noted above, went beyond the holding in the case.

In a more recent case, Agur v. Agur, 32 A.D.2d 16, 298 N.Y.S.2d 772 (1969) (Second Department), the Appellate Division reviewed the cases in this field, modified an order of Special Term and directed a prompt hearing at Special Term on the issues of custody, counsel

fee and support.   In effect, this decision reversed Special Term which had granted a stay and had directed arbitration as provided in a separation agreement.   The appellate court found that the arbitration clause in the separation agreement encompassed the custody dispute but held that in such matters the State acts as *parens patriae* and quoted the famous passage from Judge Cardozo's opinion in Finlay v. Finlay, 240 N.Y. 429, 433–434, 148 N.E. 624, 626: The court "is not adjudicating a controversy between adversary parties   *   *   *"
The appellate court then continued in *Agur,* supra:

"He (the Court) acts as *parens patriae* to do what is best for the interest of the child   *   *   *

"Thus it is that agreements by parents as to custody of their children are never final but subject always to the supervening power of the court (People ex rel. Rowe v. Rowe, 11 A.D.2d 759, 202 N.Y.S. 2d 371;   Bleck v. Bleck, 1 A.D.2d 839, 148 N.Y.S.2d 786;   Van Dyke v. Van Dyke, 278 App.Div. 446, 106 N.Y.S.2d 237)   *   *   *

"An agreement to arbitrate custody is not distinguishable from an agreement to give custody.   The process of arbitration is useful when the mundane matter of the amount of support is the issue (cases cited).   It is less so when the delicate balancing of the factors composing the best interests of a child is the matter at hand   *   *   *" (32 A.D.2d pp. 19–20, 298 N.Y.S.2d p. 777).

The appellate court thus squarely held that although the separation agreement included a provision that any issue of custody should be referred to arbitration, such provision would not be enforced and that the court continued to have the duty, despite such provision, to hear and determine what was in the best interest of the child.   The court stated:

"Nor can the arbitrators' award, once made in accord with formal requirements, be reviewed except under the narrowly limited grounds of the statute (CPLR 7511, subd. [b]).   The court may not vacate the award because of a mistake of fact (cases cited) or a 'perverse misconstruction' of law" (cases cited) (32 A.D.2d p. 20, 298 N. Y.S.2d p. 777).

The limited judicial review allowed following an arbitration award involving the custody of a child was thus not seen as satisfying the obligations of the State as *parens patriae* to determine and safeguard the best interests of a child.   In *Agur,* supra, the court further expressed grave doubts about what it described as the two-stage procedure discussed in *Sheets,* supra, under which the issue of child custody could first be determined by arbitration and subsequently be reviewed by a court which would then have the power to nullify the determination if it were found contrary to the child's best interests.

In the *Agur* case, supra, the court also took the position that arbitration stressed the settlement of a private dispute between the two contesting parties, whereas the judicial process was more broadly shaped and could decide that in the best interests of a child, neither parent should have custody. In reaching its decision in this case, the court also found that the restrictions in the clause limiting the area of decision to religious law and the choice of arbitrators to those versed in religious law, the duress alleged by the wife in regard to her signing of the separation agreement, and the factors involving the welfare of the child satisfied the court that "this case does not present cause for the use of the arbitration process." (32 A.D.2d p. 21, 298 N.Y.S.2d p. 778).

In the case now before this Court, the petitioner seeks enforcement of the separation agreement under the Family Court Act (Secs. 421 and 422) and modification of such agreement for the support of the children on the ground of change in circumstance under the Family Court Act (Sec. 461). Absent the provision for arbitration of any disputes between the wife and the husband arising out of the separation agreement, there is no question of petitioner's right to an adjudicatory hearing and determination on her petition. Incidental to and flowing from the hearings in such a case, this Court would have the power and duty to determine whether a change in custody or visitation as provided in the separation agreement was required in the best interest of the three children.

The existence of the arbitration clause does not constitute a ground for dismissal of the action for support. It certainly cannot remove the authority of this Court to proceed to hear and determine the petition seeking enforcement of support through the court and modification of the support agreement so far as the children are concerned in the absence of an order staying the proceedings by the appropriate court. It is highly questionable whether if the question of support was referred for arbitration, the arbitrators would have the power to consider the petition for modification as authorized by the Family Court Act under section 461. To have the dispute on enforcement of support heard by arbitrators and the petition for modification heard by this Court would only result in waste of time and funds, since such fragmentation would necessitate submission of the same relevant financial evidence.

In the light of the New York decisions concerning the effect of agreements to arbitrate disputes concerning custody and visitation, there is grave doubt that the provision in this case is enforceable so far as custody and visitation are concerned. In addition, in the instant case, the custody of the children, their welfare, and their support are so inextricably interrelated that the need for a judicial process to determine all issues seems clearly indicated under the doctrine of *parens patriae.*

The motion of counsel to refer all questions to the American Arbitration Association is denied. The temporary order of $300 monthly entered by consent without prejudice to either side is continued. The case is adjourned to November 24, 1970 for hearing on all issues.

NOTES AND QUESTIONS

1. For a discussion of the use of arbitration provisions in separation agreements see Holman and Noland, Agreement and Arbitration: Relief to Overlitigation in Domestic Relations Disputes in Washington, 12 Willamette L.J. 527 (1976); Spencer & Zammit, Mediation-Arbitration: A Proposal for Private Resolution of Disputes Between Divorced or Separated Parents, 1976 Duke L.J. 911; 1 A. Lindey, Separation Agreements and Antenuptial Contracts § 29 (1967). General works on arbitration include M. Domke, The Law and Practice of Commercial Arbitration § 13.09 (1968); S. Eager, The Arbitration Contract and Proceedings § 34 (1971).

The Uniform Arbitration Act, 7 Unif.L.Ann. 4 (1978) is in force in almost half the states and provides a procedure for arbitration and for the enforcement of arbitration awards. It does not, however, contain provisions dealing specifically with arbitration of domestic relations cases.

2. N.Y.Civ.Prac.L. & R. § 7511(b) (1963), referred to in the *Fence* opinion, limits judicial review of arbitration awards to such matters as fraud, partiality of the arbitrator and certain procedural claims. This would not include contentions that the arbitrator was mistaken as to the law or facts of the dispute.

3. Did the court in *Fence* hold that in no event may questions relating to the support and custody of children be referred to arbitration by a separation agreement? Or did the court hold only that in the circumstances of this case the arbitration provision would not be enforced? If so, what circumstances led to this conclusion?

4. Why should the courts take the position that matters of custody may not be referred to arbitration? Are the advantages of speed, informality and reduced expense which are often attributed to arbitration proceedings not of importance in custody cases? The N.Y.Civ.Prac.L. & R. § 7501 (1963), provides, "A written agreement to submit any controversy thereafter arising or any existing controversy to arbitration is enforceable without regard to the justiciable character of the controversy and confers jurisdiction on the courts of the state to enforce it and to enter judgment on an award." Does this literally cover an agreement to arbitrate custody disputes?

5. Suppose that H and W sign a separation agreement which provides that W is to have custody of their child, and that all questions arising under the agreement shall be submitted to arbitration. H later finds that W is living with another man, becomes enraged, removes the child from W's custody and refuses to return him. W and H refer their dispute to arbitration and the arbitrator awards custody to H on the ground that W is immoral. W then files a petition for habeas corpus seeking custody of the child, and proves that in all ways she is an excellent mother, with great affection for the child, and that the child is much upset by being taken from her. If H should defend against the petition on the ground of the arbitration award, should his defense prevail? Or should the court take ev-

idence and enter a decree in accordance with its own ideas of what the child's interests require?

6. Suppose in the case described in the preceding paragraph H had agreed in the separation agreement to pay to W $50 per month as child support, and stopped the payments when W began living with the other man and when he (H) removed the child from W's custody. If the court were not bound by an arbitration award as to custody, should it be bound by such an award concerning child support? If W should be able to prove that she needed more than $50 per month for the child's needs, and if H were able to pay it, could she obtain it from an arbitrator? Could a court give it to her notwithstanding the arbitration provision in the contract? Cf. Schneider v. Schneider, 17 N.Y.2d 123, 216 N.E.2d 318, 269 N.Y.S.2d 107 (1966).

7. Should the arbitration procedure be held especially useful in custody disputes, rather than unenforceable? For example, would it be useful for the child's parents, at the time of the divorce, to appoint a committee to decide disputes about custody, the committee to consist of a pediatrician, a child psychiatrist or child analyst, an educator or an impartial lawyer or clergyman? Cf. Kubie, Provisions For the Care of Children of Divorced Parents: A New Legal Instrument, 73 Yale L.J. 1197 (1964), and Note, Committee Decision of Child Custody Disputes and the Judicial Test of "Best Interests", 73 Yale L.J. 1201 (1964).

8. Other non-judicial methods of dealing with domestic relations disputes are conciliation and mediation. Conciliation is generally understood to involve an attempt, through conferences in which the spouses participate with an impartial conciliator, to resolve their differences and preserve the marriage. For at least twenty years now there have been attempts to set up conciliation services within the structure of family courts or divorce courts. Bodenheimer, The Utah Marriage Counseling Experiment: An Account of Changes in Divorce Law and Procedure, 7 Utah L.Rev. 443 (1961) describes one such attempt. At one time the New York divorce statutes imposed a "mandatory" counselling or conciliation requirement. McLaughlin, Court-Connected Marriage Counselling and Divorce—The New York Experience, 11 J.Fam.L. 517 (1972). The most widely publicized of these programs is the Conciliation Court of Los Angeles County, California. An extensive study of this Court concluded that it had little effect in reducing the divorce rate. Maddi, The Effect of Conciliation Court Proceedings on Petitions for Dissolution of Marriage, 13 J.Fam.L. 495 (1973). This does not mean that such programs have no value, since they may be helpful in enabling spouses to adjust to the distress and anxieties of divorce.

Mediation generally refers to an informal process by which the mediator, an impartial person who may or may not be a professional, helps the parties reach agreement on the problems created by their desire for a divorce. The mediator does not arbitrate disputes but rather tries to help the parties resolve them so that attorneys for the parties may later embody the resolution in a separation agreement. The American Arbitration Association can refer divorcing spouses to marital mediators who will function in this way. The bar associations in some states have also set up mediation programs in the hope of making divorce less expensive and reducing court time. For a brief description of the American Arbitration Association's programs, see 2 Fam.L.Rep. 3083 (1976).

9. If a separation agreement contains a provision by which the husband agrees to pay $100 per month for child support, may the child enforce that provision? Is the child a third party beneficiary of the contract? If so, is he a donee or a creditor beneficiary? May the child prevent a later modification or rescission of the separation agreement by his parents? Forman v. Forman, 17 N.Y.2d 274, 217 N.E.2d 645, 270 N.Y.S.2d 586 (1966); Schneider v. Schneider, 17 N.Y.2d 123, 216 N.E.2d 318, 269 N.Y.S. 2d 107 (1966); Quinn v. Thigpen, 266 N.C. 720, 147 S.E.2d 191 (1966); Smith v. Smith, 7 Ohio App.2d 4, 218 N.E.2d 473 (1964); Price v. Price, 197 S.W.2d 200 (Tex.Civ.App.1946); 4 A. Corbin, Contracts § 782 (1951); Note, 33 Bklyn.L.Rev. 290 (1967).

10. May the separation agreement include provisions which the courts would not be authorized to order as part of a decree for maintenance or for division of property? For example, may the parties provide that the husband shall keep in force a policy of life insurance with the wife or children as beneficiaries, in a state which does not permit such a provision to be ordered by the courts? Or could the husband agree to pay all of a child's college expenses, in a state which would not order him to make such payments beyond the child's age 21? If such a provision is included, will the courts enforce it? Cf. Genda v. Superior Court, 103 Ariz. 240, 439 P.2d 811 (1968); Robrock v. Robrock, 167 Ohio St. 479, 150 N.E.2d 421, 5 O.O. 2d 165 (1958); Nokes v. Nokes, 47 Ohio St.2d 1, 351 N.E.2d 172 (1976); Bugay v. Bugay, 53 Ohio App.2d 285, 373 N.E.2d 1263 (1977); Blackburn v. Blackburn, 526 S.W.2d 463 (Tenn.1975).

11. What should be the consequence for the effectiveness of a separation agreement of the parties' reconciliation? For example, suppose that the agreement provides that H will pay to W the lump sum of $60,500 in monthly installments of $500 over the next 121 months. W agrees to accept these payments in full satisfaction of all her claims to maintenance or a share of H's property, and to waive all rights of inheritance from H. Three months after the agreement is signed, they become reconciled and resume living together. Six months after that the reconciliation fails and they again separate. During the period of reconciliation H makes no payments. After their second separation W sues H for the payments called for in the agreement. What result? What should be the result if they were reconciled, lived together as husband and wife for fifteen years, at the end of which H died, and H's collateral relatives, relying upon the separation agreement, asserted claims to his estate to the exclusion of W? Cf. Simpson v. Weatherman, 216 Ark. 684, 227 S.W.2d 148 (1950); Larson v. Goodman, 28 Colo.App. 418, 475 P.2d 712 (1970); Travis v. Travis, 227 Ga. 406, 181 S.E.2d 61 (1971); Frana v. Frana, 12 Md.App. 273, 278 A.2d 94 (1971); In re Estate of Whiteford, 35 A.D.2d 751, 314 N.Y.S.2d 811 (3rd Dep't 1970); Peterson v. Peterson, 583 S.W.2d 707 (Ky.App.1979); Murphy v. Murphy, 295 N.C. 390, 245 S.E.2d 693 (1978); Matter of Estate of Adamee, 291 N.C. 386, 230 S.E.2d 541 (1976). Should the separation agreement contain a provision prescribing the effect of a reconciliation? If so, what should it say?

LEVITT v. LEVITT

Supreme Court of California In Bank, 1965.
62 Cal.2d 477, 42 Cal.Rptr. 577, 399 P.2d 33.

[This case is reproduced supra at page 911. The portions of it relating to the modification of alimony decrees incorporating separation agreements should be reread at this point.]

NOTES AND QUESTIONS

1. The California Civil Code has been amended since the *Levitt* decision so as to read as follows:

West's Ann.Cal.Civ.Code § 4811 (Supp.1979):

§ 4811. Property settlement agreements; severability of support provisions; power of court to modify or revoke

(a) The provisions of any agreement between the parties for child support shall be deemed to be separate and severable from all other provisions of such agreement relating to property and support of the wife or husband. All orders for child support shall be law-imposed and shall be made under the power of the court to make such orders. All such orders for child support, even when there has been an agreement between the parties on the subject of child support, may be modified or revoked at any time at the discretion of the court, except as to any amount that may have accrued prior to the date of filing of the notice of motion or order to show cause to modify or revoke.

(b) The provisions of any agreement for the support of either party shall be deemed to be separate and severable from the provisions of the agreement relating to property. All orders for the support of either party based on such agreement shall be deemed law-imposed and shall be deemed made under the power of the court to make such orders. The provisions of any agreement or order for the support of either party shall be subject to subsequent modification or revocation by court order, except as to any amount that may have accrued prior to the date of filing of the notice of motion or order to show cause to modify or revoke and except to the extent that any written agreement, or, if there is no written agreement, any oral agreement entered into in open court between the parties, specifically provides to the contrary.

(c) This section shall be effective only with respect to property settlement agreements entered into on or after * * * January 1, 1970, and shall not be deemed to affect agreements entered into prior thereto, as to which the provisions of Chapter 1308 of the Statutes of 1967 shall apply. (Amended by Stats.1970, c. 1545, p. 3140, § 4.)

The amendment would not change the result in the *Levitt* case, but it does broaden the class of cases in which divorce decrees based upon separation agreements may be modified.

2. The question raised in the *Levitt* case is a deceptively simple one: May a divorce decree which incorporates provisions as to property, maintenance of the wife, and custody, support and visitation of the children

agreed upon by the parties in their separation agreement, be modified subsequently upon proof of changed circumstances? The responses which some courts have made are anything but simple, in large part due to their failure to define the question and state their conclusions with any precision. Most courts do understand, however, that the crucial factor is which section of the decree the party is seeking to modify.

Of course the California statute just quoted provides an answer to this question. The Uniform Marriage and Divorce Act § 306(f) provides a somewhat different answer, as follows:

> "(f) Except for terms concerning the support, custody, or visitation of children, the decree may expressly preclude or limit modification of terms set forth in the decree if the separation agreement so provides. Otherwise, terms of a separation agreement set forth in the decree are automatically modified by modification of the decree."

Thus to some extent both California's statute and the Uniform Act allow the parties to limit or forbid modification of maintenance. The Uniform Act, in § 316, forbids modification of the provisions of a decree concerning the disposition of property. But § 306(f) seems to mean that if the parties wish the property division to be modifiable, and they so provide in their agreement and the agreement is set forth in the decree, then it may be modifiable.

In the absence of statute, certain aspects of the question seem clear:

(a) If the divorce decree would not be modifiable regardless of the presence or absence of a prior separation agreement, on the ground, for example, that the part sought to be modified concerned the division of property rather than the support of the spouse, then it is not modifiable when it is based upon or incorporates a separation agreement. The non-modifiable nature of property divisions has been discussed, supra, at page 917. Certainly the non-modifiability of property divisions, if that is the local rule cannot be affected by the fact that the proportion of the division is agreed upon by the parties, unless of course the agreement expressly states that the division may be modified in some way and the decree reserves jurisdiction to make such a modification. A case which seems to confuse the non-modifiability of property divisions with a much broader rule that decrees incorporating agreements may not be modified is Irwin v. Irwin, 150 Colo. 261, 372 P.2d 440 (1962). A case which recognizes the issue and deals with it correctly is Salomon v. Salomon, 196 So.2d 111 (Fla.1967).

(b) In the converse case, where a party is seeking to modify the decree's provisions for child custody, visitation or support, and those provisions have incorporated similar arrangements from the parties' separation agreement, modification may always be granted upon proof of a change in the relevant circumstances notwithstanding the contractual origin of the disposition. There are two reasons for this. First, the children are not parties to the agreement and their rights may not be foreclosed by an agreement to which they are not parties. Second, and more important, the state exercises a supervisory function over the welfare of children which is not controlled by the wishes of the parents, although of course the wishes of the parents, whether or not expressed in a separation agreement, are taken into account by the courts and often influence the outcome. In fact even if the separation agreement is not incorporated in the divorce decree it will not be permitted to control the custody and support of the children where the court finds that some other disposition will better serve the children's interests. Many cases have therefore held that custody and support provisions of divorce decrees are modifiable even though they originate in an agreement of the parents. E. g., Curley v. Curley, 588 P.2d 289 (Alaska 1979); Forrester v. Buerger, 241 Ga. 34, 244 S.E.2d 345 (1978) (child's right to increase payments may not be bargained away by the parents, but father may by agreement waive his right to reduce the payments); Knox v. Remick, 371 Mass. 433, 358 N.E.2d 432 (1976); Boden v. Boden, 42 N.Y.2d 210, 397 N.Y.S.2d 701, 366 N.E.2d 791 (1977), 27 Buff.L.Rev. 411 (1978) (child support provisions in the agreement should not be disturbed except upon proof of "an unanticipated and unreasonable change in circumstances"); Morris v. Morris, 216 Va. 457, 219 S.E.2d 864 (1975); Annot., 61 A.L.R.3d 657 (1975).

The more difficult question is whether provisions for the maintenance of a spouse, originating in a separation agreement and then incorporated in the divorce decree, may be modified upon the same basis as if they had merely been ordered by the court without an agreement of the parties. A majority of courts have held that such provisions may be so modified, their reasoning being that when incorporated in the divorce decree, the agreement is "merged", thereby losing its independent force as a contract. The rights and obligations of the parties, according to these cases, are then governed solely by the divorce decree. This logically implies that the alimony provisions are modifiable, as they would be if arrived at as a result of litigation rather than agreement. This result has the virtue not only of logic but also of encouraging the parties to negotiate their financial affairs rather than litigating them, with the awareness that once arrived at, the decision will have the same effect as if litigated. Cases adopting this view include Binder v. Binder, —— Mass.App. ——, 390 N.E.2d 260 (1979); Smith v. Smith, 72 N.J. 350, 371 A.2d 1 (1977); Wolfe v. Wolfe, 46 Ohio St.2d 399, 350 N.E.2d 413, 75 O.O.2d 474, (1976), 37 Ohio St.L.J. 382 (1976); Garnett v. Garnett, 270 Or. 102, 526 P.2d 549 (1974); Corbin v. Corbin, —— W.Va. ——, 206 S.E.2d 898 (1974). Other cases are collected in H. Clark, Law of Domestic Relations 558 (1968), and Annot., 61 A.L.R.3d 520 (1975). Florida has a statute which even permits the modification of alimony provisions in separation agreements when the agreement has not been incorporated in the decree, the statute being held constitutional in Frizzell v. Bartley, 372 So.2d 1371 (Fla.1979).

A minority of courts have held that alimony decrees based upon separation agreements are not modifiable, on the ground that modification would in some way impair the obligation of contracts. See Lay v. Lay, 162 Colo. 43, 425 P.2d 704 (1967); Law v. Law, 248 Ark. 894, 455 S.W.2d 854 (1970), 24 Ark.L.Rev. 557 (1971) (distinguishing between decrees based upon "stipulations" which are modifiable, and decrees based upon "independent agreements" which are not); Rice v. Rice, 219 Kan. 569, 549 P.2d 555 (1976); Stuart v. Stuart, 555 P.2d 611 (Okla.1976); Knodel v. Knodel, 14 Cal.3d 752, 122 Cal.Rptr. 521, 537 P.2d 353 (1975) (Virginia law); Annot., 61 A.L.R.3d 520, 559 (1975). The New York courts seem to have adopted the rule that when a separation agreement is incorporated in a divorce decree, the alimony provision of the decree may be modified, but the alimony provision in the agreement may not be modified. This has the distinction of achieving the worst results of all possible rules. For a citation of the New York cases see 2 H. Foster and D. Freed, Law and The Family New York § 28:64 (1966 and Supp.1979).

Still another qualification has to be mentioned. Where the separation agreement does not become a part of the decree, it continues in existence as a contract, and like other contracts, it is not modifiable with respect to its alimony provisions unless it expressly allows for modification or, as in Florida, unless a statute specifically authorizes modification. It follows that the question whether the agreement has become a part of the decree, has "merged" in the decree, is a crucial one in deciding whether modification is permissible. Here again the language of many courts is unclear. Ordinarily a verbatim incorporation of the agreement in the decree would be enough to "merge" the agreement. But there are cases in which the agreement is said to have been incorporated but not merged. McMains v. McMains, 15 N.Y.2d 283, 206 N.E.2d 185, 258 N.Y.S.2d 93 (1965). On the other hand, there are cases holding that the agreement is "merged" in the decree when it is merely incorporated by reference. Flynn v. Flynn, 42 Cal.2d 55, 265 P.2d 865 (1954), 42 Cal.L.Rev. 524 (1954), per Traynor, J., contains the best judicial exposition of what is meant by "merger" and how it occurs. The *McMains* case, supra, injects a further uncertainty into the problem by holding that even if the agreement is not merged, the alimony provided for by the agreement may be increased if the wife is unable to support herself on the amount provided and is in danger of becoming a public charge.

A line of California cases which has had some following in other states formerly held that where a separation agreement was an "integrated property settlement", that is, contained provisions for both a property division and alimony, in which the alimony was an integral and inseverable part of the division of property, the alimony provision could not be modified. This seems to mean that when the alimony and property are reciprocal consideration for each other, the agreement and derived decree take on the character of a property division and modification is foreclosed. See Fox v. Fox, 42 Cal.2d 49, 265 P.2d 881 (1954); Dexter v. Dexter, 42 Cal.2d 36, 265 P.2d 873 (1954); Flynn v. Flynn, 42 Cal.2d 55, 265 P.2d 865 (1954); Lincoln v. Lincoln, 24 Ariz.App. 447, 539 P.2d 921 (1975); White v. White, 296 N.C. 661, 252 S.E.2d 698 (1979); Annot., 61 A.L.R.3d 520, 589 (1975). The California cases have been overruled by the statute quoted supra, in paragraph 1.

BRADLEY v. SUPERIOR COURT OF THE STATE OF CALIFORNIA, IN AND FOR THE CITY AND COUNTY OF SAN FRANCISCO

Supreme Court of California, In Bank, 1957.
48 Cal.2d 509, 310 P.2d 634.

SCHAUER, Justice. A writ of certiorari was issued for the purpose of reviewing an order of the superior court adjudging petitioner to be in contempt for refusing to make certain payments to his former wife in accordance with the provisions of their property settlement agreement and decree of divorce, and directing that petitioner be imprisoned if he fails to comply with the court's order of payment. We have concluded that although upon the record before us certain of petitioner's contentions concerning interpretation of the provisions of the property settlement agreement cannot be upheld, the order directing his imprisonment for contempt upon his continued failure to make payment should nevertheless be annulled as in violation of the constitutional prohibition against imprisonment for debt. (Cal. Const., art. I, § 15.)

In May, 1946, petitioner and his then wife, Frances, entered into a property settlement agreement in which it is declared that the parties owned both community and separate property, and that they desired to agree to a separation and to settle and determine their respective property rights and to provide for the care and custody of their two minor children. The agreement further declares that it "is intended as a Property Settlement Agreement and to *refer only to property rights.* * * * " (Italics added.) The wife then instituted divorce proceedings in the state of Nevada and in June, 1946, was awarded a default divorce decree. Such decree by its terms purports to order, among other things, that the written property settlement agreement between the parties dated May 14, 1946, is "hereby approved, ratified, confirmed and adopted by the Court, and by reference made a part of this judgment and decree * * * and each of the parties is hereby ordered to carry out * * * each and all of the provisions by him or her respectively required under the terms of said agreement * * * ".

In September, 1952, the Nevada decree was established in California as a decree of respondent superior court and such California decree declares that "the parties are hereby ordered to perform each and every obligation provided for by" the Nevada decree. The California decree was affirmed on appeal and became final in June, 1954. *final*
* * *

Under the property settlement agreement petitioner agreed, among other things, to transfer certain real and personal property to the wife, Frances, and to place in escrow as security for performance of his obligations under the agreement certificates evidencing 40,000 shares of stock of Bradley Mining Company, which stock is the property of petitioner; under certain circumstances the stock could be sold with the proceeds going to Frances. Petitioner further agreed to pay to Frances "forty per cent. (40%) of his net income, commencing January 1st, 1947, exclusive of capital gains and losses and distributions out of capital, but before deduction of income taxes or charitable contributions, less one per cent. (1%) of such net income for each 1,000 shares of said 40,000 shares of capital stock of Bradley Mining Company placed in escrow which have been sold with the consent of First Party [Frances] pursuant to * * * this contract."

Following the Nevada divorce, petitioner remarried in March, 1948, and Frances remarried in October, 1948. * * *

In February, 1955, Frances instituted the present contempt proceeding, asserting that since June 16, 1951, petitioner has wilfully failed and refuse to pay to her forty per cent of his net income, except for a payment of $15,000 on account, and that as of February, 1955, he owed her an additional $37,969.30. Petitioner defended on the ground that the term "net income" should be construed so as to permit him to make various deductions and that one-half his salary (i. e., one-half of the community income of himself and his present wife) should be excluded on the theory that it was not his income but belonged to such wife.

The evidence which was presented to the trial court consisted in part of the judgment roll in the California action. In addition testimony was submitted in the form of affidavits. The court found that in using the term "net income" the parties had not intended that petitioner be allowed any of the deductions for which he contended or that a half of the community income be excluded in case he remarried. Judgment was rendered accordingly, and petitioner was held in contempt and ordered imprisoned unless he made installment payments to Frances pursuant to a schedule set forth in the order of contempt and commitment. This petition for review followed.

* * *

Following the rule stated, it appears that the evidence supports the trial court's interpretation of the agreement here involved, based upon its finding as to the intent of the parties. Such supporting evidence consists of affidavits of Frances and of the attorney who drafted the agreement, the language of the agreement itself, and petitioner's own conduct. Inasmuch as petitioner argues the weight of the evidence rather than seriously urging that there is no evidence whatsoever supporting the trial court's construction of the agreement, no useful purpose would be served by here relating the evidence in detail. Petitioner's argument that since his remarriage his present wife's community (one-half) interest in his earnings must be deducted before computation of the forty per cent payable to Frances, likewise is without merit in view of the trial court's determination that such a deduction was contrary to the intentions of petitioner and Frances at the time they executed their contract. * * *

Petitioner further contends that to imprison him for failure to make payments to Frances under the property settlement agreement here involved would violate the provisions of the state Constitution forbidding imprisonment for debt. (Cal.Const., art. I, § 15.) This contention is sound. In the California action it was specifically and finally determined, as between the parties, that the payments here involved are "an inseverable part of an integrated adjustment of all property relations of the parties and not * * * a severable provision for alimony," and that therefore section 139 of the Civil Code did not apply so as to terminate, upon the remarriage of Frances, petitioner's obligation to make such payments. * * * And as already mentioned herein, the property settlement agreement itself declares that it "is intended * * * to refer only to property rights. * * *" It is, of course, also the rule that a decree is subject to *Rule* modification if the payments therein provided are for alimony, maintenance or support, even though based on a property settlement agreement, but not if, as already determined in this case, they in themselves are an integral part of an adjustment of property rights. * * * Neither the court nor the Legislature may impair the obligation of a valid contract (Cal.Const., art. I, §§ 1, 16) and a court cannot lawfully disregard the provisions of such contracts or deny to either party his rights thereunder. * * *

Although, "As in the case of all constitutional provisions designed to safeguard the liberties of the person, every doubt should be resolved in favor of the liberty of the citizen in the enforcement of the constitutional provision that no person shall be imprisoned for debt" (11 Am.Jur. 1128, § 327; * * *), a court may nevertheless punish by imprisonment as a contempt the willful act of a spouse (or former spouse) who, having the ability and opportunity to comply, deliberately refuses to obey a valid order to pay alimony or an allowance for the support of the other spouse (or former other spouse). It is held that the obligation to make such payments is not a "debt" within the meaning of the constitutional guaranty against imprisonment for debt. * * *

Where, however, the payments provided in a property settlement agreement constitute an adjustment of property interests, rather than alimony, support, or maintenance, the more generally prevailing rule is stated to be that decrees based thereon are not enforceable by contempt proceedings. * * *

* * * In Miller v. Superior Court (1937), supra, 9 Cal.2d 733, 737, 72 P.2d 868, enforcement by contempt was allowed of the provisions of a property settlement agreement providing for the payment of $75 a month. However, the court there pointed out (at page 739 of 9 Cal.2d, at page 872 of 72 P.2d) that "The basis of the obligation in the case of an approval [of a property settlement agreement] and order to pay, as in the case of an award of allowance not based on agreement, is the statutory obligation of *marital support* which is not a 'debt' within the meaning of the constitutional provision. We are of the view that the order to *pay a monthly allowance,* even though in accordance with the agreement of the parties, is not a 'debt' within the meaning of the constitutional prohibition." (Italics added.) That is to say, there may be situations in which the fact that a party has agreed to pay some fixed or ascertainable amount as alimony does not change or control the character of the obligation sought to be enforced by the other. Merely adding the consensual element of agreement to pay support does not obliterate an existing le-

gal duty. In the absence of a waiver by the contracting spouses (expressly or by necessary implication) of reciprocal rights to support other than as provided in the agreement, either party may properly seek to enforce in the divorce proceeding the obligations imposed by law as incidents of the marriage. But where the parties bargain with each other and agree that the terms of their contract shall thereupon and thenceforth grant, delimit and exclusively define their respective rights and obligations *inter se,* then it is to the contract alone, and to conventional civil proceedings for the enforcement of contract rights, that they must look for a remedy in the event of breach. Inclusion of such a contract in a judgment of divorce may furnish a basis for subsequent proceedings leading to issuance of a writ of execution but cannot support a commitment to imprisonment for failure to pay the judgment debt.

* * *

It is to be recognized that the term "alimony" does not contemplate a settlement of property interests or general endowment of wealth. "Like the alimentum of the civil law, from which the word was evidently derived, it has for its sole object the provision of food, clothing, habitation, and other necessaries for * * * support." (17 Am.Jur. 406, and cases cited, note 12.) It is to attain that "sole object" that the law imposes an obligation which is regarded as something other than a debt and which may be enforced by contempt proceedings upon appropriate showing. Here the judgment manifestly purports to sanction a negotiated agreement rather than an obligation imposed by law.

We are satisfied that the better view is that payments provided in a property settlement agreement which are found to constitute an adjustment of property interests, rather than a severable provision for alimony, should be held to fall within the constitutional proscription against imprisonment for debt. That is, if the obligation sought to be enforced is contractual and negotiated, as distinguished from marital and imposed by law, even though the contract relates to marriage obligations, the remedy must be appropriate to the right asserted. Payments which fall into the category of law-imposed alimony or separate maintenance are based upon the statutory obligation of marital support, may be modified by the court upon a proper showing, ordinarily terminate with the death of either party, and may properly be held not to constitute a "debt" within the meaning of the constitutional provision. No such case for special exemption from the constitutional proscription can be made where the payments represent the result of a bargain negotiated by the parties in adjustment of their respective interests * * *.

Inasmuch, as it has been finally determined, as between these parties, that the payments to be made by petitioner to Frances in the present case constitute "an inseverable part of an integrated adjustment of all property relations of the parties and not * * * a severable provision for alimony"   * * *   we conclude that enforcement of such payments by contempt proceedings is forbidden by the constitutional prohibition against imprisonment for debt.   *   *   *

For the reasons above stated, the order holding petitioner in contempt is annulled.

*   *   *

NOTES AND QUESTIONS

1. The *Bradley* case is noted in 37 B.U.L.Rev. 531 (1957); 45 Cal.L. Rev. 782 (1957); 42 Minn.L.Rev. 929 (1958); 34 N.D.L.Rev. 170 (1958); and 10 Stan.L.Rev. 321 (1958). It has been followed in Stone v. Stidham, 96 Ariz. 235, 393 P.2d 923 (1964) and Cocke v. Cocke, 13 Ariz.App. 57, 474 P.2d 64 (1970), among other cases.

2. In Decker v. Decker, supra, page 920 it was held that a division of property may be enforced by contempt proceedings. Is that case correct, or is the *Bradley* case correct? Does the answer depend upon the characterization of the payments as debts or upon some other consideration? Is the answer affected by the fact that the division of property ordered by the court was based upon an agreement of the parties rather than having been arrived at by litigation?

3. If contempt could be used to enforce the decree, would that imply that inability to pay would be a defense? Ex parte Preston, 162 Tex. 379, 347 S.W.2d 938 (1961), 41 Tex.L.Rev. 141 (1962).

4. What is the relation between the rule of this case and the question whether alimony or property decrees based upon separation agreements are modifiable?

5. Should a decree for the support or maintenance of a spouse based upon a separation agreement be enforceable by contempt? H. Clark, Law of Domestic Relations § 16.12 (1968).

6. Should a decree for the support of a child based upon a separation agreement be enforceable by contempt?

7. Is the *Bradley* case overruled by the California statute reproduced, supra, page 1010?

8. What should be the result under this case if the parties clearly labeled their agreement, and the decree, "a division of property", but in fact it was concerned only with the support of the spouse? Does the parties' characterization of the obligation control the form of enforcement available? See State ex rel. Stirewalt v. Stirewalt, 7 Or.App. 544, 492 P.2d 802 (1972).

JORGENSEN v. JORGENSEN

Supreme Court of California, In Bank, 1948.
32 Cal.2d 13, 193 P.2d 728.

TRAYNOR, Justice. The parties were married in 1924. They separated in 1944, and executed a property settlement agreement providing that following their divorce the husband would pay to the wife $30,000 annually for her support and that of their children. The wife thereafter brought an action for divorce in which the husband made no appearance. She obtained an interlocutory decree in which the property settlement agreement was approved and adopted, and a final decree was subsequently entered. In the present action plaintiff seeks to set aside the provisions of the interlocutory decree relating to the property settlement agreement, on the grounds of fraud and mistake. She alleged in her amended complaint that some of the assets listed in the agreement as separate property of the husband were community property and that defendant procured her consent to the agreement by fraudulently representing those assets as his separate property. Plaintiff further alleged that she and the attorney who represented her when the property settlement agreement was made, relying exclusively upon defendant's representations, did not investigate whether the assets in question were community or spearate property. Plaintiff alleged as an alternative cause of action that defendant made his representations by mistake upon the advice of his counsel.

The agreement recites that it "is based upon a full disclosure of all real and personal properties and shall constitute a final settlement, adjustment and division of the property and the financial matters of the parties." Plaintiff alleges that she consented to this statement and was satisfied with the contract because she was persuaded by the representations of defendant that under the agreement she received half the community property; that defendant had exclusive control and management of the property of the parties throughout their married life and was therefore aware that the property listed in the agreement as his separate property was community property; that she was not familiar with the facts, since she was preoccupied with her duties as housewife and mother; that in making the agreement and submitting it to the court she relied on defendant's honesty and the truthfulness of his representations; and that the attorney who represented her in the negotiations with respect to the property settlement agreement and had previously represented her in the negotations with respect to a voting trust agreement with defendant was recommended to her by defendant, who paid the fee for his services.

In his answer defendant denied that the property settlement agreement classified as his separate property any assets in which the wife had a community interest or that he made false representations regarding any assets mentioned in the agreement. He also filed a cross-complaint praying that his title to the assets in question be quieted. At the trial defendant objected to the introduction of any evidence by plaintiff, on the ground that her amended complaint was insufficient to state a cause of action. The court sustained this objection, and after defendant had introduced into evidence the property settlement agreement and the interlocutory and final decree of divorce, entered a judgment for defendant on the complaint and cross-complaint.

Since the court entered judgment on the pleadings with respect to plaintiff's amended complaint, it must be assumed for the purposes of this appeal that the allegations therein are true. With regard to the partition of the community property plaintiff alleged that before the property settlement agreement was executed, the parties agreed that each was to receive half the community property and that defendant represented to her that the agreement, drafted by his attorneys, gave her half the community property, whereas actually it deprived her of her community property interest in certain shares of stock, namely, half the outstanding stock of the Earle M. Jorgensen Company (hereafter referred to as Jorgensen Company) and all the outstanding stock of the Earle M. Jorgensen-Forge Division (hereafter referred to as Forge Division).

[The plaintiff's contention was that stock in certain corporations was community property rather than the husband's individual property, as he claimed and had indicated to her at the time the separation agreement was signed. She knew of the property's existence and nature, but she claimed she did not know that it was community property.]

* * *

Plaintiff contends that the part of the interlocutory decree approving and adopting the property settlement agreement was induced by defendant's false representations and that they constitute extrinsic fraud or mistake entitling her to equitable relief from the decree. Defendant on the other hand contends that if he perpetrated any fraud it was intrinsic and therefore there can be no equitable relief from the decree. * * *

Taylor v. Taylor, 192 Cal. 71, 218 P. 756, 51 A.L.R. 1074 (1950), and Milekovich v. Quinn, 40 Cal.App. 537, 181 P. 256 (1919), as well as Howard v. Howard, 27 Cal.2d 319, 163 P.2d 439 (1945), recognize that when equitable relief from a final judgment is sought, it makes an important difference whether the fraud or mistake is intrinsic or extrinsic to the issues involved in the case in which the judgment was entered. The public policy underlying the princple of res judicata that there must be an end to litigation requires that the issues involved in a case be set at rest by a final judgment, even though a party has persuaded the court or the jury by false allegations supported by perjured testimony. This policy must be considered together with the policy that a party shall not be deprived of a fair adversary proceeding in which fully to present his case. * * * The terms "intrinsic" and "extrinsic" fraud or mistake are generally accepted as appropriate to describe the two different categories of cases to which these policies of the law apply. * * * They do not constitute, however, a simple and infallible formula to determine whether in a given case the facts surrounding the fraud or mistake warrant equitable relief from a judgment. * * * It is necessary to examine the facts in the light of the policy that a party who failed to assemble all his evidence at the trial should not be privileged to relitigate a case, as well as the policy permitting a party to seek relief from a judgment entered in a proceeding in which he was deprived of a fair opportunity fully to present his case.

The latter policy applies when a party's adversary, in violation of a duty arising from a trust or confidential relation, has concealed from him facts essential to the protection of his rights, even though such facts concerned issues involved in the case in which the judgment was entered. "The failure to perform the duty to speak or make disclosures which rests upon one because of a trust or confidential relation is obviously a fraud, for which equity may relieve from a judgment thereby obtained, even though the breach of duty occurs during a judicial proceeding and involves false testimony, and this is true whether such fraud be regarded as extrinsic or as an exception to the extrinsic fraud rule." 3 Freeman, Judgments, 5th Ed., p. 2576 * * *. In this state equitable relief has been granted from final judgments settling the accounts of guardians, administrators, or executors who withheld information that would have enabled the beneficiaries to attack the accounts. * * * The same principle applies to decrees distributing the estate of a decedent adversely to the rights of beneficiaries who have been precluded from pursuing their rights by concealment of facts by the fiduciary, * * * and to other probate decrees obtained under similar circumstances. * * *

The same principle also applies in the cases concerning equitable relief from judgments approving and adopting property settlement agreements relied on by plaintiff. In Milekovich v. Quinn, 40 Cal. App. 537, 181 P. 256 (1919), the wife alleged in a divorce action that her husband held securities worth $60,000 which were community property. The husband denied her allegation, stating in his answer and in an affidavit filed in reply to an application of the wife for alimony pendente lite that the securities held by him were worth not more than $2,000. Relying on these representations, the wife entered into a property settlement agreement specifying the community property assets that she was to receive and providing that the husband should receive the remainder of the community property. The agreement was approved and adopted by the court in an interlocutory divorce decree. The wife sought equitable relief from the provisions of the decree relating to the agreement, since the husband had concealed from her bonds in the par value of $45,000 acquired with community property funds, which he had withdrawn from his safe-deposit box and delivered to a custodian after the commencement of the divorce action.

In Taylor v. Taylor, 192 Cal. 71, 218 P. 756, 51 A.L.R. 1074 (1923), the wife entered into a property settlement agreement wherein she released all obligations of the husband as to support and alimony and disclaimed all her rights to community property in consideration of the payment of $500 to her by the husband. She sought equitable relief from a divorce decree approving and adopting this agreement, on the ground that the husband had concealed from her the existence of certain real property acquired with community property funds placing it in the name of his brother.

As the manager of the community property the husband occupies a position of trust (Civ.Code, secs. 172–173, 158), which is not terminated as to assets remaining in his hands when the spouses separate. It is part of his fiduciary duties to account to the wife for the community property when the spouses are negotiating a property settlement agreement. The concealment of community property assets by the husband from the wife in connection with such an agreement is therefore a breach of a fiduciary duty of the husband that deprives the wife of an opportunity to protect her rights in the concealed assets and thus warants equitable relief from a judgment approving such agreement. When community property is entrusted to the wife, she likewise occupies a position of trust. It has therefore been held that a husband may obtain equitable relief from a divorce decree incorporating a property settlement agreement obtained by the fraud of the wife in concealing community assets entrusted to her control. Boullester v. Superior Court, 137 Cal.App. 193, 195, 30 P.2d 59 (1934). It is immaterial whether the husband or the wife has submitted the property settlement agreement to the court for approval; the fraud of one spouse in concealing the assets, if not discovered by the other, precludes the latter from protecting his or her rights as to the concealed assets in the divorce proceeding.

        *   *   *

The issue in the present case is whether under the facts stated in her amended complaint, the wife was deprived of a fair opportunity to submit her case fully to the court because of a breach of a fiduciary duty of the husband. There is no allegation in the complaint that defendant concealed assets that were part of the community property. The assets were disclosed, and the complaint is based on the theory that defendant fraudulently claimed certain community property as his separate estate. The classification of property as separate or community is frequently difficult. A husband at the time of divorce or separation is entitled to take a position favorable to his own interest in claiming as his separate property assets that a court might hold to be community property. Confronted with the assertion by the husband that certain assets are his separate property the wife must take her own position and if necessary investigate the facts. Champion v. Woods, 79 Cal. 17, 20, 21 P. 534, 12 Am.St.Rep. 126 (1889); Dowling v. Spring Valley Water Co., 174 Cal. 218, 222, 162 P. 894 (1917); Haviland v. Southern California Edison Co., 172 Cal. 601, 609, 158 P. 328 (1916); see, Brown v. Brown, 170 Cal. 1, 5, 147 P. 1168 (1915); Lindley v. Hinch, 57 Cal.App.2d 717, 719, 135 P.2d 421 (1943). If the wife and her attorney are satisfied with the husband's classification of the property as separate or community, the wife cannot reasonably contend that fraud was committed or that there was such mistake as to allow her to overcome the finality of a judgment. In the present case plaintiff alleged that she and her attorney relied exclusively on her husband's representations that the shares in question were his separate property and that her attorney made no examination or investigation to ascertain whether the shares were community property. She did not allege that her attorney intentionally failed to protect her interests. Plaintiff is barred from obtaining equitable relief by her admission that she and her attorney did not investigate the facts, choosing instead to rely on the statements of the husband as to what part of the disclosed property was community property.

The judgment is affirmed.

* * *

NOTES AND QUESTIONS

1. What is the California Supreme Court's position on the case which arises when the husband conceals community property assets from his wife during the course of the negotiations leading to the separation agreement? Would the situation be the same in a non-community property state?

2. What should be the result if the wife brought an action for deceit, rather than one to set aside the property aspects of the divorce decree, alleging misrepresentations in the negotiations leading to the execution of the separation agreement? Holm v. Shilensky, 388 F.2d 54 (2d Cir. 1968); Hood v. Hood, 335 F.2d 585 (10th Cir. 1964), 67 W.Va.L.Rev. 243 (1965); Schoonover v. Schoonover, 172 F.2d 526 (10th Cir. 1949); United States Nat. Bank v. Bartges, 120 Colo. 317, 210 P.2d 600 (1949), aff'd on second appeal, 122 Colo. 546, 224 P.2d 658 (1950), cert. den. 338 U.S. 955 (1949); Weintraub v. Weintraub, 302 N.Y. 104, 96 N.E.2d 724 (1951), 37 Corn.L.Q. 84 (1951). What would be the measure of damages in such an action? Would punitive damages be obtainable?

For other cases upholding attack on decrees for fraud in the making of the underlying separation agreement see Nicolaides v. Nicolaides, 39 Cal. App.3d 192, 114 Cal.Rptr. 56 (1974); Pactor v. Pactor, —— Ind.App. ——, 391 N.E.2d 1148 (1979); Feinberg v. Feinberg, 96 Misc.2d 443, 409 N.Y.S. 2d 365 (Sup.Ct.1978).

3. Herbert and Wilma Jones were married twenty years ago. Herbert is now forty-eight years old and Wilma is forty-three. Before marriage Wilma was a school teacher, but her teaching credentials are no longer in effect. They have two children, Mary who is seventeen and John who is fifteen. Until about two years ago the marriage was a reasonably satisfactory one, but then Herbert began seeing his secretary after working hours, Wilma heard about it, and some violent quarrels resulted. Herbert has now decided that he is in love with his secretary, an attractive divorcee of thirty-two with two children of her own, aged eight and ten, and he wishes a divorce in order to marry her. Wilma at first strongly resisted any discussion of divorce, but now is resigned to losing her husband. She is insisting that if they do obtain a divorce their two children should live with her, while Herbert feels very strongly that John should be in his custody.

At present Herbert and Wilma live in Salmon Falls, New York, but Herbert has just been appointed assistant sales manager for the Beta Corporation whose headquarters are in San Francisco, to which he must move in the next ninety days.

Herbert has been working as a salesman for the Beta Corporation in New York for the past several years under an arrangement which gave him a salary of $20,000 per year, but with a provision for commissions in addition to the salary. Due to the contingent nature of this arrangement, his total earnings have fluctuated in the past years. Up until eight years ago his earnings never exceeded $21,000. For the past eight years his total earnings have been (before income taxes) $22,000; $24,000; $21,000; $25,000; $24,000; $25,000; $23,000; $22,000. The product which Herbert sells is a new rivetting tool used in construction work, a device which is still in the relatively early stages of exploitation, but which may turn out to be useful and popular in the future.

The position of assistant sales manager to which Herbert has just been appointed will pay a salary of $30,000, with guaranteed annual raises of $2,500 (if he works out satisfactorily) until $40,000 is reached. In addition Herbert will become entitled to participate in the company's stock option plan for executives, under which he will be entitled to buy five hundred shares of stock in the corporation each year at a price 10% below the going market price. At present this stock is selling at $10 per share. He will remain entitled to these stock options for five years, on condition he continues as assistant sales manager. He will also qualify for the corporation's pension plan, under which the corporation will make annual contributions to a trust fund in the amount of 15% of Herbert's salary, the plan providing that this will entitle him to a retirement income commencing at age sixty-five in the amount of one-half of his then salary, again on the assumption that he continues to be employed by Beta Corporation to that time. If he should die or resign before then, he will be entitled to the sum of the payments made by the corporation to the fund to that date, without interest.

Herbert and Wilma own the following property:

1. A house and lot purchased fifteen years ago for $20,000, on which there is a mortgage with $7,500 remaining unpaid. Payments on the mortgage total $200 per month, which covers interest, amortization, insurance and taxes. The property is held in joint names with survivorship. It has recently been appraised by a real estate man at $100,000.

2. Two automobiles, both owned in joint names, one a year-old Pontiac on which $2500 is still owed to the finance company, the other a three-year old Chevrolet Vega, with $500 still unpaid and owing to the same finance company. Payments on the two cars total about $150 per month.

3. A joint savings account in a local savings and loan association in the amount of $500, and a joing checking account in the local First National Bank which fluctuates between $2000. and 0 during each month.

4. Five hundred shares of General Motors common stock, currently selling at $80 per share, left to Herbert by his grandfather. The stock is held in Herbert's name and pays dividends of $3.40 per share per year.

5. Seventy-five acres of country land outside Salmon Falls, also left to Herbert by his grandfather and held in Herbert's name. The land is valued for property tax purposes at $7,500, the annual taxes being about $250. The land is presently vacant and is rented by Herbert to a local farmer for pasture, bringing an annual return of $300.

6. Wilma is the life beneficiary of a trust set up in her mother's will, of which the two children, Mary and John, are the remaindermen. The trust contains securities worth $100,000 and has been producing a net income of about $4,000 per year which Wilma has been using for family expenses.

7. Herbert has a policy of ordinary life insurance in the amount of $25,000, on which Wilma and the children are beneficiaries. It has a present cash value of $1200.

Wilma's health has in general been good, but the marital difficulties have had a serious effect on her nervous and emotional welfare, to such an extent that she has been seeing a local psychiatrist once a week, at a cost of $75 per visit. He has told her that she needs to continue therapy for at least another six months and perhaps longer. The children have also been essentially healthy, but John has been having his teeth straightened at a cost of $600 per year, payable monthly, with two years still to go.

The expenses of the family have in the past always completely exhausted the family income, including Wilma's trust income. In some years the family has been in debt over and above the amounts owing on house and cars, since Herbert enjoys golf and the country club life, while Wilma likes the theatre. One of their ways of getting along together was that each indulged his own taste in recreation at considerable expense. At the moment, however, there are outstanding only an account at a local clothing store, for Wilma's and the children's clothes, in the amount of $500 and an account at the country club for dues, drinks, meals etc. in the amount of $2,000.

Assume that you represent either Herbert or Wilma as they contemplate divorce, and draft a separation agreement on behalf of either one or the other settling the controversies and potential controversies that you perceive in the situation. Would you have this agreement incorporated in the divorce decree, or what would you do with it?

SECTION 8. CHILD CUSTODY: JURISDICTION AND SUBSTANTIVE LAW IN CONNECTION WITH DISSOLUTION OF MARRIAGE.*

INTRODUCTORY NOTE

The custody aspect of a divorce action differs in several ways from the other aspects of the case. Some of these differences are so obvious that it would be embarrassing to mention them if it were not

---

* Both jurisdictional issues and issues on the merits of custody proceedings are combined in this section because in a very large proportion of the cases as they arise both kinds of issues will occur, often inextricably entangled. This is particularly true where the Uniform Child Custody Jurisdiction Act is in force.

for the fact that lawyers and courts often overlook them. The first such difference is the most obvious of all. The custody case is concerned with the welfare, possession, care, and education of a child. The issue is not which of the parties is to have a piece of property or a sum of money, but what disposition will best promote the child's welfare. Many of the attitudes and assumptions appropriate to the usual litigation over property or money are totally inappropriate to the custody case. For example, in the case of May v. Anderson, reproduced infra at page 1029, there is no suggestion anywhere in the case that the Court recognized that it was dealing with a child's future. In fact the analogies upon which the Court drew for guidance were analogies to suits over money and property. Many other cases make the same mistake.

At the same time it is true that parents or other contending parties in custody cases have claims which must be heard and respected. The court as an agency of the state is not, under our legal system, given unlimited authority to do whatever it sees fit to benefit the child. It must act in the context of litigation between individual claimants, on the basis of evidence before it. There may often be situations in which the general precept that the child's welfare controls will be in conflict with the claims of parents and the demands of fair procedure. Such conflicts have to be faced and resolved. It is not only useless but harmful to pretend that they do not exist. In their resolution courts too often take refuge in moralizing, as where the adulterous mother is denied custody of her child. This should be avoided but not at the risk of abandoning all attempts at evaluating the parents' conduct. After all, the judge's duty is judging, not therapy.

Still another source of difficulty in custody litigation is that, unlike the usual lawsuit which is concerned with establishing in some more or less acceptable way what occurred in the past, the custody decree must make a prediction about the future. That would be difficult enough in ordinary circumstances, but there is the additional obstacle that the circumstances are anything but ordinary. The child's existing world has disintegrated and the court is being asked which of two or more concededly unsatisfactory dispositions will best serve his welfare. Past events are of little help in the prediction because the child faces a set of circumstances radically different from those in his past. It is hardly surprising that the results are often unhappy, and that judges continually characterize custody litigation as the most taxing and frustrating part of their work.

In the face of so many difficulties one response is to look outside the law for assistance. It is conceivable that the social sciences, primarily psychology or psychiatry, might offer two kinds of help, first, some information on child development which could be the basis for statutory or judicial principles of general application in custody cases, and, second, evidence in specific cases which would illuminate the situation of the child then before the court. Unfortunately, although there is a large body of learning on child development, virtually none of it is useful in formulating legal principles of general application. Studies of the consequences of the "broken home" or "father-separation" are not sufficiently precise to tell us anything about whether and under what circumstances a child should be placed with his father or his mother after a divorce. In addition many of the studies are not very rigorous and have been challenged by other investigators. Basing legal rules on such doubtful sources would be neither safe nor sensible. For further discussion of this point see Ellsworth, A Review of the Psychological Literature Relevant to Child Custody Litigation, in R. Levy, Uniform Marriage and Divorce Legislation: A Preliminary Analysis, I–1 (1968). This same review makes the statement that except for instances where the child is overtly rejected by a parent, or where there are rather obviously adverse circumstances such as alcoholism, promiscuity or criminality of the parent, all of which (to no one's surprise) have been shown by studies to be harmful to children, "psychology has little to contribute to custody decisions." Somewhat similar views are expressed in Okpaku, Psychology: Impediment or Aid in Child Custody Cases, 29 Rut.L.Rev. 1117 (1976).

This is not a view which is universally held. A note in the Yale Law Journal, relying upon interviews with Anna Freud and upon published work of Erik Erikson, suggests that the courts should concentrate on the psychological well-being of the child, and in order to determine this should investigate the child's existing structure of relationships. The assertion is that without a "psychologically adequate relationship" also referred to as an "affection-relationship," between child and custodian, the custodian "could not substantially further the child's well-being by aiding his psychological development or assisting in the resolution of personality crises." Note, 73 Yale L.J. 151, 158 (1963). Only this sort of relationship, it is argued, can produce the emotional trait of basic trust, in Erikson's opinion the hallmark of the successful personality. The criterion of the child's welfare often adopted by the courts is rejected as too vague, and as including such irrelevancies as the race, politics, religion, morality and financial abilities of the parties. Similar views are more fully stated in J. Goldstein, A. Freud, A. Solnit, Beyond the Best Interests of the Child (1973). Whether a court would be able to determine which claimant for custody could better provide a psychologically adequate relationship for the child any more easily or more satisfactorily than it can determine which would better serve the child's welfare is a matter which will very likely never be proved.

Another article, Bradbrook, The Relevance of Psychological and Psychiatric Studies to the Future Development of the Laws Governing the Settlement of Inter-Parental Child Custody Disputes, 11 J. Fam.L. 557 (1972), purports to find that some of the common assumptions made by courts in custody decisions are borne out by sociological and psychological studies. These assumptions are that a young child should normally be in the custody of its mother, a girl should normally be in the custody of her mother, and a boy should normally be in the custody of his father unless the child is very young. These rules of thumb are found to be supported by studies showing the adverse effects of maternal and paternal deprivation. The studies referred to were made on children in institutions who were cared for by "overworked nurses". Such children were found to be retarded in the acquisition of various skills, and in emotional and psychological development. Other studies seemed to show a correlation between absence of the father and incidence of juvenile delinquency among males. Would you agree that these kinds of study bear out the judicial rules of thumb?

At least one precept for custody cases does seem to be pretty generally agreed on. This is the need for continuity and permanence in the child's relationships and environment. The constant shifting between custodians which can sometimes occur is detrimental to his welfare, especially where the child is older than one or two years. Ellsworth, op. cit. supra, at I–55; Note, 73 Yale L.J. 151, 161 (1963); A. Watson, Psychiatry For Lawyers, 159, 197 (1968).

The second question, whether the law can look for assistance from other disciplines in specific cases rather than for general principles, has been answered in a number of ways. In many cases counsel representing the parties will introduce testimony by psychologists, psychiatrists or social workers concerning the merits of the contestants for custody. Sometimes this sort of testimony is helpful, sometimes not, depending upon the sort of questions asked, the opportunity which the witness has had for familiarizing himself with the child and the parties, and the sensitivity of the expert. One rather obvious fact should be emphasized. The function of a psychiatrist is therapy, not prediction. The fact that a given psychiatrist is a successful therapist does not make him an infallible predicter of future events in the life of a child. The decision in the most criticized custody case of recent years, Painter v. Bannister, 258 Iowa 1390, 140 N.W.2d 152 (1966), reproduced infra at page 1091, was based upon the testimony of a psychologist, who, according to the court, testified that the chances were very high that the child would "go wrong if he is returned to his father". The testimony was given after twenty-five hours of evaluation of the child and the grandparents who sought custody, but without ever interviewing the child's father. Custody was given to the sixty-year-old grandparents and within two years the child returned to his father. It would seem that the principle of continuity might have been considered by the psychologist when he recommended that custody be given to persons of that age. In any event the case illustrates that psychological testimony in custody cases is not a panacea.

Another form of non-legal assistance in specific cases is available under the statutes of many states which authorize investigations and reports by welfare departments, social agencies or probation officers when requested by the courts in custody cases. This procedure gives the court an impartial and supposedly unbiased insight into the background of the case. It is not, however, without its dangers. The report may be full of hearsay, rumor and gossip. It may also reflect biases of the investigator which can be very difficult to expose. And finally, it may tempt the judge to abdicate the onerous task of judging by going along with the report's express or unspoken recommendations, without giving the case the careful scrutiny it should have.

There is one further way in which the decision of custody cases can be given valuable albeit indirect non-legal help. If the parties are willing to participate in counselling with a marriage counsellor, psychiatrist or other trained person, even though their marriage may not be "saved", they may come to see the suffering and harm which they will inflict on their child if they engage in a custody battle. Indeed this seems to be the chief value of marriage counselling at the divorce stage. Many counsellors refer to their work as divorce counselling rather than marriage counselling, their most important goal being to reduce the hostility of the parties and minimize the damage to any children of the marriage. If the result is an agreement between the parties concerning custody, which can be accepted and respected while the child grows up, this is clearly the best possible resolution of the custody dilemma.

MAY v. ANDERSON

Supreme Court of the United States, 1953.
345 U.S. 528, 73 S.Ct. 840, 97 L.Ed. 1221.

Mr. Justice BURTON delivered the opinion of the Court.

The question presented is whether, in a habeas corpus proceeding attacking the right of a mother to retain possession of her minor children, an Ohio court must give full faith and credit to a Wisconsin decree awarding custody of the children to their father when that decree is obtained by the father in an *ex parte* divorce action in a Wisconsin court which had no personal jurisdiction over the mother. For the reasons hereafter stated, our answer is no.

This proceeding began July 5, 1951, when Owen Anderson, here called the appellee, filed a petition for a writ of habeas corpus in the Probate Court of Columbiana County, Ohio. He alleged that his former wife, Leona Anderson May, here called the appellant, was illegally restraining the liberty of their children, Ronald, Sandra and James, aged, respectively, 12, 8 and 5, by refusing to deliver them to him in response to a decree issued by the County Court of Waukesha County, Wisconsin, February 5, 1947. With both parties and their children before it, the Probate Court ordered that, until this matter be finally determined, the children remain with their mother subject to their father's right to visit them at reasonable times.

After a hearing "on the petition, the stipulation of counsel for the parties as to the agreed statement of facts, and the testimony," the Probate Court decided that it was obliged by the Full Faith and Credit Clause of the Constitution of the United States to accept the Wisconsin decree as binding upon the mother. Accordingly, proceeding to the merits of the case upon the issues presented by the stipulations of counsel, it ordered the children discharged from further restraint by her. That order has been held in abeyance and the children are still with her. The Court of Appeals for Columbiana County, Ohio, affirmed. * * * The Supreme Court of Ohio, without opinion, denied a motion directing the Court of Appeals to certify its record for review, and dismissed an appeal on the ground that no debatable constitutional question was involved. * * *

The parties were married in Wisconsin and, until 1947, both were domiciled there. After marital troubles developed, they agreed in December, 1946, that appellant should take their children to Lisbon, Columbiana County, Ohio, and there think over her future course. By New Year's Day, she had decided not to return to Wisconsin and, by telephone, she informed her husband of that decision.

Within a few days he filed suit in Wisconsin, seeking both an absolute divorce and custody of the children. The only service of process upon appellant consisted of the delivery to her personally, in Ohio, of a copy of the Wisconsin summons and petition. Such service is authorized by a Wisconsin statute for use in an action for a divorce but that statute makes no mention of its availability in a proceeding for the custody of chidren. Appellant entered no appearance and took no part in this Wisconsin proceeding which produced not only a decree divorcing the paties from the bonds of matrimony but a decree purporting to award the custody of the children to their father, subject to a right of their mother to visit them at reasonable times. Appellant contests only the validity of the decree as to custody. * * *

Armed with a copy of the decree and accompanied by a local police officer, appellee, in Lisbon, Ohio, demanded and obtained the children from their mother. The record does not disclose what took place between 1947 and 1951, except that the children remained with their father in Wisconsin until July 1, 1951. He then brought them back to Lisbon and permitted them to visit their mother. This time, when he demanded their return, she refused to surrender them.

Relying upon the Wisconsin decree, he promptly filed in the Probate Court of Columbiana County, Ohio, the petition for a writ of habeas corpus now before us. Under Ohio procedure that writ tests only the immediate right to possession of the children. It does not open the door for the modification of any prior award of custody on a showing of changed circumstances. Nor is it available as a procedure for settling the future custody of children in the first instance.

"It is well settled that *habeas corpus* is not the proper or appropriate action to determine, as between parents, who is entitled to the custody of their minor children.

"The agreed statement of facts disclosed to the Court of Appeals that the children were in the custody of their mother. There being no evidence that the appellant had a superior right to their custody, that court was fully warranted in concluding that the children were not illegally restrained of their liberty." In re Corey, 145 Ohio St. 413, 418, 61 N.E.2d 892, 894–895 (1945).[4]

* * *

Separated as our issue is from that of the future interests of the children, we have before us the elemental question whether a court of a state, where a mother is neither domiciled, resident nor present, may cut off her immediate right to the care, custody, management and companionship of her minor children without having jurisdiction over her *in personam*. Rights far more precious to appellant than property rights will be cut off if she is to be bound by the Wisconsin award of custody.

"[I]t is now too well settled to be open to further dispute that the 'full faith and credit' clause and the act of Congress passed pursuant to it do not entitle a judgment *in personam* to extraterritorial effect if it be made to appear that it was rendered without jurisdiction over the person sought to be bound." Baker v. Baker, Eccles & Co., 242 U.S. 394, 401, and see 403, 37 S.Ct. 152, 155, 61 L.Ed. 386; Thompson v. Whitman, 18 Wall. 457, 21 L.Ed. 897; D'Arcy v. Ketchum, 11 How. 165, 13 L.Ed. 648.

In Estin v. Estin, and Kreiger v. Kreiger, this Court upheld the validity of a Nevada divorce obtained *ex parte* by a husband, resident in Nevada, insofar as it dissolved the bonds of matrimony. At the same time, we held Nevada powerless to cut off, in that proceeding, a spouse's right to financial support under the prior decree of another state. In the instant case, we recognize that a mother's right to custody of her children is a personal right entitled to at least as much protection as her right to alimony.

In the instant case, the Ohio courts gave weight to appellee's contention that the Wisconsin award of custody binds appellant be-

---

4. This limitation contrasts with the procedure in states where a court, upon securing the presence before it of the parents and children in response to a writ of habeas corpus, may proceed to determine the future custody of the children. See e. g., People of State of New York ex rel. Halvey v. Halvey, 330 U.S. 610, 67 S. Ct. 903, 91 L.Ed. 1133 (1947) (New York procedure).

cause, at the time it was issued, her children had a technical domicile in Wisconsin, although they were neither resident nor present there.[7]

We find it unnecessary to determine the children's legal domicile because, even if it be with their father, that does not give Wisconsin, certainly as against Ohio, the personal jurisdiction that it must have in order to deprive their mother of her personal right to their immediate possession.[8]

The judgment of the Supreme Court of Ohio, accordingly, is reversed and the cause is remanded to it for further proceedings not inconsistent with this opinion.

Mr. Justice FRANKFURTER, concurring.

The views expressed by my brother JACKSON make it important that I state, in joining the Court's opinion, what I understand the Court to be deciding and what it is not deciding in this case.

What is decided—the only thing the Court decides—is that the Full Faith and Credit Clause does not require Ohio, in disposing of the custody of children in Ohio, to accept, in the circumstances before us, the disposition made by Wisconsin. The Ohio Supreme Court felt itself so bound. This Court does not decide that Ohio would be precluded from recognizing, as a matter of local law, the disposition made by the Wisconsin court. For Ohio to give respect to the Wisconsin decree would not offend the Due Process Clause. Ohio is no more precluded from doing so than a court of Ontario or Manitoba would be, were the mother to bring the children into one of these provinces.

---

7. By stipulation, the parties recognized her domicile in Ohio. See also, Estin v. Estin, supra; Kreiger v. Kreiger, supra; Williams v. North Carolina, 317 U.S. 287.

For the general rule that in cases of the separation of parents, apart from any award of custody of the children, the domicile of the children is that of the parent with whom they live and that only the state of that domicile may award their custody, see Restatement, Conflict of Laws (1934), §§ 32 and 146, Illustrations 1 and 2.

8. "* * * the weight of authority is in favor of confining the jurisdiction of the court in an action for divorce, where the defendant is a nonresident and does not appear, and process upon the defendant is by substituted service only, to a determination of the *status* of the parties. * * * This rule of law extends to children who are not within the jurisdiction of the court when the decree

is rendered, where the defendant is not a resident of the state of the seat of the court, and has neither been personally served with process nor appeared to the action. * * * [Citing cases.]

"By the authority of the cases supra, a decree of the custody of a minor child under the circumstances stated is void." Weber v. Redding, 200 Ind. 448, 454–455, 163 N.E. 269, 271. See also, Sanders v. Sanders, 223 Mo.App. 834, 837–838, 14 S.W.2d 458, 459–460; Carter v. Carter, 201 Ga. 850, 41 S.E.2d 532.

The instant case does not present the special considerations that arise where a parent, with or without minor children, leaves a jurisdiction for the purpose of escaping process or otherwise evading jurisdiction, and we do not have here the considerations that arise when children are unlawfully or surreptitiously taken by one parent from the other.

Property, personal claims, and even the marriage status, * * * generally give rise to interests different from those relevant to the discharge of a State's continuing responsibility to children within her borders. Children have a very special place in life which law should reflect. Legal theories and their phrasing in other cases readily lead to fallacious reasoning it [sic] uncritically transferred to determination of a State's duty towards children. There are, of course, adjudications other than those pertaining to children, as for instance decrees of alimony, which may not be definitive even in the decreeing State, let alone binding under the Full Faith and Credit Clause. Interests of a State other than its duty towards children may also prevail over the interest of national unity that underlies the Full Faith and Credit Clause. But the child's welfare in a custody case has such a claim upon the State that its responsibility is obviously not to be foreclosed by a prior adjudication reflecting another State's discharge of its responsibility at another time. Reliance on opinions regarding out-of-State adjudications of property rights, personal claims or the marital status is bound to confuse analysis when a claim to the custody of children before the courts of one State is based on an award previously made by another State. Whatever light may be had from such opinions, they cannot give conclusive answers.

Mr. Justice JACKSON, whom Mr. Justice REED joins, dissenting.

The Court apparently is holding that the Federal Constitution prohibits Ohio from recognizing the validity of this Wisconsin divorce decree insofar as it settles custody of the couple's children. In the light of settled and unchallenged precedents of this Court, such a decision can only rest upon the proposition that Wisconsin's courts had no jurisdiction to make such a decree binding upon appellant. * * *

A conclusion that a state must not recognize a judgment of a sister commonwealth involves very different considerations than a conclusion that it must do so. If Wisconsin has rendered a valid judgment, the Constitution not only requires every state to give it full faith and credit, but 28 U.S.C. § 1738, 28 U.S.C.A. § 1738, referring to such judicial proceedings, commands that they "shall have the same full faith and credit in every court within the United States and its Territories and Possessions as they have by law or usage in the course of such State, Territory or Possession from which they are taken." The only escape from obedience lies in a holding that the judgment rendered in Wisconsin, at least as to custody, is void and entitled to no standing even in Wisconsin. It is void only if it denies due process of law.

The Ohio courts reasoned that although personal jurisdiction over the wife was lacking, domicile of the children in Wisconsin was a sufficient jurisdictional basis to enable Wisconsin to bind all parties interested in their custody. This determination that the children were domiciled in Wisconsin has not been contested either at our bar or below. Therefore, under our precedents, it is conclusive. * * * The husband, plaintiff in the case, was at all times domiciled in Wisconsin; the defendant-wife was a Wisconsin native, was married there and both were domiciled in that State until her move in December 1946, when the parties stipulate that she acquired an Ohio domicile. The children were born in Wisconsin, were always domiciled there, and were physically resident in Wisconsin at all times until December 1946, when their mother took them to Ohio with her. But the Ohio court specifically found that she brought the children to Ohio with the understanding that if she decided not to go back to Wisconsin the children were to be returned to that State. In spite of the fact that she did decide not to return, she kept the children in Ohio. It was under these circumstances that the Wisconsin decree was rendered in February 1947, less than two months after the wife had given up her physical residence in Wisconsin and held the children out of the State in breach of her agreement.

The husband subsequently went to Ohio, retrieved the children and took them back to Wisconsin, where they remained with him for four years. Then he voluntarily brought them to Ohio for a visit with their mother, whereupon she refused to surrender them, and he sought habeas corpus in the Ohio courts. In this situation Wisconsin was no meddler reaching out to draw to its courts controversies that arose in and concerned other legal communities. If ever domicile of the children plus that of one spouse is sufficient to support a custody decree binding all interested parties, it should be in this case. * * *

I am quite aware that in recent times this Court has been chipping away at the concept of domicile as a connecting factor between the state and the individual to determine rights and obligations. We are a mobile people, historically on the move, and perhaps the rigid concept of domicile derived by common law from feudal attachment to the land is too rigid for a society so restless as ours. But if our federal system is to maintain separate legal communities, as the Full Faith and Credit Clause evidently contemplates, there must be some test for determining to which of these a person belongs. If, for this purpose, there is a better concept than domicile, we have not yet hit upon it. Abandonment of this ancient doctrine would leave partial vacuums in many branches of the law. It seems to be abandoned here.

The Court's decision holds that the state in which a child and one parent are domiciled and which is primarily concerned about his welfare cannot constitutionally adjudicate controversies as to his guardianship. The state's power here is defeated by the absence of the other parent for a period of two months. The convenience of a leave-taking parent is placed above the welfare of the child, but neither party is greatly aided in obtaining a decision. The Wisconsin courts cannot bind the mother, and the Ohio courts cannot bind the father. A state of the law such as this, where possession apparently is not merely nine points of the law but all of them and self-help the ultimate authority, has little to commend it in legal logic or as a principle of order in a federal system.

*   *   *

In spite of the fact that judges and law writers long have recognized the similarity between the jurisdictional requirements for divorce and for custody, this decision appears to equate the jurisdictional requirements for a custody decree to those for an *in personam* money judgment. One reads the opinion in vain to discover reasons for this choice, unless it is found in the remark that for the wife "rights far more precious than property will be cut off" in the custody proceeding. The force of this cardiac consideration is self-evident, but it seems to me to reflect a misapprehension as to the nature of a custody proceeding or a revision of the views that have heretofore prevailed. *   *   *

The difference between a proceeding involving the status, custody and support of children and one involving adjudication of property rights is too apparent to require elaboration. In the former, courts are no longer concerned primarily with the proprietary claims of the contestants for the *"res"* before the court, but with the welfare of the *"res"* itself. Custody is viewed not with the idea of adjudicating rights *in* the children, as if they were chattels, but rather with the idea of making the best disposition possible for the welfare of the children. To speak of a court's "cutting off" a mother's right to custody of her children, as if it raised problems similar to those involved in "cutting off" her rights in a plot of ground, is to obliterate these obvious distinctions. Personal jurisdiction of all parties to be affected by a proceeding is highly desirable, to make certain that they have had valid notice and opportunity to be heard. But the assumption that it overrides all other considerations and in its absence a state is constitutionally impotent to resolve questions of custody flies in the face of our own cases. *   *   *

I fear this decision will author new confusions. The interpretative concurrence, if it be a true interpretation, seems to reduce the law of custody to a rule of seize-and-run. I would affirm the decision of the Ohio courts that they should respect the judgment of the Wisconsin court, until it or some other court with equal or better claims to jurisdiction shall modify it.

*   *   *

NOTES AND QUESTIONS

1. May v. Anderson is noted in 67 Harv.L.Rev. 121 (1953), 52 Mich. L.Rev. 594 (1954) and other reviews. For a thorough critique of the case see Hazard, May v. Anderson: Preamble to Family Law Chaos, 45 Va.L. Rev. 379 (1959).

2. The Supreme Court faced the problem of full faith and credit to custody decrees on one occasion before it decided May v. Anderson, in People ex rel. Halvey v. Halvey, 330 U.S. 610 (1947). In that case W obtained a Florida divorce ex parte, the decree giving her custody of her child. H, without her knowledge, took the child to New York, where W then sought habeas corpus, arguing that New York was bound to enforce the Florida custody order under the Full Faith and Credit Clause. The Supreme Court held that since the Florida decree was modifiable in Florida, not merely for changed circumstances but also for proof of facts not presented in the earlier proceeding, New York could modify it on the same basis. The Full Faith and Credit Clause was held to mean that what Florida might do in the way of modification, New York could do. Therefore the New York court was not bound to give automatic enforcement to the Florida order and could impose modifications. The Court did not discuss the question whether the lack of in personam jurisdiction in Florida excused recognition of the decree in other states.

Two cases subsequent to May v. Anderson also dealt with full faith and credit to custody decrees. In one, Kovacs v. Brewer, 356 U.S. 604 (1958) the Court held, as in *Halvey*, that since New York could modify its custody decree upon proof of changed circumstances, North Carolina could do as much, remanding the case for findings on whether the circumstances had in fact changed. A similar holding, that the second state need give no broader effect to the custody decree than the first state would give to its own decree, was announced in the other case, Ford v. Ford, 371 U.S. 187 (1962). Mr. Justice Frankfurter, dissenting in Kovacs v. Brewer, supra, 356 U.S. at 613 urged that the Full Faith and Credit Clause should have no application at all to custody decrees. The same view is expressed in Bachman v. Mejias, 1 N.Y.2d 575, 154 N.Y.S.2d 903, 136 N.E.2d 866 (1956). For a reasoned conclusion that full faith and credit need not be given to custody decrees, with an extensive citation of authorities, see Borys v. Borys, 76 N.J. 103, 386 A.2d 366 (1978).

3. Is Mr. Justice Frankfurter right in saying that May v. Anderson raises no due process issue? How can we square this view with the majority opinion's statement that the mother's right to custody is a personal right as important as her right to alimony? What is Mr. Justice Jackson's view on this issue?

4. What are the implications, both negative and positive, of May v. Anderson? For example, is the case to be taken as meaning that personal jurisdiction over the parties is the *only* prerequisite to full faith and credit? Does the case mean that if there had been personal jurisdiction Ohio would have been required to enforce the Wisconsin decree? Or does the case just leave open the question whether domicile, or residence, or physical presence are also required before a decree must be given full faith and credit? What significance does the Court's footnote 2 have, apparently citing

with approval the first Restatement's rule that domicile is the *only* basis for custody jurisdiction? Does the case also leave open the question whether full faith and credit has any application at all to custody decrees? Some of the difficulties in these issues are illustrated by Lennon v. Lennon, 252 N.C. 659, 114 S.E.2d 571 (1960); McAninch v. McAninch, 39 N.C.App. 665, 251 S.E.2d 633 (1979), review denied 297 N.C. 300, 254 S.E.2d 920 (1979); Williams v. Williams, 44 Ohio St. 28, 336 N.E.2d 426, 73 O.O.2d 121 (1975).

5. Has May v. Anderson been overruled sub silentio by Stanley v. Illinois, 405 U.S. 645 (1972), reproduced supra at page 432? In particular consider footnote 9 from Mr. Justice White's opinion:

> [9] We note in passing that the incremental cost of offering unwed fathers an opportunity for individualized hearings on fitness appears to be minimal. If unwed fathers, in the main, do not care about the disposition of their children, they will not appear to demand hearings. If they do care, under the scheme here held invalid, Illinois would admittedly at some later time have to afford them a properly focused hearing in a custody or adoption proceeding.
>
> Extending opportunity for hearing to unwed fathers who desire and claim competence to care for their children creates no constitutional or procedural obstacle to foreclosing those unwed fathers who are not so inclined. The Illinois law governing procedure in juvenile cases, Ill.Rev.Stat., c. 37, § 704–1 et seq., provides for personal service, notice by certified mail, or for notice by publication when personal or certified mail service cannot be had or when notice is directed to unknown respondents under the style of "All whom it may Concern." Unwed fathers who do not promptly respond cannot complain if their children are declared wards of the State. Those who do respond retain the burden of proving their fatherhood.

Is Mr. Justice White saying that the father of the illegitimate child may be deprived of rights far more precious than property rights merely on the basis of service by mail or by an advertisement in a newspaper addressed "to whom it may concern"? Does that mean that a court not having personal jurisdiction may cut off such rights? And certainly he could not have been assuming, could he, that such a procedure would do for the parent of the illegitimate child, while something more would be required for the parent of the legitimate child? But that is an odd way of overruling a case is it not, especially since he cites May v. Anderson, and even quotes the phrase about precious rights, 405 U.S. at page 651? What then can we make of all this?

6. Some cases which have refused to give full faith and credit to the custody decrees of other states, in partial or entire reliance upon May v. Anderson, include Calhoun v. Calhoun, 46 Ala.App. 381, 243 So.2d 37 (1970); Batchelor v. Fulcher, 415 S.W.2d 828 (Ky.1967), 37 U.Cin.L.Rev. 191 (1968), 13 Vill.L.Rev. 406 (1968); McLam v. McLam, 81 N.M. 37, 462 P.2d 622 (1969); McAninch v. McAninch, 39 N.C.App. 665, 251 S.E.2d 633 (1979), review denied 297 N.C. 300, 254 S.E.2d 920 (1979); In re Messner, 19 Ohio App.2d 33, 249 N.E.2d 532, 48 O.O.2d 31 (1969); Dieringer v. Heiney, 10 Or.App. 345, 497 P.2d 1201 (1972); Miller v. Shufeldt, 2 Or. App. 243, 467 P.2d 971 (1970); Weber v. Weber, 6 Wash.App. 722, 496 P.

2d 576 (1972); Pickler v. Pickler, 5 Wash.App. 627, 489 P.2d 932 (1971). Since the same result might have been reached in several of these cases without reliance upon May v. Anderson, due to the non-final nature of custody decrees and the rule that full faith and credit does not prevent such non-final decrees from being revised in a second state, the practical significance of May v. Anderson is not as great in custody cases as might appear from the mere citation of cases which rely upon it.

7. H and W were divorced when H deserted W, leaving no address. Since W had no information concerning H's whereabouts, service was by publication. The decree gave W the divorce, and also gave her custody of C, the only child of the marriage. Some time later W remarried and H–2 wished to adopt C. H had not supported the child and in fact had not been heard from since the divorce. A petition for adoption was filed, service again was by publication and the adoption decree was entered, terminating H's parental rights on the ground of abandonment as authorized by statute. A year later H turned up and brought suit to set aside the adoption decree for lack of personal jurisdiction over him, citing May v. Anderson. W and H–2 filed a motion to dismiss. What arguments might be made for and against this motion? See Hazard, loc. cit. supra, paragraph 1, 45 Va.L. Rev. 379, 395 (1959).

8. One of the obvious deficiencies of May v. Anderson is its ignoring of other cases and other writing on custody jurisdiction. One important earlier case is Sampsell v. Superior Court, 32 Cal.2d 763, 197 P.2d 739 (1948) in which Mr. Justice Traynor wrote the opinion. This case held that (a) the courts of two or more states may have concurrent jurisdiction over the custody of a child; (b) custody jurisdiction may be based upon personal jurisdiction over the child's parents; (c) custody jurisdiction may be based upon the child's domicile; (d) custody jurisdiction may be based upon the child's physical presence within the state; and (e) the fact that two or more states may have jurisdiction does not require that both exercise it, since one court may decide that another state has a more substantial interest in the child and may choose not to exercise jurisdiction. Mr. Justice Traynor also recognized in this case that custody decrees are generally modifiable upon a showing of changed circumstances and that the decrees of other states should be treated with the same respect as would be given to the forum's own decrees.

In addition to *Sampsell* there were three important articles on custody jurisdiction providing background for the subject. Stumberg, The Status of Children in the Conflict of Laws, 8 U.Chi.L.Rev. 42 (1940); Stansbury, Custody and Maintenance Across State Lines, 10 L. & Contemp.Prob. 818 (1944); Ehrenzweig, Interstate Recognition of Custody Decrees, 51 Mich. L.Rev. 345 (1953). More recent treatment of the subject can be found in Ratner, Child Custody in a Federal System, 62 Mich.L.Rev. 795 (1964); Ratner, Legislative Resolution of the Interstate Child Custody Problem: A Reply to Professor Currie and a Proposed Uniform Act, 38 So.Cal.L.Rev. 183 (1965); Bodenheimer, The Uniform Child Custody Jurisdiction Act: A Legislative Remedy for Children Caught in the Conflict of Laws, 22 Vand. L.Rev. 1207 (1969); H. Clark, Law of Domestic Relations § 11.5 (1968).

9. There may be local law requirements for jurisdiction in custody cases which of course must be observed in such suits. For example, the

question may be raised whether, when a divorce is denied either for lack of jurisdiction or for failure to prove grounds, the court may go on to decide the custody issue. This depends on the divorce statute in force in the state. Some statutes permit a custody order in this situation. See, e. g., Atwood v. Atwood, 229 Minn. 333, 39 N.W.2d 103 (1949), 34 Minn.L.Rev. 347 (1949); Sauvageau v. Sauvageau, 59 Idaho 190, 81 P.2d 731 (1938); Annots. 113 A.L.R. 901, 905 (1938), 151 A.L.R. 1380, 1381 (1944), and 7 A.L.R.3d 1096 (1966). Others may only authorize custody orders "when a divorce has been decreed." See Johnson v. Levis, 240 Iowa 806, 38 N.W.2d 115 (1949), 35 Iowa L.Rev. 111 (1949), 35 Va.L.Rev. 921 (1949); Holderle v. Holderle, 11 Ohio App.2d 148, 229 N.E.2d 79 (1967); Newell v. Newell, 21 Ohio Misc. 239, 257 N.E.2d 90 (1969), rev'd on other grounds, 23 Ohio App.2d 149, 261 N.E.2d 278 (1970). Under these statutes, when the divorce is denied, a wholly new action to determine custody must be brought, thereby wasting the time and money of everyone concerned.

There may also be local rules concerning the county or the court in which custody disputes must be litigated. See, e. g., Commonwealth ex rel. Hickey v. Hickey, 216 Pa.Super. 332, 264 A.2d 420 (1970).

10. It should be obvious that in all custody cases there must be adequate notice and an opportunity to be heard. MacMillan v. MacMillan, 174 Colo. 20, 482 P.2d 107 (1971). See Armstrong v. Manzo, 380 U.S. 545 (1965).

11. The form of proceeding in which custody questions are raised also varies from state to state. They are most commonly raised in divorce actions. Under statutes in some states they may also be raised in an ordinary civil proceeding commenced by a petition in equity. This is essentially the form of suit authorized by the Uniform Marriage and Divorce Act, § 401(d), 9A Unif.L.Ann. 194 (1979).

In many states custody disputes are the subject of petitions for habeas corpus, the parent or person seeking custody asking that the writ issue to compel someone else to turn over the custody of the child. The use of habeas corpus for this purpose developed in English law out of the Crown's obligation to protect children, the obligation often referred to as the doctrine of parens patriae. By an anaolgy to the ordinary writ of habeas corpus, which lies to obtain the release of a person being illegally held by the state, the writ came also to be used when the allegation was that the petitioner was being illegally detained by a private person rather than the state. Only a moderate further extension of the procedure made the writ available to a person seeking to have a child's custody transferred from another to himself. The proceeding so begun came to be a well-established heading of equity jurisdiction. For discussions of the history of habeas corpus as a remedy in custody disputes, see New York Foundling Hospital v. Gatti, 203 U.S. 429 (1906); Pukas v. Pukas, 129 W.Va. 765, 42 S.E.2d 11 (1947).

In most states the petition for habeas corpus opens up the entire question of the child's welfare and what custodial arrangements will best serve that welfare. Pukas v. Pukas, supra; Miracle v. Miracle, 208 Kan. 168, 490 P.2d 638 (1971). In a few states, however, the courts in habeas corpus are limited to determining the bare legal right to custody. See, e. g., May v. Anderson, 345 U.S. 528 (1953), stating Ohio law.

12. Has May v. Anderson's apparent insistence upon personal jurisdiction as the only basis for custody decrees been reaffirmed by *Kulko*, reproduced supra, at page 851, and by Shaffer v. Heitner, cited supra, at page 863? In view of *Kulko's* statement that the "minimum contacts" standard applies to domestic relations cases, is it, or should it be, the rule that a court may not enter a custody order without in personam jurisdiction over the child's parents? And may in personam jurisdiction be obtained by compliance with a "long-arm" statute like that involved in *Kulko?* If so, what is the effect of *Kulko's* remark that a stricter application of the "minimum contracts" standard must be made in domestic relations cases than in commercial contract cases? For a thorough discussion of these issues, see Bodenheimer & Neeley-Kvarme, Jurisdiction Over Child Custody and Adoption after Shaffer and Kulko, 12 U.C.D.L.Rev. 229 (1979). State courts have reached differing results on the application of long-arm statutes to custody cases, depending in the first instance on the language of the statute. In re Marriage of Myers, 92 Wash.2d 113, 594 P.2d 902 (1979) held that the long-arm statute did apply to give in personam jurisdiction over a father who had left the state, the basis for its application being living together in the marital relationship in Washington. The long-arm statute was held not to apply to custody cases in Worland v. Worland, 89 N.M. 291, 551 P.2d 981 (1976) and State ex rel. Muirhead v. District Court, 169 Mont. 535, 550 P.2d 1304 (1976), the court also saying that, under May v. Anderson, a parent's custody may not be terminated in the absence of in personam jurisdiction.

13. W divorced H in State X, serving H by publication because he had deserted her and she did not know where he was. The decree gave custody of the parties' child, C, to W. She moved to State Y, where H turned up within the year. H petitioned for habeas corpus, seeking custody of C. W put the X decree in evidence and the court indicated a disposition to decide on the basis of that decree, without going into the merits, since the case had been thoroughly explored so recently in State X. H contended that this could not be done without violating the principle of May v. Anderson, arguing that the court of X was without jurisdiction and therefore the court of Y would be violating the Due Process Clause in giving any effect to the X decree. What should be the outcome? Cf. Eule v. Eule, 9 Wis.2d 115, 100 N.W.2d 554 (1960), cert. den. 362 U.S. 988 (1960); Cooper v. Cooper, 229 Ark. 770, 318 S.W.2d 587 (1958).

MARRIAGE OF SETTLE

Supreme Court of Oregon, 1976.
276 Or. 759, 556 P.2d 962.

HOLMAN, Justice. This case involves a dispute between a mother and a father over the custody of their two minor children. The trial court granted custody to the mother and upon appeal the Court of Appeals reversed the trial court and gave custody to the father. We granted review to determine whether the Uniform Child Custody Jurisdiction Act adopted by the 1973 Legislative Session necessitates a result which would appear to be inconsistent with our last opinion on the subject, Hawkins v. Hawkins, 264 Or. 221, 504 P. 2d 709 (1972).

Father and mother were married in Elkhart, Indiana, in 1968. Their two children are Tracy, an 8-year-old girl, and James, Jr., a 4-year-old boy. Tracy was born to mother in a previous marriage and adopted by father. In August 1973 mother left Elkhart with the children and a man by the name of Ross Fuller and eventually came to Oregon. During their absence father began a relationship with Beverly Walston, who was then the wife of David Walston and the mother of three children, one of whom was conceived by Walston and the other two by Fuller at a time when she was cohabiting with him.

In November 1973 mother returned to Elkhart from Oregon with the children and Fuller. In December she filed a suit for divorce and was given temporary custody of the children by the court pursuant to an agreement by the parties. On March 5, 1974, father filed an answer requesting that he be given the divorce and custody of the children. In the latter part of March mother again left Elkhart with the children and returned to Oregon. She made no attempt to let either the court or father know where she had gone. She claims she had no knowledge at the time she left Elkhart of father's request for custody of the children and that such request was not the reason for her leaving. She was not able to convince the trial court and the Court of Appeals that she had no such knowledge and she has been no more able to convince this court. Fuller joined her in Oregon sometime during the following month.

The final hearing in the Indiana divorce proceeding took place in May 1974, mother's lawyer having withdrawn from the case due to his client's absence. The court heard testimony of father and others to the effect that mother had had intercourse with Fuller in the presence of the children while staying with friends. The court found that mother was an unfit person to have custody and granted custody to father, who, unbeknown to the court, was then living with Beverly Walston and the father of her unborn child.

Mother learned of the divorce in June 1974 and promptly married Fuller while residing in Oregon. Thereafter father attempted to locate the children and eventually found them in Oregon. He thereupon came to Oregon and instituted a habeas corpus proceeding based upon his award of custody by the Indiana decree. Shortly prior to the institution of that proceeding mother had registered the Indiana decree in Oregon and had filed a petition for a change of custody of the children from father to herself. The two proceedings were consolidated for trial, thus setting the stage for the present litigation.

Two or three weeks prior to the hearing in the trial court father married Beverly Walston, who, by that time, had secured a divorce from Donald Walston and had given birth to father's child. The hearing in the trial court was held on September 3, 1975—20 months from the time the children had last seen father—and both parents and their spouses appeared and testified.

In addition to the facts recited, the evidence shows that father has a television repair business in Elkhart which he has operated for approximately 14 years and which provides adequate income with which to support the children. He has two additional children, not previously mentioned, by still another marriage, one of whom is in the custody of its mother and the other of whom lives with its grandparents. Ross Fuller is shown to be an itinerant, emotional incompetent. He does not consistently hold a job and for a short time he was in a mental hospital. Apparently he had a drinking problem at one time which he has since overcome. In addition to his two children born out of wedlock by father's present wife, formerly Beverly Walston, Fuller had a third child by a woman not heretofore mentioned. He supports none of these children. He and mother have also had a child born to them since their marriage. Since the group living with Fuller have been in Oregon, they have applied for public assistance and have lived in several different places. There is no evidence that Fuller has mistreated the children, and the trial judge remarked that Fuller appeared to have a personality warmer than father's. One of Tracy's school teachers testified that Tracy was an outgoing and happy child who came to school clean and well groomed, and that although she had some trouble due to a short attention span, she was making good progress, was amenable to instruction and showed no serious signs of emotional impairment. At the time of trial James, Jr., had not as yet had contact with the school system.

The trial judge reached several conclusions, including the following:

1. The Indiana decree was punitive and was made by an incompletely informed court;

2. Mother committed an act of misconduct by taking the children from Indiana and secreting them in Oregon;

3. Oregon had become the home state of the children and the more convenient and appropriate forum for considering their best interests;

4. There had been a substantial change in circumstances following the Indiana decree;

5. There were no affirmative reasons to award custody to either parent, and, under those circumstances, the court would leave the children where it found them.

Accordingly, the court denied the writ of habeas corpus and modified the Indiana decree by awarding custody to the mother. The Court of Appeals reversed, * * *.

The first question which arises is whether the Oregon court has jurisdiction. We turn to ORS 109.730(1)(a) and (b) (Section 3(a) (1) and (2) of the Uniform Act), which is as follows:

[At this point the court quoted from the Uniform Child Custody Jurisdiction Act § 3(a)(1) and (2), which is reproduced, infra, at page 1049.]

From the above it is apparent that the Oregon court has jurisdiction. Oregon is the children's "home state" under ORS 109.730(1)(a) since they lived with a parent in Oregon for more than six consecutive months immediately prior to the commencement of these proceedings. The court also has jurisdiction under subsection (1)(b) of the same section because the children and their mother have a significant connection with Oregon, and there is available in Oregon substantial evidence concerning the children's present and future care, protection, training and personal relationships.

The more troublesome issue is whether the court *should exercise* its jurisdiction. * * * In order to exercise jurisdiction in such a situation, two hurdles must be overcome. The first one is ORS 109.840(1) (Section 14(a)(1) and (2) of the Uniform Act) which is as follows:

[At this point the court quoted from the Uniform Child Custody Jurisdiction Act § 14(a)(1) and (2), reproduced, infra, at page 1053.]

Because of the above provision, we must again look to the jurisdictional subsections, ORS 109.730(1)(a) and (b), to determine whether, under the circumstances here, Indiana also presently would have jurisdiction under the Act. If it would, Oregon courts may not exercise their jurisdiction. It is clear that Indiana would not have jurisdiction under subsection (1)(a) (regardless of whether or not it has jurisdiction under the laws of the State of Indiana) because Indiana cannot now qualify as the children's "home state," since the children have not lived in Indiana for 18 months.

Subsection (1)(b) offers more difficulty. One parent certainly has a significant connection with Indiana, and there is available there substantial evidence concerning the children's relationship with that parent and, thus, their future care, protection, training and personal relationships if they are to be returned to Indiana. However, at the time of the hearing by the trial court the children had no significant connection with Indiana because of the length of time they had been away. In the lives of children 4 and 8 years of age, 18 months is a long time. Furthermore, the children had had no contact with their father for 20 months. The Commissioners' Note, 9 Uniform Laws Annotated 107, 108, § 3 (Master ed. 1973) contains the following comment:

"Paragraph (2) [Subsection (1)(b) of ORS 109.730] perhaps more than any other provision of the Act requires that it be interpreted in the spirit of the legislative purposes expressed in section 1. The paragraph was phrased in general terms in order to be flexible enough to cover many fact situations too diverse to lend themselves to exact description. But its purpose is to limit jurisdiction rather than to proliferate it. The first clause of the paragraph is important: jurisdiction exists only if it is in the *child's* interest, not merely the interest or convenience of the feuding parties, to determine custody in a particular state. The interest of the child is served when the forum has optimum access to relevant evidence about the child and family. There must be maximum rather than minimum contact with the state. The submission of the parties to a forum, perhaps for purposes of divorce, is not sufficient without additional factors establishing closer ties with the state. Divorce jurisdiction does not necessarily include custody jurisdiction. See Clark, Domestic Relations 578 (1968)." (Emphasis in original.)

It is clear that the Commissioners intended to prevent the proliferation of jurisdiction. It is also clear, however, that they did not intend that the existence of "home state" jurisdiction in one state (in the present case, Oregon) should automatically preclude the existence of jurisdiction in another state (in the present case, Indiana). Jurisdiction in another state will exist when it is in the best interests of the children because they and a parent have a significant connection with that state and because there is available in that state substantial evidence concerning the children's present or future circumstances. The above comment indicates that the requirement of the availability of "substantial evidence" should be understood to require optimum access to relevant evidence. It appears that at the time of the commencement of the proceedings in Oregon, Indiana, the state from which the children had been absent for 18 months, no longer had optimum access to relevant evidence. As to the requirement of a "significant connection," the existence of the custody decree issued after a hearing by the court in Indiana may be a factor favoring continued jurisdiction in Indiana. Commissioners' Note, 9 Uniform Laws Annotated 122 (Master ed. 1973). That factor is weakened, however, by the failure of the decree ever to take effect and by the passage of time since its issuance. Under the facts here, we conclude that under the Act there is neither "significant connection" nor "substantial evidence" in Indiana. Under the Act both must exist. It would therefore, not be in the best interests of the children for Indiana to assume jurisdiction, and Indiana therefore does not now have jurisdiction under the Act.

Having decided that the Oregon court qualifies to exercise jurisdiction under the provisions of ORS 109.840(1), we must next turn to ORS 109.780(2) (Section 8(b) of the Uniform Act) to see if the court also is qualified to exercise its jurisdiction thereunder. The Commissioners' Note at page 116, Section 8, makes it clear that when the petitioner for modification has wrongfully removed the children from another state which had jurisdiction, the provisions of both the jurisdictional statute and this statute must be met before the courts of the state to which the children have been removed may exercise its jurisdiction. ORS 109.780(2) states:

[At this point the court quoted from the Uniform Child Custody Jurisdiction Act § 8(b), reproduced, infra, at page 1052.]

The above subsection incorporates the "clean hands doctrine" as it applies to this case. Mother contends that this subsection has no application because she had legal custody of the children at the time she came to Oregon and did not remove the children from the physical custody of another person who was entitled to custody or violate any other provision of a custody decree. The contention is not valid because her acts in removing the children are within the intent, if not the literal provision, of the statute. She had only *temporary* custody of the children, subject to further court order upon the trial of the divorce proceeding. She was a temporary caretaker for the court and did not have custody that entitled her to remove the children from the court's jurisdiction. Her act was just as culpable as if she had removed the children from the legal and physical custody of father or retained them after a visit and then taken them from Indiana. It is the *kind of act* which the Act intended should preclude the exercise of jurisdiction—unless the best interests of the children otherwise require.

* * *

This case thus presents the hard choice of whether, under the Act, a court should exercise modification jurisdiction when it is presented with the following circumstances:

1. Mother, contrary to authority, removes the children of young age from their state of residence and secretes them for the purpose of avoiding a custody proceeding;

2. A court of the state of original residence grants custody to father after mother absconds, because the information available to that court dictates that such a disposition is proper;

3. Father is unable to find the children until after mother and children have established a residence of long duration in another state;

4. Legal proceedings are commenced in the state of the children's new residence for modification of the custody decree, and the court has all parties before it and optimum access to relevant evidence about the children and their family, and the children now have maximum contact with their new state of residence;

5. The court granting the original decree had incomplete information concerning the best interests of the children because of mother's wrongful act in leaving that state with the children; and

6. It is probable that the court of the state of original residence will never have an opportunity to litigate custody with the full facts before it because mother will be unable to afford it.

Two of the principal purposes of the Act are to discourage forum shopping and to protect the best interests of children. It cannot be denied that by allowing the Oregon court to exercise its jurisdiction we would put a premium upon an improper removal of children from their state of original residence. Mother will have been permitted to enjoy the jurisdiction of a court which may treat her more favorably than would the court of the state of original residence. The success and duration of the secretion of the children will have made the children's removal from mother more difficult because she has become the only parent the children really know. On the other hand, the best interests of the children require that at some time a determination be made upon all relevant facts without respect to prior parental disregard of court proceedings, and the present proceeding is probably the only opportunity which will ever exist to make such a determination.

A close reading of the Act discloses a schizophrenic attempt to bring about an orderly system of decision and at the same time to protect the best interests of the children who may be immediately before the court. When put to the test of a factual situation presenting an irreconcilable conflict between those two interests, we read the Act as making predominate the best interests of the children before the court. It is our conclusion that the best interests of the children require a hearing at some time on the full facts, that in this case the present proceeding is the only opportunity which is likely ever to exist, and that the trial court therefore properly exercised jurisdiction.

The Court of Appeals based its decision primarily upon the Commissioners' Note, 9 Uniform Laws Annotated 122–23 (Master ed. 1973), which follows Section 14 of the Uniform Act (ORS 109.840). The note, in part, is as follows:

" * * * [I]f the father * * * continued to live in state 1 [state of original residence], but let his wife keep the children [in another state] for several years without asserting his custody rights and without visits of the children in state 1, modification jurisdiction of state 1 would cease. Compare Brengle v. Hurst, 408 S.W.2d 418 (Ky.1966). The situation would be different if the children had been abducted and their whereabouts could not be discovered by the legal custodian for several years. The abductor would be denied access to the court of another state under section 8(b) * * *."

As the Court of Appeals states, 25 Or.App. at 583–84, 550 P.2d 445, this would seem to fit the situation in the present case. However, when we look at Section 8(b) of the Uniform Act (ORS 109.780(2)), to which the above set-forth language of the Commissioners' Note obviously refers, we see that it commences with the language, *"Unless required in the interest of the child,* the court shall not exercise its jurisdiction * * *."* (Emphasis ours.) In the Commissioners' Note under Section 8(b) of the Uniform Act, 9 Uniform Laws Annotated 115, 116 (Master ed. 1973), we find the following language:

" * * * In the case of illegal removal or retention refusal of jurisdiction is mandatory unless the harm done to the child by a denial of jurisdiction outweighs the parental misconduct. * * *." *Rule*

The seeming inconsistency between the two Commissioners' Notes is confusing at best. We conclude that the language of Section 8(b) and the comment thereunder should control the scope of that section rather than the comment under a different section which appears not to be properly qualified.

This leaves the sole question of whether the trial court, after correctly exercising jurisdiction, properly found a change of circumstance justifying a grant of custody to mother. Had this been the only issue in the case we would not have taken review. The trial judge found there had been a substantial change of circumstance, and with this finding we agree. In the determination of a case of this kind so much depends upon observation by the trial judge of the people involved that, although we try the matter anew on the record, we are not inclined to overrule the trial judge unless it clearly appears that he is wrong. This is not a case where the action by the trial judge appears to have been wrong. Albeit that neither of the parents is one that we would choose to rear children, an unenviable choice must be made. For practical purposes, mother's association with the children has been much closer than father's. We believe it would be a colossal mistake and detrimental to the children to take them away from mother, who has reared them from infancy, and to give them to a father they hardly know, when there is no evidence that the children have suffered from mother's custody. The Court of Appeals overruled the trial court because it believed not that father would make a better parent but because the Uniform Act required such a result. We believe the Court of Appeals was in error, and we reverse its determination and remand the case to the Court of Appeals with directions to reinstate the decree of the trial court.

NOTES AND QUESTIONS

1. The Uniform Child Custody Jurisdiction Act pursuant to which the *Settle* case was decided is, at latest count, in force in the following thirty-eight states: Alaska, Arizona, Arkansas, California, Colorado, Connecticut, Delaware, Florida, Georgia, Hawaii, Idaho, Illinois, Indiana, Iowa, Kansas, Louisiana, Maine, Maryland, Michigan, Minnesota, Missouri, Montana, Nebraska, Nevada, New Hampshire, New Jersey, New York, North Carolina, North Dakota, Ohio, Oregon, Pennsylvania, Rhode Island, South Dakota, Virginia, Washington, Wisconsin, Wyoming.

As the court's approach in *Settle* shows, the Act is complex and several of its sections may be relevant to the decision in a particular case. Its major sections follow:

"§ 1.   [Purposes of Act; Construction of Provisions]

"(a) The general purposes of this Act are to:

"(1) avoid jurisdictional competition and conflict with courts of other states in matters of child custody which have in the past resulted in the shifting of children from state to state with harmful effects on their well-being;

"(2) promote cooperation with the courts of other states to the end that a custody decree is rendered in that state which can best decide the case in the interest of the child;

"(3) assure that litigation concerning the custody of a child take place ordinarily in the state with which the child and his family have the closest connection and where significant evidence concerning his care, protection, training, and personal relationships is most readily available, and that courts of this state decline the exercise of jurisdiction when the child and his family have a closer connection with another state;

"(4) discourage continuing controversies over child custody in the interest of greater stability of home environment and of secure family relationships for the child;

"(5) deter abductions and other unilateral removals of children undertaken to obtain custody awards;

"(6) avoid re-litigation of custody decisions of other states in this state insofar as feasible;

"(7) facilitate the enforcement of custody decrees of other states;

"(8) promote and expand the exchange of information and other forms of mutual assistance between the courts of this state and those of other states concerned with the same child; and

"(9) make uniform the law of those states which enact it.

"(b) This Act shall be construed to promote the general purposes stated in this section."

"§ 2.   [Definitions]

"As used in this Act:

"(1) 'contestant' means a person, including a parent, who claims a right to custody or visitation rights with respect to a child;

"(2) 'custody determination' means a court decision and court orders and instructions providing for the custody of a child, including visitation rights; it does not include a decision relating to child support or any other monetary obligation of any person;

"(3) 'custody proceeding' includes proceedings in which a custody determination is one of several issues, such as an action for divorce or separation, and includes child neglect and dependency proceedings;

"(4) 'decree' or 'custody decree' means a custody determination contained in a judicial decree or order made in a custody proceeding, and includes an initial decree and a modification decree;

"(5) 'home state' means the state in which the child immediately preceding the time involved lived with his parents, a parent, or a person acting as parent, for at least 6 consecutive months, and in the case of a child less than 6 months old the state in which the child lived from birth with any of the persons mentioned. Periods of temporary absence of any of the named persons are counted as part of the 6-month or other period;

"(6) 'initial decree' means the first custody decree concerning a particular child;

"(7) 'modification decree' means a custody decree which modifies or replaces a prior decree, whether made by the court which rendered the prior decree or by another court;

"(8) 'physical custody' means actual possession and control of a child;

"(9) 'person acting as parent' means a person, other than a parent, who has physical custody of a child and who has either been awarded custody by a court or claims a right to custody; and

"(10) 'state' means any state, territory, or possession of the United States, the Commonwealth of Puerto Rico, and the District of Columbia.

"§ 3. [Jurisdiction]

"(a) A court of this State which is competent to decide child custody matters has jurisdiction to make a child custody determination by initial or modification decree if:

"(1) This State (i) is the home state of the child at the time of commencement of the proceeding, or (ii) had been the child's home state within 6 months before commencement of the proceeding and the child is absent from this State because of his removal or retention by a person claiming his custody or for other reasons, and a parent or person acting as parent continues to live in this State; or

"(2) it is in the best interest of the child that a court of this State assume jurisdiction because (i) the child and his parents, or the child and at least one contestant, have a significant connection with this State, and (ii) there is available in this State substantial evidence concerning the child's present or future care, protection, training, and personal relationships; or

"(3) the child is physically present in this State and (i) the child has been abandoned or (ii) it is necessary in an emergency to protect the child because he has been subjected to or threatened with mistreatment or abuse or is otherwise neglected [or dependent]; or

"(4)(i) it appears that no other state would have jurisdiction under prerequisites substantially in accordance with paragraphs (1), (2), or (3), or another state has declined to exercise jurisdiction on the ground that this State is the more appropriate forum to determine the custody of the child, and (ii) it is in the best interest of the child that this court assume jurisdiction.

"(b) Except under paragraphs (3) and (4) of subsection (a), physical presence in this State of the child, or of the child and one of the contestants, is not alone sufficient to confer jurisdiction on a court of this State to make a child custody determination.

"(c) Physical presence of the child, while desirable, is not a prerequisite for jurisdiction to determine his custody.

[Section 4 of the Act requires reasonable notice and an opportunity to be heard to parents and those having custody of a child. Section 5 specifies the methods of giving notice in a manner reasonably calculated to give actual notice, including personal delivery outside the state, or by mail, or by publication where other methods are ineffective.]

"§ 6.　[Simultaneous Proceedings in Other States]

"(a) A court of this State shall not exercise its jurisdiction under this Act if at the time of filing the petition a proceeding concerning the custody of the child was pending in a court of another state exercising jurisdiction substantially in conformity with this Act, unless the proceeding is stayed by the court of the other state because this State is a more appropriate forum or for other reasons.

"(b) Before hearing the petition in a custody proceeding the court shall examine the pleadings and other information supplied by the parties under section 9 and shall consult the child custody registry established under section 16 concerning the pendency of proceedings with respect to the child in other states. If the court has reason to believe that proceedings may be pending in another state it shall direct an inquiry to the state court administrator or other appropriate official of the other state.

"(c) If the court is informed during the course of the proceeding that a proceeding concerning the custody of the child was pending in another state before the court assumed jurisdiction it shall stay the proceeding and communicate with the court in which the other proceeding is pending to the end that the issue may be litigated in the more appropriate forum and that information be exchanged in accordance with sections 19 through 22. If a court of this State has made a custody decree before being informed of a pending proceeding in a court of another state it shall immediately inform that court of the fact. If the court is informed that a proceeding was commenced in another state after it assumed jurisdiction it shall likewise inform the other court to the end that the issues may be litigated in the more appropriate forum.

"§ 7.　[Inconvenient Forum]

"(a) A court which has jurisdiction under this Act to make an initial or modification decree may decline to exercise its jurisdiction any time before making a decree if it finds that it is an inconvenient forum to make a custody determination under the circumstances of the case and that a court of another state is a more appropriate forum.

"(b) A finding of inconvenient forum may be made upon the court's own motion or upon motion of a party or a guardian ad litem or other representative of the child.

"(c) In determining if it is an inconvenient forum, the court shall consider if it is in the interest of the child that another state assume jurisdiction. For this purpose it may take into account the following factors, among others:

"(1) if another state is or recently was the child's home state;

"(2) if another state has a closer connection with the child and his family or with the child and one or more of the contestants;

"(3) if substantial evidence concerning the child's present or future care, protection, training, and personal relationships is more readily available in another state;

"(4) if the parties have agreed on another forum which is no less appropriate; and

"(5) if the exercise of jurisdiction by a court of this state would contravene any of the purposes stated in section 1.

"(d) Before determining whether to decline or retain jurisdiction the court may communicate with a court of another state and exchange information pertinent to the assumption of jurisdiction by either court with a view to assuring that jurisdiction will be exercised by the more appropriate court and that a forum will be available to the parties.

"(e) If the court finds that it is an inconvenient forum and that a court of another state is a more appropriate forum, it may dismiss the proceedings, or it may stay the proceedings upon condition that a custody proceeding be promptly commenced in another named state or upon any other conditions which may be just and proper, including the condition that a moving party stipulate his consent and submission to the jurisdiction of the other forum.

"(f) The court may decline to exercise its jurisdiction under this Act if a custody determination is incidental to an action for divorce or another proceeding while retaining jurisdiction over the divorce or other proceeding.

"(g) If it appears to the court that it is clearly an inappropriate forum it may require the party who commenced the proceedings to pay, in addition to the costs of the proceedings in this State, necessary travel and other expenses, including attorneys' fees, incurred by other parties or their witnesses. Payment is to be made to the clerk of the court for remittance to the proper party.

"(h) Upon dismissal or stay of proceedings under this section the court shall inform the court found to be the more appropriate forum of this fact or, if the court which would have jurisdiction in the other state is not certainly known, shall transmit the information to the court administrator or other appropriate official for forwarding to the appropriate court.

"(i) Any communication received from another state informing this State of a finding of inconvenient forum because a court of this State is the more appropriate forum shall be filed in the custody registry of the appropriate court. Upon assuming jurisdiction the court of this State shall inform the original court of this fact.

"§ 8.   [Jurisdiction Declined by Reason of Conduct]

"(a) If the petitioner for an initial decree has wrongfully taken the child from another state or has engaged in similar reprehensible conduct the court may decline to exercise jurisdiction if this is just and proper under the circumstances.

"(b) Unless required in the interest of the child, the court shall not exercise its jurisdiction to modify a custody decree of another state if the petitioner, without consent of the person entitled to custody, has improperly removed the child from the physical custody of the person entitled to custody or has improperly retained the child after a visit or other temporary relinquishment of physical custody. If the petitioner has violated any other provision of a custody decree of another state the court may decline to exercise its jurisdiction if this is just and proper under the circumstances.

"(c) In appropriate cases a court dismissing a petition under this section may charge the petitioner with necessary travel and other expenses, including attorneys' fees, incurred by other parties or their witnesses.

[Section 9 of the Act requires each party in a custody case to give certain information under oath in or with his first pleading, including information on any other proceedings concerning the same child in this or other states. Section 10 provides for the joinder of other parties who have custody or claims to custody of the child. Section 11 authorizes the court to require the appearance of parties and the child.]

"§ 12.   [Binding Force and Res Judicata Effect of Custody Decree]

"A custody decree rendered by a court of this State which had jurisdiction under section 3 binds all parties who have been served in this State or notified in accordance with section 5 or who have submitted to the jurisdiction of the court, and who have been given an opportunity to be heard. As to these parties the custody decree is conclusive as to all issues of law and fact decided and as to the custody determination made unless and until that determination is modified pursuant to law, including the provisions of this Act.

"§ 13.   [Recognition of Out-of-State Custody Decrees]

"The courts of this State shall recognize and enforce an initial or modification decree of a court of another state which had assumed jurisdiction under statutory provisions substantially in accordance with this Act or which was made under factual circumstances meeting the jurisdictional standards of the Act, so long as this decree has not been modified in accordance with jurisdictional standards substantially similar to those of this Act.

"**§ 14.　[Modification of Custody Decree of Another State]**

"(a) If a court of another state has made a custody decree, a court of this State shall not modify that decree unless (1) it appears to the court of this State that the court which rendered the decree does not now have jurisdiction under jurisdictional prerequisites substantially in accordance with this Act or has declined to assume jurisdiction to modify the decree and (2) the court of this State has jurisdiction.

"(b) If a court of this State is authorized under subsection (a) and section 8 to modify a custody decree of another state it shall give due consideration to the transcript of the record and other documents of all previous proceedings submitted to it in accordance with section 22."

[Section 15 of the Act provides a procedure for the filing and enforcement of custody orders of other states, a procedure similar to that of the Uniform Enforcement of Foreign Judgments Act, 13 Unif.L.Ann. 173 (1975). Section 16 sets up in each court a registry of custody decrees of other states which have been filed, and records of communications with other states. Section 17 provides for communication of copies of custody decrees to other states. Section 18 authorizes taking testimony in other states. Section 19 authorizes the courts to request courts of other states to hold custody hearings, have social studies made, and order parties to appear in custody hearings in this state. Section 20 provides reciprocal assistance to other states when requested under section 19. Section 21 provides for the preservation of documents and for forwarding them to other states. Section 22 authorizes courts to request court records from other states. Section 23 extends the policies of the Act to the recognition and enforcement of decrees of other nations. Sections 24 through 27 contain formal provisions dealing with expedition in handling custody cases, severability of provisions, the title to the Act and repeal of other statutes.

The Uniform Act is found in 9 Unif.L.Ann. 116 (1979).

The Act has received extensive commentary. Professor Bodenheimer, who drafted it, has written the article cited infra, in paragraph 3, and another important article, Progress Under the Uniform Child Custody Jurisdiction Act and Remaining Problems: Punitive Decrees, Joint Custody, and Excessive Modifications, 65 Cal.L.Rev. 978 (1977). See also Jarrett, Jurisdiction in Interstate Child Custody Disputes, 12 Gonzaga L.Rev. 423 (1977); Foster and Freed, Child Snatching and Custodial Fights: The Case for the Uniform Child Custody Jurisdiction Act, 28 Hast.L.J. 1011 (1977); Note, Temporary Custody Under the Uniform Child Custody Jurisdiction Act: Influence Without Modification, 48 U.Colo.L.Rev. 603 (1977); Note, Uniform Child Custody Jurisdiction Act: An Attempt to Stop Child Rustling, 12 Willamette L.J. 623 (1976).

2.　Does the *Settle* case reach a result which is in accord with the letter and purpose of the Uniform Act? Does it have the effect of rewarding the parent who seizes the child in one state and runs off to another state in the hope of gaining an advantage in the custody dispute? See Etter v. Etter, 43 Md.App. 395, 405 A.2d 760 (1979), reaching a similar result on somewhat similar facts.

3.　Is the Uniform Act constitutional under May v. Anderson, especially section 3, the basic jurisdiction section, and section 5 which permits service outside the state by personal delivery, mail or as a last resort, by publication? See Bodenheimer, The Uniform Child Custody Jurisdiction Act: A Legislative Remedy for Children Caught in the Conflict of Laws, 22 Vand. L.Rev. 1207, 1232 (1969).

4. H and W were divorced in State X, the decree giving custody of their child, C, to W. W and C then moved to State Y and W acquired a domicile there. H remarried and filed a motion for modification of the X custody decree in the court of X which granted the divorce. W was served by registered mail in State Y.

(a) Does the X court have jurisdiction to modify its own decree? What does the Uniform Act have to say about this situation? Is this a question not of jurisdiction but of whether jurisdiction should be exercised?

(b) If X should modify its decree, giving custody to H, would State Y's courts be required to recognize the modification, either under the Full Faith and Credit Clause, or under the Uniform Act? Could they recognize it if they wished to? Would it matter how long C had been in W's custody?

Some cases dealing with these questions include Cox v. Cox, 457 F.2d 1190 (3d Cir. 1972); Hodgen v. Byrne, 105 Colo. 410, 98 P.2d 1000 (1940); Roberts v. District Court, —— Colo. ——, 596 P.2d 65 (1979) (under the Uniform Act); Keena v. Keena, 245 So.2d 665 (Fla.App.1971); Word v. Word, 236 Ga. 100, 222 S.E.2d 382 (1976); Odom v. Odom, 345 So.2d 1154 (La.1977); Potter v. Rosas, 111 N.H. 169, 276 A.2d 922 (1971); Jones v. Jones, 54 Wis.2d 41, 194 N.W.2d 627 (1972). See also Restatement, Second, Conflict of Laws § 26 (1971).

MARTIN v. MARTIN

New York Court of Appeals, 1978.
45 N.Y.2d 739, 408 N.Y.S.2d 479, 380 N.E.2d 305 reargument denied
45 N.Y.2d 839, 381 N.E.2d 630.

PER CURIAM. Petitioner father seeks permanent custody of two boys, now aged seven and eight, alleging that the mother, his second wife, who was awarded custody under the terms of a separation agreement incorporated into a Florida judgment of divorce, is an unfit parent (Domestic Relations Law, § 70). Special Term denied the father's application, declining to exercise jurisdiction. The Appellate Division [52 A.D.2d 144, 383 N.Y.S.2d 2] reversed, and ordered a hearing, at which the father was awarded custody. The mother appeals directly from the judgment at Supreme Court pursuant to CPLR 5601 (subd. [d]) raising only the correctness of the reversal by the Appellate Division and the direction of a hearing.

The issue involves only application of the principles most recently expressed by this court in Matter of Nehra v. Uhlar, 43 N.Y.2d 242, 401 N.Y.S.2d 168, 372 N.E.2d 4. Since the children have been in New York largely because of the father's repeated disregard of the terms of the Florida judgment, the judgment appealed from and the order of the Appellate Division brought up for review should be reversed, with costs, and the petition dismissed.

The father's allegations of misconduct by the mother need not be detailed. It suffices to note that her conduct, if the charges are true, would likely make her an unfit parent, although despite these grave charges the father returned the children at least once after having retained them unlawfully. Not justified, however, was the father's resort to self-help. He has, on three separate occasions, unlawfully taken or retained custody of the children in violation of the Florida divorce judgment. Moreover, even if the father is assumed to have been motivated by the interests of his children, the record reveals that the father several times left the children with his first wife in New Jersey or with his daughter in a college dormitory also in New Jersey.*

The best interest of the children is, of course, the prime concern. That the children's best interest must come first, however, does not mean that the courts of this State should disregard the prior Florida judgment and determine, as if writing on a clean slate, who would make a better parent. Except for interludes caused by the father's wrongful retention of the custody of the children, the Martin boys lived in Florida from the time of their parents' separation in 1970, when the younger boy was newborn, to the time of the father's most recent abduction in December, 1976. If their mother be an unfit parent, that is a matter for the Florida courts to decide. Florida is where the boys have been raised, and where the witnesses are most

---

* Explicit reference in the dissent to the charges of misconduct by the mother, however irrelevant, suggests response.

The couple had met when the mother was employed as a clerical assistant by a professor of law in the same university in which the father was a professor in the business school. She is much younger than the father and moved to Florida with the children only upon breakup of the marriage.

The misconduct detailed in the father's affidavit is not "unquestioned"; it is disputed. The mother denies, in her answering papers, most of the "affairs" alleged by the father. She also denies any police raid on her home. And she denies sleeping with male friends in the presence of the children.

Moreover, the mother's affidavit, if believed, indicates that the father may be a less than fit parent. The father, a man then over 50, divorced his wife of many years only two months before marrying petitioner. At the time of their marriage, the couple's oldest child was already born, and the mother had had two abortions as a result of her relations with the father. In response to allegations that the mother smoked marihuana in front of the children, the mother accuses the father of doing the same. The father appears to be something of a "nomad", and, as noted, when inconvenient to care for the children himself, he has left them out of State with his first wife or his daughter, then a college student.

None of this is relevant on the limited appeal before the court. The charges and countercharges have never been resolved. The determination at the hearing referred to in the dissent is not brought up for review on this appeal pursuant to CPLR 5601 (subd. [d]). At Supreme Court the only witnesses who testified were the father and a single hostile neighbor of the mother in Florida. The mother, evidently because the hearing was held in New York far from all witnesses, did not participate in the hearing and called no witnesses. Thus, the inferences drawn in the dissent are unsupported in the evidentiary record before this court.

likely to be found. It is not appropriate for the courts of this State, on the present record, to presume to say that the children would be better off with their father.

This deference to the determination of the Florida courts, contrary to assertions in the dissent, is not impliedly or expressly an application of *forum non conveniens*. Instead, principles of comity require that the Florida judgment not be lightly cast aside. *Forum non conveniens* is concerned with the convenience of parties and courts; the comity principle here is concerned with the welfare of children and restraint on abuse of the judicial process.

Certainly, it is beyond cavil that in custody cases principles of comity may not be rigidly applied to the detriment of the children. But that is not the point. The point is rather that successive contradictory determinations by courts of sister States, even if with "jurisdiction", are unseemly and intolerable in a Federal union. Such contradictory determinations are hardly justified by the flexibility of *res judicata* and full faith and credit principles in child custody matters. That is the sense of the holding in the *Nehra* case and of the Uniform Child Custody Jurisdiction Act adopted by many of the States to rid child custody matters of the incubus of child-snatching and forum-shopping.

The policy articulated in the *Nehra* case (supra) and in the Uniform Child Custody Jurisdiction Act, to become effective in New York on September 1, 1978, is a strong one (L.1977, ch. 493; Domestic Relations Law, § 75–i, subd. 2). Of course, it is not an absolute so long as the paramount concern remains the best interest of the child rather than the dignity of courts. A different case would be presented if the immediate physical and mental welfare of children required, vitally and directly, that the children be retained in this jurisdiction and that the courts in this State determine who shall have custody of them. Factors raising those difficult issues are not present in this case. It is the courts of Florida that should adjudicate the ultimate custody dispute if "priority * * * be accorded to the judgment of the court of greatest concern with the welfare of the children" and "[d]enigrated in rank * * * be the consequences of child-snatching" (Matter of Nehra v. Uhlar, 43 N. Y.2d 242, 251, 401 N.Y.S.2d 168, 173, 372 N.E.2d 4, 9, supra). There is nothing presented in this case which suggests that the courts of the sister State are not competent or ready to do justice between the parties and for the children.

Accordingly, the judgment appealed from and the order of the Appellate Division brought up for review should be reversed, with costs, and the petition dismissed.

FUCHSBERG, Judge (dissenting).

The majority does not dispute either the settled proposition that the physical presence of the children was sufficient to confer jurisdiction upon our courts nor that the Florida decree, while entitled to great weight, is subordinate to the best interests of the children—the issue of "paramount concern". Instead, in what smacks of an implicit and unwarranted obeisance to *forum non conveniens* and comity principles, its decision jeopardizes the children's best interests.

The pertinent facts, not seriously disputed, speak for themselves:

Petitioner, a full professor, at whose current post at New York University he has been engaged since about 1962, married the respondent in 1969. Two children, currently ages seven and eight, were born of the marriage. In December, 1970, shortly after the birth of the second child, respondent abandoned her husband and set up a residence in Clearwater, Florida. Her departure eventually led to divorce, prior to which the parties entered into a separate agreement in which they agreed that the children, who were then still close to the baby stage, were to be in the custody of the mother with visitation rights for the father. This provision was incorporated in the final decree in 1972.

In December, 1974, the father requested that the children come to visit him for the Christmas holidays. The respondent then sent them to New York willingly, although it is claimed that an oral agreement to return them in January was violated when the petitioner kept the children in Washington, D. C., and in New Jersey until they were returned to Florida in June, 1975. The children next came to New York in November, 1975, once again voluntarily. It was on that occasion that the petitioner commenced this action seeking custody. Thus, at no time prior to this custody proceeding had the father removed the children from their Florida domicile.[1]

In the intervening time, many troubling things about the wife's life-style, whose nature was such that it was bound to have a most pernicious effect upon the children, had come to the father's attention. We can no more ignore that now than he did then. Certainly that his marriage to the respondent *nine years ago* was preceded by the unorthodox relationship under which they previously had lived together did not require him to abdicate his concern as a father these many years later. And the majority's gratuitous characterization of him as a "nomad" simply because his work as a consultant in his field would at times take him out of town hardly changes the graphic picture of the mother image in this case.

As the petition describes in detail, at one point the mother was evicted from her apartment because of her wholesale practice of en-

1. The majority's statement that the petitioner "abducted" the children in 1976 by having them flown to New York ignores the fact that, by that time, though its judgment had not been formally entered, the Supreme Court had filed its opinion awarding custody to the father. Moreover, since the order of the Appellate Division which had found that New York had jurisdiction preceded that event, it should not now be considered as a basis for a reversal.

tertaining male visitors, most of whom were transients or drug addicts. The eviction brought no metamorphosis; additional affairs with at least 10 different men, each identified in the record by name, are reported. According to a neighbor, respondent admitted sleeping in the same bed as her "boyfriends" and her children in order to help them become "sexually uninhibited". She has been linked to the sale of marihuana and introduced its use to the children. On one occasion, her house was included in a successful police "raid" for drugs. On another, a complaint was filed against her after the police had been called to her locked car, where the children, then three and one-half and one and one-half, had become hysterical while she was sojourning at a bar. Her denial of only some of these incidents—and that by affidavit only, though she did not hesitate to come to New York on other occasions—covers but some of the tiles in this unhappy mosaic.

Thus, it is difficult to imagine, in the context of a still viable and ongoing custodial relationship, circumstances more clearly adverse to the best interests of formative children. If ever great weight is to be afforded that consideration in determining whether to exercise jurisdiction, this case demands it. For, "not acceptable as simply an 'alternative life-style' which people in an open society are entitled to follow, and courts are required to adopt as appropriate for the rearing of a little child" is the life-style allegedly led by the mother of the children with whom we are here concerned.

It is not surprising then that Special Term, after holding the factual hearing[2] which in its discretion the Appellate Division understandably believed was urgently required in the interests of the children, found that in this instance the mother's "conduct apparently is one in which she has lived a life which appears not to be a proper one for the bringing up of children of tender and adolescent age * * * [I]t would not be in the best interests of the children to remain in the custody of the respondent."[3]

Especially under these circumstances, I perceive no basis for overturning the Appellate Division's order on the ground that our courts should have declined to exercise jurisdiction in the first instance. Indeed, in Irrigation & Ind. Dev. Corp. v. Indaq S. A., 37 N. Y.2d 522, 525, 375 N.Y.S.2d 296, 298, 337 N.E.2d 749, 751, we noted that it is our established policy not to "interfere with the Appellate Division's exercise of discretion in granting or denying a motion to dismiss on the ground of *forum non conveniens* unless there has been an abuse of discretion as a matter of law or unless the Appellate Division, in exercising that discretion, has failed to take into account all

---

2. Though this hearing took place subsequent to the entry of the Appellate Division order from which the wife appeals, we are not required to ignore it.

3. By choosing to appeal under CPLR 5601 (subd. [d]) respondent waived appellate review of these findings.

the various factors entitled to consideration". We "do not substitute our evaluation of the weight to be attached to such factors, singly or in combination, for that of the lower courts" (Hadjioannou v. Avramides, 40 N.Y.2d 929, 931, 389 N.Y.S.2d 833, 835, 358 N.E.2d 516, 518).

If such a discretion is not to be lightly interfered with in a commercial context, how much more important is it that it not be disregarded where the stakes are the best interest of young children? In particular, the relegation of the New York-domiciled husband to a custody suit in Florida in the factual and legal posture of this case is an interference with discretion in which I do not believe we should engage.

Indeed, the welfare of infants "transcends the rule of comity" as well. Therefore, it matters not that the majority apparently expects the result in Florida to be consistent with that of Special Term. The vagaries and cost of duplicative litigation 1,500 miles away are not inconsequential. Most important, to shuttle the children, who have now been in the care of the father for a considerable time, back to the mother and the milieu in which she has chosen to live, could not be less desirable.

The point is that, under whatever rubric may be brought to bear —be it comity, *forum non conveniens* or other—the particular mix of factual and legal considerations in this case makes it an especially inappropriate one in which to substitute our judgment as to whether jurisdiction should be accepted for that of the Appellate Division of our court of general jurisdiction.

In short, unless we are to subscribe to the proposition that a determination as to whether the courts of this State should retain jurisdiction of custody matters must be made without any factual inquiry beyond the papers presented, the judgment and the order of the Appellate Division brought up for review should be affirmed.

NOTES AND QUESTIONS

1. The court in *Martin* was influenced by the Uniform Act, which, as the opinion indicates, had been adopted in New York but was not yet in effect. If the Act had been in effect, should the case have been decided the same way? Was Florida the child's "home state", under section 3 of the Act? Or did the other provisions of section 3 indicate that Florida still had jurisdiction? Was New York the "home state"? Or did the New York courts have jurisdiction under other provisions of section 3? For example does the "emergency" provision of section 3(a)(3)(ii) apply to this case?

The court in Martin was also influenced by Nehra v. Uhlar, which it cites on page 1054. In that case a Michigan court gave custody to the husband, but later the wife abducted the children, brought them to New York, and, partly because of delays in getting trials and appeals heard, managed to keep them for four years. Notwithstanding the long period of custody and the children's expressed desire to remain with their mother, the court gave custody to the husband, chiefly in reliance upon the wife's improper conduct and upon the prior Michigan decree. Would you agree with this result? Is it required by the Uniform Act?

2. Is the *Martin* approach inconsistent with that in *Settle?* If so, which approach is preferable?

3. How should the following cases be decided, under the Uniform Act and with some consideration for the principles announced in May v. Anderson and in the *Sampsell* case, supra, page 1038?

(a) H and W were married and lived in California. They had one daughter, six months old. When, shortly after the birth of the child, their marital relations deteriorated, W took the child one day and returned to the home of her parents in New York, without telling H that she was leaving. H then sued for divorce in California, asking that he be given custody of the child, and alleging that W had neglected their daughter and had been running around with other men, drinking heavily.

(i) Would it matter in this case if W thereupon employed an attorney in California who filed an answer in the action denying the allegations respecting custody? Cf. Willmore v. Willmore, 273 Minn. 537, 143 N.W.2d 630 (1966), cert. den. 385 U.S. 898 (1966); Speck v. Speck, 5 N.C.App. 296, 168 S.E.2d 672 (1969).

(ii) Would it matter that a statute is in force in California providing that "A court of this state may exercise jurisdiction on any basis not inconsistent with the Constitution of this state or the United States"? Cal.Civ. Pro.Code § 410.10 (1973). See Titus v. Superior Court, In and For the County of Contra Costa, 23 Cal.App.3d 792, 100 Cal.Rptr. 477 (1972); Restatement, Second, Conflict of Laws § 27 (1971); Kulko v. Superior Court, supra, page 851; and the authorities cited in paragraph 12, supra, page 1040.

(iii) What should be the result if, before bringing the California proceeding, H employed private detectives who went to New York, took possession of the baby when she had been left alone for a few moments in W's car, and brought her back to California, so that when the proceeding was brought the child was physically present in the state? Cf. Brown v. Brown, 105 Ariz. 273, 463 P.2d 71 (1969); In re Marriage of Verbin, 92 Wash.2d 171, 595 P.2d 905 (1979).

(iv) Assume you were consulted by H just after his wife's departure with the child. H told you, in addition to the facts leading to the separation, that W had returned to a small town in New York where her father was the president of the local bank and a leading citizen. He also told you that he had received letters from W stating that she intended to get a divorce and a custody decree in New York and that she was going to make sure that H never again saw the baby. What would you advise H to do?

(b) H and W were traveling in State X with their son, S, when they had a serious automobile accident in which they were killed and S seriously hurt. U, a maternal uncle of S, brought a custody proceeding in the appropriate court of X, asking that he be given custody of the boy. Service was made by registered mail upon GM and GF, the boy's paternal grandparents in State Y, the state of their domicile. The grandparents were the only other relatives. The grandparents did not appear in the suit. Walden v. Johnson, 417 S.W.2d 220 (Ky.1967); Bacon v. Bacon, 3 Or.App. 85, 472 P.

2d 283 (1970) ; Falco v. Grills, 209 Va. 115, 161 S.E.2d 713 (1968). Would the result be different if U made no effort to serve or otherwise notify GM and GF?

(c) H and W lived in Connecticut. They had marital difficulties and H left home, taking up residence at his New York club. W and their two children remained at the Connecticut home. W brought a custody proceeding in New York, serving H personally there. Alves v. Alves, 262 A.2d 111 (D.C.Ct.App.1970) ; Green v. Green, 351 Mass. 466, 221 N.E.2d 857 (1966).

4. H and W lived in California and had a son, S. When H was jailed on narcotics charges and W was an outpatient in a heroin addiction clinic, they were unable to care for S, and so G, H's mother, was appointed guardian of the person of S by a California court. About two years later G and her husband decided to move to Colorado. When H and W learned of this, they obtained a temporary restraining order prohibiting G from taking S out of California. G and her husband left California before the order could be served on them and acquired a domicile in Colorado. H and W then filed a petition to terminate the guardianship in California, and the California court granted the petition, after G had appeared in the proceeding and been heard on the merits. The court also ordered that S be turned over to the custody of H and W. H and W came to Colorado to pick up S, but G refused to hand him over, in the course of which H and G's husband got into a fight. At this point S had been living in Colorado about eight months, and with G about three years. H and W then filed a petition in the appropriate Colorado court seeking the enforcement of the California decree and asking for custody of S.

(a) What should be the result of the Colorado proceeding? Fry v. Ball, 190 Colo. 128, 544 P.2d 402 (1975). Cf. Griffith v. Griffith, —— Hawaii ——, 592 P.2d 826 (1979) ; Barcus v. Barcus, 278 N.W.2d 646 (Iowa 1979). Would it matter that although G was represented in the California hearing which terminated the guardianship, she did not testify, and no evidence concerning S's current circumstances was presented to the California court? Would it matter that at the time of the Colorado proceeding S told a psychologist who was examining him that he wanted to stay with G, and did not want to go back to "the bad guy", meaning H?

(b) Could G be held in contempt in California? Brown v. Brown, 183 Colo. 356, 516 P.2d 1129 (1974).

(c) Are any legal sanctions, other than contempt, available to H and W against G for taking S out of California? Pickle v. Page, 252 N.Y. 474, 169 N.E. 650 (1930) ; Harris v. Turner, 329 F.2d 918 (6th Cir. 1964) ; Annot., 77 A.L.R. 317 (1932).

(d) Is a criminal offense committed by a person, either a parent or one not a parent, who takes a child from its custodian in violation of a custody decree? State v. Kracker, 123 Ariz. 294, 599 P.2d 250 (App.1979) ; State v. Musumeci, 116 N.H. 136, 355 A.2d 434 (1976) ; Ark.Stat.Ann. § 41-2411 (1977) ; Model Penal Code § 212.4 (Proposed Official Draft 1962).

(e) Congress is presently considering legislation which would make it a federal crime for a parent to take his child across a state line in violation of a right of custody or visitation arising out of a custody decree or written agreement, with certain additional qualifications. See S.1437, Criminal Code Reform Act of 1978 § 1624.

5. H and W lived in State X with their son, S. When S was eight years old W got a divorce from H in X, custody being awarded to W, with rights of visitation to H. H then moved to State Y where he established his home. S lived with W until he was thirteen years old, visiting H in Y for a month each summer. At that time W married H–2, with whom S could not get along at all. S then ran away from X, came to Y and begged H to let him stay with him. H was glad to have S live with him, arranged quarters in his apartment for S, placed him in a local school and did all he could to provide a suitable home. H did not notify W that S was with him, and in fact when she called him up in considerable distress to ask if he had heard from S, he lied to her, said he had not, and that he did not know where S was.

After S had been living with H in Y for about six months, he went to the local Legal Services Office without telling H or anyone else, and asked if the lawyers there could arrange for him to stay permanently with H. An attorney in that office, acting on S's behalf, filed a petition in the appropriate court of Y alleging the foregoing facts and asking the court to enter a decree under section 2 of the Y statutes giving custody of S to his father, H. Notice of the proceeding was sent to W by registered mail, and H was personally served in Y. What should be the outcome of this proceeding? Section 2 of the Y statutes provides as follows: "The juvenile courts of this state shall have exclusive jurisdiction in proceedings concerning any child in need of supervision, that is, any child who has run away from home or is otherwise beyond the control of his parent, guardian, or other legal custodian."

Both X and Y have enacted the Uniform Child Custody Jurisdiction Act.

6. H and W were maried in California and then moved to Australia, where they had two children. Shortly thereafter H and W were divorced in Australia, with custody of the children to W and visitation rights to H. The decree forbade W to remove the children from Australia without leave of court. Five years later both H and W had remarried, W having lived a short time in California with H's agreement, and then returned to Australia with her new husband. Some changes in custody were then made, giving H more extensive visitation. Four years later the decree was again modified to give H the children on certain weekends, holidays and school vacations. Two years after that W left Australia for California, taking the children and not telling either H or the Australian court where she was going. After she left, H got a order for temporary custody from the Australian court, service being on W's solicitors, who responded that they could not locate W and had no instructions from her. Australian law provided for service on solicitors of record and for ex parte custody orders in cases of urgency. Some months later H located W and the children in Los Angeles and filed a petition in the appropriate California court seeking enforcement of the Australian custody decree. How should the California court rule on the petition? Miller v. Superior Court of Los Angeles County, 22 Cal.3d 923, 151 Cal.Rptr. 6, 587 P.2d 723 (1978).

IN RE MARRIAGE OF BOWEN

Supreme Court of Iowa, 1974.
219 N.W.2d 683.

McCORMICK, Justice. This appeal involves a parental dispute over child custody. The marriage of the parties, petitioner Catherine Bowen, now Catherine Moore (Catherine), and respondent Lloyd C. Bowen, Jr. (Clay), was dissolved February 14, 1972. Catherine is now 39; Clay is 41. Temporary custody of their two children, Mary, now 11, and Lloyd C. III (Clay III), now 10, was awarded to the Henry Court Department of Social Services with directions for placement with the mother on a six month trial basis. On September 14, 1973, after further hearing, a supplemental decree was entered awarding custody of the children to the mother. The father appealed. We reverse and remand.

The parties met about 1960 in Houston, Texas. Clay resided there. Catherine moved there from Arkansas with her four children after leaving her first husband. Those children are Richard, Jim, Anne, and Christopher, now ages 21, 19, 18, and 14. During the first few months of their acquaintanceship Catherine represented herself to Clay as a widow. Then she revealed her true status. Subsequently she divorced her first husband and in November 1961 married Clay.

Mary was born December 9, 1962, and Clay III was born February 16, 1964. The family moved to Mount Pleasant in 1965. Clay has worked for Mason & Hanger-Silas Mason Co., Inc., as an engineer at the Iowa Army Ammunition Plant in Burlington since 1964. Catherine worked for three years prior to the dissolution, two at the ammunition plant and one as assistant to a Mount Pleasant accountant.

Serious problems occurred in the marriage as early as 1964. The parties argued frequently.

Clay testified he learned in March 1967 that Catherine was involved with another man. Later she started playing in a band with several teenage males. She spent several evenings each week practicing with them. On one occasion, when Clay was out of town, one of them, Danny Hull, about 16 or 17, stayed overnight in the home. Although Clay did not think she was guilty of sexual misconduct with the boy, he asserted her attitude toward discipline of the children suddenly changed. Whereas she previously had been quite strict, Clay said she became very permissive, explaining to him she realized from her association with Danny that her own teenagers were no longer children. According to Clay she began to dress and behave as a teenager herself and turned over many household responsibilities to her daughter Anne. Danny Hull and his brother Robert, 19, were frequently her guests in the home.

Catherine testified there was "very little intimacy" between Danny and her except "such that occurs on the bandstand, or a little kiss or something like this   *   *   *." She acknowledged adulterous involvement with Robert Hull, but, even though he spent many evenings in the home, she did not think the children were aware of it. However, Clay testified he caught Catherine's teenage sons in the upstairs bath one night listening at a vent to the whispering of Catherine and Robert who were together in the living room. One of the boys asked Clay why he put up with her conduct.

On another occasion Clay got up at night, noticed a candle flickering in the living room, and discovered Catherine and Robert there on the couch partially undressed. These and similar incidents occurred while all six children were in the home. Catherine also admitted she spent a night with Robert in an Illinois motel.

She testified she experimented with marijuana in the home with another friend, Paul Whipple, age 18, but did not like it.

The parties were often at odds over Catherine's conduct, discipline of the children, and other issues. Rather than prolong an argument, Clay would withdraw to his room. Catherine moved to a separate bedroom in early summer 1970.

Mary and Clay III lived in the home with the children of Catherine's first marriage and regarded them as siblings. Richard left home while still in high school and drifted around until entering military service. Jim ran away at 16 because he was upset with the home environment. Anne and Christopher were still in the home at the time of the November 1971 dissolution hearing. Catherine brought Anne, then 16, to the hearing. She testified Anne was a confidant as well as daughter. She admitted she volunteered advice to Anne about contraception one day during an outing in a park in the presence of Anne's first boy friend. She acknowledged she depended on Anne to prepare the evening meal and take much of the responsibility for care of the younger children.

Clay testified Catherine had frequent outbursts of temper and was abusive of the children at times. He related an incident when he said he had to restrain her from beating Anne with a broomstick when Anne was an hour late getting home from a church project.

Mary was an above average student. She was upset by parental arguments but seemed to sympathize with her father. Clay III was doing average school work, below his ability, was hyperactive, and reacted to parental conflict by building a dream world of his own.

The parties visited several marriage counselors and each received some psychiatric therapy prior to the dissolution. Clay III was under treatment by a psychologist during the school year preceding the dissolution.

After consuming a non-lethal overdose of sleeping pills in February 1971, Clay was taken to the hospital and on advice of his psychiatrist did not return to the home. Catherine started the dissolution action in March.

During the period of separation Catherine often saw John Moore, a younger man but not a teenager. He was frequently an overnight guest in the home, and Catherine admitted a sexual relationship with him. She and the children went on camping trips with him. Clay refused Catherine's request that he pay half the cost of a tent for these trips.

Clay saw his children almost daily during the separation and had them with him almost every weekend. He took active part in their school activities. Catherine asserted he had not shown as much interest in them before the separation.

Catherine testified she intended to keep her job with the accountant and remain in Mount Pleasant. She described her relationship with John Moore as a "low level" romance. She said she last saw Moore in October 1971, thought he lived in Fairfield, but no longer had any relationship with him, and had no plan to marry anyone. She expressed a desire to have custody of the children because she loved them and thought they wanted to be with her but said she would be willing for Clay to have them if she could not.

Three witnesses were called by Clay in support of his request for custody. They were Lena J. Masden and Myrna Leu, family friends, and Q. Gerald Roseberry, minister of the family church. Mrs. Masden met the Bowens in 1965. She and her husband shared their interest in music. She considered herself a close friend of the family and often babysat with the children. They called her grandma. She described a change in Catherine and thought she put her own interests ahead of the best interests of the children. She thought Clay should have custody because he would put the children's interests ahead of his own, provide a religious home, and exercise a firm hand in raising them.

Mrs. Leu was better acquainted with Clay than with Catherine. Clay and her husband got together frequently to play musical instruments, and Clay often brought his children with him. She believed Clay should be awarded their custody because he would provide them a stable home.

Pastor Roseberry had counselled with the parties. He thought Catherine's discipline was erratic and less constructive than Clay's, but he was concerned about Clay's moods of depression. He gave what he called a qualified opinion that Clay should have custody. He thought the children related well to their father, and Clay would do everything he could to provide them a proper environment.

The attorney for the children offered the testimony of Harry D. Harper, Jr., a psychiatrist who had counselled with the parties, treated Clay, and examined Clay III. He described Catherine as a person who has difficulty in controlling her impulses, is sensitive to rejection, and who responds to frustration in inappropriate ways. He said she attempts to hurt those whom she blames for her frustrations and becomes quite irritable, aggressive and impulsive.

He described Clay as overly self-critical and very intense, with a tendency to scrutinize matters beyond the point of reasonableness. He saw him as depressed and pessimistic, in part because of his inability to control the conduct of others.

Clay III was described as hyperactive, bright and curious, but with little behavior control.

Dr. Harper testified Clay showed more stability than Catherine, more persistence, and more willingness to take advice. He believed Catherine was not able to handle stress in a mature manner. Yet, because Clay did not function as well as a parent should, he suggested the children be placed outside the home until one of the parents demonstrated sufficient stability to receive their custody.

Clay testified he loved the children, feared for their welfare if Catherine was given custody, and would care for them with the assistance of a housekeeper if he obtained custody.

In its decree of February 14, 1972, the court dissolved the marriage, divided the modest property of the parties, gave temporary custody of the children to the Henry County Department of Social Services with directions they be placed with their mother for six months, ordered Clay to pay debts of the parties and child support, and provided for eventual further hearing on the issue of final award of custody. Trial court did not believe either parent was then a suitable custodian but expressed three reasons the children should be placed temporarily with the mother. They were the inference a mother is ordinarily best suited to care for children of tender years, the belief it would be less upsetting emotionally for the children to remain in the home where they were living, and the fact they would be in the home with Anne who was a stabilizing and helpful influence.

Subsequent hearing was held July 19, 1973. The intervening period had been stormy and eventful. It turned out Catherine's relationship with John Moore had not ended. She continued to see him. The prospect of her remarriage upset Mary and Clay III. She quit her job with the accountant and went to work for the city as a secretary. She planned to marry Moore. He had held four jobs in the last five years and was being trained in grocery store management. He took a job in Chillicothe, Illinois.

On January 30, 1973, Anne ran away from Catherine's home. She first went to Clay and, upon his advice, went the next day to the department of social services. She said Catherine had attacked her with a board during an argument. She reported her mother had an uncontrollable temper and kept the home in turmoil. Anne was quite bitter. She believed Catherine was unreasonable at times, put too much responsibility on her, and she did not like John Moore.   She was placed in foster care so she could finish high school.   She refused to see Catherine.

Clay seemed obsessed with his desire for custody of the children. There is evidence he kept close watch on Catherine and the department of social services, with whose supervision he was dissatisfied. He took the children to Texas on one occasion in 1972 for three weeks, and Catherine had to come after them.   Clay's excuse for not returning them was a subterfuge.

For six weeks from mid-April through May 1973 Catherine denied him visitation for fear the children would reveal her marriage plans to him.

Sandra K. Shaull, a county social worker, interviewed Mary and Clay III in March 1973.   At that time Mary was not happy about the impending marriage but Clay III did not seem to object.   Catherine reported receiving threatening letters and phone calls.   She and Moore were married May 13 and moved to Chillicothe when school was out.   She quit her job in Mount Pleasant and did not seek employment in Illinois.

At the July 19, 1973, hearing Miss Shaull testified both children had recently told her they wanted to live with their father.   She said this had always been Mary's desire.   She also reported Clay's mother was living with him in Mount Pleasant.   Clay testified his mother was planning to reside permanently with him.   He said she was 57, in good health, and able and willing to help care for the children.   He wanted to purchase Catherine's one-half interest in their former home and move there with the children.

The social worker was requested to prepare a supplemental report which the parties agreed could be received and considered by the court in reaching its final custody decision.   This report was furnished August 23, 1973.   In it Miss Shaull repeated in detail the tumultuous events of the prior eight months and discussed the then-current situation in each household.   She said Mary and Clay III were unhappy in Chillicothe.   They told her there was considerable fighting in the household, they did not like Moore, they did not like the town, and they wanted to live with their father and grandmother. Clay took the children home with him every other weekend.

The report described the grandmother as divorced from her fourth husband but established in Mount Pleasant with an intent to remain there to maintain a home for Clay and the children.   She was said to believe in firm and consistent discipline.   Miss Shaull wrote, "[S]he shows a great deal of patience and understanding in dealing with the children.   The children respect her and have a great deal of affection for her."

Trial court entered its supplemental decree on September 14 awarding custody of the children to Catherine.   The court grounded it decision on findings the children seemed to be making a satisfactory adjustment, Clay's emotional problems had not ended, the children were too young to have their preference accorded much weight, it was too early to tell if Catherine's remarriage would work out, and the court did not have an opportunity to see or question Clay's mother.

This appeal by Clay followed. In addition to the usual problems attendant to a difficult custody case, we have an appeal in which the father represents himself and the mother has not participated at all.

Parts of Clay's brief are devoted to criticism of trial court's findings relating to his emotional state and the way this case was handled by the court, department of social services, and others involved. This criticism only confirms Dr. Harper's statement that Clay tends to scrutinize matters to the point of being unreasonable. The court's observations as to Clay's emotional problems are fully supported by the record, and although we disagree with the result, we have no criticism of the procedure employed by those involved in the frustrating task of attempting to find a satisfactory solution to the perplexing custody problem in this case.

Two relevant questions are presented. They are: (1) should we abandon the inference that the best interests of children of tender years are better served by awarding custody to their mother and (2) should custody have been awarded to the father in this case?

We must decide these questions in the context of several well-settled principles. Our review is de novo. Although we are not bound by trial court findings we give them weight. The status of children should be quickly fixed and, thereafter, little disturbed. Siblings should not usually be separated. No hard and fast rule governs which parent should have custody. It is not a matter of reward or punishment. The issue is ultimately decided by determining under the whole record which parent can minister more effectively to the long-range best interests of the children.

Factors to be considered include the characteristics and needs of the children, the environments involved, the characteristics of those seeking custody, their respective abilities to provide for the material, social, moral and emotional needs of the children, available alternatives, and whatever other relevant matters the evidence in a particular case may disclose. Moral misconduct by a parent is one factor affecting that parent's fitness to have custody.

It is wrong to treat a parental custody decision as merely an adjudication of parental rights. Children are innocent victims of marital bankruptcy. Their welfare is paramount. Custodial claims of contending parents are subservient to the rights of their children to grow to maturity in a proper environment.

I. *The inference.* The father challenges the inference, relied upon by trial court, that the best interests of younger children are served by placing them in their mother's custody. This inference is partly based on the assumption a mother keeps the home, performs household duties, and will have more time to devote to the children and their welfare. When the evidence in a case shows such assumption is not justified we have held the inference readily yields.

Modern redefinition and adjustment of traditional parental roles has greatly diluted the strength of the inference.

The constitutionality of the inference was attacked in the Carey case, but, because the trial court decree was not shown to be based on it, the issue was not resolved. 211 N.W.2d at 344–345. At least one court has concluded the inference unconstitutionally denies fathers equal protection of the laws under Amendment 14, United States Constitution. State ex rel. Watts v. Watts, 350 N.Y.S.2d 285 (N.Y.C. Fam.Ct.1973). This result was reached after finding the inference is based on sex, a suspect classification purportedly subject to strict judicial scrutiny. See Frontiero v. Richardson, 411 U.S. 677, 93 S.Ct. 1764, 36 L.Ed.2d 583 (1973).

Clay attacks both the constitutionality and the wisdom of the inference. We find it unnecessary to decide the constitutional issue because we hold the inference is no longer wise. It is simply not justified as an *a priori* principle. It tends to obscure the basic tenet in custody cases which overrides all others, the best interests of the children. The real issue is not the sex of the parent but which parent will do better in raising the children. Resolution of that issue depends upon what the evidence actually reveals in each case, not upon what someone predicts it will show in many cases. If past decisions teach us anything, "it is that each case must be decided on its own peculiar facts." In re Marriage of Dawson, supra, 214 N.W.2d at 132.

We do not think either parent should have a greater burden than the other in attempting to obtain custody in a dissolution proceeding. It is neither necessary nor useful to infer in advance that the best interests of young children will be better served if their custody is awarded to their mothers instead of their fathers. We previously emphasized the weakness of the inference; we now abandon it.

II. *The custody award in this case.* At the time of the initial award of temporary custody of the children to the county department of social services for placement with the mother, trial court relied upon three factors, the inference discussed in Division I, a desire to keep the children in the home where they had been living, and the stabilizing influence of their half-sister Anne. It is also obvious trial court accepted Catherine's representation that she would mend her ways and put the children's interests ahead of her own.

By the time of the second hearing 19 months later the projected image of a stable environment for the children had been shattered. Catherine continued to see and later married the paramour with whom she testified she no longer had any relationship. Her fits of temper and immature dependence drove Anne from the home in the pattern followed by her two older sons at about the same age. She moved the children from their home in Mount Pleasant to Illinois. The children's lives were put in turmoil. They complained of conditions in the mother's home and asked that they be allowed to live with their father.

What Catherine has done speaks with greater force of her qualities as a parent than what she has said she will do. She has demonstrated she does not put the best interest of the children ahead of her own self interest. Leaving the children in her custody would be hazardous and possibly disastrous.

Trial court observed that none of its alternatives for custody was completely satisfactory. We agree.

Clay suffered from depression during the time the marriage was breaking down. Perhaps to some extent this can be attributed to damage to his ego and self-esteem produced by Catherine's conduct. We do not know whether his erratic behavior since then demonstrates misguided concern for the best interests of the children or simply concern for his own self-image. In any event he has not always acted responsibly or maturely.

The determinative factor is that throughout these difficulties he has maintained what appears to be a wholesome and constructive relationship with the children. His past conduct as a parent speaks well of his ability and willingness to put the children's best interests ahead of his own. He has been a loving father. He was a faithful husband. He has held a responsible job for many years. He has a satisfactory plan to provide a stable and loving home for the children. The prospects for the children are better with him than with their mother.

Although not controlling nor entitled to much weight, it is relevant that the children have stated a preference to be in their father's custody. We are disappointed that children so young have been asked so often to express themselves on the subject, but this preference on their part coupled with close association with their father during the pendency of this case provides some assurance their lives will not be unduly disturbed now by an award of custody to him.

We hold custody of the children should have been awarded to their father. The case is reversed and remanded for entry of a modified decree awarding custody of the children to Clay subject to reasonable visitation by Catherine, elimination of the decretal provision relating to child support, and fixing the fee of the attorney for the children on appeal. Such fee and all appeal costs are taxed to respondent Lloyd C. Bowen, Jr. We also ask trial court to include a provision in the modified decree for supervision by the court of Clay's custody of the children on such terms and for such period as to the court in its discretion seems reasonable.

NOTES AND QUESTIONS

1. There are many general treatments of the legal problems of custody cases. Some of these are: Sayre, Awarding Custody of Children, 160 Annals 66 (1932), reprinted in Association of American Law Schools, Selected Essays on Family Law, 588 (1950); Kay and Phillips, Poverty and the Law of Child Custody, 54 Cal.L.Rev. 717 (1966); Weinman, The Trial Judge Awards Custody, 10 Law & Contemp.Prob. 721 (1944); Podell, Peck and First, Custody—To Which Parent? 56 Marq.L.Rev. 51 (1972); Foster and Freed, Child Custody, 39 N.Y.U.L.Rev. 423, 615 (1964); Carpenter, The Parent-Child Dilemma in the Courts, 30 Ohio St.L.J. 292 (1969); Bodenheimer, The Multiplicity of Child Custody Proceedings—Problems of California Law, 23 Stan.L.Rev. 703 (1971); Watson, The Children of Armageddon; Problems of Custody Following Divorce, 21 Syra.L.Rev. 55 (1969); Note, The "Adversary" Process in Child Custody Proceedings, 18 West.Res. L.Rev. 1731 (1967); Banta, Divorce—The Welfare and Best Interest of the Child, 5 Willamette L.J. 82 (1968); Batt, Child Custody Disputes: A Developmental-Psychological Approach to Proof and Decisionmaking, 12 Willamette L.J. 491 (1976); Solnit, Child-Rearing and Child Advocacy, 1976 B. Y.U.L.Rev. 723; Weitzman and Dixon, Child Custody Awards: Legal Standards and Empirical Patterns for Child Custody, Support and Visitation After Divorce, 12 U.C.D.L.Rev. 471 (1979).

Perhaps the most widely cited of recent works on custody has been J. Goldstein, A. Freud, A. Solnit, Beyond the Best Interests of the Child (1973). The major thesis of this book is that the child's psychological and developmental needs should control the custody decision. Rather than trying to achieve the child's best interests, the courts should try to adopt the "least detrimental available alternative" custody disposition. In doing so it is the child's psychological needs which predominate over his material needs. In the authors' view the most important factor for the child's psychological well-being is continuity of relationships. This implies that custody decisions once reached should be final and unconditional and that the child should not be shifted about from one custodian to another. The authors also assert that once custody is awarded, the custodian alone, free of court control, should decide the conditions of the child's care. The noncustodial parent should have no right to visit the child except as permitted by the custodial parent.

Critical reviews of the Goldstein, Freud, Solnit book are published in 83 Yale L.J. 1304 (1974) by Judge Dembitz; in 74 Colum.L.Rev. 996 (1974) by P. and J. Strauss, and in 12 Willamette L.J. 545 (1976) by Professor Henry H. Foster, Jr.

Professors Goldstein, Freud and Solnit may be retreating somewhat from the rigid positions they took in Beyond the Best Interests of the Child. They have recently published a sequel which provides some evidence of a change in their views. J. Goldstein, A. Freud, A. Solnit, Before the Best Interests of the Child (Free Press, New York, 1979).

2. The Uniform Marriage and Divorce Act § 402, 9A Unif.L.Ann. 197 (1979), has this to say about custody decisions:

"§ 402. [Best Interest of Child]

The court shall determine custody in accordance with the best interest of the child. The court shall consider all relevant factors including:

"(1) the wishes of the child's parent or parents as to his custody;

"(2) the wishes of the child as to his custodian;

"(3) the interaction and interrelationship of the child with his parent or parents, his siblings, and any other person who may significantly affect the child's best interest;

"(4) the child's adjustment to his home, school, and community; and

"(5) the mental and physical health of all individuals involved.

"The court shall not consider conduct of a proposed custodian that does not affect his relationship to the child."

3. Would the *Bowen* case have been decided in the same way under the Uniform Act?

4. At common law the father's claim to custody was paramount, to be rejected only where the father was corrupt or endangering the child. H. Clark, Law of Domestic Relations 584 (1968). As was formerly true in Iowa, many American courts raised a presumption that the child of "tender years" will best be cared for in the custody of his mother. This is the so-called tender years doctrine. It is presently on the wane in many jurisdictions, but it still is found useful in close cases by some courts.

(a) Can the tender years doctrine withstand constitutional attack after Orr v. Orr, supra, page 868? State ex rel. Watts v. Watts, 77 Misc.2d 178, 350 N.Y.S.2d 285 (Fam.Ct.1973); Gordon v. Gordon, 577 P.2d 1271 (Okl. 1978), cert. den. 439 U.S. 863 (1978); J. B. v. A. B., —— W.Va. ——, 242 S. E.2d 248 (1978). In any event it could not survive in a state having an Equal Rights Amendment in its constitution, could it? Cox v. Cox, 532 P. 2d 994 (Utah 1975); Thompson v. Thompson, 57 Ala.App. 57, 326 So.2d 124 (1975), cert. den. 295 Ala. 425, 326 So.2d 129 (1976).

(b) Even if the doctrine is not unconstitutional, should it be abolished, as in *Bowen*? Does the Uniform Act abolish it? Johnson v. Johnson, 564 P.2d 71 (Alaska 1977), cert. den. 434 U.S. 1048 (1978); McAndrew v. McAndrew, 39 Md.App. 1, 382 A.2d 1081 (1978); McCreery v. McCreery, 218 Va. 352, 237 S.E.2d 167 (1977); Annot., Modern Status of Maternal Preference Rule or Presumption in Child Custody Cases, 70 A.L.R.3d 262 (1976); Jones, The Tender Years Doctrine: Survey and Analysis, 16 J. Fam.L. 695 (1978).

5. The court in *Bowen* gave some consideration to the mother's "moral misconduct". The general question whether a mother's adultery or her sexual relations with men other than her husband should disqualify her for custody of her children, or whether it should be considered at all by the

court deciding the custody dispute, has been much litigated. See Lauerman, Nonmarital Sexual Conduct and Child Custody, 46 U.Cin.L.Rev. 647 (1977).

(a) Would evidence of the mother's "moral misconduct" be admissible in evidence under the Uniform Act? Moore v. Moore, 577 S.W.2d 613 (Ky.1979).

(b) To what extent, if any, should the mother's sex life be considered in awarding custody? See, e. g., Dalton v. Dalton, 214 Kan. 805, 522 P.2d 378 (1974); Davis v. Davis, 280 Md. 119, 372 A.2d 231 (1977) (collecting many cases); Dahlman v. Dahlman, 20 Or.App. 375, 531 P.2d 909 (1975); Commonwealth ex rel. Myers v. Myers, 468 Pa. 134, 360 A.2d 587 (1976); Brown v. Brown, 218 Va. 196, 237 S.E.2d 89 (1977). Should the father's "moral misconduct" be considered on the same terms as the mother's? DeVita v. DeVita, 145 N.J.Super. 120, 366 A.2d 1350 (1976); Krueger v. Stevens, 244 N.W.2d 763 (S.D.1976).

Is there any accepted standard of sexual morality in contemporary American society? If so, what is it? Is adultery immoral today, for example? Are sexual relations between unmarried adults? Is it immoral to have an illegitimate child?

(c) Should the fact that either the mother or father is a homosexual be considered a relevant circumstance by a court in a custody case, either under the Uniform Act or ordinary common law principles? Does homosexuality amount to "moral misconduct" in our society today? See, e. g., M. P. v. S. P., 169 N.J.Super, 425, 404 A.2d 1256 (1979); In re J. S. & C., 129 N.J.Super. 486, 324 A.2d 90 (1974); DiStefano v. DiStefano, 60 A.D.2d 976, 401 N.Y.S.2d 636 (4th Dep't 1978); Newsome v. Newsome, 42 N.C. App. 416, 256 S.E.2d 849 (1979); Schuster v. Schuster, 90 Wash.2d 626, 585 P.2d 130 (1978).

(d) Are the foregoing questions affected by the constitutional doctrines of Griswold v. Connecticut, supra, page 73 and Zablocki v. Redhail, supra, page 83, and the cases which followed them? Note, The Avowed Lesbian Mother and the Right to Child Custody: A Constitutional Challenge That Can No Longer Be Denied, 12 San D.L.Rev. 799 (1975).

6. Psychiatric testimony was offered in the *Bowen* case by the attorney for the children. How helpful would you say his testimony about Catherine was? (E. g., " * * * a person who has difficulty in controlling her impulses, is sensitive to rejection, and who responds to frustration in inappropriate ways. * * * she attempts to hurt those whom she blames for her frustrations and becomes quite irritable, aggressive and impulsive.") Do you know many people who, in the midst of a marital crisis, could not be described in that way? Do you suppose that this testimony influenced the court in its award of custody to the father?

7. If the court had applied the psychological best interest test of the Goldstein, Freud, Solnit book and had emphasized the principle of continuity and the search for the least detrimental available alternative, would the *Bowen* case have come differently?

CARLE v. CARLE

Supreme Court of Alaska, 1972.
503 P.2d 1050.

RABINOWITZ, Chief Justice. This appeal concerns the superior court's determination of child custody in a divorce proceeding between George Carle, appellant, and Charlotte Carle, appellee. As part of its decree of divorce, the trial court awarded custody of George Carle, Jr., the parties' 7-year old son, to his mother Charlotte Carle. George Carle has appealed from the superior court's custody determination.

George Carle and Charlotte Carle were married in 1963, when George was 21 and Charlotte 16. George is a Haida Indian whose family is from Hydaburg. Charlotte is a Tlinget Indian with family ties at Klawock.[1] George's primary source of income is employment on commercial fishing boats, although he has worked at other jobs. During the fishing off-season, he leads the traditional subsistence existence of village Alaska, hunting, trapping, fishing, and picking berries. Since the marriage of the parties, Charlotte has held many different jobs and has also attended school. At the time the custody hearing was held in this case, she had been employed in Juneau for some 6 months.

When the matter was before the trial court, Charlotte was living in Juneau with Tom Hughes, a non-Native, with whom she had been living since shortly after she separated from George in 1965. Charlotte and Hughes expressed their intent to marry after her divorce. They also indicated that they hoped to be able to bring Hughes' three children from an earlier marriage into their home in addition to George Jr., and two children of their own union. Hughes and Charlotte work alternate shifts at their respective employments and have outside help for the brief period when their shifts overlap and neither can be home.

George Jr. was born at Mt. Edgecumbe, Alaska, December 20, 1964. He first lived with Charlotte's grandmother in Klawock when Charlotte was working in a cannery for a short time in the summer of 1965. He returned to this home when his father brought him back from San Diego where Charlotte had taken him in 1965, and remained there until 1968. In October, 1968, Charlotte's grandmother

---

1. From the time of their marriage in 1963 through the summer of 1965, George and Charlotte live in Klawock off and on with Charlotte's grandmother. From 1966 to 1968, when the grandmother was taking care of his son, George spent the off-seasons in her home also. In September 1970, George took his son with him to Hydaburg where the boy lived with two of George's sisters—with one during the fall fishing season and with the other from the end of the season through the time of the custody hearing. The custody decree left the child with the latter married sister temporarily so that the boy could finish the year in the Headstart program he had been attending.

became ill, so one of her daughters took the boy to Charlotte in Juneau. He stayed with Charlotte about 9 months until her financial situation became so bad that she could not adequately care for her two children.[2] To see that they were properly cared for, she sent them to her grandmother who was at home again in Klawock.[3] George Jr. remained in Klawock until after the 1970 fishing season. His father then came to get him because the grandmother was too old and sick to be able to care for the child any longer. After visiting various relatives, George Sr. took his son to Hydaburg to live with one of the boy's paternal aunts briefly during the fishing season. At the end of the season, George Sr. made more permanent living arrangements for the boy, placing him with another aunt and her family where he could live next door and participate in the boy's upbringing. Had custody been awarded to the father, the boy would have continued to live with his married aunt indefinitely.

In our jurisdiction it is well established that the trial court is possessed of broad discretion to determine where custody should be placed. We will disturb the trial court's resolution of custody issues only if convinced that the record shows an abuse of discretion, or if controlling findings of fact are clearly erroneous. King v. King, 477 P.2d 356, 357 (Alaska 1970); Sheridan v. Sheridan, 466 P.2d 821, 824 (Alaska 1970). In the case at bar, the trial court recognized that the paramount consideration in any custody determination is what appears to be for the best interests of the child.[4]

The facts have been set forth in some detail because of appellant George Carle's contentions that the trial court erred in its evaluation of the relevant facts for the purpose of deciding what custody disposition would be in the best interests of the minor child, George Jr. George Carle's argument before this court is two-pronged: first, that the trial court failed to give adequate consideration to the "actual in-

---

2. By that time she and Hughes had had one baby. Hughes had gone to Hawaii to work in the summer of 1969, but did not stay much more than a month because of Charlotte's financial status.

3. When Charlotte sought the return of the two children two weeks later, her grandmother would only send back the baby. The grandmother had refused to give up George Jr. to Charlotte once before in 1967. Recognizing her grandmother's great attachment to the boy, Charlotte did not insist on recovering custody either time.

4. AS 09.55.205 provides that in deciding custody, the trial court should be guided by the following considerations:

(1) by what appears to be for the best interests of the child and if the child is of a sufficient age and intelligence to form a preference, the court may consider that preference in determining the question;

(2) as between parents adversely claiming the custody neither parent is entitled to it as of right.

The legislative standard parallels the standard articulated by this court. King v. King, 477 P.2d 356 (Alaska 1970); Sheridan v. Sheridan, 466 P.2d 821 (Alaska 1970); Harding v. Harding, 377 P.2d 378 (Alaska 1962); Rhodes v. Rhodes, 370 P.2d 902 (Alaska 1962).

terests" of the child, defined essentially as his psychological well-being; and second, that the trial judge's custody decision was the result of his cultural bias against the Native village way of life. In regard to this latter argument, appellant contends that the trial judge erroneously employed a presumption that the Native village culture is "inevitably succumbing" to the caucasian, urban culture.

We turn first to the asserted failure of the trial court to consider the actual interests or psychological well-being of the child. George Carle contends that the interests of the child in a custody dispute merit constitutional protection and that due process requires courts to "determine custody according to criteria which assure full and meaningful consideration of the child's actual interest." [5] According to the father, this would mean focusing primarily on "the actual psychological interests of the child," and more particularly, on "the existence and quality of * * * emotional relationships between the child and his possible custodian." We agree that the nature of the child's existing relationships should be a significant factor in choosing his custodian. Nevertheless, we believe that the "best interests" criterion adequately encompasses this factor.

Even were we to adopt the father's position and focus primarily on the actual psychological interests of the child the evidence does not clearly require a different result as to the choice of custody. The child's most stable, continuous, and longlasting relationship was with his greatgrandmother who can no longer care for him. He has spent relatively little time in 7 years with his mother, but his contacts with his father have been transitory also.[6] The child has related well to both parents and to the respective living situations they offered him. Moreover, the trial court's decision frequently touched on elements of the child's relationship with others—with his aunt and her family, with Hughes, with his school in Hydaburg. In fact, it was precisely his concern for the child's psychological development that led the judge to place him with his mother in Juneau. In his decision the trial judge found that the child's mother had obtained stable employment and possessed the means of providing good care for the child;

---

5. Whether or not a constitutional right of the child is involved, parents have standing to challenge on appeal a determination of what is in the best interests of the child. See, e. g., Sheridan v. Sheridan, 466 P.2d 821 (Alaska 1970); Bass v. Bass, 437 P.2d 324 (Alaska 1968); Rhodes v. Rhodes, 370 P.2d 902 (Alaska 1962). We deem this an appropriate occasion to reiterate the point we made in Sheridan v. Sheridan, 466 P.2d 821, 825 n. 16 (Alaska 1970) to the effect that in contested custody cases the trial court, in its discretion, is empowered to appoint a guardian ad litem to represent the interests of the minor child. See Alaska Civ.R. 17(b); Alaska R. Child P. 11.

6. While there might be some preference for leaving the child in the custody of the person with whom he has most recently and continuously resided, we decline to establish such a presumption lest it lead to pre-hearing maneuvering for possession of the child. In any event such a rule would have been no help in the instant case where neither parent actually has lived with George Jr. for long or continuous periods.

that the mother and Hughes provided a sense of family and home for the child, "a settled place of security and safety"; that the paternal aunt could not fulfill the necessary filial relationship; that placing the child in the mother's custody provided greater assurance of a settled, stable, family environment for the child; and that the mother was in a position to materially aid the child's development of a sense of identity, worth, and self confidence. The trial court was also of the view that the transition from the village to urban way of life could be more easily accomplished while the child was still young than if delayed until his character and personality were more rigidly formed.[7] In short the trial court concluded that the child would be emotionally and economically more secure in an urban setting.

The father asserts that the trial court failed "to give sufficient recognition to the traditional manner of care and upbringing of Native children" in weighing the custody alternatives available to the minor child of the parties. This assertion is not borne out by the record. Throughout the custody hearing the trial judge allowed evidence bearing on the nature and quality of village life. Before hearing final argument, the trial judge indicated what he thought was the most important question for counsel to discuss. In doing so, he said that the custody alternatives offered were perhaps somewhat unique and that

> I'm most fundamentally faced with a decision whether this child is to be reared in a Native culture in a village or in the Anglo-Saxon culture in a developed community. And I'm concerned about the basic differences between the environmental circumstances of the village life on the one hand, where his family associations are offered, apart from the specific capabilities of the [father], and on the other hand, the advantages and disadvantages of a different way of life.

Finally, in his oral decision the trial judge explicitly recognized that it is common in villages for members of the extended family to assist the natural parents of a child in his rearing and that the village offered certain advantages to children raised there.[8] More particularly,

---

7. As to the quality of emotional relationships between the child and his possible custodian, in his decision the trial judge alluded to the fact that the father's hearing loss and speech difficulties hampered his ability to readily communicate; that the father's occupation as a commercial fisherman requires that he be absent for several months during fishing season; that the father did not have a home of his own in which to care for the child; that the father's capacity to provide the necessities of life for himself and his son was limited; and that the father's married sister cared for and loved the child and that it was not an unusual facet of Native village culture to provide care and a home when the child's natural parents are unable to do so.

8. The trial court's findings of fact, where pertinent, read as follows:

> The evidence indicated that it is not unusual in the village culture for the relatives of a child, such as the paternal aunt here, to provide a home and care for a child where for some reason the natural parents are not suitably situated to do

the trial court recognized that George Jr. was then being well and lovingly cared for in his aunt's home.

From an overall appraisal of the record, it appears that the trial court's decision to award custody to the mother was influenced by the view that there existed a great probability of a more stable home, emotionally and economically, if the mother was awarded custody.

This brings us to appellant's second argument to the effect that the trial court's custody decision was dictated by the court's cultural bias against the Native village way of life and denied the child the "right of cultural survival." This contention arises out of the trial judge's statement made in the course of his decision that

> Inevitably, the village way of life is succumbing to the predominate [sic] caucasian, urban society of the land, and of necessity the youth of the villages must confront and adjust to this new life style. That transition can more easily be accomplished in the case of this child at his young age than if delayed until his character and personality are more rigidly formed.

In light of these comments, the closeness of the custody question and the fact that the child's best interests were not independently protected by the appointment of a guardian ad litem,[9] we have concluded, that the case should be remanded for further proceedings. We are reluctant to finalize the decree in this case, given the possibility that an improper criterion was employed by the court in its resolution of the custody issue. Admittedly, the precise meaning of the trial judge's assertion that "the village way of life is succumbing to the predominate [sic] caucasian, urban society" is not free of ambiguity. Similarly, it is not clear whether the trial judge was suggesting that the Native youth must necessarily adopt urban life-styles. Yet, on the basis of the trial judge's questioned remarks, we think a cogent argument can be advanced that the custody issue here was decided in part through the utilization of an impermissible criteria.

Both judicial decision and statutory provision mandate that the paramount consideration in any custody determination is "what ap-

so. In this case, the boy does appear to be loved and accepted in his aunt's home and family in Hydaburg. The evidence also indicated that he is currently doing well in a so-called 'Headstart' program in the village school.

* * *

From the evidence it may be said there are, indeed, some significant and praiseworthy values in the Native village cultural environment in which the boy would be reared under defendant's custody. These include a rapport with nature and with a community of people which is perhaps less characteristic of urban life. The village environment may well nurture a sense of pride and self-worth in this Native child which a community such as Juneau could tend to suppress in his status as a member of a minority race.

9. See n. 5, supra. During the course of the trial the trial judge remarked that the issue before him "really concerns a party who is in a sense not represented in this suit." Although counsel was not appointed to represent the child, the trial judge alluded to the fact that in the past he contemplated such appointments.

pears to be for the best interests of the child." We think it is not permissible, in a bicultural context, to decide a child's custody on the hypothesis that it is necessary to facilitate the child's adjustment to what is believed to be the dominant culture. Such judgments are, in our view, not relevant to the determination of custody issues. Rather, the focus should be on the fitness of the parent and the parent's ability to accord the child the most meaningful parent-child relationship. It is not the function of our courts to homogenize Alaskan society. Recently we had occasion to observe that, "The United States of America, and Alaska in particular, reflect a pluralistic society, grounded upon such basic values as the preservation of maximum individual choice, protection of minority sentiments, and appreciation for divergent lifestyles." Since we are unable to conclude with any degree of certainty that custody was decided without taking into consideration impermissible factors, we hold that the case must be remanded for further proceedings.

We think it necessary to comment on one other facet of the proceedings below. Here the differing lifestyles flowing from the two cultures have significance in determining which parent could provide the best possible parent-child relationship. In such circumstances, we deem it inappropriate to decide the custody issue on the basis of cultural assumptions which are not borne out by the record. Rational decision-making requires, as a necessary prerequisite, a solid evidentiary base upon which evaluation can be made of these factors as they relate to the primary question of what custody disposition is in the best interests of the child.

We therefore reverse and remand to the superior court for further proceedings not inconsistent with the foregoing. Upon remand, the superior court is empowered to appoint a guardian ad litem for the child, and to take such other steps as are deemed appropriate, including the taking of additional evidence in the event any party raises issues as to changed circumstances arising since trial that bear on the custody issue.

NOTES AND QUESTIONS

1. There seem to be suggestions in the footnotes to the *Carle* case that there may be a constitutional right on the part of a child in a custody case to have counsel representing him. Would you agree that this is so, with the cost to be paid for by his parents if they are able and by the state if they are not? Section 310 of the Uniform Marriage and Divorce Act 9A Unif. L.Ann. 172 (1979) permits but does not require counsel to be appointed by the court to represent the child. See In re B, supra, page 506. Exactly what would counsel for the child do in a custody case? Cf. the remarks of an experienced and distinguished family court judge in Dembitz, Beyond Any Discipline's Competence, 83 Yale L.J. 1304, 1312 (1974) (a review of the Goldstein, Freud, Solnit book): "The authors refrain from recommending participation by psychiatrists and other experts in a custody decision, but they do advocate independent legal representation for the child in all

cases involving child placement. To attack such a sacred and apparently in-nocuous cow is doubtless heresy. Nevertheless, the New York Family Court's extensive experience with counsel for the child indicates that the authors have an exaggerated and unrealistic view of the utility of such counsel in custody cases. * * * There is little that counsel for the child can contribute to the fact finding unless by some mere fortuity he is better prepared on the case than the other attorneys or is a more competent inter-rogator. * * * [T]he authors' own desire for speedy determinations in child placement cases may be frustrated by independent representation for the child. The proliferation of attorneys generally presents practical diffi-culties which prevent calendaring cases with dispatch. Securing counsel for the child thus is a detriment to the child, if the counsel is unlikely to con-tribute more than a superficial endorsement of the position of one of the adult parties. Admittedly, this ostensibly unbiased endorsement may serve as a crutch for a judge who wishes support for his decision to award the child to that one party. Nonetheless, routine appointment of counsel for the child in all custody matters, as the authors recommend, would result in a ritualistic and unconstructive use of the lawyer. It should be avoided." (Footnotes omitted.)

2. Counsel for the father in *Carle* urged the court to adopt the psy-chological best interest test outlined supra page 1071, in deciding the custody issue. Is the court correct in responding that the general test of the child's best interests is the equivalent? Would the psychological best interest test involve the court in determining which of the two competing life-styles would be most conducive to this child's psychological well-being?

3. The Alaska statute cited by the court authorizes the court to con-sider the child's preference as to his custody, if he is of sufficient age and intelligence to form a preference. Should the court in this case consult the child's preference? If so, how much weight should be given his prefer-ence? For example, if the child expressed a strong preference for one par-ent, should the court refuse to honor that preference only where the parent is shown to be unfit to have custody? See, e. g., Smith v. Smith, 15 Utah 2d 36, 386 P.2d 900 (1963); Annot., Child's Wishes as Factor in Awarding Custody, 4 A.L.R.3d 1396 (1965). How is the child's preference to be deter-mined? May the court interview the child out of the presence of the par-ties? Lincoln v. Lincoln, 24 N.Y.2d 270, 299 N.Y.S.2d 842, 247 N.E.2d 659 (1969).

4. The court in *Carle* holds that it is not permissible "in a bicultural context" to award custody to one claimant or the other on the ground that it is best for the child to become adjusted to the dominant culture.

(a) Does the United States Constitution have any bearing on this problem?

(b) Does the court's decision mean that in no circumstances may com-peting cultures or life-styles be considered in determining which parent is to be given custody? How should this case be decided on the remand?

(c) H and W had an agreement that their children should be brought up in the Jewish faith. H was Jewish and W a Gentile. They were divorc-ed and W married X, a Gentile, going with him to live in Idaho in a town one hundred miles from the nearest Jewish temple. H remained in New Jersey, where ample opportunity for training in and celebration of the Jewish religion existed. In a custody dispute over the parties' child, should the court take into account the relative opportunities of the parent to bring up the child in the Jewish faith? May the court take this into account under the Constitution? If so, what weight should be given to this factor? Would the result be different if there had been no agreement concerning the religion in which the children were to be brought up? Would it be different if both H and W were Jewish? See, e. g., Bonjour v. Bonjour, 592 P.2d 1233 (Alaska 1979); Lynch v. Uhlenhopp, 248 Iowa 68, 78 N.W.2d 491 (1956); Wilhelm v. Wilhelm, 504 S.W.2d 699 (Ky.1974); Robert Q. v. Judy E., 90 Misc.2d 439, 395 N.Y.S.2d 351 (Fam.Ct.1977); Schwarzman v. Schwarzman, 88 Misc.2d 866, 388 N.Y.S.2d 993 (Sup.Ct.1976); Welker v. Welker, 24 Wis.2d 570, 129 N.W.2d 134 (1964); Munoz v. Munoz, 79 Wash. 2d 810, 489 P.2d 1133 (1971); Wilson v. Wilson, 473 P.2d 595 (Wyo.1970); Note, 50 Yale L.J. 1286 (1941); Annot., 66 A.L.R.2d 1410, 1432 (1959).

(d) What should be the custody award if the mother of a child were eligible as a custodian, but the evidence showed that she was a member of a small and unusual religious sect which believed that blood transfusions and other medical and surgical procedures were wrong and should not be employed and which shunned all social relationships and activities except with members of the sect? Can such religious considerations be taken into account under the First Amendment of the United States Constitution? See Johnson v. Johnson, 564 P.2d 71, 76 (Alaska 1977); Smith v. Smith, 90 Ariz. 190, 367 P.2d 230 (1961); Quiner v. Quiner, 59 Cal.Rptr. 503 (Ct. App.1967); Levitsky v. Levitsky, 231 Md. 388, 190 A.2d 621 (1963), 36 U. Colo.L.Rev. 589 (1964); Harris v. Harris, 343 So.2d 762 (Miss.1977); Waites v. Waites, 567 S.W.2d 326 (Mo.1978).

(e) H and W were divorced, both of them being white. They had two small children. While the divorce was pending, W began living with X, a black man. H sought custody of the two children. In the course of the proceedings W testified that she intended to marry X as soon as possible after the divorce decree was entered, and asked that custody of the children be given to her. The evidence indicated that X was fond of the children, that he and W had an adequate home for the children, and that H was also fond of the children and able to care for them. May the factor of X's race be constitutionally considered in deciding on custody? If so, what weight should be given to it? Fountaine v. Fountaine, 9 Ill.App.2d 482, 133 N.E.2d 532 (1956); Boone v. Boone, 90 N.M. 466, 565 P.2d 337 (1977); Commonwealth ex rel. Lucas, v. Kreischer, 450 Pa. 352, 299 A.2d 243 (1973); Grossman, A Child of a Different Color: Race as a Factor in Adoption and Custody Proceedings, 17 Buff.L.Rev. 303 (1968).

5. (a) Where custody is awarded to one parent, it is customary to grant rights of visitation to the other parent. Thus the mother may be given custody but with the right given to the father to have the child visit him on weekends and during school holidays. On rare occasions visitation may be refused or terminated, as, for example, where its effects are seriously detrimental to the child. E. g., Taraboletti v. Taraboletti, 56 Ill.App.3d 854, 14 Ill.Dec. 350, 372 N.E.2d 155 (1978); Baehr v. Baehr, 56 Ill.App.3d 624, 14 Ill.Dec. 401, 372 N.E.2d 412 (1978); Annot., 88 A.L.R.2d 148 (1963); Note, 13 Stan.L.Rev. 108, 111 (1961). McCurdy v. McCurdy, 363 N.E.2d 1298 (Ind.App.1977) held that the trial court should have ordered the wife to permit the children to visit their father in prison.

(b) There has lately arisen a movement for the recognition of grandparents' rights of visitation, producing in a few states statutes which permit orders of this kind where dictated by the child's best interests. E. g., N.J.Stat.Ann. § 9:2–7.1 (1976). Under what circumstances should a court award visitation rights to grandparents? For example, in the *Carle* case, if the father were given custody on the remand, should the maternal grandmother have visitation rights? Or in a case in which custody goes to the child's mother, with rights of visitation to the father, should the paternal grandparents also have visitation rights? Or if the father has custody but has quarrelled with his parents, should they have visitation rights, assuming the child's mother also has visitation rights? See, e. g., J. v. M., 157 N.J.Super. 478, 385 A.2d 240 (1978); In re Adoption by M, 140 N.J.Super. 91, 355 A.2d 211 (1976); Looper v. McManus, 581 P.2d 487 (Okl.App. 1978); Dolman v. Dolman, 586 S.W.2d 606 (Tex.Civ.App.1979); Annot., Grandparents' Visitation Rights, 90 A.L.R.3d 222 (1979).

(c) Closely related to visitation is the question whether and under what circumstances a parent will be permitted to remove the child from the jurisdiction. Courts in the past have been reluctant to give custody to a parent who proposed to take the child into another state, or to permit the person who has already been awarded custody to remove the child from the state. See cases cited in Annot., 15 A.L.R.2d 432 (1951), and Tanttila v. Tanttila, 152 Colo. 445, 382 P.2d 798 (1963). More recently some courts at least have been less reluctant, where the child's welfare is not prejudiced by the move and there is some good reason for it on the part of the custodian. This is so even though such a move may result in the deprivation or curtailment of the visitation rights of the non-custodial parent. See, e. g., Johnson v. Johnson, 105 Ill.App.2d 399, 245 N.E.2d 580 (1969); Whitman v. Whitman, 28 Wis.2d 50, 135 N.W.2d 835 (1965); Note, 21 Baylor L.Rev. 121 (1968). Cf. Barstad v. Barstad, 74 Wash.2d 295, 444 P.2d 691 (1968), in which the court denied custody to a mother who had removed the child from the state in violation of a restraining order. For cogent arguments against restricting the custodial parent's right to move, see Bodenheimer, Equal Rights, Visitation, and the Right to Move, 1 Fam.Advocate 18 (1978).

DODD v. DODD

Supreme Court of New York, New York County, 1978.
93 Misc.2d 641, 403 N.Y.S.2d 401.

FELICE K. SHEA, Justice. In this action for divorce, the Court must determine whether or not to order joint custody of the parties' infant daughters, ages 5 and 7. The plaintiff mother seeks sole custody of the children, with liberal visitation to the defendant father. Defendant urges that custody be awarded jointly and that the children divide their time equally between the two homes. In the alternative, the father requests that he be the custodial parent.

Joint custody is an appealing concept. It permits the Court to escape an agonizing choice, to keep from wounding the self-esteem of either parent and to avoid the appearance of discrimination between the sexes. Joint custody allows parents to have an equal voice in making decisions, and it recognizes the advantages of shared responsibility for raising the young. But serious questions remain to be answered. How does joint custody affect children? What are the factors to be considered and weighed? While the Court should not yield to the frivolous objections of one party, it must give thought to whether joint custody is feasible when one party is opposed and court intervention is needed to effectuate it. In the end, as in every child custody decision, it is the welfare of the children which governs and each case will turn on its individual facts and circumstances.

Plaintiff and defendant are both 30 years old and had been married eight years when they separated. The father is a doctor; the mother is a college graduate who works as a customer service representative in a bank. Dr. Dodd lives in a comfortable 8-room apartment near his daughters' schools. Mrs. Dodd has remained in the marital apartment. At the insistence of the father, the children have, for the past year, spent exactly half their time with each parent—Mondays, Wednesdays and alternate weekends from Friday through Sunday with the father; Tuesdays, Thursdays and alternate week-ends with the mother.

Defendant did not contest plaintiff's fitness to have custody at trial. His position is that joint custody promotes close nurturing by both parents. He describes himself as stable and competent whereas he views the children's mother as nervous, indecisive and easily frustrated. Defendant seeks joint responsibility and equal voice in the decisions affecting his daughters, as well as a continued 50–50 division of the children's time. He maintains that the children have flourished under the shared custody arrangement and asks the Court to order its continuance.

Plaintiff, on the other hand, testified to the friction between the parties, the threats, harassment and intimidation she has suffered, the father's unwillingness to share in the care of the children while he lived at home, and his exposure of the children to his romance with her erstwhile friend. Plaintiff sees the joint custody arrangement, in which she acquiesced with reluctance, as failing to meet the needs of the children and she asks the Court to award her sole custody with liberal visitation to defendant.

The Court finds that the marriage of Dr. and Mrs. Dodd has been troubled almost from the start and that the hostility between the parties is deep and of long duration. The Court also finds that both parents have a loving and close relationship with the children and that both are fit in that they are free of significant emotional problems and willing and able to function well as parents. Joint custody can be considered only where both parties are fit parents.

No statute expressly authorizes an award of joint custody. However, Domestic Relations Law § 240 provides that the divorce court "must give * * * direction, between the parties, for the custody

* * * of any child of the parties, as * * * justice requires, having regard to the circumstances of the case and of the respective parties and to the best interests of the child. In all cases there shall be no prima facie right to the custody of the child in either parent." [1] In the few reported cases where joint custody has been found to be in the child's best interests, the courts have not hesitated to infer, expressly or impliedly, the power to give custody jointly to both parents. See, e. g., Perotti v. Perotti, 78 Misc.2d 131, 355 N.Y.S.2d 68; Woicik v. Woicik, 66 Misc.2d 357, 321 N.Y.S.2d 5; Ross v. Ross, 4 Misc.2d 399, 149 N.Y.S.2d 585; R. v. R., 91 Misc.2d 792, 399 N.Y.S.2d 93; Krois v. Krois, N.Y.L.J. 10–14–77, p. 13, col. 5; Levy v. Levy, N. Y.L.J. 1–29–76, p. 11, col. 3; Schack v. Schack, N.Y.L.J. 8–21–74, p. 15, col. 8.

Joint custody has been defined as giving both parents "legal responsibility for the child's care and alternating companionship." [2] An examination of the joint custody cases in New York [3] reveals that there has been no uniform application of the term "joint custody" and no single arrangement which results when a joint award is made. Joint or divided custody decrees generally give both parents legal responsibility for the child's care, but when physical or actual custody is lodged primarily in one parent custody may be "joint" in name only.

In the *Perotti* case, the parents were given shared responsibility, with physical custody to the father, visitation to the mother. In *Woicik,* the child was to be in boarding school in the winter, camp in the summer, with the parents sharing only the child's vacation time. In *Ross,* custody was awarded to both parties on a temporary basis, apparently to "afford the child an opportunity to adjust himself, in due time, to one or both parents". Ross v. Ross, 4 Misc.2d 399, 405, 149 N.Y.S.2d 585, 591. The actual division of time was left to the parties, and if the parties were unable to agree, then sole custody was to be given to the father with week-end visitation rights to the mother. In R. v. R., the court directed the parties to make all decisions jointly for the benefit of the children, but divided physical custody by allowing the children to live with their father and visit their mother.

1. See also Domestic Relations Law §§ 70, 80, 81.

2. Bodenheimer, Progress Under the Uniform Child Custody Jurisdiction Act and Remaining Problems: Punitive Decrees, Joint Custody and Excessive Modifications, 65 Cal.L.Rev. 978, 1009 (1977). Cf. 1 Lindey, Separation Agreements and Ante-Nuptial Contracts 14–60 to 14–61 (1977) differentiating between joint custody (child resides most of year with one parent, spouses have joint control), divided custody (each spouse has child for part of year and control while child is in his or her custody) and split custody (children split between parents).

3. Joint custody cases in other jurisdictions are collected in Note, Divided Custody of Children After Their Parents' Divorce, 8 J.Fam.L. 58, 65–68 (1968); Clark, Law of Domestic Relations 590–91 (1968) and Annot., 92 A.L.R.2d 695 (1963).

In *Krois,* there was court ordered joint guidance for a boy of 17 and a handicapped girl of 20, but both children were to remain physically with the father. In the *Levy* case, the court gave joint control of a 13 year old boy to both parents, but directed that he stay with his mother for two years to give him a chance to decide where to live. In the *Schack* case, where joint custody was awarded, the children were to live with the mother from Monday through Friday, the father on Saturday and Sunday, with vacations to be split.

It is well recognized that the children of divorce are subjected to severe strain, and that children often experience loss of security and feelings of rejection as a concomitant of their parents' separation.[4] Experts in the field have expressed opposition to divided custody on the ground that change and discontinuity threaten the child's emotional well-being.[5] It is argued that "joint custody between parents usually requires that 'shuttling back and forth' of children which must inevitably lead to the lack of stability in home environment which children require." [6] Moreover, joint or divided custody may exacerbate the adults' use of the children to defeat each other in defiance of the children's interest in stability, serenity and continuity. In attempting to maintain positive emotional ties to two hostile adults, children may become prey to severe and crippling loyalty conflicts.[7]

The proponents of joint custody contend that fathers relegated to seeing their children only intermittently experience feelings of deep loss and often react by limiting their involvement with their children.[8] They argue further that there is no scientific data for the *de facto* preference in favor of the mother [9] and that fathers in today's dual career families are equally nurturant and competent to care for their offspring.[10] They contend that a child needs a sustained involvement with both his parents and that the conventional single parent custody arrangement "tends to make ex-parents of fa-

4. Roman, The Disposable Parent, 15 Conciliation Courts Review, No. 2, Dec. 1977, at 6; Gardner, Separation of the Parents and the Emotional Life of the Child, 40 Mental Hygiene 53 (1956).

5. Goldstein, Freud and Solnit, Beyond the Best Interests of the Child 37–38 (1973).

6. 2 Foster and Freed, Law and the Family § 29:6A (Supp.1976).

7. Goldstein et al., supra note 5, at 12.

8. Grief, Child Absence: Fathers' Perceptions of their Relationship to their Children Subsequent to Divorce. Un-

published doctoral dissertation. Adelphi University, 1977. Of the 40 fathers interviewed for this study, 10 had joint custody, none pursuant to court order.

9. See Roth, The Tender Years Presumption in Child Custody Disputes, 15 J.Fam.L. 423 (1977); People ex rel. Watts v. Watts, 77 Misc.2d 178, 350 N.Y.S.2d 285; Annot., 70 A.L.R.3rd 262 (1976).

10. See, e. g., Molinoff, Joint Custody: Victory for All?, N.Y. Times, 3–6–77, XXII, 18:1, and Baum, What to Do When You Both Want Custody, New Woman Magazine, Sept.–Oct. 1977 at 32.

thers, painfully deprived creatures out of the children and overburdened people out of mothers." [11]

These are persuasive arguments. No post-divorce custody arrangement will give to children two loving parents, living together, devoted to each other and to the children's welfare. Joint custody, under the proper circumstances, may be the closest it is possible to come to the shattered ideal. The courts, in dealing with the difficult issues raised by child custody litigation, should consider joint custody as an option, particularly in performing their little noted but frequently exercised role as mediator before trial.

However, when one parent resists joint custody and refuses to be persuaded that it is workable, what will be the result for the children when it is ordered by the Court? There appear to be no social science studies that will answer this question. The most ardent professional proponents of joint custody assume cooperation between parents and agreement about child rearing practices as basic requirements for joint custody.[12] It is hardly surprising that joint custody is generally arrived at by consent.

As is noted, infra, the parties herein have made child rearing a battleground; agreement has been totally absent. Defendant urges that a court order, together with an admonition to the parties that they should cooperate in the children's interest, will end the hostilities. No authorities, legal or otherwise, have been cited in support of this proposition. The fact seems to be that court decreed joint custody often comes back to court for modification. See, e. g., Perotti v. Perotti, 78 Misc.2d 131, 355 N.Y.S.2d 68, relitigated and custody awarded to defendant father in unreported decision dated July 18, 1975; Rechtschaffen v. Rechtschaffen, N.Y.L.J. 1–6–78, p. 7, col. 1; see also Soto v. Soto, 57 A.D.2d 818, 395 N.Y.S.2d 169; Lyritzis v. Lyritzis, 55 A.D.2d 946, 391 N.Y.S.2d 133; Calder v. Woolverton, 50 A.D.2d 587, 375 N.Y.S.2d 150.

Joint custody has been tried by the Dodd family, and in the Court's view, it has failed. For fourteen months, the parents have lived apart without either a separation agreement or a court order of custody. During that time they have shared in all decisions, and for most of that time they have divided physical custody equally. In all areas, in matters both major and minor, there has been conflict. There have been disagreements over medical care and psychotherapy, over the children's clothing, over discipline, over money, over the children's attendance at family functions. Overt, bitter hostility,

11.   Roman, supra note 4, at 5.

12.   See, e. g., Roman, supra note 4, at 7; O'Neil & Leonoff, Joint Custody: An Option Worth Examining, Perception, Nov./Dec. 1977, at 28, 29, state: "[Joint Custody] is a decision that must be arrived at by the couple themselves—obviously a court could not order a joint arrangement." The articles in the popular press cited in note 10, supra, describe successful joint custody arrangements mutually arrived at.

criticism of each other, as well as angry words and obscenities have been observed repeatedly by the children.

Dr. Dodd has been uncompromising and Mrs. Dodd, while a participant in the frequent acrimonious quarrels, has acquiesced to her husband's demands in large measure out of fear that her husband's threats to remove the children, to prove her an abusive mother and to withhold support, could be carried out with impunity.

The court heard testimony from two psychiatrists. Dr. A, called by the plaintiff, examined both parents and both children. In contrast, the defendant's expert, Dr. B., examined only the defendant and the two girls. For this reason primarily, but also because of Dr. A.'s long and distinguished career in the field of child psychiatry, it is his testimony that is entitled to the greater weight.

Dr. A. testified that the children were anxious and not coping well with their complex and shifting routines. Although he saw no evidence of serious emotional problems, he found signs of precocity related to stress in both children and sleep and behavior problems in Helen. Both children are receiving therapy. Dr. B, who is Eliza's therapist, testified that Eliza is sad, lonely, unable to make friends, has anger which she has repressed, suffers a great deal and is concerned over the relationship between her parents. He found both girls troubled. In Dr. A.'s opinion, joint custody is unworkable for the Dodds, and he recommended one principal home with Mrs. Dodd as the custodial parent. Dr. B. agreed that the present joint custody situation is not working well, but viewed it as the least detrimental alternative.

The evident distress of Eliza and Helen is an unfortunate fact of life for the children of divorce. It is hard, indeed impossible, for the Court to separate out the part played in their misery by their parents' separation and the part played by the joint custodial arrangement. The physical shuttling back and forth, the parents' tensions and constant arguments, exacerbated by a situation in which neither has the deciding voice, surely must be responsible in part.

To the Court, it is clear that for this family, joint custody has been a failure and that court ordered joint custody would be equally doomed. The question then to be decided is which of two fit parents will be the better custodian. The Court finds that Mrs. Dodd is the more suitable.

In the first place, Mrs. Dodd has been the primary caretaking figure to these little girls since birth. Dr. Dodd's extensive involvement in the lives of his children is relatively recent, dating from the parties' separation. Award of custody to Mrs. Dodd will preserve the children's well-recognized need for continuity.

Moreover, the Court believes that placing custody with Mrs. Dodd will maximize the role which both parents should play in their children's lives. The testimony reveals that Dr. Dodd has a low opinion of his wife as a person and as a mother, which he has not hesitated to convey to his daughters. With the final right to make decisions lodged with Dr. Dodd, it can be expected that he would give very little weight to the views of his ex-wife. Mrs. Dodd, on the other hand, is entirely competent to act as the final arbiter in matters affecting the children, and in addition, she respects her husband, knows him to be a good father, and would rely on him for valuable assistance in making decisions as to education, medical and psychiatric care and general welfare. Mrs. Dodd has also shown herself to be the more flexible and conciliatory with regard to physical custody of the children and can be expected to cooperate fully with liberal visitation and frequent contact between her daughters and their father.

In addition, the Court concludes that of the two parents, it is Mrs. Dodd who is the more sensitive to the needs of the children. The credible evidence shows that upon leaving his family, Dr. Dodd plunged immediately into an intimate relationship with a neighbor who was a former family friend, that the friend was present much of the time while the children were with their father, and that she slept at Dr. Dodd's home overnight while the children were also there. According to Dr. A., Dr. Dodd's seeing another woman in the presence of his children intensified the stress they experienced from the separation. The Court expresses no moral judgment on Dr. Dodd's extra-marital relationship. However, choosing to have his paramour stay overnight when his children were with him demonstrated a disregard for his daughters' need for time to adjust to the transfer in their father's affection away from their mother to another woman. Mrs. Dodd, on the other hand, has shown maturity in coping with her own problems and an ability to put her children's welfare ahead of her own.

Defendant challenged Dr. A.'s testimony that one of the reasons for favoring Mrs. Dodd as the custodial parent was that she serves her daughters' needs as a role model. The Court is persuaded that the role of the father is no less important in his daughters' lives than that of the mother. Girls need to learn not only what it will be like to be a woman, but what to look for and expect in a man. In the Dodd family, the father has dominated the mother, has forced his views on her, threatened her and belittled her. It is important, for the children's emotional health, that they view their mother as the competent person she has shown herself to be and their father as a person who can treat women with kindness and respect. With Mrs. Dodd as the custodial parent, the girls will have a better chance to form positive images of both parents.

The children were interviewed separately *in camera* in the absence of counsel. While the wishes of children must be considered the weight to be given to their desires is in the Court's discretion and the custodial preferences of young children are not determinative.

Eliza and Helen each expressed the desire to live with both parents and both said they were satisfied with the present scheme of shared custody. These views are consistent with the children's love for both parents, and with what the plaintiff's expert characterized as a typical childish wish that separated parents will reunite. The interviews with the children reinforce the Court's finding that neither parent is unfit and that both parents should be involved in their upbringing, but the children, at ages 5 and 7, are too young to guide the Court on the issue of what custodial arrangement will best serve their needs.

No court can decree an arrangement in which the children of divorced parents can be guaranteed to flourish. As the Court of Appeals has said, speaking of children in a case before it, "The courts cannot assure the happiness and stability of these children; that only their parents could have done, and, hopefully, can still do." Nehra v. Uhlar, 43 N.Y.2d 242, at 252, 401 N.Y.S.2d 168 at 173, 372 N.E.2d 4 at 9 (filed December 15, 1977).

Custody is awarded to the plaintiff who shall have the right to make all decisions affecting the children upon consultation with the defendant. The defendant is to have liberal visitation. If the parties cannot agree on visitation, the Court will make appropriate direction in the judgment to be settled herein.

NOTES AND QUESTIONS

1. The subject of joint custody has been much discussed in the law reviews and in popular articles and books. Some of these are cited in the *Dodd* case. A book which argues for joint custody, primarily from the "father's rights" point of view, is M. Roman, W. Haddad, The Disposable Parent: The Case for Joint Custody (1978). Another argument for joint custody's more frequent use, with extensive citation of articles, cases and statutes is Folberg and Graham, Joint Custody of Children Following Divorce, 12 U.C.D.L.Rev. 523 (1979). See also Note, Joint Custody: An Alternative for Divorced Parents, 26 U.C.L.A.L.Rev. 1084 (1979), and Bratt, Joint Custody, 67 Ky.L.J. 271 (1978–1979).

2. A few states have enacted statutes expressly authorizing joint custody, although, as the *Dodd* case indicates, it is generally held that courts have authority to award joint custody under the usual custody statute. See, e. g., Or.Rev.Stat. § 107.105 (1977); Wis.Stat.Ann. § 247.24 (Supp.1979–1980), authorizing joint custody when the parties agree and it is in the child's best interests. This statute also defines joint custody as meaning that both parties have equal rights and responsibilities respecting the child and neither's rights are superior to the other's.

Would you favor the enactment of some such statute as the following? This is Cal.Civ.Code § 4600.5, effective January 1, 1980, Fam.L.Rep. 305.-0015 (December 18, 1979):

"4600.5. (a) There shall be a presumption, affecting the burden of proof, that joint custody is in the best interest of a minor child where the parents have agreed to an award of joint custody or so agree in open court at a hearing for the purpose of determining the custody of the minor child or children of the marriage.

"If the court declines to enter an order awarding joint custody pursuant to this subdivision, the court shall state in its decision the reasons for denial of an award of joint custody.

"(b) Upon the application of either parent, joint custody may be awarded in the discretion of the court in other cases. For the purpose of assisting the court in making a determination whether an award of joint custody is appropriate under this subdivision, the court may direct that an investigation be conducted pursuant to the provisions of Section 4602. If the court declines to enter an order awarding joint custody pursuant to this subdivision, the court shall state in its decision the reasons for denial of an award of joint custody.

"(c) For the purposes of this section, "joint custody" means an order awarding custody of the minor child or children to both parents and providing that physical custody shall be shared by the parents in such a way as to assure the child or children of frequent and continuing contract with both parents; provided, however, that such order may award joint legal custody without awarding joint physical custody.

"(d) Any order for joint custody may be modified or terminated upon the petition of one or both parents or on the court's own motion if it is shown that the best interests of the child require modification or termination of the order. The court shall state in its decision the reasons for modification or termination of the joint custody order if either parent opposes the modification or termination order."

3. (a) Was the *Dodd* case correctly decided? Would it be decided in the same way under the California statute?

(b) Should joint custody be awarded in the following case?

H and W were divorced and under a separation agreement incorporated in the divorce decree custody of the daughter, 8, and the son, 4, went to their mother. Six years later the father brought a proceeding for custody. He had married in the meantime and had two children by the second marriage. During the six years W had been a devoted mother who gave the children good care, but at the same time she had a psychiatric illness variously characterized by the experts who testified as "acute schizophrenia with paranoid treads" [sic], or "latent schizophrenia". Another psychiatrist testified that she had not been afflicted with these illnesses and would not require prolonged therapy. The evidence showed that H was fond of the children and the children indicated a desire to live with their father, but they also indicated a love for their mother. H's business required that he travel extensively from time to time. Odette R. v. Douglas R., 91 Misc. 2d 792, 399 N.Y.S.2d 93 (Fam.Ct.1977). If joint custody were ordered in such a case, should the order include a prohibition upon removal of the child from the state by either parent?

(c) If joint custody were ordered in this case, and later the parents were unable to agree on whether the child should attend public or parochial school, what, if any, remedy would be available to the parents? Cf. Asch v. Asch, 164 N.J.Super. 499, 397 A.2d 352 (1978). If the disagreement were serious or irreconcilable, should the joint custody be terminated? Cf. Bohn and Bohn, 43 Or.App. 561, 603 P.2d 781 (1979).

4. If, after joint custody has been awarded, one of the parents moves to another and distant state, taking the child with him or her, will the other parent be able to have the joint custody order enforced in the second state? Does the Uniform Child Custody Jurisdiction Act have any provision dealing with this situation? Bodenheimer, *Progress Under the Uniform Child Custody Act and Remaining Problems: Punitive Decrees, Joint Custody, and Excessive Modifications,* 65 Cal.L.Rev. 978, 1011 (1977).

5. Is the philosophy underlying joint custody in conflict with that of the Goldstein, Freud, Solnit book outlined in paragraph 1, page 1071, supra? If so, how would you characterize the conflict? And which point of view contains the greatest potential for the satisfactory solution of custody disputes?

6. For a judicial defense of joint custody see the dissent in Starkeson v. Starkeson, 119 N.H. 78, 397 A.2d 1043 (1979). For cases which reject joint custody in a variety of circumstances see Davis v. Davis, 63 Ill.App.3d 465, 20 Ill.Dec. 437, 380 N.E.2d 415 (1978); In re Marriage of Burham, 283 N.W.2d 269 (Iowa 1979); Braiman v. Braiman, 44 N.Y.2d 584, 407 N. Y.S.2d 449, 378 N.E.2d 1019 (1978); Fuhrman v. Fuhrman, 254 N.W.2d 97 (N.D.1977); Lumbra v. Lumbra, 136 Vt. 529, 394 A.2d 1139 (1978).

7. In which of the cases reproduced or stated in this section would you favor joint custody as a solution to the parties' conflict or the child's welfare?

PAINTER v. BANNISTER

Supreme Court of Iowa, 1966.
258 Iowa 1390, 140 N.W.2d 152, cert. den. 385 U.S. 949,
87 S.Ct. 317, 17 L.Ed.2d 227 (1967).

STUART, Justice. We are here setting the course for Mark Wendell Painter's future. Our decision on the custody of this 7 year old boy will have a marked influence on his whole life. The fact that we are called upon many times a year to determine custody matters does not make the exercising of this awesome responsibility any less difficult. Legal training and experience are of little practical help in solving the complex problems of human relations. However, these problems do arise and under our system of government, the burden of rendering a final decision rests upon us. It is frustrating to know we can only resolve, not solve, these unfortunate situations.

The custody dispute before us in this habeas corpus action is between the father, Harold Painter, and the maternal grandparents, Dwight and Margaret Bannister. Mark's mother and younger sister were killed in an automobile accident on December 6, 1962 near Pullman, Washington. The father, after other arrangements for Mark's care had proved unsatisfactory, asked the Bannisters, to take care of Mark. They went to California and brought Mark to their farm home near Ames in July, 1963. Mr. Painter remarried in November, 1964 and about that time indicated he wanted to take Mark back. The Bannisters refused to let him leave and this action was filed in

June, 1965. Since July 1965 he has continued to remain in the Bannister home under an order of this court staying execution of the judgment of the trial court awarding custody to the father until the matter could be determined on appeal. For reasons hereinafter stated, we conclude Mark's better interests will be served if he remains with the Bannisters.

Mark's parents came from highly contrasting backgrounds. His mother was born, raised and educated in rural Iowa. Her parents are college graduates. Her father is agricultural information editor for the Iowa State University Extension Service. The Bannister home is in the Gilbert Community and is well kept, roomy and comfortable. The Bannisters are highly respected members of the community. Mr. Bannister has served on the school board and regularly teaches a Sunday school class at the Gilbert Congregational Church. Mark's mother graduated from Grinnell College. She then went to work for a newspaper in Anchorage, Alaska, where she met Harold Painter.

Mark's father was born in California. When he was 2½ years old, his parents were divorced and he was placed in a foster home. Although he has kept in contact with his natural parents, he considers his foster parents, the McNelly's as his family. He flunked out of a high school and a trade school because of a lack of interest in academic subjects, rather than any lack of ability. He joined the navy at 17. He did not like it. After receiving an honorable discharge, he took examinations and obtained his high school diploma. He lived with the McNelly's and went to college for 2½ years under the G.I. bill. He quit college to take a job on a small newspaper in Ephrata, Washington in November 1955. In May 1956, he went to work for the newspaper in Anchorage which employed Jeanne Bannister.

Harold and Jeanne were married in April, 1957. Although there is a conflict in the evidence on the point, we are convinced the marriage, overall, was a happy one with many ups and downs as could be expected in the uniting of two such opposites.

We are not confronted with a situation where one of the contesting parties is not a fit or proper person. There is no criticism of either the Bannisters or their home. There is no suggestion in the record that Mr. Painter is morally unfit. It is obvious the Bannisters did not approve of their daughter's marriage to Harold Painter and do not want their grandchild raised under his guidance. The philosophies of life are entirely different. As stated by the psychiatrist who examined Mr. Painter at the request of Bannisters' attorneys: "It is evident that there exists a large difference in ways of life and value systems between the Bannisters and Mr. Painter, but in this case, there is no evidence that psychiatric instability is involved. Rather, these divergent life patterns seem to represent alternative normal adaptations."

It is not our prerogative to determine custody upon our choice of one of two ways of life within normal and proper limits and we will not do so. However, the philosophies are important as they relate to Mark and his particular needs.

The Bannister home provides Mark with a stable, dependable, conventional, middleclass, middlewest background and an opportunity for a college education and profession, if he desires it. It provides a solid foundation and secure atmosphere. In the Painter home, Mark would have more freedom of conduct and thought with an opportunity to develop his individual talents. It would be more exciting and challenging in many respects, but romantic, impractical and unstable.

Little additional recitation of evidence is necessary to support our evaluation of the Bannister home. It might be pointed out, however, that Jeanne's three sisters also received college educations and seem to be happily married to college graduates.

Our conclusion as to the type of home Mr. Painter would offer is based upon his Bohemian approach to finances and life in general. We feel there is much evidence which supports this conclusion. His main ambition is to be a free lance writer and photographer. He has had some articles and picture stories published, but the income from these efforts has been negligible. At the time of the accident, Jeanne was willingly working to support the family so Harold could devote more time to his writing and photography. In the 10 years since he left college, he has changed jobs seven times. He was asked to leave two of them; two he quit because he didn't like the work; two because he wanted to devote more time to writing and the rest for better pay. He was contemplating a move to Berkeley at the time of trial. His attitude toward his career is typified by his own comments concerning a job offer:

"About the Portland news job, I hope you understand when I say it took guts not to take it; I had to get behind myself and push. It was very, very tempting to accept a good salary and settle down to a steady, easy routine. As I approached Portland, with the intention of taking the job, I began to ask what, in the long run, would be the good of this job: 1, it was not *really* what I wanted; 2, Portland is just another big farm town, with none of the stimulation it takes to get my mind sparking. Anyway, I decided Mark and myself would be better off if I went ahead with what I've started and the hell with the rest, sink, swim or starve."

There is general agreement that Mr. Painter needs help with his finances. Both Jeanne and Marilyn, his present wife, handled most of them. Purchases and sales of books, boats, photographic equipment and houses indicate poor financial judgment and an easy come easy go attitude. He dissipated his wife's estate of about $4300, most of which was a gift from her parents and which she had hoped would be used for the children's education.

The psychiatrist classifies him as "a romantic and somewhat of a dreamer". An apt example are the plans he related for himself and Mark in February 1963: "My thought now is to settle Mark and myself in Sausilito, near San Francisco; this is a retreat for wealthy artists, writers, and such aspiring artists and writers as can fork up the rent money. My plan is to do expensive portraits ($150 and up), sell prints ($15 and up) to the tourists who flock in from all over the world * * *."

The house in which Mr. Painter and his present wife live, compared with the well kept Bannister home, exemplifies the contrasting ways of life. In his words "it is a very old and beat up and lovely home * * *". They live in the rear part. The interior is inexpensively but tastefully decorated. The large yard on a hill in the business district of Walnut Creek, California, is of uncut weeds and wild oats. The house "is not painted on the outside because I do not want it painted. I am very fond of the wood on the outside of the house."

The present Mrs. Painter has her master's degree in cinema design and apparently likes and has had considerable contact with children. She is anxious to have Mark in her home. Everything indicates she would provide a leveling influence on Mr. Painter and could ably care for Mark.

Mr. Painter is either an agnostic or atheist and has no concern for formal religious training. He has read a lot of Zen Buddhism and "has been very much influenced by it." Mrs. Painter is Roman Catholic. They plan to send Mark to a Congregational Church near the Catholic Church, on an irregular schedule.

He is a political liberal and got into difficulty in a job at the University of Washington for his support of the activities of the American Civil Liberties Union in the university news bulletin.

There were "two funerals" for his wife. One in the basement of his home in which he alone was present. He conducted the service and wrote her a long letter. The second at a church in Pullman was for the gratification of her friends. He attended in a sport shirt and sweater.

These matters are not related as a criticism of Mr. Painter's conduct, way of life or sense of values. An individual is free to choose his own values, within bounds, which are not exceeded here. They do serve however to support our conclusion as to the kind of life Mark would be exposed to in the Painter household. We believe it would be unstable, unconventional, arty, Bohemian, and probably intellectually stimulating.

Were the question simply which household would be the most suitable in which to raise a child, we would have unhesitatingly chosen the Bannister home. We believe security and stability in the home are more important than intellectual stimulation in the proper development of a child. There are, however, several factors which have made us pause.

First, there is the presumption of parental preference, which though weakened in the past several years, exists by statute. Code of Iowa, Section 668.1; Finken v. Porter, 246 Iowa 1345, 72 N.W.2d 445 (1955); Kouris v. Lunn, Iowa, 136 N.W.2d 502; Vanden Heuvel v. Vanden Heuvel, 254 Iowa 1391, 1399, 121 N.W.2d 216 (1963). We have a great deal of sympathy for a father, who in the difficult period of adjustment following his wife's death, turns to the maternal grandparents for their help and then finds them unwilling to return the child. There is no merit in the Bannister claim that Mr. Painter permanently relinquished custody. It was intended to be a temporary arrangement. A father should be encouraged to look for help with the children, from those who love them without the risk of thereby losing the custody of the children permanently. This fact must receive consideration in cases of this kind. However, as always, the primary consideration is the best interest of the child and if the return of custody to the father is likely to have a seriously disrupting and disturbing effect upon the child's development, this fact must prevail. Vanden Heuvel v. Vanden Heuvel, supra; In re Guardianship of Plucar, 247 Iowa 394, 403, 72 N.W.2d 455 (1955); Carrere v. Prunty, Iowa, 133 N.W.2d 692, 696 (1965); Finken v. Porter, supra; Kouris v. Lunn, supra, R.C.P. 344(f) 15.

Second, Jeanne's will named her husband guardian of her children and if he failed to qualify or ceased to act, named her mother. The parent's wishes are entitled to consideration. Finken v. Porter, supra.

Third, the Bannisters are 60 years old. By the time Mark graduates from high school they will be over 70 years old. Care of young children is a strain on grandparents and Mrs. Bannister's letters indicate as much.

We have considered all of these factors and have concluded that Mark's best interest demands that his custody remain with the Bannisters. Mark was five when he came to their home. The evidence clearly shows he was not well adjusted at that time. He did not distinguish fact from fiction and was inclined to tell "tall tales" emphasizing the big "I". He was very aggressive toward smaller children, cruel to animals, not liked by his classmates and did not seem to know what was acceptable conduct. As stated by one witness: "Mark knew where his freedom was and he didn't know where his boundaries were." In two years he made a great deal of improvement. He now appears to be well disciplined, happy, relatively secure and popular with his classmates, although still subject to more than normal anxiety.

We place a great deal of reliance on the testimony of Dr. Glenn R. Hawks, a child psychologist. The trial court, in effect, disregarded Dr. Hawks' opinions stating: "The court has given full consideration to the good doctor's testimony, but cannot accept it at full face value because of exaggerated statements and the witness' attitude on the stand." We, of course, do not have the advantage of viewing the witness' conduct on the stand, but we have carefully reviewed his testimony and find nothing in the written record to justify such a summary dismissal of the opinions of this eminent child psychologist.

Dr. Hawks is head of the Department of Child Development at Iowa State University. However, there is nothing in the record which suggests that his relationship with the Bannisters is such that his professional opinion would be influenced thereby. Child development is his specialty and he has written many articles and a textbook on the subject. He is recognized nationally, having served on the staff of the 1960 White House Conference on Children and Youth and as consultant on a Ford Foundation program concerning youth in India. He is now education consultant on the project "Head Start". He has taught and lectured at many universities and belongs to many professional associations. He works with the Iowa Children's Home Society in placement problems. Further detailing of his qualifications is unnecessary.

Between June 15th and the time of trial, he spent approximately 25 hours acquiring information about Mark and the Bannisters, including appropriate testing of and "depth interviews" with Mark. Dr. Hawks' testimony covers 70 pages of the record and it is difficult to pinpoint any bit of testimony which precisely summarizes his opinion. He places great emphasis on the "father figure" and discounts the importance of the "biological father". "The father figure is a figure that the child sees as an authority figure, as a helper, he is a nutrient figure, and one who typifies maleness and stands as maleness as far as the child is concerned."

His investigation revealed: "* * * the strength of the father figure before Mark came to the Bannisters is very unclear. Mark is confused about the father figure prior to his contact with Mr. Bannister." Now, "Mark used Mr. Bannister as his father figure. This is very evident. It shows up in the depth interview, and it shows up in the description of Mark's life given by Mark. He has a very warm feeling for Mr. Bannister."

Dr. Hawks concluded that it was not for Mark's best interest to be removed from the Bannister home. He is criticized for reaching this conclusion without investigating the Painter home or finding out more about Mr. Painter's character. He answered:

"I was most concerned about the welfare of the child, not the welfare of Mr. Painter, not about the welfare of the Bannisters. In as much as Mark has already made an adjustment and sees the Bannisters as his parental figures in his psychological makeup, to me this is the most critical factor. Disruption at this point, I think, would be detrimental to the child even tho Mr. Painter might well be a paragon of virtue. I think this would be a kind of thing which would not be in the best interest of the child. I think knowing something about where the child is at the present time is vital. I think something about where he might go, in my way of thinking is essentially untenable to me, and relatively unimportant. It isn't even helpful. The thing I was most concerned about was Mark's view of his own reality in which he presently lives. If this is destroyed I think it will have rather bad effects on Mark. I think then if one were to make a determination whether it would be to the parents' household, or the McNelly household, or X-household, then I think the further study would be appropriate."

Dr. Hawks stated: "I am appalled at the tremendous task Mr. Painter would have if Mark were to return to him because he has got to build the relationship from scratch. There is essentially nothing on which to build at the present time. Mark is aware Mr. Painter is his father, but he is not very clear about what this means. In his own mind the father figure is Mr. Bannister. I think it would take a very strong person with everything in his favor in order to build a relationship as Mr. Painter would have to build at this point with Mark."

It was Dr. Hawks' opinion "the chances are very high (Mark) will go wrong if he is returned to his father". This is based on adoption studies which "establish that the majority of adoptions in children who are changed, from ages six to eight, will go bad, if they have had a prior history of instability, some history of prior movement. When I refer to instability I am referring to where there has been no attempt to establish a strong relationship." Although this is not an adoption, the analogy seems appropriate, for Mark who had a history of instability would be removed from the only home in which he has a clearly established "father figure" and placed with his natural father about whom his feelings are unclear.

We know more of Mr. Painter's way of life than Dr. Hawks. We have concluded that it does not offer as great a stability or security as the Bannister home. Throughout his testimony he emphasized Mark's need at this critical time is stability. He has it in the Bannister home.

Other items of Dr. Hawks' testimony which have a bearing on our decision follow. He did not consider the Bannisters' age any way disqualifying. He was of the opinion that Mark could adjust to a change more easily later on, if one became necessary, when he would have better control over his environment.

He believes the presence of other children in the home would have a detrimental effect upon Mark's adjustment whether this occurred in the Bannister home or the Painter home.

The trial court does not say which of Dr. Hawks' statements he felt were exaggerated. We were most surprised at the inconsequential position to which he relegated the "biological father". He concedes "child psychologists are less concerned about natural parents than probably other professional groups are." We are not inclined to so lightly value the role of the natural father, but find much reason for his evaluation of this particular case.

Mark has established a father-son relationship with Mr. Bannister, which he apparently had never had with his natural father. He is happy, well adjusted and progressing nicely in his development. We do not believe it is for Mark's best interest to take him out of this stable atmosphere in the face of warnings of dire consequences from an eminent child psychologist and send him to an uncertain future in his father's home. Regardless of our appreciation of the father's love for his child and his desire to have him with him, we do not believe we have the moral right to gamble with this child's future. He should be encouraged in every way possible to know his father. We are sure there are many ways in which Mr. Painter can enrich Mark's life.

For the reasons stated, we reverse the trial court and remand the case for judgment in accordance herewith.

Reversed and remanded.

NOTES AND QUESTIONS

1. The *Painter* case attracted a large amount of public attention. It was noted in 8 Ariz.L.Rev. 163 (1966); 35 U.Chi.L.Rev. 478 (1968); 79 Harv.L.Rev. 1710 (1966); 51 Iowa L.Rev. 1114 (1966); and 20 Okla.L.Rev. 203 (1967). The father of the child whose custody was at stake wrote a book about the experience. H. Painter, Mark I Love You (1967). In August, 1968, a California court gave Mr. Painter custody of his son and the decision was not appealed by the grandparents. Civil Liberties, No. 258, October 1968, p. 12, col 3.

2. Is the reasoning of this case with respect to the different "lifestyles" of the parties inconsistent with the reasoning in the *Carle* case? If so, which case is correct?

3. Apparently psychiatric testimony played an important part in the court's decision. Of what value was the testimony of the psychiatrist who examined Mr. Painter? If you had represented either Mr. Painter or the Bannisters, could you have elicited testimony of any greater value? Of what value was the testimony of Dr. Glenn R. Hawks? The trial court seems to have given it little weight. Does the Iowa Supreme Court persuade you that the trial court was mistaken in this? So far as appears from the court's opinion had Dr. Hawks ever examined Mr. Painter?

4. Early in its opinion the court refers to a presumption of parental preference. The strength of this "presumption" varies greatly from court to court and even from case to case. At its strongest it is expressed by the "rule" that where the contest for custody of a child lies between a parent and a person who is not a parent, the parent should be given custody unless the evidence shows him to be "unfit". This is sometimes also called the "parental right doctrine". For cases announcing this rule see Turner v. Pannick, 540 P.2d 1051 (Alaska 1975); Heath v. Martin, 225 Ga. 181, 167 S.E.2d 153 (1969); In re Custody of Eden, 216 Kan. 784, 533 P.2d 1222 (1975); Ross v. Hoffman, 280 Md. 172, 372 A.2d 582 (1977) (presumption is overcome if the parent is unfit or "exceptional circumstances" make parental custody detrimental to the child); Matter of Guardianship of Doney, 174 Mont. 282, 570 P.2d 575 (1977) (natural parent may not be deprived of custody except on proof of dependency, abuse or neglect); Perales v. Nino, 52 Ohio St.2d 89, 369 N.E.2d 1047, 6 O.O.3d 293 (1977) (parent may be deprived of custody only where unsuitable).

Other courts have adopted weaker versions of the parental right theory, putting the issue in terms of a presumption, but weakening its force by saying merely that it is presumed that the child's welfare will be best served by placing him in the custody of a parent. E. g., Stevenson v. Stevenson, —— Ind.App. ——, 364 N.E.2d 161 (1977); Custody of a Minor, 5 Mass.App. 741, 370 N.E.2d 712 (1977); Eravi v. Bohnert, 201 Neb. 99, 266 N.W.2d 228 (1978); Hoy v. Willis, 165 N.J.Super. 265, 398 A.2d 109 (1978); Doe v. Doe, 92 Misc.2d 184, 399 N.Y.S.2d 977 (Sup.Ct.1977). A collection of cases and classification of jurisdictions is made in Note, Psychological Parents vs Biological Parents: The Courts' Response to New Directions in Child Custody Dispute Resolution, 17 J.Fam.L. 545 (1979). See also the *Scarpetta* case supra, page 496. A case which seems to decide the contest exclusively on the ground of the child's best interests is Root v. Allen, 151 Colo. 311, 377 P.2d 117 (1962), 73 Yale L.J. 151 (1963). Other cases are collected in Annots., 25 A.L.R.3d 7 (1969) and 31 A.L.R.3d 1187 (1970).

Some states may have statutes which affect this issue. For example, the Uniform Marriage and Divorce Act § 401(d)(2), 9A Unif.L.Ann. 194 (1979) provides that a person other than a parent may bring a custody proceeding only if the child is not in the physical custody of one of his parents. Riphenburg v. Henderson, 174 Mont. 1, 568 P.2d 177 (1977). And Cal. Civ.Code § 4600 (Supp.1979) provides that a parent may be deprived of custody only if his custody is found to be detrimental to the child and an award to the non-parent would be in the child's best interests. In re B.G., 11 Cal.3d 679, 114 Cal.Rptr. 444, 523 P.2d 244 (1974).

(a) What force does Painter v. Bannister give to this presumption? Does the court accept Dr. Hawks' view that the "father figure" is important, while the "biological father" is not?

(b) Does the United States Constitution, as interpreted by Stanley v. Illinois, supra, page 432, Quilloin v. Wallcott, supra, page 443, and Caban v. Mohammad, supra, page 451, require that the doctrine of parental right be adhered to in awarding custody of a child? Cf. Custody of a Minor, —— Mass. ——, 389 N.E.2d 68 (1979); Sorentino v. Family and Children's Society of Elizabeth, 74 N.J. 313, 378 A.2d 18 (1977).

5. If the thesis of the Goldstein, Freud, Solnit book, outlined supra, page 1071, paragraph 1, were applied in *Painter*, how would the case come out?

6. Is it a crucial factor in Painter v. Bannister that Mark had lived with his grandparents for about a year and four months at the time Mr. Painter asked to have him returned, and had lived with them about two and one-half years when the Iowa Supreme Court gave its opinion? Should the court's decision have been affected by the fact that the placement of Mark with his grandparents had clearly been temporary, and that in refusing to return him to his father the grandparents were apparently violating their understanding with Mr. Painter? What effect should the Bannisters' age have on the court's decision?

7. H and W–1 were married and had two children. They were divorced in Georgia, custody being awarded to H. H later married W–2 and lived with her and the children of the first marriage for three years in California. H's second marriage then broke up and in the ensuing divorce proceeding W–2 sought custody of the children. How should her claim be disposed of?

8. Jane Smith was divorced from her husband and given custody of their two sons, ages seven and eight. She was then thirty-two years old. She wanted to finish her education, so she left the children with her parents who were in their seventies and who lived on a farm in rural Pennsylvania, they agreeing to care for the boys until Jane should finish her education and be able to support them. Jane then enrolled in the University of Pennsylvania and in two years received the A.B. degree, supporting herself by working at night as a waitress. She was unable to furnish any support for the children and her former husband sent her no support. She visited the children occasionally on weekends. After graduating from Pennsylvania, Jane entered the Yale University School of Architecture, where she studied for three years. During this time she was able to visit the children only about once a month. At the end of this time, she received a graduate degree in architecture and obtained a good position with a firm of architects in New Haven. She then asked her parents to let her have the children, but they refused, and she filed a petition for habeas corpus. At the trial, in addition to the foregoing facts, it was proved that she had had various affairs with men while in college and in graduate school, and during her last year at Yale she shared an apartment with her "best friend", a male graduate student. At the time of the trial she was no longer living with him and had no intention of resuming living with him. At the request of the court a New Haven social agency investigated her and reported that she had smoked marijuana with her friend frequently just as others might enjoy a social cocktail, that she was a person of superior intelligence, that she was a stable and contented individual capable of managing her personal life to her own satisfaction, and that she had little or no regard for conventional moral or social standards. The grandparents were proved to be conventional, rather old-fashioned people living comfortably on their farm, who were extremely fond of the children. The boys were happy and well adjusted, attending a nearby private school and doing well in their school work. At the time of the trial they were eleven and twelve years old. Both boys expressed to the judge a strong desire to remain with their grandparents, say-

ing they liked their school and their mother had no free time to spend with them.

What should be the result of this custody litigation? Cf. Commonwealth ex rel. Holschuh v. Holland-Moritz, 448 Pa. 437, 292 A.2d 380 (1972).

9. As has been indicated in the cases dealing with interstate custody conflicts, custody decrees are modifiable, either by the court which entered the decree or by other courts. Of course the courts of one state are not able directly to modify the decrees of courts in other states, but they may and do enter orders making different provisions for the child, as the interstate cases demonstrate. The power to modify is not diminished by the fact that the original decree was based upon an agreement of the parties. Annot., 73 A.L.R.2d 1444 (1960).

The death of a party to the divorce action may, according to the law of some states, deprive the court of jurisdiction to modify its custody order, the rationale being that this abates the divorce action for lack of parties. Woodford v. Superior Court, 82 Ariz. 181, 309 P.2d 973 (1957). This merely means that a new suit must be started in order to obtain a new disposition of custody, however. The writ of habeas corpus is generally held to be appropriate as a device for obtaining the modification of custody decrees. Annot., 4 A.L.R.3d 1277 (1965).

The usual basis for modification of custody decrees is that the circumstances have changed since the original decision. In re Marriage of Carney, 24 Cal.3d 725, 157 Cal.Rptr. 383, 598 P.2d 36 (1979) puts the rule this way: "It is settled that to justify ordering a change in custody there must generally be a persuasive showing of changed circumstances affecting the child. * * * And that change must be substantial: a child will not be removed from the prior custody of one parent and given to the other 'unless the material facts and circumstances occurring subsequently are of a kind to render it essential or expedient for the welfare of the child that there be a change.' "

The Uniform Marriage and Divorce Act § 409, 9A Unif.L.Ann. 211 (1979), was drafted with the purpose of limiting the courts' power to modify custody decrees, or, as the comments to the section state, to "maximize finality * * * without jeopardizing the child's interest." It provides as follows:

"Section 409. [*Modification.*]

"(a) No motion to modify a custody decree may be made earlier than one year after the date of the initial decree. If a motion for modification has been filed, whether or not it was granted, no subsequent motion may be filed within 2 years after disposition of the prior motion, unless the court decides on the basis of affidavits (Section 410), that there is reason to believe that the child's present environment may endanger his physical health or significantly impair his emotional development.

"(b) [If a court of this state has jurisdiction pursuant to the Uniform Child Custody Jurisdiction Act,] the court shall not modify a prior custody decree unless it finds, upon the basis of facts that have arisen since the prior decree or that were unknown to the court at the time of the prior decree, that a change has occurred in the circumstances of the child or his custodian and that the modification is necessary to serve the best interests of the child. In applying these standards the court shall retain the custodian established by the prior decree unless:

    "(1) the custodian agrees to the modification;

    "(2) the child has been integrated into the family of the petitioner with the consent of the custodian; or

    "(3) the child's present environment endangers his physical health or significantly impairs his emotional development and the harm likely to be caused by a change of environment is outweighed by the advantage of a change to the child."

    10. H and W were divorced, with an award of custody of their two children to W. Three years later W, having remarried and had a small child by her second husband, found it difficult to care for the two children. W therefore placed them in the care of her parents, age 70 and 68, who were living in a three-bedroom home having retired on social security and a monthly pension. W was working as part of the daytime cleanup crew at the Poison Apple Disco. H had also remarried and had two more children by his second wife. He was an assembly line worker in an auto plant and lived in a three-bedroom home with his second wife who did not work and was willing to care for the children. H moved for a modification of the decree which would give custody to him. What should be the result if the evidence was as indicated above, either under the usual rule, or under the Uniform Act? See In re Custody of Harne, 77 Ill.2d 414, 33 Ill.Dec. 110, 396 N.E.2d 499 (1979).

    11. Herbert and Wilma Campbell were divorced after ten years of marriage, custody of their two children Robert, aged seven and Jane, aged nine, going to Wilma, with Herbert to pay child support. The decree provided that Herbert should have the right to have the children every week from noon on Saturday until 5:00 p.m. on Sunday, and for a month in the summer. For two and one-half years Wilma kept custody, and Herbert regularly exercised his visitation rights. Herbert also paid the required child support and gave the children presents at Christmas and on their birthdays. During that period, however, Wilma often criticized Herbert to the children, told them he was a weakling, not a real man, etc. During this time Wilma also was uncooperative many times when Herbert came to get the children, not having them ready, or making excuses for not letting him see them. A year after the divorce Herbert married again, and a year later his second wife had a baby. At the end of the two and a half years Wilma married again, her second husband being an engineer employed by a firm with many foreign contracts. Herbert heard about this and also heard that Wilma and her new husband would be leaving for Saudi Arabia where her husband was assigned to a large construction job. When he next had the children with him, which was during the summer months, Herbert refused to return them to Wilma, and she and her new husband had to leave the country without them. At the first opportunity, which was a year later when her husband had his first leave, Wilma filed a petition for habeas corpus asking for the return of the children and the enforcement of the original custody decree. The evidence established the foregoing facts, and in addition that the children now preferred to remain with Herbert, and that Wilma had, before the

original divorce action, been guilty of adultery on at least three occasions, a fact not known to Herbert at that earlier time. What arguments would you make for Herbert and Wilma, and how should the case be decided?

(a) Under the language quoted from the *Carney* case, supra, paragraph 9?

(b) Under the philosophy of the Goldstein, Freud, Solnit book, as indicated supra, page 1071, paragraph 1?

(c) Under the Uniform Marriage and Divorce Act?

For a discussion of similar problems, see King v. King, 477 P.2d 356 (Alaska 1970); Stickler v. Stickler, 57 Ill.App.2d 286, 206 N.E.2d 720 (1965); Warren v. Warren, 191 N.W.2d 659 (Iowa 1971); Smith v. Smith, 282 Minn. 190, 163 N.W.2d 852 (1968); Garrett v. Garrett, 464 S.W.2d 740 (Mo.App. 1971).

12. Custody orders, like child support orders, are enforceable by contempt. One useful method for ensuring the performance of custody decrees where there is a likelihood that the child will be removed from the state is to require the custodian to post security against any violation of the decree. This is authorized by the statutes of some states, as in Mass.Gen.L.Ann. c. 208, § 30 (1969), but presumably it is within the courts' inherent equity power in any proper case. For a case in which security was required, see Brooks v. Brooks, 300 A.2d 531 (Vt.1973).

SECTION 9.   SOME ASPECTS OF DIVORCE PROCEDURE

INTRODUCTION

Due to the way in which divorce developed in this country, its procedure today is a mixture of equity, statutory law and some remnants of ecclesiastical law. Since the distinction between law and equity has been abolished in most states, divorce is generally governed by the same procedural rules as other civil actions except where statute or rule of court dictate otherwise. These rules vary from state to state and an extensive selection of them cannot be provided here. This section focuses on a few procedural problems peculiar to divorce and of interest for what they reveal about divorce policy.

Parties

Normally only the spouses are proper parties to the divorce action. Very rarely there may be a statute allowing the corespondent in an adultery divorce to be made a party but this is seldom done.

The children of the marriage are generally not made parties to the divorce action even though the outcome will affect their interests. But some states are now beginning to authorize the appointment of an attorney for the child, to protect his interests to the extent that they may be affected by the divorce proceeding, even though the child is not a party to the action. See, e. g., Uniform Marriage and Divorce Act § 310, authorizing the court to appoint an attorney to represent the child's interests with respect to custody, support and visitation; Wis.Stat.Ann. § 247.045 (Supp.1972–1973); Note, A Case for Independent Counsel to Represent Children in Custody Proceedings, 7 N.Eng.L.Rev. 351 (1972); and Note, Guardianship Ad Litem in Texas Divorce and Custody Cases, 20 Bay.L.Rev. 433 (1968). In some states the guardian ad litem may be an investigator rather than a representative. Eaton v. Karr, 251 A.2d 640 (App.D.C.1969).

In fact one case has held that if the child's status is involved, presumably as distinguished from mere custody, due process requires that he made a party to the suit. Roe v. Roe, 49 Misc.2d 1070, 269 N.Y.S.2d 40 (Sup.Ct.1966). If this case is correct, why should it not also apply to cases where the child's custody is at stake? Cf. problem 5, page 508, supra.

In some jurisdictions the state's interest in the divorce suit is represented by an attorney who appears in the action under prescribed circumstances, as when the case is undefended or children are involved. His function is to prevent collusion and make sure that the children's interests receive due consideration. See Connolly, Divorce Proctors, 34 B.U.L.Rev. 1 (1954); Cox, The Divorce Proctor, 33 Tenn.L.Rev. 439 (1966). With the abolition of the defense of collusion and the adoption of non-fault grounds for divorce, the divorce proctor becomes superfluous.

On rare occasions other persons may be made parties to divorce actions, where this is necessary to provide complete relief in the case, as where one of the spouses has allegedly made a fraudulent conveyance. But usually such third parties are not permitted to intervene. Dick v. Dick, 238 So.2d 469 (Fla.App.1970); Yedinak v. Yedinak, 383 Mich. 409, 175 N.W.2d 706 (1970).

The death of a party pending the divorce action generally abates the action. H. Clark, Law of Domestic Relations 384 (1968). But there may be situations where property rights of the parties are left in doubt even after the death of one of them. If so, the action may be held not to abate, but be continued against the deceased's personal representative. Taylor v. Wells, 265 So.2d 402 (Fla.App.1972); Goldman v. Walker, 260 Md. 222, 271 A.2d 639 (1970). Drafting and counseling steps which may avert hardship caused by the death of a party are outlined in Bonanno, Death Before Entry of a Final Divorce Decree in California: Some Preventive Law Considerations, 3 U.S.F.L.Rev. 261 (1969).

It is generally held that a conservator may not bring a divorce action on behalf of an incompetent person, the reason being that the relationship of marriage is so personal in nature that it may not be terminated without the consent of the spouse himself. See cases cited in Annot., 6 A.L.R.3d 681 (1966). But see Newman v. Newman, 42 Ill.App.2d 203, 191 N.E.2d 614 (1963), 25 Ohio St.L.J. 412 (1964).

Arbitration

Agreements between the spouses for the arbitration of matrimonial disputes are becoming more common in some states, especially New York. For a discussion of this question, see Fencc v. Fence, supra page 1002 and appended notes.

Discovery

It is generally true that divorces may not be granted on depositions alone, due to the state's interest in making sure that there is adequate proof of grounds. Even under the new statutes on marriage breakdown, such as the Uniform Marriage and Divorce Act § 305(a) a hearing is contemplated, which presumably implies that the divorce could not be granted solely on the basis of depositions. See also McKim v. McKim, 6 Cal.3d 673, 493 P.2d 868, 100 Cal.Rptr. 140 (1972), requiring the appearance and personal testimony of the petitioner in all but exceptional cases.

Although this *use* of depositions may understandably be forbidden, there is no apparent reason why the *taking* of depositions in divorce cases for a variety of purposes other than the proof of grounds should not be permitted. Of course the language of the particular state's statute or rule of procedure determines this in the first instance, and some do limit the taking of depositions. Rheaume v. Rheaume, 107 R.I. 500, 268 A.2d 437 (1970). For cases permitting the taking of depositions in divorce see H. Clark, Law of Domestic Relations § 13.5 (1968), and Note, 22 U.Miami L.Rev. 195 (1968).

Where the plaintiff in the divorce suit refuses to respond to a question in a deposition on the ground that it may tend to incriminate him, recent cases have held that the court may then dismiss his suit. Minor v. Minor, 240 So.2d 301 (Fla.1970); Christenson v. Christenson, 281 Minn. 507, 162 N.W.2d 194 (1968), 55 Minn.L.Rev. 348 (1970); Molloy v. Molloy, 46 Wis.2d 682, 176 N.W.2d 292 (1970). This result may be correct for civil cases generally, but it seems at last doubtful for divorce cases, if the right to hearing in such cases is given the preferred status described in Boddie v. Connecticut, supra, page 779.

Preliminary Orders

Where necessary to preserve the status quo during divorce litigation, the courts will enter preliminary injunctions forbidding transfers of property in fraud of the spouse, preventing harm or interference with the person of a spouse or children of the marriage, excluding a party from the family home and in extreme cases forbidding departure from the jurisdiction where that is necessary to ensure effective relief. Such orders are only granted upon verified pleadings and evidence showing that the injunction is needed to protect the applicant from immediate threat of injury. See, e. g., Uniform Marriage and Divorce Act § 304(b). The grant or denial of such orders lies in the sound discretion of the trial court. The orders terminate automatically upon the conclusion of the main suit.

"Cooling-Off" Statutes

Statutes have been passed in some states imposing a mandatory delay between the commencement of the divorce suit and the trial, in the hope of giving the parties one last opportunity to become reconciled and preserve their marriage. Where adopted, they replace the older devices of the interlocutory decree or the prohibition on remarriage, which had as part of their purposes the encouragement of reconciliation. The idea is that providing the time for reconciliation before the bitterness aroused by the divorce trial rather than after it might offer greater chances for success. How well the cooling off period succeeds is impossible to measure. To the extent that it is based upon an assumption that people sue for divorce hastily and without serious reflection, what studies there are indicate that it is mistaken. See, e. g., W. Goode, After Divorce 138 ff (1956), finding that the decision to seek divorce normally follows a long period of deliberation by both parties and very often a period of separation.

The length of the cooling-off period varies from twenty days to six months, with thirty or sixty days being most common. The Uniform Marriage and Divorce Act § 305 authorizes but does not require the court to continue the case for not less than thirty nor more than sixty days where the parties disagree as to whether the marriage has broken down, and may suggest that the parties seek counseling during this period.

Trial and Evidence

1. Since it is well settled that divorce decrees may not be granted by default, some sort of hearing must be held in all cases. It has been indicated in the discussion of grounds for divorce that the hearing may be perfunctory when the suit is uncontested. Statutes or judicial decisions in some states attempt to prevent divorce hearings from being perfunctory by requiring that the testimony of one or both spouses be corroborated. The general principle of corroboration in divorce was borrowed from the English ecclesiastical practice, but in this country it has assumed many forms. In some states the rule is that any confession of wrongdoing by the divorce defendant must be corroborated. In others corroboration of the testimony of either spouse must be offered, the purpose being to prevent collusion. Relatively slight corroboration may be held sufficient therefore if the case is strongly contested or if there is plainly no collusion. The amount of corroborative evidence to be required in a particular case varies from state to state and seemingly from court to court. See, e. g.,

Eyer v. Eyer, 17 Ariz.App. 31, 495 F.2d 156 (1972); Fortman v. Fortman, 250 Md. 355, 243 A.2d 517 (1968); Wanser v. Wanser, 119 N.J.Super. 190, 290 A.2d 741 (1972). In general corroboration means that the testimony of the plaintiff has been made more credible or more probable by other evidence, either direct or circumstantial. Of course to the extent that the ground of marriage breakdown is adopted and the divorce defenses are abolished, the whole notion of corroboration loses significance. For a more complete discussion of the requirement, see H. Clark, Law of Domestic Relations 399–402 (1968).

Two different principles of evidence may apply to disqualify the spouses as witnesses. The first, now largely but not entirely abolished by statute, has it that each spouse has a privilege not to have the other testify against him. VIII Wigmore, Evidence 250 (McNaughton rev. 1961); C. McCormick, Evidence 144–145 (1954). The second privilege is that relating to confidential communications between spouses. These are privileged against disclosure as a way of preserving marital confidence. The privilege is usually held to belong to the spouse by whom the communication was made. This privilege has also been so limited by statute that it often does not apply in divorce actions. II Wigmore, Evidence 488 (3d ed. 1940); C. McCormick, Evidence 177 (1954); Poppe v. Poppe, 3 N.Y.2d 312, 165 N.Y.S.2d 99, 144 N.E.2d 72 (1957). But see Ellis v. Ellis, 472 S.W.2d 741 (Tenn.App.1971). There is a third principle which may prevent spouses from testifying in divorce actions, but it is a rule of competence rather than a privilege. It is known as Lord Mansfield's Rule, and states that neither spouse may testify in such a manner as to bastardize a child born after the marriage occurred. It may also be defined as a rule that neither party may testify to non-access where such testimony would make the child illegitimate. For criticism and case law see VII Wigmore, Evidence §§ 2063, 2064 (3d ed. 1940); C. McCormick, Evidence 146 (1954); Vasquez v. Esquibel, 141 Colo. 5, 346 P.2d 293 (1959), citing other cases.

The physician-patient privilege may also be invoked in divorce actions, particularly where child custody is in issue and psychiatric tests have been made. See Annot., 44 A.L.R.3d 24 (1972) for a collection of cases.

The problems of court congestion and delay in the hearing of divorce cases are serious in many states and are obviously affected by the method of trial. Usually trial is to the court, but in some states the parties may demand a jury, thereby increasing the congestion and delay. In order to increase efficiency other states have authorized divorces to be referred to referees or masters for trial, sometimes the entire case, sometimes only particular aspects of the case. The Pennsylvania system, perhaps the best known, by which divorce suits are heard by masters appointed by the court, is described in Note, The Administration of Divorce: A Philadelphia Study, 101 U. Pa.L.Rev. 1204 (1953). See also Annot., Propriety of Reference in

Connection With Fixing Amount of Alimony, 85 A.L.R.2d 801 (1962); Pokorney v. Pokorney, 348 Ill.App. 364, 109 N.E.2d 254 (1952); Strandberg v. Strandberg, 27 Wis.2d 559, 135 N.W.2d 241 (1965).

2. The Uniform Marriage Divorce Act § 404, 9A Unif.L.Ann. 203 (1979) provides as follows:

> **"§ 404.   [Interviews]**
>
> "(a) The court may interview the child in chambers to ascertain the child's wishes as to his custodian and as to visitation. The court may permit counsel to be present at the interview. The court shall cause a record of the interview to be made and to be part of the record in the case.
>
> "(b) The court may seek the advice of professional personnel, whether or not employed by the court on a regular basis. The advice given shall be in writing and made available by the court to counsel upon request. Counsel may examine as a witness any professional personnel consulted by the court."

Susan Knox sued Bruce Knox for divorce on the ground of irretrievable breakdown of the marriage. The court, pursuant to § 404(b) of the Uniform Act, directed its staff marriage counselor to conduct a custody investigation. There was one child of the marriage, Sally, who was four years old. Pending the suit Sally was living with Susan. The divorce was not contested but both parents sought custody of Sally.

The marriage counselor visited both Susan and Bruce and talked with them both at some length. She also visited the day care center which cared for Sally (since Susan was working) and interviewed the woman who ran it. Interviews were also had with the parents of both Susan and Bruce, a woman neighbor of Susan's, and two men who worked in the same office with Bruce and who said they knew him well. The marriage counselor's report to the court gave detailed accounts of all these interviews. It turned up information that Bruce had a woman living with him, and when he was asked about that, he said that he did not necessarily intend to marry her but that he believed everyone should have healthy heterosexual relationships. Bruce's mother informed the marriage counselor that she thought that Susan was a lesbian and that that was the real reason for the breakup of the marriage and the sexual difficulties which Susan and Bruce had had while married. Susan denied this. The marriage counselor then interviewed a psychiatrist whom Susan and Bruce had consulted before they decided on divorce and he indicated he did not think Susan was a lesbian, but that the parties' sexual difficulties had arisen from Susan's anger at Bruce because Bruce was more controlling, more passive-aggressive and played at being superior in order to cover up his own inner inadequacies.

The marriage counselor filed a report with the court which recounted the foregoing facts and views and contained the following concluding paragraph:

"Although I believe that either Susan or Bruce would function effectively as a single parent, I recommend that Susan be given custody of Sally. Susan is a more loving, caring, giving kind of person who is more together. She knows where she is going in life. Bruce, on the other hand is a controlling, rigid person, who does, however, have a warm, caring relationship with Sally. He said that he wanted to help Sally learn things and be a success in life. I think it more important that a parent love a child for what the child is rather than for what the child can become. This recommendation is shared by the psychiatrists who saw Bruce and Susan before the divorce who also expressed the hope that Susan could get some therapy for her anger and Bruce for his inner insecurity. Since Bruce has had a close relationship with Sally and has cared for her as much as Susan before the breakup, I also recommend that he be given generous visitation rights."

(a) If you represented Bruce in this case, and this report was delivered to you in advance of the hearing, what would you do? Would you plan on a vigorous cross-examination of the counselor who made the report? Would you call the various people who were interviewed and put them on the stand? Or would you leave the report to speak for itself and merely present other evidence on Bruce's behalf?

(b) If you were the judge in this case, how would you view this report? To what extent, if any, would it influence your decision? Would you prefer your staff to file reports which merely gave the facts and did not contain a recommendation concerning custody? Or would you want to have their views on the ultimate question of who should get custody?

Interlocutory and Final Decrees

A few states still preserve the device of the interlocutory divorce decree which does not become a final divorce until the expiration of the statutory period. See Cal.Civ.Code §§ 4512, 4513, 4514 (1970 and Supp.1979); Mass.Ann.L. ch. 208, § 21 (Supp.1979), providing for a six-month interlocutory period. The purpose is apparently to provide one last opportunity for reconciliation, although the efficacy of the device for this purpose seems very doubtful. During the interlocutory period the parties are considered still to be married to each other although authorized to live apart. In some states, like Massachusetts, the interlocutory decree automatically becomes a final decree upon expiration of the statutory time, while in others a final decree must be entered. In the latter states a final decree nunc pro tunc may be entered where the court finds that necessary to avoid hardship. See Kern v. Kern, 261 Cal.App.2d 325, 67 Cal.Rptr. 802 (1968); Annot., 19 A.L.R.3d 648 (1968).

The logical implications of the interlocutory decree are that (a) the parties may properly and legally resume cohabitation and if they do, the decree may be set aside; and (b) if one of the parties attempts to marry someone else, either within or without the state, that marriage is bigamous and invalid, as in the *Spellens* case, supra, page 805.

In a very few states, rather than an interlocutory decree, the statutes authorize a final decree of divorce which contains a prohibition upon the remarriage of one or both of the parties for a prescribed time. The purpose of these statutes seems partly to encourage reconciliation and partly to punish divorce or marital misconduct. See, e. g., Tex.Fam.Code § 3.66 (1975) forbidding remarriage for thirty days after divorce. The Pennsylvania statute seems to be unique in forbidding the defendant in a divorce granted for adultery to marry the corespondent during the lifetime of the plaintiff. Pa. Stat.Ann. tit. 48, § 169 (Supp.1979–1980). If a marriage is contracted within the state in violation of the prohibition, it is generally held invalid. But at least some cases hold such a marriage to be valid when contracted in a state other than the one in which the divorce was granted.

The final decree of divorce is of course a civil judgment and should dispose of the issues raised by the case, including the dissolution of the marriage, the award of alimony or property where appropriate and the disposition of child custody and support questions. In addition the divorce court may be asked to include in the decree a provision changing the wife's name and the names of the children. See, e. g. Cal.Civ.Code § 4362 (Supp.1979); Uniform Marriage and Divorce Act § 314(d), 9A Unif.L.Ann. 180 (1979). Where the wife desires to resume her maiden name, some courts seem oddly reluctant to approve, giving as a reason that the children in her custody will have a different name. See, e. g., W v. H, 103 N.J.Super. 24, 246 A. 2d 501 (1968). It would seem that this is a gratuitous frustration of the wife's desires, and clearly improper under the Equal Rights Amendment, quoted supra at page 21. The courts are even more reluctant to permit the wife to change the names of the children, either to her maiden name, or to the name of their stepfather where the wife remarries and has custody of the children. The courts generally say that such a change in the children's names will only be permitted where it is in the affirmative best interests of the children, and they generally find that it is not, on the ground that the change would be likely to weaken the bond between the child and his natural father. E. g., Application of Trower, 260 Cal.App.2d 75, 66 Cal.Rptr. 873 (1968); Worms v. Worms, 252 Cal.App.2d 130, 60 Cal.Rptr. 88 (1967); Lazow v. Lazow, 147 So.2d 12 (Fla.App.1962); Application of Baldini, 17 Misc.2d 195, 183 N.Y.S.2d 416 (City Ct.1959); Dolgin v. Dolgin, 1 Ohio App.2d 430, 205 N.E.2d 106 (1965); Annot., 53 A. L.R.2d 914 (1957). The wife's attempt to change the child's name de facto was enjoined in Degerberg v. McCormick, 41 Del.Ch. 46, 187 A. 2d 436 (1963). A Texas case has held that such a change of name is permissible, and that a guardian ad litem for the child need not be appointed in such a case. Newman v. King, 433 S.W.2d 420 (Tex. 1968), 22 S.W.L.J. 649 (1968). Here, too, it would seem that the Equal Rights Amendment should give the child's mother as much right to control the child's name as the father, but it provides no guidance for resolving the conflicts between them.

SECTION 10. THE LAWYER'S FUNCTION IN DIVORCE PROCEEDINGS

INTRODUCTORY NOTE

In earlier sections of this book there have been problems, questions and some discussion of the lawyer's duties in specific domestic relations contexts. At this point we raise some questions concerning the lawyer's functions in representing divorce clients.

One fact has to be recognized at the outset, a fact with which some laymen are not familiar. This is that a great many lawyers refuse to take divorce cases. In the large cities few or none of the largest law offices would accept such cases, in many instances not even for regular clients. Even in smaller cities it is common for a large segment of the Bar to avoid divorce work. This may be regrettable, since it narrows the client's choice of representative by eliminating many competent lawyers, but it is nonetheless a fact. The reasons are both plain and understandable. The divorce lawyer's work imposes far heavier burdens upon him and produces substantially less rewards, both financial and psychological, than other legal work. More precisely divorce litigation makes severe emotional demands on the lawyer who undertakes it, it is conducted in a highly charged atmosphere, it may take a great deal of time both in and out of office hours, time which really cannot be billed to the client, and at best the chances of producing a happy result for the client are not great. An experienced English solicitor, quoting from another solicitor with approval, says, "In no other branch of civil litigation is the emotional strain on the client and the solicitor greater than in matrimonial disputes. One is dealing with the most important things in life—children, home, the whole financial future.", B. Mortlock, The Inside of Divorce 94 (1972).

One of the factors which contributes no little to the difficulties faced by the divorce lawyer is that his client very often tries to place the lawyer in a role which the lawyer cannot fill, one which no mere mortal could fill adequately. The client wants not just legal advice and representation but a perceptive psychiatrist, a wise and understanding friend, a repository for his fears and frustrations, sometimes a parent, and a powerful and tireless champion. It is not surprising that the lawyer facing such demands longs for the relative calm and security of a tax or corporate practice, or that the client is distressed when he finds that his lawyer is just a lawyer and not all the other persons the client would have him be. In short a major shortcoming of our present system for handling divorces is that it demands many and great skills, both legal and non-legal, of the general practitioner while it provides him with few incentives, either monetary or psychological, for acquiring and using those skills.

From the client's point of view the emotional strain is compounded by the difficulties of choosing a lawyer and worries about the expense involved. Many divorce clients have their first contact with the law and lawyers when they decide they want a divorce. Choosing a lawyer for this purpose is particularly difficult because of the importance of the case to the client, the intimate nature of the matters which have to be discussed, and the client's total lack of criteria for judging lawyers' activities. Some divorce clients have not sufficient financial resources to pay for any legal services, while others can only pay relatively modest amounts. Even the simplest, most routine divorce may cost upwards of five hundred dollars in some cities, too much for many pocketbooks. On the other hand, the work involved, if valued at a reasonable rate, will very often produce a fee larger than the lawyer can realistically charge. In some places legal aid or other publicly supported offices may provide representation for the poor in divorce actions. And local bar associations sometimes set up programs offering legal services, including divorce representation, for people not able to pay the full cost of such representation, but not qualified for legal aid. Helpful as these agencies may be, they face an additional obstacle in that their clients are often suspicious and fearful, and identify lawyers with authority to such an extent that the lawyer may have great difficulty in establishing the relationship of trust which must exist if the client is to have effective representation.

With full recognition of the difficulties, what functions should the lawyer in a divorce action expect to perform? In the first place there is the obvious requirement that he have and exercise professional competence. In the extensive discussion which sometimes occurs around the issues of whether the lawyer should attempt reconciliation and whether he should be trained in the skills of psychology and social work we sometimes lose sight of the fact that after all he is consulted for his legal training, experience and judgment. The least that the client has the right to expect is that he will provide that training, experience and judgment. This involves a thorough knowledge of the divorce and related law of the jurisdiction as well as knowledge of the detailed aspects of divorce practice in the particular locality. It also implies an interest in the client's problems, care in collecting the information necessary for thorough consideration of all legal issues involved and the expenditure of enough time and effort to provide that consideration and to achieve solutions.

One gets the impression that some lawyers accept divorce cases only unwillingly or reluctantly, perhaps out of feelings of social obligation or from economic necessity. The consequence is that they may relegate their divorce clients to second class status which is reflected in a reduced time and effort expended on their cases. Many divorce clients seem to be dissatisfied with the quality of representation they have received, more dissatisfied than clients whose legal work has been of other types. The reason for this may be in part at least that their lawyers did dislike divorce work and did not undertake it with the same energy as other kinds of law practice. It would be preferable for the lawyer who feels this way about divorce litigation to reject it entirely.

Any consideration of the lawyer's function in divorce must confront the issue of reconciliation, which takes the form of a deceptively simple question, should the lawyer attempt to reconcile the parties? The issue is rarely dealt with sensibly. The most common approach is to propose it as a choice between becoming a marriage counselor on the one hand, or, on the other, filling out the blanks in a divorce complaint form as soon as the client in the first interview supplies the vital facts. This is a pernicious over-simplification of a complex issue. A moment's thought about the matter should make a few things obvious. The first is that the amount of counseling which a divorce lawyer does depends above all upon the extent to which he feels comfortable in such work and competent to do it. Not all divorce lawyers feel equally at home in discussing the personal and psychological problems of their divorce clients. Each lawyer should, however, be aware of his own inclinations on the subject, and should make those inclinations his standard rather than be guided by what some external "authority" tells him he ought to do. This of course also implies that he let his clients know what he expects to do in the case. There would seem to be no objection if the lawyer tells his client he does not engage in counseling of a non-legal kind. If the client finds that an obstacle to effective representation, he is free to go to some other lawyer, or to consult a psychiatrist or marriage counselor.

The second point which ought to be clear but often is not is that the lawyer who does attempt to explore the events and feelings which underlie the client's thoughts about divorce must be keenly aware of both the emotions which the client is expressing and the emotions which he, the lawyer, is feeling as he hears the client's story. This is more easily said than done of course but it is nonetheless essential.

Unless it is done any advice, whether legal or non-legal, offered to the client may be mistaken or actively harmful because inconsistent with the client's needs.

A corollary of this is the fundamental point well known to most experienced divorce lawyers that what the client says she or he wants is very often not what will best serve the client's interests. Perhaps the most familiar example is the wife who consults a lawyer with a request for a divorce merely as a way of opening up communications with her husband, in the hope that by enlisting a lawyer's help she can persuade her husband to listen to what she has to say. There are many similar but more obscure situations, in which the client's needs are not known even to himself and may not be discernible, if at all, without extensive conversations between lawyer and client. At all times in such circumstances the lawyer must keep in mind his own aims and his own limits. Interviews with divorce clients can very easily get beyond the competence of the most experienced lawyer. He must be ready to recognize this and to refer the case to someone better able to deal with the problems as he perceives them, a psychologist, a psychiatrist, a mental health clinic, a marriage counselor, a physician, a welfare worker, a priest, minister or rabbi. For this purpose every divorce lawyer should have at hand a directory of such persons and of other community resources which might be consulted by his clients. Referrals of course must be made with tact and care, whatever the purpose, but it is most important that they not be evaded when their necessity appears.

Implicit in the foregoing discussion is the view that if the lawyer wishes to explore the possibilities of reconciliation with his client, if he feels competent to do so and if he thinks there are reasonable prospects of success, then of course he should make the attempt. If he does not feel competent or wish to do so, a referral for this purpose also can be made. In some localities the courts themselves provide marriage counseling and conciliation services to which clients may be referred. Whether the lawyer does or does not decide to attempt reconciliation interviews and conferences, it is generally if not always useful for him to describe to the client in the most precise terms the difficulties and disadvantages to be encountered after divorce, including the consequences for the children of the marriage, the added expense of maintaining two households and the social and emotional consequences of living alone, the latter often greater for the woman than the man.

Whatever the lawyer's attitude toward non-legal types of counseling, he does have an obligation in all divorce cases to do what he can to minimize the hostility of the parties, not only for the benefit of his client, but also in order to keep control of the case in his own hands. In most instances hostility and anger toward the other spouse will have developed to a substantial degree before the lawyer is consulted. Too many lawyers take overly aggressive adversary positions which only increase these emotions, precisely contrary to the real interests of both clients and of the children if there are any. Instead the lawyer should try to reduce hostility, should insist upon settling all issues by negotiation and agreement if at all possible, and should do his best to convince his client that in the last analysis a one-sided result will only breed further conflict and litigation in the future. Of course where litigation is necessary he has an obligation to give his divorce client the same vigorous representation he would give to any other client. Some clients may be so bent on self-destruction that no amicable or reasonable settlement of their dispute is possible and the lawyer must then decide whether he wishes to continue with the case. In making that decision he may have to consider whether his client is willing to meet the expenses which intransigence generally entails. Even if he decides to withdraw, he must consider the rules of ethics regulating withdrawal, which, among other things, require him to avoid prejudice to the client and to give the client due notice. In some cases withdrawal may not ethically be open to him. American Bar Association Code of Professional Responsibility DR2–110 (1969).

One failing of many lawyers in divorce cases is a direct cause of legitimate client dissatisfaction and can easily be remedied. To a surprising extent these lawyers fail to keep their clients informed. When one remembers that the divorce client is emotional to begin with because of his marital conflicts, and is very often entirely unused to and ignorant of the operations of the law, it is understandable that he becomes fearful and suspicious when his lawyer fails to keep him informed about the case. At the initial interview the client should be told what the probable course of the litigation will be. Certainly fees should be fully discussed and agreed upon either in terms of a stated amount or by reference to some standard, such as an hourly charge. A written agreement or a letter containing the fee arrangements should be given the client. As the case progresses the client should be told what has gone on and what is coming. This might be done by submitting periodic itemized bills showing what has been done in the case. Finally when the divorce is granted, the client should be given a copy of the decree and should be written a letter describing in detail the rights and obligations which the decree imposes. In a shocking number of cases the failure to do this has led clients to violate decrees or act in ignorance of them with disastrous consequences to themselves, for example by marrying in violation of a prohibition in the decree, or by making informal agreements about alimony or child support inconsistent with the decree.

Legal malpractice

SMITH v. LEWIS

Supreme Court of California, 1975.
13 Cal.3d 349, 118 Cal.Rptr. 621, 530 P.2d 589.

MOSK, Justice.   Defendant Jerome R. Lewis, an attorney, appeals from a judgment entered upon a jury verdict for plaintiff Rosemary E. Smith in an action for legal malpractice.   The action arises as a result of legal services rendered by defendant to plaintiff in a prior divorce proceeding.   The gist of plaintiff's complaint is that defendant negligently failed in the divorce action to assert her community interest in the retirement benefits of her husband.

Defendant principally contends, inter alia, that the law with regard to the characterization of retirement benefits was so unclear at the time he represented plaintiff as to insulate him from liability for failing to assert a claim therefor on behalf of his client.[1]   We conclude defendant's appeal is without merit, and therefore affirm the judgment.

In 1943 plaintiff married General Clarence D. Smith.   Between 1945 and his retirement in 1966 General Smith was employed by the California National Guard.   As plaintiff testified, she informed defendant her husband "was paid by the state * * * it was a job just like anyone else goes to."   For the first 16 years of that period the husband belonged to the State Employees' Retirement System, a contributory plan.[2]   Between 1961 and the date of his retirement he belonged to the California National Guard retirement program, a noncontributory plan.   In addition, by attending National Guard reserve drills he qualified for separate retirement benefits from the federal government, also through a noncontributory plan.   The state and federal retirement programs each provide lifetime monthly benefits which terminate upon the death of the retiree.   The programs make no allowance for the retiree's widow.

On January 1, 1967, the State of California began to pay General Smith gross retirement benefits of $796.26 per month.   Payments under the federal program, however, will not begin until 1983, i. e., 17 years after his actual retirement, when General Smith reaches the

---

1. Defendant alternatively contends the state and federal military retirement benefits in question cannot properly be characterized as community property, and hence his advice to plaintiff was correct.   As will appear, the contention is manifestly untenable in light of recent decisions by this court.   (In re Marriage of Fithian (1974) 10 Cal.3d 592, 111 Cal.Rptr. 369, 517 P.2d 449; Waite v. Waite (1972) 6 Cal.3d 461, 99 Cal.Rptr. 325, 492 P.2d 13; Phillipson v. Board of

Administration (1970) 3 Cal.3d 32, 89 Cal.Rptr. 61, 473 P.2d 765.)

2. A contributory plan is one in which the member contributes to his retirement fund, normally through payroll deductions.   A noncontributory plan is one in which no such contributions are made.

The State Employees' Retirement System is now referred to as the Public Employees' Retirement System (Gov. Code, § 20000 et seq.).

age of 60. All benefits which General Smith is entitled to receive were earned during the time he was married to plaintiff.

On February 17, 1967, plaintiff retained defendant to represent her in a divorce action against General Smith. According to plaintiff's testimony, defendant advised her that her husband's retirement benefits were not community property. Three days later defendant filed plaintiff's complaint for divorce. General Smith's retirement benefits were not pleaded as items of community property, and therefore were not considered in the litigation or apportioned by the trial court. The divorce was uncontested and the interlocutory decree divided the minimal described community property and awarded Mrs. Smith $400 per month in alimony and child support. The final decree was entered on February 27, 1968.

On July 17, 1968, pursuant to a request by plaintiff, defendant filed on her behalf a motion to amend the decree, alleging under oath that because of his mistake, inadvertence, and excusable neglect (Code Civ.Proc., § 473) the retirement benefits of General Smith had been omitted from the list of community assets owned by the parties, and that such benefits were in fact community property. The motion was denied on the ground of untimeliness. Plaintiff consulted other counsel, and shortly thereafter filed this malpractice action against defendant.

Defendant admits in his testimony that he assumed General Smith's retirement benefits were separate property when he assessed plaintiff's community property rights. It is his position that as a matter of law an attorney is not liable for mistaken advice when well informed lawyers in the community entertain reasonable doubt as to the proper resolution of the particular legal question involved. Because, he asserts, the law defining the character of retirement benefits was uncertain at the time of his legal services to plaintiff, defendant contends the trial court committed error in refusing to grant his motions for nonsuit and judgment notwithstanding the verdict and in submitting the issue of negligence to the jury under appropriate instructions.[3]

3. The jury was instructed as follows: "In performing legal services for a client in a divorce action an attorney has a duty to have that degree of learning and skill ordinarily possessed by attorneys of good standing, practicing in the same or similar locality and under similar circumstances."

"It is his further duty to use the care and skill ordinarily exercised in like cases by reputable members of his profession practicing in the same or a similar locality under similar circumstances, and to use reasonable diligence and his best judgment in the exercise of his skill and the accomplishment of his learning, in an effort to accomplish the best possible result for his client."

"A failure to perform any such duty is negligence."

"An attorney is not liable for every mistake he may make in his practice; he is not, in the absence of an express agreement, an insurer of the soundness of his opinions."

The law is now settled in California that "retirement benefits which flow from the employment relationship, to the extent they have vested, are community property subject to equal division between the spouses in the event the marriage is dissolved." Because such benefits are part of the consideration earned by the employee, they are accorded community treatment regardless of whether they derive from a state, federal, or private source, or from a contributory or noncontributory plan. In light of these principles, it becomes apparent that General Smith's retirement pay must properly be characterized as community property.

We cannot, however, evaluate the quality of defendant's professional services on the basis of the law as it appears today. In determining whether defendant exhibited the requisite degree of competence in his handling of plaintiff's divorce action, the crucial inquiry is whether his advice was so legally deficient when it was given that he may be found to have failed to use "such skill, prudence, and diligence as lawyers of ordinary skill and capacity commonly possess and exercise in the performance of the tasks which they undertake." We must, therefore examine the indicia of the law which were readily available to defendant at the time he performed the legal services in question.

The major authoritative reference works which attorneys routinely consult for a brief and reliable exposition of the law relevant to a specific problem uniformly indicated in 1967 that vested retirement benefits earned during marriage were generally subject to community treatment.[5] A typical statement appeared in The California Family Lawyer, a work with which defendant admitted general familiarity: "Of increasing importance is the fact that pension or retirement benefits are community property, even though they are not paid or payable until after termination of the marriage by death or divorce." (1 Cal.Family Lawyer, supra, at p. 111.)

Although it is true this court had not foreclosed all conflicts on some aspects of the issue at that time, the community character of retirement benefits had been reported in a number of appellate opinions often cited in the literature and readily accessible to defendant. In *Benson*, decided four years before defendant was retained herein, we stated directly that "pension rights which are earned during the course of a marriage are the community property of the employee and his wife." (60 Cal.2d at p. 359, 33 Cal.Rptr. at p. 259, 384 P.2d at p. 651.) In *French*, decided two decades earlier, we indicated that "retire[ment] pay is community property because it is compensation for services rendered in the past." (17 Cal.2d at p. 778, 112 P.2d at p. 236.) The other cases contain equally unequivocal dicta.

*   *   *

5. In evaluating the competence of an attorney's services, we may justifia- bly consider his failure to consult familiar encyclopedias of the law.

On the other hand, substantial uncertainty may have existed in 1967 with regard to the community character of General Smith's *federal* pension. The above-discussed treatises reveal a debate which lingered among members of the legal community at that time concerning the point at which retirement benefits actually vest. * * * Because the federal payments were contingent upon General Smith's survival to age 60, 17 years subsequent to the divorce, it could have been argued with some force that plaintiff and General Smith shared a mere expectancy interest in the future benefits. Alternatively, a reasonable contention could have been advanced in 1967 that federal retirement benefits were the personal entitlement of the employee spouse and were not subject to community division upon divorce in the absence of express congressional approval. In fact, such was the conclusion reached in 1973 by Judge B. Abbott Goldberg in his scholarly article Is Armed Services Retired Pay Really Community Property? (1973) 48 State Bar Journal 12. Although we rejected Judge Goldberg's analysis in In re Marriage of Fithian (1974) supra, 10 Cal.3d 592, 597, 111 Cal.Rptr. 369; 517 P.2d 449, footnote 2, the issue was clearly an arguable one upon which reasonable lawyers could differ.

Of course, the fact that in 1967 a reasonable argument could have been offered to support the characterization of General Smith's federal benefits as separate property does not indicate the trial court erred in submitting the issue of defendant's malpractice to the jury. The *state* benefits, the large majority of the payments at issue, were unquestionably community property according to all available authority and should have been claimed as such. As for the *federal* benefits, the record documents defendant's failure to conduct any reasonable research into their proper characterization under community property law.[7] Instead, he dogmatically asserted his theory, which he was unable to support with authority and later recanted, that all noncontributory military retirement benefits, whether state or federal, were immune from community tretament upon divorce. The jury could well have found defendant's refusal to educate himself to the appli-

---

7. At trial defendant testified that prior to the division of property in the divorce action, he had assumed the retirement benefits were not subject to community treatment, despite the fact General Smith had already begun to receive payments from the state; that he did not at that time undertake any research on the point nor did he discuss the matter with plaintiff; that subsequent to the divorce plaintiff asked defendant to research the question whereupon defendant discovered the *French* case which contained dictum in support of plaintiff's position; that the *French* decision caused him to change his opinion and conclude "that the Supreme Court, when it was confronted with this [the language in *French*] may hold that it [vested military retirement pay] is community property." On the basis of *French* defendant filed his unsuccessful motion to amend the final decree of divorce to allow plaintiff an interest in the retirement benefits. Defendant admitted at trial, "I would have been very willing to assert it [a community interest] on her behalf had I known of the dictum in the *French* case at the time."

cable principles of law constituted negligence which prevented him from exercising informed discretion with regard to his client's rights.

As the jury was correctly instructed, an attorney does not ordinarily guarantee the soundness of his opinions and, accordingly, is not liable for every mistake he may make in his practice. He is expected, however, to possess knowledge of those plain and elementary principles of law which are commonly known by well informed attorneys, and to discover those additional rules of law which, although not commonly known, may readily be found by standard research techniques. If the law on a particular subject is doubtful or debatable, an attorney will not be held responsible for failing to anticipate the manner in which the uncertainty will be resolved. But even with respect to an unsettled area of the law, we believe an attorney assumes an obligation to his client to undertake reasonable research in an effort to ascertain relevant legal principles and to make an informed decision as to a course of conduct based upon an intelligent assessment of the problem. In the instant case, ample evidence was introduced to support a jury finding that defendant failed to perform such adequate research into the question of the community character of retirement benefits and thus was unable to exercise the informed judgment to which his client was entitled.

We recognize, of course, that an attorney engaging in litigation may have occasion to choose among various alternative strategies available to his client, one of which may be to refrain from pressing a debatable point because potential benefit may not equal detriment in terms of expenditure at time and resources or because of calculated tactics to the advantage of his client. But, as the Ninth Circuit put it somewhat brutally in Pineda v. Craven (9th Cir. 1970) 424 F.2d 369, 372: "There is nothing strategic or tactical about ignorance * * *." In the case before us it is difficult to conceive of tactical advantage which could have been served by neglecting to advance a claim so clearly in plaintiff's best interest, nor does defendant suggest any. The decision to forego litigation on the issue of plaintiff's community property right to a share of General Smith's retirement benefits was apparently the product of a culpable misconception of the relevant principles of law, and the jury could have so found.

Furthermore, no lawyer would suggest the property characterization of General Smith's retirement benefits to be so esoteric an issue that defendant could not reasonably have been expected to be aware of it or its probable resolution. * * * Certainly one of the central issues in any divorce proceeding is the extent and division of the community property. In this case the question reached monumental proportions, since General Smith's retirement benefits constituted the only significant asset available to the community. In undertaking professional representation of plaintiff, defendant assumed the duty to familiarize himself with the law defining the character of retirement benefits; instead, he rendered erroneous advice contrary to the best interests of his client without the guidance through research of readily available authority.

* * *

In any event, as indicated above, had defendant conducted minimal research into either hornbook or case law, he would have discovered with modest effort that General Smith's state retirement benefits were likely to be treated as community property and that his federal benefits at least arguably belonged to the community as well. Therefore, we hold that the trial court correctly denied the motions for nonsuit and judgment notwithstanding the verdict and properly submitted the question of defendant's negligence to the jury under the instructions given. For the same reasons, the trial court correctly refused to instruct the jury at defendant's request that "he is not liable for being in error as to a question of law on which reasonable doubt may be entertained by well informed lawyers." Even as to doubtful matters, an attorney is expected to perform sufficient research to enable him to make an informed and intelligent judgment on behalf of his client.

[At this point the court found that the damage award of $100,000 was not excessive and was supported by the evidence.]

* * *

The judgment is affirmed.

* * *

NOTES AND QUESTIONS

1. Justice Clark dissented from the majority opinion in Smith v. Lewis, joined by Justice McComb. The position of the dissent was that the law had been sufficiently uncertain in 1967 that a careful lawyer would have avoided litigation over pension rights and would instead have sought a compensating alimony award, which is what the defendant did. Therefore the record did not establish the probability that any negligence of the defendant in failing to investigate the law had caused the plaintiff to lose rights to her husband's pension.

2. It would be ironical, but certainly not much comfort to Mr. Lewis, if it should turn out that military pensions are *not* divisible on divorce as a result of *Hisquierdo* and the cases cited supra, in paragraph 4, page 908. Gorman v. Gorman, 90 Cal.App.3d 454, 153 Cal.Rptr. 479 (1979) adhered to the view that the military pension *is* divisible, finding that the failure to assert a claim to it was malpractice, notwithstanding *Hisquierdo*.

Would Mr. Lewis have been exposed to malpractice liability if he had just never learned about the husband's pension rights, and for that reason had never asserted a claim for a share of them on behalf of his client? How can a lawyer protect himself in this situation?

3. Other cases raising questions of malpractice in divorce representation include Kuehn v. Garcia, 608 F.2d 1143 (8th Cir. 1979) (malpractice in failing to contact the client and failing to appear for a hearing resulting in

a default); Dunn v. McKay, Burton, McMurray & Thurman, 584 P.2d 894 (Utah 1978) (any negligence which might have occurred did not cause the loss). Pinkerton v. West, 353 So.2d 102 (Fla.App.1977), cert. den. 365 So. 2d 715 (Fla.1978) held that the statute of limitations had not run, the negligence being erroneous advice that alimony claims would be dischargeable in bankruptcy. See also Annot., 78 A.L.R.3d 255 (1977).

4. (a) L, an attorney, represents W in her divorce suit against H. W and H have one child, C, whose custody is in issue in the case. The day before the trial of the custody issue, W took C and left the state, telling L where she was going, but telling no one else and insisting that L tell no one else. At the hearing the next day L appeared for his client, told the court she had departed with the child, but refused to reveal her whereabouts. Can L be compelled to disclose where W is, under pain of contempt proceedings? Would the case be different if W had left after a decree had been entered giving custody to H? In re Jacqueline F., 47 N.Y.2d 215, 417 N. Y.S.2d 884, 391 N.E.2d 967 (1979). See also Livingston v. Livingston, 572 P.2d 79 (Alaska 1977).

(b) You represented H in his divorce suit against W, in the course of which you drafted a separation agreement which the parties signed and which was incorporated in their divorce decree. Later, after the divorce was granted, you learn that H failed to disclose to you or to W that he owned a valuable block of corporate securities. If this property had been disclosed, it is likely that W would have been able to negotiate a better property settlement than she did. Do you have any obligation to W, or the court, or to anyone upon learning these facts? A.B.A. Code of Professional Responsibility, DR 7–102 (B)(1); Crystal, Ethical Problems in Marital Practice, 30 S.C.L.Rev. 321, 348 (1979).

5. Disciplinary proceedings have been initiated against Jones, a lawyer licensed to practice in the State of Holmes, for unethical conduct. The facts are not disputed. On several occasions Jones either advised clients that their right to a divorce in the State of Holmes was very doubtful or that they could obtain a divorce in Holmes only after rather long delays and with some unfavorable publicity. In each such case Jones told the client that he could obtain a Nevada divorce which would be valid throughout the United States if his (Jones') instructions were strictly followed. He explained that one spouse would have to live in Nevada for six weeks, pretend that he was staying indefinitely, and testify in the divorce action that he was domiciled in Nevada. It would be important to do nothing inconsistent with the intent to stay longer, and for example, the client should not buy a round-trip ticket to Nevada. Jones referred each of his clients to Sartor, a Nevada attorney who would handle the case for one spouse and who would arrange for another lawyer to represent the other spouse who would usually stay in Holmes. Jones would usually draft the separation agreement governing custody, child support and alimony and have the parties execute it before the plaintiff left for Nevada. For his services Jones regularly charged between $500 and $2,000. What arguments would you make for or against Jones in these proceedings?

In dealing with this problem you may wish to consult American Bar Association Code of Professional Responsibility, Canons DR 1–102, DR 7–102 (1969); In re Feltman, 51 N.J. 27, 237 A.2d 473 (1968); Drinker, Problems of Professional Ethics in Matrimonial Litigation, 66 Harv.L.Rev.

443 (1953); Adams and Adams, Ethical Problems in Advising Migratory Divorce, 16 Hast.L.J. 60 (1964); Annot., 13 A.L.R.3d 1010 (1967); and the following opinions: Opinion No. 123, of September 27, 1929 of the Association of the Bar of the City of New York, reprinted in Opinions on Professional Ethics (Wm. Nelson Cromwell Foundation, 1956); Opinion No. 188 of July 1, 1931, id. at 91; Opinion No. 622 of September 9, 1942, id. at 355; Opinion No. 723 of December 6, 1948, id. at 436; New York County Lawyers Opinion No. 100, id. at 568.

6.   The State of Holmes, in which you practice as an attorney, has the following statute: "It is the underlying purpose of the divorce act to strengthen and preserve the integrity of marriage, and to safeguard family relationships, and to promote the amicable settlement of disputes which have arisen between spouses." You are consulted by Nina Titus, who says that she has decided she must have a divorce. She suspects her husband, Fred, of being interested in another woman and is upset and depressed in consequence. They have been married eight years and have two children. You are mindful of the statute and decide to try to find out whether Nina has made any attempt at talking this over with Fred and whether they both want the divorce. Your interview with Nina leaves you with some doubts and you ask her whether Fred would be willing to come in for a conference. It turns out that he is willing, and three more long interviews with both of them are held, in which they discuss, under your sympathetic influence, their married life in all its ramifications. It turns out that Fred has been seeing another woman, but that he feels Nina has lost interest in him and that home is no longer a pleasant place. He also is discouraged by a series of setbacks in his work which made him moody and irritable, taking out his bad temper on Nina. When the feelings on both sides have been aired, Nina and Fred agree that they would like to give their marriage another chance, and they leave your office appearing to be reconciled.

(a) Can you send Nina a bill computed on the basis of your regular hourly charge, for the time spent on conciliation conferences? Cf. Weiner v. Weiner, 119 N.J.Super. 109, 290 A.2d 307 (1972).

(b) A year later Nina returns to your office saying that the reconciliation just did not work out and that now she knows she wants a divorce from Fred. Will you agree to represent her? Would your answer to this question be different if you were an attorney in an O.E.O. Legal Services Office and Nina and Fred were without funds and therefore qualified clients of your office? See Note, 20 Am.U.L.Rev. 30 (1970); In re Braun, 49 N.J. 16, 227 A.2d 506 (1967); In re Blatt, 42 N.J. 522, 201 A.2d 715 (1964); American Bar Association Code of Professional Responsibility, DR 5–105(B), EC 5–14, DR 4–101, EC 4–1 (1969). In answering this question you may want to consider whether you or any lawyer is capable of, and comfortable in, the shift in roles from that of adversary and champion to mediator or conciliator and then back to adversary again.

7.   You are an attorney in the State of California in general practice. You and your wife have been friends for some years with Paul and Norma New, seeing them in a social way every month or so, and playing tennis with them frequently. During one summer they go off to Europe on an extended trip and on their return Paul calls you for an appointment. Paul and Norma both come to your office at the appointed time and inform you that they have decided they cannot continue living together and wish to get

a divorce. The California statute authorizes divorces on the ground of irreconcilable differences. Paul and Norma say they are perfectly amicable in recognizing their differences, that they expect no problems about the divorce since they have no children and no property other than a car, an equity in their house, a savings account containing $10,000 and some stock that Norma inherited from her father worth about $30,000. You know that Paul makes about $18,000 a year and that they have been married six years. They ask you two questions:

(a) Could they get the divorce themselves, without the expense of a lawyer? They have read a book called "The $27 Divorce", which explains how, under the new marriage breakdown statute, spouses can have a do-it-yourself divorce, and an article, Johnson, The Family Law Act: A Guide to the Practitioner, 1 Pacific L.J. 147 (1970), which provides a clear, step by step guide for getting a divorce under the new law. If, in getting the divorce themselves, they should make a costly mistake, could they later have the mistake corrected? Kelley v. Kelley, 73 Cal.App.3d 672, 141 Cal.Rptr. 33 (1977). For an extensive account of pro se divorce in one state, drawing conclusions not favorable to the legal profession, see Note, The Unauthorized Practice of Law and Pro Se Divorce: An Empirical Analysis, 88 Yale L.J. 104 (1976).

(b) If you should begin by representing one of the two spouses, but your client runs out of funds, could you withdraw and let the client continue the case pro se? See Kriegsman v. Kriegsman, 150 N.J.Super. 474, 375 A.2d 1253 (1977).

(c) There is evidence that the sharp increase in the divorce rate has imposed heavy burdens on the courts, leading in some states to long delays in getting cases heard. Wall Street Journal, January 28, 1980, p. 1, col. 1. Would increased incidence of pro se divorce worsen these conditions? See, e. g., Board of County Commissioners of the County of Boulder v. Barday, ── Colo. ──, 594 P.2d 1057 (1979).

(d) The sale of books or "divorce kits" to aid those wishing to obtain divorces without legal representation is generally held not to constitute the unauthorized practice of law. See Schneider v. Hill, 223 Kan. 425, 573 P.2d 1078 (1978) (decision by an equally divided court); In re Thompson, 574 S.W.2d 365 (Mo.1978); Oregon State Bar v. Gilchrist, 272 Or. 552, 538 P. 2d 913 (1975); Annot., 71 A.L.R.3d 1000 (1976). But personal assistance in filling out forms or giving advice may constitute unauthorized practice. Delaware State Bar Ass'n v. Alexander, 386 A.2d 652 (Del.1978), dismissed for want of jurisdiction and cert. den. 439 U.S. 808 (1978); The Florida Bar v. Brumbaugh, 355 So.2d 1186 (Fla.1978).

(e) If you think it inadvisable for them to try to obtain the divorce themselves, would you represent them both and get them the divorce? They point out that you know them well and they would feel much more secure having you handle the matter for them than to employ some strange attorney they do not know and in whom they would have no confidence. Or, Paul suggests, if there is some difficulty about representing them both, would you just represent him, since Norma would feel that you would not do anything contrary to her interests? American Bar Association Code of Professional Responsibility, DR 5–105, EC 5–14, EC 5–15, EC 5–16 (1969); Ishmael v. Millington, 241 Cal.App.2d 520, 50 Cal.Rptr. 592 (1966); B.

Mortlock, The Inside of Divorce 93–100 (1972); Opinion No. 47, Colorado Bar Association Ethics Committee, 1 Colo. Lawyer 59 (1972); Ethics Opinion No. 478, Committee on Professional Ethics of the New York State Bar Assn., 4 Fam.L.Rep. 2233, February 1, 1978 (lawyer may prepare a separation agreement negotiated between the spouses if he is just a scrivener, can transmit it to an unrepresented party for signature, and if the matter is litigated, may negotiate with an adverse party who is acting pro se).

(f) Would your answers to any of these questions differ if Paul and Norma were a couple with an income of $5,000 per year and no property? These and other problems are discussed in Crystal, Ethical Problems in Marital Practice, 30 S.C.L.Rev. 321 (1979).

8. You are appointed to represent the child in a custody case. How would you conceive of your function in such an appointment? Just what would you attempt to do and how would you do it? Note, Lawyering for the Child: Principles of Representation in Custody and Visitation Disputes Arising From Divorce, 87 Yale L.J. 1125 (1978).

9. Contingent fee contracts have traditionally been forbidden in divorce actions, the reasons being that they give the attorney a personal motive for getting the divorce and thereby contribute to the breakup of marriages, and that they take from the wife funds essential for her support. These reasons often do not seem very persuasive. See Note, 113 U.Pa.L. Rev. 278 (1964). The American Bar Association Code of Professional Responsibility does not seem to prohibit contingent fees in divorce actions, but it does say that "Because of the human relationships involved and the unique character of the proceedings, contingent fee arrangements in domestic relations cases are rarely justified." EC 2–20. The chief justification for the contingent fee is that it enables persons to obtain representation and bring suits when they would otherwise be financially unable to do so. In divorce cases, however, the wife is usually entitled to have her attorney fees paid by her husband. Therefore if he is able to pay the fees, the need for the contingent fee does not exist. In any event many cases characterize contingent fees in divorce as illegal. See, e. g., Avant v. Whitten, 253 So.2d 394 (Miss.1971), 43 Miss.L.Rev. 406 (1972), citing other cases. For cases involving special facts see McInerney v. Massasoit Greyhound Ass'n, 269 N. E.2d 211 (Mass.1971); Burns v. Stewart, 290 Minn. 289, 188 N.W.2d 760 (1971), 56 Minn.L.Rev. 979 (1972). An attorney may be paid a reasonable fee even though his attempt to obtain a contingent fee is illegal. Hay v. Erwin, 244 Or. 488, 419 P.2d 32 (1966).

10. The following is a list of useful books and articles on the lawyer's tasks and problems in matrimonial cases. In consulting them the student should of course maintain a critical attitude toward the views expressed.

Bodenheimer, New Approaches of Psychiatry: Implications for Divorce Reform, 1970 Utah L.Rev. 191: A clear and concise account of some phychiatric approaches to marital conflict, useful for informing the student of possible alternatives to conventional Freudian analysis.

Burke, The Role of Conciliation in Divorce Cases, 1 J.Fam.L. 209 (1961): An account of the Los Angeles conciliation court's work by the judge who was instrumental in setting up that court.

Eisenstein, ed., Neurotic Interaction in Marriage (1956): A collection of papers describing various kinds of neurotic behavior by married persons and indicating what might and might not be accomplished by counseling married persons.

Elkins, A Counseling Model for Lawyering in Divorce Cases, 53 Notre Dame L. 229 (1977). This article suggests insights from psychology to help lawyers in interviewing, advising and counseling clients.

Foster, Conciliation and Counseling in the Courts in Family Law Cases, 41 N.Y.U.L.Rev. 353 (1966): A discussion of the conciliation and counseling services provided by the courts in Ohio, Wisconsin, Utah, Maine, New Jersey, Los Angeles, Michigan, New York and some other places. The more recent New York conciliation scheme is described in H. Foster and D. Freed, The Divorce Reform Law 26 (1969), which is published as a supplement to Law and the Family-New York by H. Foster and D. Freed.

H. Freeman, Legal Interviewing and Counseling (1964): This is an interviewing casebook, containing accounts of interviews of clients by their lawyers, with comments on the interviews by experts who are also lawyers. Chapter 6 contains interviews relating to marital and family problems.

Harper and Harper, Lawyers and Marriage Counseling, 1 J.Fam.L. 73 (1961): A description of counseling and conciliation as related to the work of the lawyer.

M. Heller, E. Polen and S. Polsky, An Introduction to Legal Interviewing (1960): Some elementary discussions of interviewing as practiced by lawyers.

D. Langsley and D. Kaplan, The Treatment of Families in Crisis (1968): A description, with some case illustrations, of an experimental method of treating emotional emergencies in families. This may give the lawyer some insight into the origins and possible handling of such emergencies.

B. Mortlock, The Inside of Divorce (1972): An experienced English divorce solicitor's criticisms of the divorce law, together with reflections about his practice. The criticisms are of little interest but the material on divorce practice is useful.

H. O'Gorman, Lawyers and Matrimonial Cases (1963): A rather undiscriminating description by a sociologist of the methods of work and attitudes of some New York lawyers engaged in matrimonial practice.

Parnas, The Response of Some Relevant Community Resources to Intra-Family Violence, 44 Ind.L.J. 159 (1969): Describes some sources of help for husband-wife violence.

Popenoe, Emotional Problems of Marriage and Divorce, in Family Law for California Lawyers 1–21 (1956): A simple, common sense discussion of the background of divorce and its effect on the parties.

A. Watson, Psychiatry for Lawyers (1968): A background discussion of personality development in Freudian terms. A more interesting attempt to do the same thing is C. Brenner, An Elementary Textbook of Psychoanalysis (1955), available as a Doubleday Anchor Book.

Trend Analysis: The "Changed Landscape" of Divorce Practice As Ethical Minefield, 3 Fam.L.Rep. 4031 (1977). This Family Law Reporter Monograph describes some of the criticisms, demands and pressures currently being aimed at divorce practitioners.

APPENDIX

HARRIS v. McRAE

Supreme Court of the United States, 1980.

— U.S. —, 100 S.Ct. —, — L.Ed.2d —.

Mr. Justice STEWART delivered the opinion of the Court.

This case presents statutory and constitutional questions concerning the public funding of abortions under Title XIX of the Social Security Act, commonly known as the "Medicaid" Act, and recent annual appropriations acts containing the so-called "Hyde Amendment." The statutory question is whether Title XIX requires a State that participates in the Medicaid program to fund the cost of medically necessary abortions for which federal reimbursement is unavailable under the Hyde Amendment. The constitutional question, which arises only if Title XIX imposes no such requirement, is whether the Hyde Amendment, by denying public funding for certain medically necessary abortions, contravenes the liberty or equal protection guarantees of the Due Process Clause of the Fifth Amendment, or either of the Religion Clauses of the First Amendment.

I

The Medicaid program was created in 1965, when Congress added Title XIX to the Social Security Act, 79 Stat. 343, as amended, 42 U.S.C. § 1396 et seq. (1976 ed. and Supp. II), for the purpose of providing federal financial assistance to States that choose to reimburse certain costs of medical treatment for needy persons. Although participation in the Medicaid program is entirely optional, once a State elects to participate, it must comply with the requirements of Title XIX.

One such requirement is that a participating State agree to provide financial assistance to the "categorically needy" with respect to five general areas of medical treatment: (1) inpatient hospital services, (2) outpatient hospital services, (3) other laboratory and X-ray services, (4) skilled nursing facilities services, periodic screening and diagnosis of children, and family planning services, and (5) services of physicians. 42 U.S.C. §§ 1396a(a)(13)(B), 1396d(a)(1)–(5). Although a participating State need not "provide funding for all medical treatment falling within the five general categories, [Title XIX] does require that [a] state Medicaid plan[ ] establish 'reasonable standards * * * for determining * * * the extent of medical assistance under the plan which * * * are consistent with the objectives of [Title XIX].' 42 U.S.C. § 1396a(a)(17)." Beal v. Doe, 432 U.S. 438, 441 [97 S.Ct. 2366, 2369, 53 L.Ed.2d 464].

Since September 1976, Congress has prohibited—either by an amendment to the annual appropriations bill for the Department of Health, Education, and Welfare [2] or by a joint resolution—the use of any federal funds to reimburse the cost of abortions under the Medicaid program except under certain specified circumstances. This funding restriction is commonly known as the "Hyde Amendment," after its original congressional sponsor, Representative Hyde. The current version of the Hyde Amendment, applicable for fiscal year 1980, provides:

> "[N]one of the funds provided by this joint resolution shall be used to perform abortions except where the life of the mother would be endangered if the fetus were carried to term; or except for such medical procedures necessary for the victims of rape or incest when such rape or incest has been reported promply to a law enforcement agency or public health service." Pub.L. No. 96–123, § 109, 93 Stat. 926. See also Pub.L. No. 96–86, § 118, 93 Stat. 662.

This version of the Hyde Amendment is broader than that applicable for fiscal year 1977, which did not include the "rape or incest" exception, Pub.L. No. 94–439, § 209, 90 Stat. 1434, but narrower than that applicable for most of fiscal year 1978, and all of fiscal year 1979, which had an additional exception for "instances where severe and long-lasting physical health damage to the mother would result if the pregnancy were carried to term when so determined by two physicians," Pub.L. No. 95–205, § 101, 91 Stat. 1460; Pub.L. No. 95–480, § 210, 92 Stat. 1586.[4]

On September 30, 1976, the day on which Congress enacted the initial version of the Hyde Amendment, these consolidated cases were filed in the District Court for the Eastern District of New York. The plaintiffs—Cora McRae, a New York Medicaid recipient then in the first trimester of a pregnancy that she wished to terminate, the New York City Health and Hospitals Corp., a public benefit corporation that operates 16 hospitals, 12 of which provide abortion services, and others—sought to enjoin the enforcement of the funding restriction on abortions. They alleged that the Hyde Amendment violated the First, Fourth, Fifth, and Ninth Amendments of the Constitution insofar as it limited the funding of abortions to those necessary to save the life of the mother, while permitting the funding of costs associated with childbirth. Although the sole named defendant was the Secretary of Health, Education, and Welfare, the District Court permitted Senators James L. Buckley and Jesse A. Helms and Representative Henry J. Hyde to intervene as defendants.

* * *

---

2. The Department of Health, Education, and Welfare was recently renamed the Department of Health and Human Services. The original designation is retained for purposes of this opinion.

4. In this opinion, the term, "Hyde Amendment," is used generically to refer to all three versions of the Hyde Amendment, except where indicated otherwise.

[At this point in its opinion the Court recited in detail the proceedings below. These included a temporary injunction by the district court; the certification of a class action including pregnant women in New York wishing an abortion in the first 24 weeks; the first appeal to the Supreme Court which was remanded in Califano v. McRae, 433 U.S. 916; and the intervention of various new parties. In the district court opinion which followed a long trial, the court held that Title XIX of the Social Security Act did not require the states to fund abortions not funded by the federal government under the Hyde Amendment. But the court held that all versions of the Hyde Amendment were in violation of the Fifth Amendment and the Free Exercise Clause of the First Amendment.]

* * *

II

* * * we turn first to the question whether Title XIX requires a State that participates in the Medicaid program to continue to fund those medically necessary abortions for which federal reimbursement is unavailable under the Hyde Amendment. If a participating State is under such an obligation, the constitutionality of the Hyde Amendment need not be drawn into question in the present case, for the availability of medically necessary abortions under Medicaid would continue, with the participating State shouldering the total cost of funding such abortions.

The appellees assert that a participating State has an independent funding obligation under Title XIX because (1) the Hyde Amendment is, by its own terms, only a limitation on federal reimbursement for certain medically necessary abortions, and (2) Title XIX does not permit a participating State to exclude from its Medicaid plan any medically necessary service solely on the basis of diagnosis or condition, even if federal reimbursement is unavailable for that service.[11] It is thus the appellees' view that the effect of the Hyde Amendment is to withhold federal reimbursement for certain medically necessary abortions, but not to relieve a participating State of its duty under Title XIX to provide for such abortions in its Medicaid plan.

The District Court rejected this argument. * * *

We agree with the District Court, but for somewhat different reasons. The Medicaid program created by Title XIX is a cooperative endeavor in which the Federal Government provides financial assist-

---

11. The appellees argue that their interpretation of Title XIX finds support in Beal v. Doe, 432 U.S. 438 [97 S.Ct. 2366, 53 L.Ed.2d 464]. There the Court considered the question whether Title XIX permits a participating State to exclude *non*-therapeutic abortions from its Medicaid plan. Although concluding that Title XIX does not preclude a State's refusal "to fund *unnecessary*—though perhaps desirable—medical services," the Court observed that "serious statutory questions might be presented if a state Medicaid plan excluded necessary medical treatment from its coverage." Id., at 444–445 [97 S.Ct., at 2370–2371] (emphasis in original). The Court in *Beal*, however, did not address the possible effect of the Hyde Amendment upon the operation of Title XIX.

ance to participating States to aid them in furnishing health care to needy persons. Under this system of "cooperative federalism," a State agrees to establish a Medicaid plan that satisfies the requirements of Title XIX, which include several mandatory categories of health services, the Federal Government agrees to pay a specified percentage of "the total amount expended * * * as medical assistance under the State plan * * *." 42 U.S.C. § 1396b(a)(1). The cornerstone of Medicaid is financial contribution by both the Federal Government and the participating State. Nothing in Title XIX as originally enacted, or in its legislative history, suggests the Congress intended to require a participating State to assume the full costs of providing any health services in its Medicaid plan. Quite the contrary, the purpose of Congress in enacting Title XIX was to provide federal financial assistance for all legitimate state expenditures under an approved Medicaid plan. * * *

Since the Congress that enacted Title XIX did not intend a participating State to assume a unilateral funding obligation for any health service in an approved Medicaid plan, it follows that Title XIX does not require a participating State to include in its plan any services for which a subsequent Congress has withheld federal funding. Title XIX was designed as a cooperative program of shared financial responsibility, not as a device for the Federal Government to compel a State to provide services that Congress itself is unwilling to fund. Thus, if Congress chooses to withdraw federal funding for a particular service, a State is not obliged to continue to pay for that service as a condition of continued federal financial support of other services. * * *

Thus, by the normal operation of Title XIX, even if a State were otherwise required to include medically necessary abortions in its Medicaid plan, the withdrawal of federal funding under the Hyde Amendment would operate to relieve the State of that obligation for those abortions for which federal reimbursement is unavailable. The legislative history of the Hyde Amendment contains no indication whatsoever that Congress intended to shift the entire cost of such services to the participating States. * * * Accordingly, we conclude that Title XIX does not require a participating State to pay for those medically necessary abortions for which federal reimbursement is unavailable under the Hyde Amendment.[16]

III

Having determined that Title XIX does not obligate a participating State to pay for those medically necessary abortions for which Congress has withheld federal funding, we must consider the constitutional validity of the Hyde Amendment. The appellees assert that the fund-

---

16. A participating State is free, if it so chooses, to include in its Medicaid plan those medically necessary abortions for which federal reimbursement is unavailable. See Beal v. Doe, supra, 432 U.S., at 447 [97 S.Ct., at 2372]; Preterm, Inc. v. Dukakis, supra, 591 F.2d, at 134. We hold only that a State *need* not include such abortions in its Medicaid plan.

ing restrictions of the Hyde Amendment violate several rights secured by the Constitution—(1) the right of a woman, implicit in the Due Process Clause of the Fifth Amendment, to decide whether to terminate a pregnancy, (2) the prohibition under the Establishment Clause of the First Amendment against any "law respecting an establishment of religion," and (3) the right to freedom of religion protected by the Free Exercise Clause of the First Amendment. The appellees also contend that, quite apart from substantive constitutional rights, the Hyde Amendment violates the equal protection component of the Fifth Amendment.[17]

It is well settled that, quite apart from the guarantee of equal protection, if a law "impinges upon a fundamental right explicitly or implicitly secured by the Constitution [it] is presumptively unconstitutional." Mobile v. Bolden, 446 U.S. ——, —— [100 S.Ct. 1490, —— 64 L.Ed.2d 47] (plurality opinion). Accordingly, before turning to the equal protection issue in this case, we examine whether the Hyde Amendment violates any substantive rights secured by the Constitution.

A

We address first the appellees' argument that the Hyde Amendment, by restricting the availability of certain medically necessary abortions under Medicaid, impinges on the "liberty" protected by the Due Process Clause as recognized in Roe v. Wade, 410 U.S. 113 [93 S.Ct. 705, 35 L.Ed.2d 147], and its progeny.

* * *

[The Court at this point cited and discussed Roe v. Wade, 410 U.S. 113, 93 S.Ct. 705, 35 L.Ed.2d 147, and Maher v. Roe, 432 U.S. 464, 97 S.Ct. 2376, 53 L.Ed.2d 484.]

The Hyde Amendment, like the Connecticut welfare regulation at issue in *Maher*, places no governmental obstacle in the path of a woman who chooses to terminate her pregnancy, but rather, by means of unequal subsidization of abortion and other medical services, encourages alternative activity deemed in the public interest. The present case does differ factually from *Maher* insofar as that case involved a failure to fund nontherapeutic abortions, whereas the Hyde Amendment withholds funding of certain medically necessary abortions. Ac-

---

17. The appellees also argue that the Hyde Amendment is unconstitutionally vague insofar as physicians are unable to understand or implement the exceptions to the Hyde Amendment under which abortions are reimbursable. It is our conclusion, however, that the Hyde Amendment is not void for vagueness because (1) the sanction provision in the Medicaid Act contains a clear scienter requirement under which good-faith errors are not penalized, see Colautti v. Franklin, 439 U.S. 379, 395 [99 S.Ct. 675, 685, 58 L.Ed.2d 596], and, (2), in any event, the exceptions to the Hyde Amendment "are set out in terms that the ordinary person exercising ordinary common sense can sufficiently understand and comply with, without sacrifice to the public interest." Broadrick v. Oklahoma, 413 U.S. 601, 608 [93 S.Ct. 2908, 2913–2914, 37 L.Ed.2d 830].

cordingly, the appellees argue that because the Hyde Amendment affects a significant interest not present or asserted in *Maher*—the interest of a woman in protecting her health during pregnancy—and because that interest lies at the core of the personal constitutional freedom recognized in *Wade*, the present case is constitutionally different from *Maher*. It is the appellees' view that to the extent that the Hyde Amendment withholds funding for certain medically necessary abortions, it clearly impinges on the constitutional principle recognized in *Wade*.

It is evident that a woman's interest in protecting her health was an important theme in *Wade*. In concluding that the freedom of a woman to decide whether to terminate her pregnancy falls within the personal liberty protected by the Due Process Clause, the Court in *Wade* emphasized the fact that the woman's decision carries with it significant personal health implications—both physical and psychological. 410 U.S., at 153 [93 S.Ct., at 726]. In fact, although the Court in *Wade* recognized that the state interest in protecting potential life becomes sufficiently compelling in the period after fetal viability to justify an absolute criminal prohibition of nontherapeutic abortions, the Court held that even after fetal viability a State may not prohibit abortions "necessary to preserve the life or health of the mother." Id., at 164 [93 S.Ct., at 732]. Because even the compelling interest of the State in protecting potential life after fetal viability was held to be insufficient to outweigh a woman's decision to protect her life or health, it could be argued that the freedom of a woman to decide whether to terminate her pregnancy for health reasons does in fact lie at the core of the constitutional liberty identified in *Wade*.

But, regardless of whether the freedom of a woman to choose to terminate her pregnancy for health reasons lies at the core or the periphery of the due process liberty recognized in *Wade*, it simply does not follow that a woman's freedom of choice carries with it a constitutional entitlement to the financial resources to avail herself of the full range of protected choices. The reason why was explained in *Maher:* although government may not place obstacles in the path of a woman's exercise of her freedom of choice, it need not remove those not of its own creation. Indigency falls in the latter category. The financial constraints that restrict an indigent woman's ability to enjoy the full range of constitutionally protected freedom of choice are the product not of governmental restrictions on access to abortions, but rather of her indigency. Although Congress has opted to subsidize medically necessary services generally, but not certain medically necessary abortions, the fact remains that the Hyde Amendment leaves an indigent woman with at least the same range of choice in deciding whether to obtain a medically necessary abortion as she would have had if Congress had chosen to subsidize no health care costs at all. We are thus not persuaded that the Hyde Amendment impinges on the constitutionally protected freedom of choice recognized in *Wade*.[19]

Although the liberty protected by the Due Process Clause affords protection against unwarranted government interference with freedom of choice in the context of certain personal decisions, it does not confer an entitlement to such funds as may be necessary to realize all the advantages of that freedom. To hold otherwise would mark a drastic change in our understanding of the Constitution. It cannot be that because government may not prohibit the use of contraceptives, Griswold v. Connecticut, 381 U.S. 479 [85 S.Ct. 1678, 14 L.Ed.2d 510], or prevent parents from sending their child to a private school, Pierce v. Society of Sisters, 268 U.S. 510 [45 S.Ct. 571, 69 L.Ed. 1070], government, therefore, has an affirmative constitutional obligation to ensure that all persons have the financial resources to obtain contraceptives or send their children to private schools. To translate the limitation on governmental power implicit in the Due Process Clause into an affirmative funding obligation would require Congress to subsidize the medically necessary abortion of an indigent woman even if Congress had not enacted a Medicaid program to subsidize other medically necessary services. Nothing in the Due Process Clause supports such an extraordinary result. Whether freedom of choice that is constitutionally protected warrants federal subsidization is a question for Congress to answer, not a matter of constitutional entitlement. Accordingly, we conclude that the Hyde Amendment does not impinge on the due process liberty recognized in *Wade*.

19. The appellees argue that the Hyde Amendment is unconstitutional because it "penalizes" the exercise of a woman's choice to terminate a pregnancy by abortion. See Memorial Hospital v. Maricopa County, 415 U.S. 250 [94 S.Ct. 1076, 39 L.Ed.2d 306]; Shapiro v. Thompson, 394 U.S. 618 [89 S.Ct. 1322, 22 L.Ed.2d 600]. This argument falls short of the mark. In *Maher*, the Court found only a "semantic difference" between the argument that Connecticut's refusal to subsidize nontherapeutic abortions "unduly interfere[d]" with the exercise of the constitutional liberty recognized in *Wade* and the argument that it "penalized" the exercise of that liberty. 432 U.S., at 474, n. 8 [97 S.Ct., at 2382]. And, regardless of how the claim was characterized, the *Maher* Court rejected the argument that Connecticut's refusal to subsidize protected conduct, without more, impinged on the constitutional freedom of choice. This reasoning is equally applicable in the present case. A substantial constitutional question would arise if Congress had attempted to withhold all Medicaid benefits from an otherwise eligible candidate simply because that candidate had exercised her constitutionally protected freedom to terminate her pregnancy by abortion. This would be analogous to Sherbert v. Verner, 374 U.S. 398 [83 S.Ct. 1790, 10 L.Ed.2d 965], where this Court held that a State may not, consistent with the First and Fourteenth Amendments, withhold *all* unemployment compensation benefits from a claimant who would otherwise be eligible for such benefits but for the fact that she is unwilling to work one day per week on her Sabbath. But the Hyde Amendment, unlike the statute at issue in *Sherbert*, does not provide for such a broad disqualification from receipt of public benefits. Rather, the Hyde Amendment, like the Connecticut welfare provision at issue in *Maher*, represents simply a refusal to subsidize certain protected conduct. A refusal to fund protected activity, without more, cannot be equated with the imposition of a "penalty" on that activity.

B

The appellees also argue that the Hyde Amendment contravenes rights secured by the Religion Clauses of the First Amendment. It is the appellees' view that the Hyde Amendment violates the Establishment Clause because it incorporates into law the doctrines of the Roman Catholic Church concerning the sinfulness of abortion and the time at which life commences. Moreover, insofar as a woman's decision to seek a medically necessary abortion may be a product of her religious beliefs under certain Protestant and Jewish tenets, the appellees assert that the funding limitations of the Hyde Amendment impinge on the freedom of religion guaranteed by the Free Exercise Clause.

1

It is well settled that "a legislative enactment does not contravene the Establishment Clause if it has a secular legislative purpose, if its principal or primary effect neither advances nor inhibits religion, and if it does not foster an excessive governmental entanglement with religion." Committee for Pub.Ed. & Rel.Lib. v. Regan, 444 U.S. ——, —— [100 S.Ct. 840, 63 L.Ed.2d 94]. Applying this standard, the District Court properly concluded that the Hyde Amendment does not run afoul of the Establishment Clause. Although neither a State nor the Federal Government can constitutionally "pass laws which aid one religion, aid all religions, or prefer one religion over another," Everson v. Board of Education, 330 U.S. 1, 15 [67 S.Ct. 504, ——, 91 L.Ed. 711], it does not follow that a statute violates the Establishment Clause because it "happens to coincide or harmonize with the tenets of some or all religions." McGowan v. Maryland, 366 U.S. 420, 442 [81 S.Ct. 1101, 1113, 6 L.Ed.2d 393]. That the Judaeo-Christian religions oppose stealing does not mean that a State or the Federal Government may not, consistent with the Establishment Clause, enact laws prohibiting larceny. Ibid. The Hyde Amendment, as the District Court noted, is as much a reflection of "traditionalist" values towards abortion, as it is an embodiment of the views of any particular religion. See also Roe v. Wade, supra, 410 U.S., at 138–141, 93 S.Ct., at 719–721. In sum, we are convinced that the fact that the funding restrictions in the Hyde Amendment may coincide with the religious tenets of the Roman Catholic Church does not, without more, contravene the Establishment Clause.

2

We need not address the merits of the appellees' arguments concerning the Free Exercise Clause, because the appellees lack standing to raise a free exercise challenge to the Hyde Amendment. * * *

C

It remains to be determined whether the Hyde Amendment violates the equal protection component of the Fifth Amendment. This challenge is premised on the fact that, although federal reimbursement is available under Medicaid for medically necessary services generally, the Hyde Amendment does not permit federal reimbursement of all medically necessary abortions. The District Court held, and the appellees argue here, that this selective subsidization violates the constitutional guarantee of equal protection.

The guarantee of equal protection under the Fifth Amendment is not a source of substantive rights or liberties, but rather a right to be free from invidious discrimination in statutory classifications and other governmental activity. It is well-settled that where a statutory classification does not itself impinge on a right or liberty protected by the Constitution, the validity of classification must be sustained unless "the classification rests on grounds wholly irrelevant to the achievement of [any legitimate governmental] objective." McGowan v. Maryland, supra, 366 U.S., at 425 [81 S.Ct., at 1104–1105]. This presumption of constitutional validity, however, disappears if a statutory classification is predicated on criteria that are, in a constitutional sense, "suspect," the principal example of which is a classification based on race, e. g., Brown v. Board of Education, 347 U.S. 483 [74 S.Ct. 686, 98 L.Ed. 873].

1

For the reasons stated above, we have already concluded that the Hyde Amendment violates no constitutionally protected substantive rights. We now conclude as well that it is not predicated on a constitutionally suspect classification. In reaching this conclusion, we again draw guidance from the Court's decision in Maher v. Roe. As to whether the Connecticut welfare regulation providing funds for childbirth but not for nontherapeutic abortions discriminated against a suspect class, the Court in *Maher* observed:

> "An indigent woman desiring an abortion does not come within the limited category of disadvantaged classes so recognized by our cases. Nor does the fact that the impact of the regulation falls upon those who cannot pay lead to a different conclusion. In a sense, every denial of welfare to an indigent creates a wealth classification as compared to nonindigents who are able to pay for the desired goods or services. But this Court has never held that financial need alone identifies a suspect class for purposes of equal protection analysis." 432 U.S., at 471 [97 S.Ct., at 2381], citing San Antonio School Dist. v. Rodriguez, 411 U.S. 1, 29 [93 S.Ct. 1278, 1294, 36 L.Ed.2d 16]; Dandridge v. Williams, 397 U.S. 471 [90 S.Ct. 1153, 25 L.Ed.2d 491].

Thus, the Court in *Maher* found no basis for concluding that the Connecticut regulation was predicated on a suspect classification.

It is our view that the present case is indistinguishable from *Maher* in this respect. Here, as in *Maher,* the principal impact of the Hyde Amendment falls on the indigent. But that fact does not itself render the funding restriction constitutionally invalid, for this Court has held repeatedly that poverty, standing alone, is not a suspect classification. See, e. g., James v. Valtierra, 402 U.S. 137 [91 S.Ct. 1331, 28 L.Ed.2d 678]. That *Maher* involved the refusal to fund nontherapeutic abortions, whereas the present case involves the refusal to fund medically necessary abortions, has no bearing on the factors that render a classification "suspect" within the meaning of the constitutional guarantee of equal protection.[26]

2

The remaining question then is whether the Hyde Amendment is rationally related to a legitimate governmental objective. It is the Government's position that the Hyde Amendment bears a rational relationship to its legitimate interest in protecting the potential life of the fetus. We agree.

In *Wade,* the Court recognized that the State has "an important and legitimate interest in protecting the potentiality of human life." 410 U.S., at 162 [93 S.Ct., at 731]. That interest was found to exist throughout a pregnancy, "grow[ing] in substantiality as the woman

---

26. Although the matter is not free from doubt, the District Court seems to have concluded that teenage women desiring medically necessary abortions constitute a "suspect class" for purposes of triggering a heightened level of equal protection scrutiny. In this regard, the District Court observed that the Hyde Amendment "clearly operate[s] to the disadvantage of one suspect class, that is to the disadvantage of the statutory class of adolescents at a high risk of pregnancy * * *, and particularly those seventeen and under." The "statutory" class to which the District Court was referring is derived from the Adolescent Health Services and Pregnancy Prevention and Care Act, 42 U.S.C. § 300a–21 et seq. (Supp. II 1979). It was apparently the view of the District Court that since statistics indicate that women under 21 years of age are disproportionately represented among those for whom an abortion is medically necessary, the Hyde Amendment invidiously discriminates against teenage women.

But the Hyde Amendment is facially neutral as to age, restricting funding for abortions for women of all ages. The District Court erred, therefore, in relying solely on the disparate impact of the Hyde Amendment in concluding that it discriminated on the basis of age. The equal protection component of the Fifth Amendment prohibits only purposeful discrimination, Washington v. Davis, 426 U.S. 229 [96 S.Ct. 2040, 48 L.Ed.2d 597], and when a facially neutral federal statute is challenged on equal protection grounds, it is incumbent upon the challenger to prove that Congress "selected or reaffirmed a particular course of action at least in part 'because of,' not merely 'in spite of,' its adverse effects on an identifiable group." Personnel Administrator of Mass. v. Feeney, 442 U.S. 256, 279 [99 S.Ct. 2282, 2296, 60 L.Ed.2d 870]. There is no evidence to support such a finding of intent in the present case.

approaches term." Id., at 162–163 [93 S.Ct., at 731–732]. See also Beal v. Doe, 432 U.S. 438, 445–446 [97 S.Ct. 2366, 2371, 53 L.Ed.2d 464]. Moreover, in *Maher*, the Court held that Connecticut's decision to fund the costs associated with childbirth but not those associated with nontherapeutic abortions was a rational means of advancing the legitimate state interest in protecting potential life by encouraging childbirth. 432 U.S., at 478–479 [97 S.Ct., at 2385]. See also Poelker v. Doe, 432 U.S. 519, 520–521 [97 S.Ct. 2391, 2392, 53 L.Ed.2d 528].

It follows that the Hyde Amendment, by encouraging childbirth except in the most urgent circumstances, is rationally related to the legitimate governmental objective of protecting potential life. By subsidizing the medical expenses of indigent women who carry their pregnancies to term while not subsidizing the comparable expenses of women who undergo abortions (except those whose lives are threatened), Congress has established incentives that make childbirth a more attractive alternative than abortion for persons eligible for Medicaid. These incentives bear a direct relationship to the legitimate congressional interest in protecting potential life. Nor is it irrational that Congress has authorized federal reimbursement for medically necessary services generally, but not for certain medically necessary abortions.[28] Abortion is inherently different from other medical procedures, because no other procedure involves the purposeful termination of a potential life.

After conducting an extensive evidentiary hearing into issues surrounding the public funding of abortions, the District Court concluded that "[t]he interests of * * * the federal government * * * in the fetus and in preserving it are not sufficient, weighed in the balance with the woman's threatened health, to justify withdrawing medical assistance unless the woman consents * * * to carry the fetus to term." In making an independent appraisal of the competing interests involved here, the District Court went beyond the judicial function. Such decisions are entrusted under the Constitution to Congress, not the courts. It is the role of the courts only to ensure that congressional decisions comport with the Constitution.

Where, as here, the Congress has neither invaded a substantive constitutional right or freedom, nor enacted legislation that purposefully operates to the detriment of a suspect class, the only requirement of equal protection is that congressional action be rationally related to a legitimate governmental interest. The Hyde Amendment satisfies that standard. It is not the mission of this Court or any other to decide whether the balance of competing interests reflected in the Hyde Amendment is wise social policy. If that were our mission, not every

28. In fact, abortion is not the only "medically necessary" service for which federal funds under Medicaid are sometimes unavailable to otherwise eligible claimants. See 42 U.S. C. § 1396d(a)(17)(B) (inpatient hospital care of patients between 21 and 65 in institutions for tuberculosis or mental disease not covered by Title XIX).

Justice who has subscribed to the judgment of the Court today could have done so. But we cannot, in the name of the Constitution, overturn duly enacted statutes simply "because they may be unwise, improvident, or out of harmony with a particular school of thought." Williamson v. Lee Optical Co., 348 U.S. 483, 488 [75 S.Ct. 461, 464–465, 99 L.Ed. 563], quoted in Dandridge v. Williams, 397 U.S. 471, 484 [90 S.Ct. 1153, 1161, 25 L.Ed.2d 491]. Rather, "when an issue involves policy choices as sensitive as those implicated [here] * * *, the appropriate forum for their resolution in a democracy is the legislature." Maher v. Roe, supra [432 U.S., at 479, 97 S.Ct., at 2385].

IV

For the reasons stated in this opinion, we hold that a State that participates in the Medicaid program is not obligated under Title XIX to continue to fund those medically necessary abortions for which federal reimbursement is unavailable under the Hyde Amendment. We further hold that the funding restrictions of the Hyde Amendment violate neither the Fifth Amendment nor the Establishment Clause of the First Amendment. It is also our view that the appellees lack standing to raise a challenge to the Hyde Amendment under the Free Exercise Clause of the First Amendment. Accordingly, the judgment of the District Court is reversed, and the case is remanded to that court for further proceedings consistent with this opinion.

        *   *   *

NOTES AND QUESTIONS

1. Justice White agreed generally with the majority opinion but wrote a brief concurrence. Justices Brennan, Marshall, Blackmun and Stevens dissented. Justice Brennan filed a dissenting opinion in which Justices Marshall and Blackmun joined. Justices Marshall, Blackmun and Stevens also filed dissenting opinions.

INDEX

References are to Pages

†